Register of Educational Research in the United Kingdom
Volume 10: 1993–95

This latest volume of the *Register of Educational Research in the United Kingdom* lists all the major research projects being undertaken in Britain during the latter months of 1992, the whole of 1993 and 1994 and the early months of 1995.

Each entry provides names and addresses of the researchers, a detailed abstract, the source and amount of the grant (where applicable), the length of the project (or the fact of its continuance) and bibliographic details of published material about the research.

Comprehensive author and subject indexes enable the reader to use the Register to its best advantage and to obtain accurate information with both speed and ease. The subject index is based on keywords selected from the British Education Thesaurus. Each entry is listed against all its keywords.

The National Foundation for Educational Research is the leading educational research body in the United Kingdom, carrying out a varied programme of research into many aspects of education.

Register of Educational Research in the United Kingdom

Volume 10: 1993–95

National Foundation for Educational Research in England and Wales

London and New York

First published 1995
by Routledge
11 New Fetter Lane, London EC4P 4EE

Simultaneously published in the USA and Canada
by Routledge
29 West 35th Street, New York, NY 10001

Typeset in Times by LaserScript, Mitcham, Surrey
Printed and bound in Great Britain by
Antony Rowe Ltd., Chippenham, Wiltshire

British Library Cataloguing in Publication Data
A catalogue record for this book is available from the British Library

Library of Congress Cataloguing in Publication Data
A catalogue record for this book has been requested

ISBN 0–415–13243–6

Contents

How to use the Register   vi

The Register   1

Author Index   339

Subject Index   351

How to use the Register

The Register entries are arranged alphabetically according to the name of the institution at which the research was carried out; within each institution, the entries are arranged alphabetically by department and within the department by researcher. The entries are also consecutively numbered.

Name and subject indexes appear at the back of the volume. The subject index is based on keywords which have been selected from the British Education Thesaurus. Each entry is listed against all of its keywords.

Although every effort has been made to check that the details of the entries supplied by the researchers are correct, there may be some errors and inconsistencies, for which we apologise.

The details of the research projects contained in this Register are stored on an IBM microcomputer at the National Foundation for Educational Research (NFER) and entries are continuously updated and new material is added as it is received. Therefore, it is possible to provide Register users with printouts of more up-to-date information. A modest charge is made for this service, which is available from:

Register of Educational Research in the UK
National Foundation for Educational Research
The Mere
Upton Park
Slough
SL1 2DQ
Berkshire
Telephone: (01753) 574123

Aberdeen University

10/0001

Department of Education, Taylor Building, King's College,
Old Aberdeen AB9 2UB
01224 272000
Flett, M. Dr; Watt, J. Dr; Sainsbury, S. Ms; Barrow, E. Ms
Young families now: a focus for learning in the community
Abstract: 'Young Families Now' is an action research project based
in an area of rapid social change within the city of Aberdeen. The
focus of the work is the development of educational opportunities for
young children and their parents, particularly their mothers. The
project aims to respond to educational needs as these are defined by
the community. It supports existing groups in the field of early
childhood care and education and helps local people identify new
needs and establish new forms of provision for children and their
mothers. The project also aims to bring together parents and professionals to look at new ways of working and to open up discussion on
how local childcare services in health, social work and education can
better meet the needs of young families. As an action research project
it also tries to bring together the community's expertise in developing
an action programme with the University's expertise in research. The
project is currently developing a training and advisory service for
professionals and para-professionals in the area of early childhood
care.
Published Material: FLETT, M. & ALEXANDER, E. (1988). 'Parent discussion groups', Network, July, p.6.; FLETT, M. (1988).
'Women and health', Bernard van Leer Newsletter, No 52, October,
pp.6-7.; FLETT, M. (1990). 'Women in transition: gender and
power', Journal of Community Education, Vol 8, No 4, pp.8-13.;
FLETT, M. (1990). 'Young families now: an introduction', British
Association for Early Childhood Newsletter, Vol 3, No 2, pp.1-3.
Status: Sponsored project
Source of Grant: Bernard Van Leer Foundation £1,000,000
Date of Research: 1984-1994
*KEYWORDS: access to education; community education; mothers;
preschool education; young children*

10/0002

Department of Education, Taylor Building, King's College,
Old Aberdeen AB9 2UB
01224 272000
Darling, J. Dr; Watt, J. Dr
**Beyond a gender stereotype: exceptional women teachers in
Scotland**
Abstract: This project is an interview study examining women teach-
ers in exceptional professional roles – headteachers of mixed com-
prehensive schools and teachers of technical subjects. The study will
try to identify factors which have assisted or hindered women in
pursuing these posts and factors which support or inhibit them in
playing such exceptional roles.
Status: Sponsored project
Source of Grant: Aberdeen University £4,500
Date of Research: 1993-1994
*KEYWORDS: gender equality; head teachers; sex stereotypes;
teaching profession; women teachers; women's employment*

10/0003

Department of Education, Taylor Building, King's College,
Old Aberdeen AB9 2UB
01224 272000
Darling, J. Dr; Glendinning, A. Mr
Gender and subject choice amongst pupils
Abstract: This project aimed to establish a baseline picture for further
study using data on presentation and performance in national examinations. At S4 (age = 15) there are marked variations in the proportions of males and females across the curriculum, although there is
equality in Mathematics and English. The polarisation is even more
marked at S5. Aggregating performance across all subjects, females
clearly do better than males at Standard Grade (S4). There is little or
no overall difference at Higher Grade (S5), but there is greater
diversity of performance according to subject.
Status: Sponsored project
Source of Grant: Grampian Region TVE £1,500
Date of Research: 1993-1993
KEYWORDS: academic achievement; choice of subjects; sex differences

10/0004

Department of Education, Taylor Building, King's College,
Old Aberdeen AB9 2UB
01224 272000
Darling, J. Dr; Glendinning, A. Mr
Gender and promotion amongst teaching staff in Grampian
Abstract: This project used existing data to explore the promotion
patterns amongst teaching staff in the Grampian Region. A research
report has been generated, indicating, amongst other findings, that in
secondary schools men are more likely to be in promoted posts even
within departments numerically dominated by women (e.g. English).
In the primary sector, size of school is a major determinant of whether
women achieve promotion to headship.
Status: Sponsored project
Source of Grant: Grampian Region TVE £1,500
Date of Research: 1993-1993
*KEYWORDS: equal opportunities – jobs; gender equality; promo-
tion – occupational; teaching profession; women teachers; women's
employment*

10/0005

Department of Education, Taylor Building, King's College,
Old Aberdeen AB9 2UB
01224 272000
Kiger, A. Dr; Campbell, D. Dr
**Learning styles of undergraduate medical students and
student nurses**
Abstract: The Entwistle-Ramsden inventory on learning styles has
been completed by 3 year cohorts of medical entrants to the University of Aberdeen (1991, 1992, 1993), about 350 in all, and to 1 cohort
of entrants to the Nursing College in Aberdeen (1991), about 60. The
academic progress of these students is being followed through to
graduation, to include degree examination results for medical students and a wider range of assessment for nursing students. These
results will be compared with inventory scores to test the predictive
value of the inventory, and to lay the basis for more complex analysis
of students' learning.
Status: Individual research
Date of Research: 1991-continuing
*KEYWORDS: learning strategies; medical education; nurse educa-
tion; predictive measurement*

10/0006

Department of Education, Taylor Building, King's College,
Old Aberdeen AB9 2UB
01224 272000
Kiger, A. Dr; Gordon, F. Mrs
**A cross-cultural study of nursing image amongst student
nurses**
Abstract: The image of nursing held by student nurses in three
contrasting cultural contexts in three countries, is being explored by
means of an open-ended questionnaire, developed from pilot focused
interviews. The samples comprise about one hundred at each of two
levels (beginning and experienced) and at two institutions in each
country.
Status: Individual research
Date of Research: 1992-1994
KEYWORDS: nurse education; nurses

10/0007

Department of Education, Taylor Building, King's College,
Old Aberdeen AB9 2UB
01224 272000
Watt, J. Dr; Nisbet, J. Prof.
Educational disadvantage in Scotland: a 1990's perspective
Abstract: The study is a follow-up to Educational Disadvantage Ten
Years On (Scottish Education Department (1984). Educational disadvantage ten years on. London: HMSO), which reviewed initiatives
in Scotland. What has happened since then? Although the impression
may be that 'disadvantage' has faded from public concern, there are
many worthwhile initiatives, from local authorities, nationally, from
the European Community, from business and voluntary bodies. The
review analyses policy and practice in Scotland over the period from
1984 to 1994.
Status: Sponsored project
Source of Grant: Scottish Office Education Department
Date of Research: 1993-1994

KEYWORDS: access to education; disadvantaged environment; educational innovation; educationally disadvantaged; Scotland

10/0008
Department of Education, Taylor Building, King's College, Old Aberdeen AB9 2UB
01224 272000
Nisbet, J. Prof.

Review of educational research in Scotland
Abstract: The study will record and analyse educational research in Scotland in the last ten years from: 1) a review of documents; 2) a postal survey to educational bodies; and 3) interviews with researchers, clients and funding agencies. The analysis will be in terms of themes, costs, modes of research, personnel and dissemination.
Status: Sponsored project
Source of Grant: Scottish Office Education Department £1,950
Date of Research: 1994-1994
KEYWORDS: educational research; Scotland

10/0009
Department of Education, Taylor Building, King's College, Old Aberdeen AB9 2UB
01224 272000
Shucksmith, J. Mrs; Philip, K. Ms

Peer educators and parent collaborators: educating about HIV in the community
Abstract: Attempts to educate young people about the risks from human immunodeficiency virus (HIV) and acquired immune deficiency syndrome (AIDS) via health promotion and school health education programmes have had only limited success. Evidence shows that knowledge may increase but young people's behaviour does not change. In addition, some groups of young people are notoriously difficult to reach in these ways. This action research project is an attempt to explore how effectively young people can be involved as educators of their own peer group. The project will build on previous studies carried out by the research team which found a variety of needs for information and advice expressed by different groups of young people. The study will focus on a group of young people from one neighbourhood within Aberdeen who will be recruited from community based groups throughout the area. This focus will enable the examination of the influence of local networks and contexts on the work of the peer educators. The project also intends to involve parents, recognising their role as informal educators and their need for support. This element of the project will be carried out alongside the work with young people.
Status: Sponsored project
Source of Grant: Grampian Health Department; Scottish Office, jointly £40,000
Date of Research: 1993-1994
KEYWORDS: acquired immune deficiency syndrome; health education; parent participation; peer teaching; sex education

10/0010
Department of Education, Taylor Building, King's College, Old Aberdeen AB9 2UB
01224 272000
Philip, K. Ms; Hendry, L. Prof.

Mentoring and youth work
Abstract: The role of mentoring, the relationship between a young person and an older non-related adult, is explored through a range of questions: 1) Who are the mentors in the lives of young people? 2) What is the content of the relationship? 3) Why do young people develop mentoring relationships? 4) Are youth workers recognised as mentors? A mix of quantitative and qualitative methods will be used. It is envisaged that 200 young people and 200 mentors will be interviewed. In addition, a postal questionnaire will be sent out around Scotland.
Status: Sponsored project
Source of Grant: Johann Jacob's Foundation £100,000
Date of Research: 1993-continuing
KEYWORDS: mentors; youth leaders; youth service

10/0011
Department of Education, Taylor Building, King's College, Old Aberdeen AB9 2UB
01224 272000

Shucksmith, J. Mrs; Kiger, A. Dr; Glendinning, A. Mr
Expanding education: the expansion of further and higher education and young people's welfare
Abstract: The expansion of the tertiary sector will raise problems for student welfare. The project examines the well-being and progress of approximately 2,500 students in 3 higher education establishments in Scotland. The study has 2 major strands: a quantitative survey of a cohort of students entering the tertiary sector, involving a clustered random sample stratified across sectors; and a qualitative study of some 20 students involving indepth interviews and keeping a diary. The intention is to explore the different needs for student support in an era when a broader cohort of students is being drawn into the system.
Status: Sponsored project
Source of Grant: Aberdeen University £17,000
Date of Research: 1992-1993
KEYWORDS: further education; higher education; sixteen to nineteen education; student health and welfare; student needs

Anglia Polytechnic University

10/0012
Anglia Business School, Danbury Park Conference Centre, Danbury, Chelmsford CM3 4AT
01245 225511
Marchant, J. Mr; Trafford, V. Dr

The management of income generation in secondary schools
Abstract: The Education Reform Act 1988 has provided schools with opportunities to manage its site and premises beyond the school day. Schools may also, now, supplement their budgets by lettings, the hire of facilities and other activities which raise funds. Income generating activities have thus developed beyond the traditional support provided by Parent Teacher Associations to something quite central to a school's financial base. Evidence shows that secondary schools which seek to generate additional income are likely – initially – to exhibit: (1) development plans which do not refer to this financial activity; (2) staff role statements which seldom include responsibility for this activity; (3) a general staff awareness of the need for this activity; (4) the absence of planned staff development for this activity; and (5) alterations being made to the traditional roles of teachers who are involved in this activity. This evidence also suggests that schools' dependence on self-generated funds will bring about internal structural change thereby consolidating the activity of income generation within the institutional management system of schools. The current research is testing the extent to which formal structural change has been introduced by secondary schools which have adopted strategic income generating policies. Follow-up questionnaires, and selective interviews, are being undertaken with twenty-five secondary schools in one local education authority. The findings will illuminate current management practices in schools which generate additional income from their own efforts.
Published Material: SMITH, M. (Ed.) (1993). Managing institutional development. Loughborough: Loughborough University Press.
Status: Sponsored project
Source of Grant: Anglia Polytechnic University £500
Date of Research: 1992-1993
KEYWORDS: educational finance; fund raising; income; money management; school funds; secondary schools

10/0013
Anglia Business School, Danbury Park Conference Centre, Danbury, Chelmsford CM3 4AT
01245 225511
Trafford, V. Dr; Evans, D. Mr

The Technical and Vocational Education Initiative (TVEI) in Essex schools and colleges: capitalising on the investment
Abstract: The Technical and Vocational Education Initiative (TVEI) extension is now four years through its seven year lifespan in the Essex Local Education Authority (LEA). The research is focused upon the schools and colleges who are participating in Phase One of the project and whose funding ceased in March 1993. The aim of the research is to identify how institutional management and curriculum practices have determined the effective delivery of TVEI. The investigation is based on responses from all 44 schools and colleges involved in Phase One (1988-93), for which purpose a questionnaire

has been designed, piloted and administered with a 5% return. Interviews were also conducted in nine schools, randomly selected. The data gathered from these schools, which includes school documentation, institutional plans, inspectors' reports etc., will provide material for case studies. Note has been taken of the literature which details how institutions respond to, adopt and then implement developmental change. This has been supplemented by drawing on information from national publications, consultants' reports and other publicly available TVEI documentation. An interim report suggests that there is strong evidence of assimilation of TVEI practices in mainstream curriculum and TVEI processes (e.g. monitoring and evaluation) in institutional management procedures. It is also evident that there is a high level of integration in those case study schools with whom good practice is associated. The final report will be published in April 1993.
Status: Sponsored project
Source of Grant: Essex County Council £8,000
Date of Research: 1992-1993
KEYWORDS: *institutional administration; TVEI*

10/0014
Anglia Business School, Danbury Park Conference Centre, Danbury, Chelmsford CM3 4AT
01245 225511
Thomas, H. Mr; *Supervisor:* Trafford, V. Dr; Jenkins, H. Prof.
The development and consequences of the University of Bristol's resource allocation system, 1986-90, with special reference to the Faculty of Engineering and its comparator universities
Abstract: In 1987 the University of Bristol changed from a centralised, historically based system of resource allocation to a system which devolved budgetary responsibility to a departmental level and based departmental allocations on a formula which reflected Universities Grants Commission (UGC) methodology (the 'Bristol Model'). The purpose of the research will be to analyse the Bristol Model with a view to formulating principles relating to the management of the resource allocation process in a university context. The work will be set within the environment of the late 1980s and early 1990s when there was an increasing emphasis throughout the public sector on public accountability and value for money. Although some research has been carried out into resource management in universities and polytechnics, the proposed work will be a major indepth case study of resource management within the university field. It will explore not only the technical/financial but also the behavioural/micro-political factors underlying the development, use, consequences and suspension of a devolved resource allocation model. The findings of the University of Bristol case study will be enhanced by being tested against the experience at comparable universities. In the United Kingdom the outcomes of the research will have implications for the management of the higher education sector as a whole. Focusing upon one faculty in the University of Bristol, documentary evidence, interviews and historical participant observation will generate case studies on the Bristol model. Interviews with staff outside the Faculty will provide further perspectives upon the reasons for, methods of and consequences from this example of financial devolution. Derived propositions from this date will be tested as hypotheses in comparator UK universities.
Status: Individual research
Date of Research: 1991-1994
KEYWORDS: *educational finance; financial support; universities; university administration*

10/0015
Anglia Business School, Danbury Park Conference Centre, Danbury, Chelmsford CM3 4AT
01245 225511
Davies, J. Prof.
Devolution in universities: a study of the devolvement of authority to faculties
Abstract: Many universities in Europe and Australia are currently engaged in devolving budgetary, academic and administrative authority to faculties, for various reasons: creation of large clusters to secure academic excellence; simplification of administrative processes; empowerment; creation of an entrepreneurial ethic; and effective management of financial reduction. The study attempts to explore: 1) reasons for devolution in various sample universities in Australia, New Zealand, Netherlands and UK; 2) manifestations of

devolution in budget, academic and administrative terms and its scope in eleven major areas of university administration; 3) consequences for faculty management; 4) consequences for the central management of the university; 5) effects in academic, administration and budgeting terms. The study is based on a number of institutional case studies which are assessed against several templates of organisational development. The results are intended to be: principles for the conception of devolution; classification of manifestations of devolution; and a template for the assessment of the effectiveness of devolution.
Status: Sponsored project
Source of Grant: Three Australian Universities; Australian Committee of Vice Chancellors
Date of Research: 1992-1993
KEYWORDS: *educational administration; universities; university administration*

10/0016
Anglia Business School, Danbury Park Conference Centre, Danbury, Chelmsford CM3 4AT
01245 225511
Lung, M. Mr; *Supervisor:* Trafford, V. Dr; Evans, D. Mr
Nursing education: the integration of an emergent discipline into the academic community
Abstract: The early and mid 1990s represent a period of significant organisational transition for nursing education in England. The colleges of nursing which move into the national higher education sector both face and, in their turn, create specific issues of academic, organisational and managerial integration. Previous research findings (Lung 1993) posited that the process of amalgamation for colleges with universities exhibited the three stages of affiliation, accreditation and coalition of integration. The proposed research concerns itself with this final stage. It sets out to test integration, as defined in the final stage, by the value sets of the academic community towards the emergence of nursing as a new, and young, discipline. A representative sample of universities and their respective amalgamating schools of nursing, will form the study area. Evidence will be accessed from documentary sources, questionnaire surveys and interviews to provide triangulations upon perceptions of integration. Use will be made of interviews with key personnel to identify and catalogue the micropolitical influences during the period of transition in certain amalgamations. This evidence will be presented through case studies from which models will be advanced to explain the mutual dynamics of institutional transition and reception.
Status: Individual research
Date of Research: 1993-continuing
KEYWORDS: *higher education; nurse education*

10/0017
Anglia Business School, Danbury Park Conference Centre, Danbury, Chelmsford CM3 4AT
01245 225511
Boddington, G. Mr; *Supervisor:* Jenkins, H. Prof.; Trafford, V. Dr
Transition from public service to market place: staff experiences in one local education authority, 1992-1995
Abstract: The research will be undertaken within one local education authority (LEA) during the period April 1992 to April 1995. The focus for the research is to trace the behaviours adopted by a group of education advisors attempting to come to terms with a major change in their working environment. The context will be the staff response to, and handling of the change-over from, the traditional LEA public service role to one where entrepreneurial values dominate. Thus the research will document, interpret and explain what happened and what can be learned from the experience of a single LEA during this unique transition in a field of study where at present no research based literature exists. The researcher is a member of the organisation to be investigated. As a result, an ethnographic approach will be used to understand the meanings and significances which staff in the LEA place upon their own behaviour and that of others. This evidence will be supplemented by the analysis of documentary materials and chronological interviews with both advisory service staff and other key members of the LEA. A triangulation of these staff perspectives on the emergent themes will provide internal and theoretical empirical validity. Findings will be presented through case studies of an incident and multiple concept nature. Sytems mapping will be used to illustrate, and then to analyse, the changing role relationships within these episodic case studies over the period of the research. This data will be rich in real life experiences, thereby

enabling grounded theory propositions to be advanced. Thus the case studies will not be offered as a model from which generalities may be drawn, rather they will provide an illumination which will relate to other local authority organisations as they move towards market orientation. Thus as a consequence of these findings the research will: 1) map the micropolitics and staff interactions during the above period, thereby identifying conjunctions of criticality in the life of the LEA and its advisory seice; 2) create models which explain the phases through which the above change processes appear to pass, noting how specific situation variables can be related together; and 3) offer a concluding commentary upon the way(s) by which one LEA prepared itself to operate in a more entrepreneurial manner in its advisory service.
Status: Individual research
Date of Research: 1993-continuing
KEYWORDS: *educational administration; local education authorities*

10/0018
Anglia Business School, Danbury Park Conference Centre, Danbury, Chelmsford CM3 4AT
01245 225511
Fenton, M. Mr; *Supervisor:* Trafford, V. Dr; Evans, D. Mr
The influence of secondary school image upon parental choice in one rural county town
Abstract: In the present market oriented climate in education the issue of institutional image is central to the success of schools. Although some research has been undertaken, there are still key questions to be satisfactorily addressed. These can be identified as demand issues, such as: 1) What is the role of parents and children in the process? 2) What is really meant by such concepts as 'happiness' and 'discipline', so frequently cited in research? 3) How does the process of choice evolve? All existing research has taken a snapshot view? 4) How far do parents make a rational choice of the 'best' school? The supply side of the equation raises such issue as: 1) How is a school's image formed and developed among its potential customers? 2) How can schools best communicate with their market? 3) How can school management best reconcile any conflict between 'putting the customer first' and received educational wisdom. Indeed, is such a conflict necessary? 4) What management strategies do schools need to employ to ensure that they are responsive to the market? Data will be collected by interview and questionnaire from a representative sample of parents during their children's final year in primary school, and one year later their reflections upon their decision to send their child to a specific secondary school will be sought. Documentary evidence, and interviews with representative senior staff in secondary schools, will be drawn upon to generate image maps and stars. These two sets of data will be compared for three cohorts of parents in order to identify those variables of secondary school generated image which appear to influence the choice by parents of a preferred school for their child. The secondary schools and their respective feeder primary schools will all be within the normal boundaries of a rural county town.
Status: Individual research
Date of Research: 1993-continuing
KEYWORDS: *access to education; parent choice; secondary schools; selection*

10/0019
Anglia Business School, Danbury Park Conference Centre, Danbury, Chelmsford CM3 4AT
01245 225511
Saskatchewan Teacher's Federation, 2317 Arlington Avenue, Saskatoon, Saskatchewan, Canada S7J 4S2
Crozier-Smith, D. Mr; *Supervisor:* Scharf, M. Dr; Jenkins, H. Prof.; Trafford, V. Dr
Identifying and meeting the needs of beginning teachers through planned transition to the profession
Abstract: Research on teacher socialisation has identified phases to the process of entry to the profession. Within the Canadian context, the process of becoming a teacher needs to be better understood by all constituent groups associated with teacher education in order to support successful induction into the profession. This research will identify the reasons for high attrition rates among teachers during their early years in the profession. It will identify the types of support expected and received by beginning teachers, developing proposals for formal programmes of induction to the teaching profession. Descriptive research methods will be employed through a survey instrument to enquire into the demographics of the beginning teacher group, their expectations and experiences during their first year and their reasons for choosing to stay in the profession or leave. Interpretive research through indepth interviews will attempt to find links between personal data (such as marital status, reliance on student loans, moving from a city to a small community) and the quality of the first year teaching experience. They will be asked to engage in post-decisional justification by providing data about what attracted them to teaching. Particular attention will be given to beginning teachers of aboriginal ancestry in Saskatchewan and teachers of minority racial groups in the United Kingdom in an attempt to discover the special needs of these groups. The hypothesis is that these teachers may experience greater needs for personal support as they attempt to integrate into both a profession and a cultural institution dominated by whites.
Status: Individual research
Date of Research: 1992-continuing
KEYWORDS: *Canada natives; ethnic groups; indigenous populations; newly qualified teachers; teacher background; teacher induction; teaching profession*

10/0020
Department of Arts and Letters, East Road, Cambridge CB1 1PT
01223 63271
Tallack, M. Mrs; *Supervisor:* Baxter, D. Mr
Anglia Polytechnic University critical studies project
Abstract: Anglia Polytechnic University Art History Division staff at Cambridge, are working with two hundred year 5 and year 6 pupils and their teachers, following these pupils through their school career until 1995. The staff provide: (1) expertise in and outside the classroom in Critical Studies work. Working alongside the primary and secondary teachers in schools, galleries, museums and other locations; (2) in-service classes for primary and secondary teachers; (3) visual and other resources for cross-curricular critical studies work drawn from Anglia Polytechnic University's own due resources, galleries, museums and the community. The aims of this Critical Studies research project are: (1) to introduce pupils to as wide a variety of art objects as possible in order to (i) generate understanding of the cultural, historical, formal and other ways of engaging with art objects; (ii) improve their artwork; (iii) extend their critical vocabulary to enable them to critically evaluate their own artwork. (2) to familiarise teachers with the innumerable ways in which Critical Studies work can enrich many areas of the school curriculum; (3) to develop and extend teachers' confidence and abilities in relation to Critical Studies work; (4) to test, and refine, cross curricular strategies, teaching methods and assessment procedures in relation to Critical Studies work in primary and secondary schools in the context of the National Curriculum.
Status: Sponsored project
Source of Grant: Calouste Gulbenkian Foundation £5,000; Eastern Arts Association £900
Date of Research: 1990-continuing
KEYWORDS: *art activities; art education; criticism; cross curricular approach*

10/0021
Department of Geography, East Road, Cambridge CB1 1PT
01223 63271
Fitzgerald, M. Ms
Education for sustainable development in the third world
Abstract: The aims are to determine the origin of and reasons for environmental education programmes (EEP) and to assess their contribution to sustainable development and disaster mitigation. A pilot EEP in Ethiopia has been evaluated. A 45% sample of participating centres has been visited and interviews conducted with students, farmers, teachers and education officers at district, regional and ministerial level. It is concluded that there are contradictions between the centralisation of programme planning and the need for environmental education to be location-specific and between the goals of providing relevant education and meeting the demand for qualifications. These arise from northern-inspired interpretations of sustainable development. They limit the potential of environmental education to produce the values and behaviour required for sustainable development.
Published Material: FITZGERALD, M. (1990). 'Education for sustainable development: decision-making for environmental education in Ethiopia', The International Journal of Educational Development, Vol 10, No 4, pp.289-302.; FITZGERALD, M. (1990). 'Environ-

mental education in Ethiopia: the sources of decision-making'. In: BANDHU, D., SINGH, H. & MAITRA, A.K. Environmental education and sustainable development. New Delhi: Indian Environmental Society.; FITZGERALD, M. (1991). 'Education for sustainable development: a long-term strategy for famine prevention in Ethiopia', Occasional Paper in Rural Studies, No 9, Anglia Polytechnic, Division of Geography.
Status: Individual research
Date of Research: 1987-continuing
KEYWORDS: developing countries; development education; environmental education

10/0022
Department of Geography, East Road, Cambridge CB1 1PT
01223 63271
Fitzgerald, M. Ms
The contribution of geography to environmental education
Abstract: The aim is to evaluate geography's contribution to education for sustainable development. The proposed method is an analysis of school syllabuses and assessment procedures in the United Kingdom and California. Initial research suggests that geography's separation of the 'human' and the 'physical' undermines its potential to synthesise ecology and environment in the ways needed to bring about new environmental ethics.
Published Material: FITZGERALD, M. (1990). 'Education for sustainable development: decision-making for environmental education in Ethiopia', The International Journal of Educational Development, Vol 10, No 4, pp.289-302.; FITZGERALD, M. (1990). 'Environmental education in Ethiopia: the sources of decision-making'. In: BANDHU, D., SINGH, H. & MAITRA, A.K. Environmental education and sustainable development. New Delhi: Indian Environmental Society.; FITZGERALD, M. (1990). 'Education for sustainable development: a long-term strategy for famine prevention in Ethiopia', Occasional Paper No 9 in Rural Studies. Anglia Polytechnic, Division of Geography.
Status: Individual research
Date of Research: 1991-1993
KEYWORDS: environmental education; geography

10/0023
Department of Management, East Road, Cambridge CB1 1PT
01223 63271
Evans, R. Mr; *Supervisor:* Jenkins, H. Prof.; Trafford, V. Dr
Organisational architecture in colleges of further education: case studies in organisational change
Abstract: Colleges of further education have, particularly in the last 10 years, been faced with an increasingly complex and turbulent environment. To meet these challenges a number of further education colleges have been making radical and innovative changes to their management structures and processes. For example, a small number of colleges have made far reaching changes from traditional hierarchical systems to new systems such as matrix and networking systems. Certainly, many colleges are seeking to move to new more responsive structures and to implement more flexible systems which can respond quickly to rapid changes in the environment. Organisational architecture is not only to do with structures and roles, but with processes, issues, leadership policies and politics which reflect the organisational culture. This research is based on the belief that there is a need to make a thorough and comparative assessment of the range of different approaches to organisational architecture and design in further education colleges. The research will examine a range of structures and processes adopted by further education colleges to seek out: 1) How structures and processes are being changed. 2) The rationales for the varying structures and processes. 3) The effectiveness of the different approaches to organisational architecture. The work will include: 1) A review of the management literature with special reference to issues related to organisational architecture and its underpinning concepts. 2) An identification of different approaches to organisational architecture within further education colleges. 3) An indepth and comprehensive analysis of the design and operation of management structures and processes employed in further education colleges by examining a number of key structural indicators and processes, e.g. vision and environmental fit; division of authority; leadership approaches and devolved power; creation and use of self-managing teams; coordination and collaboration processes; business/academic strategies; resource location and budgetary arrangements; information systems; patterns and policies for staff development; systems for dealing with students; quality systems. An

assessment will be made of factors underlying any change in structures such as the linkage between structural and cultural changes.
Status: Individual research
Date of Research: 1993-continuing
KEYWORDS: college administration; colleges of further education; educational administration; further education; institutional administration; organisational change

10/0024
Department of Management, East Road, Cambridge CB1 1PT
01223 63271
Billington, J. Mr; *Supervisor:* Jenkins, H. Prof.; McNay, I. Prof.; Evans, D. Mr
A policy analysis of the issues of accessibility to baccalaureate level studies in the Province of Saskatchewan
Abstract: The purpose of the study is to conduct a prospective policy analysis, to determine if there is an acceptable policy solution to accommodate the perceived need of extending baccalaureate level studies in Saskatchewan. In addition, the investigation, using the same policy analysis techniques, will study issues and options related to providing more educational opportunities at the university level for Aboriginal and Metis residents of the Province. The research will be a qualitative case study of the position of key policy stakeholders, in the post-secondary education system in Saskatchewan, regarding the extension of baccalaureate level studies in the Province. The study will describe the major factors perceived to affect the need to increase accessibility and whether it is desirable and/or feasible to provide university level education at institutions other than the two universities and their associated colleges. In addition, the desirability and/or feasibility of other models or policies to increase accessibility will be described. The most acceptable policy solution will be identified and recommendations for policy formation will be developed from the findings.
Status: Individual research
Date of Research: 1993-continuing
KEYWORDS: access to education; Canada natives; educational policy; qualifications

10/0025
Department of Management, East Road, Cambridge CB1 1PT
01223 63271
Charles, L. Mrs; *Supervisor:* Jenkins, H. Prof.; Morgan, S. Mr
The effect of the competency movement on management development and the concept of the learning organisation
Abstract: This research project investigates the impact of the competency approaches to training on management development policies and processes within companies, and the effect to which competency approaches help or hinder the concept of the learning organisation. The research will examine and monitor two on-going alliances which the Business School of Anglia Polytechnic University has already established with two large international industrial companies. It will analyse the on-going process of setting up the alliances which involves (amongst other things) the accreditation of in-company programmes on a competency basis and examines the effects on in-company management development policies and staff. The concept of the learning organisation will be used to consider whether the competency approaches lead to increased learning within organisations or whether the approach is restricted and reduces opportunities to learn.
Status: Individual research
Date of Research: 1993-continuing
KEYWORDS: competency based education; management development

10/0026
Department of Sociology, East Road, Cambridge CB1 1PT
01223 63271
Webster, A. Dr
The role of hybrid coalitions in the commercialisation of academic research
Abstract: The principal objective of the study was to provide a sociological analysis of new forms of collaboration between academia and industry, that is, long-term strategic research alliances (SRAs) between a single company and an academic research group. Comparative case studies were conducted in the UK and USA. The study identified the emergence of 'hybrid' structures, their relative success compared with other linkages, and their long-term stability which is shown to be problematic.

Published Material: WEBSTER, A. (1990). 'Institutional stability: engineering and environment for biotechnology', Science and Public Policy, Vol 17, No 6, pp.381-386.; WEBSTER, A. & SWAIN, V. (1991). 'The pharmaceutical industry: towards a new innovation environment', Technology Analysis and Strategic Management, Vol 3, No 2.; WEBSTER, A. (1993). 'University-corporate ties and the construction of research agendas', Sociology, (in press). Policy, Vol 17, No 6, pp.381-386.
Status: Sponsored project
Source of Grant: Economic and Social Research Council £40,000
Date of Research: 1989-1992
KEYWORDS: cooperative programmes; corporate support; industry-higher education relationship; research

10/0027
> Department of Sociology, East Road, Cambridge CB1 1PT
> 01223 63271
> Webster, A. Dr

Patenting in academic research
Abstract: This project explores the way in which academics (in conjunction with industrial liaison officers) have become increasingly involved in patenting. It compares academics' notions of novelty and inventiveness with those embodied in the intellectual property law. A national survey of UK universities has been completed (for the first time) and research on biotechnology and pharmacology departments will form the focus of the fieldwork.
Status: Sponsored project
Source of Grant: Economic and Social Research Council £50,000
Date of Research: 1992-continuing
KEYWORDS: industry-higher education relationship; intellectual property; patents; research

10/0028
> Division of Chemistry and Geology, East Road, Cambridge CB1 1PT
> 01223 63271
> Dray, A. Dr; *Supervisor:* Emmett, T. Dr

Computer-assisted learning packages in the earth sciences
Abstract: This research and software development project has been supported by the Higher Education Funding Council via a Teaching and Learning Technology Program's Earth Sciences Courseware Consortium. Earlier projects that attempted to introduce computer-aided learning (CAL) into the Earth Sciences have floundered because of: a) insufficient liaison with end-users (i.e. lecturers and students); and b) unsuitability and/or technological immaturity of the hardware and software. By taking advantage of recent advances in Graphical User Interface (GUI) based authoring software packages, this project allows the main developmental and research effort to be applied to the content and nature of the material to be presented. Great care has been taken to focus on material that is most amenable to the CAL medium, and crystallography and the interpretation of ancient environments ('palaeoenvironments') have been selected as the most favourable areas for development. An extensive programme of consultation has been undertaken to ensure that the subject content of the modules is as widely acceptable as possible. Each of the modules will consist of 4-5 hours of presentation, and each will include extensive use self-testing procedures. All the CAL material produced has or will be fully tested and evaluated, both informally and formally (the latter in cooperation with the Open University). The objective of testing and evaluation is to ensure that the final modules are useful, intuitive and easy to use, error-free, and that they make the best use of the CAL presentation medium.
Status: Sponsored project
Source of Grant: Higher Education and Funding Council: Teaching and Learning Technology Program £16,000
Date of Research: 1993-1994
KEYWORDS: computer-assisted learning; computer uses in education; earth science; educational software

10/0029
> Faculty of Health and Social Work, Duke House, Victoria Road South, Chelmsford CM1 1LL
> 01245 493131
> Winter, R. Prof.; Maisch, M. Ms; Guise, S. Ms

The Accreditation and Support for Specified Expertise and Training (ASSET) Programme
Abstract: The aim of the ASSET Programme is to attempt to apply the principles of competency based education developed by the National Council for Vocational Qualifications (NCVQ) to the delivery of an inservice honours degree for professionals in full-time work. The first group of workers are professional social workers, the second group are design engineers with the Ford Motor Company. Substantial amendments to the NCVQ format for the presentation of competences are proposed, including the use of Core Assessment Criteria derived from a theoretical and empirical survey..
Published Material: WINTER, R. & MAISCH, M. (1991). The ASSET Programme, Volume 1, Handbook. Chelmsford: Anglia Polytechnic University/Essex Social Services Department.; WINTER, R. & MAISCH, M. (1992). The ASSET Programme, Volume 2, Handbook. Chelmsford: Anglia Polytechnic University/Essex Social Services Department.; WINTER, R. (1992). 'Quality management or the educational workplace', Journal of Further and Higher Education, Vol 16, No 3.; WINTER, R. (1992). 'The ASSET Programme', Competence and Assessment, No 20.
Status: Sponsored project
Source of Grant: Department of Employment £393,000
Date of Research: 1990-1994
KEYWORDS: competency based education; degrees – academic; inservice education; professional education

Associated Examining Board

10/0030
> Stag Hill House, Guildford GU2 5XJ
> 01483 506506
> Delap, M. Dr; Eason, S. Mr; Taylor, M. Mr; *Supervisor:* Cresswell, M. Mr

Examinations research programme
Abstract: The Research and Statistics Group carries out a continuing programme of research into fundamental problems associated with educational measurement together with work on specific examinations. Particular areas of study being pursued in 1993, 1994 and 1995 are: grading processes; achieved weights; open-book examinations; estimated grades; aggregation. The Group is also involved in development work associated with the assessment of the National Curriculum. A further aspect of the work involves collaborative studies with other United Kingdom examining boards and groups to establish that all the General Certificate of Secondary Education (GCSE) and General Certificate of Education (GCE) examinations are set, marked and graded to comparable standards.
Published Material: CRESSWELL, M.J. (1991). 'A multilevel bivariate model'. In: PROSSER, R., RASBASH, J. & GOLDSTEIN, H. (Ed). Data analysis with ML3. London: London University, Institute of Education.; CRESSWELL, M.J. & HOUSTON, J.G. (1991). 'Assessment of the National Curriculum – some fundamental considerations', Educational Review, Vol 43, No 1, pp.63-78.; CRESSWELL, M.J. (1994). 'Aggregation and awarding methods for National Curriculum assessments in England and Wales': a comparison of approaches proposed for Key Stages 3 and 4, Assessment in Education, Vol 1, No 1, pp. 45-61.; DELAP, M. (1994). 'An investigation into the accuracy of A level predicted grades', Educational Research, Vol 36, No 2, pp.135-148.; A full list of publications is available from the researcher.
Status: Sponsored project
Source of Grant: Associated Examining Board
Date of Research: 1983-continuing
KEYWORDS: assessment; evaluation; examinations; moderation – marking; National Curriculum

Aston University

10/0031
> Aston Triangle, Birmingham B4 7ET
> 0121 359 3611
> Wright, S. Dr; *Supervisor:* Ager, D. Prof.

Educational achievement and bilingualism: a study of three hundred 16-18 year olds in Birmingham schools and colleges
Abstract: This study aimed firstly to investigate current patterns of language use amongst young bilinguals in Birmingham and secondly

to examine the relationship between this language use and educational achievement. The research then focused on various practices, customs and attitudes which would favour the attrition or survival of minority languages in the British situation. The data necessary to address this question was provided by a sample of three hundred and seventy-four 16-19 year olds, studying in Birmingham schools and colleges during the period 1987-1990 and drawn from the main linguistic minority communities in Birmingham. The research methods chosen were both quantitative and qualitative. The study found evidence of ethnolinguistic vitality amongst many of the linguistic minority communities in Birmingham: a number of practices and a range of attitudes indicate that linguistic diversity may continue and that a stable diglossic situation may develop in some instances, particularly where demographical and religious factors lead to closeness of association. Where language attrition is occurring it is often because of the move from a less prestigious minority language or dialect to a more prestigious minority language in addition to pressures from English. The educational experience of the sample indicates that literacy and formal language study are of key importance if personal bilingualism is to be experienced as an asset; high levels of oral proficiency in the first and second language do not, on their own necessarily correlate with positive educational benefit. The intervening variable associated with educational achievement appears to be the formal language learning process and literacy. A number of attitudes and practices, including the very close associations maintained with some of the countries of origin of the families, were seen to aid or hinder first language maintenance and second language acquisition.
Published Material: AGER, D. & WRIGHT, S. (1990). 'Two's and three's: research methodologies in community identification and language contact', Acta Linguistica, Vienna.; WRIGHT, S. & AGER, D. (1991). 'Assimilation, stable diglossia or separatism: possible outcomes of complexity and diversity in Britain today', Innovation, Vienna.; WRIGHT, S. (1991). 'The currency of community language qualifications', Language Learning Journal, No 4, September.
Status: Individual research
Date of Research: 1987-1993
KEYWORDS: *academic achievement; bilingualism; diglossia; ethnic groups; language usage*

10/0032
     Aston Triangle, Birmingham B4 7ET
     0121 359 3611
     Fletcher, J. Dr; Upton, C. Dr
Transcription and analysis of the domestic accounts of Merton College, Oxford, for the Tudor period
Abstract: College domestic accounts remain as one of the last largely unexplored sources of university academic, social, political and economic history for the Tudor period. Those of Merton College are particularly full for this century. The project will transcribe and publish these accounts. At the same time, a series of articles will describe and evaluate the material they contain and, where possible, link it with that available from other similar educational institutions. The work is expected to show in detail the various problems that Oxford colleges met at this period in their relations with secular and ecclesiastical authorities and to provide some insight into the management of college finance. Since Merton College was an establishment of middle size, with a stable position and well established links with the outside world, this study will also throw light on the role of the educated elite in Tudor society and the reactions of that society to problems of the provision and control of higher education in a world affected by changes of the Renaissance and Reformation.
Published Material: FLETCHER, J.M. & UPTON, C.A. (1983). 'Destruction, repair and removal: an Oxford college chapel during the Reformation', Oxoniensia, No 48, pp.119-130.; FLETCHER, J.M. & UPTON, C.A. (1984). 'A short description of the sixteenth century domestic accounts of Merton College, Oxford'. In: Die Geschichte der Universitäten un ihre Erforschung, Leipzig, pp.54-67.; FLETCHER, J.M. & UPTON, C.A. (1987). 'Monastic enclave' or 'open society'? A consideration of the role of women in the life of an Oxford college community in the early Tudor period', History of Education, No 16, pp.1-9.
Status: Sponsored project
Source of Grant: Economic and Social Research Council; Merton College; British Academy – jointly £5,000
Date of Research: 1980-continuing
KEYWORDS: *educational history; institutional administration; universities*

10/0033
     Aston Triangle, Birmingham B4 7ET
     0121 359 3611
     Fleming, W. Mr; *Supervisor:* Fleetwood-Walker, P. Dr; Townson, M. Dr; Fowler, C. Dr
The training and development of teaching support staff
Abstract: The purpose of this project is to create materials which can be used across the higher education system to enhance the skills and teaching expertise of teaching support staff (TSS) in relation to the courses to which they contribute. The project is a collaborative endeavour between the departments of Staff Development, Vision Sciences and Modern Languages at Aston University. Small group teaching is used extensively in learning languages and optometry and both departments involve practitioners either practising opticians or native speakers, in their courses. The project has a number of phases: 1) Identify current training needs and key management issues. 2) Devise induction and other training programmes and materials. 3) Implementation and evaluation. 4) Revise and refine materials. The materials will be designed to provide support for a variety of activities and functions including: 1) TSS induction to the higher education, the department and teaching roles; 2) TSS recruitment and selection; 3) involving TSS in internal department self-evaluation, audit, quality and teaching initiatives; 4) TSS career development; 5) TSS management issues; and 6) teaching techniques – especially in small groups. The materials will be set within a framework for professional learning and will enable users to identify their own professional learning wants and needs as teachers and select materials to help meet these. The analytical framework of situated learning and legitimate peripheral participation in communities of practice is being used to examine the work of these teacher practitioners and their contribution to student learning.
Published Material: FLEETWOOD-WALKER, P., FLEMING, W., FOWLER, C., TOWNSON, M. (1993). 'Cops and robbers: enhancing the quality of theft'. Proceedings of Fifth International Conference on Assessing Quality in Higher Education. Indiana University – Purdue University Indianapolis, July 1993, pp.113-115.
Status: Sponsored project
Source of Grant: Higher Education Funding Council: Flexibility in Learning Initiative £114,130
Date of Research: 1992-1994
KEYWORDS: *staff development; support staff*

10/0034
     Department of Modern Languages, Aston Triangle, Birmingham B4 7ET
     0121 359 3611
     Young, A. Miss; *Supervisor:* Ager, D. Prof.
Sociolinguistic factors affecting attitudes and motivation in foreign language learning at school: an Anglo-French comparative study
Abstract: This study will attempt to identify the differing attitudes held by English and French school children towards foreign language learning with particular reference to their sociolinguistic environment. The issue will be considered from a sociolinguistic, rather than from a psycholinguistic perspective, giving primary importance to environmental, as opposed to individual factors. In particular, emphasis will be placed upon the differing sociolinguistic environments of the two areas concerned (Mulhouse, France and Walsall, England), in an attempt to shed light upon the linguistic attitudes, orientations and motivation of the children living within these communities and to identify the underlying factors which may consequently affect motivation. Three aspects of the pupils' sociolinguistic environment – parental opinion; peer pressure and the learning environment are believed to exert significant influence and will be given special attention, as it is believed that they play an important role in the formation of attitudes. A structured sample drawn from pupils attending schools in Mulhouse and Walsall will supply the data base for this research. The main thrust of the study will be quantitative in approach, involving the distribution of about 500 questionnaires to pupils in both towns. This will be followed up by the use of qualitative methods, in the form of indepth interviews with an individually matched sample of 50 French/English pupils, whose purpose will be to modify and check the quantitative data.
Status: Sponsored project
Source of Grant: Aston University
Date of Research: 1991-1994
KEYWORDS: *comparative education; modern language studies; pupil attitudes*

Banstead Mobility Centre

10/0035
Damson Way, Orchard Hill, Queen Mary's Avenue,
Carshalton SM5 4NR
0181 770 1151
Ponsford, A-S. Mrs; *Supervisor:* Simms, B. Dr
Learner drivers with cerebral palsy
Abstract: Many individuals with Cerebral Palsy (CP) are unable, or find it too exhausting, to use public transport. Being able to drive, therefore, can help them to achieve independence and enhance the opportunities for both employment and social life. This is confirmed by the results of the current study which considers CP learners and drivers of average cognitive ability. The majority of those who drove were also in employment. Although it is the case that some CP individuals may not be aware of the facilities available for driving ability assessment, it is disappointing that a 1990 report found that only a small number of those who had been assessed had begun tuition. These studies have suggested that the reasons for not beginning tuition include a reluctance to buy a suitable (often adapted) car before tuition and the lack of local experienced driving instructors. The results indicate two areas which need further investigation. The first concerns awareness of facilities for driving assessment amongst the CP population. The second centres on those who are assessed as able to drive, but who do not do so. The proposed study investigates the availability of information regarding driving assessment units, experienced driving instructors and adapted cars based at educational establishments. To obtain a measure of awareness of driving potential, a nationwide survey of 100 young people (16-20 years) with Cerebral Palsy, in further education or vocational training, will be made. The difficulties some potential drivers experience following driving assessment will be explored by face-to-face, semi-structured interviews with 20-30 CP individuals, previously assessed at the Banstead Mobility Centre. By identifying areas of need in relation to driving, it is hoped that the provision of support or facilities in local areas will increase the chances of CP individuals becoming safe and competent drivers.
Status: Sponsored project
Source of Grant: Spastics Society £13,255
Date of Research: 1991-1993
KEYWORDS: *cerebral palsy; driver education*

Bath College of Higher Education

10/0036
Newton Park, Newton St Loe, Bath BA2 9BN
01225 873701
Bristol University, School of Education, 22 Berkeley Square,
Bristol BS8 1JA
01179 303030
Towler, L. Ms; *Supervisor:* Broadfoot, P. Prof.
Profiling in the primary school: extension of self-assessment in primary schools 1989-1991 – collaborative approach to assessment
Abstract: This project investigates the background and issues surrounding the introduction of Records of Achievement, or profiles, to the primary school and, in particular, the principle of involving children and parents as partners, with teachers, in the assessment process. It explores the contribution made by the literature and research into Records of Achievement in the secondary context, in order to develop both a rationale for, and a critique of, self-assessment and examines ways in which these may prove applicable to primary children. The issues examined include the development of skills necessary for effective review and analysis of achievement and the extent to which young children may be empowered through ownership of their profile. The effect of individual differences in respect of age, gender, attainment and culture are also explored, and the implications for school policy on assessment considered. A qualitative case study of the introduction of profiling in one primary school was carried out in order to determine the extent to which children of ten and eleven years may be capable of taking responsibility for their own learning and benefit from involvement in their own self-assessment.

The research also included using questionnaires and interviews, to gain the reaction and response of parents to the introduction of profiles as a method of reporting on achievement and to the request for their involvement in the process. The conclusions drawn indicate that a coherent school policy for assessment, which is supported by the commitment of teachers and parents, can ensure that the principle of assessment as first and foremost the responsibility of the learner is both valid and can be realistically applied in education from the early years.
Published Material: BROADFOOT, P., et al (1991). 'Implementing National Assessment: issues for primary teachers', Cambridge Journal of Education, Vol 21, No 2, pp.153-168.; TOWLER, L. & BROADFOOT, P. (1992). 'Self-assessment in the primary school', Educational Review, Vol 44, No 2, pp.137-151.
Status: Individual research
Date of Research: 1993-continuing
KEYWORDS: *assessment; primary schools; profiles; pupil responsibility; records of achievement; school reports; self evaluation – individuals*

10/0037
Newton Park, Newton St Loe, Bath BA2 9BN
01225 873701
Bristol University, School of Education, 35 Berkeley Square,
Bristol BS8 1JA
01179 303030
Feiler, A. Mr; *Supervisor:* Webster, A. Dr
Support arrangements for primary school children who experience difficulty learning to read – help or hindrance?
Abstract: One aim of this research will be to establish how much help is provided for children with reading difficulties in primary schools and the nature of this help. A related aim will then be to establish the effect that internal and external arrangements for helping such children have on the amount and quality of support provided. In other words does the presence of 'special arrangements' (either internal or external to the school) result in class teachers providing levels of support similar to those before these arrangements were made, more help, or less? A related aim will be to explore the quality of support once help is provided. Does this tend to result in children being given tasks that are less stimulating, where the emphasis is on de-coding and on processing texts for information rather than on reading texts that are imaginative and expressive? It is intended that teachers and children from 6 primary schools will participate in this investigation – which will be carried out by interviewing, observation and analysing school records.
Status: Individual research
Date of Research: 1992-continuing
KEYWORDS: *primary education; reading difficulties; reading teaching; remedial programmes; remedial reading; special educational needs*

10/0038
Newton Park, Newton St Loe, Bath BA2 9BN
01225 873701
London University, Institute of Education, Department of International and Comparative Education, 20 Bedford Way,
London WC1H OAL
0171 580 1122
Coulby, D. Dr; Jones, C. Mr
Urban civic culture and the school curriculum
Abstract: The research identifies two possible directions for curricular systems in the European Community (EC) in the light of developing European Civic Culture. The first of these – the traditional – seeks to identify European achievement in the arts and science and conflate these with human achievement per se. The second – the international – looks to the way in which European achievement in science and the arts has been influenced by forces beyond Europe. It further identifies scientific and artistic achievement entirely beyond Europe. The research seeks to investigate this polarity in curricular in EC countries. It seeks to establish ways in which international views of European civic culture may be encouraged.
Published Material: COULBY, D. (1992). 'European civic culture and education'. In: COULBY, D. & JONES, C. (Eds). (1992). The world yearbook of education in 1992: urban education. London: Kogan Page.; COULBY, D. (1993). 'Cultural and espistemological relativism and European curricula', European Journal of Intercultural Studies, Vol 3, Nos 2/3, pp.7-18.
Status: Individual research

Date of Research: 1991-continuing
KEYWORDS: *cultural activities; curriculum; European Community; sciences*

10/0039
> Newton Park, Newton St Loe, Bath BA2 9BN
> 01225 873701
> London University, Institute of Education, Department of Mathematics, Statistics and Computing, 20 Bedford Way, London WC1H 0AL
> 0171 580 1122
> Harries, T. Mr; *Supervisor:* Sutherland, R. Dr

LOGO and the development of algebraic skills
Abstract: The main aim of the research is to develop an understanding of the algebraic perceptions of pupils who are perceived to be 'low attainers' in mathematics. This involves investigating not only their algebraic perceptions but also their understanding of number and how this understanding can be used to articulate numerical algorithms. Some of the specific questions being investigated are: (1) Is algebraic thinking closed to some of the pupils in our schools or is their lack of understanding more a reflection of the environment in which they are introduced to it? (2) Is the apparent lack of understanding of algebraic symbols due in part to a lack of facility with number? (3) Is it possible to create an environment within LOGO which will enable pupils to explore number, and naturally build up a facility to generalise and use variables? The research is being carried out over a period of 4 terms, with year 8 pupils in one school. The progress of the pupils as they work through a series of activities will be monitored through observation and the use of 'dribble' files. Also there will be regular individual structured interviews.
Status: Individual research
Date of Research: 1992-continuing
KEYWORDS: *algebra; computer uses in education; logo; low achievement; mathematics education*

Bath University

10/0040
> School of Education, Claverton Down, Bath BA2 7AY
> 01225 826826
> Ritchie, R. Mr; *Supervisor:* Denley, P. Dr

Evaluating the effectiveness of a practitioner's use of a constructivist approach for developing scientific knowledge and understanding in primary students during their initial training and primary teachers on inservice courses
Abstract: Implementing the National Curriculum for Science requires primary teachers to develop pupils' knowledge and understanding in science, particularly through exploration and investigation, and assess their progress. For many teachers this is proving difficult because they lack appropriate background knowledge and understanding in science themselves. Recent research (Kruger & Summers, 1989) has confirmed that many primary teachers have no formal qualifications in science. Present recruits to teacher training are not required to have a qualification in science and existing cohorts in institutions include many students with limited scientific backgrounds. Consequently, the training of teachers and successful inservice education of teachers (INSET) requires trainers to adopt approaches that will develop scientific knowledge and understanding in teachers. Considerable research in the secondary sector, and limited research in the primary sector, have shown the importance of adopting a constructivist approach to science education. The purpose of the research is to examine the effectiveness with adult learners of the use of such an approach. Focused observation and analysis of personal practice results in modifications to teaching and evaluation of changes. Effectiveness is assessed in terms of improved knowledge and understanding of scientific ideas. The project will look for evidence of improved understanding and the impact of this on the learning opportunities provided for children in the classroom. Formal and informal methods have been used to validate the research.
Status: Individual research
Date of Research: 1989-1993
KEYWORDS: *inservice teacher education; preservice teacher education; primary education; science education; student teachers*

10/0041
> School of Education, Claverton Down, Bath BA2 7AY
> 01225 826826
> MacPherson, K. Ms; *Supervisor:* Harvey, T. Dr

Curriculum differentiation with special reference to National Curriculum English attainment targets 4 and 5 for pupils with special learning difficulties
Abstract: Current policy is to reduce special needs withdrawal to a minimum. Hence mainstream teachers need to understand and develop strategies for differentiation to help, in particular, special needs and low ability pupils. The aim of the research is to identify and analyse factors which influence the successful implementation of a differentiated curriculum. The research will involve: (a) observation and indepth interviews with teachers of special needs pupils; (b) development and evaluation of strategies; and (c) case studies of particular pupils.
Status: Individual research
Date of Research: 1992-continuing
KEYWORDS: *differentiated curriculum; English studies curriculum; learning disabilities; low achievement; mainstreaming; special educational needs*

10/0042
> School of Education, Claverton Down, Bath BA2 7AY
> 01225 826826
> Jamieson, I. Prof.

Models of progression in teacher placements in industry
Abstract: This is a study of the role of industrial placements in the professional development of student teachers and teachers. A sample of 50 teachers and student teachers at various stages in their careers/courses are being studied in three different locations via qualitative interviewing.
Status: Sponsored project
Source of Grant: Department of Employment £16,000
Date of Research: 1992-1993
KEYWORDS: *industrial secondments; industry education relationship; preservice teacher education; teacher development*

10/0043
> School of Education, Claverton Down, Bath BA2 7AY
> 01225 826826
> Treweek, J. Mr; *Supervisor:* Jamieson, I. Prof.

An investigation into the development of supported self-assessment for core skill requirements in progression routes into higher education
Abstract: Adult returners often without formal qualifications frequently return to learning by entry to GCSE, A or A/S GCE, or by direct entry to higher education (HE). In parallel circumstances in the USA similar students would need to achieve suitable scores in 'minimum competency' tests in reading, composition and mathematics. The aim of the research is to investigate the possibility that there are key/core skills which are basic to success in GCSE/GCE/HE; and to determine whether these can be measured so as to guide students to starting levels needed for returning to learn. It is fundamental to 'adult access' that barriers to returning to learn are minimised and therefore the measuring instrument being investigated and developed will need to be a self-assessment tool, rather than a 'test'.
Status: Individual research
Date of Research: 1991-1994
KEYWORDS: *access to education; adult education; adult learning; basic skills; mature students; self evaluation – individuals*

10/0044
> School of Education, Claverton Down, Bath BA2 7AY
> 01225 826826
> Sweeney, S. Mr; *Supervisor:* Thompson, J. Prof.

Music in the National Curriculum: implications of assessment for pupils, teachers and schools
Abstract: The implementation of a National Curriculum for Music in schools will have significant implications for a subject that is characterised by a wide diversity of practice in relation to teaching and learning styles, and assessment. Assessment being a central feature of the new legislation, this at present is one of the less well developed areas of practice in music education. The research identifies and evaluates, on the basis of materials provided to schools, some of the pertinent issues relating to the assessment of music learning across the five to sixteen age-range. The research includes a review of the

relevant literature, and a survey of existing practice in music education within sixty-three schools in the south and south-west of England. A trial and evaluation of some of the proposed material for the National Curriculum for Music was carried out in eight schools, using case study techniques, involving pupils from across the five to sixteen age-range, with particular reference to composing and notation. Evidence collected during the period of research supports the existence of a wide diversity of practice in schools and it confirms that assessment of pupils' musical development, via the quality of their classwork, is an underdeveloped area of practice. The research suggests that teachers in schools, via the class activities of performing, composing, listening and appraising, should reinforce children's understanding of musical skills and concepts. Assessment will serve as an invaluable vehicle for monitoring and evaluation in this respect.
Status: Individual research
Date of Research: 1989-1993
KEYWORDS: assessment; music education; National Curriculum

10/0045
School of Education, Claverton Down, Bath BA2 7AY
01225 826826
Harris, A. Ms
Experiential learning in higher education
Abstract: In 1991 Universities Funding Council (UFC) funding was obtained to conduct a research project into experiential learning in higher education. The project was initially envisaged as a three year research programme which focused upon the ways in which experiential learning was conceptualised and realised within the specific context of professional training. In the first year it was intended to explore the perceptions of students, tutors and supervisors about the role and purpose of experiential learning in training. It was decided to compare two different areas of professional training which were similar in their professional demands. The areas of teaching and social work were chosen because of the fact that teachers and social workers have to deal continually with unfamiliar, new and complex situations with pupils and clients. The emphasis in both professions is very much upon individual responsiveness to a situation which is immediate and has important repercussions for the learner and the client. The training processes in the courses of teachers and social workers and the understanding of that development by tutors and supervisors comprise the core of this research. Central to this investigation is an examination of the role experience plays in professional learning and development. Consequently, students, supervisors and tutors have been interviewed about their understanding of learning from experience. The first year of the project has mainly focused upon students' pre-experience perceptions and understanding of the training process. In particular it has investigated the types of experiences students' expect to encounter in their professional training and how they think they might learn from these experiences. The relationship between theory and practice has also been explored with students, tutors and supervisors as well as their views on what experiences might assist in the process of professional development.
Status: Sponsored project
Source of Grant: Universities Funding Council £84,000
Date of Research: 1991-1993
KEYWORDS: experiential learning; preservice teacher education; prior learning; social work studies

10/0046
School of Education, Claverton Down, Bath BA2 7AY
01225 826826
Hayden, M. Ms; *Supervisor:* Thompson, J. Prof.
An investigation of the characteristics of international education and associated implications for curriculum development and assessment in an international context
Abstract: Although the concept of the international school has become increasingly familiar in recent years, there is little similarity between schools claiming to be 'international', some of which are simply national schools abroad, while others attempt to offer what they consider to be a truly 'international' education to their students. Much of the literature referring to 'international education' deals with comparative education systems, or with national systems operating away from their home context. This research attempts to define the concept of an international education programme and to identify its characteristics, within the context of the secondary age range, initially by interacting with educators and administrators concerned with international education on a worldwide basis. The initial definition will be tested by using questionnaires and interviews with teachers,

students, school administrators, higher education administrators and admission officers. The research will also be informed on an ongoing basis by long term case studies undertaken within a number of schools which offer 'international' programmes. Ultimately the 'taxonomy of characteristics of international education' developed will be applied in the analysis of a number of programmes currently operating in an international context.
Status: Individual research
Date of Research: 1992-continuing
KEYWORDS: international education; international programmes; international schools

10/0047
School of Education, Claverton Down, Bath BA2 7AY
01225 826826
Coyle, P. Mr; *Supervisor:* Cloke, C. Dr; Richards, P. Dr
Telecommunications in education – an investigation of the factors that contribute to its development
Abstract: While teaching in various forms has been in schools for several decades, recent developments in electronic communication systems have greatly enhanced the possible contribution of telecommunications to education. Experimental systems in this country and overseas have indicated some of the benefits and limitations of global telecommunications – Campus 2000, Global Lab, National Geographic's Kid's Net, BreadNet and the Massachusetts Corporation for Educational Telecommunications (MCET) have all had varying degrees of success. Online systems can quickly link students to remote peers for bi-directional sharing of: knowledge; experience and attitudes; offering immediate access to remote learning resources; and providing a gateway to a world perspective. Teachers also benefit by gaining more and varied information plus resources for implementing student-centred learning. The research is designed to: 1) Review and analyse the potential aims of global communications for education in schools. 2) Determine the relative significance of contributory factors to the effective use of telecommunications in a school's curriculum, in particular to assess the value of: training programmes; technical support; resources; and administrative support. 3) Consider the implications for the curriculum as: a part of students' learning of information technology skills; the use of information technology across the curriculum; and a tool to enhance student learning.
Status: Individual research
Date of Research: 1992-continuing
KEYWORDS: computer uses in education; information networks; information technology; telecommunications

10/0048
School of Education, Claverton Down, Bath BA2 7AY
01225 826826
Fenner, R. Mr; *Supervisor:* Richards, P. Dr
The relationship between learning strategy and learning outcomes from Fire Service command and control simulations
Abstract: The education and training provided by the Fire Service College is closely integrated with the operational work of fire officers and this strongly influences both the curriculum content and the teaching style adopted. It is also extremely wide-ranging, covering such areas as science, technology, operational procedures, command and control, finance, law and personnel matters. The research aims to develop an understanding of the influences that diversity of background and individuals' different attitudes and learning styles have on the outcomes of learning in a command and control module of training. Data will be gathered from up to 100 officers who follow the Intelligent Command and Control Acquisition Review Using Simulation (ICARUS) procedures in a computer-based command and control simulation. The research will involve: 1) Identification of appropriate performance features and individual variations in aptitude and approach. This will involve the literature-based work, observations, discussions and interviews with personnel within and outside the Fire Service, and scrutiny of the extant and ongoing evaluation and development work in the Fire Service College. 2) Use of qualitative and quantitative methods for gathering relevant data and for identifying and analysing relationships between factors. Some of the data-gathering methods will themselves be computer-based. 3) To make recommendations for training procedures including the possibility of pre-training in relation to modes of response.
Status: Individual research
Date of Research: 1993-continuing
KEYWORDS: fire service; learning strategies; professional education; teaching methods

10/0049

School of Education, Claverton Down, Bath BA2 7AY
01225 826826
Bullock, K. Ms; *Supervisor:* Jamieson, I. Prof.; James, C. Dr

A novice-expert study of educational managers

Abstract: The aim of this study is to explore the nature of managerial knowledge in an educational context, and to investigate the ways in which that knowledge is acquired. It is intended that this study will guide the teaching of educational management and indicate areas where deeper investigation is warranted. The research design is to use indepth interview techniques to compare teachers who have just acquired a school management post with teachers who have substantial experience in similar posts. The groups have been carefully selected to represent a range of variables, including seniority, primary and secondary sectors, gender and subject area. Fifteen novice managers have been identified through job advertisements in the educational press and have been interviewed. This group will be matched as closely as possible by expert managers, identified by means of the School of Education's network of partnership and other schools. Specific research questions for both novice and expert managers focus on the development of personal practical knowledge, and concentrate on prior experiences, good and poor role models in education and other work areas, conceptualisation of the management role, and individual perceptions and intentions.

Status: Sponsored project
Source of Grant: Bath University £21,581
Date of Research: 1993-1994
KEYWORDS: *administrators; educational administration; management in education; teacher-administrator relationship*

10/0050

School of Education, Claverton Down, Bath BA2 7AY
01225 826826
Jamieson, I. Prof.; Harris, A. Dr; Chambers, J. Ms

Development of education – business policy and structures

Abstract: Research in schools, colleges and businesses about the most appropriate structures for education-business liaison. The focus is on student learning and cost as two key variables. Data gathering will be via a structured interviewing programme.

Status: Sponsored project
Source of Grant: Lancashire Local Education Authority; East Lancashire Training and Enterprise Council; Lancashire Area West Training and Enterprise Council, jointly £18,500
Date of Research: 1993-1993
KEYWORDS: *industry-education relationship; training and enterprise councils*

10/0051

School of Education, Claverton Down, Bath BA2 7AY
01225 826826
Bullock, K. Ms; Harris, A. Dr; *Supervisor:* Jamieson, I. Prof.

Student action-planning in schools and colleges

Abstract: An evaluation of action-planning (personal development planning) in Wiltshire schools and colleges. The evaluation will use a sample of 500 students drawn from schools and colleges within Wiltshire, focusing on years 11, 12 and 13. There is a small control group. Research is via questionnaires, and interviews of students, tutors, and project organisers. The evaluation is designed to test some of the claims made of action-planning e.g. that it aids career decision making.

Status: Sponsored project
Source of Grant: Wiltshire Training and Enterprise Council £25,000
Date of Research: 1993-1994
KEYWORDS: *career planning; individual development; planning; profiles*

10/0052

School of Education, Claverton Down, Bath BA2 7AY
01225 826826
Al-Alawi, K. Mr; *Supervisor:* Powell, R. Dr; Morgan, C. Dr

The teaching of English as a foreign language at third secondary education in Oman

Abstract: This research represents an attempt to investigate the teaching of English as a foreign language (EFL) in Oman with special reference to: 1) Pupil experience and perceptions of learning EFL; 2) EFL curriculum in relation to the reading materials and reading skills; 3) EFL teachers' methods; 4) EFL teachers' perceptions; and 5) EFL learning difficulties and the possible reasons for these difficulties. For the purposes of this research, questionnaires were designed taking into consideration the above mentioned issues, and administered to 959 pupils (476 males and 483 females) and 80 third secondary EFL teachers (42 males and 38 females). The sample of the present study was randomly selected from 20 secondary schools representing the nine different administrative regions of the Sultanate of Oman. Interviews were carried out with 6 EFL regional inspectors, 2 EFL teacher trainers, 10 Omani EFL teachers, and 3 experts from three different higher education institutions. Within the overall study, there is a case study which attempted to investigate Oman third secondary pupils' reading strategies, and the difficulties they face in reading. For the purposes of the case study, 16 pupils were selected randomly from different third secondary classes at Alkhansa Girls' Secondary School. The study has shown that, contrary to public opinion and teacher assumptions, the Omani third secondary pupils in this research project had a positive perception of the learning of EFL. As the results show, this perception is in part derived from parental recognition of the importance of EFL. The results indicate that there was no significant difference between male and female pupils in their perceptions of learning EFL. The results, however, demonstrated a significant difference between pupils coming from different language backgrounds, their place in secondary streams, and parental knowledge of English. Socio-economic status, as measured by occupation of head of household, appeared to have no effect. Overall, this research suggests that, despite the positive opinions displayed by pupils, their level of achievement in EFL is determined by the challenging nature of the English language itself, the skills they are expected to perform during their courses, by the syllabuses and the materials used, and the teaching methods employed.

Status: Individual research
Date of Research: 1991-1994
KEYWORDS: *English – second language; Oman; second language teaching*

10/0053

School of Education, Claverton Down, Bath BA2 7AY
01225 826826
Graham, S. Mrs; *Supervisor:* Powell, R. Dr; Morgan, C. Dr

Foreign language learning processes in post-compulsory education

Abstract: This investigation examines some of the learning processes undergone by Year 12 students of French and German as they move from the General Certificate of Secondary Education (GCSE) to A-level studies. It focuses on: learners' perceptions of the difficulties they experience at this stage; the learning strategies they employ to overcome such difficulties; the relationship between learning difficulties and learning strategies, and learner variables such as gender, anxiety and motivation; teachers' perceptions of their students' difficulties and the measures they take to ease the transition to A-level work. Following a review of factors affecting foreign language learning, the study presents and analyses data relating to a wide range of students and teachers, gathered by means of a variety of research instruments including questionnaires, learner diaries and retrospective and think-aloud interviews. The data provides insights into some of the differences between individual students and the cognitive and affective processes which seem to facilitate language learning at Advanced Level. Moreover, it emphasises that while students use a broad range of learning strategies, these are not always implemented in the most appropriate manner. The study concludes by making recommendations in terms of learning and teaching strategies, and syllabus design. It suggests that many of the cognitive and affective difficulties experienced by students can be mitigated by more explicit teaching of the proficient use of learning strategies. Above all, it argues for the need to encourage greater reflection among students about their own learning behaviour, in order to promote learning that is truly self-directed and hence more fulfilling.

Published Material: GRAHAM, S. & POWELL, R. (1992). 'From GCSE to A-Level: a natural progression?', Language Learning Journal, September, Vol No 6, pp.62-65.
Status: Individual research
Date of Research: 1991-1994
KEYWORDS: *a level examinations; learning strategies; modern language studies; sixteen to nineteen education*

10/0054

School of Education, Claverton Down, Bath BA2 7AY
01225 826826
Cleves, I. Mr; *Supervisor:* Richards, P. Dr

An examination of the factors affecting the adoption of 'workplace-related' materials in the secondary mathematics classroom

Abstract: During the past several years a variety of 'workplace-related' materials have been produced by a range of agencies. The materials are an attempt to provide resources which, based on and using the inspiration of the workplace, will enthuse both teachers and pupils. They aim to enhance classroom activity, providing a range of 'novel' approaches to make the mathematics studied more relevant to the pupils, and engage them to a greater degree. It is hoped in this fashion to improve the standard of achievement of the pupils. These materials have met with varying degrees of success in both uptake and usage. The aim of this project is to examine the factors that facilitate or inhibit the take-up of such materials. The research will be designed to elicit responses from: 1) teachers and their pupils, the teachers having varying degrees of experience in the classroom, from probationer to head of department; 2) mathematics advisory staff; 3) 'workplace' representatives; from local education authorities (LEAs) in the South-West of England. The group of established teachers will be structured to include some who are undergoing, or have undergone, some form of inservice training aimed at developing their use of this type of material. It is envisaged that twenty to thirty teachers from each of five or six authorities will be sampled, together with a sample of some three hundred pupils.

Published Material: CLEVES, I. (Ed.). (1993). Maths, the school and the workplace: a professional development resource. BP Practical Mathematics Project. BP/Mathematical Association.

Status: Individual research

Date of Research: 1988-continuing

KEYWORDS: educational materials; industry-education relationship; mathematics education

10/0055

School of Education, Claverton Down, Bath BA2 7AY
01225 826826
Abdulraman, A. Mr; *Supervisor:* Scott, W. Dr

Technical and vocational education in the Sudan

Abstract: This research is an attempt to provide a foundation for tackling the problems which hinder the development of technical and vocational education (TVE) in the Sudan. Questionnaires and interviews were used for collecting data which relates to these issues. The sample size was 700 students, 176 staff and 48 higher education staff. The study has revealed: 1) that whilst there are positive perceptions of TVE, parents advise their children against studying it, and 2) that there are wide differences in perception of TVE between students of different ages, and the type of curriculum followed. The results of the research suggest: 1) the reluctance of students to study TVE courses is not due to low perceptions of TVE, but is due to other reasons; 2) the existing secondary school system is the main cause of the high unemployment rate amongst secondary school leavers and the shortage of skilled people in the labour market; and 3) the incorporation of TVE into the secondary school curriculum will make a contribution to the reduction of the high rate of unemployment amongst school leavers.

Status: Individual research

Date of Research: 1990-1994

KEYWORDS: Sudan; technical education; vocational education

10/0056

School of Education, Claverton Down, Bath BA2 7AY
01225 826826
Harris, A. Dr; Russ, J. Ms

A pathway to school improvement: the relationship between equal opportunities and underachievement

Abstract: The aim of the research is to investigate the relationship between equal opportunity and underachievement. Semi-structured interviews will be the main source of data collection and a sample of seven schools from an inner-city will participate. Interviews will be held with the senior management teams, staff, and pupils at each school. The outcome of the research will be an occasional paper outlining the main findings from the study. In addition, there will be a set of materials produced for schools which contain practical examples of strategies which promote equal opportunities and create achievement among pupils.

Status: Sponsored project

Source of Grant: Training, Enterprise and Education Directorate £11,000

Date of Research: 1994-1994

KEYWORDS: academic achievement; equal education; school effectiveness; underachievement; urban schools

10/0057

School of Education, Claverton Down, Bath BA2 7AY
01225 826826
Loxley, A. Mr; *Supervisor:* Jamieson, I. Prof.

The effects of markets and market ideology on the policy and practice of special educational needs

Abstract: The recent changes in educational policy and legislation, most notably the introduction of a quasi-market, created by such mechanisms and structures as local management of schools, pupil-led funding, open enrolment and market information systems, i.e. league tables, has radically altered the structure of English and Welsh education since 1988. The continuing drive towards greater financial and managerial delegation within schools has created an even more problematic situation for special needs than that which previously existed. Compounded by the loss of many services provided by local education authorities (LEAs), schools now have to manage the learning of children with special educational needs (SEN) in an environment which is cash limited. This presents schools with the problem of prioritising the needs of all children and, given that the education of SEN children is marginally more expensive than their 'normal peers', schools now have to provide resources, which were previously centrally controlled, from out of their own budgets. The focus of this research is to analyse and generate theoretical insights in relation to the impact of the above. The methods used in this project are essentially qualitative, which are further linked to the grounded theory methods of Glasser and Strauss. The sample used in the research is that of two junior schools within the south west of England to allow for cross-case comparisons. This is further linked to wider changes that are occurring within the school's LEA, and then contextualised in relation to wider changes at the national level.

Status: Individual research

Date of Research: 1992-continuing

KEYWORDS: educational administration; educational change; educational policy; school-based management; special educational needs; support services

Berkshire County Council

10/0058

Education Department, Strategic Planning and Information Systems, Shire Hall, Shinfield Park, Reading RG2 9XE
01734 233425
Lawrance, R. Mr

Analysis of examination results

Abstract: Information is received from National Consortium for Examination Results (NCER) and examination results are analysed by subject, sex and school and a combination of the three. These are in the form of detailed tabulations and summary measures of performance. Results for examinations taken at different times are matched together to produce overall summaries of attainment. Information on the ethnic origin of candidates is added to the results, which are also analysed by ethnicity. Work on contextualising the results with socio-economic data is underway.

Status: Sponsored project

Source of Grant: Berkshire County Council

Date of Research: 1981-continuing

KEYWORDS: examination results; institutional evaluation; performance indicators

10/0059

Education Department, Strategic Planning and Information Systems, Shire Hall, Shinfield Park, Reading RG2 9XE
01734 233425
Lawrance, R. Mr

Berkshire school pupil forecasting system

Abstract: The objective of the Berkshire school pupil forecasting system is to predict numbers of pupils of each age group in every Berkshire school, for up to 10 years ahead. The basic approach in forecasting is the 'cohort trend' method, where changes observed to cohorts of pupils over previous years are applied in the future. Recent enhancements to the system include: (1) the prediction of primary

school entry (i.e. 5 year old) age pupils by relating intakes to the past and predicted resident population of the school catchment area, using data from the Research and Intelligence Unit's Population Estimation and Projection Models; and (2) prediction of intakes to secondary schools by using data from the Education Department's computerised Secondary School Allocation System. Forecasts are produced annually using pupil numbers in January.
Status: Sponsored project
Source of Grant: Berkshire County Council
Date of Research: 1976-continuing
KEYWORDS: long range planning; prediction; pupil numbers; regional planning

10/0060

Education Department, Strategic Planning and Information Systems, Shire Hall, Shinfield Park, Reading RG2 9XE
01734 233425
Eno, R. Mr; Symonds, G. Mr
Survey of ethnic origin, first language and religion
Abstract: A survey of pupils of specified ages in all schools in Berkshire to identify the ethnic origin, first language and religion of each pupil.
Status: Sponsored project
Source of Grant: Berkshire County Council
Date of Research: 1990-continuing
KEYWORDS: ethnic origins; mother tongue; pupils; religion; surveys

10/0061

Education Department, Strategic Planning and Information Systems, Shire Hall, Shinfield Park, Reading RG2 9XE
01734 233425
Wright, J. Mrs; Lawrance, R. Mr
Survey of individual educational needs
Abstract: Each year a survey of the numbers of pupils in Berkshire with individual educational needs is undertaken. The results are used to help allocate discretionary teaching resources to schools.
Status: Sponsored project
Source of Grant: Berkshire County Council
Date of Research: 1980-continuing
KEYWORDS: individual needs; pupils; special educational needs; surveys

10/0062

Education Department, Strategic Planning and Information Systems, Shire Hall, Shinfield Park, Reading RG2 9XE
01734 233425
Godwin, J. Mrs; Reece, D. Mr
Survey of pupils with language needs
Abstract: Each year a survey of the numbers of pupils in Berkshire in need of additional language support is undertaken. The results are used to help allocate discretionary teaching resources to schools.
Status: Sponsored project
Source of Grant: Berkshire County Council
Date of Research: 1989-1992
KEYWORDS: individual needs; language proficiency; pupils; surveys

10/0063

Education Department, Strategic Planning and Information Systems, Shire Hall, Shinfield Park, Reading RG2 9XE
01734 233425
Lawrance, R. Mr
Survey of disruptive children in Year 1
Abstract: An annual survey of Year 1 pupils to monitor severe disruptive or non-conforming behaviour. The results are used to identify trends and to contribute to the development of effective strategies for dealing with such children.
Status: Sponsored project
Source of Grant: Berkshire County Council
Date of Research: 1993-continuing
KEYWORDS: behaviour problems; discipline problems; disruptive pupils; infant school pupils; primary school pupils; problem children; surveys

Birmingham University

10/0064

Department of Public Health and Epidemiology Medical School, Edgbaston, Birmingham B15 2TT
0121 414 3344
MacArthur, C. Dr; Knox, E. Prof.; Pearson, L. Dr
Stopping smoking in pregnancy and child's subsequent physical and intellectual development
Abstract: The main element of this study is an examination of the long-term effects of smoking during pregnancy on physical and intellectual development. The population is a complete year of antenatal bookings in a large maternity hospital during 1981-1982. The smokers at booking took part in a randomised controlled trial of the effect of anti-smoking health education on birthweight. In this follow-up study the long-term effects of the intervention experiment on the children will be examined. In addition, a comparison will be made of long-term effects in women who stopped smoking some time during pregnancy, compared with those who smoked throughout, and with a sample of the non-smokers. Assessments consist of the children completing a set of British Ability Scales (BAS) appropriate to their age (9-10 years) and a short neurological assessment. A detailed parental interview is completed as well as a short self-completed teachers' assessment form. Around 1800 children comprised the original population at birth and over 1200 have been traced and full assessments completed. Analysis is presently being conducted and the first results of the study will be available in January 1994.
Status: Sponsored project
Source of Grant: Medical Research Council £91,248
Date of Research: 1990-1994
KEYWORDS: child development; cognitive ability; health education; intellectual development; intelligence quotient; pregnancy; smoking

10/0065

School of Continuing Studies, Edgbaston, Birmingham B15 2TT
0121 414 3344
Seeley, M. Rev.; *Supervisor:* Tann, J. Prof.
How clergy learn: a study of formal and informal continuing education of clergy in the Church of England
Abstract: In the past decade there has been a substantial increase in the provision of continuing education courses for Church of England clergy. This has happened with little apparent awareness of the effectiveness of such an approach, or understanding of the nature of clergy learning. The aim of this study is to investigate the factors which facilitate and inhibit clergy learning using the insights of learning organisation theory. The study will consider the nature of formal and informal education among clergy, the role of the structure of the Church of England in relation to patterns of power and value within the Church, the continuing role of social class, the function of theological models, and the changing social profile of clergy.
Status: Individual research
Date of Research: 1993-continuing
KEYWORDS: clergy; continuing education; learning processes; professional education; religious education; theological education

10/0066

School of Continuing Studies, Edgbaston, Birmingham B15 2TT
0121 414 3344
Ross, K. Dr; Bowl, R. Mr
The education and training needs of users of adult services and their carers
Abstract: The aims of this research project were, broadly, to investigate the reality behind the rhetoric of user involvement as outlined in recent legislation such as the Citizen's Charter and the National Health Service and Community Care Act. Explicitly, the project aimed to explore the extent to which users of adult services are encouraged to have a voice in the services they receive, particularly in day centre settings. In addition, the project intended to look at the development of user forums and their effectiveness. The study wanted to identify what education and training needs existed amongst user groups which, if met, would enable users (and carers) to take a more proactive role in the planning and delivery of services. A total of 300 individuals took part in the study and care staff were also

contacted for their views relating to user participation. Informal discussions took place with groups of users about their particular experiences in day-care settings, using informal methods of note-taking, but focusing on the issues concerning users rather than imposing the researcher's own agenda. The project focused on people with physical disabilities, people with learning difficulties and people experiencing mental distress, across three local authority areas in the West Midlands. Key findings include the fact that irrespective of client group or location, by far the most pertinent influence on user empowerment was the specific culture of the day-centre they attended and, more importantly, the management style of the senior staff group. Recommendations of the research include the desirability of providing training opportunities to adult users to encourage greater confidence in participating in decision-making processes.
Status: Sponsored project
Source of Grant: Universities Funding Council
Date of Research: 1992-1993
KEYWORDS: *adult day centres; caregivers; educational needs; services; special educational needs*

10/0067

School of Continuing Studies, Edgbaston, Birmingham
B15 2TT
0121 414 3344
Smith, M. Mrs; *Supervisor:* Tann, J. Prof.
Training and other factors contributing to the well-being of Catholic priests
Abstract: The research takes as its starting point: 1) the shortage of Roman Catholic priests in England, and 2) their increasing age-profile; factors which together increase the pressure on the 'work force'. It asks to what extent the initial and ongoing training of priests facilitates their ministry, and looks in particular at points of transition. The study broadly follows Abraham Maslow's motivation theory based on seven innate needs. Of these, freedom of enquiry and expression, and the need to acquire knowledge and understanding are seen as essential for the other five sets of needs. He thus implies that education, training and personal development are highly important as a means to self-actualisation. This concept is central to the current research in enabling the priest 'to become the priest God wants me to be'. Postal questionnaires have been sent out to all the priests (diocesan and religious) of one diocese – a total of 385 priests. This will yield a database covering initial seminary and ongoing training, educational background, workload, leisure, health, friendships and spiritual life. Indepth interviews with priests at different stages of their ministry, including some involved in specialist ministries, will give a deeper understanding of the processes at work. The analysis will include relationships between education and training, and present levels of stress and satisfaction with the priesthood.
Status: Individual research
Date of Research: 1991-1994
KEYWORDS: *Catholics; clergy; priests; professional education; religious education; theological education*

10/0068

School of Continuing Studies, Edgbaston, Birmingham
B15 2TT
0121 414 3344
Tann, J. Prof.; Ross, K. Dr; Lyon, D. Ms
Vocation, training and the management of transition – the first women priests
Abstract: The vote in favour of the ordination of women to the priesthood taken in Synod in 1992, followed by the approval of both Houses of Parliament in 1993, has opened the way for the ordination of women to the priesthood. The first women to be ordained in 1994 will have entered theological training with no immediate expectation of ordination beyond the deaconate. The women to be priested in 1994 will include those who have been deacons since 1985 when women were admitted to the deaconate as well as those who have been deacons for no longer than their male counterparts. The scope of the project consists of a detailed study of four dioceses, two largely in favour of the ordination of women and two against. In addition, four theological colleges – two which have been admitting women for some time and two which are against the ordination of women, will be studied from the point of view of changes in the curriculum as a consequence of the admission of women to the priesthood. All women priests and deacons in the four selected dioceses will be approached to participate in semi-structured interviews to ascertain their experiences at theological college, in post-ordination training,

in their first curacy. Those responsible for the development of priests and deacons subsequent to theological college will be approached to ascertain the extent to which changes have been made or will be made in the curriculum. In particular, those responsible for continuing ministerial education will be surveyed to ascertain the extent to which changes will be introduced nationally. It is intended that the results of this study will be fed back to those responsible for the education and training of ordinands as well as to those with a concern for change within the Anglican church.
Date of Research: 1994-continuing
KEYWORDS: *priests; professional education; religious education; theological education; women*

10/0069

School of Continuing Studies, Edgbaston, Birmingham
B15 2TT
0121 414 3344
Tann, J. Prof.
Evaluation of a programme of interventions on clinical pharmacy for community pharmacists
Abstract: The project arose out of the recognition that clinical training is needed for community pharmacists to be able, effectively, to extend working relationships with general practitioners (GPs) and to participate in joint liaison groups. It was believed that post-registration clinical pharmacy training, modelled on suitably modified programmes run for hospital pharmacists, was needed. The project commenced with a training needs analysis using a diagnostic workshop technique validated by a telephone survey. This was followed by phase 2 during which training materials on six topics were produced. The evaluation project was designed to: 1) review the appropriateness of the methodology of training needs analysis; 2) review participants' use of and reactions to distance learning materials prepared on two topics; and 3) make recommendations to the project team for subsequent distance learning materials and to assess the overall intervention. The methodology included observation, team meetings, an interim survey and a final telephone survey of all community pharmacists who had participated at some stage in the programme. The evaluation identified important content and process outcomes of the clinical pharmacy interventions. Feedback during the course of the project contributed to increasingly well produced distance learning materials, to effective tutor manuals, and to case studies. The process outcomes included: 1) the development of staff who had been involved in the project; 2) greater confidence and a more proactive approach to clinical practice amongst the participants, together with improved relationships with GPs; and 3) lateral networking with group members. The most important longer term outcome of the intervention was the clinical orientation of the participants.
Status: Sponsored project
Source of Grant: Centre for Pharmacy Postgraduate Education
Date of Research: 1991-1993
KEYWORDS: *clinical experience; distance education; pharmaceutical education; pharmacists; professional training; programme evaluation*

10/0070

School of Continuing Studies, Edgbaston, Birmingham
B15 2TT
0121 414 3344
Tann, J. Prof.
Provision and uptake of training for hospital pharmacists
Abstract: Recent changes in the National Health Service (NHS), particularly the emergence of hospital trusts have produced changes in the provision and uptake of training amongst hospital pharmacists. The project was established to ascertain the range and volume of provision of training and development for hospital pharmacists and the extent to which this range and level have changed since the reorganisation of the NHS. This was considered with reference to the Royal Pharmaceutical Society of Great Britain's Guidance on Continuing Education within Medicines, Ethics and Practice. The scope of the investigation is all hospital pharmacists and senior pharmacy managers in England. The objectives of the study are to: 1) ascertain the context for the provision of hospital pharmacists' training and development; 2) identify the extent to which hospital pharmacists are encouraged to have, and do have, a personal development plan; 3) identify those with a responsibility for, or an interest in, the identification of training needs; 4) evaluate the variance in training and development provision in different units, trusts or regions of England;

and 5) locate impediments to the uptake of training and development. It was an objective to ascertain the extent to which continuing education was discussed with a mentor or line manager. The methods include the design and testing of a questionnaire to be sent to every hospital pharmacist and senior pharmacy manager in England, together with community services pharmacists. The draft questionnaire was approved by a small working party of the Standing Committee on Pharmacy Education, it was circulated to identified interest groups and piloted in a regional health authority before being mailed out nationally. In particular, it is intended to ascertain the extent to which hospital pharmacists seek and have the opportunity to study for higher qualifications, to locate impediments to training and development, and the contribution of training and development to job satisfaction.
Status: Sponsored project
Source of Grant: Department of Health £12,500
Date of Research: 1993-1994
KEYWORDS: *pharmaceutical education; pharmacists; professional training*

10/0071
School of Continuing Studies, Edgbaston, Birmingham
B15 2TT
0121 414 3344
Tann, J. Prof.; Hanson, S. Mr
Evaluation of the introduction of pharmaceutical audit
Abstract: Amongst the National Health Service (NHS) reforms arising from the implementation of the White Paper of 1989, has been the introduction of medical audit for clinicians, general practitioners and nurses. The report of the Joint Working Party on the Future Role of the Community Pharmaceutical Services (1992) recommended the implementation of professional audit within community pharmacy. A working party on audit was established by the Royal Pharmaceutical Society of Great Britain (RPSGB), the recommendation being the concept of self and peer-audit through community and hospital pharmacy. The RPSGB appointed an audit fellow to introduce the concept of audit in pharmacy and simultaneously the Department of Health funded a number of family health services authorities projects on pharmaceutical audit, as well as several in hospitals. The Centre for Pharmacy Postgraduate Education has developed a distance learning module on audit for pharmacists and this has been distributed to all pharmacists in the autumn of 1993. The first named researcher was commissioned by the Department of Health to evaluate community pharmacists' awareness of professional audit and the effectiveness of the separate initiatives indicated above. The scope of the study was England. The project is being conducted in two stages. The first stage consists of a survey of one regional health authority as proxy for the 14 in England, the sample frame being all pharmacists residing within that authority. The objective of the first stage is to ascertain the level of knowledge of audit. The second stage consists of an evaluation of the process and impact of the spread of awareness of audit. This evaluation will explore the extent to which the Department of Health funded projects, and the distance learning package on audit, lead to an increase in awareness and knowledge of audit, and the transfer of that learning to the workplace through the establishment of self-audit and peer-audit as recommended by the RPSGB.
Status: Sponsored project
Source of Grant: Department of Health £50,000
Date of Research: 1993-continuing
KEYWORDS: *peer evaluation; pharmacists; pharmacy; self evaluation – individuals*

10/0072
School of Continuing Studies, Edgbaston, Birmingham
B15 2TT
0121 414 3344
Lyon, D. Ms; *Supervisor:* Tann, J. Prof.
Continuing education and training in Britain and France
Abstract: This project is concerned with the relationship between education and job-related training, and the possibilities for progression in manufacturing companies and the labour market in general. It is a comparative study of Birmingham in the UK and Lyon in France. Thirty face-to-face interviews with a variety of personnel have been conducted in four manufacturing companies in France, and similar fieldwork is expected to be carried out in Britain. This research is particularly interested in the different career paths of men and women, and the factors which may shape them. Training is considered as a factor within this, and as a possible tool for challenging existing inequalities.

Status: Sponsored project
Source of Grant: Universities Funding Council £38,300
Date of Research: 1993-1994
KEYWORDS: *career ladders; careers; equal opportunities – jobs; France; job training; work-education relationship*

10/0073
School of Continuing Studies, Edgbaston, Birmingham
B15 2TT
0121 414 3344
Queen Elizabeth Medical Centre, School of Physiotherapy, Edgbaston, Birmingham B15 2TH
0121 472 1311
Cross, V. Mrs; *Supervisor:* Hicks, C. Dr
Predictors of student learning outcomes in clinical education and their effects on clinical and academic staff/student development programmes
Abstract: For academic institutions involved with education in medicine and allied health professions, clinical education presents the most problematical component of courses. Inconsistency and inequity in the quality of students' learning experiences, lack of validity and reliability in assessment of students' clinical performance, poor standards of clinical teaching and low levels of motivation amongst clinical educators and lack of time and staff devoted to clinical education by clinical managers, all give rise to continuing concern within academic institutions. Central to their concern is the detrimental effect of such findings on student learning outcomes. These outcomes may take the form of performance assessment grades, clinical examination results, patient satisfaction ratings etc. Five groups of individuals exert an influence on clinical education: academic staff; clinical managers; clinical educators; students; and patients. However, development programmes have focused on the assumption that improving the quality of clinical teaching by changing the attitudes and developing the facilitation and teaching skills of clinical educators is the key to improving learning outcomes. The proposed research will investigate the validity of this assumption in relation to undergraduate physiotherapy education. Are the actions and attitudes of clinical educators as pivotal as they have been made to appear? Are other factors equally or more influential in ensuring successful student learning outcomes from clinical education? The aims of the research are to formulate, implement and evaluate a staff/student development programme designed to optimise student learning in clinical education, on the basis of identified best predictors of student learning outcomes.
Status: Individual research
Date of Research: 1993-continuing
KEYWORDS: *clinical experience; medical education; outcomes of education*

10/0074
School of Education, Edgbaston, Birmingham B15 2TT
0121 414 3344
Davies, L. Dr; Harber, C. Dr
School management in conditions of stringency
Abstract: Managers of schools in countries with limited or declining budgets for education face conditions and problems in their institutions which are rarely addressed by conventional educational administration literature. Shortages of resources of all kinds (teachers, training, textbooks, equipment, furniture), levels of pay which can compromise full commitment to the work of teaching, and communication and transport problems may characterise a number of Third World countries as well as some declining First World ones. Together with widely divergent expectations of authority and the role of the headteacher, this may mean that images of school management are called for which are radically different from the models in much administrative theory. There is little systematically collected evidence either about problems faced by schools operating in economically constrained circumstances or about the management strategies which are actually used for coping with them. However, it is probable that the internal reality of very tightly budgeted schools will depart significantly from the prescriptions for 'effective' management found in Western-based management textbooks. The research aims to gather case-study evidence on the reality of school organisation in selected Third World countries. Clearly, there can be no single objective and valid view of how a school operates. Rather, the same features of school organisation will be viewed and assessed by different participants in the process. The research therefore uses qualitative methods to examine the perceptions of key participants

within school management – headteachers, deputies and senior teachers. A cumulative bank of such case studies of schools can develop a grounded theory around themes relevant for future management training. The aim is therefore to encourage portrayal of the real contexts of school life in order to (a) critically challenge the imposition of western based educational administration principles; and (b) derive relevant management images and strategies which do not necessarily rely on full levels of school financing.
Published Material: DAVIES, L. (1990). Equity or efficiency? school management in an international context. London: Falmer Press.; HARBER, C. (1989). Politics in African education. London: Macmillan.
Status: Sponsored project
Source of Grant: Birmingham University
Date of Research: 1990-continuing
KEYWORDS: *developing countries; educational administration; educational environment; educational finance*

10/0075
School of Education, Edgbaston, Birmingham B15 2TT
0121 414 3344
Thomas, H. Dr; Bullock, A. Dr
The funding of schools after the Education Reform Act 1988
Abstract: The principal aims of this study are to: 1) describe and analyse the pattern of resource distribution in local education authorities; 2) examine the change in priorities as the system moves from one method of funding to another; 3) investigate the relationship between the resource priorities of the local education authority and those of the school; and 4) inquire into the rationale of resource decisions. The methods used are: quantitative analysis of local education authority budgetary data; and school level budgetary data.
Published Material: BULLOCK, A.D. & THOMAS, H. (1992). Pupil numbers and school budgets: an exmination of formula allocations to schools of different size. Birmingham: University of Birmingham, School of Education.; THOMAS, H. & BULLOCK, A.D. (1992). 'Local management funding formulae and LEA discretion'. In: SIMKINS, T., ELLISON, L. & GARRETT, V. (Eds). Implementing educational reform: the early lessons. Harlow: Longmans.; BULLOCK, A.D. & THOMAS, H. (1993). 'Comparing school formula allocations: an exploration of some problems'. In: WALLACE, G. (Ed). Local management, central control: schools in the market place. Bournemouth: Hyde Publications.; BULLOCK, A.D. & THOMAS, H. (1993). 'Pupil-led funding and local management funding formulae'. In: SMITH, M. & BUSHER, H. (Eds). Managing schools in an uncertain environment: resources, marketing and power. Sheffield: Sheffield Hallam University.; THOMAS, H. (1994). 'Markets, collectivities and management', Oxford Review of Education, Vol 20, No 1, pp.41-56.
Status: Sponsored project
Source of Grant: Leverhulme Trust £42,000
Date of Research: 1990-1993
KEYWORDS: *educational finance; financial policy; financial support; local management of schools*

10/0076
School of Education, Edgbaston, Birmingham B15 2TT
0121 414 3344
Thomas, H. Dr; Arnott, M. Ms; Bullock, A. Dr
The impact of Local Management of Schools
Abstract: The project aims to describe and analyse the impact of Local Management of Schools (LMS). From a national questionnaire, two follow-up surveys and visits to 40 schools, data have been gathered on a range of issues including: 1) headteachers' perceptions of their changing role, and the benefits and unwelcome consequences of LMS; 2) impact on learning; 3) workload; 4) changes in staffing patterns; 5) changing pupil numbers; 6) formula, finance and budgets; 7) management and planning; and 8) the role of local education authorities and governing bodies.
Published Material: ARNOTT, M., BULLOCK, A.D. & THOMAS, H. (1992). The impact of local management on schools: a source book. Birmingham: University of Birmingham, School of Education.; BULLOCK, A.D., THOMAS, H. & ARNOTT, M. (1993). 'The impact of local management on schools: a view from head teachers', Local Government Policy Making, Vol 19, No 5, pp.57-61.; ARNOTT, M., BULLOCK, A.D. & THOMAS, H. (1993). 'The potential for both disaster and success is great: issues arising from head teachers' attitudes to local management of schools'. In: WALLACE, G. (Ed). Local management, central control: schools in the market place. Bournemouth: Hyde Publications.; WALLACE, G. (Ed). Local

management, central control: schools in the market place. Bournemouth: Hyde Publications.; THOMAS, H. & BULLOCK, A.D. (1994). The impact of local management on schools. Lichfield: Q Ed Publications.
Status: Sponsored project
Source of Grant: National Association of Head Teachers £62,000
Date of Research: 1991-1993
KEYWORDS: *educational change; head teachers; local management of schools; school based management*

10/0077
School of Education, Edgbaston, Birmingham B15 2TT
0121 414 3344
Berry, J. Mr; *Supervisor:* Evans, W. Mr
Genre theory and writing functions
Abstract: The research arises out of current debates about genre theory and its appropriateness to English education. The aim is to examine the theory and its applicability to English classroom situations. Examination of samples of writing done in classrooms in four or five contrasting schools will attempt to establish the number of functions of writing commonly covered by children at National Curriculum Key Stages 1 and 2 in those schools, and whether they can be related to any identifiable genres. Depending on these results, specific teaching ploys might be invented to test genre ideas and apply them to the teaching of writing. The usefulness of the ideas, the need for action (or otherwise) and the nature and outcome of the experiments will be discussed with statements of the National Curriculum (Writing) in mind. Australian genre teaching materials and the experience of Australian self-help groups will enter into the study for consideration and to provide a framework for experiment.
Status: Individual research
Date of Research: 1991-continuing
KEYWORDS: *creative writing; English studies curriculum; literary genres; National Curriculum; writing – composition; writing skills*

10/0078
School of Education, Edgbaston, Birmingham B15 2TT
0121 414 3344
Layton, L. Mrs; *Supervisor:* Upton, G. Prof.
Phonological awareness of nursery-school children
Abstract: The project aims at the development and evaluation of a structured programme of phonological training materials designed to enhance phonological awareness in pre-school aged children in general and in particular those children whose phonological skills are under-developed. The first phase of the project involved assessing the phonological skills of a group of 50 pre-school aged children and a detailed examination of phonological training in a sample of 10 nursery schools. The second phase involves the development of the training pack and the evaluation of its effectiveness. The pack is being designed for use with all children but a particular focus of the study will be on its use with children whose phonological skills are under-developed and who are considered to be at risk of developing a specific learning difficulty. A follow-up of these children is planned two years after the completion of the present study.
Published Material: LAYTON, L. & UPTON, G. (1992). 'Phonological training and the pre-school child', Links, Vol 17, No 2, pp.6-8.; LAYTON, L. & UPTON, G. (1991). 'In my view', Child Education, Vol 68, No 9.
Status: Sponsored project
Source of Grant: Department for Education; Oak Foundation; Via Hereford and Worcester Dyslexia Association £54,000
Date of Research: 1991-1994
KEYWORDS: *nursery schools; phonology; preschool children; preschool education; speech handicaps*

10/0079
School of Education, Edgbaston, Birmingham B15 2TT
0121 414 3344
Shepherson, D. Mr; *Supervisor:* Thomas, H. Dr
Economic decision-making models on non-advanced further education
Abstract: An investigation of the relationship between resource decisions and curriculum decision processes will be examined in the context created by the local authority role in creating a framework for strategic planning, as influenced by the Local Authority Act and the Education Reform Act 1988. At the centre of the analysis will be an opportunity cost model of decision making. It is expected that

quantitative data will be collected reflecting commonly used performance indicators. This will be analysed in the context of qualitative data, based upon interviews, relating to the perceptions of individuals on their valuations of resource and curriculum alternatives.
Status: Individual research
Date of Research: 1989-1993
KEYWORDS: educational finance; educational planning; local education authorities

10/0080

School of Education, Edgbaston, Birmingham B15 2TT
0121 414 3344
Richmond, J. Mr; *Supervisor:* Thomas, H. Dr
Problems and possibilities of managing small secondary schools (circa 400) as a result of the Education Reform Act 1988
Abstract: The Education Reform Act 1988 has implications for the management and size of schools within a local authority, Her Majesty's Inspectorate having suggested that four-form entry schools may be the minimum under Local Management of Schools yet many secondary schools fall below this minimum. In order to examine the problems and possibilities for the management of such schools, the proposed research will be both qualitative and quantitative in approach. Key issues of the 1988 Act will be reviewed and consideration given to the requirements of the Government through the Department for Education and Science, those of the local education authority as well as the needs of small schools themselves.
Status: Individual research
Date of Research: 1990-1993
KEYWORDS: Education Reform Act 1988; local management of schools; school size; small schools

10/0081

School of Education, Edgbaston, Birmingham B15 2TT
0121 414 3344
Ranson, S. Prof.; Thomas, H. Dr; Ribbins, P. Dr
The new government and management of education
Abstract: The implementation of the 1988 Education Reform Act over four to five years provides a unique opportunity to study the emergence of a new system of government for education. This research proposes to develop knowledge and understanding of the new system of government for education. It will focus upon understanding the tension within the new system between its principal characteristics of administrative regulation and public choice and accountability. The research will analyse the emerging patterns of administration (financial staffing and curriculum procedures) and public choice (open enrolment, opting out and accountability systems) in the new system of government as it is implemented. A theoretical model will be developed which seeks to explain the development and change of the new system of government by identifying key factors; their purposes and strategies; their resource ownership and interests; their roles and relationships in the system; patterns of conflict and cooperation; and the emerging structure of power, influence and control. The unique opportunity to study a system as it develops over time requires a longitudinal research design which enables the team to understand 'diachronic' as well as 'synchronic' characteristics of the emerging system. This research intends to clarify types of emergent system of educational government and will enable a study of how the nature of institutional management may be shaped by the context in which they are located. This subsequent study will wish to investigate the effects of the changes on the roles of governors, headteachers and staff, the distribution of educational opportunities and standards of pupil achievement.
Status: Sponsored project
Source of Grant: Economic and Social Research Council £54,000
Date of Research: 1990-1994
KEYWORDS: Education Reform Act 1988; educational administration; educational change; educational finance; grant maintained schools; open entry; parent choice; school-based management

10/0082

School of Education, Edgbaston, Birmingham B15 2TT
0121 414 3344
McCall, S. Mr; Stone, J. Mrs
Moon as a route to literacy for blind children with learning difficulties
Abstract: The project is concerned with investigating the teaching of literacy to blind children with additional learning difficulties. Moon is an alternative to Braille, a tactile code based on a simplified raised line version of the Roman print alphabet rather than on dots. The characters are large and bold and Moon has traditionally found a valuable role amongst elderly blind people, many of whom cannot cope with the demands of learning Braille but go on to read fluently through Moon. There has been very little research done into the question of whether Moon presents access to literacy for blind children with learning difficulties who are unable to manage Braille. Although a few teachers have attempted to experiment with Moon, their efforts have inevitably been hampered by the lack of appropriate material and information and the results of their efforts have not been evaluated. The general aim of the project is to investigate whether Moon offers a viable alternative to Braille in the teaching of literacy to educationally blind children and young people who have additional learning difficulties. Specifically the project will address the following objectives: (1) to investigate current practices in the teaching of reading and writing to blind children with additional learning difficulties; (2) to develop packages of materials for the teaching and learning of Moon; (3) to trial and refine these materials with the assistance of teachers and children from a variety of educational settings; and (4) to evaluate the effectiveness of Moon in developing the literacy of blind children and young people with learning difficulties.
Status: Sponsored project
Source of Grant: Leverhulme Trust £51,000
Date of Research: 1992-1994
KEYWORDS: blindness; Braille; learning disabilities; literacy education; raised line drawings; sensory aids; special educational needs

10/0083

School of Education, Edgbaston, Birmingham B15 2TT
0121 414 3344
Lacey, P. Mrs; *Supervisor:* Upton, G. Prof.
The workings of multidisciplinary teams in special education
Abstract: This is an investigation into the workings of multidisciplinary teams in special education. The emphasis will be on how they function, the amount of collaboration possible, the way in which the curriculum is influenced by such a team and the training necessary for effective cross-discipline work. The main aims for the research are: (1) to investigate the workings of multidisciplinary teams in the field of special education, and (2) to draw together examples of good practice for dissemination through courses and written work. Methods of research will include observation and interview of team members and pupils in schools and local education authorities. Questionnaires will also be used but the main emphasis will be on case studies and accounts. As the Education Reform Act 1988 is likely to have a considerable effect upon the financing of specialist professionals in special education, there will be due emphasis on the changes monitored over the four years given to this research.
Status: Sponsored project
Source of Grant: Birmingham University
Date of Research: 1991-continuing
KEYWORDS: cross curricular approach; special education teachers; special educational needs; support services; team teaching

10/0084

School of Education, Edgbaston, Birmingham B15 2TT
0121 414 3344
Harber, C. Dr; Davies, L. Dr
Educational management in developing countries
Abstract: This is a qualitative research project that uses observation, semi-structured interviews and documentation to explore the realities of school management in developing societies. It pays particular attention to the social, economic, political and cultural context in which schools operate and the ways in which this affects the attitudes and behaviour of key participants including headteachers, teachers, parents and pupils.
Published Material: DAVIES, L. (1990). Equity and efficiency: school management in an international context. London: Falmer Press.; HARBER, C. (1989). Politics in African education. London: MacMillan.; DADEY, A. & HARBER, C. (1991). Training and professional support for Headship in Africa. London: Commonwealth Secretariat.
Status: Individual research
Date of Research: 1990-continuing
KEYWORDS: developing countries; educational administration; educational policy; politics education relationship; school systems

10/0085
School of Education, Edgbaston, Birmingham B15 2TT
0121 414 3344
Merrett, F. Dr
Behavioural approach to teaching project
Abstract: Empirical research has been employed to investigate the kinds of behaviours that teachers find most troublesome and the sort of responses they make to these behaviours. This has been extended to include samples from Hong Kong and Singapore. Packages used to teach teachers' methods of classroom behaviour management based on surveys and on experimental work in primary and secondary classrooms have recently been revised and upgraded. Observational research is now being focused upon the differential response rates of male and female teachers to boys and girls and the effects brought about on pupil on-task behaviour by manipulation of teachers' response ratios (i.e. the ratio between their positive and negative response rates). Another new move is the application of correspondence training to the improvement of pupils' social behaviour at the secondary level.
Published Material: MERRETT, F. & WHELDALL, K. (1990). 'Positive teaching in the primary school', (Research Paper). London: Paul Chapman.; WHELDALL, K. & MERRETT, F. (1991). General manual for the positive teaching packages. Cheltenham: Positive Products.; WHELDALL, K. & MERRETT, F. (1991). Teaching manual for the positive teaching package (primary version). Cheltenham: Positive Products.; MERRETT, F. & WHELDALL, K. (1991). Teaching manual for the positive teaching package (secondary version). Cheltenham: Positive Products.; MERRETT, F. & WHELDALL, K. (1991). 'Teachers' use of praise and reprimands to boys and girls', Educational Review, (in press).
Status: Individual research
Date of Research: 1980-continuing
KEYWORDS: behaviour problems; classroom discipline; classroom management; pupil behaviour; teacher behaviour; teacher-pupil relationship

10/0086
School of Education, Edgbaston, Birmingham B15 2TT
0121 414 3344
Martin, J. Ms; *Supervisor:* Thomas, H. Dr
The effectiveness of schooling and educational resource management
Abstract: This is a national survey of 18 sample scondary schools (both Locally Managed and Grant Maintained) to illuminate aspects of good practice in terms of the relationship between resource management and school effectiveness. This will be followed by selection of 3 case study schools which exemplify good practice in the relationship and where the changed responsibilities and contexts of the school are being used to secure improvement. A concluding analysis will interpret field study material in relation to the characteristics of school reform in England and Wales.
Status: Sponsored project
Source of Grant: Department for Education £45,000
Date of Research: 1992-1993
KEYWORDS: educational administration; educational finance; educational software; resource allocation; school effectiveness

10/0087
School of Education, Edgbaston, Birmingham B15 2TT
0121 414 3344
Lock, R. Dr; Miles, C. Dr
Biotechnology and genetic engineering: pupil knowledge and attitudes
Abstract: The research investigates the knowledge and attitude of General Certificate of Secondary Education (GCSE) students to biotechnology and genetic engineering. Biotechnology and genetic engineering are part of the National Curriculum (key stage 4), and knowledge of these subjects will be important to understand future opportunities for the biology-based industries. A 5 page questionnaire was administered to 188 GCSE students (112 male and 76 female) of mixed ability in 6 schools. Four open questions were asked to examine student knowledge of biotechnology and genetic engineering. Attitudes were investigated using a series of questions where students were instructed to tick the relevant box to indicate the extent of their agreement/disagreement with each statement. The research revealed that: 1) One third of the sample, and more males than females, did not know what biotechnology was, and nearly half of the sample did not give an example of biotechnology. When an example of biotechnology was given, it was more likely to be traditional rather than modern. 2) One third of the sample did not know what genetic engineering was, and nearly half of the sample did not give an example of genetic engineering. 3) There was broad approval of genetic engineering applied to microbes and plants, but a strong disapproval of genetic engineering applied to animals. Females were particularly unsupporting of genetic engineering in animals. 4) When the purpose of genetic engineering was to produce pharmaceutical products, a majority supported its use in microbes, but up to 33% disapproved where farm animals were involved. 5) Many students were uncertain about eating the products of genetic engineering. 6) Internal consistency of attitudes was high. Attitudes were found to be influenced by terminology used in the statements referring to the use of animals. Terms such as biotechnology and selective breeding led to lower levels of student disagreement than phrases such as changing/altering genes.
Published Material: LOCK, R. & MILES, C. (1993). 'Biotechnology and genetic engineering: students' knowledge and attitudes', Journal of Biological Education, Vol 27, No 4, pp.101-106.
Status: Sponsored project
Source of Grant: Birmingham University; Agricultural and Food Research Council
Date of Research: 1992-1994
KEYWORDS: biotechnology; genetic engineering; pupil attitudes; science education

10/0088
School of Education, Edgbaston, Birmingham B15 2TT
0121 414 3344
Chitty, C. Dr; Benn, C. Dr
An investigation into the changing nature and character of the British comprehensive school
Abstract: The research consists of a survey of all existing comprehensive schools, seeking to establish their educational practice and policy over a wide area. The ensuing report will be published in early summer 1995, on the 30th anniversary of the promulgation of circular 10/65 by the then Labour Government of Harold Wilson. The book will be a sequel to 'Half way there' by Caroline Benn and Brian Simon, first published by McGraw-Hill in 1970. The new project will involve sending out a lengthy questionnaire to 4,000 secondary schools followed by an indepth study of a selection of these schools. Only non-selective schools will be included in the survey.
Status: Individual research
Date of Research: 1994-continuing
KEYWORDS: comprehensive schools; secondary schools

10/0089
School of Education, Edgbaston, Birmingham B15 2TT
0121 414 3344
Murdoch, H. Ms; *Supervisor:* Harris, J. Dr
Repetitive motor behaviours in children with sensory impairments and multiple disabilities
Abstract: This study aims to investigate rhythmic motor behaviours in children with sensory impairments, with or without additional disabilities. The premise is that all behaviour is an adaptive response to the perceived environment. This premise will be explored by collecting information on the prevalence, forms and apparent functions of rhythmic behaviours among children with sensory impairments. The study may suggest ways of modifying interactions between children and the environment to make them more functional for the child.
Status: Individual research
Date of Research: 1991-continuing
KEYWORDS: behaviour; deaf blind; disabilities; motor reactions; multiple disabilities; sensory deprivation

10/0090
School of Education, Edgbaston, Birmingham B15 2TT
0121 414 3344
Manning, J. Miss; *Supervisor:* O'Hanlon, C. Dr; Hull, J. Prof.
University applications by students with special needs 1993/1994
Abstract: The application form used by students applying to enter universities in 1993 includes, for the first time, detailed questions relating to special educational needs. Students are asked to indicate the nature of any disability, and to describe any special educational support which might be required. Amongst the disabilities listed are visual impairments, hearing impairments, mobility problems, mental health problems, and others. This information is intended to enable

the receiving university to have a fuller picture of any special needs of its incoming students. The inclusion of the questions also makes it possible, for the first time, to monitor applications to higher education from people who are disabled or have special learning needs. The Leverhulme Trust has now agreed to fund an enquiry into the range and types of disability reported by applicants in relation to the acceptance or rejection of their applications. Patterns or acceptance relating to individual institutions and specific disabilities will be explored. A sample of applicants in various categories will be interviewed in order to acquire knowledge and understanding of the educational significance of particular disabilities for higher education. Samples of most successful, and least successful, applicants will be studied. In particular, students will be interviewed in order to ascertain their understanding of the admissions procedures and its implications for their career decisions. The project report will include case studies derived from the interviews as well as quantitative material. It is anticipated that recommendations will emerge which will lead to an improvement of application policies and procedures.
Status: Sponsored project
Source of Grant: The Leverhulme Trust £25,160
Date of Research: 1993-1994
KEYWORDS: *access to education; disabilities; higher education; special educational needs; student needs; universities; university admission*

10/0091

School of Education, Edgbaston, Birmingham B15 2TT
0121 414 3344
Wade, B. Dr; Moore, M. Dr
Babies into books
Abstract: The pilot 'Bookstart' project (Wade and Moore 1993) showed the benefit of early exposure to books. The 'Babies into Books' project investigates home activities, with a focus on book-sharing. Home-visits, observation, intonational analysis and questionnaire methods seek to discover what differences (if any) there are between a sample (30) of families who received Bookstart packs and a control group (30) who did not.
Published Material: WADE, B. & MOORE, M. (1993). Bookstart in Birmingham. London: Book Trust.
Status: Individual research
Date of Research: 1993-1993
KEYWORDS: *books; early childhood education; early experience; early reading; infants; parent participation*

10/0092

School of Education, Edgbaston, Birmingham B15 2TT
0121 414 3344
Wade, B. Dr; Moore, M. Dr; Pastor, C. Prof.; Berdousi, E. Ms
European perspectives on viewpoints of pupils with special educational needs
Abstract: Published work (Wade, B. and Moore, M. (1993). The experience of special education. Milton Keynes: Open University) reports the views of a sample of New Zealand and British school children with special educational needs. It is argued that information provided by clients on such topics as teachers, lessons, peer groups, parents, and feeling different, is important for providing for pupils with special educational needs using the original questionnaires and sentence completion instruments in translation, comparative studies are being made in Greece (Corinthus) and Spain (Sevilla) with samples of children (80 in each country) in special schools and mainstream classrooms.
Published Material: WADE, B. & MOORE, M. (1993). The experience of special education. Milton Keynes: Open University.
Status: Individual research
Date of Research: 1993-continuing
KEYWORDS: *comparative education; disabilities; mainstreaming; pupil attitudes; special educational needs; special schools*

10/0093

School of Education, Edgbaston, Birmingham B15 2TT
0121 414 3344
Miller, C. Ms; *Supervisor:* Booth, A. Mr
The efficacy of distance education in the professional development of teachers of pupils with speech and language difficulties
Abstract: This project is a case study of an approach to the professional development of teachers working with children who experience speech and language difficulties. Following an investigation of

the needs of the teachers (Miller, 1991), a distance learning course was set up. Through questionnaires, interviews and participant activities the project aims to assess the impact on the teachers' practice, in addition to reviewing the operational systems of the course. Although the main part of the study focuses, in the first instance, on teachers, there are implications for other professionals, and for opportunities for development for mixed professional groups.
Published Material: MILLER, C. (1991). Project to develop a distance learning course for teachers of children with speech and language disorders: final report to the Department of Education and Science. Birmingham: University of Birmingham/HMSO.; MASON, H., MILLER, C. & LOMAS, J. (1993). 'Professional courses at a distance for teachers of children with special educational needs', Open Learning, Vol 8, No 3, pp.46-50.
Status: Individual research
Date of Research: 1992-continuing
KEYWORDS: *distance education; language handicaps; special education teachers; special educational needs; speech handicaps; teacher development*

10/0094

School of Education, Edgbaston, Birmingham B15 2TT
0121 414 3344
British Institute of Learning Disabilities, Wolverhampton Road, Kidderminster, Worcestershire DY10 3PP
01902 850251
Cook, M. Mrs; *Supervisor:* Upton, G. Prof.; Harris, J. Dr
Developing school-based services for children with severe learning difficulties and challenging behaviour
Abstract: The general aim of the project is to improve the quality of school-based services for children with severe learning difficulties who present various forms of challenging behaviour. More specifically it involves: a) collaboration with teachers and care staff in special schools for children with severe learning difficulties in the design and implementation of a range of strategies for the management and amelioration of challenging behaviour in schools; b) monitoring and evaluating different intervention strategies to identify those which can be most effectively employed in schools; and c) developing an in-service training programme which will assist teachers and other staff in working more effectively with children with challenging behaviour. The study is being carried out in two phases. In the first phase five schools are involved in the development of the intervention strategies which will be evaluated in phase two in a further five schools.
Status: Sponsored project
Source of Grant: Mental Health Foundation £62,000
Date of Research: 1992-1993
KEYWORDS: *behaviour modification; behaviour problems; severe learning difficulties; special education teachers; special educational needs; special schools*

10/0095

School of Education, Edgbaston, Birmingham B15 2TT
0121 414 3344
Sandwell Metropolitan Borough Council, Child Guidance Centre, 12 Grange
Road, West Bromwich, West Midlands B70 8PD
0121 553 7411
Bovair, K. Mr; Smith, C. Mr; Watts, P. Mr; *Supervisor:* Upton, G. Prof.
Disruptive behaviour in schools: post Elton Project Sandwell Initiative
Abstract: The aim of this project is to collect quantitative and qualitative data, in order to further illuminate the nature, causes and consequences of disruptive behaviour in schools. An assessment will be made of the impact of the Elton Report (Discipline in schools: the report of the Committee of Enquiry chaired by Lord Elton. Department of Education and Science, 1989) on responses to disruptive behaviour in schools. A detailed examination of developments in one local education authority over a period of one school year will be carried out. The study will combine survey and case study analyses. The consequences of disruption will be examined in terms of school/local education authority responses and subsequent pupil placements.
Status: Sponsored project
Source of Grant: Birmingham University £2,000
Date of Research: 1991-1993
KEYWORDS: *antisocial behaviour; discipline; disruptive pupils; pupil behaviour; pupil placement*

10/0096

School of Education, Edgbaston, Birmingham B15 2TT
0121 414 3344
Sheffield University, Division of Education, Sheffield
S10 2TN
01142 768555
Ulster University, Faculty of Public Administration and
Legal Studies, Coleraine Campus, Cromore Road, Coleraine,
County Londonderry BT52 1SA
01265 44141
Ranson, S. Prof.; Martin, J. Mrs; Nixon, J. Dr; McKeown, P. Ms

The new management of education: a project within the Economic and Social Research Council Local Governance Initiative

Abstract: The radical reconstruction of education since the late 1980s has been designed not only to improve 'a service', but also to play a central role in the wider reform of the polity (in the realm of ideas as well as practice). The post-war world constituted a political order of social democracy based upon the principles of justice and equality of opportunity and designed to ameliorate class disadvantage and class division. Public goods were conceived as requiring collective choice and action. Thus the significance of systems of administration planning (the local education authority) (LEA) and institutional organisation (the comprehensive school). Now these beliefs are called into question. A new political order of neo-liberal consumer democracy is being constituted based upon different principles of rights and choice designed to enhance the agency of the individual. The public (as consumer) is being empowered at the expense of the (professional) provider. Public goods are conceived as aggregated private choices. Individual (negative) freedom will, it is purported, better deliver the goals of opportunity and social change. An education study provides this Initiative with a timely opportunity to examine the emerging patterns of differentiating governance, consumer choice and devolved institutional management in order to test the new benefits of active participation but also the limits of individual choice in the creation of public goods for all. The research seeks to undertake empirical and theoretical analysis which examines the development of school and college management within the emerging patterns of local market formation that increasingly characterises local governance. Any such study will need to examine the kinds of interaction among diverse forms of institution, including colleges as well as schools of different kinds – public, voluntary and private. This research, therefore, intends to focus upon the specific needs of the 14 to 19 age group because they will best illuminate the issues of contextual restructuring, differentiated governance and devolved management that are central to this Initiative. The principal research questions for the study focus upon the triangle of relationships between institutional management, educational consumers, and the pace and extent of market formation: 1) What forms of institutional organisation and management have emerged in the context of this new local governance of internal markets? In what ways will schools and colleges become more entrepreneurial, flexible and responsive to their publics, but also will their policies for admissions, curriculum and pedagogy become more selective and restrictive as they define their distinctive identities and mission in the market? Will the processes of internal management become more participative or more hierarchical in the face of pressures from market competition? What is the changing relationship between the growing power of the customer and the practices of quality management? 2) What governs the pace and extent to which educational consumers take up their new rights and powers in relation to institutions? What rights and choices are exercised and by whom and how? What are the attitudes of consumers towards choice, participation and accountability? What is the relationship between increasing agency within a service and public and political activity generally? 3) What is the impact of market formation upon institutions, provision and the educational experience, opportunities and 'life chances' of different class communities? Who gains and who loses? What understanding can develop of the values and conditions (individual and collective) required for the creation of public goods? What is the necessary balance between individual choice and collective welfare (need) within the public domain. The central task of the research is to enquire whether and how the nature of institutional management, in contexts of advantage and disadvantage, varies according to the market context (the segment) in which it is located. The research strategy will be to create a study which is comparative and longitudinal, allows study of structures and of the meanings through the collation of qualititative and quantitative data.

Status: Sponsored project
Source of Grant: Economic and Social Research Council £107,000
Date of Research: 1993-continuing

KEYWORDS: *educational administration; educational change; educational policy; governance; local education authorities; management in education; politics education relationship*

10/0097

School of Education, Centre for Religious Education
Development and Research, Edgbaston, Birmingham
B15 2TT
0121 414 3344
Hull, J. Prof.; Reeve, J. Miss

Cathedrals through touch and hearing

Abstract: The aim of the project is to explore the problems of presenting architecture to visually handicapped people. Cathedrals in England are being equipped with special facilities including wooden models, ground plans, tactile illustrations, cassette recordings and braille guides. The project was mainly confined to West Midlands cathedrals during 1988/89 but will work in more than 20 cathedrals nationwide during the following years. The work is sponsored by the Archbishop of York.

Published Material: HULL, J.M. (1990). Touching the rock: an experience of blindness. London: SPCK (Society for the Promotion of Christian Knowledge).; HULL, J.M. (1990). 'On being a whole body seer: an epistemic condition for the education of the blind', British Journal of Visual Impairment, pp.62-63.; HULL, J.M. (1990). 'The God of the blind', The New Beacon, Vol 74, No 877, pp.200-204.; REEVE, J. (1991). 'Keeping in touch with cathedrals', British Journal of Visual Impairment, Autumn.
Status: Sponsored project
Source of Grant: Industrial and charitable sources £162,179
Date of Research: 1986-1993
KEYWORDS: *architectural education; blindness; educational equipment; special educational needs; visual impairments*

10/0098

School of Education, Centre for Religious Education
Development and Research, Edgbaston, Birmingham
B15 2TT
0121 414 3344
Hull, J. Prof.

The education of the church and the pleasures of capitalism

Abstract: The project has to do with the education of the religious consciousness of adults under the conditions of industrial modernity and late capitalism. The approach is multi-disciplinary, drawing particularly upon sociology, social psychology and theology to create an understanding of the barriers to religious maturity for modern adults. Special emphasis is placed upon ideology and false consciousness, and resources are being drawn from Marxist and Freudian theory (critical theory).

Published Material: HULL, J.M. (1983). What prevents Christian adults from learning? London: SCM Press.
Status: Individual research
Date of Research: 1985-1994
KEYWORDS: *adult education; capitalism; Christianity; church and education; religious education; secularisation*

10/0099

School of Education, Centre for Religious Education
Development and Research, Edgbaston, Birmingham
B15 2TT
0121 414 3344
Hammersley, P. Rev.; *Supervisor:* Hull, J. Prof.

Rigidity and loss: a study in adult religious education

Abstract: Men and women training for Readership in the Church of England, in six dioceses of the West Midlands, on a two year part-time training programme 1991-93, have completed a battery of test instruments relating to their openness to new theological learning. A second cohort, 1993-95, is now being studied. Subjects who register at the extremes of a 'rigidity' test instrument are being individually interviewed, in order to test the hypothesis that rigidity in adult theological learning is related to loss, or fear of loss, originating at earlier points of the lifecycle. The impact of the Readership training programme upon the attitudes of these men and women will also be studied.

Status: Sponsored project
Source of Grant: Diocese of Worcester and Yapp Education Trust £3,100
Date of Research: 1990-continuing

KEYWORDS: church and education; religious education; theological education

10/0100

School of Education, Research Centre for the Education of the Visually Handicapped, Edgbaston, Birmingham B15 2TT
0121 414 3344
Hull, T. Mr; Mason, H. Mrs

The speed of tactile information processing in blind pupils

Abstract: The project aims to produce and standardise a tactile version of an existing psychometric test, and investigate its use with the educationally blind population. The researchers have produced a tactile version of the Speed of Information Processing scale of the Differential Ability Scales (which is a test of speed of scanning numbers and small diagrams), transcribed the numeric parts of the test into Braille, and produced a tactile facsimile of the diagrams. The resulting test has been standardised on the blind population of Britain and Ireland, the results published and the test made available to any interested parties. The test appeared to be viable for use with this population, with the exception of the portions involving diagrams, which did not convert well to tactile presentation and hence had a high failure rate. The second phase of the project, from September 1992 until August 1994, seeks to develop an alternative version of this part of the test which will be easier to complete, especially for children with other difficulties in addition to their blindness. The standardisation of this test is continuing, and the final report will be written in the summer of 1994.
Published Material: HULL, T. & MASON, H.L. (1992). Speed of information processing in blind pupils: administration and scoring instructions. Birmingham: University of Birmingham.; HULL, T. & MASON, H.L. (1993). 'Issues arising from the standardisation of psychometric tests on the blind population', Journal of Visual Impairment and Blindness, Vol 87, No 5, pp.149-150.; HULL, T. & MASON, L. (1993). 'The Speed of Information Processing Test for the blind in a tactile version', British Journal of Visual Impairment, Vol 11, No 1, pp.21-23.; HULL, T. & MASON, H.L. 'The conversion of a psychometric test for use with the blind', Educational Psychology in Practice. (in press).
Status: Sponsored project
Source of Grant: Leverhulme Trust £85,000
Date of Research: 1990-1994
KEYWORDS: blindness; tactual perception; tactual visual tests; tests; visual impairments

10/0101

School of Education, Research Centre for the Education of the Visually Handicapped, Edgbaston, Birmingham B15 2TT
0121 414 3344
Tobin, M. Dr; Hill, E. Mrs

Visually impaired people in their mid-twenties: educational, vocational, and personal ambitions and needs

Abstract: This research forms part of a project concerning young visually handicapped people and those over the age of 60. It is a five year investigation into the changing skills, abilities, ambitions, life styles, and needs of such people with a visual handicap. The methodology consists of postal questionnaires, telephone and face-to-face interviews. Initially a core group of some 50 to 100 subjects will be assembled. The sample will be increased from time to time to deal with specific, ad hoc topics of concern to the population of visually impaired people.
Published Material: TOBIN, M.J. & HILL, E. (1990). 'The ageing process and visual disability: investigating change', The New Beacon, Vol LXXIV, No 881, pp.381-385.; TOBIN, M.J. & HILL, E. (1992). 'Blindness in later life', The New Beacon, Vol LXXVI, No 894, pp.1-4.
Status: Sponsored project
Source of Grant: Guide Dogs for the Blind Association; Royal National Institute for the Blind; Birmingham University
Date of Research: 1990-continuing
KEYWORDS: aspiration; life style; skills; special educational needs; visual impairments; vocational education

10/0102

School of Education, Research Centre for the Education of the Visually Handicapped, Edgbaston, Birmingham B15 2TT
0121 414 3344
Hull, T. Mr; *Supervisor:* Humphreys, G. Prof.; Riddoch, M. Dr

The nature and development of spatial processing in blind children and young adults: an approach based on the use of tactile maps

Abstract: This project has examined the ability of blind children and young adults to perceive and process spatial information derived from tactile maps and graphics. It consists of seven experimental studies, covering the basic skills necessary for map reading, an examination of subjects' mental models of the layout of a map, and tests of both spatial and verbal short term memory (STM). The concept of tactile-spatial STM, for which a new test is developed, is explored in terms of its development with age, the effects of mental rotation and possible representational systems which might underlie it. A successful attempt is made to improve STM by the use of mnemonics. The results of this project have implications both for theory and for the practice of designing tactile maps.
Published Material: HULL, T. (1992). 'Children's understanding of tactile maps'. Proceedings of the Ninth Quinquennial Conference of the International Council for the Education of the Visually Handicapped. Bangkok, Thailand, 1992.; HULL, T. & MASON, H.L. 'The development of short term memory in blind children', Journal of Visual Impairment and Blindness. (in press).
Status: Individual research
Date of Research: 1990-1993
KEYWORDS: blindness; maps; memory; raised line drawings; spatial ability; tactile adaptation; visual impairments

10/0103

School of Education, Research Centre for the Education of the Visually Handicapped, Edgbaston, Birmingham B15 2TT
0121 414 3344
Tobin, M. Dr; Greaney, J. Dr; Hill, E. Mrs

Reading by the blind: Braille and Moon

Abstract: A series of experiments are being undertaken on various aspects of tactile reading by blind children and adults. Experimental comparisons are being made among alternative letter shapes with the aim of producing a more legible tactile code for older adults and for those with poor tactual ability. For Braille, measurements are being made of Braille reading speed, accuracy, and comprehension among blind school children; experimental comparisons are also being made to evaluate alternative 'papers' on to which Braille can be embossed. Trials are also being conducted on methods to enable sighted adult volunteers to teach reading and writing of Moon-type to newly-blinded adults.
Published Material: COOPER, A., DAVIES, B.T., LAWSON-WILLIAMS, N. & TOBIN, M.J. (1985). 'An examination of natural and synthetic papers for embossing Braille', The New Beacon, Vol LXIX, No 823, pp.325-328.; TOBIN, M.J., BURTON, P., DAVIES, B.T. & GUGGENHEIM, J. (1986). 'An experimental investigation of the effects of cell size and spacing in Braille – with some possible implications for the newly-blind adult learner', The New Beacon, Vol LXX, No 829, pp.133-135.; TOBIN, M.J. & HILL, E.W. (1989). 'Harnessing the community: Moonscript, the Moon-writer and sighted volunteers', British Journal of Visual Impairment, Vol VII, No 1, pp.3-5.
Status: Sponsored project
Source of Grant: Birmingham University; Royal National Institute for the Blind
Date of Research: 1985-continuing
KEYWORDS: blindness; Braille; reading teaching; sensory aids; tactile adaptation; tactual perception

10/0104

School of Education, Research Centre for the Education of the Visually Handicapped, Edgbaston, Birmingham B15 2TT
0121 414 3344
Bozic, N. Mr; Douglas, G. Dr; Gamble, A. Mr; *Supervisor:* Tobin, M. Dr

Development of microcomputer software for educational and vocational applications (for blind and partially sighted persons)

Abstract: The Research Centre has a programme of individual research and development projects concerned with using and adapting microcomputer technology to allow visually handicapped children and adults to have access to databases, educational materials, and word processing systems. Software has been developed so that output can be produced in Braille, large print, computer graphics and synthetic speech. Details of software are provided by means of regular newsletters, information sheets, and software documentation, all of which is available on request from the Research Centre.

Published Material: SPENCER, S. & ROSS, M. (1988). 'Visual stimulation using microcomputers', European Journal of Special Needs Education, Vol 3, No 3, pp.173-176.; TOBIN, M.J. & HILL, E. (1992). 'Microcomputers in education: their use by blind and partially sighted learners', Computer Education, No 70, pp.30-31.; BOZIC, N. (1992). 'Talking grass: a database for visually impaired children', Visability, No 4, p.9.; BOZIC, N. (1993). 'Text to braille translation programs', Visability, No 7, pp.20-22.; A full list of publications is available from the researcher.
Status: Sponsored project
Source of Grant: Royal National Institute for the Blind; Blatchington Court Trust
Date of Research: 1983-continuing
KEYWORDS: *blindness; computer-assisted reading; computer software; computer system design; educational materials; partial vision; visual impairments*

10/0105
School of Education, Research Centre for the Education of the Visually Handicapped, Edgbaston, Birmingham B15 2TT
0121 414 3344
Tobin, M. Dr
Longitudinal investigation of cognitive development and educational achievement in blind and partially sighted children
Abstract: This investigation, begun in 1973, aims to monitor aspects of the psychological and educational development of blind and partially sighted children attending special schools for the visually handicapped in England and Wales. The sample of 120 is estimated as constituting some 47% of the age group, the visual activities of the children ranging upwards from nil to 4/36 plus (as measured on the Snellen chart). The subjects are tested at least once every year by the researcher and a team of assistants. Among the major variables being measured are: (1) print and Braille reading; (2) mathematics attainment; (3) short-term memory; (4) verbal and non-verbal reasoning; (5) speed of information processing; (6) various 'Piagetian' constructs; (7) personality and self-concept. Degree of residual vision, cause of visual defect, age of onset and social class constitute some of the major independent variables.
Published Material: TOBIN, M.J. (1979). 'A longitudinal study of blind and partially sighted children in special schools in England and Wales', Insight, Vol 1, No 1.; TOBIN, M.J. (1987). 'Special and mainstream schooling: some teenagers' views', The New Beacon, Vol LXXI, No 837, pp.3-6.; TOBIN, M.J. & HILL, E. (1988). 'Visually impaired teenagers: ambitions, attitudes and interest', Journal of Visual Impairment and Blindness, Vol 82, No 10, pp.414-416.; TOBIN, M.J. & HILL, E. (1989). 'The present and the future: the concerns of visually impaired teenagers', British Journal of Visual Impairment, Vol 7, No 2, pp.55-57.; TOBIN, M.J. (1993). 'The educational implications of visual impairment'. In: FIELDER, A.R., BEST, A.B., & BAX, M.C.O. The management of visual impairment in childhood. London: MacKeith Press.
Status: Sponsored project
Source of Grant: Birmingham University; Royal National Institute for the Blind
Date of Research: 1973-continuing
KEYWORDS: *academic achievement; blindness; cognitive development; longitudinal studies; outcomes of education; partial vision; special schools; visual impairments*

10/0106
School of Education, Research Centre for the Education of the Visually Handicapped, Edgbaston, Birmingham B15 2TT
0121 414 3344
Birmingham University, Department of Ophthalmology, Birmingham and Midland Eye Hospital, Church Street, Birmingham B3 2NS
0121 236 4911
Dorn, L. Dr; Ross, S. Dr; *Supervisor:* Tobin, M. Dr; Fielder, A. Prof.
The development of neonates and young blind and visually disabled children
Abstract: The project aims: to develop methods of investigating perceptual, cognitive, social, and motor skills of severely visually impaired neonate and young children; and to test hypotheses about the infants' self-initiated behaviour and responsiveness to stimulation.
Published Material: DORN, J. (1993). 'The mother/blind infant relationship: a research programme', British Journal of Visual Impairment, Vol 11, No 1, pp.13-16.

Status: Sponsored project
Source of Grant: Economic and Social Research Council
Date of Research: 1992-continuing
KEYWORDS: *blindness; child development; infants; visual impairments; young children*

10/0107
School of Education, Research Centre for the Education of the Visually Handicapped, Edgbaston, Birmingham B15 2TT
0121 414 3344
Greaney, J. Dr; *Supervisor:* Tobin, M. Dr
Development of a Braille reading test
Abstract: To develop a new Braille reading test for visually impaired children. There are currently three published tests for measuring Braille reading skills. These are now somewhat out-of-date in terms of content and it is intended that the updated test will furnish teachers with information about the speed, accuracy, and comprehension abilities of Braille readers. In addition, diagnostic information will be provided that may be helpful in indentifying weaknesses in reading skills.
Status: Sponsored project
Source of Grant: University of Birmingham; Royal National Institute for the Blind
Date of Research: 1993-continuing
KEYWORDS: *blindness; Braille; reading tests; visual impairments*

10/0108
School of Psychology, Edgbaston, Birmingham B15 2TT
0121 414 3344
Stones, E. Prof.
Psychology and pedagogy: investigations into the relationships between principles of psychology of human learning and practical teaching and the supervision of practical teaching in teacher training
Abstract: The work comprises a variety of investigations by experienced teachers into different aspects of pedagogy and employing different approaches. Qualitative as well as quantitative data are sought for. Surveys of current practice are complemented by empirical work exploring the effects of theory based practical pedagogical intervention into the teaching of a wide variety of subjects. Experiments are predominantly naturalistic, clinical, learning based and outcome-oriented case studies involving small groups of teachers or student teachers and their pupils.
Published Material: STONES, E. (1984). Supervision in teacher education: a counselling and pedagogical approach. London: Methuen.; STONES, E. (1987). 'Teaching practice supervision: bridge between theory and practice', European Journal of Teacher Education, Vol 10, No 1, pp.67-69.; STONES, E. (1989). 'Pedagogical studies in the theory and practice of teacher education', Oxford Review of Education, Vol 15, No 1, pp.3-15.; STONES, E. (1992). Quality teaching: a sample of cases. London: Routledge.
Status: Individual research
Date of Research: 1983-continuing
KEYWORDS: *educational theories; learning theories; psychology; teacher education; teaching experience; teaching practice; teaching process*

Bishop Grosseteste College

10/0109
Newport, Lincoln LN1 3DY
01522 527347
Prenton, K. Mr; *Supervisor:* Moore, J. Dr
Improving the quality of primary teaching in third world countries: an analytical evaluation of a World Bank-funded inservice teacher training programme in Sindh Province, Pakistan
Abstract: Since July 1992, the researcher has worked on an Overseas Development Administration (ODA) funded teacher training programme (the British Government's contribution to the World Bank sponsored Sindh Primary Education Development Project), which involves developing a pilot inservice training programme in teacher training and supervision, to equip master trainers for running courses to improve the skills of teachers. The project also involves identifying criteria for evaluating teaching performance in order to be able to

evaluate the effectiveness of the training courses. The aims of the research are: 1) To identify those features of primary teaching which are educationally effective in the Pakistan context in terms of: a) retention of pupil numbers and levels of attendance; b) raising levels of literacy; and c) meeting the aims of the curriculum. 2) To incorporate those features identified into a teacher training programme, intended to increase teacher effectiveness in terms of (a), (b) and (c). 3) To identify methods of evaluating changes in teachers' teaching approaches and professional behaviour resulting from the teacher training courses. The practical part of the research is intended to be eclectic. Some research will be experimental but much will be in the action-research tradition. The purpose of the researcher's role in Pakistan is essentially interventionist. In developing a teacher education programme, the need is to continually reflect upon and evaluate the effectiveness of the courses that are organised. The research aims to identify and evaluate good primary teaching and classroom practice which is effective in the local context. It is then intended to disseminate this 'good practice' through inservice teacher training. The courses will be continually evaluated through both quantitative and qualitative research methods including: questionnaires, pre/post tests, case study observation, and interviews. Before and after the courses, it is planned to observe samples of classroom practice, using local researchers to observe up to 100 teachers. This collection of data will include both open and structured observation as well as interviews and questionnaires where appropriate. These will be analysed and assessed against agreed performance criteria. Performance of trained teachers will be compared with a control group of teachers at intervals. The research will also encompass a review of other teacher training and primary education projects in Pakistan and in other developing countries.
Status: Individual research
Date of Research: 1992-continuing
KEYWORDS: developing countries; educational improvement; inservice teacher education; Pakistan; primary education; programme evaluation

10/0110
Newport, Lincoln LN1 3DY
01522 527347
Leeds University, School of Education, Leeds LS2 9JT
01132 431751
Bates, R. Dr; *Supervisor:* Shorrocks, D. Dr; Beard, R. Dr
Children's writing strategies in the early years of schooling
Abstract: This is a classroom based study which explores young children's uses of drawing, talking, question generation, note-making and the use of a matrix grid as pre-text-forming planning strategies for writing in the early years of schooling. It also considers the linguistic choices that they make, and the particular difficulties that they face when composing in non-chronological modes. The study is set against the theoretical frameworks of the nature of written composition as revealed especially by cognitive analyses of writing behaviours, and models of primary school writing development. Data were collected from two groups of pupils in small rural primary schools in neighbouring Midlands local education authorities (LEAs); and analysis demonstrated marked differences in the favoured composing behaviours of individual children. The study would seem to indicate that young children's abilities to write continuous texts in non-chronological modes may have been underestimated; but that the current emphases on drawing, talking and some structured forms of prewriting activities may not in fact be so straightforward or so useful as many other studies of early writing would seem to suggest. The study concludes by suggesting that these findings have important implications for the nature of the support that is offered to young children whilst they are learning to write; and especially in view of the now legal requirements of the National Curriculum for English at key stages 1 and 2 which make use of the distinction between chronological and non-chronological writing.
Status: Individual research
Date of Research: 1984-1992
KEYWORDS: prewriting; writing – composition; writing research; writing skills; young children

10/0111
Newport, Lincoln LN1 3DY
01522 527347
Liverpool University, Department of Education, PO Box 147, Liverpool L69 3BX
0151 794 2000
Hopkins, S. Dr; *Supervisor:* Harlen, W. Prof.; Thomas, D. Mr

Teaching and learning science in the primary school: towards a model of reflective pedagogy
Abstract: The purpose of the study was to develop a model of teaching which could be used by teachers and student teachers as an heuristic for helping them to improve classroom practice through the process of reflection. A model is developed which provides a conceptualisation of the relationship between teachers' and student teachers' knowledge, actions and the process of reflection-on-action. According to this model teachers and student teachers 'act' within the classroom context in ways which are determined by their knowledge of the influences which affect successful teaching and learning and in response to their perception of 'cues' which act as indicators of the successfulness or unsuccessfulness of the teaching/learning process in the classroom. The study describes the research programme which was undertaken in order to arrive at: the indicators used by teachers and student teachers to judge the successfulness and unsuccessfulness of primary school teaching/learning episodes devoted to science; the factors which they perceived as influencing these indicative pupil responses. The research was also aimed at comparing the teachers and the student teachers as groups in order to derive insights into possible consequences for teacher training programmes. A research instrument was developed to gather data from 150 teachers and 150 student teachers. Data-reduction resulted in a set of indicator and influence categories. The frequency of category use by the teachers and the student teachers enabled chi-squared values to point towards significant differences between them. The findings suggest that the model of reflective pedagogy developed in the study has potential as a heuristic for supporting teachers' deliberative thinking about classroom teaching and learning. The comparison between teachers and student teachers with regard to their use of indicators and their influence constructs suggests possible implications for teacher education programmes.
Status: Individual research
Date of Research: 1986-1992
KEYWORDS: heuristics; learning processes; primary education; teaching methods

Bolton Institute of Higher Education

10/0112
School of Education and Health Studies, Chadwick Campus, Chadwick Street, Bolton BL2 1JW
01204 28851
Phillips, T. Dr; Farrel, V. Mr; Ross, R. Ms; Norman, M. Ms
Patterns of teaching and learning in the post-compulsory sector of education in the 1990's
Abstract: Over the past ten years there have been some very basic changes in the curriculum for the post-compulsory sector of education. One immediate consequence of this is a need for some examination to be made of the kinds of teaching that may now be found in this sector, these may be new or a development on what has gone before. The issue comes into sharp focus when teacher trainers are engaged in supervising teaching practice and find their students engaged in many activities in the name of teaching which traditional notions of teaching has not prepared them for. This project will seek to open up this area for conceptualising with observational studies playing an important role. The proposal is for an initial study at Bolton which might hopefully pave the way for a larger project later with other providers of post-compulsory education teacher training. The aims are: (1) to carry out a small scale survey of patterns of teaching and learning characteristics of work in contemporary post-compulsory education; and (2) to review literature on conceptions of teaching and learning that may be adequate to describe such patterns.
Status: Sponsored project
Source of Grant: Bolton Institute of Higher Education £5,000
Date of Research: 1991-1993
KEYWORDS: further education; open education; teaching methods

10/0113
School of Education and Health Studies, Chadwick Campus, Chadwick Street, Bolton BL2 1JW
01204 28851
Ross, R. Ms

Case study of Accreditation of Prior Learning (APL) in further education

Abstract: One of the objectives of the National Council for Vocational Qualifications (NCVQ) is to encourage and enable previous learning to be accredited against national standards. This process is known as Accreditation of Prior Learning (APL). The aim of the project is to look at current practices within a small cross section of further education institutions, compare their various systems and contrast these with traditional methods of assessment and accreditation. The research will be conducted through interviews and observation. It is envisaged that the results will help to: (1) identify good practice; (2) highlight any problem areas; and (3) determine the effect of APL procedures on the role of the tutor.
Status: Sponsored project
Source of Grant: Bolton Institute of Higher Education £1,200
Date of Research: 1992-1993
KEYWORDS: *achievement; assessment; experiential learning; further education; National Vocational Qualifications; prior learning*

10/0114

School of Education and Health Studies, Chadwick Campus, Chadwick Street, Bolton BL2 1JW
01204 28851
Harris, R. Mr; Roberts, R. Ms
Learning support in further education
Abstract: The term 'learning support' is being used for various types of provision in further education colleges. Initial investigation suggests that the term is used in different ways to reflect different sizes and types of systems. This project aims to: (1) investigate the different meanings given to and usage of the term learning support in colleges; (2) explore the scale and organisation of learning support systems; and (3) map out strategies for further development. A two stage approach has been developed for the investigation. Stage 1 is a postal questionnaire to managers and coordinators of 'learning support' provision in further education colleges to gain a picture of organisation, coverage, management and funding. Stage 2 is an indepth series of interviews with personnel in selected colleges based on data obtained in Stage 1. Through analysis of this material the intention is to identify common themes, note significant differences, and draw out appropriate models of practice.
Status: Sponsored project
Source of Grant: Bolton Institute of Higher Education £4,500
Date of Research: 1993-1994
KEYWORDS: *further education; special educational needs; support services*

10/0115

School of Education and Health Studies, Chadwick Campus, Chadwick Street, Bolton BL2 1JW
01204 28851
King, J. Mr; Kenny, C. Miss
The use of CD ROM in the curriculum in further and higher education: students' attitudes and perceptions
Abstract: CD ROM applications are increasingly being used in further and higher education institutions to enable students to research material for assignments. This initial study aims to identify the asttitudes of students to using this method of investigation and also to elicit from the students whether they use different search strategies with CD ROM applications than they do with paper based material. A sample of 200 students on further education and higher education courses will be used in the initial study. For the initial investigation a free response questionnaire will be used to elicit differences in search strategies and a variation of Osgood's semantic differential table will be used to ascertain attitudes to CD ROM use. Following the initial study it is intended to extend the work to other sample groups to ascertain whether there are differences according to the course being followed. In addition, the research will examine to what extent staff setting assignments are taking expected differences in search strategies into account when deciding on assessment criteria.
Status: Sponsored project
Source of Grant: National Council for Educational Technology £1,500
Date of Research: 1992-1993
KEYWORDS: *further education; higher education; information retrieval; information systems; optical data discs; search strategies; student attitudes*

10/0116

School of Education and Health Studies, Chadwick Campus, Chadwick Street, Bolton BL2 1JW
01204 28851
Fisher, K. Dr; Pearson, M. Dr
In pursuit of quality delivery for new vocational qualifications: an exploratory study of trainers' perspectives on aspects promoting and inhibiting quality
Abstract: The aim of this small scale research project is to elucidate attributes which are facilitating and inhibiting the delivery of high quality training. A considerable amount has been written about 'quality' and about its importance and attainment in training processes, especially in relation to training designed to meet national standards. While theoretical models and policy statements are necessary ingredients in training design, it is also essential to explore the operationalisation of those models and statements in training delivery. Through semi-structured interviews with trainers delivering National Vocational Qualifications (NVQs), and General National Vocational Qualifications (GNVQs), it is proposed to obtain trainers' perceptions of 'quality' and what contributes to, and detracts from, it during the training process. Thus, from the data gathered, quality indicators will be presented and a strategy for identifying high quality provision for NVQs and GNVQs will be suggested.
Status: Sponsored project
Source of Grant: Bolton Institute of Higher Education
Date of Research: 1993-continuing
KEYWORDS: *educational quality; national vocational qualifications; performance indicators; vocational education*

10/0117

School of Education and Health Studies, Chadwick Campus, Chadwick Street, Bolton BL2 1JW
01204 28851
Sheffield University, Division of Education, 388 Glossop Road, Sheffield S10 2JA
01142 768555
Whittaker, J. Mr; *Supervisor:* Quicke, J. Dr
The effective inclusion of students described as having severe learning disabilities within the mainstream of further education
Abstract: Increasing numbers of students described as having severe learning disabilities have been enrolled in colleges of further education over the last ten years. The Education Reform Act 1988 reinforced this trend by putting an obligation on local education authorities, for the first time, to 'have regard' for such students over the post-compulsory school leaving age. The response by the further education sector has been to continue with segregated models of provision – separate groups of students placed together under the heading of 'learning disability', and new curriculum designed and delivered solely for students so described. The main aim of this piece of research is to develop an effective instrument for evaluating the effectiveness of further education provision for students who have been described as having severe learning disabilities and highlight ways in which the existing mainstream provision might be adapted for the benefit of all students. Significant features to be considered in the further education sector will include: (1) Personal destinations of students. Eight students described as having severe learning disabilities. Using, when necessary, 'Citizen Advocacy' and 'Self Advocacy' to facilitate more effective communication. (2) Evaluation instrument. Designing an instrument for effective evaluation of provision within this sector of education. Evaluations took place in three colleges. (3) The role of support staff. Questionnaires and interviews with 'support workers' during two residential periods. (4) Teacher education. 'The Inclusive Education Option'. A model used with two cohorts of student teachers during 2 one-year courses, to raise awareness of issues relating to 'learning disability'.
Published Material: WHITTAKER, J. (1991). 'Three surprising ways of impeding the integration of students with special needs in further education and how inclusive education can help on this', The Vocational Aspect of Education, Vol 43, No 3, pp.225-230.
Status: Individual research
Date of Research: 1989-continuing
KEYWORDS: *further education; mainstreaming; severe learning difficulties; special educational needs; support services*

Bradford University

10/0118
Access Unit, 12 Claremont, Bradford BD7 1DP
01274 733466
Neville, C. Mr; *Supervisor:* Murray, R. Dr; Glandon, N. Dr
Experiences of male students on Access courses in West Yorkshire
Abstract: The research is concerned with the experiences of male students on Access Courses in West Yorkshire. It will highlight the backgrounds, motivations and experiences of study, as well as future career aspirations of 124 male students. The experiences of male students will be compared with those of female Access Course students. The research used questionnaires and follow-up discussions with respondents. Initial findings suggest that 1 in 10 of both male and female students are seriously isolated from the support of their immediate family.
Published Material: NEVILLE, C. (1993). 'Lost for words: developing core skills', Journal for Access Studies, Vol 8, No 2, pp.265-273.
Status: Individual research
Date of Research: 1991-1994
KEYWORDS: *access programmes; higher education; mature students; men; student experience*

10/0119
Centre for Continuing Education, 12 Claremont, Bradford BD7 1DP
01274 733466
Field, J. Dr
Lifestyle, values and educational participation among adults
Abstract: Most studies of participation in adult education focus upon socio-economic and demographic factors, such as social class, age or gender. However, participation rates also vary widely within categories, and this study is concerned to discover whether lifestyle patterns can be related to educational participation among the adult population. Two major methods will be used to explore the extent to which educational participation can be explained with reference to life cycle patterns. They are: (a) surveys of adult learners in personal development courses and in craft-based courses, using an established lifestyle analysis; and (b) semi-structured interviews to explore the degree of inner-directedness within adult learners' value systems, and to investigate the role of material factors in influencing decisions to participate. Outcomes will be analysed using a conceptual framework that will draw upon the work of Pierre Bourdieu as well as of market research theorists and critics of post-modernist sociology.
Published Material: FIELD, J. (1991). 'Out of the adult hut: Institutionalisation, individuality and new values in the education of adults'. In: RAGGATT, P. & UNWIN, L. (Eds). Change and intervention: vocational education and training. London: Falmer Press.
Status: Individual research
Date of Research: 1992-1993
KEYWORDS: *adult education; life style; participation*

10/0120
Centre for Continuing Education, 12 Claremont, Bradford BD7 1DP
0274 733466
Field, J. Dr
National Vocational Qualifications – the industrial relations implications
Abstract: The research is exploring the implications of the workplace context for the implementation of the National Vocational Qualifications (NVQs) system. It is particularly concerned with identifying the perceptions and behaviour of key actors: trades unions; personnel managers; human resource developers and trainers; supervisors; and assessors. The intention is to establish the extent to which the sociology of the workplace determines the nature of the implementation process, and establish whether any distortion of policy goals has occurred as a result.
Published Material: FIELD, J. (1991). 'Competency and the pedagogy of labour', Studies in the Education of Adults', Vol 22, No 1.; FIELD, J. & WELLER, P. (1992). 'Trades unions and NVQs', The Industrial Tutor, Vol 6, No 1.; FIELD, J. 'The industrial relations implications of NVQs', The Industrial Tutor, (in press).
Status: Individual research
Date of Research: 1991-1994

KEYWORDS: *industry education relationship; national vocational qualifications; work attitudes; work education relationship*

10/0121
Centre for Continuing Education, 12 Claremont, Bradford BD7 1DP
01274 733466
Jowitt, J. Mr
Lifelong learning – the cultural constraints on the development of a learning society in the UK
Abstract: This study will analyse the role that business, the public sector and other institutions are playing in the development of learning situations, in particular the development of support for non-vocational education and training. The analysis will rest on a series of qualitative interviews with firms and the public sector in two regions of the UK (Yorkshire – Humberside and East Anglia) with a small amount of comparative work in other member states of the European Community.
Published Material: JOWITT, A. (1992). 'Science parks, academic research and economic regeneration'. In: HILPERT, U. (Ed). Regional innovation and decentralisation. London: Routledge.
Status: Sponsored project
Source of Grant: Universities Funding Council £30,000
Date of Research: 1992-1993
KEYWORDS: *access to education; adult education; continuing education; lifelong learning*

10/0122
Centre for Continuing Education, 12 Claremont, Bradford BD7 1DP
01274 733466
Allen, S. Prof.; Mitchell, G. Dr
Drop-out rates among potential and existing first year undergraduates
Abstract: Drop-out rates are assuming a growing importance throughout higher education as the pressure to expand student numbers and provide learning experiences of high quality increases. However a satisfactory methodology by which such rates can be monitored needs to be devised. This project has two major objectives. The first is to monitor drop-out rates within the University of Bradford, the second is to test possible methodologies by working on a sample of drop-out students in the same institution. The sample includes the following categories: those who gain a place, but reject it; those who accept a place but do not appear; those who drop-out within the first year. It will utilise and review existing data from 1990 onwards which is held centrally in registry and in departments. It will also test questionnaires, face to face and telephone interviews as a means by which information relating to the specific reasons for drop-out can be gathered.
Status: Sponsored project
Source of Grant: Bradford University £1,500
Date of Research: 1992-1994
KEYWORDS: *dropout research; dropouts; enrolment; higher education; student behaviour*

10/0123
Centre for Continuing Education, 12 Claremont, Bradford BD7 1DP
01274 733466
Allen, S. Prof.; Mitchell, G. Dr
The role of the personal tutor in relation to the needs of students from non-traditional backgrounds
Abstract: The University of Bradford aims to widen access to its full-time and part-time courses. To this end, a number of support services for students are provided, including the allocation of a personal tutor for all undergraduates. This study concentrates upon the roles and responsibilities of such tutors, particularly in relation to full-time and part-time studies from groups normally under represented in higher education. It focuses selectively upon departments drawn from the Boards of Studies in Engineering, Social Sciences and Natural and Applied Sciences. Data was collected from questionnaires sent to 90 personal tutors and a proportion of student views were elicited by the same means.
Status: Sponsored project
Source of Grant: Bradford University £2,125
Date of Research: 1991-1993
KEYWORDS: *access to education; higher education; nontraditional education; student counselling; student health and welfare*

10/0124

Centre for Continuing Education, 12 Claremont, Bradford BD7 1DP
01274 733466
Friedrich-Schiller University, Jena, Germany
Ruhr University, 4630 Bochum, Germany
Jowitt, J. Mr; Hilpert, U. Prof.; Eichener, V. Dr
Economic restructuring and social marginalisation: education, training and skills – Anglo-German comparisons
Abstract: An Anglo-German comparative study of the educational and training responses to economic restructuring. By this is meant the decline or demise of staple industries with large scale structural unemployment; the development of new industries requiring less labour but of a more highly skilled nature; the development of service industries requiring a greater proportion of seasonal, part-time or casual workers. The study will take 3 areas – Bradford in West Yorkshire, Jena in Thuringer and the Ruhr, and examines: (1) changes in schooling associated with economic objectives; (2) developments in post-school vocational education; (3) provision of retraining; (4) changes in workplace education; and (5) initiatives aimed at developing a learning culture.
Status: Sponsored project
Source of Grant: Anglo-German Society
Date of Research: 1992-1994
KEYWORDS: *comparative education; economic change; economics-education relationship; Germany; industry-education relationship; structural unemployment; training; work-education relationship*

10/0125

Centre for Continuing Education, 12 Claremont, Bradford BD7 1DP
01274 733466
University of Wroclaw, Institut Pedagogiki, 50 527
Wroclaw, Poland Field, J. Dr; Malewski, M. Dr
Citizenship and consumer culture in the education of adults
Abstract: Citizenship is being redefined across Europe, and its educational implications are controversial conceptually and politically. Building on earlier studies of self-directed learning in citizen movements of various kinds in the UK and Sweden, the project is now exploring the balance between citizenship and consumerism as influences upon the formal adult education system. The study will explore both the institutional and the participants' perspectives on educational activities. The increasing role of the market in determining education provision will be studied in the context of both teachers' and learners' value systems and lifestyles. Outcomes are being analysed using a conceptual framework that draws upon the work of Pierre Bourdieu as well as of market research and of neo-Weberian criticisms of post-modernist sociology. The work is being undertaken in both the UK and in Poland at present. However, the project is also part of the research network on citizenship and adult education of the European Society for Research into the Education of Adults.
Published Material: FIELD, J. (1991). 'Out of the adult hut: institutionalisation, individuality and new values in the education of adults'. In: RAGGATT, P. & UNWIN, L. (Eds). Change and intervention: vocational education and training. London: Falmer Press.
Status: Individual research
Date of Research: 1992-1994
KEYWORDS: *adult education; citizenship; comparative education; consumer economics; educational policy; Poland*

10/0126

Management Centre, Emm Lane, Bradford BD9 4JL
01274 733466
McClements, R. Mr; *Supervisor:* Gilding, D. Dr; Peacock, A. Dr
Learning resource centres for executive development
Abstract: This project will develop and evaluate different forms of flexible delivery of management education, that allow structured self-learning. A pilot 'Learning Resource Centre' will be established with an industrial partner. The project will study: (1) the place of student centred learning in the management development process; (2) the design and production of suitable modules of learning material; (3) the 'learning and technology' required; (4) the physical facilities needed; (5) the management of learning resource centres; (6) effectiveness of multimedia.
Status: Sponsored project
Source of Grant: Bradford University £60,000
Date of Research: 1991-continuing
KEYWORDS: *educational media; learner-centred methods; learn-*

ing resources centres; management development; management studies; multimedia approach

10/0127

Management Centre, Emm Lane, Bradford BD9 4JL
01274 733466
Marsland, J. Mr
Comparison of examination results of Business Studies students who have/have not intercalated a year to see if the extramural experience affects results
Abstract: This research is a comparison of the results of courses run by the Management Centre at Bradford University. For several years the department has run both traditional and 'sandwich' undergraduate courses in parallel. Direct comparison of results from the two is difficult since the syllabuses are not identical. However, in recent years an appreciable number (10-15%) of the three-year course students have voluntarily intercalated a year of industrial experience. Examination marks and degree classifications will be examined to see whether performance in the final year of the course is affected by the break for practical experience.
Status: Individual research
Date of Research: 1989-continuing
KEYWORDS: *attendance patterns; business education; course evaluation; examination results; outcomes of education; sandwich courses; undergraduate study*

Brighton University

10/0128

Chelsea School Research Centre, Gaudick Road, Eastbourne BN20 7SR
01273 600900
Lee, M. Dr
Ethical issues in sport: measurement of values in sport
Abstract: This research is carried out as part of an ongoing project sponsored by the Sports Council and conducted within the framework of the Council of Europe which aims to investigate standards of conduct and the prevailing values in children's sports. The Council has previously commissioned a bibliography and review of English language literature dealing with fair play in children's sports which was delivered in September 1989. This document places values as the central construct in determining attitudes and behaviour, and clarifies the notion of values and the difficulties associated with identifying them. The purpose of the research is to identify instruments which have commonly been used to assess values in society in general and to evaluate their use within the sports field, secondly, to deduce principles for the development of an instrument to measure values in sport. The major emphasis is placed upon the Rokeach Value Survey which is described in detail and used as a basis for the evaluation of further instruments. These include the Webb Professionalisation Scale, Colberg's Measurement of Moral Judgement, Zavalloni's Multi Stages Identity Enquiry and Triandis' Antecedent-Consequent Method of establishing attitude values. Sport specific research which is considered includes cognitive developmental theory as applied by Breidemeier and Kroll's Scaling of Sports Ethics. Recommendations for future research are proposed and plans for a coordinated research strategy across Europe are outlined. Four reports have been produced for the Sports Council: Ethical aspects of sport; The measurement of values; Identification of values in young football and tennis players; and Measurement of value systems in young athletes.
Status: Sponsored project
Source of Grant: Sports Council £23,300
Date of Research: 1989-continuing
KEYWORDS: *ethics; sports; sportsmanship; values*

10/0129

Chelsea School Research Centre, Gaudick Road, Eastbourne BN20 7SR
01273 600900
Whitehead, J. Dr
The generalizability of achievement orientations across young people's success and failure experiences in sport
Abstract: The first study of subjective achievement orientations in sport (Ewing, 1981) employed the critical incident method, in which

subjects recall a subjective success experience, in order to avoid experimenter bias in defining success. Subjective achievement orientations were then determined by factor analysis of Likert items, which subjects responded to with reference to the critical incidents they had selected. However, Ewing did not report the correspondence between the critical incidents and the Likert ratings, and it is unclear to what extent a subject-selected meaningful incident relates to a goal perspective which generalizes across different sporting experiences. The present study, conducted with 890 subjects in middle and upper schools, explores the relationship between Ewing's ability, mastery, social approval and sportventure orientations, and subjects' critical incidents and attributions for success and failure. Differences in age and gender sub-groups are reported, and recommendations made for improved methodology and further research.
Published Material: WHITEHEAD, J. (1993). 'Why children choose to do sports or stop'. In: LEE, M.J. (Ed). Watching children in sport: principles and practices. London: E. & F.N. Spon.; WHITEHEAD, J. 'Multiple achievement orientations and participation in youth sport: a cultural and developmental perspective', International Journal of Sports Psychology. (in press).
Status: Individual research
Date of Research: 1992-1993
KEYWORDS: achievement; failure; motivation; sports

10/0130
Chelsea School Research Centre, Gaudick Road, Eastbourne
BN20 7SR
01273 600900
Whitehead, J. Dr
Development of a questionnaire on multiple goal perspectives in youth sport
Abstract: Maehr and Nicholls (1980) proposed that success is a state of mind, dependent on people's perceptions that they have reached their goals, and their attributions for achieving them. On theoretical grounds they suggested the existence of three achievement orientations: task mastery; demonstrations of ability; and social approval. Subsequent research has confirmed the existence of these orientations in sport, and the present study has developed from previous work with samples of 890, 1198 and 1273 young people aged 9 to 16 years. Exploratory and confirmatory factor analyses have been employed to construct an instrument which assesses 6 goal perspectives: ability; victory; task mastery; breakthrough; social approval; and teamwork. Further work is currently in progress to improve the reliability of the scales for different age groups.
Published Material: WHITEHEAD, J. (1992). 'Toward the assessment of multiple goal perspectives in children's sport'. Conference proceedings of Olympic Scientific Congress, Malaga, Spain.
Status: Individual research
Date of Research: 1994-1994
KEYWORDS: achievement; sports

10/0131
Chelsea School Research Centre, Gaudick Road, Eastbourne
BN20 7SR
01273 600900
Wood, S. Mrs; *Supervisor:* Fleming, S. Dr; Tomlinson, A. Prof.
The physical education curriculum in higher education: a study of the gender dimensions of socialisation in the physical education profession
Abstract: The study will analyse the socialisation processes in the gender relations of the professional practice of physical education (PE) teacher's educators. Part of the investigation will be of the socialisation into sport that physical education/sports students experience prior to their entry into higher education, and the way in which these experiences affect students' abilities to recognise and challenge gender stereotyping in their own sports experiences. A further consideration will be the impact of coeducational training upon physical education professional practice, particularly for women and physical education students in initial teacher education. Information will be gathered through: questionnaires to a cohort of first year students entering teacher training in physical education; through interviews with selected women students and school physical education teachers; and participant observation in coeducational and physical practice and in informal interaction.
Status: Individual research
Date of Research: 1993-continuing
KEYWORDS: physical education teachers; preservice teacher education; socialisation; teacher educators

10/0132
Faculty of Education, Sport and Leisure, Falmer, Brighton
BN1 9PH
01273 600900
Blake, M. Mrs;
Supervisor: Bolwell, L. Dr
An investigation into the role of guidance and counselling for students in higher education
Abstract: The aims of the investigation are to: (1) critically analyse the theory and practice of guidance and counselling for students in higher education through a review of the pertinent literature; (2) identify and examine the practice of guidance and counselling through a case study of selected practice at Brighton University; (3) construct a taxonomy of guidance and counselling practices and thus to inform the theory of counselling as it relates to the experience of students in higher education.
Status: Individual research
Date of Research: 1993-continuing
KEYWORDS: educational guidance; higher education; student counselling

10/0133
Faculty of Education, Sport and Leisure, Falmer, Brighton
BN1 9PH
01273 600900
Bolwell, L. Dr; Allen, J. Miss
Mentorship in schools
Abstract: This is the monitoring and evaluation of a mentorship scheme managed by Essex Local Education Authority and accredited jointly by the Universities of Brighton, Greenwich, Anglia and Homerton College, Cambridge. Semi-structured interviews will be conducted in sample primary and secondary schools. The results will be published in a final response to Essex County Council and in appropriate journals.
Published Material: ALLEN, J. et al. (1993). Video: mentorship in secondary schools. Brighton: University of Brighton.
Status: Sponsored project
Source of Grant: Essex Local Education Authority £5,000
Date of Research: 1994-1994
KEYWORDS: mentors; teacher development; teacher education; teacher induction

10/0134
Faculty of Education, Sport and Leisure, Falmer, Brighton
BN1 9PH
01273 600900
Austin, S. Mr; *Supervisor:* Fox, C. Dr; Laing, S. Dr
Collaborative narrative discourse in the primary school: what happens when children write collaboratively?
Abstract: The aim of this research is the observation and analysis of the processes and outcomes of collaborative written and oral utterances within the framework of narrative. It will compare and contrast the strategies adopted in various models of collaborative and individual discourse creation. Evidence will be collected from children of pre-school age, together with children in Reception classes, Year 1, Year 2, Year 4, Year 5, Year 6, and Year 7 in local primary, first and middle schools in West and East Sussex. Work by children working as individuals, in pairs, in small groups, and larger units will be used to investigate the journeys that their writing, and their tellings, take towards a point where they feel satisfied with a product that they themselves regard as finished. The research is naturalistic and ethnographic, based in active classrooms, during ongoing work, and related to the social context inside and outside the school, with the researcher as the teacher. The title and mode of analysis are based on Genette's 'Narrative Discourse'.
Status: Individual research
Date of Research: 1991-continuing
KEYWORDS: children as writers; group work; narration; primary school pupils; story telling; writing – composition

10/0135
Faculty of Education, Sport and Leisure, Falmer, Brighton
BN1 9PH
01273 600900
London University, Institute of Education, Department of English and Media
Studies, 20 Bedford Way, London WC1H 0AL
0171 580 1122

Martin, W. Ms; *Supervisor:* Dombey, H. Dr; Kress, G. Prof.; Fox, C. Dr
A study of linguistic coherence within young children's role play
Abstract: This investigation is based on audio and video recordings of Nursery, Reception and Year 1 children engaging in voluntary social role play, showing a wide variety of themes being played out. It will examine how in each episode of role play, the players create a new text, locating themselves flexibly in positions deriving from their knowledge of discursive practices. It will seek to characterise the linguistic coherence of such role play episodes and to examine the processes whereby that coherence is achieved. It will consider how in the play language is used as a tool, medium and resource for creation, rather than as a static, neutral reproduction of perceived role speech: role play is not just about events, but about how they are made to happen. This research will examine the ways in which players may construct roles for themselves and others, considering: the presumption or imposition of shared knowledge; the control of the developing storyline; the relationship between the 'duality of contexts' of play and not play; the threads of power, solidarity and resistance running through the play. It will recognise that the play observed takes place in school: there may be less jockeying for position in sibling play at home.
Status: Individual research
Date of Research: 1991-1994
KEYWORDS: language usage; role playing; young children

10/0136
Faculty of Education, Sport and Leisure, Falmer, Brighton BN1 9PH
01273 600900
London University, Institute of Education, Department of English and Media Studies, 20 Bedford Way, London WC1H 0AL
0171 580 1122
Evershed, J. Mr; *Supervisor:* Fox, C. Dr; Kress, G. Prof.; Dombey, H. Dr
The expression of a range of discursive roles and positions in young children's voluntary pretend play
Abstract: The aim of the investigation is to discover and describe the functions and meanings of particular discourse features in the role play between children; to explore in particular children's apperceptions of social practices in creating, sustaining and delimiting a range of power relations in the course of pretend play. The children to be studied will be in the age range 4 to 6 years. Observations of play will occur within the confines of Nursery and Reception class Home Corners. Data collection will be by means of tape recordings made of play, these being transcribed for analysis. Where appropriate video recording will be used to incorporate the use of gesture and body language where this is deemed to be important. Field notes will be taken of context, situation etc. as a necessary tool for the interpretation of tape recordings and transcripts. An approach deriving from social semiotics will be followed in the analysis of data.
Status: Individual research
Date of Research: 1991-1994
KEYWORDS: language usage; role playing; young children

10/0137
Faculty of Education, Sport and Leisure, Falmer, Brighton BN1 9PH
01273 600900
Sussex University, Institute of Continuing and Professional Education, Falmer, Brighton BN1 9RH
01273 606755
Ashenden, C. Ms; *Supervisor:* Bastide, D. Mr; Yates, P. Dr; Modgil, S. Dr
Christianity and the primary school
Abstract: An ethnographic study of Christianity as experienced in contemporary communities, to critique the presentation of Christianity in primary schools. The rationale arises out of concern about the teaching of Christianity in primary schools. The problem of teaching Christianity is seen as follows: 1) Religious Education (RE) has been widely neglected, but has attracted attention since the Education Reform Act 1988. 2) Presentation of Christianity within RE is narrow and marginalised – Christianity is largely restricted to Biblical studies and festivals, neglecting practices and beliefs of contemporary Christians. 3) There is widespread misunderstanding that the purpose of teaching Christianity is confessional. Consequently, the subject is either neglected or taught implicitly with over emphasis on moral

development. 4) It is more difficult to present Christianity phenomenologically, because of the cultural proximity of teachers and pupils. In order for teachers to represent Christianity as a world religion, i.e. as experienced in community and conceived of as a cultural form, the researcher is carrying out an ethnographic study of 3 diverse Christian communities. The methods used are participant observation and indepth interviews. The purpose of this is to describe contemporary Christianity as it is understood by its adherents.
Status: Individual research
Date of Research: 1991-1994
KEYWORDS: Christianity; primary schools; religious education

Bristol University

10/0138
School of Education, 35 Berkeley Square, Bristol BS8 1JA
01179 303030
Grant, M. Dr; Came, F. Mr; Bowker, P. Mr; Noble, J. Mrs
Special educational needs and the GCSE
Abstract: The programme of research and development work reviewed the efficacy of existing General Certificate of Secondary Education (GCSE) provision for pupils with special educational needs and low-attaining pupils, and showed how better access to assessment and certification could be achieved. In September 1991, the project was expanded to include approaches adopted by a sample of examining bodies, other than GCSE examining groups, to provision made for pupils with special educational needs. Methods used included a questionnaire survey of 55 mainstream schools in England and Wales; interviews in 30 special schools; interviews with a range of representatives of examining groups, examining bodies, special educational needs (SEN) interest groups/interested parties and indepth research and development work in two case study local education authorities (LEAs). The research report identified developments in practice which have improved opportunities for pupils with special educational needs to gain accreditation at 16+. The report was accompanied by support materials designed to provide techniques and procedures through which teachers and examiners could monitor and improve aspects of their assessment strategies. The project centred upon five National Curriculum subjects: English; mathematics; science; technology; and geography.
Status: Sponsored project
Source of Grant: School Examinations and Assessment Council £340,000
Date of Research: 1991-1993
KEYWORDS: assessment; examinations; General Certificate of Secondary Education; low achievement; special educational needs

10/0139
School of Education, 35 Berkeley Square, Bristol BS8 1JA
01179 303030
Osborn, M. Ms; Black, E. Ms
Delivering the National Curriculum at key stage 2: the implications for primary schools
Abstract: The general aim of the study is to explore the implications for primary schools of delivering the National Curriculum at key stage 2. More particularly, the research has four main elements: 1) Curriculum-led staffing and its implications for teachers: The study will explore the extent to which schools are moving towards a curriculum-led staffing model and the implications of pressures to move towards more specialist subject teaching for the work of the classroom teacher. 2) Whole-school strategies for changes: The study will investigate developments in whole-school approaches to curriculum planning, strategies used for the implementation of institutional development plans, and the role of curriculum coordinators/subject specialists. 3) Collegiality and collaboration amongst primary school teachers: The study will explore the impact of current changes on teachers' working relationships with colleagues both within and beyond the classroom. 4) The impact of assessment at key stage 2: The study will examine the changes made by Years 5 and 6 teachers to their working patterns in preparation for the first national assessment of eleven year olds. The study will be conducted in two parts. The first will consist of interviews with headteachers and teachers of pupils in Years 5 and 6 in primary schools in Avon, Somerset and the West Midlands. The second part will consist of a wider survey based on a postal questionnaire.

Published Material: OSBORN, M. & BLACK, E. (1994). Delivering the National Curriculum at key stage 2: the changing nature of teachers' work. Final Report to the National Association of Schoolmasters/Union of Women Teachers (NAS/UWT). Birmingham: NAS/UWT, Hillscourt Education Centre, Rednal, Birmingham.
Status: Sponsored project
Source of Grant: National Association of Schoolmasters/Union of Women Teachers £15,000
Date of Research: 1992-1993
KEYWORDS: *curriculum development; educational change; National Curriculum; primary education; primary school teachers; primary schools; teacher role; teacher workload*

10/0140

School of Education, 35 Berkeley Square, Bristol BS8 1JA
01179 303030
Kyle, J. Dr; McEntee, L. Dr; Ackerman, J. Ms
British Sign Language acquisition (deaf children developing sign)
Abstract: Despite growing interest and research in sign language, as yet we know relatively little about deaf children's acquisition. The Centre for Deaf Studies, at Bristol University, has accumulated ten years of sign language data of deaf children interacting with deaf and hearing parents and it is now involved in developing a linguistic analysis capable of coding semantic, pragmatic and syntactic aspects of early sign language development and mother/child interaction. There is sufficient data to permit both cross-sectional and longitudinal analyses of child language to be undertaken across various interactional modalities (e.g. free play, reading), permitting both individual and comparative analyses of the data to be undertaken. It is envisaged that data taken from approximately thirteen hearing and deaf children of deaf parents will be analysed. At present a semantic and pragmatic coding system has been developed, adapted from Bristol Language Development Scales (BLADES) (Gutfreund, Harrison and Wells 1989), and linguistic coding will be entered into a database (currently under construction) making data both accessible and manageable. It is hoped that in time syntactic coding will be added to this coding chart. In addition to the development of the profile and coding of the data, when and wherever possible, contact with families of deaf children is maintained enabling further video data to be accumulated, contributing to the archive currently available within the Centre.
Status: Sponsored project
Source of Grant: Leverhulme Trust £99,869
Date of Research: 1993-continuing
KEYWORDS: *deafness; language acquisition; sign language*

10/0141

School of Education, 35 Berkeley Square, Bristol BS8 1JA
01179 303030
Koumi, I. Miss; *Supervisor:* Meadows, S. Dr;
Beveridge, M. Prof.
Self-values and academic self-concept of Greek secondary school pupils
Abstract: Previous research has shown that global self-esteem is a multidimensional, hierarchically organised psychological construct, and that academic self-concept (one of the dimensions of global self-esteem) is also a multidimensional and hierarchically organised psychological construct. Based on this evidence, the present study has sought to examine whether the academic self-concept of Greek adolescent pupils is also a multidimensional and hierarchically organised construct. The study has also examined whether the way in which the hierarchical structure of the academic self-concept is organised and is affected by the psychological principle of self-values. The sample consisted of 168 fourteen year old pupils in schools on the Greek island of Chios. Quantitative data (via Pearson Correlation Analyses and Factor Analyses) confirmed that the academic self-concept is a multidimensional, hierarchically organised construct. Content analysis of qualitative information (answers to an open-ended question in one of the 4 questionnaires, and to interviews) clarified that the reason for the particular organisation of the hierarchy for the sample (a core academic and non-core academic were identified as general dimensions) was the pupils' self-values and goals. The findings posit the importance of self-values for the formation of the structure of the academic self-concept (and suggest that self-values constitute an important factor for the formation of global self-esteem, as well). The research also posits the compatibility of quantitative and qualitative research methods.
Status: Individual research

Date of Research: 1991-1994
KEYWORDS: *Greece; self concept; self esteem*

10/0142

School of Education, 35 Berkeley Square, Bristol BS8 1JA
01179 303030
Crossley, M. Dr; Bennett, A. Mr
The impact of the Belize Primary Education Development Project: case studies
Abstract: This is essentially a qualitative study of the impact of the Belize Primary Education Development Project in selected schools. Case studies involving collaboration between school and external personnel (from both Belize and the University of Bristol) will be conducted, focusing upon the documentation of the nature and quality of teaching and learning. Nine to twelve schools will be involved and the development of local research capacity will also be included through research training workshops.
Status: Sponsored project
Source of Grant: Belize Primary Education Development Project
Date of Research: 1994-continuing
KEYWORDS: *Belize; developing countries; development education; educational quality; primary education*

10/0143

School of Education, 35 Berkeley Square, Bristol BS8 1JA
01179 303030
Crossley, M. Dr; Thomas, H. Mr; Clarke, G. Ms; Tabi, T. Mr
Modularisation in higher education: trans-national issues
Abstract: The implementation of modularisation at two universities (Bristol and Ghana) is compared through two detailed, qualitative, case studies. Focus is placed upon the administrative perspective and motivating factors, both internal and external. External pressures for modularisation in Ghana resulted in rapid change, but the results of this has not been empirically evaluated. The University of Bristol has adopted a more cautious strategy and involved academic staff more fully in the planning and implementation process. The views of academic staff in both contexts requires further documentation and analysis.
Published Material: CROSSLEY, M., CLARKE, G., TABI, T. & THOMAS, H. 'Implementing the process of modularisation in higher education: some trans-national issues', Higher Education Quarterly. (in press).
Status: Sponsored project
Source of Grant: British Council
Date of Research: 1992-1993
KEYWORDS: *comparative education; Ghana; higher education; modular courses; universities*

10/0144

School of Education, 35 Berkeley Square, Bristol BS8 1JA
01179 303030
Crossley, M. Dr
Textbook provision in developing countries
Abstract: The study is based upon a critical review and classification of the literature relating to textbook development and provision in developing countries. Four models have been identified: 1) adopt; 2) adapt; 3) develop in country; and 4) develop in country with external support. This framework is now being used to help evaluate textbook development strategies in Belize.
Published Material: CROSSLEY, M. & MURBY, M. (1994). 'Textbook provision and the quality of the school curriculum in developing countries: issues and policy options', Comparative Education, Vol 30, No 2, pp.99-114.
Status: Individual research
Date of Research: 1992-continuing
KEYWORDS: *Belize; developing countries; educational materials; material development; textbooks*

10/0145

School of Education, 35 Berkeley Square, Bristol BS8 1JA
01179 303030
Marangou, A. Mrs; *Supervisor:* Webster, A. Dr; Meadows, S. Dr
The transition from home to school: a study of social, cultural and emotional factors in Greek children
Abstract: The transition from the pre-school to the actual school years

in Greece is not, at present, considered as a period during which children deserve special treatment or provision. Many demands are placed upon the children with serious consequences on their school performance, relationships and emotional development. The research will primarily look at the quality and quantity of time spent on selected teacher/pupil verbal and non-verbal interactions, pupils' activities and pupils' physical movements while at school, during the transitional period (i.e. the 5 1/2 to 6 1/2 year old age group). The aim of this research is to draw attention to a period of children's lives which, the researcher believes, is crucial, but which has not received adequate attention. Hopefully, the conclusions will be used as recommendations to teachers and adults responsible for children's lives at this delicate stage.
Status: Individual research
Date of Research: 1994-continuing
KEYWORDS: early childhood education; Greece; preschool to primary transition; primary school pupils; school readiness

10/0146
School of Education, 35 Berkeley Square, Bristol BS8 1JA
01179 303030
Moschovaki, E. Miss; *Supervisor:* Meadows, S. Dr
Classroom story reading with young children
Abstract: Although it is generally accepted that classroom story reading is important, nevertheless research on reading stories with young children is still limited and mainly descriptive. Thus an indepth study is needed on how story reading styles influence young children's cognition in a classroom context. The research questions of this project are mainly concerned with the following areas: 1) Are there significant differences among teachers' strategies when reading aloud different books (i.e. information/narrative/familiar/unfamiliar) for identifying distinctive story reading styles? 2) What is the relationship between the affective and congnitive dimensions of story reading for empowering children to demonstrate higher cognitive demand thinking and more complex verbal behaviour? 3) What assists children in taking initiatives during the process of reading stories which lead story reading interaction from being teacher-regulated to becoming group-regulated? 4) Is there a relationship between teachers' story reading styles and children's emergent behaviour in the classroom library? One hundred and forty story readings will be collected from thirty schools, and classroom observations of children's behaviour will take place as well as interviews of teachers. Hopefully, the research outcomes will identify effective ways for classroom story reading and better understanding of teaching styles. Moreover, it may clarify the effects on children's interest towards books and their literacy development. This will assist teachers in becoming aware of the significance of their own behaviour when interacting with children, in modelling specific linguistic and literacy patterns, and how they can complement family literacy in order to achieve successful transition to primary school.
Status: Individual research
Date of Research: 1993-continuing
KEYWORDS: children's literature; early childhood education; reading aloud to others; story reading; teacher-pupil relationship

10/0147
School of Education, 35 Berkeley Square, Bristol BS8 1JA
01179 303030
Jackson, D. Mr; Day, D. Mr; *Supervisor:* Kyle, J. Dr
Deaf studies at a distance: Horizon II project
Abstract: The aims of the research are: 1) The development of distance-learning modules of British Sign Language (BSL) courses. This will be in conjunction with prepared texts on disks, written materials and existing videos. Many of these courses include 'Bilingualism at home and at school'; 'Sign Interpreting'; 'Sign Linguistics'; 'Sociolinguistics'; and 'Deaf Education' etc. 2) The development of distance-learning materials for current text modules: a) video-recording of support materials for courses such as Bilingualism and the linking of video clips with text and graphics on computer and in booklets; and b) (longer term) development of these facilities on CD-ROM. 3) The development of a Sign Dictionary database on computer to aid comprehension of British Sign Language. The reasons for these developments are to ensure that potential students who were unable to study in Bristol are able to study the courses at home at their convenience. Many of these people come from all over the world. Two main software packages are used – Asymetrix's Tool-Book to develop the distance learning packages and Microsoft's Access to develop the sign language dictionary. Other software

(Microsoft's Video for Windows) and hardware (Indeo video card) are also used to grab video clips from existing and new videos. These clips are imported to both developments. New videos are produced to help supplement the two areas (distance learning and dictionary). The Educational Technology Service within the University is involved in providing the project with expert help.
Status: Sponsored project
Source of Grant: European Union Horizon
Date of Research: 1993-1994
KEYWORDS: deafness; distance education; material development; sign language; special educational needs

10/0148
School of Education, 35 Berkeley Square, Bristol BS8 1JA
01179 303030
Woll, B. Dr; Allsop, L. Ms; Brauti, J. Mr
A study of the grammatical and lexical features of International Sign
Abstract: The aims of this project are to: 1) describe the grammatical and lexical features of International Sign as used by deaf people from different countries at international meetings; 2) explore changes over time in International Sign from 1985 to the present; 3) compare the features found in International Sign as used by British signers with those found in the International Sign of deaf people from other countries; 4) suggest explanations for the particular grammatical and lexical features found in International Sign; and 5) explore attitudes to and awareness of International Sign.
Status: Sponsored project
Date of Research: 1993-continuing
KEYWORDS: deafness; sign language

10/0149
School of Education, 35 Berkeley Square, Bristol BS8 1JA
01179 303030
Wallace, M. Dr; *Supervisor:* Hoyle, E. Prof.
The role of the mass media in the education policy process
Abstract: The aim of this research is to explore how the mass media contribute to the generation and implementation of education policy within a context of national education reform. It will conceptualise how the media form an integral component of the education policy process, and identify major influences on media production and output and their link with education policy. Research methods consist of monitoring selected broadcasts and national press output, focusing on policy related to schooling; interviews with media professionals and representatives of other groups concerned with education policy and the media; and a case study of the national debate about progressive education, especially in primary schools, in 1991 and 1992.
Published Material: WALLACE, M. (1993). 'Discourse of derision: the role of the mass media within the education policy process', Journal of Education Policy, Vol 8, No 4, pp.321-337.
Status: Sponsored project
Source of Grant: Leverhulme Trust £41,000
Date of Research: 1993-continuing
KEYWORDS: educational change; educational policy; mass media effects; press opinion; public opinion

10/0150
School of Education, 35 Berkeley Square, Bristol BS8 1JA
01179 303030
Beveridge, M. Prof.; Webster, A. Dr; Reed, M. Mr
Mapping the literacy curriculum in primary and secondary school
Abstract: The research has investigated the range and functional demands made on children's use of literacy as they progress through school. The research has a particular interest in teachers' perceptions of the nature of literacy and whether secondary subject teachers view literacy as a domain of learning which lies outside their own subject expertise. Consequently, using a direct observation framework, it has plotted pupils' use of literacy across the curriculum, focusing on the nature of challenges set, and the strategies of adults as they collaborate with children to foster learning. Some of the early results of this work indicate that pupils are not sustained in their engagement with a wide range of reading and writing forms as they move through secondary school, which has an increasingly subject content focus. The researchers have worked with schools to audit the literacy curriculum and develop methods for embedding literacy within subject areas. In other words, to reinstate literacy as 'the curriculum',

rather than viewing this area as something which lies outside the curriculum for older pupils.
Published Material: WEBSTER, A., BEVERIDGE, M. & REED, M. Managing literacy curriculum. London: Routledge. (in press).
Status: Sponsored project
Source of Grant: Bristol University
Date of Research: 1992-continuing
KEYWORDS: *curriculum; literacy education; reading skills; secondary school curriculum; writing skills*

10/0151
School of Education, 35 Berkeley Square, Bristol BS8 1JA
01179 303030
Barnes, S. Dr; *Supervisor:* Satterly, D. Dr
Individual differences in learning to use word processing systems
Abstract: The efficient use of a word processing system can be viewed as a combination of four factors: factors common to all types of learning; factors specific to word processing tasks; factors specific to the sample being studied; and factors or individual differences that were not measured in the present study. Previous research on the acquisition of word procesing skills has focused on the limitations of the systems under investigation or the training strategies used. This study departs from previous research and focuses on how the personal characteristics of the users affect their use of the word processing system. Learning to use a word processing system is viewed within the framework of an information processing approach to learning. This study describes a short-term longitudinal investigation of university secretaries learning to use Microsoft Word 5. Thirty-one secretaries participated in a four week study which included the carrying out of editing tasks using Microsoft Word 5. Background characteristics, approaches to learning, conditions for learning, and scores on the Eysenck Personality Questionnnaire were also elicited from the subjects. Statistical analyses (including repeated measures ANOVAs, factor analyses, and cluster analysis) were carried out to explore individual differences in efficient use of the word processing system and to investigate styles of word processing use. The results suggest that although all secretaries made progress through the course of this investigation, none of them had reached a level of expert use of Microsoft Word 5 and the majority were still 'finding their way'. Styles of word processing use were related to characteristics of the individuals' personal backgrounds and personality. There was no evidence to support the notion of the need for optimal conditions for learning as proposed by adult learning theories.
Status: Individual research
Date of Research: 1986-1993
KEYWORDS: *adult learning; human-computer interaction; learning strategies; secretaries; word processing*

10/0152
School of Education, 35 Berkeley Square, Bristol BS8 1JA
01179 303030
University of Wales College of Cardiff, School of Education, Senghennydd Road, Cardiff CF2 4AG
01222 874000
Wallace, M. Dr; *Supervisor:* Bolam, R. Prof.
The role of the senior management team in secondary schools
Abstract: The aim of this research is to examine how senior management teams manage secondary schools within a context of educational reform and to identify approaches to teamwork which appear to be effective. Senior managers in secondary schools may face a greater need than hitherto to co-ordinate their work so as to effectively orchestrate the implementation of multiple innovations. The research will be conducted in two local education authorities (LEAs). In each LEA, case studies will be carried out during the summer of 1991 in three schools where all members of the senior management team express a strong commitment to teamwork. A longitudinal case study will be undertaken in one of these schools.
Status: Sponsored project
Source of Grant: Economic and Social Research Council £57,000
Date of Research: 1991-1993
KEYWORDS: *educational administration; educational change; management teams; school-based management; secondary schools*

10/0153
School of Education, 35 Berkeley Square, Bristol BS8 1JA
01179 303030

University of the West of England, Faculty of Education, Redland Campus, Redland Hill, Bristol BS6 6UZ
01179 741251
Osborn, M. Ms; Abbott, D. Ms; *Supervisor:* Broadfoot, P. Prof.; Pollard, A. Prof.; Croll, P. Prof.
Primary assessment, curriculum and experience
Abstract: The project aims to describe and analyse the responses of pupils and teachers in infant schools and infant departments to the National Curriculum and related innovations. This includes a consideration of the views of headteachers and teachers of the new reforms and their impact on the school and, in particular, an analysis and evaluation of the development of strategies for change. The study aims to contribute to theoretical perspectives on teacher professionalism and on the control and impact of educational change. It is designed too to consider the impact of the National Curriculum on the curriculum and pedagogy of the infant school. Issues of teacher aims and expectations, curriculum content and time allocation, teaching methods and pupil classroom experience, are being addressed. As well as considering the impact of the National Curriculum on teachers and pupils, the study will provide baseline data on contemporary infant practice. The project will also evaluate materials in action and their impact on pupils. The operation of the assessments in classrooms will be studied and pupil responses to the assessment tasks considered. Conflicting claims about pupil perceptions of and reactions to being tested are being considered. The research involves interviews with 150 teachers drawn from 48 schools in 8 local education authorities plus four rounds of detailed classroom studies in a sub-sample of nine classrooms to study curriculum change and pupil experience in more depth. Classroom studies are also being conducted during the implementation of the first unreported and reported Standard Assessment Tasks in these nine schools.
Status: Sponsored project
Source of Grant: Economic and Social Research Council £149,973
Date of Research: 1989-1993
KEYWORDS: *assessment; educational change; infant school curriculum; infant school education; National Curriculum; primary school teachers; pupil attitudes*

10/0154
School of Education, 35 Berkeley Square, Bristol BS8 1JA
01179 303030
University of the West of England, Faculty of Education, Redland Campus, Redland Hill, Bristol BS6 6UZ
Osborn, M. Ms; Broadfoot, P. Prof.; Pollard, A. Prof.
Primary teachers and policy change
Abstract: In recent years there have been major policy changes in education in France and England. The Education Reform Act 1988 in England moved towards more central control with the introduction of a National Curriculum and national assessment. In striking contrast the 'Loi d'Orientation Sur L'Education' of 1989 in France aimed at making schools more responsive to local needs and putting individual children at the centre of the learning process. In this research, using quantitative data from eighty teachers in four regions of France, as well as qualitative data based on classroom observation and interviews, will explore whether French teachers' views of their professional priorities and their classroom practice have changed as a result of these policy initiatives. It forms part of a wider investigation into teachers' views of their professional responsibilities, as it provides a comparative dimension to the Economic and Social Research Council (ESRC) funded Primary Assessment, Curriculum and Experience (PACE) project now in its second phase, which uses a concurrent matched junior school sample of teachers in England to study the impact of recent policy change on English teachers. Both these studies use as base-line data the 'Bristaix' project (1984-1987) which was a comparative study of the professional perspectives of teachers in England and France. As part of a comparative and long-term study, this research will shed light on the relative significance of policy change and other influences on teachers' views of their professional responsibility and will provide insights into the effect of policy change on classroom practice.
Status: Sponsored project
Source of Grant: Economic and Social Research Council £28,000
Date of Research: 1993-continuing
KEYWORDS: *comparative education; educational change; France; primary school teachers; teacher attitudes; teaching profession*

10/0155

School of Education, 35 Berkeley Square, Bristol BS8 1JA
01179 303030
University of the West of England, Faculty of Education,
Redland Campus, Redland Hill, Bristol BS6 6UZ
01179 741251
Osborn, M. Ms; Abbott, D. Ms; *Supervisor:* Broadfoot, P.
Prof.; Pollard, A. Prof.; Croll, P. Prof.

Primary assessment, curriculum and experience: Phase 2

Abstract: This is a continuation of the earlier Primary Assessment,
Curriculum and Experience project. Phase 2 focuses upon primary
school pupils and teachers.
Published Material: BROADFOOT, P., ABBOTT, D., CROLL, P.,
OSBORN, M., POLLARD, A. & TOWLER, L. (1991). 'Implement-
ing national assessment: issues for primary teachers', Cambridge
Journal of Education, Vol 21, No 2, pp.153-168.; BROADFOOT, P.
& ABBOTT, D., CROLL, P., OSBORN, M. & POLLARD, A.
(1991). 'Look back in anger? Primary teachers' experience of SATs',
PACE Working Paper 8. Bristol: Bristol University, School of Edu-
cation.; OSBORN, M., ABBOTT, D., BROADFOOT, P., CROLL,
P. & POLLARD, A. (1992). 'The impact of current changes in
English primary education on teacher professionalism', Teachers'
College Record, Vol 95, No 1, pp.138-151.; ABBOTT, D., BROAD-
FOOT, P., CROLL, P., OSBORN, M. & POLLARD, A. (1992).
'Classroom studies manual', PACE Working Paper 9. Bristol: Bristol
University, School of Education.; POLLARD, A. (1993). 'Balancing
priorities: children and curriculum in the 90s'. In: CAMPBELL, R.J.
(Ed). Breadth and balance in the primary curriculum. London: Falmer
Press.
Status: Sponsored project
Source of Grant: Economic and Social Research Council
Date of Research: 1993-1994
*KEYWORDS: assessment; educational change; National Curricu-
lum; primary education; primary school curriculum; primary school
teachers; pupil attitudes*

10/0156

School of Education, 35 Berkeley Square, Bristol BS8 1JA
01179 303030
University of Wales College of Cardiff, School of Education,
Senghennydd Road, Cardiff CF2 4AG
01222 874000
Create Consultants, 109 West End Lane, London NW6 4SY
0171 328 8619
Bolam, R. Prof.; McMahon, A. Ms; Pocklington, K. Mr;
Weindling, R. Mr

National evaluation of the headteacher mentoring pilot schemes

Abstract: The broad aim of the research was to carry out a formative
evaluation of the Department for Education (DFE) funded national
mentor support programme for new headteachers, during its initial
period of operation up to March 1993. The focus of the evaluation
was upon: 1) the overall organisation and management of the
schemes; 2) the organisation, content, methods, implementation and
effectiveness of training; and 3) the roles and tasks of mentors and
the effectiveness of the mentoring process in helping new headteachers adapt to their role. Data were collected through: initial visits to 12
consortia organising schemes and interviews with key personnel; a
questionnaire to mentors and new headteachers, which had a response
rate of 303 mentors (68%) and 238 (65%) new headteachers; a
questionnaire to regional organisers with a response rate of 68
(51.5%); and interviews with 16 pairs of successful mentors and new
headteachers. The participants concluded that mentoring was of
practical benefit to new headteachers and that it should be continued
and made more widely available. Other recommendations were that
the arrangements for organisation and funding needed to be improved, and that preparatory training for mentors was necessary.
Specific conclusions were drawn about the nature of the mentoring
process.
Published Material: BOLAM, R., McMAHON, A., POCK-
LINGTON, K. & WEINDLING, D. (1993). National evaluation of
headteacher mentoring pilot schemes. London: Department for Education.
Status: Sponsored project
Source of Grant: Department for Education
Date of Research: 1992-1993
*KEYWORDS: head teachers; mentors; programme evaluation;
teaching profession*

British Institute of Traffic Education Research

10/0157

Kent House, Kent Street, Birmingham B5 6QF
0121 622 2402
Clayton, A. Dr; Platt, C. Mrs; Butler, G. Mr; Menzies, I. Mrs

**A child-based approach to the development and evaluation of
a road safety education package for 8-11 year olds**

Abstract: A representative sample of 120 8-11 year-old children will
be interviewed to obtain their views on their own road behaviour and
those situations which they consider to be safe and risky. On the basis
of these and other data, a draft educational resource will be produced.
It will be aimed at upper primary school children and is designed to
fit within the National Curriculum and Scottish Curriculum Guidelines. This age group was chosen as they have one of the highest
number of road casualties. In early 1994, the resource will be piloted
with around 150 pupils. At this time, various measures to evaluate its
effectiveness in terms of changes in knowledge, attitudes and behaviour will be used. After revision, the resource will then be tested using
a sample of about 350 children in 7 schools. This work is planned for
the summer of 1994. Children will be tested before they are taught
and on two occasions afterwards. Their results will be compared with
a matched control sample of 350 children who did not receive any
teaching. The results will be analysed to provide an evaluation of the
effectiveness of the resource in enhancing road safety knowledge,
attitudes, skills and behaviour. The resource will also be evaluated in
terms of its acceptability and value as perceived by teachers.
Status: Sponsored project
Source of Grant: AA Foundation for Road Safety Research £181,000
Date of Research: 1993-continuing
*KEYWORDS: primary school pupils; pupil attitudes; safety educa-
tion; traffic safety*

10/0158

Kent House, Kent Street, Birmingham B5 6QF
0121 622 2402
Clayton, A. Dr; Menzies, I. Mrs

Road user education in Scottish secondary schools

Abstract: The aims of the research are to: determine the level of road
user education in Scottish maintained and independent secondary
schools; and monitor the secondary schools' use of materials published by The Scottish Road Safety Campaign. The research is being
carried out in two stages. In Stage 1, questionnaires were sent to all
465 Scottish secondary schools to determine: a) where road user
education was being taught, to whom and by whom; and b) the
awareness of the existence of materials produced by the Scottish
Road Safety Campaign. Stage 1 was completed in July 1993. Stage
2 involves interviewing staff in approximately 50 schools to obtain
more detailed information on policy, methodology and resources.
Status: Sponsored project
Source of Grant: Scottish Road Safety Campaign/Scottish Office
£32,500
Date of Research: 1993-1994
*KEYWORDS: safety education; Scotland; secondary education; traf-
fic safety*

Brunel University

10/0159

Centre for the Study of Human Learning, Uxbridge UB8 3PH
01895 274000
Brunel University, Faculty of Education and Design,
Runnymede Campus, Cooper's Hill, Egham TW20 OJZ
01784 431341
Sepehr, H. Dr; *Supervisor:* Harri-Augstein, S. Dr;
Harris, D. Prof.

**A conversational research into self-organisation and literacy
learning by pupils with emotional and behavioural difficulties**

Abstract: This research aims to support the development of a conversational pedagogy for self-organised learning. In order to undertake
such a task, the need for an appropriate theory of learning within the

self-organisation paradigm is emphasised. Learning Conversations for Self-Organised Learning (Thomas and Harri-Augstein 1985) has been adopted as the research strategy. A focus on developing learning conversations with individual pupils has provided the experimental environment. The children's special educational needs (SEN) had led to their placement at a primary, residential school for children with emotional and behavioural difficulties (EBD). Nine 'conversational case studies' have been carried out and reported. The pupils were those identified by their teachers as experiencing greater specific difficulties in literacy learning. Through the pilot and the experimental periods of the research, elements of a conversational methodology have been identified and elaborated. A heuristic and a tentative taxonomy of learning activities for the management of the learning conversations has been proposed. The theoretical and action frameworks seem to have made a more 'holistic' approach possible. Conversational tools for recording and analysis of processes and outcomes have been developed. A review of processes and outcomes aims to illuminate aspects of conversational practice, and has helped develop practitioner skills. The framework of the Personal Learning Biography (Harri-Augstein and Thomas 1991) has been used to evaluate pupils' learning. Within the period of the research, important changes in pupils' learning and behaviour have been observed and reported. Possible implications for educational and psychological support and provision are discussed.
Published Material: SEPEHR, H. et al. (1994). 'An inquiry into a conversational framework to support literacy learning in an EBD school'. In: LITTLEFAIR, A.B. (Ed). Literacy for life. Widnes: United Kingdom Reading Association.
Status: Individual research
Date of Research: 1991-1994
KEYWORDS: *behaviour disorders; classroom communication; conversation; learning activities; literacy education; special educational needs*

10/0160
Centre for the Study of Human Learning, Uxbridge UB8 3PH
01895 274000
Kingston University, Faculty of Education, Kingston Hill Centre, Kingston Hill, Kingston upon Thames KT2 7LB
0181 549 1141
Johnson, G. Mr; *Supervisor:* Harri-Augstein, S. Dr; Thomas, L. Prof.
Teaching competence – a personal construct investigation
Abstract: The research involves the elicitation of personal constructs of teaching competencies from teacher training staff and students with a view to re-designing teaching/school experience criteria for assessment. The major research tool is repertory grids and feedback for learning programmes linked to learning conversations between staff (c.12) and students (c.50).
Status: Individual research
Date of Research: 1990-1994
KEYWORDS: *competence; competency-based teacher education; discussion – teaching technique; personal construct theory; repertory grid test; teacher effectiveness*

10/0161
Department of Government, Centre for the Evaluation of Public Policy and Practice, Uxbridge UB8 3PH
01895 274000
Le Metais, J. Dr; *Supervisor:* Kogan, M. Prof.
Conservative values and education policy 1979-1990
Abstract: This study provides a systematic description of the Conservative Government's education policies and their initial implementation during the period 1979-1990. It charts elements of coherence between the Government's values and policies and examples of dissonance. By analysing the underlying values, it identifies conflicts which go some way toward explaining the apparent contradictions. Government policy reflects a market switch in emphasis from regionalised provision to institutional provision within a strong, centralised framework which reflects a move from communal provision in response to individual needs to a market model where individual effort is intended to bring its own rewards. This analysis reveals the way in which policies apparently concerned with separate aspects of public services (structure, management, funding and mechanisms of reporting and accountability) culminated in the creation of a mixed market economy as a basis for transferring responsibility for the provision of welfare services from the state to commercial and voluntary agencies, as well as to individuals and their families. Whilst

responsibility for the provision of education has not itself been delegated to parents, their involvement through choice, participation and voluntary financial contributions has steadily increased throughout the period in question. The transfer from State to the commercial and voluntary agencies is also evident in the provision of services to schools (meals, maintenance, cleaning) by commercial agencies under contract and the delegation to voluntary, lay governors of many of the responsibilities formerly exercised by local education authorities.
Status: Individual research
Date of Research: 1987-1992
KEYWORDS: *educational change; educational policy; politics education relationship*

10/0162
Department of Government, Centre for the Evaluation of Public Policy and Practice, Uxbridge UB8 3PH
01895 274000
Kogan, M. Prof.; Cordingley, P. Ms
Governing the reformed system of education
Abstract: An analysis of the range of governing patterns set in train by the legislation of 1988 and 1993. The research analyses these models against intended outcomes of values, needs and functions. The research was conducted in three local education authority areas and through a series of consultations at which emerging conceptualisations were tested and developed.
Published Material: CORDINGLEY, P. & KOGAN, M. (1993). In support of education: the functioning of local Government. London: Jessica Kingsley Publishers.
Status: Sponsored project
Source of Grant: Joseph Rowntree Foundation £70,000
Date of Research: 1991-1993
KEYWORDS: *educational administration; educational change; educational policy; governance; governing bodies; local education authorities; management in education*

10/0163
Department of Government, Centre for the Evaluation of Public Policy and Practice, Uxbridge UB8 3PH
01895 274000
Southbank University, Department of Social Science, 103 Borough Road, London SE1 0AA
0171 928 8989
Charlwood, A. Mr; *Supervisor:* Kogan, M. Prof.; David, M. Prof.
An analysis of the events leading up to the establishment of the National Advisory Body for Local Authority Higher Education and the reason for its demise and replacement by the Polytechnics and Colleges Funding Council
Abstract: To investigate the political and other reasons for the establishment of the National Advisory Body for Local Authority Higher Education (NAB) in 1982 and subsequently its short life. It was abolished at the end of 1988. Research was conducted through the medium of a literature search and through use of NAB papers produced during 1982-1988. Interviews were sought with about 95 individuals including politicians (central and local); officials of the Department of Education and Science, local authority oficers; officers of NAB; and leaders of higher education institutions. In all some 45 interviews were conducted using open ended interviewing techniques. Conclusions are still to be reached.
Status: Individual research
Date of Research: 1989-1994
KEYWORDS: *educational finance; educational policy; higher education; local education authorities*

10/0164
Department of Government, Centre for the Evaluation of Public Policy and Practice, Uxbridge UB8 3PH
01895 274000
Marshall, L. Mrs; *Supervisor:* Kogan, M. Prof.
Employer involvement in higher education with particular reference to Enterprise in Higher Education
Abstract: This research will examine: (1) The relationships between higher education institutions (HEIs) and employers, promoted by initiatives such as PEGASUS, the Royal Society of Arts (RSA), Higher Education for Capability (HEC) and in particular Enterprise in Higher Education (EHE) which focus on personal, transferable and life (or enterprise) skills. (2) The background to employer/HEI links

indicating the possible influence of government in bringing these initiatives about. The following issues will also be addressed: (1) What are the benefits deriving from employer/higher education partnerships? (2) Is funding in kind increasing, decreasing or remaining at the same level as in previous years? (The present recession is obviously a key factor). (3) How can employers, academics and students assess/quantify/measure to their own satisfaction the value of joint activities? and (4) Would closer working relationships between employers and HEIs have come about without initiatives such as EHE? The research will be carried out by interviews and questionnaires, with responses sought from: (a) employers ranging from large multinationals to small and medium sized companies; (b) individual academics responsible for departmental programmes with employer involvement; (c) HEIs with government funded EHE and other programmes; and (d) HEIs which have programmes similar in aim to EHE but without government funding. The principal aim of the research is to establish the nature, quality and benefits of higher education programmes run in partnership with employers, particularly those programmes which focus on the development and application of personal, transferable, life skills within academic disciplines.
Status: Individual research
Date of Research: 1992-continuing
KEYWORDS: *corporate support; employers; enterprise education; industry-higher education relationship; transfer of learning*

10/0165
    Department of Government, Centre for the Evaluation of Public Policy and Practice, Uxbridge UB8 3PH
    01895 274000
    Dunne, J. Mr; *Supervisor:* Kogan, M. Prof.
The application of market mechanisms to education: consumerism in education
Abstract: This study will examine the theoretical foundation of market ideologies and consumerist theories with particular reference to education. The relationship of such theories to the reorganisation of the governance of education resulting from the Education Reform Act 1988 and subsequent education acts will also be examined. The study will comprise an examination of the literature and interviews of those involved in education (local officials, headteachers, parents, national officials, local and national politicians). The study will make conclusions on the nature of consumerist/market forces operating in education and on the consequences of such forces.
Status: Individual research
Date of Research: 1993-continuing
KEYWORDS: *consumer economics; educational administration; educational change; educational finance; educational policy; politics education relationship*

10/0166
    Department of Government, Centre for the Evaluation of Public Policy and Practice, Uxbridge UB8 3PH
    01895 274000
    Sussex University, Institute of Continuing and Professional Education, Sussex House, Falmer, Brighton BN1 9RH
    01273 606755
    Becher, T. Prof.; Henkel, M. Ms; Kogan, M. Prof.
Graduate education in Britain
Abstract: The research followed six disciplines in eighteen departments in twelve institutions through interviews and study of documentation. It analysed research, graduate education, funding and policies at the national level, and the processes of recruiting, training and assessing graduate students.
Published Material: BECHER, T., HENKEL, M. & KOGAN, M. (1993). Graduate education in Britain. London: Jessica Kingsley Publishers.
Status: Sponsored project
Source of Grant: Nuffield Foundation £5,000
Date of Research: 1990-1993
KEYWORDS: *graduate study; higher education; student recruitment*

10/0167
    Department of Human Sciences, Uxbridge UB8 3PH
    01895 274000
    Richardson, J. Prof.
Cognitive processes in student learning
Abstract: Over the last 20 years, cognitive psychologists have made considerable advances in the development of theories of human learning and memory. Nevertheless, it is commonplace that such models cannot easily encompass the sort of learning that occurs in real life situations. During the same period, researchers into higher education have carefully investigated the knowledge and skills relevant to a variety of academic disciplines. Their findings have major implications for policy and practice in higher education, but they need to be interpreted within clearly articulated models of the cognitive processes underlying student learning. This research attempts to integrate these two areas of investigation. It will provide cognitive psychologists with a rich and qualitatively different body of evidence against which to evaluate the validity and generality of their theories of human learning and development; it will provide researchers into higher education with sophisticated theoretical descriptions of the strategies and processes employed in academic contexts; and it will provide teachers in higher education with statements of the practical applications of this research.
Published Material: RICHARDSON, J.T.E. (1983). 'Student learning in higher education', Educational Psychology, Vol 3, Nos 3 & 4, pp.305-311.; RICHARDSON, J.T.E., EYSENCK, M.W. & PIPER, W.D. (Eds). (1987). Student learning: research in education and cognitive psychology. Milton Keynes: Open University Press.
Status: Individual research
Date of Research: 1983-continuing
KEYWORDS: *cognitive processes; cognitive psychology; epistemology; higher education; learning processes; memory*

10/0168
    Department of Human Sciences, Uxbridge UB8 3PH
    01895 274000
    King, E. Ms; *Supervisor:* Richardson, J. Prof.
An investigation into the learning experiences of mature students entering higher education
Abstract: The life histories of 25 mature students are investigated to identify possible significant influences on their developing sense of self and social identity. The links are explored between being a mature student and the influence of prior lifelong learning and how different dimensions of social identity may interact with particular learning conditions to curtail or enhance learner identity and possibility. The inter-related cycles of the emergent research design include: (1) Indepth life story interviews during the participants' first year of a degree course, supplemented by written material and impromptu discussions. (2) Follow-up interviews one year later. In addition to idiographic updating, participants are invited to respond to the patterns and themes given as arising from their own transcript and those generated from the study in general. (3) Discussions with a range of other mature students, thus broadening the search for paradox and contradiction, in addition to aiding clarification and explanation. (4) Group discussions with original participants as the final cycle to help ensure the emerging theory fits the data well. Adopting a grounded approach, this research aims to contribute towards constructing a language of experience reflecting differences in individual perspectives.
Published Material: RICHARDSON, J.T.E. & KING, E. (1991). 'Gender differences in the experience of higher education: quantitative and qualitative approaches', Educational Psychology, Vol 11, Nos 3 & 4, pp.363-382.
Status: Individual research
Date of Research: 1991-continuing
KEYWORDS: *higher education; learning experience; mature students*

10/0169
    Faculty of Education and Design, Runnymede Campus, Cooper's Hill, Egham TW20 0JZ
    01784 431341
    Harris, N. Prof.; Walker, M. Mr
Development of postgraduate surgical education
Abstract: A study of postgraduate surgical education in two phases: 1) analysis of the current situation; and 2) development of good practice. The analysis involves documentary analysis, interviews with learners, teachers and those responsible for postgraduate education. The development will involve reporting good practice, providing support and assistance in the development of good practice.
Status: Sponsored project
Source of Grant: National Health Service via St George's Hospital, Tooting £26,245
Date of Research: 1993-1994
KEYWORDS: *medical education; surgery*

10/0170

Faculty of Education and Design, Runnymede Campus,
Cooper's Hill, Egham TW20 0JZ
01784 431341
Hussain, N. Ms; *Supervisor:* Down, B. Dr; Harris, N. Prof.

Perceptions of a sample of female students towards their higher educational opportunity in Lahore, Pakistan

Abstract: The research is concerned to discuss why such a high proportion of female students fail to take the opportunity to pursue higher education qualifications in Lahore, Pakistan. As such, the study concentrates on a specific area of gender equal opportunities with regard to Pakistani education. Women's enrolment at university, since the independence of Pakistan in 1947, has shown variation; having visibly declined during the period 1978-88. In this context, it was thought important to explore the perceptions of females at college, towards their future educational opportunities. This was a complex task as Muslim women lead lives of partial or total seclusion and are not easily available for questioning and research. Moreover, much of the research carried out was politically, socially and religiously sensitive. The research was designed to gain insight into the attitudes, beliefs and feelings of a small group of females already studying at college, into their prospects of higher education. Assessment of all questions needed evaluation by different means. Thus quantitative and qualitative analysis of the data derived from the research was necessary depending on the nature of the questions posed. Questionnaires and interviews were the research methods employed for this study. An attempt was made to construe the lived culture or gender opportunity at a particular time and place in Pakistan through available research, selective Islamic and cultural tradition, and through discursive and political discussion. The results of the research reflected socio-cultural influences on female students' perceptions of their ability to pursue higher education.
Status: Individual research
Date of Research: 1988-1994
KEYWORDS: *access to education; equal education; higher education; Pakistan; women's education*

Buckinghamshire School Library Service

10/0171

Unit 9, Abbey Centre, Weedon Road, Aylesbury HP19 3NS
01296 398978
Alsford, V. Mrs; Hill, J. Mrs; Smith, S. Mrs; *Supervisor:* Ryan, M. Mr

Pilot scheme for chartered librarians in primary schools

Abstract: Three experienced chartered librarians have been employed on a two year project to work in a small sample of Buckinghamshire primary schools (total of 5 schools). The purpose of the scheme is to demonstrate the improved quality of education that derives from their work in the schools, particularly with regard to: 1) the development of the role of the library in the curriculum; 2) the promotion and effective management of library resources; 3) the implementation of an information skills curriculum; 4) the encouragement of reading. The scheme is being managed and monitored by Buckinghamshire School Library Service. A range of performance measures have been devised and it is intended that a member of Her Majesty's Inspectorate will participate in the final evaluation.
Status: Sponsored project
Source of Grant: Buckinghamshire County Library Service; Participating Schools
Date of Research: 1993-continuing
KEYWORDS: *primary schools; school librarians; school libraries*

Cambridge University

10/0172

Department of Education, 17 Trumpington Street,
Cambridge CB2 1QA
01223 332888
Newstead, K. Ms; *Supervisor:* Anghileri, J. Dr

Investigating mathematics anxiety in children aged nine and ten

Abstract: Children taught in a manner compatible with socio-constructivist theory will be compared, in terms of the amount and nature of their mathematics anxiety, with those taught in a manner which emphasises teacher demonstration and individual drill and practice. Less anxiety is expected to be present in the former. Mathematics anxiety will be measured using a questionnaire designed for this purpose. Validation studies have been carried out on this instrument and it is reliable (alpha = 0.84). Factor analysis will be carried out to investigate dimensionality and to see if anxiety profiles vary according to teaching approaches used. The correlation between mathematics anxiety and mathematics performance will be calculated, and is expected to be negative and significant. Mathematics anxiety will be further investigated, especially causes, effects and specificity, using interviews with children aged nine and ten.
Published Material: NEWSTEAD, K. (1993). 'Hair-raising experiences', Times Educational Supplement, 8 October.; NEWSTEAD, K. (1993). 'Investigating children's mathematics anxiety: the effect of teaching approaches'. Proceedings of the Annual Conference of the British Society for Research in Learning Mathematics.
Status: Individual research
Date of Research: 1992-continuing
KEYWORDS: *mathematics anxiety; mathematics education; teaching methods*

10/0173

Department of Education, 17 Trumpington Street,
Cambridge CB2 1QA
01223 332888
Wells, R. Ms; *Supervisor:* Hunt, M. Dr

An investigation into representations of girlhood in girls' popular magazines and school textbooks, 1900-1930.

Abstract: Education plays a crucial role in transmitting ideologies of gender, and its prescriptions and practices are indications of how society views girls and women. Although classroom practice enables us to identify some changes in the conceptualisation of girlhood, an historical record of that practice cannot easily be reconstructed. However, an examination of school textbooks can provide some account, since they represent evidence of what authority believed ought to be taught in classrooms. Through their prescriptions, textbooks provide a commentary on how girlhood was viewed and what assumptions about feminine characteristics surrounded it. They can tell us how the content of girls' education was changing, and which commonly held beliefs about their schooling had a particular effect on that education. They are also highly revealing about the ways in which the education of girls differed from that of boys. Finally, they give some account of the purposes for which girls were being educated and the adult roles for which they were being prepared. A concentrated analysis of the experience of girlhood through educational resources produces only a partial picture since it excludes other important sites of socialisation. It is therefore necessary to investigate other areas where representations of girlhood are to be found. Magazines for girls are one such site in which adult characterisations of girlhood are implicit in production and, like textbooks, they are highly prescriptive in nature. The magazines examined show how prescriptions and advice were offered to readers on behaviour, appearance, activities, employment prospects and adult destinies. Their broad scope gives an account of who adolescent girls were thought to be, and who they were expected to become in adult life. An examination of English, mathematics and science and domestic-science textbooks used in elementary and secondary schools between 1900-1910 and 1920-1930 will be compared with an analysis of the content of magazines published for adolescent girls dung the same period, 1900 to 1930. The magazines examined are: Girls' Realm and Girl's Own Paper (issues between 1900 and 1910) and School Friend, Schoolgirls' Weekly, The Schoolgirl, Girl's Own Paper and Every Girl's Paper (issues between 1920 and 1930).
Status: Individual research
Date of Research: 1988-1993
KEYWORDS: *children's literature; comics – publications; educational history; girls; popular culture; sex role; textbooks; women's education*

10/0174

Department of Experimental Psychology, Downing Site,
Downing Street, Cambridge CB2 3EB
01223 333550
Swan, D. Miss; *Supervisor:* Goswami, U. Dr

Co-occurence of poor reading and object naming deficits: metaphonological and neuropsychological correlates
Abstract: It has consistently been observed that dyslexic children are slower and less accurate in producing names for pictures of familiar objects than normal readers (e.g. saying 'snake' to a picture of a SNAKE). It is suggested that this naming deficit, which extends to other alphanumeric stimuli such as digits, is caused by a failure in a central neurological temporal processing mechanism. In order to name objects efficiently (and to read), children must be fast processors of information. The current project began by taking the simple step of measuring whether dyslexic children could read the words that they had difficulty in naming. Surprisingly, prior research has not examined this important link. It found that dyslexic children were significantly better at reading the printed form of a word like SNAKE than at producing the name for a picture of a snake. Normal controls (RL and CA) did not show these effects. The project also investigated the phonological structure of the names that the dyslexic children had difficulty with, and found that long names (TELEVISION) were more difficult to produce than short names (FLAG), and that low frequency names (CLOG) were more difficult than high frequency ones (PIPE). Thus, the findings so far indicate that naming difficulties occur because dyslexic children have poorly specified phonological representations of words, rather than because of a central timing deficit. This finding is in line with other research suggesting that the fundamental deficit for dyslexic readers is a phonological one.
Status: Individual research
Date of Research: 1991-1994
KEYWORDS: dyslexia; reading difficulties

10/0175
Faculty of Oriental Studies, Sidgwick Avenue, Cambridge CB3 9DA
01223 337733
Stafford, C. Dr
Education and the family in Taiwan and China
Abstract: Anthropological fieldwork was carried out in Taiwan to investigate the relationship between families and the state. Particular attention was paid to education and to family religion as competing discourses within a small fishing village. The schools promote identification with the nation, and encourage sacrifice to the point of martyrdom for national goals. Families, through religious practices involving spirit mediums, seek to protect children from all harm for the sake of the family goals. The researcher is in the process of writing articles based on this fieldwork, and in the next year will expand the project to include material from mainland China.
Published Material: STAFFORD, C. (1992). 'Good sons and virtuous mothers: kinship and Chinese nationalism in Taiwan', MAN, June. (forthcoming).
Status: Sponsored project
Source of Grant: Wenner-gren Foundation £4,286; Taiwan History Field Research Project £7,143; University of London Central Research Fund £1,000
Date of Research: 1991-continuing
KEYWORDS: family life; nationalism; religion; state schools

10/0176
Faculty of Social and Political Sciences, Sociological Research Group, Free School Lane, Cambridge CB2 3RQ
01223 334549
Blackburn, R. Dr; Jarman, J. Dr
Class and gender inequality in access to higher education
Abstract: The last fifty years have seen fundamental changes in education throughout the industrial world, including the United Kingdom. While these changes have affected education at all levels, they have been most dramatic in higher education. There has been massive expansion of provision which has transformed its character and social significance. This research examines, and attempts to explain, the changing patterns of class and gender inequalities in UK higher education. The focus is on access to what may be regarded as the top segment of higher education, full-time university degree courses. Sources include British Labour Force Surveys, and the sample for the Oxford Mobility Study, as well as various forms of published data, mainly from UK government publications.
Published Material: BLACKBURN, R.M. & JARMAN, J. (1992). 'Changing inequalities in access to higher education', Working Paper 12. Cambridge: Cambridge University Sociological Research Group.; BLACKBURN, R.M. & JARMAN, J. (1993). 'Changing inequalities in access to British universities', Oxford Review of Education, Vol 19, No 2, pp.197-215.
Status: Individual research
Date of Research: 1992-1993
KEYWORDS: access to education; equal education; gender equality; higher education; social class

10/0177
Homerton College, Hills Road, Cambridge CB2 2PH
01223 411141
Nottingham University, Faculty of Education, University Park, Nottingham NG7 2RD
01159 515151
Whitebread, D. Mr; *Supervisor:* Youngman, M. Dr
An investigation of cognitive factors involved in the development of problem-solving strategies by young children
Abstract: The study explores the development of young children's problem-solving abilities, and the cognitive factors which might be related to this. Such development is conceptualised in terms of the emergence of increasingly sophisticated and powerful cognitive strategies. Children's performance on an inductive reasoning task (the multidimensional discrimination learning (MDL) task was examined). The sample consisted of 72 Leicestershire primary school children, comprising three equal groups of 24 children aged 6, 8 and 10 years. The children were also tested on a number of cognitive factors theoretically predicted to influence performance on reasoning and problem-solving tasks. These predictors included working memory capacity, metacognitive awareness and control, style of attribution, and two measures of cognitive style (cognitive tempo and field dependence-independence). Cluster analysis of strategic components revealed a pattern of 7 clusters of increasingly complex strategic behaviours used by the children on the MDL task. These strategy clusters appeared to be principally differentiated by an increasing ability to integrate information gained from different trials. Two stylistic variations were also identified which were related to the number of hypotheses verbalised on each trial. Further investigation involving multiple regression analyses revealed that the major factor which predicted strategic behaviour and performance on the MDL task was metacognitive awareness and control. However, correlational analyses of subgroups revealed interactions between predictors, and between predictors and strategies, in relation to performance. No significant effects were revealed relating to gender, but age effects in relation to predictors, strategies and performance were indicated. The implications for future research and for the development of children's thinking and problem-solving skills within educational contexts are discussed.
Status: Individual research
Date of Research: 1985-1993
KEYWORDS: cognitive processes; cognitive style; learning strategies; problem solving

10/0178
Institute of Education, Shaftesbury Road, Cambridge CB2 2BX
01223 69631
Ainscow, M. Mr; Hopkins, D. Dr; Southworth, G. Dr; West, M. Mr
Improving the quality of education for all
Abstract: The aim of this study is to produce and evaluate a model of school development, and a programme of support, that strengthens a school's ability to provide quality education for all its pupils. Currently the project involves 25 schools in the South East of England and in Yorkshire. The team from Cambridge provide training and support for school coordinators who, in turn, support project activities in other schools. Current research questions are: (1) What strategies facilitate policy development in schools? (2) What are the social experiences that characterise the cultures of 'moving schools'? (3) What is the impact of our intervention? Work is also going on to explore new methodologies to map the process of change in schools.
Published Material: AINSCOW, M. & HOPKINS, D. (1992). 'Aboard the "moving school"', Educational Leadership, Vol 50, No 3, pp.79-83.; HOPKINS, D., AINSCOW, M. & WEST, M. (1994). School improvement in an era of change. Poole: Cassell.
Status: Sponsored project
Source of Grant: Local Education Authority contributions; Participating schools; Cambridge University: Institute of Education
Date of Research: 1990-1994
KEYWORDS: educational improvement; educational innovation; educational quality; school effectiveness

10/0179

> Institute of Education, Shaftesbury Road, Cambridge
> CB2 2BX
> 01223 69631
> Ainscow, M. Mr

Special needs in the classroom

Abstract: The aim of this project is to develop and disseminate teacher education materials that can be used to help student teachers and experienced teachers cater for pupil diversity in mainstream schools. The research involves an international resource team. Intensive action research was carried out in 1990-91 in eight countries. This has led to the development of a resource pack, video programmes and a coordinator's guide. On the basis of this formative research the materials are now being used in over 30 countries. Major national action research projects involving the project materials and ideas are currently underway in China, India, Spain and Thailand. Developments are also being introduced in the Middle East, South America and Africa. All of these developments involve further action research to refine the theoretical basis of the materials.

Published Material: AINSCOW, M. (1990). 'Special needs in the classroom: the development of teacher education resource pack', International Journal of Special Education, Vol 5, No 1, pp.13-20.; AINSCOW, M. (1993). 'Teacher education as a strategy for developing inclusive schools'. In: SLEE, R. (Ed). The politics of integration. London: Falmer Press.; AINSCOW, M. (1993). 'Teacher development and special needs: some lessons from the UNESCO project "Special needs in the classroom"'. In: MITTLER, P. et al. (Eds). World yearbook of education. London: Kogan Page.; AINSCOW, M. (1994). Special needs in the classroom: a teacher education guide. London: Jessica Kingsley Publishers.

Status: Sponsored project

Source of Grant: UNESCO

Date of Research: 1988-continuing

KEYWORDS: comparative education; educational materials; mainstreaming; special educational needs; teacher education

10/0180

> Institute of Education, Shaftesbury Road, Cambridge
> CB2 2BX
> 01223 69631
> Ainscow, M. Mr; Hart, S. Ms; Fielding, M. Mr

Developing successful learning

Abstract: This is an action research project which is seeking to develop effective approaches to school-based staff development. The work was prompted by concerns about how to support teachers in meeting the needs of all pupils within the National Curriculum. Specifically the research is exploring the use of partnerships within which teachers support one another in reflecting upon and developing their professional practice. Currently the findings of the research are now being introduced into a further group of schools using materials that have been developed. Experience so far suggests that adopting a partnership approach to professional development helps to create a collaborative culture in schools.

Published Material: AINSCOW, M. & HART, S. (1992). 'Moving practice forward', Support for Learning, Vol 7, No 3, pp.115-120.

Status: Sponsored project

Source of Grant: Bedfordshire Local Education Authority; Sharnbrook School; Samuel Whitbread School; Cambridge University: Institute of Education

Date of Research: 1990-continuing

KEYWORDS: cooperative learning; staff development; teacher development

10/0181

> Institute of Education, Shaftesbury Road, Cambridge
> CB2 2BX
> 01223 69631
> Gibson, R. Dr

Shakespeare: from school to higher education

Abstract: A study of the continuity of the Shakespeare experience of students moving from school, sixth form college or further education into higher education. The research arises out of the work of the Shakespeare and Schools project based at the University of Cambridge, Institute of Education. A considerable amount of data has been collected for the period 1986-1993. This will be analysed together with data on teaching methods and students' experience in the period April 1993-July 1994.

Published Material: GIBSON, R. (1993). 'Teaching Shakespeare'.

In: BRINDLEY, S. et al Teaching English. Milton Keynes: Open University Press.; GIBSON, R. (1993). 'A black day will it be to somebody', Cambridge Journal of Education, Vol 23, No 1.; GIBSON, R. (Ed). (1993/4). Romeo and Juliet, Macbeth, Twelfth Night, Hamlet, The Two Gentlemen of Verona, King John, Cambridge School Shakespeare Series. Cambridge: Cambridge University Press.; GIBSON, R. (1994). 'Transforming INSET into classroom practice'. In: BRADLEY, H. et al. (Eds). Making INSET effective for the school. London: David Fulton.; A full list of publications is available from the researcher.

Status: Individual research

Date of Research: 1992-continuing

KEYWORDS: developmental continuity; English literature; higher education; sixteen to nineteen education; teaching methods

10/0182

> Institute of Education, Shaftesbury Road, Cambridge
> CB2 2BX
> 01223 69631
> Dadds, M. Dr

The nature and use of the enquiry project in short award-bearing courses for primary school teachers

Abstract: The research is exploring the variety of classroom and school development issues upon which primary school teachers focus when conducting their self-chosen project on short courses at the Cambridge Institute of Education. The research is also studying the practical links that teachers make between their self-chosen projects and the work of colleagues in their schools where links are being made, the research looks at the demands which this places on the inservice teachers as disseminators and change agents. It is seeking to understand what knowledge, personal skills, personal qualities and competences are needed for teachers to make successful links. The research also seeks to identify factors within the inservice course and the school that support, or hinder, teachers in these demands. Questionnaires have raised data from students on four short award-bearing courses. Follow-up interviews with a small sample of teachers are being conducted over a period of a year. Interviews will be sought with a small sample of colleagues in the inservice teachers' schools.

Status: Sponsored project

Source of Grant: Cambridge University: Institute of Education £3,530

Date of Research: 1992-continuing

KEYWORDS: inservice teacher education; primary school teachers; teacher development

10/0183

> Institute of Education, Shaftesbury Road, Cambridge
> CB2 2BX
> 01223 69631
> Bradley, H. Mr

Evaluation of a mentor scheme for headteachers

Abstract: There are three phases, containing 16, 32 and 96 mentor/mentee pairs respectively. By questionnaire and interview, the mentors are followed through their training. Then by interview of a sample of both mentors and mentees, the implementation of the mentor programme will be monitored. In Phase 1 about a 50% sample is being followed for evaluation purposes, reducing to about 25% in Phase 2 and 10% in Phase 3.

Status: Sponsored project

Source of Grant: School Management Task Force; Department for Education; Local Education Authorities, jointly £220,000

Date of Research: 1992-1994

KEYWORDS: head teachers; management in education; mentors

10/0184

> Institute of Education, Shaftesbury Road, Cambridge
> CB2 2BX
> 01223 69631
> Rouse, M. Mr

Special needs in primary schools

Abstract: This project investigates the effects of the government funded National Priority Area (NPA) courses designed to help schools in meeting special educational needs. A collaborative initiative was established six years ago between higher education (Cambridge Institute of Education) and a number of local education authorities (LEAs). The initiative linked individual development for teachers with institutional development for their schools with the active participation of the LEAs. Follow up evaluation by survey,

case study and other ethnographic methods across five LEAs has indicated successful implementation of school change and growth for individual participants.
Published Material: ROUSE, M. & BALSHAW, M. (1991). 'Collaborative INSET and special educational needs'. In: UPTON, G. (Ed). Staff development for special educational needs. London: David Fulton.; ROUSE, M. (1991). 'Effective INSET: the role of the outsider'. In: McLAUGHLIN, C. & ROUSE, M. (Eds). Supporting schools. London: David Fulton.
Status: Sponsored project
Source of Grant: Six participating Local Education Authorities
Date of Research: 1989-continuing
KEYWORDS: *local education authorities; mainstreaming; primary schools; special educational needs; teacher development*

10/0185

Institute of Education, Shaftesbury Road, Cambridge
CB2 2BX
01223 69631
McLaughlin, C. Ms
Evaluation of teacher appraisal in Havering
Abstract: The project aims to evaluate the training and implementation of teacher appraisal in a London Borough. The schools in the Borough were divided into 2 cohorts and the evaluation covers both cohorts. Headteacher appraisal was also evaluated. The methods used were as follows: Questionnaires to all participants and then interviews in the sample schools. In Cohort 2 sample schools volunteers also kept diaries of the process. In Cohort 1 the interviewed sample was 4 out of a total of 20 primary schools, 1 special school and 2 out of a total of 4 secondary schools. The same sample was in Cohort 2. The evaluation is now completed and a report published.
Status: Sponsored project
Source of Grant: Havering Borough Council
Date of Research: 1992-1993
KEYWORDS: *teacher effectiveness; teacher evaluation*

10/0186

Institute of Education, Shaftesbury Road, Cambridge
CB2 2BX
01223 69631
Rouse, M. Mr; Florian, L. Dr
The development of inclusive schools in the London Borough of Newham
Abstract: The London Borough of Newham has committed itself to the development of an inclusive education system in which all pupils will be educated in mainstream primary and secondary schools. This research will review progress made to date, consider the difficulties faced, and intends to make recommendations on future developments. Site visits, observations of inclusive classrooms, and interviews with key staff and parents, have been carried out. A series of case studies of inclusive schools will provide the data for analysis. This research replicates a similar project carried out in Utah (US) by the same researchers in 1992. Dissemination of findings will take place through publications,a day conference and an Anglo-American symposium held in Cambridge in July 1994.
Status: Sponsored project
Source of Grant: London Borough of Newham £2,000; University of Cambridge Institute of Education £3,000
Date of Research: 1994-continuing
KEYWORDS: *institutional evaluation; mainstreaming; special educational needs; whole school approach*

10/0187

Institute of Education, Shaftesbury Road, Cambridge
CB2 2BX
01223 69631
Ainscow, M. Mr; Hargreaves, D. Prof.; Hopkins, D. Dr
Mapping the process of change in schools
Abstract: This study aims to develop five new research techniques for investigating the processes of innovation and change in schools and for understanding school cultures. Existing research carried out by the Cambridge team is leading to a better understanding of the patterns of interaction that characterise 'moving schools'. This present study is concerned with the development of techniques which will capture the perspectives of those involved in the change process in organisations such as schools. Specifically these techniques should collect data in ways that are more efficient for the researcher, more

interesting for the subjects, and more penetrating in terms of the quality of data than has been possible with existing techniques. It is not the intention to devise a methodology that will separately measure some of the key concepts in organisational change, such as structure, cultures, strategy or change capacity. Rather the study seeks to develop approaches that will capture high quality data that span such concepts.
Status: Sponsored project
Source of Grant: Economic and Social Research Council £24,580
Date of Research: 1993-1994
KEYWORDS: *change strategies; educational environment; educational research; organisational change; research methodology*

10/0188

Institute of Education, Shaftesbury Road, Cambridge
CB2 2BX
01223 69631
London University, King's College London, Cornwall House Annexe, Waterloo Road, London SE1 3TY
0171 836 5454
Walsh, A. Ms; *Supervisor:* Brown, M. Prof.
The calculator as a catalyst for change – children and number
Abstract: Although the electronic calculator is well accepted as a tool in society and with young children, very little is known about the possible potential of the effective use of a calculator to support the learning of number within mathematics for children in the primary years, and thus also its possible potential as a 'catalyst for change'. This research study uses an ethnographic methodology to follow the development of four schools in their attempts to integrate the calculator into the teaching and learning of number with children from 6/7 years upwards, which began as part of the work of Primary Initiatives in Mathematics Education project in which the research played a leading role. The study will cover a five year period of development. Some evidence presented to date calls into question the general perception of how and when children acquire particular number concepts and skills and their ability to deal with them. The research study involves a detailed analysis of these findings with particular reference to the development of place value and further research focusing on the children's understanding of and ability to use and apply number. It is intended to address issues related to implications for teaching.
Status: Individual research
Date of Research: 1987-1993
KEYWORDS: *arithmetic and number education; calculators; mathematics education; primary education*

10/0189

Institute of Education, Shaftesbury Road, Cambridge
CB2 2BX
01223 69631
National Council of Educational Research and Training, Sri Aurobindo Marg, New Delhi, India
Ainscow, M. Mr; Jangira, N. Prof.; Ahuja, A. Mrs
Effective schools for all: a multi-site action research project in India
Abstract: This initiative grew out of the United Nations Economic, Scientific and Cultural Organisation (UNESCO) international project 'Special Needs in the Classroom'. It involves representation of 22 teacher education institutions from different regions of India and explores the use of active learning approaches in teacher education as a means of encouraging teaching for diversity. Data is being collected using a variety of instruments. The intention is that the findings will be used as a basis for wider dissemination activities involving some further 400 training institutions. Additional indepth studies are also being carried out in a small number of primary schools in the Delhi area.
Status: Sponsored project
Source of Grant: United Nations Economic, Scientific and Cultural Organisation; UNESCO); United Nations International Children's Emergency Fund (UNICEF)
Date of Research: 1991-1993
KEYWORDS: *India; mainstreaming; special educational needs; teacher education*

10/0190

Institute of Education, Shaftesbury Road, Cambridge
CB2 2BX
01223 69631

University of East Anglia, School of Education, Norwich
NR4 7TJ
01603 456161
Southworth, G. Dr; *Supervisor:* Nias, J. Prof.;
MacDonald, B. Prof.

Primary school headship: an analysis derived from an ethnographic study of a single headteacher

Abstract: An ethnographic study was conducted into the work of a single, male headteacher. Using participant observation and interviews over the course of a school year (one day per week) data were collected and then analysed and written-up as a case study. The case study offers a portrait of the headteacher at work. Whilst a number of themes emerge from the study the main issue centres upon the power of the headteacher. The researcher is critical of the headteacher's power in the school and analyses why the headteacher is powerful and how this might be altered and headship reconceptualised.
Published Material: SOUTHWORTH, G. (1995). Looking into primary headship: a research based interpretation. Basingstoke: Falmer Press Ltd.
Status: Individual research
Date of Research: 1987-1993
KEYWORDS: head teachers; primary schools; school organisation; teaching profession

10/0191

Institute of Education, Shaftesbury Road, Cambridge
CB2 2BX
01223 69631
University of Utah, Department of Special Education, Milton Bennion Hall, Salt Lake City, Utah 84112, USA
0101 801 581 8122
University of Maryland, College Park, Department of Special Education, Maryland 20742, USA
0101 301 405100
Rouse, M. Mr; Hardman, M. Dr; Florian, L. Dr

Towards the effective inclusive school

Abstract: The State of Utah (USA) has been committed for a number of years to the development of inclusive schools in which all pupils, regardless of disability will be educated. This evaluation and research project by the State investigated the outcomes of the initiative and the progress made to full inclusion. Initial findings indicate progress in a range of significant areas in certain parts of the State. Barriers to change, as well as an account of innovative practice, are included in the final report.
Published Material: FLORIAN, L. & ROUSE, M. (1993). 'Utah's inclusive schools': a report to the Utah State Department of Education, Salt Lake City, Utah.
Status: Sponsored project
Source of Grant: State of Utah £8,451
Date of Research: 1992-1993
KEYWORDS: institutional evaluation; mainstreaming; special educational needs; United States of America; whole school approach

10/0192

Research Centre for English and Applied Linguistics, Trumpington Street, Cambridge CB2 1QA
01223 332340
Williams, J. Dr

Bilingual lexical processing

Abstract: The project examines two aspects of lexical processing in non-fluent bilinguals (first year undergraduates studying French, and upper intermediate and advanced foreign learners of English from various language backgrounds): (i) the content of the semantic representations automatically activated by words, and whether words in the bilingual's two languages have representational elements in common; (ii) the mechanisms by which the bilingual controls of language is accessed by a written word, and whether there are circumstances under which no such control can be exercised. Both sets of studies employ experimental methodologies and theoretical models from psycholinguistic research on monolingual lexical processing. Preliminary results show that (i) words in the two languages share 'core semantic' features (e.g. those determining the relations between SUITCASE and BAG), whereas the information supporting 'schematic' relations (e.g. KING – CROWN) is either not automatically activated (even in the monolingual) or is not shared by words in different languages; and (ii) even when performing a task entirely in one language a bilingual's semantic knowledge of the other language

is still active (e.g. when a French-English bilingual is performing a reading task entirely in English the word PAIN can be shown to automatically and unconsciously activate the concept BREAD. Current experiments are investigating whether language selective-processing is influenced by language dominance and the degree of phonological processing involved in the task.
Status: Individual research
Date of Research: 1993-1993
KEYWORDS: bilingualism; lexicology; word recognition

10/0193

Research Centre for English and Applied Linguistics, Trumpington Street, Cambridge CB2 1QA
01223 332340
Brown, G. Prof.

The map task paradigm: a study of deixis and reference

Abstract: The study investigates the extent of deictic usage in spoken language and how deictic interpretation is essential to enable the listener not only to identify the speaker's referent but to be able to adopt the same perspective on the referent as the speaker. Once the notion of deictic interpretation is fully taken on board, a sharp and restricted account of the notion of context can be provided. The data which is studied includes conversations between 14-16 year olds and undergraduate subjects as they work together to complete cooperative tasks. The tasks either involve spatial relations (where, for instance, one subject instructs another how to draw a route on a map), or temporal relations (where groups of subjects who have watched different scenes of a short video attempt to relate the individuals and incidents which they have observed). The data permits the investigation of the deictic categories of space, time and person.
Status: Individual research
Date of Research: 1992-1994
KEYWORDS: conversation; language; speech communication; verbal communication

Canterbury Christ Church College of Higher Education

10/0194

North Holmes Road, Canterbury CT1 1QU
01227 767700
Howlett, K. Mr; *Supervisor:* Parsons, C. Dr

The experience of excluded primary school children

Abstract: The numbers of pupils excluded from primary schools is increasing. The research aims to contribute to debate about exclusions, to seek alternatives to exclusions and to look for ways of minimising the harm to children and their families once exclusion has happened. In particular, the research set out to: 1) describe events leading up to exclusion and the role of the school, parents and others; 2) gather perceptions of the pupil's experience of school from all those involved; 3) describe the experience of the child and his/her family while out of school; 4) assess the availability of services to support the child while excluded; 5) examine the legal framework within which exclusion decisions and actions take place; and 6) estimate the costs of exclusion to other social welfare agencies. The study focused on eleven primary school age children in three local education authorities in the south-east of England. These children had been, or were at the time, excluded from their primary schools. Interviews were carried out with the child and with others involved in caring for, supporting or educating the child – parents, teachers and headteachers, education department officers, educational psychologists, educational welfare officers, social workers, home tutors and people in voluntary organisations. The major findings of the research were in three areas: in documenting the experience of the children themselves and their families; in an examination of the legislation relating to safeguarding the education and care of young excluded children; and in costing exclusions. The experience of exclusion is stressful and distressing for all concerned, most particularly for the parents. Long, continued exclusion occurs in a number of cases but remediation and support services are sometimes slow to respond. Legislation protects these children very little and recent acts and circulars offer very little improvement. Exclusions are costly when measured in simply financial terms.
Published Material: ABBOTTS, P. & PARSONS, C. (1993). 'Chil-

dren's rights and exclusions from primary schools', Therapeutic Care and Education, Vol 2, No 3, pp.416-421.
Status: Sponsored project
Source of Grant: Joseph Rowntree Foundation £26,250
Date of Research: 1993-1994
KEYWORDS: expulsion; primary school pupils; pupil experience; suspension

10/0195
North Holmes Road, Canterbury CT1 1QU
01227 767700
Nicholls, G. Dr
Energy 9-16 project
Abstract: The Energy 9-16 Project involves the development of computer software and teaching material based on pupils' prior conceptions and cognitive development.
Published Material: (1992). Keep Warm. Energy teaching package for the National Curriculum key stage 1 and 2. Incorporating computer software, pupils' notes and teachers' notes on the teaching of energy for 9 to 11 year olds. Leicester: British Gas Publications.; NICHOLLS, G. (1992). 'Primary pupils' ideas of energy, fact or fiction?', Evaluation and Research in Education Journal, Vol 6, Nos 2 & 3, pp.85-93.; NICHOLLS, G. (1993). 'Primary pupils' ideas of "energy, fact or fiction"'. In: NEWTON, L.D. (Ed). Primary Science: The Challenge of the 1990's. Clevedon: Multilingual Matters Ltd.; NICHOLLS, G. & OSBORN, J. (1993). 'Dimensions of children's conceptions of energy', International Journal of Science Education, Vol 15, No 1, pp.73-81.; (1994). Energy Transfer. Energy teaching package for the National Curriculum key stage 3 and 4. Incorporating computer software, pupils' activity sheets, and teachers' notes. Leicester: British Gas Publications. A full list of publications is available from the researcher.
Status: Sponsored project
Source of Grant: British Gas £110,000
Date of Research: 1991-1994
KEYWORDS: computer software; educational materials; energy education; material development; science education

10/0196
North Holmes Road, Canterbury CT1 1QU
01227 767700
Alfrey, M. Mrs; Coe, J. Mr; Gooding, S. Ms
Children's learning: early attainment in reading (CLEAR)
Abstract: The study is concerned with the factors outside and inside school which have a major impact on children making a competent start to reading. Recent surveys have indicated that the overall level of attainment in reading, as assessed at the end of National Curriculum key stage 1, has been maintained, or even improved, up to the present time. However, there is now evidence that there has been a decline in attainment among children of low ability coming from disadvantaged backgrounds. The children's learning: early attainment in reading (CLEAR) research project has established that this decline has taken place since the mid 1980s and has confirmed that the decline is not related to teaching methods since, in general, these have not changed over the period in question. Currently the research seeks to establish the most important factors affecting the children's early progress, and could go on to attach relative weighting to school factors as compared to those related to home and outside school. It is envisaged that the last phase of the research will devise and publish strategies and practical approaches to reverse the decline in early attainment.
Status: Sponsored project
Source of Grant: Canterbury Christ Church College of Higher Education £30,000; European Funding £10,000
Date of Research: 1993-continuing
KEYWORDS: early reading; home-school relationship; reading achievement; reading difficulties

10/0197
North Holmes Road, Canterbury CT1 1QU
01227 767700
Clift, S. Dr; Stears, D. Mr; Clark, N. Miss; Black, P. Miss
Travel, lifestyles and health project
Abstract: The project is engaged in a variety of studies to explore the connections between travel, tourism and health risks (particularly risks of human immunodeficiency syndrome (HIV) infection and sexually transmitted diseases associated with sexual behaviour), and

to consider the role of health promotion and health education in this area. A survey of health precautions, behaviours and health problems among approximately 800 British tourists on Malta was undertaken in Spring 1993. A survey of local health promotion unit campaigns on travel and health has also been completed. Currently research is underway investigating students' experiences of holidays in the UK, and abroad, and work is planned on the travel experiences and sexual risk behaviours of patients attending genito-urinary medicine clinics.
Published Material: CLARK, N., CLIFT, S. & PAGE, S. (1993). A safe place in the sun? The health precautions, behaviours and health problems of British tourists in Malta. Canterbury: Canterbury Christ Church College of Higher Education.; STEARS, D. (1993). Travel health promotion: a survey of the work of district health promotion units in the UK. Canterbury: Canterbury Christ Church College of Higher Education.
Status: Sponsored project
Source of Grant: South East Thames Regional Health Authority; Canterbury Christ Church College of Higher Education, jointly £70,000
Date of Research: 1992-continuing
KEYWORDS: acquired immune deficiency syndrome; health education; health promotion; sexuality; sexually transmitted diseases; tourism; travel

10/0198
North Holmes Road, Canterbury CT1 1QU
01227 767700
Holliday, A. Dr; Hyde, M. Mr; Taylor, R. Mr; Bax, S. Mr; Kyeyune, R. Mr
Cultural transferability of British approaches to international contexts in English language education
Abstract: English language education in both foreign and second language contexts throughout the world is dominated by technologies originating in Britain, North America and Australasia. The research project investigates the appropriacy of this technology transfer in a variety of activities in which British teachers, teacher educators, curriculum developers or curriculum project managers work with students, teachers and educational administrators from other countries. Data is being collected through observation of classroom and other events, and interviews with and reports from students, teachers and administrators. Sources include English teaching and teacher education within the Department of Language Studies at Canterbury Christ Church College of Higher Education, projects with which the Department is involved in Cyprus, South Africa, Mexico, Malaysia and Syria, and professional contacts in a range of other countries. Students within the Department are also encouraged to carry out small-scale research in this area. A main focus is the investigation of what happens at the interface between different regional, professional-academic, institution, classroom and educational cultures. The research methodology is interpretive, sometimes employing applied ethnography.
Published Material: HOLLIDAY, A.R. (1991). 'From materials development to staff development: an informed change in direction in an EFL project', System, Vol 19, No 3.; HOLLIDAY, A.R. (1992). 'Intercompetence: sources of conflict between local and expatriate ELT personnel', System, Vol 20,No 2.; HOLLIDAY, A.R. (1992). 'Tissue rejection and informal orders in ELT projects: collecting the right information', Applied Linguistics, Vol 13, No 4, pp.404-24.; TAYLOR, R. (1992). 'The production of training packs in in-service teacher training', ELT Journal, Vol 46, No 4, pp.356-61.; HOLLIDAY, A.R. (1994). 'The house of TESEP and the communicative approach', ELT Journal, Vol 14, No 1, pp.3-11. A full list of publications is available from the researcher.
Status: Individual research
Date of Research: 1991-continuing
KEYWORDS: comparative education; English – second language; international educational exchange; second language teaching

10/0199
North Holmes Road, Canterbury CT1 1QU
01227 767700
Sharpe, K. Dr
French primary schooling in action
Abstract: This research project focuses on the operation of France's national curriculum in primary schools in a northern French town. In particular, two contrasting schools were selected for long-term ethnographic study, one located in an affluent area near the centre and the other situated on a run down municipal housing estate on the outskirts in an officially designated educational priority zone. During

the period of the fieldwork (1989-1992) a variety of methodological strategies was used to assemble a diverse array of evidence to investigate the extent of educational homogeneity existing between the two schools. Through the examination of official and unofficial documentation, observation in the classroom and around the schools, and interviews, discussions and conversations with teachers and pupils, it became clear that, despite their widely divergent economic and cultural situations, the two schools provided largely homogeneous educational experience for two socially heterogeneous populations. It is contended in the latter part of the study that theoretical analysis of the data gathered indicates that this educational homogeneity arises not from the mere existence of national programmes of study designed to ensure a basic curricular entitlement, but rather out of the whole 'national context' in which French primary schooling is embedded.
Published Material: SHARPE, K. (1991). 'Coming off a strict diet', Times Educational Supplement, 6 December 1991, p.22.; SHARPE, K. (1992). 'Catechistic teaching style in French primary education: analysis of a grammar lesson with seven year olds', Comparative Education, Vol 28, No 3, pp.249-268.; SHARPE, K. (1992). 'Educational homogeneity in French primary education: a double case study', British Journal of Sociology of Education, Vol 13, No 3, pp.329-348.; SHARPE, K. (1992). 'French recipes', Times Educational Supplement, 25 September 1992.
Status: Sponsored project
Source of Grant: Economic and Social Research Council £9,000
Date of Research: 1989-1993
KEYWORDS: *comparative education; France; primary education*

10/0200
    North Holmes Road, Canterbury CT1 1QU
    01227 767700
    Cant, R. Mr; Alcindor, L. Ms
The needs of mature students in higher education
Abstract: There is an ever increasing number of students now entering higher education (Department for Education, 1992) who did not follow the traditional route of entry at eighteen. Government initiatives have argued for a substantial expansion of student numbers by the year 2000 and, in response to demographic changes, have indicated that this can only be achieved by widening access to previously under-represented groups (Department of Education and Science, 1987). The project aims to identify the expressed and perceived educational, supportive and psycho-social needs of such under-represented groups and evaluate the extent to which such needs are currently being provided for within institutions of higher education. It is suggested that possibly unrealistic expectations and resultant pressures and tensions associated with higher education may adversely affect mature students' stability and personal relationships. A self-administered questionnaire will be issued across a stratified sample of mature students, undertaking a first degree course, at a range of institutions of higher education. Subsequently, individual indepth interviews will be carried out with mature students who report role conflict and stress related problems. It is intended that the project will establish a clearer understanding of the attitudes and experiences of mature students and will attempt to analyse how the individual policies, practices and support mechanisms at each of a range of institutions will promote and support the personal, social and intellectual progress of mature students.
Status: Individual research
Date of Research: 1992-continuing
KEYWORDS: *higher education; mature students; student attitudes; student needs*

10/0201
    North Holmes Road, Canterbury CT1 1QU
    01227 767700
    Nene College, Moulton Park, Northampton NN2 7AL
    01604 735500
    Bridge, C. Mr; *Supervisor:* Thomas, P. Mr; Matthews, M. Dr
The development of geographical understanding in the primary school child
Abstract: The National Curriculum has raised the profile of geography teaching in the primary classroom. Both teachers and children are faced with a geographical vocabulary which fronts an understanding of concepts and processes with which most are unfamiliar. Research into children's understanding of maps or places has illustrated the slow and partial development of holistic views plus the high level of abstraction and generalisation required. This study will:

review the range of conclusions drawn in recent research into environmental perception; make comparisons with current curricular demands in geography in the primary school; and consider desirable outcomes of young children's learning in geography. It is hoped that this preliminary investigation will reveal the range of conceptual demand being made on young children. The focus will be on aspects of physical and human geography which are within the child's own experience. The data collection aspect of the study will seek to involve two to three hundred children. It will investigate the quality of children's responses to key geographical concepts and processes across significant age bands in the primary school.
Status: Individual research
Date of Research: 1993-continuing
KEYWORDS: *geographic concepts; geography education; primary education*

10/0202
    North Holmes Road, Canterbury CT1 1QU
    01227 767700
    Southampton University, Faculty of Educational Studies, Department of Health Education, Highfield, Southampton SO9 5NH
    01703 595000
    Robinson, S. Ms; *Supervisor:* Weare, K. Ms
Children's perceptions of eating and body image
Abstract: Current research suggests that the incidence of eating disorders (from anorexia nervosa to extreme obesity) is increasing sharply among young adolescents, and that the determining factors may develop before adolescence. This has created a need to increase knowledge about children's perceptions of their body image and eating. The aim of the research is to explore children's perceptions of their body image with particular attention to whether they perceive thinness to be a more positive body image than being ordinary or fat. It will analyse children's understanding of any link between body size and the food they eat. It will seek to discover how much control children feel they have over their food, as children may be encouraged or discouraged from achieving a healthy body image depending on their accessibility to certain foods. The research will be analysed in terms of gender, in particular, as previous studies show that food has a different social meaning for men and women, and eating disorders are common to both.
Status: Individual research
Date of Research: 1992-continuing
KEYWORDS: *body image; eating habits; food; health; self concept*

Cardiff Institute of Higher Education

10/0203
    School of Physical Education, Sport and Leisure, Cyncoed Centre, Cardiff CF2 6XD
    01222 551111
    University of Wales College of Cardiff, School of Education, Senghenydd Road, Cardiff CF2 4AG
    01222 874000
    Lancey, K. Mr; *Supervisor:* Durojaiye, S. Dr
Gender differences in motor performance from infancy to adolescence
Abstract: The aim of the research is to identify gender differences in the motor performance of children of primary school age, and to account for those differences.
Date of Research: 1990-continuing
KEYWORDS: *motor development; primary school pupils; sex differences*

Centre for International Studies

10/0204
    Meadowlea House, 86 Littleham Road, Exmouth EX8 2QT
    01395 264902
    Vallance, T. Mr

Who's who in international education in Europe
Abstract: The research aims to identify persons, courses and all bodies concerned with the promotion of international and development education throughout the European Union member states. A directory will be produced on computer disk, and also in written form, to examine the place and contribution of European bodies in the context of national educational surplus and curricula demands.
Status: Sponsored project
Source of Grant: Commission of European Communities; International Foundation for Education, jointly £89,000
Date of Research: 1993-1994
KEYWORDS: Europe; international education; international educational exchange

Cheltenham and Gloucester College of Higher Education

10/0205
Faculty of Education and Health, The Park, Cheltenham GL50 2QF
01242 532700
Charlton, A. Dr; Leo, E. Ms; Indoe, D. Mr; James, J. Ms
Evaluation of a teacher training package designed to enhance pupils' self-image
Abstract: The research involves an evaluation of an inservice teacher training package constructed by the researchers. The package – EASI Teaching Package (Enhancement Approaches with the Self-Image) – is designed to assist teachers to improve the self-image of their pupils. Evaluation will incorporate a pre-/post-intervention design. Seventy-two teachers (drawn from nine primary schools) are to constitute the intervention group. They will receive the EASI Teaching Programme (4 one and a half hour meetings) over a 4 week period. A comparison group (similar size/type to the intervention group) will receive no special treatment. Pre-/post-evaluations will utilise indices of teachers' classroom behaviour, and pupils' self-image reports and behavioural functioning.
Date of Research: 1990-1993
KEYWORDS: inservice teacher education; programme evaluation; pupil development; self concept

10/0206
Faculty of Health and Education, The Park, Cheltenham GL50 2QF
01242 532700
Corbett, P. Mr; Noyes, P. Dr
The development of oracy and literacy
Abstract: The Oracy and Literacy Research Centre was formed in 1990 to draw together research into language development. The research involved College staff, students and teachers. The aim is to research identified aspects of language development including: the development of spelling through emergent writing; process writing; reading/writing links; using visits to develop language; and the value of process writing in developing literacy skills in children experiencing learning difficulties. Sample sizes vary. Methodology includes: observation; tape recording; video; diaries; analysis of samples; survey and questionnaire. Results will be disseminated through conference, journal articles and monographs.
Status: Sponsored project
Source of Grant: Cheltenham and Gloucester College of Higher Education
Date of Research: 1991-continuing
KEYWORDS: language skills; literacy; oracy; reading skills; special educational needs; spelling; writing skills

Chester College of Higher Education

10/0207
Cheyney Road, Chester CH1 4BJ
01244 375444

Alston, P. Dr; Ellis, V. Mrs; McQueen, A. Mr; Derby, J. Mrs; Boxall, V. Mrs
Music for the generalist primary teacher, with reference to the National Curriculum
Abstract: The aim of the project is to develop a model for combined skill, concept and affective learning in listening, performing and composing. This theoretical model will then be translated into classroom practice by the devising of materials to assist the generalist primary teacher to cope with the demands of the National Curriculum in Music at key stage 1 and key stage 2. All materials will be on trial in classrooms before being published. This work will then feed back into the theoretical model which will need to be revised and refined. A final report will comment on the practicability of teaching the National Curriculum in Music at key stage 1 and key stage 2 through a model of skill, concept and affective learning.
Published Material: A list of publications is available from the researchers.
Status: Sponsored project
Source of Grant: University of Liverpool Board of College Studies £565; Chester College £200
Date of Research: 1990-continuing
KEYWORDS: music education; National Curriculum; primary school teachers

10/0208
Cheyney Road, Chester CH1 4BJ
01224 375444
Alston, P. Dr; Carhart, J. Rev.; Robertson, D. Mr; Pegg, R. Dr; Major, D. Mr; Jackson, S. Dr; Lunt, P. Dr
Work based learning for academic credit
Abstract: The aim of the project is to work in collaboration with three higher education institutions (Chester College of Higher Education, Liverpool Polytechnic and Liverpool University), to develop the use of work placements as academic components of first degree programmes as an option for students not on designated sandwich courses. The project will: (1) provide them with experience of the world of work, opportunities for taking initiatives and developing their independence; (2) provide them with the opportunity of gaining academic credit towards their degree from learning derived from experience in an employer site; (3) provide additional examples of ways to extend the range of main stream curricula with higher education to meet the requirements of employment; and (4) to enhance partnerships between higher education and employers.
Status: Sponsored project
Source of Grant: Learning from Experience Trust
Date of Research: 1990-1994
KEYWORDS: credits; experiential learning; industry-higher education relationship; job placement; work-education relationship

10/0209
Cheyney Road, Chester CH1 4BJ
01244 375444
Pickford, A. Mr
Developing information technology in a primary Post Graduate Certificate of Education course
Abstract: The aim of the project is to identify the factors affecting student competence in information technology in relation to the teaching practice experience of Post Graduate Certificate of Education (PGCE) students. The research will also consider the kinds of positive interventions which can be made by a teacher training institution and those personal characteristics of students which might lead to the development of information technology capability. The sample size is approximately 50 PGCE students (primary). The study uses questionnaires and direct observation by tutors.
Status: Individual research
Date of Research: 1992-1994
KEYWORDS: information technology; preservice-teacher education; student teachers; teaching practice

10/0210
Cheyney Road, Chester CH1 4BJ
01224 375444
Exeter University, School of Education, St Luke's, Exeter EX1 2LU
01392 263263
Heaney, S. Ms; *Supervisor:* Golby, M. Dr
Developing a curriculum in reflective practice: a narrative case study in primary teacher education

Abstract: This study examines the development of a particular primary postgraduate course in initial teacher education over the five year period from 1987 to 1992. The case record and accompanying narratives illustrate ways in which the concept of the reflective practitioner has been realised in the work of student teachers; showing also those aspects of the course which have contributed to the achievement of this model of the teacher in the students' work. The case study examines the relative roles and responsibilities of students, teachers and tutors in school-based teacher education and addresses the related issues of competence and effectiveness regarding the newly qualified teacher. Recommendations are drawn from the study for the establishment of successful partnership arrangements between schools and institutions of higher education which share in the preparation of new entrants to the teaching profession.
Status: Individual research
Date of Research: 1987-continuing
KEYWORDS: *preservice teacher education; primary school teachers; probationary teachers; professional development; student teachers; teaching profession*

Chichester Institute of Higher Education

10/0211
The Dome, Upper Bognor Road, Bognor Regis PO21 1HR
01243 865581
Jacques, K. Ms; Ferguson, J. Ms; Davies, R. Dr
Teacher professionalism: the role of initial training in the professional development of teachers
Abstract: The lack of any recent research on the competences and notions of professionalism held by practising teachers means that the construction of competences for the beginning teacher – and our understanding of their links with induction and continuing professional development – is being conducted on the basis of limited information. The project will provide important data about teacher perceptions of their professionalism; the role of initial teacher education in their professional development; and the sequencing of their training. The key research issues are: 1) How do teachers define 'teacher professionalism'? 2) What contribution did their initial training make to their professionalism? 3) How do they draw on their experiences as beginning and experienced teachers when mentoring trainee teachers? The research will be conducted in two phases and will incorporate quantitative and qualitative research methods. A survey questionnaire will be administered to a sample of 150 teachers at the beginning and end of the research project. The sample will be drawn from partnership schools across West Sussex and will include teachers from both school phases and a variety of school types. A sample of 75 teachers, with varying lengths of professional experience, will be drawn from the survey respondents. Qualitative research techniques (focus groups and interviews) will be used to gather data on teacher perceptions of professionalism (phase 1) and professional development (phase 2) from the sample of 75 teachers.
Status: Sponsored project
Source of Grant: Chichester Institute of Higher Education £9,430
Date of Research: 1994-continuing
KEYWORDS: *preservice teacher education; professional development; teacher attitudes; teacher development; teaching profession*

10/0212
The Dome, Upper Bognor Road, Bognor Regis PO21 1HR
01243 865581
Batho, R. Mr; *Supervisor:* Benton, M. Dr
Teaching Shakespeare at key stage 3
Abstract: This investigation has arisen out of the introduction, for the first time ever, of the compulsory study and examination of Shakespeare for all 13/14 year olds. Its aims are to: 1) Identify the different perceptions of teachers and pupils to the teaching of Shakespeare; 2) Investigate the range of teaching of Shakespeare at key stage 3, and whether the introduction of the compulsory testing of Shakespeare at key stage 3 has altered teachers' approaches and practices. It is intended to survey the teaching of Shakespeare in English departments in approximately fifty secondary schools, initially through a postal survey sent to English teachers in these schools. This is to be followed-up by interviews of teachers and pupils involved in the teaching and study of Shakespeare at key stage 3 in some of the schools, ensuring representation from rural, urban and inner-city schools.
Status: Individual research
Date of Research: 1993-continuing
KEYWORDS: *English literature; English studies curriculum; literature studies*

10/0213
The Dome, Upper Bognor Road, Bognor Regis PO21 1HR
01243 865581
Batho, R. Mr
An investigation into lower secondary school pupils' comparative use of CD ROMs and other reference material in English
Abstract: The aims of the project are to: 1) discover if and to what extent the use of CD-ROMs assist Year 7 pupils in attaining National Curriculum English Attainment Target 2 (AT2) (Reading) requirements; and 2) compare their use of CD-ROMs with their use of more conventional sources of information. The project involved a group of twelve Year 7 boys using CD-ROMs and other sources of information and means of presentation to further, complete and present an English project on one aspect of 'The Romans'. The outcomes will be of greatest relevance to initial teacher education courses, particularly subject study at middle and secondary school level. They include: 1) That pupils are attracted to using CD-ROMs to search and browse for information to meet the demands of subject study. 2) Access to and use of CD-ROMs in English is likely to help pupils meet certain parts of English AT2 requirements. 3) Access to CD-ROMs is likely to help pupils in other subject areas with similar requirements for information retrieval. 4) Staff development in the use and application of CD-ROMs in the areas indicated is necessary. Overall evaluation conclusions are that: 1) use of CD-ROMs by pupils in Year 7 did assist them in meeting English AT2 requirements; 2) when using CD-ROMs, pupils preferred trial and error first, and teacher advice second, rather than consulting the 'User Guide'; 3) pupils used a variety of CD-ROM discs effectively with minimal teacher intervention, and displayed many information technology and reading skills; 4) pupil difficulty included selecting effective keyword/phrase, and false expectations of the capabilities of CD-ROMs; 5) paired work with CD-ROMs was more effective than individual; 6) pupils showed a preference to work with CD-ROMs over other sources of information; the main advantages being CD-ROMs' capabilities in speed of finding information, cross-referencing and word processing. The results of the project will be published as part of a wider research report into CD-ROM use in schools and higher education institutions with initial teacher training courses.
Status: Sponsored project
Source of Grant: National Council for Educational Technology £1,000
Date of Research: 1992-1992
KEYWORDS: *computer uses in education; English studies curriculum; information technology; optical data discs*

10/0214
The Dome, Upper Bognor Road, Bognor Regis PO21 1HR
01243 865581
Blake, D. Mr; Hanley, V. Dr; Jennings, M. Mr
Change in teacher education: interpreting and experiencing new professional roles
Abstract: The project aims to investigate ways in which changes in teacher education are being interpreted. In its first year the project focused on the implementation and evaluation of a school-based Postgraduate Certificate in Education (PGCE) secondary course operating under the arrangements set in train by the Department for Education Circular 9/92. The research surveyed the views of students, mentors, teachers and college tutors on the operation of school-based initial teacher education. Interviews were conducted with a sample of respondents in twenty-four school locations. In the second phase of the project (1994-95) attention has switched to school-based and school-centred training arrangements in the primary sector.
Status: Sponsored project
Source of Grant: Chichester Institute of Higher Education £6,690
Date of Research: 1993-continuing
KEYWORDS: *mentors; postgraduate certificate in education; preservice teacher education; school based teacher education; student teacher attitudes; teacher attitudes*

10/0215

> The Dome, Upper Bognor Road, Bognor Regis PO21 1HR
> 01243 865581
> Lansdell, J. Ms; Gatrell, M. Mrs

A longitudinal study into the nature of progression in mathematical learning and the role of language in that progression

Abstract: There seems to be no clearly articulated and widely used theoretical framework for understanding the incremental learning processes in which children engage. This project aims to further develop the theory of complex learning originated by Norman and Rumelhart in 1978 in order to assist teachers in matching tasks more effectively to children's learning needs. This indepth longitudinal study of six children's learning in mathematics is qualitative. Using mathematical tasks, observation, informal and structured interviews, baseline information is obtained about the children's existing knowledge and understanding of particular aspects of mathematics. Mathematical activities are then designed and introduced to promote progression in the children's learning. The data collected as they work through the tasks indicates which learning processes are in operation. Primary sources for data collection will be the teaching activities themselves and the diagnosis of the children's learning. Data collection techniques will include observation (participant and non-participant) and interviews (informal and structured). Recording the data will involve use of field notes, audio and video tapes, children's drawings and written evidence. Preliminary findings indicate that children's progression in the learning of mathematics is dependent upon: 1) the learning experiences on offer; 2) the opportunity to verbalise their existing learning; 3) effective diagnosis and task matching; and 4) recognition of children's difficulties and a constructive response to them.

Published Material: GATRELL, M. & LANSDELL, J. (1993). 'A small-scale study into the nature of progression in the mathematical learning of three six-year old children'. Conference Paper presented at British Educational Research Conference, Liverpool, September 1993.; GATRELL, M. & LANSDELL, J. 'The nature of progression in mathematical learning', Research in Education. (in press).
Status: Sponsored project
Source of Grant: West Sussex Institute of Higher Education £4,000; Leverhulme Trust £4,100
Date of Research: 1993-continuing
KEYWORDS: learning activities; learning processes; mathematics education

10/0216

> The Dome, Upper Bognor Road, Bognor Regis PO21 1HR
> 01243 865581
> George, R. Ms

Ethnic minority representation in teacher education: an institutional perspective

Abstract: The project aims to investigate the reasons why ethnic minority students in the Crawley area of West Sussex appear not to apply for places on the teacher education course based at Crawley. The under representation of 'visible minority' teachers in the UK has been highlighted by the Community Relations Council in 1977 and the Swann Report (Great Britain. Department of Education and Science. (1985). Education for all: the report of the committee of enquiry into the education of children from ethnic minority groups. London: HMSO). Research in this area suggests that the reason many ethnic minority individuals and groups shun teacher education is personal experiences of racism suffered in and out of school. An analysis of the Graduate Teacher Training Registry suggests the situation remains the same. The figures for 1989 showed that black UK citizens made up only 2.06% of the total applying for Post Graduate Certificate in Education and that black graduate trainees are statistically more than five times as likely to fail the course. Crawley and the immediate environs has a large Asian community and Crawley College of Further Education recruits a significant number of students from ethnic minority groups onto their courses. It is important to analyse the post-tertiary destinations of these students and to examine the reasons why they shun the teacher education course situated on the same campus. Given the fact that Crawley College has a successful Access course from which many students are recruited to the Bachelor of Education (B.Ed.), the absence of ethnic minority students is cause for concern. The results of the research will be put forward for publication in a refereed journal.

Status: Sponsored project
Source of Grant: Chichester Institute of Higher Education £2,000
Date of Research: 1994-continuing
KEYWORDS: ethnic groups; preservice teacher education

10/0217

> Bishop Otter College, College Lane, Chichester PO19 4PE
> 01243 787911
> Southampton University, Faculty of Educational Studies,
> Highfield, Southampton SO9 5NH
> 01703 595000
> Laws, C. Mr; *Supervisor:* Evans, J. Dr

Individualism and curriculum development in physical education

Abstract: The word individualism is often used by educational writers and teachers without conscious precision as to its meaning. The research project attempts to discover whether teachers' commitment to individualism is expressed in their practice of teaching. Data have been utilized from a four year case study at one secondary school. The emphasis of the research focuses on the interpretative paradigm adopting the qualitative principles associated with ethnography. Initial analysis of data indicates that while individualistic approaches are expressed in the formal intended curriculum, they are not always evident in the practice of teaching. Issues of equality of opportunity, equal worth, and value were recognised by teachers but their practice did not express their commitment to these issues. The capacity of teachers to achieve an individualistic approach in their practice was also related to the distribution of power in schools and the limits inherent in the philosophy of individualism.

Published Material: LAWS, C.J. (1990). 'Individualism and teaching games: a contradiction of terms?', British Journal of Physical Education, Vol 21, No 4, Winter. Research supplement, No 8, pp.2-6.
Status: Individual research
Date of Research: 1986-1993
KEYWORDS: curriculum development; individualism; physical education; teaching methods; theory-practice relationship

10/0218

> Bishop Otter College, College Lane, Chichester PO19 4PE
> 01243 787911
> Sussex University, Institute of Continuing and Professional Education, Sussex House, Falmer, Brighton BN1 9RH
> 01273 606755
> Paton, R. Mr; *Supervisor:* Cooper, B. Dr

Renewal in music and education

Abstract: This is a theoretical and empirical study of musical learning and its role in the changing nature of musical functions and forms. It includes epistemology of music, psychological aspects of musical learning, improvisation and "holding forms" (containment structures for improvised musical acts). There will be empirical back-up from workshops with students, children and people with learning disabilities, also study of new-style methods and courses elsewhere.

Status: Individual research
Date of Research: 1986-1993
KEYWORDS: learning; music; music education

10/0219

> The Dome, Upper Bognor Road, Bognor Regis PO21 1HR
> 01243 865581
> London University, Institute of Education, Department of Policy Studies, Health and Education Research Unit, 20 Bedford Way, London WC1H OAL
> 0171 580 1122
> Hill, D. Mr; *Supervisor:* Whitty, G. Prof.

A comparative study of school based, school focused and college based approaches to teacher education

Abstract: This research aims to examine and evaluate contemporary developments in teacher education, and to explore the possibilities of developing a left radical analysis of teacher education policy, using a model of the critical reflective practitioner and teacher educator as 'transformative intellectual'. The main objectives of this study are to: (1) ascertain and evaluate the nature of a variety of routes to teacher education; (2) critique radical left, radical right and liberal perspectives on teacher education and schooling; (3) elicit novice teachers' reactions to key elements and issues in their training programmes; (4) identify elements and approaches that facilitate the development of critical reflective approaches to teacher education and schooling; (5) assist in the development of radical left policies for teacher education.

Published Material: HILL, D. (1990). 'Thatcherism, teacher education and the suppression of critical thought', Liberal Education and General Educator, Issue 64, pp.36-39.; CLAY, J., COLE, M. & HILL, D. (1990). 'Black achievement in initial teacher education: how do

we proceed into the 1990's', Multicultural Teaching, Vol 8, No 3, pp.31-35.; HILL, D. (1990). 'Local management of schools', New Socialist, October/November.; HILL, D. (1991). 'The Hillcole Group', Forum, Vol 33, No 2, pp.58-59.; HILL, D. (1992). 'What the radical right is doing to teacher education: a radical left critique', Multicultural teaching, Vol 10, No 3, pp.31-34. A full list of publications is available from the researcher.
Status: Individual research
Date of Research: 1990-continuing
KEYWORDS: political influences; politics education relationship; teacher education

10/0220
> The Dome, Upper Bognor Road, Bognor Regis PO21 1HR
> 0243 865581
> London University, King's College, Centre for Educational Studies, Cornwall House Annexe, Waterloo Road, London SE1 3TY
> 0171 836 5454
> Gaine, C. Mr; *Supervisor:* Ball, S. Prof.

Race and education: perspectives of primary BEd students
Abstract: This is a study of the perspectives about race and education held by primary Bachelor of Education (B.Ed) students, and whether these change in any way during their course, and whether critical or anti-racist perspectives persist after two years of working as teachers.
Published Material: GAINE, C. (1987). No problem here. London: Hutchinson Publishing Co.; GAINE, C. (1989). 'On getting equal opportunities policies'. In: COLE, M. (Ed). Education for equality. Basingstoke: Falmer Press.; GAINE, C. (1991). 'The effect of LMS on black children', Multicultural Teaching, Vol 9, No 2, pp.21-22, Spring.
Status: Individual research
Date of Research: 1989-continuing
KEYWORDS: antiracism education; probationary teachers; racial attitudes; student teacher attitudes; student teachers; teacher education

10/0221
> The Dome, Upper Bognor Road, Bognor Regis PO21 1HR
> 01243 865581
> London University, King's College, Centre for Educational Studies, Cornwall House Annexe, Waterloo Road, London SE1 3TY
> 0171 836 5454
> Jacques, K. Ms; *Supervisor:* Ball, S. Prof.

School-based routes into teacher education
Abstract: The past ten years has seen a shift dramatically away from notions of teacher education to a more pragmatic approach emphasising teacher training, with the focus on skills and competencies and learning-on-the-job. The aim of the study is to examine the political and educational context in which this shift has taken place and determine whether new forms of school-based teacher training achieve their stated goals, and what, if anything, has been lost. Seventy-five teachers will be interviewed about the effectiveness of their own teacher training. In addition, fifteen articled teachers are tracked from 1990, when they began their school-based training, to 1994 two years after completing their course.
Published Material: JACQUES, K.A. (1992). 'Mentoring in initial teacher education', Cambridge Journal of Education, Vol 22, No 3, pp.337-349.
Status: Individual research
Date of Research: 1990-continuing
KEYWORDS: preservice teacher education; school based teacher education; teacher attitudes

10/0222
> The Dome, Upper Bognor Road, Bognor Regis PO21 1HR
> 01243 865581
> Southampton University, Faculty of Education, Highfield, Southampton SO9 5NH
> 01703 595000
> Forth, I. Mr; *Supervisor:* Grenfell, M. Mr

The effects of language competence and language awareness on decision making and teaching strategies in the foreign language classroom
Abstract: The practical starting point for this study concerns the professional language needs of non-native speaker teachers of English. In certain teaching contexts, (i.e. the case of primary teachers of

English in Portugal and Italy) teachers have been told almost 'overnight' that they are to become English language teachers. In such circumstances, there is a considerable gulf between the methodological demands of the coursebook and the teachers' actual command and knowledge of English. The research will focus on the decision making and teaching strategies of non-native speaker teachers whose competence in English does not match the demands of the curriculum/coursebook in use in their teaching context. It is envisaged that in this way the research will be able to explore and understand some of the links between language competence/knowledge about language, and teaching behaviour in the foreign language classroom. In particular, via field work and qualitative data obtained from practising overseas teachers, it is envisaged that the research will describe the thinking and actions of a small sample of 'language-inexperienced' English language teachers in coping with various areas of planning, analysis, and classroom management. The research will ask to what extent does the 'language-inexperienced' non-native speaker teacher of English: 1) modify or adapt the coursebook and in what specific ways is this done? 2) employ compensatory or avoidance strategies in planning and implementation of classes? 3) evaluate and choose language tasks? 4) make decisions about levels of textual difficulty? 5) explain areas of the language code to learners? 6) make judgements concerning student error? 7) deal with spontaneous, unplanned features of classroom discourse? 8) improve their command of the language through the use of resources and interaction with classes?
Status: Individual research
Date of Research: 1994-continuing
KEYWORDS: English – second language; language proficiency; language teachers; second language teaching

10/0223
> The Dome, Upper Bognor Road, Bognor Regis PO21 1HR
> 01243 865581
> Southampton University, Faculty of Educational Studies, Highfield, Southampton SO9 5NH
> 01703 595000
> Pinel, A. Mr; *Supervisor:* Evans, J. Dr

Embedded teacher development
Abstract: The central interest 'embedded teacher development' refers to processes through which teachers develop perceptions of their task, while continuing as classroom practitioners. The major concerns are how they learn more about the capabilities and powers of their pupils and how they attempt to provide more opportunities for the release of these powers through reflecting on and re-structuring their approaches to them and to their teaching material. The medium is (mainly) mathematics. The teachers are primary teachers.
Status: Individual research
Date of Research: 1987-1993
KEYWORDS: primary school teachers; teacher behaviour; teacher development; teacher role; teaching methods

10/0224
> The Dome, Upper Bognor Road, Bognor Regis PO21 1HR
> 01243 865581
> University of Georgia, School of Education, Department of Curriculum of Supervision, Athens, Georgia, U.S.A.
> Fulcher, G. Mr; *Supervisor:* Phillips, A. Prof.

An analysis of the social, political and economic factors with reference to the formation of core curricula in diverse countries
Abstract: The research examines the social, political and economic conditions in the United Kingdom, Netherlands and Zambia, with reference to the core curricula developed in the above countries. The methodology attempts a comparative analysis by the review of international and national reports and documentation in relation to the core curricula found within the educational systems. An attempt is made to generate a theoretical model which seeks to identify and explain the diversification seen in core curricula as exemplified by the United Kingdom, Netherlands and Zambia.
Status: Individual research
Date of Research: 1989-1992
KEYWORDS: comparative education; core curriculum; National Curriculum; Netherlands; Zambia

City University

10/0225
Continuing Education Research Unit, Northampton Square, London EC1V 0HB
0171 477 8000
Capizzi, E. Ms; Lindsay, A. Mr; *Supervisor:* Davies, P. Ms
Database enhancement
Abstract: The current Access Course Register (ACRG) and the Educational Counselling and Credit Transfer Information Systems (ECCTIS) registers contain only limited information on the Access programmes included. City University Continuing Education Research Unit has been asked to produce a computerised database of the Access programmes listed as validated in the 1992 ACRG register but incorporating further information on curriculum, assessment structures, and progression routes and links. The system and structure in use will also provide for the future addition of other fields of information and has the advantage of permitting searching and retrieval of both the records of individual Access programmes and information on topics for all Access programmes. The aims of this project are to: (1) improve the information available to students, educational guidance advisors, and staff in further, adult and higher education whether Access tutors, development workers, higher education admission tutors, or researchers; and (2) contribute to the development of systems for the collation, management, presentation and dissemination of information on Access programmes. The objectives are: (1) enhancement of the information available on those Access programmes listed as validated in the 1992 ACRG register; (2) a contribution to the methodology and techniques for the analysis and coding of Access programme structures and features for information and research purposes; and (3) the dissemination of ideas and good practice for the establishment, development and use of information on the structure and features of Access programmes. The project will include: (1) Survey of Access Validating Agencies (AVAs) and/or the designated Access programme contact for courses listed as validated in the 1992 ACRG register to confirm existing programme details and obtain further information on curriculum, assessment structure and progression routes and links; (2) through collaboration with ACRG and ECCTIS, the productionof a compatible database with additional fields; and (3) production of a computer database structure permitting the searching and analysis of records and information fields, the production of reports in diverse formats, and the inclusion of further fields of information for future needs and development. The outcomes of the project will be: (1) the enhancement of ACRG and ECCTIS databases; (2) a database structure for records of Access programmes that provides for future development and enhancement; and (3) a report on the database system, methods of collation, recording and analysis.
Status: Sponsored project
Source of Grant: Council for National Academic Awards on behalf of the Higher Education Quality Council (HEQC)
Date of Research: 1992-1994
KEYWORDS: *access programmes; adult education; databases*

10/0226
Continuing Education Research Unit, Northampton Square, London EC1V OHB
0171 477 8000
Capizzi, E. Ms; *Supervisor:* Davies, P. Ms
Progress and performance of Access students
Abstract: Several important institutional and regional projects have examined the social composition and the progress and performance of Access students. However, there remains the need for a national context within which such studies can be located. Recent projects have also identified the need for a clearer map of the location and format of data on Access programmes and students. The methodological issues of such survey research and the conceptualisation and measurement of progress and performance would also benefit from investigation on a larger and longer scale. The aims of this project are to: (1) produce a national snapshot of the social characteristics and patterns of progression of Access students on programmes listed as validated in the 1992 Access Course Register (ACRG); (2) conduct a national cohort study of a sample of Access students on such programmes in 1992-1993. The objectives are to: (1) collect currently available data on Access students who completed such programmes in July 1992 and draw a profile of their characteristics and progression; (2) collect currently available data on Access students enrolling on such Access programmes in September 1992 and draw a profile
on their characteristics; (3) investigate in greater depth a representative sample of these 1992 enrolments in relation to social characteristics, performance and progression; and (4) map the current location, means and forms of data collection on Access students and programmes. The project will cover Access programmes in England, Wales and Northern Ireland and will be conducted using a variety of methods. It is restricted to programmes listed as validated in the current ACRG register, and covers as and where indicated, students completing programmes in July 1992 or enrolling in September 1992. Methods will include (1) the collection of documents and statistics from Access Validating Agencies (AVAs) and where necessary institutions; (2) secondary analysis of existing institutional, AVA and Department for Education statistical data; (3) questionnaire survey of a sample of Access tutors; and (4) questionnaire survey of a sample of Access students. The proposed outcomes will be: (1) a written report on the research process, the findings and proposals for further research; (2) a cohort record that can be used for further research, and in particular will form the basis of a follow-up study of students through their first year in higher education; (3) a written report on the variety of practices in record keeping for Access programmes (categories used, methods, timing and point of data collection); and (4) the dissemination of examples of good practice in record systems.
Status: Sponsored project
Source of Grant: Universities Funding Council
Date of Research: 1992-1994
KEYWORDS: *access programmes; adult education; mature students; student development*

10/0227
Continuing Education Research Unit, Northampton Square, London EC1V OHB
0171 477 8000
Carter, J. Ms; Webb, S. Ms; *Supervisor:* Davies, P. Ms
Wider participation for adults and the role of professional bodies in the finance sector
Abstract: The project has mapped the education and training routes to professional qualifications and membership across the finance sector and has identified the scale and scope of the involvement of professional bodies and associations particularly in relation to the control of qualifications and the recognition of courses and establishments. It has reviewed opportunities for adult learners and returners to pursue professional qualifications at initial level and considered the impact of national frameworks for vocational qualifications and of European developments.
Published Material: CARTER, J. & WEBB, S. (1993). Professional education in the finance sector: open to all? London: City University.
Status: Sponsored project
Source of Grant: Universities Funding Council £25,000
Date of Research: 1992-1993
KEYWORDS: *access to education; finance occupations; mature students; professional education*

10/0228
Continuing Education Research Unit, Northampton Square, London EC1V OHB
0171 477 8000
Parry, G. Mr; *Supervisor:* Davies, P. Ms
Adult learners and national databases in further and higher education
Abstract: The project has reviewed the range of information held on national databases in relation to adults in further and higher education and identified the strengths and weaknesses of individual databases. It has investigated the categories and processes involved in the construction of information about adults and assessed the use of these databases in policy, planning and research. It has also considered alternative models and future needs.
Status: Sponsored project
Source of Grant: Universities Funding Council £9,500
Date of Research: 1992-1994
KEYWORDS: *adult education; databases; further education; higher education; mature students*

10/0229
Continuing Education Research Unit, Northampton Square, London EC1V OHB
0171 477 8000
Davies, P. Ms

Access and participation of adults in higher education in Germany

Abstract: This project is designed to outline arrangements in Germany for the participation of adults in higher education. It has identified ways in which government policies and higher education institutions provide for access, participation and progression. A comparative approach has been adopted focusing on concepts and definitions of 'adults', 'access' and 'higher education' exploring patterns of participation with reference to different categories of learners and examining contemporary issues and debates which inform policy and practice.
Status: Sponsored project
Source of Grant: Universities Funding Council £36,800
Date of Research: 1993-1994
KEYWORDS: *access to education; adult education; Germany; higher education; mature students; student participation*

10/0230
> Continuing Education Research Unit, Northampton Square, London EC1V 0HB
> 0171 477 8000
> Davies, P. Ms

Access and participation of adults in higher education in France
Abstract: This project is designed to outline arrangements in France for the participation of adults in higher education. It has identified ways in which government policies and higher education institutions provide for access, participation and progression. A comparative approach has been adopted focusing on concepts and definitions of 'adults', 'access' and 'higher education' exploring patterns of participation with reference to different categories of learners and examining contemporary issues and debates which inform policy and practice.
Status: Sponsored project
Source of Grant: Universities Funding Council £45,000
Date of Research: 1991-1994
KEYWORDS: *access to education; adult education; France; higher education; mature students; student participation*

10/0231
> Continuing Education Research Unit, Northampton Square, London EC1V OHB
> 0171 477 8000
> Carter, J. Ms; Lindsay, A. Mr; *Supervisor:* Davies, P. Ms

Employer sponsorship of continuing professional development
Abstract: The aim of the research is to examine patterns of employer sponsorship and employee participation in postgraduate continuing professional development. The methods used include a questionnaire survey of students on part-time postgraduate courses in business management and financial services, group interviews with students, and interviews with employers.
Status: Sponsored project
Source of Grant: Universities Funding Council
Date of Research: 1993-1994
KEYWORDS: *employers; financial support; professional continuing education; sponsorship; staff development*

10/0232
> Social Statistics Research Unit, Northampton Square, London EC1V OHB
> 0171 477 8000
> Steedman, J.; *Supervisor:* Bynner, J. Prof.

Birth Cohort Study 70: basic skills element
Abstract: The Birth Cohort Study 70 (BCS 70) is a longitudinal study owned by City University. The Adult Literacy and Basic Skills Unit (ALBSU) sponsored an inclusion of questions on basic skills to this large sample group (12,000 people born in April 1970) to be undertaken during 1991-1992. Cohort members were asked attitudinal questions on their perceived ability in basic skills. A sub-sample of 1,650 individuals was selected to undertake a 30 minute assessment in reading and number skills. These were linked to nationally recognised competences in basic skills designed by ALBSU. ALBSU is sponsoring a continuing programme of data analysis based on this work, currently running until the end of 1994.
Status: Sponsored project
Source of Grant: Adult Literacy and Basic Skills Unit £100,000
Date of Research: 1970-continuing
KEYWORDS: *adult literacy; basic skills; cohort analysis; numeracy*

College of St Mark and St John

10/0233
> Centre for Physical Education, Health and Recreation, Derriford Road, Plymouth PL6 8BH
> 01752 777188
> Cardiff Institute of Higher Education, School of PE, Sport and Leisure, Cyncoed Centre, Cardiff CF2 6XD
> 01222 551111
> Jones, G. Mr; *Supervisor:* Treadwell, P. Mr

The comparative affects of the National Curriculum (Physical Education) on the provision of physical education
Abstract: The study aims to investigate, evaluate and formulate the affects of the implementation of a National Curriculum in Physical Education on the teaching and learning of primary school physical education. Through this study, an attempt to construct theoretical paradigms and/or a series of criteria of recommended best practice will be made via on-going case studies. The research methodology involved in this proposed study includes the quantitative and qualitative assessment of key issues, namely the teaching and learning strategies that relate to primary school physical education teachers, teachers' perceived competence in teaching primary school physical education, and pupils' perceived physical competence in the activity specific programmes of study. The changing role of the curriculum leader for physical education in the primary school will also be investigated. The opportunities for a comparative study (e.g. West Devon/South Glamorgan) may also prove a useful focus. The August 1992 implementation of a National Curriculum in Physical Education in years 1, 3 and 7 allow this study to run chronologically with the implementation in remaining primary years. Creative research methods will include a sophisticated research design and education research paradigms, and a case study methodology that precedes surveys and data collection in a quest to identify important questions to test generally, or to facilitate data collection. The research will aim to help primary schools to provide a 'broad, balanced, relevant, progressive and differentiated' physical education curriculum.
Published Material: JONES, G.M. (1990). 'Fitting Everything In', Sports Teacher, June.; JONES, G.M. (1990). 'Jumping Off Points', Junior Education, Vol 14, No 10, pp.30-31.; JONES, G.M. (1990). 'Fitting Everything In', Primary Supplement, British Journal of Physical Education, Vol 21, No 3.; JONES, G.M. (1991). 'Know, Understand, Do – and Appreciate', Sports Teacher, December.
Status: Individual research
Date of Research: 1993-continuing
KEYWORDS: *National Curriculum; physical education; primary education*

Coopers and Lybrand Associates

10/0234
> 1 Embankment Place, London WC2N 6NN
> 0171 213 2892
> Thompson, Q. Mr; *Supervisor:* D'Armenia, M. Ms

Investment appraisal of Education Support Grant XXX for the training of youth leaders in the inner cities in England and in the valleys in Wales
Abstract: The Department of Education and Science commissioned Coopers and Lybrand to carry out an investment appraisal of Education Support Grant (ESG) XXX for the training of youth leaders in the inner cities in England and in the Valleys in Wales. The appraisal estimated the total investment in the local scheme; assessed the extent of support from other sources; compared costs with those of other forms of youth worker training; assessed the costs and benefits of the schemes; and evaluated the efficiency of the ESG mechanism. This was one of a number of evaluation exercises of the ESG, the combined results of which will allow the Department to assess the overall value of the programme and its viability as a model for future youth training.
Status: Sponsored project
Source of Grant: Department of Education and Science £53,500
Date of Research: 1991-1993
KEYWORDS: *financial support; inner city; investment; training; youth leaders; youth service*

10/0235

> 1 Embankment Place, London WC2N 6NN
> 0171 213 2892
> Lakin, J. Mr; *Supervisor:* Thompson, Q. Mr

Local Management of Schools (LMS) and small schools

Abstract: The study was to produce a good management guide for small schools operating under Local Management of Schools (LMS). Research was carried out in four local education authorities (LEAs) with samples of schools with less than 200 pupils. Schools were visited and headteachers, governors and non-teaching staff interviewed. LEA officers were also consulted. A good management guide was then produced and circulated to all small schools in England and Wales.

Status: Sponsored project
Source of Grant: Department for Education £56,000
Date of Research: 1993-1993
KEYWORDS: educational administration; local management of schools; school based management; small schools

Council for Environmental Education

10/0236

> Reading University, London Road, Reading RG1 5AQ
> 01734 756061
> Midgley, C. Ms

Building support for environmental education (Phase II)

Abstract: The overall aim is to develop a coherent strategy for the development of information provision in the field of environmental education. Specific objectives are to: 1) support the formation of local structures and networks for information provision, distribution and communication; 2) develop communication and cooperative working between environmental education information providers; 3) provide training and support for information providers; 4) support users by increasing their awareness of available sources of information; 5) develop criteria for the evaluation of materials and to apply these as appropriate; 6) provide comprehensive information on training opportunities for environmental education; and 7) strengthen and enhance the Council for Environmental Education (CEE's) information services into a National Information Centre for Environmental Education.

Status: Sponsored project
Source of Grant: Department of the Environment £21,000; Esso UK plc £15,000
Date of Research: 1994-continuing
KEYWORDS: educational resources; environmental education; information needs; information sources

10/0237

> Reading University, London Road, Reading RG1 5AQ
> 01734 756061
> Loughborough University of Technology, Department of Information and Library Studies, Loughborough LE11 3TU
> 01509 263171
> Midgley, C. Ms

Building support for environmental education (Phase I)

Abstract: The overall aim is to improve the provision and use of support for environmental education. The main objectives of the project are to: (1) increase awareness amongst practitioners of the sources of support; (2) encourage discerning use and evaluation of information by users; (3) improve and extend the means of dissemination of/access to information; (4) improve the applicability of the support provided; (5) establish mechanisms for maintaining the currency of information disseminated; and (6) recommend further initiatives, depending on the results of the research. Phase I was a survey of the information needs of environmental education practitioners, carried out by questionnaire and semi-structured interviews. A consultation period followed the publication of the report of the survey. Based on the findings of the survey and the consultation exercise, a strategy has now been produced to facilitate the development of information provision for environmental education.

Published Material: JAMES, B. (1992). Environmental education information: meeting the needs. Reading: Council for Environmental Education.; MATTHEWS, G. & STEPHENS, D. (1992). Environ-

mental education information needs: a report of a survey of environmental education information needs in schools and youth work. Reading: Council for Environmental Education.; COUNCIL FOR ENVIRONMENTAL EDUCATION (1993). Information in action: the Council for Environmental Education's information strategy. Reading: Council for Environmental Education.

Status: Sponsored project
Source of Grant: Department of the Environment £45,000; Esso UK plc £3,000
Date of Research: 1991-1994
KEYWORDS: educational resources; environmental education; information needs; information sources

Coventry University

10/0238

> Coventry School of Art and Design, Priory Street, Coventry CV1 5FB
> 01203 631313
> Flynn, S. Mrs; *Supervisor:* Richards, C. Dr

Interactive multimedia for teaching numeracy with an emphasis on the dyslexic

Abstract: The aim of the research is to establish whether the use of multimedia and fast access to data can be an effective method of teaching those with learning difficulties or whose ways of learning and knowing do not fall into what has come to be known as the normal process of learning. Sixty per cent of dyslexic people have a problem with numeracy. Most dyslexics have a problem with memory. It is these two elements which will be addressed in this research. The aim is to produce a multimedia system, which could be used to create personal 'landscapes' from which associative links can be made.

Status: Individual research
Date of Research: 1992-continuing
KEYWORDS: computer assisted learning; dyslexia; interactive video; learning disabilities; multimedia approach

10/0239

> Coventry School of Art and Design, Priory Street, Coventry CV1 5FB
> 01203 631313
> Wright, A. Mr; *Supervisor:* Syson, A. Dr; Richards, C. Dr

Computer aided learning in design education

Abstract: This is an enquiry into the didactic potential of computer aided instruction when based on the heuristic paradigms of the traditional design project. The use of computers in teaching gives students control over their own learning. As the pedagogic tradition of art and design education relies heavily on heuristic practice graphic design students should benefit from computer driven programmes of independent learning. Most design students are computer literate, have an empathy with screen imagery and are familiar with the process of learning-by-doing, therefore the introduction of computer aided learning (CAL) would seem to be axiomatic. Courseware prepared by teachers is of variable quality and needs the development of skills not found within traditional teaching practice. A prerequisite for good courseware design is the revision and refinement of current teaching practices. Presently, good courseware design is inhibited by the absence of any authoritative guide lines, production standards or evaluation criteria. HyperCard software is used for authoring the courseware for a pilot study. This simulates a tutorial/project based structure for teaching basic time based media concepts to first year graphic design students. The students involved in the pilot study find CAL techniques an acceptable alternative to traditional teaching methods, they willingly accept an increased responsibility for taking the initiative in the acquisition of knowledge and quickly adopt appropriate study skills. It is difficult to make an accurate evaluation of the learning outcomes but the initial knowledge gain is good. It is concluded that computer based education can offer design students the benefits of individual tutelage and a self-discovery learning base which relates strongly to their heuristic heritage.

Status: Individual research
Date of Research: 1991-1994
KEYWORDS: computer assisted learning; design education; hypermedia

10/0240

School of Health and Social Sciences, Priory Street,
Coventry CV1 5FB
01203 631313
Heames, R. Mrs; Green, M. Mrs

Investigation into course evaluation (module)

Abstract: A course evaluation programme has been tested, modified
and used with some success in the B.Sc Occupational Therapy course
at Coventry University. The aims of the present small study are to:
(1) review present provision; (2) produce a scheme of evaluation
which might be generally useful (across different disciplines); (3)
investigate the most effective and efficient method of data analysis.
Letters of enquiry have initially been sent to all seven higher education institutions linked in the Midlands through staff development
programmes. Two other institutions (known to have been involved
in course evaluation) have also been contacted. Information collected
from these sources and within Coventry University will determine
visits to be made to clarify the areas/topics evaluated, the methodology used, the method of processing data and subsequent action taken.
A pilot evaluation will be produced and tested, followed by a final
version. Systems of data handling will be considered from the beginning and will, to some extent determine the design.
Status: Sponsored project
Source of Grant: Coventry University: Learning Systems Development Fund £2,244
Date of Research: 1992-1993
KEYWORDS: course evaluation; educational quality

10/0241

School of Health and Social Sciences, Priory Street,
Coventry CV1 5FB
01203 631313
Wildman, S. Mr; Weale, A. Mr; Rodney, C. Mr;
Pritchard, J. Mrs

**The impact of the diploma in professional studies in nursing on
professional development and clinic practice as perceived by
past and present students**

Abstract: The Diploma in Professional Studies in Nursing (DPSN)
has been part of the move in nursing and other health professions to
develop the academic level of practitioners. In nursing this has
gathered momentum through the development of pre-registration
nurse education to diploma level arising from Project 2000. A new
emphasis on clinical practice has emerged in the 1990's which is
influencing the development of post-registration courses to address
this issue. The proposed study would evaluate some of the ways in
which a diploma level course can inform practitioners, influence their
careers and make a difference to their practice. This appears to be an
under researched area and is important in order to contribute to
appropriate course development. This is an initial study of a diploma
level course and could point the way towards evaluation studies of
courses at undergraduate and postgraduate level. Data will be generated by postal questionnaire to both past and present students. All
students who have successfully completed the DPSN since 1988 (n
= approximately 90) and the current two cohorts (n = 88) are eligible
for inclusion in the study.
Status: Sponsored project
Source of Grant: Coventry University
Date of Research: 1994-1994
KEYWORDS: nurse education; professional education

10/0242

School of International Studies and Law, Priory Street,
Coventry CV1 5FB
01203 631313
Jones, D. Mr; Orsini-Jones, M. Mrs

Multi-media course in Italian language

Abstract: The aim is to prepare a course for the teaching of Italian
language which would be suitable for use in this institution. It will
need to make use of audio and video recording facilities and computer
programs as well as written material, and to be usable with limited
input from teaching staff. Work is currently progressing on a beginners course, but it is hoped ultimately to produce an integrated course
for three years.
Status: Sponsored project
Source of Grant: Coventry University
Date of Research: 1986-continuing
*KEYWORDS: course content; educational materials; Italian; mod-
ern language studies; multimedia approach*

Dartington Social Research Unit

10/0243

Foxhole, Dartington Hall, Totnes TQ9 6EB
01803 862231
Bristol University, Department of Social Policy and
Planning, 8 Woodlands Road, Bristol BS8 1TN
01179 251424
Cleaver, H. Mrs; *Supervisor:* Millham, S. Prof.

A continued evaluation of 'Catch 'em Young'

Abstract: The study will explore the possible long term benefits for
children who were involved in 'Catch 'em Young', a 3 year scheme
established to prevent delinquency and behaviour problems in secondary school children. The report submitted to the Department of
Education and Science in 1989 scrutinised children's behaviour as
they transferred from primary to secondary school. The long term
follow up study allows us to focus on the study group of 495 children
as they pass through school, make important career decisions and
enter the adult world. The previously applied methodology, which
used both extensive and intensive dimensions, will be utilised. Thus,
the research will continue to combine an overview resulting from a
survey of the experiences of the study children with insights and
perceptions of a small group of children, their teachers and parents.
When linked with the earlier research findings, it will provide an
opportunity to explore how family, school and peer group influences
interact in the transitions of adolescents.
Published Material: CLEAVER, H. (1991). Vulnerable children in
schools: a study of Catch 'em Young – a project helping 10 year olds
transfer school. Aldershot: Dartmouth Publishing Company.
Status: Sponsored project
Source of Grant: Department of Education and Science £30,000
Date of Research: 1990-continuing
*KEYWORDS: antisocial behaviour; behaviour problems; delin-
quency prevention; longitudinal studies; secondary school pupils;
transfer pupils*

De Montfort University

10/0244

37 Lansdowne Road, Bedford MK40 2BZ
01234 351966
Whitehead, M. Dr; Lockwood, A. Ms

**The contribution of Physical Education to National
Curriculum cross-curricular themes, dimensions and skills**

Abstract: Bedford College is supporting a research project looking at
the role of Physical Education in National Curriculum cross-curricular themes, dimensions and skills. The initial stimulus to the project
was the result of a perceived mismatch between the potential Physical
Education has to make a significant contribution to cross-curricular
work and the lack of recognition of this potential in National Curriculum documentation. The research has three strands: (a) a literature
search of references outside the National Curriculum; (b) a detailed
examination of National Curriculum documentation; and (c) an investigation to ascertain how far schools already acknowledge the
potential for Physical Education in this area. The first of the strands
is still in process while the second and third are complete.
Status: Sponsored project
Source of Grant: Bedford College of Higher Education
Date of Research: 1992-1993
*KEYWORDS: cross curricular approach; National Curriculum;
physical education*

10/0245

37 Lansdowne Road, Bedford MK40 2BZ
01234 351966
Smith, J. Ms

Interactive video dance disc 2

Abstract: A research project based at Bedford College of Higher
Education between 1988 and 1989 culminated in the production of
an interactive video laser disc for the teaching of dance in secondary
schools and colleges. The college team's major breakthrough was
recognised by the British Interactive Video Association in October
1989 when the silver award in honour of excellence in production of

interactive video to achieve educational aims was presented. Most of the discs made have been sold to schools, colleges and resource centres. Building on the knowledge gained from the work in choreography and design of the content for the above disc, the researcher is currently working with a professional choreographer, Siobhan Davies, with the aim of producing a compact interactive video disc and accompanying educational materials based upon a new work to be choreographed between March and May 1993. The intention is to produce a teaching resource pack to develop students' artistic and aesthetic appreciation of the Siobhan Davies dance work. The design and content of the pack is informed by the resource-based teaching methodology for dance education developed over the past ten years.
Published Material: SMITH, J. (1991). 'Teaching dance performance in secondary education', British Journal of Physical Education, Vol 22, No 4, pp.14-17.
Date of Research: 1988-continuing
KEYWORDS: dance education; interactive video

10/0246

Polhill Avenue, Bedford MK41 9EA
01234 351671
Sampson, J. Mr; Stephenson, H. Ms; Wooldridge, I. Mrs;
Supervisor: Yeomans, R. Mr
Teacher education and mentorship
Abstract: The aims of the research are: to clarify the nature of mentorship and the skills mentors use in working with students; to identify similarities and differences within various systems; and to suggest the conditions which are conducive to successful mentoring outcomes in primary teacher education. The project uses case studies of twelve mentors across three forms of primary teacher education with Bedford College programmes: Postgraduate Certificate in Education (PGCE); Articled teachers scheme; and year three of the Bachelor of Education (B.Ed.) course. Each researcher has acted as participant observer within one or more of the schools over a period of at least seven months (with the exception of B.Ed. four week school experience). Case studies are in the process of being written, using field diaries, documentary sources, and semi-structured interviews. The whole is subject to an ethical code governing participant rights. Once draft data has been cleared with participants, issues will be generated across case studies. The scheme has now been extended to include secondary schools.
Published Material: SAMPSON, J.S. & YEOMANS, R.M. (1994). Primary school mentorship in action. Lewes: Falmer Press.
Status: Sponsored project
Source of Grant: Paul Hamlyn Foundation £7,500; Bedford College of Higher Education £7,500
Date of Research: 1991-1993
KEYWORDS: mentors; preservice teacher education; primary school teachers; secondary school teachers

10/0247

Polhill Avenue, Bedford MK41 9EA
01234 351671
Leask, M. Ms; *Supervisor:* McLean, M. Dr
The search for quality in education: international comparisons
Abstract: The first stage of the research involved an indepth analysis of attempts to improve the quality of the UK education system. The findings of this work provide the framework for the research. Seven areas are identified as providing foci for improving the quality of a system: (1) The structure of the education system. (2) Traditional, current and legislative demands in the areas of curriculum and assessment and approaches to teaching and learning. (3) Teacher education. (4) Teacher quality and qualifications. (5) Management development. (6) Evaluation, accountability and motivation. (7) Resources (delegation of/allocation of). As decision making processes within a system govern the process of introducing and managing changes, other education systems have been investigated to illuminate alternative structures for decision making. This was the second stage of the research. Using these findings, it was decided to study the Australian system in parallel to the UK system. The practice in both countries in the above areas provides the focus for the third stage of the research.
Published Material: GODDARD, D. & LEASK, M. (1992). The search for quality: planning for improvement and managing change. London: Paul Chapman Publishing.
Status: Individual research
Date of Research: 1990-continuing
KEYWORDS: comparative education; educational quality

10/0248

37 Lansdowne Road, Bedford MK40 2BZ
01234 351966
Rix, C. Mr; Boyle, M-L. Miss; *Supervisor:* Grugeon, E. Mrs
The role of language in children's acquisition of knowledge in science
Abstract: Building on recent research as part of the National Oracy Project, the present project explores the role of language in the acquisition of knowledge in specific curriculum areas, with special reference to the science curriculum in primary schools. The main focus will be: primary school children's language in science; the development of related concepts; the role of talk in learning; and the development of non-chronological writing. The project will be based on the observation and recording of children's talk and writing in primary schools, and will include the development of a suitable database. It is hoped to extend the project in subsequent years to the history curriculum area.
Status: Individual research
Date of Research: 1993-continuing
KEYWORDS: child language; classroom communication; language of instruction; language research; primary school pupils; science education

10/0249

Polhill Avenue, Bedford MK41 9EA
01234 351671
Hull University, School of Mathematics, Hull HU6 7RX
01482 46311
Simpson, A. Mr; Duffin, J. Mrs
Natural, conflicting and alien: implications for teaching and learning
Abstract: The research is an attempt by the researchers to build a personal framework for understanding the learning process. Critical incidents involving a wide variety of learners ranging from school pupils and university undergraduates to teachers in initial and inservice training as well as ourselves, have been examined. The methodology has been analysis of, and reflection on, such incidents. Based on the belief that all learners develop individual mental structures to account for experience, the work has identified three types of experiences: 'natural' experiences which fit the learner's current mental structures, 'conflicting' experiences which jar on those structures and 'alien' which do not connect at all with current structures. The research has gone on to distinguish between experience and the learner's response to it. A major outcome from the work has been the recognition of the place of introspection in the building of the theory and the fact that examination of one's own learning, as that to which one has the most direct access, can provide a powerful tool for examining the learning of others. It is hoped that the continuation of the work, by looking at, for example, the question of 'intersubjectivity' and the meaning of the word 'understanding' will enable the theory to provide a route towards greater understanding of how best to effect learning.
Published Material: DUFFIN, J. & SIMPSON, A. (1992). 'Natural, conflicting and alien: a forum for discussion'. Proceedings of the British Society for Research into Learning and Mathematics, 21 November 1992.; DUFFIN, J. & SIMPSON, A. (1993). 'Three case studies: analysis, links, speculations and questions'. Proceedings of the British Society for Research into Learning and Mathematics, 22 May 1993.; DUFFIN, J. & SIMPSON, A. (1993). 'Natural, conflicting and alien: concepts for analysing the learning process'. Proceedings of British Congress on Mathematical Education 2, Leeds.; DUFFIN, J. & SIMPSON, A. (1993). 'Natural, conflicting and alien', Journal of Mathematical Behaviour, Vol 12, No 4, pp.313-328.
Status: Individual research
Date of Research: 1990-continuing
KEYWORDS: learning processes; mathematics education; thinking skills

10/0250

Polhill Avenue, Bedford MK41 9EA
01234 351671
Hull University, School of Mathematics, Hull HU6 7RX
01482 46311
Simpson, A. Mr; *Supervisor:* Cutland, N. Prof.
Undergraduate attitudes to a degree course in mathematics
Abstract: The project is based on semi-structured interviews with undergraduates on traditional mathematics degree courses at universities in northern England. The interviews were conducted over two

years and analysis of them has attempted to classify developing attitudes students have about mathematics and their degree course. A theoretical basis of radical construction has been developed and a stage theory related to the work of William G. Perry constructed to help account for the results of analysis.
Published Material: DUFFIN, J. & SIMPSON, A. (1991). 'Interacting reflections on a young pupil's work', For the Learning of Mathematics, Vol 11, No 3, pp.10-15.; DUFFIN, J. & SIMPSON, A. (1993). 'Natural conflicting and alien', Journal of Mathematical Behaviour, Vol 12, No 4.
Status: Individual research
Date of Research: 1989-1994
KEYWORDS: course evaluation; degrees – academic; mathematics education; student attitudes

10/0251

School of Arts and Humanities, Centre for Postgraduate Teacher Education, The Gateway, Leicester LE1 9BH
01162 551551
Rice, J. Mrs; O'Sullivan, T. Mr; Saunders, C. Ms
Communication and professional competencies in a modular humanities programme
Abstract: The Communication and Professional Studies (CPS) programme plays a key role in the degree scheme in arts and humanities (DSAH) at De Montford University. In brief, its function is two-fold: (1) it is designed to equip students with the core skills necessary to participate effectively within a flexible, modular arts degree; and (2) it begins to develop in students some of the key vocational and future career skills relevant to their undergraduate studies. This project was completed in August 1993. A summary of the aims include open learning packages; developing tutoring and student-centred delivery skills for staff; research on teaching and learning requirements generated by DSAH and staff development to support these needs; provide a model for development for open learning packages on the Level 1 DSAH programme. The conclusions reached by the project team were that the diversity of student needs can be best accommodated by offering a variety of teaching and learning experiences. There was a marked difference between mature students and 'traditional' post A-level entrants. The former were keen on the flexibility that open learning offered them but were concerned about their study skills; the latter were less inclined to open learning but were confident in their study skills abilities which were fresh to them from recent studying. The majority of students preferred learning in a context of practical, applied situations rather than lectures. The open learning packages were welcomed but students also wanted staff support in conjunction with them. Staff's responses to the idea of open learning packages were favourable if guarded. There was a recognition of the amount of time needed to assemble a successful package. Some staff took the opportunity to attend staff development sessions on the application of computer aided learning.
Status: Sponsored project
Source of Grant: De Montfort University £19,000
Date of Research: 1991-1993
KEYWORDS: communication skills; competency based education; humanities; minimum competencies; modular courses; open education

10/0252

School of Arts and Humanities, Centre for Postgraduate Teacher Education, The Gateway, Leicester LE1 9BH
01162 551551
Iwano, M. Miss; *Supervisor:* Mason, R. Dr
Curriculum reform in Japanese art education: the case for multiculturalism
Abstract: This research investigated, analysed and evaluated Japanese art curriculum at primary, secondary and high school levels. It explored the possibility of curriculum reform in Japanese art education with reference to theory and practice of multicultural education. The researcher used the hypothesis that controversy in aesthetics is a potential source of curriculum development in art education. The notion of controversy was explored with reference to diverse 'kinds' of theory: educational research; art history and criticism in art education; general philosophy; aesthetics of criticism; literature education; and curriculum. An analysis was made of 'standard oppositions' in philosophy and aesthetics with particular reference to the divide between the analytical and continental philosophical traditions. Underlying theoretical frameworks were identified and speculations made about the kinds of critical strategies that might arise from them. Teaching about intention in literature education was explored in

detail with the aim of discovering strategies for metacriticism that might be applied to art. The research also addressed the problem of translating discipline-based content in respect of controversy into a pedagogy of metacriticism. Following an examination of pedagogical models in general education theory, it was concluded that fundamental controversy (in aesthetics) implies a paradoxical, though not illogical, alignment of 'commitment' and 'impartiality' in respect of art education subject content and wider educational goals. Arguments were synthesized to formulate a set of principles for teaching metacriticism with reference to relevant classes of artworks, which linked theoretical frameworks with key distinctions in art criticism (notably, intrinsic/extrinsic evidence, descriptive/interpretive statements, moral/aesthetic judgments, and intentionalisms/anti-intentionalism). The implications of teaching aesthetics and criticism as an interactive whole were discussed in respect of curriculum development and teacher training at both national and institutional levels. The study concluded with a reflective criticism of the research method and suggestions for future research.
Published Material: IWANO, M. (1992). 'Some issues on Japanese multicultural education', Conference Paper NAEA, Phoenix.; IWANO, M. (1991). 'Towards multicultural curriculum reform', The case for Japanese multicultural education, National Research Conference, Brighton.
Status: Individual research
Date of Research: 1989-1994
KEYWORDS: art education; Japan

10/0253

School of Arts and Humanities, Centre for Postgraduate Teacher Education, The Gateway, Leicester LE1 9BH
01162 551551
Mason, R. Dr; Maughan, C. Mr
The artists-in-education training project
Abstract: This pilot project was set up in 1990 by the Arts Council working in conjunction with three regional arts associations and Leicester Polytechnic (now De Montfort University). Its aims were 'to provide performing artists, visual artists, craftspeople, writers and composers with the skills they need to work with confidence in education today'. The programme implemented in 1991 covered a ten day period and included residential training weekends staffed by a combination of artists, teachers and educators and six day placements in primary or secondary schools. The progress of the project was systematically documented and evaluated by a project officer specifically appointed for this purpose. The evaluation report identified strengths and weaknesses of the programme of training and of the residencies in terms of the contribution they made to arts learning in schools.
Published Material: ILLSLEY, R. (1991). Artists-in-education training project: external summative evaluation. Leicester: Leicester Polytechnic.; THOMAS, S. (1991). Artists-in-education training project: artists' report I. Leicester: Leicester Polytechnic.; THOMAS, S. (1992). Artists-in-education training project: artists' report II. Leicester: De Montfort University.; MASON, R. (1993). Artists-in-education training project: final report. Leicester: De Montfort University.
Status: Sponsored project
Source of Grant: Arts Council of Great Britain £30,000
Date of Research: 1990-1993
KEYWORDS: artists; peripatetic teachers; training

10/0254

School of Arts and Humanities, Centre for Postgraduate Teacher Education, The Gateway, Leicester LE1 9BH
01162 551551
Allison, B. Prof.
Research in art and design in the United Kingdom
Abstract: The Allison Research Index of Art and Design (ARIAD), has been developed as the UK national database for research in art and design with support from and in collaboration with all the major bodies associated with art and design, (Arts Council of Great Britain, Chartered Society of Designers Conference for Higher Education in Art and Design, Council for National Academic Awards, Design Council and the National Society for Education in Arts and Design) as well as with government departments. ARIAD originated and grew out of the Index of British Studies in Art and Design Education published by Gower Press in 1986 to meet the present and future needs of students, teachers, researchers and practitioners across all the art and design fields in both education and industry. The ARIAD includes information on research submitted for the academic awards of UK universities and the CNAA as well as that carried out by

individuals and research teams in industry, local and national organisations and in professional and private practice. The ARIAD is published in hard copy electronically in Apple Macintosh Hypercard and MS Dos.

Published Material: ALLISON, B. (1991). Allison Research Index of Art and Design. Project No 32. London: Council for National Academic Awards.; ALLISON, B. (1992). Allison Research Index of Art and Design. Leicester: Leicester Expertise.
Status: Sponsored project
Source of Grant: Department of Trade and Industry £21,000
Date of Research: 1990-continuing
KEYWORDS: *art; databases; design; information sources; research*

10/0255
School of Arts and Humanities, Centre for Postgraduate Teacher Education, The Gateway, Leicester LE1 9BH
01162 551551
Tyers, J. Mr; *Supervisor:* Allison, B. Prof.
A study of personality and other attributes, qualities and opinions of 'A' level design students
Abstract: Recent research identified subjective claims that students studying 'A' level design possessed certain qualities, attributes and abilities not found in students who studied other academic 'A' level examination subjects. The principle aim of the research was to objectively: (1) Identify and quantify the differences between the structure and content of the 'A' level design examination course and other 'A' level examination courses. (2) Identify and compare the personality characteristics, attributes, abilities and opinions of 'A' level design students with those who study other 'A' level subjects. (3) Identify and compare the personality characteristics, attributes and abilities of potential 'A' level design students with those who chose to study the subject. (4) Determine the relationship between the personality characteristics, attributes and abilities of 'A' level design students and: (a) success in the final examination; (b) general intelligence; (c) arts/science bias; (d) gender. (5) Determine the extent to which, if any, an 'A' level design examination course develops certain personal qualities, attributes, abilities and opinions in students. (6) Determine the validity of teacher assessment of those personal qualities which lead to success in the final examination. The following methodologies were used: (a) descriptive studies; (b) causal-comparative cross-sectional studies; (c) quasi-experimental longitudinal studies. The instruments used included: (a) descriptive questionnaires; (b) unstandardised single pole 'designing' attributes rating scale; (c) AH4 and AH6 general ability tests; (d) Cattell's 16 Personality Factor Questionnaire. The subjects included: (a) cluster sample of 200 'A' level design students; (b) sample of 100 other 'A' level students; (c) sample of 30 'A' level design teachers; (d) sample of 5 other 'A' level teachers. The data was subjected to statistical analysis based on: (a) differences between means; (b) analysis of variance; (c) correlation. A number of significant differences were oectively shown to exist between the groups of students and teachers which provides a firmer basis for the understanding of the effects on students of specialised study in design. The data also provided standardised 16PF norms for British 'A' level students.
Status: Individual research
Date of Research: 1988-1993
KEYWORDS: *A level examinations; design education; learner characteristics; student attitudes*

10/0256
School of Arts and Humanities, Centre for Postgraduate Teacher Education, The Gateway, Leicester LE1 9BH
01162 551551
Kypreou, I. Ms; *Supervisor:* Allison, B. Prof.; Mason, R. Dr
Assessment in fine art at first degree level: a comparative study of the principles and methods underlying assessment of fine art students in Athens and Leicester
Abstract: Evaluation of worth in art historically has been a contentious issue, particularly when affected by fashion or taste. Nonetheless, assessment of quality or worth has been a necessary element in national competitions and central in education at all levels. In undergraduate and postgraduate fine art courses, assessment is a central element in determining levels of award. Two degree courses in fine art, in Britain and in Greece are compared in terms of the procedures and criteria employed for the assessment of students' work. In both institutions the assessment of students at first degree level is based principally on their practical work. A major difference between the two institutions is that whilst in Greece the final assessment is made

by tutors in discussion without written or specified criteria, in Britain the assessment is based on explicit documented criteria. However, in both institutions there is no doubt that underpinning all assessment is the consideration of the extent to which the individual students are able to demonstrate their capability as professional artists and it is likely that, implicitly, the assessment in both institutions is based on commonly held concepts of fine art activity and shared beliefs about the nature of artistic production. The study aims to determine: (i) the role theories of art play in the assessment of fine art students at first degree level; (ii) whether the assessment procedures in two fine art institutions in Britain and in Greece respectively, can be described relative to theories of art and art criticism; and (iii) the extent to which the differing procedures of assessment utilised in the two institutions are subject to or affected by the theoretical positions adopted by individual tutors. In order to achieve this, a triangulation model is pursued to determine the relationships between explicated criteria, assessors'/tutors' theoretical positions and students' perceptions of assessment. More specifically, the objectives of the study are to determine: (iv) the tutors' pspectives of teaching in fine art, of curriculum, assessment procedures and criteria and whether their personal artistic inclinations affect the above; (v) the students' perspectives of teaching in fine art, curriculum, assessment procedures and criteria and whether these perceptions are affected by factors such as achievement or gender; (vi) the researcher's perspective of the structure, teaching and curricula of the fine art courses, the procedures and criteria for assessment and the level of objectivity operating in the assessment of painting students. Some of the methodological problems and concerns and a sample of the findings of this ongoing research as well as a selection of visual examples of students' work from both institutions will be presented.
Status: Individual research
Date of Research: 1989-1993
KEYWORDS: *art education; assessment; comparative education; degrees – academic; fine arts; Greece*

10/0257
School of Arts and Humanities, Centre for Postgraduate Teacher Education, The Gateway, Leicester LE1 9BH
01162 551551
Bruntlett, S. Mr; *Supervisor:* Allison, B. Prof.
The use of computer based technology in the development of teaching and learning strategies in art and design education
Abstract: The action research project will begin with a preliminary survey of existing practice in Computer Aided Art and Design (CAAD) teaching and learning. This qualitative research project will be accomplished by a series of visits and a search of the literature. Teachers' narratives (experienced or beginners in terms of CAAD), will be gathered from taped or otherwise documented interviews and conversations with a dozen art educators from a wide variety of art and design backgrounds. Hard copy relating to 'best methods', curricula or schemes of work for CAAD will be compiled, analysed and interpreted. These will be compared with schemes of work in National Curriculum (Art) and differences or similarities accounted for. Examples of work will be collected to show what is currently being achieved using teaching and learning strategies. This will lead to a structured critical analysis of CAAD practice and form the basis of a specific CAAD curriculum which may be based on competence, objectives, process or other models. Such a curriculum will be tested by both experienced and inexperienced teachers to see if there is a demonstrable need for a separate curriculum, or whether existing art and design curricula can accommodate new technologies as they develop as is claimed by some theories of art. The results of such testing will determine the best use of new technology in art and design education which will be formulated in a series of recommendations relating to the appropriateness or otherwise of new technology across art and design experience in secondary education.
Published Material: A full list of publications is available from the researcher.
Status: Individual research
Date of Research: 1994-continuing
KEYWORDS: *art education; computer assisted design; computer uses in education; design education*

10/0258
School of Arts and Humanities, Centre for Postgraduate Teacher Education, The Gateway, Leicester LE1 9BH
01162 551551
Nakase, A. Prof.; *Supervisor:* Mason, R. Dr; Bruntlett, S. Mr

Teaching craft inheritance in Britain and Japan
Abstract: The three year project is a joint venture between research teams in Joetsu and De Montfort Universities to investigate the use of computers to develop a resource base for crafts, and as a teaching/learning strategy for delivering crafts input into the National Curriculum (Art) in schools. The proposed outcomes of the research are two prototype bilingual multimedia applications for teaching crafts heritage in schools, which are part of a larger crafts resource. Access to collections of domestic and rural crafts has been secured in Tokyo and Leicestershire Museums, and the project has been set up as a collaborative venture involving museum educators and teachers and pupils in schools. The programme of research is built on previous investigations by team members into computer applications in art and design, teaching crafts heritage and education for international understanding.
Published Material: IWANO, M. (1991). 'Museum education in school', Museum Education Studies, Vol 2, No 1, pp.10-11.; BRUNTLETT, S. (1992). 'Uses of CD ROM in the art and design classroom as a teaching learning resource', Micro User, Vol 10, No 4, p.26.; SUSUMAGO, K. (1993). 'The present state of crafts teaching in Japanese schools'. Paper presented at De Montfort University Research Colloquia, March 1993.
Status: Sponsored project
Source of Grant: De Montfort University £1,000; DAIWA Foundation £2,000
Date of Research: 1993-continuing
KEYWORDS: *arts education; computer uses in education; cultural education; handicrafts; museums; visual arts*

10/0259
School of Arts and Humanities, Centre for Postgraduate Teacher Education, The Gateway, Leicester LE1 9BH
01162 551551
London University, Imperial College of Science, Technology and Medicine, Department of Mechanical Engineering, Exhibition Road, London SW7 2AZ
0171 589 5111
Nagata, T. Mr; *Supervisor:* Allison, B. Prof.; Coe, B. Mr; Kennaway, A. Prof.
An investigation into the spatial visualisation ability and psychopedagogical strategies for training designers
Abstract: This project includes: (1) A review of literature relating to spatial abilities to determine indicators of maturity in terms of developmental level and susceptibility for training in visual spatial representation. Critical review of strategies for the development of abilities to represent visual spatial form from a cognitive viewpoint. Critical review of the potential effect of related factors including the visual/haptic (Lowenfeld, 1964) and field-dependency/independency (Witkin et al 1949) dichotomies. (2) The development of a pedagogical strategy designed to develop visualisation and representational skills and the generation of aptitude measures applicable to higher education students in the design fields. (3) The validation of the strategy and aptitude measures with a pilot sample of higher education design students. It is hypothesised that the anticipated variations in the students' performances on pre-test and post-test criterial tasks will be due, in particular, to differences in spatial abilities. (4) Experimental design, in particular: (a) development of test battery – spatial abilities and representational skills; (b) instructional treatments – traditional drawing methods and experimental drawing methods; (c) selection of experimental and control groups drawn from graphic design, industrial design and engineering students. (5) Implementation of research design. Pre-tests; experimental teaching programmes; post-tests. Protocol analysis on the basis of comparison of psychopedagogic strategies. (6) Analysis of data and conclusions.
Status: Individual research
Date of Research: 1992-continuing
KEYWORDS: *design education; designers; spatial ability; visualisation*

10/0260
School of Arts and Humanities, Centre for Postgraduate Teacher Education, The Gateway, Leicester LE1 9BH
01162 551551
Leicester University, School of Education, University Road, Leicester LE1 7RH
01162 522522
Stuart, J. Mrs; *Supervisor:* Allison, B. Prof.; Merry, R. Dr
Art critical abilities: modes of reasoning and intellectual development

Abstract: The present study seeks to continue an enquiry into the nature of the relationship between artistic and intellectual development, through the vehicle of art criticism in art and design education. The intention is to extend the findings of a replication of Hickey's (1975) enquiry which established such a relationship through a study of art critical abilities both in Hickey's terms of cognitive and perceptual functions and also through modes of reasoning measure. Therefore the present aim is to elaborate the modes of concrete and formal reasoning measure in conjunction with a programme of study to promote modes of reasoning through art critical development in secondary education. The theoretical framework to examine cognition-perception and modes of reasoning was derived from educational psychology and critical studies in art education. Theories of cognitive development were derived from Piaget's model of logical operations (Inhelder and Piaget, 1964), modified by Bruner's (1967) theory of instruction; and perception from Arnheim's (1954) theory of visual perception. Feldman's (1971) theoretical art critical strategy of Description, Analysis, Interpretation and Evaluation, interpreted as art critical abilities, examined the role of cognition-perception through an hypothetical model of reasoned explanation. The modes of reasoning measure combined the theories of Peel's (1971) transference of the Piagetian model to concrete and formal judgements with Bernstein's (1961) theory of language as an indicator of cognitive development, to provide a measure in art critical terms. The measure allows analysis of critical thinking in a subject specific area (McPeck, 1981). The research methodology involves the provision, testing and evaluation of the contribution of the critical strategy programme of study, to cognitive development through modes of reasoning. The programme will be tested with two samples of pupils aged twelve years and sixth-formers, with tests for operational levels; critical abilities and modes of reasoning r statistical analysis of data. The educational advantages will be: (a) an empirically tested programme which promotes and objectively measures artistic development in terms of concrete and 'higher' level cognitive thinking through modes of reasoning; and (b) a contribution to the debate about the nature and merits of critical thinking in specific subject areas.
Status: Individual research
Date of Research: 1989-1994
KEYWORDS: *art education; criticism; intellectual development; reasoning*

10/0261
School of Arts and Humanities, Centre for Postgraduate Teacher Education, The Gateway, Leicester LE1 9BH
01162 551551
University of Central England in Birmingham, Perry Barr, Birmingham B42 2SU
0121 331 5000
Eastwood, J. Ms; *Supervisor:* Mason, R. Dr; Denscombe, M. Dr; Shute, C. Dr
An investigation into the therapeutic relationship and implications for speech language therapy training
Abstract: Student training in speech-language therapy comprises theoretical and practical components. Theories are largely borrowed from other disciplines such as psychology, linguistics and medicine, but practical work with communicatively-impaired individuals is an important part of training. The theory of therapy is, however, poorly understood. This research will examine the theory or philosophy and practice of therapy in the literature and in a variety of in situ settings where communicatively-impaired individuals receive treatment from speech-language therapists. The aim of the research is to analyse and clarify existing theories of therapy and to develop new systems and methods or models for training speech-language therapy students.
Published Material: EASTWOOD, J. (1988). 'Qualitative research methodology – an additional research method for speech pathology?', British Journal of Disorders of Communication, Vol 23, No 2, pp.171-184.; SHUTE, C., EASTWOOD, J., FREEMAN, M. & WHITEHOUSE, J. (1989). Supervised work experience in speech therapy. Birmingham: Birmingham Polytechnic.; C.N.A.A. Briefing Paper No. 23 (1990). A survey of supervised work experience in speech therapy.
Status: Individual research
Date of Research: 1990-continuing
KEYWORDS: *speech therapy; speech training; therapists; training methods*

Derby University

10/0262
Western Road, Mickleover, Derby DE3 5GX
01332 47181
Wallace, G. Dr
Local Management of Schools: database of research
Abstract: The aim of this research is to establish and maintain a database of Local Management of Schools (LMS) related research with the objective of: (a) ensuring ready access to an overview of LMS research and findings for British Educational Research Association (BERA) members and other researchers; (b) widening such access beyond what is normally published, e.g. dissertations, and theses at Masters level; (c) identifying and disseminating successful practice; (d) identifying and disseminating issues of interest or concern to policy makers and the media.
Published Material: WALLACE, G. (Ed). (1991). Local management of schools. London: Multilingual Matters. British Educational Research Association. (BERA Dialogues Series, No 6).
Status: Sponsored project
Source of Grant: Derby University £3,700; British Educational Research Association £600
Date of Research: 1990-continuing
KEYWORDS: databases; local management of schools; research

Dundee University

10/0263
Centre for Continuing Education, Dundee DD1 4HN
01382 223181
Hartley, J. Dr
An analysis of government policy for teachers' professional development in Scotland: 1979-1990
Abstract: An analysis of government documentation and research on teachers' continuing professional development, informed by critical theory.
Published Material: HARTLEY, J.D. (1986). 'Structural isomorphism and the management of consent in education', Journal of Education Policy, Vol 1, No 3, pp.229-237.; HARTLEY, J.D. (1990). 'Tests, tasks and Taylorism: a model T approach to the management of education', Journal of Education Policy, Vol 5, No 1, pp.67-76.; HARTLEY, J.D. (1989). 'Beyond collaboration: the management of professional development in Scotland', British Journal of Education for Teaching, Vol 10, No 2, pp.253-261.; HARTLEY, J.D. (1990). 'Beyond competency: a socio-technical model of continuing professional education', British Journal of Inservice Education, Vol 16, No 1, pp.66-70.
Status: Individual research
Date of Research: 1986-continuing
KEYWORDS: academic staff development; educational policy; inservice teacher education; professional development; Scotland

10/0264
Centre for Continuing Education, Dundee DD1 4HN
01382 223181
Kaskaris, I. Mr; *Supervisor:* Hartley, J. Dr
The Gramscian theory of education: a critical study of the development of educational theory
Abstract: This research aims to generate a theory of education which, firstly, provides a critical analysis of the positivism underlying much educational theory; secondly, to analyse the post-modern semiotic reaction to this, with a view to pointing up its largely de-politicised, ahistorical essence; and to suggest a convergence of Gramscian theory and critical theory.
Status: Individual research
Date of Research: 1988-continuing
KEYWORDS: educational theories; sociology of education

10/0265
Centre for Continuing Education, Dundee DD1 4HN
01382 223181
Murray, R. Mr; *Supervisor:* Hartley, J. Dr

The development of managerialism in Scottish education since 1945
Abstract: The study examines the increasing tendency in Scottish education to use industrial and corporate modes of management in education since 1945.
Status: Individual research
Date of Research: 1988-1993
KEYWORDS: educational history; management in education; Scotland

10/0266
Centre for Continuing Education, Dundee DD1 4HN
01382 223181
Neale, F. Miss; *Supervisor:* Cooke, A. Mr
Assessment of adult education needs in the Carse of Gowrie area
Abstract: In conjunction with Tayside Regional Council, the research will attempt to give an impression of the Carse of Gowrie area geographically, statistically and educationally, to review current adult education provision, and consider how feasible it is to set up an Adult Education Association, and how this would fit into existing patterns of provision. Questions to be addressed include: 1) What changes have there been in population, occupations, patterns of travel in recent years? 2) Is a sense of 'community' still important, and is 'local provision' meaningful to the residents of The Carse? 3) How far has informal education survived change? 4) How far has education become a 'consumer product'? Methods to be used include statistical analysis, questionnaire, and interview.
Status: Individual research
Date of Research: 1993-continuing
KEYWORDS: adult education; community education; rural areas

10/0267
Centre for Continuing Education, Dundee DD1 4HN
01382 223181
Owen, M. Mrs; *Supervisor:* Cooke, A. Mr; Spackman, A. Dr
Policy frameworks for access in three European educational systems
Abstract: Access has become a prominent issue on the higher education agenda. This study has focused on policy making for access programmes in three contrasting systems including the educational criteria used in formulating policy. This is to test the hypothesis that different countries ask different questions and set different criteria for the development of educational programmes. This in turn affects whether new or existing delivery systems and curricula are adopted in programmes initiated by central and local government. In Scotland, the study has focused on the Scottish Wider Access programme which began in 1988. In Denmark, a much longer established Higher Preparatory programme which encompasses both adults and younger people has operated since the early 1970's. In the Netherlands, there is no dedicated programme for adult access to higher education. The aims and objectives of the project are to: a) identify policy differences and similarities in the three countries in relationship to adult access programmes initiated by central or local government; b) explore what educational purposes and criteria have been used to develop effective programmes of adult access to higher education; c) explore how far current programmes prepare adults for access to higher education within the single market; d) assess the implications of the findings of the study for future policies for adult access programmes. The investigation was based on a literature survey of the three countries, supplemented by interviews with approximately 20 people in each country concerned with educational policy making including politicians, civil servants and educationists from universities, further and adult education colleges.
Status: Sponsored project
Source of Grant: University Funding Council £34,000; Scottish Higher Education Funding Council £8,000
Date of Research: 1992-1994
KEYWORDS: access programmes; access to education; adult education; comparative education; higher education; mature students

10/0268
Centre for Medical Education, Ninewells Hospital and Medical School, Dundee DD1 9SY
01382 660111
Mulholland, H. Dr
Assessment of competence in general practice
Abstract: The research was designed to improve the reliability and

validity of the Membership Examination of the Royal College of General Practitioners (RCGP). Results of the last five years were analysed (for approximately 2,000 candidates each year) and recommendations made as to changes in numbers and types of questions in the existing papers. Two new types of test were developed: (1) The Critical Reading Paper in which candidates have to read, critically evaluate and discuss applications of scientific journal articles and of printed material of a variety of forms. (2) The simulated surgery in which candidates are placed in conditions which simulate as far as possible real surgery conditions and are assessed on their competence in consultation. This part of the research is now being continued with funding from the European Community.
Published Material: LOCKIE, C. (1990). (Ed). 'The MRCGP Examination', Occasional Paper, No 46. London Royal College of General Practitioners.
Status: Sponsored project
Source of Grant: Royal College of General Practitioners; Department of Health; European Community
Date of Research: 1988-1993
KEYWORDS: assessment; competence; examinations; medical education; medicine; physicians

10/0269
> Centre for Medical Education, Ninewells Hospital and
> Medical School, Dundee DD1 9SY
> 01382 660111
> McAleer, J. Dr; *Supervisor:* Harden, R. Prof.; Laidlaw, J. Miss

A programme to encourage and facilitate doctors' participation in clinical audit
Abstract: The need for audit as one aspect of clinical practice is now generally accepted throughout the medical profession. Its adoption requires a change in behaviour of doctors – one which will be successful and long lasting. This distance learning programme intends to provide a more indepth training about audit by using a 5 stage approach – awareness, interest, appraisal, trial and adoption. The programme will be designed to relate audit to the doctor's (both hospital and community) day to day practice and encourage further learning about audit on-the-job. It comprises a resource book which contains key information about audit. In addition participants will receive a series of 'doctors' diaries' in which audit activities will be described in a problem based format. Responses to these problems will be collected and feedback provided – using comparisons between decisions made and those of colleagues. There will also be a number of practical audit activities linked to the diaries. The programme will be offered on a national basis. The wealth of information collected as part of the distance learning programme will be analysed with the key findings published in report form. Another feature of the study is concerned with an evaluation of the complete package.
Published Material: ARNOLD, C. et al (1992). Moving to audit: what every doctor needs to know about audit. Dundee: University of Dundee; The Postgraduate Office.
Status: Sponsored project
Source of Grant: Scottish Office Home and Health Department
Date of Research: 1991-1993
KEYWORDS: distance education; institutional evaluation; medical services; professional continuing education

10/0270
> Centre for Medical Education, Ninewells Hospital and
> Medical School, Dundee DD1 9SY
> 01382 660111
> Lindsay, G. Mr; Hesketh, A. Mrs; *Supervisor:* Harden, R. Prof.

An individualised patient education programme for community pharmacy practice
Abstract: This project aims to develop and study a practical system to provide patient education via the community pharmacy. This will involve the use of new technology to provide user-friendly interactive patient education materials. An important aspect of the project will look at ways of developing and studying a liaison between pharmacists, general practitioners, and patients, as well as studying their attitudes to the community pharmacist giving out this type of information.
Status: Sponsored project
Source of Grant: Scottish Office Home and Health Department
Date of Research: 1990-1994
KEYWORDS: health education; medical services; patient education; pharmacists; pharmacy

10/0271
> Centre for Medical Education, Ninewells Hospital and
> Medical School, Dundee DD1 9SY
> 01382 660111
> Thomson, L. Mrs; Rogerson, E. Mrs; *Supervisor:* Harden, R. Prof.

Diploma in advanced nursing studies
Abstract: The Diploma Course aims to equip the individual with the knowledge and ability necessary to provide a high standard of individualised nursing care which is research based and reinforces individual accountability of the practitioner. Furthermore, the course aims to embrace the dynamics of change and emphasise the necessity for continuing professional updating and educational development.
Published Material: ROGERSON, E. et al (1992). Nursing in the 90's. Dundee: University of Dundee; Centre for Medical Education.; ROMNEY-ALEXANDER, D. (1992). Quality of life. Dundee: University of Dundee; Centre for Medical Education.
Status: Sponsored project
Source of Grant: University of Dundee; Tayside Health Board
Date of Research: 1990-continuing
KEYWORDS: distance education; nurse education; professional continuing education; professional development

10/0272
> Centre for Medical Education, Ninewells Hospital and
> Medical School, Dundee DD1 9SY
> 01382 660111
> Davis, M. Dr; *Supervisor:* Harden, R. Prof.

The Wound Programme
Abstract: The Wound Programme is a learning resource for medical undergraduates in the UK, Europe and North America. It comprises a resource book, a student study guide and a teachers' guide. It is designed to inform undergraduates about recent advances in the field of skin wound healing and can be employed by medical schools wishing to implement one or more of the following curriculum strategies, student centred learning, problem based learning and integration of the curriculum, both horizontal and vertical. The resource book employs a new format, based on a hypertext layout, and a new approach to the assessment of patients with wounds – the wound healing matrix.
Status: Sponsored project
Source of Grant: ConvaTec
Date of Research: 1990-1994
KEYWORDS: educational materials; learning strategies; medical education; medical students

10/0273
> Centre for Medical Education, Ninewells Hospital and
> Medical School, Dundee DD1 9SY
> 01382 660111
> Harden, R. Prof.; Smyth, J. Dr

Technology based learning in medicine: beyond courseware
Abstract: A consortium of seven medical schools comprising Dundee, Aberdeen, Belfast, Edinburgh, Glasgow, Liverpool, and Newcastle-upon-Tyne, with Dundee as the lead centre are collaborating in the development of a system of technology based learning. Using personal computers, students will assess the computer based system, each charting an individualised learning pathway and availing of all the resources and information to which they will have access. The project includes: (1) Utilisation of the computer as a vehicle of delivery for sophisticated study guides, important aids to effect efficient learning and teaching. (2) Encouraging students to keep a computer based record of progress of tasks accomplished and of their clinical experiences. (3) Access to personal timetables provided by the Faculty Office and stored on computer which will enable students to schedule their time with regard to learning and other activities. (4) Personal databases used to store and retrieve information including abstracts of primary or secondary sources, perhaps annotated by the tutor as well as lecture and tutorial notes and 'handouts' made available in hypertext format. Students will be able to add their own annotations to resource materials provided. (5) Students using self-assessment instruments with feedback. (6) The use of word processing for writing up reports and assignments encouraged; a system of E-mail will allow both inter and intra institutional communication; use of an on-line medical thesaurus will facilitate development, with understanding of medical terminology and vocabulary. This will be particularly helpful when students are based off the main campus. The programme will be implemented in the clinical phase of the

medical curriculum, in particular in relation to clinical method courses where the features described above offer significant advantages in terms of efficiency and effectiveness. The project will be evaluated by the Scottish Council for Research in Education (SCRE).
Status: Sponsored project
Source of Grant: Universities Funding Council
Date of Research: 1992-continuing
KEYWORDS: computer assisted learning; computer uses in education; individualised methods; information technology; medical education

10/0274
Centre for Medical Education, Ninewells Hospital and Medical School, Dundee DD1 9SY
01382 660111
Davis, M. Dr
The wound programme – assessment procedure
Abstract: The Wound Programme is self-learning material for medical students on the management of patients with wounds. Its evaluation employs a student and a teacher questionnaire, multiple choice questions, and Objective Structured Clinical Examination (OSCE) stations. The aim of the research is to discover how students and teachers used the programme, their attitudes to it, and how different utilisation influenced student learning measured by the examination questions.
Published Material: DAVIS, M.H. et al (1992). The wound programme. Dundee: University of Dundee, Centre for Medical Education.
Status: Individual research
Date of Research: 1990-1994
KEYWORDS: educational material evaluation; educational materials; medical education

10/0275
Centre for Medical Education, Ninewells Hospital and Medical School, Dundee DD1 9SY
01382 660111
Mulholland, H. Dr
Evaluation of a medical school curriculum
Abstract: This project consists of the development of a method for evaluating the curriculum of a medical school. Observation and interviews were used to generate questionnaires which have been extensively pilot tested within the Faculty and with control groups from other faculties. The final form of the questionnaire is now being translated into an optically scanned version.
Status: Sponsored project
Source of Grant: University of Dundee: Centre for Medical Education
Date of Research: 1987-1994
KEYWORDS: curriculum evaluation; medical education

10/0276
Centre for Medical Education, Ninewells Hospital and Medical School, Dundee DD1 9SY
01382 660111
Mulholland, H. Dr
Study of experimental learning approaches in distance learning
Abstract: The study consists of evaluation of distance learning at Certificate and Diploma & Master programmes, all of which incorporate elements of experimental learning. The methods used are questionnaire and analysis of tutor-student correspondence. The sample used is 500 health profession teachers.
Status: Individual research
Date of Research: 1991-1994
KEYWORDS: distance education; medical education; programme evaluation

10/0277
Centre for Medical Education, Ninewells Hospital and Medical School, Dundee DD1 9SY
01382 660111
Mulholland, H. Dr
Evaluation in interactive video tutorials in anatomy
Abstract: The project consists of qualitative and quantitative evaluation of the effectiveness of interactive video tutorials in Anatomy. Methods used are pre- and post-tests, interaction analysis and questionnaire. Individual and group use of the tutorials are being evaluated.

Status: Sponsored project
Source of Grant: Rheumatism and Arthritis Council £3,000
Date of Research: 1991-1993
KEYWORDS: human computer interaction; interactive video; medical education

10/0278
Centre for Medical Education, Ninewells Hospital and Medical School, Dundee DD1 9SY
01382 660111
Mulholland, H. Dr
Assessment of vocational training in general practice
Abstract: The project consists of a survey of methods of assessment currently in use in the Northern Region in the Vocational Training Schemes for General Practice.
Status: Sponsored project
Source of Grant: Regional Adviser in General Practice, Northern Region
Date of Research: 1992-1993
KEYWORDS: medical services; training

10/0279
Centre for Medical Education, Ninewells Hospital and Medical School, Dundee DD1 9SY
01382 660111
Mulholland, H. Dr
Evaluation of clinical teaching
Abstract: The project consists of the development of a questionnaire for evaluating clinical teaching. Observation of teaching and interviews with staff and students were used to generate a preliminary questionnaire which asked students to compare their best and worst placements on a range of criteria. Those criteria which distinguish between good and bad placements will be built into a final questionnaire which will be used to evaluate clinical teaching.
Status: Sponsored project
Source of Grant: Dundee University: Faculty of Medicine
Date of Research: 1992-1994
KEYWORDS: clinical experience; medical education; medical students

10/0280
Centre for Medical Education, Ninewells Hospital and Medical School, Dundee DD1 9SY
01382 660111
Mulholland, H. Dr
Evaluation of the Universities Funding Council funded computer assisted learning (CAL) project 'Fully Evaluated Problem-Centred Practical and Tutorial Courseware for the Life Sciences'
Abstract: The project consists of qualitative and quantitative evaluation of computerised modules in practical life science classes and a comparison of the new technology with the methods which it replaced. Methods used will be gain scores, interaction analysis, questionnaire and interview.
Status: Sponsored project
Source of Grant: Universities Funding Council £17,000
Date of Research: 1992-continuing
KEYWORDS: biological sciences; computer assisted learning; medical education

10/0281
Centre for Medical Education, Ninewells Hospital and Medical School, Dundee DD1 9SY
01382 660111
Dundee Dental Hospital, Department of Orthodontics, Dundee DD1 4HW
01382 226041
Davis, M. Dr; *Supervisor:* Clark, J. Mr; Harden, R. Prof.
Clinical audit: scenarios for evaluation and study
Abstract: The aim of this project is to provide a picture of national payment management practice in orthodontics through a series of patient management problems. All UK hospital-based orthodontists will participate in the study, coordinated by regional advisers. Answers to the six problems will be collated in Dundee, analysed and the findings distributed to every region with educational material related to the topics. Individual practitioners can compare their own patient management with that of their colleagues in the region and in

other regions. National and regional trends in patient management will be highlighted by the study.
Status: Sponsored project
Source of Grant: Royal College of Surgeons of Edinburgh £9,000
Date of Research: 1992-1993
KEYWORDS: dentistry; medical education

10/0282
    Centre for Medical Education, Ninewells Hospital and Medical School, Dundee DD1 9SY
    01382 660111
    Leicester University, Department of General Practice, Leicester General Hospital, Gwendolen Road, Leicester LE5 4PW
    01162 584873
    Mulholland, H. Dr; Fraser, R. Prof.; *Supervisor:* McKinlay, R. Dr
Assessment of consultation competence in general practice
Abstract: This is the second stage of the 'Assessment of competence in general practice' project. The project consists of a series of studies into the validity and reliability of the Leicester Assessment Package. The criteria on which assessment is to be based were validated by submission to 100 course organisers. An experiment was undertaken in which five doctors carried out six standardised patient consultations and were assessed by six markers. Another study investigated the correlation between scores based on video and those based on live consultations. A further study will investigate the effects on scores if assessors are allowed to question candidates about the reasons for their actions.
Published Material: HARDEN, R.M. et al (Eds). (1992). Approaches to the assessment of clinical competence. Dundee: University of Dundee; Centre for Medical Education.
Status: Sponsored project
Source of Grant: Department of Health; Royal College of General Practitioners
Date of Research: 1991-1993
KEYWORDS: assessment; competence; examinations; medical education; medicine; physicians

10/0283
    Department of Social Work, Dundee DD1 4HN
    01382 223181
    Kendrick, A. Dr; Fraser, A. Dr
An examination of the factors that promote the development of an integrated child care strategy
Abstract: This is an overview study of current policies and developments in Scottish Social Work Departments which relate to the integration of residential and community child care services between agencies (particularly Social Work and Education) and with Social Work Departments. The study will be carried out by content analysis of policy and planning documents and by interviews with key social work personnel. In three selected local authorities the nature of the integration of child care services will be studied in more detail over two years. A cohort study will look at career patterns of children in care and will focus on the outcomes of particular social work placements. Collection of data will be by questionnaire, analysis of case files and interviews with children and young people. Interviews will be carried out with personnel involved with the cohort of children to examine the relationship between organisational structures policies and practice as perceived by social work staff, Children's Panel Members and Reporters to the Children's Panel. To provide information about the level of inter-agency integration, educational staff will be interviewed. A questionnaire survey of residential establishments used for children in the care of Social Work Departments will be carried out to establish the extent and range of residential services in Scotland and their links with complementary child care services.
Status: Sponsored project
Source of Grant: Social Work Services Group £200,000
Date of Research: 1990-1993
KEYWORDS: child welfare; community services; residential care; Scotland; social services; social work

10/0284
    MicroCentre, Park Wynd, Dundee DD1 4HN
    01382 223181
    Beattie, W. Mr; Booth, L. Mrs; Morris, C. Dr; *Supervisor:* Newell, A. Prof.; Ricketts, I. Dr; Gregor, P. Dr

The use of predictive software in education
Abstract: Predictive Adaptive Lexicon (PAL), a predictive word processing system has been developed at Dundee University and was originally designed to assist physically disabled people to type. For the period April 1990 to February 1992 the research was widened to include the client group, those with spelling and language dysfunction. This research was conducted in collaboration with two special education teachers who worked with the funded research staff. This part of the project was funded by TEED and supported: (1) The continued evaluation of PAL within schools in Tayside and with adults with physical, spelling and language disabilities, together with the provision of client assessment and inservice training. (2) The further development of PAL and of other related software, including: (a) PALSTAR, (a word processor designed to work with PAL and to be particularly appropriate for people with special needs); (b) a speech output facility for the PAL/PALSTAR combination; (c) SPELLER, a spelling corrector designed to be compatible with PAL/PALSTAR to aid people whose spelling problems were so severe that standard spelling correctors would not perform adequately; (d) a prototype 'syntax PAL' designed for people with language problems as well as spelling dysfunction. PAL and PALSTAR are commercially available through Lander Software plc of Glasgow, and SPELLER is undergoing customer acceptance testing. A National Training Award was presented to the University by the Department of Employment for this work. It is proposed that the PAL predictive software and further developments of it could be of significant value to adult literacy training, this would include: (a) development of training structures and packages using predictive software within adult literacy, and evaluating the usefulness of predictive software within adult literacy training; and (b) further development of the software, particularly for the adult literacy market.
Published Material: A full list of publications is available from the researcher.
Status: Sponsored project
Source of Grant: Department of Trade and Industry; Scottish Office Education; Department £100,000; Training, Enterprise and Education Directorate £240,000; Scottish Enterprise and Mathews Trust £100,000
Date of Research: 1983-1994
KEYWORDS: computer software; computer uses in education; learning disabilities; special educational needs; spelling; writing difficulties

Durham University

10/0285
    Business School, Enterprise and Industry Education Unit, Mill Hill Lane, Durham DH1 3LB
    0191 374 2268
    Ma, S. Miss; *Supervisor:* Gibb, A. Prof.; Cotton, J. Mrs
The relationship of enterprising modes of learning to enterprising behaviours and the fulfilment of educational goals
Abstract: After a decade's hot debate on the rationale and the process of enterprise education, researchers are assessing its outcomes in the light of personal growth, educational standards and economic development. However, limited theoretical research has been done to extrapolate individual elements of learning, such as motivation, monitoring, memory, and transferability of knowledge, etc, of an enterprising approach from other teaching and learning approaches. Therefore, a lack of generally agreed definition of 'enterprise education' has led to controversial and non-integrative findings. The research to be undertaken will attempt to distinguish between enterprising and non-enterprising modes of learning in terms of the psychology of learning. Having established the theoretical construct for enterprising modes of learning, a control experiment will then be carried out in a classroom setting. Students from schools which adopt enterprising modes of learning will be subjects in the experimental group, and students from traditional didactic modes of learning will act as control. Subjects will be matched according to their age, academic achievement or IQ etc. Measurement will be made against knowledge acquisition (e.g. literacy and numeracy skills), enterprising behaviours (e.g. social skills and need for achievement) and personal development (e.g. self-esteem and career anxiety).
Status: Sponsored project
Source of Grant: Durham University Business School £27,000
Date of Research: 1993-continuing

KEYWORDS: *enterprise education; industry-education relation-ship; learning strategies; motivation; skill development; transfer of learning*

10/0286

School of Education, Leazes Road, Durham DH1 1TA
0191 374 2000
Breet, F. Ms; *Supervisor:* Byram, M. Dr; Thompson, L. Ms
Verbal interaction in mathematics lessons in four secondary schools in Anglophone Cameroon
Abstract: The study examines the role of classroom language in the learning mathematics through English as a second language. Teach-ers of English and mathematics will be trained to work together and change classroom practices. Consequences for children's learning will be monitored.
Status: Sponsored project
Source of Grant: Overseas Development Administration
Date of Research: 1990-1993
KEYWORDS: *Cameroon; cross curricular approach; English – sec-ond language; language of instruction; mathematics education*

10/0287

School of Education, Leazes Road, Durham DH1 1TA
0191 374 2000
Dexter, G. Mr; *Supervisor:* Gilliland, J. Mr; McGuiness, J. Mr
Training in communication skills and counselling techniques and its influence on participants' personal constructs
Abstract: A study of the effectiveness of counsellor training, involv-ing a review of intentions, content and processes involved in coun-sellor training courses. The research, in its early stages, will sample a range of short and long courses. The effects and effectiveness of courses will be evaluated by use of a range of qualitative measures including structured interviews, personal diaries, with some pre- and post-structured assessment, possibly involving the use of repertory grid techniques and where appropriate, case studies.
Status: Individual research
Date of Research: 1989-1994
KEYWORDS: *communication skills; counselling techniques; coun-sellor training; course evaluation*

10/0288

School of Education, Leazes Road, Durham DH1 1TA
0191 374 2000
Davis, A. Dr
Inquiry into key psychological concepts used to characterise features of learning and teaching, especially in mathematics
Abstract: This research argues that learning may be seen as the acquisition of knowledge and understanding, and/or the acquisition of abilities, capacities and skills. Research into the degree to which the curriculum offered to pupils 'matches' their current level of knowledge etc. relies on certain conceptions of knowledge, belief, understanding, ability, skill, and so on. Ideas behind the National Curriculum, especially with regard to assessment, also rely upon certain characteristics of the changes in pupils that occur when learning takes place. The research consists of a wide ranging concep-tual/philosophical investigation into the adequacy of these concep-tions and characterisations. Empirical research of others is sometimes reviewed and referred to but the argument being pursued is that at least some of this research is an expensive irrelevance, based tacitly on conceptually inadequate foundations.
Published Material: DAVIS, A.J. (1986). 'Learning and belief', Journal of Philosophy of Education, Vol 20, No 1.; DAVIS, A.J. (1988). 'Ability and learning', Journal of Philosophy of Education, Vol 22.; DAVIS, A.J. (1990). 'Logical defects of the TGAT Report', British Journal of Educational Studies, Vol XXXVIII, No 3, pp.237-250.; DAVIS, A.J. 'Matching and assessment', Journal of Curricu-lum Studies, (forthcoming).
Status: Individual research
Date of Research: 1987-continuing
KEYWORDS: *cognitive processes; learning processes; learning theories; mathematics education*

10/0289

School of Education, Leazes Road, Durham DH1 1TA
0191 374 2000
Robson, M. Ms; *Supervisor:* Cook, P. Mr; Gilliland, J. Mr

Stress in children
Abstract: The aim of this research is to investigate stress as it is perceived by adolescents in secondary schools and to build a para-digm of this perception. It is also proposed to design an intervention system that could be used in schools to teach adolescents to cope more successfully with stress. The cognitive paradigm that is useful in understanding the stress process seems incomplete without an ack-nowledgement of the role of unconscious learning and perception and this research aims to extend the model to include this. It is hoped that the role played by our unconscious in the perception of, and reaction to, stress may be incorporated in the model of the stress process as well as in the intervention system. The size and composition of the sample has not yet been established although exploratory pilot studies suggest that stress is a meaningful concept in the adolescents' world. From these exploratory studies, stressors seem many and various and the individual's perception of the stress appears to rest upon factors which include learned responses, social support and personality. Coping strategies are also many and various and likewise appear to rest upon the same mediating factors, as well as the individual's perceived control over the stressors.
Status: Individual research
Date of Research: 1990-continuing
KEYWORDS: *secondary school pupils; stress – psychological; stress management*

10/0290

School of Education, Leazes Road, Durham DH1 1TA
0191 374 2000
Abu-Jalala, F. Mrs; *Supervisor:* Byram, M. Dr
The cultural dimension of English as a Foreign Language in the Arabian Gulf States
Abstract: The research aims to examine the possibility of introducing English as a foreign language (EFL) together with its western culture in an Arabic/Islamic culture, and to what extent. The study falls into two branches. Firstly, investigating the experts' (university staff, English language Inspectors, the curriculum planning department and teachers) opinion using the 'Delphi Technique', questionnaire method. Secondly, pupils at the secondary stage are involved in interviews and questionnaires to give their opinions about the same issue. The size of the sample is governed by the size of the population of teachers and pupils – this will include English language staff in secondary schools and the University of Qatar, and secondary school pupils.
Status: Sponsored project
Source of Grant: British Council in Doha £1,700
Date of Research: 1989-1993
KEYWORDS: *Arab states; English – second language; second lan-guage teaching*

10/0291

School of Education, Leazes Road, Durham DH1 1TA
0191 374 2000
Grace, G. Prof.; McGuiness, J. Mr
Headteachers: the impact of radical reform upon senior professionals
Abstract: An empirical and theoretical study of changing conceptions of leadership in English schooling with reference to transitions from the headteacher (as moral leader), the headteacher (as senior profes-sional) and the headteacher (as chief executive). The study is based upon taped interviews with a sample of infant, junior and secondary headteachers in the north-east of England. A target sample of 100 is proposed. Accounts will be analysed in relation to local education authority (LEA) locations, level of school and possible gender differ-ences in reaction to the development of managerialism in education.
Status: Sponsored project
Source of Grant: Durham University: Research and Initiatives Committee
Date of Research: 1990-1994
KEYWORDS: *head teachers; leadership; leadership styles; local management of schools; management in education; school based management*

10/0292

School of Education, Leazes Road, Durham DH1 1TA
0191 374 2000
Byram, M. Dr

Culture and civilisation studies for advanced language learners – an experiment in French and English schools
Abstract: The purpose of the research is to develop curricula, teaching and assessment methods for advanced language learning with reference to cultural studies, i.e. acquiring knowledge and understanding of the way of life and thinking of a foreign people and country. The research takes place in England and France and is based on existing approaches to teaching culture at GCE 'A' level and Baccalaureate. The design involves, in both countries, a team of teachers and researchers who develop, operate and evaluate an experimental curriculum and assessment. The curriculum has two main emphases: that learners should acquire knowledge and understanding of selected dimension of French/English culture (defined as above); and that learners should acquire the research tools – largely those of ethnography – to carry out their own investigations of a foreign culture. The cooperation of teams working in parallels in France (at the Institut National de Recherche Pedagogique) and in England provides for mutual information on research and development methods, on teaching techniques and on evaluation. The report will include, as well as a description of the research process, a specimen curriculum and materials to illustrate the principles underpinning the experiment.
Status: Sponsored project
Source of Grant: Leverhulme Trust £90,700
Date of Research: 1990-1993
KEYWORDS: *comparative education; cultural education; educational materials; second language learning; teaching methods*

10/0293
School of Education, Leazes Road, Durham DH1 1TA
0191 374 2000
Qattous, K. Mr; *Supervisor:* Byram, M. Dr
English language teaching – an evaluation of an industrial training programme
Abstract: The English for Specific Purposes (ESP) course for workers in the Aramco petroleum company will be analysed and evaluated as an example of programme development and ESP in industrial settings.
Status: Individual research
Date of Research: 1988-1993
KEYWORDS: *Arab states; English – second language; English for specific purposes; programme evaluation*

10/0294
School of Education, Leazes Road, Durham DH1 1TA
0191 374 2000
Gates, J. Mrs; *Supervisor:* Smith, R. Mr
Professional development of teachers
Abstract: This is a qualitative research project using case study method. It focuses upon a small group of primary school teachers at varying career stages and in differing cultural settings. Using research strategies of action research, biographical and journal writing and career profiles, the growth of reflectivity is examined. The research aims to identify the explicit and implicit values, attitudes and assumptions that govern the rationale of teachers in both their 'talk about teaching' and their practice. From an analysis of these it is planned to move to a consideration of implications in terms of initial and inservice teacher training.
Status: Individual research
Date of Research: 1990-1994
KEYWORDS: *primary school teachers; professional development; teacher attitudes*

10/0295
School of Education, Leazes Road, Durham DH1 1TA
0191 374 2000
Byram, M. Dr
Education for international understanding through foreign language teaching: a German – British collaborative project
Abstract: The purpose of the project is to investigate the contribution of foreign language teaching to international understanding through the images of a country purveyed in language teaching. The focus is on the images purveyed by textbooks for teaching English in Germany and German in England. The design involves a team of teachers and researchers at the Universities of Durham and Braunschweig (Germany). Working in German-English pairs, the teams analyse the images of German-English life portrayed in textbooks for secondary schools according to criteria including representativity, accuracy, realism and appropriateness to learners. Each textbook analysis includes a detailed account of the content of the book as well as an evaluation. The project also involves theoretical development of criteria for evaluation and discussion of the relationship between language teaching and teaching for international understanding or 'politische Erziehurig'.
Published Material: DOYE, P. (Ed). (1990). Grossbritannien: seine Darstellung in duetschen Schulbuchern für den Englischunterricht. Frankfurt: Deisterweg.
Status: Sponsored project
Source of Grant: Durham University £2,000; British Council £2,800
Date of Research: 1990-1993
KEYWORDS: *cultural awareness; English – second language; German; modern language studies; textbook evaluation*

10/0296
School of Education, Leazes Road, Durham DH1 1TA
0191 374 2000
Stockdale, C. Mr; *Supervisor:* French, M. Mr
The Mechanics Institution movement in the North East of England
Abstract: This research looks at the history of the development of the Mechanics Institutions in the North East of England between 1820 and 1902. It includes comparisons of contemporary and recent literature about the Movement. The Movement's activities will be evaluated within the context of the social and economic climate of the period, together with the legacy of educational, literary and social development in terms of failure and success. The research includes consultation of contemporary records existing within the region and also those of institutions in other parts of the country. Standard texts have been used to support the political, social, economic and cultural background against which the Movement evolved.
Status: Individual research
Date of Research: 1990-1993
KEYWORDS: *adult education; educational history; mechanics institutes*

10/0297
School of Education, Leazes Road, Durham DH1 1TA
0191 374 2000
Ashton, E. Miss; *Supervisor:* Smith, R. Mr
Religious education and primary school children
Abstract: The research project arose out of observations of primary school children's modes of thinking and ways in which they conceptualize. Wide reading, at the moment, is being carried out in the fields of educational psychology, philosophy and theology. Practical teaching projects and schemes of work are to be planned and executed in the classroom, which will be assessed according to certain evaluation criteria. It is anticipated that the research will lead to the publication of educational material for both teachers and children.
Status: Individual research
Date of Research: 1991-continuing
KEYWORDS: *primary education; religious education*

10/0298
School of Education, Leazes Road, Durham DH1 1TA
0191 374 2000
Awiria, O. Mr; *Supervisor:* Gilliland, J. Mr; McGuiness, J. Mr
Comparative study of disruptive behaviour and discipline in schools in the United Kingdom and Kenya
Abstract: This study, in its early stages, seeks to examine aspects of disruptive behaviour and discipline in selected secondary schools in the United Kingdom and Kenya. In both countries, disruption in schools is currently an issue of considerable concern to teachers, parents and government (e.g. Discipline in schools: report to the Committee of Enquiry chaired by Lord Elton, HMSO, 1989). The present study will examine aspects of definition, theory and explanation as they apply to different levels of organisation in the two countries. Data collection will be by means of sample surveys of attitudes among administrators, teachers, student teachers and pupils. It is hoped to include qualitative data obtained through individual and group interviews. Other research techniques are likely to be used as the project develops.
Status: Sponsored project
Source of Grant: St Christopher's Trust £4,000; British Foreign Schools Society £1,400; The Leathersellers' Company £1,000
Date of Research: 1991-1994
KEYWORDS: *behaviour problems; comparative education; discipline; disruptive pupils; Kenya; secondary schools*

10/0299

School of Education, Leazes Road, Durham DH1 1TA
0191 374 2000
Cornelius, M. Mr
Graduate numeracy
Abstract: This is an investigation into the mathematical needs of new graduates in employment. The methods used include a sample of new graduates being investigated through employers via questionnaires and interviews to ascertain what mathematical skills are needed in employment and what deficiencies exist. The conclusions are likely to be of interest to both institutions of higher education and employers.
Published Material: CORNELIUS, M.L. (1991). 'Numeracy in a university and beyond', Education and Training, Vol 33, No 3, pp.28-31.; CORNELIUS, M.L. (1991). 'Just a few questions', Times Higher Education Supplement, April.; CORNELIUS, M.L. (1991). 'Degree of panic', Times Educational Supplement, May.; COR-NELIUS, M.L. (1991) 'Graduate numeracy', Teaching Mathematics and its Applications, Vol 10, No 4, pp.151-153.
Status: Sponsored project
Source of Grant: Enterprise in Higher Education
Date of Research: 1990-continuing
KEYWORDS: *employer attitudes; graduate employment; graduates; mathematical ability; numeracy; work education relationship*

10/0300

School of Education, Leazes Road, Durham DH1 1TA
0191 374 2000
Palmer, J. Dr
Emergent environmentalism: subject knowledge and concern for the environment
Abstract: Phase One of this project is currently proceeding and has led to the accumulation of a substantial amount of data. Questionnaires have been circulated to environmental educators throughout the UK asking for information and supporting autobiographical statements explaining key factors influencing the development of personal concern for the environment. The aim is to identify significant life events/life experiences which have contributed towards people's concern for and interest in environmental matters. If a major goal of environmental education is to produce informed and environmentally active citizens, then presumably environmental educators should know the kinds of learning experiences which help to influence the development of environmental care and concern. Statements have been collected from a sample of over 200 educators. They will be used to make recommendations on the implications of significant learning experiences for the designing of educational programmes and approaches to the inclusion of environmental education in the formal curriculum. The pilot study for Phase Two of the project will involve the collection of autobiographical (audio taped) statements/discussion from nursery children in the USA on their understanding of common environmental issues (ranging from the immediate environment to global concerns). Analysis of this should reveal issues for further investigation, suggest preliminary categories of response and allow for subsequent comparison with nursery age children in the UK.
Status: Sponsored project
Source of Grant: Durham University £3,412
Date of Research: 1991-1994
KEYWORDS: *conservation – environment; environmental education; natural resources*

10/0301

School of Education, Leazes Road, Durham DH1 1TA
0191 374 2000
Cotton, P. Ms; *Supervisor:* McGuiness, J. Mr; Gilliland, J. Mr
Comparative study of writing development in French and English primary schools
Abstract: This research will be looking at the effect of early visual exposure to cursive script on children's writing, and is a comparative study of writing development in England and France. From this it is hoped to add theoretical substance to the rapidly increasing desire for schools to change from print to joined writing when children begin school. Initially, theoretical aspects of the differences between print and cursive script will be investigated, looking at the theoretical rationale of French researchers such as Lilian Lurcat and her influence on children's writing in France. These will be compared with research that has influenced British children's writing, beginning with Edward Johnson in 1913, who wanted all children to print because he thought it would help with their reading. Practical aspects

will be observed from school entry until the later primary years. Children will be carefully monitored in terms of their attitudes to writing and their self-image as writers. Specific areas to be targeted will be legibility, speed, accuracy, spelling, flow of ideas, creativity, and handwriting as part of the whole writing process. A small sample of about six schools will be monitored in detail over a period of about three years. This will necessitate involvement with all classes in all schools. Alongside this, a nationwide developmental survey will be conducted, and a National Register set up of all schools who are introducing or have already introduced joined writing on school entry. This development has been prompted by the numerous responses from an article written in 'Child Education'.
Published Material: COTTON, P. (1988). Handwriting Review, p.15.; COTTON, P. (1990). Handwriting Review, p.57.; COTTON, P. (1990). United Kingdom Reading Association Journal, Vol 24, No 1, p.2, April.; COTTON, P. (1991). United Kingdom Reading Association Journal, Vol 25, No 1, p.27, April.; COTTON, P. (1992). Child Education, p.53, April.
Status: Sponsored project
Source of Grant: Kingston University
Date of Research: 1990-continuing
KEYWORDS: *comparative education; creativity; France; handwriting; writing research; writing skills*

10/0302

School of Education, Leazes Road, Durham DH1 1TA
0191 374 2000
Morrison, K. Mr; *Supervisor:* Gilliland, J. Mr
Developing emancipatory curricula in primary schools
Abstract: The study critiques the work of Jurgen Habermas and indicates how it may be used to inform a debate on developing emancipation through primary school curricula. Issues in the sociology of knowledge are addressed which bridge the gap between Habermasian theory and school curricula. A case study of the National Curriculum of England and Wales is undertaken, focussing particularly on cross-curricular issues. A short empirical research is undertaken to attempt to complete an analysis of the contribution of Habermas to curriculum theory and practice.
Published Material: MORRISON, K. (1989). 'Bringing progressivism into a critical theory of education', British Journal of Sociology of Education, Vol 10, No 1, pp.3-18.
Status: Individual research
Date of Research: 1990-1993
KEYWORDS: *educational theories; primary school curriculum*

10/0303

School of Education, Leazes Road, Durham DH1 1TA
0191 374 2000
Galloway, D. Prof.; Smith, M. Mr
Evaluation of education and prevention of crime project (EPOC)
Abstract: This is a Home Office funded evaluation of a project carried out by the National Association for the Care and Resettlement of Offenders (NACRO), with funds from the Department for Education, on Education and Prevention of Crime (EPOC). The aims of the evaluation are: (1) To provide EPOC workers, and the Project's Steering and Advisory Committees, with an independent perspective on the progress of the project, with particular reference to its success in meeting its stated objectives. (2) To provide the Home Office with independent evidence on: (a) the extent to which the project has succeeded in reducing levels of juvenile crime and related problems, for example exclusion from school on disciplinary grounds and truancy, in each of the four areas; (b) criteria for successful implementation of juvenile crime prevention policies, and ways of overcoming obstacles.
Status: Sponsored project
Source of Grant: Home Office £30,000
Date of Research: 1992-1994
KEYWORDS: *crime prevention; delinquency; discipline problems; expulsion; programme evaluation; truancy*

10/0304

School of Education, Leazes Road, Durham DH1 1TA
0191 374 2000
Mahmoud, T. Mr; *Supervisor:* Galloway, D. Prof.
Making efficient use of microcomputers in teaching mathematics to gifted children in the Jordanian primary schools

Abstract: The study offers a critical examination of concepts of giftedness, in the context of mathematics. It presents a framework for the development of computer based programmes of individualized education for the mathematically gifted. It tests the framework by pilot studies in a sample of schools in Jordan.
Status: Individual research
Date of Research: 1989-1993
KEYWORDS: *computer uses in education; gifted; individualised methods; Jordan; mathematics; primary education*

10/0305
School of Education, Leazes Road, Durham DH1 1TA
0191 374 2000
Gilliland, J. Mr; Steele, J. Mr
A survey of computer literacy in initial teacher education
Abstract: Nationally, information technology (IT) has been given an increasingly high profile in schools, from the early Department of Education and Science/Department of Trade and Industry initiatives and the Microelectronics in Education Project (MEP) to its inclusion now as a cross-curricular issue in the National Curriculum. Schools of Education are required therefore to offer computer literacy courses which meet professional school orientated needs and also enhance personal skills through IT in response to computer literacy programmes in higher education. This research is gathering survey data from students following courses of initial teacher education and students following some higher degree courses. Access, confidence and competence are assessed on entry to the course and the project seeks to monitor changes in these three aspects during and on exit from the course. First results from pre- and post-course surveys show differences between groups and positive effects of introductory courses and the IT environment made available to students in the School of Education of Durham University. The range of competence, confidence and experience on entry is extremely wide and creates educational and logistic problems for the delivery and management of courses in IT and the IT environment. Activities, responses and results to date suggest the need for an application of more sophisticated models of teaching and instruction.
Published Material: GILLILAND, J. & STEELE, J. (1990). 'Computer literacy in an initial teacher training student population'. In: McCARTAN, A. (Ed). Computer literacy for every graduate – strategies and challenges for the early 1990s, pp.30-33. Oxford: CTISS Publications.
Status: Sponsored project
Source of Grant: Durham University: School of Education
Date of Research: 1989-continuing
KEYWORDS: *computer literacy; computer uses in education; information technology; preservice teacher education*

10/0306
School of Education, Leazes Road, Durham DH1 1TA
0191 374 2000
Aubrey, C. Ms
An investigation of teachers' mathematical subject knowledge and the processes of instruction in reception classes (phase 2)
Abstract: Using the applicants' existing data on children's informal mathematical knowledge as the basis of a framework for analysing teachers' pedagogical subject knowledge, the aim is to explore the coordination and utilisation of teacher and pupil knowledge in the complexities of reception classrooms. The project will follow a cohort of children through their first year in school to investigate the learning and teaching. Classroom processes will be documented by recording discourse occurring during activities and by observing teachers' structure and management of mathematical content, children's behaviour and response, and roles of teacher and pupil as learning progresses. By these means it is hoped to establish goals and processes associated with teaching and learning early years mathematics.
Published Material: AUBREY, C. (1993). 'An investigation of the mathematical knowledge and competencies which young children bring into school', British Educational Research Journal, Vol 19, No 1, pp.27-41.; A full list of publications is available from the researcher.
Status: Sponsored project
Source of Grant: Economic and Social Research Council £34,690
Date of Research: 1992-1993
KEYWORDS: *early childhood education; infant school teachers; mathematics education; reception classes*

10/0307
School of Education, Leazes Road, Durham DH1 1TA
0191 374 2000
01482 46311
Hull University, Department of Education, Hull HU6 7RX
Warburton, P. Mr; Sleap, M. Mr; Cale, L. Mrs
Physical activity patterns of primary school children
Abstract: There is now wide recognition of the positive effect regular exercise can have on our health. The main aim of this observation study is to monitor the exercise activity levels of children aged between 5 and 11 years. This observation study forms part of a wider evaluation of the Happy Heart Resource Materials which was undertaken between February 1991 and June 1992. The method of observation to be used will be based on a paper presented by O'Hara and Colleagues (1988) which validated a minute by minute observation procedure against heart rate. Between 60 and 70 children were observed in the spring of 1991 and again during the same period in 1992. Half of the children will act as a control group whilst the other half will receive regular input from the Happy Heart Resource Materials. The children will be observed both in school and at home. The results from the study will be used to assess the impact of the Happy Heart Resource Materials with regard to possible changes in children's activity patterns.
Status: Sponsored project
Source of Grant: Health Education Authority £16,000
Date of Research: 1990-1993
KEYWORDS: *educational materials; exercise; health activities; health promotion; heart rate; physical activities; primary school pupils*

10/0308
School of Education, Leazes Road, Durham DH1 1TA
0191 374 2000
Roskilde University, PO Box 260, Marbjergvej 35, DK 4000, Roskilde, Denmark Byram, M. Dr; Risager, K. Ms
The changing identity of foreign language teachers in the European integration process
Abstract: This project is set against national and international changes in society in general and foreign language teaching in particular. The project will establish and analyse language teachers' views of how their work should contribute to European integration, especially through the teaching of culture and cultural awareness. Changes in the curricula of England and Denmark provide an opportunity for reassessment of the aims of language teaching and a comparative dimension will throw further light on this. Data will be gathered by question and interview and analysed quantitatively and qualitatively and comparisons will be made across the two countries.
Status: Sponsored project
Source of Grant: University of Durham Research and Initiatives Committee £2,215; Danmarks Humanistik Forskningsrad £2,930
Date of Research: 1992-continuing
KEYWORDS: *comparative education; cultural awareness; Denmark; Europe; modern language studies*

10/0309
School of Education, Leazes Road, Durham DT1 1TA
0191 374 2000
University of Qatar, Doha, PO Box 2713, Qatar
974 83-2222
Hassan, F. Mr; *Supervisor:* Byram, M. Dr
Sociocultural aspects of teaching English to Arabic speaking students
Abstract: In foreign language learning the learner's affective variables seem to be playing a very crucial role. For example, the learner's own attitude towards learning the target language can be influenced by his/her attitudes towards the native speakers of this language and their culture. There is accumulating evidence that prejudice or active dislike diminishes motivation and interferes with learning. The attitudes of the Arab students in the Gulf towards the English language people and culture have never been investigated before. In doing so, the present research aims to find out: (a) if these students come into the English language class with already acquired perceptions of the target language, people and culture and what these perceptions are; (b) what the students' attitudes towards the English people and culture are and whether these tend to be stereotypical; (c) if there is an association between these perceptions and attitudes and if the association is significant; and (d) investigate the relationship between the students' attitudes and perceptions on the one hand, and the

learners' achievement in the target language on the other. The study sample consists of 60 male and 120 female students starting their first year in Qatar University. The research tools are: self-report writing, questionnaires, interviews, semantic differential tests and results of final achievement examinations kept in the university records.
Status: Individual research
Date of Research: 1989-1993
KEYWORDS: Arab states; cultural awareness; English – second language; foreign culture; native speakers; second language learning

Edinburgh University

10/0310
    Centre for Educational Sociology, Old College, South
    Bridge, Edinburgh EH8 9YL
    0131 650 1000
    Paterson, L. Dr; *Supervisor:* McPherson, A. Prof.
The efficient use of talent in the expansion of Scottish higher education
Abstract: The object of the research is to investigate the scope for exploiting untapped talent among young people (aged under 20) as a result of the fundamental changes affecting Scottish higher education.
Published Material: A full list of publications is available from the Research Administrator
Status: Sponsored project
Source of Grant: The Leverhulme Trust £25,632
Date of Research: 1992-1993
KEYWORDS: access to education; educational change; further education; higher education; sixteen to nineteen education

10/0311
    Centre for Educational Sociology, Old College, South
    Bridge, Edinburgh EH8 9YL
    0131 650 1000
    Paterson, L. Dr; Lamb, J. Dr; Howieson, C. Ms; Croxford, L.
    Ms; Middleton, L. Ms; Raffe, D. Prof.; *Supervisor:*
    McPherson, A. Prof.
Scottish Young People's Survey
Abstract: Regular multi-purpose surveys of school leavers and young people in Scotland, which collect data on their secondary, further and higher education, training, employment and unemployment, and on the various transitions among them. The surveys also cover the family backgrounds of young people, their household formation and other aspects of the transition to adulthood, and various attitudes. A postal survey, the Scottish Young People's Survey (SYPS) currently comprises two arms: a biennial survey, conducted in the spring of each odd-numbered year, of school leavers from the previous session; and a biennial series of longitudinal survey of school year groups, each of which is first contacted in the spring after fourth year and followed up after about 30 months at age 19-plus. Samples for the leavers survey and the (first-sweep) year-group survey overlap. Sample fractions are usually 10% giving target samples of about 7,000 for each survey arm, and achieved samples of about 5,500. The basic survey design is periodically enhanced to boost coverage in particular regions or for groups of interest (e.g. TVEI students).
Status: Sponsored project
Source of Grant: Scottish Office Education Department; Industry Department for Scotland; Department of Employment; Economic and Social Research Council
Date of Research: 1971-continuing
KEYWORDS: further education; higher education; school to work transition; unemployment; vocational education; youth employment

10/0312
    Centre for Educational Sociology, Old College, South
    Bridge, Edinburgh EH8 9YL
    0131 650 1000
    McPherson, A. Prof.; Raffe, D. Prof.; Lamb, J. Dr;
    Middleton, L. Ms
Continuation of Scottish Young People's Survey
Abstract: The biennial series of surveys of Scottish school leavers is to be continued.
Published Material: A bibliography of published work is available from the Research Administrator, Joan Hughes, at Edinburgh University.

Status: Sponsored project
Source of Grant: Scottish Education Department £120,000
Date of Research: 1990-continuing
KEYWORDS: school leavers; school to work transition; Scotland; secondary education; surveys

10/0313
    Centre for Educational Sociology, Old College, South
    Bridge, Edinburgh EH8 9YL 031 650 1000
    McPherson, A. Prof.; Raffe, D. Prof.; Lamb, J. Dr;
    Middleton, L. Ms
Establishing a performance indicator system for Grampian Region secondary schools
Abstract: To describe the characteristics, experiences and attainments of Grampian school leavers on a school-by-school basis in order to establish the boost or added value that each school gives to the attainment of its pupils and to their other outcomes.
Published Material: A full list of publications is available from the Research Administrator.
Status: Sponsored project
Source of Grant: Grampian Regional Council £230,068
Date of Research: 1992-continuing
KEYWORDS: outcomes of education; performance indicators; school effectiveness; school leavers; secondary schools

10/0314
    Centre for Educational Sociology, Old College, South
    Bridge, Edinburgh EH8 9YL
    0131 650 1000
    Raffe, D. Prof.; Howieson, C. Ms
The effectiveness of new curriculum models for initial vocational training: Phase 2 – Partnership on modularisation
Abstract: To provide information and analysis to support policy makers in European Community member states who seek to pursue policy objectives in initial vocational training through modularisation.
Published Material: A full list of publications is available from the Research Administrator.
Status: Sponsored project
Source of Grant: European Community: Petra Programme £74
Date of Research: 1992-1993
KEYWORDS: comparative education; curriculum development; European Community; modular courses; vocational education

10/0315
    Centre for Educational Sociology, Old College, South
    Bridge, Edinburgh EH8 9YL
    0131 650 1000
    McPherson, A. Prof.; Raffe, D. Prof.; Bagnall, G. Dr; Lamb,
    J. Dr; Middleton, L. Ms
A survey of young people in the Central Region
Abstract: To conduct a 10% survey of young people in the Scottish Central Region.
Published Material: A full list of publications is available from the Research Administrator.
Status: Sponsored project
Source of Grant: Central Regional Council £8,365
Date of Research: 1992-1993
KEYWORDS: school leavers; school to work transition; sixteen to nineteen education; surveys; youth

10/0316
    Centre for Educational Sociology, Old College, South
    Bridge, Edinburgh EH8 9YL
    0131 650 1000
    McPherson, A. Prof.; Raffe, D. Prof.; Bagnall, G. Dr; Lamb,
    J. Dr; Middleton, L. Ms
A survey of Strathclyde 16-19 year olds
Abstract: To conduct a survey of a 10% sample of school leavers from Strathclyde Region secondary schools.
Published Material: A full list of publications is available from the Research Administrator.
Status: Sponsored project
Source of Grant: Strathclyde Regional Council £30,000
Date of Research: 1992-1993
KEYWORDS: school leavers; school to work transition; sixteen to nineteen education; surveys; youth

10/0317

Centre for Educational Sociology, Old College, South Bridge, Edinburgh EH8 9YL
0131 650 1000
McPherson, A. Prof.; Raffe, D. Prof.

Aiming for a college education: Scottish evaluation
Abstract: To advise on British Petroleum's (BP's) 'Aiming for a College Education' programme.
Published Material: A full list of publications is available from the Research Administrator.
Status: Sponsored project
Source of Grant: British Petroleum Exploration Operating Company Ltd £30,000
Date of Research: 1992-continuing
KEYWORDS: access to education; further education; higher education; programme evaluation

10/0318

Centre for Educational Sociology, Old College, South Bridge, Edinburgh EH8 9YL
031 650 1000
Howieson, C. Ms

Longitudinal study of Women Onto Work course participants
Abstract: To carry out a follow-up survey of three cohorts of former students from community based pre-employment courses for women returners, including women with disabilities and women from minority ethnic groups.
Published Material: A full list of publications is available from the Research Administrator.
Status: Sponsored project
Source of Grant: Edinburgh District Council: Women Onto Work Ltd. £15,482
Date of Research: 1992-1994
KEYWORDS: adult vocational education; followup studies; outcomes of education; retraining; women's education; women's employment

10/0319

Centre for Educational Sociology, Old College, South Bridge, Edinburgh EH8 9YL
0131 650 1000
Jones, G. Dr

Family support for young people
Abstract: The aims of the project are to: 1) identify the types of help which young people perceive as support; 2) inform social policy and practitioners working with young people and their families; and 3) provide a basis for further research at European level on these issues.
Published Material: A full list of publications is available from the Research Administrator.
Status: Sponsored project
Source of Grant: Joseph Rowntree Foundation £20,961
Date of Research: 1993-1994
KEYWORDS: family income; family influence; financial support; parent-child relationship; parent role; youth

10/0320

Centre for Educational Sociology, Old College, South Bridge, Edinburgh EH8 9YL
0131 650 1000
Raffe, D. Prof.; McPherson, A. Prof.; Lamb, J. Dr

A follow-up survey of 19 year olds in Scotland
Abstract: The 5% follow-up survey of 19 year olds in Scotland will fill a four-year gap in a series of surveys of 19 year olds in Scotland.
Published Material: A full list of publications is available from the Research Administrator.
Status: Sponsored project
Source of Grant: Economic and Social Research Council £56,330
Date of Research: 1993-1994
KEYWORDS: cohort analysis; followup studies; longitudinal studies; school leavers; school to work transition; Scotland; sixteen to nineteen education; youth

10/0321

Centre for Educational Sociology, Old College, South Bridge, Edinburgh EH8 9YL
0131 650 1000

Howieson, C. Ms; Bagnall, G. Dr; Raffe, D. Prof.

Guidance in secondary schools
Abstract: This project will examine the guidance needs of secondary school pupils, the organisation of guidance provision, and the effectiveness of this provision in meeting pupils' needs.
Published Material: A full list of publications is available from the Research Administrator.
Status: Sponsored project
Source of Grant: Scottish Office Education Department £79,911
Date of Research: 1993-continuing
KEYWORDS: career counselling; guidance; secondary schools; vocational guidance

10/0322

Centre for Educational Sociology, Old College, South Bridge, Edinburgh EH8 9YL
0131 650 1000
Scottish Council for Research in Education, 15 St John Street, Edinburgh EH8 8JR
0131 557 2944
McPherson, A. Prof.; Munn, P. Mrs

School discipline: explanations and effects
Abstract: The project, looking at secondary schools, will attempt to explain variations among teachers and among pupils in their perceptions of the incidence of indiscipline, and the relationships between indiscipline and pupils' other experiences at school, including their attainment and attendance.
Published Material: A full list of publications is available from the Research Administrator.
Status: Sponsored project
Source of Grant: Economic and Social Research Council £70,260
Date of Research: 1994-1994
KEYWORDS: attendance; discipline; discipline problems; pupil attitudes; secondary schools; teacher attitudes

10/0323

Centre for Educational Sociology, Old College, South Bridge, Edinburgh EH8 9YL
0131 650 1000
Strathclyde University, Department of Statistics and Modelling Science, Glasgow G1 1XQ
0141 552 4400
McPherson, A. Prof.; Robertson, C. Dr

Schools' effects on attainment in school and higher education
Abstract: The project will show whether attainment in higher education is influenced by the student's school, and whether any such effect can be explained by characteristics of that school, including the school's effectiveness at secondary level.
Published Material: A full list of publications is available from the Research Administrator.
Status: Sponsored project
Source of Grant: Economic and Social Research Council £26,665
Date of Research: 1992-1993
KEYWORDS: academic achievement; higher education; school effectiveness; secondary schools

10/0324

Department of Artificial Intelligence, Old College, South Bridge, Edinburgh EH8 9YL
0131 650 1000
Bull, S. Miss; *Supervisor:* Pain, H. Dr; Brna, P. Dr

A collaboratively constructed student model for intelligent computer assisted language learning
Abstract: This research focuses on the student model of an intelligent computer assisted language learning (ICALL) system which is based on current theories in the field of second language acquisition (SLA). The following four issues were selected as important questions in SLA, while also being implementable in the ICALL environment: 1) the acquisition order of the target rules; 2) language learning strategies; 3) language transfer; and 4) language awareness. The first three points are represented in the student model. A learner's language awareness is enhanced by explicit user/system discussion of these issues and the target constructions, and also by cooperative construction and repair of the student model. The project aims both to test the suitability of these theories in the context of ICALL, and at the same time develop a system which demontrates guidelines for the creation of more successful and acceptable ICALL systems. Thus the aims

can be summarised as: 1) Creation of a more accurate student model by taking account of issues affecting SLA, and allowing the student to become an active agent in the construction and repair of the model. 2) Fostering learner reflection through this collaborative process, resulting in enhanced awareness and learning. 3) Gather more data and test theories from the field of second language acquisition.
Published Material: BULL, S. (1993). 'Towards user/system collaboration in the development of a student model for intelligent computer assisted language learning', Recall, No 8.; BULL, S., PAIN, H. & BRNA, P. (1993). 'Student modelling in an intelligent computer assisted language learning system: the issues of language transfer and learning strategies'. Proceedings of International Conference on Computers in Education, Taiwan, December 1993.; BULL, S., PAIN, H. & BRNA, P. (1993). 'Collaboration and reflection in the construction of a student model for intelligent computer assisted language learning'. Proceedings of the Seventh International PEG Conference (Vol 1), Edinburgh, July 1993, pp.48-56.
Status: Individual research
Date of Research: 1991-1994
KEYWORDS: computer assisted language learning; educational software; models

10/0325

Department of Education, Old College, South Bridge, Edinburgh EH8 9YL
0131 650 1000
Aitken, S. Dr; Millar, S. Ms; Nisbet, P. Mr; Sutherland, E. Ms; *Supervisor:* Entwistle, N. Prof.
Communication Aids for Language and Learning (CALL)
Abstract: This is a research and development project, including service delivery, offering help in assessing what communication aids or teaching programmes are needed for learners with disabilities. Development work includes investigation of how these aids might be incorporated within, and contribute towards, curriculum development. Research is carried out into a wide range of aspects of communication difficulty and technology, with development of a new micro-electronic and computing systems to exploit new technologies. Support is given to clients and carers in tailoring and using the chosen system. Activities cover a Scotland-wide assessment service; information, demonstrations and advice and loan services. Training is offered through the media of seminars, awareness training, short and long term secondments for training of professionals including teachers, psychologists, social workers, programmers and technicians. 1991/92 projects include assessment related work; training related work; smart wheelchair-related work; and functional communication related work.
Published Material: AITKEN, S. (1987). 'Me and my therapists', The Scottish Child, Winter, pp.16-17.; AITKEN, S. (1988). 'Computer aided instruction with the multiply impaired', Journal of Mental Deficiency Research, No 32, pp.257-263.; BUULTJENS, M. & AITKEN, S. (1987). 'Assessment of vision in multiply impaired children', British Journal of Special Education, No 14, pp.112-114.; A comprehensive report pack and a set of research papers are available from the researcher.
Status: Sponsored project
Source of Grant: Scottish Office Education Department £110,000
Date of Research: 1986-continuing
KEYWORDS: communication aids – for disabled; disabilities; educational materials; special educational needs

10/0326

Department of Education, Old College, South Bridge, Edinburgh EH8 9YL
0131 650 1000
Smith, C. Mr; *Supervisor:* Entwistle, N. Prof.
Understanding in educational contexts
Abstract: Understanding is a much used term in education but what it is to understand in an educational context has received surprisingly little attention to date. If an aim of education is that students should achieve understanding, it seems that this deficit should be remedied. In fact, a growing interest in the nature of understanding is beginning to emerge. A difference in conceptualisation between authors can be detected in which understanding is described either as a phenomenon of personal experience or as a target set in some way by the contextual conditions around the individual. A more appropriate description for education seems to require some sort of combination of these two views in which the relationships between the targets for understanding set by the curriculum and the experiences of the students can be examined. Accordingly, an attempt has been made to develop a

conceptualisation of understanding which enables this type of issue to be examined and attention is now being turned to examining the relationship between the target for understanding set by the curriculum (in terms of course outlines and aims, assessment materials and course delivery) and the understanding experiences of the students (probably by surveying responses to assessments and interviews).
Status: Individual research
Date of Research: 1991-1994
KEYWORDS: comprehension; learning

10/0327

Department of Education, Old College, South Bridge, Edinburgh EH8 9YL
0131 650 1000
Percy, S. Ms; *Supervisor:* Donn, G. Dr; King, K. Prof.
'Curriculum and Assessment in Scotland: A Policy for the 90s', impact of this initiative in a rural secondary and primary school
Abstract: This research aims to trace the process of change and the impact on assessment and teaching of English language in Scottish schools following the publication of Scottish Office Education Department (1987) Curriculum and Assessment in Scotland: A Policy for the 90s. Using a rural secondary school (510 pupils and 44 staff) and its feeder primary school (220 pupils and 11.8 staff) as a sample, the study involves oral history, ethnographic interviews, documentation and participant observation.
Status: Individual research
Date of Research: 1990-1994
KEYWORDS: curriculum development; educational assessment; educational change; English studies; Scotland

10/0328

Department of Education, Old College, South Bridge, Edinburgh EH8 9YL
0131 650 1000
Weiyuan, Z. Mr; *Supervisor:* King, K. Prof.; Thomson, G. Dr
Comparative research on career guidance between Britain and China
Abstract: Career guidance is increasingly becoming an important task in a changing world. The aim of this research is to compare students' career needs, including students' value criteria and choices of various occupations; the relationship between their career goals and school activities; and their needs in regard to career choice. In China, the researcher has selected and surveyed four junior-senior secondary schools (grades 7-12) and two junior secondary schools (grades 7-9). In each of these schools, classes were randomly chosen from each grade level. The total participants in the study were 674 students, 722 parents, and 127 teachers. A further study will select and survey using the same questionnaire, similar schools and students, parents and teachers, in Scotland. Through comparative research on need assessment between British students and Chinese students, the study will discuss problems and give recommendations on how career guidance can be best implemented.
Published Material: A full list of publications is available from the researcher.
Status: Individual research
Date of Research: 1991-1994
KEYWORDS: career counselling; China; comparative education; Scotland; vocational guidance

10/0329

Department of Education, Old College, South Bridge, Edinburgh EH8 9YL
0131 650 1000
Dyer, C. Dr
British resource on international training and education (BRITE) inventory
Abstract: The inventory of the British Resource on International Training and Education (BRITE) is intended as a document that summarises the varied nature and scope of Britain's institutional expertise in that area. The principal beneficiaries will be research and training institutes and agencies, and private and non-governmental organisations. BRITE points towards the location of expertise, and subject and area-wise specialisations in a format that can be regularly updated.
Status: Sponsored project
Source of Grant: British Council £4,000
Date of Research: 1993-1993
KEYWORDS: information sources; international education

10/0330

Department of Education, Old College, South Bridge,
Edinburgh EH8 9YL
0131 650 1000
Morris, J. Mr; *Supervisor:* Entwistle, N. Prof.; McPherson,
A. Prof.

**The work of the Scottish Council for Research in Education
1928-1993**

Abstract: This is a study of the Scottish Council for Research in
Education which was one of the earliest research councils to be found
in Europe. Its history is traced from total independence relying on
voluntary but professional labour, to that of a group of professional
researchers still having independence but within the bounds of a
market economy. The main themes will be testing shading into
assessment; outreach i.e. dissemination of findings to the teaching
force and in international activity; policy where customer-contractor
and even negotiated research works within a range of constraints. The
methodology will be that of archive search with the Founder Institutions, the Education Institute of Scotland and the Association of
Directors of Education, Scotland, and other appropriate bodies such
as the Scottish Office Education Department, the Public Record
Office, West Register House, Edinburgh and the archive of the
Council itself. It will include taped interviews with leading Council
Members and officials, past and present. Four of its five Directors
and all its Chairmen for the past 40 years are still alive. The researcher
has had an association with the Council, first as a subject in one of
its projects in 1932 and subsequently in a variety of roles including
that of assessor.
Status: Individual research
Date of Research: 1991-1993
KEYWORDS: *educational history; educational research; Scotland*

10/0331

Department of Education, Old College, South Bridge,
Edinburgh EH8 9YL
0131 650 1000
Davis, J. Mr; *Supervisor:* Donn, G. Dr; Thomson, G. Dr

**Sport for all in education: an inquiry into PE and sport in
schools, what constitutes good practice and its relation to the
role of culture and culture within schools**

Abstract: The project can be separated into two sections. The first is
policy based and aims to outline teaching methods, lesson structure,
share of the curriculum, methods of evaluation and other areas that
relate to physical education (PE) in schools. It will describe how these
affect and are perceived by children of different age, sex and ethnic
background. In doing so it will illustrate the present aim of PE policy,
how this relates to children at different stages of development and
how this is affected by issues such as time and resources. In short the
present practice existing in schools with regard to PE, will be brought
forth with the aim of defining good practice in PE as viewed by
parents, teachers and pupils. The second part of the proposal will use
the first section as a practical core around which to develop the
theoretical nature of the project. By viewing the school as a social
microcosm the project will illustrate PE as it relates to other areas of
the school and is affected by the structure of the school. Central to
this will be the examination of the role of culture and cultures within
the school.
Status: Sponsored project
Source of Grant: Carnegie Trust for Universities of Scotland £2,275;
Scottish Office Education Department £10,750
Date of Research: 1991-1994
KEYWORDS: *educational policy; educational practices; physical
education; sports*

10/0332

Department of Education, Old College, South Bridge,
Edinburgh EH8 9YL
031 650 1000
Dyer, C. Dr; *Supervisor:* King, K. Prof.; Donn, G. Dr

**Operation Blackboard: policy implementation in Indian
elementary education**

Abstract: In the search to achieve universal elementary education,
India's 1986 National Policy on Education initiated a qualitative
improvement in elementary education. A major strategy was Operation Blackboard, a programme for upgrading physical facilities in
small Indian elementary schools, which this thesis takes as a case
study. This examination of public policy implementation in India's
complex federal polity contextualises Operation Blackboard within
the historical development of the elementary sector. It draws on
policy science based implementation research and educational innovations literature to develop a theoretical framework, but finds they
cannot fully explain the dichotomy between 'appearance', or policy
rhetoric, and the 'reality' of contexts beyond the policy making
environment. A critical analysis of Indian policy documents straddles
that gap by revealing their implicit and explicit rationales, which may
conflict once policy moves into 'reality', where implementors operate
in the domain of this unresolved conflict. The methodology of
'backwards mapping' starts from three case study sites in Gujarat and
works backwards through local administrations, to New Delhi. The
study finds that centralised national policy does not allow for the
varying capacity of teachers in different socio-economic contexts to
absorb an innovation, while bureaucrats attach greater importance to
operating norms than outcomes of their actions. The centrality of
teachers to the education process is acknowledged but not acted upon;
education policy is used as a lever in centre State relations. For
universal elementary education to be achieved, the State must reap-
propriate its own educational policy arena; and struggles for control
must be replaced by centre State dialogue.
Published Material: DYER, C. (1992). 'Networking: a possible
approach to Centre-State policy dialogue in India', Norrag News, No
13, pp.72-73.
Status: Individual research
Date of Research: 1989-1993
KEYWORDS: *educational policy; India; primary education*

10/0333

Department of Education, Old College, South Bridge,
Edinburgh EH8 9YL
0131 650 1000
Dyer, C. Dr

**Literacy for migrants: an ethnography of literacy acquisition
by Gujarati nomads**

Abstract: Gujarat's average literacy rate is among the highest in India,
but there are in the State some communities with scarcely any literate
members. Among those are migrants, whose way of life does not
allow them to be accommodated in either existing formal or non-
formal modes of education. The rapidly deteriorating economic situation
of Gujarat's pastoral nomads is very precarious and their autonomy
is increasingly affected by the literate world on whose margins they
live. Literacy skills are now seen by nomads as imperative for survival
but their lifestyle appears incompatible with gaining access to them.
Working very closely with the community, researchers will devise
literacy teaching materials drawn from the oral culture of nomads,
and formulate an appropriate methodology for imparting them. Researchers will migrate with one group, constructing an ethnography
of literacy acquisition. The project will seek to generate a pool of
future teachers within the nomadic community who can carry on the
work initiated; and to stimulate policy dialogue and greater awareness
in the policy community of the literacy and educational needs of
non-mainstream communities
Status: Sponsored project
Source of Grant: Economic and Social Research Council £87,620
Date of Research: 1993-continuing
KEYWORDS: *India; literacy; nomads*

10/0334

Department of Education, Old College, South Bridge,
Edinburgh EH8 9YL
0131 650 1000
Anderson, C. Mr; *Supervisor:* Entwistle, N. Prof.

A study of university tutorial groups in social science subjects

Abstract: This piece of research aims to: 1) provide a fine-grained
analysis of the nature of talk in university tutorials; 2) present and
interpret students' perceptions of their experience of tutorials; 3)
describe tutors' reflections on their aims and practice in small group
teaching; and 4) consider a number of theoretical issues concerning
the negotiation of understanding in educational settings. The methods
used are non-participant observation of tutorials conducted in four
university departments by nine different tutors (covering all the years
of undergraduate teaching), the analysis of audio-tapes of these
tutorials, and semi-structured interviews with undergraduate students
and academic staff.
Status: Individual research
Date of Research: 1988-1993
KEYWORDS: *individual teaching; small group teaching; teaching
methods; tutorials; university teaching*

10/0335

> Department of Education, Centre for Research on Learning
> and Instruction, Old College, South Bridge, Edinburgh
> EH8 9YL
> 0131 650 1000
> Entwistle, N. Prof.; Napuk, A. Mrs; Dickie, S. Ms;
> Normand, B. Mrs

English language monitoring

Abstract: This is the fourth round of a three-yearly rolling programme. The main aim is to assess national standards in Scotland of
attainment across the language outcomes of reading, writing, listening and talking. A representative national sample will be drawn from
pupils at P4, P7 and S2 and assessed using appropriate test materials
which reflect the 5-14 guidelines. Some tests used in the 1992 survey
will be repeated to provide a basis of comparison over time.
Status: Sponsored project
Source of Grant: Scottish Office Education Department
Date of Research: 1994-continuing
*KEYWORDS: assessment; attainment tests; English studies; lan-
guage tests; Scotland*

10/0336

> Department of Education, Centre for Research on Learning
> and Instruction, Old College, South Bridge, Edinburgh
> EH8 9YL
> 0131 650 1000
> Tait, H. Dr; Speth, C. Dr; *Supervisor:* Entwistle, N. Prof.

Identifying and advising students at academic risk

Abstract: This project aims to develop prediction rules via a Revised
Approaches to Studying Inventory (RASI) which will identify students who might be at risk of academic failure, due to deficient study
strategies or skills, before they actually fail. Computer software is
being developed to import the RASI data, identify those at risk and
provide tailored advice geared to the students' individual needs. It is
hoped that failure rates could be reduced, and that staff in departments
could gain a greater insight into the ways in which their students
studied and the types of problems they faced.
Published Material: ENTWISTLE, N.J., TAIT, H. & THOMPSON,
S. (1991). 'Improving student achievement through promoting effective learning'. Final Report to the Scottish Office Education Department. Edinburgh: University of Edinburgh, Centre for Research on
Learning and Instruction.; ODOR, J.P. (1991). 'Studentview: an
interactive graphical system for analysing and exploring student
questionnaire data'. User handbook (preliminary version). Edin-
burgh: University of Edinburgh, Centre for Research on Learning and
Instruction.
Status: Sponsored project
Source of Grant: Universities Funding Council £250,000
Date of Research: 1992-continuing
*KEYWORDS: academic failure; higher education; intervention; stu-
dent problems; underachievement*

10/0337

> Department of Education, Centre for Research on Learning
> and Instruction, Old College, South Bridge, Edinburgh
> EH8 9YL
> 031 650 1000
> Tait, H. Dr; *Supervisor:* Entwistle, N. Prof.

**Students' perceptions of teaching in relation to their
approaches to studying**

Abstract: The programme of reported research in this thesis comprised a series of five factor analytic studies which aimed to explore
the relationships between students' perceptions of teaching and their
approaches to studying. It was found that different types of perceptions existed, some of which were rather general and reflected broad
views shared by a majority of students sharing similar learning
environments, while others were highly specific and enhanced individual differences in response. Following this finding, items were
developed which asked students to reflect on their preferences for
different types of teaching and it was found that interesting and
meaningful empirical relationships were apparent. Deep approach
(seeking personal understanding) was linked with preferences for
types of teaching likely to encourage and support such an approach
while surface approach (seeking to reproduce course material) was
linked with contrasting preferences. Further analyses revealed that
students entering higher education with 'instrinsic' motives also
endorsed a deep approach and had preferences for 'deep' teaching,
whereas those entering with 'extrinsic' motives endorsed a surface

approach and had preferences for 'surface' types of teaching. This
suggested that orientation leads to intention, intention to process, and
process to outcome, with the learning environment intervening to
some extent to alter students' intentions.
Published Material: ENTWISTLE, N.J. & TAIT, H. (1990). 'Approaches to learning, evaluations of teaching and preferences for
contrasting academic environments', Higher Education, No 19,
pp.169-194.; ENTWISTLE, N.J., MEYER, J.H.F. & TAIT, H.
(1991). 'Student failure: disintegrated patterns of study strategies and
perceptions of the learning environment', Higher Education, No 21,
pp.249-261.
Status: Individual research
Date of Research: 1987-1992
*KEYWORDS: higher education; learning strategies; learning theo-
ries; student attitudes; teaching methods*

10/0338

> Department of Education, Centre for Research on Learning
> and Instruction, Old College, South Bridge, Edinburgh
> EH8 9YL
> 0131 650 1000
> Entwistle, D. Dr; *Supervisor:* Entwistle, N. Prof.

Understanding academic understanding

Abstract: This study is being used to extend a previous study (Understanding understanding, Entwistle, 1991) which looked at the
revision strategies of students in their final year of a degree. The
current study is looking at the study strategies and attempts to develop
conceptual understanding of final year social science students taking
courses in social and business history. Fifteen students were interviewed in depth about their ways of tackling, first, essay writing and,
subsequently, revision and final examinations. A re-analysis of the
earlier work has led to the concept of 'knowledge objects' to describe
the experience of tightly integrated and elaborate academic understanding. This concept is being further examined in the current work,
particularly in relation to the organisational principles involved in
constructing essays.
Published Material: ENTWISTLE, N.J. & MARTON, F. 'Knowledge objects: understandings constituted through intensive academic
study', British Journal of Educational Psychology, Vol 64. (in press).
Status: Sponsored project
Source of Grant: Godfrey Thomson Trust
Date of Research: 1992-continuing
*KEYWORDS: comprehension; essays; examination techniques;
higher education; learning strategies; review – reexamination; study
skills; writing – composition*

10/0339

> Department of Education, Old College, South Bridge,
> Edinburgh EH8 9YL
> 0131 650 1000
> London University, Institute of Education, Department of
> International and Comparative Education, 20 Bedford Way,
> London WC1H 0AL
> 0171 580 1122
> McGrath, S. Mr; Leach, F. Dr; *Supervisor:* King, K. Prof.;
> Carr-Hill, R. Prof.

Education and training for the informal sector

Abstract: The Overseas Development Administration (ODA) is currently sponsoring a study of the Education and Training Needs of the
Informal Sector. The study is being undertaken by researchers at
Edinburgh University and the Department of International and Comparative Education at London University, Institute of Education.
Within the general theme, several subthemes will be targeted, including a rough distinction between more viable and more marginal
enterprises within the informal sector. The study will look at: 1)
Diversification/vocationalisation of secondary education and prevocational programmes/projects in primary education. 2) Training for
people already engaged in viable informal sector activities. 3) Orien-
tation/preparation for the informal/microenterprise sector within
post-secondary education institutions. 4) Programmes focusing specifically on education and training for the more marginal levels of the
informal sector, e.g. projects targeted at income generation. 5) Identification and encouragement of people in formal sector employment
who are interested in entering the informal or microenterprise sector.
Status: Sponsored project
Source of Grant: Overseas Development Administration £17,000
Date of Research: 1993-1994
KEYWORDS: small businesses; vocational education

10/0340

Department of Mathematics and Statistics, Old College, South Bridge, Edinburgh EH8 9YL
0131 650 1000
Triadafillidis, T. Mr; *Supervisor:* Searl, J. Dr; Entwistle, N. Prof.

Practical work in the mathematics classroom

Abstract: This research arises from the oft asserted claim that practical activities are an essential element in creating a learning environment in the mathematical classroom. A number of practical activities have been developed for pupils aged 12-14 and these, together with activities developed elsewhere, are being evaluated in a number of schools. The illuminative evaluation approach will be used.
Status: Individual research
Date of Research: 1990-1994
KEYWORDS: learning activities; mathematical applications; mathematics education; secondary education

10/0341

Department of Mathematics and Statistics, Old College, South Bridge, Edinburgh EH8 9YL
0131 650 1000
Searl, J. Dr

Mathematics 16-20

Abstract: This project will analyse the different patterns of learning and teaching adopted in school and university (and polytechnics) for mathematics. The reasons for undergraduates abandoning their mathematical studies will be examined by means of personal interview and questionnaire. Students will be matched by sex, age and qualification in an attempt to elucidate the factors which contribute to success in mathematics in tertiary education.
Status: Individual research
Date of Research: 1991-1994
KEYWORDS: higher education; learning motivation; learning strategies; mathematics achievement; sixteen to nineteen education; undergraduate study

10/0342

Department of Mathematics and Statistics, Old College, South Bridge, Edinburgh EH8 9YL
0131 650 1000
Grant, F. Ms; *Supervisor:* Searl, J. Dr

Group work in mathematical education

Abstract: This investigation concerns the role of group work in mathematical education at every level and its use in inservice training. Illuminative evaluation will be used.
Status: Individual research
Date of Research: 1990-1994
KEYWORDS: group work; mathematics education

10/0343

Department of Mathematics and Statistics, Old College, South Bridge, Edinburgh EH8 9YL
0131 650 1000
Ballantyne, H. Mrs; *Supervisor:* Searl, J. Dr

Personal technology in undergraduate mathematics education

Abstract: The purpose of this research is to investigate how personal technology (e.g. graphic calculators, audio cassette players, and videotapes) can be harnessed to enrich and support the learning of mathematics by undergraduates. The progress of 500 first year undergraduates will be monitored each year and up to 10% of the students interviewed. Appropriate learning materials will be developed and evaluated.
Status: Individual research
Date of Research: 1992-continuing
KEYWORDS: audiovisual education; calculators; equipment; mathematics education; undergraduate students

10/0344

Department of Social Anthropology, Old College, South Bridge, Edinburgh EH8 9YL
0131 650 1000
Cambridge University, Department of Social Anthropology, New Museum Site, Free School Lane, Cambridge
01223 334599
De La Gorgendiere, L. Dr; *Supervisor:* Hart, J. Dr

Education and development in Ghana (an Asante village study, linked to education and development more generally in Ghana)

Abstract: The aim of the research was to examine the link between education and the process of development in Ghana. The research covered developmental issues in contemporary Ghana and sought to understand the link between education and the process of development. Through an indepth village study, the research concluded that the effects of out-migration for the purposes of seeking further education, employment, and/or extending networks tended to have a negative effect on rural development. Education becomes a means of 'individual' development and advancement, not a means of 'mobilization of the collectivity' for development. The problems of the educational system in Ghana are vast and not readily explainable outside the context of the current socio-political situation. The policies for education that have been shaped by the implementation of structural reforms to the economy (International Monetary Fund/World Bank) have served to push formal education out of the reach of many through the institution of 'cost-recovery measures', thus widening the gap between those who can or cannot afford to educate their children.
Status: Individual research
Date of Research: 1990-1993
KEYWORDS: developing countries; development education; Ghana

10/0345

Department of Social Policy and Social Work, Old College, South Bridge, Edinburgh EH8 9YL
0131 650 1000
Scottish Council for Research in Education, 15 St John Street, Edinburgh EH8 8JR
0131 557 2944
Adler, M. Mr; Raab, C. Mr; Munn, P. Mrs; Arnott, M. Mrs; Moore, C. Ms

Devolved management of schools

Abstract: This project aims to: (a) compare the effects of the devolved management of schools (DMS)/local management of schools (LMS) on parents, teachers, schools, local education authorities and central government in England and Scotland. (b) Compare parents' attitudes towards, and participation in, DMS in different local and national education systems. (c) Analyse and compare governing bodies (in England) and school boards (in Scotland) in terms of their internal workings and their external relations with other levels of decision making, using analytical frameworks drawn from the field of policy studies. (d) Analyse changes in the relationships among participants and in the networks of government and management of education which have resulted from recent legislation. (e) Contribute to the theoretical understanding of a major innovation in education policy and of its implications for the realisation of a range of values and outcomes. The analytic framework is drawn from current work in the social sciences that bear upon issues concerning public policy and implementation, management, interorganisational and network relations, learning systems, and public/parental participation. Research will be carried out in four secondary schools in each of three education authorities (Strathclyde and Lothian regions, and Newcastle-upon-Tyne); amongst councillors and officials in the authorities; and amongst officials and HMIs at the national level. Methods include semi-structured, face-to-face interviewing, structured telephone interviewing, observation and documentary analysis. The main samples for interview are: c. 50 members (total) of school boards and governing bodies; c. 50 (total) of headteachers and teachers; telephone survey of c.600 parents.
Status: Sponsored project
Source of Grant: Economic and Social Research Council £159,720
Date of Research: 1992-1994
KEYWORDS: educational administration; educational change; local management of schools; parent participation; school based management; school boards – Scotland; school governing bodies

Education for Development

10/0346

Woodmans, Westwood Row, Tilehurst, Reading RG3 6LT
01734 426772
Holland, D. Ms; Street, B. Dr; Millican, J. Ms; Edwards, V. Dr; Eade, F. Mr; Norrish, P. Dr; Skidmore, G. Ms; *Supervisor:* Rogers, A. Prof.

Post-literacy materials production
Abstract: A research project into the processes of production of post-literacy materials in Third World countries, based on case-studies in India, South Africa, Kenya, Egypt, Uganda, Bangladesh etc. The project is run as team exercise. Searches in the literature at UIE Hamburg, CESO The Netherlands, Institute of Development Studies at the University of Sussex, and the University of Reading have been conducted.
Published Material: HOLLAND, D. & ROGERS, A. (1993). BALID Newsletter, Vol 8, No 2. (special edition on post-literacy).
Status: Sponsored project
Source of Grant: Overseas Development Administration £20,000
Date of Research: 1992-1993
KEYWORDS: developing countries; development education; educational materials; literacy; material development; reading materials

Essex University

10/0347
> Contemporary Japan Centre, Wivenhoe Park, Colchester
> CO4 3SQ
> 01206 872543
> Okazaki, T. Mr; Widdows, S. Mr; *Supervisor:* Neary, I. Prof.

Teaching and testing Japanese and similar languages in schools
Abstract: The aim of this research project is to undertake an investigation into methodologies appropriate for the teaching of 'hard languages', such as Japanese, Chinese and Arabic in schools in the UK. In the course of the research the Research Fellow will develop teaching materials, schemes of work and assessment techniques which will be used initially in the teaching of Japanese to groups of children from three schools in Colchester, namely the Sixth Form College, the Royal Grammar School and the County High School for Girls. The first stage of the research will consist of a survey of the courses already being used to teach Japanese, Chinese and Arabic in this country. New teaching materials for experimental Japanese classes will be devised according to the results of the preliminary survey, then they will be modified in response to the experiences within the classroom throughout the three year project.
Status: Sponsored project
Source of Grant: Department for Education and Science £90,000
Date of Research: 1991-1994
KEYWORDS: Arabic; Chinese languages; educational materials; Japanese; non western languages; second language learning

Exeter University

10/0348
> School of Education, St Luke's, Heavitree Road, Exeter
> EX1 2LU
> 01392 263263
> Preece, P. Dr

Learning and the pace of lessons
Abstract: An algebraic model relating the rate of learning to the pace of teaching and to pupil ability has been developed. The model accounts well for prior data on learning at different speeds and accurately predicts the learning deficit for able pupils taught in heterogeneous classes. The model can predict the changes of pace and learning from lesson to lesson. A direct investigation of the interrelationship of learning, ability and pace has been carried out with 40 undergraduate education students, using foreign language vocabulary items. Some qualitative features of the theoretical model were supported.
Published Material: PREECE, P.F.W. (1990). 'Learning and the pace of lessons: a theoretical model', British Journal of Mathematical and Statistical Psychology, Vol 43, pp.1-6.; PREECE, P.F.W. (1990). 'Imitatio Physicae', British Educational Research Journal, Vol 16, pp.297-304.; PREECE, P.F.W. (1991). 'Foreign language vocabulary learning and the pace of instruction', The Teacher Trainer, Vol 5, No 2, pp.21-22.
Status: Individual research
Date of Research: 1989-continuing
KEYWORDS: ability; learning; mixed ability; pacing; time factors – learning

10/0349
> School of Education, St Luke's, Heavitree Road, Exeter
> EX1 2LU
> 01392 263263
> Somers, J. Mr

The nature of learning in educational drama
Abstract: Very little evidence exists about the nature of learning in educational drama. Given the current status of drama in the National Curriculum, it is timely that we attempt to prove that, in addition to aesthetic learning, drama also permits participants to engage with, and change their attitudes towards, the issues and concepts which form the content of the drama. The research team, which included 4 secondary drama teachers, has devised, piloted and evaluated a research lesson pack which is now in use in 74 schools nationally. Data is being sent to Exeter for analysis and it is expected that early results will be available by Summer 1994. The data collection includes the use of attitude and social distance scales and teacher and pupil observation and evaluation. It is hoped that the work may pave the way for a more focused qualitative project. Research lessons deal with attitudes of mental handicap; old age and gender stereotyping as well as the use of photographs as a stimulus for making drama and children's awareness of story form.
Status: Sponsored project
Source of Grant: Exeter University Research Fund £3,000
Date of Research: 1989-1993
KEYWORDS: curriculum development; drama; educational materials; learning experience

10/0350
> School of Education, St Luke's, Heavitree Road, Exeter
> EX1 2LU
> 01392 263263
> Preece, P. Dr

Student attitudes regarding effective teaching behaviours – a teaching practice study
Abstract: An anglicized version of the Teaching Behaviors Questionnaire is to be given to 200+ Postgraduate Certificate in Education (PGCE) secondary students before teaching practice (TP). After TP, quantitative ratings on each student for each category on the standard assessment schedule will be obtained. This should permit the investigation of the factorial structure of the instrument and provide TP performance scores for correlating with scores on the attitude inventory. In a related intervention exercise, half of the science student group will receive feedback on the research evidence concerning teaching behaviour covered in the inventory. By using the other half of the group as a control, the effect of the intervention on TP performance will be investigated.
Status: Sponsored project
Source of Grant: Exeter University: School of Education
Date of Research: 1991-1994
KEYWORDS: postgraduate certificate in education; preservice teacher education; student attitudes; student teacher evaluation; teacher behaviour; teaching practice

10/0351
> School of Education, St Luke's, Heavitree Road, Exeter
> EX1 2LU
> 01392 263263
> Biddle, S. Dr; Fox, K. Dr; Armstrong, N. Dr

Psychological aspects of children and physical activity
Abstract: Children aged 11-12 years (N=250) have been tested on physical activity and psychological constructs to see if activity levels and choices can be related to the psychology of the child. Preliminary evidence indicated that more active boys were intrinsically motivated towards physical education and sport, whereas girls required more extrinsic motivation. Active and less active children could also be discriminated on the basis of motivational orientations and physical self-perceptions. Ongoing research is following up these findings and is investigating achievement cognitions and self-perceptions.
Published Material: BIDDLE, S. & ARMSTRONG, N. (1992). 'Children's physical activity: An exploratory study of psychological correlates', Social Science and Medicine, Vol 34, No 3, pp.325-331.
Status: Sponsored project
Source of Grant: Exeter University £4,000; Northcott Medical Foundation £14,000
Date of Research: 1990-continuing
KEYWORDS: child psychology; exercise; health; physical activities; physical activity level

10/0352

School of Education, St Luke's, Heavitree Road, Exeter
EX1 2LU
01392 263263
Fines, J. Dr; Nichol, J. Dr
Primary history project
Abstract: The primary history project is enquiring into possible approaches to implementing the National Curriculum in History in 25,000 primary schools where there is little expertise.
Status: Sponsored project
Source of Grant: Nuffield Foundation £20,000
Date of Research: 1991-1994
KEYWORDS: history; National Curriculum; primary education

10/0353

School of Education, St Luke's, Heavitree Road, Exeter
EX1 2LU
01392 263263
Hughes, M. Dr
Feedback, peer-interaction and adult-intervention in initial logo learning
Abstract: The overall aim of the research is to increase our understanding of children's learning, and of the effects on learning of outside agencies such as feedback, peers and adults. The research will study children learning to control the Logo Turtle in view of the theoretical and curricular relevance of this activity. The specific research objectives are to: (1) to compare children learning in four conditions (a) alone (b) with a peer (c) with an adult and (d) with an adult and a peer, looking at the effects of these conditions on task performance and on aspects of learning; (2) to examine the nature of the feedback provided by the system and to look at its effect on children's learning in the individual condition; (3) to analyse the interaction taking place within the peer and adult conditions, looking in particular at interaction concerned with planning and feedback, and to assess its effects on learning; (4) to examine the effects of age and gender on the above issues, by using children aged 4, 7 and 11, and by including same-sex and mixed-sex pairs in the peer conditions.
Status: Sponsored project
Source of Grant: Economic and Social Research Council £90,550
Date of Research: 1990-1994
KEYWORDS: computer uses in education; feedback; interaction; learning processes; peer teaching; teacher-pupil relationship

10/0354

School of Education, St Luke's, Heavitree Road, Exeter
EX1 2LU
01392 263263
Golby, M. Dr
Perspectives on the government of schools at local level
Abstract: The School Governors Research Group and the Governors Support Centre mounts a range of research conducted both by individual members of the Group and as a collective. The research includes local studies, regional studies and international comparative studies. Central interests are in the extent of parental involvement, the internal processes of deliberation and judgement and the relation to local education authorities. Theoretical work on key constructs underpins the work.
Published Material: GOLBY, M. (1990). The new governors speak: Exeter papers in school governorship No 1. Tiverton: Fairway Publications.; GOLBY, M. (1990). 'In their own words', School Governors, pp.11-18, April.; GOLBY, M. & APPLEBY, R. (1991). School governors today: in good faith. Tiverton: Fairway Publications.
Status: Sponsored project
Source of Grant: Leverhulme Trust; Universities Funding Council; Exeter University Research Fund; Exeter Society for Curriculum Studies
Date of Research: 1986-continuing
KEYWORDS: educational administration; school governing bodies; school governors

10/0355

School of Education, St Luke's, Heavitree Road, Exeter
EX1 2LU
01392 263263
Ernest, P. Dr
A social constructivist theory of mathematics
Abstract: This is a basic, theoretical research project extending a previous project which concerned the philosophical foundations of the mathematics curriculum and mathematical pedagogy (see ERNEST, P. (1991). 'The philosophy of mathematics education'). The current project is intended to extend the theoretical foundations. The contributions of Imre Lakatos and Ludwig Wittgenstein form a basis, but parallels in educational, psychological, sociological theory (e.g. constructivism) are drawn upon and utilised. The central thesis is that mathematics is a human construction, which is fallible, corrigible and ever changing. The project concerns working out this theory rigorously.
Published Material: ERNEST, P. (1991). The philosophy of mathematics education. London: Falmer Press.
Status: Sponsored project
Source of Grant: Leverhulme Trust £11,400
Date of Research: 1991-1994
KEYWORDS: educational philosophy; mathematics

10/0356

School of Education, St Luke's, Heavitree Road, Exeter
EX1 2LU
01392 263263
Hazlewood, P. Mr; *Supervisor:* Wragg, E. Prof.
The influence of teacher appraisal on secondary school management
Abstract: The imminent introduction of formal teacher appraisal into schools based on the premises that appraisal would monitor teacher performance, improve practice and enhance the overall management of schools provides a platform for considerable debate. The principal aim of this investigation is to consider the influence that teacher appraisal has on the management of secondary schools. A range of hypotheses relating to management of schools are being tested. Based on case studies of four similar sized secondary schools (for 11-16 age group) in similar localities, the research used unstructured interview as the primary methodology. Validity is currently being established through group discussion and other methods. A detailed questionnaire is being utilized to test hypotheses arising from the interviews. Approximately 45 teachers in various management positions were interviewed and questionnaires were sent to a range of 198 teachers in six schools. The results are currently being analyzed.
Status: Sponsored project
Source of Grant: Wiltshire Local Education Authority; Pool School
Date of Research: 1989-1993
KEYWORDS: educational administration; secondary schools; teacher evaluation

10/0357

School of Education, St Luke's, Heavitree Road, Exeter
EX1 2LU
01392 263263
Watson-Broughton, A. Mrs; *Supervisor:* Copley, T. Mr; John, M. Prof.
The aims of the Education Reform Act 1988 for acts of worship in secondary schools
Abstract: The aim of this research is to discover the most practical, sensitive, interesting, dynamic, relevant way to deliver the aims of the Education Reform Act 1988 with reference to daily acts of worship. To promote the spiritual aspects of a balanced curriculum in the secondary school, a working definition of 'spiritual' needs to be drawn. This needs to address the current secular nature of society. Since symbols have always played an important role in religion it was thought useful to pursue research in the area of aesthetics. A study of National Curriculum art documents was made which was very beneficial. Particular artists from history were highlighted and their ideas, aims and aspirations related to recent legislation on acts of worship in schools. A distinction was drawn at all times between ecclesiastical worship and educational worship.
Status: Sponsored project
Source of Grant: College of St Hild and St Bede Durham Bursary £2,000
Date of Research: 1991-continuing
KEYWORDS: Education Reform Act 1988; religion and education; school worship; symbolism

10/0358

School of Education, St Luke's, Heavitree Road, Exeter
EX1 2LU
01392 263263
Desforges, C. Prof.; Hughes, M. Dr

Parents and assessment at National Curriculum key stage 1
Abstract: The aim of the proposed research is to study the effect that
parents' conceptions of teaching, learning and assessment may have
on the assessment and reporting procedures currently being introduced into schools, and to study the effect that these procedures may
in turn have on parents. It is hypothesised that two important mediating factors could be the accuracy of teachers' perceptions of parents' views, and the extent to which parents are directly involved in
the assessment process. The specific research questions to be addressed are: (1) What are parents' conceptions of teaching, learning
and assessment? (2) How accurately are these conceptions perceived
by teachers? (3) How far do teachers' perceptions of parents influence
their actual assessment behaviour? (4) How far do teachers actually
involve parents in the assessment process, and to what effect? (5)
What do teachers select to report to parents at the end of the assessment process? (6) What do parents make of these reports, and what
effects do they have on their conceptions of teaching, learning and
assessment, and on their relationship to the school? (7) What effects
do the assessment and reporting processes have on teachers' perceptions of parents' conceptions, and on teachers' classroom practice?
Status: Sponsored project
Source of Grant: Economic and Social Research Council £55,943
Date of Research: 1991-1993
KEYWORDS: *academic records; parent aspiration; parent-school
relationship; school-based assessment*

10/0359
School of Education, St Luke's, Heavitree Road, Exeter
EX1 2LU
01392 263263
Trotter, A. Mrs; Bennett, S. Prof.
**Differential provision for children with special educational
needs in ordinary schools**
Abstract: The aim of the study is to investigate the effects of various
kinds of provision made for children with special educational needs
at secondary level. Three main systems were investigated – the
support base, withdrawal, and in-class support. Children were selected at primary level who were deemed to be in need of special
educational needs provision at secondary school. Their entry into
secondary school and subsequent performance was closely monitored. Along with details of their academic performance, the research
includes the views of their parents and the children themselves.
Published Material: BENNETT, N. & CASS, A. (1989). From
special to ordinary schools: case studies in integration. London:
Cassell.
Status: Sponsored project
Source of Grant: Economic and Social Research Council
Date of Research: 1986-1988
KEYWORDS: *mainstreaming; secondary education; special educa-
tional needs; support services*

10/0360
School of Education, St Luke's, Heavitree Road, Exeter
EX1 2LU
01392 263263
Kennett, D. Mr; Al-Seaidy, H. Mr; Supervisor: Burghes, D. Prof.
Further development on interactive video
Abstract: The main aim of the research is to evaluate a mathematics
teaching interactive video package called School Disco. The evalu-
ation concentrates on the motivational and attainment based aspects.
For the purpose of conducting the evaluation process, several tests
have been applied. Technical and educational points which might
have a direct or indirect effect on pupil motivation have been detected.
Other aims of the research are to explore the extent to which interac-
tive video material could be employed within an educational system.
Status: Sponsored project
Source of Grant: Exeter University £2,000
Date of Research: 1990-continuing
KEYWORDS: *interactive video*

10/0361
School of Education, St Luke's, Heavitree Road, Exeter
EX1 2LU
01392 263263
Savage, J. Mrs; Supervisor: Desforges, C. Prof.
The role of informal assessment in teachers' practical action
Abstract: The main aims of the research are to: (1) understand more

about the way in which informal assessment is generated from
teachers' intuitive theories; and (2) understand more about the way
that this influences teaching acts. An opportunity sample of nine or
ten teachers, who are working with 5-7 year olds, is being used. There
will be several parts to the research. Firstly, the teachers will record
some classroom action on videotape. Nine pieces of action of not
more than 20 minutes in length will be recorded by each teacher.
Secondly, each teacher will reflect upon this action, through the
method of stimulated recall, in order to gain their informal assessments. Unstructured interviews will be used. Thirdly, these informal
assessments will be organised and related to each teacher's views of
teaching and learning. A more structured interview will then take
place. Fourthly, the data will be analysed in terms of whether or not
any action is taken as a result of the informal assessments. This data
will include both the classroom action on videotape and teachers'
reflections of that action on audiotape. The research is examining and
analysing two types of process – teachers' thinking (the processes in
their heads) and the processes that occur over a period of time in terms
of action.
Status: Individual research
Date of Research: 1989-1994
KEYWORDS: *assessment; classroom observation techniques;
teacher response*

10/0362
School of Education, St Luke's, Heavitree Road, Exeter
EX1 2LU
01392 263263
Greenhough, P. Ms; Supervisor: Hughes, M. Dr; Preece, P. Dr
**The inter-relationship of cognitive abilities, attitudes, social
interaction and performance in early logo learning**
Abstract: This research investigates the inter-relationship of cognitive abilities, attitudinal factors, social interaction and performance
in young children. The context of the research is paired learning with
a computer and in the first instance focuses on early Logo activities.
Seventy-two, Year 3 children worked either in same-sex or mixed
pairs for five sessions with the floor Turtle on drawing or driving
activities. They also worked for two sessions individually. Prior to
the work with the Turtle, the children were assessed on five British
Abilities Scales. Prior, during and after the sessions their attitudes to
the task, their partner, and gender stereotypes were assessed. All
sessions were videotaped and the social interaction transcribed.
Status: Sponsored project
Source of Grant: Nuffield Foundation £25,000
Date of Research: 1990-1993
KEYWORDS: *cognitive ability; computer assisted learning; interac-
tion; logo; turtles – robots*

10/0363
School of Education, St Luke's, Heavitree Road, Exeter
EX1 2LU
01392 263263
Peacock, A. Dr
Parents' understanding of science in the National Curriculum
Abstract: The research is a longitudinal study of parents of children
entering school in Autumn 1989 in 11 representative primary schools
in one local authority. The sample is identical to that being used for
a larger study (Parents and the National Curriculum, sponsored by
Leverhulme Trust, director Dr M. Hughes) and the current study
works closely with Dr Hughes' team. The study uses semi-structured
interviews on a serial basis with parents, teachers and head teachers,
to ascertain the flow of information to parents about their children's
science work at National Curriculum Key Stage 1, and to evaluate
parents' understanding of the information received. The study has so
far highlighted clear differences of perception between parents and
teachers about what parents know and need to know; and is currently
investigating parents' interpretations of the reports received after the
1991 Standard Assessment Tasks.
Published Material: PEACOCK, A. & BOULTON, A. (1991). 'Parents' understanding of science at Key Stage 1', Education 3-13, Vol
19, No 3, pp.26-29, October.
Status: Sponsored project
Source of Grant: Exeter University Research Committee Grant
£5,000
Date of Research: 1990-1993
KEYWORDS: *National Curriculum; parent attitudes; parent-school
relationship; primary education; science education*

10/0364

School of Education, St Luke's, Heavitree Road, Exeter
EX1 2LU
01392 263263
Cousins, J. Ms; *Supervisor:* Desforges, C. Prof.; Hughes, M. Dr
The place of reflection in teachers' processes of change
Abstract: This is an ethnographic study of teachers' theories about the language of young children when they start school and how these influence their classroom practice. It is based on a piece of action research carried out with 10 reception teachers for a year and examines the development of their own theories and the courses of change.
Status: Individual research
Date of Research: 1986-1993
KEYWORDS: change; child language; classroom management; teacher attitudes

10/0365

School of Education, St Luke's, Heavitree Road, Exeter
EX1 2LU
01392 263263
Wragg, C. Ms; *Supervisor:* Wragg, E. Prof.; Ackland, J. Mr
Classroom management in the primary school
Abstract: This PhD project is part of the Leverhulme Primary Project which received total funding of £268,000. This particular research focused on classroom management in the primary school and was divided into three studies. Study One involved non-participant observations of 239 lessons and interviews with 60 teachers. Forty-eight teachers were experienced practitioners, the remaining 12 were student teachers on their first teaching practice. Two quantitative observation schedules were used. The first focused on pupil deviancy and any subsequent teacher responses, the second on deviancy and on-task involvement levels. In addition to this, freehand notes were also taken and 'critical events' were recorded. These 'events' were any that appeared to be illustrative of a particular teacher's class management style. Study Two consisted of interviews with 430 pupils selected from the classes of 20 of the teachers in Study One. Pupils were interviewed using a semi-structured interview schedule and photographs depicting classroom incidents. Study Three involved observations of a further 33 lessons to enable a special case of questioning to be studied. Seven teachers were observed and data on over a thousand questions was collected. The data combined both quantitative and qualitative methodologies and therefore a process of triangulation was used to analyse the findings. Excessive talk was found to be the most frequently observed form of deviance and pupils continually mentioned it as being an unacceptable mode of behaviour. The results of the interviews with pupils and teachers suggested that pupils' perceptions of the way teachers responded to deviance was closer to that observed by the researcher, than to the teachers' views of their actions.
Published Material: WRAGG, E.C. (1993). Primary teaching skills. London: Routledge.; BROWN, G. & WRAGG, E.C. (1993). Questioning. London: Routledge.; WRAGG, E.C. & BROWN, G. (1993). Explaining. London: Routledge.; WRAGG, E.C. (1993). Class management. London: Routledge.
Status: Individual research
Date of Research: 1990-1994
KEYWORDS: classroom management; classroom research; primary schools

10/0366

School of Education, St Luke's, Heavitree Road, Exeter
EX1 2LU
01392 263263
Wikeley, F. Mrs; *Supervisor:* Hughes, M. Dr; Golby, M. Dr
Parental choice of school
Abstract: This research involves the use of case study to identify criteria used by parents in choosing schools and to explore how these can help schools in marketing themselves.
Status: Individual research
Date of Research: 1991-1994
KEYWORDS: institutional advancement; marketing; parent choice; parent-school relationship; selection

10/0367

School of Education, St Luke's, Heavitree Road, Exeter
EX1 2LU
01392 263263

Hughes, M. Dr; *Supervisor:* Golby, M. Dr
Parents and National Curriculum: criteria of parental choice of primary school
Abstract: In the present political climate it is becoming increasingly important for schools to make themselves attractive to parents. In order to do this it would be advantageous for them to know how parents choose a school and on what criteria that choice is based. The research will concentrate on parental choice of primary school. It will select from the sample being used by the wider research project 'Parents and the National Curriculum', some parents for a case study approach. The whole sample consists of a wide range of parents in differing socio-economic circumstances. They all have a child who started school in the year 1988/89 and have been interviewed four times over the past two years. The complete interview, which was semi-structured, covered several aspects of the changes taking place in their children's schooling at the present time. This research will look in depth at the criteria they used, and how those criteria were chosen in their decision as to which primary schools their children would attend. It is hoped that by looking closely at the cases of a few parents it will be possible to identify differences in the choice process. In this way it is hoped to develop a paradigm which illuminates the process and would enable schools to better target potential parents.
Published Material: HUGHES, M., WIKELEY, F. & NASH, P. (1990). Parents and the National Curriculumm: an interim report. Exeter University.; HUGHES, M., WIKELEY, F. & NASH, P. (1991). Parents and SATs: a second interim report from the project Parents and the National Curriculum. Exeter University, School of Education.; HUGHES, M., WIKELEY, F. & NASH, P. (1991). 'Parents in the new era: myth and reality'. In: MERTHENS, F. & VASS, J. (Ed). Impact Issues: Discursive Interruptions in Curriculum Practice. London: Falmer.; HUGHES, M., WIKELEY, F. & NASH, P. (1990). 'Business partners', Times Educational Supplement, 5 January.
Status: Sponsored project
Source of Grant: Leverhulme Trust
Date of Research: 1989-continuing
KEYWORDS: access to education; Education Reform Act 1988; parent choice; primary schools

10/0368

School of Education, St Luke's, Heavitree Road, Exeter
EX1 2LU
01392 263263
Neather, E. Mr
Foreign language training for initial teacher training (ITT) students
Abstract: The aim of this project is to: (1) establish a detailed register of current language experience and competence amongst all undergraduate and Postgraduate Certificate in Education (PGCE) students at the School of Education; (2) enquire into the aspirations and wishes of students in terms of foreign language learning, and their perception of the place of foreign languages in their careers, and in the future lives of the children they teach; (3) relate the pattern of such wishes and aspirations to the pattern of main subject courses followed by students with a view to establishing what language courses could best be offered to which groups of students; (4) investigate the resources and timetabling of access courses for students wishing to pursue individual programmes of less common languages, such as Greek and Portuguese, for which class tuition might not be available; (5) discuss with course tutors the role and function of foreign languages in the course profile of students with a view to integrating foreign language modules into the overall course structure on a rational and planned basis; (6) investigate the practice followed by other institutions of teacher training, and to make comparisons with foreign languages in teacher training establishments in other countries of the European Community; and (7) explore the needs and aims of foreign languages teaching in primary and middle schools in Devon. It is proposed that the project should last three terms from October 1992. This would give time to carry out surveys and put in place a carefully considered pilot scheme at the start of the new academic year in October 1993. Proposals and recommendations would then be made in December 1993 for possible implementation of a full programme in October 1994. The research will involve questionnaire surveys and interviews with students (sample=420 postgraduate students and 917 undergraduate students) and staff colleagues; visits to other institutions and attendance at European conferences.
Status: Sponsored project
Source of Grant: Department for Education £4,590
Date of Research: 1992-1993

KEYWORDS: *modern language studies; preservice teacher education; student teachers*

10/0369

School of Education, St Luke's, Heavitree Road, Exeter
EX1 2LU
01392 263263
Vosho, M. Mr; *Supervisor:* Davis, N. Dr
Beyond the fantasy are the rules: mental models and computer games
Abstract: Computer games are motivating but why and what are the users doing? This research looks at the mental models of novice and experienced game players in education.
Status: Individual research
Date of Research: 1990-1993
KEYWORDS: cognitive processes; computer games

10/0370

School of Education, St Luke's, Heavitree Road, Exeter
EX1 2LU
01392 263263
Owen, G. Mr; *Supervisor:* Davis, N. Dr; Sparkes, A. Dr
The role of the information technology coordinator
Abstract: Information technology (IT) is used across the National Curriculum, therefore the role of the secondary school IT coordinator can be seen as a key position. This research looks at the coordinator's role through policies, case studies and IT innovations.
Status: Individual research
Date of Research: 1989-1994
KEYWORDS: coordinators; information technology; secondary schools; staff role

10/0371

School of Education, St Luke's, Heavitree Road, Exeter
EX1 2LU
01392 263263
Kirkman, C. Mr; *Supervisor:* Davis, N. Dr; Wragg, E. Prof.
The influence of the National Curriculum on information technology in schools
Abstract: The role and development of information technology (IT) is changing rapidly with the National Curriculum. This research reviews examination entries, teacher professional development, and the attitude and experience of students over a three year period during which National Curriculum information technology was introduced.
Status: Individual research
Date of Research: 1989-1994
KEYWORDS: computer uses in education; information technology; National Curriculum

10/0372

School of Education, St Luke's, Heavitree Road, Exeter
EX1 2LU
01392 263263
Wragg, E. Prof.; Wikeley, F. Mrs; Wragg, C. Ms;
Haynes, G. Mrs
Leverhulme teacher appraisal project
Abstract: This research addresses one of the most vital and central aspects of teacher appraisal, namely the observation of lessons in the classroom, a compulsory requirement of all appraisal schemes. The project has been carried out in 3 ways: 1) Collection of information about local education authority appraisal schemes. All 109 local education authorities in England were contacted and asked about the classroom observation element of their scheme. 2) A national questionnaire of 500-1000 primary and secondary teachers. The sample was randomly selected, although structured to ensure that it was balanced to reflect the national regions and different sizes and situations of school. It asks teachers about the pattern of appraisal within their school; what kind of classroom observation took place and who observed them; the timing and type of feedback received; any documentation used during the observation; and the effect the teacher felt subsequently on his/her classroom practice. 3) Case studies of 12 schools, 30 individual teachers at both the primary and secondary levels. These included large, medium and small schools. The sample teachers volunteered, but represented all age groups and positions of responsibility, although headteacher appraisal was not included. Each teacher was observed in their classroom before, during and after (both immediately and a term later) their appraisal. All other parts of their appraisal process were also observed and discussions recorded and transcribed for analysis. Appraisees and their appraisers and headteachers were interviewed at various points during the process to ascertain attitudes to appraisal and opinions of their appraisal experience.
Status: Sponsored project
Source of Grant: Leverhulme Trust £132,450
Date of Research: 1992-1994
KEYWORDS: classroom management; classroom observation techniques; teacher evaluation; teaching profession

10/0373

School of Education, St Luke's, Heavitree Road, Exeter
EX1 2LU
01392 263263
Golby, M. Dr; Delve, R. Mr; Olek, H. Mrs
JEP-TEMPUS 'ADEPT'
Abstract: This is the 2nd year of a 3 year project. The JEP-TEMPUS 'ADEPT' is a proposal incorporating a negotiated response by universities in the United Kingdom, Denmark and Spain to approaches made to the Centre of Secondary and Tertiary Inservice Training at the University of Exeter School of Education by the Ministry of National Education in Poland. These approaches relate to the Ministry's request for advice, help and practical support in creating a new initial and inservice teacher training system and curricula for the secondary sector. Project 'ADEPT' is designed to provide the maximum initial support, training, opportunities and experiences needed to empower key personnel to research and develop their own new programmes for teacher trainers. The Advisory Team and other European Community (EC) expert educationalists would assist in a variety of ways through offering opportunities for visits to EC institutions, and providing training sessions, seminars, tutorials and workshops, encouraging the key trainers to develop their own strategies and programmes. It is hoped that the project will involve, directly, 180 key trainers and, indirectly, all Polish teacher trainers over the three year project period. The development of a national Teacher Training and Inservice Resource Support Centre is seen as fundamental to procure, store and disseminate a large variety of modern international educational information, literature, resources and material. This would form the basis for the Centre to develop its own resource production, designed to meet the specific needs of the developing trainers. It is the aim that this Centre would provide a future base for satellite centres.
Published Material: KONARZEWSKI, K. (Ed). (1992/3). Ksztalcenie Nauczycieli, Vols 1 (1); 1 (2); 1 (3). Warsaw: Centralnego Osrodka Doskonalenia Naucsycieli (CODN).
Status: Sponsored project
Source of Grant: European Community: TEMPUS £185,261
Date of Research: 1993-1994
KEYWORDS: inservice teacher education; international educational exchange; international programmes; Poland; preservice teacher education; teacher education

10/0374

School of Education, St Luke's, Heavitree Road, Exeter
EX1 2LU
01392 263263
Hughes, M. Dr; Desforges, C. Prof.; Mitchell, C. Miss;
Carre, C. Dr
Using and applying mathematical knowledge: an action research project
Abstract: This research has arisen directly from an enquiry into primary mathematics which is currently being supported by the Nuffield Foundation. Two major themes which have emerged from this enquiry are that the application of mathematical knowledge is a major problem in early mathematics learning, and that practising teachers should be centrally involved in any future project. These two themes are brought together in the research project. The specific objectives are to: 1) develop conceptions of knowledge use which are manageable in classrooms; and 2) develop methods of teaching children to use mathematical knowledge and skills in a variety of settings and across a range of problems. The objectives will be met by carrying out an action-research project involving two groups of primary teachers over a period of one year. In addition, visits to other countries will be made to investigate how the problem is being addressed elsewhere.
Status: Sponsored project

Source of Grant: Nuffield Foundation £45,000
Date of Research: 1993-1994
KEYWORDS: comparative education; mathematics education; primary education

10/0375
School of Education, St Luke's, Heavitree Road, Exeter
EX1 2LU
01392 263263
Wray, D. Mr; Lewis, M. Mrs
Extending literacy in the junior school
Abstract: The project has the ultimate aim of producing materials which will assist teachers of junior school children to develop more effectively the literacy of their pupils. It is founded upon several key ideas: 1) Learning to read and to write are only the first steps in the process of becoming fully literate. They are complemented by the activities of reading and writing to learn. 2) The use of reading and writing in this way are, by definition, curriculum-wide processes. 3) In their use of reading and writing across the curriculum, children can naturally encounter and should be expected to produce a wide range of text types. 4) These real-life interactions with texts tend to be characterised by several features, that is, they are purposeful, they demand the use of a range of strategies in the text user, they make reference to, and rely upon, knowledge of other texts and they have definite outcomes. 5) Children learn to interact critically and purposefully with texts by engaging in critical and purposeful behaviour; that is, the process is not that of practising the 'skills' of being a critical and effective user of text which they then apply to real texts, but rather one of learning through activities which are authentic in their own rights. Some materials have already been produced which aim to support teachers' attempts to develop children's use of information and reference books in this authentic way, i.e. Wray, D. (1991). The Project Research Pack, Cheltenham: Stanley Thornes Publishers. These materials work through the ubiquitous primary school 'project' and provide activities which require children involved in project work to identify, locate, consult, extract information from and evaluate reference materials. The materials thus give teachers a means of directly teaching particular aspects of information handling through authentic and motivating children's activities. They also provide guidance on strategies by which teachers can make contextualised assessments of children's abilities in these information skills. These materials give a model for other materials which will be produced, trialled and developed during the project.
Published Material: WRAY, D. & LEWIS, M. (1994). 'Extending literacy: the EXEL project'. In: LITTLEFAIR, A. Literacy for life. Widnes: United Kingdom Reading Association.
Status: Sponsored project
Source of Grant: Nuffield Foundation £71,839
Date of Research: 1992-1994
KEYWORDS: information seeking; literacy; primary education; reading skills; writing skills

Glamorgan University

10/0376
Business School, Pontypridd, Mid Glamorgan CF37 1DL
01443 480480
Thomas, R. Ms
The impact of the introduction of staff appraisal on women academics' career opportunities in higher education
Abstract: Staff appraisal is new to higher education and its introduction can be seen to reflect wider changes in public sector industrial relations. Stemming from the 23rd Report from Committee A (Committee of Vice Chancellors and Principals (CVCP) (1987)), appraisal is being presented to staff as a formal procedure for staff development, "...directed towards developing staff potential, assisting in the improvement of performance and enhancing career and promotion opportunities..." (para 43). The assumption arising from this is that the introduction of staff appraisal will serve to improve women's opportunities of gaining senior positions due to the bureaucratisation of the promotion process and the provision of career planning. However, to some, its introduction is being heralded as an extension of managerial control which at best will have little impact on women's career opportunities and at worse will be detrimental to them, merely formalising and legitimising existing discriminatory practices. Longitudinal research of indepth case studies in higher education institutions, accompanied by wider questionnaire analysis, aims to establish women academics' experience of appraisal and its impact on their careers.
Status: Individual research
Date of Research: 1990-continuing
KEYWORDS: career development; institutes of higher education; teacher evaluation; teaching profession; women teachers; women's employment

10/0377
Business School, Pontypridd, Mid Glamorgan CF37 1DL
01443 480480
Farrell, C. Miss; *Supervisor:* Boyne, G. Dr; Baker, C. Prof.
Territorial justice and nursery education provision in England and Wales
Abstract: The aim of this project is to measure the need for, and the provision of, nursery education facilities in local authority areas in England and Wales. This involves the construction of a model of service need and service provision, and the evaluation of the extent of territorial justice. This assessment is based on a statistical analysis of the relationship between service need and service provision. The project examines the reasons for spatial variations in provision and assesses the impact of local financial resources, party politics, private sector provision and day care services upon the level of local authority provision of nursery education.
Status: Individual research
Date of Research: 1990-continuing
KEYWORDS: early childhood education; nursery school education; preschool education; regional characteristics; regional planning

10/0378
Centre for Language Studies, Pontypridd, Mid Glamorgan CF37 1DL
01443 480480
Price, A. Mr; *Supervisor:* Davies, C. Mr; Davies, W. Mr
An analysis of errors in the written and spoken language of advanced Welsh learners
Abstract: With the establishment of examinations at GCSE Ordinary and Advanced level by the Welsh Joint Education Committee, which are specifically designed for adult learners, a large corpus of written and oral material has become available for analysis. The aim of this research is to analyse the nature of the errors incurred, classify them, and devise materials to help learners to avoid known pitfalls. The research will examine carefully defined attainment categories, and will compare the nature of oral and written errors.
Status: Individual research
Date of Research: 1993-continuing
KEYWORDS: error analysis – language; second language learning; Welsh

10/0379
Centre for Language Studies, Pontypridd, Mid Glamorgan CF37 1DL
01443 480480
Packer, Rh. Miss; *Supervisor:* Davies, C. Mr; James, A. Mr
The development of Welsh-medium education in South East Wales
Abstract: This work will examine the development of Welsh-medium education post 1939. It will look at the reasons for growth, the social background of those demanding Welsh provision, the attitude of local education authorities, the educational pros and cons, the development of teaching/learning materials, and staff development. The uneven level of demand will be examined, together with factors leading to surges in demand at various times. Finally the study will look at the educational attainments of Welsh-medium schools and speculate on future developments.
Status: Individual research
Date of Research: 1994-continuing
KEYWORDS: educational development; language of instruction; language policy; mother tongue; Wales; Welsh; Welsh speaking schools

10/0380
Department of Computer Studies, Pontypridd, Mid Glamorgan CF37 1DL
01443 480480
Edwards, R. Dr

Community projects in student learning

Abstract: A computer based database of 100 local voluntary or non-profit making organisations is held and maintained. These organisations are sources of student group or individual projects, and teaching staff are encouraged to use these projects in their teaching.
Published Material: EDWARDS, R.M. (1993). 'Community Enterprise at the University of Glamorgan'. In: BUCKINGHAM-HAT-FIELD, S. (Ed). Community enterprise in higher education in the 1990s'. London: Community Service Volunteers.
Status: Sponsored project
Source of Grant: Glamorgan University: Enterprise Unit; Department of Employment: Enterprise in Higher Education Unit
Date of Research: 1989-continuing
KEYWORDS: community organisations; databases; student projects

10/0381

Department of Computer Studies, Pontypridd, Mid Glamorgan CF37 1DL
01443 480480
Edwards, R. Dr
Student centred learning
Abstract: Currently, teaching methods are being investigated through a totally self-assessed course (PAD1) in the Department of Business and Administrative Studies at Glamorgan University. Publication on this work is in preparation. Also in connection with the research field, a workshop on simulation and role playing was presented in Glasgow in December 1989.
Published Material: EDWARDS, R.M. & WARE, A.J. (1989). 'Case study: an approach to the teaching and assessment of introductory computing', Education and Training Technology International, Vol 26, No 1, pp.68.; EDWARDS, R.M. (1989). 'An experiment in student self assessment', British Journal of Educational Technology, Vol 20, No 1, pp.5.; EDWARDS, R.M. & SUTTON, R.A. (1992). 'A practical approach to student centred learning', British Journal of Educational Technology, Vol 23, No 1, pp.4.
Status: Individual research
Date of Research: 1989-continuing
KEYWORDS: assessment; higher education; learner centred curriculum; self evaluation – individuals; teaching methods

10/0382

Department of Property and Development Studies, Pontypridd, Mid Glamorgan CF37 1DL
01443 480480
Jiang, L. Mr; *Supervisor:* Plimmer, F. Ms; Hibberd, P. Prof.; Gronow, S. Mr
Education and training of property valuers in China
Abstract: In the light of China's economic reform and the development of an 'open policy', the emergence of a property market has produced the need for property valuation skills in China. The research has investigated the needs of China for property valuation skills and, based on United Kingdom experience, is investigating ways in which computer-aided teaching can be used to provide appropriate professional education and training for valuers in China.
Published Material: JIANG, L., PLIMMER, F., HIBBERD, P. & GRONOW, S. (1993). 'Land reform in China', Journal of Property Management (forthcoming).; JIANG, L., PLIMMER, F., HIBBERD, P. & GRONOW, S. (1993). 'Education and training of valuers in China', Journal of Property Research (forthcoming).
Status: Sponsored project
Source of Grant: Royal Institution of Chartered Surveyors
Date of Research: 1991-1993
KEYWORDS: China; housing; professional education

10/0383

Department of Property and Development Studies, Pontypridd, Mid Glamorgan CF37 1DL
01443 480480
Williams, T. Mr; *Supervisor:* Hughes, T. Mr; Hibberd, P. Prof.; Gronow, S. Mr
The application of quality management principles to learning
Abstract: In vocational courses there are two principle customers whose needs are to be satisfied; the students and the employers. Research has shown that these needs are difficult to define and equally difficult to satisfy. The aims of the research are therefore to: (1) identify the key personal and technical skills necessary in professional quantity surveying practice; (2) develop a simulation based teaching vehicle on the basis of (1) above; and (3) use quality management principles to monitor and improve the learning experience.
Published Material: HUGHES, T. & WILLIAMS, T. (1991). Quality Assurance, a Framework to Build on. Oxford: Blackwell Scientific Publications.; HUGHES, T. & WILLIAMS, T. (1991). 'Learning by experience: integrated learning materials based on a construction project', Building Technology and Management, Vol 18, pp.56-64, Kuala Lumpur, Building Technology Society.
Status: Sponsored project
Source of Grant: Department of Employment: Enterprise in Higher Education Initiative £9,000
Date of Research: 1991-1993
KEYWORDS: educational quality; industry higher education relationship; quality control; vocational education; work education relationship

10/0384

Enterprise Unit, Pontypridd, Mid Glamorgan CF37 1DL
01443 480480
Saunders, D. Mr; Kingdon, R. Mr
Student and peer tutoring in Wales
Abstract: The student and peer tutoring in Wales initiative involves four higher education centres which are sending their students into schools to help teachers in the delivery of the curriculum as well as provide positive role models for pupils. The project examines assessment issues and strategies emerging from student and peer tutoring, as well as numerous other developments emerging out of links between universities or institutes and local schools.
Published Material: SAUNDERS, D. (1992). 'Peer tutoring in higher education', Studies in Higher Education, Vol 17, No 2, pp.211-217.
Status: Sponsored project
Source of Grant: BP (Chemicals) Baglan Bay £30,000
Date of Research: 1991-1994
KEYWORDS: peer teaching; role models; student-school relationship; Wales

10/0385

Enterprise Unit, Pontypridd, Mid Glamorgan CF37 1DL
01443 480480
Saunders, D. Mr
Developing a portfolio of personal development
Abstract: A cross-section of students is engaged in a longitudinal study involving self-assessment of study and transferable skills. Academic and personal achievement are also recorded, and the final stage of the project involves the preparation of one-page profile sheets for use with curriculum vitae.
Published Material: SAUNDERS, D. (1990). 'The assessment of prior experiential learning', Simulation Games for Learning, Vol 20, No 1, pp.76-85.; SAUNDERS, D. (1992). 'Profiling in higher education', Journal of the National Association for Staff Development, No 26, pp.51-57.
Status: Sponsored project
Source of Grant: Department of Employment: Enterprise in Higher Education Initiative
Date of Research: 1990-1993
KEYWORDS: higher education; profiles; records of achievement; resumes – personal; self evaluation – individuals; skill development

10/0386

Enterprise Unit, Pontypridd, Mid Glamorgan CF37 1DL
01443 480480
Rogers, S. Ms; *Supervisor:* Hawkins, P. Prof.; Gornal, L. Ms
Attitudes towards women in the management of schools
Abstract: This study attempts to explore the nature of organisations by comparing two management styles, 'transformational' and 'transactional'. Using a 'prescriptive model' it explores the relationship between management theory and management practice. The male nature of the organisational world provides the major lens through which females are viewed – serving at one level to suggest the absence of women from positions of responsibility in senior management teams; while at another level to cast images of females in management positions in a contradictory light. The study explores the link between gender-related stereotyping and attitudes towards women in school management. It recognises that cultural dimensions of organisational life through positive affirmative action play a vital part in creating equal opportunities for the upward mobility of female staff into senior management teams in today's schools in the UK.

Status: Individual research
Date of Research: 1993-continuing
KEYWORDS: *educational administration; head teachers; management in education; sex differences; teaching profession; women's employment*

10/0387

Enterprise Unit, Pontypridd, Mid Glamorgan CF37 1DL
01443 480480
Race, P. Prof.; Saunders, D. Mr; Edwards, R. Dr

Developing 'learning-centred' approaches to assessment and teaching

Abstract: The aim of the research is to extend the principles of student-centred learning into teaching and assessment procedures. In particular, it is planned to develop the use of the researcher's model of learning based on four key processes ('wanting, doing, feedback, digesting') to help teaching and training staff design learning resources, teaching processes, and assessment instruments which relate directly to the quality of the learning experience. The research will be conducted in the context of a programme of staff development work with colleagues at the University of Glamorgan and elsewhere, and also in the context of the extensive study-skills development work undertaken with a wide range of the University's student population. The products of the research will take the form of pamphlets and other publications aiming to help teaching and training practitioners design learning-centred approaches and resources, and to help learners and trainees structure their learning more effectively and productively. In particular, it is hoped to evolve recommendations for the design of assessment processes and instruments which are in harmony with students' learning experiences, to replace traditional assessment methods such as 3-hour written examinations which are rarely useful learning experiences for learners (and from which the amount of feedback learners derive is minimal).
Published Material: RACE, P. & BOURNE, T. (1990). How to win as a part-time student: study skills guide. London: Kogan Page.; RACE, P. (1992). 53 interesting ways to write open learning materials. Bristol: Technical and Educational Services Ltd.; RACE, P. (1992). 'Ten worries about assessment', British Journal of Educational Technology, Vol 23, No 22, p.141.; RACE, P. (1993). The open learning handbook: promoting quality in designing and delivering flexible learning. 2nd Edition. London: Kogan Page.; RACE, P. (1993). 'Never mind the teaching – feel the learning', Quality Assurance in Higher Education, Vol 1, No 2, pp.40-43. A full list of publications is available from the researcher.
Status: Sponsored project
Source of Grant: Glamorgan University
Date of Research: 1993-continuing
KEYWORDS: *assessment; higher education; learner-centred methods; open education; self evaluation – individuals; teaching methods*

10/0388

Enterprise Unit, Pontypridd, Mid Glamorgan CF37 1DL
01443 480480
Saunders, D. Mr; Race, P. Prof.; McNorton, M. Ms

Investigating student experiences in higher education

Abstract: Three broad categories of student experience are recognised by the research group, these being: academic learning; study skills; and social and pastoral well-being. For each category, sub-groups of academic staff from across departments within the University will identify a range of successful and less successful outcomes for particular student groups with especial reference to the following: comparisons within and between levels of study within higher education; comparisons between subject and discipline areas; induction activities and outcomes; methods of assessment; traditional and non-traditional students; modes of study and attendance; class sizes; reactions to student-centred learning initiatives; entrance qualifications; inclusion or exclusion of supervised work experience; deep and surface learning; staff perceptions and awareness of students' approaches to learning; and students' experiences within 'old' vs 'new' university sectors. The research programme will involve an eclectic theoretical approach on topics including: deep and surface learning; experiential learning cycles; learning taxonomies; learning hierarchies; learning stages; and self-actualised learning. As theoretical perspectives vary, so do favoured methodological processes for the collection and interpretation of data and evidence. A unifying perspective within the team is that of action research based on cross-disciplinary collaboration.
Published Material: SAUNDERS, D. (1992). 'Community enter-

prise and higher education', Journal of Further and Higher Education, Vol 16, No 2, pp.50-59.; SAUNDERS, D. (1992). 'Peer tutoring in higher education', Studies in Higher Education, Vol 17, No 2, pp.211-218.; SAUNDERS, D. (1994). (Ed). The complete student handbook. Oxford: Blackwell.
Status: Sponsored project
Source of Grant: Higher Education Funding Council for Wales; BP Chemicals, jointly £46,000
Date of Research: 1992-continuing
KEYWORDS: *higher education; learner characteristics; learning experience; learning strategies; student experience*

Glasgow Caledonian University

10/0389

Department of Biological Sciences, City Campus, Cowcaddens Road, Glasgow G4 OBA
0141 331 3000
Leitch, A. Mrs; *Supervisor:* Richardson, K. Dr; Knowler, J. Prof.

Experimental study on improving study skills in undergraduates

Abstract: A model based on discriminant analysis was devised to identify frist year biology students at risk of failing, using data from the 1990-91 cohort. Predictor variables included gender, school performance, and aspects of study skill behaviour assessed by means of a questionnaire. The criterion variable was performance in first diet examinations. In subsequent years of the study, the model was used to identify potentially weak students at the sixth week of their first semester. They were then allocated to experimental and control groups that were matched by gender, age and probability of failure derived from the model. The experimental treatment consisted of a tutorial programme designed to enhance metalearning, to improve academic self-confidence and to increase the score on predictor variables, such as organisation. The experimental groups performed better in most subject areas, though the results were only significant at the 10% level. Throughout the study, the predictive validity of the model has been tested on data from students not taking part in the experimental programme. Although the success rate for prediction of performance was 80% in the initial split-half procedure used on the 1990 data, the rate dropped to about 50% for subsequent cohorts. Recent work has included semi-structured interviews with weak students. It is hoped that the qualitative data yielded will facilitate the development of a variety of improved predictive models, designed to identify different categories of weakness.
Status: Individual research
Date of Research: 1990-1994
KEYWORDS: *higher education; learning strategies; study skills; undergraduate students*

10/0390

Department of Psychology, City Campus, Cowcaddens Road, Glasgow G4 OBA
0141 331 3000
Wrennall, M. Mr; Tuohy, A. Dr; McQueen, R. Mr

The use of computer simulation in the teaching of occupational/industrial psychology

Abstract: The Committee of Scottish University Principals on Teaching and Learning (1992) highlighted the need for re-appraising course delivery in higher education. Increasing demands on staff time, rising student numbers and the need for cost effectiveness is placing a strain on traditional course structures; a problem which can no longer be alleviated simply by increasing class sizes. To address these issues, the researchers have developed a computerised simulation for use on business and commerce degree courses, which replaces a conventional small group seminar system with a more student directed learning situation, where the individual controls the interaction and learning process and which at the same time enhances the teaching of occupational/industrial psychology on these degrees. The use of computer simulation has enabled staff to move to a more student centred learning approach and to provide students with the degree of complexity which is required to make case studies meaningful learning experiences, tapping a range of skills and abilities. The simulation requires the user to adopt the role of an occupational/industrial psychologist tasked with solving a number of organisational problems. Using Hypercard stacks, the user can move through an organ-

isation, consulting personnel records, memoranda, minutes of meetings and review interviews, and consider job satisfaction and attitudinal data. By this process various problems can be identified relating to psychological issues. Access is also available to theoretical material, references and suggested readings. As currently used, the student is required to write a consultant's report, identifying problems, highlighting causes and offering recommendations. Ongoing evaluation of the package with a variety of students, has shown qualitative and quantitative gains in performance, in addition to which, that students appreciate the realism and complexity of the issues involved. Further case studies are being developed and evaluated.
Status: Sponsored project
Source of Grant: Glasgow Caledonian University £10,000
Date of Research: 1991-1994
KEYWORDS: *computer simulation; computer uses in education; industrial psychology; psychology*

10/0391
    Department of Psychology, City Campus, Cowcaddens Road, Glasgow G4 OBA
    0141 331 3000
    Siann, G. Dr
Vocational guidance: with special reference to the needs of ethnic minorities
Abstract: The research study is concerned with identifying, instituting and evaluating measures designed to meet the vocational needs of secondary school pupils in two target groups: a) ethnic minority pupils, particularly females; and b) pupils from socially disadvantaged backgrounds in schools to be identified by equal opportunities advisors. The aims of the study over three years are to: 1) compare the take up of vocational guidance services by ethnic minority and ethnic majority pupils in the selected schools; 2) identify possible modifications in vocational guidance within these schools in order to improve the service to the target groups; 3) identify channels of communication with parents of pupils in the target groups in such a way as to increase parents' knowledge of the educational opportunities on offer to pupils after the completion of secondary school; 4) help institute and monitor changes in vocational guidance practice based on the findings in the selected schools; and 5) evaluate the changes in vocational guidance instituted in the selected schools.
Status: Sponsored project
Source of Grant: Project schools £5,000; Glasgow Caledonian University £60,000
Date of Research: 1993-continuing
KEYWORDS: *career counselling; ethnic groups; minority groups; secondary school pupils; vocational guidance*

10/0392
    Faculty of Health, Southbrae Campus, Southbrae Drive, Jordanhill, Glasgow G13 1PP
    0141 337 4000
    Alexander, H. Mrs; *Supervisor:* Bell, F. Prof.; Duncan, E. Dr; Garven, F. Mrs
An evaluation of a physiotherapy student clinical education assessment instrument
Abstract: The hypothesis tested in this research project was that physiotherapy clinical tutors and visiting lecturers at Glasgow Caledonian University evaluated students rather than just assessing their performance on clinical placement. A distinction was drawn between assessment of student performance and evaluative judgements based on subjective impressions of personal factors. It was contended that these evaluation judgements influenced the grades awarded to students when the assumption of the assessment system was that they did not. It was suggested that this led to problems with the clinical education assessment instrument. This hypothesis emerged from anecdotal and observational evidence which had suggested that there were problems with the assessment instrument and that it required to be evaluated. An eclectic approach was adopted which utilised three studies to determine whether or not the anecdotal and observational evidence was supported, and a fourth study to explore an explanation for any problems found. Methodology included semi-structured interviews, questionnaires, analysis of cohort statistics, and qualitative data collection by means of clinical placement diaries. Results have shown that there were problems with the clinical education assessment instrument in both its design and its actual use. Results of the fourth study found evidence that clinical tutors and visiting lecturers made evaluation judgements of the students. Hence the proposed hypothesis of this research was supported by this data. Further work

will test the representativeness of these results for other groups in the hope that this hypothesis may become established as a principle in a new theory of physiotherapy clinical education.
Status: Individual research
Date of Research: 1988-1994
KEYWORDS: *assessment; clinical experience; medical education; physical therapy*

10/0393
    Faculty of Health, Southbrae Campus, Southbrae Drive, Jordanhill, Glasgow G13 1PP
    0141 337 4000
    Monk, E. Mrs; *Supervisor:* Williams, C. Prof.; Mahmood, Z. Dr
Student mental health: a study of the relationship between stressors, the mental health of students and their academic performance
Abstract: Research over the past 25 years has shown that student casualties are very much a reality. Stressors result in a diversity of responses within the student population, these being dependent on ability to cope or otherwise. This study attempts to ascertain: 1) What stressors affect students? 2) How, why and to what degree they affect? 3) With what frequency they occur among the student population studied? and 4) What steps, if any, the students take to remedy the resultant problems? A pilot study involving oral and written questionnaires gave indicators as to the direction the main study should follow. It involved a small sample (12) of male and female students within the under and over 21 years groupings. The main study involved 200 students within the same categories. A package of 3 separate written questionnaires was administered. Frequency tables and factor analysis are the main indicators of the findings. Patterns in both the pilot and main study appear to be similar. Students do have problems which are causing them distress. Many of them are doing little to alleviate this. It is further proposed to follow up for 1 academic year a small number of students who are highly stressed, together with a similar number who do not seem to be adversely affected by any stressors they may have.
Status: Individual research
Date of Research: 1992-continuing
KEYWORDS: *higher education; stress – psychological; stress management; stress variables; student health and welfare*

Glasgow University

10/0394
    Department of Education, Glasgow G12 8QQ
    0141 339 8855
    Dunn, W. Mr; Holroyd, C. Mr
National standards for training and development within masters programmes in education: Glasgow University
Abstract: The project aims to assess the appropriateness of incorporating the National Standards for Training and development with Masters Degrees in Education. Work at the feasibility stage has shown that students on M.Ed courses recognise the Training and Development Lead Body (TDLB) key roles, units and elements of competence as applicable within their work as education professionals. In 1992-1993 two courses within the Glasgow M.Ed programme will be developed in ways which allow students to demonstrate which of the TDLB standards they meet; it is intended that it will be clarified which parts of M.Ed provision can NOT be described in terms of the TDLB competences/standards.
Published Material: Four papers are available on request from the researchers.; Paper 1. Recognition of TDLB key roles by M.Ed. students (November 1991).; Paper 2. Staff views on basic issues (November 1991).; Paper 3. Recognition of TDLB units and elements by M.Ed. students (September 1992).
Status: Sponsored project
Source of Grant: Department of Employment
Date of Research: 1991-continuing
KEYWORDS: *competency based education; education courses; higher education; masters courses; qualifications; standards*

10/0395

Department of Education, Glasgow G12 8QQ
0141 339 8855
Kirk, R. Ms; *Supervisor:* Wilkinson, J. Dr

Daycare in Tayside: its impact on family relationships and well-being

Abstract: Based on a sample of 100 families using social work daycare in Tayside, the study is an indepth investigation of the impact of the daycare on children and families. The study is using instrumentation (reliable and valid schedules) to examine parents' social support networks and children's development. The study is an attempt to cast light on the extent to which daycare can help families with a child 'at risk' or the subject of abuse.

Published Material: KIRK, R. (1990). Parents and their perceptions of family centres on Tayside. Dundee: Tayside Regional Council.

Status: Individual research

Date of Research: 1991-continuing

KEYWORDS: *children at risk; community services; day care; family problems; family relationship*

10/0396

Department of Education, Glasgow G12 8QQ
0141 339 8855
Wilkinson, J. Dr

The functioning of family centres in Tayside Region

Abstract: The aim of this study is to examine the use and functioning of Family Centres in Tayside Region. Based on interviews with families, both users and non-users, and analysis of the work of the centres, an attempt will be made to ascertain the value of such provision and its possible impact on families with children 'at risk'.

Status: Sponsored project

Source of Grant: Tayside Regional Council £27,500

Date of Research: 1993-1994

KEYWORDS: *child rearing; children at risk; community services; family programmes; programme evaluation; quality control*

10/0397

Department of Education, Glasgow G12 8QQ
0141 339 8855
Wilkinson, J. Dr

A research and evaluation study of community nurseries in Strathclyde Region 1989-1992

Abstract: The study is a research and evaluation study into the strengths and weaknesses of new types of establishments (community nurseries) for families with young children set up in Strathclyde Region following publication of the Member/Officer Group Report, Under Fives (1985). Based on two pilot community nurseries and a conventional nursery school, the evaluation was conducted at a number of levels: (1) achievement of aims and objectives with explanations for successes and failures; (2) assessment of quality of the nursery environment; (3) children's developmental progress; (4) development of the nurseries; (5) effects of the nurseries on families; (6) inter-agency liaison; (7) applications and admissions. Methods used were: interview; observation; children's assessments and analysis of documents. The study shows that quality in the community nurseries is high; most children and families are benefiting and that the nurseries are targeted at the most needy.

Published Material: WILKINSON, J.E., KELLY, B. & BRADY, J. (1990). 'Pre-five evaluation: research in Scotland', Forum on Educational Research in Scotland, No 6, The school in its community. Edinburgh: SCRE.; WILKINSON, J.E. & STEPHEN, C. (1992). Evaluating ourselves. Glasgow: University of Glasgow, Department of Education.; WILKINSON, J.E., KELLY, B. & STEPHEN, C. (1993). Flagships: an evaluation/research study of community nurseries in Strathclyde 1989-1992. Glasgow: University of Glasgow, Department of Education.

Status: Sponsored project

Source of Grant: Strathclyde Regional Council £85,000

Date of Research: 1989-1993

KEYWORDS: *agency cooperation; child caregivers; community services; day care centres; early childhood education; programme evaluation; quality control*

10/0398

Department of Education, Glasgow G12 8QQ
0141 339 8855
Grant, N. Prof.

Comparative education: international perspectives in policy studies

Abstract: This project builds upon a body of publication already generated, which since 1971 has been shifting its emphasis to: (1) ways in which international studies can enhance our understanding of our own systems (Bell, R.E. & Grant, N.D.C. (1973), A mythology of British education, Panther) and (2) the mechanisms by which educational systems interact (Bell, R.E. & Grant, N.D.C. (1975) Patterns of education in the British Isles, Allen & Unwin). The present stage seeks to expand this work, directed particularly at the non-specialist in comparative studies. The work currently in preparation examines the nature and uses of comparative education; methodologies, area studies (Europe, North America and developing countries), national case studies (USSR/CIS, USA, France, Germany, Denmark, Spain, Switzerland, Latin America, South Africa); the interaction of educational systems in the British Isles, North America and Europe, and policy perceptions in the light of international experience. Contributions from Emeritus Professor L.J. Brown, Dr David Matheson, Messrs L. Tikly and F.J. Docherty.

Published Material: GRANT, N.D.C. (1988). 'Future roles for comparative education'. In: CORNER, T.E. (Ed). Learning opportunities for adults. MIEU. Glasgow University, Department of Education.; GRANT, N.D.C. (1990). 'Other people's curricula', Compare, Vol 19, No 1, pp.47-64.

Status: Individual research

Date of Research: 1971-1994

KEYWORDS: *comparative education; educational policy; educational practices; international education*

10/0399

Department of Education, Glasgow G12 8QQ
0141 339 8855
Grant, N. Prof.

Education in the former USSR and the Commonwealth of Independent States

Abstract: This project builds upon an accumulation of publication on education in the Soviet Union and Eastern Europe since 1914. This stage dates from 1989, when the decline of the USSR was more widely perceived to be terminal. A number of field studies have been carried out, and more are plannned, as is the revision of a book, Soviet Education (last edition 1979) as a largely historical work. The stages leading up to the collapse of the USSR, and the collapse itself in 1991, have already been studied, and more such study is planned, using book-based study, documentation and field study. The emphasis is now shifting to the post-Soviet period, and the economic, ideological, ethnic and linguistic problems facing education in the successor states.

Published Material: GRANT, N.D.C. (1989). 'Mechanisms: policy formation and implementation'. In: KIRKWOOD, M. (Ed). Language planning in the Soviet Union. London: Macmillan.; GRANT, N.D.C. (1990). 'Current Soviet educational reform in comparative perspective'. In: COWEN, R. & JONES, C. (Eds). Essays in honour of J.J. Tomiak. DICE, University of London, Institute of Education.; GRANT, N.D.C. (1991). 'Soviet Union: vocational education and training'. In: STEEDMAN, H. (Ed). Pergamon encyclopaedia of education. Oxford: Pergamon Press.; GRANT, N.D.C. (1992). 'Education in the USSR: the last phase', Compare, Vol 22, No 1, pp.69-90.

Status: Individual research

Date of Research: 1989-continuing

KEYWORDS: *Commonwealth of Independent States; communist education; educational change; ideology; politics education relationship; social change; USSR*

10/0400

Department of Education, Glasgow G12 8QQ
0141 339 8855
Grant, N. Prof.

Scottish education: history, politics and the international context

Abstract: This project, which is book and document based, seeks to examine and demythologise certain aspects of the history, ethos and governance of Scottish education, it seeks to relate the perceptions thus gained to contemporary and future educational policy, and to set the discussion in a European and wider international context. It will deal with some contemporary political and educational controversies, and make recommendations for action, both within Scotland and in conjunction with our European and international partners.

Published Material: GRANT, N.D.C. et al (1989). Scottish education: a declaration of principles. Edinburgh: Scottish Centre for

Economic and Social Research/Advisory Council for the Arts in Scotland.; GRANT, N.D.C. (1990). 'La formación profesional y ocupational en Escocia'. En: FERRÁNDEZ, A. & PEIRO, J. (directores) Formación para el empleo. Zaragoza: Universidad Popular/Editorial Humanitas.; GRANT, N.D.C. (1991). 'The education of an international Scot'. In: CORNER, T.E. & VAN de BUNT-KOK-HUIS, S. (Eds). The space between words: cross cultural studies in education. Tilburg University Press.; A full list of publications is available from the researcher.
Status: Individual research
Date of Research: 1975-continuing
KEYWORDS: comparative education; educational history; educational policy; Scotland

10/0401
    Department of Education, Glasgow G12 8QQ
    0141 339 8855
    Grant, N. Prof.
Multicultural education and the education of minorities
Abstract: This project is a series of investigations into cultural pluralism and its educational implications, both in Scotland and internationally, and seeks to make contributions to the educational debate on racism, bilingual education, language maintenance and survival and the multicultural aspects of the curriculum. The research was book based but also included archival material and field studies. It has already produced some publications and the development of a course at Masters' level. A general textbook is in progress.
Published Material: GRANT, N.D.C. (Ed). (1988). 'Education and minority groups', Comparative Education, Special Edition No 11, Vol 24, No 2.; GRANT, N.D.C. The education of minority and peripheral cultures: introduction. Loc. cit., pp. 155-166.; GRANT, N.D.C. (1989). 'Education for a pluralist world: some considerations of language and culture'. In: KORNER, A. (Hrsg.), Bildungspolitische Perspektiven in Nord und Westeuropa. Giessen: Verlag des Ferber'schen Universitatsbuchhandlung.; GRANT, N.D.C. (1992). 'L'educazione multiculturale in Scozia e in altri paesi della periferia europea'. In: TASSINARI, G., CURRIERI, G.C. & GIUSTI, M. (a cura di), La scuola e societa multiculturale. La Nuova Italia, Firenze.; GRANT, N.D.C. (1992). ''Scientific' racism: what price objectivity?', Scottish Educational Review, Vol 24, No 1, pp.24-31.
Status: Individual research
Date of Research: 1985-continuing
KEYWORDS: bilingual education; minority groups; multicultural education; multiculturalism

10/0402
    Department of Education, Glasgow G12 8QQ
    0141 339 8855
    MacKenzie, M. Mr
The future of Scottish Toryism with particular reference to Scottish education and culture
Abstract: The research is based on many years of publication, research and advisory work in the fields of politics and education with specific reference to the Scottish Conservative Party. The approach involves the analysis of policy documents and discussions with leading politicians. The role of pressure groups such as the Scottish Tory Reform Group and the Adam Smith Society is analysed and described. The research is primarily theoretical in character, with the aim of relating political and cultural thinking to policy, and exploring the political dimensions of educational thought.
Published Material: MACKENZIE, M.L. (1986). The intellectual roots of Conservative 'reforms', Tory Reform Group.; MACKENZIE, M.L. (1988). Scottish Toryism, identity and consciousness, Tory Reform Group.; MACKENZIE, M.L. (1989). Scottish Toryism and the Union: a phenomenological approach, Tory Reform Group.
Status: Individual research
Date of Research: 1986-continuing
KEYWORDS: conservatism; politics education relationship; Scotland

10/0403
    Department of Education, Glasgow G12 8QQ
    0141 339 8855
    MacKenzie, M. Mr
The thoughts of Parker Palmer with specific reference to the teaching of religious education in Scotland
Abstract: The research will: (1) analayse Palmer's thoughts, specifically as explained in his book 'The company of strangers: Christians

and the renewal of America's public life' (New York: Crossroad 1990); and (2) compare this thinking with Scottish politics, education systems and the thinking emanating from the Association of Teachers of Religious Education in Scotland (ATRES) a body of which the researcher is a member. The aim is a synthesis of political, educational and religious thought in Scotland based on a comparison with the United States, focused on the work of that country's foremost religious thinkers.
Status: Individual research
Date of Research: 1992-1993
KEYWORDS: religion and education; Scotland

10/0404
    Department of Education, Glasgow G12 8QQ
    0141 339 8855
    Humes, W. Dr
Partnership: a conceptual analysis
Abstract: The concept of partnership is frequently invoked in educational discourse. This study attempts to disentangle its various meanings using a range of examples covering home/school relations, education/industry links and central/local government responsibilities. The question of whether it is simply a rhetorical device designed to disguise differential power will be considered.
Status: Individual research
Date of Research: 1992-1993
KEYWORDS: government – administrative body; home-school relationship; industry education relationship

10/0405
    Department of Education, Glasgow G12 8QQ
    0141 339 8855
    Grant, N. Prof.; Humes, W. Dr
Scottish education after the 1696 Education Act
Abstract: This study is part of a larger project for publication entitled 'Scotland: a concise cultural history'. The project as a whole will cover literature, science, the law, the arts and religion as well as education. The chapter on education will deal with legislation, access and expansion, democracy and equality, and the changing nature of the policy process. Several recurring myths about Scottish education will be challenged.
Status: Individual research
Date of Research: 1992-1993
KEYWORDS: educational history; Scotland

10/0406
    Department of Education, Glasgow G12 8QQ
    0141 339 8855
    Humes, W. Dr
The management of morale
Abstract: This is a small scale project which attempts to review recent research on teacher morale and to consider its implications for educational managers. Among the topics to be considered are communication systems, decision making processes, promotion, innovation and professional autonomy. The question of whether central and local government are expecting educational managers to do an impossible job will be addressed.
Published Material: HUMES, W. (1993). 'Scottish ideas for managing morale', Management in Education, Vol 7, No 3, pp.9-10.
Status: Individual research
Date of Research: 1992-1993
KEYWORDS: educational administration; teacher morale; teaching profession

10/0407
    Department of Education, Glasgow G12 8QQ
    0141 339 8855
    Morrison, D. Mr; *Supervisor:* Wilkinson, J. Dr
The effective secondary school
Abstract: The study explores in ideological, political and educational terms, parental and pupil perceptions about what constitutes an effective secondary school. Using data on school performance in external examinations, the study focuses on 12 secondary schools – 6 performing above the 'norm' and 6 below, in order to identify school based factors that contribute to their effectiveness. These factors will be related to parent support and aspirations, and to pupils' own perceptions and behaviour, by asking parents and pupils to

complete an extensive questionnaire prior to the pupils taking external examinations in May 1993.
Status: Individual research
Date of Research: 1991-continuing
KEYWORDS: examination results; school effectiveness; secondary schools

10/0408
Department of Education, Glasgow G12 8QQ
0141 339 8855
Walker, L. Ms; *Supervisor:* Dunn, W. Mr
Access and completion rates in higher education
Abstract: This research explores some of the implications of widening access to higher education on non-completion rates. The project has three main aims: (1) To examine the academic performances and perceived problems in higher education of students from socio-economic groups which are traditionally under-represented at university but which are increasingly the target of policies for wider access, i.e. certain socio-economic groups and non-traditional entrants; (2) To investigate the reasons for non-completion of their degree courses by a general cross section of students; (3) To identify possible predictors of success or failure in undergraduate performance. Preliminary findings indicate that students who have attended the Pre-University Summer School – a pre-university preparation course at the University of Glasgow run for students from areas of deprivation – are more likely to obtain degrees, despite socio/economic disadvantages, than a random sample of entrants. Work is proceeding at present to establish the academic progress of students with similar socio-economic backgrounds who did not attend the Pre-University Summer School, in order to determine the value added by this type of preparation course. Methods include reviews of academic transcripts, statistical analysis of demographic make-up of entrants, longitudinal surveys of academic performances and problems encountered during degree courses including the financial effects of student grants and loans, semi-structured interviews with sample groups, and discussions with 'experts' such as student advisors, admissions officers and tutors.
Published Material: A full list of publications is available from the researcher.
Status: Individual research
Date of Research: 1991-continuing
KEYWORDS: access to education; dropout research; higher education; nontraditional education; summer schools; university admission; university preparation

10/0409
Department of Education, Glasgow G12 8QQ
0141 339 8855
Munro, J. Mr; *Supervisor:* MacBeth, A. Dr
Preconceptions about the roles of parents in education and schooling since the Plowden Report: how such preconceptions influence the professional decision-maker and the parent in their attitudes towards home-school practice
Abstract: This study explores the relationship between preconceptions of what constitutes education and the role of parents in education. Political trends of the past 25 years are assessed with regard to both use of language about parents in education and assumptions associated with such language. The study recognises current developments as constituting a significant period of transition. Methodology will include analysis of official and other documents and interviews with key personnel who have influenced policy changes with regard to the role of parents in education.
Status: Individual research
Date of Research: 1990-continuing
KEYWORDS: educational history; parent participation; parent-school relationship

10/0410
Department of Education, Glasgow G12 8QQ
0141 339 8855
Kirkham, J. Mr; *Supervisor:* MacKenzie, M. Mr
A critical analysis of Thomas Greenfield's subjective approach to the field of educational administration in the context of an interdisciplinary initiative to the field, drawing on sociology of education, anthropology, philosophy and organisation theory in general
Abstract: This project includes: (1) an analysis of all relevant docu-

mentation following Greenfield's paper to the 1974 International Intervisitation Programme in Bristol; (2) an examination of the resulting subjective/systems debates; (3) a detailed review of the relevant literature; (4) an exploration of the justificatory philosophical sources used by Greenfield and his critics; (5) comparison of Greenfield's 'new perspective' with the 'new directions' movement in the sociology of education; (6) an examination of the importance of anthropological and ethnographic research methods in educational administration; (7) an examination of ambiguity models in relation to systems and subjective approaches; (8) the relevance of the Inlogou Report; (9) a critical examination of the possibility of resolving the subjective/systems debate.
Status: Individual research
Date of Research: 1988-1993
KEYWORDS: educational administration; organisational theories

10/0411
Department of Education, Glasgow G12 8QQ
0141 339 8855
Marker, W. Mr; *Supervisor:* MacKenzie, M. Mr
Policy making in teacher education in Scotland 1959-1981
Abstract: This project includes: (1) a study of the policy process, involving interviews and analysis of original documentation; (2) a UK analysis which compares policy in England with that of Scotland; (3) examination of demographic and economic factors, as well as political and pressure group considerations with regard to major decisions such as college closure. Conclusions and analysis takes place within a theoretical framework. The research illuminates key issues and processes concerning teacher education in Scotland during the period studied.
Status: Individual research
Date of Research: 1987-1993
KEYWORDS: comparative education; educational history; educational policy; Scotland; teacher education

10/0412
Department of Education, Glasgow G12 8QQ
0141 339 8855
Boyd, B. Dr; *Supervisor:* MacKenzie, M. Mr
'Let a hundred flowers blossom...': a study of educational policy making in Scotland in the 1970's, 1980's and early 1990's: formulation, implementation and dissemination, using the 10-14 report as a case study
Abstract: This project includes: (1) an examination of the primary and secondary scene in Scotland by means of a case study of the 10-14 initiative; (2) a study of local government reorganisation; (3) a look at the School as an important element in the policy implementation process and a consideration of why the 10-14 initiative failed to be implemented as a policy and was instead replaced by the Government's 5-14 Development Programme. Data is used from the 10-14 Committee. In addition, interviews with members of the policy community are presented as commentary both on the 10-14 initiative and on the policy making process generally. Various papers, including memos and letters from participants in the 10-14 initiative are examined. Thus 10-14 is offered as a case study of the Scottish educational policy making process. The influence of 'New Light' ideology is also examined.
Status: Individual research
Date of Research: 1988-1993
KEYWORDS: educational innovation; educational policy; middle school education; Scotland

10/0413
Department of Education, Glasgow G12 8QQ
0141 339 8855
Cavanagh, J. Mr; *Supervisor:* MacKenzie, M. Mr
Quality assurance in secondary education
Abstract: The aim of this project is to examine the relevance of the British Standard BS 5750 and other quality assurance procedures to the work of secondary schools. A secondary school in the south of Scotland has been selected as a case study. This will involve analysis of documents, interviews and participant observer approaches. Inter-regional comparisons will be made of policies and decision making with regard to quality assurance. The theoretical, conceptual aspects of the problem will be a major thrust of the research.
Status: Individual research
Date of Research: 1992-continuing

KEYWORDS: educational quality; quality assurance; school effectiveness; secondary schools

10/0414

Department of Education, Glasgow G12 8QQ
0141 339 8855
Tikly, L. Mr; *Supervisor:* Humes, W. Dr
Education policy in South Africa since 1948
Abstract: This study examines the changing nature of educational policy in South Africa since 1948. It shows how the orthodoxies of apartheid were challenged and transformed by major economic forces. Debates both within the National Party and the African National Congress are examined critically. Interviews with leading political and educational figures are used to explain the context and recommendations of key documents (such as the De Lange Report). The implications of the reform process for future policy are considered.
Status: Individual research
Date of Research: 1990-1993
KEYWORDS: educational history; educational policy; politics education relationship; South Africa

10/0415

Department of Education, Glasgow G12 8QQ
0141 339 8855
Sinclair, N. Miss; *Supervisor:* Humes, W. Dr
The history of education in Caithness since 1872
Abstract: This study attempts to trace the development of education in Caithness following the Education (Scotland) Act, 1872. The effect of subsequent legislation is considered and, in particular, the difficulty of successfully implementing national policy in a remote area with special geographical, economic and manpower problems. Extensive use is made of primary sources in the shape of school logbooks, education committee minutes and correspondence between the local authority and the Scottish Office Education Department.
Status: Individual research
Date of Research: 1992-continuing
KEYWORDS: educational change; educational history; Scotland

10/0416

Department of Education, Glasgow G12 8QQ
0141 339 8855
Skelton, F. Ms; *Supervisor:* Humes, W. Dr
The influence of Juan Luis Vives on the educational ideas of John Locke
Abstract: This study examines the ideas of the Spanish humanist, Juan Luis Vives, and their impact on subsequent writers on education, in particular John Locke. Vives' empirical approach to educational enquiry and his views on psychological development are given detailed analysis. Locke's indebtedness to Vives is shown to be indirect rather than direct in the sense that it is mediated through other writers. The importance of Vives in the history of educational thought is also evident in the work of the Scottish Common Sense school of philosophy.
Status: Individual research
Date of Research: 1992-continuing
KEYWORDS: educational history; educational psychology; educational theories

10/0417

Department of Education, Glasgow G12 8QQ
0141 339 8855
Matheson, D. Dr; *Supervisor:* Grant, N. Prof.
Post-compulsory education in Suisse Romande – a comparison of formal and non-formal education, vocational and non-vocational, in the Francophone areas of Switzerland
Abstract: This project examines the various sectors of post-compulsory education in Suisse-Romande. It is set in its historical context, and pays particular attention to the operation of educational systems which are almost totally controlled (and differ considerably) at Cantonal level, not federal. Some conclusions are reached regarding confederal organisation of education.
Published Material: MATHESON, D.J. (1991). 'Non-vocational, non-formal further education in Highland Region in Scotland and the Canton of Valais in Switzerland', Comparative Education, Vol 27, No 2, pp.153-164.
Status: Individual research

Date of Research: 1989-1992
KEYWORDS: further education; Switzerland

10/0418

Department of Education, Glasgow G12 8QQ
0141 339 8855
Mouhoubi, R. Ms; *Supervisor:* Grant, N. Prof.
Sociolinguistic study of minority languages in education
Abstract: This is a comparative study of education and language policy in Scotland, where some recognition for Gaelic has been achieved, and Algeria, where none has been accorded to Tamazight (Berber). The study is set in the context of a sociolinguistic study of bilingualism and a study of the historical, demographic, cultural and political backgrounds of the minorities in both countries. Field studies have been carried out in Scotland and Algeria, and archival research in Glasgow, Algiers and Paris.
Status: Individual research
Date of Research: 1991-1994
KEYWORDS: Algeria; bilingualism; comparative education; Gaelic; language policy; mother tongue; Scotland

10/0419

Department of Education, Glasgow G12 8QQ
0141 339 8855
Yekta, Z. Mrs; *Supervisor:* Grant, N. Prof.; Shanley, E. Dr
The development of the curriculum in nursing education in Iran
Abstract: This is a study of the development of the curriculum for nursing education in Iran, and the implementation of government policy. Comparisons are drawn with work in the United States and the United Kingdom.
Status: Individual research
Date of Research: 1990-1994
KEYWORDS: Iran; nurse education

10/0420

Department of Education, Glasgow G12 8QQ
0141 339 8855
Rajanaorison, A. Mr; *Supervisor:* Grant, N. Prof.
Evaluation of an international curriculum
Abstract: This is a book and document based study of attempts to encourage international awareness through the curriculum of the general school system in various countries in Europe and elsewhere. An attempt to evaluate success to date, will also be made.
Status: Individual research
Date of Research: 1990-1994
KEYWORDS: cultural awareness; international education

10/0421

Department of Education, Glasgow G12 8QQ
0141 339 8855
Stapa, S. Mrs; *Supervisor:* Grant, N. Prof.; Barr, A. Mr
The development of teaching materials for teaching English in developing countries with special reference to secondary schools in Malaysia
Abstract: This is a study of the development of teaching materials for teaching English in Malaysian secondary schools, with particular reference to written English, and set in the context of a linguistic study of writing in a second language. Field studies have been carried out and questionnaires and interviews conducted.
Status: Individual research
Date of Research: 1990-1994
KEYWORDS: English – second language; Malaysia; secondary schools

10/0422

Department of Education, Glasgow G12 8QQ
0141 339 8855
Ariffin, S. Mrs; *Supervisor:* Grant, N. Prof.; Barr, A. Mr
Characteristics of secondary schools in Pulau Penang, Malaysia
Abstract: This project examines the implementation of a scheme for the teaching of English in Malaysian schools, recently introduced by the Government, and the effectiveness of this implementation. Field studies have been carried out in Malaysia with questionnaires on teachers' experience of inservice training for the purpose, and their attitudes towards it.

Status: Individual research
Date of Research: 1990-1993
KEYWORDS: English – second language; Malaysia; secondary schools

10/0423

Department of Education, Glasgow G12 8QQ
0141 339 8855
Canen, A. Mrs; *Supervisor:* Grant, N. Prof.; MacKenzie, M. Mr

The role of teachers in society – a comparative study of Brazil and the UK
Abstract: The project seeks to investigate perceptions of teachers (particularly of science), of the role of teachers in their respective societies, and how they are regarded by society at large.
Status: Individual research
Date of Research: 1993-continuing
KEYWORDS: Brazil; comparative education; public opinion; teacher role

10/0424

Department of Education, Glasgow G12 8QQ
0141 339 8855
Emara, H. Mrs; *Supervisor:* Grant, N. Prof.; Barr, A. Mr

The effects of language difficulties on the achievements of Arab students
Abstract: Many higher education courses (e.g. medicine) in Saudi Arabia are taught in English, and difficulties have emerged in students' performance. This project examines the psycholinguistic issues that arise in the course of studying through a language not native to either the teacher or the learner, and some of the difficulties that emerge in the particular circumstances of Saudi universities. Documentary and fieldwork has been used in this project.
Status: Individual research
Date of Research: 1988-1993
KEYWORDS: English – second language; higher education; language of instruction; Saudi Arabia

10/0425

Department of Education, Glasgow G12 8QQ
0141 339 8855
Dunn, W. Mr; Hamilton, D. Dr

The pre-university summer school
Abstract: The pre-university summer school is a research and development project which has two main aims: 1) To give the young people and adults who attend (all of whom hope to enter university later in the year) confidence in themselves and in their ability to cope with university. 2) To allow those who do not reach the required standards, designated by admissions officers, the opportunity to have their entry application reconsidered on the basis of their summer school performance. Two hundred and fifty students will attend the summer school for nine weeks. They will come from areas of priority treatment in Strathclyde Region. Week One is an introduction to academic life at a university. In Weeks Two to Nine, the students will study three subjects of their choice. They will choose those subjects they intend to take in their first year at university, and they will be taught by university staff who will select aspects of the first year syllabus for those eight weeks of study. Those students who will need the summer school as an entry mechanism to higher education will have their performance assessed by their tutors. The tutors will be asked – "on the basis of the work you have seen over the summer, is this student likely to complete your first year course?" Those students not offered a university place will be given career advice and assistance. The students' careers in higher education will be carefully monitored with the main aim being to compare their progress with that of students from a similar background who did not attend the summer school.
Status: Sponsored project
Source of Grant: Strathclyde Regional Council; University of Glasgow, jointly £120,000
Date of Research: 1993-1994
KEYWORDS: access to education; higher education; summer schools; transition education; university admission; university preparation

10/0426

Department of Education, Glasgow G12 8QQ
0141 339 8855
Sarkar, R. Mrs; *Supervisor:* Grant, N. Prof.; Wilkinson, J. Dr

The teaching of community languages in Scotland
Abstract: This is a study of the teaching of community languages in Scotland, especially among the Asian community. The problem of policy and practice will be addressed and likely future developments will be considered.
Status: Individual research
Date of Research: 1993-continuing
KEYWORDS: Asians; bilingualism; ethnic groups; language maintenance; language policy; minority groups; mother tongue

10/0427

Department of Education, Glasgow G12 8QQ
0141 339 8855
Humes, W. Dr

The policy process in Scottish education: towards a revised model
Abstract: This study re-examines the models of the policy process in Scottish education offered by two earlier studies – Humes (1986) and McPherson and Raab (1988). It suggests that political developments within the Scottish Office (in particular Michael Forsyth's period as the minister responsible for education) require a modification of earlier conceptualizations. A five-dimensional model involving ideology, people, structures, issues and culture is proposed.
Published Material: HUMES, W. (1993). 'The policy process in Scottish education: towards a revised model', Education in the North, New Series, No 1, pp.1-9.
Status: Individual research
Date of Research: 1993-1994
KEYWORDS: educational policy; politics education relationship; Scotland

10/0428

Department of Education, Glasgow G12 8QQ
0141 339 8855
Humes, W. Dr; MacKenzie, M. Mr

The management of educational policy: a Scottish perspective
Abstract: This project aims to explore the interface between policy and management in education with reference to a range of examples covering primary, secondary, further and higher education. The outcome will be a collection of essays which seek to avoid a narrow 'systems' approach by showing how management issues are closely tied up with value questions deriving from the worlds of politics, ideology and culture.
Status: Sponsored project
Source of Grant: British Educational Management and Administration Society
Date of Research: 1993-1994
KEYWORDS: educational administration; educational policy; management in education; politics education relationship; Scotland

10/0429

Department of Education, Glasgow G12 8QQ
0141 339 8855
Humes, W. Dr

The General Teaching Council of Scotland: an independent professional body?
Abstract: This study examines whether the hopes expressed about teacher professionalism, when the General Teaching Council (GTC) was established in Scotland in 1965, have been realised. The recent creation of a comparable body in British Columbia, Canada (the College of Teachers), and the 1992 conclusions of a Government sponsored policy review of the GTC, suggest that such an investigation is timely. Initial findings point to a discrepancy between perspectives on the GTC held by observers outside Scotland and those of Scottish teachers themselves.
Status: Individual research
Date of Research: 1993-1994
KEYWORDS: national organisations; professional associations; Scotland; teaching profession

10/0430

Department of Education, Glasgow G12 8QQ
0141 339 8855
Campbell, P. Mr; *Supervisor:* Grant, N. Prof.;
MacKenzie, M. Mr
Nordic folk high schools and their possible application to Scotland
Abstract: This is a study of the development and function of the Folk High Schools in Denmark, Norway, Sweden and elsewhere in Scandinavia, examining the different patterns in the various countries. An attempt will be made to examine the salient features, and to consider how some of them could be adapted and introduced to Scotland.
Status: Individual research
Date of Research: 1993-continuing
KEYWORDS: *adult education; comparative education; lifelong learning; mature students; people's universities; Scandinavia*

10/0431

Department of Education, Glasgow G12 8QQ
0141 339 8855
Kobenhavns Universitet, Institut for Paedagogik, Filosofi og Retorik, Njalsgade 80, 2300 Copenhagen S, Denmark
Grant, N. Prof.; Slowey, M. Prof.; Winther-Jensen, Th. Dr
Popular enlightenment and the Danish Folk High School: international influences in lifelong learning
Abstract: This is a new project, to be carried out by the Universities of Glasgow and Copenhagen, which aims to examine the experience of provision of access for mature students to higher education in Scotland and Denmark, the changing role of the Folk High Schools (FHS), and their cultural and social function. Also examined will be the influence of the Danish FHS in Norway, Sweden, Iceland and Germany, and the prospects and possibilities of adopting any of their experience in Scotland.
Status: Sponsored project
Source of Grant: British Council
Date of Research: 1993-1994
KEYWORDS: *adult education; comparative education; Denmark; lifelong learning; mature students; people's universities*

10/0432

Department of Education, Glasgow G12 8QQ
0141 339 8855
St Andrew's College of Education, Duntocher Road, Bearsden, Glasgow G61 4QA
0141 943 1424
O'Brien, J. Mr; *Supervisor:* MacBeth, A. Dr
A study of the origins, concepts, development and procedures of school boards in Scotland, encompassing political, educational and managerial aspects
Abstract: This study initially considers concepts associated with the context for the development of Scottish School Boards (counterparts to English Governing Bodies). Such concepts include: democracy, especially in its representative and participatory forms; bureaucracy; accountability; professionalism; management. The focus moves from general to school issues, with emphasis placed on the historical development of school boards in light of analysis of the above concepts. Documentary evidence from the official government consultative procedures on the pre-existing school councils, the government's proposals for school boards and the recent proposals for devolved management of schools in Scotland and other sources both before and after enactment of the School Boards (Scotland) Act, 1988 are analysed with a view to identifying trends and relationships with political, managerial and educational aspects. Consideration will be given to ways by which school boards may develop through functions which they may adopt within the terms of the Act.
Status: Individual research
Date of Research: 1990-continuing
KEYWORDS: *educational administration; school boards – Scotland; school governing bodies; Scotland*

10/0433

Department of Education, Glasgow G12 8QQ
0141 339 8855
St Andrew's College of Education, Department of Learning Difficulties, Duntocher Road, Bearsden, Glasgow G61 4QA
0141 943 1424
Smith, C. Ms; *Supervisor:* Wilkinson, J. Dr; Hayward, L. Ms

The effectiveness of peripatetic teaching services to hearing impaired children in Scotland
Abstract: The research focuses on peripatetic services supporting pupils with hearing impairment in mainstream secondary schools in Scotland. The investigation will cover the historical development of such services; the range of policies adopted by central and local government and an indepth study of practices in one Region, i.e. Strathclyde. Longitudinal case studies are being set up of two different support systems and compared with provision for hearing impaired children in a special school. Aspects such as: social integration; staff deployment; parental and pupil perspective; and resources will be examined in detail. Based on the data, an attempt will be made to evaluate the effectiveness of peripatetic services.
Status: Individual research
Date of Research: 1993-continuing
KEYWORDS: *educational quality; hearing impairments; mainstreaming; peripatetic teachers; special educational needs; support teachers; teacher effectiveness*

10/0434

Department of Sociology, Lilybank House, Glasgow G12 8RT
0141 339 8855
Littlewood, P. Mr
A sociological evaluation of the relationship between expectations and outcomes concerning parental inclusion on School Boards
Abstract: The establishment of School Boards in Scotland under the Education Reform Act 1988 took place amid considerable controversy as to the possible consequences of so increasing the participative role of parents in decision making and policy formulation of schools. The study seeks to assess the nature and extent of the impact of this increased participation, and how the perceptions of the principal actors have been affected by the first two years of School Board activity. The study is based on a sample of 6 secondary schools in Glasgow, and involves, a) sustained observation of their meetings, b) interviews and questionnaires with all members and head teachers of the school in the sample, and c) collection of data from the Regional and Scottish Education Departments regarding policies relating to School Boards.
Published Material: LITTLEWOOD, P. (1990). 'The return of the board? 'Parent power' and participation in the Scottish school system', Critical Social Policy, No 27, pp.96-109.
Status: Sponsored project
Source of Grant: Glasgow University: John Robertson Bequest £755
Date of Research: 1990-1994
KEYWORDS: *parent control; parent-school relationship; school boards – Scotland; school governing bodies*

Greenwich University

10/0435

School of Primary Education, Avery Hill Campus, Bexley Road, Eltham, London SE9 2PQ
0181 316 8000
Mayes, J. Ms; Barron, P. Mr; Doggett, A. Ms
Science evaluation project
Abstract: This project involves a targeted evaluation of the Science component of the B.Ed (Hons) Degree in the light of recent changes in the requirements for the science curriculum in schools (through the National Curriculum) and for the training of primary school teachers in sciences.
Status: Sponsored project
Source of Grant: Greenwich University £2,000
Date of Research: 1991-continuing
KEYWORDS: *B. Ed. degrees; preservice teacher education; science curriculum; science education*

10/0436

School of Primary Education, Avery Hill Campus, Bexley Road, Eltham, London SE9 2PQ
0181 316 8000
Williams, G. Dr; Street-Porter, R. Ms; Clayton, A. Mr; Draper, M. Mr
European cooperation through media-based learning technology

Abstract: This project is being run, and partially funded, in conjunction with the School staff examining three distinct but interrelated areas of collaboration associated with the training of early years teachers in Sweden. The first will undertake a feasibility study of teacher needs; the second will explore the potential provided by more flexible approaches to academic and award structures (e.g. accreditation for developing European cooperation at a more formal level, and the third will examine course delivery methodology through media-based learning technology. The outcomes of the project are intended to provide an operational framework for developing the School's Inservice education of teachers (INSET) work within the broader market of Europe.
Status: Sponsored project
Source of Grant: Greenwich University; Gothenburg University, Sweden – jointly £9,700
Date of Research: 1991-continuing
KEYWORDS: distance education; educational media; infant school teachers; inservice education; international educational exchange; Sweden; telecommunications

10/0437

School of Primary Education, Avery Hill Campus, Bexley Road, Eltham, London SE9 2PQ
0181 316 8000
Harland, L. Ms; Taylor, P. Ms; Townsend, R. Ms; Brook, D. Mr
Seminar leadership: the development of performance indicators
Abstract: This project is exploring the possibilities and limitations of formulating performance indicators in the area of seminar leadership skills. It will look at the process of small-group tutors interactions, widening its scope to involvement in other departments of the University. The research methodology is twofold: (i) in the form of collaborative action research; (ii) in the form of observation and feedback or collaborative evaluation. The collaboration is between the research and the seminar leader.
Status: Sponsored project
Source of Grant: Greenwich University £2,000
Date of Research: 1991-1993
KEYWORDS: leadership; performance indicators; seminars; small group teaching; teacher effectiveness; teaching methods; university teaching

10/0438

School of Primary Education, Avery Hill Campus, Bexley Road, Eltham, London SE9 2PQ
0181 316 8000
Harland, L. Ms; Taylor, P. Ms; Brook, D. Mr; Hancock, R. Mr
Reflective teaching and learning
Abstract: The project's broad aim is to have practical consequences throughout the University in the improvement of teaching techniques in seminars, and the development of teaching skills which will encourage and promote independent learning among students. The project will involve pairs of tutors working together, monitoring and evaluating seminar leadership, and will use action research, a collaborative model, observation, student interviews and post-seminar joint evaluation.
Status: Sponsored project
Source of Grant: Greenwich University £2,000
Date of Research: 1990-1992
KEYWORDS: leadership; seminars; small group teaching; teaching methods; university teaching

10/0439

School of Primary Education, Avery Hill Campus, Bexley Road, Eltham, London SE9 2PQ
0181 316 8000
Harland, L. Ms
Work-based learning in teacher education
Abstract: This is a pilot project which is exploring the possibilities and problems of student teaching practice supervision by mentor teachers in schools. While acknowledging and synthesising previous work in this area, the project will place the issues within the context of Greenwich University and the two London Boroughs involved (Greenwich and Tower Hamlets) and through case study establish frameworks for future organisation of work-based learning.
Status: Sponsored project
Source of Grant: University of Gothenburg £2,000

Date of Research: 1991-1992
KEYWORDS: mentors; preservice teacher education; student teacher supervisors; teaching practice

10/0440

School of Secondary Education, Avery Hill Campus, Bexley Road, Eltham, London SE9 2PQ
0181 316 8000
Ingham, A. Dr; Fisher, G. Mr
The development and evaluation of new teaching and learning styles in higher education: an international venture
Abstract: Recent years have seen considerable changes in teaching and learning styles in all sectors of education in the UK, particularly in higher education. Less is known of the work done in other European institutions involved in initial teacher training. The aims of the project are: (1) An initial comparison of teaching and learning styles currently employed in two institutions: Thames Polytechnic (now Greenwich University), London, UK and the Central Netherlands Polytechnic, Utrecht. (2) Production of distance learning and other materials related to science and/or language programmes of the Central Netherlands Polytechnic. Initial communication between the two institutions will involve electronic communication methods. Evaluation of teaching and learning styles will be carried out by a variety of methods including: seminar/lecture observations; semi-structured interviews with staff and students; and repertory grid analysis. At a later stage in the project, the focus will be an evaluation of electronic communication in an international research project in higher education.
Status: Sponsored project
Source of Grant: Greenwich University; Central Netherlands Polytechnic
Date of Research: 1992-continuing
KEYWORDS: comparative education; distance education; higher education; international educational exchange; learning activities; Netherlands; teaching methods; telecommunications

10/0441

School of Secondary Education, Avery Hill Campus, Bexley Road, Eltham, London SE9 2PQ
0181 316 8000
Goodger, B. Dr; Goodger, J. Dr
Cultural transmission and change in sport, with special reference to judo
Abstract: The research is concerned with the processes of cultural transmission and change in sports, using judo in Britain as a major case study. Emphasis has been placed on changing social composition and selection, pedagogy and mass media influences on processes of socialisation within sports. Further, the sources of such changes have been sought in both the specific nature, and circumstances, of particular sport cultures and the wider social context in which growing individualism, rationalism and awareness of social arrangements are seen as being of particular significance. In this context, judo is thought to be of special interest since its Japanese origin has resulted in high degrees of insulation from more mainstream sport cultures. The recent penetration of its distinctive culture, organisation and pedagogy, therefore, provides a particularly interesting example of the ways in which contact with larger, often international, organising bodies, administrative demands arising from expansion, the experience of pedagogical practices outside judo, and the influence of television coverage of sport (and the desire for such coverage), have opened the way for more typically modern, western, social organisation and culture to become dominant. It is not, however, suggested that judo is unique in this respect and it is seen to be important that the possible applications of this approach to the study of other sports and, indeed, educational institutions are explored.
Published Material: GOODGER, B.C. (1980). 'Sociology of sports: some implications from instruction in judo', Focus on Learning, USA, Vol 7, No 1, pp.30-38.; GOODGER, J.M. (1985). 'Collective representations and the sacred in sport', International Review for Sociology of Sport, Vol 20, No 3, pp.179-187.; GOODGER, J.M. (1986). 'Pluralism transmission and change in sport', Quest, Vol 38, No 2, pp.135-147.; GOODGER, J.M. (1986). 'Ritual sociology and sport', Acta Sociologica, Vol 29, No 3, pp.219-224.; GOODGER, B.C. & GOODGER, J.M. (1989). 'Transformed images: representations of judo on British television', Play and Culture, Vol 2, pp.340-353.
Status: Individual research
Date of Research: 1974-continuing
KEYWORDS: judo; physical activities; sports

10/0442
School of Secondary Education, Avery Hill Campus, Bexley Road, Eltham, London SE9 2PQ
0181 316 8000
Ingham, A. Dr; Oliver, M. Prof.
Widening access to practical subjects at Thames Polytechnic (now Greenwich University) with particular reference to handicapped students
Abstract: Throughout a disabled person's life it is considered almost unimaginable to go to a university or a polytechnic. Reasons to account for the small number of disabled students following practical courses at further education (FE) and higher education (HE) are complex and may include: facilities provided by the institutions; the perceptions of the students themselves, the teachers and FE/HE admissions tutors. The project will focus initially on three areas within Thames Polytechnic (now Greenwich University): (i) the facilities available for disabled students; (ii) the advertising and promotion of courses applicable to disabled students; (iii) admissions procedures and perceptions of admissions tutors towards disabled students; with a view to: (i) assessing the need for staff development; (ii) increasing provision and widening access at Thames and subsequently other London higher education institutions; (iv) improving recruitment. Factual data will be obtained by questionnaires to all course directors within Thames Polytechnic, and follow-up interviews (semi-structured) will obtain information on perceptions and thought processes of staff concerning disabilities, and access.
Status: Sponsored project
Source of Grant: Greenwich University £5,000
Date of Research: 1991-1992
KEYWORDS: access to education; accessibility – for disabled; disabilities; equal education; higher education; student recruitment

10/0443
School of Secondary Education, Avery Hill Campus, Bexley Road, Eltham, London SE9 2PQ
0181 316 8000
Reeves, C. Mr; *Supervisor:* Cooper, M. Dr; Head, J. Dr
Transition from primary to secondary school and the role of physical education
Abstract: The aim of the research is to study children during the transition from primary to secondary school. For some children this is a stressful time and disaffection, underachievement and absenteeism are some ways stress is exhibited, (HARGREAVES, D.H. (1984). Improving secondary schools. ILEA). Attitudes towards physical education appear to be universally positive at both primary and secondary level (ILEA (1985). Secondary transfer project 1-17, ILEA; Macintosh, P. (1988). 'My favourite subject', ILEA). A greater understanding of how these attitudes arise and why they are held is necessary so that the findings may enable children to cope with the stress of transfer and combat disaffection. Fifty boys (aged 10-11) at two primary schools completed questionnaires designed to examine anxiety, global and specific esteem, attitude to physical education and physical activity levels. Body mass index and skinfold measures were recorded and each subject was tested for general motor ability. Correlation coefficients across the variables are currently being calculated. It is envisaged that a sample of boys recently transferred to secondary school be studied to identify comparisons with the original sample.
Status: Individual research
Date of Research: 1989-1994
KEYWORDS: developmental continuity; physical activity level; physical education; primary secondary education

10/0444
School of Secondary Education, Avery Hill Campus, Bexley Road, Eltham, London SE9 2PQ
0181 316 8000
Wasp, D. Mr
Primary/secondary transition
Abstract: This is a joint project involving the School of Secondary Education (Greenwich University) and the London Borough of Greenwich. The project examines the issues raised by the transition of pupils from primary to secondary school. Course members include teachers from one secondary, four primary and one special school within the Borough. Areas covered include: (1) recommendations for good practice in transition; (2) science practice across the phases; (3) school visit reports; (4) the recording and reporting of information; (5) cross-curricular work; (6) special educational needs; (7) pupils' views of transition.
Status: Sponsored project
Source of Grant: London Borough of Greenwich; Greenwich University – jointly £10,000
Date of Research: 1991-1992
KEYWORDS: developmental continuity; primary secondary education

10/0445
School of Secondary Education, Avery Hill Campus, Bexley Road, Eltham, London SE9 2PQ
0181 316 8000
Sussex University, Institute of Continuing and Professional Education, Sussex House, Falmer, Brighton BN1 9RH
01273 606755
Goddard, W. Mr; *Supervisor:* Cooper, B. Dr
Redefinitions and reconstructions of technical education in secondary schools in England and Wales 1944-1989
Abstract: This research investigates the influences and developments which have caused curriculum development to take place in the secondary school subject area which represents Technical. Attention is given to key actors in the field as well as to subject associations, research projects and government initiatives. The project will show how the interaction between these various segments have fostered new developments in the subject area.
Status: Individual research
Date of Research: 1985-1993
KEYWORDS: curriculum development; educational history; secondary education; technical education

Guildford Educational Services Limited

10/0446
32 Castle Street, Guildford GU1 3UW
01483 579454
Ward, C. Mrs; Twining, J. Mr; Botcherby, C. Miss
Exploratory policy study on the development of national codes of practice for developers of computer assisted assessment systems
Abstract: The project built on earlier work, specifically another Department of Employment funded project, to establish the potential for using computer assisted assessment in the assessment of National Vocational Qualifications. In the current project, codes of practice for awarding bodies, software developers and centres involved in computer assisted assessment, were drafted and discussed with interested organisations. Consultations were both face-to-face, and by a postal questionnaire, and covered the content of the draft codes and methods of implementation and enforcement. The project outcomes were revised draft codes and a report to the Department of Employment recommending a two-year trial of the codes, to cover the use of computer assisted assessment in both National Vocational Qualifications and other UK qualifications.
Published Material: A full list of publications is available from the researcher.
Status: Sponsored project
Source of Grant: Department of Employment
Date of Research: 1993-1994
KEYWORDS: assessment; computer assisted testing; computer uses in education; National Vocational Qualifications

Harris City Technology College

10/0447
The Dyslexia Centre, 9 Maberley Road, Upper Norwood, London SE19 2JH
0181 771 2261
Canterbury Christ Church College, North Holmes Road, Canterbury CT1 1QU
01227 767700
Tod, J. Ms; *Supervisor:* Jones, L. Mr; Abbott, P. Mr
Dyslexia research project
Abstract: A three year research project has been set up at the Dyslexia

Centre of Harris City Technology College in Upper Norwood, South London. The research body is Harris City Technology College in conjunction with Christchurch College, Canterbury. The aim of the new centre is the development of best practice in the teaching of dyslexic students. The provision of special teacher training in this area of learning difficulty and the undertaking of research and development in the use of technology and materials appropriate to the teaching of dyslexic students. The aims of the project are: (1) to measure the progress over three academic years of a group of pupils entering the Harris CTC in September 1990, diagnosed as having the specific learning difficulty known as dyslexia, using a range of approaches designed to enable these pupils to participate fully and effectively in the City Technology College curriculum which includes access to the National Curriculum; (2) to devise new approaches and resource materials in order to test their value for pupils in the Harris CTC and to enable the Centre to develop resource materials for a wide use with the CTC age group (11-18); (3) to develop the use of information technology and work with dyslexic pupils in the Harris CTC and to disseminate good practice in this respect. The project runs from 1 November 1990 to 31 October 1993.
Status: Sponsored project
Source of Grant: Department for Education £250,000
Date of Research: 1990-1993
KEYWORDS: *city technology colleges; dyslexia; educational materials; learning disabilities; special educational needs; teaching methods*

Health Promotion Wales

10/0448
Research and Development Division, Ffynnon-las, Ty Glas Avenue, Cardiff CF4 5DZ
01222 752222
Smith, C. Mr; Frankland, J. Ms; Playle, R. Ms; Moore, L. Dr
An evaluation of Life Education Centres
Abstract: Life Education Centres (LEC's) were established in Australia in 1979 as a drug education/prevention project for young schoolchildren. The project aim was to develop skills and build self-esteem which would enable children to make responsible decisions concerning themselves and their bodies. The Centres are mobile classrooms staffed by trained educators which visit schools for several days at a time. They contain sophisticated audio-visual aids, including illuminated models of body systems and organs. They also use more traditional educational methods such as games, films and role play. The lessons which last between 30 and 60 minutes are primarily for children aged between 5 and 11 years. Since June 1990 Health Promotion Wales has coordinated a pilot project of LEC's in the Principality. This includes an evaluation of the effects of LEC's visits to primary schools. The study will examine any changes in school curriculum content, changes in pupils' knowledge, attitudes or skills and school policy development. A multi-stage evaluation design has been adopted involving teachers, pupils and parents. In the first stage of this design, a sample of 171 teachers and 509 pupils were asked to complete pre and two post test questionnaires. Primary findings suggest that both teachers and pupils have favourable views on participating in an LEC visit, and that attendance at an LEC was a predictor of greater drug knowledge and understanding of techniques used in advertising cigarettes.
Status: Sponsored project
Source of Grant: Health Promotion Wales
Date of Research: 1993-continuing
KEYWORDS: *health education; health promotion; primary schools*

10/0449
Research and Development Division, Ffynnon-las, Ty-Glas Avenue, Cardiff CF4 5DZ
01222 752222
Smith, C. Mr; Frankland, J. Ms; Playle, R. Ms; Moore, L. Dr
Health promotion in Welsh primary schools, 1993
Abstract: This study provides data on health promotion activity in Welsh primary schools. It covers the organisation and provision of health education teaching, the implementation of health related policies and the involvement of outside agencies and professionals in the planning and delivery of health promotion. The data are drawn from a self-completion questionnaire of 493 randomly selected primary

schools in Wales which was undertaken in the summer of 1993. The results from the 62% (308) of schools who returned questionnaires show a widespread commitment to, and a sound base for, the further expansion of health promotion activity. For example, all the schools reported teaching health education, whilst the vast majority of schools reported covering a wide range of important health topics (particularly physical health, nutrition, growth and development, environment and health, dental health and exercise) within the curriculum, having policies on bullying by pupils and smoking by adults on school premises, and believing that health education has an important role in promoting knowledge, skills and attitudes for healthy living. However, it is recommended that greater attention should be given to the continuing education of primary school teachers in health promotion, the development of policies on smoking, nutrition and sex education and the integration of community resources into school health promotion programmes.
Published Material: SMITH, C., FRANKLAND, J., PLAYLE, R. & MOORE, L. (1994). Health promotion in Welsh primary schools. Health Promotion Wales. Technical Report No 6. Cardiff: Health Promotion Wales.
Status: Sponsored project
Source of Grant: Health Promotion Wales
Date of Research: 1993-1994
KEYWORDS: *health education; health promotion; primary schools*

Heriot-Watt University

10/0450
Department of Business Organisation, Riccarton Campus, Currie, Edinburgh EH14 4AS
0131 449 5111
McKay, K. Ms; Tinklin, T. Ms; *Supervisor:* Keenan, A. Prof.
Career outcomes of engineers and their relationships to education, training and early work experiences
Abstract: The research follows up a sample of two hundred professional engineers into mid career. Extensive data are already held on them from a previous study covering the first five years at work. The investigation is looking at the predictive power of the earlier data in terms of a variety of career outcomes.
Status: Sponsored project
Source of Grant: Science and Engineering Research Council £74,000
Date of Research: 1992-1994
KEYWORDS: *career development; engineering education; engineers; training; work education relationship*

10/0451
Moray House Institute of Education, Holyrood Road, Edinburgh EH8 8AQ
0131 556 8455
Francis, E. Mrs; *Supervisor:* Perfect, H. Mr
Research on values education (ROVE)
Abstract: The project is concerned with the identification of approaches to teaching and learning which are beneficial to the development of values education for students over the age of 16 years. The aim of the project is to highlight the philosophical and methodological issues which should be addressed whenever the development of a values curriculum is contemplated. The focus will be the language currently used by educationalists in curriculum guidelines and educational settings which conveys a sense of values and approaches to teaching and learning which enable values education. The enquiry is being conducted with: teachers; lecturers in teacher education and other academic disciplines; curriculum developers; and educational administrators in central and local government. A network committed to the study of values in education will be created to enhance discussion of values education in Scotland for the 16+ age group. A number of unpublished working papers are available on request from the project team.
Status: Sponsored project
Source of Grant: Gordon Cook Foundation £40,000
Date of Research: 1991-1993
KEYWORDS: *curriculum development; sixteen to nineteen education; values education*

10/0452

Moray House Institute of Education, Holyrood Road,
Edinburgh EH8 8AQ
0131 556 8455
Tymms, P. Mr; Cosford, B. Mr; Dunnett, A. Mrs; Draper, J.
Mrs; Knowles, I. Mr
Institutional ethos
Abstract: The aim of the project is to investigate the 'ethos' of the
Institute with a view to (a) establishing how people who work in it
experience the Institute, with a particular emphasis on how shared or
distinct perceptions of ethos are; and (b) identifying a set of performance indicators upon which a long term strategy to monitor Institutional ethos can be designed. Data was initially collected through
interview from a range of people including students and academic
and support staff. This interview data has been analysed to highlight
key issues and as the basis for the development of questionnaires on
ethos issues which will be circulated to: (a) Institute staff (academic
and support); (b) Institute students; (c) staff and students at two other
institutions (one a university, one a two campus college) for comparative purposes. Associations will be sought between views on the
Institute regarding relationships, academic atmosphere and social
opportunities role within the organisation and other, individual characteristics.
Status: Sponsored project
Source of Grant: Moray House Institute of Education
Date of Research: 1991-continuing
KEYWORDS: *attitude measures; institutes of higher education; institutional environment; organisational climate; student attitudes;
teacher attitudes*

10/0453

Moray House Institute of Education, Holyrood Road,
Edinburgh EH8 8AQ
0131 556 8455
Diniz, F. Mr; Reid, G. Mr
Specific learning difficulties (Dyslexia) project
Abstract: The aims of the research are to investigate the potential for
developments in teacher education to meet the needs of those con-
cerned about the education of children with specific learning diffi-
culties associated with dyslexia.
Status: Sponsored project
Source of Grant: Scottish Dyslexia Trust
Date of Research: 1990-1993
KEYWORDS: *dyslexia; learning disabilities; reading difficulties;
special educational needs; teacher education*

10/0454

Moray House Institute of Education, Holyrood Road,
Edinburgh EH8 8AQ
0131 556 8455
Crowther, N. Mr
Development of curriculum based resources
Abstract: Since 1982 a series of filmstrips for schools have been
published under the collective title 'Habitats in Scotland'. Each is
accompanied by a teacher's booklet. Initially the publications were
made to meet the curriculum resource needs of specialist teachers of
outdoor and environmental education. Increasingly in recent years
the resource needs of primary teachers, identified by the Primary
Education Development Project (PEDP) has been a major outlet for
sales. Work continues on reprinting and updating previous titles in
addition to the completion of the remaining titles in the series. The
focus of continuing research is the production of teaching resources
for the 5-14 Environmental Studies Syllabus.
Published Material: CROWTHER, N. (1984). Seashore and coastal
habitats. Edinburgh: Moray House.; CROWTHER, N. (1985).
Mountains and moorlands. Edinburgh: Moray House.; CROW-
THER, N. (1987). Freshwater habitats. Edinburgh: Moray House.;
CROWTHER, N. (1988). Woodlands in Scotland. 2nd edition. Ed-
inburgh: Moray House.
Status: Sponsored project
Source of Grant: Resources for Environmental and Social Studies
Teaching (RESST); Moray House Institute of Education
Date of Research: 1982-continuing
KEYWORDS: *educational materials; environmental education; out-
door education; publications; resource materials*

10/0455

Moray House Institute of Education, Holyrood Road,
Edinburgh EH8 8AQ
0131 556 8455
Masterton, T. Mr; Simpson, A. Mr
**Environmental Development Unit and Resources for
Environmental and Social Studies Teaching (RESST)**
Abstract: The aims of the Environmental Development Unit are to:
(1) act as a non-course related focus for environmental developments
with the Institute; (2) create and manage an Institute environmental
and social studies publications system; (3) assist with help – products
specific to particular courses.
Published Material: A full list of RESST publications and videos can
be obtained from the researchers on request.
Status: Sponsored project
Source of Grant: Moray House Institute of Education
Date of Research: 1983-continuing
KEYWORDS: *educational materials; environmental education; publications; social studies*

10/0456

Moray House Institute of Education, Holyrood Road,
Edinburgh EH8 8AQ
0131 556 8455
Drame, M. Mr; *Supervisor:* Dickinson, L. Mr;
McMichael, P. Dr
**An investigation of an interactive process model for
implementing an English Language Teaching (ELT) syllabus
in secondary schools in French speaking Africa**
Abstract: In post-independence Africa there is concern about the
mismatch between educational curricula and inappropriate teaching
materials used to implement them. For example, in Senegal a national
syllabus has been designed and yet the incongruity between this
syllabus which teaches English as communication and the inappropriate audiolingual textbook used for its implementation remains an
urgent issue to be addressed. The project aims to address this issue
and proposes to investigate an interactive process model for syllabus
implentation. A draft set of materials appropriate to the Senegalese
threshold level communicative syllabus will be designed. This package of materials will be trialled, revised and retrialled in Senegal with
a view to investigating a proposed model for teacher development on
syllabus implementation. The project will include three stages: (1) a
planning phase (1991-1992) in which a draft set of materials suitable
to the Senegalese syllabus will be developed in addition to the data
collection instruments (observation schedules, questionnaires, interviews) to be used during the implementation phase to take place in
Senegal during the second year; (2) an implementation phase (1992-
1993) in which the draft set of materials will be trialled, revised and
retrialled in Senegal with a view to investigating the effectiveness of
the proposed interactive process model for syllabus implementation;
and (3) an evaluation and reporting phase (1993-1994) in which all
data including questionnaires, interviews, observation schedules,
teachers' diaries and samples of pupils' test scores will be collected
and analysed qualitatively and quantitatively with the objective of
assessing the empirical validity of the proposed procedure. The
research findings will be assessed and the possible applications
considered with regard to the educational context in Senegal in
particular and in French speaking Africa in general.
Status: Sponsored project
Source of Grant: The British Council
Date of Research: 1991-1994
KEYWORDS: *curriculum development; educational materials; English – second language; second language teaching; Senegal*

10/0457

Moray House Institute of Education, Holyrood Road,
Edinburgh EH8 8AQ
0131 556 8455
Hamilton, J. Dr
Language medium teaching
Abstract: The aim of the research is to examine the effects of language
medium teaching on learner motivation and foreign language profi-
ciency within the Scottish context.
Status: Sponsored project
Source of Grant: Moray House Institute of Education
Date of Research: 1990-1993
KEYWORDS: *learning motivation; modern language studies; Scot-
land; second language teaching*

10/0458
> Moray House Institute of Education, Holyrood Road,
> Edinburgh EH8 8AQ
> 031 556 8455
> Tymms, P. Mr

The long term influence of effective and ineffective A level departments
Abstract: The short-term effectiveness of schools can be measured by immediate outputs such as examination results, attitudes and aspirations. But what about the long-term effects of schools? The project will extend an existing database to answer that question.
Status: Sponsored project
Source of Grant: Economic and Social Research Council £10,000
Date of Research: 1992-1994
KEYWORDS: *A level examinations; accountability; examination results; outcomes of education; performance indicators; programme effectiveness; school effectiveness*

10/0459
> Moray House Institute of Education, Holyrood Road,
> Edinburgh EH8 8AQ
> 0131 556 8455
> Macintyre, C. Dr

Student teachers' perceptions of stressful situations in schools
Abstract: Most student teachers expect to have anxious, even stressful times during their weeks on school placement as they build relationships with teachers, children and tutors, learn to teach and have continuous assessment. Some cope very well; they may even find short periods of anxiety or stress stimulating if there is a fairly immediate and successful outcome. But others find that stress builds to an unacceptable level, that of distress, and they fail to cope. This can have devastating and possibly long lasting results. What then are the factors which cause student teachers stress/distress? Are there ways (coping strategies) in which they can be helped to cope? This research intends to address these questions by asking student teachers to reflect on their practice and report their level of anxiety stress/distress, to articulate if they can name the factors that caused them stress and to evaluate the coping strategies they used. Having identified the students' perceptions and their successful coping strategies the research will then find if these can usefully be shared with other students to alleviate their problems. Finally the student teachers in the next cohort at Moray House will be asked whether knowledge of coping strategies helped them to select appropriately and so helped them to reduce the level of stress to at least an acceptable degree.
Status: Sponsored project
Source of Grant: Moray House Institute of Education
Date of Research: 1991-1994
KEYWORDS: *preservice teacher education; stress – psychological; stress variables; student teachers; teaching experience; teaching practice*

10/0460
> Moray House Institute of Education, Holyrood Road,
> Edinburgh EH8 8AQ
> 0131 556 8455
> Glasgow University, Department of Psychology, Glasgow
> G12 8QQ
> 0141 339 8855
> Reid, G. Mr; *Supervisor:* Hinton, J. Dr

Teacher stress and organisational climate
Abstract: The results from four pilot studies already undertaken show a need for examination of teacher stress from the perspectives of personal organisation, school organisation and organisational climate. The study will, therefore, develop some strands identified in the pilot studies including the following: (1) the implications of personal organisation for inservice programmes including aspects such as time management, staff support and staff training; (2) the effect of school organisation on communications, staff support, interpersonal links, role factors, curriculum development and curriculum and organisational changes; (3) the nature of the school organisational climate and its importance in relation to school management – staff morale, motivation, sociability and efficiency. Reading has revealed stress factors such as role overload; time management; administration; fragmentation; interpersonal relations; interpersonal support; openness of staff discussions; leadership skills; school communications network; role conflict and locus of control. The problem it appears with identifying stress contributory factors such as the list above, is that it is acknowledged that teacher stress is a multi-faceted phenomenon and the identification of isolated factors can be misleading and unhelpful for the development and delivery of a school inservice stress management programme. The study examines the theme of organisation, aiming to support the following hypothesis: (a) personal organisation, school organisation and organisational climate are influential factors in stress generation among teachers in schools; (b) stress management inservice programmes need to address these issues for enhanced effectiveness; and (c) the theoretical model of psychological stress (Hinton 1991) is a valid model of examining perceived stress among teachers.
Published Material: REID, G. (1991). 'Supporting the support teacher: stress factors in teaching children with specific learning difficulties', Links, Vol 16, No 3, pp.18-20.
Status: Individual research
Date of Research: 1989-continuing
KEYWORDS: *educational environment; institutional environment; stress – psychological; stress management; stress variables; teacher morale*

10/0461
> Moray House Institute of Education, Scottish Centre for
> Education Overseas, Holyrood Road, Edinburgh EH8 8AQ
> 0131 556 8455
> Ahrens, P. Mrs

An investigation into the difficulties of introducing innovation in English language teaching in developing countries
Abstract: This research grew out of work for a presentation at the British Council Dunford House Conference in 1990 on the topic of sustainability in the design of English language teaching projects. A database of difficulties was compiled in consultation with overseas Master of Arts (MA) students and used at the conference. This will be expanded and put into a hierarchy, in consultation with current overseas students, to form a questionnaire which will be sent to previous students, now seeking to introduce various innovative practices in their home systems. The results will be an ordered list of difficulties actually encountered by practitioners in the field. Later research might seek to identify ways of coping with these difficulties.
Status: Sponsored project
Source of Grant: Moray House Institute of Education £250
Date of Research: 1992-1993
KEYWORDS: *developing countries; English – second language; second language teaching*

10/0462
> Moray House Institute of Education, Scottish Centre for
> Education Overseas, Holyrood Road, Edinburgh EH8 8AQ
> 0131 556 8455
> Ahrens, P. Mrs; Dickinson, N. Ms

Teaching foreign languages at primary level
Abstract: This piece of research looks at English language teaching in Europe and at the teaching of foreign languages in Scotland at the primary level. It relates to the increased interest in and demand for foreign language learning at primary level. Data has been collected and is still in the process of being collected on the problems teachers of a foreign language at primary level face. From existing data a checklist of common difficulties has been designed. This has been trialled and refined. Copies of this checklist have been sent to contacts in various countries. The data from the checklists will be analysed. Visits have been made within Edinburgh to selected primary schools where a foreign language is being taught. A report will be written on the different models of teaching a foreign language at primary level in use and teachers will be asked to fill in a checklist about their specific problems. The analysis of the data should show the main areas that cause problems to teachers at this level. Further research will set out to identify and collect teachers' coping strategies.
Status: Sponsored project
Source of Grant: Moray House Institute of Education £500
Date of Research: 1991-1993
KEYWORDS: *modern language studies; primary education; problems; second language teaching; teaching methods*

Hertfordshire University

10/0463

School of Humanities and Education, Wall Hall Campus,
Aldenham, Watford WD2 8AT
01707 284000
Campbell, R. Prof.

Hearing children read

Abstract: Now in its second phase, this study aims to explore the effectiveness of various teacher responses to the mistakes of early beginning readers. An indepth case study of two children reading to their teacher throughout a school year has been conducted. Interactions were audio-recorded and subsequently transcribed. Results have suggested that a word cueing strategy was particularly helpful to the reader. However, effectiveness needs to be explored at various levels and recent articles have debated this topic. Differences between infant and junior school teachers are being explored.

Published Material: CAMPBELL, R. (1987). 'Oral reading errors of two beginning readers', Journal of Research in Reading, Vol 10, No 2, pp.144-155.; CAMPBELL, R. (1988). 'Is it time for USSR, SSR, SQUIRE, DEAR or ERIC?', Education, Vol 16, No 2, pp.3-13.; CAMPBELL, R. (1988). Hearing children read. London: Routledge.; CAMPBELL, R. (1990). Reading together. Buckingham: Open University Press.; CAMPBELL, R. (1992). 'Shared reading within an apprenticeship approach to reading', Educational Studies, Vol 18, No 2, pp.173-183.

Status: Individual research

Date of Research: 1980-continuing

KEYWORDS: *beginning reading; early reading; oral reading; reading skills; teacher-pupil relationship*

10/0464

School of Humanities and Education, Wall Hall Campus,
Aldenham, Watford WD2 8AT
01707 284000
Jackson, A. Dr

Microcomputer use in the primary school

Abstract: This is an extension of research commenced at postgraduate level. It investigates some of the psychological variables which influence children's performance during microcomputer based problem solution when working alone or in groups. It also considers the current uses of microcomputers in primary education, and factors which affect use. Previous surveys have revealed that microcomputers are primarily used for group rather than individualised instruction in the primary school. This research addresses the question of why, and whether groups of children show superior performance compared to children working alone. Previous research investigated mathematical problem solving amongst 10/11 year old children. This is now being extended to examine problem solving and peer tutoring at the computer with 5/6 year old children.

Published Material: JACKSON, A., FLETCHER, B.(C) & MESSER, D.J. (1986). 'A study of microcomputer use and provision in primary school', Journal of Computer Assisted Learning, Vol 2, No 1, pp.45-55.; MESSER, D.J., JACKSON, A. & MOHAMEDALI, M. (1987). 'Influences on computer based problem solving: help facilities, intrinsic orientation, gender and home computing', Educational Psychology, Vol 7, No 1, pp.33-46.; JACKSON, A., FLETCHER, B.(C) & MESSER, D.J. (1988). 'Effects of experience on microcomputer use in primary schools: results of a second survey', Journal of Computer Assisted Learning, Vol 4, No 4, pp.214-226.; JACKSON, A. (1988). 'Are three heads better than one? An investigation of children solving microcomputer based problems', Paper presented to the XXIV International Congress of Psychology, Sydney, Australia, August.; JACKSON, A., FLETCHER, B.(C) & MESSER, D.J. (1992). 'When talking doesn't help: an investigation of microcomputer based group problem solving', Learning and Instruction, Vol 2, No 3, pp.185-197. A full list of publications is available from the researchers.

Status: Individual research

Date of Research: 1988-continuing

KEYWORDS: *computer uses in education; group work; microcomputers; primary schools; problem solving*

10/0465

School of Humanities and Education, Wall Hall Campus,
Aldenham, Watford WD12 8AT

01707 284000
Thornton, M. Dr

The educational division of labour as it relates to subject specialism and gender in primary schools

Abstract: This study is a follow-up to Ph.D research work on specialisation and the primary curriculum. It aims to explore, map and explain gender differences across areas of subject responsibility and management in primary schools. The study involves data collection in over 100 schools including documentary analysis and interviews.

Published Material: THORNTON, M. (1990). 'Primary specialism', Early Years, Vol 11, No 1, pp.34-38.

Status: Individual research

Date of Research: 1992-continuing

KEYWORDS: *primary school teachers; primary schools; sex differences; teacher role; teaching profession*

10/0466

School of Humanities and Education, Wall Hall Campus,
Aldenham, Watford WD2 8AT
01707 284000
Birmingham University, School of Education, Edgbaston,
Birmingham B15 2TT
0121 414 3344
Powell, S. Dr; Jordan, R. Ms

Investigation of the development of social cognition in autism

Abstract: This research investigates the development of social cognition with special regard to individuals who fall within the autistic continuum. The researchers have conducted experimental studies with individuals with autism on the development of a 'theory of mind'. Action research is being conducted into ways in which individual learning can be facilitated within the curriculum by means of cognitive approaches. Computer programs were used to derive principles that underpin the pedagogy of a 'cognitive curriculum', that encompasses the needs of all children. The programs were evaluated in an experimental study with autistic individuals and the principles are being evaluated, and have been revised, through classroom-based action research in a variety of educational settings.

Published Material: JORDAN, R.R. & POWELL, S.D. (1990). 'Autism and the National Curriculum', British Journal of Special Education', Vol 17, No 4, pp.140-142.; POWELL, S.D. & JORDAN, R.R. (1991). 'A psychological perspective on identifying and meeting the needs of exceptional pupils', School Psychology International, Vol 12, No 4, pp.315-327.; POWELL, S.D. & JORDAN, R.R. (1992). 'Putting principles into practice – remediating the thinking of pupils with autism', Journal of Autism and Developmental Disorder, Vol 22, No 3, pp.413-418.; POWELL, S.D. & JORDAN, R.R. (1993). 'Diagnosis, intuition and autism', British Journal of Special Education', Vol 20, No 1, pp.26-29.; RIDING, R.J. & POWELL, S.D. (1993). 'Thinking and education', Educational Psychology, Vol 13, Nos 3-4, pp.217-227.

Status: Sponsored project

Source of Grant: Inge Wakehurst Trust £500

Date of Research: 1987-continuing

KEYWORDS: *autism; cognitive ability; curriculum research; social cognition*

Homerton College

10/0467

Cambridge CB2 2PH
(see also under Cambridge University, Homerton College)
01223 411141
Open University, Mathematics Faculty, Centre for
Mathematics Education, Walton Hall, Milton Keynes
MK7 6AA
01908 274066
Rowland, T. Mr; *Supervisor:* Pimm, D. Mr

Language and conceptual development in mathematics

Abstract: This work arises from earlier work by the researcher in 1986/1988 in connection with Calculator-Aware Number Curriculum (CAN), a dimension of the Schools Computer Development Centre/National Curriculum Council (SCDC/NCC) PrIME project, based at Homerton College 1986/1990. Young children were observed to develop individual, idiosyncratic, approaches to solving elementary number problems. Drawing on individual schemes for

number concepts and operations, developed in an environment which allowed them free access to a four-function calculator. The current research sets out to describe and illuminate such schemes. Early attempts to access them through soliciting information about associated mental imagery proved to be disappointing, however discourse analysis of transcript material revealed the potential of language as an alternative 'window' on children's mathematical thinking. For example, analysis of children's use of pronouns in 'maths talk' is proving to be a fruitful, indeed a novel, means of accessing aspects of mathematical thought. Substantial case studies with three children are being pursued, their purpose being to exemplify and to examine linguistic consistency indepth, and also to generate and refine conjectures about the way children (age 9-12) might reveal their thinking about, and their awareness of, mathematical propositions of a general nature. The second phase (1992-1993) of the research will validate and develop such conjectures by gathering and analysing speech-data derived from some 20-30 children, who work in pairs on a task (the same for each pair) which requires the production of mathematical generalisations for the solution of a specific problem. The intended outcome (to be published as a thesis) is enhanced understanding of linguistic (and possibly other) pointers to children's conceptual thinking. This might contribute to a raising of awareness in researchers and classroom teachers of the potential of specific linguistic clues to the presence of concepts and generalisations in children's thking.
Published Material: ROWLAND, T. (1992). 'Pointing with pronouns', For the Learning of Mathematics, Vol 12, No 2, pp.44-48.
Status: Individual research
Date of Research: 1990-1994
KEYWORDS: *classroom communication; concept teaching; mathematical concepts; mathematics education*

Hull University

10/0468

Computer Centre, Hull HU6 7RX
01482 46311
Reese, R. Mr; *Supervisor:* Moore, J. Dr
Thesis production in UK universities – the role of information technology
Abstract: The project aims to: 1) survey the changes in research practice brought about by making word processing and other desktop computer facilities readily available to students; 2) see if the changes have allowed improvements in the quality and presentation of research and have speeded up the production of theses and/or reduced the costs; 3) review current and earlier standards laid down for theses and suggest improvements for printed work, in typography and structure, language use and graphics; 4) consider the acceptability to students of the patterns of work with and without information technology; and 5) consider the implications of Electronic Document Delivery and suggest how and when this might impact upon the conduct and reporting of research.
Status: Individual research
Date of Research: 1993-continuing
KEYWORDS: *computer uses in education; information technology; research reports; theses*

10/0469

Department of Education, Hull HU6 7RX
01482 46311
McNamara, D. Prof.
Focused mentoring for the National Curriculum
Abstract: The study aims to explore the contributions which teacher trainers (tutors) and teachers responsible for the student teachers during periods of school practice (mentors) make to students' practical preparations for teaching. The study addresses teaching the National Curriculum with an emphasis upon the primary sector. A case study and critical incident design has been adopted supplemented by classroom observation and focused interviews. A final report is available from the researcher.
Status: Sponsored project
Source of Grant: Paul Hamlyn Foundation £8,000
Date of Research: 1992-1994
KEYWORDS: *mathematics education; mentors; National Curriculum; preservice teacher education; student teacher supervisors; teaching practice*

10/0470

Department of Education, Hull HU6 7RX
01482 46311
McClelland, V. Prof.
History of the Roman Catholic involvement in education in England and Wales since 1935. (Within a general history of the Roman Catholic church in England and Wales since 1935)
Abstract: The project re-evaluates the origins of the dual system in education since 1944 and locates educational policy in the Roman Catholic church in England and Wales within the general ecclesiastical development of the period since 1935. The work will estimate the effect of the Second Vatican Council upon educational development and will examine the social upheaval within the Catholic community since 1965. It will also provide indications of the future of the current partnership between church and state in educational provision.
Published Material: McCLELLAND, V. (1988). 'Sensus Fidelium': the developing concept of Roman Catholic effort in education in England and Wales'. In: TULASIEWICZ, W. & BROCK, C. (Ed). Christianity and educational provision. London: Routledge.; McCLELLAND, V. (1991). 'The effect of the Council on Catholicism: Great Britain and Ireland'. In: HASTINGS, A. (Ed). Modern Catholicism: Vatican II and after. London: SPCK.; McCLELLAND, V. (1991). 'Gravissimum Educationis'. In: HASTINGS, A. (Ed). Modern Catholicism: Vatican II and after. London: SPCK.
Status: Sponsored project
Source of Grant: The National Catholic Fund
Date of Research: 1989-continuing
KEYWORDS: *Catholic schools; church and education; church-state relationship; educational history; educational policy; Roman Catholic church*

10/0471

Department of Education, Hull HU6 7RX
01482 46311
Richmond, M. Mr; *Supervisor:* Whitehead, M. Dr
The transition to democracy and educational change in contemporary Chile and post-Franco Spain
Abstract: Located within two main sub-fields of educational inquiry (comparative education and the politics of education), the study aims to ascertain and understand the effects of transitions to democracy upon education and also the role of education within such transitions. Given its vital involvement in social and cultural reproduction, education may reveal itself to be a particularly sensitive field for registering the changes associated with a shift away from authoritarianism towards more democratic forms of polity. This sensitivity (its extent and character) will constitute the primary focus of the study. An examination of Chile and Spain affords an opportunity to explore whether or not there are structural similarities or parallels within the process of democratic transition and associated educational change in different countries. Study of the two national experiences is further justified by the possibility that Spain's transition may have furnished lessons for later transitions in Latin America in particular, such as that in Chile. Fieldwork in both countries will focus upon the main primary and secondary written sources of information and upon interviews with government officials and significant personnel within non-governmental organisations.
Status: Individual research
Date of Research: 1990-continuing
KEYWORDS: *change; comparative education; democracy; development education; politics education relationship*

10/0472

Department of Education, Hull HU6 7RX
01482 46311
Mitchell, S. Ms; *Supervisor:* Andrews, R. Dr
The teaching and learning of argument in sixth forms and higher education
Abstract: The project arose from recent research interest in the ability of students to conduct argument. It has taken a case study approach to work in a number of disciplines in both the humanities and sciences at sixth form and undergraduate level. Comparison between disciplines reveals both similarities and differences in the conduct and forms of argument within particular contexts. Successful argument is understood to be heavily context dependent, and to be a form of social, as well as cognitive activity. Both spoken and written forms of argument are examined, as well as the relationship between them. As a result of the research a number of suggestions for improvement

of practice have emerged. The research has also involved collaboration with teachers who are introducing new schemes and approaches relating to argumentative skill.

Published Material: MITCHELL, S. (1992). The teaching and learning of argument in 6th forms and higher education: interim report. Hull: University of Hull.; MITCHELL, S. (1992). Questions and schooling: classroom discourse across the curriculum. Occasional Paper 1. Hull: University of Hull, Centre for Studies in Rhetoric.; MITCHELL, S. (1993). 'The aesthetic and the academic: are they at odds in English literature at A level?', English in Education, Vol 27, No 1, pp.19-28.; MITCHELL, S. (1993). 'Learning to be critical and correct: forms and functions of argument at A level', Curriculum, Vol 14, No 1, pp.48-56.; MITCHELL, S. & ANDREWS, R. 'Learning to operate successfully in Advanced Level History'. In: FREEDMAN, A. & MEDWAY, P. (Ed). Learning and Teaching Genre. Oxford: Heinemann. (in press).

Status: Sponsored project
Source of Grant: Leverhulme Trust £89,000
Date of Research: 1991-1994
KEYWORDS: *argument; criticism; higher education; sixth form education; writing processes; writing skills*

10/0473

Department of Education, Hull HU6 7RX
01482 46311
Bennett, J. Mr; *Supervisor:* Webster, D. Rev.
Personal, social, moral and religious education in primary schools. The impact and implications of the Education Reform Act 1988 and the National Curriculum
Abstract: The introduction of the National Curriculum and the implications of the Education Reform Act 1988 have serious consequences for the formal subject curriculum in primary schools, and for the informal curriculum defined to some degree as moral, personal and social education. Alongside this, the status of religious education in the basic curriculum, but not the National Curriculum, and the legal standing of the subject in the light of the Education Reform Act poses problems and possibilities for the subject within the curriculum as a whole. An analysis of these four interconnected areas of the curriculum will provide insights into their place and purpose in the primary school curriculum and a backdrop for an exploration of the impact of recent changes in education. The following will be considered: (a) the natures of the four subject areas, aims, objectives and philosophical implications in primary schools; (b) the implications and effects of the Education Reform Act 1988; (c) the implications and effects of the National Curriculum; and (d) the interconnective nature of the four subject areas.
Status: Individual research
Date of Research: 1989-1994
KEYWORDS: *Education Reform Act 1988; individual development; moral education; National Curriculum; primary schools; religious education; social development*

10/0474

Department of Education, Hull HU6 7RX
01482 46311
Okpanachi, J. Mr; *Supervisor:* Mawer, M. Mr; Hornby, G. Mr
An investigation into the effects of inservice training (the knowledge, attitudes and understanding) of primary school teachers in the Kaduna state of Nigeria towards the integration of children with special educational needs in physical education
Abstract: The 20th century has witnessed many educational innovations aimed at improving the quality of life for all children. The significant improvement among these is the education of children with special educational needs who for so long have been neglected and even forgotten. With several legislative acts and through the support of various philanthropic organisations, children with special needs are moving towards taking their proper place in society. To begin with, special schools were built to cater for the welfare of these children but with time it has been realised that special schools can only serve those with severe learning difficulties while others could be integrated into ordinary schools. Children with special educational needs have greater problems in physical education than other school subjects because of difficulties in movement. The main concern of this research is to find out how best these children can be helped to participate in physical education lessons in spite of their movement difficulties and how others with different problems can also be helped. Participation and sense of belonging are not the only goals for these children; their acceptance by others is equally important.

Through integrated programmes all children should be able to work, play and learn together successfully. To be able to achieve this successfully, teachers working with children with special needs should be provided with further education in the form of inservice training in order to improve their skills and knowledge towards an integration programme. Inservice training is essential because the initial training had failed to make provision for teachers' needs in order to gain their support for the integration programme. Some of the findings made in this study tend to suggest that teachers lack adequate knowledge in the practice of integration programme in most Nigerian schools and this seems to account for the absence of such mainstream education. It has, therefore, been suggested that the practice of an integrational physical education programme should be made a matter of policy in Nigeria and should be part of mainstream education so that children with special educational needs can receive adequate attention in the school physical education curriculum. In addition, the Government should provide teachers with appropriate knowledge and skill required in the solution of the learning problems of children with special needs in Nigeria.
Status: Individual research
Date of Research: 1990-1994
KEYWORDS: *disabilities; mainstreaming; moderate learning difficulties; Nigeria; physical education; special educational needs*

10/0475

Department of Education, Hull HU6 7RX
01482 46311
Smith, J. Mr; *Supervisor:* McClelland, V. Prof.
The educational influence of the Wesleyan Methodist church in the second half of the 19th century (1850 – 1902) with particular reference to the work of Dr James Harrison Rigg
Abstract: A survey of the influence of the Methodist church on education in the second half of the 19th century, with particular reference to the work of Dr J.H. Rigg. The influence of Methodist thought and pressure groups on the framing of legislation relating to education between 1870 and 1902.
Status: Individual research
Date of Research: 1991-continuing
KEYWORDS: *church and education; church-state relationship; educational history; educational legislation; nonconformity; religion and education*

10/0476

Department of Education, Hull HU6 7RX
01482 46311
Sharma, C. Mr; *Supervisor:* Andrews, R. Dr
Multimedia approach to teaching literature
Abstract: This research is an attempt to find what makes an expression a work of art, especially a literary expression and how these can be read by readers from different cultural backgrounds. All the signs and symbols that an author uses have an individual as well as social significance. A combination of media (media-mix) on the one hand and hypermedia on the other may help us gain a better understanding of the signs used in the texts. Technology in education would be helpful because of its varied presentational mode, immense retention capacity and easy accessibility. The purpose of stylistic analysis is to analyse and make simple the elements in a text which 'limit freedom of perception in the process of decoding'. To suggest new approaches through the help of media first hand information from teachers teaching English literature as non-native; foreign literature has been collected. From the field study (i.e. informants) the research is able to delimit the usefulness of different media in teaching of an interpretation based discipline (as against information based discipline) like literature. Individual responses have helped collect ideas for analysing symbols necessary to decode non-native literary texts. These symbols might not be linearly connected but join together to make the text. A hypermedia programme encompassing all the 'modes' with different approaches to the text is being developed.
Published Material: SHARMA, C.B. (1993). 'Teaching foreign literature through multimedia', The Electronic Library, Vol 11, No 1.
Status: Individual research
Date of Research: 1991-1994
KEYWORDS: *hypermedia; literary criticism; literature studies; multimedia approach*

10/0477

Department of Education, Hull HU6 7RX
01482 46311
Warner, M. Mr; *Supervisor:* Webster, D. Rev.

Developmental concepts of Christianity in a person with a mental handicap

Abstract: The majority of the research in this particular field, and to a large extent in the field of Christianity and education, has been done from a western, secular, academic approach. It is the intention of the study to 'plug this gap' by having the emphasis on Christianity and the development of thinking in terms of Faith, Jesus, God, Heaven, Hell, Holy Spirit, Salvation, death, angels, demons etc, in a person with a mental handicap. Gilliferd, an authoritative work in this field, highlights the concern. He quotes in this work a study by D. Answorth (1961) 'it is likely that until 9 or 10 years of age, any story (biblical and in particular parables) will probably be interpreted literally, and that the details of the text and incidents of the story will be of paramount importance to the child'. The research hypothesises that this highlights a child's Faith; Matthew's Gospel chapter 18, v. 3 states 'Assuredly, I say to you, unless you are converted and become as little children, you will by no means enter the Kingdom of Heaven' NKJ. This implies a simplicity of Faith uncomplicated by adult intellect and doubt. The research starts from the premise that if a child can accept love, then they can accept the love of God. No child/adult, irrespective of the degree of intellectual handicap, is unable to receive love. Secondly, if we accept that we are body, soul and spirit in 'design', then a person with a mental handicap is injured in body and soul. However, God communicates through the spirit, hence the experience they have of God is as real as my own. The problem is that they may be unable to express this experience in the physical. The intention of this research is to establish what is understood by such a person, to identify the development of thinking in this area, and propose ways in which we might teach and encourage their Beliefs and Faith.
Status: Individual research
Date of Research: 1991-continuing
KEYWORDS: beliefs; Christianity; mental retardation; religious education; special educational needs

10/0478

Department of Education, Hull HU6 7RX
01482 46311
Biggs, M. Mr; *Supervisor:* Spence, B. Dr

Education in the United Arab Emirates: an examination of selected themes and issues with reference to the 'small country' context

Abstract: The United Arab Emirates (UAE) is a group of seven small sheikdoms, previously known as the Trucial States whilst under British tutelage. Since their independence in 1971, and aided by the oil wealth of certain emirates, the UAE has undergone a period of unprecedented growth and modernisation. It has progressed from relative obscurity and poverty into a modern well serviced country of international recognition with one of the highest per capita incomes in the world. Education has always been assigned an important role in this process of modernisation. This research outlines educational provision in the UAE in both an historical and contemporary context. It further discusses important factors that influence the style of educational provision at all levels in both the state and private sectors such as Islam; demography, gender; manpower, multi-culturalism; and 'small country' issues.
Status: Individual research
Date of Research: 1989-continuing
KEYWORDS: Arab states; developing countries; development education; educational policy

10/0479

Department of Education, Hull HU6 7RX
01482 46311
Pereiro, J. Rev.; *Supervisor:* McClelland, V. Prof.

The teaching office of the church

Abstract: H.E. Manning's years as Archbishop of Westminster coincided with a renewed interest in the 'Education Question'. The civilizing value of education, the social and economic benefits which would follow from its wider extension, were themes dear to Victorian England. The interest in education and the rapid nationwide development of the educational structures soon led to an all important debate about the respective roles of the individual, the Church and the State in this area. H.E. Manning played a prominent part in the 'Education Question'. On the one hand, he made a considerable contribution to the setting up of the Catholic Educational System. He also intervened quite decisively in the above-mentioned debate through his connections with men in power and his involvement in the official commissions set up to examine present policy and to offer solutions to the educational problems of the times. The research concentrates on the philosophical principles from which he draws his suggestions to solve the problems and tensions of the age, as well as for the setting up of the educational system on a proper basis to assure its greater effectiveness.
Status: Individual research
Date of Research: 1990-1993
KEYWORDS: church education relationship; educational history; educational philosophy

10/0480

Department of Education, Hull HU6 7RX
01482 46311
Waugh, D. Mr; *Supervisor:* Gorwood, B. Dr

A study of the management and implementation of educational change in primary schools

Abstract: The research involves a study of primary schools of different sizes, but is concerned principally with those with 100 pupils or fewer. Case studies will be made and a questionnaire has been used to enable comparisons to be drawn between schools of varying sizes and the effects of educational reform upon them. The following will be considered: management of curriculum change; collaboration with other schools; resources and facilities; scope for delegation of responsibility by headteachers; the role of the headteacher; professional development of teaching staff; secretarial and other ancillary assistance; and classroom and school organisation.
Status: Individual research
Date of Research: 1990-1994
KEYWORDS: educational change; primary schools

10/0481

Department of Education, Hull HU6 7RX
01482 46311
Lanade, J. Mr; *Supervisor:* Spence, B. Dr

An investigation into parent teacher association activities and their effectiveness in secondary schools in Kwara State, Nigeria

Abstract: The argument that parents and teachers must work together for the overall educational development of children was far from unanimous all over the world but particularly in Kwara State, Nigeria. Teachers wanted parents in the State mainly because the financial aids to schools were far from adequate. Parents for their part only wanted to participate in schools as long as it did not involve them financially. The worsening economic condition of the entire country and particularly Kwara State made both the administrators of schools and teachers to think of strategies to use to involve parents to want to contribute generously towards the up-keep of children in schools, particularly in secondary schools where nearly all scientific equipment is imported.
Status: Individual research
Date of Research: 1989-1994
KEYWORDS: Nigeria; parent-school relationship; parent-teacher associations; secondary schools

10/0482

Department of Education, Hull HU6 7RX
01482 46311
Uzoigwe, F. Mrs; *Supervisor:* Brookes, K. Mr

Education and social change with special reference to Nigeria – women (particularly the Igbo)

Abstract: Nigeria embraced western style education in the early 1940s. Unlike many developing countries, Nigeria is a very big country with a population of well over a million people. There are over 200 languages in Nigeria and the main ethnic groups are: the Hausa/Fulani in the north, the Yoruba in the west and the Igbo in the east. Since the advent of western education no serious study has been undertaken with a view to determining whether or not Nigerian women and girls have had the same educational opportunities as men and boys, and also whether western style education has enhanced or jeopardised the status of women in Nigeria. In this study, therefore, a vigorous attempt is being made to assess the educational status of women – firstly in global terms, in order to understand and appreciate more realistically the Nigerian situation; bearing in mind the findings

of the United Nations, which show that women constitute the greater percentage of the world's illiterates and that the rate is much higher among the women in the developing countries. In the case of Nigeria for instance, in 1984 the Federal Ministry of Education indicated that the adult illiteracy rate stood at 65%. It should, however, be borne in mind that in Nigeria a number of factors including heavy domestic chores and child marriages have, over the years, militated against the formal education of women and girls. Generally, the women in the northern part of Nigeria have lagged behind their counterparts in other parts of the country educationally, because the north is predominantly Moslem and certain demands are made on the women. For example, some women have to go into complete seclusion (purdah) and some girls are withdrawn from educational institutions at puberty. Significantly, it has been highlighted that in the north girls' education is being hindered by child marriage and parents' fear of pregnancy, should their daughters remain in schools beyond puberty. The Fulani, owing to their nomadic way of life, have negative attitudes towards formal education. However, it is noteworthy that any measures designed to reduce female illiteracy rates in Nigeria (there are more illiterate women than men) must take into account informal methods of education, including adult education, especially with regard to rural women. It is important to note that the writer, at this stage, can justifiably report that there is hardly any country in the world, where women have not suffered any form of educational disadvantage. In the developing world, the problems are more challenging. With regard to Nigeria, profound changes are taking place. The most far reaching of these changes is the 'Better Life Programme for the Rural Woman', spearheaded by the First Lady, Mrs. Babangida. It is interesting to note that under this programme, even the nomadic Fulani are starting to embrace formal education which has eluded them over the years, because of their lifestyle.
Status: Individual research
Date of Research: 1989-continuing
KEYWORDS: Nigeria; women's education

10/0483
Department of Education, Hull HU6 7RX
01482 46311
Gonzalez, B. Mr; *Supervisor:* Gorwood, B. Dr
The teaching and learning of geography in schools in Gibraltar
Abstract: Examination results over the last 10 years have given much concern in Gibraltar with regard to geography. There have been several visible trends which suggest a decrease in importance and status of the subject in the school curriculum. The research aims to identify the factors which have been responsible for this downward trend. In British schools geography is one of the more popular subjects and the results obtained compare quite favourably with the results obtained in other diciplines. Why is there such a marked contrast with the results obtained in Gibraltar? The research will concentrate on the learning of the subject and the importance of environmental stimulus or lack of it, and an indepth analysis of the existing geographical curriculum taught in schools at all levels.
Status: Individual research
Date of Research: 1989-1993
KEYWORDS: geography education; Gibraltar

10/0484
Department of Education, Hull HU6 7RX
01482 46311
Douglas, F. Mr; *Supervisor:* McClelland, V. Prof.
A study of pre-school education in the Republic of Ireland with particular reference to those pre-schools which are listed by the Irish Pre-School Playgroups Association in Cork City and County
Abstract: This study was undertaken in order to investigate the activities which took place in Irish pre-schools other than those within the formal school system. The principle focus of the research concerned the degree to which pre-school children were being 'cognitively stretched' by the curriculum in which they were engaged. The social, linguistic, physical and creative development of these children was also considered. Twenty-three pre-schools were taken at random from the membership list in Cork City and County of the Irish Pre-School Playgroups Association. One pre-school which was not a member was added. This study, which took place between 1986 and 1990 was eclectic in nature, employing a multi-faceted approach encompassing a target child observational schedule, interviews, a study of classrooms, a questionnaire, and an interaction and analysis system. Among other things, the results showed that the 157 children

engaged in this study were being 'cognitively stretched' for approximately one-quarter of the time if they were in a playgroup and approximately one half of the time if they were in a Montessori setting.
Status: Individual research
Date of Research: 1989-1993
KEYWORDS: early childhood education; Ireland; Montessori method; play groups; preschool education

---

10/0485
Department of Education, Hull HU6 7RX
01482 46311
Mitchell, S. Ms; *Supervisor:* Andrews, R. Dr
The place of aesthetic response in the academic study of literature
Abstract: The aim of the research is to elucidate the place of aesthetic response in the academic study of literature. This involves an understanding and characterisation of what is meant by aesthetic response and of the academic discipline. The suitability and compatibility of these two approaches to literature is then possible. The particular conditions for the communication of academic and aesthetic responses are considered, with particular attention to language and institutional framing. The research involves an extensive review of the literature on aesthetic response and the use of current thinking on disciplinary discourses and genres. It will use empirical data collected from literature students and teachers at advanced levels, including interviews and spoken and written work.
Published Material: MITCHELL, S. (1993). 'The aesthetic and the academic – are they at odds in English literature at A level?', English in Education, Vol 27, No 1, pp.19-28.
Status: Individual research
Date of Research: 1992-continuing
KEYWORDS: aesthetic values; literary criticism; literature studies

---

10/0486
Department of Education, Hull HU6 7RX
01482 46311
Waugh, D. Mr; *Supervisor:* Gorwood, B. Dr
Implementing educational changes in primary schools with particular reference to small schools
Abstract: The research takes the form of questionnaire and survey work on the methods used, and problems encountered, when primary schools attempt to meet the requirements of the Education Reform Act 1988. A survey of around 200 schools has been undertaken and a number of case studies made. The aim of the research is to determine whether school size affects the ability to implement change. It is hoped that recommendations can be made, which will draw upon examples of 'good practice', to enable schools to fulfil legal requirements in an educationally acceptable way.
Status: Individual research
Date of Research: 1990-1993
KEYWORDS: Education Reform Act 1988; educational change; educational legislation; educational planning; primary schools; school size; small schools

---

10/0487
Department of Education, Hull HU6 7RX
01482 46311
Alaydarous, A. Mr; *Supervisor:* McClelland, V. Prof.
Adolescents in Makkah: a study of creative thinking in relation to certain variables
Abstract: Creativity is an important intellectual activity which develops through adolescence. Although the Saudi educational curriculum places great importance on creative development, there have been no studies focusing on this area. This study will attempt to fill this gap, and will use verbal and figural creative tests, verbal and figural intelligence tests, a logical thinking test, an ideal student check-list and family background sheet. The study will investigate: 1) the creative abilities in adolescents aged from 13-18 in Makkah, Saudi Arabia; 2) the relationship between their creative thinking and cognitive development, intelligence, age, gender, grade level and family background; and 3) teachers' views of creativity.
Status: Sponsored project
Source of Grant: Saudi Arabian Government
Date of Research: 1989-1994
KEYWORDS: cognitive ability; creative thinking; Saudi Arabia

10/0488

Department of Education, Hull HU6 7RX
01482 46311
Chandler, W. Mr; *Supervisor:* Wright, N. Mr
The impact of the National Curriculum on history studies in small schools in the East Riding division of Humberside Local Education Authority, with specific reference to oral history
Abstract: This research began with the general implementation of the National Curriculum in small schools, with issue definition and rating by all the schools. A database of this information has been constructed. The research included a series of six sample structured interviews of headteachers. Oral history projects have been developed in three schools and the results published. Further questionnaires and interviews specific to history studies will now be carried out.
Status: Individual research
Date of Research: 1992-continuing
KEYWORDS: history studies; National Curriculum; oral history; small schools

10/0489

Department of Education, Hull HU6 7RX
01482 46311
Clifford, J. Ms; *Supervisor:* McClelland, V. Prof.
The religious education of young adults attending university
Abstract: This research will look at: 1) the relationship between the secular university and religion; 2) the place and relationship of the Church in an academic community; 3) the role of institutionally appointed professional religious leadership in a modern university; 4) the organisational aspects of a campus ministry; 5) the aims of religious education for the university student; 6) a survey of religious experiences, attitudes and expectations of university students; and 7) a programme of religious ministry to university students.
Status: Individual research
Date of Research: 1993-continuing
KEYWORDS: higher education; religion and education; religious education; universities

10/0490

Department of Education, Hull HU6 7RX
01482 46311
Fields, J. Miss; Sharma, C. Mr
The teaching and learning of English/English Literature as a second language through the media of hypercard/information technology
Abstract: It was apparent that, although Indian students spoke English fluently, there was, however, perceived lack of understanding of the written idiom of English Literature within the context of various novels. It was decided to write a self-edifying information technology programme using hypercard. The main thrust being that the student can delve further into the meanings of words in context using a database of relevant information to explain idiom and common usage.
Status: Individual research
Date of Research: 1993-continuing
KEYWORDS: computer uses in education; English – second language; second language learning

10/0491

Department of Education, Hull HU6 7RX
01482 46311
Exeter University, School of Education, St Luke's, Heavitree Road, Exeter EX1 2LU
01392 263263
Williams, V. Ms; *Supervisor:* Webster, D. Dr; Priestley, J. Dr
The silent eye: a study of the relationship between the spiritual, art and religious education
Abstract: The nature of religious education in recent times has been dominated by words, conceptual analysis and rational argument. Somehow the non-rational has lost its credibility and perceived importance. In contrast, the nature of the spiritual is non-rational, concerned with an alternative view of reality and therefore difficult to define. Although rational thinking is important for understanding that which can be 'potential dynamite', good or evil, there is a need to 'glimpse' the spiritual through non-rational means. Art is able to provide that non-rational medium and can offer access to the alternative reality of the world of the spiritual. However, it is not just the existence of certain types of artistic image with certain features which can be analysed which provides this window onto the spiritual world, but the response of the onlooker who is evoked to gaze, and to reflect. The experience of the spiritual when described verbally often includes visual terms. The visions, dreams and revelations of the mystics and contemplatives are examples and others include the miracles, transformations, occasions of enlightenment and transportations which are frequently recorded in the lives of holy people. The arts offer a creative human attempt to experience the spiritual. The nature of art has been defined in many ways. This Ph.D thesis will present an argument which emphasises art as an 'ideal' form which allows the spiritual to be glimpsed. The argument will be supported by reference to a range of philosophical and aesthetic writing: Plato, Abbot Suger, Hildegard, Ruskin, Wordsworth, Coomaraswamy, etc. There are two ways of considering 'the visual': 1) from the point of view of what is seen – the image itself (shapes, colour, mood, configuration, distance, blurr, content, story, association etc); and 2) what might be described as the inward eye, that which sees beyond, what is physically present. It will be argued that by looking reflectively or 'gazing', the observer is able to glimpse beyond what is physically present. Such issues as the psychology of gazing will be considered as well as the contribution offered by scientists and poets. The nature of the spiritual may be opaque but opaqueness in itself has visual quality if only metaphorical in form. It will be argued that certain works of art by their form, content, context or intention provide 'windows onto the spiritual world'. This will be supported by reference to a range of examples. The thesis will examine the educational relevance of the theoretical framework and offer a teaching model, essential conditions and criteria for the selection of images which encourage and develop the process of gazing and spiritual appreciation in the classroom.
Published Material: A full list of publications is available from the researcher.
Status: Individual research
Date of Research: 1989-1994
KEYWORDS: art; religious education

Institute for the Study of Drug Dependence

10/0492

1 Hatton Place, London EC1N 8ND
0171 242 1878
South, N. Dr; Murji, K. Mr; Henderson, S. Dr; Oliver, L. Ms; James, B. Ms; Lee, M. Dr; *Supervisor:* Dorn, N. Dr
Prevention aspects of work of ISDD's Research and Development Unit
Abstract: Studies include a review of the international English language literature on drug prevention (literature review); qualitative research on the needs of carers of women with Human Immunodeficiency Virus or Acquired Immune Deficiency Syndrome (HIV/AIDS) (group discussion, indepth interviews); action research to explore issues involved in policing the giving to offenders information about welfare facilities or referral opportunities (action research in several police forces); and analysis of development of drug policies within the context of the European communities.
Published Material: DORN, M. & MURJI, K. (1992). Drug prevention: a review of the English language literature. ISDD Research Monograph Series, Vol 5. London: ISDD Publications Unit.; DORN, N., HENDERSON, S. & SOUTH, N. (Eds). (1992). AIDS: Women, drugs and social care. London: Falmer Press.; DORN, N. (1993). 'Health policies, drug control and the EC'. In: NORMAND, C. & VAUGHAN, P. (Eds). Europe without frontiers: implications for health. Chichester: John Wiley.; DORN, N. 'Three faces of police referral', Policing and Society. (in press).
Status: Sponsored project
Source of Grant: Home Office; Department of Health; Charitable Trusts
Date of Research: 1986-continuing
KEYWORDS: acquired immune deficiency syndrome; drug abuse; drug education; health education; welfare services

Institute of Child Health

10/0493
The Wolfson Centre, Mecklenburgh Square, London
WC1N 2AP
0171 837 7618
Pennington, L. Ms; *Supervisor:* McConachie, H. Dr; Jolleff,
N. Ms; Wisbeach, A. Ms
Putting training into practice: evaluating 'My Turn to Speak'
Abstract: The current project has two parts to it. Firstly, the development team for 'My Turn to Speak' will run study days to familiarise speech therapists, teachers and others who might wish to use the published training package. The study days will include some of the activities of the workshop, and discussion on how best to implement the approach in various schools and with children who have various levels of severity of physical disorder. The second part of the current project involves evaluating the workshops that have been run by the development team, and comparing their process and outcome with workshops run by new tutors, often past participants. One aim of the package is to facilitate the setting up of a rolling programme of training throughout a school. In addition a multiple baseline, single case study is being undertaken to look at the implementation of the team approach to communication with one child.
Published Material: PENNINGTON, L., JOLLEFF, N., McCON-ACHIE, H., WISBEACH, A. & PRICE, K. (1993). My Turn to Speak: A Team Approach to Augmentative Communication. London: Institute of Child Health, distributed by Winslow Press.
Status: Sponsored project
Source of Grant: The Viscount Nuffield Auxiliary Fund £11,683
Date of Research: 1993-1993
KEYWORDS: communication aids – for disabled; communication disorders; programme evaluation; special educational needs; workshops

10/0494
The Wolfson Centre, Mecklenburgh Square, London
WC1N 2AP
0171 837 7618
Pennington, L. Ms; *Supervisor:* McConachie, H. Dr
The communication skills of severely physically disabled children
Abstract: The study involves designing an assessment tool which will enable speech and language therapists to describe the communication skills of non-verbal children who have severe physical disabilities, and to evaluate the effectiveness of intervention. This assessment of functional communication skills will be suitable for use with children who have a broad range of communication skills and who may be using any type of augmentative and alternative communication (AAC) system e.g. symbol charts; speech synthesisers. The assessment will: 1) give a baseline of the child's communication strengths and weaknesses; 2) profile the patterns of communication used by the child's usual communication partners, e.g. parents and teachers; 3) evaluate change after intervention, such as a therapy programme or the introduction of an augmentative communication system; 4) provide a basis for planning individual intervention programmes. As part of the validity testing of the assessment procedures, verbal children with and without physical disabilities will be included, to examine how developmentally appropriate is the attempt to elicit a broad range of communication skills. Comparison of these groups with non-verbal physically disabled children will allow the separation of the effects of physical disability (and physical dependency) and severe speech difficulties on communication development. The comparison will thus permit preliminary investigation of the question of whether non-verbal physically disabled children are pragmatically less able than one would expect given their developmental level and degree of physical disability.
Status: Individual research
Date of Research: 1993-continuing
KEYWORDS: communication skills; nonverbal communication; physical disabilities; severe disabilities; special educational needs; speech handicaps

Keele University

10/0495
Department of Education, Keele ST5 5BG
01782 621111
Wakelin, M. Mrs; *Supervisor:* Wringe, C. Dr
The use of performance indicators in the evaluation of educational institutions
Abstract: Current use of performance indicators is to be surveyed and evaluated in relation to currently proposed educational aims. Their validity as a measure of educational effectiveness and their affect on the performance of teachers and institutions will be assessed.
Status: Individual research
Date of Research: 1989-1994
KEYWORDS: educational objectives; institutional evaluation; organisational effectiveness; performance indicators

10/0496
Department of Education, Keele ST5 5BG
01782 621111
Sang, J. Mr; *Supervisor:* Bale, J. Mr
School, sport and society in Kenya
Abstract: This project seeks to explore the development of athletics in Kenya by adopting a world systems approach. The role of educational organisations both inside Kenya and abroad will be fully evaluated but it is recognised that other agencies in a very wide range of cultures and nations cannot be ignored in explaining the emergence of sport in a 'developing' nation.
Status: Individual research
Date of Research: 1990-1994
KEYWORDS: Kenya; sports

10/0497
Department of Education, Keele ST5 5BG
01782 621111
Burgess, R. Mr; *Supervisor:* Gleeson, D. Prof.
Research and evaluation of Cheshire LEA's Technical and Vocational Education Initiative (TVEI), Inservice Education of Teachers (INSET) & Education Support Grant (ESG) programmes
Abstract: The aim is to provide an up-to-date case study analysis of a small group of schools (secondary, primary and special) and a further education institution, in order to evaluate the impact of Technical and Vocational Education Initiative (TVEI), Inservice Education of Teachers (INSET) and Education Support Grant (ESG) initiatives on staff development and teaching and learning processes.
Status: Sponsored project
Source of Grant: Cheshire Local Education Authority £35,000
Date of Research: 1989-1993
KEYWORDS: education support grants; inservice teacher education; programme evaluation; TVEI

10/0498
Department of Education, Keele ST5 5BG
01782 621111
Russell, V. Mr; Gleeson, D. Prof.
Evaluation of a local education inspectorate
Abstract: This project involves an investigation of the changing role of the inspectorate in one local education authority using interview and observation approaches.
Status: Sponsored project
Source of Grant: Hereford & Worcester Local Education Authority
Date of Research: 1989-continuing
KEYWORDS: inspection; inspectors – of schools; local education authorities

10/0499
Department of Education, Keele ST5 5BG
01782 621111
Russell, V. Mr; Gleeson, D. Prof.
Evaluation of Technical & Vocational Education Initiative developments
Abstract: This is an evaluation of the Technical & Vocational Education Initiative (TVEI) in a local education authority, with the

specific purpose of initiating and supporting practitioner research.
Status: Sponsored project
Source of Grant: Hereford & Worcester Local Education Authority
Date of Research: 1989-continuing
KEYWORDS: TVEI

10/0500

Department of Education, Keele ST5 5BG
01782 621111
Powell, G. Mr
The order of knowledge
Abstract: The study will offer a radical re-assessment of the development of education, especially since the Renaissance. It will involve a new interpretation of the significance of Plato's analysis of the classical conceptual system which has dominated our education.
Status: Individual research
Date of Research: 1988-1993
KEYWORDS: educational history; educational theories; philosophy

10/0501

Department of Education, Keele ST5 5BG
01782 621111
Thompson, D. Mr
The history and promotion of geological and earth-science education in the United Kingdom and elsewhere in the world
Abstract: The history of geological and earth science education in the United Kingdom reveals the important part that geology, geologists and the geological profession played in the early days of the growth of science education from 1830 to 1900 in both schools and vocational courses, e.g. of the Department of Science and Arts. The wives of geologists were in the van of women's education and extra mural education. A decline to a nadir in the 1930s has been followed by a steady rise in the growth of interest, culminating in the formation of the Association of Teachers of Geology (1967) (now the Earth Science Teachers' Association (1988)), and the acceptance of Earth Science in Science in the national curriculum of the UK and many other countries.
Published Material: THOMPSON, D.B. (1993). 'Highlights from the history of the geological curriculum in schools, colleges and universities', Teaching Earth Sciences, Vol 18, No 3, p.113.; THOMPSON, D.B. (1993). Geoscience education in schools worldwide – a summary report on the presentations at the International Geoscience Education Conference, Southampton', Teaching Earth Sciences, Vol 18, No 4, pp.123-129.
Status: Individual research
Date of Research: 1970-continuing
KEYWORDS: earth science; educational history; geology education; physical sciences; science education

10/0502

Department of Education, Keele ST5 5BG
01782 621111
Marques, L. Mr; *Supervisor:* Thompson, D. Mr
Children's alternative ideas about earth-science concepts, e.g. continental drift and plate tectonics
Abstract: Children's alternative ideas relating to earth-science concepts have been only modestly researched. Following work on children's ideas of the origin of the earth, the origin of life and the nature and origin of volcanoes, the research has now turned to children's views of the origin of continents, oceans and the possible wandering of the former. Following a pilot study with pupils and teachers and indepth interviews with pupils, a questionnaire survey of the views of 300 Portuguese children has been administered. It is conjectured that the many garbled ideas of students accrue from watching television, reading newspapers and attempting to use ideas drawn from science and geography lessons at school. So far 30 or so alternative ideas have been noted and curriculum strategies which challenge many of them been developed and trialled.
Published Material: THOMPSON, D.B. (1993). 'Portuguese and English students' ideas on the nature and origin of earth, life, volcanoes, earthquakes and soil'. First International Geoscience Education Conference, Southampton, April 1993.
Status: Individual research
Date of Research: 1989-1994
KEYWORDS: comprehension; earth science; oceanography; physical sciences; plate tectonics

10/0503

Department of Education, Keele ST5 5BG
01782 621111
Thompson, D. Mr
Curriculum materials for earth-science teaching in the National Curriculum
Abstract: Earth Science is new to the science curriculum in the United Kingdom. Curriculum materials need to be written, trialled and published quickly. Trials are to be carried out on whole classes of 20-30 pupils. Materials are designed for variety and balance of approach and a concentration on pupil activity including practical experimental work. Publication is via the Earth Science Teachers' Association 'Science of the Earth' and 'Project Earth'.
Published Material: A list of Earth Science Teachers Association publications is available from Geo Supplies Ltd, 11 Station Road, Chapeltown, Sheffield S30 4XH.
Status: Individual research
Date of Research: 1988-continuing
KEYWORDS: earth science; educational materials; material development; National Curriculum; physical sciences; science education

10/0504

Department of Education, Keele ST5 5BG
01782 621111
Barber, M. Prof.; Gough, G. Dr; Johnson, M. Mr; Glover, D. Dr
Successful schooling
Abstract: The project aims to establish further information and knowledge about 'successful schooling', by means of questionnaires and indepth interviews with pupils, parents and teachers.
Status: Sponsored project
Source of Grant: Local Education Authorities £25,000
Date of Research: 1990-continuing
KEYWORDS: educational quality; outcomes of education; parent school relationship; school effectiveness; success

10/0505

Department of Education, Keele ST5 5BG
01782 621111
Mardle, G. Mr; Colclough, P. Mr; Shain, F. Ms; Modiba, M. Ms
Equal opportunities policies in schools and colleges post local management developments from the Education Reform Act 1988 and the Education Act 1992.
Abstract: In the past, policy initiation in the education system has in general been the responsibility of either the government or the local education authority. Under the Education Reform Act 1988 and the Education Act 1992 this has changed. Secondary schools and further education colleges now have control over their budgets and also a far higher degree of control over certain policy initiatives. Within the context of many other pressures this has led to a degree of inertia in certain areas. In particular, the development of equal opportunity policies has been affected. The aim of this investigation is to examine, via questionnaire and case study material, the effects of current legislation on the area of equal opportunity policy in schools and colleges. The focus of attention starts with the political aspects of the problem. It then goes on to examine the way in which such policy in the areas of gender, race and disability is seen by the participants, developed in the institutions and the methods deployed in putting it into practice. It is hoped the results and conclusions of the study will enable more institutions to develop and implement such policies.
Status: Individual research
Date of Research: 1991-continuing
KEYWORDS: educational policy; equal education; gender equality; nondiscriminatory education

10/0506

Department of Education, Keele ST5 5BG
01782 621111
Tolley, J. Ms; *Supervisor:* Wringe, C. Dr
Evaluation of foreign language teaching objectives (with particular reference to the teaching of French)
Abstract: An empirical investigation of factors determining the choice of objectives for the teaching of French at school level. These include pupil motivation and communication needs for the individual and for industry and commerce.
Status: Individual research
Date of Research: 1986-1994
KEYWORDS: educational objectives; French; modern language studies

10/0507

Department of Education, Keele ST5 5BG
01782 621111
Toy, K. Mr; *Supervisor:* Wringe, C. Dr

Educational management, teacher evaluation and teacher autonomy

Abstract: This is principally a conceptual and library study. Theories of educational management and teacher evaluation are to be explored in relation to a concept of teacher autonomy. Historical and current expectations and practice will be examined in the light of available documentary evidence, and a small number of exemplary case studies may be undertaken.

Status: Individual research
Date of Research: 1986-1994
KEYWORDS: management in education; teacher evaluation; teacher role

10/0508

Department of Education, Keele ST5 5BG
01782 621111
Kim, J. Mr; *Supervisor:* Wringe, C. Dr

Well-being and education

Abstract: This is a philosophical study examining the concept of well-being as an educational aim. Various conceptions of well-being will be examined, a distinction established between material welfare and a broader conception of well-being, and the links between this conception of well-being and education explored.

Status: Individual research
Date of Research: 1991-1994
KEYWORDS: educational objectives; educational philosophy; quality of life; well being

10/0509

Department of Education, Keele ST5 5BG
01782 621111
Parkhouse, P. Mr

Undergraduate physicists' and post-graduate scientists' (undergoing teacher training) understanding of the nature of science

Abstract: The current research is concerned with students' understanding of the nature of science. It is in two principle parts: one concerned with undergraduate physicists and the other with postgraduate science students undergoing a course of training for teaching at Keele University. Some of the post-graduate science students will be followed during their teaching practice to see if their teaching exemplifies their beliefs and whether the researcher is able to influence this by heightening their awareness through prolonged contact with them. The approach is ethnographic and the stimulus of a free-response questionnaire followed by recorded interviews elucidating their responses has been adopted. In addition both samples have to interact with specially prepared practical materials designed to reveal further their philosophical standpoints.

Status: Individual research
Date of Research: 1991-continuing
KEYWORDS: comprehension; philosophy of science; science education; scientific concepts; student attitudes

10/0510

Department of Education, Keele ST5 5BG
01782 621111
Miller, D. Mr

Curriculum development in mathematics: using and applying mathematics

Abstract: The aims of this research are to extend the breadth of the secondary school mathematics curriculum, within the context of the National Curriculum, with particular reference to the use and application of mathematics, and to influence and enrich mathematics teachers' current methodologies. The nature of the research is to provide teachers of mathematics with new, or unfamiliar, activities and contexts for using and applying mathematics. These activities and contexts include mathematics as it is used by different cultures, topics from the history of mathematics, cross-curricular material and micro-computer and calculator applications. The results will be detailed in appropriate journals, the materials wil be published in a suitable format.

Published Material: MILLER, D.J. (1990). Activity Maths, Level 5. Ormskirk: Causeway Press Ltd. (Teachers' book also available).; MILLER, D.J. (1990). Micromathematics: levels 5 and 6. Ormskirk:

Causeway Press Ltd. (Teachers' book also available).; MILLER, D.J. (1991) Activity Maths: levels 6 and 7. Ormskirk: Causeway Press Ltd. (Teachers' book also available).; MILLER, D.J. (1991). Micromathematics: levels 7 and 8. Ormskirk: Causeway Press Ltd. (Teachers' book also available).; MILLER, D.J. (1992). Micromathematics: levels 9 and 10. Ormskirk: Causeway Press Ltd. (Teachers' book also available). A full list of publications is available from the researcher.

Status: Individual research
Date of Research: 1989-1994
KEYWORDS: curriculum development; information technology; mathematics education; secondary education

10/0511

Department of Education, Keele ST5 5BG
01782 621111
McLean, M. Mrs; *Supervisor:* Gleeson, D. Prof.

Local evaluation of Technical and Vocational Education Initiative (TVEI), TVEI-Related Inservice Training (TRIST) and Grant Related INSET (GRIST)

Abstract: The study looks at the background and development of Technical and Vocational Education Initiative (TVEI) and TVEI-Related Inservice Training (TRIST) in local institutions. The research adopts an action oriented approach to evaluation, involving formative methods of reporting. Reports will be sent to the schools and colleges involved.

Published Material: GLEESON, D. (1988). TVEI and secondary education. Buckingham: Open University Press.; GLEESON, D. (1989). The paradox of training: making progress out of crisis. Buckingham: Open University Press.

Status: Sponsored project
Source of Grant: Staffordshire LEA; Training, Enterprise & Education Directorate £221,000
Date of Research: 1985-1994
KEYWORDS: inservice teacher education; TVEI

10/0512

Department of Education, Keele ST5 5BG
01782 621111
Miller, D. Mr

Mathematics and pupils and information technology (MAPIT)

Abstract: The aim of this research is to improve secondary school pupils' learning and understanding of mathematics by developing strategies which will enable mathematics departments to exploit more fully the potential of information technology within the mathematics classroom. The research is concerned with all aspects of computer use in mathematics classrooms, however, one area of particular interest is the use of notebook computers. The nature of the research is to: (1) provide appropriate training for teachers involved in the research; (2) collect case study data at regular intervals from the schools; and (3) provide formative and summative reports for the schools. In addition, information has been collected from Postgraduate Certificate in Education (PGCE) mathematics students on teaching practice. The interim reports and final results will be detailed in appropriate journals.

Status: Sponsored project
Source of Grant: Keele University: Department of Education £1,500
Date of Research: 1992-continuing
KEYWORDS: computer uses in education; information technology; mathematics education; microcomputers; secondary schools

10/0513

Department of Education, Keele ST5 5BG
01782 621111
Miller, D. Mr

The use of computers in mathematics lessons

Abstract: The aim of this research is to examine the use of computers in secondary school mathematics lessons. Information has been collected by questionnaire from 100 secondary schools in England and Wales. The survey requested information about the computer equipment in school; the time spent by pupils using computers in mathematics; the programs in use in the school; the views of the head of mathematics on the use of computers; and the training needs of the mathematics department. The results will be detailed in appropriate journals.

Status: Individual research
Date of Research: 1992-1993
KEYWORDS: computer uses in education; information technology; mathematics education; secondary schools

10/0514

Department of Education, Keele ST5 5BG
01782 621111
Mardle, G. Mr; Glover, D. Dr

Examination of the structural implications of changes in teacher education and mentoring for schools

Abstract: Recent changes in government policy towards teacher education has given greater prominence to the role of schools in the process. In particular, the need to involve teachers more thoroughly in the role of mentoring those in training. As a consequence, there have been rapid changes and developments of the relationship between higher education institutions and schools across a range of settings. The Esmee Fairbairn sponsored research project on mentoring is part of a national framework of research in the area involving six universities, namely Keele, Oxford, Leicester, Sussex, Manchester Metropolitan and Swansea. The Keele project, whilst contributing to the wider aims of the main project, has a specific focus in looking at the structural framework of the process and how it is being embedded within the normal workings of the school organisation. It is, therefore, mainly concerned with the following: 1) Approaches by institutions to the changing roles of teachers within initial teacher training. 2) Changing institutional structures. 3) Long term development and training needs. 4) Management relationships and facilitation of mentoring. 5) Individual career profiles of mentors. 6) Financial implications for schools. 7) Partnership developments with higher education institutions.
Status: Sponsored project
Source of Grant: Esmee Fairbairn Foundation £35,000
Date of Research: 1993-continuing
KEYWORDS: *institutes of higher education; mentors; preservice teacher education; school based teacher education; student teacher supervisors*

10/0515

Department of Education, Keele ST5 5BG
01782 621111
Powell, G. Mr

Educating the educators

Abstract: At a time when teacher education has given way to the exclusive claims of training, the study will set out to construct an educational scheme to prepare future educators. In particular, it will explore the nature of the specific knowledge needed by educators to respond to individual differences.
Status: Individual research
Date of Research: 1994-continuing
KEYWORDS: *preservice teacher education; teacher educators*

10/0516

Department of Education, Keele ST5 5BG
01782 621111
Barber, M. Prof.

The making of the Education Act, 1944

Abstract: The aim was to research and write a new, readable account of the Education Act 1944. The research, involving sifting existing secondary sources as well as primary sources, also involved the reinterpretation of the events between 1941 and 1944 in the light of what is now known about policy making and implementation. Overwhelmingly, however, the aim was to retell a story in a way which was both accessible and entertaining in time for the 50th anniversary.
Published Material: BARBER, M. (1994). The making of the 1944 Education Act. London: Cassell.; BARBER, M. (1994). 'The prime of R.A. Butler', Times Educational Supplement, 14 January.; BARBER, M. (1994). 'The battleground that was Butler's legacy', Sunday Times, 16 January.; BARBER, M. (1994). Guardian Education, 18 January.
Status: Individual research
Date of Research: 1993-1994
KEYWORDS: *educational change; educational history; educational policy*

10/0517

Department of Education, Keele ST5 5BG
01782 621111
Ozga, J. Prof.

Women managers in higher and further education

Abstract: The aim of the project is to build on work completed for the publication 'Women in education management' (Ozga, 1993) in order to provide detailed case studies of women in management in higher and further education. A small sample of senior managers has been selected for work shadowing, and the study will develop detailed accounts of their work parties over a six month period. It will also make use of life history methods to develop detailed accounts of women's experience of management and of their experience of 'careers'. The data will be analysed in order to explore the extent to which it supports claims of productive gender-related difference in management styles.
Published Material: OZGA, J. (Ed). (1992). Women in education management. Buckingham: Open University Press.
Status: Individual research
Date of Research: 1993-continuing
KEYWORDS: *administrators; educational administration; further education; higher education; management in education; women; women's employment*

10/0518

Department of Education, Keele ST5 5BG
01782 621111
Open University, School of Education, Walton Hall, Milton Keynes MK7 6AA
01908 274066
Ozga, J. Prof.

Elites in education policy making

Abstract: The aim of the project was to explore the nature of policy making in education, in England, in the post-war period and to use that exploration as the basis for interrogation of major theoretical approaches to the study of policy making, especially pluralism and sexism. A further aim was to ensure that the role of permanent officials in policy making was recorded and discussed, and to do this through the use of life history methods. The study was undertaken using a variety of methods, including document analysis, exploration of archives, and extended interviews with members of the policy elite. The identification of this group was a considerable part of the project, and included the tracing of connections among them. The conclusions of the project indicated the strong influence exerted on policy by permanent officials at the centre and in the localities, and indicated their interconnectedness and their adherence to particular forms of provision. This in turn suggested that some modification of conventional pluralism approaches to education policy making was necessary.
Published Material: GERVITZ, S. & OZGA, J. (1990). 'Partnership, pluralism and education policy: a reassessment', Journal of Education Policy, Vol 5, No 1, pp.37-48.; OZGA, J. (1990). 'Policy research and policy theory: a comment on Fitz and Halpin', Journal of Education Policy, Vol 5, No 4, pp.359-362.; GERVITZ, S. & OZGA, J. (1994). 'Interviewing the education policy elite'. In: WALFORD, G. (Ed). Doing research on the powerful in education. London: University College London Press.; OZGA, J. & GERVITZ, S. 'Sex lies and audiotape'. In: HALPIN, D. & TROYNE, B. (Eds). Researching education policy: ethical and methodological issues. Basingstoke: Falmer Press. (in press).
Status: Sponsored project
Source of Grant: Open University Research Committee £30,000
Date of Research: 1988-continuing
KEYWORDS: *educational planning; educational policy; policy formation; policy makers*

10/0519

Department of Education, Keele ST5 5BG
01782 621111
University of the West of England, Faculty of Education, Redland Campus, Bristol BS6 6UZ
01179 741251
Ozga, J. Prof.; Nicholls, P. Mr; Pollard, A. Prof.

Quality in the marketplace: a study of the impact of market forces on small-scale providers. (Primary schools, nursing homes and restaurants)

Abstract: The project is designed to explore the impact of the market on the provision of primary education, care for the elderly, and fast food. There is a particular interest in finding out about possible connections between marketization and management practice. Any changes in workforce, training and structuring are also of interest. The different small providers were selected in the hope of achieving instructive contrasts and parallels. The research is being conducted in an English county town, initially through surveys and questionnaires, but mainly through detailed case studies of a small sample of each of the organizations under examination. The case studies include

semi-structured interviews with management and staff, and non-participant observation.
Status: Sponsored project
Source of Grant: Higher Education Funding Council £140,000
Date of Research: 1993-continuing
KEYWORDS: *economic factors; educational quality; management in education; marketing; primary schools*

10/0520
Department of Psychology, Keele ST5 5BG
01782 621111
Afzalnia, M. Mr; *Supervisor:* Hartley, J. Prof.
Reading, listening and television viewing: a study in children's cognition
Abstract: This research is concerned with the relationships between children's television viewing and their school performance with an emphasis on their reading, listening and viewing comprehension skills. Seventy eight 9-10 year olds were selected from a local school to take part. Tests of reading, intelligence and listening skills, together with questionnaires, were used to collect information about the children's abilities and their parents' and teachers' attitudes towards their reading and listening habits. While the results of the test studies supported the assumption that predicted that children's general reading and listening skills would relate to their viewing comprehension, the obtained data did not produce much support for the hypothesis that assumed a positive relationship between children's sensitivity to the audio channel of television and their verbal receptive achievements. The assumption that there would be a positive relationship between children's background variables and their reading, listening and viewing skills was mostly supported. However, the data indicated that some variables (such as library membership) were more important than the others. It was found that children with low achievements in reading and listening also had some difficulty with their overall cognition which was shown in their difficulty in general learning.
Published Material: AFZALNIA, M.R. (1993). 'Television literacy and young children's promotion of mental health'. In: TRENT, D. (Ed). Promotion of mental health, Aldershot: Avebury.; A full list of proposed publications is available from the researcher.
Status: Sponsored project
Source of Grant: Government of Iran
Date of Research: 1988-1993
KEYWORDS: *academic achievement; cognitive ability; listening skills; reading achievement; television research; television viewing*

10/0521
Department of Psychology, Keele ST5 5BG
01782 621111
Hartley, J. Prof.
Designing instructional text
Abstract: This research focuses on the design of instructional text – mainly in the form of printed materials – which enables the reader to do or to understand something. The research covers three areas: (1) the layout of such materials; (2) the language of such materials; and (3) the use of structural devices which enable people to find their way about a piece of text. Work with layout stresses the importance of using the 'white-space' systematically in order to convey the underlying structure of text. Work with language suggests the importance of simpler wording. Work with 'access structures' indicates how devices such as headings and summaries can aid recall. Recently the research has broadened its focus of interest to include work with braille, audio-taped instruction, and electronic text.
Published Material: HARTLEY, J. (1990). 'Textbook design: current status and future directions', International Journal of Educational Research, Vol 14, pp.533-541.; HARTLEY, J. (1990). 'Author, printer, reader, listener: four sources of confusion when listening to tabular/diagrammatic information', British Journal of Visual Impairment, Vol VIII, pp.51-53.; HARTLEY, J. (1991). 'Psychology, writing and computers', Visible Language, Vol 25, pp.339-375.; HARTLEY, J. (Ed). (1992). Technology and writing: readings in the psychology of written communication. London: Jessica Kingsley Publishers.; HARTLEY, J. (1994). 'Text design for the visually impaired: a British perspective', Educational Technology, Vol 34, pp.58-64.
Status: Individual research
Date of Research: 1970-continuing
KEYWORDS: *educational materials; educational media; low vision aids; printing; textbooks*

10/0522
Department of Psychology, Keele ST5 5BG
01782 621111
Seale, J. Mrs; Newberry-Tarrier, S. Mrs; Topping, M. Mr; *Supervisor:* Hegarty, J. Dr
Computer applications to special education
Abstract: The aim of the research is to support users of microcomputers in special education, particularly those who work with adults who have severe learning difficulties. The work combines research, development of software and hardware devices, consultancy and staff training. There are three major research projects: (1) Staff development – a detailed study of 11 centres using micros has revealed the dimensions of effective management of the computer as an educational resource. The research has produced a management profile (AMMASE) which can be used to identify weaknesses and strengths in management and create goals. (2) Expert Systems Project – detailed observational research of adults with a mental handicap whilst shopping for groceries has produced a specification for a computer aid which will help them produce their own shopping lists based on the grocery stocks normally required for their weekly needs. The software is now written for a hand-held microcomputer with integral touch screen and printer which allows clients who cannot read or write to input the current grocery stocks and thus create a shopping list (which is graphical). Evaluation of the system is in progress. (3) A robotic device to allow people to eat unassisted has been developed. This low cost device is now in use and is being evaluated.
Published Material: COLLINS, R. (1989). 'Computers and special education for adults'. In: HARTLEY, J. & BRANTHWAITE, J.A. (Eds). The Applied Psychologist. Buckingham: Open University Press.; HEGARTY, J.R. (1991). Into the 1990s: the Present and Future of Microcomputers for People with Learning Difficulties. Market Drayton: Change Publications.
Status: Sponsored project
Source of Grant: Various public and charitable sources
Date of Research: 1985-continuing
KEYWORDS: *computer system design; computer uses in education; severe learning difficulties; special educational needs*

10/0523
Department of Psychology, Keele ST5 5BG
01782 621111
Trueman, M. Mr
Attitudes towards computers
Abstract: A series of four studies has been carried out using the Lloyd and Gressard (1984) Computer Attitude Scale to measure computer anxiety, computer liking and computer confidence. A study of undergraduate students showed that males had more experience in using computers and liked computers more than females did. However, there were no sex differences in computer anxiety or computer confidence. A second study of undergraduates found that males had more experience of using computers, liked computers more and were more confident with computers than females in the study. This study also showed a correlation between higher neuroticism scores and found that males had more experience with computers and were more likely to have access to a computer than females were. Males were more confident about using computers and they liked computers more than females. The final study looked at the relationship between androgeny (as assessed by the Personal Attributes Questionnaire, Spence & Helmreich, 1978) and the Computer Attitude Scale in a sample of 4th form school children. There were no sex differences in computer anxiety, computer liking or computer confidence. However, androgynous individuals had higher computer liking scores than masculine, feminine or undifferentiated individuals. Also, there were a series of significant sex and androgeny interactions in which androgenous males and masculine females were less anxious, liked computers more and were more confident about computers than the other groups.
Published Material: TRUEMAN, M. (1989). 'Attitudes towards computers', Paper presented to the 5th Annual Wolverhampton Polytechnic Educational Research Conference. Ibiza: San Antonio.; TRUEMAN, M. (1990). 'The effects of gender and computer experience on attitudes towards computers', CORE (Collected Original Resources in Education), Vol 14, No 3. (Fr. B01 on No 1 of 9 microfiches).
Status: Individual research
Date of Research: 1985-continuing
KEYWORDS: *attitudes; computer literacy; computers; sex differences*

10/0524
Department of Psychology, Keele ST5 5BG
01782 621111
Loumidis, K. Mr; *Supervisor:* Hill, A. Dr
Social problem solving and learning disabilities (mental handicap): evaluation of a therapeutic training programme
Abstract: There is evidence to suggest that Social Problem Solving Training can help people with learning disabilities (Loumidis, 1992). The study reported here had three parts. In the first part, 22 people with learning disabilities living at a residential hospital and 24 people who lived in the community were assessed to establish baseline measures of intellectual, adaptive and maladaptive functioning. Social problem solving skills were assessed on the basis of people's ability to solve hypothetical but personally relevant social and interpersonal problems. The responses obtained from this measure were rated on the basis of eleven scoring criteria, providing a rigorous and detailed analysis of people's abilities. During the second part of the study, 29 people were selected for training and these were assigned to two residential groups and two community groups, each group receiving an average of 15 hours of training. While maintaining the traditional components of social problem solving programmes, significant modifications in the process of training were required. The remaining 17 people of the sample formed two control groups. At the end of training the measures initially used to establish baseline performance were re-administered to obtain post treatment-scores. In the third part of the study the effects of training were assessed by comparing performance on the measures of problem solving and adaptive/maladaptive behaviour.
Published Material: LOUMIDIS, K.S. (1992). 'Can "Social Problem Solving Training" help people with learning difficulties?'. In: TRENT, D.R. (Ed). The promotion of mental health: Volume 1. Aldershot: Avebury Press.; LOUMIDIS, K.S. (1992). 'Evaluating social problem solving groups for people with learning disabilities'. In: LOUMIDIS, K.S. (Chair): Cognitive behavioural approaches for people with learning disabilities. Symposium presented at the British Psychological Society Conference, London.
Status: Individual research
Date of Research: 1990-1993
KEYWORDS: moderate learning difficulties; problem solving; severe learning difficulties; social skills; special educational needs

10/0525
Department of Psychology, Keele ST5 5BG
01782 621111
O'Neill, S. Ms; *Supervisor:* Sloboda, J. Prof.
Factors influencing children's motivation and achievement during the first year of music tuition
Abstract: Why do some children persevere at the task of mastering a musical instrument while other children with seemingly equal ability and potential make little progress or even abandon musical study altogether? Research within the past decade has made significant progress in developing and testing social-cognitive theories of achievement motivation which have focused primarily on children's conceptions of ability and recovery from failure in intellectual-academic situations. The current one-year longitudinal study examines several of these theoretical perspectives with a group of children who are beginning instrumental music tuition for the first time. The results will be presented with reference to the initial pilot results which indicated that children's implicit theories of ability (as stable or malleable) varied across different domains and that although most children held the belief that physical skill could be improved, just under half the children believed this was not possible with musical skill. This factor, together with musical self-concept, appears to have an important initial influence on children's interest in playing an instrument and their subsequent enrolment with an instrumental teacher.
Status: Individual research
Date of Research: 1992-continuing
KEYWORDS: achievement; motivation; music education; musical instruments

10/0526
Department of Psychology, Keele ST5 5BG
01782 621111
Isa, P. Mrs; *Supervisor:* Hartley, J. Prof.
Academic achievement motivation and locus of control of Malaysian college students
Abstract: The purpose of this study was to examine a) the academic motivation, academic locus of control, and academic performance of Malay and Chinese college students in Malaysia; and b) the effects of race, gender and other students' background characteristics on academic motivation and academic locus of control. Four academic motivation scales and an Academic Locus of Control Scale were all developed specifically for use in this study. Three hundred and forty Malay college students and three hundred and sixty-two Chinese college students completed the scales. It was predicted, on the basis of previous research, that: 1) the Malay students would be lower in academic motivation than the Chinese students; 2) the Malay students would be more 'externally controlled' than the Chinese students; 3) there would be significant effects of socioeconomic status, gender and other background characteristics on a) students' academic motivation and b) academic locus of control; 4) students with high academic motivation would have better grades than students with lower academic motivation; and 5) students with an internal locus of control would have better grades than students with an external locus of control. The analyses of the data showed that none of the hypotheses was fully supported. The Malay students scored higher than the Chinese ones on two of the motivation scales, and they had a higher internal locus of control. Women students scored higher than men students on two of the motivation scales, but not on the academic locus of control scale. There were no socio-economic status differences on the academic motivation scales or the academic locus of control scale. Unfortunately it did not prove possible to obtain a meaningful comparative measure of academic performance for the two groups, so the results obtained on the scales could not be related to academic performance. However, the scales developed for this study have clear factorial structures and high reliability, so they can be used for future research in the Malaysian cont.
Status: Individual research
Date of Research: 1990-continuing
KEYWORDS: academic aspiration; locus of control; Malaysia; motivation tests; student motivation

10/0527
Department of Psychology, Keele ST5 5BG
01782 621111
Exeter University, Department of Psychology, Washington Singer Laboratory, Exeter EX4 4QJ
01392 263263
Sloboda, J. Prof.; Davidson, J. Dr; Howe, M. Prof.
The biographical determinants of excellence in young musicians
Abstract: This project aims to extend our understanding of the circumstances in which high levels of musical ability are acquired. Existing theories tend to be based upon often unreliable biographical anecdotes collected decades after the events or circumstances to which they refer. There is a lack, therefore, of systematic evidence to provide accurate descriptions of the events which actually take place in the formative years of young people who are given opportunities to learn to become musicians. Such 'natural histories' are prerequisites if a full explanation of the causes of superior abilities is to be achieved. In order to do this, the researchers have undertaken a retrospective study based on factual evidence (examination certificates, school term dates) of 100 young musicians who attend a specialist music school and 100 control subjects. The controls were of similar social backgrounds and whilst all 100 began music lessons, only 50 have persisted. In addition, the day to day musical activities of the 50 players in the control group and 50 of the talented group were traced. This was based on a diary of musical activities kept for one year. The aim of this part of the study was to discover to what extent the distribution of current musical activities can be predicted by previous musical life-events, and whether current musical activity can be predictive of future progress. It is a particularly important issue to examine, as what little information about practice already exists is somewhat contradictory.
Published Material: HOWE, M.J.A. & SLOBODA, J.A. (1991). 'Young musicians' accounts of significant influences in their early lives. 1. The family and the musical background', British Journal of Music Education, Vol 8, No 1, pp.39-52.; HOWE, M.J.A. & SLOBODA, J.A. (1991). 'Young musicians' accounts of significant influences in their early lives. 2. Teachers, practising and performing', British Journal of Music Education, Vol 8, No 1, pp.53-63.; SLOBODA, J.A. & HOWE, M.J.A. (1991). 'Biographical precursors of musical excellence: an interview study', Psychology of Music, No 19, pp.3-21.
Status: Sponsored project
Source of Grant: Leverhulme Trust £85,200

Date of Research: 1991-continuing
KEYWORDS: *biographical inventories; music activities; musical ability; musicians*

Kent University

10/0528
Department of Sociology, Canterbury CT2 7NZ
01227 764000
Ainley, P. Dr
A comparison of student and staff experiences at two contrasted higher education institutions
Abstract: A cross section of 51 final year undergraduates at Kent University has been interviewed for comparison with a geographical selection of 50 final year undergraduates at the University of East London. This is intended to bring out the differences and similarities in the experience of higher education by 'stereotypical' – 18-21 year old middle class students moving from school to work and home to living away via residential higher education; and the 'new' – mature female, ethnic minority and working class students living at home whilst studying. The student interviews are supplemented by staff interviews at the two higher education institutions.
Published Material: AINLEY, P. (1994). Degrees of difference: higher education in the 1990s. London: Lawrence and Whishart.
Status: Sponsored project
Source of Grant: Department of Employment: Enterprise in Higher Education Initiative
Date of Research: 1991-1993
KEYWORDS: *academic staff; ethnic groups; higher education; mature students; middle class students; student attitudes; student experience; working class*

10/0529
Department of Sociology, Canterbury CT2 7NZ
01227 764000
Davey, B. Mr; *Supervisor:* Ainley, P. Dr
The student charter project
Abstract: The report starts with working definitions for a charter and other related terms, compact and contract. It then traces some early developments in charters and examines why there has been renewed interest in the concept in recent years. The link between charters and quality is examined, followed by the results of a survey of all higher education institutions in the UK with case studies of charter implementation in three of them. The different types of charters are set against the Institute of Public Policy Research's definitions of quality.
Published Material: DAVEY, B. (1992). 'The student charter project report'. Canterbury: Enterprise Kent, University of Kent.
Status: Sponsored project
Source of Grant: Department of Employment: Enterprise in Higher Education Initiative £12,000
Date of Research: 1992-1993
KEYWORDS: *educational quality; higher education; institutional role; performance contracts*

10/0530
School of Continuing Education, Canterbury CT2 7NZ
01227 764000
West, L. Mr; Lea, M. Ms
An indepth study of adult student motivation in access programmes and higher education
Abstract: The research will explore the motivation of mature students embarking on higher education via indepth, qualitative, autobiographical research with a sample of 30 students chosen to include both sexes, a range of occupational, social and ethnic groups, ages and backgrounds. The research examines the importance of self-narrative in making sense of, and creating meaning during, periods of change and fragmentation. A multi-disciplinary perspective will be used in the work, drawing on sociology, psychology, psychoanalysis, ethnography, as well as critical linguistics and critical discourse analysis in interpreting text and theorising its meaning. The methodology involves the use of semi-structured interviews, notes and diaries.
Published Material: WEST, L., LEA, M. & ALEXOPOULOU, F. (1993). 'On keeping a diary, a new approach to reflective practice'. In: MILLER, N. & JONES, D. (Eds). Research Reflecting Practice,

SCUTREA Conference Papers, Manchester.; MILLER, N. & JONES, D. (1993). 'Epistemological issues in reflective practice'. In: MILLER, N. & JONES, D. (Eds). Research Reflecting Practice, SCUTREA Conference Papers, Manchester.
Status: Sponsored project
Source of Grant: Higher Education Funding Council £60,000
Date of Research: 1992-continuing
KEYWORDS: *access programmes; access to education; higher education; mature students; nontraditional education; student motivation*

10/0531
School of Continuing Education, Canterbury CT2 7NZ
01227 764000
Alexander, B. Ms; Burnett, F. Dr; West, L. Mr
An evaluation of the performance of mature, non-traditional students at the University of Kent, 1990-93
Abstract: The research involves a two-stage evaluation of mature students' academic performance using quantitative and qualitative research methods. Its purpose is to compare the academic performance of mature, non-traditional students with traditional students at Kent University, and to identify and assess subjectively-reported factors associated with academic outcome. The methods involve a comparison of data on academic performance of the two groups and interviews with a sample of mature students to identify and evaluate their subjective experiences of being a mature student at Kent University.
Status: Sponsored project
Source of Grant: Kent University £5,000
Date of Research: 1993-1994
KEYWORDS: *academic achievement; access programmes; higher education; mature students; nontraditional education; performance*

King Alfred's College of Higher Education

10/0532
Sparkford Road, Winchester SO22 4NR
01962 841515
Boyce-Tillman, J. Dr
Gender issues in the composing process
Abstract: The background to the research is accounts by women composers of their own processes and observation of gender differences in the classroom. The investigation will compare these accounts with classroom behaviour. The methodology will include critical studies of texts and a classroom observation project, probably extended to a variety of schools. It will identify individual pupils and use questionnaires for more detailed work. It will compare this with interviews with contemporary women composers. It will examine issues like cooperative work, the use of traditional material and already existing material, the use of the unconventional and the choice of instruments and the use of the voice.
Published Material: BOYCE-TILLMAN, J.B. (1993). 'Women's ways of knowing', British Journal of Music Education, Vol 10, No 3, pp.153-61.
Status: Individual research
Date of Research: 1993-continuing
KEYWORDS: *music education; musical composition; sex differences*

10/0533
Sparkford Road, Winchester SO22 4NR
01962 841515
Penny, A. Dr; Hall, C. Mrs; Threadingham, M. Mrs; Jessop, T. Ms
Educating the educators: a study of partnership programmes in initial teacher education
Abstract: The changes in central government policy on initial teacher education is the background for this research. It aims to focus on the mentor/student relationship as the axis of training, and on aspects of the devolution of control, financial academic and professional. The research will cover a sample of institutions in the south of England. Methods will include: case studies of institutions; case profiling of students and mentors; and surveys of documenting conceptual bases of partnership programmes.

Status: Sponsored project
Source of Grant: King Alfred's College of Higher Education
Date of Research: 1995-continuing
KEYWORDS: *cooperative programmes; mentors; preservice teacher education*

10/0534
Sparkford Road, Winchester SO22 4NR
01962 841515
Ryan, C. Dr; Cremin, P. Mr; Dupre, A. Mr
The European dimension in primary education
Abstract: This group project is an analysis of the development of a European dimension in the primary school. Intensive programmes are organised with final year teacher education students from the European Union. They are supported in an action research project to devise, test and evaluate appropriate materials and approaches in the primary school. This student teacher activity generates a range of data types: diaries, videotape, written evaluation, interviews, and questionnaires. These are collected from pupils, student teachers and teacher educators. The data is analysed using a variety of frameworks particularly those produced by the Council of Ministers of the European Union.
Published Material: CREMIN, P. & RYAN, C. (1993). 'Developing the European dimension in teacher education – a case study in European education'. In: LEINO, A-L., HELLGREN, P. & HAMALAINEN. Integration of technology and reflection in teaching: a challenge for European teacher education. Helsinki: Hakapaino Oy/University of Helsinki.
Status: Sponsored project
Source of Grant: Eurydice: Network of Teacher Training Institutes; Reseau d'Institutions de Formation (RIF)
Date of Research: 1990-continuing
KEYWORDS: *comparative education; European studies; preservice teacher education*

10/0535
Sparkford Road, Winchester SO22 4NR
01962 841515
Homerton College, Cambridge CB2 2PH
01223 411141
Derby Tertiary College, Japanese Resources Centre, Mackworth, Derby DE3 4LR
01332 519951
Carr, M. Dr; Kinmont, A. Mrs; Barker, T. Mr; Jones, M. Miss
Daiwa primary initiative project
Abstract: The aim of the project is to promote the study of Japan within the primary school curriculum through a range of materials, approaches and methodologies. It involves the development and production of resources and materials with associated pilot studies and trials. In the first year, four researchers worked independently to produce key texts, supported by one freelance consultant. Based in Winchester, Cambridge, Bath and Derby, there is now joint development work in progress. School-based investigations are being supported by conferences and presentations for both teachers and students. The research project is intended to lead towards the production and publication of materials, resources and texts.
Status: Sponsored project
Source of Grant: Daiwa Anglo/Japanese Foundation £22,500
Date of Research: 1992-1994
KEYWORDS: *Japanese studies; primary education*

Lancaster University

10/0536
Department of Applied Social Science, Cartmel College, Bailrigg, Lancaster LA1 4YW
01524 65201
Wilkinson, H. Miss; *Supervisor:* Deem, R. Prof.; Finch, J. Prof.
An investigation into the concept of parental choice within special needs education
Abstract: The background to the project was an 18 month pilot study for The Spastics Society which examined the location of, and provision for, primary aged pupils with movement disabilities (Hadley, R. & Wilkinson, H. 1993). From this project, and within the current market-orientated developments in education as a whole, the question of the relevance of choice for parents whose children have special educational needs led to the current project. How the ideologies of special needs relates to the current ideologies around market-led education will be an element of the research. The sample is taken from 3 local education authorities and will involve the longitudinal observation of a number of pupils and parents during the process of statementing and choice of schools. Methods will be based on a range of quantitative and qualitative techniques.
Status: Individual research
Date of Research: 1993-continuing
KEYWORDS: *access to education; parent choice; special educational needs*

10/0537
Department of Educational Research, Cartmel College, Bailrigg, Lancaster LA1 4YW
01524 65201
Simco, N. Mr; *Supervisor:* Smith, L. Dr
Initial teacher training and professional development within dimensions of classroom activity ambiguity
Abstract: The research seeks to illuminate aspects of the professional development of students undergoing initial teacher training. In particular it aims to richly describe classrooms where students are operating and to draw from this description common strands of professional progress made by beginning teachers. The study has, as a central focus, the development made along two dimensions of 'ambiguity', namely the degree of activity openness enabled and the degree of teacher clarity in delivering activity. In this respect activity will be described in four 'cells': activity which is open and clear; activity which is closed and clear; activity which is open and vague; activity which is closed and vague. The empirical work has an ecological approach, allowing issues to emerge for semi-structured observation and pre and post activity interviews with student teachers and children. In essence it is a longitudinal study which focuses on the professional progress of four students during teaching practices at various times in their training. These case studies represent the first stage of the research. This stage attempts to be purely descriptive. From this description a second prescriptive stage is likely to emerge.
Status: Individual research
Date of Research: 1990-continuing
KEYWORDS: *ambiguity; class activities; preservice teacher education; student teachers; teaching practice; teaching styles*

10/0538
Department of Educational Research, Cartmel College, Bailrigg, Lancaster LA1 4YW
01524 65201
Helsby, G. Ms; Saunders, M. Dr
Lancaster Technical and Vocational Education Initiative evaluation programme
Abstract: The focus of the work has varied over the lifetime of the project, being based upon a consortium of 15 local education authorities (LEAs) under Technical and Vocational Education Initiative (TVEI) pilot, and a consortium of seven LEAs under TVEI extension. During TVEI pilot the researchers investigated the effect of TVEI upon students, teachers and institutions. This work included wide-scale student surveys amongst some 7,000 TVEI and non-TVEI students, as well as qualitative inquiry. Areas of particular interest included profiling, work experience, technology, cross-curriculum developments and teaching and learning strategies. During TVEI extension the focus was particularly upon the use of teacher-generated performance indicators as a route into self-evaluation. More recently the researchers have undertaken an investigation of the TVEI effect, including its impact upon whole institutional working and its influence upon change.
Published Material: HELSBY, G. & SAUNDERS, M. (1993). 'Taylorism, Tylerism and performance indicators: defending the indefensible?', Educational Studies, Vol 19, No 1, pp.55-77.; HELSBY, G. & SAUNDERS, M. (1993). 'Evaluating the influence and legacy of TVEI: an overview', Evaluation and Research in Education, Vol 7, No 2, pp.45-50.; HELSBY, G. (1993). 'Creating the autonomous professional or the trained technician? Current directions in inservice teacher support', Evaluation and Research in Education, Vol 7, No 2, pp.65-82.; SAUNDERS, M. (1993). 'TVEI and the National Curriculum: culture clash between use and exchange value', Evaluation and Research in Education, Vol 7, No 2, pp.107-115.
Status: Sponsored project

Source of Grant: LEAs Consortium; Employment Department/(MSC/Training Agency)
Date of Research: 1984-continuing
KEYWORDS: programme evaluation; TVEI

10/0539
Department of Educational Research, Cartmel College,
Bailrigg, Lancaster LA1 4YW
01524 65201
Summerfield, P. Dr
Gender, training and employment: an historical analysis 1939-50
Abstract: This is a study of the relationships between the training and employment of women during the Second World War and the immediate post-war period. The central research question is whether wartime training altered the position of women in the labour market on either a temporary or a permanent basis. In pursuit of answers the research scrutinizes the formulation and outcomes of training and employment policy in the period 1939-50.
Published Material: SUMMERFIELD, P. (1989). 'What women learned from the second world war', History of Education, Vol 18, No 3, pp.213-230.; SUMMERFIELD, P. & CROCKETT, N. (1992). '"You weren't taught that with the welding": lessons in sexuality in the second world war', Women's History Review, Vol 1, No 3, pp.435-454.; SUMMERFIELD, P. (1992). 'Gender training and employment: a historical analysis 1939-1950'. Final Report to Economic and Social Research Council, November 1992.; SUMMERFIELD, P. (1993). 'The patriarchal discourse of human capital: women's work and training in the second world war', Journal of Gender Studies, November.
Status: Sponsored project
Source of Grant: Economic and Social Research Council £43,000
Date of Research: 1990-1993
KEYWORDS: educational history; training; women's education; women's employment

10/0540
Department of Educational Research, Cartmel College,
Bailrigg, Lancaster LA1 4YW
01524 65201
Tinkler, P. Dr
Young women and leisure, 1920-1950
Abstract: This research has two aims. Firstly it explores the structural and ideological context within which young women's leisure was situated in terms of the social and economic conditions in which girls grew up and the influences which young women were exposed to through the family, schooling, paid work, formal leisure provision, media and popular culture. Secondly, it aims to uncover the actual leisure practices of young women during the period 1920-50. The research is structured in two parts reflecting these dual aims. The first part of this research addresses the social, economic and ideological context of young women's leisure activity. It draws upon a range of sources including official documentation, academic and popular literature; census material and Board/Ministry of Education statistics; a range of data relating to the conditions of life of young women including that pertaining to schooling, paid work, housing and home conditions, health, courtship and sexuality. Three main themes structure this part of the research – access to leisure, the temporal dimensions of leisure, and the question of suitable leisure activity. The second part of the research explores young women's experience and understanding of leisure using oral history sources as well as autobiographies, diaries, contemporary studies and material from the Mass Observation Archive (Sussex University).
Status: Sponsored project
Source of Grant: British Academy
Date of Research: 1990-1993
KEYWORDS: girls; leisure time; recreational activities; women's studies

10/0541
Department of Educational Research, Cartmel College,
Bailrigg, Lancaster LA1 4YW
01524 65201
Rimmershaw, R. Dr
Collaborative writing
Abstract: This is a study of the collaborative writing practices of writers in the academic community. The main focus is on why they are involved, how they manage the collaboration, and how they deal with issues of identity and power in collaborating. The sample comprises 20 academic writers from eight disciplines, and from undergraduate to professional status. The main source of data is indepth interviews. Additional sources used are observation and tape-recordings of collaborations in progress, and written reports by collaborators on the production of specific pieces of writing.
Published Material: RIMMERSHAW, R.E. (1992). 'Collaborative writing practices and writing support technologies'. In: SHARPLES, M. (Ed). Computers and Writing: Issues and Implementations. Dordrecht: Kluwer Academic Publishers.
Status: Individual research
Date of Research: 1990-1993
KEYWORDS: authors; cooperation; writing – composition

10/0542
Department of Educational Research, Cartmel College,
Bailrigg, Lancaster LA1 4YW
01524 65201
Rimmershaw, R. Dr
Reading and writing in student learning
Abstract: This research into students' reading and writing development is in two phases. In the first phase undergraduate students worked with the researcher to reflect on and analyse their own reading and writing development before and during their courses at Lancaster University. In the second phase a cohort of 16 non-traditional students were followed through the three years of their degree programme. The methods used include individual interviews, group discussions and deconstruction of particular reading and writing tasks as the students perform them.
Published Material: RIMMERSHAW, R.E. (1993). 'Students' changing conceptions of academic writing'. In: EIGLER, G. & JECHLE, T. (Eds). Writing: current trends in European research. Freiburg: Hochschul Verlag.; BENSON, N., GURNEY, S., HARRISON, J. & RIMMERSHAW, R.E. (1994). 'The place of academic writing in the whole-life writing experiences of three university students'. In: HAMILTON, M., BARTON, D. & IVANIC, R. (Eds). Worlds of Literacy. Language and Education Library, Vol 5. Clevedon: Multilingual Matters.
Status: Individual research
Date of Research: 1989-continuing
KEYWORDS: critical reading; reading; student development; study skills; writing – composition; writing skills

10/0543
Department of Educational Research, Cartmel College,
Bailrigg, Lancaster LA1 4YW
01524 65201
Serafingos, J. Mr; Supervisor: Rogers, C. Dr
Teachers planning and evaluation of mathematics in Greek high schools
Abstract: This project is an examination of the ways in which a sample of Greek mathematics teachers think about their subject and their teaching, and how these understandings influence the kinds of experiences that are selected and presented to children in the mathematics curriculum. This is of particular interest in Greek education because of the high emphasis that is placed upon high school teachers' subject degree studies and the lack of any significant professional training for high school teaching.
Status: Sponsored project
Source of Grant: Greek Ministry of Education scholarship
Date of Research: 1988-1993
KEYWORDS: Greece; mathematics education; mathematics teachers; teacher education

10/0544
Department of Educational Research, Cartmel College,
Bailrigg, Lancaster LA1 4YW
01524 65201
Heath, S. Ms; Supervisor: Summerfield, P. Dr; Mason, J. Dr
Preparation for life: TVEI and equal opportunities (gender)
Abstract: From its inception, the Technical and Vocational Education Initiative (TVEI) included, as a central objective, a commitment to the promotion of equal opportunities for boys and girls within pilot schemes. Using a triangulated case study approach, this research seeks to explore, within a theoretical framework informed by feminist research and theory on gender and education, the development, implementation and impact of TVEI equal opportunities policy and

practice in one local education authority (LEA), from the dual perspectives of (a) policymakers (both at local authority and school level) and (b) the young people involved in the second year of the pilot scheme. With regard to the former perspective, methods have included the analysis of archive documentation and interviews with key local authority personnel; and with regard to the latter, the analysis of careers service destinations data, questionnaire data and data from indepth interviews, conducted at various stages up to two-and-a-half years after leaving school. In particular, the research seeks to understand the nature of the underlying philosophy/philosophies reflected in the equal opportunities developments of the LEA in question, and the impact this has had on the young people involved, and the implications of this for the promotion of equal opportunities work within a feminist framework.
Published Material: NEW, S.J. (1990). The destinations of 1989 leavers from the five TVEI pilot schools. (Working Paper). City of Salford Education Department (14-19 Development Unit).; NEW, S.J. (1990). The Salford school leavers survey: a report based on the experiences of 1989 leavers from the five TVEI pilot schools. (Working Paper). City of Salford Education Department (14-19 Development Unit).
Status: Individual research
Date of Research: 1990-1993
KEYWORDS: equal education; gender equality; transition education; TVEI

10/0545
> Department of Educational Research, Cartmel College,
> Bailrigg, Lancaster LA1 4YW
> 01524 65201
> Fulton, O. Prof.

Enterprise in higher education: evaluation
Abstract: This is a rolling evaluation of enterprise in higher education at Lancaster University. The first year investigated organisational and implementation issues, using interviews with staff. The second year focused on student experiences, using interviews with students. The third year looked at institutional diffusion and impact using staff and student interviews and student questionnaires.
Status: Sponsored project
Source of Grant: Training, Enterprise and Education Directorate £35,000
Date of Research: 1988-1993
KEYWORDS: enterprise education; higher education; programme evaluation; work-education relationship

10/0546
> Department of Educational Research, Cartmel College,
> Bailrigg, Lancaster LA1 4YW
> 01524 65201
> Knight, P. Dr

A comparative study of outcomes and process in English higher education
Abstract: This is a comparative study of the outcomes of higher education institutions and universities. Although there has been plentiful research into student learning in higher education, and consequent recommendations for effective teaching, it does not readily allow explanation of the performance of public sector institutions in the 1980s. In a decade where student expenditure has remained below that of the university sector (allowing for research funding), when public sector student numbers have burgeoned, and when staff-student ratios have become less favourable, the number and proportion of 2:1 and 1st class degrees have also grown on a sector-wide basis as compared to universities. The study attempts to find out why this should be. The focus is upon academic departments teaching the same subject. The usual forms of input and process data are to be collected, but close attention is being given also to the structure of courses; to observation of teaching; and to the assessment of student performance leading to degree classification. The working hypothesis is that there are general, distinct differences in the teaching/learning processes in the two sectors (university:public).
Status: Individual research
Date of Research: 1991-1993
KEYWORDS: college effectiveness; higher education; outcomes of education; universities and colleges

10/0547
> Department of Educational Research, Cartmel College,
> Bailrigg, Lancaster LA1 4YW
> 01524 65201
> Goodyear, P. Dr

JITOL: Just In Time Open Learning
Abstract: Just in time open learning (JITOL) aims to explore the use of electronic communications networks and multimedia computer conferencing in order to support continuing professional development and upating by skilled workers distributed throughout Europe. The lead partner in the project is NeuropeLab (in Archamps, France). Other partners include Logica, DEC, Credit Agricole, Dida*el and the universities of Lisbon and Namur.
Published Material: LEWIS, R., GOODYEAR, P. & BODER, A. (1992). Just In Time Open Learning: a DELTA project outline. Archamps, France: NeuropeLab. (Occasional Paper 92/1) (obtainable from Dr Goodyear at Lancaster University)
Status: Sponsored project
Source of Grant: European Community DELTA Programme £453,600
Date of Research: 1992-1994
KEYWORDS: communications; distance education; networks; open education; teleconferencing

10/0548
> Department of Educational Research, Cartmel College,
> Bailrigg, Lancaster LA1 4YW
> 01524 65201
> Johnson, R. Mr; Goodyear, P. Dr

DISCOURSE: Design & Interactive Specification of Courseware
Abstract: The goal of DISCOURSE is to build a set of computer-based tools to help the producers of computer-based learning materials work through the early stages of courseware design. Tools will be built to help with representing subject matter, teaching strategies and characteristics of target learners. Courseware designers will be able to work with a variety of presentational possibilities, including multimedia simulations. The project builds on earlier work in the EC DELTA projects TOSKA and Simulate. The lead partner for DISCOURSE is Dornier (part of Deutsche Aerospace).
Status: Sponsored project
Source of Grant: European Community DELTA Programme £256,900
Date of Research: 1992-1994
KEYWORDS: artificial intelligence; computer assisted learning; educational materials; material development

10/0549
> Department of Educational Research, Cartmel College,
> Bailrigg, Lancaster LA1 4YW
> 01524 65201
> Machell, J. Ms; *Supervisor:* Saunders, M. Dr

The reconstruction and transfer of learning: teaching for effective learning in higher education
Abstract: 'Transfer of learning' is a much used but misused phrase. 'Transfer' represents a facile, inflexible and surface approach to learning which has limited use value. In contrast 'reconstructing learning' – applying previous learning creatively in new contexts – offers far more potential benefits and it is this ability, rather than simple transfer, which instructional strategies should aim to develop. The research will (1) identify the key differences between transfer and reconstruction; (2) establish connections between current educational concerns and reconstruction; (3) examine key theories of learning which contribute to an understanding of reconstruction; (4) explore the ways in which teaching in higher education facilitate reconstruction; (5) discuss the implications of reconstructions for teaching methods in higher education.
Status: Individual research
Date of Research: 1989-1993
KEYWORDS: higher education; prior learning; transfer of learning

10/0550
> Department of Educational Research, Cartmel College,
> Bailrigg, Lancaster LA1 4YW
> 01524 65201
> Rogers, C. Dr; *Supervisor:* Rogers, C. Dr; Galloway, D. Prof.

Learned helplessness and self-worth motivation in children with special educational needs

Abstract: The project aims to identify: (1) the prevalence of the motivational styles of mastery orientation, self-worth motive and learned helplessness in pupils in two secondary schools and their feeder primary schools; (2) the degree to which the distribution of styles varies in children with special needs contrasted to whole populations; (3) changes in prevalence of style over time in a longitudinal sample; (4) changes in prevalence across year groups with cross-sectional samples; (5) differences between curriculum areas with regard to the prevalence of motivational styles; and (6) to examine the degree to which factors associated with school (e.g. school attended, teacher) influence the prevalence of each style. Theoretical developments by Weiner, Nicholls and Covington provide a general background to the research. The sample consists of all children in the final year of 12 primary schools who are followed into years seven and eight in two secondary schools. Further cross-sectional samples are obtained with pupils in years nine and eleven in the secondary schools. Information about motivational style is obtained from analysis of children's performance on curriculum related tasks in mathematics and English. Additional information is obtained from questionnaires completed by pupils and teachers. Pupil attainment data is used to identify children with special needs and also to allow comparisons between motivational style and achievement levels. A sub-sample of children have been interviewed. Data analysis has been, largely, completed. Initial results suggest increases in maladaptive motivational styles consequent upon transfer to secondary schools, and differences in proportion of pupils showing maladaptive styles as a function of the curriculum subject.
Status: Sponsored project
Source of Grant: Economic and Social Research Council £84,280
Date of Research: 1991-1993
KEYWORDS: *helplessness; motivation; self-esteem; special educational needs*

10/0551
Department of Educational Research, Cartmel College,
Bailrigg, Lancaster LA1 4YW
01524 65201
McCulloch, G. Prof.

Tripartism and education in 20th century Britain

Abstract: This research project is designed to explore the tripartite distinctions in educational provision in 20th century Britain, and how they have been reconstructed and developed in the final decades of the century. The theme of 'education for leadership' originally associated with the 19th century public school has been one focus of the research. The attempts to promote a 'respectable' form of technical education, for example through the post-war secondary technical schools, has provided another. Lastly the tradition of working class schooling seen in the central schools and secondary modern schools is an important theme for further research. Continuities and shifts in emphasis underlying policy documents such as Hadow in the 1920s, Spens in the 1930s, Norwood in the 1940s, and Crowther in the 1950s. The relationships between these and the educational policies of the 1980s-90s are another aspect of the research project.
Published Material: McCULLOCH, G. (1989). The secondary technical school: a usable past? London: Falmer Press.; McCULLOCH, G. (1991). Philosophers and kings: education for leadership in modern England. Cambridge: Cambridge University Press.
Status: Individual research
Date of Research: 1987-continuing
KEYWORDS: *educational administration; educational history; educational policy; public education; secondary education; tripartite system*

10/0552
Department of Educational Research, Cartmel College,
Bailrigg, Lancaster LA1 4YW
01524 65201
Jackson, C. Ms; *Supervisor:* Rogers, C. Dr

Is the sex-type of an individual an influencing factor in teacher-pupil interaction and motivational style amongst school children?

Abstract: Evidence demonstrating sex-differences in motivational style and teacher-pupil interaction is now well documented. The aim of this research is to consider the importance of sex-type (masculine, feminine, androgynous or undifferentiated, as defined by the BEM Sex Role Inventory, 1978), on these two areas. Is sex-type a more useful and predictive concept than biological sex? The tests developed by Craske (1988) are the intended tool to identify motivational style amongst samples of secondary school children in the two key areas of mathematics and English. The BEM Sex-Role Inventory is selected to identify sex-type. Teacher perceptions of the sex-type of children may be identified using a short pupil rating scale completed by the teacher.
Status: Individual research
Date of Research: 1991-continuing
KEYWORDS: *motivation; sex differences; sexual identity; teacher-pupil relationship*

10/0553
Department of Educational Research, Cartmel College,
Bailrigg, Lancaster LA1 4YW
01524 65201
Armstrong, D. Mr; *Supervisor:* Galloway, D. Prof.

The assessment and statementing of children with emotional and behavioural difficulties: child and parent perspectives

Abstract: A sample of 29 children, who were being assessed under the Education Act 1981 because of emotional and behavioural difficulties, was identified for an indepth case study of the assessment procedures. The research focused in particular on the perspectives of the children and their parents. The research had 3 aims: (1) to examine the perspectives of children and their parents on the procedures for assessing special educational needs; (2) to describe and provide a theoretical account of the concept of emotional and behavioural difficulties informed by the perspectives of children and their parents; (3) to describe and provide a theoretical analysis of sources of conflict and agreement between clients and professionals and to consider the implications of these for conceptualisations of the client-professional relationship.
Published Material: ARMSTRONG, D., GALLOWAY, D. & TOMLINSON, S. (1991). 'Decision-making in psychologists' professional interviews', Educational Psychology in Practice, Vol 7, No 2, pp.82-87.; ARMSTRONG, D. & GALLOWAY, D. (1992). 'On being a client: conflicting perspectives on assessment'. In: BOOTH, T., SWANN, W., MASTERSON, M. & POTTS, P. (Eds). Policies for diversity in education. London: Routledge/Open University.; ARMSTRONG, D. & GALLOWAY, D. 'Who is the child psychologist's client? Responsibilities and Options for psychologists in educational settings', Association for Child Psychology and Psychiatry Newsletter. (forthcoming).; Details of proposed publications are available from the researcher.
Status: Individual research
Date of Research: 1989-1993
KEYWORDS: *behaviour disorders; emotional disturbances; special educational needs; statements – special educational needs*

10/0554
Department of Educational Research, Cartmel College,
Bailrigg, Lancaster LA1 4YW
01524 65201
McCulloch, G. Prof.

Education and the working class: history, theory, policy and practice

Abstract: The project seeks to identify and explore a tradition of working class secondary education in modern Britain. It will assess its origins, its character, its wider influence, and its longer-term significance. The working hypothesis is that this tradition has been related to different forms of educational provision that have been developed over the past century, especially in the higher grade schools, the central schools, and the secondary modern schools. The aim is to study the curriculum, pedagogy, pupils, examinations and class relationships that developed in each of these types of schools, as well as changing policies and attitudes towards them. The underlying continuities are related to policy and provision especially in secondary education but also at other levels of educational provision in the 1990s, to examine how far the forms, assumptions and relationships that underlay these earlier types of provision have survived to play a part in our current outlooks and methods.
Status: Sponsored project
Source of Grant: Leverhulme Trust £42,400
Date of Research: 1992-continuing
KEYWORDS: *educational history; educational policy; educational principles; school systems; secondary education; secondary modern schools; tripartite system; working class*

10/0555

Department of Educational Research, Cartmel College,
Bailrigg, Lancaster LA1 4YW
01524 65201
Ding, D. Mr; *Supervisor:* Fulton, O. Prof.

Enterprising higher education: links between higher education institutions and industrial, commercial sectors

Abstract: As a comparative study, this research focuses on mapping out the main trends over the past decade of higher education institutions (HEIs) links with industrial and commercial sectors in Britain and China, examining the rationales and attempting to find appropriate models for each. Through interviews with a selective sample of personnel numbering nearly 60 in HEIs in both countries; together with documentation review, this qualitative study illustrates a diversified picture of the present links respectively, where some interesting similarities are found. Meanwhile, differences of the links are also paid attention and probed, as obvious gaps remain between the two nations' fundamental social structures as well as educational systems. In sum, the current linkage at all levels would, against resistance, continue to exist since there is a growing recognition that this link is not only a channel eventually generating funds for the much needed HEI pool, particularly in a time when its main, central funding sources are dwindling in real terms, but also a vitality which animates higher education progress. However, at present the links have formulated a challenge in both HE frameworks, since its behaviours are generally alien, unfamiliar to many, and still on a trial base. This controversy has inevitably confronted traditional ethos long established in higher education. Currently found issues show that unless some all-round strategies and policies are available and in effect, the links for some HEIs would cause quality problems and put the health of those linking institutions in jeopardy.

Status: Sponsored project
Source of Grant: Overseas research studentship; Lancaster University studentship
Date of Research: 1989-1993
KEYWORDS: *enterprise education; industry-higher education relationship; institutes of higher education*

10/0556

Department of Educational Research, Cartmel College,
Bailrigg, Lancaster LA1 4YW
01524 65201
Nwaokolo, P. Mr; *Supervisor:* Saunders, M. Dr

Public construction of the status of teachers and teaching in Nigeria with special interest in vocational teachers: a case study of the Delta and Edo States of Nigeria

Abstract: This study arose following complaints as evidenced in the literature about poor public image and poor status of teachers in Nigeria. Its aim is to ascertain the extent of the problem, explore its nature and why it exists, with a view to proffering suggestions for the solution of the problem. The enquiry was carried out as a case study of the Edo and Delta States of Nigeria between January 1991 and September 1992. A total of 171 teachers, student-teachers, educational administrators, business and public administrators, professionals, clerks/artisans and typical village peasant farmers were interviewed in 9 major towns of Edo and Delta States. A questionnaire was also administered on 150 subjects, mainly to teachers and student-teachers. Its principal aim was to locate the teacher and the teaching profession on an occupational prestige ladder. Secondly, it aimed at identifying the social standing of the vocational teacher among colleagues in the same secondary school system. Data on the subject matter was also generated through documents, and more unobtrusive means such as monitoring radio commentaries and casual discussion with members of the public. The data is now being analysed but it is already clear that the poor status of teachers in Nigeria is traceable to unattractive conditions of service such as poor pay; salary irregularity; the unhelpful attitude of civil servants implementing policies that favour teachers; poor working environment; presence of a large number of unqualified teachers in the system; poor promotion, denial and/or delayed fringe-benefits; and non-professionalisation of teaching. Other factors which are a consequence of the earlier ones include poor teacher dedication to duty and unimpressive appearance and attitude that portray teaching as synonymous with poverty.

Published Material:
Status: Sponsored project
Source of Grant: European Community
Date of Research: 1990-1993
KEYWORDS: *Nigeria; professional recognition; status need; teacher attitudes; teachers; teaching profession*

10/0557

Department of Educational Research, Cartmel College,
Bailrigg, Lancaster LA1 4YW
01524 65201
Konting, M. Mr; *Supervisor:* Knight, P. Dr

Study of teacher effectiveness in the Malaysian secondary school

Abstract: Despite voluminous research findings in the literature on teacher effectiveness, its contribution, particularly from the theoretical and practical aspects is still being debated. This research is undertaken with the assumptions that teachers make a difference and that true knowledge of teaching is achieved by practice and experience in the classroom. The objectives of the study are to: (a) identify and determine the notion of teacher effectiveness; (b) examine and describe the effective teacher's teaching, and (c) study the planning and implementation of the teacher education programme, particularly on how the programme takes into account the notion of teacher effectiveness. A total of 41 effective lower secondary school teachers, nominated by educational authorities, who teach National Language (12 teachers), English (13 teachers), and Mathematics (16 teachers) are asked, through open-ended questionnaire and interview, to identify and to list the characteristics of an effective teacher, and to explain why such a characteristic is important for the teacher to be an effective teacher. They are also asked about what they do and do not do in teaching, and why. Classroom teaching of the subjects is also observed using a systematic classroom observation schedule. The results of the study indicate that there exists peculiar characteristics of effective teacher and specific effective teacher's teaching styles.

Status: Sponsored project
Source of Grant: Universiti Pertanian, Malaysia £2,400
Date of Research: 1991-1994
KEYWORDS: *Malaysia; secondary school teachers; teacher behaviour; teacher effectiveness; teaching styles*

10/0558

Department of Educational Research, Cartmel College,
Bailrigg, Lancaster LA1 4YW
01524 65201
Bray, R. Mr; *Supervisor:* Fulton, O. Prof.

An evaluation of career development courses in higher education

Abstract: There is evidence of a significant growth in careers education provision in higher education in recent years. Contributory causes may include: transfer from the experiences of secondary and further education (e.g. Technical and Vocational Education Initiative); influence of the Enterprise in Higher Education project with its focus on transferable personal skills; and policy responses to graduate unemployment. This research aims to identify the reasons for such growth, the nature of the provision and likely future trends. The research will involve two stages. Stage 1 involves a questionnaire to all United Kingdom institutions of higher education investigating extent of careers education content and aims. Stage 2 uses Stage 1 results to select a sample (6-10) of institutions for indepth follow up: interviews with management, teaching staff and students concerning course aims, content and outcomes.

Status: Individual research
Date of Research: 1991-continuing
KEYWORDS: *career education; higher education; vocational guidance*

10/0559

Department of Educational Research, Cartmel College,
Bailrigg, Lancaster LA1 4YW
01524 65201
Fulton, O. Prof.

Mature students' perceptions and performance of polytechnic degree courses

Abstract: Because of the increasing number of places available, coupled with the drop in birth rate more mature students enter higher education. However, they often face difficulties such as poor educational background and a more complex personal background. Such difficulties have been studied but not acted upon because mature students have been seen as an homogeneous group and their problems considered accordingly. Although research has shown that mature students' examination results compare favourably with traditional entry students, the researcher believes that they could perform better and, equally importantly, could enjoy their courses more if their particular needs were considered. Using a broadly phenomenological perspective, the researcher contends that within polytechnics many mature students do not get the type of education that best fits their needs, needs which have been created by their past experiences. By

studying different types of courses, with their contrasting styles and philosophies of teaching, in relation to categories of mature students we may better understand their needs. The research will involve statistically analysing questionnaires from around 600 mature degree students. Students' perceptions of higher education courses and the teaching styles used will be examined, and these perceptions related to their social and academic backgrounds and degree classification in order to establish any relationship between them. The findings will be used to assess through modelling the strength of the relationships between the various elements of the research, and thus gain an overview of the effects of specific types of courses on categories of mature students.
Status: Sponsored project
Source of Grant: Economic and Social Research Council
Date of Research: 1991-1994
KEYWORDS: academic achievement; educational experience; higher education; mature students; student attitudes

10/0560
> Department of Educational Research, Cartmel College,
> Bailrigg, Lancaster LA1 4YW
> 01524 65201
> McHugh, G. Ms; *Supervisor:* Saunders, M. Dr

Evaluation of the Lancashire Licensed Teachers Scheme
Abstract: This is a brief evaluation of the Lancashire Licensed Teachers Scheme which has been jointly delivered by Lancashire Local Education Authority and the two collaborating colleges of education, which has been running since September 1991.
Status: Sponsored project
Source of Grant: Lancashire Local Education Authority £37,000
Date of Research: 1992-1993
KEYWORDS: licensed teachers; preservice teacher education; programme evaluation; teacher qualifications; teaching profession

10/0561
> Department of Educational Research, Cartmel College,
> Bailrigg, Lancaster LA1 4YW
> 01524 65201
> Sambili, H. Dr; *Supervisor:* Saunders, M. Dr

Do school based vocational programmes work? a case study of employment related experiences of Kenya's 8-4-4 graduates
Abstract: Unemployment in Kenya was seen to be rising the fastest among school leavers; those most affected being from poor socio-economic backgrounds as they faced high parental expectations. The study sets out to investigate the employment related experiences of the first cohort of Kenya's recently adopted 8-4-4 vocationalised school curriculum. Three specific questions addressed were: (1) How did the value attribution tendency to their educational qualifications and experiences vary with time? (2) What were the relative roles of economic and cultural support factors (enabling factors) in the attempted application of the acquired functional skills by the school leavers? (3) What is the school leavers' perspective of the new system's potential in solving the unemployment problem? More than three hundred school leavers from a representative number of schools in one of Kenya's eight Provinces were contacted by postal questionnaires, using their home addresses (17 months after leaving school). Two hundred questionnaires were returned. Thirty four leavers were later interviewed (27 months after leaving school) in the field during the second phase of fieldwork. The conclusion of the research is that the new system was shown to be popular amongst most of the leavers but the application of any acquired skills was greatly constrained by the lack of economic and cultural support and that student behaviour is strongly influenced by socio-cultural factors such as the cultural stigmatisation against self-employment.
Status: Sponsored project
Source of Grant: Kenyan Ministry of Education £30,000
Date of Research: 1990-1993
KEYWORDS: Kenya; school leavers; school to work transition; unemployment; vocational education; youth employment

10/0562
> Department of Educational Research, Cartmel College,
> Bailrigg, Lancaster LA1 4YW
> 01524 65201
> Helsby, G. Ms; Rogers, C. Dr

Process and pressures in post-16 science uptake
Abstract: This investigation aims to explore the factors affecting the uptake of science courses post-16, particularly with regard to gender differences. Data will be gathered through a questionnaire, targeted at a sample group of Year 11 students, and through semi-structured interviews with students and science teachers in four schools.
Status: Sponsored project
Source of Grant: Blackpool TVEI Consortium £3,000
Date of Research: 1994-1994
KEYWORDS: choice of subjects; course selection – students; science education; sex differences; sixteen to nineteen education

10/0563
> Department of Educational Research, Cartmel College,
> Bailrigg, Lancaster LA1 4YW
> 01524 65201
> Helsby, G. Ms; Knight, P. Dr; McCulloch, G. Prof.;
> Saunders, M. Dr; Warburton, T. Mr

The professional culture of teachers and the secondary school curriculum
Abstract: The aims of this investigation are to: 1) develop a grounded theory of 'teacher professionalism' in its social, historical and comparative contexts; 2) gather data and information on how perceived changes in the control of secondary school curriculum policy and practice relate to the professional culture of teachers; 3) explore methodological issues relating to the gathering and analysis of teachers' views of their own 'culture' and 'professionalism'; 4) contribute to our knowledge of changes and continuities in the role of school teachers in the education system; 5) contribute to our understanding of the relationship between changing education policies and the development of professional practices in schools. Data will be gathered through documentary research and interviews with key informants at national level, as well as through indepth interviewing of 180 teachers in 3 chosen subject areas.
Status: Sponsored project
Source of Grant: Economic and Social Research Council £100,000
Date of Research: 1994-1994
KEYWORDS: educational change; secondary education; secondary school curriculum; secondary school teachers; teacher role; teaching profession

10/0564
> Department of Educational Research, Cartmel College,
> Bailrigg, Lancaster LA1 4YW
> 01524 65201
> Frank, F. Ms; Hamilton, M. Dr; McHugh, G. Ms

Evaluation of European funded initiatives, at Knowsley Community College, Merseyside
Abstract: This project is a rolling programme of evaluation for Knowsley Community College, covering European Community funded courses in progress at the College. Evaluation is formative and built into development of the courses so as to provide feedback at every stage. Methods include interviews, group discussions and questionnaires with students, tutors and management, collecting documentation of course outcomes and aims. The first phase of the project will be completed by the end of March 1994 and covers 4 courses – 2 Horizon courses, 1 new opportunities for women and 1 Euroform course. Approximately 50 students are covered by these courses.
Status: Sponsored project
Source of Grant: Knowsley Community College £10,000
Date of Research: 1994-continuing
KEYWORDS: colleges of further education; community colleges; course evaluation; European Community; international programmes

10/0565
> Department of Educational Research, Cartmel College,
> Bailrigg, Lancaster LA1 4YW
> 01524 65201
> Trowler, P. Mr; *Supervisor:* Fulton, O. Prof.; Saunders, M. Dr

Paradigm change or Robbins trap? Implementing aspects of a mass higher education system
Abstract: A single site case study of the implementation of the aspects of a mass higher education system in the UK, focusing on the credit framework. The study uses qualitative methodological techniques and is designed to elicit linkages between the various attitudes and perspectives of academic staff towards specific changes in higher education, their disciplinary background and their work practices.
Status: Individual research

Date of Research: 1991-continuing
KEYWORDS: access to education; credit transfer; educational change; higher education

10/0566

Department of Educational Research, Cartmel College, Bailrigg, Lancaster LA1 4YW
01524 65201
Kang, B. Mr; *Supervisor:* Goodyear, P. Dr
Automating key processes in instructional design: a requirements and evaluations study
Abstract: The research proposed will centre on an investigation of the scope and nature of automated instructional design (ID). ID is a complex task, with high-order cognitive demands. Much ID work is carried out by people who have relatively unsophisticated skills in the design of learning activities or learning events. Instruction can be even more complicated when the delivery medium is computer-based, as in traditional Computer Assisted Instruction/Computer Based Training (CAI/CBT) or in the use of simulations or multimedia learning environments. Yet computer-aided learning environments offer great potential, if properly used and efficiently developed, especially in the areas of technical training. In recent years, there have been a number of developments intended to reduce the demands placed on the designer of computer-based learning systems. An important distinction in this field is between tools which replace the work of the instructional designer (a strong interpretation of automation) and tools which empower the instructional designer by taking over some of the cognitive load of design work (a weaker interpretation of automation). This research project will include: a) a survey of the state-of-the-art in automated ID; b) the development of several models of ID practices; c) use of a state-of-the-art ID system, and design of some representative examples of computer-based learning materials; d) through (c), development of some scenarios within which key aspects of the usability of the system can be investigated; e) carrying out a carefully selected subset of such investigations; and f) synthesis of results from such investigations in order to (i) generate recommendations for future automated ID systems, and (ii) refine the available models of ID practices, particularly their cognitive demands.
Status: Individual research
Date of Research: 1993-continuing
KEYWORDS: computer assisted learning; computer system design; computer uses in education

10/0567

Department of Educational Research, Cartmel College, Bailrigg, Lancaster LA1 4YW
01524 65201
Lancaster University, Faculty Board of Teacher Education and Training, Charlotte Mason College, Ambleside, Cumbria LA22 9BB
01539 433066
Knight, P. Dr; Huggins, M. Mr
Looking at liaison: a study of the history curriculum liaison between National Curriculum key stages 2 and 3
Abstract: In 1995 the first cohort of primary pupils will have taken National Curriculum History through both key stages. If secondary schools are to achieve progression, effective liaison will be vital. An assessment of such links will be of interest to the Office for Standards in Education (OFSTED), schools and the wider community. The objectives of the research are: 1) identification of the extent to which systems of liaison are in place; 2) evaluation of effectiveness; 3) identification of problems and difficulties; 4) identification of models of good practice. The sample will be 18 secondary schools plus their feeder primary schools in contrasting urban and rural contexts. The timetable of the research project will be as follows: Spring 1994 – Pilot interviews with primary teachers. Summer 1994 – Pilot interviews with heads of department in 6 secondary schools; framing of questionnaire for primary schools. Summer 1995 – Interviews with further 12 secondary schools; sending of primary feeder school questionnaires; interviews with feeder primary schools; collection of data on liaison meetings, examples of records etc.; interim analysis and writing up. Autumn 1995 – Questionnaire for children in Year 7 secondary classes, examining the rhetoric and reality of continuity and progression; final analysis and writing up of work.
Status: Sponsored project
Source of Grant: Lancaster University £10,000
Date of Research: 1994-continuing

KEYWORDS: cooperation; developmental continuity; history; national curriculum; primary secondary education

10/0568

Department of Educational Research, Cartmel College, Bailrigg, Lancaster LA1 4YW
01524 65201
London University, Goldsmiths College, Department of Advanced and Continuing Education, New Cross, London SE14 6NW
0171 919 7171
Bergin, S. Ms; Hamilton, M. Dr; O'Mahony, C. Ms; Moss, W. Ms
Open learning in adult basic education
Abstract: The open learning project has involved students, teachers and organisers in adult basic education (ABE) to explore: 1) how people make choices about the places and ways they learn; 2) what helps or blocks learning in ABE; 3) what makes learning 'open' or 'closed'; how specially funded open learning centres offer different ways of learning from the more established ABE programmes. The researchers carried out a national questionnaire survey of open learning centres and established ABE programmes and chose six case study sites to work with in depth using student and staff interviews, observation and discussion groups. Staff conferences and a residential writing weekend for students involved in the research were an integral part of the project.
Published Material: BERGIN, S. & HAMILTON, M. (1994). 'Who's at the centre: open learning in adult basic education'. In: THORPE, M. & GUDGEON, D. (Eds). Open learning at the centre. Harlow: Longmans.
Status: Sponsored project
Source of Grant: Higher Education Funding Council £44,000
Date of Research: 1991-1994
KEYWORDS: adult basic education; open education

10/0569

Department of Educational Research, Cartmel College, Bailrigg, Lancaster LA1 4YW
01524 65201
Reading University, Faculty of Education and Community Studies, Department of Education and Management Studies, Bulmershe Court, Woodlands Avenue, Earley, Reading RG6 1HY
01734 875123
Deem, R. Prof.; Brehony, K. Dr; New, S. Ms
Reforming school governing bodies: a sociological investigation
Abstract: School governing bodies in England and Wales were reshaped in the autumn of 1988 as a result of the 1986 (No 2) Education Act, with greater parental representation and more co-opted governors (including those from the business community). The 1986 Act and the 1988 Education Act have also given governors more power over schools than previously. The project is an indepth study of ten school governing bodies (four primary and six secondary) in two local education authorities. A pilot study ran from October 1988 to January 1990. The research has monitored what coping strategies governing bodies are using to deal with the tasks and responsibilities given to them by the new educational legislation and has also focused on the identification of power relations (including gender and race/ethnicity), decision making processes and networks of influence operating in the eight governing bodies. The project also, in addition, seeks to discover whether co-opted governors and parent governors (widely described as 'consumer') come to predominate over those sometimes termed 'producer' governors (teacher and local education authority representative) and headteachers. The work has been done through observation of formal, informal and sub-committee meetings, questionnaires and interviews.
Published Material: DEEM, R. (1993). 'Education reform and school governing bodies in England: old dogs, new tricks or new dogs, new tricks?'. In: PREEDY, M. & GLATTER, R. (Eds). Managing the effective school. London: Paul Chapman.; DEEM, R. & BREHONY, K.J. (1993). 'Governing bodies and local education authorities: who shall inherit the earth?', Local Government Studies, Vol 19, No 1, pp.56-76.; DEEM, R. & BREHONY, K.J. (1993). 'Consumers and education professionals in the organisation and administration of schools: partnership or conflict?', Educational Studies, Vol 19, No 3, pp.339-355.; DEEM, R., BREHONY, K.J. & NEW, S. (1993). 'Education for all? Three schools go to market'. In: WALLACE, G. (Ed). Decentralised management in education. Bournemouth: Hyde

Publications.; NEW, S. (1993). 'The token teacher: school governing bodies and teacher representation', International Studies in the Sociology of Education, Vol 3, No 1, pp.69-90.
Status: Sponsored project
Source of Grant: Economic and Social Research Council £56,720
Date of Research: 1990-1993
KEYWORDS: local management of schools; parent participation; participative decision making; school-based management; school governing bodies; school governors

10/0570

Department of Management Learning, Gillow House, Bailrigg, Lancaster LA1 4YX
01524 65201
Armitage, S. Ms

Management learning from computer-based management simulations/games

Abstract: This research has arisen from an initial study carried out by the researcher that identified computer-based simulations/games as the main use of information technology (IT) in UK business schools. The research focuses on participant perceptions of learning from computer-based management simulations in cases taken from three European business schools in the UK, France and the Netherlands. A current lack of qualitative research regarding participant views of their learning from simulations is highlighted and the need for such research is argued. This leads to the central research question explored: "What are participant perceptions of learning and experiences of computer-based management simulations?" The qualitative methodology involved in gathering the data made use of semi-structured interviews with a small number of participants and the tutors in each institution. Open ended questionnaires were distributed to other participants to gather supplementary data. An understanding of student learning from the general literature on learning is developed and claims made in the specific literature regarding student learning from simulations are then examined. Comparison between tutors' intentions for student learning and students' perceptions of their own learning is made. Three biases in students' perceptions of their learning emerge from the data: 1) technique; 2) people/self; 3) unbiased. A number of unexpected emphases in outcome and unexpected outcomes are identified from data regarding the experience of the simulation. Possible causes for this are proposed. Illustrations from the data are used to support the arguments made and the implications for management educators is explored. The role of management simulations in management education is also explored.
Published Material: ARMITAGE, S. 'Guidelines for enhancing learning opportunities in computer-based management simulations'. In: JONES, K. Icebreakers: sourcebook of innovative simulations, exercises, puzzles and games. London: Kogan Page. (in press).
Status: Individual research
Date of Research: 1992-continuing
KEYWORDS: business education; computer simulation; computer uses in education; management studies

10/0571

Department of Psychology, Cartmel College, Bailrigg, Lancaster LA1 4YW
01524 65201
Ridgway, J. Dr; Passey, D. Mr

Supporting technology across the curriculum

Abstract: This project aims to accelerate the use of information technology (IT) in schools. It has involved collaboration with local education authorities (LEAs), schools, and government bodies, notably the National Council for Educational Technology. It sets out to identify key factors in the range of current and projected support mechanisms at a national level, in LEAs and in schools – loosely characterised as levers for change, and barriers to success. A wide variety of information sources have been used, notably: surveys and interviews in and across schools, with trainee teachers, advisory teachers and advisers, as well as analyses of published documents. Resource materials and procedures (such as maps of the loci of IT in the National Curriculum; inservice teacher education (INSET) guides; distance learning materials to support whole school development; and assessment schemes) have been developed in order to promote appropriate forms of innovation, via extensive experimentation, school consultancies, and in-situ observation. These resources share the common characteristics of providing detailed feedback to different agents (teachers, departments, coordinators, whole schools, advisory teachers, advisers) about success and failure in different

domains (classroom practice, pupil attainment, policy coherence, INSET provision) and offer supportive documentation and guidance to improve current practices. They have all been subjected to robust trialling in schools.
Published Material: RIDGWAY, J. & PASSEY, D. (1991). Effective inservice education for teachers in information technology: a school's guide. Coventry: National Council for Educational Technology.; DUNN, S. & RIDGWAY, J. (1991). 'Computer use during primary school teaching practice: a survey', Journal of Computer Assisted Learning, Vol 7, No 1, pp.7-17.; DUNN, S. & RIDGWAY, J. (1991). 'Naked into the world: IT experiences on a final primary school teaching practice: a second survey', Journal of Computer Assisted Learning, Vol 7, No 4, pp.229-240.; PASSEY, D. & RIDGWAY, J. (1992). Effective inservice education for teachers in information technology: a resource for INSET providers. Newcastle: Northern Micromedia.; PASSEY, D. & RIDGWAY, J. (1992). 'Consultancy: supporting schools through interesting times', Computer Education, No 70, pp.8-14.
Status: Sponsored project
Source of Grant: Training Agency £300,000; Contracts: NCET; NCC; commercial companies; LEAs; individual schools
Date of Research: 1988-continuing
KEYWORDS: computer uses in education; cross curricular approach; curriculum development; information technology

10/0572

Faculty Board of Teacher Education and Training, Charlotte Mason College, Ambleside, Cumbria LA22 9BB
01539 433066
Light, R. Mr

Mathematics – shape & space: mathematics & art

Abstract: The project looks at cross-curricular links for mathematics and art, studying children's spatial development in the context of both their mathematics and drawing abilities, the development of spatial representation within art history and their relationship with cognitive development.
Status: Individual research
Date of Research: 1991-continuing
KEYWORDS: art; art history; cognitive development; cross curricular approach; mathematics; spatial ability

10/0573

Faculty Board of Teacher Education and Training, Charlotte Mason College, Ambleside, Cumbria LA22 9BB
01539 433066
Hegarty, P. Dr; Hegarty, P. Mrs

The Two Degrees – a comparative study of former students and first post headteacher satisfaction with initial teacher education at Charlotte Mason College

Abstract: The Council for the Accreditation of Teacher Education (CATE) criteria for primary initial teacher education have occasioned very significant changes in B.Ed. applied teacher education courses. This study aims to illuminate the levels of student and first post headteacher satisfaction with students' initial training. The methods include surveys of the whole output from Charlotte Mason College of the last two cohorts of Applied B.Ed. and the first two cohorts of Subject Studies B.Ed., and observations and interviews with a small sample each year.
Status: Sponsored project
Source of Grant: Charlotte Mason College £300
Date of Research: 1989-1993
KEYWORDS: B.Ed. degrees; participant satisfaction; preservice teacher education; probationary teachers; student teachers; teaching experience

10/0574

Faculty Board of Teacher Education and Training, Charlotte Mason College, Ambleside, Cumbria LA22 9BB
01539 433066
Alker, D. Mr; *Supervisor:* Postle, M. Dr

The identification of prerequisites for effective teacher mobility between Germany and the United Kingdom

Abstract: The project will develop, implement, monitor and evaluate a training programme in consultation with local education authorities (LEAs) for the induction and transfer training of European Community (EC) trained teachers. The aims of the training programme are: (1) to introduce an appropriate range of teaching methods and styles

to obtain a better match in teaching approaches; (2) to familiarise EC teachers with the National Curriculum; (3) provide support in meeting the language demands in both general communication skills and the language of the classroom; (4) develop confidence in coping with the demands of cultural and social difference. A major focus of the training programme will be school-based training in association with participating schools and LEAs
Status: Sponsored project
Source of Grant: Department of Education and Science £20,000
Date of Research: 1989-1993
KEYWORDS: European Community; Germany; teacher mobility; teacher transfer; training

10/0575
  Office of Adult Continuing Education, The Storey Institute, Lancaster LA1 1TH
  01524 849494
  Geale, J. Mr; *Supervisor:* Percy, K. Dr
Stimulating the demand for Continuing Professional Development (CPD) by young professionals in the north west of England
Abstract: The project is development rather than research. It will identify, design and pilot specific activities which support qualified professionals in continuing their personal and career development. Some 150 young professionals will participate in the development of at least 5 activities which cut across occupational boundaries.
Status: Sponsored project
Source of Grant: Training, Enterprise and Education Directorate £73,000
Date of Research: 1993-continuing
KEYWORDS: continuing education; lifelong learning; professional continuing education; professional development

10/0576
  Office of Adult Continuing Education, The Storey Institute, Lancaster LA1 1TH
  01524 849494
  Withnall, A. Ms; Percy, K. Dr
Good practice in the education and training of older adults
Abstract: The aims of the project were to: 1) review and analyse the literature on targeted educational provision for older adults in order to define good practice; 2) identify and document good practice through a review of 7 selected case studies, drawn from the fields of statutory, voluntary and commercial provision; 3) evaluate these case studies in order to construct guidelines for good practice. The conclusions were that: 1) the term 'older adults' is insufficient to describe the post-work population; 2) learning opportunities should be available to all who are post-work; 3) older people's experience and capabilities for self-help and mutual support are the key factors in the design of learning opportunities; and 4) educational provision must take account of the changing context in which older people live and the changing experiences of different cohorts as they move into later life.
Published Material: WITHNALL, A. & PERCY, K. (1994). Good practice in the education and training of older adults. Aldershot: Avebury Press.
Status: Individual research
Date of Research: 1993-1994
KEYWORDS: adult education; older adults

10/0577
  Office of Adult Continuing Education, The Storey Institute, Lancaster LA1 1TH
  01524 849494
  Withnall, A. Ms; Percy, K. Dr; Hamilton, M. Dr
Older adults' needs and usage of numerical skills in everyday life
Abstract: The project aims to: 1) explore what numerical skills older adults (over 60) most commonly use in everyday life; 2) investigate whether there are points at which older people need to acquire new numerical skills; 3) make recommendations about the role which adult continuing education could most usefully play in facilitating learning opportunities in numerical skills for older adults. The methodology will include: 1) Diary keeping by sample of 10 older people of different ages to ascertain skills most often required. 2) Interviews with 3 groups of older people (10 in each group) in 3 different locations (urban, rural, seaside) in the north west of England. 3) Analysis of newspaper reporting of the 1993 Budget (November) and older people's understanding of it (sub-project).

Status: Sponsored project
Source of Grant: Universities Funding Council
Date of Research: 1992-1994
KEYWORDS: adult education; life skills; numeracy; older adults

10/0578
  Office of Adult Continuing Education, The Storey Institute, Lancaster LA1 1TH
  01524 849494
  Percy, K. Dr; Withnall, A. Ms; Burton, D. Dr
Adult self-directed learning and implications for formal providers of continuing education
Abstract: The aims of this project are to: 1) examine the prevalence and conditions of adult self-directed learning among adults in the United Kingdom in different social strata; 2) explore the inter-relationships between adult self-directed learning and learning in formal and non-formal settings; and 3) identify implications of the findings for formal providers of continuing education. Key questions shaping empirical work include: 1) Why do adults choose to learn on their own? 2) What are the processes of adult self-directed learning? 3) Do adults in different social strata and different life situations engage in self-directed learning differently? 4) How does one evaluate quality in self-directed learning? The main study is focusing upon the self-directed learning activity of two groups of adults: a) informal carers in the community; and b) adults who are largely housebound. There will be 15 interviewees in each group.
Status: Sponsored project
Source of Grant: Universities Funding Council
Date of Research: 1992-1994
KEYWORDS: adult education; adult learning; caregivers; disabilities; independent study; lifelong learning

Leeds Metropolitan University

10/0579
  Faculty of Cultural and Education Studies, Teacher Education Studies, Beckett Park, Leeds LS6 3QS
  01132 832600
  Abou El-Khir, M. Mr; *Supervisor:* Perkin, R. Dr; Long, J. Mr; Duffield, B. Mr
The use of resources in the development of learning through drama in education in primary schools
Abstract: The study seeks to examine the assertion that the use of theatre resources (such as lighting, costume, properties, sound effects etc.) enhances the symbolic fictitious world created in educational drama sessions thereby influencing learning outcomes. A localised survey followed by selective interviews will provide data relating to the attitudes of primary teachers to the assertion. The assertion itself will be tested through action research and participant observation, culminating in a case study of drama practice with a particular class of primary children.
Status: Sponsored project
Source of Grant: Egyptian Education Bureau
Date of Research: 1990-1994
KEYWORDS: drama education; dramatics; learning processes; primary education; theatre arts

10/0580
  Faculty of Cultural and Education Studies, Teacher Education Studies, Beckett Park, Leeds LS6 3QS
  01132 832600
  Zeng, J. Ms; *Supervisor:* Martin, P. Mr; Roper, E. Mr; Long, J. Mr
Ethnic minority students' participation in higher education in the UK
Abstract: The aims of the research are to: a) examine trends in ethnic minority students' applications and admissions to UK higher education institutions, through an analysis of relevant research; b) analyse relevant policies (marketing, access, equal opportunities etc) at institutional level; and c) explore the experiences of ethnic minority students, and identify the factors that affect their experiences, in a sample of higher education institutions. Pilot studies will be carried out in two contrasting higher education institutions, to be followed by a national survey (the sample size and focus will depend on the

outcome of the pilot studies). Surveys, indepth interviews, group discussion and the analysis of documents will be used according to purpose at different stages of the research. It is intended that the findings of the research inform those responsible for decision-making in higher education institutions in relation to the participation of members of ethnic minorities, through a book to be published by the Higher Education Information Services Trust (HEIST).
Status: Sponsored project
Source of Grant: Higher Education Information Services Trust (HEIST) £9,000
Date of Research: 1993-continuing
KEYWORDS: access to education; equal education; ethnic groups; higher education; student experience; student recruitment

10/0581
Faculty of Cultural and Education Studies, Teacher Education Studies, Beckett Park, Leeds LS6 3QS
01132 832600
Welch, S. Ms; *Supervisor:* Roper, E. Mr; Sharp, A. Dr; Hall, A. Dr
Student teachers' learning about teaching and learning: the roles of reflection and personal theories
Abstract: The study seeks to investigate the relationship between students' approaches to learning and the process of reflecting on personal and public theories of teaching and learning. Of particular interest is the area of possible conflict between public and private theories and how students react to this conflict. Monitoring a group of nine B.Ed. primary students over the four years of their course will provide data relating to influences on their learning and ways they make sense of public and private theories. Methods of eliciting and analysing data will be within a personal construct theory framework.
Status: Individual research
Date of Research: 1993-continuing
KEYWORDS: learning strategies; learning theories; preservice teacher education; student teachers

10/0582
Faculty of Cultural and Education Studies, Teacher Education Studies, Beckett Park, Leeds LS6 3QS
01132 832600
Bird, D. Mr; *Supervisor:* Welch, S. Ms; Thomas, R. Mr; Shaw, M. Dr
The development and use of an expert system-based training tool for strategic management
Abstract: The aim is to create an expert system-based training tool for students of strategic management. Few expert systems are currently used as teaching tools and there is little discussion of success in facilitating the learning of users. The hypothesis behind this research is that expert systems are effective tools in the learning facilitation of strategic management and that a system of tests can ascertain whether a certain method of learning facilitation is more successful than another. Detailed aims of the research are to: 1) establish a method of integrating expert systems into teaching module; 2) discover the extent to which learning is affected by availability of an expert system in a teaching environment; and 3) discover the importance of student personality characteristics as factors affecting learning with expert systems. The experiment will be a group of 50 undergraduate hospitality students. The assessment methods used will provide a method of identifying the best method of integrating an expert system, and whether such a method of learning favours a certain type of personality. The tests implemented in the experiment will ascertain whether any link exists between case study results and the use of the expert system. They will also assess the level of learning which the expert system contributes to. The results will show whether this method of integrating expert systems into teaching regimes is effective, and what lessons can be drawn for other teaching regimes where incorporation of expert systems is considered.
Published Material: BIRD, D. (1992). 'Creating an expert system-based training tool for strategic management decision makers in the hospitality industry'. Proceedings of the International Association of Hotel Management Schools, Manchester, 1992.
Status: Individual research
Date of Research: 1991-1994
KEYWORDS: computer-assisted learning; computer uses in education; expert systems; management studies

10/0583
Faculty of Cultural and Education Studies, Teacher Education Studies, Beckett Park, Leeds LS6 3QS
01132 832600
Majid, M. Mrs; *Supervisor:* Valli, Y. Miss; Martin, P. Mr; Talbot, M. Prof.
Parental involvement: Asian parents and their children's schooling
Abstract: The aims of the research are to examine: 1) the views of Asian parents on parental involvement in their children's schooling; and 2) the role played by a school in involing Asian parents in their children's schooling. The research is in two stages. The first stage is an issue formulation stage where six primary schools will be studied to get an initial insight into parental involvement. The second stage will consist of a case study of one primary school using broad ethnographic principles of observation, semi-structured interviews and document analysis. Staff, pupils and parents will all be interviewed and, where appropriate, parents will be interviewed in their own languages.
Status: Individual research
Date of Research: 1993-continuing
KEYWORDS: Asians; ethnic groups; parent participation; parent-school relationship

10/0584
Faculty of Cultural and Education Studies, Teacher Education Studies, Beckett Park, Leeds LS6 3QS
01132 832600
Bramwell, A. Mrs; *Supervisor:* Bennett, H. Mr; Roper, E. Mr; Sharp, A. Dr
Teacher appraisal: comparative school case studies in one small, urban local education authority
Abstract: All the teachers within the particular local education authority have undergone a two-day training programme to be both appraisers and appraisees. The programme has been run by the same team from a university's department of education. The process for the two yearly cycle is laid down by the local authority (in line with the nationally agreed framework) and has been agreed with the local teaching unions. The hypothesis to be tested is that attitudes to appraisal, and the climate for a successful appraisal system, depend upon the management of the process within each school, and that despite a common framework there will be a vast range of experiences of appraisal amongst the teachers in the authority. The study will identify the differences in attitudes to appraisal, the differences in the management of the appraisal process and, where possible, the differences in the outcomes of the appraisal process in six different institutions within the authority. Selection of the schools is based on the broad variable of phase in addition to the narrower variables of size and culture. Questionnaires and interviews will be used in this naturalistic research and an executive summary of the six case studies will constitute the results of the enquiry.
Status: Individual research
Date of Research: 1994-continuing
KEYWORDS: teacher development; teacher effectiveness; teacher evaluation; teaching profession

10/0585
Faculty of Cultural and Education Studies, Teacher Education Studies, Beckett Park, Leeds LS6 3QS
01132 832600
Ball, D. Mr; *Supervisor:* Flintoff, A. Dr; Gilchrist, D. Ms; Talbot, M. Prof.
Educational change: the new right and the implications for equality of opportunity in a secondary school
Abstract: In recent years, education has become more politicised. It is an ideological arena in which the disparate tenets of the New Right are increasing their influence. Secondary schools have experienced swift and wide-ranging changes which may not be in the best interests of all pupils, or indeed staff. Therefore, the aim of the research is to understand the changing school culture, and to establish how those within the secondary sector ensure the disadvantaged and the powerless pupils are not further marginalised in these processes of educational change. The study is primarily ethnographic, focusing upon one school and its various constituencies. Methods used will include observation, indepth interview and document analysis.
Status: Individual research
Date of Research: 1993-continuing

KEYWORDS: educational change; educational policy; education-ally disadvantaged; equal education; politics education relationship; secondary schools

Leeds University

10/0586
Adult Education Centre, 37 Harrow Road, Middlesbrough, Cleveland TS5 5NT
01642 814987
O'Rourke, R. Ms; *Supervisor:* Croft, A. Dr
Creative writing in adult education
Abstract: This project is to compile an evaluative survey of creative writing activity in the Cleveland, North Yorkshire and West York-shire regions. The main point of contact is with the existing writers groups and WRITEAROUND, Cleveland's festival for readers and writers. A small scale survey of random responses to elicit how much local knowledge there is about creative writing opportunities has also been planned. The research is concerned with the experience of teaching and learning within creative writing and explores the differ-ent sites within which such activity takes place, and what its value is to participants. The research is exploring the extent to which creative writing activity can best be understood and evaluated as an arts or an educational activity. The research methods include interviews, group discussions, participant observation, and a literature search
Status: Sponsored project
Source of Grant: Universities Funding Council £32,103
Date of Research: 1992-1993
KEYWORDS: adult education; creative writing

10/0587
Centre for Studies in Science and Mathematics Education, Leeds LS2 9JT
01132 431751
University of Botswana, Department of Mathematics and Science Education, Postbag 0022, Gaborone, Botswana
Towse, P. Mr; Prophet, R. Mr; Kurup, P. Mr
Language in the learning of science
Abstract: This is a study exploring just some of the problems of learning science in a second language, including oral as well as written communication. Initial work is concentrating on the use of non-technical words in science. The study was first conducted among secondary pupils in Botswana and among Asian children in the Leeds/Bradford area of the UK, as well as among first language English speakers. Some of the early results caused the study to be extended to India and there are plans to extend it further in Southern Africa in the near future.
Status: Individual research
Date of Research: 1992-continuing
KEYWORDS: Botswana; language of instruction; languages for specific purposes; science education; scientific vocabulary; second language learning

10/0588
Centre for Studies in Science and Mathematics Education, Leeds LS2 9JT
01132 431751
Bassett, J. Mr; *Supervisor:* Wain, G. Mr
Key stage 1 of the National Curriculum in mathematics as it relates to infant schools in Huddersfield
Abstract: This research study will investigate the mathematics cur-riculum of 70 schools engaged in key stage 1 of the National Cur-riculum in Huddersfield. It will cover the background to the setting up of the National Curriculum and the philosophy which underpins it. It will involve looking at infant/first school models of the curric-ulum and, in particular, the mathematics curriculum and to relate these to the National Curriculum. The content of key stage 1 of the National Curriculum will be analysed and compared with the pre National Curriculum mathematics curriculum. Similarly the assessment com-ponent will be analysed in terms of assessment theory and pre National Curriculum assessment procedures in school. The influence of the Standard Assessment Tasks of school internal curriculum assessments and approaches to teaching methods will be ascertained. The results of the first unreported Standard Assessment Tasks and

the first reported Standard Assessment Tasks will be analysed in terms of what they mean in themselves and the affect on schools. The effects of the National Curriculum on the content of the mathematics curriculum in schools, internal assessment, and approaches to mathe-matics teaching will be assessed by means of a teacher questionnaire. This will be sent to all teachers involved in Key Stage 1 in 70 Huddersfield schools. A separate questionnaire will be sent to mathe-matics co-ordinators in the same schools. Selective interviews in a sample of the schools will be used to support the questionnaires. The questionnaires cover teacher opinions on effectiveness of National Curriculum INSET (Inservice Education of Teachers), areas where further training is needed, areas in which teachers feel confident/lack-ing confidence and resource needs to implement National Curriculum Mathematics.
Status: Individual research
Date of Research: 1989-1993
KEYWORDS: assessment; first schools; infant schools; mathematics curriculum; mathematics teachers; standard assessment tasks

10/0589
Centre for Studies in Science and Mathematics Education, Leeds LS2 9JT
01132 431751
Asoko, H. Mrs; Scott, P. Mr
Teaching and conceptual change study
Abstract: This project is undertaking research into teaching ap-proaches in science which are designed to take into account students' initial thinking and promote conceptual development or change. The study is informed by constructivist views of learning and is being carried out in collaboration with teachers at both primary and secon-dary school levels. The research is based upon detailed case studies which document both the thinking behind the teaching and also the conceptual development of the pupils during the teaching. At secon-dary level, studies are under way with key stage 3 (11-14 years) pupils in the topic areas of air pressure, chemical change and interdepen-dency. At primary level, key stage 2 (7-11 years) pupils have been involved in learning about light. The aim of the research is to develop better insights into the intellectual demands involved for pupils in developing science concepts and to explore how such analysis might aid planning and implementing science instruction.
Published Material: SCOTT, P.H., ASOKO, H.M., DRIVER, R.H. (1991). 'Teaching for conceptual change: a review of strategies'. In: DUIT, R., GOLDBERG, F. & NIEDDERER, H. (Eds). Research in physics learning: theoretical issues and empirical studies, Kiel, Ger-many.; SCOTT, P.H., ASOKO, H.M., DRIVER, R.H. & EMBER-TON, J. (1992). 'Working from children's ideas: an analysis of constructivist teaching in the context of a chemistry topic', Proceed-ings of an International Writing Workshop at Monash University, Australia, June.; ASOKO, H.M. (1993). 'First steps in the construc-tion of a theoretical model of light: a case study from a primary classroom'. In: NOVAK, J. (Ed). Proceedings of the Third Interna-tional Seminar: Misconceptions and Educational Strategies in Sci-ence and Mathematics. USA: Cornell University, Ithaca.; SCOTT, P.H. (1993). 'Overtures and obstacles: teaching and learning about air pressure in a high school classroom'. In: NOVAK, J. (Ed). Proceedings of the Third International Seminar: Misconceptions and Educational Strategies in Science and Mathematics. USA: Cornell University, Ithaca.
Status: Sponsored project
Source of Grant: Leeds University: School of Education £10,000
Date of Research: 1991-continuing
KEYWORDS: science education; scientific concepts; teaching methods

10/0590
Centre for Studies in Science and Mathematics Education, Leeds LS2 9JT
01132 431751
Scott, P. Mr; *Supervisor:* Driver, R. Prof.; Donnelly, J. Dr
Constructivist approaches to teaching and learning
Abstract: This research is investigating the interaction between teach-ing informed by a social constructivist perspective on learning and the development of science concepts by high school students. The methodology is based upon a multiple case study design and covers teaching and learning in three specific concept areas. The aim of the research is to develop better insights into the intellectual demands involved for students in developing science concepts and to explore how such analysis might aid planning and implementing science instruction.

Published Material: SCOTT, P.H., ASOKO, H.M. & DRIVER, R.H. (1991). 'Teaching for conceptual change: a review of strategies'. In: DUIT, R., GOLDBERG, F. & NIEDDERER, H. (Eds). Research in physics learning: theoretical issues and empirical studies, Kiel, Germany.; SCOTT, P.H., ASOKO, H.M. & DRIVER, R.H. & EMBERTON, J. (1992). 'Working from children's ideas: an analysis of constructivist teaching in the context of a chemistry topic', Proceedings of an international writing workshop at Monash University, Australia, June.
Status: Individual research
Date of Research: 1991-continuing
KEYWORDS: science education; scientific concepts; sociology of education; teaching methods

10/0591

Centre for Studies in Science and Mathematics Education, Leeds LS2 9JT
01132 431751
Scott, P. Mr; *Supervisor:* Driver, R. Prof.; Donnelly, J. Dr

An analysis of pedagogical processes relating to the development of science concepts in secondary school classrooms from a socio-cultural perspective

Abstract: The aim of this study is to draw upon a Vygotskian perspective on development and learning to interpret the ways in which high school students' understandings of particular science concepts develop through the influence of science teaching. The Vygotskian position maintains that all higher psychological processes, including particular forms of reasoning and the ability to understand and to apply concepts, originate in social interactions. It follows from this position that learning higher processes must therefore involve a process of internalisation; what initially exists in the social interactions of a particular culture must be internalised by the individual. In emphasising the transition from social to personal values and the part played by semiotic mechanisms in that process, the Vygotskian perspective on learning demands that the prime focus of investigation should be upon the interactions of the classroom. The focus is upon how pupils' understandings develop in the social, interactive environment of the classroom. The methodology is based upon an ethnographic case study approach in which the interactions of short sequences of lessons, focusing on the teaching and learning of particular science concepts, are documented in some detail. Two science concept areas (air pressure and rusting) are focused upon and two different classes of 13/14 year olds followed through each lesson sequence. It is anticipated that the outcomes of the research will be two-fold: 1) to better understand the processes involved in teaching and learning science concepts in a classroom environment by drawing upon Vygotskian theory; and 2) to develop and elaborate that theory through its application to contemporary science classroom contexts.
Published Material: SCOTT, P. (1993). 'Overtures and obstacles: teaching and learning about air pressure in a high school classroom'. In: NOVAK, J. (Ed). Misconceptions and educational strategies in science and mathematics. Proceedings of the Third International Seminar, Cornell University, Ithaca, USA, 1993.; SCOTT, P., ASOKO, H., DRIVER, R. & AMBERTON, J. (1994). 'Working from children's ideas: an analysis of constructivist teaching in the context of a chemistry topic'. In: FENSHAM, P.J., GUNSTONE, R. & WHITE, R. (Eds). The content of science: a constructivist approach to its teaching and learning. Basingstoke: Falmer Press.
Status: Individual research
Date of Research: 1991-continuing
KEYWORDS: concept formation; learning theories; science education; scientific concepts

10/0592

Centre for Studies in Science and Mathematics Education, Leeds LS2 9JT
01132 431751
Twigger, D. Mr; *Supervisor:* Driver, R. Prof.

A longitudinal study of the development of selected science concepts by pupils

Abstract: The overall aim of this study is to document and interpret the development of individual children's conceptual understandings. A fundamental question for consideration relates to whether or not different children pass through similar sequences or steps in their learning. The study will monitor the development of children's conceptual understanding in 2 selected topics in science (Light and The Earth in Space) throughout their secondary schooling. The input of classroom learning opportunities will be monitored. The data

obtained will be analysed relative to alternative models of progression in learning science. The central objective is to study the progress of a sample of 20 children from the ages of 11-16 through their secondary schooling, documenting their progress in conceptual understanding in the selected topics in science and comparing this progress to 'maps' established from previous cross-age studies. Tasks will be used to assess their conceptual understanding in the selected domains. These will be administered through interviews, which will be videotaped and transcribed. The tasks will be designed to elicit pupils' conceptions relating to presented phenomena by asking for predictions and/or explanations of events. In addition, the study aims to collect information about the learning experiences in science to which the children are exposed over the 5 year period in order to interpret progress in the light of learning opportunities.
Status: Individual research
Date of Research: 1992-continuing
KEYWORDS: concept formation; longitudinal studies; science education; scientific concepts

10/0593

Centre for Studies in Science and Mathematics Education, Leeds LS2 9JT
01132 431751
Kent, D. Mr; Byard, M. Mr; Holder, K. Mr

Education business partnerships

Abstract: The aims of the project were to: 1) increase the awareness and understanding between education and industry; 2) develop in newly qualified teachers the concept of workplaces as sites for learning; 3) develop long-term liaison between newly qualified teachers, schools and companies; 4) develop a range of classroom resource materials for use at National Curriculum key stages 3 and 4. The project involved four consortia consisting of three Postgraduate Certificate in Education (PGCE) technology students, an experienced teacher of technology and company mentors. The four companies were: Elida Gibbs, Yorkshire Water, J. Sainsbury PLC, and Calderdale Tourist Services. The partnership lasted for six months during which time both students and teachers spent time working both in and with the company/mentors. The four cohorts each developed a package of classroom resource materials based on a multimedia presentation. However, the personal and professional development of the participants was as important as the tangible products. The project was formally evaluated using semi-structured interview techniques.
Status: Sponsored project
Source of Grant: Teacher Placement Service; Unilever PLC; Leeds Training and Enterprise Council, jointly £5,000
Date of Research: 1993-1994
KEYWORDS: industrial secondments; industry education relationship; teacher development

10/0594

Centre for Studies in Science and Mathematics Education, Leeds LS2 9JT
01132 431751
University of Cape Coast, Department of Science Education, Cape Coast, Ghana Towse, P. Mr; Anamuah-Mensah, J. Dr

Science and technology in action in Ghana

Abstract: For too long, the science taught in schools and the science practised in industry have been perceived as quite different. Moreover, through a lack of awareness of what goes on in industry, teachers have tended to oversimplify the application of scientific knowledge and concepts. The time is right to bridge the gap between school and industry, and bring industrial applications of science and technology more into the mainstream of science teaching, particularly at the secondary level. To this end the aim is to help practising teachers by producing resource materials, both for teacher background reading and for classroom use, which put the science taught in school into an everyday context and link it more realistically with the practice of science in everyday life.
Published Material: TOWSE, P. & ANAMUAH-MENSAH, J. (1991). 'Science and technology in action in Ghana', Science Education International, Vol 2, No 2, pp.31-34.
Status: Sponsored project
Source of Grant: African Forum for Children's Literacy in Science and Technology £32,579
Date of Research: 1991-continuing
KEYWORDS: Ghana; industry-education relationship; science education

10/0595

Centre for Studies in Science and Mathematics Education,
Leeds LS2 9JT
01132 431751
University of Dar Es Salaam, Faculty of Education,
Department of Curriculum and Teaching, PO Box 35048,
Dar Es Salaam, Tanzania
010 255 5148135
Kent, D. Mr; Mushi, P. Mr

The education and training of artisans in the informal sector of Tanzania

Abstract: The aims of the project are to: 1) Identify and examine initiatives designed to assist in the development of the informal sector of the Tanzanian economy; 2) Examine the process(es) by which artisans are trained; 3) Examine the ways in which the training articulates in realistic ways with community and market needs; and 4) Make recommendations relating to the training needs of artisans to government and non-governmental agencies. A literature search, coupled with semi-structured interviews, will be employed to map this provision of training within Tanzania. Ethnographic instruments will be employed to gain an understanding of training methods. The study will use representative samples of training institutes drawn from three categories of providers: governmental, non-governmental, and private, and will include both rural and urban centres. The focus of the study is the training of mechanical and electrical artisans, although in the policy defining stage 'the training of artisans' will consider a broad range of skills/trades.

Status: Sponsored project
Source of Grant: Overseas Development Administration £30,000
Date of Research: 1994-continuing
KEYWORDS: skilled workers; Tanzania; training; vocational education

10/0596

Centre for Studies in Science and Mathematics Education,
Leeds LS2 9JT
01132 431751
York University, Department of Educational Studies,
Heslington, York YO1 5DD
01904 430000
Driver, R. Prof.; Scott, P. Mr; Millar, R. Dr; Leach, J. Mr

The development of children's understanding of the nature of science from 9 to 16

Abstract: Concern has been expressed about the growing gap in understanding and awareness between scientists on the one hand and the general public on the other. The aim of this study was to investigate the ways in which students of school age understood the workings of the scientific community and its relationship to society, and the nature and status of scientific knowledge. The study focused on the ways in which students represented various features of science. Five interview tasks were designed in which 30 pairs of students at ages 9, 12 and 16 discussed various features of science in familiar school science contexts. Groups of 16 year old students worked on tasks in which information about scientists was presented and discussed, as part of science lessons. Data analysis involved three stages: (i) identification of particular representations of science used in particular contexts; (ii) identification of age-related trends; (iii) identification of broader trends across a range of contexts. We identified a number of portrayals of scientific knowledge and enquiry, ranging from naive realism through correlational modelling to theoretical modelling. The most common view at each age tended to be correlational modelling (knowledge emerges from finding correlations between variables and phenomena). These views of scientific knowledge and enquiry influenced students' interpretations of the functioning of the scientific community. Findings from this study can inform curriculum decisions about sequencing and the nature of curricular interventions, as well as theoretical issues about the nature of progression in learning and the purposes of the science curriculum.

Published Material: Various publications are available from the Leeds University/York University Science Education Group.
Status: Sponsored project
Source of Grant: Economic and Social Research Council £70,000
Date of Research: 1991-1993
KEYWORDS: comprehension; science education; scientific concepts; scientific literacy

10/0597

Department of Adult Continuing Education, Leeds LS2 9JT
01132 431751

Payne, J. Dr; *Supervisor:* Ward, K. Mr; Forrester, K. Dr

The Leeds adult learners at work project

Abstract: The aims of the project are to study work-based learning to: (1) identify existing schemes and facilities by which employers cater for the continuing general education and training of their employees; (2) determine the factors that affect the success of such schemes; (3) explore the theoretical issues emerging which relate to adult learning at the workplace; (4) examine the policy issues relating to the development of lifelong learning; and (5) make international comparisons. In practical terms this will involve: gathering information about existing schemes; visiting existing schemes, together with interested individuals and organisations; and selecting a number of schemes in different kinds of enterprise for more detailed evaluation. Journal articles and a final report will be produced. An international conference on this topic will be held in Leeds from July 13-15 1993.

Status: Sponsored project
Source of Grant: Universities Funding Council
Date of Research: 1991-1993
KEYWORDS: adult education; labour force development; works schools

10/0598

Department of Adult Continuing Education, Leeds LS2 9JT
01132 431751
Taylor, R. Prof.

Continuing education practice in Canada and the United Kingdom: a case study of Calgary and Leeds Universities

Abstract: Continuing education provision in Canada and the United Kingdom operates on different models. This research analyzes assumptions, priorities, models, financing, curriculum approaches and outcomes in the two countries, using case study material for Calgary and Leeds.

Status: Sponsored project
Source of Grant: Alberta/Leeds Exchange Scheme £1,800
Date of Research: 1988-1994
KEYWORDS: adult education; Canada; comparative education; continuing education

10/0599

Department of Adult Continuing Education, Leeds LS2 9JT
01132 431751
Malcolm, J. Ms; *Supervisor:* Zukas, M. Ms; Gardiner, J. Ms

Policy and outcomes in women's education

Abstract: The aim of this research is to discover how policies on women's education have evolved over the last fifteen years; how far practice and outcomes have fulfilled policy aims; and the extent of the impact of courses for women on 'mainstream' continuing education. The research falls into two parts: (a) an analysis of policy initiatives over the period in question, relating these both to different strands of feminist thought and developments in other areas of social and educational policy; (b) a survey of current and past students on courses for women outside higher education, and of staff with responsibility for this provision, which will assess its effects both on individuals and on institutions.

Published Material: MALCOLM, J. (1992). 'The culture of difference: women's education re-examined'. In: MILLER, N. & WEST, L. (Eds). Changing cultures and adult learning. Canterbury: University of Kent, Standing Conference on University Teaching and Research into the Education of Adults, (SCUTREA).
Status: Individual research
Date of Research: 1991-continuing
KEYWORDS: access programmes; continuing education; educational benefits; educational objectives; women's education

10/0600

Department of Adult Continuing Education, Leeds LS2 9JT
01132 431751
Taylor, R. Prof.; Steele, G. Dr

An examination of the inter-relationship between the development of adult education, Gandhian philosophy, the Congress Party, and the legacy of the British Raj, in India between 1935 and 1955, and an analysis of subsequent developments in adult education in the period up to the 1980s

Abstract: This project concerns the influence of British cultural values, practices and structures on the development of adult education in India from the 1930s to the 1980s. British cultural legacy was not homogeneous, as with the industrial British society from which it sprang, its imperial strands were diverse and often conflicting. A major theme of the study will be to disentangle these various elements and to match them up both to the empirical development of adult education structures in India, and to the political dimensions of British culture in the UK. An essential concern will be the relationship between Gandhian philosophy and adult education development. Linked to this will be a study of the educational dimension to the emerging Congress Party as the dominant political force in India before, during and after Indian independence.

Published Material: TAYLOR, R. (1992). 'Contested concepts: The development of education in British India from the early years to 1920'. In: HAKE, B.J. & MARRIOTT, S. (Ed). Adult education between cultures: encounters and identities in European adult education since 1890, Leeds Studies in Continuing Education, Cross Cultural Studies in the Education of Adults, No 2. Leeds: University of Leeds.; TAYLOR, R. (1993). 'Educational policy and social development in India from 1947 to 1964: the ideology of Nehru and the Congress Party'. In: HAKE, B.J. & MARRIOTT, S. (Eds). Adult education between cultures: encounters and identities in European Adult Education since 1890. Leeds: University of Leeds, School of Education, Study of Continuing Education Unit.; TAYLOR, R. & STEELE, G. (1994). 'Against modernity: Gandhi and adult education', International Journal of Lifelong Education, Vol 13, No 1, pp.33-42.; TAYLOR, R. & STEELE, G. 'From empire to industry: the burden of modernisation in Indian adult education', International Journal of Lifelong Education. (in press).
Status: Sponsored project
Source of Grant: Universities Funding Council £42,000
Date of Research: 1989-1994
KEYWORDS: adult education; educational history; India

10/0601

Department of Adult Continuing Education, Leeds LS2 9JT
01132 431751
James, J. Mr; *Supervisor:* Forrester, K. Dr; Thorne, C. Mr
Training matters
Abstract: The objectives of the retail training project are to: (a) identify Union of Shop, Distributive and Allied Workers (Usdaw) members' awareness of and attitudes towards their vocational education and training (VET) needs; (b) report on the members' assessment of their vocational training experience, including the Retail Certificate and company specific schemes; (c) conduct a training needs analysis of Usdaw lay representatives and full-time officers to establish the skills and knowledge required to promote vocational training; (d) develop an action programme at national and local level designed to publicise the VET opportunities available in retailing and to encourage members to take up these opportunities; (e) produce suitable materials and pilot appropriate training courses for the Union's full-time officers and senior lay officials in order to familiarise them with the Retail Certificate (NVQ levels 1 – 4); (f) help increase the number of retail employees gaining recognised vocational training qualifications. Phase I (15 months) will involve the production of a major report resulting from a survey of members' attitudes, experience and perceptions of vocational training. This must cover NVQ/Scotree training, in-house company specific training and areas where training is limited or non-existent. Phase II (21 months) will consist of the production and piloting of material for promoting vocational education and training. The 'raw materials' for this phase will be the Phase I report together with the associated research.
Status: Sponsored project
Source of Grant: Distributive Industry Training Trust; Union of Shop, Distributive and Allied Workers, jointly £100,000
Date of Research: 1992-continuing
KEYWORDS: distributive trades education; National Vocational Qualifications; retailing; training; vocational education

10/0602

Department of Adult Continuing Education, Leeds LS2 9JT
01132 431751
Taylor, R. Prof.; Steele, G. Dr
Adult education, working class histories and popular culture 1945-1965
Abstract: The aim of this study is to understand the origins, nature and influence of the new approaches to working class history, popular formations, the 'national' culture and socialist politics which were produced in the work of adult educators in the post-war period. The pedagogic practice and publications of E.P. Thompson, Richard Hoggart and Raymond Williams during this period will be of special

interest as the 'founding fathers' of British cultural studies but they will be contextualised within the broader milieu. The work of other significant figures in adult education such as Thomas Hodgkin, Sidney Raybould, J.F.C. Harrison and Roy Shaw and their interrelationships will also be germane to the study. Methodologically, the study will examine a number of related aspects: (1) The milieu and practice of adult education in the immediate pre-war and post-war period, focusing on the departments of Leeds, Hull and Oxford and the debates in the Workers Educational Association (WEA) over class based versus 'popular' education and the sociological approach to arts teaching. (2) The privileging of the 'literary' and textual criticism as modes of political and social analysis in, for example, the Leavises and Scrutiny's agenda, George Orwell and a 'common culture' and Marxist cultural theory. Literary studies at Leeds and Cambridge. (3) The political context of adult education: the Cold War, the Labour government and the formation of the New Left.
Status: Sponsored project
Source of Grant: Universities Funding Council £80,000
Date of Research: 1992-1994
KEYWORDS: adult education; educational history; social history; working class

10/0603

Department of Adult Continuing Education, Leeds LS2 9JT
01132 431751
Salveson, P. Dr; *Supervisor:* Ward, K. Mr
Wyther Action Project: a community economic development plan for the Wyther estate in Leeds
Abstract: The project was based on detailed consultation with local residents to identify both skills and needs, of people on a deprived housing estate in west Leeds. Local people were involved in both the research and management of the project. Discussions were also held with local employers, government agencies and church/voluntary groups. The report made 19 key recommendations covering community business, training, youth projects, and cultural initiatives.
Published Material: SALVESON, P. (1992). Wyther Action Project: a community economic development plan for the Wyther Estate, Leeds.
Status: Sponsored project
Source of Grant: Leeds City Council: Department of Community Benefits and Rights £25,000
Date of Research: 1992-1992
KEYWORDS: community development; community programmes

10/0604

Department of Continuing Professional Education, Leeds LS2 9JT
01132 431751
Todd, F. Dr; Neale, P. Mrs
United Kingdom professions and the European challenge
Abstract: This is a 3 year, real-time study of British professionals, their employers and their institutions in a period of change. It has been examining the links established with other professional organisations within the European Community to analyse developing policies and practices towards Europe and how these might be affected by cross-national working relations. The first phase of this project was a comprehensive survey of 77 professional institutions whose members are affected by the First General Directive on the Mutual Recognition of Qualifications. The response rate was 74%. The second phase involved case studies of selected institutions and particular issues raised by the professions' response to Europe. The final stage included a follow-up survey of the original respondents to monitor change. The project culminated in an international conference 'Facing the European Challenge – the Role of the Professions in a Wider Europe', held in Leeds in July 1993. Data analysis suggests that the advent of the Single European Market is not as significant as one might have predicted for all the professions surveyed. Many have taken an international stand on their professional activities on behalf of their members for a substantial number of years. Professional institutions are aware of the opportunities and problems that may arise for their practitioners in the next few years and they are becoming increasingly active, particularly through European networks, on behalf of their members and of the publics they serve. There is also evidence of growing cross-border practice for a wide range of occupations.
Published Material: TODD, F. & NEALE, P. (1992). 'Professions without frontiers? The 'European Project' and UK professional associations', International Journal of Sociology and Social Policy, Vol

12, No 3, pp.26-57.; NEALE, P. (1993). 'Engineering change in the European Community', International Journal of Sociology and Social Policy, Vol 13, No 5-6, pp.1-21.
Status: Sponsored project
Source of Grant: Universities Funding Council £114,091
Date of Research: 1990-1994
KEYWORDS: European Community; professional associations; professional continuing education; qualifications; Single European Market

10/0605
Department of Social Policy and Sociology, Leeds LS2 9JT
01132 431751
Harrison, M. Dr; Law, I. Dr
Ethnic monitoring of undergraduate admissions processes and performance
Abstract: This research involved statistical analysis and interviews focused on entry to case study degree schemes at Leeds University. A paper has been produced for the University's Department of Social Policy and Sociology Working Papers series and is available, price four pounds fifty pence (including postage and packing).
Status: Sponsored project
Source of Grant: Leeds University
Date of Research: 1992-1993
KEYWORDS: equal education; ethnic groups; student recruitment; university admission

10/0606
School of Education, Leeds LS2 9JT
01132 431751
Marriott, J. Prof.
Hudson Shaw and the university extension movement
Abstract: This research is a biography of G.W. Hudson Shaw. Although Shaw was always acknowledged as one of the greatest figures of the Oxford Extension Movement, he has not received serious biographical attention. The study will set the record right about his origins, his early life and personal/family circumstances. It will treat him as the eiptome of the Oxford Extension Movement, and examine the origins and character of his educational beliefs and commitments. Leading sub-themes will be: use of the ideas of John Ruskin; the attitude to working-class education and the effects of a changing political climate; relations to the early Workers' Educational Association (WEA); his position as an ordained clergyman of the Church of England; his relationship to Maude Royden, feminist and advocate of female ordination. The method of research is conventionally historical and biographical.
Published Material: MARRIOTT, J.S. (1985). 'Shaw, George William Hudson 1859-1944'. In: THOMAS, J.E. & ELSEY, B. (Eds). International biography of Adult Education. Nottingham University.
Status: Individual research
Date of Research: 1988-continuing
KEYWORDS: adult education; biographies; educational history; extension education; universities; working class

10/0607
School of Education, Leeds LS2 9JT
01132 431751
Marriott, J. Prof.
University extension and national education
Abstract: This research is a policy and organisational study of the university extension system (1873-1914) which argues that the movement cannot be adequately understood in terms of the later concept of 'adult education'. The aspirations and efforts of extension are presented in the context of changing attitudes towards secondary, technical and higher education, and in the light of its aims of becoming a recognised element within 'national education'. Also emphasised is the implicit shaping of policy by the internal organisational problems of the movement. Sub-themes include: the search for financial aid from the State; the relation to technical instruction; the relation to secondary education and the training of teachers; involvement in local institutes for higher education; historical application of organisation theory. The method used is historical; the analysis draws additionally on the sociology of organisations.
Published Material: MARRIOTT, J.S. (1981). 'State Aid', Studies in Adult Education, No 13.; MARRIOTT, J.S. (1981). 'The University Extension movement and the education of teachers', History of Education, No 10.; MARRIOTT, J.S. (1981). A backstairs to a degree. Leeds: Leeds University; MARRIOTT, J.S. (1983). 'The

whiskey money and the University Extension movement', Journal of Educational Administration and History, No 15.
Status: Individual research
Date of Research: 1988-continuing
KEYWORDS: adult education; educational history; educational policy; extension education; working class

10/0608
School of Education, Leeds LS2 9JT
01132 431751
Chambers, G. Mr; *Supervisor:* Sugden, D. Prof.; Tomlinson, P. Dr
Problems of motivation in foreign language learning: a comparative study
Abstract: The National Curriculum makes the implementation of a 'Languages for All' policy, a requirement in all schools teaching key stages 3 and 4. For some schools this is an innovation. Teachers are concerned about not only teaching the less able, but equally the less motivated for a 5 year period between the ages of 11 and 16. Is it true that German pupils are generally more motivated to learn foreign languages than the British? If so, why? The purpose of the study is to investigate problems of motivation relating to foreign language learning in Leeds, focusing on German, and Kiel, Germany, focusing on English and French. The investigation takes the form of an accelerated longitudinal study. In 1992 400 year 7 pupils from four Leeds comprehensive schools, 300 in year 9 and 200 in year 11 fill in questionnaires. 10% of those surveyed are subsequently interviewed. In 1993 the same procedure is followed in two Kiel comprehensive schools. The questions cover the following areas: attitude to language learning brought from home; pupil-perception of importance of language learning; ethnocentricity; importance of language learning environment; role of the teacher and teaching methods. In 1994-95 the same pupils are surveyed and interviewed again to examine how motivation and attitudes may have changed and why.
Status: Individual research
Date of Research: 1991-continuing
KEYWORDS: language attitudes; language teachers; learning motivation; modern language studies

10/0609
School of Education, Leeds LS2 9JT
01132 431751
de Medeiros, C. Mrs; *Supervisor:* Orton, A. Dr
An investigation into errors made in attempts to solve mathematical problems
Abstract: The study aims to investigate teacher perceptions of pupils' errors in elementary arithmetic with a view to developing teacher training techniques which will enable teachers to improve their teaching methods. Selected groups of young pupils have been tested using simple problems and their errors have been classified by teachers in training, in a preparatory study aimed at clarifying the issues and problems. A further study of pupils' problem solving has yielded data which is currently being analyzed.
Status: Sponsored project
Source of Grant: Brazilian Government
Date of Research: 1988-1993
KEYWORDS: arithmetic; mathematical ability; mathematics education; problem solving; teacher education; teaching methods

10/0610
School of Education, Leeds LS2 9JT
01132 431751
McAuley, J. Mr; *Supervisor:* Orton, A. Dr
Cognitive style and learning mathematics
Abstract: The implications of cognitive styles such as field dependence and field independence in learning mathematics have not been widely investigated. This study aims to focus on such styles and the implications in learning matrices. It is expected that pupils will be assessed and classified on a field dependence/field independence spectrum and the effects of different teaching styles will be measured.
Status: Individual research
Date of Research: 1989-continuing
KEYWORDS: cognitive processes; cognitive style; field dependence independence; learning; mathematics; teaching styles

10/0611

School of Education, Leeds LS2 9JT
01132 431751
Child, D. Prof.; Baker, R. Mr

Survey of communication practices in schools for the hearing impaired in the United Kingdom

Abstract: In 1987 a survey was carried out with a number of schools for the hearing impaired in England and Scotland using a total communication approach. When the findings were circulated, suggestions were made by several headteachers for a further study to explore in more detail the ways in which different modes of communication are used, demand for resource materials, training of staff and parents in communication skills and the roles of deaf people in the schools. It has subsequently been suggested that a new survey be carried out to establish exactly what range of approaches are used throughout all the schools at the present time. A questionnaire was designed which asks for communication approaches in use, in order to provide a base of information for planning for future needs. At the same time, it goes more deeply into aspects of practices in schools using a total communication approach, in response to the requests already made by headteachers. The questionnaire has now been circulated and a 100% return obtained. The data have been analysed and the findings circulated to all participants. Two papers have appeared in the Journal of The British Association of Teachers of the Deaf.
Status: Sponsored project
Source of Grant: Northern Counties School for the Deaf £4,000
Date of Research: 1990-1993
KEYWORDS: communication skills; deafness; hearing impairments; hearing therapy; special schools; total communication

10/0612

School of Education, Leeds LS2 9JT
01132 431751
Lewis, I. Mr; *Supervisor:* Jenkins, E. Prof.; Donnelly, J. Dr

A study of technological capability as manifest in secondary school pupils' project work

Abstract: The study is an exploration of 'the technology project' with particular attention being given to its origination, development and closure. An attempt is made to establish the criteria used by pupils in, for example, choosing one solution/design criteria in preference to another, evaluating/appraising their project as it develops. The work is based on an ethnographic study of pupils in classes in five Sheffield schools. Three schools are likely to be involved.
Status: Sponsored project
Source of Grant: Leeds University: School of Education; Sheffield Local Education Authority
Date of Research: 1989-1993
KEYWORDS: ability; projects – learning activities; pupil projects; secondary education; technology education

10/0613

School of Education, Leeds LS2 9JT
01132 431751
Moncur, D. Mr; *Supervisor:* Orton, A. Dr

Students' understanding of literal algebraic equations and formulae

Abstract: This research has been devised to compare the ability of pupils and students to solve numerical and literal equations in order to analyze why many learners find the step from numerical to literal so difficult. A preliminary study based on group testing was carried out using pupils from four schools in different parts of Britain. In some schools the literal equations were placed before the numerical. The main part of the research is based on individual interviews with a large sample of pupils, and transcription of this data is currently taking place.
Status: Individual research
Date of Research: 1987-1993
KEYWORDS: algebra; cognitive processes; comprehension; mathematical formulas; mathematics education

10/0614

School of Education, Leeds LS2 9JT
01132 431751
Marriott, J. Prof.; Coles, J. Mrs

'University extension' across the English-speaking world, 1867-1914

Abstract: The project is a contribution to a larger research programme in the University of Leeds on inter-cultural influences in the field of adult education. It complements previous work on Anglo-German relations in adult education and on the significance of the English model of 'university extension' for the development of 'popular universities' in continental Europe. This project investigates the export of ideas and practices in university extension to the USA, Canada, Australia, New Zealand and South Africa. It considers why the English model attracted attention, and what happened to it after transplantation to a different social and cultural environment.
Published Material: COLES, J. (1992). 'University extension in the United States'. In: HAKE, B.J. & MARRIOTT, S. (Eds). Adult education between cultures. Leeds: University of Leeds, Studies in Cross Cultural Communication in the Education of Adults, No 2.
Status: Sponsored project
Source of Grant: Leverhulme Trust £18,750
Date of Research: 1991-1993
KEYWORDS: adult education; comparative education; educational history; extension education

10/0615

School of Education, Leeds LS2 9JT
01132 431751
Zachos, I. Mr; *Supervisor:* Orton, A. Dr; Carter, D. Mr

Problem solving in Euclidean geometry in Greek schools

Abstract: The solution of Euclidean geometry problems is difficult for pupils in Greek schools, as it has always been for all pupils where Euclidean geometry has been taught. The aim is to produce a new scheme for teaching the subject, based on worked examples but theoretically underpinned by recent research on the writing of geometry proofs. Matched control and experimental groups will be used, the matching being carried out by using van Hiele levels and a specially constructed test. Pupils in Greek schools will be taught and tested in groups, with a large sample also having individual interviews.
Status: Individual research
Date of Research: 1990-1994
KEYWORDS: geometry education; Greece; mathematics education; problem solving

10/0616

School of Education, Leeds LS2 9JT
01132 431751
Chambers, G. Mr

Diversification of first foreign language in Leeds schools

Abstract: Traditionally French has been dominant as the first foreign language in Leeds secondary schools. German, as a second foreign language has been squeezed into as few as 5 terms in years 10 and 11. In line with recommendations of the National Curriculum, up to 20 Leeds schools have plans to introduce German as either first foreign language or first equal foreign language with French from year 7, as part of a diversification scheme. The purpose of the research is to examine the problems posed by this major change in policy and to seek some tentative solutions, insofar as this is possible, given the constraints of circumstances within individual schools. Interviews will be conducted with the local education authority (LEA) adviser for modern languages to establish the LEA approach to presenting diversification to schools, problems of resourcing and the implications of the reorganisation of secondary education in Leeds. Interviews will also be conducted in 15-20 schools committed to diversification as well as those which are delaying reform and those which have determined to retain the status quo of French as the first foreign language. The views of headteachers, heads of modern languages and class teachers are being sought on reasons for diversifying, staffing implications, training issues, resourcing and problems of transfer and continuity and other related matters. Outcomes of the research will be published in an extensive report in July 1993.
Status: Sponsored project
Source of Grant: Leeds University: School of Education £8,300
Date of Research: 1992-1993
KEYWORDS: French; German; modern language studies; National Curriculum

10/0617

School of Education, Leeds LS2 9JT
01132 431751
Demsetz, E. Ms; *Supervisor:* Tomlinson, P. Dr; Scott, P. Mr

Developing and evaluating a characterization of thought in a microanalysis of students' learning in science

Abstract: A theory of learning is developed using the basic principles of network modelling, and the usefulness of the theory in analyzing science education research data is evaluated. The theory portrays learning as a structuring of knowledge occurring through two processes, termed 'conceptualization' and 'symbolization'. The structured knowledge is capable of supporting three types of thought, termed 'conceptual reasoning', 'intuitive thought', and 'procedural thought'. This characterization of thought is operationalized to allow the theory of learning to be 'trialled' in analyzing science education data. Data for this trial analysis is obtained using a 'non-comparative', open-interview methodology to probe the understandings of two sixth-form physics students learning about electricity. The usefulness of the theory is evaluated by examining the results of the trial analysis to identify issues which the analysis did and did not address. A set of guidelines is developed to allow the science education researcher to characterize research questions in terms of these issues, thereby determining whether the theory of learning will be useful to a particular research study.

Status: Individual research
Date of Research: 1991-1993
KEYWORDS: electricity; learning processes; physics education; science education; sixth form education

10/0618

School of Education, Leeds LS2 9JT
01132 431751
Watson, P. Mr

The role of cognitive styles in the arithmetic of 15 and 50 year old students

Abstract: This project is the extension of earlier research (Watson, 1991) which looked at cognitive styles and their role in arithmetic of school students. The current phase of the research compares the findings from the work of the school students with results from work of students aged 50 plus. Field dependence, impulsivity and flexibility will be examined along with other psychological variables. These are studied mainly in relation to variables in simple arithmetic.

Published Material: WATSON, P. (1991). 'Cognitive styles and errors in simple arithmetic', British Journal of Educational Psychology, Vol 61, No 1, pp.110.
Status: Individual research
Date of Research: 1992-continuing
KEYWORDS: arithmetic; cognitive style; mathematics education; mature students; secondary school pupils

10/0619

School of Education, Leeds LS2 9JT
01132 431751
Wain, G. Mr; Monaghan, J. Dr; Roper, T. Mr

The use of symbol manipulators in teaching algebra to year 10 pupils in secondary schools

Abstract: The development of new systems for computers and calculators which manipulate algebraic symbols and perform calculus procedures have enormous potential for the teaching of algebra and calculus in secondary schools. This research project is aiming to explore the use of symbol manipulators with year 10 students in local secondary schools. The project is a pilot for a larger project which is hoped to be mounted in the future and will be concerned with middle ability and high ability pupils in two comprehensive schools. Each class will be taught a section of the algebra curriculum with the use of symbol manipulators either on hand-held calculators or on computers, and at the same time control groups will be taught the same material without the use of the technology. The pupils will be given a pre-test of the material, and a post-test shortly after the teaching and again after about six weeks. A number of the pupils involved will also be interviewed to find out some of the processes by which they had come to their solutions. The teaching will be observed by one person other than the teacher, and, for the classes that use the technology, a video recording will be made of the display on the screens. The observer will keep a diary about the teaching process and together with the videos an overview of the way that the teaching has been conducted will be compiled. This will be compared with the results of the tests on the pupils and interview material.

Status: Sponsored project
Source of Grant: University of Leeds: Academic Development Fund £20,000
Date of Research: 1992-1993

KEYWORDS: algebra; calculators; computer uses in education; mathematics education; secondary education

10/0620

School of Education, Leeds LS2 9JT
01132 431751
Constable, H. Ms; *Supervisor:* Anning, A. Ms

Technology capability in primary schools

Abstract: The project is the second stage of a small scale investigation into capability in design and technology in National Curriculum key stages 1 and 2. The first stage of the project (1990-1991) sought to: (1) observe and record the strategies of children engaged in technology activities at key stages 1 and 2 and to collect evidence of development in their capabilities in design and technology over a period of one year in the first instance; (2) establish a database of examples of key stages 1 and 2 technology in action in the classrooms; (3) compare the data with expectations of pupil performances set out in the National Curriculum Council Technology curriculum for key stages 1 and 2. Methods used to collect data from twelve schools in two local education authorities (LEAs) included: (1) interviews with headteachers, technology coordinators, class teachers of years 1 and 3, advisers and advisory teachers; (2) close observations in Autumn term 1990 in two year 1 and two year 3 classrooms of children engaged in design and technology activities using tape recorders, video recorders, field notes, and records of children's work; (3) structured tasks for the same groups of children in Summer term 1991 to investigate particular features of capability – close observations and records of their performance. The second stage of the project (1993) will focus on four particular developmental features of capability: (1) graphicacy-communicating/and thinking through drawing; (2) technical skills – fine motor control and the ability to handle tools and equipment; (3) technical knowledge – understanding characteristics of materials and physical laws; (4) evaluation – ability to conceive and work towards alternative solutions.

Published Material: ANNING, A. (1992). 'Factors affecting design and technology capability at key stages 1 and 2', Design and Technology Teaching, Vol 24, No 3, pp.10-15.; ANNING, A. (1992). 'Who's afraid of the technology order?', Journal of TACTYC, Vol 13, No 1, pp.24-32.; ANNING, A. (1993). 'Learning design and technology in primary schools'. In: HARRISON, M.H., McCORMICK, R. & MURPHY, P. (Eds). Teaching and learning in technology. Buckingham: Open University Press.
Status: Sponsored project
Source of Grant: Leeds University: School of Education £10,000
Date of Research: 1993-1994
KEYWORDS: ability; design and technology; national curriculum; primary education; technology education

10/0621

School of Education, Leeds LS2 9JT
01132 431751
Wanjala, E. Mr; *Supervisor:* Orton, A. Dr; Gibbs, W. Mr

Secondary school pupils' errors in algebra and teacher strategies in identifying and counteracting the errors

Abstract: Secondary school pupils in Kenya will complete algebra test papers and will take part in individual interviews designed to reveal errors and difficulties. Inspection of lessons and pupils' work books will reveal the ways errors are dealt with by teachers. Interviews with teachers will investigate possible teaching strategies. It is hoped that attainment can be enhanced as a result of the study.

Status: Individual research
Date of Research: 1992-continuing
KEYWORDS: algebra; Kenya; mathematics education; pupil problems

10/0622

School of Education, Leeds LS2 9JT
01132 431751
Walton, R. Mr; *Supervisor:* Jenkins, E. Prof.

Children's understanding of force in an informal setting

Abstract: Interviews and video techniques will be used to explore young children's understanding of the concept of force as exemplified by the objects and activities in a hands-on science museum.

Status: Individual research
Date of Research: 1992-continuing
KEYWORDS: force; museums; science activities; science education; science teaching centres; scientific concepts

10/0623

School of Education, Leeds LS2 9JT
01132 431751
Donnelly, J. Dr; Jenkins, E. Prof.; Welford, A. Mr

Realising policy: attainment target 1 and science education in National Curriculum key stages 3 and 4

Abstract: The aim of the study is to identify the forces and processes which contribute the establishment of pedagogic and assessment practices in relation to attainment target 1 (AT1) for the National Curriculum for science. The study will: (a) characterise the representation of 'scientific investigation' (AT1 of the National Curriculum for science) within official and professional discourse; (b) investigate how the representations identified above are reinterpreted at other levels in the educational system (local education authorities, school, department), and ultimately realised as pedagogic practice(s) in science classrooms at key stages 3 and 4, and thus to conceptualise the mediations between public discourse (including governmental policy) and classroom practice; (c) document the procedures and activities used in the assessment of AT1 at key stage 3, their relationship to 'everyday' classroom practice and to statutory and other guidance, and thus to examine the interaction and accommodation between the system of national assessment and the practices identified above; (d) examine, in similar terms to (b) and (c), the institutional and other shifts by which the existing assessment of practical science within GCSE is transformed into that at key stage 4 of the National Curriculum; (e) develop and implement a methodology for validating the findings of the study by the use of 'consultation conferences' of teachers.

Published Material: DONNELLY, J.F., BUCHAN, A.S., JENKINS, E.W. & WELFORD, A.G. (1993). Investigations in science education policy: science in the National Curriculum for England and Wales. Leeds: University of Leeds: School of Education, Centre for Policy Studies in Education.
Status: Sponsored project
Source of Grant: Economic and Social Research Council £130,000
Date of Research: 1993-continuing
KEYWORDS: assessment; National Curriculum; school-based assessment; science education

10/0624

School of Education, Leeds LS2 9JT
01132 431751
Buchan, A. Miss; *Supervisor:* Jenkins, E. Prof.; Donnelly, J. Dr

Practical assessment of science at GCSE level: the realisation of policy in school

Abstract: This research aims to identify the origins of the recent emphasis on the assessment of practical skills in school science examinations at 16+. It will examine how the policy to assess pupils' practical competences has been realised both at examination group level and within schools themselves. The historical background to the policy will be charted by means of a literature search and documentation relating to examining groups' practices will be also studied. The main focus of the work, the realisation of the policy within school science departments, will be investigated by means of extensive field work in a sample of ten secondary schools. Data will be gathered by means of semi-structured interviews and through classroom observation. The interviews will seek the views of science teachers, technicians and pupils regarding the implementation of the policy. Members of senior management teams with curriculum and pastoral responsibilities will also be interviewed to provide a wider perspective. Classroom observation will take place when teachers are assessing the practical skills of pupils. Analysis of the data will also consider the effects the policy has had on science education.

Published Material: BUCHAN, A.S. & JENKINS, E.W. (1992). 'The internal assessment of practical skills in science in England and Wales, 1960-1991: some issues in historical perspective', International Journal of Science Education, Vol 14, No 4, pp.367-380.; BUCHAN, A.S. (1992). 'Practical assessment in GCSE: the diversity of the examination groups' practices', The School Science Review, Vol 73, No 265. pp.19-28.; BUCHAN, A.S. (1993). 'Policy into practice: the operation of practical assessment in the GCSE', The School Science Review, (forthcoming).; BUCHAN, A.S. & WELFORD, A.G. (1993). 'Policy into practice: the effects of practical assessment on the teaching of science', Research in Science and Technological Education, (forthcoming).; BUCHAN, A.S. (1993). 'Policy into practice: internal assessment at 16+: standardisation and moderation procedures', Educational Research, Vol 35, No 2, pp.171-179.
Status: Individual research

Date of Research: 1990-continuing
KEYWORDS: assessment; General Certificate of Secondary Education; practical science; science activities; science education

10/0625

School of Education, Leeds LS2 9JT
01132 431751
Donnelly, J. Dr; Jenkins, E. Prof.; Welford, A. Mr

Practical assessment in secondary science

Abstract: The aim of the study is to evaluate the implementation of the policy requirement that GCSE science examinations should include an element of practical assessment. The main methods used were: a survey of public documentation, including examination syllabuses; a national questionnaire involving analysis of responses from 500 schools, and fieldwork of an ethnographic kind in 10 local schools. The findings of the study cast doubt on the nature of policy as a category in this kind of educational context. If a wide definition of policy is adopted (i.e. including semi-official prescriptions of 'good practice') what goes on in schools bears little resemblance to it. This stems from the fact that such prescriptions take little account of teachers real situations and that situation is heavily constrained. They also operate a centre-periphery model. Changes in practice used to be constructed by teachers themselves. To do this teachers need appropriate professional structures of mutual support and a body of 'theoretical' knowledge. Neither of these is in place for practical assessment.

Published Material: BUCHAN, A.S. & JENKINS, E.W. (1992). 'The internal assessment of practical skills in science in England and Wales, 1960-1991: some issues in historical perspective', International Journal of Science Education, Vol 14, No 4, pp.367-380.; JENKINS, E.W. (1992). 'Policy into practice: internal assessment at 16+: standardisation and moderation procedures', Educational Research, Vol 35, No 2, pp.171-179.; BUCHAN, A.S. & WELFORD, A.G. (1993). 'Policy into practice: the organisational, financial and curricular setting of practical assessment in science in the GCSE', The School Science Review (forthcoming).; BUCHAN, A.S. & WELFORD, A.G. (1993). 'Policy into practice: the effects of practical assessment on the teaching of science', Research in Science and Technological Education, (forthcoming).
Status: Sponsored project
Source of Grant: Economic and Social Research Council £67,000
Date of Research: 1990-1992
KEYWORDS: assessment; General Certificate of Secondary Education; practical science; science activities; science education

10/0626

School of Education, Leeds LS2 9JT
01132 431751
Leach, J. Mr; *Supervisor:* Wood-Robinson, C. Mr; Driver, R. Prof.

Progression in understanding of ecological concepts by students aged 5-16

Abstract: This cross-sectional study aims to document the ideas used by children about phenomena related to cycles of matter, flows of energy and interdependence of organisms, and how these change from age 5 to age 16. The nature of the changes in explanations with age is being considered, addressing in particular the entities from which explanations are constructed and the underlying epistemology of the explanations. These changes are evaluated in terms of various theoretical positions on the nature of learning. The diagnostic tasks used were generally phenomenologically framed, the stimulus material being some kind of natural phenomenon rather than a particular conceptual term. Analysis was ideographic, emphasising the content of subjects' responses rather than the extent to which they corresponded to canonical science. In addition, some diagnostic tasks were designed to investigate the nature of subjects' understandings of particular representations of natural phenomena used in science, such as food webs. Data were collected by interview and written tasks, and the same tasks were used with 499 students across the 5 to 16 age range. Findings from the study relate to the ontological and epistemological features of students' explanations of ecological phenomena at characteristic ages, and the associated familiarity with ecological phenomena drawn upon in framing explanations. Characteristic representations of the nature of ecosystems and ecological processes such as photosynthesis, respiration and decay at particular ages are described.

Published Material: LEACH, J.T., DRIVER, R.H., SCOTT, P.H. & WOOD-ROBINSON, C. (1992). Progression in understanding of

ecological concepts by pupils aged from 5 to 16. Leeds: University of Leeds, Centre for Studies in Science and Mathematics Education.; LEACH, J.T., DRIVER, R.H., SCOTT, P.H. & WOOD-ROBINSON, C. 'The development of children's ideas from age 5 to age 16 about the interdependency of organisms in ecosystems 1: methodology', International Journal of Science Education. (in press).; LEACH, J.T., DRIVER, R.H., SCOTT, P.H. & WOOD-ROBINSON, C. 'The development of children's ideas from age 5 to age 16 about the interdependency of organisms in ecosystems 2: matter cycling', International Journal of Science Education. (in press).; LEACH, J.T., DRIVER, R.H., SCOTT, P.H. & WOOD-ROBINSON, C. 'The development of children's ideas from age 5 to age 16 about the interdependency of organisms in ecosystems 3: interpendency', International Journal of Science Education. (in press).
Status: Individual research
Date of Research: 1990-1994
KEYWORDS: comprehension; ecology education; science education; scientific concepts

10/0627

School of Education, Leeds LS2 9JT
01132 431751
Malcolm, J. Ms; Jones, H. Ms
European community funding and the education of adults
Abstract: This is a two year project investigating the policy of the European Community (EC) with regard to the education and training of adults, and the uses to which EC funding is put within continuing education in Britain. The research covers: (1) the relationships between EC, national and local policy priorities as they affect continuing education; (2) the implementation of EC policy in selected programmes of education and training for adults in Britain (e.g. through the European Social Fund); (3) monitoring and evaluation of EC funded programmes; and (4) the impact of such programmes on other forms of provision, with particular regard to the concept of 'additionality'. The project focuses on continuing education programmes in west and south Yorkshire, and involves some collaboration with the University of Sheffield.
Status: Sponsored project
Source of Grant: Universities Funding Council £42,000
Date of Research: 1992-1994
KEYWORDS: adult education; continuing education; educational finance; educational policy; European Community; financial support

10/0628

School of Education, Leeds LS2 9JT
01132 431751
Orton, J. Mrs; *Supervisor:* Orton, A. Dr
Children's perception and conception of pattern in mathematics
Abstract: Human beings both perceive and create patterns in their interactions with their environment. The National Curriculum (mathematics) of England and Wales makes assumptions about children's perceptions and conceptions of pattern. This study is part of a collection of studies aimed at clarifying how children develop in terms of seeing, using and generating patterns in mathematics. It is hoped that more will be learned about (a) whether the school curriculum is realistic; and (b) whether more could be developed from patterns in mathematics.
Status: Sponsored project
Source of Grant: University of Leeds: School of Education
Date of Research: 1993-1994
KEYWORDS: cognitive processes; mathematics education; National Curriculum; pattern recognition

10/0629

School of Education, Leeds LS2 9JT
01132 431751
Williams, R. Mr; Yeomans, D. Mr
A longitudinal study of the impact on the curriculum of selected secondary schools of the Technical and Vocational Education Initiative
Abstract: The research aims to investigate and analyse the medium-term impact of the Technical and Vocational Education Initiative (TVEI) in ten English secondary schools. The schools, which all participated in the TVEI pilot scheme, were first visited in 1985 and 1986 as part of the National Evaluation of the TVEI Curriculum Project which was conducted in the School of Education, University of Leeds. The schools were revisited in 1991 and 1992. During both

series of visits broadly ethnographic methods of data gathering were employed involving interviews, classroom observation and document collection. In addition to investigation of the more general effects of TVEI upon the schools, particular emphasis was placed upon developments in the curriculum areas of Design and Technology, Information Technology and Business Studies. The preliminary findings indicate complex interplay between TVEI, itself subject to considerable change over the period of study, other national initiatives, sugject cultures, changing and variable school environments and institutional histories, cultures and imperatives.
Published Material: WILLIAMS, R. & YEOMANS, D. (1993). 'The fate of TVEI in a pilot school: a longitudinal case study', British Educational Research Journal, Vol 19, No 4, pp.421-434.; YEOMANS, D. & WILLIAMS, R. (1993). 'Then and now: technology in ten of the original TVEI pilot schools'. Education for Capability Research Group, Occasional Publication No 5. Leeds: University of Leeds, School of Education.
Status: Individual research
Date of Research: 1991-1994
KEYWORDS: educational change; longitudinal studies; TVEI

10/0630

School of Education, Leeds LS2 9JT
01132 431751
Jiya, M. Mrs; *Supervisor:* Orton, A. Dr; Gibbs, W. Mr
Change of attitude and performance of Ciskei High School pupils as a result of a new curriculum
Abstract: It is proposed to introduce a new geometry curriculum into high schools in Ciskei (South Africa) with the intention of making the curriculum more appropriate and more motivating. Post-test results will be compared, not only with pre-test, but also with results obtained from pupils studying the old curriculum. The implications for teaching and for retraining teachers will also be considered.
Status: Individual research
Date of Research: 1992-continuing
KEYWORDS: curriculum development; geometry; mathematics education; secondary education; South Africa

10/0631

School of Education, Leeds LS2 9JT
01132 431751
Peacock, M. Dr; *Supervisor:* Beard, R. Dr; Tomlinson, P. Dr
Evaluating word processed pupil writing
Abstract: This thesis is concerned with the effects and implications of the use of word processors on the writing of secondary school pupils. It enquires into aspects of both teacher and pupil responses. An initial overview of the field of Information Technology in schools, and a detailed review of the research literature, together highlight several issues which are examined in a series of empirical studies. One feature of reactions to the advent of the new technologies has been the consistent and widely publicised expectation of beneficial educational effects. This evidence is analysed and an assessment study conducted that presents evidence that presentation alone can account for a significant proportion of teachers' improved marks for pupils' word processed writing, although it is found that less directly, pupil work is related to an external referent (a novel, poem or text-book, for example), the more likely it is that word processing will enhance its apparent quality relative to equivalent handwritten work. It is also found that the work of average and low achieving pupils tends to be enhanced more than the work of high achieving pupils. Additionally, a substantial survey reveals recurrent in-school problems hampering use of word processors. However, empirical work with pupils using 'laptop' word processors suggests that handwriting remains popular and quicker for most classroom writing tasks, neither planning nor constructive reflection on language seem to be enhanced, typing speeds remain very slow, and repeated loss of work is commonplace. Nevertheless, there is evidence that for some of the pupils the connotations of the word 'writing' are beginning to alter in line with the medium of production. This is one of the most significant inferences of the study, and systematic examination of this change finds that although – as might be expected – experienced pupil word processor users tend to attach less importance to the 'surface' features of their writing than do the handwriting control groups, there is no evidence of any corresponding concern with the compositional features of their writing. Finally, the findings and conclusions are summarised and discussed and some possibilities for classroom work are outlined and reviewed, with examples. Consideration is also given to a model of the writing process adapted from neuro-psychological

research findings: a model which is felt to hold promise of being of practical use in attempting to account for several features of writing behaviour.
Published Material: PEACOCK, M.J. (1990). 'Evaluating the evidence', Interchange, University of Leeds.; PEACOCK, M.J. & BREESE, C. (1990). 'Pupils with portable writing machines', Educational Review, Vol 42, No 1, pp.41-56.; PEACOCK, M.J. & NAJARIAN, B. (1992). 'What's important in writing?: some differences in attitude between word processing and handwriting pupils'. In: MONTEITH, M. (Ed). Writing and computers. Walton-on-Thames: Nelson (Thomas) & Sons Ltd.
Status: Individual research
Date of Research: 1987-1992
KEYWORDS: computer uses in education; secondary school pupils; word processing; writing skills

10/0632
School of Education, Leeds LS2 9JT
01132 431751
Garrick, R. Mrs; *Supervisor:* Threlfall, J. Dr; Orton, A. Dr
The development of pattern-related abilities through play activities in young children
Abstract: The development of young children's abilities to perceive and create patterns will be studied, with particular relation to progression through the early years of learning mathematics.
Status: Individual research
Date of Research: 1992-continuing
KEYWORDS: early childhood education; mathematics education; pattern recognition; play; young children

10/0633
School of Education, Leeds LS2 9JT
01132 431751
Healy, M. Ms
An examination of the process of appraisal of headteachers in phase one of its implementation in one local education authority
Abstract: The programme of headteacher appraisal is part of a national statutory programme involving all teachers. This research project involves a close consideration of the process as it affects a core group of ten headteachers. It is complemented by a study of the support offered by the local education authority (LEA) together with a survey of the larger cohort of headteachers in a LEA undertaking the process for the first time. Methods used involve: direct observation of the process of appraisal in the case of the core study; interviews with core study headteachers, peer appraisers and LEA appraisers; and a questionnaire to other headteachers in the cohort. Results are still emerging. Present indications suggest that important insights are to be gained as to the following issues: (1) the role of the LEA in appraisal; and (2) the headteachers' understanding of issues of accountability and their concept of the task of management.
Status: Sponsored project
Source of Grant: Leeds University Research Fund £2,350
Date of Research: 1992-1993
KEYWORDS: head teachers; teacher evaluation

10/0634
School of Education, Leeds LS2 9JT
01132 431751
Jenkins, E. Prof.; Donnelly, J. Dr
School technology at National Curriculum key stage 4: knowledge and action
Abstract: The project is a pilot study of technology education in three schools in a northern city. A researcher on full-time secondment observed technology teaching in these schools, interviewed staff and pupils and collected appropriate documentation. The case studies based on this research are used to explore a variety of dimensions of technology education, notably the relationship between knowledge and action and the influence of patterns of assessment on the realisation of school technology.
Published Material: DONNELLY, J.F. & JENKINS, E.W. (1992). 'GCSE technology: some precursors and issues', Education for Capability Research Group, No 4, University of Leeds
Status: Sponsored project
Source of Grant: University of Leeds: School of Education £10,000; Sheffield Local Education Authority £10,000
Date of Research: 1990-1992

KEYWORDS: National Curriculum; school-based assessment; secondary education; technology education

10/0635
School of Education, Leeds LS2 9JT
01132 431751
Jenkins, E. Prof.
School science education in England and Wales, 1960-1990
Abstract: The study seeks to take forward a full length account of science education in schools in England and Wales completed in 1960. It will explore the social history and politics of the school science curriculum from the introduction of the Nuffield Science Teaching Projects in the early 1960s to the advent of the National Curriculum of the late 1980s.
Published Material: JENKINS, E.W. (1989). 'Processes in science education: an historical perspective'. In: WELLINGTON, J. (Ed). Skills and processes in science education: a critical analysis. London: Routledge.; JENKINS, E.W. (1992). 'School science education: towards a reconstruction', Journal of Curriculum Studies, Vol 24, No 3, pp.229-246.
Status: Individual research
Date of Research: 1992-continuing
KEYWORDS: educational history; science education

10/0636
School of Education, Leeds LS2 9JT
01132 431751
Leger, E. Ms; *Supervisor:* Marriott, J. Prof.; Watson, P. Mr
Mature students' perceptions of stress on return to learning
Abstract: Stress is part of life. Returning to learn creates additional demands on adults who already have responsible roles in society, family and workplace. If returning to learn creates demands on stressors then to what degree are mature students affected and what variables factor into their perceived stress levels? This work develops a model for viewing the perceptions of stress (demands) of mature students who return to learn. The components of this model are a theoretical framework and findings from a process of indepth interviews of students, aged thirty to fifty-five, who have returned to learn. This is a comparative study of mature students in Britain (West Yorkshire) and the United States (Minnesota), using a sample of about 40 students in each country. Implications for this model are understanding and facilitating the returning learner into higher education institutions while supporting their multiple roles as student, family/society member and employee. The interviews having been completed and analysed, a questionnaire is being developed using the interview findings. This will be administered to larger samples in both countries to attempt to confirm and extend findings from the interviews.
Published Material: LEGER, E. 'Perceived stressors of mature students', Abstract in: Proceedings of the Annual Conference of the British Psychological Society, Education Section, British Journal of Educational Psychology. (in press).
Status: Individual research
Date of Research: 1989-1994
KEYWORDS: higher education; mature students; stress – psychological; stress variables

10/0637
School of Education, Leeds LS2 9JT
01132 431751
Driver, R. Prof.; Drake, F. Dr; Jenkins, E. Prof.; Wood-Robinson, C. Mr; Leach, J. Mr
Public understanding of global atmospheric change
Abstract: Global environmental changes (GEC) due to human activity involving such factors as stratospheric ozone depletion and global warming have been investigated by natural scientists. A compelling case has been made for socioeconomic change, whereby changes in the practices of individuals and institutions could lead to a reversal of GEC. Little attention has been paid to the public understanding of science that underpins attitudes to GEC at all levels in society, and which will be central to the changes required to harmonise socioeconomic development with the environment. This study aims to provide baseline data on the public understanding of global atmospheric changes. Pilot work is underway on a survey instrument to elicit the popular understanding of: (1) the scientific process involved in global warming and stratospheric ozone depletion as they relate to GEC; and (2) the relationship between individual, institutional and societal

action relating to such global atmospheric changes.
Status: Sponsored project
Source of Grant: University of Leeds £6,000
Date of Research: 1993-continuing
KEYWORDS: climate; global approach; physical environment; scientific attitudes; social attitudes

10/0638

School of Education, Leeds LS2 9JT
01132 431751
Shorrocks, D. Dr
Mathematics assessment at National Curriculum key stage 2: development of new assessment materials
Abstract: The aim of the project is to develop, trial and pre-test new assessment materials in National Curriculum Mathematics, for key stage 2 (11 year olds). These materials will be developed and deployed nationally with all 11 year olds in the years 1994, 1995 and 1996. Their use and outcomes will be monitored and evaluated throughout. In each year, the proposed materials will be developed and pre-tested with a national, representative sample (England and Wales) of about 2,000 children. Once the materials are deployed with the whole age cohort (approximately 500,000 children) during the years 1994-1996, evaluation and monitoring samples will be selected each year, in order to collect data that will facilitate improved assessment in subsequent years. Each year two reports will be submitted to the funding body, outlining the ongoing evaluations. The project is overseen by a supervisory group, selected by the funding body, and made up of senior HMI and representatives of National Curriculum Council (NCC), Curriculum Council for Wales (CCW) and members of Schools Curriculum and Assessment Authority (SCAA).
Status: Sponsored project
Source of Grant: School Examinations and Assessment Council £493,000
Date of Research: 1992-continuing
KEYWORDS: assessment; mathematics education; National Curriculum; school-based assessment

10/0639

School of Education, Leeds LS2 9JT
01132 431751
Southworth, A. Mrs; *Supervisor:* Williams, R. Mr
The evaluation of a whole school curriculum enhancement project across the high schools of a local education authority
Abstract: The design, implementation and management of the Technical and Vocational Education Initiative (TVEI) scheme in one local education authority are critically evaluated. The processes of internal and external evaluation employed in the project are reviewed and compared to other evaluations of TVEI and curriculum change more generally.
Published Material: WILLIAMS, R.P. & SOUTHWORTH, A. (1991). 'Evaluation of Leeds LEA TVEI (ELLEAT) summative report'. Leeds: University of Leeds, School of Education.
Status: Individual research
Date of Research: 1990-1994
KEYWORDS: local education authorities; programme evaluation; TVEI

10/0640

School of Education, Leeds LS2 9JT
01132 431751
Stephens, W. Dr
Education in Britain in its economic setting, 1780-1902
Abstract: The aim of this project is to provide a survey of education in England, Scotland and Wales, 1780-1902 in its social and economic setting, stressing inter-relationship of educational change and socio-economic development.
Status: Individual research
Date of Research: 1993-continuing
KEYWORDS: educational history

10/0641

School of Education, Leeds LS2 9JT
01132 431751
Stephens, W. Dr
Local history for the National Curriculum
Abstract: The aim of this project is to provide a guide for teachers of children aged 7-16 on uses of local history (now a compulsory

element in the National Curriculum History syllabus), with special reference to the nature, availability and uses of original source material.
Status: Individual research
Date of Research: 1991-continuing
KEYWORDS: history studies; local history; National Curriculum

10/0642

School of Education, Leeds LS2 9JT
01132 431751
Alexopolou, E. Miss; *Supervisor:* Driver, R. Prof.;
Tomlinson, P. Dr
Small group discussion in physics: interaction and development of students' physics ideas
Abstract: The study investigates the effect of group discussion on secondary students' understanding in three physics domains. The discussion processes are analysed in terms of social interaction as well as argument construction. The dynamics of change in students' physics reasoning are investigated. The results show that gender, group size, the forms of argument used as well as the type of social confrontation between group members all affect both the course and the outcomes of the discussion in terms of individual conceptual change.
Published Material: ALEXOPOLOU, E., DRIVER, R. & TOMLINSON, P. (1992). 'Small group discussion in physics: interaction and development of students' physics understanding': Psychological and educational foundations of technology-based learning environments, Proceedings of the NATO Advanced Study Institute, Crete.
Status: Individual research
Date of Research: 1989-1993
KEYWORDS: group discussion; group work; physics education; science education

10/0643

School of Education, Leeds LS2 9JT
01132 431751
Willcocks, J. Mr; *Supervisor:* Shorrocks, D. Dr
Aspects of linguistic influence of primary school teachers on their pupils
Abstract: Using a newly devised original system of analysis, the study focuses on lexical and syntactic features of the every day discourse of primary school teachers and their pupils. It is particularly concerned with matters of consistency during the course of a school year, individual differences between teachers in the same school, differences between classes of children of similar age in the same and different catchment areas, and children's informal learning through imitation of their teachers.
Status: Individual research
Date of Research: 1991-continuing
KEYWORDS: classroom communication; primary school teachers; teacher behaviour; teacher-pupil relationship; verbal communication

10/0644

School of Education, Leeds LS2 9JT
01132 431751
Hayes, D. Mr; *Supervisor:* Coleman, P. Mr
Inservice education programmes and teacher change: an investigation of the effects of inservice training courses on teachers' beliefs and classroom behaviour with specific reference to the teaching of English as a foreign language in Thailand
Abstract: There has been much research in English language teaching in recent years into classroom teaching/learning processes. This, allied to developments in theories of second/foreign language learning, has led to an increase in inservice training programmes focusing on the introduction or promotion of the communicative language teaching approach and learner-centred methodology. Such a programme is currently operating in all provinces of Thailand. However, little has been done to assess: a) the efficacy of such inservice teacher education (INSET) programmes in terms of whether or not teachers adopt innovations introduced to them; b) whether teachers themselves perceive the training to be relevant or useful to them in the context of their everyday working lives. These issues will be investigated via a primarily qualitative research programme. Extensive visits will be made to inservice courses in Thailand, in order that the researcher can attend the courses and conduct in-school follow-up classroom observation and interviews with trainers and selected

teachers. These interviews/observations will provide varied perspectives of the training events. The scope of the interviews will consider the wider social context of teachers' lives and work. The researcher will also interview and/or administer questionnaires to selected students in order to discover attitudes to the learning of English and their perceptions of teaching-learning activities in classes before their teachers attended the training course and whilst they were attending them.
Status: Individual research
Date of Research: 1993-continuing
KEYWORDS: English – second language; inservice teacher education; language teachers; second language teaching; Thailand

10/0645
　　　School of Education, Leeds LS2 9JT
　　　01132 431751
　　　Sugden, D. Prof.; Utley, A. Ms
Manual skills in children with hemiplegic cerebral palsy
Abstract: The overall aim of this project is to improve manual functions in children with hemiplegic cerebral palsy (CP) so that they can have total access to the National Curriculum. This includes: 1) providing a 'vocabulary' of grips that CP children use and adaptations they make; 2) describing reaching and grasping in CP children; 3) analysing the effect of the lesser involved side on the hemiplegic limb (interlimb coupling); and 4) analysing how this interlimb coupling is best achieved. The methods used in the study include: normal real live video analysis; and three dimensional kinematic analysis.
Published Material: SUGDEN, D.A., & UTLEY, A. (1993). Manual skills in children with hemiplegic cerebral palsy. Report to the Spastics Society.
Status: Sponsored project
Source of Grant: Spastics Society £21,000; Action Research £37,000; Leeds University
Date of Research: 1992-1993
KEYWORDS: cerebral palsy; mobility aids; neurological impairments; psychomotor skills; special educational needs

10/0646
　　　School of Education, Leeds LS2 9JT
　　　01132 431751
　　　Sugden, D. Prof.; Beveridge, S. Dr; Baron, A-M. Dr; Collins, J. Mrs
Curricular entitlement at National Curriculum key stages 2 and 3 for children with special educational needs
Abstract: The overall aims of this research are: 1) To examine the values, assumptions and decisions underlying both policy and processes in schools that have been identified as exhibiting good practice in the area of special educational needs (SEN). 2) To examine the delivery and assessment of the National Curriculum for pupils with SEN at key stages 2 and 3 within these schools. Collection of data will be through semi-structured interviews, observational techniques, both naturalistic and systematic, and analysis of documentary materials.
Status: Sponsored project
Source of Grant: Leeds University
Date of Research: 1993-continuing
KEYWORDS: mainstreaming; pupil needs; school effectiveness; special educational needs

10/0647
　　　School of Education, Leeds LS2 9JT
　　　01132 431751
　　　Moorcroft-Cuckle, P. Dr; *Supervisor:* Broadhead, P. Dr; Dunford, J. Dr; Hodgson, J. Ms
Investigating the design and implementation of school development plans in the primary school
Abstract: Relatively little is known about the ways in which School Development Plans (SDP) evolve, their subsequent implementation and general management. This project will investigate conditions necessary for successful implementation and consider the implications of outside involvement in this process. The first phase involves a large cohort of primary schools across three authorities. Questionnaires will be used to ascertain procedures and examples of SDP's will be collected. Phase two will involve semi-structured interviews on a smaller number of contrasting schools involving headteachers, deputies, governors and class teachers. In these schools (drawn from phase one responses) the project will look more closely at roles,

contributions and management. Phase three will involve the co-directors each working with two schools (six in total) as outsider consultants. The research fellow will investigate this insider-outsider partnership. During the third phase a support package will be developed and trialled, designed to assist a whole school approach to the implementation of whole school development plans.
Status: Sponsored project
Source of Grant: Leeds University
Date of Research: 1994-continuing
KEYWORDS: development plans; educational planning; planning; primary schools; whole school approach

10/0648
　　　School of Education, Leeds LS2 9JT
　　　01132 431751
　　　Foster, E. Dr; Williams, R. Mr
Industrial placement in the initial training of secondary school teachers
Abstract: Since 1986, all secondary Postgraduate Certificate in Education (PGCE) students at the University of Leeds (250-400 per annum) have undertaken a period of at least one week of industrial placement. The project is a continuation of previous work in researching and evaluating this experience. Over the period 1986-93 a data bank of student evaluation questionnaires, de-briefing reports and records of interviews with students and host employers has been compiled. Using the data bank the project will seek to document and analyse changing placement patterns, attitudes and experience of participants and perceived outcomes. This changing local experience will be set against changing national debate and policy on teacher education in general and placing student teachers in industry in particular. Further data will be gathered on the range and quality of student teacher placement activity in present, more school based, initial teacher training.
Published Material: FOSTER, E.J. & WILLIAMS, R.P. (1993). 'Business placements for teachers in training'. In: BLOOMER, G. & SCOTT, W. (Eds). Partnership in teacher education: economic and industrial understanding. Southampton: Bassett Press.
Status: Sponsored project
Source of Grant: Leeds University £11,500
Date of Research: 1994-continuing
KEYWORDS: enterprise education; industrial secondments; industry-education relationship; placement; preservice teacher education; student teachers

10/0649
　　　School of Education, Leeds LS2 9JT
　　　01132 431751
　　　Chambers, G. Mr; Asher, C. Dr
Special educational needs: policy and provision
Abstract: The Statutory Orders of the National Curriculum require all pupils, with the exception of those few who are 'disapplied', to learn a foreign language from the age of 11 to 16 years. The purpose of the research is to examine the implications of this major innovation for pupils with special educational needs (SEN) in special and mainstream schools participating in the Leeds University Secondary School Partnership scheme. It is proposed to adopt the following approach, some aspects of which will have been set in place before October 1993: 1) The Local Education Authority (LEA) policy documents relating to special educational needs and modern foreign languages are to be examined. This will be followed by interviews with relevant representatives from the advisory division. 2) A sample of special and mainstream schools will be identified as case studies in policy implementation. This involves interviews with school management and teachers as well as observation of classroom practice. Areas to be the focus of special investigation include: a) the practical implications of 'disapplication'; b) timetable provision for modern languages for pupils with SEN; c) resource implications – material and human; and d) teachers' qualifications and levels of competence, experience of teaching foreign languages, and nature of support-teacher provision. It is intended that the research should represent the first phase of a more ambitious project which would adopt an experimental approach to the study of the most effective teaching of languages to pupils with SEN.
Status: Sponsored project
Source of Grant: Leeds University £2,000
Date of Research: 1993-1994
KEYWORDS: modern language studies; special educational needs

10/0650

School of Education, Leeds LS2 9JT
01132 431751
Donnelly, J. Dr; Healy, M. Ms; Roper, T. Mr; Sugden, D.
Prof.; Welford, A. Mr; Whitelaw, S. Ms
Classroom management project
Abstract: The project seeks to identify those classroom management capabilities which student teachers develop during initial teacher training. It further seeks to identify the circumstances in which this development takes place. Methods include: questionnaire, observation and interview, together with written accounts by student teachers.
Status: Sponsored project
Source of Grant: Leeds University £29,500
Date of Research: 1993-1994
KEYWORDS: *classroom management; preservice teacher education; student teachers*

10/0651

School of Education, Leeds LS2 9JT
01132 431751
Jenkins, E. Prof.; Swinnerton, B. Dr
Primary science in England: a social and political history
Abstract: The study explores the factors that have shaped the science curriculum in elementary and primary schools in England in the twentieth century. The research will draw upon published and private sources and, for the more recent period, will make use of interviews with key personnel. The various primary science 'projects' of the 1960's will be fully documented and an attempt made to explore policy realisation in the schools themselves.
Status: Sponsored project
Source of Grant: Leeds University
Date of Research: 1993-continuing
KEYWORDS: *educational history; primary education; science curriculum; science education*

10/0652

School of Education, Leeds LS2 9JT
01132 431751
Daniels, S. Mrs; *Supervisor:* Shorrocks, D. Dr; Redfern, E. Dr
Multi-level statistical models in the analysis of birthdate effects on pupils' school performance
Abstract: The area of research interest was defined as 'multi-level models applied to performance data in order to explore the nature and extent of birthdate as an exploratory variable of the variation in performance outcomes between groups of pupils over a wide range of ages'. Two main data sets were used in the research. One that had been collected as part of the Evaluation of National Curriculum and Assessment at Key Stage 1 Project (Shorrocks et al, 1992) and the second was collected for the Testing and Assessing 6 and 7 Year Olds: The Evaluation of the 1992 Key Stage 1 National Curriculum Assessment (Shorrocks et al, 1993). The proposed method of addressing this research is by multi-level modelling of the performance outcomes of pupils. Predominantly key stage 1 children will be studied but with reference to findings from a range of ages. A variety of tests and assessments will be considered in terms of factors appropriate to each age group but with particular reference to possible confounding effects, namely: social background, previous educational history or achievement (where appropriate) and other pupil background information; birthdate and length of schooling; nursery experience and age etc. Information about local education authority (LEA) admissions policies, school and class background data will be collected and used to set the research problems in context.
Published Material: SHORROCKS, D., DANIELS, S. (1992). Evaluation of national curriculum assessment at key stage 1: final report. London: School Examinations and Assessment Council.; SHORROCKS, D., DANIELS, S., STAINTON, R. & RING, K. (1993). Testing and assessing 6 and 7 year olds: the evaluation of the 1992 key stage 1 National Curriculum assessment: final report. London: National Union of Teachers.
Status: Individual research
Date of Research: 1992-continuing
KEYWORDS: *academic achievement; achievement; birth; performance; school entrance age*

10/0653

School of Education, Leeds LS2 9JT
01132 431751
Francis, M. Ms; *Supervisor:* Shorrocks, D. Dr; Threlfall, J. Dr
Factors influencing the perception and generalisation of number patterns in children aged from 7 to 13
Abstract: A developmental study of children identifying and generalising patterns in number. The study will explore children's understanding of, and responses to, tasks involving different kinds of number pattern in contrasting representative modes (symbolic; pictorial; concrete; and graphical). The effectiveness of selected teaching approaches will also be investigated.
Status: Individual research
Date of Research: 1993-continuing
KEYWORDS: *mathematics education; number concepts; numbers*

10/0654

School of Education, Leeds LS2 9JT
01132 431751
Bradford & Ilkley Community College, Great Horton Road, Bradford BD1 1AY
01274 753166
Robinson, P. Mr; *Supervisor:* Marriott, J. Prof.
Attitudes towards 'economic course' provision in the public further education sector
Abstract: During the 1980s the further education (FE) sector has come under increasing pressure to operate within the context of a 'New Right Market Economy'. The purpose of this research is to enquire into and collect information about people's perceptions of how economic course provision within FE can be developed more effectively. Given a context of increasing competitiveness from other public and private agencies, the research aims to examine the attitudes of staff in terms of their willingness to embrace this current entrepreneurial philosophy, as well as to further consider present management and administrative structures in order to assess the degree to which these existing structures may hinder or facilitate flexible responses to commercial demands. The research has an ethnographic base and will aim to interview respondents from four sample areas: college managers and administrators; college staff academic and technical, other local training providers; and industrial managers. An initial pilot project took place within Bradford & Ilkley Community College during the academic year 1989/90 and five subsequent research projects were developed during the following 18 months.
Status: Sponsored project
Source of Grant: Bradford & Ilkley Community College £4,800
Date of Research: 1989-1993
KEYWORDS: *course evaluation; economics education relationship; educational administration; educational economics; entrepreneurship; further education*

10/0655

School of Education, Leeds LS2 9JT
01132 431751
London University, Institute of Education, Department of English for Speakers of Other Languages, 20 Bedford Way, London WC1H OAL
0171 580 1122
Cameron, L. Ms; *Supervisor:* Cook, G. Dr
The development of metaphor in children
Abstract: The aims of this research are to examine and extend what is known about children's developing understanding and use of metaphor. This requires an examination of theories of metaphor for their adequacy in explaining development. The empirical part of the study uses ethnographic data collected at home and at school. The classroom based data focuses on an individual 10 year old, and was collected by audio recording and observation, with all written texts used by the child over 5 days also collected. The naturalistic data is supplemented by structured investigations of responses to texts, analysed using thinking-out-loud protocol analysis. Other analysis techniques are drawn from conversation/discourse analysis. Initial results indicate that a child's understanding of text and talk depends on an understanding of metaphorical structuring of conceptual domains. Explicit labelling and understanding of the notion of metaphor is possible from 6-7 years of age. Metaphor is a viable tool for cognitive development but may be used in unexpected and not immediately recognisable ways by children.
Published Material: CAMERON, L. (1991). 'Off the beaten track: implications for teachers of recent developments in the study of metaphor', English in Education, Vol 25, No 2, pp.4-15.
Status: Individual research
Date of Research: 1990-1994
KEYWORDS: *child language; figurative language; metaphors*

10/0656

School of Education, Overseas Education Unit, Leeds
LS2 9JT
01132 431751
Coleman, H. Mr
Language learning in large classes research project
Abstract: The project is primarily concerned with the learning and teaching of English as a second language or foreign language in the context of large classes. It has four aims: to develop links with individuals and institutions concerned with large classes (LCs), to organize meetings and other events for the purpose of discussing current research, undertake and promote research into specific aspects of language learning and teaching in LCs, and to develop and maintain a bibliography. A series of project reports is now being published, and more reports will appear in the future. Colloquia have been organized in Chicago (1988), Warwick (1989), San Antonio (1989), Dublin (1990), San Francisco (1990), New York (1991) and Exeter (1991). A Specialist Conference was organised in Karachi, Pakistan, in 1991. The specific issues being investigated include the following: (1) the aetiology of large classes, the definition of a 'large class', patterns of teacher and learner behaviour in large classes, teachers' perceptions of large classes, learners' perceptions of large classes, and approaches to the management of large classes; (2) relationship between class size and language acquisition, and teachers' and learners' strategies in large classes.
Published Material: A complete list of publications is available from the researchers.
Status: Sponsored project
Source of Grant: The British Council £1,500; The Bell Educational Trust £300; The Centre for British Teachers £500
Date of Research: 1986-continuing
KEYWORDS: class size; English – second language; second language learning; second language teaching

Leicester University

10/0657

Department of Psychology, University Road, Leicester
LE1 7RH
01162 522522
Gillett, R. Dr
Sample size determination in replication attempts
Abstract: A replication attempt is a study undertaken to establish whether an earlier finding represents a genuine effect. Sample size determination can prove difficult if the theory motivating the original experiment is insufficiently precise to provide strong predictions about the expected magnitude of the experimental effect. A method is being developed to determine sample size in a replication attempt when there is uncertainty about the magnitude of the experimental effect. The method uses information provided by the original study to construct a distribution of probable effect sizes. The sample size to be employed in a replication attempt is that which supplies an expected power of the desired amount over the distribution of probable effect sizes.
Published Material: GILLETT, R. (1986). 'Sample size determination in replication attempts: the standard normal Z test', British Journal of Mathematical and Statistical Psychology, Vol 39, No 2, pp.190-207.
Status: Individual research
Date of Research: 1983-continuing
KEYWORDS: research methodology; sample size

10/0658

Department of Psychology, University Road, Leicester
LE1 7RH
01162 522522
Gillett, R. Dr
Matching: an exact test procedure
Abstract: Studies using the matching paradigm aim to establish whether a one-to-one pairing of objects or people from two groups contains more pairing of a particular kind than expected under the null hypothesis. By applying the combinatorial technique of Rook methodology, a flexible and general framework for constructing exact tests in the matching paradigm is being developed. Among the practical benefits of the approach are (a) a more sensitive test of individual matching performance, (b) the assessment of broad agreement when raters are uncertain, and (c) a solution to the problem of infeasible pairings.
Published Material: GILLETT, R. (1985). 'The matching paradigm: an exact test procedure', Psychological Bulletin, Vol 97, No 1, pp.106-118.; GILLETT, R. (1985). 'Nominal scale response agreement and rater uncertainty', British Journal of Mathematical and Statistical Psychology, Vol 38, No 1, pp.58-66.; GILLETT, R. (1985). 'Allowing for infeasible pairings in the matching paradigm', Psychometrika, Vol 50, No 3, pp.265-274.
Status: Individual research
Date of Research: 1983-continuing
KEYWORDS: models; predictive validity; probability; statistical inference

10/0659

Department of Psychology, University Road, Leicester
LE1 7RH
01162 522522
Annett, M. Dr
Phonological and visuospatial processing at the left and right of the laterality distribution
Abstract: The right shift (RS) theory of handedness has led to the hypothesis that there are specific risks for cognitive processing, associated with the rs— and rs++ genotypes. The genotypes cannot be identified directly, but are more frequent at the left and right of the continuum of right minus left (R-L) hand skill. Those at the left are at risk because they lack something which assists the growth of speech in the left hemisphere. Those at the right are at risk because they carry a double dose of a factor which appears to work by handicapping the right hemisphere. Annett and Manning (1990) have shown that reading ability varies with laterality in normal school children such that children at both extremes are likely to be poorer readers than those in the centre. The purpose of the research is to show that a double dissociation between people specifically at risk for phonological and visuospatial processing is associated with the left and right of the R-L hand skill distribution; and that this dissociation is relevant to subtypes of dyslexia. Among poorer readers, error patterns associated with 'phonological' versus 'surface' or 'dyseidetic' dyslexias could be more prevalant at the left and the right of the laterality distribution respectively.
Published Material: ANNETT, M. & MANNING, M. (1990). 'Reading and a balanced polymorphism for laterality and ability', Journal of Child Psychology and Psychiatry, Vol 31, No 4, pp.511-529.; ANNETT, M. (1992). 'Phonological processing and right minus left hand skill', Quarterly Journal of Experimental Psychology, No 44, pp.33-46.; ANNETT, M. (1991). 'Reading upside down and mirror text in groups differing for right minus left hand skill', European Journal of Cognitive Psychology, No 3, pp.363-377.
Status: Sponsored project
Source of Grant: Wellcome Trust £50,545
Date of Research: 1991-1994
KEYWORDS: brain hemisphere functions; dyslexia; handedness; lateral dominance; reading difficulties; visual perception

10/0660

Department of Psychology, University Road, Leicester
LE1 7RH
01162 522522
Sluckin, A. Mrs; Foreman, N. Dr; Milloy, N. Dr
The aetiology and treatment of selective mutism (children who do not talk in school)
Abstract: This research is undertaken by members of the Leicester Selective Muslim Information and Research Association (SMIRA). The research analyses the phenomenon of the child who does not talk in school despite having age-appropriate speech at home. Data on 25 such cases, including details of home background, exposure to more than one language, age at referral and number of school terms spent mute, has been accumulated. The research also involves scrutinisation of the treatment programmes to which children were exposed, in particular the extent to which behavioural treatment methods were incorporated. Statistical analysis revealed that those children having made little progress at follow-up were those having a clinical psychopathology in the immediate family (often maternal depression), and those having been given standard remedial programmes in school without a behavioural component. The results suggest that a subgroup of selective mute children can be identified that is likely to persist in selectivity of speaking, and that would benefit from the early appli-

cation of treatment methods having a behavioural content. Current research is aimed at extending the data to a larger sample, analysing more closely the quality of speech shown by selective mute children in the home environment, and assessing quality of speech in the school environment on recovery. It is hoped to develop procedures for assessing the possible role of behavioural inhibition in the aetiology of the condition. The research group is linked to a registered charity devoted to researching selective mutism and offering support to the parents, teachers and other professionals currently having to deal with selectively mute children. The group is currently producing a video that will be distributed to parents and professionals throughout the UK on request. The work of this group may have special relevance to the difficulties of children who are difficult to test under National Curriculum arrangements due to their reluctance to speak. The group has links with Norway and the USA.
Published Material: SLUCKIN, A., FOREMAN, N. & HERBERT, M. (1991). 'Behavioural treatment programmes and selectivity of speaking at follow-up in a sample of twenty-five selective mutes', Australian Psychologist, Vol 26, pp.132-137.
Status: Individual research
Date of Research: 1975-continuing
KEYWORDS: *behaviour problems; elective mutism; inhibition; psychopathology; speech communication*

10/0661

Department of Psychology, University Road, Leicester
LE1 7RH
01162 522522
Foreman, N. Dr; Wilson, P. Dr
The development of spatial awareness in children with physical handicaps, particularly those integrated in mainstream schools
Abstract: Children's spatial awareness has been tested using a variety of paradigms, and the development of cognitive mapping skills charted across the preschool and primary school age-range. Using search tasks with groups of 10-20 infants, it has been shown that spatial awareness develops especially rapidly between 2 and 5 years (Foreman et al, 1984), and that reference memory develops in advance of working memory for visited places (Foreman, Warry & Murray, 1990). The research has also found, in groups of 30-40 able-bodied children, that independent spatial choice is necessary for the development of spatial awareness (Foreman, Foreman et al, 1990). In disabled children integrated in mainstream schools (N=10) it was found that mobility status determined accuracy in using cognitive spatial representations of the classroom and school campus compared with a matched control group (Foreman et al, 1989; Foreman & Gell, 1990). This work was carried out collaboratively between the Psychology Department of Leicester University and the Advisory Service for Physically Impaired Pupils in Mainstream Schools, based at Westbrook Special School, Long Eaton, Derbyshire. Current research is extending the earlier work, investigating whether locomotion in space and/or spatial choice in able-bodied pupils specifically affects working or reference components of spatial memory, and whether spatial skill relates to other areas of intellectual development such as reading, mathematical or technical ability. The research attempts to develop desk-top procedures and computerised tasks which measure spatial development. This will enable schools to identify spatial disabilities and offer appropriate remedial help. Within special education, the researchers are currently exploring the use of 'virtual reality' computerised environments as a possible means of remediating spatial difficulties in more severely disabled pupils, and in relating spatial difficulties to particular forms of cerebral dysfunction. The research currently focuses upon the use of computer-simulated spatial environments (3-D Virtual Reality) to enhance and assess spatial skills in disabled children, using a variety of interface devices.
Published Material: FOREMAN, N., ARBER, M. & SAVAGE, J. (1984). 'Spatial memory in preschool infants', Developmental Psychobiology, Vol 17, pp.129-137.; FOREMAN, N., FOREMAN, D., CUMMINGS, A. & OWNES, S. (1990). 'Locomotion, active choice, and spatial memory in children', Journal of General Psychology, Vol. 117, pp.215-232.; FOREMAN, N. & BERRYMAN, M. (1990). 'Kids in space (Access, Mobility and Motability Section)', Special Children, No 35, pp.20-21.; FOREMAN, N., ORENCAS, C., NICHOLAS, E., MORTON, P. & GELL, M. (1989). 'Spatial awareness in seven to 11-year-old physically handicapped children in mainstream schools', European Journal of Special Needs Education, Vol 4, No 3, pp.171-180.; FOREMAN, N. (Ed). (1993). 'Virtual reality', Special Children, No 68, pp.26-27.

Status: Individual research
Date of Research: 1983-continuing
KEYWORDS: *cognitive processes; mainstreaming; spatial ability; special educational needs*

10/0662

Department of Psychology, University Road, Leicester
LE1 7RH
01162 522522
Colley, A. Dr; *Supervisor:* Hargreaves, D. Dr
Gender differences in educational computing in the humanities
Abstract: Although Information Technology (IT) has become an important part of education at all levels, there is clear evidence that girls receive less benefit from IT. Research shows that boys are more interested in computers, and that they use them more at home and at school. Computers are widely used in the male-dominated areas of science and technology but they are now making a significant impact in the arts, in subject areas which traditionally have attracted girls. This project uses a large scale survey method (N=1,500) to investigate secondary school boys' and girls' interest in, attitudes towards and use of IT in English and music in which new technologies are increasingly being used. Previous research has found that girls are likely to perform better in science and technology subjects in single-sex schools, where they do not feel in competition with their male peers. A comparison will therefore be made between pupils in co-educational and single sex schools. Gender stereotyping has prevented many girls from developing an interest in science and technology. The project will provide valuable information which can be used to ensure that girls do not miss out on technological advancements in the humanities.
Status: Sponsored project
Source of Grant: Leverhulme Trust £41,593.12
Date of Research: 1991-1993
KEYWORDS: *computer uses in education; gender equality; humanities; information technology; sex differences*

10/0663

School of Education, University Road, Leicester LE1 7RH
01162 522522
Fogelman, K. Prof.; Reeder, D. Dr; Crook, D. Mr
Processes and outcomes of the introduction of comprehensive schools in England and Wales
Abstract: This research looks at the processes and outcomes of the introduction of comprehensive schools in England and Wales. Ten representative authorities are being studied and Duke University, North Carolina (collaborating in the project) is working on data gathered by the National Child Development Study.
Status: Sponsored project
Source of Grant: Spenser Foundation
Date of Research: 1991-1993
KEYWORDS: *comprehensive schools; educational change; educational history; secondary education*

10/0664

School of Education, University Road, Leicester LE1 7RH
01162 522522
Dobson, N. Mr; *Supervisor:* Aplin, R. Mr; Wortley, A. Mrs
The use of outdoor pursuits in schools in England and France
Abstract: Outdoor pursuits have grown greatly in importance in the educational programme of school children in England and France since World War Two. In 1951 the first local authority residential outdoor pursuits centre in England and Wales was opened, and the first class of elementary school children was taken to the Alps for a month of half-time skiing and half-time normal lessons. After a slow start the number of children being taken, through the education authorities of both countries, to experience outdoor pursuits, has expanded enormously. This study will attempt to describe this movement and to discover what value the authorities, parents, teachers and children ascribe to outdoor pursuit activities.
Status: Individual research
Date of Research: 1991-continuing
KEYWORDS: *activities; comparative education; France; outdoor pursuits; physical education*

10/0665

School of Education, University Road, Leicester LE1 7RH
01162 522522
Tomley, D. Mr

Individual action plan project

Abstract: The project aims to introduce the process of Action Planning within the Postgraduate Certificate of Education (PGCE) courses at Leicester University. The project will follow the PGCE students who secure posts locally for two years, to see how individual action planning is built upon during their induction period.

Status: Sponsored project
Source of Grant: Training, Enterprise & Education Directorate
Date of Research: 1991-1994
KEYWORDS: planning; postgraduate certificate in education; teacher education

10/0666

School of Education, University Road, Leicester LE1 7RH
01162 522522
Brown, M. Mrs; *Supervisor:* Wright, C. Dr; Fogelman, K. Prof.

Multicultural education: images at primary level

Abstract: Is concern about minority pupils a worthy matter or are there more pressing problems in education? What does multicultural education mean in terms of actual school practice? Who is referred to when we use the term 'ethnic minority'? In this study an observational research will be conducted, with the aim of analysing attitudes and views of teachers and pupils of given primary schools. Three types of schools will be researched and formal and informal interviews with individuals and groups of teachers and pupils will be conducted. Records and reports will also be assessed in order to discover views on multicultural education and to ascertain if school experiences of ethnic minority pupils in the various schools are similar. It will also be decided whether the internal system of the schools and their teaching methods have differential effects on the pupils of ethnic minority. The three different types of school examined are: (a) large primary schools in inner city areas (Birmingham and London) where there exists a high percentage of pupils from ethnic minority backgrounds. In these schools multicultural educational techniques are used to an extreme to cater for 'supposed needs' especially in the area of language development; (b) primary schools in developing towns (Northampton and Cambridge) where pupils of multiethnic backgrounds attend on a smaller scale, and multicultural teaching methods and practices are incorporated in the curriculum successfully; (c) rural primary schools where heads and teachers alike believe that multicultural education is not needed in their school as no pupils of multiethnic backgrounds attend and they find multicultural education baffling, misleading and foreign. The study prompts questions in relation to the degree of multicultural awareness and practices observed in schools.

Status: Sponsored project
Source of Grant: Overstone Park Kindergarten & Preparatory School
Date of Research: 1988-1993
KEYWORDS: ethnic groups; multicultural education; primary schools

10/0667

School of Education, University Road, Leicester LE1 7RH
01162 522522
Martin, J. Mrs; *Supervisor:* Lofthouse, M. Dr

Management and development of teacher education in Jamaica (the Caribbean) and England 1938-1988

Abstract: This research will take an historical look at teacher training in the Caribbean and in Jamaica, in particular. Some indicators will be pointed up to present policy. The level is all through ages 5-16, but emphasis is upon adolescence and the tailoring of initial teacher training (ITT) towards it.

Status: Individual research
Date of Research: 1989-1993
KEYWORDS: educational history; Jamaica; preservice teacher education

10/0668

School of Education, University Road, Leicester LE1 7RH
01162 522522
Galton, M. Prof.; Hargreaves, L. Dr

Implementation of the National Curriculum in clusters of small rural schools

Abstract: This project is furthering the research already carried out on small schools in rural areas. It will look at the effects of the National Curriculum requirements on small schools and the advantages/disadvantages of clusters of small schools.

Status: Sponsored project
Source of Grant: Economic and Social Research Council £51,000
Date of Research: 1992-1994
KEYWORDS: cooperation; National Curriculum; rural schools; small schools

10/0669

School of Education, University Road, Leicester LE1 7RH
01162 522522
White, S. Mr; *Supervisor:* Aplin, R. Mr

Rushey Mead: a study of school effectiveness

Abstract: An indepth study of a secondary school in Leicester. Its management, effectiveness, and delivery of the National Curriculum is investigated. Partnership relations with the local teacher training school of education are included in the research.

Status: Individual research
Date of Research: 1990-1994
KEYWORDS: educational administration; National Curriculum; preservice teacher education; school effectiveness; secondary schools

10/0670

School of Education, Centre for Citizenship Studies in Education, University Centre, Barrack Road, Northampton NN2 6AF
01604 30180
Fogelman, K. Prof.; Edwards, J. Mrs

Citizenship project

Abstract: A centre established to investigate the teaching of citizenship, particularly in the National Curriculum. An annotated bibliography, inservice teacher education (INSET) work, teacher training and case studies are all in hand. A book is planned and market research will be undertaken.

Status: Sponsored project
Source of Grant: Barclaycard; ESSO
Date of Research: 1991-1994
KEYWORDS: citizenship education; cross curricular approach; National Curriculum

10/0671

School of Education, Educational Management Development Unit, University Centre, Barrack Road, Northampton NN2 6AF
01604 30180
Drane, J. Mrs; *Supervisor:* Lofthouse, M. Dr

The changing role of secondary headteachers

Abstract: This research focuses upon the changing role of secondary headteachers following the Education Reform Act 1988. The main area of interest is the centralisation v decentralisation conflict within recent legislation and the effect this has had on the role of the headteacher. Questions of interest are: (1) headteachers and governors – their working relationship; (2) headteachers or chief executives; (3) headteachers and power/authority – enhanced or diminished; and (4) headteachers and their senior management teams – real or imagined team work.

Status: Individual research
Date of Research: 1990-continuing
KEYWORDS: administrator role; educational change; head teachers; management in education; role conflict; secondary schools; teacher role

10/0672

School of Education, Educational Management Development Unit, University Centre, Barrack Road, Northampton NN2 6AF
01604 30180
Bush, T. Prof.; Coleman, M. Mrs

Educational Management Development Unit research into educational management

Abstract: This is a centre established to investigate all aspects of educational management, particularly quantitative and qualitative aspects. Emphasis will be on Local Management of Schools (LMS) and Grant Maintained Status (GMS). A series of reports will result.

Published Material: BUSH, T. & COLEMAN, M. (1992). The

financial implications of mass opting out. Northampton: Leicester University, Educational Management Development Unit.
Status: Sponsored project
Source of Grant: Digital (DEC); Northamptonshire Local Education Authority
Date of Research: 1992-continuing
KEYWORDS: *educational administration; grant maintained schools; local management of schools; management in education; school-based management*

10/0673
> School of Education, Educational Management Development Unit, University Centre, Barrack Road, Northampton
> NN2 6AF
> 01604 30180
> Bush, T. Prof.; Coleman, M. Mrs; West-Burnham, J. Mr; Wall, D. Ms

Mentoring of headteachers and mentoring in middle management
Abstract: Leicester is one of six universities (the others being: Keele; Sussex; Manchester Metropolitan; Oxford and Swansea) included in a research project on mentoring. The distinctive feature of the Leicester team's research is the emphasis on mentoring in continuing professional development, rather than mentoring in initial teacher training (ITT). During the academic year 1993-94, two sets of interviews will be undertaken. The research on the mentoring of headteachers comprises interviews with, and observations of, seven pairs of mentors and new headteachers from two different local education authorities. Headteachers are also asked to complete a log indicating the number and purpose of meetings. The pilot research on the mentoring of middle managers will take place in three schools: one primary; one middle; and one secondary. Interviews with newly qualified teachers (NQTs) and mentors are taking place in six schools in the two authorities, involving 13 NQTs and 11 mentors. It is anticipated that a book and journal articles will be written to disseminate the results of the research.
Status: Sponsored project
Source of Grant: Esmee Fairbairn Foundation £35,000
Date of Research: 1993-continuing
KEYWORDS: *head teachers; mentors; middle management; professional continuing education; teacher development; teaching profession*

10/0674
> School of Education, Educational Management Development Unit, University Centre, Barrack Road, Northampton
> NN2 6AF
> 01604 30180
> Bush, T. Prof.; Coleman, M. Mrs; Glover, D. Dr

The management of grant-maintained schools
Abstract: Research focused on the experience of the first one hundred schools to become grant maintained. Five questionnaires were sent to each of these schools to be completed by the headteacher, the chair of governors, a parent governor, a teacher governor and a teacher union representative. Detailed case studies were undertaken at five of the schools, one selective, three comprehensive and one primary. Both survey and case studies investigated the reasons for opting out and also considered the benefits and disadvantages perceived by the individuals within the schools. The research investigated management of admissions policies, finance, staff, curriculum, external relations and the relationship with governors. The conclusions were that grant maintained status has been efffective in raising morale within the schools studied. Three major weaknesses were identified, relating to preferential financing, the opportunity for grant maintained schools to introduce selection and the lack of accountability of the governors to the local community.
Published Material: BUSH, T. & COLEMAN, M. (1992). The financial implications of mass opting out. Leicester: University of Leicester.; BUSH, T., COLEMAN, M. & GLOVER, D. (1993). Managing autonomous schools: the grant maintained experience. London: Paul Chapman Publishing.; BUSH, T., COLEMAN, M. & GLOVER, D. (1993). 'Managing grant maintained primary schools', Educational Management and Administration, Vol 21, No 2, pp.69-78.; COLEMAN, M., BUSH, T. & GLOVER, D. (1993). 'Researching autonomous schools: a survey of the first 100 GM schools', Educational Research, Vol 35, No 2, pp.107-126.; GLOVER, D., BUSH, T. & COLEMAN, M. (1993). 'The early experience of grant maintained Church schools', Research in Education, No 50, pp.27-37.

Status: Sponsored project
Source of Grant: Leverhulme Trust
Date of Research: 1992-1993
KEYWORDS: *educational administration; educational change; grant maintained schools; management in education; school-based management*

Liverpool John Moores University

10/0675
> School of Education and Community Studies, I M Marsh Campus, Barkhill Road, Liverpool L17 6BD
> 0151 231 2121
> Fenwick, G. Mr

Ten year old pupils reading preferences
Abstract: The aims of the research are to: 1) discover the nature of the material which primary pupils read; and 2) record their reading preferences and the time which they devote to reading. Very little work has been done in this field in recent years. This survey seeks to update, in a modest way, the findings of Whiteheads Schools Council research (1977). The sample to be used is 450+ Year 5 pupils in 18 schools in 4 neighbouring local education authorities. The survey used a questionnaire, with follow-up interviews. The data is still being worked, but to date the findings are: 1) Fiction predominates. Non-fiction preferred by a minority. This applies to both boys and girls. 2) Poetry relatively popular, more particularly with girls. 3) Knowledge of poets wideranging but varies greatly from school to school. A paper on preliminary findings was delivered at the International Reading Conference at Lancaster in September 1993.
Status: Sponsored project
Source of Grant: Liverpool John Moores University
Date of Research: 1992-1994
KEYWORDS: *books; children's literature; fiction; poetry; primary school pupils; reading; reading material selection*

10/0676
> School of Education and Community Studies, I M Marsh Campus, Barkhill Road, Liverpool L17 6BD
> 0151 231 2121
> Peel, J. Dr; Burns, M. Mrs

Self-esteem enhancement programmes
Abstract: Six week self-esteem enhancement programmes were trialled on three sets of adolescent girls: girls who had been sexually abused; girls drawn from remedial classes in schools; and girls who were about to sit for GCSE examinations. These programmes demonstrated short-term positive effects, but few long-term gains. Stage 2 of the research will be to trial modified programmes with pupils in mainstream schools. In Stage 1 specialist counsellors and therapists were used to run the programmes. In Stage 2 non-specialist trainee teachers will run the programmes.
Status: Sponsored project
Source of Grant: Liverpool John Moores University £950
Date of Research: 1992-1994
KEYWORDS: *attitude change; motivation techniques; pupil needs; self-concept; self-esteem*

10/0677
> School of Education and Community Studies, I M Marsh Campus, Barkhill Road, Liverpool L17 6BD
> 0151 231 2121
> Roberts, R. Ms; Mullins, P. Ms; *Supervisor:* Spalding, R. Mr

Entitlement within the National Curriculum: issues of identification and differentiation for children with special educational needs
Abstract: The aims of the research are to: 1) monitor current progress in a number of local education authorities in the North West towards differentiation with the National Curriculum; 2) investigate differing rates of progress in these developments and the reasons for them; 3) evaluate the variety of materials and approaches being used for their relative success as measured against a variety of criteria; 4) develop a bank of good and effective practice in the identification of specific difficulties and differentiation for them within the framework offered

by the National Curriculum; and 5) disseminate the results in the form of publications and open learning packs for use in initial and inservice teaching training. The methodology includes: 1) survey of current practice via local authority sources, questionnaire and fieldwork; 2) systems analysis of institutions in terms of the factors which facilitate and hinder such developments; 3) participant observation, and observational analysis techniques; 4) measurement of pupil progress against learning outcomes, and other criteria, both cognitive and affective; 5) comparative studies using set criteria of a variety of materials and approaches on matched populations; and 6) individual case studies.

Status: Individual research
Date of Research: 1993-1994
KEYWORDS: *differentiated curriculum; individual needs; mainstreaming; National Curriculum; special educational needs*

10/0678

> School of Education and Community Studies, I M Marsh Campus, Barkhill Road, Liverpool L17 6BD
> 0151 231 2121
> Fidler, L. Miss; *Supervisor:* Latham, J. Mr

Multicultural education and the National Curriculum in primary schools
Abstract: The period since the Education Reform Act 1988, has seen much despondency in the field of multicultural education in the primary school, as a consequence of the marginalisation or omission of multicultural education and equal opportunities issues in the Statutory Orders for most subjects of the National Curriculum. A crucial question not yet substantially theorised or answered practically, in the context of the National Curriculum, is that of appropriate strategies for taking forward multicultural issues in the school classroom. Moreover, the primary school curriculum, which is traditionally more flexible and process-oriented than that of many secondary schools, has been particularly overlooked. This research is designed to provide theoretical underpinnings, and to draw out practical implications to address this evolving situation. The Cross-Curricular Dimensions of Equal Opportunities and Multicultural Education offer opportunities for some curriculum-development, and these have begun to be explored in the literature. An even more fruitful avenue for exploration is, however, the Cross-Curricular Theme of 'Education for Citizenship', and in particular its references, albeit brief and undeveloped, to pluralism and human rights education. The small literature which at present treats the educational implications of this subject includes formal documents, background academic works and a small number of obscure school textbooks. An important objective of this research is to review and augment this literature, in addition to developing practical guidelines for teachers.
Status: Individual research
Date of Research: 1993-continuing
KEYWORDS: *cross curricular approach; multicultural education; National Curriculum; primary education*

10/0679

> School of Education and Community Studies, I M Marsh Campus, Barkhill Road, Liverpool L17 6BD
> 0151 231 2121
> MacLeod, M. Mr; *Supervisor:* Huddart, D. Dr; Griffiths, T. Mr

Strategies for the wider implementation of environmental education in higher education
Abstract: The aims of this research are: 1) A 'cross-curricular greening' of the students' curriculum and the establishment of an Environmental Education entitlement in all teacher training courses. 2) A development policy for Environmental Education across the curriculum and an action plan for its implementation. 3) The development of a wider strategy for the development of Environmental Education within the Institution and the development of excellent environmental practices. 4) The adoption of a comprehensive environmental policy statement, an action plan for its implementation, and the adoption of a policy for the development of Environmental Education within this Institution. The project will involve: action research; questionnaire surveying; discussions; curriculum development; and evaluation.
Status: Individual research
Date of Research: 1993-continuing
KEYWORDS: *curriculum development; environmental education; higher education*

10/0680

> School of Education and Community Studies, I M Marsh Campus, Barkhill Road, Liverpool L17 6BD
> 0151 231 2121
> Martin, D. Mr; *Supervisor:* Huddart, D. Dr; Griffiths, T. Mr

An evaluation of earth education programmes as alternative methods of environmental education in schools and outdoor centres
Abstract: Earth Education developed from Acclimatization which was a special introductory programme of carefully crafted, structured learning experiences based on discovery and experiential learning. This was based around structured programmes using a wide variety of activities. These programmes could be an important alternative method of Environmental Education but their success in imparting knowledge, giving an accurate view of ecological concepts, and in changing attitudes and behaviour has not been evaluated. The project includes: action research; questionnaire surveying; discussions; and curriculum evaluation in schools and centres which run Earth Education programmes. Short (a few days to a month) and longer term (1, 2 and 3 year) evaluations of the programme's success will be undertaken.
Status: Individual research
Date of Research: 1993-continuing
KEYWORDS: *earth science; environmental education; learning activities*

10/0681

> School of Education and Community Studies, I M Marsh Campus, Barkhill Road, Liverpool L17 6BD
> 0151 231 2121
> Mennell, D. Ms; *Supervisor:* Leaman, O. Dr; James, P. Dr

Death and schools: problems and possibilities
Abstract: Positivists (White 1977; Maccoby and Martin 1983; Minuchin & Shapiro 1983), Symbolic Interactionalists (Sarason 1972), Psychologists and Sociologists (Mead 1934; Freud 1948; Cooley & Mead 1934), have all suggested their own ideas on how human beings are socialised. All the approaches have had their critics and their supporters. However, the Positivist model of socialisation provides useful sub-divisions for the purpose of research. For example, the approach claims that the major socialisation agents of human beings are the 'family' and 'schools'. To date theorists and researchers have focused on the concept of death from a number of different standpoints, and all the information and ideas has added to our knowledge of human beings in relation to the concept of death, however they have failed to investigate the concepts of socialisation and death in relation to children. By building on the Positivist model of socialisation, this research aims to investigate the influence of: schools; the family; television programmes; children's books; poetry; computer games; religious philosophy; and comic books on children's understanding of death. This will be achieved by literature searches, interviews with 48 children, 12 teachers and 30 parents. Interviews will be conducted in independent, State, Church of England, Roman Catholic, Jewish and rural schools.
Status: Individual research
Date of Research: 1993-continuing
KEYWORDS: *attitude formation; bereavement; childhood attitudes; death*

10/0682

> School of Education and Community Studies, I M Marsh Campus, Barkhill Road, Liverpool L17 6BD
> 0151 231 2121
> Porter, J. Dr

Environment and polymers
Abstract: The aim of the research is to develop curriculum plans and materials on the theme of environment and polymers including those contained within the National Curriculum. The plans will be aimed at the key stages in the National Curriculum and will include a consideration of cross-curricular planning in relation to cross-curricular areas and cross-curricular themes. Plastics are used widely by individuals, families and industry. In the UK very little plastic is recycled; most plastics are dumped in landfill sites where they take years to decay. The curriculum development will focus on: 1) Increase of awareness of the problems of disposal in our 'throwaway' society – the role of education and the media in changing attitudes so waste products are valued/re-used. 2) The importance of plastics in our society and an exploration of the reasons for this – economic and scientific. 3) Novel innovation ideas for the recycling and re-use of plastics.

Status: Sponsored project
Source of Grant: BP Chemicals £2,500
Date of Research: 1991-1992
KEYWORDS: cross curricular approach; curriculum development; environmental education; National Curriculum; polymers

10/0683

School of Education and Community Studies, I M Marsh Campus, Barkhill Road, Liverpool L17 6BD
0151 231 2121
Stanley, N. Mr; Mason, M. Mrs
CD-ROM in education: effective use
Abstract: Experience in the classroom has indicated that when children are presented with a large amount of information, they find difficulty in extracting the relevant subset that will enable them to solve a problem, describe a characteristic or answer a question. This can also be observed to some extent in students at a different level. Working with children, and observing student teachers working with children, has shown that particular skills and strategies are necessary to extract the relevant information from written sources such as reference books. There is a tendency to attempt to present all the information which is offered, rather than to use, analyse and distill that which is relevant. Many children given a reference book will simply try to copy the contents. Students are encouraged to help children to develop strategies to overcome this when working with written materials. The research will focus on identifying strategies for the intelligent use of CD-ROM and investigating ways in which such strategies could be developed in learners at all stages of education. Obviously a small scale project such as this can only use a limited amount of research time and resources. In the light of this it is planned to utilise opportunities already scheduled to facilitate the enquiry. In addition, the research will try to identify what makes a 'good' CD-ROM.
Status: Sponsored project
Source of Grant: National Council for Educational Technology £1,500
Date of Research: 1992-1993
KEYWORDS: computer uses in education; optical data discs

10/0684

School of Education and Community Studies, I M Marsh Campus, Barkhill Road, Liverpool L17 6BD
0151 231 2121
Deeside College, Department of Art and Design, Kelsterton Road, Connah's Quay, Deeside CH5 4BR
01224 831531
Jones, C. Ms; Supervisor: Leaman, O. Dr; Clarke, J. Mr; Parkinson, F. Ms
The work related further education needs of Deeside, Clwyd: training requirements, funding and marketing
Abstract: As a result of the Government's White Paper in May 1991, further education colleges and sixth form colleges have been granted autonomy from local education authorities (LEAs). These independent colleges are now responsible for designing and creating relevant and attractive courses to entice a range of clients to their college rather than their rival college. Funding will come via the Funding Councils and the Training and Enterprise Councils (TECs) which will hold funds for work related further education (WRFE) programmes. The TECs objectives are to link vocational education to the local labour market needs. In an effort to promote retraining in the changing market place, the Government launched the Professional, Industrial and Commercial Update (PICKUP) Programme in 1982. The PICKUP Programme is designed to help increase, improve and meet the updating, retraining and educational needs of adults at work. Colleges need to define areas of retraining and skills updating, compile suitable and relevant WRFE courses, locate the funding, and sell the benefits of such training to employers using effective marketing strategies and printed marketing material. This thesis will research the training needs of five employers on Deeside, Clwyd, with the view to: establishing the present training levels of their workforce; defining the companies short and long term objectives; and analysing the training needs of tomorrow's employees. An investigation will be undertaken into WRFE training providers and funding opportunities; model courses will be put forward for pilot schemes; suitable marketing strategies will be compiled; and promotional material will be designed and produced and their effectiveness evaluated. The outcomes of the research will include: a definition of the historical and demographic characteristics of Deeside; a description of local

WRFE training providers; a definition of the training needs; recognition of the need for skills updating; the accreditation of prior learning for experienced staff; establishment of training levels of the current workforce; feasibility studies of funding opportunities for pilot courses; an evaluation of present WRFE courses and, as a result, a framework for future WRFE courses; a definition of the specific marketing strategies; and sample marketing material required for the promotion of WRFE. The methods will include: 1) An investigation of the historical and demographic characteristics of Deeside. 2) Case studies of five major employers. 3) A survey in the form of (anonymous) postal questionnaires to all employees to ascertain their present skills levels. 4) Feasibility studies carried out into the content of current WRFE courses and an evaluation of their effectiveness in the form of face-to-face questionnaires. 5) Interviews with TEC officials, PICKUP agents, Welsh Office representatives, trade union representatives, and employees. 6) Model WRFE courses piloted and their effectiveness evaluated – via confidential opinion questionnaires to employers, employees, course providers, trade union representatives, and funding bodies. Sample marketing material specifically for the promotion of WRFE will be designed and produced, including an evaluation of their effectiveness.
Status: Individual research
Date of Research: 1993-continuing
KEYWORDS: further education; industry-further education relationship; training; vocational education

Liverpool University

10/0685

Department of Education, PO Box 147, Liverpool L69 3BX
0151 794 2000
Beattie, N. Dr
The Freinet Movement in its international context
Abstract: The aim is to explore the Freinet Movement, which has been central to most 'progressive' developments in French education, over the period 1920 to the present day and to describe and discuss its cross-national impact. This has been considerable in some areas (e.g. Italy post-1945, Portugal post-1974) and nil in others (e.g. United Kingdom). By placing a very broad movement of opinion and practice in its cultural and historical context, this long-term enquiry should produce some clarification of elusive culture-bound ideas such as 'progressive' and 'international' dissemination.
Status: Individual research
Date of Research: 1987-1993
KEYWORDS: comparative education; educational history; educational theories; progressive education

10/0686

Department of Education, PO Box 147, Liverpool L69 3BX
0151 794 2000
Meakin, D. Mr
Philosophy of the curriculum with particular reference to moral, religious, physical education and personal and social education
Abstract: This research has been within the area of the philosophy of the curriculum with particular reference to moral, religious, aesthetic and physical education. It has mainly been concerned with three questions: (i) how these kinds of education are to be characterised; (ii) how, if at all, they might be justified; (iii) whether any general criteria can be established for including subjects and activities in the school curriculum.
Published Material: MEAKIN, D.C. (1983). 'On the justification of physical education', Momentum, Vol 8, No 3, pp.10-17.; MEAKIN, D.C. (1986). 'The moral status of competition: an issue of concern to physical educators', Journal of Philosophy of Education, Vol 20, No 1, pp.59-67.; MEAKIN, D.C. (1988). 'The justification of religious education reconsidered', British Journal of Religious Education, Vol 10, No 2, pp.92-96.; MEAKIN, D.C. (1989). 'Personal, social and moral education and religious education': the need for conceptual clarity', British Journal of Religious Education, Vol 11, No 1, pp.15-21.; MEAKIN, D.C. (1990). 'How physical education can contribute to personal and social education', Physical Education Review, Vol 13, No 2, pp.108-119. A full list of publications is available from the researcher.
Status: Individual research

Date of Research: 1973-continuing
KEYWORDS: curriculum development; educational philosophy; individual development; moral education; physical education; religious education

10/0687
Department of Education, PO Box 147, Liverpool L69 3BX
0151 794 2000
Stewart, R. Mr; Walsh, S. Ms; *Supervisor:* Martland, J. Mr
Developing navigational skills in young children
Abstract: The aim of the project is to: a) examine the ability of children, aged 7-11 years, to acquire and use map and compass skills in orienteering and navigation; b) explore the teaching and coaching problems encountered and to develop instructional materials. The project has worked with over 450 children aged 7-11 years in Merseyside schools. The children were required to use a map to complete a route following task across a 40 feet square grid. The research identified that orientation of the map and oneself is a key skill in navigation. The research revealed an apparent developmental pattern in orientation in that seven year olds tried to use a finger pointing strategy to pinpoint their own location, equivalent to saying, "I am here", without reference to their route or large scale locational information. They then proceeded by trial and error to complete the task. Eight, nine and ten year olds tend to use a simple map turning strategy. In a follow up study, 83 seven year olds in four intact classes were presented with strategies for orientation. One group was presented with an intervention programme based on the use of landmarks, a second group used a compass strategy, a third used both with the fourth acting as a control group. All groups, except the control, showed significant improvement in route following tasks. Sixty-two percent of the group offered both strategies chose to use the compass based strategy. The results suggest that children of seven years of age are able to complete potentially disorientating route following tasks when using a simple compass to maintain orientation.
Published Material: MARTLAND, J.R., STEWART, R.R. & WALSH, S.E. (1991). 'How do we teach our young orienteers to use the compass more effectively?', Scientific Journal of Orienteering, Vol 7, No 1/2, pp.104-114.; MCNEILL, C., MARTLAND, J.R. & PALMER, P. (1992). Orienteering in the National Curriculum: a practical guide for teachers. Harveys Map Services.; WALSH, S.E. & MARTLAND, J.R. (1993). 'The development of orientation strategies with young children'. In: Orientation and navigation: birds, humans and other animals. Royal Institute of Navigation.; WALSH, S.E. & MARTLAND, J.R. (1993). 'The orientation and navigational skills of young children: an application of two intervention strategies', Journal of Navigation, Vol 1.46, No 1, pp.63-68.; A full list of publications is available from the researcher.
Status: Sponsored project
Source of Grant: Sports Science Education Programme £54,000
Date of Research: 1989-1994
KEYWORDS: geography education; mathematics education; navigation; orientation; orienteering; outdoor pursuits; primary education

10/0688
Department of Education, PO Box 147, Liverpool L69 3BX
0151 794 2000
Marsden, W. Prof.
An Anglo-Welsh teaching dynasty, 1840's-1930's
Abstract: 'An Anglo-Welsh teaching dynasty' traces the contribution of three generations of teachers in the Adams family (two of whom were headteachers at Fleet Road School). It illuminates the history of education in England and Wales over one hundred years by exploring the meritocratic advances of a family, starting with a Pembrokeshire milller in the 1840s and ending with his grandson, a Cambridge graduate and MBE who ended his educational career in the 1930s. The family included six headteachers and a School Board clerk; and the institutions covered included a national school; British and Foreign Society schools; training colleges; Board Schools, secondary schools; a private school; the Army Education Service; and two universities. Locations ranged from Pembrokeshire to industrial South Wales; the London Metropolitan area; Hampshire and Kent. The project extends previous historical research through bibliographic study.
Published Material: MARSDEN, W.E. (1991). Educating the respectable; a study of Fleet Road Board School, Hampstead, 1879-1903. London: The Woburn Press.; GOODENOW, R.K. & MARSDEN, W.E. (1992). (Eds). The city and education in four nations. Cambridge: Cambridge University Press.; MARSDEN,

W.E. An Anglo-Welsh teaching dynasty: the Adams family, 1840s-1930s. London: The Woburn Press. (in press).
Status: Sponsored project
Source of Grant: Liverpool University Research Fund; Woburn Press
Date of Research: 1990-continuing
KEYWORDS: educational history; head teachers

10/0689
Department of Education, PO Box 147, Liverpool L69 3BX
0151 794 2000
Ferguson, S. Mr
School/Industry Compacts: the translation of an American model to England
Abstract: The Boston Compact has been used as a model for school/industry compacts in the United Kingdom which have been promoted by government, industry and local authorities since late 1987. This research builds upon first-hand knowledge of the original Boston Compact to make comments upon the applicability of this American model to the English education setting.
Status: Individual research
Date of Research: 1988-continuing
KEYWORDS: comparative education; industry-education relationship; United States of America; work education relationship

10/0690
Department of Education, PO Box 147, Liverpool L69 3BX
0151 794 2000
Beattie, N. Dr
The educational impact of Celestin Freinet in France, and internationally (especially Italy, Germany and the United Kingdom)
Abstract: Celestin Freinet (1896-1966) was an important innovator in French education, especially primary education, over the period from 1920 until his death. His work continues through an Institute he founded in Cannes. He had wide international contacts and influence, and he was politically on the left. Research will be conducted by library work interviews. It will place Freinet against his French background and explore the extent and significance of his international outreach, especially in Italy and Germany, and his failure to have any impact in the English speaking world. There is thus a comparative dimension to the work. A book is planned.
Status: Individual research
Date of Research: 1994-continuing

10/0691
Department of Education, PO Box 147, Liverpool L69 3BX
0151 794 2000
Hamilton, D. Prof.
Modernism and schooling
Abstract: A study of European schooling in the period 1400-1700.
Status: Individual research
Date of Research: 1993-1994
KEYWORDS: educational history

10/0692
Department of Education, PO Box 147, Liverpool L69 3BX
0151 794 2000
Pearce, J. Ms; Garrigan, P. Ms; Stewart, R. Mr; Ferguson, S. Mr
The application of syndicate group work and competency profiling to an undergraduate programme of professional study
Abstract: Tutors from Liverpool University, Department of Education, who have for some years used Syndicate Group Work methods in the Postgraduate Certificate in Education (PGCE) course, are working collaboratively with tutors in the University School of Architecture to develop such methods with their students. The project aims to improve the effectiveness of group work teaching and learning, to increase the efficiency of the course by developing the roles of facilitation among tutors, and to devise appropriate competency-based profiling methods for student assessment. Outcomes so far include: the production of materials which introduce students to group work; a report to the School of Architecture on current assessment procedures; a review of student perceptions of conventional teaching on the course; and a learning pack ('Building Analysis') which groups of students are currently using. The development of assessment methods is proceeding.
Status: Sponsored project

Source of Grant: Higher Education Funding Council £88,000
Date of Research: 1992-1994
KEYWORDS: *assessment; competency based education; group work; higher education; teaching methods*

10/0693

Department of Education, PO Box 147, Liverpool L69 3BX
0151 794 2000
Hesford, L. Mrs; *Supervisor:* Harrop, S. Mrs
Women in the professions: their early education and training
Abstract: This is an historical project, relating in the first instance to the late nineteenth and early twentieth centuries. The University of Liverpool provided education for female teachers in the nineteenth century. This was followed by education for female doctors, dentists, engineers, lawyers and architects since the twentieth century. This research project intends to ask such questions as: 1) Which young women trained to read for degrees in professional subjects? 2) From which areas and schools did they come? 3) What did they do with their training? 4) What was their role in the rise of the professional society? Comparative material will be sought from the University of Birmingham's Leverhulme Project on its social and economic history, and from the libraries and archives of the relevant professional bodies. Contact will also be made with international scholars known to be working in this field.
Status: Individual research
Date of Research: 1993-continuing
KEYWORDS: *educational history; higher education; professional education; universities; women's education; women's employment*

10/0694

Department of Education, PO Box 147, Liverpool L69 3BX
0151 794 2000
Pearce, J. Ms; Johnston, K. Ms
Involving teachers in the design of work-based learning in a secondary PGCE course
Abstract: The project's aim is to involve a group of teachers from a cross-section of Liverpool University's Department of Education's 'partner' schools in planning part of a new, 66% work-based course of training for student teachers. It is hoped that by involving teachers the programme devised will make as full a use as possible of the potential provided by workplace-based learning. The main task of the group is to design, pilot and evaluate six 'self-study' packs, which secondary Postgraduate Certificate in Education (PGCE) students will use as a basis for the study of 'whole-school' issues during their course. The packs will be designed for use by individual students, by student groups (working as syndicates), or by teacher mentors working with students in school.
Status: Sponsored project
Source of Grant: Liverpool University: Enterprise in Higher Education Unit £3,150
Date of Research: 1993-1994
KEYWORDS: *postgraduate certificate in education; preservice teacher education; school-based teacher education*

10/0695

Department of Education, PO Box 147, Liverpool L69 3BX
0151 794 2000
Skidmore, P. Ms; *Supervisor:* Harrop, S. Mrs; Woodcock, G. Dr
Local radio and adult education
Abstract: This study examines the use of local radio for educational work with adults. It tests the view that local radio is able to cater for an adult audience in a way which is different from other media, being able to focus on the involvement of the local community. Included in the research is the emergence of local radio in the history of radio broadcasting; the development of educational broadcasting in general; and the specific contribution of local radio to the education of adults. Methods used include: a documentary study; interviews with key personnel in national and local radio, and in adult education; and a case study of the policies and programmes of Radio Merseyside from the 1970s to the early 1990s, with an evaluation of their effectiveness. Provisional conclusions are as follows: i) Local radio has a unique contribution to make to adult education; ii) The demands made by involving members of the local community in programming are very heavy; iii) Personalities play a key role in the success or otherwise of educational policy.
Status: Sponsored project
Source of Grant: Universities Funding Council £20,000

Date of Research: 1991-1993
KEYWORDS: *adult education; educational broadcasting; educational radio; local radio; mass media; radio*

10/0696

Department of Education, PO Box 147, Liverpool L69 3BX
0151 794 2000
Hall, K. Mr; *Supervisor:* Derricott, R. Mr
Corporate identity in secondary schools
Abstract: This research arises out of marketing within the management of institutions. It focuses on the creation and promotion of corporate identity in state secondary schools. The aim is to determine whether this activity, as practised in profit and other non-profit organisations, affects the success of schools, and notably their ability to attract pupils. The resulting thesis will include: a general introduction on the concept of corporate identity; a major section, within an historical survey, on attempts to achieve a national identity in Germany; following a literature review, a chapter on school marketing; and a report on preliminary research interviews in commercial and non-commercial institutions. The main research constitutes a questionnaire to a one-third sample of state secondary schools in England and Wales. This survey, with a 43.6% response, was followed up with visits to 41 schools of special interest. Because of the link between architecture and identity, the research included interviews with the Hampshire County architect and visits to 3 recommended schools in that county. The thesis will also include a case study based on two pupils in a local school, the aim of which is to clarify how clients (e.g. pupils, parents) form an image of an institution. The thesis thus progresses from culture, through identity, to image. As well as research in British schools and institutions, the study also included research in Boston, USA, and in the Bundesarchiv, Koblenz, Germany.
Status: Individual research
Date of Research: 1991-1994
KEYWORDS: *marketing; secondary schools*

10/0697

Department of Education, PO Box 147, Liverpool L69 3BX
0151 794 2000
Cambridge University, Local Examinations Syndicate, 1 Hills Road, Cambridge CB1 2EU
01223 61111
Schilling, M. Dr; Russell, T. Mr; Massey, A. Mr; McCarty, C. Mr; Boden, J. Mrs; Chatfield, J. Mrs
The development of National Curriculum key stage 2 standard tests for science
Abstract: The Centre for Research in Primary Science and Technology (CRIPSAT) and the University of Cambridge Local Examinations Syndicate (UCLES) are the appointed agency to develop the standard tests for science which will be used at the end of Key Stage 2. Tests are developed, trialled with Y6 children, evaluated by National Pre-testing, and cover levels 1-6 of the National Curriculum in science. Test materials, evaluation reports and non-statutory materials are published with a School Curriculum and Assessment Authority (SCAA) copyright.
Status: Sponsored project
Source of Grant: School Curriculum and Assessment Authority £540,000
Date of Research: 1992-continuing

10/0698

Department of Education, Centre for Research in Primary Science & Technology, PO Box 147, Liverpool L69 3BX
0151 794 2000
Russell, T. Mr; Qualter, A. Dr
Evaluation of the implementation of science in the National Curriculum
Abstract: The evaluation rests on a number of issues which have been raised by Her Majesty's Inspectorate, the National Curriculum Council, and by others. There are three main ones: (1) coverage; (2) progression; and (3) differentiation. In relation to coverage, it has been observed that teachers are to some extent failing to cover certain aspects of the National Curriculum in science; they may be overlooking them; or they may be deferring them. The reasons why this is the case are being explored with a focus on planning for teaching science. The second study, on progression, involves a consideration of the match between the levels in the National Curriculum intended to

represent progression in learning, and the order in which pupils develop their understanding in science. The third issue involves the study of the appropriateness of the order for less able, and more able and talented pupils. A mixture of individual interviews of teachers and pupils, national questionnaire, group interviews and classroom observation is used in meeting the not inconsiderable challenges of this project.
Status: Sponsored project
Source of Grant: National Curriculum Council £345,000
Date of Research: 1991-1993
KEYWORDS: curriculum development; National Curriculum; science education

10/0699
> Department of Education, Centre for Research in Primary Science & Technology, PO Box 147, Liverpool L69 3BX
> 0151 794 2000
> Cambridge University, Local Examinations Syndicate, Syndicate Buildings, 1 Hills Road, Cambridge CB1 2EU
> 01223 61111
> Schilling, M. Dr; *Supervisor:* Daniels, R. Mr

Development of National Curriculum standard tests in science for key stage 2
Abstract: The project is designing test materials for early trials in autumn 1992, in 80 schools across 13 local education authorities (LEAs). Analysis of children's responses to test items and of teachers' questionnaires will inform the modification of tests for national pilot tests in May 1993. Monitoring of testing in 2% of schools (at National Curriculum key stage 2) will further inform the writing of test questions and mark schemes, for 1994. Continuing trials and modifications as a result of teachers' feedback, will inform test development for 1995 and 1996.
Status: Sponsored project
Source of Grant: School Examinations and Assessment Council
Date of Research: 1992-continuing
KEYWORDS: assessment; National Curriculum; school-based assessment; science education

10/0700
> Department of Education, Environmental Education Research Unit, PO Box 147, Liverpool L69 3BX
> 0151 794 2000
> Boyes, E. Dr; Stanisstreet, M. Dr

Development of the ideas of secondary school children concerning the ozone layer
Abstract: The understanding of pupils between the ages of 11 and 16 about the ozone layer – what it is, what will damage it, and what will be the likely result of such damage – has been studied. Following the use of a preliminary open-form questionnaire, the ideas of a large cohort of children (over 1700) have been probed by closed-form questionnaire and by interviews with a subset of this group. Children seem aware that the ozone layer is a layer of gas around the earth, but less sure what that gas is. They also know that it protects the earth from ultra-violet rays from the sun, and that further depletion will allow more ultra-violet to earth and cause more skin cancer. Most also know that one cause of depletion is the use of chlorofluorocarbons (CFCs), but may confuse the depletion of the ozone layer with the greenhouse effect and other forms of atmospheric pollution. The research provides evidence to suggest that such confusion between ideas is strongly held and that, even with this relatively new and abstract phenomenon as far as the children are concerned, ideas are held in a consistent and similar framework by most pupils. Similar research is being conducted in Greece and in the USA.
Status: Individual research
Date of Research: 1992-1993
KEYWORDS: air pollution; conservation – environment; environmental education; misconceptions; scientific concepts; secondary school pupils

10/0701
> Department of General Practice, PO Box 147, Liverpool L69 3BX
> 0151 794 2000
> Al-Shehri, A. Dr; *Supervisor:* Derricott, R. Mr

Learning by reflection in general practice
Abstract: The most prevalent criticism of any professional educational programme is the diversity between theory and practice. This

is true in the medical profession generally and in general practice particularly. For example, it has been recognised that continuing medical education (CME) for general practitioners (GPs) has little relevance to their daily experience. In order to bridge this gap between theory and practice, professional learning programmes need to be linked to daily experience. Experiential, or experience-based, learning seems to be the way forward. However, many educational theorists maintain that experiential learning cannot take place without reflection. Reflection and reflective practice enable practitioners to step back and examine their work critically so that they become more competent, professionally. Many methods and approaches have been used to promote reflection and reflective practice, but personal professional journals seem to be the most cost-effective method. This study examines this notion of reflection and reflective practice by using personal professional journals in the context of medical general practice. Nineteen established general practitioners have been involved in pre-test/post-test experimental design to determine whether there is any association between reflection and professional competence. Using structured document devised by the researcher, GPs are asked to write their reflection daily for one week each month over six months. These documents will be analyzed to see development of reflection for each participant over the study period. Parameters such as learning approaches of GPs, referral and prescribing rates, are used to assess participants before and after the study to assess their competence and learning.
Status: Individual research
Date of Research: 1991-continuing
KEYWORDS: critical thinking; experiential learning; medical education; professional continuing education; professional development; reflective teaching

10/0702
> Department of Psychology, PO Box 147, Liverpool L69 3BX
> 0151 794 2000
> Faber, D. Mrs; *Supervisor:* Lovie, A. Dr

Binet's work and achievement: the first intelligence scales of 1905
Abstract: The area of this research is the history of psychology. Although Binet is recognised as the pioneer of intelligence testing and his influence has been very great, the genesis of his scales is often misrepresented. The researcher's aim is to explain the achievement of Alfred Binet (1857-1911) with reference to his Intelligence Scales of 1905, the first 'true' tests of intelligence. The research involves identifying Binet's changing conceptions of intelligence and its developmental aspects, and tracing the origins of the test items in his experimental work in the 20 years preceding 1905. This also necessitates an examination of Binet's view of psychology as a science, his conception of a psychological experiment and the nature and role of introspections. The social and cultural contexts are important contributing factors to Binet's achievement, and are explained with reference to testing in other countries. In France, political forces and an immediate educational problem led to the Minister of Education's decision to have Paris school children tested or screened for ineducability. Binet's work, particularly that in association with the 'Société Libre pour L'Etude Psychologique de l'Enfant', was known by the authorities in 1904. The commission was entrusted to Binet; his earlier work and later collaboration with Simon resulted in the finally produced Scales of 1905, amply justifying their trust in the psychological work of Binet.
Status: Individual research
Date of Research: 1988-1993
KEYWORDS: educational history; France; intelligence tests; psychological testing; psychology

10/0703
> Department of Sociology, Social Policy and Social Work Studies, PO Box 147, Liverpool L69 3BX
> 0151 794 2000
> Roberts, K. Prof.

Young people and economic change in Poland
Abstract: This project involves surveys of over 1,800 17-25 year olds, plus depth interviews with smaller numbers of young people and other key informants in Gdansk, Katowice and Suwalki in Poland. The enquiries are intended to clarify the impact of 'the reforms' on Poland's young people and to indicate the need for policy initiatives in education, training and employment. The research has been designed so that some of the findings will be comparable with data from the Economic and Social Research Council (ESRC) 16-19 initiative and an associated study of young people in Germany.

Status: Sponsored project
Source of Grant: Economic and Social Research Council £60,000;
European Union £50,000
Date of Research: 1992-1994
KEYWORDS: economic change; educational needs; educational policy; Poland; social change; youth

London Borough of Wandsworth

10/0704
Education Department, Professional Centre, Franciscan
Road, Tooting, London SW17 8HE
0181 682 3759
Strand, S. Dr
Baseline assessment at age 4+
Abstract: Wandsworth LEA (local education authority) is instigating
a baseline assessment for every pupil starting full-time education in
a reception class in a Wandsworth school. The aims of the assessment
are (i) to provide structured materials to support teachers in identifying children with problems in their first term of school (ii) to identify
children for further diagnostic assessment or referral to LEA support
agencies (e.g. Integrated Support Service, Educational Psychology
Service) (iii) to act as a baseline against which to evaluate the child's
progress at the end of National Curriculum Key Stage 1. Baseline will
consist of two elements: (i) a teacher completed checklist giving
detailed background information on the child, and an assessment of
the child's social and emotional development, motor skills, attainment in oral language, early reading and writing, mathematics and
science; (ii) a shortened form on the Linguistic Awareness for Reading Readiness (LARR) Test. Both assessments will be completed by
the classroom teacher during the course of the child's first term in
school. A borough-wide pilot involving over 2,000 pupils in 63
schools started in Autumn term 1992. The LEA will evaluate the
reliability and concurrent validity of baseline in an interim report in
1993. This will include investigating the relationship between pupil
attainment and gender, home language/s, ethnic group, family size,
birth order and age (summer born). The final report, evaluating the
predictive validity of baseline, will be compiled when the cohort have
completed their Key Stage 1 assessment in 1994.
Published Material: Copies of Baseline materials are available from
the researcher.
Status: Sponsored project
Source of Grant: Wandsworth Local Education Authority £10,000
Date of Research: 1991-1994
*KEYWORDS: assessment; pupil development; pupil evaluation; re-
ception classes; school entrance age; screening tests*

London University

10/0705
Birkbeck College, Department of Psychology, Malet Street,
London WC1E 7HX
0171 580 6622
Van der Lely, H. Dr
**A psycholinguistic investigation into the underlying cause of
specific language impairment in children**
Abstract: Specific language impaired (SLI) children suffer from
language disorder in the absence of any other impairments. The
underlying nature and cause of this disorder, affecting an estimated
500,000 children, is still poorly understood. This research proposes
a hypothesis about the underlying deficit in SLI children based on the
findings from expression and comprehension. The extent of the
hypothesised 'domain specific' language deficit will be tested by
investigating grammatical, general linguistic and non-linguistic (domain neutral) representations. This will give a better understanding
of SLI children and of the mechanisms of language acquisition in
general.
Published Material: VAN DER LELY, H.K.J. & DEWART, H.
(1986). 'Sentence comprehension strategies in specifically language
impaired children', British Journal of Disorders of Communication,
No 21, pp.291-306.; VAN DER LELY, H.K.J. & DEWART, H.
(1987). 'How do specifically language impaired children understand

sentences?', Proceedings from the First International Symposium for
Specific Speech and Language Disorders in Children, London: As-
sociation for All Speech Impaired Children (AFASIC).; VAN DER
LELY, H.K.J. & HARRIS, M. (1990). 'Specifically language im-
paired children's comprehension of reversible sentences', Journal of
Speech and Hearing Disorders, Vol 55, No 1, pp.101-117.
Status: Sponsored project
Source of Grant: British Academy £64,000
Date of Research: 1991-1994
*KEYWORDS: language acquisition; language handicaps; learning
disabilities; psycholinguistics*

10/0706
Goldsmiths' College, Faculty of Education, Lewisham Way,
New Cross, London SE14 6NW
0171 919 7171
Mace, J. Ms; Gregory, E. Dr
**Literacy at home and at school: the relationship between
literacy practices in the households of children in two inner
city primary schools and those of their classrooms**
Abstract: The aims of this project were to: (1) investigate and report
on the literacy practices in the households of children in two inner
city primary schools; (2) compare these with those used by teachers
in the schools; (3) test out a home-school event which would bring
the two together. This was a pilot six month project, jointly supervised
by two academics with, respectively, expertise in adult and primary
literacy, and employing two part-time research assistants, working in
two East London schools. A total sample of 10-12 households will
have been used; half of the sample are bilingual Sylheti-speaking
households; the other half, speakers of English as a first language.
Parents in both groups include some with expressed literacy difficulties. The methods used included interviews, observations, and participatory events. So far the results show evidence of under-
expectation by school of children from Sylheti households; and
interest in the role of television as a barrier to or inspiration for
children's literacy. A successful grant application to the Economic
and Social Research Council will mean a further one-year sequel to
this study (1991-95).
Status: Sponsored project
Source of Grant: Goldsmiths' College research grant £4,195
Date of Research: 1992-1993
*KEYWORDS: adult literacy; home-school relationship; literacy;
literacy education; mother tongue; native speakers; primary education; teaching methods*

10/0707
Goldsmiths' College, Faculty of Education, Lewisham Way,
New Cross, London SE14 6NW
0171 919 7171
Mace, J. Ms
**Reminiscence and the uses of literacy: transitions between oral
and written narrative in reminiscence work with elderly people**
Abstract: The project (1) used oral history techniques with a community of pensioners sharing a common work history; and (2) explored
the writing development issues of reminiscence work. This was a
one-year study, commissioned by the Cottage Homes Charity, which
provides accommodation on an estate in Mill Hill for 250+ retired
staff from the retail trade. The research project involved a total of 50
of these residents. The methods used include tape-recorded individual interviews; group meetings; editorial individual/group meetings
based on the tape transcripts; and publication of an anthology by the
participants, documenting recollected life in department stores (1910
– 1985).
Published Material: MACE, J. (Ed). (1993). Call yourself a draper:
memories of life in the trade. London: Cottage Homes.
Status: Sponsored project
Date of Research: 1993-1993
*KEYWORDS: literacy; memory; older adults; oral history; personal
narratives*

10/0708
Goldsmiths' College, Faculty of Education, Lewisham Way,
New Cross, London SE14 6NW
0171 919 7171
Hurst, V. Ms; Blenkin, G. Ms
Monitoring and evaluation in workplace nurseries
Abstract: The project aims to gain an insight into the evaluation

procedures used by workplace nurseries, in particular the role of the 'outsider'. Ethnographic action research, based on two nursery centres, will investigate how staff may be supported in the monitoring and evaluation of their practice.
Published Material: BLENKIN, G.M. & KELLY, A.V. (1992). (Eds). Assessment in early childhood education. London: Paul Chapman.
Status: Sponsored project
Source of Grant: London University: Goldsmiths' College £3,700
Date of Research: 1990-1993
KEYWORDS: *employer supported day care; evaluation methods; institutional evaluation; self evaluation – groups*

10/0709
Goldsmiths' College, Faculty of Education, Lewisham Way, New Cross, London SE14 6NW
0171 919 7171
Matthews, B Mr; Thumpston, G. Ms
Collaborative learning and equal opportunities
Abstract: There has been an increasing emphasis on collaborative learning in all aspects of education. Within the National Curriculum, evaluation of pupils discussing and taking part in group work is now statutory. In particular, recent research projects have shown how important the discussion of ideas is to children learning about science and other subjects. The action research is to find ways of: studying interactions; finding strategies that will enable pupils to be aware of their interactions; finding strategies that will enable pupils to change the ways they discuss; encouraging greater learning of all pupils; encouraging girls and boys to see each other as full people, rather than to relate to each other through stereotypes; encouraging pupils from all ethnic backgrounds to see each other as full people, rather than to relate to each other through stereotypes. The project is focused on all curriculum areas in primary and secondary schools, but will also apply to adults. As it is an action research project set in the classroom it is possible that local education authorities will be interested.
Published Material: MATTHEWS, B. (1994). 'Promoting equal opportunities: starting girls and boys communicating', Journal of Teacher Development, Vol 3, No 3, pp.149-158.
Status: Individual research
Date of Research: 1991-continuing
KEYWORDS: *discussion; group work; interaction; intergroup education; learning activities*

10/0710
Goldsmiths' College, Faculty of Education, Lewisham Way, New Cross, London SE14 6NW
0171 919 7171
Clyne, P. Mr; *Supervisor:* Coben, D. Ms
Professional development of adult educators in south east London
Abstract: This project seeks to research the need for professional development of adult educators in south east London. This will be done through consultation with other providers of adult and continuing education in a range of settings including the new local education authorities, health authorities; social services and others. The aim will be to develop the curriculum and appropriate accreditation and transferability and to begin to provide short courses.
Status: Sponsored project
Source of Grant: Universities Funding Coucil £15,000
Date of Research: 1991-1993
KEYWORDS: *adult education teachers; adult educators; professional development*

10/0711
Goldsmiths' College, Faculty of Education, Lewisham Way, New Cross, London SE14 6NW
0171 919 7171
Gibbs, L. Ms
Research into the professional development and training of private music teachers
Abstract: An initial survey of private music teachers, qualified and unqualified, to examine kinds of training/preparation teachers may or may not have received. Data from almost 600 questionnaires has been analysed, together with 60 follow-up interviews. Musical training is shown to be variable and lacking strongly on improvisation, composing and aural training. Training for teaching is also variable

and external qualifications for teaching do not actually endorse teaching expertise. Teachers generally teach what they themselves have been taught. Survey interviews include information on private music teachers' perceptions of their effectiveness and their recommendations for further training and accreditation.
Published Material: GIBBS, L. (1990). 'Private lives', Music Teacher, Vol 69, No 8, pp.11,13.; GIBBS, L. (1990). 'How good are private music teachers', Journal of the Incorporated Society of Musicians, Vol 53, No 3, pp.78.; GIBBS, L. (1991). 'Research into the professional development and training of private music teachers', Journal of the European Piano Teachers Association, Vol 12, No 36, pp.36.; GIBBS, L. (1993). Private lives: report on the survey of private music teachers and their professional development and training. London: University of London, Goldsmiths' College.; GIBBS, L. (1993). 'Private life and work: getting inside private music teaching', ISM Music Journal, August, pp.92-93.
Status: Sponsored project
Source of Grant: Universities Funding Council £20,000
Date of Research: 1991-1993
KEYWORDS: *music teachers; professional development; professional training; teacher education*

10/0712
Goldsmiths' College, Faculty of Education, Lewisham Way, New Cross, London SE14 6NW
0171 919 7171
Adams, T. Dr
Investigation into what factors pre-dispose students to seek counselling with special reference to: subject bias, special categories of college entry and history of mental instability
Abstract: Data collected by Goldsmiths' Counselling Service over the last three years profiles a number of factors which the case-load presents. With regard to strategies of resourcing and academic pastoral support the data moves beyond an equation of student numbers and counselling hours. Relevant factors so far identified are that subject bias can appear to influence student stability; that special categories of students (e.g. mature) can cause considerable stress on the counselling provision; and that aspects of the psychological backgrounds of vulnerable students can lead to the service responding to problems that are reactivated through study. In order to address then the essential responsibilities of the Counselling Service provision the present study aims to evaluate students' specific needs by investigating what factors pre-dispose students to seek counselling. By appropriating the preliminary data, special reference is given in the study to subject bias, categories of college entry and history of mental instability. Research on student counselling services has been largely conducted by practising counsellors upon their own services. Such relatively small-scale research has resulted in a dearth of comparative studies across services. The present study is a comparative study made of the case-loads of counselling services in three institutions in the first instance. On identifying the small sample of services, students' specific needs are accessed by means of a semi-structured interview schedule, through which a base of information evolves and from which the final field work questions can be structured. The design of the pilot questionnaires will incorporate attitudes to and expectations of the counselling service, i.e. how the perception of student counselling consumerism affect the service provision. As a pilot study this research initiative will be broadened in scope at a national level.
Status: Sponsored project
Source of Grant: London University: Goldsmiths' College £1,600
Date of Research: 1991-1993
KEYWORDS: *counselling services; higher education; pastoral care – education; student counselling; student needs*

10/0713
Goldsmiths' College, Faculty of Education, Lewisham Way, New Cross, London SE14 6NW
0171 919 7171
Tomlinson, S. Prof.
Alternative policies in education
Abstract: The research stemmed from the view that post 1988 educational reforms could lead to a divided and divisive education system based on competitive individualism and on inappropriate market ideology. The project analysed the policy and ideological base of reforms, and attempted to suggest alternative policies based on consensus and cooperation which would still serve both individual development and economic needs. The methodology was library

work and participatory action research in policy making left-of-centre groups.

Published Material: TOMLINSON, S. (1991). 'Teaching by numbers', Fabian Review, Vol 103, No 2.; TOMLINSON, S. (1992). 'Back to the future: streaming and selection', ACE Bulletin, No 45, pp.6-7.; TOMLINSON, S. (1993). 'Education: vision, principles and policies', Renewal, No 1, pp.47-56.; TOMLINSON, S. (1993). 'A nationalistic curriculum for white superiority?', ACE Bulletin, No 51, pp.10-11.; TOMLINSON, S. (Ed) (1994). Educational reform and its consequences. London: Rivers Oram Press.
Status: Sponsored project
Source of Grant: Leverhulme Trust £20,500
Date of Research: 1990-1993
KEYWORDS: Education Reform Act 1988; educational change; educational policy; politics education relationship

10/0714
Goldsmiths' College, Faculty of Education, Lewisham Way, New Cross, London SE14 6NW
0171 919 7171
Jones, L. Ms
Continuity in curriculum learning experience (CICLE)
Abstract: This project is monitoring the progress of a group of children from Year 6 through to Year 7, focusing on mathematics, science and design technology. The children were selected from a number of 'feeder' primary schools, feeding into the comprehensive school which they presently attend. They keep a weekly diary, recording their curriculum experiences and their personal observations. Teachers and children have been interviewed. The content of the curriculum experience will be analysed and categorised using a content analysis schedule. Record keeping systems will be analysed and data collected about the curriculum materials used in each school.
Published Material: JONES, L. & JONES, L.P. (1992). 'Spiralling upwards: progression across the interface', British Journal of Curriculum and Assessment, Vol 3, No 1, pp.10-12.; JONES, L.P. & JONES, L. (1993). 'Keeping up the momentum: improving continuity', Education 3-13, Vol 21, No 3, pp.46-50.; GRIFFITHS, J. & JONES, L. (1994). 'And you have to dissect frogs!', Forum, Vol 36, No 3, pp.83-84.
Status: Sponsored project
Source of Grant: University of London Central Research Fund
Date of Research: 1991-continuing
KEYWORDS: curriculum development; developmental continuity; primary secondary education

10/0715
Goldsmiths' College, Faculty of Education, Lewisham Way, New Cross, London SE14 6NW
0171 919 7171
Blenkin, G. Ms; Whitehead, M. Ms; Hurst, V. Ms; Yue, N. Dr
Principles into practice: improving the quality of children's early learning
Abstract: The main aims of the project are to: 1) identify key aspects of professional ability which are crucial to the quality of children's early learning; 2) generate criteria for promoting the development of these aspects of professional ability; and 3) generate consequent criteria for improving professional practice in the early years. During the first funded year, research activities will include: 1) A major survey of institutions and groups caring for young children throughout England and Wales (a questionnaire has been sent to a representative sample of heads of these institutions and groups). 2) A pilot study involving structured interviews with heads of institutions and groups caring for young children (pilot sample of 12 in the London area). 3) A pilot study involving action research to evaluate professional practice (pilot sample of 8 institutions in the London area). It is hoped to secure funds for the 2nd and 3rd year of the project (April 1994 to March 1996).
Status: Sponsored project
Source of Grant: Esmee Fairbairn Charitable Trust £90,000
Date of Research: 1993-continuing
KEYWORDS: early childhood education; preschool education

10/0716
Goldsmiths' College, Faculty of Education, Lewisham Way, New Cross, London SE14 6NW
0171 919 7171
Gregory, E. Dr
A family literacy project in Tower Hamlets, London
Abstract: This is part of a longitudinal project to investigate the home literacy practices of a group of Year 1 children of Bangladeshi origin and their families. The aim of the project is to devise language and literacy programmes which build both upon the child's knowledge from home, and accepted principles for successful second language learning. Programmes will be used by teachers, parents and community language teachers. Phase 1 of the project (1992/93) is an investigation into the reading practices of the Year 1 children outside school, and a comparison with those in the English classroom, in terms of: scope; materials used; and participation structures. Phase 2 is the development of early literacy programmes for use at home and in school which take account of the information gathered in Phase 1. Inservice education in the school runs parallel with this. Size and composition of the sample will be 6 families of Year 1 children of Bangladeshi origin. The project will use ethnographic and ethnomethodological approaches such as interviews, mini-surveys, participant observation, discourse analysis etc. Results of Phase 1 show contrasts in the types of material used during literacy events in and outside school, and also in the participation structures and the scope of events taking place. The children's interpretation of 'reading' in the different domains has also been highlighted. The nature of the child's role as 'reader' at home and at school has been documented.
Published Material: GREGORY, E. (1993). 'What counts as reading in the early years' classroom?', The British Journal of Educational Psychology, Vol 63, No 2, pp.214-30.; GREGORY, E. (1993). 'Reading between the lines', Times Educational Supplement, No 4033, October 15, p.4.; GREGORY, E., LATHWELL, J., MACE, J. & RASHID, N. (1993). Literacy at home and at school. Literacy Research Group Report. London: University of London, Goldsmiths' College.
Status: Sponsored project
Source of Grant: Paul Hamlyn Foundation £7,700
Date of Research: 1993-1994
KEYWORDS: bilingual education programmes; English – second language; ethnic groups; home-school relationship; literacy education; parent participation; reading teaching; second language learning

10/0717
Imperial College of Science, Technology and Medicine, Humanities Programme, Mechanical Engineering Building, Exhibition Road, London SW7 3BX
0171 589 5111
Hughes, J. Mr; *Supervisor:* Goodlad, S. Dr
Tutoring from colleges to schools
Abstract: The aim of the project is to promote peer tutoring schemes, similar to Imperial College's 'Pimlico Connection', around the United Kingdom. This is when volunteer students from further or higher education act as tutors in local primary and secondary schools often in science, mathematics and technology lessons. The professional teacher uses them as an extra, and valuable, teaching resource. The student tutors provide positive role models to the school pupils and in doing so it is hoped to increase the aspiration for them to stay on in education and training beyond age 16. Students acquire communication, organisational and problem-solving skills as well as self-confidence. Student tutoring involves volunteer students going into local primary and secondary schools on a sustained and systematic basis. From the original Pimlico Connection Scheme the number has risen to 96 similar programmes.
Published Material: GOODLAD, S. & HIRST, B. (1989). Peer tutoring: a guide to learning by teaching. London: Kogan Page.; GOODLAD, S. & HIRST, B. (1990). Explorations in peer tutoring. Oxford: Blackwell.; HUGHES, J.C. (1992). Tutoring: students as tutors in school. London: BP Educational Service.; HUGHES, J.C. (1991) (Ed). Tutoring Resource Pack. London: BP Educational Service.
Status: Sponsored project
Source of Grant: British Petroleum (BP) Aiming for a College Education Initiative £300,000
Date of Research: 1990-1993
KEYWORDS: mathematics education; peer influence; peer teaching; science education; student volunteers; technology education

10/0718
Imperial College of Science, Technology and Medicine, School of Management, 53 Prince's Gate, London SW7 2PG
0171 589 5111
Hall, J. Mr; *Supervisor:* Cox, B. Dr

Computer aided management education
Abstract: Computer aided management education in the School of
Management at Imperial College consists of an experiential learning
mechanism where groups of executives work on a business problem,
aided by the computer and led by a tutor. This research aims to
improve the software used in such education by enhancing information technology (IT) through the provision of participant and tutor
support. Experiments have been carried out to determine the educational effectiveness of the software, both with and without the enhancements. Results to date have been encouraging. The objective of
the enhanced software is to provide: 1) controlled management of
learning; 2) efficiency and consistency in leraning; 3) participant
satisfaction; and 4) tutor satisfaction. The research separates into 3
elements: fuzzy feedback; tutor support systems; and participant
support systems. Fuzzy feedback provides software generated feedback that is timely and apposite to the current learning need. Tutor
support provides a means of explaining simulation results, indicating
learning needs and opportunities. Participant support is an extension
of the normal decision support system in a manner that supports the
participant's learning process.
Published Material: HALL, J. & COX, B. (1992). 'Computerised
management games: a servo-mechanism analog'. Proceedings of the
SAGSET Conference, Edinburgh, August, 1992.; HALL, J. & COX,
B. (1993). 'Computerised management games: the feedback process
and servo-mechanism analogy'. In: PERCIVAL, F. et al. (Eds). The
simulation and gaming yearbook. London: Kogan Page.
Status: Individual research
Date of Research: 1991-1994
*KEYWORDS: computer assisted learning; computer uses in educa-
tion; educational software; management studies*

10/0719
Imperial College of Science, Technology and Medicine, St
Mary's Hospital Medical School, Norfolk Place, Paddington,
London W2 1PG
0171 723 1252
McManus, I. Dr; Richards, P. Prof.; Vincent, C. Dr
Three longitudinal studies of medical student selection
Abstract: This project is an assessment of the process of medical
student selection at five medical schools, for admission in October
1981 with follow-up of the entrants between October 1981 and
October 1986
Status: Sponsored project
Source of Grant: Leverhulme Trust
Date of Research: 1990-1994
*KEYWORDS: admission criteria; medical schools; medical students;
selective admission*

10/0720
Institute of Education, Centre for Multicultural Education, 20
Bedford Way, London WC1H 0AL
0171 580 1122
Gundara, J. Dr
**Diversity of educational expectations of young
gypsies/travellers, their teachers and educational institutions**
Abstract: This project aims to raise the awareness in the classroom
of the cultural influences affecting educational expectations and
performance of gypsies/travellers aged 14-18 and those responsible
for their education. Information will be gathered from the Advisory
Council for the Education of Romany and other travellers (ACERT),
Essex Travellers Education Service, Inner London Travellers Education Team, and the gypsy/traveller community. A seminar will be
held to further explore and exchange experiences. It is hoped that this
pilot study will lead to a collaborative action research project in three
member states – UK, Eire and Holland.
Status: Sponsored project
Source of Grant: European Community £2,112
Date of Research: 1992-1992
*KEYWORDS: cultural influences; gypsies; minority group children;
performance factors; travellers – itinerants*

10/0721
Institute of Education, Centre for Multicultural Education, 20
Bedford Way, London WC1H 0AL
0171 580 1122
Gundara, J. Dr
Diversity of expectations and influences on educational

achievement of young gypsies/travellers aged 14-18
Abstract: To examine the nature of such expectations and influences
via exchanges with young people themselves, their parents, teachers
and other practitioners concerned.
Status: Sponsored project
Source of Grant: Centre de Recherches Tsiganes £2,783
Date of Research: 1993-1993
*KEYWORDS: cultural influences; gypsies; minority group children;
performance factors; travellers – itinerants*

10/0722
Institute of Education, Department of Child Development
and Primary Education, 20 Bedford Way, London
WC1H 0AL
0171 580 1122
Moore, T. Prof.; *Supervisor:* Hindley, C. Prof.
**Data analysis of the longitudinal research project: changes in
general ability, personality, attitudes, values etc. of normal
children from infancy to adolescence**
Abstract: The research began in 1949 as a collaborative project
between the Institute of Education and Department of Child Health
at London University. There is thus a parallel research under Professor J.M. Tanner on the physical development of the same subjects.
As representative a sample as possible of the London West Central 1
area was recruited from 1949 to 1952. 223 subjects were recruited,
and 186 were in the sample at 18 months. For many purposes the
researchers have around 110 subjects with records complete enough
for general use up to 14 years; and 84 plus, up to 17 years. Subjects
were seen at 8 days, 6 weeks, 3, 6, 9, 12 and 18 months, and then
annually from 2 to 18 years. The aim was to obtain reasonably
comprehensive information, which includes: (1) regular interviews
with mothers about their child's behaviour and parental methods; (2)
testing of abilities, personality, etc; (3) assessment of interests, attitudes, personal values; and (4) interviews with adolescent subjects.
Data on social and family background have been obtained throughout. The researchers interests have been: (i) comparison of child-rear-
ing methods and early locomotion across collaborating European
samples; (ii) infant sleep and the effects of anoxia at birth; (iii) effects
of daily substitute care; (iv) stability and change in IQs and personality using individual curve fitting in addition to correlations etc; (v)
factors influencing development – family, social, life events, school
etc; and (vi) children's views of themselves or school, of their future
and their correspondence with outcome.
Published Material: A full list of publications is available from the
researchers.
Status: Sponsored project
Source of Grant: Leverhulme Trust £60,250
Date of Research: 1949-1988
*KEYWORDS: ability; child development; developmental continuity;
longitudinal studies; personality development*

10/0723
Institute of Education, Department of Child Development
and Primary Education, 20 Bedford Way, London
WC1H 0AL
0171 580 1122
Nunes, T. Dr
Children's understanding of the concept of area
Abstract: An analysis of the effects of different tools for measuring
on children's understanding of area.
Published Material: NUNES, T., LIGHT, P., MASON, J. & ALLER-
TON, M. (1994). 'The role of symbols in structuring reasoning:
studies about the concept of area'. Annual Meeting of the Interna-
tional Group for the Study of the Psychology of Mathematics Edu-
cation, Lisbon, 1994.
Status: Sponsored project
Source of Grant: Economic and Social Research Council £24,530
Date of Research: 1992-1993
*KEYWORDS: area; concept formation; mathematics education;
measurement equipment*

10/0724
Institute of Education, Department of Child Development
and Primary Education, 20 Bedford Way, London
WC1H 0AL
0171 580 1122
Sylva, K. Prof.

Early learning: its form and impact
Abstract: A study to investigate the effects of early learning experience. The work is mainly in libraries, but also includes some interviews of staff.
Published Material: SYLVA, K. (1992). 'Quality care for the under fives: is it worth it?', RSA Journal, October 1992, pp.683-690.; SYLVA, K. & WILTSHIRE, J. (1993). 'The impact of early learning on children's later development: a review prepared for the RSA inquiry "start right"', European Early Childhood Education Research Journal, Vol 1, No 1, pp.17-40.
Status: Sponsored project
Source of Grant: Royal Society for the Arts, Manufacture and Commerce £19,934
Date of Research: 1993-1994
KEYWORDS: early childhood education; preschool education

10/0725
Institute of Education, Department of Child Development and Primary Education, 20 Bedford Way, London
WC1H 0AL
0171 580 1122
Bryant, B. Prof.; Nunes, T. Dr
Development of orthographic and syntactic knowledge in children
Abstract: A longitudinal study of children's morphological and syntactic awareness and the development of spelling.
Published Material: NUNES, T., BRYANT, P.E. & BINDMAN, M. (1994). 'Is it "soft" or "sofed"?'. Biennial Meeting of International Society for the Study of Behavioural Development, Amsterdam, 1994.
Status: Sponsored project
Source of Grant: Medical Research Council £48,090
Date of Research: 1992-continuing
KEYWORDS: grammar; morphology – languages; semantics; spelling; syntax

10/0726
Institute of Education, Department of Child Development and Primary Education, 20 Bedford Way, London
WC1H 0AL
0171 580 1122
Nunes, T. Dr
The role of feedback and collaboration in learning
Abstract: A comparison between 9/10 year olds solving mathematics problems individually and in pairs.
Status: Sponsored project
Source of Grant: Nuffield Foundation £3,000
Date of Research: 1993-1993
KEYWORDS: feedback; group work; mathematics education; problem solving

10/0727
Institute of Education, Department of Curriculum Studies, 20 Bedford Way, London WC1H 0AL
0171 580 1122
Hull, B. Mrs; *Supervisor:* Gipps, C. Prof.
The effects of the National Curriculum on infant teachers and their practice
Abstract: The research aims to investigate the extent to which infant teachers respond to change, in particular the requirements of the National Curriculum. Case studies involving six teachers in two schools were carried out, employing techniques of participant observation and interviewing over a two year period. The results have been written up for submission as a Ph D thesis which examines the image of teachers of young children through history and literature. This theme is developed into an examination of the growth of professionalism with regard to infant teachers, and with particular reference to gender inequalities in education, posing the hypothesis that infant teaching has suffered from low status because of its relationship to the education of girls and the social position of women in society.
Published Material: HULL, B. (1990). 'The National Curriculum: its effects on infant teachers and their practice', Early Years, Vol 2, No 1, pp.39-44.
Status: Individual Research
Date of Research: 1989-1993
KEYWORDS: infant school teachers; National Curriculum; professional recognition; teaching profession

10/0728
Institute of Education, Department of Curriculum Studies, 20 Bedford Way, London WC1H 0AL
0171 580 1122
Lawton, D. Prof.
National Council for Vocational Qualifications (NCVQ) Fellowship
Abstract: This project is to examine impact and take-up of the new framework for National Vocational Qualifications (NVQs); it examines and supports the technical processes required to develop and implement NVQs as well as providing a critique of policy and strategy formation in vocational qualifications in the United Kingdom.
Status: Sponsored project
Source of Grant: National Council for Vocational Qualifications £216,669
Date of Research: 1990-1994
KEYWORDS: National Vocational Qualifications; qualifications; vocational education

10/0729
Institute of Education, Department of Curriculum Studies, 20 Bedford Way, London
0171 580 1122
Gipps, C. Prof.
Towards a theory of educational assessment
Abstract: This is an attempt to draw together developments and writing in educational assessment to re-work the theoretical and conceptual underpinnings.
Status: Sponsored project
Source of Grant: Nuffield Foundation £21,441
Date of Research: 1992-1993
KEYWORDS: assessment

10/0730
Institute of Education, Department of Curriculum Studies, 20 Bedford Way, London WC1H 0AL
0171 580 1122
Thomas, S. Dr; Mortimore, P. Prof.
National Curriculum key stage 1 analysis
Abstract: The major aim of the project is to analyse the National Curriculum assessment results at key stage 1 of all schools in the Lancashire Local Education Authority, against a variety of background variables, to identify schools doing particularly well or badly.
Status: Sponsored project
Source of Grant: Lancashire County Council £32,340
Date of Research: 1992-1993
KEYWORDS: assessment; educational quality; National Curriculum; school effectiveness

10/0731
Institute of Education, Department of Curriculum Studies, 20 Bedford Way, London WC1H 0AL
0171 580 1122
Sammons, P. Dr; Thomas, S. Dr; Mortimore, P. Prof.; Hind, A. Ms
Differential school effectiveness: departmental variations in GCSE attainment
Abstract: This 30 month project, funded by the Economic and Social Research Council (ESRC), is investigating four crucial issues of differential secondary school effectiveness: 1) departmental differences at GCSE (in English, Mathematics, Science, History and French); 2) differential academic achievement of groups of pupils (by sex and ethnic group); 3) stability over time of departmental and school effects on GCSE performance; and 4) school and departmental processes affecting GCSE attainment. The investigation analyses examination results for secondary schools in eight London local education authorities (LEAs) over a two year period using multilevel modelling techniques. In addition, detailed qualitative case studies of six selected schools are being undertaken, and some process information is being collected from a further 50 schools.
Published Material: SAMMONS, P., MORTIMORE, P. & THOMAS, S. (1993). 'Do schools perform consistently across outcomes and areas?'. Paper presented to the ESRC School Effectiveness and School Improvement Seminar Series, Sheffield, July 1993.
Status: Sponsored project
Source of Grant: Economic and Social Research Council £122,870

Date of Research: 1993-continuing
KEYWORDS: departments; differential performance; examination results; outcomes of education; school effectiveness; secondary schools

10/0732
 Institute of Education, Department of Curriculum Studies, 20 Bedford Way, London WC1H 0AL
 0171 580 1122
 Gipps, C. Prof.
Study of teacher feedback to young children
Abstract: This is a small-scale study investigating two questions: 1) What sort of feedback do teachers give to infant school children? 2) How do children interpret, understand and act on this feedback? The aim is to establish a grounded typology of teacher feedback with more explanatory power than current models.
Status: Sponsored project
Source of Grant: Economic and Social Research Council £101,600
Date of Research: 1993-continuing
KEYWORDS: classroom communication; feedback; infant school education; infant school teachers; teacher-pupil relationship; teacher response

10/0733
 Institute of Education, Department of Curriculum Studies, 20 Bedford Way, London WC1H 0AL
 0171 580 1122
 Greenwich University, Avery Hill Campus, Bexley Road, Eltham, London SE9 2PQ
 0181 316 8000
 Harland, L. Ms; *Supervisor:* Gipps, C. Prof.
Supporting teachers, supporting children with special educational needs: an exploration of the partnership between class teachers and support teachers
Abstract: The role of the support teacher is changing extensively. It is assumed that the move from withdrawing children with special educational needs from the classroom, towards working within the classroom, with the accompanying need to advise/consult the class teacher, has resulted in a qualitative improvement of educational provisions for these children. Questions are proposed which will explore the nature of the partnership between support teacher and class teachers. It is intended to uncover some of the tensions which accompany the work of the support teacher. So far there has been little evaluation of any possible improvement in educational provision for children with special educational needs which may have been accounted for by support teacher/class teacher collaboration.
Status: Individual research
Date of Research: 1986-continuing
KEYWORDS: special educational needs; support teachers; teachers

10/0734
 Institute of Education, Department of Curriculum Studies, 20 Bedford Way, London WC1H 0AL
 0171 580 1122
 London University, Institute of Education, Thomas Coram Research Unit, 20 Bedford Way, London WC1H 0AL
 Sammons, P. Dr; Mortimore, P. Prof.; Owen, C. Mr; Thomas, S. Dr
Assessing school effectiveness: developing measures to put school performance in context
Abstract: This project, commissioned by the Office for Standards in Education (OFSTED), is exploring ways of developing measures to put school performance in context. It is examining how better account can be taken of the impact of schools' intakes on their pupils, examination performance at GCSE, by investigating the feasibility of grouping schools based on measures of their intakes known to be associated with educational attainment. A review of research into school effectiveness, educational disadvantage and priority, and educational indicators is being used to guide the choice of measures. The study is constrained by the need to utilise nationally available sources of data about schools' intakes and is examining the value of using 1991 Census data concerning schools' (probable) catchment areas.
Status: Sponsored project
Source of Grant: Office for Standards in Education £38,816
Date of Research: 1993-1994
KEYWORDS: achievement; educational quality; performance factors; performance indicators; school effectiveness

10/0735
 Institute of Education, Department of Curriculum Studies, 20 Bedford Way, London WC1H 0AL
 0171 580 1122
 London University, King's College, Department of Education, Strand, London WC2R 2LS
 0171 836 5454
 Gipps, C. Prof.; Brown, M. Prof.
National assessment in primary schools: phase two
Abstract: This project is an evaluation of the introduction of national assessment focusing on teachers' developing practices in relation to standard assessment tasks (SATs) and teacher assessment, and the interpretation and use of results by teachers, parents and local education authorities (LEAs).
Published Material: GIPPS, C., McCALLUM, B., McALLISTER, S. & BROWN, M. (1991). 'National assessment at seven: some emerging themes'. In: GIPPS, C. (Ed). Developing assessment for the National Curriculum, Bedford Way series. London: Kogan Page.; McCALLUM, B. (1991). 'SATs and rites of passage', British Journal of Curriculum and Assessment, Vol 2, No 1, pp.14-16.; McCALLUM, B. et al. 'Something to gain? creative responses to national assessment'. University of Hull: Aspects of Education. (forthcoming).
Status: Sponsored project
Source of Grant: Economic and Social Research Council £201,010
Date of Research: 1990-continuing
KEYWORDS: assessment; National Curriculum; primary schools; standard assessment tasks

10/0736
 Institute of Education, Department of Economics, Geography and Business Education, 20 Bedford Way, London WC1H 0AL
 0171 580 1122
 Manchester University, School of Education, Oxford Road, Manchester M13 9PL
 0161 275 2000
 Thomas, L. Dr; Hodkinson, S. Mr
The Economic Awareness Teacher Training Programme (ECATT)
Abstract: The Economic Awareness Teacher Training Programme which began in 1986 is a response to calls for the introduction of economic awareness programmes into schools and colleges. The initiative was initially based upon a partnership between the Department of Education and Science, the Department of Trade & Industry, teacher training institutions, local education authorities and industrial and commercial organisations. British Petroleum, Banking Information Service, the Department of Trade & Industry, Unilever and the Esmee Fairbairn Trust Fund have provided funds to allow the appointment of academic and administrative staff. Initially, the Institute of Education and the University of Manchester took responsibility for coordinating the programme, which included: the development, piloting and evaluation of training programmes, schemes of work and training materials; the establishment of a forum to help local education authorities to identify their training needs and to devise strategies to meet these needs; promoting and supporting the development of teacher groups of advisers, coordinators and advisory teachers across local education authority boundaries as well as the development of links between training institutions, local education authorities and industry and commerce; the extension of the initiative to institutions in other areas of the country.
Published Material: DUNNILL, R. (1990). 'Three of a kind? a review of three LEA publications on Economic Awareness', Economic Awareness, Vol 2, No 2.; JOHNSON, C. & CLARKE, P. (1990). 'Coal: an economic awareness lesson in humanities', Economic Awareness, Vol 2, No 3, pp.15-19.; DAVIES, P. (1990). 'Industrial change – a lower school geography lesson', Economic Awareness, Vol 2, No 3, pp.20-22.; THOMAS, L. & WOOD, K. et al (1991). 'What is slavery anyway? – the economic awareness implications of work on a theme in history', Economic Awareness, Vol 3, No 2.; HODKINSON, S. (1991). 'Modern foreign languages and economic awareness: a comment', Economic Awareness, Vol 4, No 1, pp.7-9. A full list of publications is available from the researcher. Over 100 articles and monographs have been produced by the programme.
Status: Sponsored project
Source of Grant: Department of Trade & Industry; Banking Information Service; British Petroleum; Unilever; Esmee Fairbairn Charitable Trust £528,000

Date of Research: 1989-1994
KEYWORDS: *cross curricular approach; curriculum development; economics education; enterprise education; teacher education*

10/0737

Institute of Education, Department of Economics, Geography and Business Education, 20 Bedford Way, London
WC1H 0AL
0171 580 1122
Thomas, L. Dr

Economics education 16-19 project

Abstract: An Economics Association project, it aims to stimulate and co-ordinate a fundamental review of the nature of economics thinking in response to the last decade's shift in the basic concerns of the discipline; by focusing on the full range of classroom contexts at 16-19, to help teachers to investigate the implications of this review for teaching, learning and assessment strategies; to develop and publish reports, materials and resources to provide access for other teachers to the expertise which will eventually be required by all.
Published Material: THOMAS, L. (1992). 'The economics education 16-19 project: setting the scene', Economics, Vol 28, Part 2, pp.81-86.; THOMAS, L. (1992). 'The economics education 16-19 project: questions and answers', Money Management Review, No 35, pp.2-3.; THOMAS, L. (1993). 'The economics education 16-19 project: more questions and answers', Money Management Review, No 37, pp.14-15.; THOMAS, L., McCORMICK, B. & VIDLER, C. (Eds). (1994). Teaching and learning the new economics. Economics 16-19 series. Oxford: Heinemann Educational.
Status: Sponsored project
Source of Grant: Economics Association £27,000
Date of Research: 1991-1994
KEYWORDS: *curriculum development; economics education; sixteen to nineteen education*

10/0738

Institute of Education, Department of Economics, Geography and Business Education, 20 Bedford Way, London
WC1H 0AL
0171 580 1122
Lines, D. Mr

Economics and business studies education

Abstract: To provide a comprehensive 16-19 curriculum package in economics and business studies, including teaching and learning aids and a post-16 assessment vehicle.
Status: Sponsored project
Source of Grant: Nuffield Foundation £110,157
Date of Research: 1991-1994
KEYWORDS: *business education; curriculum development; economics education; sixteen to nineteen education*

10/0739

Institute of Education, Department of Economics, Geography and Business Education, 20 Bedford Way, London
WC1H 0AL
0171 580 1122
Dyer, D. Mr; Lines, D. Mr

Cambridge Business Studies Project

Abstract: This project has six objectives: (1) to foster the development of business education courses at 16+ and 18+ level, giving advice and support to teachers; (2) to develop and disseminate teachers' aids and materials primarily of value for 16+ and 18+ courses; (3) to develop inservice training courses for intending teachers and others wishing to extend their expertise; (4) to liaise with examining bodies and others for appropriate curriculum development, to foster dialogue between teachers and others interested in business education; (5) to liaise with business and industry; and (6) to monitor work and interpret and report as required.
Published Material: DYER, D.M. & CHAMBERS, I. (1987). Business Studies: an introduction. Harlow: Longman.; WHITEHEAD, D. & DYER, D.H. (1991). 'New developments in economics and business education': handbook for teachers. London: Kogan Page.; A list of teaching materials and syllabuses is available from the researchers.
Status: Sponsored project
Source of Grant: Cambridge Business Studies Trust
Date of Research: 1967-1990
KEYWORDS: *business education; curriculum development; inservice teacher education*

10/0740

Institute of Education, Department of Economics, Geography and Business Education, 20 Bedford Way, London
WC1H 0AL
0171 580 1122
Thomas, L. Dr

Tower Hamlets College

Abstract: This project will use Tower Hamlets College as a case study for an investigation of the implications of industry and work related activities for staff development and training needs.
Published Material: CLARKE, P. (1993). The implications of work experience programmes for staff development and training. A case study: Tower Hamlets College. London: Institute of Education, The Economic Awareness Teacher Training Programme.
Status: Sponsored project
Source of Grant: London East Training and Enterprise Council £2,500
Date of Research: 1992-1993
KEYWORDS: *colleges of further education; industry-further education relationship; staff development; work experience programmes*

10/0741

Institute of Education, Department of Economics, Geography and Business Education, 20 Bedford Way, London
WC1H 0AL
0171 580 1122
Slater, F. Dr; Job, D. Mr

Earth Sciences Process Laboratory

Abstract: The Earth Science Process Laboratory is designed to enable students to conduct simple but powerful educational experiments. The facilities include a rainfall simulator, wave tank, wind tunnel, flumes and a sediment laboratory. It expands the Institute's teacher training opportunities at initial training level and for inservice courses. It is also planned to develop the centre as a research facility.
Published Material: JOB, D.A., with SLATER, F.A. & POINTON, K. (1992). 'Investigating earth science processes in Central London', Teaching Earth Sciences, Vol 17, No 3, pp.114-115.; JOB, D.A. 'Learning through models – recent developments at the Earth Science laboratory, Institute of Education', Teaching Geography. (in press).; A full list of publications is available from the researcher.
Status: Sponsored project
Source of Grant: Nuffield Foundation; Sir John Cass Foundation – jointly £141,286
Date of Research: 1990-1994
KEYWORDS: *earth science; laboratories; laboratory experiments; physical environment; physical geography; simulated environment*

10/0742

Institute of Education, Department of Economics, Geography and Business Education, 20 Bedford Way, London
WC1H 0AL
0171 580 1122
Whitehead, D. Dr

Standardisation of the test of economic knowledge in the UK

Abstract: The project aims to provide norming data for the test of economic knowledge, a US origin standardised test for 14/15 year olds.
Status: Sponsored project
Source of Grant: Nuffield Foundation £5,000
Date of Research: 1992-1994
KEYWORDS: *economics education; secondary school pupils*

10/0743

Institute of Education, Department of Economics, Geography and Business Education, 20 Bedford Way, London
WC1H OAL
0171 580 1122
Thomas, L. Dr

The contribution of staff in industry and education to the success of work related activities

Abstract: The overall aim of the study was to conduct a case study of Tower Hamlets College to investigate the implications of industry and work related activities for staff development and training needs.
Status: Sponsored project
Source of Grant: London East Training and Enterprise Council; Unilever; Grand Metropolitan, jointly £2,500
Date of Research: 1992-1993

KEYWORDS: industry-education relationship; teacher development; work experience programmes

10/0744

Institute of Education, Department of Educational Psychology and Special Educational Needs, 20 Bedford Way, London WC1H 0AL
0171 580 1122
Haines, C. Dr

Effect of perceptuo-motor difficulty on early handwriting speech and reading

Abstract: In an earlier study, children entering school routinely completed neurodevelopmental tasks in the entrant school medical examination. To study the effect of difficulties with these on later school activities in and around the classroom, teachers completed a questionnaire in final year infant and first year junior classes, and children copied a sentence from the blackboard. Some four thousand children were involved. Now the geometric shapes copied at school entry, and the sentence copied from the blackboard are being assessed in greater detail to test the effect of perceptuo-motor difficulties on early handwriting skills.

Published Material: HAINES, C. (1992). 'Young children's difficulty with capital letters', Handwriting Review, pp.44-54.
Status: Sponsored project
Source of Grant: Nuffield Foundation £2,560
Date of Research: 1992-continuing
KEYWORDS: *handwriting; motor development; perceptual motor coordination; reading; speech*

10/0745

Institute of Education, Department of Educational Psychology and Special Educational Needs, 20 Bedford Way, London WC1H 0AL
0171 580 1122
Henderson, S. Dr; Dubowitz, L. Dr

Motor and perceptual competence in prematurely born children

Abstract: The focus of this study, which is being carried out jointly with the Royal Postgraduate Medical School, is on children who were born prematurely, both with and without brain damage. The study has two distinct objectives; the first is to investigate the progress of these children in school. The second is to investigate the specific perceptual and motor difficulties which many of the children experience.

Status: Sponsored project
Source of Grant: Medical Research Council £87,326; Nuffield Foundation £5,000
Date of Research: 1989-1993
KEYWORDS: *child development; motor development; neurological impairments; perceptual handicaps; premature infants; special educational needs*

10/0746

Institute of Education, Department of Educational Psychology and Special Educational Needs, 20 Bedford Way, London WC1H 0AL
0171 580 1122
Wedell, K. Prof.; Norwich, B. Dr; Lunt, I. Ms; Evans, J. Ms

Clusters project

Abstract: The project will describe the functioning of the cluster from an organisational point of view and look at the impact of the cluster organisation on special educational needs provision. Clusters of schools will be visited in four LEAs (local education authorities) and interviews of headteachers, teachers, educational psychologists (EPs) and other LEA personnel will be carried out.

Status: Sponsored project
Source of Grant: Economic and Social Research Council £46,760
Date of Research: 1991-1993
KEYWORDS: *cluster grouping; educational cooperation; special educational needs; special schools*

10/0747

Institute of Education, Department of Educational Psychology and Special Educational Needs, 20 Bedford Way, London WC1H 0AL
0171 580 1122
Henderson, S. Dr

A new look at perceptuo-motor disorders in cerebral palsied children

Abstract: The focus of the project is on children who find it difficult to negotiate their way around in the environment i.e. children who cannot judge the size of doorways, who cannot perceive distances accurately etc. Such children are handicapped in a school setting because they need so much help from others with their wheelchairs, in PE lessons, on the way to school etc. The aim of the study will be to try to establish what causes these problems – lack of motor experience, visual disorders such as squints which lead to absence of stereopsis and types of brain disorder will be investigated.

Status: Sponsored project
Source of Grant: Spastics Society £29,683
Date of Research: 1991-1993
KEYWORDS: *cerebral palsy; disabilities; motor reactions; perceptual handicaps; perceptual motor coordination; special educational needs*

10/0748

Institute of Education, Department of Educational Psychology and Special Educational Needs, 20 Bedford Way, London WC1H 0AL
0171 580 1122
Cowan, R. Dr

Children's development of number competence

Abstract: The research aims to develop an accurate account of how children's understanding of number develops from 4 to 7 years. Studies have been conducted to refine tasks used to assess children's understandings of number and procedures such as counting and sharing, to determine the causes of children's nonconserving responses, to explore whether children with severe language disorders show a qualitatively different pattern of development, and to identify what experiences make children more likely to count.

Published Material: COWAN, R. (1991). 'The same number'. In: DURKIN, K. & SHIRE, B. (Eds). Language in mathematical education: research and practice. Milton Keynes: Open University.; A full list of publications is available from the researcher.
Status: Individual research
Date of Research: 1974-continuing
KEYWORDS: *arithmetic; cognitive development; number concepts; numbers; numeracy; primary education*

10/0749

Institute of Education, Department of Educational Psychology and Special Educational Needs, 20 Bedford Way, London WC1H 0AL
0171 580 1122
Cowan, R. Dr

Primary school children's understanding of heat and temperature

Abstract: Assessment of Performance Unit surveys suggest that few 11-year-olds understand much about heat and temperature and how to measure them. Studies have been conducted to assess children's knowledge of temperature phenomena in connection with daily life; i.e. body temperature, ice cream and swimming pools. In addition, 9-11-year olds have been interviewed to assess their understanding of the two common temperature scales. Children between 7 and 12 have been tested on verbal and numerical versions of temperature prediction tasks. The researchers found confusion over temperature was common even when no reference to numerical temperatures was made.

Published Material: COWAN, R. & SUTCLIFFE, N. (1991). 'What children's temperature predictions reveal of their understanding of temperature', British Journal of Educational Psychology, Vol 61, Part 3, pp.300-309.
Status: Individual research
Date of Research: 1987-continuing
KEYWORDS: *cognitive development; comprehension; heat; primary education; science education; temperature*

10/0750

Institute of Education, Department of Educational Psychology and Special Educational Needs, 20 Bedford Way, London WC1H 0AL
0171 580 1122
Kambouri, M. Dr; Supervisor: Francis, H. Prof.

Dropout and progression in basic skills

Abstract: The study aims to focus on the extent and reasons for dropout

and progression from basic skills programmes and the level and nature of progression from programmes. It utilises questionnaires to tutors and students who have moved on or out of basic skills. In addition registers and patterns of attendance are monitored and data accumulated, coded and analysed. A final report will be published in 1993.
Status: Sponsored project
Source of Grant: Adult Literacy and Basic Skills Unit £49,943
Date of Research: 1992-1993
KEYWORDS: *achievement; adult basic education; adult dropouts; basic skills; dropout research*

10/0751

Institute of Education, Department of Educational Psychology and Special Educational Needs, 20 Bedford Way, London WC1H 0AL
0171 580 1122
Dee, L. Ms
Assessment of students with disabilities or learning difficulties
Abstract: An investigation into current assessment procedures used by colleges of further education (FE) to identify the learning support needs of young people and adults with disabilities or learning difficulties, with a view to producing guidelines for good practice.
Status: Sponsored project
Source of Grant: Further Education Unit £20,000
Date of Research: 1992-1993
KEYWORDS: *assessment; colleges of further education; diagnostic assessment; disabilities; further education; moderate learning difficulties; special educational needs*

10/0752

Institute of Education, Department of Educational Psychology and Special Educational Needs, 20 Bedford Way, London WC1H 0AL
0171 580 1122
Wedell, K. Prof.; Lunt, I. Ms; Norwich, B. Dr; Evans, J. Ms
Clusters Project (Extension)
Abstract: This is an extension of the Clusters Project funded by the Economic and Social Research Council.
Status: Sponsored project
Source of Grant: Waldburg Foundation £20,000
Date of Research: 1993-1994
KEYWORDS: *cluster grouping; educational cooperation; special educational needs; special schools*

10/0753

Institute of Education, Department of Educational Psychology and Special Educational Needs, 20 Bedford Way, London WC1H 0AL
0171 580 1122
Wedell, K. Prof.; Norwich, B. Dr
Developing policy in the field of special educational needs for the 1990's
Abstract: The preparation and publication of policy papers on special educational needs provision.
Status: Sponsored project
Source of Grant: B & G Cadbury Trust; Economic and Social Research Council
Date of Research: 1992-continuing
KEYWORDS: *educational policy; special educational needs*

10/0754

Institute of Education, Department of Educational Psychology and Special Educational Needs, 20 Bedford Way, London WC1H 0AL
0171 580 1122
Wolf, A. Mrs
A bibliography and digest of basic skills in industrialised countries
Abstract: The project will utilise existing database information to compile a digest of research into basic skills (in industrialised countries) undertaken since 1973. The project will produce a full bibliography and digest of research relevant to basic skills. It will concentrate on work undertaken in English speaking countries but reference to other relevant research will be made.
Status: Sponsored project
Source of Grant: Adult Literacy and Basic Skills Unit (ALBSU)

£31,000
Date of Research: 1993-1993
KEYWORDS: *basic skills; educational research*

10/0755

Institute of Education, Department of Educational Psychology and Special Educational Needs, 20 Bedford Way, London WC1H 0AL
0171 580 1122
Daniels, H. Dr; Norwich, B. Dr; Anghilieri, N. Ms
Evaluating teacher support teams
Abstract: This project aims to evaluate Teacher Support Teams (TSTs) in primary schools as an organisational response to enabling schools to extend their capabilities to provide for children with special educational needs. This will provide systematic information about the processes of setting up TSTs and the effects of TSTs on the school and the individual teachers and children involved in TST work. The results of the project will be disseminated to interested groups via publications and inservice training programmes.
Published Material: NORWICH, B. & DANIELS, H. (1992). 'Support from the team', Managing Schools Today, Vol 1, No 6, pp.30-31.; DANIELS, H. & NORWICH, B. (1993). Teacher support teams in 3 Enfield primary schools: an evaluation report. London: London University, Institute of Education.; DANIELS, H., NORWICH, B. & ANGHILIERI, N. (1993). 'Teacher support teams: an evaluation of a school based approach to meeting special educational needs', Support for Learning, Vol 8, No 4, pp.169-173.
Status: Sponsored project
Source of Grant: Economic and Social Research Council £68,680
Date of Research: 1992-1994
KEYWORDS: *primary schools; special educational needs; support services*

10/0756

Institute of Education, Department of Educational Psychology and Special Educational Needs, 20 Bedford Way, London WC1H 0AL
0171 580 1122
Evans, J. Ms; Lunt, I. Ms; Young, P. Dr; Vincent, C. Ms
Local Management of Schools and special educational needs
Abstract: The project will continue work on the effects of Local Management of Schools (LMS) on special educational provision by means of a questionnaire survey and more detailed studies of a sample of local education authorities and schools.
Published Material: VINCENT, C., EVANS, J. LUNT, I. & YOUNG, P. (1994). 'The market forces? The effects of Local Management of Schools in special educational needs provisions', British Educational Research Journal, Vol 20, No 3, pp.261-277.
Status: Sponsored project
Source of Grant: Economic and Social Research Council £55,420
Date of Research: 1992-1994
KEYWORDS: *educational administration; local management of schools; school-based management; special educational needs*

10/0757

Institute of Education, Department of Educational Psychology and Special Educational Needs, 20 Bedford Way, London WC1H 0AL
0171 580 1122
Norwich, B. Dr
Seminar series on policy analysis and policy options for special educational needs in the 1990's
Abstract: A series of six policy seminars on key topics in special educational needs organised over a two year period. Each seminar resulting in the publication of a policy paper.
Status: Sponsored project
Source of Grant: Economic and Social Research Council £3,300
Date of Research: 1993-1994
KEYWORDS: *educational policy; seminars; special educational needs*

10/0758

Institute of Education, Department of Educational Psychology and Special Educational Needs, 20 Bedford Way, London WC1H 0AL
0171 580 1122
Blatchford, P. Dr

Pupils' academic self assessment and attitudes to school work: follow up at 16 years
Abstract: This study will re-interview pupils at 16 years, who had earlier been interviewed at 7 and 11 years as part of the Thomas Coram Research Unit longitudinal study. Interviews at 7 and 11 years provided information on pupils' attitude to school work and academic self assessment, just prior to important transitions into junior and secondary school. It will therefore provide a unique opportunity to obtain information from the same children over the whole of their primary and secondary education.
Published Material: BLATCHFORD, P. (1992). 'Children's attitudes to work at 11 years', Educational Studies, Vol 18, No 1, pp.107-118.; BLATCHFORD, P. (1992). 'Academic self-assessment at 7 and 11 years: its accuracy and association with ethnic group and sex', British Journal of Educational Psychology, Vol 62, No 1, pp.35-44.
Status: Sponsored project
Source of Grant: Economic and Social Research Council £29,980
Date of Research: 1993-1994
KEYWORDS: *longitudinal studies; pupil attitudes; school activities; self evaluation – individuals; sixteen to nineteen education*

10/0759
Institute of Education, Department of Educational Psychology and Special Educational Needs, 20 Bedford Way, London WC1H 0AL
0171 580 1122
Henderson, S. Dr; Demetre, J. Dr
Perceptuo-motor difficulties in prematurely born children
Abstract: Perceptuo-motor difficulties in prematurely born children – do these problems affect the children's self-concept and do teachers notice? The focus of this study is on children with perceptuo-motor difficulties, a group whose special educational needs are often neglected. The aim of the study is twofold. The first objective is to investigate the way six year old children with such difficulties perceive themselves. The second objective is to determine whether infant school teachers recognise and are sensitive to these difficulties at such a young age. The investigation forms part of a much larger study of 200 prematurely born children whose development has been extensively documented over a six year period.
Published Material: JONGMANS, M., HENDERSON, S.E., DE VRIES, L. & DUBOWITZ, L. (1993). 'Duration of periventricular densities in pre-term infants and neurological outcome at six years', Archives of Diseases in Childhood, Vol 69, pp.9-13.
Status: Sponsored project
Source of Grant: Nuffield Foundation £4,820
Date of Research: 1993-1993
KEYWORDS: *perceptual motor coordination; self-concept; special educational needs*

10/0760
Institute of Education, Department of Educational Psychology and Special Educational Needs, 20 Bedford Way, London WC1H 0AL
0171 580 1122
Dubowitz, L. Dr; Henderson, S. Dr
Clumsiness in premature and full term children
Abstract: The aim of this project is to improve our understanding of the aetiology, developmental progression, and consequences of mild to moderate perceptuo-motor impairment in children. Two groups of seven to ten year old children with such impairment will participate in the study, one will be full term. Using magnetic resonance imaging (MRI) scanning techniques, we plan to evaluate the current brain status of those children whose perceptuo-motor difficulties were identified at different points in time and were presumably of different origins. Using psychometric measures and educational assessment, our aim is to elaborate on the patterns of functional impairment that such children exhibit and determine how well they are coping with the demands of the new National Curriculum.
Status: Sponsored project
Source of Grant: Waldburg Foundation; Action Research, jointly £11,558
Date of Research: 1993-1994
KEYWORDS: *clumsy children; perceptual motor coordination; psychomotor skills; special educational needs*

10/0761
Institute of Education, Department of English, Media and Drama, 20 Bedford Way, London WC1H 0AL
0171 580 1122
Burgess, T. Dr; Kress, G. Prof.
Books in schools
Abstract: This is an investigation of the quality of access to books in schools for current secondary pupils and of how decisions about choosing books are arrived at by teachers in the light of new curriculum and financial arrangements.
Published Material: Books in schools: Book Trust report. (1992). London: Book Trust.
Status: Sponsored project
Source of Grant: Book Trust £3,000
Date of Research: 1992-1992
KEYWORDS: *books; secondary schools*

10/0762
Institute of Education, Department of English, Media and Drama Studies, 20 Bedford Way, London WC1H 0AL
0171 580 1122
Grahame, J. Ms; Buckingham, D. Mr
Making media: a research and development project
Abstract: Classroom-based case studies of the use of practical media production (video, photography, desk-top publishing etc.) in a range of curriculum areas.
Status: Sponsored project
Source of Grant: Calouste Gulbenkian Foundation £9,000
Date of Research: 1993-1994
KEYWORDS: *educational media; mass media; material development; production techniques*

10/0763
Institute of Education, Department of English, Media and Drama Studies, 20 Bedford Way, London WC1H 0AL
0171 580 1122
Moss, G. Ms
Negotiated literacies: how children make sense of texts in different setting
Abstract: The project is designed to explore children's informal literacies, i.e. the literary practices children develop outside of formal schooling and often associated with the 'new' technologies such as video, television and computers. Particular attention is given to the ways in which children negotiate and establish these practices through talk and how these practices are embedded in different social contexts.
Status: Sponsored project
Source of Grant: Economic and Social Research Council £74,480
Date of Research: 1993-continuing
KEYWORDS: *incidental learning; literacy; mass media; popular culture*

10/0764
Institute of Education, Department of English for Speakers of Other Languages, 20 Bedford Way, London WC1H 0AL
0171 580 1122
Flavell, R. Dr
Impact of English by radio broadcasts on Mozambican English learners
Abstract: The project aims to measure the impact of BBC English language broadcasts on the English skills and levels of the target audience.
Status: Sponsored project
Source of Grant: British Broadcasting Corporation £29,500
Date of Research: 1993-1994
KEYWORDS: *English – second language; Mozambique; radio; second language learning*

10/0765
Institute of Education, Department of History, Humanities and Philosophy, 20 Bedford Way, London WC1H 0AL
0171 580 1122
Dickinson, A. Mr; Lee, P. Mr
Concepts of history and teaching approaches at National Curriculum Key Stages 2 & 3
Abstract: The project is concerned with the teaching and learning of

history in National Curriculum Key Stages 2 and 3, and falls into three phases. In phase 1 the development of children's understandings of the concepts of evidence and explanation in history will be investigated. Phase 2 will seek to categorise teaching approaches according to their attention to progression in children's ideas. Phase 3 will explore relationships between teaching approaches and learning outcomes. Enhancement funding has been granted for a study of the progression paths followed by children moving from year 3 to year 6.
Status: Sponsored project
Source of Grant: Economic and Social Research Council £71,127
Date of Research: 1991-continuing
KEYWORDS: history; history studies; National Curriculum; teaching methods

10/0766
Institute of Education, Department of History, Humanities and Philosophy, 20 Bedford Way, London WC1H 0AL
0171 580 1122
Silto, W. Mr; *Supervisor:* Gordon, P. Prof.
The origins, development and failure of the Day Continuation School Movement in England and Wales
Abstract: This research deals with the background behind the rise of Continuation Schools following the First World War. The importance of the 1918 Education Act and the Oxford school of idealist philosophers are described. The development and failure of the movement are traced in examination of local records of the seven LEAs which implemented Day Continuation Schools: this will also involve a study of Public Record Office files in order to ascertain the views of the Board of Education as well as the political papers of the main supporters of the movement and other interest groups.
Status: Individual research
Date of Research: 1990-continuing
KEYWORDS: adult education; continuing education; educational history

10/0767
Institute of Education, Department of History, Humanities and Philosophy, 20 Bedford Way, London WC1H 0AL
0171 580 1122
Lee, P. Mr; *Supervisor:* Gordon, P. Prof.
Some aspects of historical understanding
Abstract: The research undertakes an analysis of concepts involved in the idea of historical understanding (rationality, intentionality, practical inference) and of related ideas (imagination, empathy, sympathy, identification, intuition, fellow-feelings, tolerance). An attempt is made to show that imagination (as supposal) is criterial to understanding in history. There is a discussion of major accounts of historical explanation (covering-law, explanation by rationale, narrativist and Marxist accounts). The relation between explanation, understanding and interpretation in history is examined, with particular attention to notions of meaning and significance. The second part of the research is concerned to argue some implications of the earlier analysis for children's thinking and, in particular, the development of their ideas (explicit and tacit) about the nature and status of history (i.e. the ideas in question are second-order as opposed to substantive). Possible consequences for teaching will also be discussed. Previous work is examined, both from wider psychological research and from the more specific research undertaken within education, bearing directly upon children's abilities and thinking in history. The argument will draw upon empirical investigations performed by the author and by research projects in which he has been involved. It is anticipated that these will provide evidence bearing on children's ideas at all ages between 7 years and 19 years.
Status: Individual research
Date of Research: 1977-continuing
KEYWORDS: comprehension; explanation; historiography; history; imagination

10/0768
Institute of Education, Department of History, Humanities and Philosophy, 20 Bedford Way, London WC1H 0AL
0171 580 1122
Dickinson, A. Mr; *Supervisor:* Gordon, P. Prof.
Children's thinking and understanding in history with special reference to the role of computer assisted learning (CAL)
Abstract: The main aims of the research are to investigate further,

children's conceptions of evidence and enquiry and to explore aspects of the contribution that computers can make to pupils' thinking and understanding in history (in particular their reflexive thinking, substantive understanding and notions of historical evidence and enquiry). A key principle underlying the work is that research into the learning and teaching of history requires analysis of the conceptual base of the discipline and empirical investigation of children's thinking and ideas (both explicit and tacit understandings). The work involves the use of video-recording techniques pioneered by the History Department at the Institute of Education with the aim of revealing the processes of children's thinking in history, pupils' strategies for making sense of the past and their understandings (explicit and tacit) of specific historical concepts (second order and substantive).
Status: Individual research
Date of Research: 1967-continuing
KEYWORDS: comprehension; computer-assisted learning; computer uses in education; history; thinking skills

10/0769
Institute of Education, Department of History, Humanities and Philosophy, 20 Bedford Way, London WC1H 0AL
0171 580 1122
Aldrich, R. Dr
Historical perspectives on educational issues in England
Abstract: To establish a database of historical material – facts, bibliography and interpretations in respect of contemporary educational issues: e.g. the control of education; the training and profession of teachers; the National Curriculum. This will be assembled in computer-based and book form.
Status: Sponsored project
Source of Grant: Leverhulme Trust £23,680
Date of Research: 1993-continuing
KEYWORDS: educational change; educational history; educational policy

10/0770
Institute of Education, Department of Inservice Training, 20 Bedford Way, London WC1H 0AL
0171 580 1122
MacGilchrist, B. Mrs
Relationship between school management training materials and development planning
Abstract: This project is linked to the development of school managed training materials on the management of teaching and learning. To assist the schools and the local education authorities (LEAs) to use such materials as part of a management development policy, two detailed case studies are to be conducted in two of the primary schools trialling the materials to demonstrate how the use of such materials can influence school development planning. The annotated studies will be used by LEAs as a basis for planning their support for development planning in schools.
Status: Sponsored project
Source of Grant: Department of Education and Science £7,620
Date of Research: 1991-1992
KEYWORDS: educational administration; educational materials; management development; management in education; material development

10/0771
Institute of Education, Department of Inservice Training, 20 Bedford Way, London WC1H 0AL
0171 580 1122
MacGilchrist, B. Mrs
Using supported self-study materials in management development
Abstract: The purpose of the project is to trial management development training materials in 10 schools across 4 local education authorities (LEAs) and to investigate the role of the LEA as supporting agency. Particular attention will be paid to the role of an 'on call tutor' and the short-term impact of this approach on the development of senior and middle managers in the project schools.
Published Material: MACGILCHRIST, B. & HALL, V. (1993). Using management development materials: a guide for schools, local education authorities and other support agencies. London: HMSO.
Status: Sponsored project
Source of Grant: Department of Education and Science £17,860

Date of Research: 1991-1992
KEYWORDS: educational administration; educational materials; management development; management in education; material development

10/0772

Institute of Education, Department of Inservice Training, 20 Bedford Way, London WC1H 0AL
0171 580 1122
MacGilchrist, B. Mrs
Development of training materials on the management of teaching and learning
Abstract: This is the second phase of a project to develop school managed training materials on the management of teaching and learning. The materials drafted in phase 1 are to be trialled in 11 primary schools across 6 local education authorities (LEAs). The aims of the project are to: (i) produce training materials for use in schools across the 6 LEAs; (ii) assess the implications for the use of such materials in relation to the roles performed by LEA staff and school staff.
Status: Sponsored project
Source of Grant: Department of Education and Science £22,380
Date of Research: 1991-1992
KEYWORDS: educational administration; educational materials; management in education; material development

10/0773

Institute of Education, Department of International and Comparative Education, 20 Bedford Way, London
WC1H 0AL
0171 580 1122
Nherera, C. Dr; *Supervisor:* Little, A. Prof.; Young, M. Dr
Vocationalisation of secondary education in Zimbabwe
Abstract: As in most developing countries, attempts to vocationalise secondary education have remained a priority in educational reform policy since the attainment of independence in Zimbabwe. Vocational education remains popular among policy makers in both developed and developing countries in spite of empirical evidence suggesting that vocational programmes do not achieve their intended goals. Increasing literature has indicated that such education is not cost effective and promotes social class disparities. The purpose of the current study is to investigate recent attempts to vocationalise secondary education in Zimbabwe. The main aspects investigated arise from the controversy surrounding the provision of such education internationally. It focuses on the Zimbabwe National Craft Certificate and National Foundation Certificate introduced successively as pilot schemes to vocationalise secondary education in the country. It examines the objectives and assumptions underlying the provision of these schemes in relation to the emerging central arguments. The investigation involves both theoretical and empirical approaches. The research questions were developed from arguments that have emerged from international literature and a critical examination of the economical and sociological arguments that have dominated the 'vocationalisation debate'. Fieldwork data were collected over a period of 4 months, from six 6 piloting the scheme in Zimbabwe. Questionnaires were administered to 180 pupils, 14 teachers and 8 education officers (EO's). Semi-structured interviews were conducted with the teachers, EO's, senior Ministry officials, and officers in the Confederation of Zimbabwe Industries, parents and some school leavers. Policy and other official documents were also collected. The study takes the premise that the viability of vocational education cannot be judged from labour market outcomes only. These seem to mask underlying economic, political, social and other dysfunctions that might influence such outcomes. Some of the fieldwork analysed so far seems to disprove the commonly held notions about vocational education. It appears the subjects pupils study influence their career choices. Most pupils want to continue with their education beyond secondary level, but their aspirations are still towards technically oriented occupations. Teachers and Ministry of Education officials seem to believe vocational education is a viable curriculum option, both on pedagogical grounds and post-school propensities.
Status: Sponsored project
Source of Grant: Association of Commonwealth Universities
Date of Research: 1991-1994
KEYWORDS: developing countries; vocational education; Zimbabwe

10/0774

Institute of Education, Department of Mathematics, Statistics and Computing, 20 Bedford Way, London WC1H 0AL
0171 580 1122
Sutherland, R. Dr
Mexican/British project on the role of spreadsheets within school-based mathematical practices
Abstract: The aims of this project are: 1) To investigate the school mathematical practices of 16-17 year old students within and across a range of science subjects. 2) To investigate the ways in which a spreadsheet supports students to make links between their informal problem solving approaches and a more formal spreadsheet-based mathematical approach.
Status: Sponsored project
Source of Grant: Spencer Foundation £87,054
Date of Research: 1993-continuing
KEYWORDS: mathematics education; science education; spreadsheets

10/0775

Institute of Education, Department of Mathematics, Statistics and Computing, 20 Bedford Way, London WC1H 0AL
0171 580 1122
Goldstein, H. Prof.
Extending multilevel models
Abstract: This project extends the work of the earlier projects entitled 'Developing the use of multilevel models' and 'Developing and disseminating multilevel models'. The three aims of the current project are: 1) to disseminate knowledge of multilevel modelling to the social science research community through conferences, seminars and training sessions in the use of statistical software developed for this form of analysis; 2) to extend existing methodology, especially in the area of time series and linear structural relations models; and 3) to study the practical application of the models to real data sets, especially with a view to increasing robustness and developing data diagnostic procedures. Work is in progress in many domains including, improving the operational efficiency of the 'Iterative Generalised Least Squares' (IGLS) algorithm used in fitting multilevel models; developing the theory of multilevel analysis with latent variables; comparing various methods for treating missing data in multilevel analysis; developing loglinear, time series and survival multilevel models.
Published Material: GOLDSTEIN, H. (1987). Multilevel models in educational and social research. London: Griffin.; GOLDSTEIN, H. & MCDONALD, R.P. (1988). 'A general model for the analysis of multilevel data', Psychometrika, No 53, pp.455-467.; GOLDSTEIN, H. (1989). 'Models for multilevel response with an application to growth curves'. In: BOCK, R.D. (Ed). Multilevel analysis of educational data. New York: Academic Press.; GOLDSTEIN, H. (1989). 'Restricted (unbiased) iterative generalised least squares estimation', Biometrika, Vol 76, No 3, pp.622-623.
Status: Sponsored project
Source of Grant: Economic and Social Research Council £177,770
Date of Research: 1990-1994
KEYWORDS: models; research tools; statistical analysis

10/0776

Institute of Education, Department of Mathematics, Statistics and Computing, 20 Bedford Way, London WC1H 0AL
0171 580 1122
Wolf, A. Mrs
Measurement and accreditation of broad skills
Abstract: Over a four-year period the project has examined the types of assessment – both written and practical – which are most effective in predicting retention of skills, and ability to generalise to other more or less closely related areas. The work has been carried out with students (aged 16-20, and adult) who are nearing completion of vocational training courses. It builds upon previous research including a large study completed for the Training Agency (now Training, Enterprise and Education Directorate – TEED) by the Institute of Education, and has implications for the development of assessment procedures for National Vocational Qualifications (NVQs), and for the design and regulation of training schemes receiving government funding. The study is longitudinal and relates to: current mastery; success, at time of mastery, in generalising to related tasks; measured retention of skills at a later date; and success in generalising to related tasks at a later date. The use of definitions and measures of 'mastery' is central to the project, reflecting the criterion-referenced nature of current reforms in vocational standards and testing.

Status: Sponsored project
Source of Grant: Training, Enterprise and Education Directorate
£197,000
Date of Research: 1990-1994
KEYWORDS: assessment; job skills; mastery tests; retention – psychology; vocational education

10/0777

Institute of Education, Department of Mathematics, Statistics and Computing, 20 Bedford Way, London WC1H 0AL
0171 580 1122
Sutherland, R. Dr

Algebraic processes and the role of symbolism

Abstract: A seminar group to coordinate and synthesise the United Kingdom work on algebraic thinking in school mathematics. The group has produced a set of clear questions and working hypotheses for future research collaboration with European colleagues.
Status: Sponsored project
Source of Grant: Economic and Social Research Council £4,950
Date of Research: 1992-1993
KEYWORDS: algebra; computer uses in education; mathematics education; symbols – mathematics

10/0778

Institute of Education, Department of Mathematics, Statistics and Computing, 20 Bedford Way, London WC1H 0AL
0171 580 1122
Mellar, H. Dr; Ogborn, J. Prof.

London Mental Models

Abstract: The European Community programme Esprit 2 funded, as a working group, an association of researchers in Denmark, Paris and London. The London group consists of the London Mental Models Group, with members from the Institute of Education, King's College London, Imperial College, and Kingston Polytechnic (now Kingston University). The work has been concerned with the nature of Explanation, particularly in Science and in History, and with the possibility of designing a computer system which provides explanations.
Status: Sponsored project
Source of Grant: European Community Esprit 2 £3,400
Date of Research: 1991-1992
KEYWORDS: explanation; reasoning; research methodology

10/0779

Institute of Education, Department of Mathematics, Statistics and Computing, 20 Bedford Way, London WC1H 0AL
0171 580 1122
Hoyles, C. Prof.

Data handling for years 5-6: teachers and pupils as research designers

Abstract: The project will develop a pack of materials to support data handling in primary schools involving the use of computer databases.
Status: Sponsored project
Source of Grant: Nuffield Foundation £84,321
Date of Research: 1992-1994
KEYWORDS: computer uses in education; data processing; databases; material development; primary schools

10/0780

Institute of Education, Department of Mathematics, Statistics and Computing, 20 Bedford Way, London WC1H 0AL
0171 580 1122
Pozzi, S. Mr

Mathematics learning and computer algebra systems

Abstract: The aim of this study is to identify the influences of computer algebra systems (CAS) on A-level students' algebraic problem solving strategies. Case studies of eight students will be developed, each one consisting of a process and a background profile. The process profile will focus on students' strategies and approaches and how these are structured by the CAS environment, while the background profile will focus on students' competencies in algebra and attitudes to CAS.
Published Material: POZZI, S. (1993). 'Computer algebra systems', Micromath, Vol 9, No 1, pp.26-27.
Status: Sponsored project
Source of Grant: Economic and Social Research Council £31,150
Date of Research: 1992-1993

KEYWORDS: algebra education; computer uses in education; mathematics education; problem solving

10/0781

Institute of Education, Department of Mathematics, Statistics and Computing, 20 Bedford Way, London WC1H 0AL
0171 580 1122
Sutherland, R. Dr

Exploiting mental imagery with computers, in mathematics education

Abstract: The aim of this NATO advanced research workshop is to bring teachers in several disciplines together to explore the role of mental images in mathematics, particularly those stimulated by computer generated graphics and to chart directions for further research.
Status: Sponsored project
Source of Grant: North Atlantic Treaty Organisation £19,417
Date of Research: 1993-1993
KEYWORDS: computer uses in education; imagery; mathematics education

10/0782

Institute of Education, Department of Mathematics, Statistics and Computing, 20 Bedford Way, London WC1H 0AL
0171 580 1122
Sutherland, R. Dr

Visualising and symbolising in a computer environment

Abstract: This collaborative Franco/British project aims to investigate the effect on learning of students' interactions with visual and symbolic representations, relating this to input from both the teacher and the computer.
Published Material: CAPPONI, B. & SUTHERLAND, R. (1992). 'Teaching trigonometry in France with Cabri', Micromath, Vol 8, No 2, pp.32-33.
Status: Sponsored project
Source of Grant: Economic and Social Research Council £2,980
Date of Research: 1992-1992
KEYWORDS: computer uses in education; mathematics education; symbols – mathematics; trigonometry; visualisation

10/0783

Institute of Education, Department of Mathematics, Statistics and Computing, 20 Bedford Way, London WC1H 0AL
0171 580 1122
Sutherland, R. Dr; Wolf, A. Mrs

Spreadsheet approach to mathematical modelling for engineering students

Abstract: The aim of this project is to develop and evaluate a mathematical modelling unit for engineering technicians (NVQ Level 2/3). These materials will use a spreadsheet approach to mathematical modelling incorporating authentic problems from industry.
Status: Sponsored project
Source of Grant: Nuffield Foundation £50,724
Date of Research: 1993-1994
KEYWORDS: engineering education; mathematical models; mathematics education; spreadsheets

10/0784

Institute of Education, Department of Mathematics, Statistics and Computing, 20 Bedford Way, London WC1H 0AL
0171 580 1122
Wolf, A. Mrs

Evaluation of the TEC Access to Assessment Initiative

Abstract: An evaluation of a government funded special programme which gives Training and Enterprise Councils (TECs) earmarked funds designed to: (1) create networks of assessors who can provide assessment services for National Vocational Qualification (NVQ) candidates; and (2) promote Accreditation of Prior Learning.
Published Material: CROWLEY-BAINTON, T. & WOLF, A. (1994). Access to assessment initiative. Sheffield: Department of Employment.
Status: Sponsored project
Source of Grant: Department of Employment £22,915
Date of Research: 1992-1993
KEYWORDS: accreditation of prior learning; assessment; National Vocational Qualifications; Training and Enterprise Councils; vocational education

10/0785

Institute of Education, Department of Mathematics, Statistics and Computing, 20 Bedford Way, London WC1H 0AL
0171 580 1122
Wolf, A. Mrs

Review of research literature relevant to oral assessment in the context of National Vocational Qualifications (NVQs) and Scottish Vocational Qualifications (SVQs)

Abstract: The project comprises a review of literature on oral assessment and the identification of good practice and research priorities.
Published Material: WOLF, A. (1992). Oral assessment: a review of the literature. Report to TEED, February. Reprinted by the International Centre for Research on Assessment. London University: Institute of Education.
Status: Sponsored project
Source of Grant: Training, Enterprise and Education Directorate £3,000
Date of Research: 1992-1992
KEYWORDS: assessment; job skills; National Vocational Qualifications; Scottish Vocational Qualifications; verbal tests

10/0786

Institute of Education, Department of Mathematics, Statistics and Computing, 20 Bedford Way, London WC1H 0AL
0171 580 1122
Wolf, A. Mrs

Study of mathematics attainment of French as compared to English apprentices

Abstract: This project comprises mathematical tests administered to 500 French and 500 English apprentices/youth trainees. The relative strengths/weaknesses were analysed and related to the structure of training systems in both France and England.
Published Material: WOLF, A. & RAPIAU, M-T. (1992). 'Apprenticeship in England and France: mathematics attainment, patterns of recruitment and their socio-economic implications'. Proceedings of the CESE Conference: IREDU, University of Dijon, France.; WOLF, A. & RAPIAU, M-T. (1993). 'The academic achievement of craft apprentices in England and France: contrasting systems and common dilemmas', Comparative Education, Vol 29, No 1, pp.29-43.
Status: Sponsored project
Source of Grant: Economic and Social Research Council £510
Date of Research: 1992-1992
KEYWORDS: comparative education; France; mathematics achievement; trainees

10/0787

Institute of Education, Department of Mathematics, Statistics and Computing, 20 Bedford Way, London WC1H 0AL
0171 580 1122
Wolf, A. Mrs

Evolution of GNVQ's: enrolment and delivery patterns and their policy implications

Abstract: A representative national survey of enrolment and delivery patterns for General National Vocational Qualifications (GNVQ's) and of progression routes for a sample of GNVQ graduates.
Status: Sponsored project
Source of Grant: Further Education Unit; Nuffield Foundation, jointly £53,130
Date of Research: 1993-continuing
KEYWORDS: employment qualifications; National Vocational Qualifications; vocational education

10/0788

Institute of Education, Department of Mathematics, Statistics and Computing, 20 Bedford Way, London WC1H 0AL
0171 580 1122
Hoyles, C. Prof.

Visualisation, computers and learning

Abstract: There is recognition that the status of the visual in both mathematics and mathematics education needs re-evaluation. Since the 1960's, there has been a decline in geometry and its replacement by numerical and algebraic approaches and more generally visualisation is assigned low priority within mathematics teaching and learning. Central to the effectiveness of advanced computer software is the use of graphic screen representations by which mathematical objects can be observed in dynamic relation. This project aims to investigate if and how computers with appropriate software can facilitate visualisation in mathematics and offer the prospect undertaken within carefully designed activities: to map the visualisation strategies of construction, justification and interpretation, to identify how links are made with symbolisation; and to analyse how both strategies and linkages are influenced by the media in which the mathematics is expressed, that is paper and pencil or computer.
Status: Sponsored project
Source of Grant: Economic and Social Research Council £112,940
Date of Research: 1993-continuing
KEYWORDS: computer uses in education; educational software; mathematics education; symbols – mathematics; visual learning

10/0789

Institute of Education, Department of Mathematics, Statistics and Computing, 20 Bedford Way, London WC1H 0AL
0171 580 1122
Warwick University, Department of Education, Coventry CV4 7AL
01203 523523
Glasgow University, Department of Education, 8 University Gardens, Glasgow G12 8QQ
0141 339 8855
Wolf, A. Mrs; Dunn, W. Mr; Duke, C. Prof.

National standards for training and development within masters programmes

Abstract: A new structure of qualifications is being put in place to encourage employers and employees to raise standards of performance in the workplace. The qualifications are called National and Scottish Vocational Qualifications (NVQs and SVQs). The qualifications are based on standards of competence which are being set by Lead Bodies. National Standards for Training and Development were published by the Training and Development Lead Body, first in January 1991, then in revised form in March 1992. These National Standards are intended to cover all work roles that have a training and development content. The whole shift towards competence-based qualifications means there is a need for standards to which the assessors of competence must work; these are included. The National Standards have a number of uses: as a basis for job descriptions; to identify training needs; to develop training programmes; as a basis for assessment; as benchmarks for development; and to form vocational qualifications. The Lead Body has defined the key purpose of training as "to develop human potential to assist organisations and individuals to achieve their objectives'. Given this broad definition, it is clear that National Standards can be applied to the work of teachers in schools and to the work of lecturers in colleges and universities. The extent to which they will be applied, and the rate of the application, is currently unpredictable. A research study has been funded by the Department of Employment to explore the delivery of the National Standards for Training and Development within Masters degree programmes. The project involves the Universities of London, Glasgow and Warwick. The three institutions involved have had distinct plans and priorities; however, the project was conceived as a consortium activity and each site has learned from the others. The current stage of the project has these aims: (1) To determine appropriate ways of drawing on the National Standards for Training and Development within Masters Degrees; (2) To secure approval for, and to prepare for the implementation of, pilot programmes; and (3) To integrate the parallel work of the three participating institutions, both internally and with other relevant developments.
Published Material: Five papers are available on request from the researchers.; Paper 1. Recognition of TDLB key roles by M.Ed. students (November 1991).; Paper 2. Staff views on basic issues (November 1991).; Paper 3. Recognition of TDLB units and elements by M.Ed. students (September 1992).; Paper 5. Final report on stage 1 of the project (March 1993).
Status: Sponsored project
Source of Grant: Training, Enterprise and Education Directorate £79,046
Date of Research: 1991-1994
KEYWORDS: competency based education; higher education; masters courses; National Vocational Qualifications; qualifications; standards

10/0790

Institute of Education, Department of Modern Languages, 20 Bedford Way, London WC1H 0AL
0171 580 1122
Roberts, A. Mr

Feasibility study into establishing a PGCE course in the teaching of Japanese as a foreign language
Abstract: To establish the viability of setting up a Postgraduate Certificate in Education (PGCE) in the teaching of Japanese as a foreign language. This involves a survey of: a) projected needs for Japanese in UK industry; b) possibilities for expansion in UK secondary schools; c) potential market for recruitment to such a course.
Status: Sponsored project
Source of Grant: Japan Foundation £9,300
Date of Research: 1993-1994
KEYWORDS: *Japanese; postgraduate certificate in education; second language teaching*

10/0791
> Institute of Education, Department of Music Education,
> 20 Bedford Way, London WC1H 0AL
> 0171 580 1122
> Swanwick, K. Prof.

Resources for music at key stage 2
Abstract: Matching existing teaching and other resources against the National Curriculum Music specification.
Status: Sponsored project
Source of Grant: Calouste Gulbenkian Foundation £10,000; Paul Hamlyn Foundation £5,000
Date of Research: 1993-1993
KEYWORDS: *educational resources; music education; National Curriculum*

10/0792
> Institute of Education, Department of Music Education,
> 20 Bedford Way, London WC1H 0AL
> 0171 580 1122
> Shiobara, M. Ms; *Supervisor:* Swanwick, K. Prof.

The effect of movement on musical comprehension
Abstract: The researcher examines the effect of movement on younger children's musical comprehension with special reference to the quality of their perception of music. Different approaches to the use of movement in the music curriculum are examined and it is shown that many of the aims and practices of the various methods have at one time or another entered the mainstream of the music curriculum. The approach of Jacques-Dalcroze in music education is discussed as a basis for the further theoretical development of this thesis. A theoretical framework for the examination of the crucial role of physical movement for musical comprehension is constructed. Background aesthetic theory is presented, and accounts are given by Piaget and others of the role of action or physical movement in the development of children's representational thought are discussed. An empirical investigation into the effect of movement on musical comprehension, and various problems associated with measurement of the child's ability to perceive and comprehend music, are discussed, and an experimental method for assessing the effect of movement on the musical perception of 7-8 year old children is proposed by the researcher. The experiments which were carried out in England and Japan are reported in detail and the results are presented. The findings indicate that movement appears to have a positive effect on the detail of musical perception. There are implications of the research for the development of the music curriculum and for further research work.
Status: Individual research
Date of Research: 1989-1993
KEYWORDS: *movement education; music education; psychomotor skills*

10/0793
> Institute of Education, Department of Music Education,
> 20 Bedford Way, London WC1H 0AL
> 0171 580 1122
> Hentschke, L. Dr; *Supervisor:* Swanwick, K. Prof.

The effect of movement on musical development
Abstract: An investigation to see if responses made through listening in audience can be mapped according to the Swanwick and Tillman Spiral of Musical Development. The work includes a review of previous studies in the field of musical abilities, aptitudes, musical development and the assessment of listening in audience and a critical outline of the Spiral Theory of Musical development and its assessment criteria. This is analysed by employing five general developmental characteristics named as Temporality, Cumulativity, Directionality, New Mode of Organisation and Increased Capacity for Self Control. The terms in which musical development have been conceived are seen as being analogical to Piaget's Theory on Play Development in early childhood. This generalisation of the analogical process to the remaining activities of performing and listening in audience is discussed along with methods employed to assess listening in audience responses, which consisted of interviewing a total of 105 children in 2 field studies (in Brazil and England) by using 2 kinds of interview – structured and semi-structured. Results suggest that the proposed development sequence can be successfully mapped on to data gained centred on response to music as audience-listener. There are implications for music education, including consideration of the positive effect of a structured music curriculum.
Status: Individual research
Date of Research: 1989-1993
KEYWORDS: *music appreciation; music education*

10/0794
> Institute of Education, Department of Policy Studies,
> 20 Bedford Way, London WC1H 0AL
> 0171 580 1122
> Williams, G. Prof.; Loder, C. Ms

Study of independent further and higher education
Abstract: The Centre for Higher Education Studies is undertaking a survey of independent further and higher education in Great Britain in order to provide information on: (1) number and type of institutions; (2) number and characteristics of students (including age, sex, mode of study and domicile); (3) range of courses offered; (4) number and range of qualifications obtained by students; and (5) sources of financial support for students (e.g. grants under PICKUP, sponsorship by employers, mandatory and discretionary awards from local education authorities and training vouchers.
Status: Sponsored project
Source of Grant: Department of Education and Science £79,075
Date of Research: 1991-1993
KEYWORDS: *further education; higher education; independent colleges; private education; private universities*

10/0795
> Institute of Education, Department of Policy Studies,
> 20 Bedford Way, London WC1H 0AL
> 0171 580 1122
> Williams, G. Prof.

Identifying and developing a quality ethos for teaching in higher education
Abstract: The primary aim of the project is to increase understanding of quality in higher education teaching by a systematic series of surveys of students, academics, administrators and employers of graduates.
Status: Sponsored project
Source of Grant: Leverhulme Trust £137,879
Date of Research: 1991-1993
KEYWORDS: *educational quality; higher education; teacher effectiveness*

10/0796
> Institute of Education, Department of Policy Studies,
> 20 Bedford Way, London WC1H 0AL
> 0171 580 1122
> Howell, D. Dr

Committee of Vice Chancellors and Principals of the UK: a study of its development and role
Abstract: A study of the Committee of Vice Chancellors and Principals of the UK (CVCP) from a political science perspective, concentrating on its current role in the higher education policy making process and its relationship with other organisations involved therein.
Status: Sponsored project
Source of Grant: Nuffield Foundation £2,860
Date of Research: 1991-1993
KEYWORDS: *advisory committees; higher education; policy formation; politics education relationship; universities*

10/0797
> Institute of Education, Department of Policy Studies,
> 20 Bedford Way, London WC1H 0AL
> 0171 580 1122
> Green, A. Dr

Formalised continuing vocational training and the training effects of the organisation of labour in British enterprises
Abstract: Part of a twelve nation study of the training effects of work reorganisation. This research involves case studies of three enterprises in the UK which have undergone substantial reorganisation.
Published Material: WALSH, K., GREEN, A. & YOUNG, M. (1992). Study of continuous vocational training. Report to CEDEFOP, August 1992.
Status: Sponsored project
Source of Grant: CEDEFOP £7,000
Date of Research: 1992-1992
KEYWORDS: industrial training; job training

10/0798
> Institute of Education, Department of Policy Studies,
> 20 Bedford Way, London WC1H 0AL
> 0171 580 1122
> Holland, J. Dr

Young heterosexuals, sexual safety and AIDS
Abstract: The Women, Risk and Acquired Immune Deficiency Syndrome (AIDS) Project research team have generated a large body of qualitative data on the sexual knowledge, understanding and practice of young men (46 depth interviews; 250 questionnaires) and young women (150 depth interviews; 500 questionnaires) in London and Manchester in two studies undertaken between 1988 and 1992. The aims of the current research are to: (i) continue and develop the analysis of the (qualitative and quantitative) data from these two studies; (ii) compare the findings from the studies; (iii) take critical findings from the data on the possibilities for and limitations on the negotiation of safer sex to: (a) inform policy and practice in sex and health education and AIDS prevention and (b) develop further proposed future research on heterosexual couples in the age group 22-40.
Published Material: A full list of publications is available from the researcher.
Status: Sponsored project
Source of Grant: Department of Health £13,871
Date of Research: 1992-1992
KEYWORDS: acquired immune deficiency syndrome; health education; sex education; sexuality; sexually transmitted diseases

10/0799
> Institute of Education, Department of Policy Studies,
> 20 Bedford Way, London WC1H 0AL
> 0171 580 1122
> Holland, J. Dr

Women, Risk and AIDS
Abstract: The Women, Risk and Acquired Immune Deficiency Syndrome (AIDS) Project has generated a large body of data on the sexual knowledge, understanding and practice of young women from depth interviews with 150 16-21 year olds. The current research aims to develop and continue the analysis of this data and dissemination of findings.
Published Material: (1992). 'The sexual knowledge and practice of young women in the context of HIV/AIDS with particular reference to different ethnic groups', Report to the Department of Health, March.; HOLLAND, J. (1993). Sexuality and ethnicity: variations in young women's sexual knowledge and practice. WRAP Paper 8. London: Tufnell Press.
Status: Sponsored project
Source of Grant: Department of Health £8,676
Date of Research: 1991-1992
KEYWORDS: acquired immune deficiency syndrome; health education; sex education; sexuality; sexually transmitted diseases

10/0800
> Institute of Education, Department of Policy Studies,
> 20 Bedford Way, London WC1H 0AL
> 0171 580 1122
> Holland, J. Dr

Young people, AIDS and the negotiation of safer sex
Abstract: A qualitative exploration of the sexual practices, beliefs and understanding of young men, and their practical implications for the practice of safer sex and the limitation of Human Immunodeficiency Virus/Acquired Immune Deficiency Syndrome (HIV/AIDS). A group of 16-21 year olds in London are being interviewed in depth. A small sample of advisers to young people will also be interviewed, and a comparison made between the responses of the young women

(investigated in 'Young women, sexuality and the limitation of AIDS') and young men in this study. The work has policy implications in the field of health, sex and AIDS education.
Published Material: A full list of publications is available from the researcher on request.
Status: Sponsored project
Source of Grant: Leverhulme Trust £19,806
Date of Research: 1991-1992
KEYWORDS: acquired immune deficiency syndrome; health education; sex education; sexuality; sexually transmitted diseases

10/0801
> Institute of Education, Department of Policy Studies,
> 20 Bedford Way, London WC1H 0AL
> 0171 580 1122
> Oakley, A. Prof.

Families and sexual health – a literature review
Abstract: A literature review of research on how families discuss sexual health matters and whether there have been any health education interventions in this area.
Published Material: OAKLEY, A. & MAUTHNER, M. (1992). Families and sexual health: a literature review: Report to the Health Education Authority.
Status: Sponsored project
Source of Grant: Health Education Authority £7,750
Date of Research: 1992-1992
KEYWORDS: family attitudes; family health; health education; sex education; sexuality

10/0802
> Institute of Education, Department of Policy Studies,
> 20 Bedford Way, London WC1H 0AL
> 0171 580 1122
> Oakley, A. Prof.

Parental influences on young people smoking
Abstract: A literature review of the relationship between parental smoking and young people's smoking with a view to suggesting appropriate family-based interventions
Status: Sponsored project
Source of Grant: Health Education Authority £5,000
Date of Research: 1992-1992
KEYWORDS: family health; family influence; smoking

10/0803
> Institute of Education, Department of Policy Studies,
> 20 Bedford Way, London WC1H 0AL
> 0171 580 1122
> Oakley, A. Prof.; Bendelow, G. Dr

Young people and cancer
Abstract: An exploratory pilot study of primary and secondary school children examining health beliefs in relation to cancer, and associated beliefs about lifestyles.
Status: Sponsored project
Source of Grant: Women's Nationwide Cancer Control Campaign £32,999
Date of Research: 1992-1993
KEYWORDS: cancer education; health education; pupil attitudes

10/0804
> Institute of Education, Department of Policy Studies,
> 20 Bedford Way, London WC1H 0AL
> 0171 580 1122
> Oakley, A. Prof.; Mayall, B. Dr

Evaluation of the 'Look After Your Heart' Regionalisation Project
Abstract: An evaluation of a Department of Health/Health Education Authority initiative to increase information about healthy lifestyles with a view to the prevention of coronary heart disease. Special staff are being appointed in the 14 Regional Health Authorities to undertake local initiatives, and this evaluation will be concerned with their work.
Status: Sponsored project
Source of Grant: Health Education Authority £162,739
Date of Research: 1991-1994
KEYWORDS: health education; heart disorders

10/0805

Institute of Education, Department of Policy Studies,
20 Bedford Way, London WC1H 0AL
0171 580 1122
Oakley, A. Prof.; Holland, J. Dr
Family Education Project: literature review and pilot study
Abstract: This is a pilot study to investigate the ways in which families discuss/deal with health education issues. It involves a literature survey and some exploratory empirical work.
Status: Sponsored project
Source of Grant: Health Education Authority £29,203
Date of Research: 1992-1992
KEYWORDS: family health; family influence; health education

10/0806

Institute of Education, Department of Policy Studies,
20 Bedford Way, London WC1H 0AL
0171 580 1122
Oakley, A. Prof.; Fullerton, D. Ms
Establishing a social science database of controlled interventions in education and social welfare
Abstract: The aims of the project are to review and classify the methodology of interventions in education and social welfare, to set up a computer database and compare the findings derived from different research designs.
Status: Sponsored project
Source of Grant: Economic and Social Research Council £28,650
Date of Research: 1993-1993
KEYWORDS: databases; intervention; pupil welfare

10/0807

Institute of Education, Department of Policy Studies,
20 Bedford Way, London WC1H 0AL
0171 580 1122
Young, M. Dr; Barnett, M. Prof.
Evaluation of the technological Baccalaureate
Abstract: The aims of this project are to investigate how pilot schools are using the Technological Baccalaureate and what the problems are of using the pilot scheme booklet. This will lead to an interim report for City & Guilds and the City Technology Colleges Trust with recommendations; a series of consultancy visits to the schools and colleges; and a final report.
Status: Sponsored project
Source of Grant: City Technology Colleges Trust £15,000
Date of Research: 1992-1993
KEYWORDS: qualifications; technology education

10/0808

Institute of Education, Department of Policy Studies,
20 Bedford Way, London WC1H 0AL
0171 580 1122
Young, M. Dr
Prevocational and vocational education continuation project (Extension)
Abstract: The project aims to assist in developing the work of the Centre for Post Sixteen Education with particular reference to inservice education of teachers (INSET) and initial teacher education. The main areas of project activity have been: (1) designing and supporting a 14-18 route within the Postgraduate Certificate of Education (PGCE) course; (2) research and development on progression (14-19) and overcoming barriers between academic and vocational learning; (3) development of short courses and conferences on Technical and Vocational Education Initiative (TVEI) related issues; (4) planning and preparation for the Centre to offer, in collaboration with other departments, a main course of study on vocational education and training within the modular MA in Educational Studies.
Published Material: A full list of working papers is available from the Centre for Post Sixteen Education.
Status: Sponsored project
Source of Grant: Training Agency £41,775
Date of Research: 1990-1992
KEYWORDS: sixteen to nineteen education; vocational education

10/0809

Institute of Education, Department of Policy Studies,
20 Bedford Way, London WC1H 0AL

0171 580 1122
Saran, R. Dr; Esp, D. Mr
Effective governors for effective schools: roles and relationships
Abstract: The study focuses on how the emerging relationships in school government, in particular between headteachers and chairs of governors, influence for better or worse the effectiveness of schools. Field work involves approximately 20 schools – primary, secondary, county, voluntary, and grant maintained.
Published Material: ESP, D. & SARAN, R. (Eds). (1995). Effective governors for effective schools. London: Longman.
Status: Sponsored project
Source of Grant: British Education Management Abstract Service; Longman Publishers
Date of Research: 1993-continuing
KEYWORDS: educational administration; governance; head teachers; school governing bodies; school governors

10/0810

Institute of Education, Department of Policy Studies,
20 Bedford Way, London WC1H 0AL
0171 580 1122
Oakley, A. Prof.; Rajan, L. Ms; Turner, H. Ms
Evaluation of NEWPIN
Abstract: An evaluation of a voluntary organisation set up to help people with parenting difficulties (and their children).
Status: Sponsored project
Source of Grant: Gatsby Charitable Foundation £142,333
Date of Research: 1993-continuing
KEYWORDS: child rearing; parent-child relationship; parenthood education; parenting skills; voluntary agencies

10/0811

Institute of Education, Department of Policy Studies,
20 Bedford Way, London WC1H 0AL
0171 580 1122
Young, M. Dr; Morris, A. Mr
Development of performing arts education for people over 16
Abstract: Development of formal systems for recognising achievement in 'informal' or 'supplementary' performing arts curriculum in post-16 education. Involves creation of modules (e.g. jazz dance, studio recording, performing arts workshop, careers in the arts) and of progression paths.
Status: Sponsored project
Source of Grant: Calouste Gulbenkian Foundation £9,000
Date of Research: 1993-1994
KEYWORDS: art education; dance; music; sixteen to nineteen education; theatre arts

10/0812

Institute of Education, Department of Policy Studies,
20 Bedford Way, London WC1H 0AL
0171 580 1122
Young, M. Dr
Unified curriculum at 16+ development phase
Abstract: The Hamlyn Post-16 Unified Curriculum Project has two overarching aims: 1) Raising levels of participation and achievement in post 16 education and training in the Hackney and Islington area. 2) Developing a national strategy for unifying the curriculum at 16+.
Status: Sponsored project
Source of Grant: Paul Hamlyn Foundation £65,000
Date of Research: 1993-1994
KEYWORDS: curriculum development; sixteen to nineteen education

10/0813

Institute of Education, Department of Policy Studies,
20 Bedford Way, London WC1H 0AL
0171 580 1122
Supervisor: Mayall, B. Dr
Evaluation of the smoking and pregnancy training manual
Abstract: An evaluation of the usefulness of a training manual designed to help community nurses work with pregnant smokers.
Status: Sponsored project
Source of Grant: Health Education Authority £17,473
Date of Research: 1993-1994
KEYWORDS: educational materials; guides; health education; nurse education; nurses; smoking

10/0814

Institute of Education, Department of Policy Studies,
20 Bedford Way, London WC1H 0AL
0171 580 1122
Young, M. Dr

Accreditation of work-based learning of teachers and trainers

Abstract: This project is concerned with developing a model of how academic accreditation might improve the quality and relevance of staff development carried out in the area of education and training in colleges, by training providers, and in private sector companies.
Status: Sponsored project
Source of Grant: City and Inner London North Training and Enterprise Council £69,980
Date of Research: 1993-1994
KEYWORDS: *on the job training; teacher development*

10/0815

Institute of Education, Department of Policy Studies,
20 Bedford Way, London WC1H 0AL
0171 580 1122
Mayall, B. Dr; Oakley, A. Prof.

Health in primary schools

Abstract: A study of the status of health in primary schools, using a postal questionnaire and case studies.
Status: Sponsored project
Source of Grant: Economic and Social Research Council £162,020
Date of Research: 1993-continuing
KEYWORDS: *health education; primary education*

10/0816

Institute of Education, Department of Policy Studies,
20 Bedford Way, London WC1H 0AL
0171 580 1122
Williams, G. Prof.

Long term study of British universities

Abstract: Statistical projections and systematic assembly of expert opinions to produce senarios of possible developments in British higher education by the early years of the next century.
Status: Sponsored project
Source of Grant: Committee of Vice-Chancellors and Principals of the Universities of the United Kingdom £23,011
Date of Research: 1993-1993
KEYWORDS: *educational development; higher education; prediction; universities*

10/0817

Institute of Education, Department of Policy Studies,
20 Bedford Way, London WC1H 0AL
0171 580 1122
Mauthner, M. Ms; Holland, J. Dr

Family health project

Abstract: A qualitative study of transmission processes and communication patterns in relation to health education information in families.
Published Material: HOLLAND, J., HEY, V. & MAUTHNER, M. (1992). The family education project pilot. Interim and Final Reports to the Health Education Authority.; HOLLAND, J., HEY, V. & MAUTHNER, M. (1993). 'Behind closed doors: researching the family'. Paper given at the British Sociological Association Annual Conference, Essex University, 5-8 April 1993.
Status: Sponsored project
Source of Grant: Health Education Authority £83,553
Date of Research: 1994-continuing
KEYWORDS: *communication research; family involvement; health education*

10/0818

Institute of Education, Department of Policy Studies,
20 Bedford Way, London WC1H 0AL
0171 580 1122
Fullerton, D. Ms; Holland, J. Dr; Oakley, A. Prof.

Towards effective interventions: a critical review of HIV prevention and sexual health education interventions

Abstract: A review of published ongoing studies of Human Immunodeficiency Virus/Acquired Immune Deficiency Syndrome (HIV/AIDS) education interventions with both low and high risk groups.
Status: Sponsored project
Source of Grant: Medical Research Council £32,290
Date of Research: 1993-1994
KEYWORDS: *acquired immune deficiency syndrome; health education; sex education; sexually transmitted diseases*

10/0819

Institute of Education, Department of Policy Studies,
20 Bedford Way, London WC1H 0AL
0171 580 1122
Warwick, I. Mr; Whitty, G. Prof.

Evaluation of HIV prevention initiatives amongst young people

Abstract: This project is examining the effectiveness of Human Immunodeficiency Virus (HIV) prevention initiatives amongst young people in schools and youth work settings in East Sussex.
Status: Sponsored project
Source of Grant: Hastings Health Authority £17,782
Date of Research: 1993-1994
KEYWORDS: *acquired immune deficiency syndrome; health education; sex education; sexually transmitted diseases; youth*

10/0820

Institute of Education, Department of Policy Studies,
20 Bedford Way, London WC1H 0AL
0171 580 1122
Oakley, A. Prof.; Holland, J. Dr

Review of effectiveness of sexual health education for young people

Abstract: A review and evaluation of sexual health education interventions for young people.
Status: Sponsored project
Source of Grant: Health Education Authority £19,695
Date of Research: 1993-1994
KEYWORDS: *health education; sex education; youth*

10/0821

Institute of Education, Department of Policy Studies,
20 Bedford Way, London WC1H 0AL
0171 580 1122
Whitty, G. Prof.

Cross-curricular work in post-primary schools in Northern Ireland

Abstract: A national survey and detailed observation in a small sample of post-primary schools were used to compare the implementation of the educational themes specified in Northern Ireland's Education Reform Order 1989, with earlier findings about the implementation of the cross-curricular themes in England and Wales.
Published Material: WHITTY, G., ROWE, G. & AGGLETON, P. (1994). 'Subjects and themes in the secondary-school curriculum', Research Papers in Education, Vol 9, No 2, pp.159-181.
Status: Sponsored project
Source of Grant: Department of Education Northern Ireland £4,335
Date of Research: 1993-1993
KEYWORDS: *cross curricular approach; curriculum development; Northern Ireland*

10/0822

Institute of Education, Department of Policy Studies,
20 Bedford Way, London WC1H 0AL
0171 580 1122
Barnett, R. Dr

Assessment of the quality of education: evaluation and review of the assessment and procedures of the Higher Education Funding Council for England (HEFCE) and the Higher Education Funding Council for Wales (HEFCW)

Abstract: An evaluation of the quality assessment exercise (1993/94) in universities in England and Wales.
Published Material: BARNETT, R. (1994). Assessment of the quality of higher education: a review and an evaluation. Report to Higher Education Funding Council in England.
Status: Sponsored project
Source of Grant: Higher Education Funding Council for England £29,375
Date of Research: 1993-1994
KEYWORDS: *assessment; educational quality; higher education*

10/0823

Institute of Education, Department of Policy Studies,
20 Bedford Way, London WC1H 0AL
0171 580 1122
Keele University, Department of Social Anthropology, Keele
ST5 5BG
01782 62111
Mayall, B. Dr; Prout, A. Dr
Childhood and society
Abstract: A seminar group which holds regular day meetings to
discuss issues in the sociology of childhood.
Status: Sponsored project
Source of Grant: Economic and Social Research Council £3,315
Date of Research: 1993-continuing
KEYWORDS: children; sociology

10/0824

Institute of Education, Department of Policy Studies,
20 Bedford Way, London WC1H 0AL
0171 580 1122
London University, Goldsmiths' College, Faculty of
Education, Lewisham Way, New Cross, London SE14 6NW
0171 919 7171
Inman, S. Ms; Whitty, G. Prof.
Promoting health in secondary schools
Abstract: This project will assess the training needs in each of the
eight new health regions in England and, in the light of this assess-
ment, will facilitate the provision of relevant training for local trainers
and those responsible for promoting health in secondary schools.
These training activities will be evaluated and a training resource on
the promotion of health in secondary schools will be produced and
disseminated.
Status: Sponsored project
Source of Grant: Health Education Authority £157,589
Date of Research: 1994-continuing
KEYWORDS: health education; health promotion; secondary schools

10/0825

Institute of Education, Department of Policy Studies, 20
Bedford Way, London WC1H 0AL
0171 580 1122
West Sussex Institute of Higher Education, The Dome,
Upper Bognor Road, Bognor Regis PO21 1HR
01243 865581
Barrett, E. Dr; Whitty, G. Prof.; Furlong, J. Prof.; Barton, L.
Prof.; Miles, S. Ms; Jacques, K. Ms
**Changing modes of professionalism: a case study of teacher
education in transition**
Abstract: It was against the background of changes in the shape of
initial teacher training (ITT), and growing political concern about its
effectiveness and its ideological bias, that this project developed. The
lack of any large scale recent research on ITT meant that much of the
policy debate was being conducted on the basis of very limited
information. The research project aims to explore: 1) the nature of
the training offered in different training routes; 2) the costs associated
with different routes; 3) trainee experience within different routes;
and 4) the outcomes of different routes. The current project will build
on work done on previous Modes of Teacher Education (MOTE)
project. Work will continue with the sample of 50 ITT courses used
on the previous project. Students completing these courses will be
followed up during their first year of teaching. The model for costing
ITT, developed in the previous project, will be refined and applied to
ITT courses. A new national survey of ITT provision will be conducted in 1995.
Published Material: BARRETT, E., BARTON, L., FURLONG, J.,
GALVIN, C., MILES, S. & WHITTY, G. (1992). Initial teacher
education in England and Wales: a topography. London: University
of London, Goldsmiths' College.; WHITTY, G., BARRETT, E.,
BARTON, L., FURLONG, J., GALVIN, C. & MILES, S. (1992).
'Initial teacher education in England and Wales: a survey of current
practices and concerns', Cambridge Journal of Education, Vol 22,
No 3, pp.293-306.; BARRETT, E., BARTON, L., FURLONG, J.,
GALVIN, C., MILES, S. & WHITTY, G. (1992). 'New routes to
qualified teacher status', Cambridge Journal of Education, Vol 22,
No 3, pp.323-335.
Status: Sponsored project
Source of Grant: Economic and Social Research Council £91,721
Date of Research: 1993-continuing

*KEYWORDS: preservice teacher education; school-based teacher
education*

10/0826

Institute of Education, Department of Policy Studies, Health
and Education Research Unit, 20 Bedford Way, London
WC1H 0AL
0171 580 1122
Warwick, I. Mr; Supervisor: Aggleton, P. Dr; Whitty, G. Prof.
**Health Education Authority HIV/AIDS and homeless young
people project**
Abstract: This is a project to identify the Human Immunodeficiency
Virus/Acquired Immune Deficiency Syndrome (HIV/AIDS) health
education needs of young homeless people. Via a programme of
national consultations involving workers from the statutory and
non-statutory sectors, it will seek to access perspectives on the
HIV/AIDS health education needs of young people who are homeless
and rootless.
Status: Sponsored project
Source of Grant: Health Education Authority
Date of Research: 1990-1994
*KEYWORDS: acquired immune deficiency syndrome; health educa-
tion; homeless people*

10/0827

Institute of Education, Department of Policy Studies, Health
and Education Research Unit, 20 Bedford Way, London
WC1H 0AL
0171 580 1122
Aggleton, P. Dr; Whitty, G. Prof.
**South East Thames regional HIV education and training
evaluation project**
Abstract: This is a project to evaluate the implementation of the South
East Thames Regional Human Immunodeficiency Virus (HIV) Education and Training Strategy at district level. It will seek to identify
via interviews with Human Immunodeficiency Virus/Acquired Immune Deficiency Syndrome (HIV/AIDS) prevention coordinators,
trainers, training providers, workers in relevant non-statutory agencies and other key informants. The aims of the project are to discover
(1) awareness of South East Thames Regional HIV Education and
Training Strategy; (2) perceptions of its appropriateness and inclu-
siveness in meeting the HIV/AIDS training needs of relevant health
authority personnel; (3) perceptions of the effectiveness and inclu-
siveness of this strategy in meeting the needs of clients and carers,
for appropriate priorities for future HIV education and training; (4)
appropriate ways in which the South East Thames Regional Health
Authority might promote and support such work and (5) appropriate
strategies by which such education and training might be monitored
and evaluated on an ongoing basis.
Status: Sponsored project
Source of Grant: South East Thames Regional Health Authority
£15,865
Date of Research: 1991-1993
*KEYWORDS: acquired immune deficiency syndrome; evaluation;
health education; training*

10/0828

Institute of Education, Department of Policy Studies, Health
and Education Research Unit, 20 Bedford Way, London
WC1H 0AL
0171 580 1122
Whitty, G. Prof.; Aggleton, P. Dr
AVERT AIDS: working with young people project
Abstract: This project extends earlier work which researched the
Human Immunodeficiency Virus/Acquired Immune Deficiency Syndrome (HIV/AIDS) training needs of adults who work with young
people in youth service settings. A number of needs were identified.
These ranged from information on social and medical issues to ways
in which young people may be helped to learn about HIV infection
and AIDS. The findings were disseminated via a resource for youth
workers. The current project aims to develop the work to include the
needs of teachers in secondary schools. It will : (1) research the needs
of teachers in relation to classroom-based activity on HIV and AIDS;
(2) compare these needs with those of workers in youth service
settings; (3) identify ways in which teachers might best support and
enable pupils in learning about the medical and social issues associated with HIV and AIDS. The projects findings will be disseminated

via an updated resource package which emphasises participatory training within a clearly defined equal opportunities framework.
Published Material: AGGLETON P. et al. (1993). AIDS: working with young people. Second Edition. Horsham: AVERT.
Status: Sponsored project
Source of Grant: AIDS Education and Research Trust (AVERT) £38,299
Date of Research: 1992-1993
KEYWORDS: acquired immune deficiency syndrome; health education; secondary schools

10/0829

Institute of Education, Department of Policy Studies, Health and Education Research Unit, 20 Bedford Way, London WC1H 0AL
0171 580 1122
Whitty, G. Prof.; Aggleton, P. Dr
Learning about AIDS Project (continuation)
Abstract: This project aims to update earlier research on the training needs of adults who educate other adults about Human Immunodeficiency Virus (HIV) infection and Acquired Immune Deficiency Syndrome (AIDS). A series of national consultative meetings identified that adult HIV/AIDS trainers have had the following concerns: (1) relevant scientific and medical issues on HIV and AIDS should continue to be clarified; (2) psychological dimensions of HIV/AIDS should be explored; (3) there should be a greater attention to 'newer issues' in HIV/AIDS works (such as children and HIV); and (4) monitoring and evaluation, pre-course planning and post-course action should be further examined. A series of interactive focus groups will be held across the country so that the above issues might be explored in greater detail. Attention will be focused on the need to develop accessible and relevant information as well as on the ways trainers might be supported in their work. Resource materials will be produced which will help trainers conduct effective HIV/AIDS education.
Published Material: AGGLETON, P. et al. (1989). Learning about AIDS: exercises and materials for adult education about HIV and AIDS. Edinburgh: Churchill Livingstone.; AGGLETON, P. et al. (1994). Learning about AIDS: scientific and social issues. Edinburgh: Churchill Livingstone.
Status: Sponsored project
Source of Grant: Health Education Authority £177,318
Date of Research: 1992-1994
KEYWORDS: acquired immune deficiency syndrome; educational materials; health education

10/0830

Institute of Education, Department of Policy Studies, Health and Education Research Unit, 20 Bedford Way, London WC1H 0AL
0171 580 1122
Whitty, G. Prof.
AIDS Education and Research Trust (AVERT) HIV/AIDS and Nursing project
Abstract: Following Phase I of this project (a qualitative study of student nurses' lay beliefs of Human Immunodeficiency and Acquired Immune Deficiency Syndrome (HIV and AIDS) conducted between September 1991 and September 1992) Phase II will: (1) Produce and disseminate policy recommendations detailing how HIV/AIDS might best be addressed on Project 2000 courses. (2) Provide curriculum guidance for lecturers, nurse tutors and clinical teachers on how HIV/AIDS might best be addressed on Project 2000 courses and in allied clinical practice. (3) Produce a booklet of information and guidance for student nurses.
Published Material: WALKER, B. & WARWICK, I. (1993). Information for nurses about HIV infection and AIDS. Horsham: AVERT.
Status: Sponsored project
Source of Grant: AIDS Education and Research Trust (AVERT) £58,042
Date of Research: 1992-1994
KEYWORDS: acquired immune deficiency syndrome; nurse education; nurses; sexually transmitted diseases

10/0831

Institute of Education, Department of Policy Studies, Health and Education Research Unit, 20 Bedford Way, London WC1H 0AL
0171 580 1122

Aggleton, P. Dr; Whitty, G. Prof.
Health Education Authority 'Men who have sex with men' project: selected examples of good practice in HIV/AIDS health promotion
Abstract: This project seeks to identify and document instances of good practice in local Human Immunodeficiency Virus/Acquired Immune Deficiency Syndrome (HIV/AIDS) education work with men who have sex with men, with a view to making this information more widely available. The aims are to identify: (1) the range of activities currently underway to prevent HIV transmission amongst men who have sex with men; (2) projects and activities that have proved most appropriate, innovative and effective within specific local contexts; (3) factors which facilitate such work; (4) factors which hinder such work. Interviews will be carried out with relevant project personnel so as to lay the foundations for a number of case studies documenting good practice in this field. The case studies will be written up and made available through two project reports.
Published Material: McKEVITT, C., WARWICK, I. & AGGLETON, P. (1994). Towards good practice: selective examples of HIV and AIDS health promotion with gay, bisexual and other men who have sex with men. London: Health Education Authority.
Status: Sponsored project
Source of Grant: Health Education Authority £24,700
Date of Research: 1992-1993
KEYWORDS: acquired immune deficiency syndrome; health education; homosexuality; sex education; sexuality; sexually transmitted diseases

10/0832

Institute of Education, Department of Policy Studies, Health and Education Research Unit, 20 Bedford Way, London WC1H 0AL
0171 580 1122
Whitty, G. Prof.; Aggleton, P. Dr
Assessing quality in cross-curricular contexts: a case study
Abstract: This project is exploring changing approaches to cross-curricular work in key stages 3 and 4 in the context of the National Curriculum. Particular attention is being paid to work relating to the National Curriculum Council's five designated cross-curricular themes. Baseline data from an earlier project conducted in 1988/1989 is being compared with a new survey of policy and practice in a sample of 1 in 4 secondary schools in England and Wales. Intensive observation and interviewing is being conducted in a sub-sample of 8 schools.
Published Material: ROWE, G. & WHITTY, G. (1993). 'Five themes remain in the shadows', Times Educational Supplement, 9 April 1993.; ROWE, G., AGGLETON, P. & WHITTY, G. (1993). 'Cross-curricular work in secondary schools: the place of careers education and guidance', Careers Education and Guidance, June, pp.2-6.; WHITTY, G., ROWE, G. & AGGLETON, P. (1994). 'Subjects and themes in the secondary school curriculum', Research Papers in Education, Vol 9, No 2, pp.159-181.
Status: Sponsored project
Source of Grant: Economic and Social Research Council £49,711
Date of Research: 1992-1993
KEYWORDS: cross curricular approach; curriculum development; educational quality; National Curriculum

10/0833

Institute of Education, Department of Science Education, 20 Bedford Way, London WC1H 0AL
0171 580 1122
MaCaskill, C. Mrs
Initial teacher training CD-ROM Scheme
Abstract: This is an investigation of how CD-ROMs can be usefully employed by teachers and pupils in National Curriculum Technology. The aim is to explore the potential of using CD-ROM in National Curriculum Technology specifically for supporting attainment targets (AT) 1 and 2 for which pupils are required to research and investigate the context of their study and also to support AT 5, Information Technology. Two questions were posed: (1) how can CD-ROM be used to support pupils' independent researching? (2) what researching strategies are normally employed by technology teachers, both in and out of the classroom, do they consider the use of CD-ROMs to be beneficial to this process.
Status: Sponsored project
Source of Grant: National Council for Educational Technology £1,000

Date of Research: 1992-1993
KEYWORDS: information seeking; information technology; National Curriculum; optical data discs; technology education

10/0834

Institute of Education, Department of Science Education, 20 Bedford Way, London WC1H 0AL
0171 580 1122
Ogborn, J. Prof.; Boohan, D. Mr
Teaching about why things change
Abstract: To develop ways of teaching about energy and the reasons for change. Working initially with a few classes of children to develop the approach – then working with Postgraduate Certificate in Education (PGCE) students and a wider range of teachers to develop inservice education of teachers (INSET) materials.
Status: Sponsored project
Source of Grant: Nuffield Foundation £97,523
Date of Research: 1992-continuing
KEYWORDS: energy education; physics education; science education

10/0835

Institute of Education, Department of Science Education, 20 Bedford Way, London WC1H 0AL
0171 580 1122
Ogborn, J. Prof.
Commonsense understanding of science
Abstract: The project is concerned with the description of fundamental dimensions of commonsense or everyday reasoning about processes and events in the natural world, and the relation of these to scientific accounts of similar processes.
Published Material: MARIANI, M. & OGBORN, J. (1990). 'Commonsense reasoning about conservation: the role of action', International Journal of Science Education, Vol 12, No 1, pp.51-66.; MARIANI, M. & OGBORN, J. (1991). 'Towards an ontology of commonsense reasoning', International Journal of Science Education, Vol 13, No 1, pp.69-85.; OGBORN, J. (1992). 'Fundamental dimensions of thought about reality: object, action, cause, movement, space and time'. In: Teaching about reference frames: from Copernicus to Einstein. Proceedings of GIREP Conference, Torun, Poland, August 1991. Torun: Nicholas Copernicus University Press.; OGBORN, J. (1992). 'Basic structures underlying some mental models'. In: Mental models and everyday activities, Proceedings of Second Interdisciplinary Workshop on Mental Models, March 23-25, 1992, Cambridge.
Status: Sponsored project
Source of Grant: Leverhulme Trust £43,567
Date of Research: 1992-1993
KEYWORDS: explanation; physical environment; public opinion; reasoning; scientific attitudes; scientific literacy

10/0836

Institute of Education, Department of Science Education, 20 Bedford Way, London WC1H 0AL
0171 580 1122
Ogborn, J. Prof.; Brosnan, T. Mr; Hann, K. Dr
Children and Teachers Talking Science (CHATTS)
Abstract: With Science now part of the National Curriculum, primary school teachers need more and more scientific knowledge. However, as a significant group in the general population, their scientific knowledge is part of the problem of public understanding of science. The project is looking at how primary school teachers are able to make sense of information about contentious public issues with a scientific dimension, through television and other media.
Published Material: HANN, K.L. (1990). 'CHATTS project for primary teachers', Education in Science, No 139, pp.42.; HANN, K.L. (1990). 'CHATTS', children and teachers talking science', Primary Science Review, No 14, pp.34.; HANN, K.L., BROSNAN, T. & OGBORN, J. (1991). 'The facts behind the issues', Questions, Vol 4, No 1, pp.26-27.; HANN, K.L., BROSNAN, T. & OGBORN, J. (1991). 'The work of the CHATTS project'. Paper presented at the Association for Teacher Education Europe Conference', Amsterdam, September 1991.; A full list of publications is available from the researcher.
Status: Sponsored project
Source of Grant: British Gas £59,719
Date of Research: 1990-1992
KEYWORDS: mass media; primary school teachers; public opinion; science teachers; scientific attitudes; scientific literacy; television

10/0837

Institute of Education, Department of Science Education, 20 Bedford Way, London WC1H 0AL
0171 580 1122
Ogborn, J. Prof.; Brosnan, T. Mr; Hann, K. Dr
Development of teaching and curriculum materials for Children and Teachers Talking About Science (CHATTS)
Abstract: The project involves developing inservice education of teachers (INSET) materials for primary school teachers to explore their understanding of science topics and point to ways of developing these in the classroom.
Status: Sponsored project
Source of Grant: British Gas £26,000
Date of Research: 1992-1992
KEYWORDS: inservice teacher education; material development; primary education; science education

10/0838

Institute of Education, Department of Science Education, 20 Bedford Way, London WC1H 0AL
0171 580 1122
Turner, S. Dr
Review of steps taken by local education authorities to encourage healthy eating in schools
Abstract: This is a review of steps taken by local education authorities (LEAs) to encourage healthy eating in schools. Information is being sought from all LEAs in England on the extent and nature of nutritional specifications used by LEAs in school meals contracts by means of questionnaires and some indepth interviews.
Published Material: COLES, A. & TURNER, S. (1993). 'Catering for healthy eating in schools'. London: Health Education Authority.
Status: Sponsored project
Source of Grant: Health Education Authority £20,933
Date of Research: 1992-1992
KEYWORDS: health education; local education authorities; nutrition education; school meals

10/0839

Institute of Education, Department of Science Education, 20 Bedford Way, London WC1H 0AL
0171 580 1122
Ogborn, J. Prof.; Kress, G. Prof.
Explanation in the science classroom
Abstract: The project is an attempt to construct a language, theoretically and empirically based, to describe the various forms and effects of explanations in science classrooms. The approach is through the analysis of discourses, and the ontologies they support or exclude.
Status: Sponsored project
Source of Grant: Economic and Social Research Council £113,430
Date of Research: 1994-continuing
KEYWORDS: explanation; science education

10/0840

Institute of Education, Directorate, 20 Bedford Way, London WC1H 0AL
0171 580 1122
Mortimore, P. Prof.; MacGilchrist, B. Mrs; Savage, J. Ms; Beresford, C. Mr
Impact of school development plans in primary schools
Abstract: School development plans provide a mechanism to link the planning of improvements with the financial and staff development planning of the school as a whole. This project aims to investigate whether these plans – and the process of planning – are having positive impacts. Schools in contrasting areas make up the sample. A mixture of research methods has been chosen for this three year study.
Published Material: BERESFORD, C., MORTIMORE, P. MacGILCHRIST, B. & SAVAGE, J. (1992). 'School development planning matters in the UK', Unicorn (Journal of the Australian College of Education), Vol 18, No 2, pp.12-16.; SAVAGE, J. (1993). 'The impact of school development planning in primary schools'. Paper presented to the British Educational Research Association, September 1993.; MORTIMORE, P., MacGILCHRIST, B., SAVAGE, J. & BERESFORD, C. (1994). 'School development planning in primary schools: does it make a difference?'. In: HOPKINS, D., HARGREAVES, D. (Eds). Development planning for school improvement. London: Cassell.; SAVAGE, J., MacGILCHRIST, B.,

MORTIMORE, P. & BERESFORD, C. (1994). 'The impact of school development planning in primary schools'. Presented at the International Congress for School Effectiveness and Improvement, January 1994.
Status: Sponsored project
Source of Grant: Economic and Social Research Council £85,120
Date of Research: 1991-1994
KEYWORDS: development plans; educational administration; planning; primary schools

10/0841
Institute of Education, Directorate, 20 Bedford Way, London WC1H 0AL
0171 580 1122
Mortimore, P. Prof.; Mortimore, J. Mrs; Thomas, H. Dr
Innovatory staffing practices in City Technology Colleges
Abstract: Recent changes in education (in particular, the introduction of the National Curriculum and Local Management of Schools) have accelerated the demand for posts to assist teachers in the provision of the curriculum and to support the management and administration of increasingly complex institutions. Building on earlier work on the innovative use of associate staff in the maintained sector, this study investigates some of its unanswered questions in the context of City Technology Colleges (CTC's), institutions which were themselves created to be innovatory. The research team will collect information on the benefits and disbenefits of the innovatory associate staff posts, and their effect on the traditional boundaries of teachers' roles, in a representative sample of CTC's. The cost effectiveness of the posts will also be explored. In addition, the researchers will seek to evaluate and extend current theories of how change is implemented in educational settings.
Status: Sponsored project
Source of Grant: Economic and Social Research Council £104,230
Date of Research: 1993-continuing
KEYWORDS: city technology colleges; school personnel; support staff; teacher aides

10/0842
Institute of Education, Directorate, 20 Bedford Way, London WC1H 0AL
0171 580 1122
Bird, C. Ms
Telling parents about education: an exercise in dissemination of information to parents
Abstract: The project will examine methods used by schools and local authorities to inform parents about national and local issues. Experiment will identify strengths and weaknesses of different approaches and work with parents to find ways of producing information of use to them.
Status: Sponsored project
Source of Grant: Paul Hamlyn Foundation £15,000
Date of Research: 1993-1994
KEYWORDS: access to information; information needs; parent-school relationship

10/0843
Institute of Education, Social Science Research Unit, 20 Bedford Way, London WC1H 0AL
0171 580 1122
Hewitt, R. Dr
Effects of teaching 'speaking and listening' in the National Curriculum
Abstract: This is an examination of how the explicit teaching of 'speaking and listening' affects the performance of pupils' communicative skills and the conduct of collaboration in oral group work. The aims are to investigate: (1) how, at key stage 2 of the National Curriculum, the foregrounding of talk as a subject of pedagogic activity in its own right affects: (a) how pupils communicate with each other in oral group work; (b) how their talk influences their group collaborations, and (2) how teachers' objectives in teaching and creating opportunities for the development of speaking and listening skills are realised or changed in practice.
Status: Sponsored project
Source of Grant: Economic and Social Research Council £29,530
Date of Research: 1991-1993
KEYWORDS: communication skills; listening skills; National Curriculum; speech communication

10/0844
Institute of Education, Technology and Education Unit, 20 Bedford Way, London WC1H 0AL
0171 580 1122
Barnett, M. Prof.
Databases for children making technological decisions
Abstract: The aims of this project are to: (1) determine whether and how various types of databases are being used in National Curriculum Technology key stages 2 and 3; (2) determine how they might be better used; (3) establish exemplary projects, and evaluate their operation in terms of outcomes for pupils; (4) create and trial relevant inservice education of teachers (INSET) material.
Status: Sponsored project
Source of Grant: Esmee Fairbairn Charitable Trust £50,000
Date of Research: 1992-1994
KEYWORDS: databases; information technology; National Curriculum; technology education

10/0845
Institute of Education, Technology and Education Unit, 20 Bedford Way, London WC1H 0AL
0171 580 1122
Barnett, M. Prof.; Kent, A. Mr
Remote sensing in the Geography National Curriculum
Abstract: This project involves the development of teacher education materials for remote sensing in the Geography National Curriculum. The geography order specifically requires that satellite images of the earth and aerial photographs should be used as resources. There are also many points where delivery would be much enhanced by the use of such images. The project aims to develop materials which will enable teachers to make wider use of all forms of remotely sensed images by illustrating how images can be integrated into the geography curriculum.
Status: Sponsored project
Source of Grant: National Council for Educational Technology £77,296
Date of Research: 1992-1993
KEYWORDS: earth science; geography education; inservice teacher education; National Curriculum

10/0846
Institute of Education, Thomas Coram Research Unit, 20 Bedford Way, London WC1N 0AL
0171 580 1122
Mooney, A. Ms; Munton, A. Dr; Rowland, L. Ms;
Supervisor: McGurk, H. Prof.
Quality of daycare provision in the United Kingdom
Abstract: The aim of this project is to develop instruments and procedures that can contribute to the monitoring, evaluation, and enhancement of the quality of centre and family based (childminding) childcare settings. The project is grounded in child development theory and informed by consideration of the perspectives and needs of parents, child care workers, and service providers. The project is being conducted in five successive phases: an instrument development phase; a pilot phase; a validatiom phase involving 100 urban, suburban and rural settings; an intervention phase in which selected settings participate in a study of quality enhancement; and a dissemination phase. The duration of the project is three and a half years. It is intended that, in addition to their research value, the instruments and procedures developed should be usable by those involved directly in the provision of child care, by the trainers of child care workers, and those with responsibility for monitoring and evaluating the quality of child care.
Status: Sponsored project
Source of Grant: Department of Health £209,716
Date of Research: 1992-continuing
KEYWORDS: child caregivers; child minding; day care; day care centres; preschool children; quality control

10/0847
Institute of Education, Thomas Coram Research Unit, 20 Bedford Way, London WC1H 0AL
0171 580 1122
Veltman, M. Ms; *Supervisor:* Plewis, I. Mr
Changes in the classroom experience of Inner London infant pupils 1984-1992
Abstract: The introduction of the National Curriculum and standardised assessment is likely to lead to major changes in the way

classrooms are organised, in the way teachers operate, and in pupils' classroom experiences. This study focuses on infant schools, where such changes are already well underway. The project will look at how much time pupils spend on different parts of the curriculum, and in particular how much of the mathematics curriculum they experience. The project will also look at classroom organisation in terms of how pupils are grouped for mathematics, how this varies over time, and how the grouping arrangements relate to academic progress. The study will make a direct comparison with data collected in 1984/1985 by an earlier project based at the Thomas Coram Research Unit, and so obtain a unique picture of how clasrooms have been changed by the Education Reform Act 1988. The sample will consist of twenty-four Inner London infant schools, as far as possible the same schools used in the earlier project. All the children in one class in each school will be studied as they progress from the end of Year 1 to the end of Year 2 (6-7 years). Data will be obtained by systematic observation techniques, teacher interviews and assessment of pupils' attainment and progress. Preliminary findings are likely to be available in Autumn 1993, and the main findings in Autumn 1994.
Published Material: TIZARD, B., BLATCHFORD, P., BURKE, J., FARQUHAR, C. & PLEWIS, I. (1988). Young children at school in the inner city. Hove: Lawrence Erlbaum Associates.
Status: Sponsored project
Source of Grant: Economic and Social Research Council £76,520
Date of Research: 1992-1994
KEYWORDS: *classroom research; curriculum research; Education Reform Act 1988; educational change; educational experience; infant schools; mathematics education*

10/0848

Institute of Education, Thomas Coram Research Unit,
20 Bedford Way, London WC1H 0AL
0171 580 1122
Petrie, P. Dr; Poland, G. Ms
Out of school services survey and evaluation
Abstract: Twelve case studies of playschemes, using a consultative approach with providers and staff, followed by a survey of 100 schemes looking at objectives and their realisation; organisation and resources.
Status: Sponsored project
Source of Grant: Department of Health £181,827
Date of Research: 1990-1993
KEYWORDS: *child care givers; community services; play; play centres; recreational activities*

10/0849

Institute of Education, Thomas Coram Research Unit,
20 Bedford Way, London WC1H 0AL
0171 580 1122
McGurk, H. Prof.; Hurry, J. Dr
Evaluation of Project Charlie: a drug prevention programme for primary school children
Abstract: Project Charlie is a drug prevention programme for primary school children, developed in 1976 in the USA and now widely implemented there. Currently being piloted in London, The Home Office requested an evaluation of the programme. The impact of Project Charlie in two Hackney primary schools is being investigated on the basis of: (a) its objectives to improve children's 'life-skills'; decision making, peer-pressure resistance, self-esteem and making relationships; and (b) its goals, to inform on drug abuse and to alter drug-related behaviour and drug use. The degree to which this programme is acceptable and workable in these Hackney schools is also being established. Approximately 200 children aged between 7 and 11 years were tested on a battery of paper and pencil measures relating to their 'life-skills' and verbal competence. The majority of these children, 175, attending one school were tested, prior to receiving Project Charlie lessons for one period weekly. Half were randomly assigned to the Project Charlie group and half to the control group. After one year of the programme both the experimental and control groups are currently being re-tested.
Status: Sponsored project
Source of Grant: Home Office £32,870
Date of Research: 1990-1993
KEYWORDS: *drug education; health education; life skills; primary education*

10/0850

Institute of Education, Thomas Coram Research Unit,
20 Bedford Way, London WC1H 0AL
0171 580 1122
Doxford, P. Ms; Fox-Lee, L. Mrs; Kennedy, B. Ms; Mirelman, H. Ms; Zuke, L. Ms; *Supervisor:* Sylva, K. Prof.; Hurry, J. Dr
Early intervention in children with reading difficulties: a comparison of local education authority (LEA) programmes
Abstract: The study will compare the progress of children in the Reading Recovery Programme with children of similar ability receiving a sophisticated phonological programme which offers a less intensive, highly focused intervention. Both groups will be compared to a control group with no formal intervention. It will address not only the effects of the interventions on reading, but also on behaviour problems and progress in other areas of the curriculum. The attitudes of school staff to the interventions and changes in policy and practice in the teaching of reading will be monitored. In addition, careful records will be kept of the full cost of the two interventions so that the outcome (in terms of gains in reading scores and other measures) may be examined in light of the cost (per child) to the local education authority (LEA) of providing the service.
Status: Sponsored project
Source of Grant: National Curriculum Council £278,000
Date of Research: 1992-continuing
KEYWORDS: *phonics; reading difficulties; reading teaching; remedial reading*

10/0851

Institute of Education, Thomas Coram Research Unit,
20 Bedford Way, London WC1H 0AL
0171 580 1122
Cameron, C. Ms; Candappa, M. Mr; Bull, J. Ms; *Supervisor:* Moss, P. Mr; Owen, C. Mr; Statham, J. Dr
Studies of English and Welsh local authorities implementation of the provisions of the Children Act 1989 on day care and preschool education
Abstract: These two projects will monitor the implementation by English and Welsh local authorities of the provisions of the Children Act on day care services for children under 8 and preschool education, and evaluate the impact of that implementation. They will also consider the effects of certain organisational differences between local authorities, including the use of Independent Inspection Units for implementation of parts of the Act and the transfer of responsibility of all under 8s services to local education authorities, and in Wales will focus on the implementation of the Act in a rural and bilingual context.
Status: Sponsored project
Source of Grant: Department of Health £434,504; Welsh Office £135,223
Date of Research: 1992-continuing
KEYWORDS: *Children Act 1989; day care; early childhood education; legislation; local government; preschool education; social services*

10/0852

Institute of Education, Thomas Coram Research Unit,
20 Bedford Way, London WC1H 0AL
0171 580 1122
Oakley, A. Prof.; Brannen, J. Dr
Adolescent health and parenting
Abstract: The project is intended to explore two main issues: The transfer of responsibility for health from parents to young people, and the experience of parenting at this stage of the life cycle. In the first part of the research questionnaires have been completed by 15-16 year olds in 5 schools. In the second part, a sample of 80 households will be studied indepth, and results of the questionnaire survey will be fed back to schools.
Published Material: OAKLEY, A., BRANNEN, J. & DODD, K. 'Young people, gender and smoking: towards a social epidemiology', Health Promotion, (forthcoming).
Status: Sponsored project
Source of Grant: Department of Health £178,114
Date of Research: 1989-1992
KEYWORDS: *adolescents; family influence; health; smoking*

10/0853

Institute of Education, Thomas Coram Research Unit,
20 Bedford Way, London WC1H 0AL
0171 580 1122
Bee, P. Ms; Heverin, A. Ms; Nobes, G. Dr; Poland, G. Ms;
Supervisor: Smith, M. Dr

Bullying and victimisation in school in relation to parental behaviour in the home

Abstract: As part of a large community-based study on parental control strategies and punishment of children in the home, teachers were surveyed about children's behaviour in school. This provided an account of the child's behaviour which was independent of those of the parents. Particular emphasis was placed on children's bullying and victimisation, in attempt to investigate the relationship between these behaviours at school and children's experience of specific parental control strategies at home. The sample consisted of 200 families, half with children aged 7 years and half with 11 year old children, drawn from an urban area near London and from South London. The children's class teachers were asked to complete a short questionnaire on the child's behaviour.
Status: Sponsored project
Source of Grant: Department of Health £207,000
Date of Research: 1990-1994
KEYWORDS: *behaviour problems; bullying; family influence; home environment; parent child relationship; parent-pupil relationship; punishment; pupil behaviour*

10/0854

King's College, Centre for Educational Studies, Cornwall House Annexe, Waterloo Road, London SE1 3TY
0171 836 5454
Head, J. Dr; Paechter, C. Dr

Power, Gender and the negotiation of the design and technology curriculum

Abstract: The study takes advantage of the current unique situation in school design and technology departments, in order to examine the process of subject sub-cultural negotiation among teachers. The researchers believe that the negotiation of the content of the design and technology curriculum, with its aspirations to gender neutrality and extended core status, highlights the relationship between gender and power. The study has two interrelated and equal aims: 1) to investigate how this new curriculum area and subject sub-culture is developed by teachers coming from different subject bases; and 2) to generate a description of how power and gender operate and inter-relate in the processes of negotiation within a professional group. The main body of research has been carried out through semi-structured interviews and observation. It has a strong ethnographic bias. Five schools are involved.
Status: Sponsored project
Source of Grant: Economic and Social Research Council £74,860
Date of Research: 1992-1994
KEYWORDS: *design and technology; sex differences; teaching profession*

10/0855

London School of Economics and Political Science,
Department of Geography, Houghton Street, London
WC2A 2AE
0171 405 7686
Bennett, R. Prof.; Wicks, P. Dr

Education-Business Partnerships (EBPs): targets and stocktake

Abstract: The objective of the report is to provide a stocktake of the current development of Education-Business Partnerships (EBPs). This has the purpose of acting like a 'church tower appeal' in that a visual impression is to be given of the current level of development in EBPs in different local education authorities (LEAs). The purpose of the stocktake is to provide a measure of the current development of EBPs against which future evolution and progress can be judged. It is intended that this will encourage existing effective EBPs whilst setting clear targets for the LEAs which have not yet developed full EBPs, and that further assessments will be made annually to stimulate the development of EBPs. The analysis assesses the progress in development of EBPs against a five level classification.
Published Material: BENNETT, R.J. (1991). Education-Business Partnerships. London: Confederation of British Industry.; BENNETT, R.J., MCCOSHAN, A. & SELLGREN, J. (1989). 'The organisation of Business/Education links: further findings from the CBI Schools Questionnaire'. (Department of Geography Research Papers). London: London University.;

Status: Sponsored project
Source of Grant: Shell UK; Confederation of British Industry £14,000
Date of Research: 1988-continuing
KEYWORDS: *industry-education relationship; local education authorities; school to work transition; vocational education*

10/0856

London School of Economics and Political Science,
Department of Social Policy and Administration, Suntory
Toyota International Centre for Economics and Related
Disciplines, Houghton Street, London WC2A 2AE
0171 405 7686
Nevison, D. Mr; Falkingham, J. Miss; Barr, N. Dr;
Supervisor: Glennerster, H. Prof.; Bennett, R. Prof.

Investing in skills

Abstract: The research fell into two parts: 1) A re-analysis of data derived from the General Household Survey (GHS) on individuals' lifetime earnings and their previous education. Estimates of individuals' earnings and education were derived from a pooled cross section of 20,000 individuals drawn from the national GHS samples in 1985-88. The results showed the lifetime returns young individuals might reasonably expect if they looked at the earnings of older generations. These showed considerable variation but, in particular, showed that higher education and academic school education produced higher returns than vocational education. 2) The second part of the research modelled various alternative ways of financing higher education and showed the implications of introducing an income related loan repayment scheme for students administered through the tax system. The research was based on a computer micro simulation model of 4000 individuals.
Status: Sponsored project
Source of Grant: British Petroleum
Date of Research: 1990-1993
KEYWORDS: *economics-education relationship; educational benefits; educational finance; employment opportunities; outcomes of education; rewards; work-education relationship*

10/0857

Royal Holloway, Department of Psychology, Egham Hill,
Egham TW20 0EX
01784 434455
Wilding, J. Dr; Tickle, S. Mrs

Learning styles and other factors associated with student performance

Abstract: Measures of students' approaches to learning, and various personality factors, are being collected in a longitudinal study of the relation of such measures to academic performance, and the nature of changes over the undergraduate course in approaches and performances.
Published Material: WILDING, J. & VALENTINE, E. (1992). 'Factors predicting success and failure in the first year examinations of medical and dental courses', Applied Cognitive Psychology, Vol 6, No 3, pp.247-261.; WILDING, J. & HAYES, S. (1992). 'Relations between approaches to studying and note-taking behaviour in lectures'. Applied Cognitive Psychology, Vol 6, No 3, pp.233-246.
Status: Individual research
Date of Research: 1988-continuing
KEYWORDS: *learning strategies; study skills*

10/0858

Royal Holloway, Department of Psychology, Egham Hill,
Egham TW20 0EX
01784 434455
Wilding, J. Dr; Valentine, E. Dr; Marshall, P. Mr

Memory ability

Abstract: Previous work on subjects with superior memory ability will form the basis for a study in a gifted teenage sample of the relation between memory ability and other cognitive abilities. A wide range of memory tasks will be employed in order to identify individual variation in specific and general memory abilities and the relation of these to aspects of imagery and to verbal and non-verbal I.Q. Memory ability of near relatives will also be examined and the relevance of early experiences to the development of memory ability will be explored.
Published Material: WILDING, J. & VALENTINE, E. (1991). 'Su-

perior memory ability'. In: WEINMAN, J. & HUNTER, J. (Eds). Memory: neurochemical and abnormal perspectives. London: Harwood Academic Publishers.; WILDING, J. & VALENTINE, E. 'Memory champions', British Journal of Psychology. (in press).
Status: Individual research
Date of Research: 1984-continuing
KEYWORDS: cognitive ability; gifted; memory

10/0859
Royal Holloway, Department of Psychology, Egham Hill, Egham TW20 0EX
01784 434455
Wilding, J. Dr
Attentional problems in children
Abstract: The research aims to identify information processing weaknesses in children rated by teachers as having poor attention. Subjects are shown four colours briefly and simultaneously, then probed by a location cue for recall of one of them. Children rated as having poor attention performed significantly worse than a control group. It is suggested that they may have difficulty in processing several locations in parallel. Ability to focus on one location following a warning signal and to maintain such focus is being explored.
Published Material: GIANNOULIS, K. & WILDING, J. (1992). 'A deficit of iconic memory in children with attentional problems assigned to nurture groups', British Journal of Developmental Psychology, Vol 10, No 2, pp.199-201.
Status: Individual research
Date of Research: 1992-continuing
KEYWORDS: attention; attention deficit disorders; concentration; hyperactivity

10/0860
Royal Holloway, Department of Psychology, Egham Hill, Egham TW20 0EX
01784 434455
Wilding, J. Dr; Saeedi,N. Mrs
Use of computers with learning-disabled subjects
Abstract: Tasks are being developed on BBC and Archimedes computers which are appropriate for levels of handicap, using concept keyboards and touch screens for response. These enable measurement of ability, training in interaction with the computer and eventually use of the computer for other types of training and activity.
Status: Individual research
Date of Research: 1990-continuing
KEYWORDS: computer assisted learning; computer uses in education; concept keyboards; human-computer interaction; learning disabilities; special educational needs; touch screens

10/0861
Royal Holloway, Department of Psychology, Egham Hill, Egham TW20 0EX
01784 434455
Crowley, K. Mr; Wilding, J. Dr
Relations between musical ability and reading ability in children
Abstract: A number of measures of musical ability and phonological competence are being collected from pre-readers in order to explore whether common underlying mechanisms exist. Follow-up measures of progress in reading will be collected and further tests are being devised to investigate communalities between the two areas of ability within a framework derived from the Working Memory Model of Baddeley and Hitch.
Published Material: BARWICK, J., VALENTINE, E., WEST, J. & WILDING, J. (1989). 'Relations between reading and musical abilities', British Journal of Educational Psychology, Vol 59, pp.253-257.
Status: Individual research
Date of Research: 1992-continuing
KEYWORDS: musical ability; phonology; reading ability

10/0862
University College London, Department of Psychology, Gower Street, London WC1E 6BT
0171 387 7050
Frederickson, N. Ms; *Supervisor:* Furnham, A. Prof.
The social acceptance of children with moderate learning difficulties in mainstream schools
Abstract: The research aims to investigate and identify factors asso-

ciated with the social acceptance of children with moderate learning difficulties who are integrated into mainstream middle schools. Methods of assessing social acceptance are first examined with a particular focus on the wide variety of methods which have been used for collecting and categorising sociometric information. A methodological study, carried out with a sample of 250 children, investigates the reliability and validity of a range of sociometric categorisation systems. The social acceptance of children with moderate learning difficulties (MLD) is then investigated through examining the distribution across sociometric categories of 114 MLD pupils aged 8-12 years and their 1,227 mainstream classmates. Changes and continuities in social acceptance are explored through a 2-year follow-up of 40% of this sample. The third study of the series examines, separately for the mainstream (N=983) and MLD (N=108) populations, the relationship between social acceptance and a number of factors hypothesised or found in previous research to be associated with it. Aspects investigated in both the mainstream and MLD populations include behaviour, as reported by peers using the Guess Who Peer Assessment procedure; classroom social climate as assessed by the My Class Inventory (Fraser et al 1982). Aspects investigated in the MLD population include social adjustment as rated by class teachers uisng the Bristol Social Adjustment Guides (Stott 1974) and the class teacher's attitude to integration, assessed using the Classroom Integration Questionnaire (Kaufman et al 1985).
Status: Individual research
Date of Research: 1987-1993
KEYWORDS: classroom environment; mainstreaming; moderate learning difficulties; pupil attitudes; pupil behaviour; social behaviour; special educational needs

10/0863
University College London, Department of Psychology, Gower Street, London WC1E 6BT
0171 387 7050
Colorado College, Department of Psychology, 14E Cache la Poudre, Colorado Springs, CO 80903
719 634 4180
Millar, W. Dr; Weir, C. Dr
The influence of stress on contingency learning and habituation in at-risk infants
Abstract: The study examines the influence of stress related behaviour during contingency learning, stimulus encoding, and stimulus discrimination of infants in the third quarter of the first year who in the neonatal period had experienced low and high risks. Previous findings suggested that the poorer performance of at-risk infants on learning and habituation factors may result from higher levels of arousal which may be associated with infant's difficulties in assimilating stimulus information. A measure of pulse rate was obtained as an index of 'stress', along with measures of visual attention and contingency learning for high risk, low risk and well babies. The findings will relate to dual process theory of habituation, and should have practical relevance to the amelioration of early learning difficulty.
Status: Individual research
Date of Research: 1992-continuing
KEYWORDS: attention; cognitive development; early experience; infant behaviour; learning; neurological impairments

10/0864
University College London, Department of Psychology, Gower Street, London WC1E 6BT
0171 387 7050
National Hospitals' College of Speech Sciences, Chandler House, 2 Wakefield Street, London WC1N 1PG
0171 837 0113
Snowling, M. Prof.; Goulandris, N. Dr
Developmental analysis of dyslexia in childhood
Abstract: The development of 24 dyslexic children (reading at the 6, 7 and 8 year levels) is being closely monitored, and compared with a control gorup of average readers. Experimental investigations have included qualitative comparisons of their literacy skills and phonological processing abilities. The consistency of their reading has been investigated to explore the status of the lexical reading system of the dyslexic and normal readers. Preliminary evidence suggests that the dyslexics are less consistent in their reading behaviour even when processing familiar words.
Published Material: SNOWLING, M., HULME, C. & GOULANDRIS, N. (1990). 'Phonological coding in deficits in dyslexia'. In:

HALES, G. (Ed). Meeting points in dyslexia. Proceedings of the First International Conference of the British Dyslexia Association. Reading: British Dyslexia Association, pp.93-97.; GOULANDRIS, N. & SNOWLING, M. 'Visual memory deficits: a plausible explanation for reading failure?' Cognitive Neuropsychology, (in press).; HULME, C. & SNOWLING, M. 'Deficits in output phonology cause developmental phonological dyslexia, Mind and Language, (in press).
Status: Sponsored project
Source of Grant: Medical Research Council £65,000
Date of Research: 1989-1994
KEYWORDS: dyslexia; language handicaps; reading difficulties

Loughborough University of Technology

10/0865
Department of Computer Studies, Loughborough LE11 3TU
01509 263171
Fish, J. Mr; *Supervisor:* Scrivener, S. Dr
Cognitive model for the design of sketching systems
Abstract: A model is proposed for the mental representation of artist's sketches. Evidence is presented to support the theory that artists' sketches are hybrid images consisting of visible precept and a cognitive component of a superimposed mental image. It is further argued that sketches amplify the mind's ability to generate imagery from long term memory by facilitating translation between descriptive and depictive modes of representation. The model is used to suggest new improved computer software packages parts of which it is hoped to implement. The implication of the model for the way in which drawing is taught and the future use of sketching systems in education is analysed.
Published Material: FISH, J.C.H. & SCRIVENER, S. (1990). 'Amplifying the mind's eye: sketching and visual cognition', Leonardo, Vol 23, No 1.
Status: Individual research
Date of Research: 1983-1993
KEYWORDS: computer-assisted design; computer graphics; drawing

10/0866
Department of Education, Loughborough LE11 3TU
01509 263171
Tyler, K. Mr
Experiential learning in initial teacher education
Abstract: This is an investigation into experiential learning in teacher education. The work will focus on the development of interpersonal skills within an experiential workshop setting with primary Post Graduate Certificate of Education (PGCE) students. The workshops, which are optional, will focus on the development of communication and counselling skills and strategies for developing positive relationships in the primary classroom. The study will measure changes in the Rosenberg Self-Esteem Scale, the Nowicki-Strickland Locus of Control Scale and the Pupil Control Ideology Scale. The relevance of this work to the students' overall preparation for teaching in a primary school will also be examined.
Status: Individual research
Date of Research: 1990-continuing
KEYWORDS: experiential learning; interpersonal competence; learning experience; preservice teacher education; student teachers; workshops

10/0867
Department of Education, Loughborough LE11 3TU
01509 263171
Reid, I. Prof.
The development and application of socio-spatial indices
Abstract: This project looks at the use of commercially based post code applications to school populations to allow for comparisons, and the construction and application of the derived scale of social advantage/social deprivation to school and pupil performance.
Status: Sponsored project
Source of Grant: Bradford Metropolitan Council, Directorate of Education
Date of Research: 1990-1993

KEYWORDS: academic achievement; performance factors; scaling; school effectiveness; social environment; socioeconomic influences

10/0868
Department of Education, Loughborough LE11 3TU
01509 263171
Demaine, J. Dr
Citizenship and education
Abstract: A study of the concept of citizenship in the context of the National Curriculum requirement for teaching in schools.
Status: Individual research
Date of Research: 1991-1993
KEYWORDS: citizenship education; National Curriculum

10/0869
Department of Education, Loughborough LE11 3TU
01509 263171
Demaine, J. Dr
Student evaluation of teaching in higher education in the UK
Abstract: An investigation into student evaluation of teaching in higher education in the United Kingdom.
Status: Individual research
Date of Research: 1991-1993
KEYWORDS: higher education; student evaluation of teacher performance; teacher effectiveness

10/0870
Department of Education, Loughborough LE11 3TU
01509 263171
Demaine, J. Dr
Local Management of Schools
Abstract: A study of the effects of Local Management of Schools (LMS) on a select group of schools in England.
Status: Individual research
Date of Research: 1991-1993
KEYWORDS: educational administration; educational change; local management of schools; school-based management

10/0871
Department of Education, Loughborough LE11 3TU
01509 263171
Demaine, J. Dr
Socio-political attitudes of teacher trainers in the United Kingdom
Abstract: An investigation into the socio-political attitudes of teacher trainers in the United Kingdom.
Status: Individual research
Date of Research: 1991-1993
KEYWORDS: political attitudes; social attitudes; teacher attitudes; teacher education; teacher educators

10/0872
Department of Education, Loughborough LE11 3TU
01509 263171
El-Laithy, S. Mrs; *Supervisor:* Smedley, D. Mr
The teaching of English as a second language in higher education institutions in the United Arab Emirates
Abstract: The thesis will survey the education system of the United Arab Emirates (UAE), especially the higher education (HE) sector and the place of Teaching English as a Second Language (TESOL) within it. It will survey the literature on TESOL – its philosophy, curriculum and pedagogy. The empirical work will be an evaluation of the present teaching of TESOL in HE institutions in UAE, carried out through a variety of methods including questionnaires, structured interviews, and document analysis. Recommendations for development and change will be made in the light of this evaluation.
Status: Individual research
Date of Research: 1991-continuing
KEYWORDS: Arab states; English – second language; higher education

10/0873
Department of Education, Loughborough LE11 3TU
01509 263171
Wild, P. Dr; Richardson, S. Mr

Evaluation of information technology systems used to support administration in schools

Abstract: A consequence of the Education Reform Act 1988 (ERA) is the need for information technology (IT) systems to support the Local Management of Schools (LMS). It is well known from research in the commercial and industrial sectors that the success rate for the implementation of such systems is as low as 20%. If the IT systems being installed in schools are to achieve their potential in helping to administer, or, more importantly, manage the working of the school then it is essential that some evaluation of the systems is carried out. A methodology developed at the Human Sciences and Advanced Technology (HUSAT) Research Institute at Loughborough University, called the User Acceptance Audit, is being modified for the school environment. A detailed task analysis is required of the management and administration within the schools so that the evaluation tool developed by HUSAT can be made context sensitive. The final outcome should be an 'evaluation package' which could be used by local education authorities and/or individual schools to assess the potential barriers to successful implementation.
Published Material: WILD, P., SCIVIER, J.E. & RICHARDSON, S.J. (1992). 'Evaluating information technology-supported Local Management of Schools: the User Acceptability Audit', Education Management and Administration, Vol 20, No1, pp.40-48.
Status: Individual research
Date of Research: 1989-continuing
KEYWORDS: computer uses in education; educational administration; information technology; local management of schools; management systems; school-based management

10/0874

Department of Education, Loughborough LE11 3TU
01509 263171
Thomas, J. Mr

History of educational psychology in Britain with special reference to university departments of education

Abstract: This project includes the development of bibliographies on individual psychologists of education and case studies of individual university departments of education. It involves the use of primary and secondary historical services. The long term aim is a monograph on the history of educational psychology in Britain, including its clinical practice.
Published Material: THOMAS, J.B. (1982). 'J.A. Green, educational psychology and the Journal of Experimental Pedagogy', History of Education Society Bulletin, No 29, pp.41-45.
Status: Individual research
Date of Research: 1982-continuing
KEYWORDS: educational history; educational psychology; teacher education

10/0875

Department of Education, Loughborough LE11 3TU
01509 263171
Thomas, J. Mr

Studies of teacher education in the Victorian day training college

Abstract: The project aims to describe and analyse the work of education departments in universities from 1890 to 1918. It consists of case studies of individual institutions, biographical studies and investigations of related areas, for example, the development of the academic study of education and the greater opportunities for the professional education of women.
Published Material: THOMAS, J.B. (1986). 'Amos Henderson and the Nottingham Day Training College', Journal of Educational Administration and History, Vol 18, No 2, pp.24-33.; THOMAS, J.B. (1986). 'University College, London, and the training of teachers', History of Education Society Bulletin, Vol 37, pp.44-49.; THOMAS, J.B. (1986). 'Students, staff and curriculum in a day training college (Cardiff)', Collected Original Resources in Education, Vol 10, No 3, Fiche 1 A04.; THOMAS, J.B. (1988). 'University College, Bristol: pioneering teacher training for women', History of Education, Vol. 17, No 1, pp.55-70.; THOMAS, J.B. (Ed). (1990). British universities and teacher education: a century of change. London: Falmer Press.
Status: Individual research
Date of Research: 1978-continuing
KEYWORDS: educational history; preservice teacher education

10/0876

Department of Education, Loughborough LE11 3TU
01509 263171
Wild, G. Dr; *Supervisor:* Hinton, R. Dr

An investigation of communication problems for blind students in higher education

Abstract: As a result of its experience in producing tactile diagrams, the department has in recent years been asked to help several blind students in higher education who are pursuing courses with a high content of visually orientated material. It has become apparent that not only are more blind students seeking to study courses which have an inherent visual content but also that courses which have in the past had a predominantly verbal structure are now making increasing use of visual resources. Resources which make it possible for a blind student to access visually orientated course work may exist but they are not always easily available or may require further development. Many existing students still struggle to obtain good quality resources and some students are refused entry to the courses of their choice partly because suitable resources are not available. The present study has been making detailed case studies of ten individual students pursuing a wide variety of courses with a significant visual content. Through maintaining contact with the students and their teaching and support staff it has: 1) established the degree and kind of support given to these students in enabling them to access the visually orientated elements of their course work; 2) advised staff on the provisions of suitable teaching materials and, where necessary, developed more effective resources; and 3) appraised the importance of such material in enabling the students to follow their courses successfully.
Published Material: WILD, G. (1992). 'Requirements for tactile diagrams of visually impaired students in higher education: preliminary findings', Educare, No 42, pp.11-14.; WILD, G. (1992). 'Tactile diagrams and visually impaired students', Intact, No 4. (Publication of Commission VII of the International Cartographic Association).
Status: Sponsored project
Source of Grant: Leverhulme Trust £16,450
Date of Research: 1991-1993
KEYWORDS: blindness; communication problems; higher education; nonverbal communication; special educational needs; visual impairments

10/0877

Department of Education, Loughborough LE11 3TU
01509 263171
Demaine, J. Dr

The future of Labour Party education policy

Abstract: A study of the British Labour Party's education policy and recommendations for future policy.
Published Material: DEMAINE, J. (1992). 'The Labour Party and education policy', British Journal of Educational Studies, Vol 40, No 3, pp.239-247.
Status: Individual research
Date of Research: 1991-continuing
KEYWORDS: educational policy; politics education relationship

10/0878

Department of Education, Loughborough LE11 3TU
01509 263171
Demaine, J. Dr

Problems with right wing education policy

Abstract: The research examines right wing arguments on educational provision, including the notion of a voucher scheme and the introduction of elements of a 'free market' into public sector education. It examines right wing argument on 'gradualism' as a means of securing educational reform. The research examines arguments put forward by the Right on the idea of a General Teaching Council, on the teacher labour market, and on the status of teachers.
Published Material: DEMAINE, J. (1988). 'Teachers' work, curriculum and the New Right', British Journal of Sociology of Education, Vol 9, No 3, pp.247-264.; DEMAINE, J. (1989). 'Privatisation by stealth: new right education policy', ACE Bulletin, No 28, pp.5-7.; DEMAINE, J. (1989). 'A General Teaching Council and the status of teachers', ACE Bulletin, No 32, pp.3-5.; DEMAINE, J. (1990). 'The reform of secondary education'. In: HINDESS, B. (Ed). Reactions to the right. London: Routledge.
Status: Individual research
Date of Research: 1987-continuing
KEYWORDS: education vouchers; educational change; educational policy; politics education relationship

10/0879

Department of Education, Loughborough LE11 3TU
01509 263171
Shepherd, D. Ms; Ayres, D. Mr

Survey of Leicestershire LEA schools into their HIV/AIDS and health education provision (11-16 age range), compared with sample of Midland schools

Abstract: The project aims were to explore the progress and curriculum provision for Human Immunodeficiency Virus/Acquired Immune Deficiency Syndrome (HIV-AIDS) education in a sample of 140 secondary schools in the East Midlands, particularly against local education authority (LEA) HIV-AIDS policy guidelines. Two questionnaires were sent to each school to extract different samples of information from headteachers and health education coordinators. Amongst the information sought was curriculum and teaching organisation and staffing, school policy and influence of governors, in-service teacher education (INSET) needs and provision, and constraints in teaching in the HIV-AIDS area.
Status: Sponsored project
Source of Grant: Leicestershire Local Education Authority; Leicestershire Health Authority
Date of Research: 1989-1993
KEYWORDS: acquired immune deficiency syndrome; health education; sex education

10/0880

Department of Education, Loughborough LE11 3TU
01509 263171
Demaine, J. Dr

Racism and multicultural education

Abstract: The research examines the arguments surrounding the notions of multicultural and antiracist education with particular reference to the pedagogic practice. The research is also concerned with the ways in which terms and categories are deployed in analyses, and discussion of differences in educational achievement between social groups whose identity is usually specified in terms of 'race' or 'ethnicity'.
Published Material: DEMAINE, J. & KADOWALA, D. (1988). 'Multicultural and antiracist education: the unnecessary divide', Curriculum, Vol 9, No 2, pp.99-102.; DEMAINE, J. (1989). 'Race, categorisation and educational achievement', British Journal of Sociology of Education, Vol 10, No 2, pp.195-214.; DEMAINE, J. (1993). 'Racism, ideology and education: the last word on the Honeyford affair?', British Journal of Sociology of Education, Vol 14, No 4, pp.409-414.
Status: Individual research
Date of Research: 1988-continuing
KEYWORDS: antiracism education; ethnic groups; multicultural education

10/0881

Department of Education, Loughborough LE11 3TU
01509 263171
Simmons, C. Mr

Adolescent attitudes in England, Saudi Arabia and Israel

Abstract: This project compares the results of two surveys, the main aim of which was to portray what young people think, feel and believe about important aspects of their lives, using as evidence own written statements. The subjects comprised 89 Saudi Arabian and 107 English adolescents aged between 13-15 years. The open-ended questionnaire comprised 10 prompts designed to elicit responses concerning ideals and least ideals, most and least preferred companions, use of solitude, summun bonum, most and least desired outcomes to life and nascent philosophies. Two methods of analysis were used. First, references to dominant themes were totalled; second, responses were assigned to six categories according to the dominant values expressed from materialistic to altruistic. Significant differences were found in the dominant themes and between the values expressed by the two samples. Most marked were the pervasive religious values in the Saudi Arabian sample and the absence of these in the English sample.
Published Material: SIMMONS, C. & SIMMONS, C. (1994). 'Personal and moral adolescent values in England and Saudi Arabia', Journal of Moral Education, Vol 23, No 1, pp.3-16.
Status: Individual research
Date of Research: 1991-1994
KEYWORDS: comparative education; cross cultural studies; educational attitudes; pupil attitudes; Saudi Arabia

10/0882

Department of Education, Loughborough LE11 3TU
01509 263171
Hough, J. Prof.

Cost-benefit analysis in education

Abstract: This project surveys techniques of cost-benefit analysis and their application to eduction and examines the practical problems and pitfalls that arise in such applications. Particular emphasis is made to cost-benefit studies in developing countries.
Status: Sponsored project
Source of Grant: Overseas Development Administration (British Government) £11,000
Date of Research: 1991-1993
KEYWORDS: cost effectiveness; developing countries; educational economics; educational finance; efficiency

10/0883

Department of Education, Loughborough LE11 3TU
01509 263171
Hough, J. Prof.

The education system in England and Wales

Abstract: This research is surveying developments in the education system in England and Wales with emphasis on changes since the Education Reform Act 1988. The research includes: The Department of Education and Science; local education authorities; the Education Reform Act 1988; the comprehensive school; the private sector of education; the education of the 16-19 age group and the further education sector; and higher education. In each case the project studies recent changes, especially those stemming directly from the Education Reform Act and considers the effects and consequences.
Published Material: HOUGH, J.R. (1992). The education system in England and Wales: a synopsis. Papers in Education Series. Loughborough: Loughborough University of Technology, Department of Education.
Status: Sponsored project
Source of Grant: Loughborough University of Technology: Department of Education
Date of Research: 1991-1993
KEYWORDS: Education Reform Act 1988; educational change; educational development; educational planning; educational policy; government role; local education authorities

10/0884

Department of Education, Loughborough LE11 3TU
01509 263171
Rovira-Garza, N. Miss; *Supervisor:* Hinton, R. Dr

Factors influencing the successful integration of children with Down's Syndrome in mainstream education

Abstract: A study of the factors influencing successful integration of children with Down's Syndrome into mainstream classes, and in particular the influence of the teacher's attitude to the child and the quality and appropriateness of the pedagogic strategies.
Status: Sponsored project
Source of Grant: National Mental Health Foundation
Date of Research: 1991-continuing
KEYWORDS: Down's Syndrome; mainstreaming; special educational needs

10/0885

Department of Education, Loughborough LE11 3TU
01509 263171
Thomas, J. Mr

The development of teacher education in British universities, including the development of education as an academic subject

Abstract: This is research using archive and secondary sources which will examine case studies of university departments, produce biographical data, and provide specific studies of special topics, e.g. the history of educational psychology.
Published Material: THOMAS, J.B. (Ed). (1990). British universities and teacher education: a century of change. London: Falmer Press.; THOMAS, J.B. (Ed). (1991). 'Educational research in the University of Wales: the half century to 1940', Welsh Journal of Education, Vol 3, No 1, pp.10-21.; THOMAS, J.B. (Ed). (1992). 'Birmingham University and teacher training: day training college to department of education', History of Education, Vol 21, No 3, pp.307-321.; A full list of publications is available from the researcher.

Status: Individual research
Date of Research: 1978-continuing
KEYWORDS: *teacher education; universities*

10/0886
Department of Education, Loughborough LE11 3TU
01509 263171
Hinton, R. Dr
Development of effective tactile overlays, support material and user-training for an audio-tactile device for blind and disabled users
Abstract: The Nomad audio-tactile device is a computer add-on which has a touch sensitive pad on which tactile diagrams and pictures can be placed for interactive use with a personal computer by blind students. It helps to overcome some of the problems of accurately linking information which would normally be in braille or tape to a clear tactile display, and of making use of the computing and data storing potential of the computer. Although this device has performed well in preliminary trials, it requires educational development to enable teachers to use it effectively with blind students following a normal curriculum. The research team will be collaborating with the mathematics, science and geography departments of Exhall Grange School, Coventry (initially to develop this device further and provide ancillary teaching resources).
Published Material: HINTON, R.A.L. (1991). 'Working with Nomad: an audio-tactile device'. In: Proceedings of the World Congress of Technology, Arlington, Virginia, December 1991, Vol VI.; HINTON, R.A.L. (1992). 'Children's reactions to Nomad', British Journal of Visual Impairment, Vol 10, No 1, pp.27-28.; HINTON, R.A.L. (1992). 'Stimulating access to graphics for visually impaired students'. Special Update, June, pp.12-13. Coventry: National Council for Educational Technology.; HINTON, R.A.L. (1992). 'Preparing for diagram use in higher education'. Paper delivered at Quinquennial Conference of International Council for the Education of the Visually Handicapped, Bangkok, 26-31 July 1992.
Status: Sponsored project
Source of Grant: Nuffield Foundation £19,989
Date of Research: 1990-1993
KEYWORDS: *blindness; low vision aids; microcomputers; sensory aids; tactile adaptation; visual impairments*

10/0887
Department of Education, Loughborough LE11 3TU
01509 263171
Clowes, P. Mr; *Supervisor:* Busher, H. Dr
Managing professionals inside and outside education
Abstract: This research project asks: 1) What are the questions and paradoxes of managing professionals in institutions? 2) What does the term 'professional' mean? 3) Who are the professional workers in education? 4) Are the terms 'professional' and 'management' compatible, and what are the key issues involved in this nexus? 5) Who are the people involved in management in education and what form does the management function take in schools?
Status: Individual research
Date of Research: 1992-continuing
KEYWORDS: *management in education; professional personnel*

10/0888
Department of Education, Loughborough LE11 3TU
01509 263171
Busher, H. Dr; Hodgkinson, K. Mr
Managing interschool liaison under Local Management of Schools
Abstract: The project will explore how schools are managing interschool liaison under Local Management of Schools (LMS). For example, how this is affecting the internal management of individual schools, and how this is affecting the staff development of teaching and ancillary staff. For the sake of brevity the term "ancillary" is used to cover all technical, clerical, cleaning and domestic staff. The project focuses upon a local cluster of schools – those in and around Loughborough and Shepshed. The aim is to interview primary, high and upper school headteachers, and deputy headteachers or vice-principals responsible for interschool liaison, in schools with a post which includes this as part of a job description. Each interview is likely to last an hour, and answers given will be treated confidentially. In addition the person interviewed will be asked to keep a diary for one week in each of the three school terms of the contacts he/she has with other schools.

Status: Sponsored project
Source of Grant: Universities Funding Council £2,000
Date of Research: 1992-1993
KEYWORDS: *educational administration; institutional cooperation; local management of schools*

10/0889
Department of Education, Loughborough LE11 3TU
01509 263171
Abdullah, S. Mr; *Supervisor:* Wild, P. Dr
The use of expert systems in assessment and testing in school science
Abstract: This project continues work started at the University Technology of Malaysia to integrate microcomputers in the field of testing, measurement and evaluation. It is hypothesised that expert system software could be used to improve computerized testing. The study will: 1) design a prototype system of intelligent computerized testing by using an expert system shell (Leonardo); 2) develop a database of items or questions in science, initially mainly physics based; 3) validate the prototype intelligent computerized testing system; 4) investigate the efficiency and effectiveness of the system by trials in schools.
Status: Sponsored project
Source of Grant: British Council £12,000
Date of Research: 1992-continuing
KEYWORDS: *assessment; data processing; expert systems*

10/0890
Department of Education, Loughborough LE11 3TU
01509 263171
Salih, L. Mrs; *Supervisor:* Hough, J. Prof.
Educational costs and resources in the Sudan
Abstract: This project surveys costs and resources of education in the Sudan and analyses consequences and implications for schools and pupils. Areas covered include: inter-regional differences; trends over time; teachers and their allocation; and effects on educational policies.
Status: Sponsored project
Source of Grant: Government of Sudan £20,000
Date of Research: 1988-1992
KEYWORDS: *educational economics; educational finance; Sudan*

10/0891
Department of Education, Loughborough LE11 3TU
01509 263171
Harvey, J. Miss; *Supervisor:* Busher, H. Dr
Marketing an independent school
Abstract: This research sets out to find out how headteachers and parents perceive a school, make choices, and give advice to potential pupils about whether or not to apply. One measure of the impact of this research on policy will be the changes in the number of pupils coming to the school. Another measure will be expressions by parents of increased satisfaction with the school. The research will include interviews with headteachers of precursor schools, and a survey of parents' views of schools.
Status: Individual research
Date of Research: 1991-1993
KEYWORDS: *independent schools; marketing; parent choice*

10/0892
Department of Education, Loughborough LE11 3TU
01509 263171
Hodgkinson, K. Mr; Wild, P. Dr
A flexible learning plan for information technology on primary school teaching practice
Abstract: The development of a detailed profile of student use of information technology (IT) on teaching practice in primary schools. It will include a pilot study of 5 students, and a full design for 60 students. Students will record their work. The flexible learning plan (FLP) will then be formally assessed and student performance in IT will be matched against the Council for the Accreditation of Teacher Education (CATE) and Trotter Report recommendations.
Status: Sponsored project
Source of Grant: Loughborough University of Technology £2,325
Date of Research: 1992-1993
KEYWORDS: *information technology; preservice teacher education; student teachers; teaching practice*

10/0893

Department of Education, Loughborough LE11 3TU
01509 263171
Costello, J. Mr
Special needs in learning mathematics
Abstract: An identification of the nature of special educational needs
in mathematics, particularly in the 11-16 age range.
Status: Individual research
Date of Research: 1994-continuing
KEYWORDS: mathematics education; special educational needs

10/0894

Department of Education, Loughborough LE11 3TU
01509 263171
Irving, B. Mr; *Supervisor:* Demaine, J. Dr
TVEI and equality of opportunity
Abstract: A study of the Technical and Vocational Education Initia-
tive (TVEI) in respect to equality of opportunity.
Status: Individual research
Date of Research: 1992-continuing
KEYWORDS: equal education; TVEI

10/0895

Department of Education, Loughborough LE11 3TU
01509 263171
Demaine, J. Dr
Citizenship, politics and education
Abstract: A study of citizenship in the context of politics and educa-
tion in a number of different countries.
Status: Individual research
Date of Research: 1991-1994
*KEYWORDS: citizenship education; comparative education; politics
education relationship*

10/0896

Department of Education, Loughborough LE11 3TU
01509 263171
Demaine, J. Dr
**Governors' responses to Local Management of Schools (LMS)
and other aspects of education reform**
Abstract: A study of effects of education reform on the attitudes of
governors in a select group of English schools.
Status: Individual research
Date of Research: 1991-continuing
*KEYWORDS: educational change; governing bodies; local manage-
ment of schools; school-based management; school governors*

10/0897

Department of Education, Loughborough LE11 3TU
01509 263171
Blease, D. Mr; Wild, P. Dr
Open learning in initial teacher education
Abstract: This is an investigation into the use of open learning in
teacher training using the personal learning plan. It is primarily
focused on science graduates on the Postgraduate Certificate in
Education (PGCE) course, using groups of 20-25 per year over a
period of up to 5 years. Open learning and computer-based learning
resources form the basis of students' individualised work, in addition
to their regular taught course.
Published Material: BLEASE, D. & WILD, P. (1990). 'Open learning in initial teacher education: meeting the needs of a National
Curriculum in science'. Proceedings of the 7th International Conference on Technology and Education, Brussels, March, 1990.
Status: Individual research
Date of Research: 1989-1994
*KEYWORDS: computer uses in education; open education; pre-
service teacher education*

10/0898

Department of Education, Loughborough LE11 3TU
01509 263171
King Saud University, The College of Education, Riyadh,
Saudi Arabia Al Rawat, H. Dr; *Supervisor:* Simmons, C. Mr
**An open university for women in Saudi Arabia: problems and
prospects**

Abstract: This study investigates the prospects of setting up an open
university for women in Saudi Arabia against the background of the
problems which Saudi women face in pursuing higher education. A
review is given of the development of modern public education for
women since its beginning in 1960, with emphasis on the more recent
development of higher education for women. The position of women
in Islam and in contemporary Saudi society is examined as this has
influenced their access to higher education. Three open universities
in the United Kingdom, Thailand and Pakistan are described (the
latter in an Islamic country). A questionnaire was devised in order to
gather data on attitudes to the setting up of an open university for
women in Saudi Arabia, on perceptions of its feasibility, and on
possible obstacles to its foundation. The questionnaire also included
a section on the most suitable model for an open university for women
in Saudi Arabia. The questionnaire was distributed in government
bodies and higher educational establishments in Saudi Arabia to
policy makers, academics and female students. An analysis of the
data reveals a very positive response to the setting up of an open
university for women in Saudi Arabia. Respondents, however, demonstrated a realistic awareness of the problems of gaining public
acceptance for a new type of higher education in a time of restrictions
on government spending. Finally, on the basis of the findings a
proposal is being made for the setting up of an open university for
women in Saudi Arabia.
Published Material: AL RAWAT, H.S. & SIMMONS, C.V. (1991).
'The education of women in Saudi Arabia', Comparative Education,
Vol 27, No 3, pp.287-295.
Status: Individual research
Date of Research: 1986-1990
*KEYWORDS: distance education; open universities; Saudi Arabia;
women's education*

10/0899

Department of Education, Loughborough LE11 3TU
01509 263171
Leicester University, School of Education, University Road,
Leicester LE1 7RH
01162 522522
Wild, P. Dr; Rogers, L. Mr
**A study of the impact of information technology on practical
science in schools**
Abstract: The aim of this project is to study the effect of the use of
the computer for measurement in practical science in secondary
schools. Through classroom observation, conventional practical ac-
tivity will be compared with newer methods employing the computer
for measurement and analysis.
Status: Sponsored project
Source of Grant: Loughborough University of Technology; Leicester
University, jointly £3,000
Date of Research: 1992-1994
*KEYWORDS: computer uses in education; practical science; science
education*

10/0900

Department of Education, Loughborough LE11 3TU
01509 263171
Royal National Institute for the Blind Vocational College,
Radmoor Road, Loughborough LE11 3BS
01509 611077
Todd, N. Mr; *Supervisor:* Hinton, R. Dr
**The integration of visually impaired students in further
education**
Abstract: This thesis is in three main parts. Part One reviews the
general literature on the integration debate and looks at the debate in
relation to the specific field of visual impairment. This examines the
issues and gives a broad context to the particular area of the visually
impaired student in mainstream further education. Part Two is a
review of the field of integration support with particular reference to
further education and individuals with visual impairment. There exist
real concerns about the ability of the mainstream to provide an
environment that will ensure that these individuals maximise their
learning potential. These concerns seem principally related to making
appropriate support services available so that the advantages of
mainstreaming are not outweighed by the disadvantages of reduced
levels of support. Part Three is a research project based on further
education colleges in the Midlands. It attempts to identify and examine the support services that enable successful integration of visually
impaired students. It also attempts to evaluate these factors to estab-

lish their relative value in this mainstreaming process. The evaluation is from the perspective of visually impaired students in further education rather than that of professionals in the visually impaired field. The survey was conducted by means of a structured questionnaire to Midlands further education (FE) colleges and a separate questionnaire to visually impaired students who were identified. Thirty-five FE colleges had visually impaired students in mainstream courses and from these eighty individual students completed the questionnaire. The statistical significance of the graded results were analysed by the Chi-square test.
Status: Individual research
Date of Research: 1988-1993
KEYWORDS: *further education; mainstreaming; special educational needs; visual impairments*

10/0901

Department of Education, Loughborough LE11 3TU
01509 263171
Warwick University, Department of Science Education, Coventry CV4 7AL
01203 523523
Melrose, J. Miss; *Supervisor:* Schwarzenberger, R. Prof.
An exploration into the notion of levels of attainment in mathematics
Abstract: This research is a comparison of young children and older low-attainers in their thinking about mathematics topics including subtraction and three dimensional visualisation. The methods employed are principally individual interviews with the children together with reflections from their teachers.
Status: Individual research
Date of Research: 1989-1993
KEYWORDS: *low achievement; mathematics achievement; mathematics education*

10/0902

Department of Physical Education and Sports Science, Loughborough LE11 3TU
01703 595000
Southampton University, Faculty of Educational Studies, Department of Physical Education, Highfield, Southampton SO9 5NH
01509 263171
Evans, J. Dr; Penney, D. Miss; Bryant, A. Miss
The impact of the National Curriculum and Local Management of Schools (LMS) on the provision of sport and physical education in schools
Abstract: The research will be conducted over a three year period to monitor the impact of the National Curriculum and Local Management of Schools (LMS) on the provision of sport and physical education (PE) in schools in England and Wales. The research will be conducted in two phases. The first will employ a qualitative methodology to survey the impact of LMS on the levels and nature of physical education and sport provision for schools. The second will use a qualitative methodology to monitor the effects of LMS and a National Curriculum for PE on processes of teaching and learning in PE and sport in schools.
Status: Sponsored project
Source of Grant: Sports Council; Southampton University; Economic and Social Research Council
Date of Research: 1990-1994
KEYWORDS: *educational change; local management of schools; National Curriculum; physical education; sports*

10/0903

Department of Social Sciences, Loughborough LE11 3TU
01509 263171
Bagilhole, B. Dr
On the inside: equal opportunities in academic life. A research report on women, ethnic minority and disabled academics
Abstract: Women academics in British universities make up a very small minority and are concentrated in the lower grades. Statistical evidence points to the fact that an important reason for this is that discrimination exists within the academic profession. However, there is very little empirical information on the nature of this discrimination and how it operates. This research study sought to identify and illuminate the processes that serve to maintain this discrimination through the experiences and perceptions of women academics them-

selves. A total of 43 women were interviewed at length using a semi-structured interview schedule. This explored issues such as recruitment and selection, probation, career development, appraisal, positions of power, the roles of women academics, the problem of being in small minorities functioning in a male environment, isolation, exclusion from male colleagues, and challenges to authority by male students. Women academics were found to have fewer support systems than their male colleagues, fewer role models or mentors, and little access to communication networks. They report problems with work relationships, and experience hostility from male colleagues and students. The majority had experienced discrimination within the university. This leads to the majority becoming convinced that the concept of a woman academic is problematic. They put pressure on themselves to perform better than their male colleagues, and avoid being identified with other women. They become 'honorary men' and as such are in no position to support other women.
Published Material: BAGIHOLE, B. (1992). On the inside: equal opportunities in academic life. A research report on women, ethnic minority and disabled academics. Loughborough: Loughborough University, Department of Social Sciences.; BAGIHOLE, B. (1993). 'How to keep a good woman down: an investigation of the role of institutional factors in the process of discrimination against women academics', British Journal of Sociology of Education, Vol 14, No 3, pp.261-274.; BAGIHOLE, B. (1993). 'Survivors in a male preserve: a study of British women academics' experiences and perceptions of discrimination in a UK university', Higher Education, Vol 26, No 4, pp.431-447.
Status: Sponsored project
Source of Grant: Loughborough University of Technology £1,000
Date of Research: 1992-1993
KEYWORDS: *academic staff; employment opportunities; equal opportunities – jobs; higher education; universities; women teachers; women's employment*

Luton University

10/0904

Centre for Educational Development, Park Square, Luton LU1 3JU
01582 34111
Fallows, S. Dr
Introduction of open learning into mainstream higher education
Abstract: Open learning is seen as one possible solution to increased student numbers in higher education without increased resources. The University of Luton is seeking to achieve 20% of course provision by open learning methods by the academic year 1994-95. This research project seeks to increase understanding of the implementation of open learning in a mainstream higher education institution. The key points of interest are the implications of the use of open learning in different educational situations and with students from different backgrounds (such as younger/older; different ethnic backgrounds; first year/final year etc). The intention is to utilise the University of Luton as an initial 'test bed' with the aim of both informing the Luton situation and contributing to the wider debate.
Published Material: FALLOWS, S.J. (1994). 'Integration of open learning into mainstream higher education'. In: KNIGHT, P. University-wide change, staff and curriculum development. Birmingham: SEDA Publications.
Status: Sponsored project
Source of Grant: Luton University
Date of Research: 1993-continuing
KEYWORDS: *higher education; open education*

10/0905

Centre for Educational Development, Park Square, Luton LU1 3JU
01582 34111
Guest, K. Mr; *Supervisor:* Fallows, S. Dr; Van den Brink Budgen, R. Dr; Dillon, M. Mr
Evaluation of critical writing assessment tests as predictions of performance in higher education
Abstract: This research stems from the development of aptitude profiling tests by the University of Cambridge Local Examination Syndicate (The MENO project), in particular those sections con-

cerned with Critical Thinking, Communications and Literacy. The researcher has been involved in the development of these tests for 3 years; producing and evaluating materials, establishing marking criteria, and piloting the tests in institutions across the UK and abroad. This specific research project seeks to address the problems of: 1) how to assess the suitability of mature, non-standard entry students (i.e. those without conventional academic qualifications) able to benefit from a degree course; and 2) what makes a successful student (i.e. the required qualities and competences, generic skills, character traits, experiential or prior learning). It includes a critical review of approaches tried so far and what is currently available – practicality, strengths and limitations – and investigates the conceptual base of MENO, the design and testing of the experimental programme (with results and analysis), and discussion of future development of aptitude profiling as a diagnostic tool.

Published Material: GUEST, K. (1992). Study skills booklet. Luton: University of Luton.
Status: Individual research
Date of Research: 1991-continuing
KEYWORDS: *aptitude; assessment; critical thinking; higher education; mature students; prediction of success; selection; student evaluation*

10/0906

Centre for Educational Development, Park Square, Luton LU1 3JU
01582 34111
Nene College, Department of Built Environment, St Georges Avenue, Northampton NN2 6JD
01604 720636
Fallows, S. Dr; Harvey, R. Dr; Ashworth, A. Mr
Evaluating and improving quality in higher education
Abstract: To develop an intelligent knowledge base system (IKBS) which is designed to provide a self-inspection system to evaluate and enhance activities and facilities, i.e. teaching and learning; accommodation; equipment and resources; staffing; staff development; curriculum; standards; quality control; students and their support; liaison and marketing; management and finance, existing and operating in higher education (HE) institutions. The knowledge base will be centred upon well established national inspection procedures; the response of the IKBS will be reactive and proactive. It will diagnose shortcomings whilst seeking to advise on improvements that could be advantageously implemented to improve the activities and facilities. In short, the IKBS provides the means by which the activities and facilities that influence quality can be inspected; it suggests improvements that will correspondingly provide further improvements to impact on the students' experience and standards of work. It will draw conclusions as to the effectiveness of the quality assurance system that operates in an HE institution and suggest strategies by which it might be improved. Upon completion of the project, the IKBS software and handbook containing the knowledge base will be available to all HE institutions.
Demonstrations/seminars will be undertaken and conference presentations made. It is judged that debate during and after implementation of the knowledge base, with the opportunity to revise and/or add to it, will generate substantial staff development on the maintenance and improvement of quality and impact upon the development of HE institutions.
Published Material: ASHWORTH, A. & HARVEY, R. (1993). Assessing quality in further and higher education. Higher Education Policy Series No 24. London: Jessica Kingsley.; HARVEY, R.C. & ASHWORTH, A. (1994). 'Indicators of quality: recommendations for the self-assessment of institutions of higher education'. First National Conference on Total Quality Management in Higher Education, York, 1994.
Status: Sponsored project
Source of Grant: Higher Education Funding Council £25,000
Date of Research: 1992-continuing
KEYWORDS: *computer software; computer uses in education; higher education; performance indicators; quality control*

10/0907

Department of Psychology, Park Square, Luton LU1 3JU
01582 34111
Berkshire County Psychological Service, Orwell House, 23 Craven Road, Reading RG1 5LE
01734 313644
Cline, T. Mr; Baldwin, S. Mrs

A retrospective study of selective mutism in childhood: stage 1
Abstract: The first stage of these studies will involve: (a) carrying out a meta-analysis of published reports on approximately 300 cases of selective mutism; (b) identifying a satisfactory study sample of selectively mute children currently known to professionals; and (c) piloting a strategy for collecting basic information about the development and treatment of the symptom from professional informants by telephone. The aim is to test linked theoretical predictions about: (1) the differences within the population of selectively mute children between those from socially isolated families and others; and (2) the relative effectiveness of treatment approaches that do and do not incorporate a stimulus fading process. The results will be interpreted in terms of a systems model of selective mutism and its treatment. As part of (a) an investigation is planned of gender imbalance in selective mutism. This developmental pattern is unusual among language problems in that it is more common among girls. The planned investigation will focus on possible cultural factors in that phenomenon.
Published Material: CLINE, T. & BALDWIN, S. (1993). Selective mutism in childhood. London: Whurr Publishers.
Status: Individual research
Date of Research: 1993-1994
KEYWORDS: *behaviour problems; communication disorders; elective mutism; problem children*

10/0908

Faculty of Management, Putteridge Bury Management Centre, Hitchin Road, Luton LU2 8LE
01582 482555
Thody, A. Dr
Nineteenth century school management
Abstract: This research has commenced with the recreation of a day in the life of a headmaster in 1887. This introduces the themes which will be developed in the course of the project. These are planning physical resources and staff management, classification and admissions, home-school relations and reputation management, financial management, initial teacher training, quality assurance and inspections, relations with school managers, managing change and defining management. In addition, the research will review sources for this topic, and reflect on the value of history in the training of school leaders today. A comparative perspective will be pursued from Australian literature to see how English and Irish ideas penetrated a related culture. Victorian school management has not previously been researched.
Published Material: THODY, A. (1994). 'Persistent dilemmas: persistent solutions – an investigation in 19th century school leadership'. Paper presented at the International Intervisitation Programme for Educational Administrators, Toronto, May 1994.
Status: Sponsored project
Source of Grant: Luton University
Date of Research: 1994-continuing
KEYWORDS: *educational administration; educational history; management in education*

10/0909

Faculty of Management, Putteridge Bury Management Centre, Hitchin Road, Luton LU2 8LE
01582 482555
Thody, A. Dr
Public sector executives: a longitudinal study of Chief Education Officers, 1986-1995
Abstract: This research reports the observed behaviour of public sector chief executives in strategic change processes set contextually and temporally. Its central methodology of direct observation offers time series data describing and analysing the daily activities of a cohort of chief education officers at two periods, 1986-88, and 1994-95, which span major developments in the public sector. This holistic documentation arises within a period of major organisational, political and functional change for local authorities and aims to provide unique and rich data to illuminate theoretical conceptualisations of strategic management. The research will include: 1) A review of the literature on chief executives in public sector management and on chief education officers; 2) Analysis of observation data, collected between 1986-88, from 25 days' shadowing of five chief education officers in four local education authorities; 3) Observing recording and analysing 25 days' activities of five chief education officers, 1994-95, in the same local education authorities; 4) Comparing the two periods, relating data to literature; 5) Assessing the value of this style of empirical field study in providing evidence for theoretical analyses of strategic management, particularly contextual, processual

and historical interpretations; and 6) Offering researchers of strategic management, new data on chief executive roles which can be used for studies of management styles, models and effectiveness.
Status: Individual research
Date of Research: 1986-continuing
KEYWORDS: *educational administration; educational administrators; local education authorities; management in education*

10/0910

Faculty of Management, Putteridge Bury Management Centre, Hitchin Road, Luton LU2 8LE
01582 482555
Thody, A. Dr

Mentoring: comparison of an intra- and extra-professional scheme
Abstract: The aim of this research is to investigate mentoring as an alternative learning method for the preparation of educative leaders by comparing two mentoring schemes – an intra-professional mentoring programme for school principals and an extra-professional mentoring scheme for senior faculty with business executives. This research examines the relationships resulting from, the training for, and the possible effects of, mentoring as a means of preparation for educative leadership. The research has its empirical foundations in two contrasting schemes of mentorship. The first involves experienced school principals mentoring newly appointed principals, thus relying on the assumption that the sharing of common role values and mandates would facilitate learning. This is reinforced by the 'normal' configuration of the learning relationship – i.e. 'age' of experience, leading unpractised 'youth'. In the second mentoring scheme analysed, the partners are a group of university faculty and a group of executives from local businesses. This partnering may denote extra professional destabilisation for either group. This research commences with a collation and comparative analysis of the elements of the two schemes, including the administration of the schemes, their underlying conceptualisations and rationales, the selection and pairing of participants, their training and the elements which each have decided to incorporate in their schemes. Structured interviews with partners will form the basis of the primary data reflecting effectiveness and a comparison of these personalised accounts will be set against the national evaluation of the principals' mentoring scheme.
Published Material: THODY, A. (1994). 'Mentoring: cultural reinforcement or extra-professional destabilisation?'. Paper presented at American Educational Research Association Conference, April 1994.
Status: Individual research
Date of Research: 1993-1994
KEYWORDS: *head teachers; management development; managerial occupations; mentors*

10/0911

Faculty of Management, Putteridge Bury Management Centre, Hitchin Road, Luton LU2 8LE
01582 482555
Thody, A. Dr; Crystal, L. Dr

Mentoring in education and employment
Abstract: The aims of the project are: 1) To investigate the effectiveness of co-mentoring by senior managers in the private and public sectors with senior academics with management responsibilities, and to evaluate the effectiveness of mentoring as a management development tool. 2) To investigate the value to final year students of being mentored by a local employer, and to assess the value of this as support for job seeking. A sample of six senior academics and six senior managers from a range of companies will co-mentor for a minimum period of six months. Six junior managers will mentor six final year students for a minimum of six months. All participants received an introduction to mentoring skills. The programme will be evaluated through questionnaires and interviews and written up as a case study with recommendations for future practice.
Status: Sponsored project
Source of Grant: Department of Employment £8,000
Date of Research: 1993-continuing
KEYWORDS: *industry-education relationship; management development; mentors; work-education relationship*

10/0912

Faculty of Management, Putteridge Bury Management Centre, Hitchin Road, Luton LU2 8LE
01582 482555

Leicester University, School of Education, Educational Management Development Unit, University Centre, Barrack Road, Northampton NN2 6AF
01604 30180
Duffield, R. Mr; *Supervisor:* Thody, A. Dr; Churcher, J. Mr; Lofthouse, M. Dr

School governance. Sharing the responsibility between governors and schools' senior managers: a comparative study of practice, policy and possible models
Abstract: The role of the school governor has undergone a considerable number of changes in the last hundred years and particularly in the last ten years. As a result of recent legislation, governors have been given increased powers, but generally it appears that they may not be exercising these powers (Brehony 1992, Cooper 1993, Deem 1993). In spite of Government led pragmatic solutions to the division of powers between headteachers and governors, there is a lack of clear definition of the power of governors and headteachers which can be unsatisfactory for the efficiency of school governance. This can lead to problems as individual governing bodies are deciding the extent of involvement in decision making. The objective of these case studies will be to analyse power sharing between governors and headteachers and to examine how the decision making roles develop over phases of schooling by the study of practices and processes in a linked family of schools. The Groby (Leicestershire) Family of Schools comprises Groby Community College, a 14 to 19 upper school and community college of 790 students which share a campus with Brookvale High School, an 11 to 14 comprehensive school of 630 students; and six contributory primary schools – Martinshaw Primary School, Groby; Elizabeth Woodville Primary School and Newtown Linfirs Primary School, Groby; Lady Jane Grey Primary School, Groby; Ratby Primary School; Kirby Muxloe Primary School. The primary schools range in size from 300 pupils to 59 pupils. A linked family of schools has been chosen to minimise the influence of socio-economic variables on the study. The schools are situated in a cluster of Leicestershire suburban villages, the population of which represent a range of social classes. In analysing appropriate models, the study focuses on particular issues of how different schools have chosen to divide responsibility between headteachers and governors on specific policy issues. Particular aspects could include: statutory responsibilities, e.g. National Curriculum; non-statutory responsibilities, e.g. public relations; pedagogy. The methodology will include: a) a literature survey and study of contextual issues; b) observation of full meetings of governing bodies of the above-mentioned schools over an 18 month period; c) observation of governors' sub-committee meetings over an 18 month period (the sub-committees selected will be those having similar responsibility); d) a questionnaire survey of all governors in the family of schools (approximately 150 governors); e) governors' diaries – a number of governors from each school and from each category of governors (e.g. parent governors, coopted governors, local education authority appointed governors); and f) semi-structured interviews with headteachers and chairs of governors in all the schools. The expected results will include: a) contextual and comparative data to provide models for comparison; b) observational, questionnaire and diary data to demonstrate the nature and context of governor involvement and to assess whether or not this varies according to different phases of schooling, different types of governorship, types of issues being discussed, the timing of involvement, variations in levels of formality and types of governor participation; c) interview data to provide perceptions of how governors and headteachers view their roles; d) analysis of data to assess degrees of commonality in emergent roles and partnership. Comparison of data with current accepted roles of governorship and with partners from other countries and periods of time; and e) creation of models from the data for the division of responsibilities for headteachers and governors and a discussion of how governors can best be prepared for appropriate roles.
Status: Individual research
Date of Research: 1993-continuing
KEYWORDS: *educational administration; governing bodies; head teachers; management in education; school governors*

10/0913

Faculty of Management, Putteridge Bury Management Centre, Hitchin Road, Luton LU2 8LE
01582 482555

Leicester University, School of Education, University Road, Leicester LE1 7RH
01162 522522
Alsop, A. Mr; *Supervisor:* Thody, A. Dr; Marry, R. Dr

The management of disruptive pupils with reference to primary secondary school liaison

Abstract: The aim of the research is to improve the management of disruptive pupils through secondary intervention in the primary phase. This research will provide alternative models in the management of disruption to those available at the present time. It will provide better structures that will offer alternatives that may keep more pupils within the education system, who might otherwise have been excluded or rejected because of their disruptive behaviour. The main objectives of the research are: 1) To illuminate and evaluate new processes of managing secondary school disruptives through interventions by secondary school staff in primary schools and through contact maintenance during transfer from primary to secondary schools. 2) To analyse and develop school policies, staff training and resources to increase the chance of maintaining a greater number of disruptive pupils for longer periods in the educational system. This would help pupils, parents and teachers by early identification, cooperation and sound effective interventions. 3) To clarify the language of definitions of disruption acceptable in both primary and secondary phases in order to facilitate identification of disruptives and appropriate intervention strategies. This study considers methods of ameliorating disturbance and concentrates on the new area of management of primary school liaison. The studies are of two secondary schools and five primary schools. The cohort consists of 150 teachers and over 2,000 pupils. The schools have been selected because they fall within a close geographical area so that it should be possible to compare different methods of coping with disruptive pupils from similar socioeconomic areas. Consideration is being given to extending the study to include schools in a rural area if the literature and local education authority surveys indicate a significant factor influencing the extent of disruption. Questionnaires, individual and group interviews and observations will be used. The research entails a longitudinal study following 4- disruptive pupils from year 5 to year 8. The researcher expects to provide results that will have investigated whether or not more effective management of disruptive pupils will help provide a better and prolonged education for those identified as being disruptive. By providing coherent management structures linked with clear, concise and negotiated information it is hoped to be able to sustain, support and suggest ways which could modify the behaviour of disruptive pupils.
Status: Individual research
Date of Research: 1993-continuing
KEYWORDS: *behaviour problems; discipline policy; discipline problems; disruptive pupils; primary-secondary education; problem children; transfer pupils*

10/0914
Faculty of Management, Putteridge Bury Management Centre, Hitchin Road, Luton LU2 8LE
01582 482555
Reading University, Faculty of Education and Community Studies, Bulmershe Court, Woodlands Avenue, Earley, Reading RG6 1HY
01734 875123
Stein-Davies, M. Mrs; *Supervisor:* Thody, A. Dr; Fidler, B. Dr; Loynes, A. Mr

A case study of the effectiveness of the school governance model as a medium for parental influence in state nursery schools

Abstract: The aim of the project is to develop models of effective state nursery school governance as a means of mediating parental views. This involves: 1) identifying the contributions of systems of nursery school governance to the mediation of parental views; 2) ascertaining views of parents and school governors across the nursery school sector concerning the extent of parental influence over the education and facilities offered in nursery schools; 3) producing case studies of parental influence in different types of nursery provision; and 4) developing models for effectively expressing parental views through systems of governance.
Status: Individual research
Date of Research: 1992-continuing
KEYWORDS: *early childhood education; governing bodies; nursery schools; parent attitudes; parent-school relationship; preschool education; school governors*

10/0915
Faculty of Management, Putteridge Bury Management Centre, Hitchin Road, Luton LU2 8LE
01582 482555

Warwick University, Department of Education, Coventry CV4 7AL
01203 523523
Duckett, H. Ms; *Supervisor:* Thody, A. Dr; Crystal, L. Dr; Bell, L. Dr

Quality assurance: fact or fiction? An investigation of external and internal perceptions of university quality control systems and the development of a model to demonstrate the variables affecting quality assurance in higher education

Abstract: To investigate how the effectiveness of systems of quality assurance operating in higher education are perceived by staff, students and externals (examiners, employers, governmental agencies etc). Through an examination of the quality measurement used by universities at course level such as the quantitative results of students' questionnaires, course reports, committee minutes, external examiner reports and completion rates and investigation as to the degree of congruence between the qualitative/quantitative data and the perceptions of the direct participants (staff, students, and externals) will be conducted. The research will determine the rationale underlying the selection of a traditionally positivist approach to quality assessment within higher education as distinct from the adoption of phenomenologies (social and relational investigation). An investigation of a sample of undergraduate and postgraduate programmes (full and part-time) will be undertaken. In order to achieve further breadth, a comparative analysis of other universities/colleges within higher education will be undertaken utilising the researchers network. In particular, a comparative study of the new and old universities will be conducted to establish differences in their respective methodologies. The research will progress into an evaluation of those variables which affect perception within higher education. A model of 'cause and effect' will be derived through allocating weightings to variables derived from research into staff, student and external perception. Preliminary investigations into the potential use of the research for linking participant perception and demand for higher education will be conducted.
Status: Individual research
Date of Research: 1993-continuing
KEYWORDS: *attitudes; higher education; quality assurance*

Manchester Metropolitan University

10/0916
Crewe & Alsager Faculty, Department of Educational Management, Hassall Road, Alsager, Stoke on Trent ST7 2HL
0161 247 2000
Hailey, A. Ms; *Supervisor:* Devlin, T. Mr

The management of school culture through pastoral care

Abstract: The context of this research was the pastoral provision in a Shropshire secondary school. The hypothesis for the research states that school culture can be changed or developed through management activities. Central assumptions were: that school culture can be changed; that teachers do have choices and are not 'passive recipients' of culture. The investigation inevitably considered: the underlying philosophy of pastoral care; school culture and the impact of internal and external pressures, structures and practices; accountability and school differences research; and the effect of career development. The research was intended to raise awareness about the issues of pastoral care, and more importantly, to move those issues forward in a developmental way for the mutual benefit of the wider school community. The 'action research' model was selected as the most appropriate for this particular investigation. Pastoral care was diagnosed as a very complex phenomenon and further investigations were necessary. Detailed information was required and the potential for bias was recognised and planned for. A range of investigative techniques were used which included: participant observations; interviews; surveys; and feedback from the county advisory service review. The research concluded that pastoral care remains very elusive to define and yet permeates all aspects of teaching and learning. The lack of clear definition of pastoral care has led to confusion and a great deal of variance in practice, and for some of the teaching sample, pastoral care is considered to be synonymous with personal and social education, and discipline. Changes did occur in school structure and organisation, which can, in part, be attributed to management activities associated with the action research.

Changes in individual attitudes and values were less evident although some consensus in understanding seems to have developed. Interactions and relationships with pupils were considered to be improving, and issues for action were identified. Career deelopment is a significant issue in moving developments on – but it also created some important limitations.
Published Material: HAILEY, E. (1990). 'Introducing a whole-school P.S.E. programme', Pastoral Care in Education, Vol 8, No 2, pp.19-25.
Status: Individual research
Date of Research: 1988-1992
KEYWORDS: educational environment; pastoral care – education; school organisation

10/0917

Crewe & Alsager Faculty, Department of Psychology and Speech Pathology, Hassall Road, Alsager, Stoke on Trent ST7 2HL
0161 247 2000
Peer, L. Ms; *Supervisor:* Alston, J. Dr
The language development and cognitive competences of bilingual children with specific learning difficulties
Abstract: There is evidence to suggest that the spoken vocabulary skills of children with specific learning difficulties are at least average. This vocabulary competence is associated with an effective knowledge of word meaning related to established auditory-visual-semantic links in working memory which facilitate effective levels of recall leading to cognitive competence in major aspects of oral verbal thinking. This leads to the cognitive profile referred to as the ACID profile. Testing carried out with bilingual children indicates that their vocabulary skills in both languages may be more variable than for native single language speakers. Pilot studies have been carried out, examining the language used by bilingual students in conditions of stress. Results show the importance of the primary language in working memory. Questions addressed in the main study include: (i) Are bilingual language learners significantly different from single language learners in their cognitive development, application and use of language skills in school? (ii) Are bilingual dyslexics significantly different from single language dyslexics in cognitive profile, and their application and use of language in their thinking processes? (iii) In bilingual dyslexics, does the development of a language skill in the first language, have significant advantages over the development of such competences in the second language? (iv) Does the development of working memory competences in first language have significant advantages over the development of such competences in the second language? To investigate these questions three groups have been established: Group 1 consists of twelve monolingual mixed sex dyslexic children in the age range 10-18; Group 2 consists of twelve mixed sex bilingual dyslexic children in the age range 10-18; Group 3 consists of twelve monolingual mixed sex non-dyslexic students in the age range 10-18, who have already been tested and have known cognitive profiles. This third group will act as a control. Results to date are encouraing and support the major thrust of the study that bilingual learners with specific learning difficulties have different cognitive profiles which significantly alter their learning and need a very carefully constructed teaching approach.
Status: Individual research
Date of Research: 1990-1992
KEYWORDS: bilingual pupils; cognitive ability; dyslexia; language acquisition; language handicaps; learning disabilities; special educational needs

10/0918

Crewe & Alsager Faculty, Health and Research Development Unit, Hassall Road, Alsager, Stoke on Trent ST7 2HL
0161 247 2000
Heathcote, G. Dr
Professional development of teachers in health education
Abstract: The research identified the inservice professional needs of teachers and lecturers of Health Education/Promotion through survey methods using a structured sample of individuals working in schools and further education colleges. Local education authority advisers and current course providers were also surveyed. Five major national questionnaires were developed and implemented, and indepth interviews (up to 3 hours) were conducted with 65 practising Health Education teachers/lecturers. A research report was published by the Health Education Authority to disseminate the research findings. A

further grant was then awarded for the development of a curriculum framework, based on a process and skills model, for use by institutions of higher education to develop appropriate inservice provision at postgraduate level. The director of research piloted one of two national courses and the evaluation findings were widely distributed. Consultancy work and publications continue in this extended dissemination phase. The project findings indicated that teachers need a structured progression of inservice courses and that this particular course with its distinctive methodologies can very adequately meet their needs.
Published Material: HEATHCOTE, G. (1989). Inservice provision for teachers of health education. London: Health Education Authority.; HEATHCOTE, G. (1989). 'Teachers, health education and inservice training', Health Education Journal, Vol 48, No 4, pp.172-175.; HEATHCOTE, G. (1992). 'Developments in INSET: Health education for teachers in the United Kingdom'. Association for Teacher Education in Europe: ATEE News, No. 37, September 10.; HEATHCOTE, G. (1992). 'The professional development of teachers in health education: issues in the delivery of inservice provision in the United Kingdom', In: PLOMP, T.J., PIETERS, J.M. & PETERIS, A. (Eds). European Conference in Educational Research: Book of Summaries, 2, University of Twente, The Netherlands, (June 22-25).
Status: Sponsored project
Source of Grant: Health Education Authority £70,000
Date of Research: 1988-1994
KEYWORDS: health education; inservice teacher education; professional development

10/0919

Crewe and Alsager Faculty, Crewe Campus, Crewe Green Road, Crewe CW1 1DU
0161 247 2000
Smith, P. Mrs
Mentor development and competency-based profiling: continuity across initial teacher training, newly qualified teacher status, and continuing professional development
Abstract: The background to the research lies in the Department for Education (DFE) Circulars 9/92 and more recently 14/93, amd the Grants for Education Support and Training (GEST) funded activities of 27/92 and 17/93, aiming to enhance continuity and progression from initial teacher training (ITT) to newly qualified teacher status (NQT) through the development of NQT competency-based profiles and mentor training and support. In 1992-93, this development work was enhanced through an additional DFE project grant of 5,000 pounds used to further establish the networking across 5 local education authorities (LEAs): Staffordshire, Tameside, Cheshire, Wirral and Shropshire. The NQT profiles developed used the Secondary Postgraduate Certificate in Education (PGCE) profile of competences as their basis. These competences were developed and refined from 9/92 and enhanced through the addition of reflexivity and detailed indicators providing an agenda for professional development discussion between mentor and student teacher/newly qualified teacher. These indicators have been further developed by professional mentors and are proving valuable in self-assessment, observation and target setting. Schools have spent 1993 piloting the use of the NQT profiles and are engaged in the initial review and evaluation of their design. Immediate feedback is leading researchers urgently into the incorporation of management development competences, to allow the profiles to be used for whole staff development purposes, including appraisal. The Management Charter Initiative (MCI) based School Management South Competences Project (Earley, P. (1992). The School Management Competences Project: Final Report. Crawley: School Management South) provides a valuable possibility for this strand of development.
Published Material: ACTON, R., KIRKNAM, G. & SMITH, P. (1992). Mentoring: a core skills pack. Crewe: Crewe and Alsager College of Higher Education.; SMITH, P. (1992). A guide to mentoring in the secondary school: a competency-based approach. Crewe: Crewe and Alsager College of Higher Education.; SMITH, P. & WEST-BURNHAM, J. (Eds). (1993). Mentoring in the effective school. Issues in School Management Series. London: Longman.
Status: Sponsored project
Source of Grant: Department for Education £51,000; Grants for Education Support and Training
Date of Research: 1992-1994
KEYWORDS: competency-based teacher education; mentors; profiles; teacher development

10/0920

Crewe and Alsager Faculty, Crewe Campus, Crewe Green Road, Crewe CW1 1DU
0161 247 2000
Keating, I. Ms; *Supervisor:* Taylorson, D. Dr
The impact of participation in a nursery on a group of socially and economically disadvantaged mothers
Abstract: The research will consider the impact of participation in a nursery on a group of socially and economically disadvantaged mothers. From background reading, it is clear that early years at schooling play a particularly significant part in child development and attitudes towards schooling. It is accepted that fathers (and other members of the community) become involved in school but it is argued that the role of mothers is particularly significant. The researcher does not intend to reiterate the debate about the value and importance of parental involvement and its impact on children, but to focus on its impact on the mothers who have become involved. The research focus is two-fold: 1) The impact of parental involvement on mothers. 2) Which forms of parental involvement are most valued by different interest groups in a nursery. The research will take place in a nursery with the research subjects identified as mothers, staff and children. It is hoped to construct cost-benefit analyses from these three distinct perspectives. The research methods are essentially interpretative ethnographic. The researcher is anxious to disassociate herself from any possibility of exploiting the women she contacts for the purpose of her research. It is hoped that advantages should arise out of the research for the women (and in particular the mothers) involved in it.
Status: Individual research
Date of Research: 1991-continuing
KEYWORDS: *early childhood education; mothers; nursery schools; parent participation*

10/0921

Crewe and Alsager Faculty, Crewe Campus, Crewe Green Road, Crewe CW1 1DU
0161 247 2000
Barnes, E. Mrs; *Supervisor:* Pumfrey, P. Prof.
A longitudinal study of the development of automaticity in children's free writing during National Curriculum key stage 1
Abstract: This longitudinal study into the teaching and learning of spelling during National Curriculum key stage 1 is set within the theoretical context of automaticity in early literacy. In particular it aims to examine children's orthographical development in relation to several popular theories of spelling development, and to examine the development of automaticity. It will also consider the development of children's spelling ability in relation to the teaching methods adopted. The research is based upon an acknowledgement that pedagogy derives, in part, from the view held by schools as institutions, and by teachers as individuals, of the nature of pupils' learning and its relationship with teaching methods. A teacher's philosophy of education, whether implicit or explicit, will directly influence the teaching and learning approaches within the classroom. This is true of pedagogy in general, and of the approaches to the teaching of writing in particular. During the last few decades there has been an increase in the number of studies relating to the teaching of writing, and a further consideration of the teaching and learning of spelling. This present study aims to build upon the work recently undertaken, in an attempt to offer further insights into how classroom practice might best support the teaching and learning of spelling. The research is focused in schools which: 1) could identify their overall approach to the teaching and learning of writing; and 2) have a written policy statement reflecting their approach. A random selection of schools was identified, two schools favouring a traditional approach, two a developmental approach and two an eclectic approach. In total some 200 children form the cohort for the study, representing the total Reception year group intake of the selected schools during the academic year 1991-92. A sample of free writing will be obtained termly from each child by the researcher, and this will be analysed using the CHILDES program. In addition, the children's knowledge of letter sounds an letter names will be assessed. Data collection will take place between September 1991 and July 1994.
Status: Individual research
Date of Research: 1990-1994
KEYWORDS: *spelling; writing skills; writing teaching*

10/0922

Crewe and Alsager Faculty, Department of Educational Management, Hassall Road, Alsager, Stoke on Trent ST7 2HL
0161 247 2000
Turnock, J. Mr; *Supervisor:* Tolly, B. Dr
The role of the Church of England in the provision of education at Worfield Endowed Church of England (Aided) Primary School from 1546 to 1991, with particular reference to the governors' responsibility for curriculum, funding and building in the light of the Education Reform Act 1988
Abstract: The aim of this research is to clarify the purpose and application of educational endowments from the Brierley Charity of 1609, Lloyd and Parker Charity of 1613 and other trust deeds which were later amalgamated into the Worfield United Charities. It will also try to establish the changing role of the Church of England and the provision of free education. The project will look at the changes which took place in local thinking and to examine the influences of the major educational reform acts of the last 150 years. The researchers will establish whether the Foundation Governors' income from endowment is still regulated by the 1909 scheme, or whether subsequent variations have been legitimised by the Charity Commissioners. Links will be established between the elected Church Foundation Governors and their associated endowments with other members of the Governing Body in order to clarify responsibility for the curriculum and the ownership of the land and buildings of Worfield Primary School. It is also hoped to clarify the powers of the whole Governing Body in the light of new legislation under the Education Reform Act 1988.
Status: Sponsored project
Source of Grant: Shropshire Local Education Authority £395
Date of Research: 1991-1993
KEYWORDS: *church-education relationship; educational history; educational legislation; financial support; free education; school governors*

10/0923

Crewe and Alsager Faculty, Department of Educational Management, Hassall Road, Alsager, Stoke on Trent ST7 2HL
0161 247 2000
James, M. Mr; *Supervisor:* Seymour, R. Mr
Managing the implementation of the National Curriculum
Abstract: This research examines the introduction of the National Curriculum as an exercise in the management of change. Literature reviews have been carried out on curriculum theory, a centrally controlled curriculum and various perspectives on the National Curriculum as well as educational change. The question of cross curricularity and subject overlap has emerged as extremely important. Five secondary schools will be studied. Interviews with the headteacher and deputy and the heads of science, geography and technology will take place. Data will then be collated and analysed to compare 'real world' perceptions and problems with the theoretical perspectives of the literature review. It is hoped that 'good practice' guidelines and additional knowledge on the management of change will emerge.
Status: Individual research
Date of Research: 1990-1993
KEYWORDS: *core curriculum; curriculum development; educational administration; educational change; educational development; interdisciplinary approach; National Curriculum*

10/0924

Crewe and Alsager Faculty, Department of Educational Management, Hassall Road, Alsager, Stoke on Trent ST7 2HL
0161 247 2000
Hemmings, N. Mr; *Supervisor:* Seymour, R. Mr
Self managing schools – a practical way forward for secondary schools
Abstract: The research aims to consider some of the practical effects of school management in the light of the Education Reform Act 1988 (ERA). In particular focusing upon the ways secondary schools have adapted to the new challenges that ERA has presented. A case study of representative schools has begun.
Status: Sponsored project
Source of Grant: Stoke on Trent Local Education Authority £150
Date of Research: 1990-1993
KEYWORDS: *Education Reform Act 1988; educational administration; educational change; local management of schools; school-based management; secondary schools*

10/0925

Crewe and Alsager Faculty, Department of Educational Management, Hassall Road, Alsager, Stoke on Trent ST7 2HL
0161 247 2000
West-Burnham, J. Mr; *Supervisor:* Seymour, R. Mr; James, L. Dr

The applicability of Total Quality Management to the management of schools

Abstract: Total Quality Management (TQM) has emerged in the 1980s as the most powerful tool for organisational review and development. This research seeks to explore the extent to which the principles of TQM are applicable to school management. The research model is based on the researcher's book (WEST-BURNHAM, J. (1992). Managing quality in schools: a TQM approach, Longman), as a basis for examining perceptions of quality, identifying and analysing existing relevant practice and developing a model that is applicable in schools. The book includes an invitation to respond to the writer – this will generate an opportunity sample. The writer has been engaged by a number of local education authorities to run courses on quality management – participants in these courses will be used as a sample for follow-up work in order to review the principles and practices identified in the book.

Published Material: WEST-BURNHAM, J. (1992). Managing quality in schools: a TQM approach. Harlow: Longman Press.
Status: Individual research
Date of Research: 1990-1994
KEYWORDS: *educational quality; management in education; school-based management*

10/0926

Crewe and Alsager Faculty, Crewe Campus, Crewe Green Road, Crewe CW1 1DU
0161 247 2000
Exeter University, School of Education, St Luke's, Heavitree Road, Exeter EX1 2LU
01392 263263
Hodkinson, P. Mr; Hodkinson, H. Mrs; Sparkes, A. Dr

Training credits in action project

Abstract: This is a longitudinal study of one of the original training credit pilot schemes. These schemes are based on the currently fashionable principles of individualisation and market forces in the context of youth training. A small number of young people were followed from leaving school and through eighteen months training. In each case the researchers interviewed the young person and other stakeholders they come in contact with several times. These stakeholders included careers teachers, careers officers, training organisations, employers, parents and Training and Enterprise Council (TEC) officials. The approach was to be critically interpretive, investigating the scheme through the perceptions of these stakeholders. Analysis is still continuing, but current findings include: 1) the development of an interactive/interactionist perspective on the transition from school to work, which complements existing but contrasting research and policy perspectives; 2) contracting the pragmatically rational way in which young people make career decisions with the technically rational assumptions of some policies and procedures; 3) a challenge to the policy conception of a customer driven market in training, which was found to be largely mythical. Training Credits in Action Project briefing papers and working papers are available from the researcher.

Published Material: HODKINSON, P. & SPARKES, A.C. (1993). 'Feedback in stakeholder based research'. In: MATHISON, S., ROSS, E.W. & COMETT, J.W. (Eds). A casebook for teaching about ethical issues in qualitative research. Washington, D.C.: Qualitative Research SIG, American Educational Research Association.; HODKINSON, P. & SPARKES, A.C. (1993). 'Young people's choices and careers guidance action planning: a case study of training credits in action', British Journal of Guidance and Counselling, Vol 21, No 3, pp.246-261.; HODKINSON, P. & SPARKES, A.C. (1994). 'To tell or not to tell? Reflecting on ethical dilemmas in stakeholder research', Evaluation and Research in Education, Vol 7, No 3, pp.117-132.; HODKINSON, P. & SPARKES, A.C. 'Taking credits: a case study of the guidance process into a training credits scheme', Research Papers in Education. (in press).
Status: Sponsored project
Source of Grant: Economic and Social Research Council £43,000
Date of Research: 1992-1994
KEYWORDS: *school to work transition; training; training credits; youth employment*

10/0927

Crewe and Alsager Faculty, Crewe Campus, Crewe Green Road, Crewe CW1 1DU
0161 247 2000
Manchester University, School of Education, Centre for Formative Assessment Studies, Oxford Road, Manchester M13 9PL
0161 275 2000
Ellis, S. Mr; *Supervisor:* Christie, T. Prof.

National Curriculum assessment in the 1990s: a critical review of the literature

Abstract: The Education Reform Act 1988 has created an unprecedented climate of rapid curricular change in both primary and secondary schools. The management of change will be crucial if the reforms are to benefit all concerned; schools will need to increasingly involve themselves in review and evaluation at whole-school level. The role of research in this area has been largely ignored especially National Curriculum assessment monitoring and evaluation. There is a need to develop our understanding of assessment theory and to move towards a national system which is not just concerned with the 'products' of assessment, but also seeks to explore the underlying 'process' rationale. The central tension and 'dilemma' is the distinction between formative (classroom-based) and summative (external) national assessment. The way in which both primary and secondary schools are managing this conflict forms the broad rationale for this research. The main style of research is pluralistic evaluation as a multi-method approach (triangulation). The collection of data falls into two contexts: 1) Broad context: The focus is 2/3 tier educational institutions exploring the development, monitoring and evaluation of whole school approaches to curricular and assessment implementation. 2) Specific context: This context aims to narrow the field and includes the interlocking variables of continuity and progression, experience of the individual child and the foundation subject geography. The outcomes of the research will provide an examination of the 'state of the art' re-assessment in the National Curriculum. Furthermore, it will provide guidelines for 'good practice' re whole-school assessment issues. Issues of progression and continuity in assessment from the child's perspective are also addressed.

Status: Individual research
Date of Research: 1993-continuing
KEYWORDS: *assessment; National Curriculum*

10/0928

Department of Applied Community Studies, Didsbury Campus, 799 Wilmslow Road, Didsbury, Manchester M20 2RR
0161 247 2000
Stokes, I. Ms; *Supervisor:* Humphries, B. Dr

Black practice teachers in social work: a study of their number and contributions in four statutory agencies in Greater Manchester

Abstract: This study is an investigation into black practice teachers in social work in three local authority social services departments and one probation service in an area of the north west of England. It attempts to identify the numbers of black practitioners who were eligible to become practice teachers and whether such practitioners were interested in practice teaching. In addition, mechanisms in the agencies which determine how individuals are chosen to become practice teachers were examined and the effectiveness of such mechanisms were explored with the research subjects. The research is based on the notion of black perspectives in terms of taking into account the reality of black people's experiences. The data was gathered through questionnaire, interviews, group sessions, and analysis of relevant literature and policy and practice documents of the agencies. The report concludes that large numbers of black practitioners in the agencies were eligible to become practice teachers and a large percentage were interested in being practice teachers. The recommendations suggest ways in which all those involved in social work practice teaching could work to develop and realise these interests, at the same time as increasing the number of black practice teachers in the system.

Status: Sponsored project
Source of Grant: Central Council for Education and Training in Social Work Practice Placement Initiative Grant £90,000
Date of Research: 1992-1993
KEYWORDS: *blacks; ethnic groups; social work teachers*

10/0929

Department of Hotel, Catering and Tourism Management, Hollings Faculty, Old Hall Lane, Manchester M14 6HR
0161 247 2000
Keele University, Department of Education, Keele ST5 5BG
01782 621111
Ineson, E. Dr; *Supervisor:* Kempa, R. Prof.

The predictive validity of criteria used in the selection of students for undergraduate courses and graduate training in hotel and catering management

Abstract: This study investigated whether selection criteria, which were predictive of undergraduate Hotel and Catering Management (HCM) students' subsequent academic performance and their recruitment into employment, could be identified. The scant findings from previous HCM studies were supplemented by evidence from HCM prospectuses, application forms and interviews with selectors. Data were collected from 469 first year and 210 final year HCM undergraduates in England and Scotland and related to a series of performance measures. The predictive qualities of the data in relation to the performance measures were evaluated by appropriate statistical techniques including ANOVA and discriminant analysis. The findings confirmed that academic criteria were predominantly the most effective single predictors of HCM degree course success. However, slightly better predictions were obtained from a combination of academic and non-academic criteria. As far as recruitment to graduate management training was concerned, academic criteria did not have significant predictive value. Instead, these recruiters relied on a preconception that all graduates had acquired certain skills and competences, then sought evidence of managerial work experience, interpersonal skills and certain personal qualities. Ambition, measured at the commencement of the final undergraduate year, was the main criterion leading to Hotel and Catering employment. It was concluded that the selection criteria in operation were not very well matched with the performance outcomes, hence it was extremely difficult for undergraduate admission tutors to take a long term perspective. This PhD project was sponsored in part by the ASE division at NFER-Nelson.

Published Material: INESON, E.M. (1987). 'The do's and don'ts of jobhunting', Hospitality, February.; CHILDS, R. (1990). Graduate and managerial assessment data supplement. Windsor: ASE – a division of NFER-Nelson.
Status: Individual research
Date of Research: 1986-1993
KEYWORDS: *hotel and catering education; hotel management education; selection*

10/0930

Didsbury School of Education, 799 Wilmslow Road, Didsbury, Manchester M20 2RR
0161 247 2000
Steiner, M. Ms

Educating for global citizenship: a world studies approach for teacher educators

Abstract: The objective of this research is to identify the ways in which courses and modules in teacher education enable teachers to bring a global dimension into their classroom work. The global dimension is defined as learning experiences to do with human rights, development, citizenship, environment, and equal opportunities. It also pertains to appropriate teaching and learning styles and teacher education in England and Wales. The research will focus upon definitions, materials and practices. It will be collaborative and cross-disciplinary. This project is working in partnership with a similar Europe-wide initiative funded by ERASMUS. It is intended to publish a Handbook of Methods and Processes for Global Citizenship in Teacher Education in additon to a research report.

Published Material: STEINER, M. (1993). Learning from experience: world studies in the primary curriculum. Stoke on Trent: Trentham Books.
Status: Sponsored project
Source of Grant: Oxfam £24,000; Christian Aid £10,000; UNICEF £5,000; Save the Children Fund £8,000; CAFOD £6,000
Date of Research: 1993-continuing
KEYWORDS: *citizenship education; global approach; teacher education*

10/0931

Didsbury School of Education, 799 Wilmslow Road, Didsbury, Manchester M20 2RR
0161 247 2000

Brown, A. Dr

Linguistics and mathematics education

Abstract: This research explores how recent advances in philosophy and psychoanalysis provide models for development within mathematics education. The study focuses on the linguistic aspects of understanding mathematics following post-structuralist writings that see developing understanding as the initiation into culturally conventional signification. By asserting mathematics as the product of human activity and as such essentially interpretive, the applicability of human scientific techniques is explored towards accounting for this activity in terms of how the mathematics engaged in is captured in language. This follows recent work carried out by writers in mathematics education on constructivism but extends this work by locating it within a broader theoretical context. Two research assistants attached to the project are exploring constructivist models of describing children's learning of mathematics in school and the determinants of teachers' beliefs about how children learn mathematics. Another member of the department is conducting related work into how staff working on initial teacher training courses see their role in influencing these beliefs.

Published Material: BROWN, T. (1991). 'Hermeneutics and the Human Sciences', Educational Studies in Mathematics, Vol 22, No 5, pp.475-480.; BROWN, T. & McNAMARA, O. (1993). 'Linguistics, post structuralism and mathematics education'. Proceedings of Conference of the British Society of Research into the Learning of Mathematics, Nottingham, 1993.; BROWN, T. (1993). 'Mathematics as an interpretive activity'. Proceedings of Conference of the British Congress of Mathematical Education, University of Leeds, July 1993.; BROWN, T. (1993). 'Symbolising experience and experiencing symbolisation'. Proceedings of Conference of the British Society of Research into the Learning of Mathematics, Manchester Metropolitan University, November 1993.; A full list of publications is available from the researcher.
Status: Individual research
Date of Research: 1992-1994
KEYWORDS: *educational philosophy; linguistics; mathematics education*

10/0932

Didsbury School of Education, 799 Wilmslow Road, Didsbury, Manchester M20 2RR
0161 247 2000
Gutteridge, K. Dr; Hatch, G. Mrs; Lingard, D. Mr

A case study to compare the experience of teacher training students in primary and secondary schools

Abstract: The research is a case study involving two secondary schools and four primary schools. The schools fall into two groups of one secondary and two primary schools in the same geographical area. The two geographical areas are contrasting in social type. All data on the student experience during a school practice forming part of year 3 of the B.Ed. course is being collected. A researcher will visit all six schools twice to observe classes and discuss the practice with the student. The latter will be taped. Student file entries will be collected together with school and tutor reports. The underlying purpose of the case study is to see whether it is possible to throw any light on the reasons that secondary students obtain lower gradings on school experience than primary students. This small-scale project may develop into a larger scale one if the current work shows any patterns which seem to merit a wider investigation.

Status: Sponsored project
Source of Grant: Manchester Metropolitan University
Date of Research: 1992-1993
KEYWORDS: *placement; preservice teacher education; primary schools; secondary schools; student teachers; teaching practice*

10/0933

Didsbury School of Education, 799 Wilmslow Road, Didsbury, Manchester M20 2RR
0161 247 2000
Hustler, D. Mr

Competences and teacher education: ESRC research seminar programme

Abstract: This is a research seminar group consisting of Mr D. Hustler, Manchester Metropolitan University; Professor J. Elliott, University of East Anglia; Mr D. McIntyre, Oxford University; Professor A. Pollard, University of the West of England; Professor L. Burton, Birmingham University; Professor S. Brown and Professor I. Stronach, Stirling University; Professor J. Rudduck, Sheffield

University; Professor M. Eraut, Sussex University; Ms P. Mahoney, Goldsmiths' College, London University; Professor R. Winter, Anglia Polytechnic University; Professor G. Whitty, Institute of Education, London University. The area of attention for the group is competence-based teacher education (initial and continuing). This area is established nationally through recent policy initiatives as a major area for development, but there is as yet no established network with a clear concern to enhance research development and advance theoretical understanding in this field. Research seminar meetings will be held in each of the six collaborating host universities, (Manchester Metropolitan University; Sheffield University; University of East Anglia; Stirling University; Oxford University; University of the West of England), allowing the work to draw strongly on non-academic practitioners from various regions. Each seminar will have a slightly different focus concerning research relating to competences and teacher education. The work of the group will lead to a series of seminar group papers.
Status: Sponsored project
Source of Grant: Economic and Social Research Council; British Educational Research Association; Host universities
Date of Research: 1993-1994
KEYWORDS: competency-based teacher education; educational research; teacher education

10/0934

Didsbury School of Education, 799 Wilmslow Road, Didsbury, Manchester M20 2RR
0161 247 2000
Hustler, D. Mr; Carter, K. Ms; Green, J. Ms; Halsall, R. Mr
An evaluation of 'The Recording Achievement and Higher Education Project'
Abstract: The Recording Achievement and Higher Education project is a collaborative project across 15 higher education institutions and 11 local education authorities (LEAs) and associated schools and colleges. The project is designed to investigate how best to link and coordinate initiatives within and across both institutions and sectors, as regard to recording achievement. Work focuses on admissions processes into higher education and on the role of recording achievement processes within higher education. The evaluation team have: participated in project events and activities; undertaken an extensive interviewing programme; and sampled a range of project products. The evaluation work has been designed so as to have both formative and summative outcomes. An interim evaluation report has been produced and a project statement drawing on this work is available.
Status: Sponsored project
Source of Grant: Department of Employment £10,000
Date of Research: 1992-1993
KEYWORDS: access to education; higher education; programme evaluation; records of achievement; student records

10/0935

Didsbury School of Education, 799 Wilmslow Road, Didsbury, Manchester M20 2RR
0161 247 2000
DeJonckheere, S. Ms; *Supervisor:* Rodger, R. Ms; Abbott, A. Ms
Quality care and education for children aged 0-5 in a range of educational and social service settings in one local education authority.
Abstract: The Rumbold Report (Great Britain, Department of Education and Science, Committee of Inquiry on the Under Fives (1990). Starting with quality. London: HMSO) the Children Act 1990 and HMI reports have identified criteria by which establishments for the education and care of children aged from 0-5 may be measured to ensure qualitative care and education. The broad aim of this research project is to describe, through case studies, a range of situations in which these qualitative criteria are in evidence, and the factors contributing to this situation. Three schools with nursery provision, a combined centre and a day nursery have been selected in consultation with a local authority as the focus for the research. The aspects of quality on which the research is concentrating are: a curriculum for children aged under three; curriculum for children aged 3-5; assessment procedures; roles and relationships; and home-school relations. An ethnographic methodology is being used with an emphasis on participant and non-participant observation, interviewing, diaries, and videotaping.
Published Material: RODGER, R.S. (1994). 'Subjects in the early years curriculum', European Early Childhood Education Research

Journal, Vol 2, No 1.
Status: Sponsored project
Source of Grant: Manchester Metropolitan University
Date of Research: 1992-1994
KEYWORDS: community services; day care; early childhood education; local government; nursery school curriculum; nursery schools; preschool education; young children

10/0936

Didsbury School of Education, 799 Wilmslow Road, Didsbury, Manchester M20 2RR
0161 247 2000
Johnson, P. Dr
The Book Art Project
Abstract: The Book Art Project was inaugurated by a Crafts Council grant of 400 pounds in 1986. The main aims of the project are to: (1) further the literacy development of children through the book arts; (2) encourage the interrelationship of verbal and visual modes of communication in the curriculum; (3) enhance the role of the book arts as a cross-curricular model of processing information in education; (4) increase children's awareness of the cultural heritage of the book concept and their place in that tradition. This research programme is conducted entirely by the project director and involves medium to long term school-based skills through the book arts. Results and conclusions are published periodically. Project publications include Book Pack 1 (1990). Structures and authorship; Book Pack 2 (1992). Books across the curriculum; Book Pack 3 (1993). Introducing illustration to children; INSET video (1992). Children making their own books. The Children's Press was established in 1992. The aim of the press is to encourage children to write and illustrate their own books by publishing a selection each year.
Published Material: JOHNSON, P. (1992). 'Children writing their own books', Books for Keeps, No 74, pp.4-5.; JOHNSON, P. (1992). Pop-up paper engineering: cross-curricular activities in design engineering technology, English and art. Basingstoke: Falmer Press.; JOHNSON, P. (1993). 'Literacy through the book arts'. London: Hodder & Stoughton.; JOHNSON, P. (1993). 'The Japanese connection', Language and Learning, Vol 15, No 2, pp.31-36.; JOHNSON, P. (1994). Books searching for authors. London: Hodder & Stoughton. A full list of publications is available from the researcher.
Status: Sponsored project
Source of Grant: Gulbenkian Foundation £5,000
Date of Research: 1990-continuing
KEYWORDS: books; children as writers; children's literature; literacy; picture books

10/0937

Didsbury School of Education, 799 Wilmslow Road, Didsbury, Manchester M20 2RR
0161 247 2000
Rowlands, M. Mr; Gibson, F. Mr; Heywood, D. Mr; Parker, J. Dr; Staniforth, J. Mr
Industrial and community placements for science students: an action research project
Abstract: The main aim of the project is to research the use of placements on initial teacher education courses, with particular reference to science. The project builds upon tutors' and students' experience of placements which has been established through prior involvement of the institution in the Enterprise Awareness in Teacher Education (EATE) project. This showed that a placement is a very complex learning experience with a range of variables affecting the nature and quality of the learning, such as: the background, attitudes and previous experience of both the person undertaking the placement and the people in the workplace; how the placement is organised; the relation between the placement's purpose and the students' course. The project intends to clarify appropriate foci for research, with a view to investigating particular learning outcomes common to a range of placements and identifying features which could, with some degree of success, contribute to the success of the placement. An action research approach has been used with a group of fifteen B.Ed. (Primary) students whose main subject on the degree is science. Data has been collected through diary notes of briefing and de-briefing sessions with students; recordings of interviews with a sample of students; recorded interviews with people at the workplace; questionnaire evaluations and written products of the students' work.
Status: Sponsored project
Source of Grant: Training, Enterprise and Education Directorate
Date of Research: 1992-1994

KEYWORDS: enterprise education; industrial secondments; industry education relationship; preservice teacher education; science teachers; student teachers

10/0938

Didsbury School of Education, 799 Wilmslow Road, Didsbury, Manchester M20 2RR
0161 247 2000
Archer, M. Mr; Hogbin, J. Mr; Pickard, A. Dr; Strahan, H. Ms; Palmerone, W. Ms

Supervision 'in action': a study of the process of supervision of initial teacher training students

Abstract: The aim of the project is to investigate the process of school experience supervision, in order to identify and prioritise those elements necessary for an effective scheme for induction into supervisory skills. This is a small scale pilot project focused on the supervisory practices utilised by the five research collaborators in their supervision of a group of students in training. Twenty students are participating in the project chosen at random from two different year groups. The approach fits within the tradition of ethnographic research. All transactions associated with the supervision of students including tutorials, classroom observation, discussion with students and teachers are being documented. All tutorials and supervision are being tape recorded. The research concerns are to identify the nature of the activities associated with each style of 'event' and to identify the supervisory issues associated with each. The research is essentially self-analytical in its stance seeking to identify the concerns, intentions and reflections of the supervisors engaged in the project. The intention is to produce illuminative materials that can be used, in the first instance, within the School of Education, at Manchester Metropolitan University to help induct new supervisors to their role. It is likely that the materials will have direct relevance to experienced supervisors and to mentors.

Status: Sponsored project
Source of Grant: Manchester Metropolitan University
Date of Research: 1992-1993
KEYWORDS: mentors; preservice teacher education; student teacher supervisors; supervision; supervisory methods; teaching practice

10/0939

Didsbury School of Education, 799 Wilmslow Road, Didsbury, Manchester M20 2RR
0161 247 2000
Harnor, M. Mr

Higher education students with epilepsy

Abstract: It might be possible that public attitudes and expectations concerning people with epilepsy are less likely to be negative if individuals with the condition can increasingly establish themselves in occupations requiring graduate and post-graduate qualifcations. University level institutions generally maintain that they have equal opportunities policies. This study is concerned with students' perceptions of their own epilepsy and a range of personal, social and educational consequences whilst they are in higher education. A sample of 40 students so far has been reached through advertisement. Each received a suitably designed and trialled questionnaire concerned with 38 variables and a sub-sample interviewed. Many wrote substantial correspondence highlighting the need for this research. Those who answered received a brochure previously co-written for students and institutions. The personal and idiosyncratic nature of epilepsy and its treatment makes suitable multivariant analysis difficult although this is being attempted. Examples of some of the many findings are given by: 60% of those who had initial attacks under 19 years doing so at or near key school examination dates. Of those having attacks during an examination or within 24 hours either way, 37% had references made to the examiners; 43% had initial attacks post 18 years; 41% of those in college accommodation had been given priority; 86% felt people regarded them as different; drugs worried many; 83% felt that these affected their academic performance; 77% felt the brochure would have been valuable to them.

Status: Sponsored project
Source of Grant: Manchester Metropolitan University
Date of Research: 1990-1994
KEYWORDS: epilepsy; higher education; student attitudes; student health and welfare

10/0940

Didsbury School of Education, 799 Wilmslow Road, Didsbury, Manchester M20 2RR
0161 247 2000
Hall, N. Mr; Robinson, A. Mrs

Using letter writing to develop young children's non-chronological writing

Abstract: This project aims to provide experiences in relation to socio-dramatic play situations where children are required to write letters which contain non-chronological text. The children involved will be aged 5-7. Within each project setting opportunities will be created where the writing of a particular text form will become a reasonable and natural thing to do. In each setting the researchers will provide real responders to the children's letters. These replies will aim to draw out the children in a variety of textual forms. The textual forms the project will aim to introduce to the children will be: (1) persuasive/argumentative (subsuming apologies, complaints and application); (2) procedural (subsuming directions, rules and instructions; (3) explanatory; (4) descriptive. Two principal kinds of data will be recorded: (1) Transcriptions of teaching undertaken by the teacher or project workers in respect of the textual forms. Thus any discussions or explanations will be recorded and analysed. This will be done in order to identify the most useful teaching points; (2) The letters written by the children. Each group of children's letters will be analysed for appropriate use of the correct textual form. The analysis will be primarily linguistic, looking at genre form and the children's use of register.

Status: Sponsored project
Source of Grant: Commercial Sources £14,000
Date of Research: 1993-1994
KEYWORDS: letters – correspondence; writing – composition; writing exercises; writing skills

10/0941

Didsbury School of Education, 799 Wilmslow Road, Didsbury, Manchester M20 2RR
0161 247 2000
Arthur, C. Ms; Hall, N. Mr; Robinson, A. Mrs

An investigation into the concepts of punctuation held by children between the ages of 6 and 8

Abstract: The intended research will focus on children's own observations of punctuation in the processes of reading, adding punctuation to existing text, and writing. It is hoped thereby to ascertain the children's concepts and understanding of punctuation, as much as possible, from the children's own statements. The difficulties with this are mainly to do with eliciting from children their knowledge about a subject which is of little significance to them, which they would not naturally talk about at all, which is inevitably extremely complex, and which requires a metalanguage of which children are largely ignorant or confused. In an attempt to alleviate some of these problems the experimental procedure will involve children working in pairs on one task. It is hoped that this will 'force' children to be explicit about many of the things that are normally simply thought about. The pairs of children will undertake a variety of tasks. They will: (1) read and respond to passages with and without punctuation; (2) place punctuation in an unpunctuated passage; (3) engage in free writing during which the punctuation of texts will be observed and will be discussed immediately afterwards; (4) discuss or explain in interviews their use or understanding of punctuation. The children will be selected from Year 2 classes (pre-National Curriculum assessment) and Year 3 classes (post-National Curriculum assessment). For each pair of children a set of data will be collected, allowing comparison between the results of the various tasks set, and across age groups. Analysis of the data will be in terms of the underlying linguistic strategies revealed by the children's statements, reading responses, and writing.

Status: Sponsored project
Source of Grant: Manchester Metropolitan University
Date of Research: 1992-1994
KEYWORDS: comprehension; punctuation; writing skills; written language

10/0942

Didsbury School of Education, 799 Wilmslow Road, Didsbury, Manchester M20 2RR
0161 247 2000
Rainer, J. Mr; Johnson, M. Mr; Black, M. Ms; Cockett, M. Mr

Research into ways in which drama teaching in primary schools may have an impact on general classroom learning and interpersonal behaviour

Abstract: The aims of the project are to: a) find whether drama teaching in primary schools has an effect on classroom behaviours and ethos; b) find whether such effects might be measured; c) find whether particular kinds of drama activity might have more effect than others; and d) devise an instrument which might measure (c). The project will use 8 teacher-researchers recruited from 5 primary schools across Greater Manchester/Cheshire to administer Professor B. Fraser's "My Class Inventory" – an instrument designed to quantify changes in classroom behaviour and ethos – before and after a programme of monitored drama activity. In addition, a research group will be set up with the task of designing an instrument which might quantify drama activity in order to assist more detailed classroom observation.
Status: Sponsored project
Source of Grant: Manchester Metropolitan University; Higher Education Funding Council
Date of Research: 1993-continuing
KEYWORDS: *classroom environment; classroom management; drama education; primary schools; pupil behaviour*

10/0943

Didsbury School of Education, 799 Wilmslow Road, Didsbury, Manchester M20 2RR
0161 247 2000
Wood, D. Mr; *Supervisor:* Goodwin, A. Mr; Langrish, J. Dr

Influences of increased school-based training in developing science teaching competences

Abstract: A case study of the influence of increasing school-based teacher training on the development of science student teacher competences. The project will look at a range of influencing factors on student development in one university department of education in the United Kingdom. The influence of course input, school experience (including mentoring), previous experience and peer relationships will all be explored using observation, interview, questionnaire and document analysis. A longitudinal comparison spanning the implementation period of the British government's reforms to secondary teacher training (1992), will be made by collecting data from courses throughout this period of change (2-3 years). The sample size will be approximately 70 students per year in each year of the study, which will run for 2-3 years in all. The whole course will be sampled using questionnaires, but smaller samples will be selected for interview and observation.
Status: Individual research
Date of Research: 1993-continuing
KEYWORDS: *preservice teacher education; school-based teacher education; science education; science teachers; student teachers*

10/0944

Didsbury School of Education, 799 Wilmslow Road, Didsbury, Manchester M20 2RR
0161 247 2000
Phillips, S. Ms; Campbell, A. Ms; Cockett, P. Ms

Accreditation of school-based professional development

Abstract: The research investigates a scheme to accredit school based professional development undertaken in relation to school development plans. It will consider why schools join the scheme and the intentions and expectations held by senior managers. The methods of supporting professional development coordinators in schools will be evaluated. The research will consider the perspectives of both teachers in schools and higher education teachers as to the criteria for accreditation of professional development. The project team will produce case studies of secondary, primary and special schools engaged in the scheme, making explicit the ways in which schools relate staff development plans to their school development plans. The research stage leading to the production of the case studies will take place Spring/Summer 1994. The research uses questionnaires and interviews with 20 coordinators involved in the scheme. The project should provide a real contribution to research into the continuing professional development of teachers at a time of great change in inservice education.
Status: Sponsored project
Source of Grant: Manchester Metropolitan University
Date of Research: 1993-1994
KEYWORDS: *inservice teacher education; professional development; teacher development; teaching profession*

10/0945

Didsbury School of Education, 799 Wilmslow Road, Didsbury, Manchester M20 2RR
0161 247 2000
Gutteridge, K. Dr; Edgar, B. Ms; Phillips, S. Ms

The identification of an appropriate curriculum for low attaining pupils at National Curriculum key stage 4

Abstract: This three year project will include: 1) a survey of secondary and special schools to identify any changes in curriculum provision since the introduction of the National Curriculum; review notions of 'alternative curricula' and where they are now in relation to low attaining pupils; 2) a review of the notions of 'alternative curricula' in relation to the National Curriculum; 3) an action research project involving Parklands (a special school for pupils with mild learning disabilities), a cluster of its local secondary mainstream schools, and local industry, in the development of an appropriate curriculum for poor attainers at key stage 4.
Status: Sponsored project
Source of Grant: Manchester Metropolitan University
Date of Research: 1993-continuing
KEYWORDS: *curriculum development; low achievement; moderate learning difficulties; special educational needs; underachievement*

10/0946

Didsbury School of Education, 799 Wilmslow Road, Didsbury, Manchester M20 2RR
0161 247 2000
Green, J. Ms; Hunt, M. Mr; Palmer, J. Ms; Peckett, J. Ms; Whiteley, M. Ms

Learning contracts and a record of professional development, responding to the issue of quality assurance in school based secondary initial teacher training

Abstract: The move towards more school based initial teacher education requires the underpinning principles and processes of courses to be designed by and be made explicit to a wider audience. The research takes an action approach, being set in the context of a rapidly developing secondary partnership. Its prime intention is to critically explore the potential of learning contracts and a record of professional development as a means of ensuring a higher quality student experience. A number of perspectives will be sought, e.g. the use of learning contracts within various subject areas, and evaluation of learning contracts as a means of students assessing whole school issues. The outcomes of these early foci will inform, along with much broader reference to national developments, the examination of issues surrounding the evolution of a record of professional development.
Status: Sponsored project
Source of Grant: Manchester Metropolitan University
Date of Research: 1993-1994
KEYWORDS: *performance contracts; preservice teacher education; records of achievement; school-based teacher education; student teachers; teacher development; teaching profession*

10/0947

Didsbury School of Education, 799 Wilmslow Road, Didsbury, Manchester M20 2RR
0161 247 2000
Schofield, A. Ms; *Supervisor:* Riseborough, G. Mr; Pickard, A. Dr

Mediating State educational policy in the inner city primary school

Abstract: The aim of the project is to produce a detailed ethnographic case study of a primary school in order to identify the critical factors and changing values which affect current primary education. There is, at present, little critical research of the impact of the recent extensive policy initiatives to which schools have to respond, both in terms of statutory requirements and their mediation. The research focuses on an inner city primary school in North Manchester over an identified period of time. Specific ideas, events, organisation, debate, curriculum, inservice teacher education (INSET), assessment and other 'in-house' activity will be described and analysed through their processes and outcomes in the setting of the school. The intention will be to reveal, describe and analyse the complex relationships which exist between the culture of the community, the staff, and State demands. It will attempt to explain the duality of 'in-house' demands against State policy in so doing, identify tensions and consensus of practicalities in implementation. In a primary school of 330 children and 25 staff, the issues become multi-faceted when set against a backdrop of inner city poverty and deprivation. The aim is to set a

cultural and detailed enquiry of an inner city primary school, in a wider social context, within a framework of State requirements.
Status: Individual research
Date of Research: 1993-continuing
KEYWORDS: educational change; educational legislation; educational policy; primary schools; urban schools

10/0948
Didsbury School of Education, 799 Wilmslow Road, Didsbury, Manchester M20 2RR
0161 247 2000
Macrory, G. Ms
Teaching and learning styles: the use of video to teach language acquisition
Abstract: The research will include collecting and editing video film which will be used to teach different aspects of language acquisition in a more coherent and holistic way, and to encourage more participative and analytic learning. Student responses will be evaluated, via observation, interview and/or questionnaire. The data on language acquisition collected by these means will be valuable for subsequent research into language acquisition itself.
Status: Sponsored project
Source of Grant: Manchester Metropolitan University
Date of Research: 1993-continuing
KEYWORDS: audiovisual aids; educational media; language acquisition; second language teaching; teaching methods; videodiscs

10/0949
Didsbury School of Education, 799 Wilmslow Road, Didsbury, Manchester M20 2RR
0161 247 2000
Naylor, S. Mr
An exploration of the value of cartoons as a teaching approach in science
Abstract: The research involves an evaluation of the use of cartoons in children's learning in science. The focus for the evaluation will include providing starting points for investigation, challenging children's ideas and assessing their ideas. Pupils from a wide age range (primary and secondary) will be studied. The research methods include participant observation and interviews with selected teachers, questionnaires and systematic reflection on the researcher's own practice.
Status: Sponsored project
Source of Grant: Manchester Metropolitan University
Date of Research: 1993-1994
KEYWORDS: cartoons; educational materials; science education

10/0950
Didsbury School of Education, 799 Wilmslow Road, Didsbury, Manchester M20 2RR
0161 247 2000
Andrews, P. Mr; *Supervisor:* Lockley, P. Mr; Hatch, G. Mrs; Woodrow, D. Mr
Information technology in the teaching of mathematics and the induction of trainee teachers of mathematics
Abstract: With the move to school based teacher training comes a need to identify the means by which aspects of a student teacher's entitlement may be guaranteed. This research is an attempt to explore how information technology (IT) as a means for teaching mathematics, might be made explicit to a student. The investigation is three pronged: 1) To explore teachers' perceptions of the availability of computer and calculator hardware for their teaching of mathematics. 2) To explore the attitudes towards IT and beliefs, of both teachers and Postgraduate Certificate in Education (PGCE) students, about its effectiveness as a tool for the teaching and learning of mathematics. 3) To explore teachers' use of IT as specified in the National Curriculum for mathematics in England and Wales, both statutory and non statutory. The above, coupled with a review of the research into the efficacy of IT as a tool for the teaching and learning of mathematics will provide, it is hoped, sufficient data for a model of both preservice and inservice education to be developed.
Status: Individual research
Date of Research: 1991-continuing
KEYWORDS: computer uses in education; information technology; mathematics education; preservice teacher education; student teachers; teacher attitudes

10/0951
Didsbury School of Education, 799 Wilmslow Road, Didsbury, Manchester M20 2RR
0161 247 2000
Procter, P. Mrs; Walker, K. Mr
Photography education
Abstract: The investigation focuses on developmental work in photography education over a three year period. The key features of the work are: 1) To develop awareness of photography as an art form with broad applications and relevance across all phases of education. 2) To establish working relationships with teachers, students and children and develop school and community based photography projects and initiatives. 3) To use photography and digital media to produce educational resources and teaching materials relating to the National Curriculum Orders and/or A level and inservice teacher education (INSET) needs. In collaboration with Viewpoint Photography Gallery, Salford, Oldham Art Gallery and targeted schools, a number of high profile projects will be coordinated and documented which will demonstrate the range of possibilities and the educational potential of photography in enhancing visual literacy. Central to the work will be issues of media representation, ways of broadening cultural enfranchisement, access and critical perspectives. The results of the work will be disseminated through contextualised exhibitions at a number of national venues and by CD ROM and/or video. Throughout the period of investigation a range of educational resources and publications will be produced to ensure national dissemination.
Status: Sponsored project
Source of Grant: Manchester Metropolitan University; Higher Education Funding Council; Arts Council; North West Arts Board
Date of Research: 1994-continuing
KEYWORDS: art education; photography; visual arts

10/0952
Didsbury School of Education, 799 Wilmslow Road, Didsbury, Manchester M20 2RR
0161 247 2000
Kelly, M. Mr; ApThomas, J. Mr; Naftalin, I. Ms
Matching management training and development provision to the needs of school managers
Abstract: The research aims to define components of education management competences for middle and senior managers in schools, and their possible usage in training and development programmes in higher education institutional courses, and in school development programmes.
Status: Sponsored project
Source of Grant: Manchester Metropolitan University; Higher Education Funding Council
Date of Research: 1993-1994
KEYWORDS: administrators; educational administration; head teachers; management development; management in education

10/0953
Didsbury School of Education, 799 Wilmslow Road, Didsbury, Manchester M20 2RR
0161 247 2000
Sheffield Hallam University, School of Leisure and Food Management, Totley Hall Lane, Sheffield S17 4AB
01142 720911
Hunt, P. Ms; Ludlow, M. Mrs; *Supervisor:* Woodcock, M. Miss; Rose, A. Miss
Home and health in the European Community
Abstract: The project's aim is to investigate the extent to which the education systems (for ages 5-16) within the European Community (EC) address two of the World Health Organisation's (European Region) targets 'Health for all by the year 2000'. The selected targets are: Target 11 – Accidents, and Target 22 – Food Quality and Safety. The work involves: (a) an indepth review of literature relating to the structure of education systems of all Member States; (b) an indepth review of the teacher/delivery of health education within primary and secondary schools of all Member States; (c) a questionnaire (translated into the appropriate EC languages) distributed to four primary and four secondary schools in all Member States, to be completed by teachers; (d) study visits to two countries to work more closely with cooperating schools (case study). It is hoped that the work will be of value/interest to the World Health Organisation – Copenhagen (strong links have been established), to the various ministries of education and to other professionals/persons interested in school health education. The work will be recorded in a detailed 'report'/'document'.

Status: Sponsored project
Source of Grant: All Saints Educational Trust £99,000
Date of Research: 1991-1993
KEYWORDS: *accidents; comparative education; European Community; food standards; health education; nutrition education; safety education*

10/0954
Didsbury School of Education, 799 Wilmslow Road,
Didsbury, Manchester M20 2RR
0161 247 2000
The David Lewis Centre for Epilepsy, Warford, Alderley
Edge, Cheshire SK9 7UD
01565 872613
Benham, K. Ms; Harnor, M. Mr; Brown, S. Dr
Educational statements of special educational needs in children with complex epilepsy referred to a residential special school
Abstract: The Education Act 1981, in England and Wales, with its equivalent in Scotland, requires that a child who appears to have a degree of difficulty which calls for special educational provision to be made for them, shall have an assessment of those needs made by the local education authority and, where appropriate, a 'statement' of those needs issued. The educational statements of 86 children referred to the David Lewis School as of December 1991 were researched. These emanated from 26 local education authorities throughout the UK. Complete statements were available for 54 (63%) children whilst the school had not actually been provided with the statements for 32 (37%). In 10 (19%) of the statements epilepsy was not mentioned at all. In another 20 (39%) descriptions were vague and inappropriate. A syndrome only was mentioned in 3 (6%). A sub-group of 16 children were chosen for comparison of statement contents with their teacher's personal perceptions of the children's needs. There was no significant difference. Multivariate statistical analysis of medical, educational and social data has initially failed to demonstrate any other consistent pattern. It was concluded that the medical portions of the statements, where present, were extremely unhelpful to clinicians. Educational aspects were variable but more adequate.
Status: Sponsored project
Source of Grant: Manchester Metropolitan University
Date of Research: 1991-1994
KEYWORDS: *epilepsy; special educational needs; special schools; statements – special educational needs*

10/0955
Didsbury School of Education, 799 Wilmslow Road,
Didsbury, Manchester M20 2RR
0161 247 2000
The David Lewis Centre for Epilepsy, Warford, Alderley
Edge, Cheshire SK9 7UD
01565 872613
Harnor, M. Mr; Owen, L. Ms; Brown, S. Dr
Effect of task nature, duration and difficulty upon the electroencephalograph (EEG) patterns of adolescents with generalised epilepsy monitored in their school setting
Abstract: It is a matter of concern that unrecognised subclinical seizure patterns chronically interrupt pupils' educational progress. These can only be determined by electroencephalograph (EEG). Studies suggest a relationship with task difficulty, concentration and inactivity but there is some lack of work carried out with pupils in familiar school locations rather than in clinical settings. Twenty adolescents known to show frequent generalised spike wave (s/w) discharges were selected over 6 years. Each carried out 15 minute tasks in number, plan drawing and picture colouring. Recently, where practical, 15 minute graded reading was added. Fifteen minute measured inactivity was always included. All sessions took place in the morning. Analysis was carried out initally using 8 channel ambulatory recording improving latterly to 16 channel with synchronised video. Four pupils showed no s/w during any tasks. Two were unmeasureable due to their continuous s/w density. Of the remainder, time into task generally increased the s/w count, in some this stabilised or decreased during the last 5 minutes. Individual variation was wide. (This was a population with generally idiosyncratic and problematic histories.) Inactivity was markedly evocative in individuals. Whilst laterality effects and variant analysis is being investigated, the results aim to demonstrate through illustrative sets of histograms, percentage of activity against time into task.
Status: Sponsored project
Source of Grant: Manchester Metropolitan University

Date of Research: 1986-1994
KEYWORDS: *adolescents; electroencephalograph; epilepsy; handicap identification*

10/0956
Didsbury School of Education, 799 Wilmslow Road,
Didsbury, Manchester M20 2RR
0161 247 2000
TVEI, Units 25 & 26, Greenhays Business Park, 10 Pencroft
Way, Manchester M15 6JJ
Howarth, C. Ms; *Supervisor:* Goodwin, A. Mr; Hustler, D. Mr;
Cockett, M. Mr
Student outcomes (TVEI, Manchester Compact Partnership and the Careers Service)
Abstract: The aim of the project is to seek evidence for the effects of the Manchester COMPACT partnership, Technical and Vocational Education Initiative (TVEI) and aspects of the Careers Service work as they are evident in student outcomes. The focus of the project will be on evaluating student outcomes. The outcomes will be determined and evaluated via young people's own perceptions of their schooling and of the transition to their first destination after school (post-16). It is the intention that information will be collected against a range of performance indicators, related to the following areas: (1) work-related curriculum including COMPACT; (2) teaching and learning styles; (3) transition and progression – including Records of Achievement; relevance of school to life after school; (4) careers education and guidance; and (5) equal opportunities. A sample of 402 school leavers from across the City of Manchester has been identified for the purposes of the research. A postal questionnaire has been sent to the whole sample to gather background information. Further data will be collected via semi-structured interviews with a sub-sample of approximately fifty young people. The data from the questionnaires is currently being analysed and the semi-structured interviews are due to begin in February 1993. The results will be used to inform the methodology for the second year of the project.
Status: Sponsored project
Source of Grant: Manchester TVEI Project; Manchester Metropolitan University
Date of Research: 1992-1994
KEYWORDS: *career counselling; outcomes of education; pupil attitudes; school leavers; school to work transition; transition education; TVEI; work-education relationship*

10/0957
Didsbury School of Education, 799 Wilmslow Road,
Didsbury, Manchester M20 2RR
0161 247 2000
University of Manchester Institute of Science and
Technology, PO Box 88, Sackville Street, Manchester
M60 1QD
0161 236 3311
Taylor, P. Mr; *Supervisor:* Kelly, M. Mr; ApThomas, J. Mr;
Cooper, C. Dr
The governance of primary schools: appropriate roles and relationships, perceived and actual, in the governing and managing of primary schools
Abstract: The study aims to establish appropriate action, roles and relationships for effective governance of primary schools, deriving from an investigation of existing practice. Structured interview are being used on a cross-section of headteachers, governors, parents, business people, support staff, teaching staff and support agencies (local education authority (LEA) members etc) for their views on the position as it now stands, and what they feel would be an effective way to conduct governor business. Secondly, a questionnaire will be designed and piloted on 'opportunity samples' of headteachers. The questionnaire will then be sent to a much larger sample of headteachers in at least 2 districts of Cheshire. At least 100 returns will be collected by this means. The study will use the data gathered from the interviews, questionnaires, wide ranging literature survey and industrial/commercial secondments to Marks and Spencer, Sainsbury's, Woolworth plc and the South East Cheshire Training and Enterprise Council (TEC), to develop proposals for good practice in the key areas of concern for the self-managing school (e.g. headteacher/governing body relations, alternative spheres of influence and action, development of bases for effective learning organisations, and possible codes of practice).
Status: Individual research
Date of Research: 1993-continuing

KEYWORDS: educational administration; governing bodies; primary schools; school governors

Manchester University

10/0958
>School of Education, Centre for Adult and Higher Education, Oxford Road, Manchester M13 9PL
>0161 275 2000
>Nichol, B. Dr; Davis, M. Mr; *Supervisor:* Miller, N. Dr; Ruddock, R. Mr

Group work in education project
Abstract: Originally concerned with an understanding of group dynamics within the context of inservice teacher education, the project is now examining the wider significance of this to education in a variety of contexts, including secondary schools, continuing professional education, and undergraduate and postgraduate education. The aim of the project is to deepen an understanding of the dynamic forces at work in educational settings, exploring such issues as group composition; formation; maintenance and decline; intergroup activity; leadership; power; cross-cultural communication. Drawing substantially on socio-psychological perspectives developed from the work of Kurt Lewin, the research is concerned with providing group workers with opportunities to gain access to some clearer insights into the complexities of group life. This approach is being supplemented by a more psychoanalytic perspective provided through contact with Group Analysis North, an organisation dedicated to training of group psychotherapists working under the tradition developed by S.H. Foulkes. A pilot survey exploring aspects of group life was carried out in Autumn 1993 in six English secondary schools chosen at random. Representatives of subject departments and four classes of pupils in each school completed survey instruments and results were analysed.
Status: Sponsored project
Source of Grant: Manchester University £2,000
Date of Research: 1993-continuing
KEYWORDS: group behaviour; group dynamics; group work

10/0959
>School of Education, Centre for Adult and Higher Education, Oxford Road, Manchester M13 9PL
>0161 275 2000
>Nottingham University, Department of Adult Education, Centre for Research in the Education of Adults, 14-22 Shakespeare Street, Nottingham NG1 4FJ
>01159 515151
>Stock, A. Prof.

Lifelong education as a significant cultural element in various European countries
Abstract: Lifelong education is a concept adopted by UNESCO, the European Union and numerous national departments of government world-wide. It is not, however, frequently evident in practice although there are signs of development in certain countries, together with substantial prominence in a few. The research examines the manifestations of lifelong education as cultural phenomena in each country where concentrated 'social-anthropological' fieldwork is undertaken in similar communities. The information and data will, in the final analysis, be subjected to rigorous comparative examination and an end report prepared accordingly.
Status: Individual research
Date of Research: 1991-continuing
KEYWORDS: adult education; comparative education; continuing education; cultural differences; Europe; lifelong learning

10/0960
>School of Education, Centre for Audiology, Education of the Deaf and Speech Pathology, Oxford Road, Manchester M13 9PL
>0161 275 2000
>Lynas, W. Dr

The educational management of children with Usher Syndrome
Abstract: The aim of the research is to develop sound principles for the educational management of children with Usher Syndrome. Diagnosed children and young people are observed in a variety of educational settings – special school for the deaf, unit, mainstream class, further education college and special provisions for deaf pupils/students with deteriorating vision are noted. The data collected include material from informal interviews with teaching staff and from the Usher pupils themselves. So far, 15 Usher children/young people have been observed.
Published Material: LYNAS, W. (1991). 'Deaf children with Usher Syndrome', Journal of British Association of Teachers of the Deaf, Vol 15, No 2, pp.33-39.; LYNAS, W. (1991). The educational management of children with Usher Syndrome. London: SENSE.
Status: Sponsored project
Source of Grant: National Deaf-Blind and Rubella Association (SENSE)
Date of Research: 1989-continuing
KEYWORDS: deafness; hearing impairments; special educational needs

10/0961
>School of Education, Centre for Audiology, Education of the Deaf and Speech Pathology, Oxford Road, Manchester M13 9PL
>0161 275 2000
>Aplin, D. Dr

Psychological assessment of cochlear implantees
Abstract: A cochlear implant has important psychological implications for recipients and usually has a major impact on the lives of implantees and their families. There have been relatively few reports of psychological assessment of patients from cochlear implant projects world-wide. Psychological assessment has formed an integral part of the Manchester multi-channel cochlear implant programme. Subjects are seen in order to assess their psychological suitability pre-implant and the progress of implantees is reviewed at regular intervals post-implant. Cognitive, educational, personality, anxiety and depression assessments are carried out. The aim of the research is to assess and monitor intellectual and personality profiles of implantees and to evaluate the psychosocial benefits of implantation. Investigation of the possible psychological predictors of audiological outcome for implantees will also be carried out. The subjects will be all cochlear implantees in the Manchester programme. Up to December 1994 over 70 adults (of whom 6 are deaf and blind) and 20 children have been implanted with multi-channel devices. As the project is on-going, the numbers in the research will continue to increase. In the adult programme subjects have ranged in age from 14 to 80.
Published Material: APLIN, D.Y. (1993). 'Psychological assessment of multi-channel cochlear implant patients', Journal of Laryngology and Otology, Vol 107, pp.298-304.; APLIN, D.Y. (1994). 'Psychological evaluation of adults in a cochlear implant program', American Annals of the Deaf, Vol 138, pp.415-419.
Status: Individual research
Date of Research: 1989-continuing
KEYWORDS: communication aids – for disabled; deafness; hearing aids; hearing impairments; psychological evaluation

10/0962
>School of Education, Centre for Curriculum Policy, Oxford Road, Manchester M13 9PL
>0161 275 2000
>Hodkinson, S. Mr; Atherton, M. Ms

Consumer education in the National Curriculum
Abstract: Consumer education was designated a role within non-statutory cross-curricular themes when a national curriculum was introduced in England and Wales. The research aims to assess the perceptions of local education authorities (LEAs) and primary and secondary schools as to its progress since 1989. All schools in two LEAs are being surveyed by postal questionnaire. Key questions consider the nature and extent of advisory support and inservice teacher education (INSET); the nature and extent of school staff responsibility for consumer education; the extent to which schools consider their practice to be effective; and the extent to which practice is informed by policy and development planning. Follow-up interviews in selected schools will provide case data on practice. The results will inform National Consumer Council policy.
Status: Sponsored project
Source of Grant: National Consumer Council £8,000
Date of Research: 1993-1994
KEYWORDS: consumer education; cross curricular approach; National Curriculum

10/0963

School of Education, Centre for Curriculum Policy, Oxford Road, Manchester M13 9PL
0161 275 2000
Davies, P. Mr; *Supervisor:* Hodkinson, S. Mr
The relationship between staff and curriculum development in economics and business studies
Abstract: The background to the project is the diversity and change in the curriculum profile and substance of economics and business studies in the 11-18 curriculum. It relates to the development of this subject area as a planning unit within the curriculum and provides a basis for reflection on ideas about stages in the development of a subject area. The objective is to establish the teaching commitments of staff with expertise in economics and business studies, how that expertise is being developed, and how that expertise bears upon planning decisions for school curricula. The first stage in the research was to review national (England and Wales) data available since 1980 on the teaching of economics and business studies. The second stage was a questionnaire survey of 600 schools in the north-west of England (which received a response rate of above 40%). The third stage will be interviews with economics and business studies teachers and deputy headteachers, reviewing the history of developments in that institution, their career histories, and their attribution of the causes of these developments.
Status: Individual research
Date of Research: 1993-continuing
KEYWORDS: business education; curriculum development; economics education; teacher attitudes; teacher development

10/0964

School of Education, Centre for Curriculum Policy, Oxford Road, Manchester M13 9PL
0161 275 2000
Davies, P. Mr; *Supervisor:* Hodkinson, S. Mr
Teacher assessment in geographical education
Abstract: The introduction of national curricula in England, Wales and Northern Ireland has thrust the assessment of 11-14 year olds into the limelight. Teachers have faced the job of interpreting statements of attainment which purport to describe strands of progression. The vailidity of describing geographical achievement in this way, the sense of the particular statements of attainment which have now been set in statute, and the reliability of teachers' assessments of pupils' work have each been called into question. The aim of this project is to identify how geography teachers differentiate between levels of achievement, this includes: (a) identifying procedures used; (b) isolating criteria adopted; (c) exemplifying criteria with evidence; (d) isolating changes in criteria used by teachers and relating such changes to possible influences; and (e) comparing the consistency of teachers' judgments when using the same criterion. Initial investigation will focus on the written tests for National Curriculum key stage 3 geography in England, Wales and Northern Ireland prepared by the Centre for Formative Assessment (CFAS) at the University of Manchester. The work of CFAS in developing statutory instruments for asessment at key stage 3 for England, Wales and Northern Ireland provides a valuable database of pupil responses and teachers' interpretation of mark schemes. The work of three groups of teachers will be studied over the period September 1993 to September 1995. There will be approximately one dozen teachers in each group drawn from Greater Manchester, North Wales and Northern Ireland.
Status: Individual research
Date of Research: 1993-continuing
KEYWORDS: assessment; assessment by teachers; geography education; National Curriculum

10/0965

School of Education, Centre for Educational Guidance and Special Needs, Oxford Road, Manchester M13 9PL
0161 275 2000
Davies, J. Mrs; *Supervisor:* Pumfrey, P. Prof.
The teaching and learning of reading at National Curriculum key stage 1 in six primary schools
Abstract: The aim of this project is to observe the effects of the National Curriculum on children's attainment in reading in Year 2 in six primary schools. A cross-sectional study was devised which gathered quantitative data on the cognitive and affective aspects of four cohorts of Year 2 children's reading (n=800+). One cohort (1988/89) was tested prior to the introduction of the National Curriculum; the others were tested subsequently. Data was also collected at the individual child level; parental occupation; pre-school experience; age; length of infant schooling; self-esteem and adjustment to school; as well as attitudes to school and school activities. The sample comprised all Year 2 children within six randomly selected primary schools within one local education authority. Each summer term the cohorts were tested using the following instruments: Primary Reading Test (France 1981); Mathematics 7 (NFER 1986); Self-Esteem (Lawrence 1981); Attitudes Towards School and School Activities ('Smiley' Scale, ILEA, 1988); Adjustment to School (Child at School Schedule, ILEA 1988). The standard assessment task (SAT) results for 1991 and 1992 were collected. One inter-correlational matrix will be drawn up for each of the four cohorts. The hypothesis covering the mean scores of cohorts 1, 2, 3 and 4 on each of the dependent variables will be tested using: a) a series of seven one-way anovas for each independent variable; b) a series of six two-way anovas each using cohort as one main effect: cohort x school; cohort x sex; cohort x parental occupation; cohort x pre-school experience.
Published Material: DAVIES, J. & BREMBER, I (1993). 'Comics or stories? Differences in the reading attitudes and habits of girls and boys in Years 2, 4 and 6', Gender and Education, Vol 5, No 3, pp.305-320.; DAVIES, J. & BREMBER, I. (1994).' The first standard assessment tasks at key stage 1: issues raised by a five school study', British Educational Research Journal, Vol 20, No 1, pp.35-40.; DAVIES, J. & BREMBER, I. (1994). 'The reliability and validity of the "Smiley" scale', British Educational Research Journal, Vol 20, No 4, pp.447-454.; DAVIES, J. & BREMBER, I. 'Attitudes to school and the curriculum in Year 2 and Year 4: changes over two years', Educational Review. (in press).
Status: Individual research
Date of Research: 1988-1994
KEYWORDS: achievement; National Curriculum; primary education; reading achievement

10/0966

School of Education, Centre for Educational Guidance and Special Needs, Oxford Road, Manchester M13 9PL
0161 275 2000
Mittler, P. Prof.
Access to the National Curriculum for pupils with severe and complex learning difficulties
Abstract: Starting with the 'broad, balanced and relevant' curriculum of the Education Reform Act 1988, indepth studies have been carried out with the aim of demonstrating ways in which programmes of study and cross-curricular elements can be integrated with core and foundation subjects to meet the individual needs of children with severe and complex learning difficulties. Statements of attainment for the core subjects have been broken down for key stage 1 of the National Curriculum.
Published Material: FAGG, S., AHERNE, P., SKELTON, S. & THORBURN, A. (1990). Entitlement for all in practice: towards a broad, balanced and relevant curriculum for pupils with severe and complex learning difficulties in the 1990s. London: David Fulton.; FAGG, S. & SKELTON, S. (1990). Science for All. London: David Fulton. (2nd edition, 1992).; AHERNE, P. & THORBURN, A. (1990). Mathematics for all: an interactive approach within level 1. London: David Fulton.; AHERNE, P. & THORBURN, A. (1990). Communication for all: a cross-curricular skill involving interactions between speaker and listener. London: David Fulton. (2nd edition, 1992).; MOUNT, H. & ACKERMAN, D. (1991). Technology for all. London: David Fulton.
Status: Sponsored project
Source of Grant: Manchester Education Committee (secondments)
Date of Research: 1989-1994
KEYWORDS: curriculum development; National Curriculum; severe learning difficulties; special educational needs

10/0967

School of Education, Centre for Educational Guidance and Special Needs, Oxford Road, Manchester M13 9PL
0161 275 2000
Pumfrey, P. Prof.
The concerns of young people
Abstract: This research concerns the psycho-social development of young persons aged from 11 to 18 years. The aim is to plot the changing concerns of males and females in relation to personal, educational and vocational issues. This is seen as a first step whereby young people can be helped to address their concerns in a variety of educational settings. Data are being collected from a variety of

educational establishments using a specially devised checklist covering 15 major aspects of psycho-social development. In the present phase of the study, the current version of the Concerns Checklist is deliberately lengthy. To date, checklists from 5,000 pupils have been obtained. This database is being further extended.
Status: Individual research
Date of Research: 1990-continuing
KEYWORDS: *adolescent attitudes; adolescent development; adolescents; educational attitudes; interests; personality development; social development; vocational interests*

10/0968

School of Education, Centre for Educational Guidance and Special Needs, Oxford Road, Manchester M13 9PL
0161 275 2000
Piotrowski, J. Mrs; *Supervisor:* Pumfrey, P. Prof.
Integration and responsibility for learning in mainstream primary schools
Abstract: This study is set within the theoretical framework of social learning theory. It comprises a cross-sectional study of about four hundred 6-11 year old boys and girls. Hypotheses concerning the relationships between the independent variables (year group, sex and special educational needs) and the dependent variables (locus of control, belief, self-concept and attendance) will be tested. The study will examine the implications of the results for integration policies and practices in mainstream primary schools.
Status: Individual research
Date of Research: 1991-continuing
KEYWORDS: *locus of control; mainstreaming; primary schools; self-esteem; socialisation; special educational needs*

10/0969

School of Education, Centre for Educational Guidance and Special Needs, Oxford Road, Manchester M13 9PL
0161 275 2000
Boreham, N. Prof.
Cognitive components of experience in professional diagnosis and decision making, with implications for professional education
Abstract: Task analyses are being carried out of diagnosis and decision making in selected professions. Using protocol analysis techniques, computable models of the cognitive processes involved are being constructed. Comparisons between experts and novices are being made, and the results are being used to suggest improvements in current professional education and training.
Published Material: BOREHAM, N.C. (1989). 'Modelling medical decision making under uncertainty', British Journal of Educational Psychology, Vol 59, Part 2, pp.187-199.; BOREHAM, N.C. (1987). 'Causal attributions by sensing and intuitive types during diagnostic problem solving', Instructional Science, Vol 16, pp.123-136.
Status: Individual research
Date of Research: 1987-continuing
KEYWORDS: *cognitive processes; decision making; professional education*

10/0970

School of Education, Centre for Educational Guidance and Special Needs, Oxford Road, Manchester M13 9PL
0161 275 2000
Boreham, N. Prof.
Cognitive components of expertise in professional judgement, with reference to factors influencing acquisition of the relevant cognitive skills
Abstract: The aim of this research is to analyse the knowledge and cognitive skills underpinning professional judgement, and to derive implications for higher education and continuing professional education. The fields encompassed include medical decision making, personnel management, fault finding and educational psychology. The methodology includes task analysis, skills analysis, cognitive simulation, expert-novice comparisons and learning experiments. The results point to the cognitive processes and structures crucial to cognitive skill acquisition, and lead to recommendations about teaching and learning.
Published Material: BOREHAM, N.C. (1987). 'Causal attribution by sensing and intuitive types during diagnostic problem solving', Instructional Science, Vol 16, pp.123-136.; BOREHAM, N.C. (1988). 'Models of diagnosis and their implications for adult profes-

sional education', Studies in the Education of Adults, Vol 20, pp.95-108.; BOREHAM, N.C., FOSTER, R.W. & MAWER, G.E. (1989). 'The phenytoin game: its effect on decision skills', Simulation and Games, Vol 20, pp.292-299.; BOREHAM, N.C. (1989). 'Modelling medical decision making under uncertainty', British Journal of Educational Psychology, Vol 59, No 2, pp.187-199.; BOREHAM, N.C. (1994). 'Error analysis and expert-novice differences in medical diagnosis'. In: HOC, J-M., CACCIABUE, P. & HOLLNAGEL, E. (Eds). Expertise and Technology, Chapter 7. Hillsdale, New Jersey: Erlbaum. A full list of publications is available from the researcher.
Status: Individual research
Date of Research: 1980-continuing
KEYWORDS: *cognitive processes; decision making; professional autonomy*

10/0971

School of Education, Centre for Educational Guidance and Special Needs, Oxford Road, Manchester M13 9PL
0161 275 2000
Davies, J. Mrs
The National Curriculum and children's attainments in reading and mathematics in key stage 2 in six primary schools
Abstract: The aim of this project is to observe the effects of the National Curriculum on children's attainments in reading and mathematics in Year 6 (end of key stage 2) in six primary schools. The project uses a cross-sectional study which was devised to gather quantitative data on the cognitive and affective aspects of five cohorts of Year 6 children's reading and mathematics. One cohort (1988/89) was tested prior to the introduction of the National Curriculum; the others were tested subsequently. A range of theoretically and practically important situational variables were also considered. The sample comprised all Year 6 children within six randomly selected primary schools from within one local education authority (n=1000). Each summer term the cohorts were tested using the following instruments: Primary Reading Test (France 1981); Mathematics 7 (NFER 1986); Self-Esteem (Lawrence 1981); Attitudes towards School and School Activities ('Smiley' Scale, ILEA 1988); Adjustment to School (Child at School Schedule, ILEA 1988). One intercorrelational matrix will be drawn up for each of the cohorts. The hypothesis covering the mean scores of cohorts 1, 2, 3, 4 and 5 on each of the dependent variables will be tested using: a) a series of seven one-way anovas for each independent variable; b) a series of six two-way anovas each using cohort as one main effect: cohort x school; cohort x sex; cohort x length of infant experience.
Status: Individual research
Date of Research: 1988-continuing
KEYWORDS: *achievement; mathematics education; National Curriculum; primary education; reading achievement*

10/0972

School of Education, Centre for Educational Guidance and Special Needs, Oxford Road, Manchester M13 9PL
0161 275 2000
North, T. Mr; *Supervisor:* Conti-Ramsden, G. Dr
Reading and writing numbers: specific language impaired mathematics poor and normal children
Abstract: This project was designed to investigate the abilities of specifically language impaired (SLI) and mathematics poor children to process numbers of two and three digits in various stimulus modalities (written, spoken and Dienes blocks). They were asked to represent the number in 1 of the other 2 modalities – for example they were shown written numbers and had to put out the correct Dienes blocks representation. Hence the flexibility of symbolic system processing in relation to understanding place value was tested. Subjects were selected from Years 2 and 3 of normal schools, language units, and special language schools, on the basis of their performance on tests of abstract reasoning (Raven's Coloured Matrices), reading (Young Group Reading Test) and mathematics (Young Group Mathematics Test). The experimental groups consisted of 15 SLI, 12 mathematics poor, and 15 control 'normal' children. It was hypothesised that SLI children would have more problems with tasks involving oral language, compared to the control group, but mathematics poor would have a deficit in all combinations of stimulus-response modality. A manoua did not reveal an interaction. The main effects found were that: 1) SLI and mathematics poor groups did significantly less well than the control group, and tasks involving the Dienes blocks proved more difficult than those not involving blocks. However, when only tasks involving written and oral stimulus were

analysed, it was found that there was an interaction between number of digits in the number and experimental group. The SLI and mathematics poor group scored significantly less well than the control group on 3 digit numbers only. Further research might examine whether this is a developmental delay.
Status: Sponsored project
Source of Grant: Economic and Social Research Council £25,960
Date of Research: 1992-1994
KEYWORDS: ability tests; language handicaps; learning disabilities; mathematical ability; mathematics education; numbers; special educational needs

10/0973
School of Education, Centre for Ethnic Studies in Education, Oxford Road, Manchester M13 9PL
0161 275 2000
Canterbury Christchurch College of Higher Education, North Holmes Road, Canterbury CT1 1QU
01227 767700
Verma, G. Prof.; Zec, P. Mr; Skinner, G. Mr; Gewirtz, D. Ms
Inter-ethnic relationships in secondary schools
Abstract: Concern with race relations in the wider community as well as with related issues in the education system in the UK prompted this research. It aimed to provide a portrait of relationships in nine secondary schools in terms of their organisation, structures and interactive processes. It attempted to characterise prevalent attitudes and behaviour, centring on those of the pupils and those who taught them. The study further sought to discover how inter-ethnic relationships are influenced by the policies and practices of individual schools. The research was intended to yield positive models and examples of good practice which might be of help to schools with multi-ethnic populations. The methodology was mixed, entailing multi-site case-studies, largely ethnographic in emphasis; and an overall quantitative analysis of results from a questionnaire administered to all the 2,300 Year 8 and Year 10 pupils across the 9 schools. Indepth interviews were conducted with 281 Year 8 and Year 10 pupils, and with 190 teachers (including headteachers). The findings included: 1) Teachers confessing relative ignorance of ethnic minority pupils' cultural backgrounds. 2) Lack of inservice training in relevant fields. 3) The perceived effectiveness and value of school policies on inter-ethnic relationships and multicultural/anti-racist education turned on questions of ownership, practical implementation and monitoring. 4) Curriculum and other processes seemed to correlate more closely with the quality of inter-ethnic relationships than did curriculum content. 5) The more ethnically diverse the school, the more pupils from different ethnic backgrounds mixed socially. 6) The most commonly reported subject matter of verbal abuse across the 9 schools was race or colour. Ethnic minority pupils were more likely than others to mention race, language or religion as the focus of experienced abuse; Muslims much more likely. 7) The more ethnically diverse the school, the better its inter-ethnic relationships were felt to be by pupils and teachers
Published Material: ZEC, P. (1993). 'Dealing with racial incidents in schools'. In: FYFE, A. & FIGUEROA, P. Education for cultural diversity. London: MacMillan.; VERMA, G.K., ZEC, P.M. & SKINNER, G. The ethnic crucible: harmony and discord in secondary schools. London: Falmer.
Status: Sponsored project
Source of Grant: Leverhulme Trust £65,000
Date of Research: 1990-1993
KEYWORDS: ethnic groups; ethnic relations; intergroup relations; multiculturalism; racial relations; school policy; secondary schools

10/0974
School of Education, Centre for Ethnic Studies in Education, Oxford Road, Manchester M13 9PL
0161 275 2000
Verma, G. Prof.; Darby, D. Mr; Chan, Y. Ms
The cultural identity of Chinese adolescents in Britain
Abstract: The research focuses on the cultural identities of Chinese adolescents in Britain and Hong Kong. The social background and the educational needs of those children and youngsters who may migrate to Britain will be examined in particular. The findings will be used to provide informal recommendations for educational policy and practice in schools. A variety of research techniques, including survey by questionnaires and interviews, will be used. The sample will be drawn from the Chinese community in Britain, a similar group of white British adolescents, and from secondary school pupils in Hong Kong.

Status: Sponsored project
Source of Grant: Leverhulme Trust £58,160
Date of Research: 1993-continuing
KEYWORDS: adolescents; Chinese; cultural background; ethnic groups; ethnicity; Hong Kong; migrants

10/0975
School of Education, Centre for Ethnic Studies in Education, Oxford Road, Manchester M13 9PL
0161 275 2000
Verma, G. Prof.; Skinner, G. Mr; Talbot, S. Ms
Primary schools with all pupils from Asian backgrounds
Abstract: Despite recent research into multi-ethnic schools, little is known about the processes and problems of the increasing number of primary schools with all or virtually all pupils drawn from South Asian communities. The research used a multi-site case study approach to study seven such schools in the north west of England. Half of the sample were Church of England schools. The main areas of interest were how schools were able to respond to the felt needs of the Asian communities, the implications of the National Curriculum, and the need to prepare all pupils for life in plural Britain.
Status: Sponsored project
Source of Grant: Leverhulme Trust £26,290
Date of Research: 1993-1994
KEYWORDS: ethnic groups; minority groups; multiculturalism; primary schools; voluntary schools

10/0976
School of Education, Centre for Formative Assessment Studies, Oxford Road, Manchester M13 9PL
0161 275 2000
Harrison, I. Mr; *Supervisor:* Christie, T. Prof.
Evaluation of distance learning materials and workshops for the professional development of community pharmacists
Abstract: National questionnaire surveys of the effectiveness of professional development courses offered to community pharmacists. The impact to be evaluated in terms of knowledge acquisition and skills development.
Status: Sponsored project
Source of Grant: Manchester University
Date of Research: 1991-continuing
KEYWORDS: pharmaceutical education; pharmacists; professional development

10/0977
School of Education, Centre for Formative Assessment Studies, Oxford Road, Manchester M13 9PL
0161 275 2000
Davies, P. Mr; Digby, B. Mr; Boyle, B. Mr; Schiavone, T. Mr; *Supervisor:* Christie, T. Prof.
Development of National Curriculum key stage 3 geography standard assessment tasks
Abstract: The aims of this project are: 1) The development of standard assessment tasks to national pilot stage (June 1993). 2) The development of national guidance for teacher assessment in geography (August-December 1993). 3) Change in focus of the development following amendments to the assessment arrangements for geography in March/June 1993.
Status: Sponsored project
Source of Grant: Schools Examination and Assessment Council £560,000
Date of Research: 1992-1993
KEYWORDS: assessment; assessment by teachers; attainment tests; geography education; National Curriculum; standard assessment tasks

10/0978
School of Education, Centre for Formative Assessment Studies, Oxford Road, Manchester M13 9PL
0161 275 2000
Ray, R. Dr; Boyle, B. Mr; Miller, S. Miss; Wright, Y. Miss; Davies, P. Mr; Schiavone, T. Mr; Dean, D.Mr
Development of assessment units and common assessment instruments in English; mathematics at key stage 1; science at key stage 3; and assessment units in geography at key stage 3 for the Northern Ireland Schools Assessment and Examination Council (NISEAC)

Abstract: Assessment items in English and mathematics (key stage 1) and science and geography (key stage 3) have been generated, developed into coherent units, trialled, evaluated and re-developed into subject specific assessment units or assessment instruments for use in Northern Ireland.
Status: Sponsored project
Source of Grant: Northern Ireland Schools Assessment and Examination Council £208,000
Date of Research: 1994-1994
KEYWORDS: assessment; attainment tests; English studies; geography education; mathematics education; National Curriculum – Northern Ireland; Northern Ireland; science education

10/0979
School of Education, Centre for Formative Assessment Studies, Oxford Road, Manchester M13 9PL
0161 275 2000
Harrison, I. Mr; *Supervisor:* Christie, T. Prof.
Development of assessment system for work-based projects in electrical engineering
Abstract: Research objectives are to establish the nature of the learning experience for students working in the group Enterprise Project Scheme organised by the Department of Electrical Engineering at Manchester University, and to develop appropriate assessment procedures and strategies for on-going teaching/learning.
Status: Sponsored project
Source of Grant: Enterprise in Higher Education £11,500
Date of Research: 1991-continuing
KEYWORDS: assessment; electrical engineering

10/0980
School of Education, Centre for Mathematics Education, Oxford Road, Manchester M13 9PL
0161 275 2000
Kyeleve, J. Mr; *Supervisor:* Williams, J. Dr
The evaluation of the mathematical modelling component of advanced level mathematics programmes
Abstract: The major purpose of this study is to assess the perception of the teachers and the attitudes of the learners to mathematical modelling. The study is designed to explore the classroom practices as they relate to the use of mathematical modelling materials, to identify any implementation problem (at classroom level) arising from the teachers' perception. Five sets of instruments will be used in the study: MMCEQ, SASMM, SOQ, interview and observation schedules. The result of the pilot study, using the MMCEQ and SASMM, indicated five factors measuring the construct of mathematical modelling as perceived and practised by the teachers and students. The effects of context, inservice teacher education (INSET), teaching experiences, courses offered, gender and grade level on the teachers' perception, and learners' attitudes will be examined. Interviews with the teachers will be conducted to dictate the direction of their perception and seek clarifications on issues raised about the teaching of mathematical modelling in the schools.
Status: Individual research
Date of Research: 1992-continuing
KEYWORDS: mathematical models; mathematics education

10/0981
School of Education, Centre for Mathematics Education, Oxford Road, Manchester M13 9PL
0161 275 2000
Amir, G. Mr; *Supervisor:* Williams, J. Dr
The influence of children's culture on their probabilistic thinking
Abstract: This research examines the influence of children's culture on their probabilistic thinking. In the first stage of the research thirty-eight 11-12 year old children wre interviewed. The interviews included discussion of their concepts of 'chance' and 'luck', their beliefs and attributions, their relevant experiences, and their probabilistic thinking. Interpretations of the concepts 'chance' and 'luck' were varied, often not involving randomness. Several distinct types of reasoning were identified. In some cases religious and superstitious beliefs appear to influence their inclination to use probabilistic thinking. Certain heuristics and approaches were common: the 'outcome approach'; 'representativeness'; 'availability'; the 'equiprobability bias'. Some children did not understand coins and dice as random devices. In the second stage a questionnaire was administered, in an attempt to further validate these results.

Status: Individual research
Date of Research: 1992-1994
KEYWORDS: cultural background; mathematics education; probability

10/0982
School of Education, Centre for Mathematics Education, Oxford Road, Manchester M13 9PL
0161 275 2000
Steeg, T. Mr
Technology enhancement programme
Abstract: The Technology Enhancement Programme is a curriculum development and evaluation project managed by the Engineering Council. The aims of the Programme include: linking students' learning in technology, science and mathematics; providing industrial contexts for work in school; and raising the quality of work done in technology. Materials are being written and trialled in partnership with around 100 schools nationally. All the schools are working closely with industrial partners. The materials have a vocational slant and are aimed at students in the 14 to 19 age range.
Published Material: SAGE, J. & STEEG, T.J. (1993). 'Linking the learning of mathematics, science and technology within key stage 4 of the National Curriculum'. Proceedings of the IDATER Conference, Loughborough, 1993.
Status: Sponsored project
Source of Grant: Engineering Council £123,500
Date of Research: 1991-1994
KEYWORDS: curriculum development; mathematics education; science education; technology education

10/0983
School of Education, Centre for Physical Education, Oxford Road, Manchester M13 9PL
0161 275 2000
Carroll, R. Mr
Assessment and examinations in physical education
Abstract: Since the 1970s there has been a movement in schools into physical education examinations, first with Certificate of Secondary Education (CSE), later General Certificate of Secondary Education (GCSE) and A-levels. There has also been a movement by the further education sector into vocational qualifications such as City and Guilds and BTEC, and physical education has widened into the leisure industries. In addition there have been developments such as Records of Achievement (ROA) and the National Curriculum. The aim of the research has been to monitor such developments. The research has taken the form of a number of small projects and has been accumulative rather than one major project. This information has been collected from all the examination boards on statistics and structure, and from teachers and pupils on the functioning of examinations and assessment methods. Examples of Records of Achievement have also been collected, and questionnaires and interviews carried out. The findings show the dramatic take-up of examinations in physical education. These statistics are continually updated and published. Analysis of GCSE and National Curriculum has been made to show the changes which will have to be undertaken in these examinations.
Published Material: CARROLL, R. (1990). 'Examinations and assessment in physical education'. In: ARMSTRONG, N. (Ed). New Directions in Physical Education. Human Kinetics, pp.137-160.; CARROLL, R. (1990). 'The twain shall meet: GCSE and the National Curriculum', British Journal of Physical Education, Vol 21, No 3, pp.29-32.; CARROLL, R. & JEPSON, J. (1991). 'ROA versus reports: what the pupils say', British Journal of Physical Education, Vol 22, No 2, pp.19-22.
Status: Individual research
Date of Research: 1986-continuing
KEYWORDS: assessment; examinations; physical education

10/0984
School of Education, Centre for Science and Technology Education, Oxford Road, Manchester M13 9PL
0161 275 2000
Reid, D. Prof.
Picture-text interaction in children's learning of science
Abstract: The Picture Superiority Effect (PSE) is ambiguous. What are the variables which contribute to it? The investigations are data driven and school based to optimise ecological validity. Typically

between 100 and 200 13-14 year old children are given memory recall tasks of science comprehension. Use of microcomputers has shown that PSE is enhanced when the material to be learned is present redundantly in both picture and text, the learning task is memory based, the structure of the picture is optimised in terms of those perceptual elements known to direct or attract attention and the learner is trained how to use pictures in relation to the text.
Published Material: A full list of publications is available from the researcher.
Status: Individual research
Date of Research: 1985-continuing
KEYWORDS: *memory; pictorial stimuli; science education; visual learning*

10/0985
School of Education, Centre for Science and Technology Education, Oxford Road, Manchester M13 9PL
0161 275 2000
Universiti Sains Malaysia, Pusat Pongajian, Ilmu Pendidikan, 11800 Nimden, Penang, Malaysia
Ahmed, S. Mr; *Supervisor:* Reid, D. Prof.
Teacher appraisal in Malaysia: towards a strategy
Abstract: Current trends in Malaysian secondary education are towards a national system of teacher appraisal. What has Malaysia to learn from the British model, and what features of the Malaysian teacher population demand special attention? A survey of 1,200 teachers in Malaysia is being used to determine the attitudes and opinions of secondary school teachers to appraisal. A strategy for appraisal will be developed on the basis of the survey.
Status: Individual research
Date of Research: 1989-1993
KEYWORDS: *Malaysians; secondary schools; teacher evaluation*

MENCAP National Centre

10/0986
123 Golden Lane, London EC1Y ORT
0171 454 0454
0171 962 1280
Further Education Unit, Spring Gardens, Citadel Place, Tinworth Street, London SE11 5EH
Griffiths, M. Mr; *Supervisor:* Hood, P. Ms
Post-school learning opportunities for people with profound intellectual and multiple impairments
Abstract: The aim of the project is to identify existing practice and the current perceptions of learning opportunities for adults with profound intellectual impairment who are likely to have multiple disabilities and to produce a curriculum framework for these learners. The project will use the following methods: (a) A nationwide survey by questionnaire (b) selection from the above and otherwise by a multi-disciplinary working group who will: (1) identify core learning experiences (2) generate a curriculum framework (3) produce and test learning material.
Status: Sponsored project
Source of Grant: Department of Health £12,500; Further Education Unit £12,500
Date of Research: 1991-1993
KEYWORDS: *access to education; adult basic education; adult learning; intelligence differences; multiple disabilities; severe learning difficulties*

Napier University

10/0987
Napier Business School, Department of Accounting and Law, Sighthill Court, Edinburgh EH11 4BN
0131 444 2266
Surrey University, Department of Educational Studies, Guildford GU2 5XH
01483 300800
Dyson, J. Mr; *Supervisor:* Denicolo, P. Dr; Brown, A. Dr

The relationship between accounting research and teaching
Abstract: This is an investigation into the impact accounting research has on teaching, and in particular, whether it is necessary to be an active researcher in order to be a good accounting teacher. In addition it is intended to ascertain whether the impact of research on teaching is greater at the individual or at the departmental level. The investigation is being conducted using case study material based on five Scottish universities' accounting departments
Status: Individual research
Date of Research: 1993-continuing
KEYWORDS: *accountancy education; business education; research; teaching methods*

National Children's Bureau

10/0988
8 Wakley Street, London EC1V 7QE
0171 278 9441
Grimshaw, R. Dr; *Supervisor:* Berridge, D. Dr; Sinclair, R. Dr
A comparative, evaluative study of residential special schools for children with emotional and behavioural difficulties
Abstract: This has been an 18 month research study to investigate the processes by which children are defined as having emotional and behavioural difficulties (EBD) and being in need of residential experience. This has been approached with particular regard to the overlap between education and social service responsibilities. The work analyzes the treatment methods, social and educational functioning and impact on children of a sample of residential EBD schools. The researcher has observed the schools for significant periods, noting daily activities and interviewing adults and pupils.
Published Material: GRIMSHAW, R. with BERRIDGE, D. (1994). Educating disruptive children: placement and progress in residential special schools for children with emotional and behavioural difficulties. London: National Children's Bureau.
Status: Sponsored project
Source of Grant: The Nuffield Foundation £75,000; The Healey Group and the National Children's Home
Date of Research: 1991-1994
KEYWORDS: *behaviour disorders; emotional disturbances; special educational needs; special schools*

National Foundation for Educational Research

10/0989
The Mere, Upton Park, Slough SL1 2DQ
01753 574123
Harland, J. Dr; Kinder, K. Ms; *Supervisor:* Bradley, J. Dr
Patterns of local education authority inservice education and training of teachers (INSET) organisation
Abstract: Recent changes in inservice education and training of teachers (INSET) funding arrangements have resulted in local education authorities (LEAs) adopting a wide range of strategies for the planning and delivery of professional development activities. The proposed research would map the major types and patterns of LEA INSET organisation with the intent of developing guidelines on good practice. A national survey of INSET coordinators was followed by case study work in five LEAs exhibiting different types of INSET policy and practice. The views of LEA and school staff were sought on the benefits, problems and effectiveness of the varying approaches to INSET. A report on the project was produced in 1993.
Published Material: HARLAND, J., KINDER, K. & KEYS, W. (1993). Restructuring INSET: privatization and its alternatives. Slough: National Foundation for Educational Research.
Status: Sponsored project
Source of Grant: National Foundation for Educational Research £64,000
Date of Research: 1991-1993
KEYWORDS: *educational administration; inservice teacher education; local education authorities*

10/0990

The Mere, Upton Park, Slough SL1 2DQ
01753 574123
Smith, P. Dr; *Supervisor:* Whetton, C. Mr
Development of a spatial ability handbook
Abstract: This project was developed as a response to the belief that the education process does not currently pay sufficient attention to the development and use of spatial skills. It aims to produce a handbook for those educators who want to develop the spatial thinking and capitalise on the spatial strengths of their pupils, but who are not sure how best to do so. The handbook will be in two parts. The first will describe the necessary background ideas in a non-technical way and will also include guidance on self-assessment and the role of parents and the home environment in developing spatial skills. The second part will include a wide range of teaching ideas and resource information, dealing with spatial memory, spatial thinking skills, spatial skills within specific subject areas and spatial presentation/study techniques. Some of the sub-sections within Part II have been written by external consultants.
Published Material: SMITH, P. & TRAYNELIS, J.F. (1991). 'Keeping memory in shape', Physics Education, Vol 26, No 5, pp.262.
Status: Sponsored project
Source of Grant: Macfarlane Smith Bequest £45,502
Date of Research: 1991-continuing
KEYWORDS: memory; perceptual development; spatial ability

10/0991

The Mere, Upton Park, Slough SL1 2DQ
01753 574123
Maychell, K. Ms; *Supervisor:* Bradley, J. Dr
Evaluation and monitoring at local education authority level
Abstract: This eighteen-month research project had three main aims: 1) to gather detailed information on the operation of a range of local education authority (LEA) monitoring and evaluation strategies; 2) to carry out a national survey of LEA's and schools that would provide useful information when developing evaluation and monitoring strategies; and 3) to provide practical information and guidance to assist LEA's in the future development of good practice in this area of their work. The research was nearing completion as the Education (Schools) Act 1992 was going through parliament. The report takes these changes into account and describes LEA inspection and other strategies for monitoring schools in the crucial period prior to the introduction of the Government's 'privatisation' of school inspection, i.e. the Office for Standards in Education (OFSTED) inspections. It emerged that 60% of LEA's already carried out a programme of full inspections, though the numbers of schools inspected were generally much lower than the 25% of all schools which OFSTED must inspect each year. Of the 830 schools in the survey, half had never experienced full inspection. However, most headteachers and LEA chief inspectors/advisers were in favour of introducing four-yearly formal inspections, though they were overwhelmingly against private inspection teams. Only one in ten LEA respondents and one in five headteachers felt that separating advice and inspection would be in the best interest of schools.
Published Material: MAYCHELL, K. (1993). Under inspection: LEA evaluation and monitoring. Slough: National Foundation for Educational Research.
Status: Sponsored project
Source of Grant: NFER Membership Programme
Date of Research: 1991-1993
KEYWORDS: evaluation; inspection; local education authorities; monitoring

10/0992

The Mere, Upton Park, Slough SL1 2DQ
01753 574123
Smith, P. Dr; *Supervisor:* Whetton, C. Mr
The analysis and use of spatial ability in educational contexts
Abstract: This project has developed two paper and pencil tests of spatial memory, suitable for use as educational and psychological research tools. One uses a drawing response and is scored for correctness of shapes and proportions. The other uses multiple choice then shape-arranging on a grid and is scored for correctness of shape, position and orientation. An experimental computerised test, which runs on IBM compatibles, has also been developed. Evidence has been gathered to support the U.S. research literature which suggests that spatial memory is the key component of spatial ability. Differential validity studies have been carried out with the paper and pencil

tests by testing large samples of eight, 12 and 16 year olds, then comparing their scores with performance measures in various achievement-based assessments. The tests are being prepared for publication by the NFER as research tools.
Published Material: SMITH, P. (1991). 'Spatial Ability', Topic, 5.; SMITH, P. (1992). 'Spatial ability and its role in United Kingdom education', The Vocational Aspect of Education, Vol 44, No 1, pp.103-106.
Status: Sponsored project
Source of Grant: MacFarlane Smith Bequest
Date of Research: 1989-continuing
KEYWORDS: assessment; memory; spatial ability

10/0993

The Mere, Upton Park, Slough SL1 2DQ
01753 574123
Stradling, R. Dr; MacDonald, A. Ms
Recognition and certification of transnational placements in the United Kingdom
Abstract: The European Commission's PETRA Programme (Pre-vocational Education and Training) offers opportunities to young people (aged 16-27) receiving initial vocational training to participate in a work experience or training placement in another Member State of the European Union. From the outset it was decided that participation should be assessed and successful completion should be recognised and certificated. In 1993 it was decided that a study should be conducted in each Member State to find out whether exchanges were being certificated, and whether the certificates were recognised and credited by employers and training colleges and agencies.
Status: Sponsored project
Source of Grant: European Commission: PETRA Programme £12,000
Date of Research: 1993-1994
KEYWORDS: degrees – academic; main subjects; postgraduate certificate in education; preservice teacher education

10/0994

The Mere, Upton Park, Slough SL1 2DQ
01753 574123
Taylor, M. Miss; Bagley, C. Dr; *Supervisor:* Stoney, S. Dr
Multicultural education after ERA: concerns and challenges for the 1990s
Abstract: The values underpinning the Education Reform Act 1988 (ERA) and the structures and targets set by the implementation of the National Curriculum and Local Management of Schools (LMS) raised new issues and challenges in the realisation of equal opportunities in the translation of multicultural antiracist policies into practice. This project sought to be diagnostic and responsive by establishing current concerns among local education authorities (LEAs) and identifying promising developmental strategies in relation to institutional, training and curricular issues. The research had three phases: a national questionnaire, interviews, and thematic case studies. Initially the project identified LEA concerns, constraints and challenges for multicultural antiracist education in post-ERA developments. As a result, four themes formed the focus of subsequent research: (1) the implementation of Section 11 changes; (2) Training and Enterprise Councils (TECs) and the Ethnic Minority Grant; (3) equal opportunities in governor training; (4) the issues of cultural diversity in Religious Education and the Standing Advisory Councils on Religious Education (SACREs). Research dissemination has occurred during the project and included ongoing publications, seminars, conference presentations and talks to various audiences.
Published Material: TAYLOR, M.J. (1992). Multicultural antiracist education after ERA: concerns, constraints and challenges. Slough: National Foundation for Educational Research.; TAYLOR, M.J. (1992). Equality after ERA? Slough: National Foundation for Educational Research.; TAYLOR, M.J. (1992). 'Empowering SACRE to support RE', Resource, Vol 15, No 1, pp.2-4.; BAGLEY, C.A. (1992). Back to the future: Section 11 of the Local Government Act 1966: Local education authorities and multicultural/antiracist education. Slough: National Foundation for Educational Research.; TAYLOR, M.J. & BAGLEY, C.A. (1995). 'Multicultural antiracist education – the LEA and TEC context'. In: TOMLINSON, S. & CRAFT, M. (Eds). Ethnic relations and schooling: policy and practice in the 1990s. London: Athlone Press. A full list of publications is available from the researcher.
Status: Sponsored project
Source of Grant: National Foundation for Educational Research £154,649

Date of Research: 1991-1993
KEYWORDS: antiracism education; Education Reform Act 1988; educational planning; equal education; local education authorities; multicultural education

10/0995

The Mere, Upton Park, Slough SL1 2DQ
01753 574123
Sims, D. Mr; *Supervisor:* Stoney, S. Dr

Evaluation of the Construction Industry Training Board's curriculum centre initiative

Abstract: The Construction Industry Training Board (CITB) has established 73 Curriculum Centres around the country with the aim of: (1) establishing 'construction' as a genuine context for cross-curricular learning; (2) providing practical facilities which will simulate real-work situations; and (3) providing a platform for a continuing dialogue between education and industry. The National Foundation for Educational Research was contracted to provide consultancy and devise materials for the self-evaluation of the initiative by the CITB and the Centres themselves. It also conducted periodic evaluative reviews of the self-evaluation outputs and of data collected independently by the Foundation. The evaluation proceeded in a series of phases. A preliminary phase (when a self-evaluation strategy and materials were devised) was completed in August 1991. The first phase of the main evaluation was completed in February 1992 and resulted in a report, published by the CITB, on the progress and outcomes of the initiative to date. During the remainder of 1992 further work (Phase 2) was conducted and resulted in an evaluation up-date report, a report on the employers' contribution to the initiative and an evaluation handbook. During Phase 3, in 1993, a series of evaluation workshops were organised in order to disseminate the evaluation findings and to support local self-evaluation.
Published Material: SIMS, D. & STONEY, S. (1992). The CITB curriculum centre initiative: evaluation report. Norfolk: Construction Industry Training Board/National Foundation for Educational Research.; SIMS, D. & STONEY, S. (1992). The CITB curriculum centre initiative: evaluation update report. Norfolk: Construction Industry Training Board/National Foundation for Educational Research.; SIMS, D. & STONEY, S. (1992). The CITB curriculum centre initiative: employer report. Norfolk: Construction Industry Training Board/National Foundation for Educational Research.; SIMS, D. & STONEY, S. (1992). The CITB curriculum centre initiative: evaluation handbook. Norfolk: Construction Industry Training Board/National Foundation for Educational Research.
Status: Sponsored project
Source of Grant: Construction Industry Training Board £10,680
Date of Research: 1991-1993
KEYWORDS: building trades education; construction – process; construction industry; cross curricular approach; technical education; vocational education

10/0996

The Mere, Upton Park, Slough SL1 2DQ
01753 574123
Earley, P. Mr; Kinder, K. Ms

The role of the local education authority in the professional development of new teachers

Abstract: Awareness of the potentially powerful role of local education authorities (LEAs) and schools in programmes of professional development for new teachers has been heightened following the introduction of the new training routes to Qualified Teacher Status (QTS), the proposed changes in the nature and content of initial teacher training courses and the abolition of probation. A growing number of LEAs and schools are offering induction and training programmes designed to ensure the continuing development of the professional skills and competencies currently required of new teachers, not least in the delivery of the National Curriculum. This 18-month study is employing both survey and case study research methods to investigate the role of the LEAs in the extension of initial training. It intends to analyse the professional development programmes offered to new teachers and seek perceptions of the range of professionals involved on their effects and outcomes. The main aim of the research is to contribute to the improvement of the quality of support offered to new teachers. More specifically, the research has three aims: (i) to gather a broad base of information from all LEAs on their structures and procedures for training and supporting new teachers; (ii) to collect more detailed information from selected authorities and schools on professional development programmes in practice; and (iii) to ascertain the perceptions of a wide range of providers and practitioners on the benefits, problems and overall effectiveness of the various approaches to the induction and development of new teachers. The research will begin with a series of exploratory interviews in several LEAs to gather initial perspectives from key training personnel on the main issues relating to the induction and professional development of new teachers. The material collected from these interviews, complemented by the findings from recent research studies, will be used to develop a questionnaire which will be sent to each authority. An interim report based on the questionnaire findings will be available by autumn 1992. In the next phase of the research, interviews will be held with LEA personnel to clarify and expand upon the questionnaire data. About six LEAs will then be chosen for case study investigation. In each case study location, interviews will be held with relevant LEA personnel and all documentation relating to the professional development of new teachers will be collected. A sample of schools will be selected to represent the primary and secondary sectors as well as grant-maintained schools within each LEA. The work in the schools will involve interviews with headteachers, INSET coordinators, staff with responsibility for the guidance and support of new teachers, and the new teachers themselves. It will, of course, be important to ensure that teachers following different routes to QTS are included in the sample. The particular emphasis during the case study phase will be on collecting more detailed information on the content and delivery of training and support programmes in the selected LEAs and schools, whilst also focusing on emerging issues. A final report, drawing on both the survey and case study evidence will be produced at the end of the project.
Published Material: EARLEY, P. (1992). Beyond initial teacher training: induction and the role of the LEA. Slough: National Foundation for Educational Research.; EARLEY, P. & KINDER, K. (1994). Initiation rights: effective induction practices for new teachers. Slough: National Foundation for Educational Research.; KINDER, K. & EARLEY, P. (1995). 'Key issues emerging from an NFER study of NQT's: models of induction support'. In: KERRY, T. & MAYES, A. Shelton. (Eds). Issues in mentoring. London: Routledge.; EARLEY, P. (1995). 'Beginning teachers' professional development and the objectives of induction training'. In: KERRY, T. & MAYES, A. Shelton. (Eds). Issues in mentoring. London: Routledge.
Status: Sponsored project
Source of Grant: National Foundation for Educational Research £135,000
Date of Research: 1992-1993
KEYWORDS: local education authorities; preservice teacher education; probationary teachers; teacher development; teacher education; teacher induction

10/0997

The Mere, Upton Park, Slough SL1 2DQ
01753 574123
Sainsbury, M. Dr; Underhay, S. Mrs

Standard tests in English for pupils at the end of the second key stages of the National Curriculum in 1994, 1995, 1996

Abstract: The purpose of this work is to provide assessments of individual pupils' attainments in National Curriculum English at the end of key stage 2 (Year 6, typical age of pupils, 11 years). The assessments will be made in relation to the statutory curriculum order for English. The tests will be predominantly written and timed. Developmental work leading up to the first full test of year 6 pupils in England and Wales in 1994 included a pre-test carried out in December 1992 in about 70 schools. A range of materials and approaches were tried in the pre-test, from which a selection was made for use in a national 2% pilot undertaken in May 1993. During the initial developmental stage of the work, the research team at the National Foundation for Educational Research worked intensively with teacher consultants, acting as material writers. Members of this panel reconvene in successive stages of the project to revise and adapt material. Draft materials are scrutinised by an internally appointed vetting panel, while the work as a whole is under regular supervision by the committees of the School Curriculum and Assessment Authority.
Status: Sponsored project
Source of Grant: School Examinations and Assessment Council
Date of Research: 1992-continuing
KEYWORDS: assessment; English studies; National Curriculum; reading achievement; standard assessment tasks; writing skills

10/0998

The Mere, Upton Park, Slough SL1 2DQ
01753 574123
Ashby, J. Mr; Sizmur, S. Mr; Hargreaves, E. Ms; Jones, E.
Ms; *Supervisor:* Sainsbury, M. Dr
Development of standard assessment tasks in mathematics and science for pupils at the end of the first key stage of the National Curriculum for 1994-1996
Abstract: A research team at the National Foundation for Educational Research (NFER) is developing standard assessment tasks in mathematics and science for pupils at the end of the first key stage of the National Curriculum. The tasks will provide valid, reliable assessments of attainment targets and be appropriate to seven-year-old children. Issues such as classroom manageability, comparability of judgements, bias and special educational needs will all be addressed. The tasks for each year will be monitored in operation and a commentary produced. The project will lead to the production of assessment materials to be used nationally in 1994, 1995 and 1996.
Status: Sponsored project
Source of Grant: School Curriculum and Assessment Authority
Date of Research: 1992-continuing
KEYWORDS: *assessment; mathematics achievement; National Curriculum; primary education; science education; standard assessment tasks*

10/0999

The Mere, Upton Park, Slough SL1 2DQ
01753 574123
Smith, P. Dr; *Supervisor:* Whetton, C. Mr
Standardisation of the LARR short-form test
Abstract: The project has standardised a new version of the Canadian 'Linguistic Awareness in Reading Readiness (LARR) test' for use with British children at the start of formal schooling. The new version, 'The LARR short-form', will be published by NFER-Nelson. The standardisation involved administering the test to nearly 500 nursery children and over 2,300 children in reception classes in schools throughout England and Wales during October 1992. The test was found to be too demanding for the nursery children but appropriate for the reception sample. Norms were created for the age range from 4 years 0 months to 5 years 3 months. The results, together with administration instructions and guidance on interpreting the test scores, were written for the test manual. In parallel with the national standardisation, the test was also given to all reception age pupils in Wandsworth schools as part of the Local Education Authority's baseline assessment. The National Foundation for Educational Research (NFER) then carried out a local standardisation for Wandsworth.
Published Material: 'LARR test of emergent literacy'. (1993). NFER-Nelson.
Status: Sponsored project
Source of Grant: NFER-Nelson; Wandsworth Local Education Authority
Date of Research: 1992-1993
KEYWORDS: *infant school pupils; nursery school pupils; reading; reading readiness; reception classes; tests*

10/1000

The Mere, Upton Park, Slough SL1 2DQ
01753 547123
Hagues, N. Mr; Courtenay, D. Ms
Item bank testing
Abstract: An item bank is a large collection of pre-trialled questions, a small proportion of which can be selected to construct a test to the user's specification and to a pre-determined level of difficulty. Because these tests are custom-made, the test is unique and hence a very high level of security can be guaranteed. The National Foundation for Educational Research maintains item banks in verbal reasoning, non-verbal reasoning, mathematics and English, and these have been used in recent years with pupils aged 8 to 14 for attainment testing, monitoring, screening and selection.
Date of Research: 1983-continuing
KEYWORDS: *assessment; item banks; screening tests; test items; test selection; tests*

10/1001

The Mere, Upton Park, Slough SL1 2DQ
01753 574123
Dickson, P. Mr; Lee, B. Ms; Harris, S. Mrs
Local education authority support for continuity and

progression in the 5-16 curriculum
Abstract: The introduction of the National Curriculum and associated assessment has provided a new context for the activities which have been traditionally undertaken to ensure curriculum continuity, within school and on transfer between school phases. The research aimed to investigate continuity from two different perspectives: the support provided by local education authorities (LEAs) and the measures taken at school level. Through the use of six case studies, based on 'families' of schools, and a questionnaire survey of LEAs, information was sought on: (1) strategies for promoting continuity in different LEA contexts; (2) collaboration and arrangements for transfer between school phases; and (3) methods used for promoting continuity within schools and subject areas. The findings of the research were disseminated through workshops for participants and a project report is in preparation. Two papers have been produced which are available from B. Lee, the Project Leader: 1) Issues Paper A. Teachers working together: the transfer of information and curriculum planning. 2) Issues Paper B. Arrangements for pupils: cross-phase activities.
Published Material: LEE, B., HARRIS, S. & DICKSON, P. Continuity and progression 5-16: developments in schools. Slough: National Foundation for Educational Research. (in press).
Status: Sponsored project
Source of Grant: National Foundation for Educational Research £129,359
Date of Research: 1992-1994
KEYWORDS: *curriculum development; developmental continuity; local education authorities; National Curriculum; primary secondary education; transfer pupils*

10/1002

The Mere, Upton Park, Slough SL1 2DQ
01753 574123
Mason, K. Mr; *Supervisor:* Whetton, C. Mr
Teacher assessment in the National Curriculum core subjects: Mathematics, Science and English
Abstract: In September 1989, following the Education Reform Act 1988, The National Curriculum was introduced in the core subjects of mathematics, science and English in all schools in England and Wales for the the cohort of pupils in Year 1. A year later saw the implementation of the National Curriculum in the core subjects in Year 3; the first year of key stage 2. National Curriculum assessment arrangements include teacher assessment (TA) based on pupils' classroom work over the course of each key stage, as well as statutory national assessments. Over the next two or three years, teachers of pupils at key stage 2 will be required to address a number of issues in their assessment practices, and to form and implement appropriate school policy. The broad aims of this project are to study the various facets of teacher assessment in the three National Curriculum core subjects, as carried out by teachers in key stage 1 and 2 classrooms, and to identify good practice. The particular aims are to: (1) investigate if and how teachers use cross-curricular or topic work to make assessments in more than one subject; (2) determine the purposes to which teachers put the results of their assessments; (3) examine the range of procedures for recording pupil attainment; and (4) make recommendations on the professional development of teachers in teacher assessment practices, and the role of the local education authority (LEA) in this regard. After an initial phase spent reviewing LEA and national documents on assessment, and contacting LEAs and primary schools, the project is to be carried out through a number of case studies of teachers. The case studies, which took place during the school year 1992/93, involved the observation of the classroom work of teachers of Years, 1, 2, 3, and 4. A final report is to be written in Spring 1995 which will point up good practice in teacher assessment, and make recommendations on the professional development of teachers in this area. A programme of dissemination will take place toward the end of the proect within the LEAs participating in the research.
Status: Sponsored project
Source of Grant: National Foundation for Educational Research £120,000
Date of Research: 1992-continuing
KEYWORDS: *assessment; core curriculum; English studies; mathematics education; National Curriculum; science education*

10/1003

The Mere, Upton Park, Slough SL1 2DQ
01753 574123
Stoney, S. Dr; Saunders, L. Ms; Morris, M. Miss

National evaluation of Compacts

Abstract: The Compacts initiative, funded by the Department of Employment from 1988, has had the main aim of raising the attainment of young people in education, training and work by guaranteeing a job with training for all young people aged 14 and over who meet their personal goals. Each Compact is a contract between employers, schools, colleges, training providers and young people, where each party makes a commitment to achieve agreed goals such as: (a) schools, colleges and training providers work with young people to improve levels of achievement; (b) young people make a commitment to attend school regularly and to complete their course work on time and to the best of their ability; (c) employers agree, wherever possible, to provide jobs with training, or training leading to a job, for young people who achieve their goals. There are currently over 50 Compacts in existence based in Urban Programme Authority areas in England and priority areas in Scotland and Wales. The National Foundation for Educational Research (NFER) was commissioned by the Department of Employment to carry out a national evaluation in England and Wales, the overall aim of which was to establish whether the Compacts initiative has been effective in meeting its stated objectives with respect to students, schools and employers. The evaluation is taking place over the period 1990-1994 and has a nation-wide focus. Although individual schemes are not being evaluated, most Compacts have been asked to provide information for the study in some way by assisting with one or more of the following: (a) an annual questionnaire to key decision-makers (Compact directors and Compact school staff), to collect factual information on the management and performance of Compacts; (b) a series of questionnaires to key participants (Compact students, parents, employers and training providers) to gather a range of viewpoints of the programme's impact; (c) questionnaires to students participating in Compacts during the four years to look at the longer-term outcomes of the prgramme for young people's decisions, qualifications and destinations; (d) questionnaires to non-Compact students and schools to provide comparisons. Additionally, 'case studies' in four contrasting travel to work areas were used to identify key issues and collect indepth data concerning the operational effectiveness of Compacts in different kinds of labour markets. Annual reports have been produced with a final report early in 1995.
Published Material: MORRIS, M., SCHAGEN, I. & STRADLING, B. (1992). Compact: Technical Report 1991. National evaluation of Compacts. Sheffield: Department of Employment.; SAUNDERS, L., MORRIS, M. & SCHAGEN, I. (1993). National evaluation of inner city Compacts: annual overview 1992. National evaluation of inner city Compacts. Sheffield: Department of Employment.; SAUNDERS, L., MORRIS, M. & SCHAGEN, I. (1993). Supporting students' needs through Compacts: thematic report for 1992. National evaluation of inner city Compacts. Sheffield: Department of Employment.; MORRIS, M., SAUNDERS, L. & SCHAGEN, I. (1993). The impact of Compacts 1992: annual report 1992. National evaluation of inner city Compacts. Sheffield: Department of Employment.; MORRIS, M., SAUNDERS, L. & SCHAGEN, I. (1994). Briefing paper 1. Motivation for success: a study of urban Compacts. Sheffield: Department of Employment. A full list of publications is available from the researcher.
Status: Sponsored project
Source of Grant: Department of Employment £447,633
Date of Research: 1990-1994
KEYWORDS: *cooperative education; school to work transition; vocational education; work-education relationship*

10/1004

The Mere, Upton Park, Slough SL1 2DQ
01753 574123
Jamison, J. Mr; *Supervisor:* Stradling, R. Dr

Developing European awareness: the role of local education authorities and schools in the 1990s

Abstract: As part of the preparation for the creation of a single European Market by the end of 1992, the Council of the European Community passed a resolution in May 1988 aimed at promoting and strengthening the European dimension at all levels of education. Although a growing number of local education authorities (LEAs) and schools are now taking steps to incorporate the European dimension, research evidence on established practice and new developments is still limited. The purpose of the evaluation therefore is to update and extend the database on LEA- and school-based initiatives on European Awareness, and to evaluate the impact of established LEA programmes on school practice. In addition, the project will determine how LEAs are supporting these activities. Finally, the project will identify successful practices and establish which initiatives are appropriate to different educational phases, ability ranges and school contexts. Methods employed will include a survey of all LEAs in England and Wales by questionnaire, concerning their policy documents and initiatives on European Awareness, and a national survey of primary and secondary schools regarding the incorporation of European Awareness into the curriculum. These will be accompanied by case study research in schools in selected LEAs. The research team plans to produce a written report on activities at LEA level and a handbook for schools and advisory staff with supporting materials which could be used for staff development.
Published Material: JAMISON, J. (1993). Developing European awareness: the role of local education authorities. Slough: National Foundation for Educational Research.
Status: Sponsored project
Source of Grant: National Foundation for Educational Research £100,000
Date of Research: 1993-1993
KEYWORDS: *curriculum development; European Community; European studies; local education authorities*

10/1005

The Mere, Upton Park, Slough SL1 2DQ
01753 574123
Sims, D. Mr; Harland, J. Dr; Tomlins, B. Dr; Twitchin, R. Mr; *Supervisor:* Stoney, S. Dr

Evaluation of the second year of the Training Credits pilot: three case studies

Abstract: This evaluation sought to explore any changes in attitudes, culture and practice amongst young people, school staff, careers staff, employers and training providers which may have occurred as a result of the introduction of the Training Credits (TC) pilot and since the first round of evaluations. The project focused on the extent to which the original aims of the Training Credits pilots had been achieved, how much progress had been made in overcoming difficulties identified from the first-year evaluations and making practical recommendations to assist in the further development of the pilots. The three case studies employed the following research methods: postal questionnaires, telephone and face-to-face interviews, and group discussions. The number in each questionnaire sample were as follows: Year 11 students (760), Year 12/13 students (162), young people (731 TC-users; 47 non-TC users) and training providers (75). Interviews were conducted with up to 50 operational personnel such as Training and Enterprise Councils (TECs), local education authority (LEA) and Careers Service staff and 311 employers (160 TC-users; 151 non-TC users). Broadly, findings indicate that TECs were making strenuous efforts to promote the Training Credits pilot but were finding that outcomes and impact were being seriously constrained by the current recession. The main outcomes from the project were three case-study reports and one overall national report.
Published Material: SIMS, D. & STONEY, S. (1993). Evaluation of the second year of training credits: final report. Slough: National Foundation for Educational Research.
Status: Sponsored project
Source of Grant: Department of Employment £87,064
Date of Research: 1992-1993
KEYWORDS: *credits; school to work transition; training; training and enterprise councils; vocational education; vocational guidance*

10/1006

The Mere, Upton Park, Slough SL1 2DQ
01753 574123
Ware, J. Mrs; *Supervisor:* Stoney, S. Dr

Environmental education: a directory and review of research

Abstract: In order to facilitate better communication between groups involved in research into environmental education, the National Foundation for Educational Research (NFER) has published a directory of organisations across the United Kingdom research community with experience in this area. The directory includes details such as name of organisation, address and area of interest/activity. It focuses on any research involving the teaching of 5-18 year olds, and includes details on all the environmental education research centres in the United Kingdom. The NFER is currently updating this information and a directory update will be published in April 1995.
Status: Sponsored project
Source of Grant: National Foundation for Educational Research £10,770
Date of Research: 1993-continuing

KEYWORDS: directories; educational research; environmental education

10/1007

The Mere, Upton Park, Slough SL1 2DQ
01753 574123
Christophers, U. Mrs; *Supervisor:* Stoney, S. Dr;
Whetton, C. Mr
Developing tools to measure the outcomes of guidance
Abstract: The aim of the project is to produce valid and reliable instruments for measuring the outcomes of vocational or careers guidance. Vocational guidance is increasingly seen as a requirement in a range of effective employment strategies. Guidance is one of a number of services offered through Training and Enterprise Councils and subject to systematic evaluation. Currently, methods of evaluating guidance rely on measures of customer satisfaction and/or numbers of clients seen. The new instruments are intended to provide alternative and more objective measures. The present-day theoretical formulation of careers guidance provided the starting point for this new approach. The process of guidance involves assisting clients themselves to achieve as good a match as may be possible between their interests and skills and their job aspirations, bearing in mind the opportunities open to them. An additional aim is to foster the transition skills which will stand clients in good stead in their job search now and at other times in their lives. Four areas, therefore, are frequently addressed in guidance: Opportunity Awareness; Self Awareness; Decision Making Skills; and Transition Skills. The new instrument probes the extent to which learning in these areas has occurred and how well this persists. A national trial involving 800 clients has been undertaken and norms have been established for the group of clients studied. The new instrument has been published under the title of the Measure of Guidance Impact (MGI). An additional aim of the project was to produce a diagnostic tool, which, when used during guidance, would assist workers in pinpointing a client's particular area of difficulty. This has been disseminated by the Department of Employment and is currently in use in a number of Training and Enterprise Councils. Its function is that of an induction instrument to provide both client and guidance workers with a starting point for their discussion. A further aim of the project is to examine the predictive validity of the new istrument, the MGI. Clients were followed-up after three, six and nine months to discover how the guidance affected their job search and employment/educational/training status.
Published Material: NATIONAL FOUNDATION FOR EDUCATIONAL RESEARCH IN ASSOCIATION WITH DEPARTMENT OF EMPLOYMENT (1994). Measure of guidance impact (MGI). Windsor: NFER-Nelson.
Status: Sponsored project
Source of Grant: Department of Employment £77,933
Date of Research: 1992-1994
KEYWORDS: career counselling; evaluation methods; guidance objectives; measurement techniques; vocational guidance

10/1008

The Mere, Upton Park, Slough SL1 2DQ
01753 574123
Powell, R. Mr; Lewis, G. Mr; Jones, Ll. Ms; Lewis, T. Mr
Development of standard assessment tasks in Welsh for key stage 3 of the National Curriculum
Abstract: This is an extension of the original contract for Welsh key stage 3 standard assessment tasks which ran from July 1989 to August 1991. The requirement is for the creation of standard assessment tasks to assess the range of attainment from Level 1 to Level 10 on both the Welsh and Welsh Second Language programmes contained in the Statutory Orders. Following pilots in 1991 and 1992 the first statutory assessment will be held in 1993. The standard assessment tasks comprise a long task for assessment of oracy and reading through oral response to be administered in the classroom over three months, and written tests for assessment of writing and reading through written response.
Status: Sponsored project
Source of Grant: School Examinations and Assessment Council £700,000
Date of Research: 1991-1993
KEYWORDS: assessment; attainment tests; National Curriculum; standard assessment tasks; Welsh studies

10/1009

The Mere, Upton Park, Slough SL1 2DQ
01753 574123
Taylor, M. Miss; *Supervisor:* Stoney, S. Dr
Values education in Europe
Abstract: This project, the first collaborative exercise of the Consortium of Institutes of Development and Research in Education in Europe/Values Education in Europe Programme (CIDREE/VEEP), was commissioned by United Nations Educational Scientific and Cultural Organisation (UNESCO). It had three parts: (1) To provide guidelines for Values Education in Europe (this work was undertaken by Ian Barr, Chair of CIDREE/VEEP at the Scottish Consultative Council on the Curriculum, Dundee, Scotland); (2) To provide an annotated bibliography on Values Education in Europe from 1985-1992; (3) To provide an overview of the state of the art in Values Education in Europe. (2) and (3) were coordinated and undertaken by the National Foundation for Educational Research (NFER). The objectives of the project were to coordinate and facilitate the exchange of information and to build a foundation for undertaking further collaborative projects on a European scale. Almost 30 countries participated in the bibliography (up to 20 entries per country) and survey. Values Education has different emphases and scope in the education systems of Europe and the overview sought to establish common ground, and review historical and ideological backgrounds, aims and objectives, aspects of provision, theoretical influences, current concerns, teacher training, teaching methods, curriculum development research and evaluation and aspects of informal education relating to Values Education. There are three publications, corresponding to the three aspects of the project: guidelines, annotated bibliography and overview of state of the art. These were launched by UNESCO at an international conference in Norway in September 1993.
Published Material: BARR, I. (Ed). (1994). A sense of belonging: guidelines for values for the humanistic and international dimension of education. CIDREE Vol 6. Dundee: Consortium of Institutions for Development and Research in Education in Europe/UNESCO.; TAYLOR, M. (Ed). (1994). Values education in Europe: a select annotated bibliography for 27 countries (1985-1992). CIDREE Vol 7. Dundee: Consortium of Institutions for Development and Research in Education in Europe/UNESCO.; TAYLOR, M. (Ed). (1994). Values education in Europe: a comparative overview of a survey of 26 countries in 1993. CIDREE Vol 8. Dundee: Consortium of Institutions for Development and Research in Education in Europe/UNESCO.
Status: Sponsored project
Source of Grant: UNESCO £4,500; CIDREE £1,000; National Foundation for Educational Research £2,770
Date of Research: 1992-1993
KEYWORDS: Europe; international educational exchange; values education

10/1010

The Mere, Upton Park, Slough SL1 2DQ
01753 574123
Rodrigues, S. Dr; *Supervisor:* Tabberer, R. Mr
Critical review of the use of new technologies in education
Abstract: The aim of this one-year National Foundation for Educational Research (NFER) funded project is to review critically the existing recent literature on the use of information technology (IT) in classroom learning. The review has four sections entitled: subject; resources; cognition; equity and attitudes. The review considers literature from the mid 1980s and critically reviews literature related to the use of IT in education published from 1989.
Status: Sponsored project
Source of Grant: National Foundation for Educational Research £30,000
Date of Research: 1994-continuing
KEYWORDS: computer uses in education; information technology; literature reviews

10/1011

The Mere, Upton Park, Slough SL1 2DQ
01753 574123
Weston, P. Mrs; Hutchison, D. Mr; MacDonald, A. Ms;
Lines, A. Mrs; Schagen, S. Dr; *Supervisor:* Stoney, S. Dr
Cohort study of TVEI students
Abstract: This is a major study of the impact of the Technical and Vocational Education Initiative (TVEI) sponsored by the Department

of Employment. Two cohorts of young people each of about 5,000 from over 100 schools have been surveyed annually by postal self-completion questionnaire. The older cohort were in Year 11 in 1991, the younger cohort in Year 10. Most of the schools have been involved in the TVEI Extension programme from 1989 or earlier; a small number have more recent involvement. Questionnaires cover curriculum experience 14-16, careers guidance and choices, transition from 16 onwards, post-16 education and training, qualifications at 16 and later, jobs and work experience/placements, and attitudes to their experience during these years. The study has two main aims: (1) to measure the impact of TVEI upon young people, charting their progress through the TVEI Extension and on to further education, training and work; and (2) to assess the development of the initiative as a whole. Results suggest that schools' participation in TVEI is associated with increased access 14-16 to balanced science courses, computer use, work experience and individual guidance. However, TVEI schools differ in their TVEI priorities, and young people's thinking is strongly influenced by their individual TVEI-related experience, in conjunction with ability and other individual characteristics.

Published Material: WESTON, P. (1992). TVEI cohort study of TVEI extension students 1991 survey. Experiencing TVEI extension 14-16 overview report. Sheffield: Department of Employment.; WESTON, P. (1993). Cohort study of TVEI extension students: TVEI and foundation target 4. TVEI Briefings No 5. Sheffield: Department of Employment.; MACDONALD, A. (1993). Cohort study of TVEI extension students: experiencing the world of work. TVEI Briefings No 6. Sheffield: Department of Employment.; WESTON, P. (1993). Guidance and destinations at 16. Cohort Study of TVEI Extension Students Briefings No 1. Sheffield: Department of Employment.; WESTON, P., HUTCHISON, D. & MACDONALD, A. (1994). TVEI and young people: 16 and beyond 1994 key findings report. Cohort study of TVEI extension students 1992 and 1993 surveys. London: Department of Employment.

Status: Sponsored project
Source of Grant: Department of Employment £567,791
Date of Research: 1990-1994
KEYWORDS: *cohort analysis; programme evaluation; school leavers; school to work transition; sixteen to nineteen education; TVEI*

10/1012

The Mere, Upton Park, Slough SL1 2DQ
01753 574123
Morris, M. Miss; *Supervisor:* Weston, P. Mrs
Calderdale and Kirklees TEC 'Next Step': (Education and Training Credits) 1994 evaluation programme
Abstract: The initial consultancy called for the development of an evaluation strategy for the pilot Training Credits programme developed and managed by Calderdale and Kirklees Training and Enterprise Council (TEC). NFER has since, as part of the strategy, undertaken specific elements of the evaluation, including a student cohort study (surveys in 1993 and 1994) and the impact on schools, colleges, training providers and employers. A report is available from Calderdale and Kirklees TEC.
Status: Sponsored project
Source of Grant: Calderdale and Kirklees Training and Enterprise Council
Date of Research: 1992-1994
KEYWORDS: *programme evaluation; training and enterprise councils; training credits; vocational education*

10/1013

The Mere, Upton Park, Slough SL1 2DQ
01753 574123
Fletcher-Campbell, F. Dr; Lee, B. Ms; *Supervisor:* Bradley, J. Dr
Good practice in assessment, recording and accreditation procedures used where pupils make small steps of progress in the National Curriculum
Abstract: The introduction of the National Curriculum as an entitlement for all pupils has been welcomed by many teachers of pupils with special educational needs as an opportunity to extend the range and breadth of their pupils' learning. However, some pupils with learning difficulties or disabilities may be working at levels below the programmes of study for their age, and may remain within the same levels for a number of years. Although they may be making progress, the current arrangements for assessment do not allow for these small steps to be formally recorded and accredited. As the

Dearing Report comments: "Such pupils may have made, in their own terms, significant progress, but there is no way of recognising this other than through the teacher's own daily assessment"). (Dearing, R. (1993). The National Curriculum and its assessment: final report. London: School Curriculum and Assessment Authority). The lack of formal accreditation becomes particularly acute at the end of key stage 4: as many students with significant learning difficulties will move either immediately, or within a couple of years, to some sort of further education, it is essential that any accreditation is of value not only as recognition of progress and attainment, per se, but as an accurate and valid account of these students' present position in order to inform further education staff, vocational trainers, future employers and support agencies concerned with their future progression. The research will focus on three main groups of pupils in both mainstream and special schools: those with complex learning difficulties and disabilities who may be working towards or at level 1 for more than one key stage; those working at levels 1, 2 or 3 for several years or more than one key stage; those at key stage 4 working at or below grade G at GCSE and at or below the lowest level for GNVQ. The research has five main aims: 1) To identify good practice in the assessment, recording and reporting of progress and achievement both within and outside the National Curriculum. 2) To evaluate the success of different approaches as perceived by teachers, pupils and parents. 3) To codify the essential features of good practice. 4) To recommend guidelines for developing effective practice. 5) To recommend ways in which the project outcomes can be effectively disseminated to and implemented in both mainstream and special schools and colleges. The research will be carried out in two phases. Phase one will involve a questionnaire survey of all local education authorities (LEAs) in England and Wales to obtain information on the policy and procedures in place to assess, record and accredit the progress of pupils with learning difficulties and disabilities. LEA advisers/inspectors will be asked for their views on what constitutes good ractice in this area and will be invited to nominate schools or colleges which, in their view, demonstrate some aspects of this practice. In addition, discussions will be held with Her Majesty's Inspectorate (HMI) and representatives of other interested professional bodies, to elicit nominations of examples of good practice and to obtain their contributions to the identification of the characteristics of effective models, in the same way as the questionnaire respondents. The nominations of examples of good practice will be evaluated against the criteria for identifying good practice, emerging from the research literature, previous work undertaken by the National Curriculum Council (NCC) and the School Examinations and Assessment Council (SEAC) and from the discussions with interested professionals. Following the survey, more detailed case study investigations will be conducted in a sample of approximately 25 schools and colleges, chosen from the nominations to represent a range of approaches to assessment, recording and reporting that match the initial set of criteria for good practice. In each case study location, indepth interviews will be conducted with relevant local authority personnel, school and college managers, governors, teachers, support staff, pupils/students and parents; relevant documentation will also be collected and analysed. Phase two will be a rigorous evaluation of the criteria and examples of good practice identified above and recommendations will be made on how the School Curriculum and Assessment Authority (SCAA) might best support institutions and teachers wishing to develop practice in this area. The evaluation and development of recommendations will be carried out by means of further discussions with key informants in participating LEAs and institutions and through the establishment of working groups of professionals/practitioners active in this area
Status: Sponsored project
Source of Grant: School Curriculum and Assessment Authority £122,000
Date of Research: 1994-continuing
KEYWORDS: *assessment; learning disabilities; low achievement; moderate learning difficulties; special educational needs*

10/1014

The Mere, Upton Park, Slough SL1 2DQ
01753 574123
Fletcher-Campbell, F. Dr; *Supervisor:* Bradley, J. Dr
The resourcing of provision for special educational needs
Abstract: Local Management of Schools and the opportunities offered in the Education Acts of 1988 and 1993 for schools to opt out of local authority control have brought significant changes to mechanisms for resourcing provision for pupils with special educational needs. Local authorities have been under pressure to delegate to

schools a greater proportion of the special needs budget but, having statutory responsibility for pupils with statements of special educational needs under the terms of the Education Act 1981, must nevertheless retain sufficient resources to meet the needs of these children. Authorities are still developing mechanisms by which resources for general, non-statemented special needs are allocated to ordinary schools. The very means of resource allocation have implications both by way of the costs of administering them and by way of the professional practices that they support. At the same time, many authorities are reporting an increase in the number of requests for formal assessment; such requests normally expect that the child will be issued with a statement, although this is, of course, not inevitable. The efficacy of the resourcing continuum for all degrees of need is critical in ensuring not only that a pupil is adequately supported without necessarily going through the time-consuming and costly process of statutory formal assessment but also that support may be available in the form and location which best meet the pupil's needs. The research seeks clarification on the following issues: 1) The distribution of the special education budget and the relative balance between the various budget heads (e.g. for statements, general special needs, units, special schools and training). 2) Procedures for the identification of needs and factors that determine allocations to schools. 3) The costs of allocation procedures and mechanisms, and their perceived advantages and disadvantages. 4) The profile of Local Management of Special Schools (LMSS) formulae. 5) Responses to the needs of pupils with special eductional needs who are educated within grant-maintained schools. 6) Differentials in the costs of services offered by various providers. 7) Local authorities' procedures for monitoring the use of monies nominally designated for the meeting of non-statemented special educational needs, and any money delegated for pupils with statements. 8) The way in which schools resource provision for pupils with special educational needs both by way of their own resources and external support 'bought in' under contract. The research will be undertaken in two phases. Phase one will involve a questionnaire survey of all local education authorities (LEAs) in England and Wales to ascertain actual spending on special education; the rationale for the distribution of spending under different budget heads; mechanisms for allocating resources to both ordinary and special schools; procedures for monitoring schools' use of special education funding; and any proposed changes to the current position. Telephone interviews will be undertaken with some respondents to clarify and amplify questionnaire returns. In phase two, case studies will be undertaken of about six authorities with contrasting patterns of expenditure on special education. Interviews will be conducted with relevant practitioners in ordinary and special schools, resourced schools and units, and within the primary and secondary phases; budgets and provision will be examined. Special education services within these authorities will also be studied and interviews conducted with special educational needs advisers/inspectors and officers.
Status: Sponsored project
Source of Grant: NFER Membership Programme £91,700
Date of Research: 1994-continuing
KEYWORDS: *educational administration; educational finance; local management of schools; mainstreaming; resource allocation; school-based management; special educational needs*

10/1015
The Mere, Upton Park, Slough SL1 2DQ
01753 574123
Fletcher-Campbell, F. Dr; Pathak, S. Ms
The training of care staff in residential special schools
Abstract: In England and Wales there are in excess of 300 residential schools in the maintained, non-maintained and independent sectors, providing for the whole range of special needs. Within residential special schools the contribution of the care staff complements that of the teaching staff in meeting the needs of the pupils. It is vital that the two groups of professionals work together and that there is an institutional approach to the monitoring and assessment of pupils' overall development and to meeting their often complex needs for which residential placement has been considered appropriate. There is anecdotal evidence that the training needs of care staff are currently being inadequately addressed. Both training that is provided by local education authorities for welfare or support assistants within the classroom and that provided by social services departments for care staff in residential children's homes is reported to be deficient in that it is directed towards different, albeit related, constituencies. Problems of recruitment and the high turnover of staff increase the need for basic initial training. In addition, it is arguable that existing care

staff need continuing education and training in exactly the same way as do practising teachers. The aims of this research are to: 1) gather statistical data on the number and profile of care staff within residential special schools; 2) ascertain the nature of the training needs of care staff within residential special schools; 3) quantify the short-term and long-term training needs within these schools; 4) identify the most appropriate means of provision; 5) delineate effective models of care staff training; and 6) examine the management implications of utilising staff effectively within the establishment when they have undergone training. A questionnaire will be sent to all residential special schools (maintained, independent and non-maintained) seeking information on the numbers of staff employed, their present qualifications and experience, and perceived trainin needs. This will be complemented by interviews with the heads of care and staff in a small sample of residential special schools which have particularly interesting training schemes or are representative of the common problems identified by respondents to the questionnaire. Relevant training providers will also be contacted.
Status: Sponsored project
Source of Grant: NFER Additional Activities Fund £15,000
Date of Research: 1994-continuing
KEYWORDS: *caregivers; child caregivers; residential schools; special schools; training*

10/1016
The Mere, Upton Park, Slough SL1 2DQ
01753 574123
Fletcher-Campbell, F. Dr
Links between special and ordinary schools
Abstract: This research followed up one of the strands of a research project undertaken at the National Foundation for Educational Research (NFER) from 1983-1986, namely the strand that explored links between ordinary and special schools. A questionnaire was sent to all special schools in England and Wales with the aim of identifying any sharing of pupils, staff or material resources between establishments; the sharing could be reciprocal or one-way. Telephone interviews were conducted with the schools which were the subject of detailed case studies in the earlier research project in order to ascertain how their link schemes had developed.
Published Material: FLETCHER-CAMPBELL, F. (1994). Still joining forces? A follow-up study of links between ordinary and special schools. Slough: National Foundation for Educational Research.; FLETCHER-CAMPBELL, F. (1994). 'Special links? Partners in provision?', British Journal of Special Education, Vol 21, No 3, pp.118-120.; FLETCHER-CAMPBELL, F. (1995). 'And where do you go to school?', Topic, Issue 13.
Status: Sponsored project
Source of Grant: NFER Additional Activities Fund £22,000
Date of Research: 1994-1994
KEYWORDS: *institutional cooperation; mainstreaming; special educational needs; special schools*

10/1017
The Mere, Upton Park, Slough SL1 2DQ
01753 574123
Fletcher-Campbell, F. Dr; Pathak, S. Ms; *Supervisor:* Keys, W. Dr
An analysis of the comparative costs of meeting the educational needs of pupils of different ages
Abstract: The changes in financial and curriculum management brought about by the Education Reform Act 1988 have entailed not only new mechanisms but also the adoption of new roles and responsibilities within all schools. These roles and responsibilities have, in turn, brought new needs vis-à-vis staffing, administration and material resources. It is increasingly questioned whether these needs are sufficiently different between the primary and secondary sectors as to justify considerable discrepancies between the financial resources that are allocated to schools via the Age-Weighted Pupil Units, in particular, the considerable differential that is present in many authorities' schemes when a pupil transfers to secondary school. On account of the lack of data as to what costs of educating pupils of different ages really are, the National Foundation for Educational Research (NFER) is undertaking a study of the comparative costs of meeting the educational needs of pupils of different ages. The aims of the study are to: 1) identify the resources required to deliver the National Curriculum to pupils of different ages; and 2) estimate the comparative costs of meeting the educational needs of pupils of different ages and on different courses. The research will be con-

ducted in two phases. In phase one, existing documentary evidence of relevant issues and alternative funding models which aim to address the problem will be examined. Phase two will involve a large-scale survey of schools; questionnaires will be designed to identify and quantify the resources needed to deliver the National Curriculum to pupils of different ages. The survey will be complemented by case studies in a small number of schools in order to develop and extend the findings of the survey.
Status: Sponsored project
Source of Grant: NFER Membership Programme
Date of Research: 1993-1994
KEYWORDS: *age differences; educational economics; educational finance; resource allocation*

10/1018

The Mere, Upton Park, Slough SL1 2DQ
01753 574123
Fletcher-Campbell, F. Dr; Kendall, L. Mrs; Drysdale, D. Dr;
Supervisor: Keys, W. Dr
Survey of discretionary awards provision
Abstract: The Education Act 1962 allows for two main types of award for students who wish to take a course of study in further or higher education. Mandatory awards are normally given to full-time UK students on designated courses of higher education (such as those leading to a degree or a Higher National Diploma); the Treasury reimburses local education authorities (LEAs) in full. Discretionary awards are given by LEAs from within their own budgets to students on non-designated courses of higher education, on further education courses, or to students on designated courses who do not personally qualify for mandatory awards. LEAs have a degree of flexibility, within delegated powers, as to the courses which they recognise for discretionary awards purposes and the proportion of fees and maintenance paid in each case. A number of organisations and establishments have expressed concern about the way in which the discretionary awards system is functioning. Although there is some hard data, most of the evidence is either anecdotal or piecemeal, gathered by particular interest groups or for particular types of courses. There is a lack of broadly based, systematic data. Thus the Gulbenkian Foundation and the Sir John Cass's Foundation, in collaboration with the Department for Education (DFE) and the Further Education Funding Council (FEFC), have commissioned a survey of discretionary grant-giving by LEAs in England and Wales in order to ascertain whether there are grounds for setting up an inquiry into the system. The main aims of the survey were to: 1) collect and compare statistics of English and Welsh LEA discretionary awards made in the academic years 1992/93, 1991/92 and 1990/91, and LEAs' planned budgets for 1993/94; and 2) collect qualitative information on changes in LEAs' discretionary awards policies and estimate the likely demand for discretionary awards. The study involved: a questionnaire survey, in two parts, of all LEAs in England and Wales; a review of previous research on discretionary awards and all relevant docuentation on LEAs' policies; and an interview programme with Senior Awards Officers in 17 LEAs. A report for the sponsors was submitted in July 1993.
Status: Sponsored project
Source of Grant: Gulbenkian Foundation; Sir John Cass Foundation; Department for Education; Further Education Funding Council, jointly £25,000
Date of Research: 1992-1994
KEYWORDS: *local education authorities; maintenance grants; student financial aid; tuition grants*

10/1019

The Mere, Upton Park, Slough SL1 2DQ
01753 574123
Christophers, U. Mrs; Lines, A. Mrs; Taylor, M. Miss;
Lewis, G. Mr; *Supervisor:* Stoney, S. Dr; Morris, M. Miss
The role of the Careers Service in careers education and guidance in schools
Abstract: Following on from other relevant research and the survey of 'The Work of the Careers Service in Schools and Colleges' carried out by the Careers Service Inspectorate, this project will seek to evaluate the activities, provision and procedures currently in operation in eleven careers service areas. These represent a range of geographical, socio-economic and operational contexts. The specific aims of the project are to: 1) establish the value, to schools, young people and other stakeholders, of the Careers Service involvement in schools; 2) establish the most appropriate role for Careers Service

involvement in careers education and guidance; and 3) assess the added value of Careers Service guidance practice. The research adopts a qualitative, case-study methodology and will be undertaken in two stages. In the first stage a review of recent reports on Careers Service involvement in school-based activities will lead to a position paper which highlights the issues and models for the investigations in stage two. In this latter stage, the research will be primarily field-based, collecting evaluative information on Careers Service inputs to careers education and guidance from a range of secondary schools in the eleven selected Careers Service areas. The main objective will be to obtain detailed, high quality information and views from all relevant participants, including Careers Service and school staff. In addition, information will be obtained from local education authority (LEA)/Training and Enterprise Council (TEC) personnel regarding school-based careers education and guidance provision in these areas.
Status: Sponsored project
Source of Grant: Department of Employment £79,313; Welsh Office
Date of Research: 1994-continuing
KEYWORDS: *career education; careers service; school to work transition; vocational guidance*

10/1020

The Mere, Upton Park, Slough SL1 2DQ
01753 574123
Taylor, M. Miss; *Supervisor:* Stoney, S. Dr
Values education in the UK: a directory of research and resources
Abstract: Following a seminar on The Future of Values Education held at the National Foundation for Educational Research (NFER) in 1992, which successfully brought together representatives of many of the key organisations in England concerned with aspects of values education, further sponsorship was received from the Gordon Cook Foundation and the NFER to compile a Directory of Research and Resources on Values Education in the UK. The project had two parts: 1) to provide a comprehensive directory of organisations, associations, centres, and courses involved in various aspects of values education, specifically listing their objectives, resourcing, main areas of work since 1988, current activities, longer-term agenda and providing a contact person and address. 2) to provide a comprehensive register of recent and current research and curriculum development, its location, duration, aims, objectives, methods outcomes and publications. Questionnaires were sent to organisations and individuals across the UK. The material was entered into a database and a key words index was generated. A directory of over 100 entries and a select bibliography was published by the NFER in 1994. Further developmental work has also been undertaken to establish a Values Education Council (VEC) for the UK, launched in 1995.
Published Material: TAYLOR, M. (Ed). (1994). Values education in the UK: a directory of research and resources. Slough: National Foundation for Educational Research.
Status: Sponsored project
Source of Grant: Gordon Cook Foundation; National Foundation for Educational Research
Date of Research: 1993-1994
KEYWORDS: *directories; moral education; reference materials; values education*

10/1021

The Mere, Upton Park, Slough SL1 2DQ
01753 574123
Froud, K. Ms; *Supervisor:* Stoney, S. Dr
Environmental education: teaching approaches and students' attitudes
Abstract: This project is being conducted as part of the Economic and Social Research Council's (ESRC) Global Environmental Change (GEC) programme of research. One of the central questions for the GEC programme is 'Can people be persuaded to make changes in behaviour – through reducing consumption, recycling or conserving resources?' The project will focus on the contribution which formal education, particularly in secondary schools, can make to the development of young people's awareness of the environment and environmental issues, and assess the extent to which classroom teaching has an impact on their attitudes and behaviour. The research aims to: 1) Investigate the relationship between teachers' different teaching approaches, their differing perceptions of the status of environmental education (EE) and their different attitudes towards environmental issues and students' learning outcomes. 2) Investigate the relation-

ship between the aims, objectives, content and teaching and learning styles for science, geography, technology and personal and social education (PSE) and students' attitudes towards knowledge about, understanding of, and skills relevant to, environmental education. 3) Assess Year 11 students' attitudes towards key environmental issues and explore students' views on the EE they have received at school and elsewhere and how it may or may not have affected their behaviour towards the environment. 4) Implement and critically appraise a research methodology for eliciting students' attitudes to the environment and, in particular, their behavioural pre-dispositions. 5) Elicit and discuss examples of effective inter-disciplinary strategies in secondary schools for the provision of EE, the delivery of appropriate inservice training/updating, and explore the philosophies and policies which have given rise to these practices. The project includes: a critical review of the literature on teacher and student attitudes towards EE, effective practice within the secondary sector and the out-of-school influences on young people's attitudes to the environment; a national representative survey of 500 secondary schools, gathering data from both senior managers and subject teachers providing detailed quantitative evidence on the nature and organisation of EE being delivered in seconary schools, teachers' attitudes to the environment, their training and background characteristics and their teaching strategies; case-study visits to about 40 schools involving interviewing school and LEA staff, classroom observations and discussions, and administration of an attitudinal and semi-protective test to a sample of Year 11 students which seeks to elicit students' knowledge of, and attitudes towards, environmental issues and to gauge the extent to which the EE they have received at school, and out-of-school influences have helped determine their attitudes and present behaviour towards the environment. It is anticipated that the outcomes of the project will include a critical review of the literature and a detailed report of the research findings and conclusions, accompanied by an appendix which will outline and appraise the methodological issues addressed by the project. There will also be a series of shorter papers on areas of specific interest and at least one workshop for the active dissemination of the project's outcomes.

Status: Sponsored project

Source of Grant: Economic and Social Research Council

Date of Research: 1993-continuing

KEYWORDS: *environmental education; pupil attitudes; secondary school pupils*

10/1022

   The Mere, Upton Park, Slough SL1 2DQ
   01753 574123
   Weston, P. Mrs; Tomlins, B. Dr; Ashby, P. Mrs;
   Supervisor: Stoney, S. Dr

An evaluation of the use made of action plans

Abstract: The enhancement of careers education and guidance services for both young people and adults is currently at the heart of the Government's strategies to make the education and training system in Britain more effective and responsive to developing labour market needs. The notion of individual action planning has been gaining prominence as a key strategy within effective careers education and guidance provision and the Department of Employment has now launched an evaluation project into the use of action plans. The study therefore evaluated how action plans are currently being used by different groups of clients (that is, young people and adults with action plans) in a range of contexts, and by those with a stake or interest in the outputs of the action planning process, including employers, training providers and post-16 education providers. The specific aims of the project were to establish the value to clients and stakeholders, of the careers guidance action plans (i.e. the document and the information contained in it); establish the stability of careers guidance action plans; suggest ways of increasing the value of action plans; and make recommendations for future policy and practice, based on the research findings. The research was carried out in five areas in England, Scotland and Wales over six months and the research design involved self-completion questionnaire surveys to clients and stakeholder groups, supplemented by indepth face-to-face or telephone interviews. Group discussions were held with a number of young people in school or college or undergoing training elsewhere. A comprehensive literature review was conducted drawing together relevant research and highlighting issues of concern.

Published Material: WESTON, P., STONEY, S. & ASHBY, J. (1994). A review of current literature on action planning. Evaluation of the Use of Action Plans Project. Sheffield: Department of Employment, Careers Service Quality Assurance Unit.; WESTON, P., TOMLINS, B., STONEY, S. & ASHBY, J. (1994). An evaluation of the

use made of action plans. Sheffield: Department of Employment, Careers Service Quality Assurance Unit.; WESTON, P. & TOMLINS, B. (1994). An evaluation of the use made of action plans: executive summary. Sheffield: Department of Employment, Careers Service Quality Assurance Unit.

Status: Sponsored project

Source of Grant: Department of Employment

Date of Research: 1993-1994

KEYWORDS: *career development; career education; career planning; school to work transition; vocational guidance*

10/1023

   The Mere, Upton Park, Slough SL1 2DQ
   01753 574123
   Christophers, U. Mrs; *Supervisor:* Stoney, S. Dr

Course and module evaluation through student feedback

Abstract: There has been growing momentum in recent years for institutions in all sectors of education to become more accountable and to demonstrate their effectiveness and cost efficiency. As part of this, attention is now focussing on the effectiveness of individual teachers and courses. The University of Westminster is seeking to strengthen its strategy for assessing course and module performance. The project will make a contribution to this process by designing a suitable instrument, help to mediate its introduction and implementation, and provide clear guidelines on its use. An additional aim is to examine the reliability of the new instrument and advise on the interpretation and use of aggregated results. The project has two phases. In the first phase, consultations with staff and students will take place to establish agreed dimensions on which to examine teacher effectiveness, followed by a small scale trial. Phase two will consist of a trial of the refined instrument with a larger sample of modules from different faculties within the University.

Status: Sponsored project

Source of Grant: University of Westminster £25,635

Date of Research: 1993-1994

KEYWORDS: *course evaluation; educational quality; higher education; performance indicators; quality control; student attitudes; teacher effectiveness; universities*

10/1024

   The Mere, Upton Park, Slough SL1 2DQ
   01753 574123
   Schagen, S. Dr; Simkin, C. Ms; Johnson, F. Ms; *Supervisor:* Stoney, S. Dr

The post-compulsory curriculum in schools with sixth forms

Abstract: In recent years there has been a marked increase in participation in post-compulsory education, and a growing emphasis on vocational education, culminating in the introduction of General National Vocational Qualifications (GNVQs). As a result of these and other factors, the character of school sixth forms is changing rapidly. The aim of the research is to analyse the effect of the changes and map the new patterns which are emerging. Issues to be addressed will include the implications of diversification for schools seeking to expand their sixth forms, and the impact of local education authority (LEA) discretionary awards on staying-on rates. The project will use both quantitative and qualitative methods in four overlapping phases: 1) An initial exploratory interview in a range of LEAs and schools to clarify concerns and identify the main issues. 2) A survey of LEAs, investigating current patterns of post-16 provision and support for schools. 3) A national survey of schools with sixth forms, to map the range of courses on offer, and the curriculum management issues which secondary schools are needing to address. 4) Indepth case-study research in a small number of schools, each with different characteristics and curriculum patterns. The final report will analyse the opportunities and challenges faced by schools and LEAs as a result of current developments. It will also illustrate attempts to bridge the academic/vocational divide and provide a unifying framework for post-16 study.

Status: Sponsored project

Source of Grant: National Foundation for Educational Research Membership Programme £131,805

Date of Research: 1993-continuing

KEYWORDS: *curriculum research; National Vocational Qualifications; sixteen to nineteen education; sixth form education; vocational education*

10/1025

The Mere, Upton Park, Slough SL1 2DQ
01753 574123
Schagen, S. Dr; Ratcliffe, S. Ms; *Supervisor:* Stradling, R. Dr
Evaluation of the piloting of the NatWest financial literacy programme
Abstract: NatWest Bank has piloted a financial literacy programme, offering a range of activities to schools in four regions of England. The aim of the research was to evaluate the pilot programme and see whether it was meeting its educational objectives. The evaluation was carried out principally by means of 12 case studies, selected to reflect the range of activities on offer, and a geographical spread across the four regions. Each case study involved visits to a bank branch and a linked school. Relevant bank staff, teachers and students were interviewed. There were telephone surveys of participating branches and school/business link coordinators. A report was prepared which summarised the research findings, and recommended further developments. The programme was subsequently launched nationally in September 1994.
Status: Sponsored project
Source of Grant: National Westminster Bank £18,899
Date of Research: 1993-1994
KEYWORDS: economics education; industry-education relationship; money management

10/1026

The Mere, Upton Park, Slough SL1 2DQ
01753 574123
Smith, P. Dr; *Supervisor:* Whetton, C. Mr
British Ability Scales revision
Abstract: The British Ability Scales are a battery of tests which are widely used by educational and clinical psychologists in the assessment of individuals aged from two and a half to seventeen and a half years. The scales were last standardised in 1975, though a revised set of scales was published in 1983 (BAS-R). A US adaptation of the scales was developed by the main BAS-R author, Colin Elliott, and published as the Differential Ability Scales (DAS). This project aims to up-date the BAS-R, building on the DAS developments and making further revisions. Revised scales have been trialled, and the full battery will be standardised during 1995 on a national random sample of around 3,000 individuals aged from two and a half to seventeen and a half years. Special studies will be conducted to evaluate the reliability and validity of the new battery, as will studies designed to ensure that the final battery is free from gender or ethnic bias.
Status: Sponsored project
Source of Grant: NFER-Nelson
Date of Research: 1993-continuing
KEYWORDS: ability tests; diagnostic assessment; intelligence tests; special educational needs

10/1027

The Mere, Upton Park, Slough SL1 2DQ
01753 574123
Ashby, J. Mr; *Supervisor:* Ruddock, G. Dr
Test of mathematical concepts for five year olds
Abstract: The research will produce a test of mathematics concepts for five year olds. The data from the test will be able to be used both as a baseline measure of performance and to guide the teaching programme in mathematics for each pupil. The content covered has been selected to be representative of the concepts likely to be familiar to many pupils from pre-school experience. The test is intended for administration a few weeks after the start of infant schooling.
Status: Sponsored project
Source of Grant: National Foundation for Educational Research; NFER-Nelson, jointly £59,303
Date of Research: 1993-1994
KEYWORDS: assessment; early childhood education; mathematical concepts; mathematics education; mathematics tests; school entrance age

10/1028

The Mere, Upton Park, Slough SL1 2DQ
01753 574123
Sims, D. Mr; *Supervisor:* Stoney, S. Dr
Evaluation of GNVQs in construction and the built environment
Abstract: The General National Vocational Qualification (GNVQ) in Construction and the Built Environment is being piloted during the academic year 1993-94. The GNVQ programme is broadly based and includes the learning of core skills (application of number, communication and information technology) in addition to vocational content in the form of mandatory and optional units. This qualification, which has A-level equivalency, was designed to provide an entry to the construction industry, mainly at technician level, or progression into higher education. The evaluation had two main aims: to monitor the implementation of the Construction and Built Environment GNVQ (intermediate and advanced levels) in pilot centres; and to ascertain the views of key stakeholders on the content, delivery and relevance of this GNVQ. The scope and methods of the evaluation were as follows: analysis of relevant documentation produced by the awarding bodies and the pilot centres; visits to 20 pilot centres to interview staff and students; a telephone interview survey of 100 employers and representatives of professional associations; and a questionnaire survey of 400 students. The two main outcomes from the project were an interim report, written in January 1994, and a final report, written in April 1994. The latter is available from the Construction Industry Training Board.
Status: Sponsored project
Source of Grant: Construction Industry Training Board; Department of Employment
Date of Research: 1993-1994
KEYWORDS: basic skills; building trades education; construction – process; construction industry; course evaluation; National Vocational Qualifications; technical education; vocational education

10/1029

The Mere, Upton Park, Slough SL1 2DQ
01753 574123
Jamison, J. Mr; Froud, K. Ms; Taylor, M. Miss; Johnson, F. Ms; *Supervisor:* Stradling, R. Dr
Evaluation of the European Network of Health Promoting Schools
Abstract: In 1993, the United Kingdom entered the European Network of Health Promoting Schools, a three-year developmental project in school health education. The Health Education Authority (HEA) has been designated as the UK National Support Centre. Up to 30 schools will be selected throughout the UK to be pilot schools, 15 of these in England. Pilot schools will be offered support and advice in developing initiatives and disseminating their experiences. The 15 pilot schools in England will be matched with a further 30 schools which will act as controls. The aim of the project is to strengthen the capacity of primary, secondary and special schools, both local authority and grant-maintained, to be healthy environments for living, learning and working. This research project is the formal evaluation of the Health Education Authority's European Network of Health Promoting Schools project. It will evaluate the effectiveness of different approaches to the development of health promoting schools. It aims to assess the benefits to pupils of a whole school approach to health promotion in terms of their knowledge of health issues and their behaviour. Main methods employed will be as follows: Stage 1 – a screening survey of all schools which apply for membership of the project, followed by an audit of 150 of the applicants to identify 15 pilot and 30 control schools. Stage 2 – monitoring of the pilot and control schools over two school years. Stage 3 – a final complete audit of the pilot and control schools starting in May 1996. Reporting and dissemination activities will take place throughout the project, increasing in intensity from autumn 1995.
Published Material: STRADLING, R. (1995). The health promoting school: a baseline survey. London: Health Education Authority.
Status: Sponsored project
Source of Grant: Health Education Authority
Date of Research: 1993-continuing
KEYWORDS: health education; health promotion; programme evaluation

10/1030

The Mere, Upton Park, Slough SL1 2DQ
01753 574123
Jamison, J. Mr; Sims, D. Mr; *Supervisor:* Stradling, R. Dr
Portable computers in schools pilot evaluation
Abstract: The Department for Education (DFE) asked the National Council for Educational Technology (NCET) to manage a pilot initiative to assess the curriculum potential of portable computers in

schools. The National Foundation for Educational Research (NFER) was commissioned by the NCET to carry out an independent national evaluation of this pilot initiative. The aims of the pilot were to investigate how different types of portable computers might support, enhance and extend pupils' learning in a particular curriculum area, and deliver aspects of information technology (IT) capability through a curriculum focus or a combination of curriculum areas. Projects based in English primary, secondary and special schools were selected from proposals submitted to NCET by local education authorities, initial teacher training institutions and grant-maintained schools during the spring of 1993. The summer months were used for staff training and familiarisation with the machines. The projects became fully operational in September 1993 and continued until April 1994. The NFER looked at a number of issues concerned with the use of portable computers and their impact on pupils' education, including the appropriateness of types of machines for different contexts, the benefits of using portables in varying numbers, the impact of using portables on pupils' learning and the key factors affecting the use of portables in school-based teacher training. The project was also intended to be forward-looking as it will consider the potential use of portable computers beyond the timescale of the pilot. Thirty schools were selected for case study. The main elements of the research design in the thirty schools comprised interviews with staff, observation of lessons and activities, the collection of more detailed information using log books compiled by teachers, and short pupil questionnaires. This data was supplemented in 8-10 schools by more detailed pupil-focused work. Project coordinators in all institutions were asked to complete questionnaires towrds the end of the pilot. A final report, written for a wide, non-specialist audience, was submitted to NCET by 30 April 1994.
Published Material: STRADLING, R., SIMS, D. & JAMISON, J. (1994). Portable Computers Pilot Evaluation Report: Executive Summary. Coventry: National Council for Educational Technology.
Status: Sponsored project
Source of Grant: National Council for Educational Technology
Date of Research: 1993-1994
KEYWORDS: computer uses in education; curriculum development; information technology; microcomputers

10/1031
> The Mere, Upton Park, Slough SL1 2DQ
> 01753 574123
> Brooks, G. Dr; *Supervisor:* Foxman, D. Mr

Reading standards in Northern Ireland
Abstract: The Department of Education in Northern Ireland (DENI) commissioned surveys of the reading standards of pupils in Northern Ireland aged 8, 11, 14 and 16, and these were carried out in 1993. The aims of the study were to establish the feasibility of monitoring levels of performance through such surveys, and to estimate the level of reading attainment of the four age groups studied. A subsidiary aim was to provide results which could be compared with those of previous surveys. Representative random samples of schools, and of pupils within schools, were drawn. The pupils were asked to attempt tests appropriate to their age, and in some cases also to take tests appropriate to their age, and in some cases also to take tests primarily intended for pupils of adjacent ages involved in the study. All the tests had been used in previous surveys. The 118 schools which participated returned 3978 tests on behalf of 1353 pupils. The tests were marked by highly experienced Northern Ireland teachers, and they provided largely favourable comments on the process. The main findings were: Girls' results were on average higher than boys'. Pupils not receiving free school meals achieved higher mean scores than those receiving free school meals. Pupils in inner-city schools tended to have lower mean scores than those in schools in other locations. The attainment of Protestant pupils was in general higher than that of Catholic pupils. The results showed satisfactory progress in reading between ages 8 and 11, and between ages 11 and 14. Progress between ages 14 and 16 was masked by ceiling effects on the tests, but did show up in the scores for particular questions. Comparisons with previous surveys suggested that attainment of Northern Irish pupils in 1993 was broadly similar to that of pupils of the same ages in England and Wales in 1991 (age 8) or in England, Wales and Northern Ireland in 1988 (ages 11 and 16). This was also suggested by the patterns of performance on questions of different levels of difficulty. (There had been no pevious surveys at age 14).
Published Material: BROOKS, G., FERNANDES, C., GORMAN, T. & WELLS, I. (1995). Reading standards in Northern Ireland revisited. Slough: National Foundation for Educational Research.
Status: Sponsored project

Source of Grant: Department of Education for Northern Ireland £48,066
Date of Research: 1993-1994
KEYWORDS: Northern Ireland; reading ability; reading research

10/1032
> The Mere, Upton Park, Slough SL1 2DQ
> 0753 574123
> Jamison, J. Mr; Johnson, F. Ms; Ratcliffe, S. Ms; *Supervisor:* Stradling, R. Dr

Parental needs as regards sex education
Abstract: The context for sex education work in schools in England has recently changed. In July 1993 the Government accepted an amendment to the Education Reform Act 1988 which had the effect of removing elements of teaching about human sexual behaviour and about human immunodeficiency virus (HIV) and acquired immune deficiency syndrome (AIDS) from the National Curriculum statutory orders for Science at key stage 3. Amongst other changes, the amendment establishes a parental right to withdraw children from those aspects of sex education which are not part of the National Curriculum. The National Foundation for Educational Research (NFER) was commissioned by the Health Education Authority (HEA) to undertake a survey of parents' views regarding the current provision of sex education in schools, what they think should be provided by the schools and what they see as their own roles. The HEA also wished to find out what kind of support might best assist parents in talking to their own children about sexual and related issues. The main aims of the research were twofold. Firstly, to identify what schools are offering in terms of sex education and what is being provided by parents. Secondly, to look at ways in which parents can be supported to work with schools and to talk about HIV and AIDS and other sexual health issues with their own children. Fifty of the schools which took part in a survey of school health education policies, conducted by the NFER for the HEA in 1992, were selected to take part in this project. Methods employed included: a questionnaire survey of the provision of sex education in those schools; interviews with key members of staff; a questionnaire survey of parents of pupils in all 4 key stages; and a follow-up survey of a sample of parents by telephone interview. A report was submitted to the HEA in May 1994. Key findings and recommendations were presented both in the main body of the report and in the form of specific learning points for relevant groups – teachers, other professionals and parents groups.
Published Material: JAMISON, J., JOHNSON, F., RATCLIFFE, S. & STRADLING, R. Parental needs as regards children's sex education. London: Health Education Authority. (in press).; JAMISON, J., JOHNSON, F., RATCLIFFE, S. & STRADLING, R. (1995). Parents, schools and sex education. Sex Education Matters: A Quarterly Newsletter of the Sex Education Forum. London: Sex Education Forum.
Status: Sponsored project
Source of Grant: Health Education Authority
Date of Research: 1993-1994
KEYWORDS: health education; parent attitudes; sex education

10/1033
> The Mere, Upton Park, Slough SL1 2DQ
> 01753 574123
> Lewis, G. Mr

Setting effective papers (differentiation) in Welsh and Welsh second language at key stage 4
Abstract: The project aimed to establish what questions and elements of papers, and which papers were most effective at differentiating pupils' performance at three ability range points – high, low and medium. Pupils' scores at these points were analysed, as were scripts, the respective mark schemes, and papers. Chief examiners were interviewed regarding best practice in setting papers.
Status: Sponsored project
Source of Grant: School Curriculum and Assessment Authority £19,000
Date of Research: 1993-1993
KEYWORDS: assessment; attainment tests; differential performance; second language learning

10/1034
> The Mere, Upton Park, Slough SL1 2DQ
> 01753 574123
> Hutchison, D. Mr; Schagen, I. Dr

Reliability and related characteristics of adaptive testing in the context of National Curriculum assessment

Abstract: This project is a follow-up of previous research which looked at measuring the reliability of National Curriculum assessment. The main emphasis of the new project is on the effect of the adaptive system currently used for key stage 1. Areas of interest include the effect of the adaptive system on reliability and efficiency of the assessment; the influence of 'out-of-level' items on the outcome; and the effects of variations in the starting level. Research has mainly been carried out using IRT-type models and simulations. With some investigation of the validity of the one-dimensional assumptions behind such models, other topics investigated include estimating item facilities for adaptive tests and computing reliabilities for aggregation systems based on total scores.
Published Material: HUTCHISON, D. & SCHAGEN, I. (Eds.) (1994). 'How reliable is National Curriculum assessment?'. Proceedings of the Symposium at BERA, 1993. Slough: National Foundation for Educational Research.; HUTCHISON, D. & SCHAGEN, I. 'Measuring the reliability of National Curriculum assessment', Educational Research. (in press).
Status: Sponsored project
Source of Grant: Economic and Social Research Council
Date of Research: 1933-1994
KEYWORDS: *adaptive testing; assessment; attainment tests; computer-assisted testing; National Curriculum; test validity*

10/1035

The Mere, Upton Park, Slough SL1 2DQ
01753 574123
Saunders, L. Ms; Schagen, I. Dr; Gallacher, S. Dr;
Supervisor: Stradling, R. Dr
Quantitative analysis for self-evaluation (QUASE)
Abstract: There is a perceived need for rigorous school self-evaluation, particularly in judging year-on-year performance on a range of outcome measures. For the purposes of self-evaluation, outcome measures need to be analysed in a way which takes into account the school context, the ability range of pupils and the 'value added' by the school over time; and are also flexible enough to measure the progress made by individual departments, year teams, etc. The National Foundation for Educational Research (NFER) has been developing a responsive package which will help schools to evaluate their own performance relative to the kind of students they have and to other key factors – in other words, a 'value added' approach' to judging achievements. The study has piloted an approach which: 1) utilises data already being collected for statutory purposes; 2) collects data felt by participating schools to be relevant in judging educational performance; 3) takes into account appropriate school/student input measures; 4) is sensitive enough to provide information at departmental/year group level. A limited sample of secondary schools participated in a feasibility study whose activities included: 1) developing appropriate ways of publicising the service to schools; 2) refining appropriate data collection instruments, including student intake measures; 3) generating a multi-level model for establishing appropriate norms against which schools and departments within schools can compare their own performance; and 4) identifying the most useful forms of feedback and follow-up for participants. The feasibility study has led to the setting up of a service to all secondary schools in England and Wales, operational from Autumn 1994.
Published Material: SCHAGEN, I. & SAUNDERS, L. (1994). 'Developing a system for school self-evaluation based on quantitative data'. Paper presented at the Annual Conference of the British Educational Research Association, Oxford, September 8-11.
Status: Sponsored project
Source of Grant: National Foundation for Educational Research £20,000; Participating schools and LEAs subscriptions
Date of Research: 1994-continuing
KEYWORDS: *educational quality; evaluation criteria; institutional evaluation; performance indicators; school effectiveness*

10/1036

The Mere, Upton Park, Slough SL1 2DQ
01753 574123
Sharp, C. Ms; *Supervisor:* Bradley, J. Dr
Evaluative reviews of alcohol research 1983-1992: alcohol education for young people
Abstract: The review aimed to present the findings from English language studies of alcohol education published between 1983 and 1992, and to identify any gaps in the literature as a guide to future research. There have been three broad shifts in approaches to alcohol education in the past three decades. Informational programmes were common in the 1960's. In the 1970's 'affective' approaches enhanced self-esteem and developed students' social skills. The 'social influences' approach in use since the mid 1980's has focused on resisting external influences to drink. Results and conclusions of the review include: 1) Factors found to be related to alcohol use in adolescence concern: the family; the personality; the peer group; and the sociocultural environment. 2) Evaluations of alcohol and drug education have found that it is easier to improve knowledge than to affect attitudes. Behavioural change is the most difficult to accomplish. 3) Social influences approaches to alcohol education have not generally proved effective in impacting on adolescent alcohol use. The fact that this approach has shown more promising results for tobacco and other drugs suggests that the relative social acceptability of alcohol may be a strong factor which cannot be easily overcome through education. 4) There is a need for more research in the UK. Large-scale, longitudinal studies of new approaches are needed, which consider the impact of programmes for different groups of participants. There is also a need for qualitative studies, particularly of peer group influence in alcohol and substance use.
Published Material: SHARP, C. (1994). Alcohol education for young people: a review of the literature 1983-1992. Slough: National Foundation for Educational Research.
Status: Sponsored project
Source of Grant: Alcohol Education and Research Council; Portman Group
Date of Research: 1993-1993
KEYWORDS: *alcohol education; drinking; health education*

10/1037

The Mere, Upton Park, Slough SL1 2DQ
01753 574123
Maychell, K. Ms; *Supervisor:* Bradley, J. Dr
Youth service provision
Abstract: The purpose of this research is to gather information that will be of use to all those working in the youth service as they plan for the future. At a time of rapid and far-reaching changes in local authorities the youth service stands at a cross-roads. It needs to be prepared with detailed information on the types of provision that have been successful in achieving positive learning outcomes for young people and that have received high rates of take-up. Phase 1 will involve a short questionnaire to all local authority Principal Youth Officers (or equivalent) seeking basic information on their policy and provision. Phase 2 will comprise interviews with the Principal Youth Officer in 15 local authorities to extend the information obtained in the questionnaire. Phase 3 will involve detailed case-studies of five local authorities. These will include interviews with all policy-makers and practioners (local authority and voluntary) as well as a sample of young people in each area. A final report will be published in summer 1995. It will provide detailed information on current youth service policy, provision, management and types of initiative that are popular and achieve positive learning outcomes.
Status: Sponsored project
Source of Grant: National Foundation for Educational Research
Date of Research: 1994-continuing
KEYWORDS: *local education authorities; voluntary service; youth leaders; youth service*

10/1038

The Mere, Upton Park, Slough SL1 2DQ
01753 574123
Maychell, K. Ms; Pathak, S. Ms; *Supervisor:* Keys, W. Dr
The impact of Local Management of Schools (LMS) on schools' patterns of expenditure
Abstract: One of the most important aspects of the Education Reform Act 1988 was the introduction of Local Management of Schools (LMS). The initiative, which was phased in between 1989 and 1994, withdrew the responsibility for managing school budgets from local education authorities (LEAs) and delegated this to school governing bodies. By increasing schools' autonomy in this way, the Government believed that it would make better use of available resources, make schools more responsive to the needs of pupils, parents and the community, and thus improve the quality of the education schools provide. This project had three main aims: 1) To identify the criteria which schools use to establish their financial priorities. 2) To discover the impact of LMS on schools' patterns of spending. 3) To provide practical information that would be of use to schools in managing

their own budgets. Phase 1 involved a questionnaire survey of a nationally representative sample of approximately 1,000 primary and secondary schools in England and Wales that sought information on their spending patterns. Phase 2 comprised case studies in seven schools. These involved interviews with headteachers, financial staff employed by the school, school governors and teachers. Aspects on which information was sought included: the use of school development plans in determining budget priorities; governor involvement in budget setting; internal monitoring and quality assurance; organisation of staffing and the impact of LMS has had on this; and any measures to take account of special circumstances relating to the school's intake or locality.

Published Material: MAYCHELL, K. (1994). Counting the cost: the impact of LMS on schools' patterns of spending. Slough: National Foundation for Educational Research.; MAYCHELL, K. (1994). Counting the cost: the impact of LMS on schools' patterns of spending. Summary of main findings for survey respondents. Slough: National Foundation for Educational Research.
Status: Sponsored project
Source of Grant: National Foundation for Educational Research
Date of Research: 1993-1994
KEYWORDS: budgeting; educational administration; educational finance; local management of schools; school-based management

10/1039

The Mere, Upton Park, Slough SL1 2DQ
01753 574123
Earley, P. Mr; *Supervisor:* Bradley, J. Dr; Keys, W. Dr
The effectiveness of school governing bodies since the Education Reform Act 1988
Abstract: The main aims of the project were to: 1) ascertain how effectively school governing bodies are fulfilling the responsibilities devolved to them as a result of the Education Reform Act 1988; 2) seek information on governors' own perceptions of their roles and responsibilities; 3) identify the most important training needs of governors; 4) seek information on any other ways in which local education authorities (LEAs) could help school governing bodies to fufil their roles more effectively. The issues addressed by the study included: the composition of school governing bodies; level of turnover of governors; arrangements and support for meetings; school governors' and Chairs' workloads; the training governors have received to date and their perceived training needs for the future; and their perceptions of their roles and responsibilities. The research began with a series of exploratory interviews with relevant personnel to explore issues of current concern. The material collected from these interviews, complemented by recent research studies, was used to develop a questionnaire. The questionnaire, after piloting, was sent to a representative sample of schools for completion by headteachers, Chairs of governing bodies and individual governors. In the next phase, a small number of schools were selected for more intensive study involving interviews with headteachers, governors, teachers and parents.
Published Material: EARLEY, P. (1994). 'Governor matters', Governors' Action, No 32, pp.2-3.; EARLEY, P. (1994). 'Room for improvement', Managing Schools Today, Vol 4, No 2, pp. 6 & 8.; EARLEY, P. (1994). School governing bodies: making progress? Slough: National Foundation for Educational Research.
Status: Sponsored project
Source of Grant: National Foundation for Educational Research Membership Programme £70,000
Date of Research: 1993-1994
KEYWORDS: educational administration; local management of schools; school-based management; school governing bodies; school governors

10/1040

The Mere, Upton Park, Slough SL1 2DQ
01753 574123
Keys, W. Dr; Harris, S. Mrs
The Third International Mathematics and Science Study (TIMSS)
Abstract: Research organisations in about 50 other countries are collaborating to carry out the Third International Mathematics and Science Study (TIMSS). TIMSS, which is coordinated by the International Association for the Evaluation of Educational Achievement (IEA) is intended to identify variations from country to country in: 1) pupils' knowledge and understanding of mathematics and science; 2) pupils' and teachers' attitudes towards these subjects; 3) mathematics and science curricula; 4) teaching conditions and practices.

The TIMSS study in England is being carried out in two stages. The first stage, which began in 1993 and finished in November 1994, consisted of pilot studies of the tests and questionnaires and a small-scale field trial. Its purpose was to develop internationally agreed versions of the tests and questionnaires. The next stage of the research, the main study, will consist of a large-scale study of about 9,000 nine year olds in about 150 primary schools and about 5,000 thirteen year olds in about 150 secondary schools in England. The main study will take place during the first half of 1995 at the same time as similar studies in other countries. The pupils taking part in the study will complete tests of mathematics and science and a brief questionnaire focusing on their learning experiences and attitudes. Questionnaires will also be completed by teachers and schools. One of the main outcomes of the study will be an international report comparing mathematics and science achievement in different countries. This will be complemented by a national report commenting on the results of the study from a national perspective. The project team is keen to provide information about TIMSS. Schools taking part in the study will receive a TIMSS newsletter once a term for the duration of the project. Articles outlining the purpose of the study and what it involves have already been published in a number of journals.
Published Material: (1994). 'How do our children compare', NFER News, No 61, p.1.; HARRIS, S. (1994). 'The Third International Mathematics and Science Study', Mathematics in School, Vol 23, No 5, pp.34-35.; HARRIS, S. (1994). 'TIMSS – an international study in mathematics and science', Mathematics Teaching, Vol 149, pp.30-31.; HARRIS, S. (1994). 'The Third International Mathematics and Science Study', Primary Science Review, No 34, pp.25-26.; KEYS, W. (1994). 'Admissible evidence', Junior Education, Vol 18, No 10, pp.16-17.
Status: Sponsored project
Source of Grant: Department for Education £400,000
Date of Research: 1993-continuing
KEYWORDS: comparative education; mathematics education; science education

10/1041

The Mere, Upton Park, Slough SL1 2DQ
01753 574123
Harris, S. Mrs; *Supervisor:* Keys, W. Dr
Analysis of schools' information technology policies
Abstract: A number of primary and secondary schools sent copies of their current information technology (IT) policies to the National Foundation for Educational Research (NFER) during a project which investigated the use of software in schools, and which was carried out on behalf of the National Council for Educational Technology (NCET). A short study was therefore set up to analyse the content of the schools' IT policies. A total of 24 primary and 53 secondary schools' IT policies were available for analysis. The analysis was carried out in four stages: 1) An initial examination of all the policies in order to identify the range of contents. 2) The contents were grouped into main categories with sub-sections to provide a series of codes. 3) The IT policies were re-examined and coded according to content. 4) Details of each policy's content were recorded on a database and the analysis was then carried out.
Published Material: HARRIS, S. (1994). Schools' IT policies. Slough: National Foundation for Educational Research.
Status: Sponsored project
Source of Grant: National Foundation for Educational Research
Date of Research: 1994-1994
KEYWORDS: computer uses in education; information technology; school policy

10/1042

The Mere, Upton Park, Slough SL1 2DQ
01753 574123
Harris, S. Mrs; *Supervisor:* Keys, W. Dr
A comparison of the attitudes towards school and education of top primary (Year 6) and first year secondary (Year 7) pupils
Abstract: The National Foundation for Educational Research (NFER) is currently undertaking a study designed to compare the attitudes towards school and education of top primary (Year 6) and first year secondary (Year 7) pupils. The findings will extend the research evidence collected in an earlier study which investigated the attitudes towards school of Year 7 and Year 9 pupils, and which was reported in the NFER publication 'What do students think about school?'. One concern identified during the earlier study was that a minority of Year 7 pupils already held negative attitudes towards

school by the end of their first year of secondary education. This raised an important question: had these pupils' negative attitudes been developed during their primary school years, or had pupils developed these attitudes since they had transferred to secondary school? The current study is intended to clarify this issue. In addition, a second phase is proposed which would follow the Year 6 pupils to their secondary schools and attempt to clarify how their attitudes towards school and education changed, if at all. The research is being carried out by means of questionnaire surveys of Year 6 and Year 7 pupils. Random samples of approximately 80 primary and 80 secondary schools were drawn so as to achieve samples of about 1,250 Year 6 pupils and about 1,000 Year 7 pupils. The main outcome of the study will be a publication highlighting any differences in attitudes towards school between top primary and first year secondary pupils. A further document would report on the second phase of the study, in which the responses of the Year 6 pupils were compared with their responses once they had transferred to secondary school.
Status: Sponsored project
Source of Grant: NFER Additional Activities Fund
Date of Research: 1994-continuing
KEYWORDS: *primary school pupils; pupil attitudes; secondary school pupils*

10/1043

The Mere, Upton Park, Slough SL1 2DQ
01753 574123
Gallacher, S. Dr; Johnson, F. Ms; *Supervisor:* Stoney, S. Dr; Hegarty, S. Dr
Review of government-funded educational research and development in Europe
Abstract: The European Commission (EC) has sponsored the Consortium of Institutions for Development and Research in Education in Europe (CIDREE) to conduct a review of government-funded educational research and development activities in EC countries, plus Switzerland. The National Foundation for Educational Research (NFER) has undertaken the work on behalf of CIDREE. The specific aims are to: 1) identify and describe the agencies which conduct research and development activities in education within each EC country (plus Switzerland) and to identify their status; 2) identify and describe the main research topics in education which have attracted government sponsorship within member countries and Switzerland over the last ten years and highlight any key findings which arise from these topics; 3) provide an overview of common trends and themes within government-funded educational research and development across member states, and identify likely future directions. The review comprised two phases. In 1993, using an agreed typology of educational research themes, initial information was sought from each country on past, present and likely future research priorities and on the main government and non-governmental agencies which fund and undertake educational research and development activities. In the second phase (in 1994) more detailed information was obtained by questionnaire, by a survey of identified research agencies and a scrutiny of relevant documentation. CIDREE colleagues played a major part in supplying the necessary information. An initial draft report was sent to the EC in April 1994 and an updated version was submitted in early 1995. The report will be published by CIDREE and the NFER in 1995 and contains four major sections: International Overview; Country Reports; Database of Research Development Agencies; Methodological Annexe.
Published Material: STONEY, S.M, GALLACHER, S. & JOHNSON, F. Review of government-funded educational research and development in Europe. Dundee: Consortium of Institutions for Development and Research in Education in Europe. (in press).
Status: Sponsored project
Source of Grant: European Commission (via CIDREE); National Foundation for Educational Research, jointly £30,000
Date of Research: 1993-continuing
KEYWORDS: *comparative education; educational research; Europe; international educational exchange; research and development*

10/1044

The Mere, Upton Park, Slough SL1 2DQ
01753 574123
Rodrigues, S. Dr; *Supervisor:* Tabberer, R. Mr
The use of new technology with very able children
Abstract: This one-year National Foundation for Educational Research (NFER) funded project aims to describe the use of information technology by able children in mainstream primary schools. The

research is predominantly qualitative with interviews and classroom observation being the main research tools.
Status: Sponsored project
Source of Grant: National Foundation for Educational Research £30,000
Date of Research: 1994-continuing
KEYWORDS: *ability; computer uses in education; gifted; information technology; primary school pupils*

10/1045

The Mere, Upton Park, Slough SL1 2DQ
01753 574123
Dickson, P. Mr; Le Metais, J. Dr; *Supervisor:* Tabberer, R. Mr
Schools' use of time: a critical review of issues and related research
Abstract: Research into school effectiveness, teacher effectiveness, teacher attitudes, teacher workload and stress, was reviewed in order to clarify: 1) how schools use time; 2) how schools might more effectively manage time; and 3) how school managers and individual teachers should collaborate best to enhance pupil achievement.
Published Material: DICKSON, P., TABBERER, R. & LE METAIS, J. (1994). Schools' use of time: a critical review of issues and related research. London: Association of Teachers and Lecturers.; TABBERER, R. (1994). 'Time for what?', Education, Vol 184, No 4, p.71.
Status: Sponsored project
Source of Grant: Association of Teachers and Lecturers £8,000
Date of Research: 1994-1994
KEYWORDS: *school effectiveness; teacher attitudes; teacher effectiveness; teacher workload; time management*

10/1046

The Mere, Upton Park, Slough SL1 2DQ
01753 574123
Tabberer, R. Mr
Survey of parents' perceptions of OFSTED's work
Abstract: Parents' participation of the Office for Standards in Education (OFSTED) are being investigated in this three-phase study. In the first phase, surveys are being undertaken of parents in schools inspected by OFSTED – secondary, primary and special schools are included. In the second phase, telephone interviews will take place with selected parents. In the third phase, parents will be interviewed face-to-face, to clarify their views of inspections, their perception of OFSTED as a whole, and to identify areas for future OFSTED development.
Status: Sponsored project
Source of Grant: Office for Standards in Education £43,000
Date of Research: 1994-continuing
KEYWORDS: *inspection; inspectors – of schools; parent attitudes*

10/1047

The Mere, Upton Park, Slough SL1 2DQ
01753 574123
Tate, A. Dr; Brooks, G. Dr; *Supervisor:* Foxman, D. Mr
Promoting core skills
Abstract: The specification and assessment of core skills has been an important development in further and higher education, but less so in secondary schools. The main aim of this project was to update and extend the information available on the implementation of core skills and cross-curricular initiatives in secondary schools. The design included a survey of local education authority (LEA) advisers (July 1992); and a telephone survey of schools identified by LEAs as showing good practice (October 1992 – March 1993). From the 56 LEA responses received, the main findings were: 1) LEA advisers were thinking in terms of 'cross-curricularity' per se rather than discrete skills, themes etc. 2) Among cross-curricular elements, skills were the 'Cinderella' area. More development work was taking place in the area of cross-curricular dimensions and themes. From the exactly 100 telephone interviews with senior secondary staff, the principal findings were: 1) Definitions of core skills abound, but have little in common. 2) Very little development work directly on skills could be identified in the secondary curriculum. 3) Skills receive less attention than cross-curricular dimensions and themes. 4) Where cross-curricular initiatives were occurring, they often addressed the problem of curricular balance and coherence. 5) Most of the initiatives encountered exhibited both good management and curriculum

enhancement. 6) A few schools were successfully tackling the development of cross-curricular skills. 7) Above all, initiatives were local and isolated, and there was little national or coordinated drive. It was concluded that the 1994 revision of the National Curriculum provides an opportunity to improve the development of both cross-curricular work in general and of core skills in particular.
Published Material: TATE, A. (1992). Pursuing core skills: a discussion paper. Slough: National Foundation for Educational Research.; TATE, A. (1994). Core skills and cross-curricular initiatives in secondary schools. Slough: National Foundation for Educational Research.
Status: Sponsored project
Source of Grant: NFER Membership Programme £40,000
Date of Research: 1992-1994
KEYWORDS: basic skills; cross curricular approach; National Curriculum; secondary education

10/1048
   The Mere, Upton Park, Slough SL1 2DQ
   01753 574123
   Brooks, G. Dr; Fernandes, C. Mr; *Supervisor:* Bradley, J. Dr
Trends in the reading attainment of 7 and 8 year olds
Abstract: In 1991, the National Foundation for Educational Research (NFER) conducted a Comparative Reading Study into the reading attainment of pupils in Year 3. This was the first occasion on which trends in the reading attainment of Year 3 pupils had been investigated using a representative national sample. The study compared attainment in 1987 and 1991, and discovered a significant decline in overall mean scores in that period. This project is repeating that investigation at a further four-year interval. The aims of the investigation are to continue to provide reliable, up-to-date and nationally valid data on the reading attainment of 7 and 8 year olds, to investigate whether the 1987-1991 trend has continued, and to relate the results to a wider range of background data. The Comparative Reading Study is being replicated; that is, NFER-Nelson Reading Ability Series Test A is again being used both with a new national sample and with as many as possible of the schools which took part in the original standardisation in 1987 and in the first replication in 1991. Testing is taking place in March 1995; the target sample is 120 schools and 3600 pupils.
Status: Sponsored project
Source of Grant: NFER Membership Programme £64,000
Date of Research: 1994-continuing
KEYWORDS: achievement; comparative testing; reading ability; reading achievement; reading research

10/1049
   The Mere, Upton Park, Slough SL1 2DQ
   01753 574123
   Brooks, G. Dr; Gorman, T. Dr; Wilkin, A. Mrs; Self, T. Mr; *Supervisor:* Bradley, J. Dr
Evaluation of the Family Literacy through Demonstration Programmes
Abstract: In late 1993, the Adult Literacy and Basic Skills Unit (ALBSU) received Department for Education and Welsh Office funding to set up Family Literacy through Demonstration Programmes. All four are deliberately based in urban areas with high levels of multiple deprivation. To be eligible, a parent must have at least one child aged between 3 and 6, and the programmes are targeted at parents with low incomes and low literacy skills. Parents participate in intensive 12-week courses, creche facilities are provided, and part of the tuition shows parents how best to engage in literacy-related behaviours with their children. The aim of the evaluation is to investigate the effectiveness of the programmes in: 1) improving parents' literacy; 2) increasing parents' skills in supporting their children's literacy; 3) establishing increased literacy practices in the family; and 4) boosting children's emerging literacy. Besides evidence of these changes, the research focuses on the process by which this is achieved. The research team is gathering both quantitative and qualitative data. Quantitative data on parents includes: background information; reading attainment; writing attainment; literacy activities undertaken at home with children; and attendance, retention, accreditation and destinations. Quantitative data on children includes: background information; early writing development; vocabulary development; and early reading development. Qualitative data includes: interviews with parents; interviews with programme coordinators; observations of teaching sessions; teachers' impressions; and documentation from the Programmes. In order to estimate the

effectiveness of the Programmes in boosting parents' and children's literacy, and in sustaining the gains made, information on literacy attainment is being gathered at several points: near the beginning of the course; just before the end of the course; 12 weeks after the end of the course; and (where possible within the timescale of the evaluation) nine months after the end of the corse.
Status: Sponsored project
Source of Grant: Adult Literacy and Basic Skills Unit £102,000
Date of Research: 1994-continuing
KEYWORDS: family involvement; family programmes; literacy; parent participation; reading skills; writing skills

10/1050
   The Mere, Upton Park, Slough SL1 2DQ
   01753 574123
   Brooks, G. Dr; Fernandes, C. Mr
Evaluation of the Knowsley Reading Project
Abstract: Knowsley Local Education Authority is mounting a reading project with Year 6 pupils, wishes to evaluate its effectiveness, and has commissioned the National Foundation for Educational Research (NFER) to provide support and advice on the design and conduct of the evaluation. About 500 pupils participating in the Reading Project were assessed at the beginning of their participation in it (June 1994) on an appropriate level (A, B, C or D, according to their teachers' judgement) of the Reading Ability Series of tests, and will be assessed again after one year in order to evaluate the Project's impact on their progress. The evaluation also involves questionnaire surveys of pupils, their teachers and the adult volunteers involved.
Status: Sponsored project
Source of Grant: Knowsley Local Education Authority £10,000
Date of Research: 1994-continuing
KEYWORDS: assessment; programme evaluation; reading ability; reading achievement

10/1051
   The Mere, Upton Park, Slough SL1 2DQ
   01753 574123
   Brooks, G. Dr
ALBSU basic skills tests, phase 2
Abstract: The Adult Literacy and Basic Skills Unit (ALBSU) commissioned the National Foundation for Educational Research (NFER) to develop tests of various elements of its Basic Skills Standards in Communication and Numeracy. These were submitted to ALBSU in November 1994, and are intended largely for research purposes.
Status: Sponsored project
Source of Grant: Adult Literacy and Basic Skills Unit £19,000
Date of Research: 1994-1994
KEYWORDS: basic skills; communication skills; numeracy

10/1052
   The Mere, Upton Park, Slough SL1 2DQ
   01753 574123
   Gorman, T. Dr; Hutchison, D. Mr; Trimble, J. Ms; *Supervisor:* Foxman, D. Mr
Avon collaborative reading study
Abstract: All too often, pupils work in groups in school, but not as groups. Effective, collaborative groupwork is uncommon. This study shows one way it can be done, and how it can raise reading standards. In 1992-93, a project was carried out in a group of inner-city schools in Avon. It was designed to improve the reading performance of children aged 10 and 12. The children tackled questions about a poem or a passage of non-fiction, discussed their answers in groups, then had the chance to revise them. Over 100 groups of children were involved – a larger total than in any previous research of this type in Britain. The main results were: 1) All groups improved their answers to the questions. 2) Poorer readers improved their answers the most, and substantially more than better readers did. 3) The pupils' reports showed they had become more reflective about their reading. 4) Most pupils enjoyed collaborative reading. 5) Over two terms, the primary school pupils involved made a significant gain in scores on a standardised reading test. So groupwork can be effective, and can help to raise reading standards, when the task is focused and specific.
Published Material: GORMAN, T., HUTCHISON, D. & TRIMBLE, J. (1993). Reading in reform: the Avon Collaborative Reading Project. Slough: National Foundation for Educational Research.
Status: Sponsored project

Source of Grant: Avon Local Education Authority £5,000
Date of Research: 1992-1993
KEYWORDS: *group work; learning activities; reading improvement; reading strategies*

10/1053
> The Mere, Upton Park, Slough SL1 2DQ
> 01753 574123
> Mason, K. Mr; Clausen, T. Dr; Evans, S. Dr; Henkhuzens, Z.
> Ms; *Supervisor:* Ruddock, G. Dr

The writing of National Curriculum key stage 3 mathematics tests for use in 1995-1997
Abstract: The project is sponsored to produce mathematics tests for the higher level of the National Curriculum and classroom-based tasks for pupils working at levels 1 and 2. The tests and tasks are for use with pupils at the end of key stage 3 of the National Curriculum, Year 9. In 1995 they are based on the old version of the National Curriculum, while those for 1996 and 1997 will reflect the revised version.
Status: Sponsored project
Source of Grant: School Curriculum and Assessment Authority
Date of Research: 1994-continuing
KEYWORDS: *achievement tests; assessment; mathematics achievement; mathematics education; National Curriculum*

10/1054
> The Mere, Upton Park, Slough SL1 2DQ
> 01753 574123
> Sims, D. Mr; Christophers, U. Mrs; *Supervisor:* Stoney, S. Dr

Reflections on guidance: a study of adult learners' experiences
Abstract: This project contributes to the existing body of knowledge on adult education and lifelong learning by carrying out independent, indepth research into what attracts adults to take full advantage of learning opportunities and into whether guidance really does make a difference and, if so, how. The aims of the project were as follows: to explore adults' reflections on their learning experiences and the critical incidents or interventions which have had an impact on their entry to study and their subsequent progress and success; to help assess, by qualitative means, the role and impact of guidance (relative to other course, college and non-college factors) on adults' learning progress and outcomes; to provide evidence which will contribute to a greater understanding being achieved of guidance and its place and impact within adult learning programmes in British and European contexts. The researchers collected qualitative data from three colleges in the Thames Valley using the following methods: face-to-face interviews with senior managers and guidance and academic staff; group discussions with adult learners; and individual indepth interviews with 30 students. The main outcomes from the project will be a report and oral feedback to each college.
Status: Sponsored project
Source of Grant: NFER Additional Activities Project £15,366
Date of Research: 1994-continuing
KEYWORDS: *adult education; adult learning; guidance; lifelong learning*

10/1055
> The Mere, Upton Park, Slough SL1 2DQ
> 01753 574123
> Sharp, C. Ms; *Supervisor:* Bradley, J. Dr

LEA responses to the 'summer born' effect
Abstract: Research has shown a consistent finding on season of birth and attainment: children born in the autumn (September to December) do best and those born in the summer (May to August) tend to do least well in school assessments. This effect has been found at different ages and in a number of countries. It has been argued that the effect could be due, at least in part, to school entry policy in this country. In some local education authorities (LEA's) and schools, entry policies mean that children born in the summer enter school later in the year than other children, and therefore spend less time in school. This hypothesis was examined in the recently published study by Sharp et al (1994). The research found that, although spending longer at school was associated with higher scores for older children, those born in the summer did not appear to benefit from increased time at school in terms of their key stage 1 results. This paper has been the subject of a great deal of interest, not least from LEA's who have found a 'summer born effect' in their own analyses of National Curriculum, GCSE and A level results. LEA officers, schools and parents are concerned about the potential disadvantage suffered by summer-born children, and are keen to explore strategies for counteracting the season of birth effect. The research has the following aims: 1) To collect information about LEA investigations into the effect of season of birth on attainment and other aspects of children's educational experience. 2) To consider the implications of these for explanations about the cause of season of birth effects. 3) To identify a range of possible strategies that could be implemented at school and LEA level, to counteract any disadvantage experienced by children born in the summer months. The research will collect information by means of a short pro-forma sent to LEA's. The pro-forma will ask for awareness of the issue and any suggested strategies for addressing the disadvantages suffered by summer-borns. Information will also be sought frm other interested parties (e.g. teachers' and parents' organisations) via requests submitted to relevant journals. Information of particular interest will be followed-up by telephone interviews. The research will result in one or more articles for publication, drawing together the available evidence and pointing to a range of suggested strategies. Although not proposed as part of the project itself, a possible further development from the research would be a seminar or conference for LEA's, headteachers and parents' organizations.
Published Material: SHARP, C., HUTCHISON, D. & WHETTON, C. (1994). 'How do season of birth and length of schooling affect children's attainment at key stage 1?', Educational Research, Vol 36, No 2, pp.107-121.
Status: Sponsored project
Source of Grant: NFER Membership Programme
Date of Research: 1995-continuing
KEYWORDS: *achievement; birth; local education authorities; school entrance age*

10/1056
> The Mere, Upton Park, Slough SL1 2DQ
> 01753 574123
> Sharp, C. Ms; Maychell, K. Ms; Walton, I. Ms

Nursing and AIDS: material matters. Issues, information and teaching materials on HIV and AIDS for nurses
Abstract: From April 1992 to March 1993 the National Foundation for Educational Research (NFER) carried out the second phase of a research study looking at information and educational materials on human immunodeficiency virus (HIV) and acquired immune deficiency syndrome (AIDS) for nurses and nurse educators. The research was funded by the Department of Health. The NFER's study built on work conducted by Akinsanya and Barnett, based at Anglia Polytechnic University. They conducted a questionnaire survey of colleges and university departments offering training on HIV/AIDS to students and qualified nurses, midwives and health visitors (collectively termed 'nurses' for the purposes of this document). The second phase of the research focused on nurse educators' decision-making processes in selecting and using materials on HIV/AIDS and looked at the information sources on HIV/AIDS currently used by nurses and nurse educators. The research also sought to identify key factors in the professional culture of nursing and nurse education which may help or hinder dissemination and knowledge utilisation in relation to HIV and AIDS.
Published Material: SHARP, C., MAYCHELL, K. & WALTON, I. (1993). Nursing and AIDS: material matters. Issues, information and teaching materials on HIV and AIDS for nurses – a research study. Slough: National Foundation for Educational Research.
Status: Sponsored project
Source of Grant: Department of Health
Date of Research: 1992-1993
KEYWORDS: *acquired immune deficiency syndrome; educational materials; nurses; sexually transmitted diseases*

10/1057
> The Mere, Upton Park, Slough SL1 2DQ
> 01753 574123
> Sharp, C. Ms; *Supervisor:* Bradley, J. Dr

The defining characteristics of educational broadcasts
Abstract: This research aimed to: 1) identify factors influencing teachers' decisions to use broadcasts; 2) identify the perceived benefits and defining characteristics of schools' broadcasts; and 3) study the effects of programme techniques on pupils' comprehension and recall of content. The methods included: a questionnaire to over 1500 primary teachers and secondary heads of department; interviews with 47 teachers; and group interviews with 240 pupils aged 4-16. The report gives details on the most popular radio and television series;

teachers' attitudes towards broadcast use; barriers to use of broadcasts; and pupils' reactions to specific programme features.
Published Material: SHARP, C. Viewing, listening and learning: the use and impact of schools' broadcasts. Slough: National Foundation for Educational Research. (in press).
Status: Sponsored project
Source of Grant: BBC Education
Date of Research: 1993-continuing
KEYWORDS: *educational broadcasting; educational radio; educational television; radio; television*

10/1058
The Mere, Upton Park, Slough SL1 2DQ
01753 574123
Harris, S. Mrs; *Supervisor:* Keys, W. Dr
The Third International Mathematics and Science Study: performance and assessment
Abstract: The Third International Mathematics and Science Study (TIMSS) is a major international project involving over 50 countries, including every member of the European Union. One of the study's main aims is to gather information about pupils' knowledge and understanding of mathematics and science: this will be done by means of written achievement tests for the 9 and 13 year-olds involved in the study, supplemented by specific practical tasks which have an emphasis on investigative skills. These practical tasks comprise the Performance Assessment element of TIMSS, and will provide information about pupils' approaches to practical mathematics and science work. The Performance Assessment will be carried out with a sub-sample of the pupils involved in the main survey (in England, about 10 pupils in 50 schools selected from the total of 150 schools with 13 year-olds). A total of 12 different tasks will be used, some focusing on mathematics skills, some on science skills and some with elements relating to both subjects. Pupils will be asked to carry out specific activities, record and analyse their results. Skills in the tasks which are related to the mathematics and science curricula include: taking and recording measurements, problem solving, designing practical investigations and carrying out fair tests. The results will form part of the national report on TIMSS, and will also contribute towards the international report, both of which are to be published in summer/autumn 1996.
Status: Sponsored project
Source of Grant: Office for Standards in Education
Date of Research: 1995-continuing
KEYWORDS: *achievement; achievement tests; assessment; comparative education; mathematics education; science education*

10/1059
The Mere, Upton Park, Slough SL1 2DQ
01753 574123
Sharp, C. Ms; *Supervisor:* Bradley, J. Dr
Handbook on instrumental music
Abstract: This small-scale project aimed to provide examples of how instrumental music services and schools are providing high-quality music tuition. Research methods include: case studies of music services and schools, including interviews with heads of service, music teachers, headteachers, pupils and parents.
Published Material: SHARP, C. (1995). Instrumental music handbook. Slough: National Foundation for Educational Research.
Status: Sponsored project
Source of Grant: Paul Hamlyn Foundation (administered by the Music Education Council).
Date of Research: 1994-1994
KEYWORDS: *guides; music activities; music education*

10/1060
The Mere, Upton Park, Slough SL1 2DQ
01753 574123
Harland, J. Dr; Kinder, K. Ms; *Supervisor:* Bradley, J. Dr
Attitudes to participation in the arts, heritage, broadcasting and sport: a literature review
Abstract: The main aim of the project is to review and examine the research evidence on the role of attitudinal factors in influencing the levels of participation in, and appreciation of, the arts, culture, heritage and sport, and, in particular, the part played by negative attitudes in affecting the level of participation. The literature review includes research carried out in the following areas: 1) The arts (including visual arts, music, literature, theatre, opera and ballet). 2)

Heritage (including the viewing and appreciation of buildings and other tangible objects of historical, aesthetic and other significance). 3) Broadcasting (with particular reference to its role in broadening access to other areas within the remit of the Department of National Heritage (DNH). 4) Sport and active recreation. Special attention is given to the following issues: 1) Positive attitudes to the above areas. 2) Negative attitudes. 3) The influences which give rise to these attitudes. 4) The degree to which negative outcomes can be overcome.
Status: Sponsored project
Source of Grant: Department of National Heritage
Date of Research: 1994-1994
KEYWORDS: *arts; attitudes; culture; mass media; music; participation; sports; theatre arts*

10/1061
The Mere, Upton Park, Slough SL1 2DQ
01753 574123
Harland, J. Dr; Weston, P. Mrs; Kinder, K. Ms; Wakefield, A. Ms; *Supervisor:* Bradley, J. Dr
The Northern Ireland curriculum cohort study: pilot phase
Abstract: The aim of the cohort study is to provide evidence of the impact of the Northern Ireland Curriculum as a total package from the perspective of the learner in terms of relevance and appropriateness; breadth, balance and coherence; enjoyment and manageability. It is also envisaged that the study would gather evidence of the extent to which the aims of the Northern Ireland Curriculum are evident in its implementation; the extent to which the objectives of cross-curricular themes are being addressed through the curriculum; and the appropriateness of methods of assessment and evaluation. Initially, the cohort study will involve groups of pupils at key stage 3. The pilot phase of the study will explore the substantive issues involved, trial different research and data collection techniques, and assess the feasibility of conducting the full cohort inquiry. Data for the pilot project will be collected from teachers and pupils in five schools spread across the province. Research methods include direct and indirect interviewing techniques, pupil pursuits and classroom observation, diary-keeping, and class-administered questionnaires.
Status: Sponsored project
Source of Grant: Northern Ireland Council for the Curriculum, Examinations and Assessment
Date of Research: 1994-continuing
KEYWORDS: *cohort analysis; curriculum development; National Curriculum – Northern Ireland; Northern Ireland; pupil attitudes*

10/1062
The Mere, Upton Park, Slough SL1 2DQ
01753 574123
Harland, J. Dr; Kinder, K. Ms; *Supervisor:* Bradley, J. Dr
Youth participation in the arts
Abstract: The project's aim is to provide a national picture of youth arts participation – both within and outside of formal education. The study portrays different patterns and experiences of young people's involvement in the arts and examines these in relation to key biographical variables (e.g. gender, age, social class, status and ethnicity). It provides evidence on leisure interests, participation in specified art forms, attitudes to the arts, experiences of the arts in primary and secondary schools, arts involvement beyond school and in youth clubs, the effects of arts participation, and the perceived needs for future opportunities in the arts. Data were collected through an interviewing programme which involved 700 young people between the ages of 14 and 24 in five regions of England. The interviews included open and closed-ended items. A report of the research will be published by the NFER in March 1995.
Published Material: HARLAND, J., KINDER, K. & HARTLEY, K. Arts in their view: a study of youth participation in the arts. Slough: National Foundation for Educational Research. (in press).
Status: Sponsored project
Source of Grant: NFER; Arts Council of Great Britain; Baring Foundation; Calouste Gulbenkian Foundation, jointly £65,000
Date of Research: 1993-continuing
KEYWORDS: *arts; arts education; attitudes; culture; leisure time; participation; youth*

10/1063
The Mere, Upton Park, Slough SL1 2DQ
01753 574123

Kinder, K. Ms; Harland, J. Dr; Wilkin, A. Mrs; Wakefield, A. Ms; *Supervisor:* Bradley, J. Dr
School attendance, truancy and exclusions
Abstract: Research on truancy and disruption has provided a number of different perspectives on the problem. Numerous studies have established that substantial differences, associated with a range of factors exist between schools in their rates of non-attendance and exclusion, and on the level of disruptive incidents reported. The project's stated aims are: 1) To investigate the interrelationships between non-attendance, disruption and exclusion. 2) To assess the effectiveness of present policies and practices for dealing with non-attendance, reducing exclusion rates and providing alternative education. 3) To identify innovative practices with a view to assisting local authorities and schools wishing to improve their practice. A range of research techniques will be used including indepth interviews with local education authority (LEA) personnel, headteachers, teachers, specialist staff, pupils and parents.
Status: Sponsored project
Source of Grant: NFER Membership Programme
Date of Research: 1994-continuing
KEYWORDS: *attendance; discipline problems; disruptive pupils; expulsion; truancy*

10/1064
The Mere, Upton Park, Slough SL1 2DQ
01753 574123
Harland, J. Dr; Kinder, K. Ms; *Supervisor:* Bradley, J. Dr
Students' perspectives on their curriculum experience: a review of the research literature
Abstract: The aim of the project is to review the main substantive findings of recent UK research into students' perspectives on the whole curriculum (including perceptions of relevance, appropriateness, coherence, progression and continuity). The review will also assess the relative merits of different methodological approaches used to collect data on students' views on the whole curriculum. It will also consider what lessons may be garnered from international studies in this area.
Status: Sponsored project
Source of Grant: National Foundation for Educational Research
Date of Research: 1994-continuing
KEYWORDS: *National Curriculum; pupil attitudes; relevance – education*

10/1065
The Mere, Upton Park, Slough SL1 2DQ
01753 574123
Lewis, G. Mr; *Supervisor:* Stoney, S. Dr; Morris, M. Miss
Careers Service new arrangements: Welsh baseline studies
Abstract: Following publication of the Trade Union Reform and Employment Rights Act (TURER) in 1993, the Secretary of State for Wales announced that, from April 1995, Careers Services in Wales will be managed under contract through the New Arrangements. This project will seek to evaluate current policies, processes and outcomes of two of the Welsh Careers Services prior to re-organisation. The specific aims of the project are to: 1) gather baseline data on provision; 2) present a detailed assessment of the Services; 3) derive a framework of indicators against which the processes and outcomes of the Services can be evaluated. The research uses a coordinated case-study approach with a uniform set of research instruments and strategies in each area. Relevant reports and documentation will be collected and scrutinised. Staff from Careers Services, schools, colleges, training providers and employer organisations, as well as relevant local education authority (LEA), Training and Enterprise Council (TEC) and Education Business Partnerships (EBP) personnel. Postal surveys of schools, young people on one-year and two-year full-time academic and vocational courses and on youth training/youth credit programmes, and of parents of young people in Year 11, will also be conducted. The main aim will be to gain high quality, objective and detailed information and views from all relevant users of the two Services in order to evaluate the Services using the indicators agreed during the early stages of the project.
Status: Sponsored project
Source of Grant: Welsh Office £9,545
Date of Research: 1994-continuing
KEYWORDS: *career education; careers service; school to work transition; vocational guidance; Wales*

10/1066
The Mere, Upton Park, Slough SL1 2DQ
01753 574123
Schagen, S. Dr; Ratcliffe, S. Ms; *Supervisor:* Stradling, R. Dr
Evaluation of the NatWest financial literacy staff tutoring scheme
Abstract: Community Service Volunteers (CSV) has been providing training for volunteer staff from the National Westminster Bank (NatWest) to go into secondary schools and work with teachers to help develop the financial literacy and money management skills of young people aged 14-19. The National Foundation for Educational Research (NFER) was commissioned by CSV to evaluate the training and the participation of the volunteer 'tutors' in schools.
Status: Sponsored project
Source of Grant: Community Service Volunteers £9,000
Date of Research: 1994-1994
KEYWORDS: *economics education; life skills; money management; volunteers*

10/1067
The Mere, Upton Park, Slough SL1 2DQ
01753 574123
Stradling, R. Dr; Weston, P. Mrs; MacDonald, A. Ms; Ratcliffe, S. Ms; Stanesby, C. Mrs; Taylor, M. Miss
The management of differentiated teaching and learning in primary and secondary schools
Abstract: While most teachers would agree that their pupils tend to learn in different ways and at different speeds, and that within any year group or class there may be marked variations in the levels of attainment that their pupils achieve, there is not the same consensus about how best to respond to this diversity. A variety of alternative strategies are now being adopted, including: ability groupings within mixed ability classes; greater use of setting by subject departments; banding, streaming and 'accelerated learning streams' for the most able; greater emphasis on teaching and learning tailored to the needs of individual pupils; greater emphasis on teaching and learning strategies which differentiate by task, outcome, pace of learning or style of learning. The research aims to evaluate these differentiation strategies through qualitative fieldwork in case study schools and through a follow-up survey of a representative sample of primary and secondary schools.
Status: Sponsored project
Source of Grant: NFER Membership Programme £140,000
Date of Research: 1994-continuing
KEYWORDS: *ability; class organisation; grouping – teaching purposes; mixed ability; pupil placement; streaming; teaching methods*

10/1068
The Mere, Upton Park, Slough SL1 2DQ
01753 574123
Bradley, J. Dr; Earley, P. Mr
Further and higher education lecturers' workload and stress
Abstract: The data on which the study was based were collected primarily by means of a questionnaire survey of further education (FE) and higher education (HE) lecturers. Following a small number of detailed discussions with college personnel and National Association of Teachers in Further and Higher Education (NATFHE) officials, and a review of the relevant literature, a questionnaire was constructed. This attempted to gather information on members' workloads, factors relating to stress and attitudes towards a range of issues of current concern. There were a number of open-ended questions inviting respondents to comment more fully on any of the issues raised. The questionnaire was despatched to a stratified random sample of 1,000 NATFHE members drawn from the Association's database. It was stratified to ensure an accurate reflection of members from all sectors of further, adult and higher education. Replies were received from 435 lecturers which represents a response rate of nearly 44%. Although the number of returns is low, the response was in fact better than expected given the time of year when the survey was undertaken – towards the end of the summer term – when many other activities compete for lecturers' time (e.g. student assessments). In fact the response rate was higher than many other postal surveys of this kind, but it should be recalled that it was a survey of NATFHE members rather than a sample of the lecturing population as a whole.
Published Material: EARLEY, P. (1994). Lecturers' workload and factors affecting stress levels. A research report from the NFER. Slough: National Foundation for Educational Research.
Status: Sponsored project

Source of Grant: National Association of Teachers in Further and Higher Education £9,000
Date of Research: 1994-1994
KEYWORDS: *academic staff; further education teachers; higher education; stress – psychological; teacher workload*

10/1069
The Mere, Upton Park, Slough SL1 2DQ
01753 574123
Bradley, J. Dr; Dee, L. Ms; Wilenius, F. Mr
Students with disabilities and/or learning difficulties in further education: a review of research
Abstract: This comprehensive review of the literature was carried out to support the work of the specialist committee set up by the Further Education Funding Council (FEFC) to consider the future development of provision for students with special needs in the further education (FE) sector.
Published Material: BRADLEY, J., DEE, L. & WILENIUS, F. (1994). Students with disabilities and/or learning difficulties in further education: a review of research. Slough: National Foundation for Educational Research.
Status: Sponsored project
Source of Grant: Further Education Funding Council £25,000
Date of Research: 1993-1994
KEYWORDS: *disabilities; further education; further education students; literature reviews; moderate learning difficulties; special educational needs*

10/1070
The Mere, Upton Park, Slough SL1 2DQ
01753 574123
Maychell, K. Ms; *Supervisor:* Keys, W. Dr
Youth service provision in London
Abstract: In recent years statutory and voluntary youth services in London have undergone a period of considerable change in terms of levels of funding and organisation. The effects of these changes have been reported by individual local authorities and some voluntary organisations, but there is no reliable information on youth service provision as a whole for the city. The purpose of this study is to provide evidence of the extent of funding changes and the impact of these on the youth service in London, as provided by the 32 London boroughs and the major voluntary youth organisations operating in London. In Phase One a questionnaire will be sent to the principal youth officer (or their equivalent) in each of the 32 London boroughs and to the main voluntary youth service providers in London. It will seek information on: changes in funding levels; the impact of these changes on youth service provision; changing patterns of service delivery; the extent to which London's young people are having their needs met by existing provision; and emerging needs for the future. Phase Two will involve follow-up interviews in ten London borough and ten voluntary organisations. These will focus on current issues of concern among service providers, with particular emphasis on identified needs of young people that currently are not being met. The findings will be presented in a report to the sponsors. It will provide information that will serve as a basis for future planning and development of London's youth services.
Status: Sponsored project
Source of Grant: Sir John Cass's Foundation £20,000
Date of Research: 1995-continuing
KEYWORDS: *local education authorities; voluntary agencies; youth leaders; youth service*

10/1071
The Mere, Upton Park, Slough SL1 2DQ
01753 574123
Jowett, S. Ms; *Supervisor:* Keys, W. Dr
Secondary school questionnaire on health and behaviour
Abstract: Meeting the needs of young people requires up-to-date information on what they think is important and the life-style they adopt. This research provided the opportunity for some of the young people in the London Borough of Newham to provide that information. Four secondary schools in Newham were selected for the research and a questionnaire was administered to all their students in Years 8 and 10. A total of 1,160 students took part. The 16-page questionnaire covered five main areas – school life (attitudes to school, discipline, truancy, parental views and homework); aspirations (plans after school-leaving, employment, continuing education,

personal relationships); health (exercise, food, weight, smoking, alcohol, drugs, sex education), out-of-school time (leisure, finances, current employment (paid and unpaid) and concerns and support services (self-esteem, perspectives on racism, police, sexuality, problems encountered and who to turn to, undisclosed problems). The evidence from this study was that while there is considerable scope for developing the services available to young people in Newham, there is also a good deal of optimism and ambition amongst this sector of the population. It is also clear that these young people have a range of unmet needs and the way ahead lies in acknowledging the achievement and strengths of both the services and the consumers in Newham, while also developing a responsive service that listens to what the latter have to say.
Published Material: JOWETT, S. (1995). Health and well-being in the 1990's: a study of young people's attitudes and behaviour in the London Borough of Newham. Slough: National Foundation for Educational Research. (Main report and summary available).
Status: Sponsored project
Source of Grant: Newham Social Services £8,000; City Challenge £4,000
Date of Research: 1994-1994
KEYWORDS: *aspiration; attitudes; health; pupil attitudes; pupil behaviour; secondary school pupils; sex education; social attitudes*

10/1072
The Mere, Upton Park, Slough SL1 2DQ
01753 574123
Jowett, S. Ms; *Supervisor:* Bradley, J. Dr
Sex education in secondary schools: the Berkshire survey
Abstract: This research was commissioned in response to recent changes in legislation regarding sex education in schools. The aim was to identify what sex education is provided, how it is being developed and what school staff see as the key issues in that development. All but 5 of the 70 secondary schools in Berkshire (including all special schools with secondary age pupils) were visited and a member of staff with responsibility for sex education was interviewed. In addition, discussion groups with a small number of Year 11 pupils will be undertaken in some schools.
Status: Sponsored project
Source of Grant: East Berkshire Community Health NHS Trust £15,000
Date of Research: 1994-continuing
KEYWORDS: *health education; secondary schools; sex education*

10/1073
The Mere, Upton Park, Slough SL1 2DQ
01753 574123
Jowett, S. Ms; Evans, C. Ms; *Supervisor:* Bradley, J. Dr
Speech and language therapy services for children
Abstract: For the last twenty years, the provision of speech and language therapy services has been the responsibility of the National Health Service (NHS). The Education Act 1993 (Section 166) and the Code of Practice on the Identification and Assessment of Special Educational Needs (Paras. 4.34 and 4.35) confirm this overall responsibility, but emphasise the importance of collaborative working relationships between the NHS, local education authorities (LEAs), schools and parents in securing the most effective provision to meet the needs of each child. The research aims to identify, describe and evaluate the key models of collaborative organisation and delivery of efficient and cost-effective speech and language therapy services. Five speech and language therapy services have been selected to represent a range of different approaches to the organisation and delivery of therapy. In each of the five locations there will be indepth interviews with all interested parties, combined with the collection of all relevant documentation. Interviewees will include local education authority and health service personnel with administrative and financial responsibilities for service delivery, speech and language therapists, headteachers and school staff, and parents.
Status: Sponsored project
Source of Grant: Department of Health; Department for Education, jointly £48,739
Date of Research: 1994-continuing
KEYWORDS: *language handicaps; speech handicaps; speech therapy*

10/1074

> The Mere, Upton Park, Slough SL1 2DQ
> 01753 574123
> Jowett, S. Ms; *Supervisor:* Bradley, J. Dr

Parental choice of secondary school

Abstract: The rights of parents to play a part in the allocation of secondary school places to their children has featured in debates about educational provision in recent times. This research investigated how parents are involved in decision about which secondary school their children will attend, and their levels of satisfaction both with the allocation of school places and (where appropriate) the appeals procedures. It was concerned with how local education authorities (LEA's) have organised the information which they must provide to parents and the procedures they have established to allocate places and deal with subsequent appeals. The role of school staff at the time of transfer was also of interest. The work was undertaken in ten LEA's in England, and ten primary schools in each were selected for inclusion in the study. Seventy nine of these one hundred schools were willing to participate and each was asked to distribute a questionnaire to the parents of children from one Year 6 class. The eight secondary schools visited were selected from LEA's representing four different systems for allocating secondary school places. Fifty-eight parents were interviewed over the telephone about the appeals procedures. Staff in the secondary schools and the LEA's were interviewed. Most parents said they were satisfied with the procedures and the outcome, although it was clear that there were no easy answers to some of the dilemmas raised by open enrolment policies. There are inevitably advantages and disadvantages to each system and care needs to be taken in developing the optimum approaches, given the diverse circumstances in which transfers to secondary school take place.

Status: Sponsored project
Source of Grant: Department for Education £50,000
Date of Research: 1993-continuing
KEYWORDS: *access to education; admission criteria; enrolment; open entry; parent choice; secondary schools*

10/1075

> The Mere, Upton Park, Slough SL1 2DQ
> 01753 574123
> Jowett, S. Ms; Payne, S. Ms; Walton, I. Ms; *Supervisor:* Bradley, J. Dr

National evaluation of demonstration schemes in pre-registration nurse education (Project 2000)

Abstract: The launch of Project 2000 in 13 Demonstration Districts in England in late 1989/early 1990 was a substantial innovation in nurse education. While there was much enthusiasm and excitement about the introduction of Project 2000, it generated a considerable amount of hard work, stress and anxiety and it is crucial that lessons for the future are identified and dissected. The research was undertaken in 6 of the 13 first round Demonstration Districts in England. The main data collection was by interviews with college of nursing staff, senior nurse managers, senior service managers, practice-based nurses, staff in higher education and students. This was a longitudinal study in which interviews with the same key personnel took place at different points in time. The findings suggested good cause for optimism, particularly from the students vis-à-vis their role as qualified staff, and from staff whose professional development has been enhanced by the changes. A great many individuals have benefited from the opportunities Project 2000 offers, with implications for their enhanced performance as practitioners and educators. Although it was widely accepted that considerable problems had been encountered, there was also broad agreement about the viability and desirability of the changes Project 2000 promised.

Published Material: JOWETT, S., WALTON, I. & PAYNE, S. (1992). The introduction of Project 2000: early perspectives from higher education. National Evaluation of Demonstration Schemes in Pre-registration Nurse Education (Project 2000). Interim Paper 4. Slough: National Foundation for Educational Research.; JOWETT, S., WALTON, I. & PAYNE, S. (1992). The introduction of Project 2000: early perspectives from the students. National Evaluation of Demonstration Schemes in Pre-registration Nurse Education (Project 2000). Interim Paper 5. Slough: National Foundation for Educational Research.; JOWETT, S. (1992). 'Project 2000: research on its implementation', Nursing Times, Vol 88, No 26, pp.40-43.; JOWETT, S., WALTON, I. & PAYNE, S. (1992). Implementing Project 2000 in an interim report. Slough: National Foundation for Educational Research.; JOWETT, S. (1995). 'Added value', Nursing Times, Vol 91, No 1, pp.55-57. A full list of publications is available from the researcher.

Status: Sponsored project
Source of Grant: Department of Health £250,000
Date of Research: 1989-1993
KEYWORDS: *nurse education; professional education*

10/1076

> The Mere, Upton Park, Slough SL1 2DQ
> 01753 574123
> Hutchison, D. Mr

ALCD Fellowship multilevel modelling contextual effectiveness

Abstract: This project is a Fellowship in conjunction with the Economic and Social Research Council (ESRC) Analysis of Large and Complex Data Sets (ALDC) programme. It is associated with the University of London, Institute of Education Multilevel Modelling Project, and is looking at 'contextual' or 'compositional' effects in education, that is, the extent to which pupils' progress is affected by the characteristics of their class- or school-mates. The statistically preferred method of carrying out 'value-added' analyses of pupils' progress in schools is via the technique of multilevel modelling, which enables one to make allowance for various pupil and school characteristics in assessing how well the school has performed with the resources at its disposal. One question which has not yet been satisfactorily settled is that of contextual or compositional effects, i.e. the extent to which the aggregated characteristics of the pupil body affect the performance of the pupils in the class, after taking account of their individual characteristics. It is a statistically important question, as well as one that has possible implications for the organisation of education provision in this country. The research would look at the question of contextual effects in a variety of ways. It is usual to conceptualise such effects as taking place by the average score in the class pulling up or down the progress of its members. However, a number of other possibilities would be investigated: for example, the possibility of differential effect on pupils of differing previous attainment; the possibility of using different measures of classroom atmosphere, such as proportion with low scores, or proportion excluded; and the extent to which such effects are more important at different ages. The work would involve secondary analyses of a number of datasets looking at pupils' learning progress in schools.

Status: Sponsored project
Source of Grant: Economic and Social Research Council £17,000
Date of Research: 1994-continuing
KEYWORDS: *achievement; classroom environment; performance factors; statistical analysis*

10/1077

> The Mere, Upton Park, Slough SL1 2DQ
> 01753 574123
> Kendall, L. Mrs; Hutchison, D. Mr

Contextualisation of school examination results

Abstract: The National Foundation for Educational Research (NFER) has recently entered into contracts with thirteen local education authorities (LEA's) to provide 'value added' analyses of the achievements of the pupils in their schools, as measured by GCSE results, including brief automated individual school reports. This work continues a programme initiated by the Association of Metropolitan Authorities in 1990. Each of the participating authorities is able to provide data on all its 16 year old pupils, including GCSE results and information relating to the background of the individual pupils such as sex and ethnicity, as well as the scores on tests taken when the pupils transferred to secondary school. In addition, variables relating to the school attended, such as size, denomination, and whether the school is coeducational or not, will be collated. The combined data set should provide comprehensive information on over 20,000 pupils. The outcomes of the project will include an overall report, giving general findings for all LEA's and schools involved, with an appendix for each LEA giving results at school level for that LEA. A series of seminars/workshops tailored to the needs of individual LEA's will also be offered, at a small additional cost. Confidentiality will be preserved, so that individual schools or LEA's can be identified only on a 'need to know' basis. The reports and seminars between them can form an integral part of an ongoing LEA process of school improvement, identifying aspects where further investigation by the LEA or the school could be targeted. Participating authorities are committed to providing data by January 1995, and it is planned that results will be reported to these authorities in May 1995.

Status: Sponsored project
Source of Grant: Participating Local Education Authorities

Date of Research: 1994-continuing
KEYWORDS: *achievement; educational quality; examination results; outcomes of education; performance factors; performance indicators; school effectiveness*

10/1078
>The Mere, Upton Park, Slough SL1 2DQ
>01753 574123
>Dickson, P. Mr

Evaluation of LINGUA in the UK
Abstract: The purpose of the evaluation was to assess progress in the UK on the implementation of the EC LINGUA programme. Interviews were carried out with those responsible for the management and administration of the programme, and a questionnaire survey sought views from those who had benefited from LINGUA grants. The information collected provided a detailed account of the work of the UK LINGUA Unit in promoting the programme, administering it and processing applications. The views of applicants threw light on the difficulties facing those seeking grants, who, nevertheless, provided evidence of the substantial benefits to be gained from the programme, not only in language learning, but also in personal and professional development.
Published Material: DICKSON, P., with MOYS, A. & WIGHTWICK, C. (1994). LINGUA: the UK perspective. Slough: National Foundation for Educational Research.
Status: Sponsored project
Source of Grant: Department for Education £35,000
Date of Research: 1993-1993
KEYWORDS: *international programmes; modern language studies; programme evaluation; second language learning; student exchange programmes*

10/1079
>The Mere, Upton Park, Slough SL1 2DQ
>01753 574123
>Hawker, J. Mrs; *Supervisor:* Dickson, P. Mr

IEA language education study (phase 1)
Abstract: The International Association for the Evaluation of Educational Achievement (IEA) is conducting an international, comparative survey language education in secondary schools throughout the world. The Language Education Study (LES) will provide: 1) overview information on national policies for education in foreign, second, and minority languages in about 30 countries; 2) descriptions of language curricula based on surveys of students, teachers, and schools representative of secondary education; 3) descriptions, using internationally-validated tests, of the proficiency for communication that students achieve in English, French, German and other commonly taught languages at (a) the end of compulsory schooling, and (b) upon completing secondary education; 4) recommendations of needs and promising options for change in school language curricula for each participating country. Results will be useful for governments, educators, businesses and industries and researchers. In this phase of the study an enquiry form will be completed and this will provide overviews of the general context and policies for language education in each country. Findings will identify key policy issues and factors in school contexts broadly influencing curricula and students' learning in specific languages. Data collection in the first half of 1995 will be reported initially in November 1995 in the form of an inventory booklet, then a more extensive compendium reference document the following year, providing international comparisons.
Status: Sponsored project
Source of Grant: International Association for the Evaluation of Educational Achievement £58,645
Date of Research: 1994-continuing
KEYWORDS: *comparative education; language policy; modern language curriculum; modern language studies; second language teaching; secondary education*

10/1080
>The Mere, Upton Park, Slough SL1 2DQ
>01753 574123
>Dickson, P. Mr

Survey of media education
Abstract: Four hundred and eighty-two schools and colleges were surveyed by questionnaire to obtain information about the provision and organisation of media education. A response rate of only 40% was achieved, but this was sufficient to establish that a substantial majority of institutions had planned elements of media education, often as a part of the curriculum for English. Nearly all respondents thought media education important, and a trend towards increased entry for examinations in media studies was identified. The survey provided evidence also of resources for media education, staffing, inservice teacher education (INSET), which was reported to be in decline, and equipment. It also yielded descriptive information about the content of media education and the views of teachers on its role in the curriculum.
Published Material: DICKSON, P. (1994). A survey of media education. London: British Film Institute.
Status: Sponsored project
Source of Grant: British Film Institute £5,000
Date of Research: 1993-1994
KEYWORDS: *mass media; media studies*

10/1081
>The Mere, Upton Park, Slough SL1 2DQ
>01753 574123
>Ridout, M. Mr; *Supervisor:* Ruddock, G. Dr

Mathematical attainment in primary schools
Abstract: The project investigates pupils' mathematical performance in relation to the curriculum taught in their schools. Eighteen schools were chosen to represent a variety of practice in nine local education authorities (LEA's). The research is concerned with a range of mathematical concepts and skills with the main focus being number and shape and space. The objectives are: 1) investigate and contrast children's knowledge and understanding of different aspects of mathematics at two primary ages – Year 1 and Year 3; 2) study children's knowledge and understanding in relation to the curriculum provided by the project schools. To gain an indication of progression in mathematics, specially developed assessment tasks were administered on two occasions during 1993-94. From each age group three pupils were selected to represent the average attainment band and two pupils each were selected as representative of higher and lower attainment bands, making a total of seven pupils for each year group. Pupils from twenty-two classes containing Year 1 pupils and twenty-five classes containing Year 3 pupils were assessed, giving a sample of one hundred and nineteen Year 1 pupils and one hundred and nineteen Year 3 pupils. The results provide more insights into aspects of young children's learning than have previously been obtained at this age. Professional issues were investigated in the context of mathematics teaching in each school. The mathematics policy was examined, key staff were interviewed about their role, classteachers completed a questionnaire and the mathematics curriculum was observed in relation to the children studied.
Status: Sponsored project
Source of Grant: NFER Membership Programme
Date of Research: 1994-continuing
KEYWORDS: *mathematics achievement; mathematics education; primary education*

10/1082
>The Mere, Upton Park, Slough SL1 2DQ
>01753 574123
>Williams, M. Mrs; Francis, M. Mrs; *Supervisor:* Powell, R. Mr

National Curriculum key stage 1 Standard Task Development for Welsh
Abstract: From the start of statutory National Curriculum key stage 1 assessment in 1989, Welsh was assessed as a component of the Core Standard Assessment Task. From 1992, when the present contract began, Welsh has been assessed separately. This contract requires the development of a classroom task assessing speaking and listening, reading and writing, and also of an optional spelling test. Materials are developed in consultation with teacher panels and the Schools Curriculum and Assessment Authority (SCAA) Test Review Group and trialled thoroughly before final copy is presented to SCAA. Responsibility for the project passes to the Assessment and Curriculum Authority for Wales (ACAC) in April 1995. During 1995 a Welsh key stage 1 Standard Task and a Welsh Spelling Test will be produced.
Status: Sponsored project
Source of Grant: Schools Curriculum and Assessment Authority
Date of Research: 1992-continuing
KEYWORDS: *assessment; attainment tests; National Curriculum; standard assessment tasks; Welsh studies*

10/1083

The Mere, Upton Park, Slough SL1 2DQ
01753 574123
Lewis, T. Mr; Breese, N. Mrs; Derbyshire, G. Mr;
Supervisor: Powell, R. Mr

National Curriculum key stage 3 tasks and tests in Welsh and Welsh Second Language

Abstract: This project is a continuation of the National Curriculum key stage 3 assessment development which began in July 1989. The present contract requires the development of Welsh and Welsh Second Language tests and classroom tasks for the end of key stage 3 in 1995, 1996 and 1997. Materials are developed in consultation with teacher panels and the Schools Curriculum and Assessment Authority (SCAA) Test Review Group and trialled thoroughly in schools before final copy is presented to SCAA. Responsibility for the project passes to the Assessment and Curriculum Authority for Wales (ACAC) in April 1995. During 1995 ACAC will publish the Welsh Task and the Welsh Second Language Task.
Status: Sponsored project
Source of Grant: Schools Curriculum and Assessment Authority
Date of Research: 1994-continuing
KEYWORDS: assertiveness; attainment tests; National Curriculum; standard assessment tasks; Welsh studies

10/1084

The Mere, Upton Park, Slough SL1 2DQ
01753 574123
Brunel University, Faculty of Education and Design, Runnymede Campus, Cooper's Hill Lane, Egham TW20 OJZ
01784 431341
Ruddock, G. Dr; Harris, D. Prof.; Tomlins, B. Dr; Brooks, G. Dr; Salt, S. Mr; *Supervisor:* Whetton, C. Mr; Foxman, D. Mr

Evaluation of National Curriculum assessment at key stage 3 in mathematics, science, English and technology

Abstract: The project evaluated the first nationwide National Curriculum assessment of fourteen year olds in science and mathematics in 1992, and in English and technology in 1993. The results of these were surveyed and the procedures used evaluated. One focus of evaluation was the validity and reliability of the results. Three elements made up the study: a statistical survey of results; case studies of schools' management of the assessment process; and review of the assessment materials used. Reports on the 1992 mathematics and science pilot have been published, while that on the 1993 English and technology is due to be available in 1995.
Published Material: RUDDOCK, G. et al. (1992). Teacher assessment in mathematics and science at key stage 3: a report. London: School Examinations and Assessment Council.; RUDDOCK, G. et al. (1993). Evaluation of National Curriculum Assessment in mathematics and science at key stage 3: the 1992 National Pilot. Final Report. London: School Examinations and Assessment Council.
Status: Sponsored project
Source of Grant: School Examinations and Assessment Council £569,000
Date of Research: 1991-1993
KEYWORDS: assessment; English studies; evaluation; mathematics education; National Curriculum; science education; secondary education; technology education

10/1085

The Mere, Upton Park, Slough SL1 2DQ
01753 574123
London University, Institute of Education, 20 Bedford Way, London WC1H 0AL
0171 580 1122
Harris, S. Mrs; Preston, C. Mrs; *Supervisor:* Foxman, D. Mr

Survey of the provision, acquisition and use of computer software in primary and secondary schools

Abstract: Information technology (IT) is one of the attainment targets of Technology in the National Curriculum. The main aim of the project was to investigate the current use of educational software in schools, in terms of what is being used, how it is being used and which aspects of the curriculum are being supported. The research was carried out by means of: 1) questionnaire surveys of a random sample of 400 primary and 600 secondary schools; 2) telephone interviews with IT coordinators in a sub-sample of primary and secondary schools selected from respondents to the survey; 3) visits to local education authority (LEA) computer centres; 4) interviews with IT coordinators in a number of 'focus' schools outside the random

sample, which explored issues covered in the questionnaire in more depth; and 5) a questionnaire survey of 50 educational software publishers. The report on the project provides: information on schools' software purchases; the software in use in schools; and the systems and strategies available to support school use of software. The contributions of LEAs and educational software publishers are also explored. Finally, some perspectives on the future (in terms of needs and possible developments) are collated from schools, LEAs and educational software publishers.
Published Material: HARRIS, S. & PRESTON, C. (1993). Software in schools: the provision, acquisition and use of computer software in primary and secondary schools. Slough: National Foundation for Educational Research.
Status: Sponsored project
Source of Grant: National Council for Educational Technology £38,000
Date of Research: 1993-1993
KEYWORDS: computer software; computer uses in education; educational software; information technology; technology education

10/1086

The Mere, Upton Park, Slough SL1 2DQ
01753 574123
London University, London School of Economics and Political Science, Department of Statistical and Mathematical Sciences, Houghton Street, London WC2A 2AE
0171 405 7686
Hutchison, D. Mr; Kendall, L. Mrs; Knott, M. Dr; Galbraith, J. Mrs; Piccoli, M. Mrs

Latent variable analysis with missing data in educational research

Abstract: Sound monitoring of national educational performance requires that a very wide range of skills is assessed, a range that is in general much too wide to be administered to any one pupil. Consequently monitoring programmes such as the Assessment of Performance Unit (APU) employed a system of multiple matrix sampling whereby all the material to be assessed is taken, but not by each pupil tested. Politicians and members of the public at large frequently want an answer to the question 'Is performance in a subject going up or down?'. However if curriculum changes mean that performance improves in some areas and deteriorates in others, then this is not a particularly useful question, and an answer in terms of smaller curriculum elements is likely to be preferable. It is important to be able to identify when a topic is fragmenting in this way, and this is generally done by means of factor analysis, comparing the factor structure at the two times, and assessing whether it has changed. While this is a fairly standard technique under normal circumstances, it is not readily applicable to matrix-sampled data, and it is necessary to develop new techniques. The proposed project aims to: a) develop new techniques to deal with data of this kind; and b) apply them to matrix-sampled data, particularly from the APU language study of 1988 and 1989.
Status: Sponsored project
Source of Grant: Economic and Social Research Council £55,000
Date of Research: 1994-continuing
KEYWORDS: educational research; performance; statistical data

10/1087

The Mere, Upton Park, Slough SL1 2DQ
01753 574123
Newcastle upon Tyne University, School of Education, St Thomas Street, Newcastle upon Tyne NE1 7RU
0191 222 6000
Hutchison, D. Mr; Fitz-Gibbon, C. Prof.

Value added in further education

Abstract: This project, which is a joint venture between the National Foundation for Educational Research (NFER), Further Education Unit (FEU) and the University of Newcastle, aims to look at the possibility of introducing 'value-added' methodology in further education (FE). It comprises two main sub-projects. The first project is looking at the work of colleges in relationship to advanced GNVQ's, and given that correlations with traditional input measures such as average GCSE results are weak, seeks further, non-traditional, intake measures. Approximately 1,000 students in 10-15 colleges, and on 4 courses, will be covered. The second project is concerned with another group for whom the current methods may not necessarily be feasible or accurate, namely adults taking A-levels. A small exploratory study of about 250-300 adults is being mounted. The methodol-

ogy for both projects is similar. Data will be collected by the FEU from the colleges on such information as student's scores on standardised tests, answers to questionnaires, and merged with Census information. The predictive value of this information will be assessed.
Status: Sponsored project
Source of Grant: Further Education Unit £34,000
Date of Research: 1994-continuing
KEYWORDS: college effectiveness; educational quality; further education; institutional characteristics; performance factors; performance indicators

10/1088
The Mere, Upton Park, Slough SL1 2DQ
01753 574123
Southampton University, Faculty of Educational Studies, Highfield, Southampton SO9 5NH
01703 595000
Hawker, J. Mrs; Hooper, J. Ms; *Supervisor:* Dickson, P. Mr; Mitchell, R. Dr
Progression in foreign language learning
Abstract: The project is a study of progression in the learning of French in the initial stages and is carried out by tracking a cohort of sixty pupils in two secondary schools. Throughout Years 7, 8 and 9 the pupils' development in spoken language is being monitored by the use of specially prepared tasks; lessons are being observed, and teachers and pupils interviewed. The analysis of the data being collected focuses on prefabrication, grammar, vocabulary and conversational development. It also aims to explore the relationship of classroom instruction with children's learning, and the relevance of the National Curriculum Order for French.
Status: Sponsored project
Source of Grant: Economic and Social Research Council £186,930; National Foundation for Educational Research £59,450
Date of Research: 1993-continuing
KEYWORDS: French; modern language studies

10/1089
The Mere, Upton Park, Slough SL1 2DQ
01753 574123
York University, Department of Chemistry, Heslington, York YO1 5DD
01904 433433
Tomlins, B. Dr; Lazonby, J. Dr; *Supervisor:* Weston, P. Mrs; Waddington, D. Prof.
Progression to post-16 chemistry: a review of current practice
Abstract: In order to build on the investment in balanced science, schools and colleges need assistance in developing effective procedures and strategies to assist students to progress from GCSE to advanced science courses such as A- or AS-level or BTEC National. The first stage of the process, addressed by this project, is to review current provision and procedures in post-16 institutions for transition to advanced science courses. The immediate aim of this project was to carry out a review of the currently available courses and institutional provision and support for post-16 advanced science. Additional aims were to: identify factors which appear to enhance or constrain effective progression from GCSE to advanced courses; inform and assist those responsible for managing advanced science courses; provide a firm foundation for possible development work with teachers and students, to improve progression and success in advanced chemistry courses. There are two main aspects to the project: a syllabus analysis and a survey of current practice. A syllabus analysis was conducted on post-16 science syllabuses which offer advanced chemistry. A questionnaire survey of a national sample of institutions providing 16-19 education (maintained, grant-maintained and independent; and post-16 colleges of all types) was administered. The sample included 57 further education/tertiary colleges, 20 sixth-form colleges and 270 schools offering post-16 courses. The report covered both the syllabus review and the questionnaire survey, and showed that while teachers were concerned that GCSE science courses do not offer an adequate foundation for A-level chemistry, dual award science was not thought to provide students with adequate knowledge and understanding. However, some post-16 staff were addressing the problem by promoting a structured introduction and appropriate support. All teachers felt that student motivation was a key factor, and the report reviews teachers' strategies for encouraging and sustaining it.
Published Material: WESTON, P., LAZONBY, J. & TOMLINS, B.

(1994). Progression to post-16 chemistry: a survey of schools and colleges. Slough: National Foundation for Educational Research.
Status: Sponsored project
Source of Grant: National Foundation for Educational Research; University of York; The Salters' Company
Date of Research: 1993-1994
KEYWORDS: chemistry education; science education; sixteen to nineteen education

National Institute for Careers Education and Counselling

10/1090
Sheraton House, Castle Park, Cambridge CB3 0AX
01223 460277
Watts, A. Mr
European careers guidance survey
Abstract: The survey is studying the educational and vocational guidance services available to young people and adults in the twelve Member States. Its aim is to illuminate the different structures and strategies adopted in these countries in a way which will enable Member States to: (a) learn from each other's experience; (b) develop stronger networks across national boundaries in support of the Single European Market. Particular attention is being paid to: (i) Changes which have taken place since the survey of guidance services for young people carried out by Watts et al. in 1985/1987; (ii) The structure of guidance services for adults, which were not examined in any detail in the earlier survey. Country-studies are being commissioned from experts in each Member State; they will be revised during a one-week study visit to the country in question by a member of the project's central team (Tony Watts, UK; Peter Plant, Denmark; Dr Jean Guichard, France; Professor Luisa Rodriguez, Spain).
Published Material: WATTS, A.G., GUICHARD, J., PLANT, P. & RODRIGUEZ, M.L. (1994). Education and vocational guidance in the European Community. Luxembourg: Office for Official Publications of the European Communities.
Status: Sponsored project
Source of Grant: European Commission – ECUs £136,500
Date of Research: 1992-1993
KEYWORDS: adult counselling; career counselling; Europe; European community; vocational guidance

10/1091
Sheraton House, Castle Park, Cambridge CB3 0AX
01223 460277
Watts, A. Mr; Hawthorn, R. Ms; Kidd, J. Dr; Killeen, J. Mr; Law, W. Dr
Rethinking careers education and guidance
Abstract: The aim of the project is to rethink the basis for policy, theory and practice in careers education and guidance in the UK. The project will include a thorough review of existing research, and its implications for policy and practice. The main outcome will be a book, designed to provide a durable reference point for the next decade, and a key text for use in the training of teachers and other guidance practitioners. There will also be briefing documents and seminars addressed to policy-makers and practitioners.
Status: Sponsored project
Source of Grant: Esmee Fairbairn Trust £30,000
Date of Research: 1993-continuing
KEYWORDS: career counselling; career education; vocational guidance

National Institute of Adult Continuing Education

10/1092
21 De Montfort Street, Leicester LE1 7GE
01162 551451
McGivney, V. Dr

Part-time and temporary workers and the national education and training targets
Abstract: The aim of the enquiry was to investigate the nature and extent of the training offered to part-time and temporary workers to see whether the National Education and Training Targets can be achieved. The study was in two parts: a context analysis using existing research; and empirical research in employing organisations, involving interviews with personnel and training managers and with part-time and temporary staff. The results showed that although large 'leading edge' companies have improved the training they offer 'peripheral' or 'atypical' workers, and reduced differentials between part-time and full-time employees, part-time workers as a whole still receive far less training than full-time workers. Their opportunities for promotion and progression also remain limited. Unless this state of affairs can be improved, the National Lifelong Education and Training Targets stand little chance of being achieved.
Published Material: McGIVNEY, V.K. (1994). Wasted potential: training and career progression for part-time and temporary workers. Leicester: National Institute of Adult Continuing Education.
Status: Sponsored project
Source of Grant: Department of Employment £21,500
Date of Research: 1993-1993
KEYWORDS: *job training; part time employment; temporary employment; training*

10/1093
    21 De Montfort Street, Leicester LE1 7GE
    01162 551451
    Hillcroft College, South Bank, Surbiton KT6 6DF
    0181 399 2688
    McGivney, V. Dr; *Supervisor:* Aird, E. Mrs
Women in education and training: barriers to access; informal starting points and progression issues
Abstract: The study involved a literature search and interviews with staff and women students in a range of education and training courses. It showed that the principal barriers that deter women from participating in education and training – lack of finance, lack of childcare, lack of confidence in their abilities – stem from cultural attitudes and expectations underpinned by social and economic structures and policies. Help with education/training costs and childcare most facilitates women's access to education/training and their progression within it. The project revealed that informal re-entry learning schemes have enabled a great number of women without qualifications to take the first step back into education, training and employment. However, the reliance on 'special' funding for women's re-entry courses, coupled with the changes brought about by the Further and Higher Education Act, have resulted in a sharp reduction in the informal learning opportunities available for women. Women are still expected to fit into a system established mainly for the benefit of men. The project showed that formal education and training providers need to adapt not only the courses they offer, but also delivery methods, teaching approaches, support structured and institutional 'ethos' in order to give women equal access to training, qualifications and employment opportunities.
Published Material: McGIVNEY, V. (1993). Women, education and training: barriers to access, informal starting points and progression issues. Leicester: National Institute of Adult Continuing Education.; McGIVNEY, V. (1994). 'Women, education and training: a research report', Adult Learning, Vol 5, No 5, pp.118-120.
Status: Sponsored project
Source of Grant: Training, Enterprise and Education Directorate
Date of Research: 1992-1993
KEYWORDS: *access to education; adult education; retraining; women's education*

National Union of Teachers

10/1094
    Hamilton House, Mabledon Place, London WC1H 9BD
    0171 388 6191
    Stainton, R. Mr; Baker, K. Ms
The new arrangements for inspecting schools
Abstract: To identify the responses of teachers and headteachers in the first 382 secondary and middle deemed secondary schools to be inspected under the new school inspection arrangements introduced following the Education (Schools) Act 1992. The research is based on two questionnaires to each school, plus visits to a small number of schools
Status: Sponsored project
Source of Grant: National Union of Teachers
Date of Research: 1993-1994
KEYWORDS: *educational change; inspection; secondary schools; teacher attitudes*

Nene College

10/1095
    Moulton Park, Northampton NN2 7AL
    01604 715000
    Silcock, P. Dr
Monitoring the implementation of the National Curriculum in primary schools
Abstract: Practitioners are interviewed each school term using a semi-structured interview, to discover: a) positive; and b) negative effects of the implementation of the National Curriculum on primary schools. Sample sizes vary from around 12-25. Results indicate increasing problems of curriculum manageability with a fairly positive view being taken of the tighter structure imposed on practitioners by the National Curriculum. Hybrid methodologies appear to be developing.
Published Material: SILCOCK, P.J. (1990). 'Implementing the National Curriculum: some teachers' dilemmas', Education 3-13, Vol 18, No 3, pp.3-10.; SILCOCK, P.J. (1992). 'The reflective practitioner in the year of the SAT', Education 3-13, Vol 20, No 1, pp.3-9.; SILCOCK, P.J. (1992). 'Primary school teacher-time and the National Curriculum: managing the impossible?', British Journal of Educational Studies, Vol XXXX, No 2, pp.163-173.
Status: Sponsored project
Source of Grant: Nene College £87,500
Date of Research: 1988-continuing
KEYWORDS: *educational change; National Curriculum; primary schools*

10/1096
    Moulton Park, Northampton NN2 7AL
    01604 735500
    Winch, C. Dr; Wells, P. Mr; Ellis, S. Ms
Student literacy in further and higher education
Abstract: The study arises from concern about standards of literacy in further and higher education. An intensive study will be conducted in one institution consisting of pilot projects, together with visits to other institutions. The pilot projects will include diagnosis and an evaluation of work undertaken to improve students' communication skills.
Status: Sponsored project
Source of Grant: Nene College
Date of Research: 1993-1994
KEYWORDS: *further education students; higher education; literacy; reading skills; writing skills*

10/1097
    Moulton Park, Northampton NN2 7AL
    01604 735500
    Clark, U. Ms
Learning about language in National Curriculum key stages 2 and 3
Abstract: This project arises from a previous research project investigating the implementation of National Curriculum English. It aims to establish: a) what and how teachers teach pupils about language; and b) the impact of the National Curriculum on such teaching. The methodology includes: teacher diaries; classroom observation; and interview. The sample will consist of two teachers in two different schools at key stage 3 to be joined by two teachers in two different schools at key stage 2.
Status: Individual research
Date of Research: 1993-continuing
Keywords: *English studies; language teachers; National Curriculum*

10/1098

Moulton Park, Northampton NN2 7AL
01604 735500
Leicester University, School of Medicine, Department of
Epidemiology and Public Health, Clinical Science Building,
PO Box 65, Leicester Royal Infirmary, Leicester LE2 7LX
01162 523206
Merriman, L. Mrs; *Supervisor:* Winch, C. Dr; Field, D. Dr
**The transition from diploma to degree in the professions allied
to medicine**
Abstract: The professions allied to medicine, in particular Occupational Therapy, Podiatry and Radiography, have made the transition
from diploma to degree course in a relatively short period of time.
The purpose of this study is to examine what, if any, educational
changes have been made to the courses in this transition. The factors
which led to the transition will also be investigated. The main
methodology adopted is case studies. Three schools have been selected, one in Podiatry, one in Occupational Therapy and one in
Radiography. Interviews are to be held with the last cohort of diploma
students, the first cohort of degree students and the lecturers who have
seen the transition from diploma to degree. Content analysis will be
undertaken on the diploma and degree documentation. As well as
these methods, interviews are being held with key people who played
an active part in gaining degree status for those professions.
Status: Sponsored project
Source of Grant: Higher Education Funding Council £15,000
Date of Research: 1992-continuing
KEYWORDS: *degrees – academic; medicine; professional education; undergraduate students*

10/1099

Moulton Park, Northampton NN2 7AL
01604 715000
Warwick University, Department of Education, Coventry
CV4 7AL
01203 523523
Duncan, D. Ms; *Supervisor:* Burgess, R. Prof.
**Mature women entrants to teaching: an analysis of the process
of adjustment to the student role in the four year BEd course**
Abstract: The research study has two distinct aims: (1) To investigate
mature candidates' previous career and work experiences and the
factors leading to a decision to pursue a career in the teaching
profession. (2) To identify the problems, resource needs and learning
needs of mature students in the first year of the BEd course. A case
study approach will be used to chart the socialisation process of 26
mature women into the student role in the first year of the BEd course
(1991-92). The research will be conducted using mainly qualitative
research methods. Much of the data will be gathered via tape recorded
interviews using a 'structured conversation' approach. Interviews
will be conducted at key points of their first year (before entry; once
in each of the three terms; and at the end of the post-examination
period of the first year) in order to identify the changes which have
occurred in their behaviour, and in their perceptions of the student
role in the first year of a teacher training course.
Status: Individual research
Date of Research: 1989-1994
KEYWORDS: *mature students; preservice teacher education; student behaviour; student teacher attitudes; student teachers; women's
education*

10/1100

Moulton Park, Northampton NN2 7AL
01604 735500
Wolverhampton University, School of Health Sciences,
62-68 Lichfield Street, Wolverhampton WV1 1DJ
01902 28528
Snape, J. Dr; Cavanagh, S. Prof.
Stress in student nurse learners
Abstract: While considerable attention has been given to aspects of
occupational stress in nursing and health care, the subject of stress
experienced by students undergoing initial nursing and midwifery
eduction has been almost totally overlooked. The introduction of the
Project 2000 scheme of education, the movement of colleges of
nursing and midwifery into higher education, a move towards an
older student and changes in job opportunities are all factors which
now face students. This is in addition to learning the skills and
complexities of a practice-based discipline. The purpose of the study
is to address: 1) What do student nurses and midwives find stressful

while completing their initial nurse training? 2) How do students react
to these stressors? 3) What are the self-reported consequences of
stress in the learning environment? 4) What strategies do students
adopt when confronted with stress in the learning environment?
Student nurses and midwives are being asked to complete a questionnaire which assesses stress and to complete log books of their
experiences while training. Both instruments have been developed
from previous research by Snape (1991), Snape and Cavanagh
(1992), and Cavanagh and Snape (1993). The questionnaire has been
optically prepared to facilitate rapid data entry and analysis. The
information from both questionnaire and logs (approximately 2000
subjects) will be collated and triangulated to produce a better understanding of the stresses which students are facing.
Status: Sponsored project
Source of Grant: Nene College; Wolverhampton University, jointly
£4,000
Date of Research: 1993-1994
KEYWORDS: *nurse education; nurses; stress – psychological*

New College Durham

10/1101

Department of Education and Administration, Neville's
Cross Centre, Darlington Road, Durham DH1 4SY
0191 3847325
Beverton, S. Dr
**Teachers' perceptions of oracy and information technology
project**
Abstract: The aim of the research is to investigate teachers' perceptions of oracy and information technology (IT) in a number of local
authorities. These two subject areas, although separate in themselves,
were chosen because of two common factors: (1) both are 'new' in
the sense of having acquired new status in the National Curriculum
with little historical background as subjects per se; (2) the National
Curriculum demands that all teachers address these themes. The
research aims to survey a wide range of perceptions to reflect the
current position of oracy and IT in the curriculum in primary and
secondary schools. A questionnaire has been designed and developed
to be used in a pilot survey. Appropriate modifications will then be
made before the questionnaire is distributed to schools in a number
of local authorities. It is envisaged that a variety of perceptions in
both areas will be revealed and that these might have implications for
classroom practice. After analysis, the questionnaires will be followed up by more indepth studies of particular teachers and schools,
with the intention of revealing the nature of the relationship between
perceptions and practice. The results will determine the current status
of oracy and IT in terms of perceptions and practice. The dissemination of these results will inform and assist teachers' practice and also
enable authorities to plan inservice education of teachers (INSET)
courses appropriately.
Status: Sponsored project
Source of Grant: New College Durham
Date of Research: 1990-continuing
KEYWORDS: *information technology; National Curriculum; oracy;
teacher attitudes*

Newcastle upon Tyne University

10/1102

Department of Psychology, Ridley Building, Newcastle upon
Tyne NE1 7RU
0191 222 6000
Lister, C. Dr; Simpson, L. Miss
The development of quantity concepts in children who are blind
Abstract: Relatively little research has been reported exploring blind
children's concepts of quantity conservation and the findings and
interpretations have been conflicting. Even fewer studies have attempted to develop such concepts in these children. It is important to
know how concepts may be built if children show developmental lags
and the importance of understanding quantity conservation is well
attested, for example as fundamental to measurement. This project
builds upon the series of investigations of sequence in development

of concepts in children with and without specific handicapping conditions carrried out by the first researcher and her colleagues. It extends the study of order in concept acquisition to work with children who are blind and it goes beyond this to examine processes in developing these children's understanding through specific forms of intervention. Pre-test tasks examining understanding of number, substance, length, weight, area and volume are being specifically adapted for blind children paying particular attention to influences on their experience of the six attributes. These will reveal the blind children's initial understanding and clarify how far there is a common sequence in development. By providing experiences and explanations designed to build the children's quantity concepts within a training study, it is possible to focus closely upon processes of development and the effect of handicapping conditions. Post-testing enables further exploration and evaluation of the development of blind children's concepts. Altogether, the project aims to provide insights into development generally as well as to contribute specifically to understanding and developing blind children's concepts.
Status: Sponsored project
Source of Grant: Leverhulme Trust £30,590
Date of Research: 1993-continuing
KEYWORDS: *blindness; concept formation; number concepts; quantity concepts*

10/1103
Department of Psychology, Ridley Building, Newcastle upon Tyne NE1 7RU
0191 222 6000
Stothard, S. Dr; *Supervisor:* Snowling, M. Prof.
The nature and origins of children's reading comprehension problems
Abstract: This research will investigate the nature of specific reading comprehension problems in children. A group of children (N=15) with adequate decoding skills but poor comprehension will be selected. These children will be aged 7-9 years. They will be compared with two control groups: a group of chronological-age controls and a group of younger comprehension-age controls. The three groups will be given a number of standardised tests to measure their reading ability, vocabulary and verbal intelligence. They will also be given experimental tests of vocabulary to explore their semantic skills. The aim of the project is to obtain detailed information about the semantic processing skills of children with comprehension problems.
Status: Sponsored project
Source of Grant: Medical Research Council £5,812
Date of Research: 1994-continuing
KEYWORDS: *learning disabilities; reading comprehension; reading difficulties; special educational needs*

10/1104
School of Education, St Thomas Street, Newcastle upon Tyne NE1 7RU
0191 222 6000
Newton, L. Mrs
The new teacher project
Abstract: The initial training of primary teachers has been subjected to criticism in recent years, both in terms of quality and variety of approach. Such criticism has seldom been based on research evidence, nor have the views of student teachers themselves been thoroughly explored. Moves towards 'training on the job', reflected in school based partnerships or school-provided training models, are based upon a view of training in which it is seen as desirable to give students more practical experience at the chalk face and less exposure to potentially radical and subversive theories which it is claimed are propounded by tutors in higher education institutions. But what of newly qualified teachers themselves? How do they feel about the balance of their training, the mix of theory and practice? A study carried out over the last five years by the University of Newcastle upon Tyne provides data which gives evidence of their needs and views. It can also guide the nature and form of evolving partnerships between schools and universities, to meet the needs of those who are most important yet least consulted in the training process, the student teachers. Analysis of the questionnaire responses of 118 past Postgraduate Certificate in Education (PGCE) students at the end of their first year of teaching highlights the value they place on the different elements of their training. In essence, the majority of the respondents were satisfied with their training as a preparation for a teaching career, and felt that the balance of theory and practice was correct. While a small percentage would have liked more time in school, it was

explicitly not at the expense of the institution based elements of their training. None of the aspects covered in training were considered inappropriate or unnecessary. For many, support in the probationary/induction year was lacking and they relied heavily on their PGCE course notes.
Published Material: NEWTON, L.D. (1991). 'Who needs trained relations?', Primary Teaching Studies, Vol 6, No 1, pp.62-67.; NEWTON, L.D. (1991). 'What comes next? The inservice needs of newly qualified primary teachers', British Journal of In-Service Education, Vol 17, No1, pp.75-80.; NEWTON, L.D. (1994). 'New teachers reflecting on their training'. In: REID, I., CONSTABLE, H. & GRIFFITHS, R. (Eds). Teacher education reform: current research. London: Paul Chapman.
Status: Sponsored project
Source of Grant: Newcastle upon Tyne University
Date of Research: 1989-1994
KEYWORDS: *preservice teacher education; probationary teachers; student teachers; teaching profession*

10/1105
School of Education, St Thomas Street, Newcastle upon Tyne NE1 7RU
0191 222 6000
Williamson, J. Mr; Hardman, F. Mr
Time for refilling the bath?: a study of primary student teachers' grammatical knowledge
Abstract: The introduction of the National Curriculum for English in England and Wales has placed an increased demand on primary teachers to promote a greater knowledge about language, including the teaching of grammar. Critics of the English curriculum believe, however, that too little attention has been paid to the teaching of grammar and proposals for a revised curriculum which place more emphasis on the teaching of grammatical structure and terminology have been put forward. This study investigates the current levels of some aspects of grammatical knowledge amongst 99 trainee primary school teachers. Results indicate a higher level of grammatical knowledge than some critics might have us suppose. There are, however, significant gaps which could affect the student teachers' ability to teach about language and grammar and suggest the need for a systematic course of study during initial teacher training and beyond.
Status: Sponsored project
Source of Grant: Newcastle upon Tyne University
Date of Research: 1994-1994
KEYWORDS: *English studies; grammar; student teachers*

Newman College

10/1106
Genners Lane, Bartley Green, Birmingham B32 3NT
0121 476 1181
Exeter University, School of Education, St Luke's, Heavitree Road, Exeter EX1 2LU
01392 263263
Davenport, A. Mr; *Supervisor:* Peacock, A. Dr; Desforges, C. Prof.
Initial Teacher Training and Inservice Education of Teachers (IT-INSET) and the higher education tutor
Abstract: This research involves an ethnographic study of the cognitive, social, pedagogical and professional pathways taken by university and college tutors involved in initial teacher training and inservice education of teachers (IT INSET). There will be continuing research into the evaluative procedures used by higher education tutors during a degree-centred INSET programme.
Status: Sponsored project
Source of Grant: Newman College
Date of Research: 1990-continuing
KEYWORDS: *academic staff; higher education; inservice teacher education; preservice teacher education; teacher educators*

NICER Research Unit

10/1107

Queen's University of Belfast, School of Education, 61
University Street, Belfast BT7 1FY
01232 245133
McLean, L. Miss; *Supervisor:* Sutherland, A. Miss
Unjustified absenteeism in Northern Ireland schools
Abstract: Following the Education Reform (NI) Order, 1989, this
project set out, firstly, to consider how data on 'unjustified' pupil
absenteeism (ie absence due not to illness or other legally permitted
cause) might be collected and disseminated in a way helpful both to
schools wishing to raise their standards and to parents making a
choice of school. In commissioning the project, the Department of
Education for Northern Ireland viewed absenteeism as a potential
behavioural performance indicator for schools. Other project aims
were to discover whether levels of persistent absenteeism had
changed since the last Northern Ireland survey in 1982, to find out
how schools monitored attendance and to review school-based and
other intervention strategies to improve attendance. Education Welfare Officers (EWOs) examined the attendance registers of all sec-
ond-level and some 200 primary schools in Northern Ireland. Pupils
absent for 14 or more days in the spring term of 1992 were identified.
If 7 or more of these days' absence were not attributable to illness,
the main other reason was noted. The incidence of persistent absenteeism was related, at individual level, to age, gender and some social
background factors and, at school level, to its type (e.g. primary,
grammar , other secondary), religious affiliation, size, the percentage
of pupils entitled to free school meals, the annual percentage attendance and to data from the published performance indicators. Information on attendance monitoring and intervention strategies was
obtained through an initial telephone survey in 92 schools, follow-up
telephone interviews and visits, a questionnaire survey, completed in
253 schools, on strategies to improve attendance and interviews and
correspondence with EWOs and others who had organised or evaluated special initiatives to improve attendance.
Published Material: SUTHERLAND, A.E. (1993). Persistent school
absenteeism in Northern Ireland in 1992. Belfast: NICER Research
Unit, School of Education, The Queen's University of Belfast.
Status: Sponsored project
Source of Grant: Department of Education for Northern Ireland
£41,000
Date of Research: 1991-1994
KEYWORDS: *attendance; attendance patterns; Northern Ireland;
pupil behaviour; truancy*

10/1108

Queen's University of Belfast, School of Education, 61
University Street, Belfast BT7 1FY
01232 245133
D'Arcy, J. Mr; Thompson, K. Miss; Leitch, C. Miss;
McMahon, J. Miss; Rainey, N. Mrs; *Supervisor:* Sutherland,
A. Miss
Annual follow-up of newly-trained teachers
Abstract: In collaboration with the teacher training institutions in
Northern Ireland, the Northern Ireland Council for Educational Research (NICER) carries out an annual survey of newly-qualified
teachers. The investigation seeks to describe the newly-qualified
teachers in terms of their subject specialism, sector emphasis and type
of training; to identify employment status by the same characteristics;
to take note of teachers' experiences in seeking teaching posts and to
examine trends in teacher employment. Data are collected by means
of an annual questionnaire survey to all teachers who qualified the
previous summer. Over the years considerable changes have been
observed in the numbers of teachers qualifying, in the percentage who
fail to find employment and in the ratio of permanent to non-perma-
nent teaching posts obtained by newly-qualified teachers.
Published Material: D'ARCY, J.M. (1990). Teachers newly-qualified in 1989. Belfast: Northern Ireland Council for Educational
Research.; THOMPSON, K. (1991). Teachers newly-qualified in
1990. Belfast: Northern Ireland Council for Educational Research.;
LEITCH, C.M. & SUTHERLAND, A.E. (1992). Teachers newly-
qualified in 1991. Belfast: NICER Research Unit, School of Education, The Queen's University of Belfast.; SUTHERLAND, A.E.,
McMAHON, J.M. & RAINEY, N.A. (1993). Teachers newly-qualified in 1992. Belfast: NICER Research Unit, School of Education,
The Queen's University of Belfast.

Status: Sponsored project
Source of Grant: Department of Education for Northern Ireland
Date of Research: 1978-continuing
KEYWORDS: *labour market; northern ireland; probationary teach-
ers; teacher employment; teacher recruitment; teaching profession*

North Cheshire College

10/1109

Padgate Campus, Fearnhead Lane, Warrington WA2 0DB
01925 814343
Lancaster University, Department of Management Learning,
Gillow House, Bailrigg, Lancaster LA1 4YX
01524 65201
Lloyd, P. Mr; *Supervisor:* Davies, J. Mrs
**Assessment of work experience in relation to management
learning**
Abstract: The aim of this research is to investigate and evaluate the
validity of supervised work experience as a degree course component
that: (1) Enables students to acquire knowledge and skills. (2) Enables
students to complement the college based learning prior to the placement period. (3) Enables students to develop appropriate and meaningful learning strategies following work experience periods. (4)
Facilitates course development through 'wash back' on existing
learning programmes. (5) Promotes staff development in terms of
updating current practices within the industrial/commercial environment. (6) Enhances host awareness and sympathy towards participation in supervised work experience programmes. (7) Accurately
assesses student development and performance in terms of: (a) per-
sonal/social skills; and (b) academic/cognitive skills. A further aim
is to test the above through a process of primary and secondary
research into short- and long-term supervised work experience programmes in several institutions offering a range of vocational related
courses. It also aims to establish the theoretical concepts via primary
and secondary sources of the notions underpinning: (1) experiential
learning; (2) education and training; (3) teaching and learning methods; (4) assessment and profiling; and (5) competence and competition.
Status: Individual research
Date of Research: 1991-1993
KEYWORDS: *industry-higher education relationship; management
studies; placement; work experience*

10/1110

Padgate Campus, Fearnhead Lane, Warrington WA2 0DB
01925 814343
Manchester University, School of Education, Centre for
Adult and Higher Education, Oxford Road, Manchester
M13 9PL
0161 275 2000
Walters, M. Mrs; *Supervisor:* Nichol, B. Dr
**To investigate whether there is a difference in the
support/counselling provision needed for the mature student
compared to younger students**
Abstract: Mature students, by re-entering education, have already
made major choices. These choices may have been influenced or
precipitated by major life incidents, some traumatic, e.g. redundancy,
divorce, bereavement, failure or loss. Students have tremendous
commitment to making a success of their venture; they may or may
not, however, have come to terms with their changing circumstances,
self-image, aspirations and present role. Their positive drive and
energy, therefore, may be dissipated by their underlying problems,
which sometimes have to be addressed and resolved to enable their
energy to be recharged and channelled into academic work. The
objective of the research is to investigate whether there is a difference
in the support/counselling provision needed for the mature student
compared to younger students. The methods used will, on the whole,
be qualitative rather than quantitative. It will involve indepth interviews of students and of student counsellors and careers advisors;
and case studies which may be journalistic, quantitative or evaluative.
Surveys will be carried out on: students' problems; students' evaluation of student services; and student services, including counsellors
and careers advisors.
Status: Individual research
Date of Research: 1991-continuing

KEYWORDS: *counselling services; higher education; mature students; student counselling*

Northbrook College of Design and Technology

10/1111
Littlehampton Road, Goring-by-Sea, Worthing BN12 6NU
01903 830057
Hayler, S. Mr; *Supervisor:* Sexton, T. Mr
Northbrook College – the influence and application of marketing planning techniques on the strategic planning process
Abstract: A general overview of the educational strategic environment will lead to an investigation of strategic planning as applied to the education sector, and then specifically, the College being investigated. The various techniques of marketing planning will be explored, moving from the general theory to practical applications in colleges, and the specific usage at Northbrook College. The optimum application of marketing planning to the College will be suggested, giving a full view of options available, and finally suggesting a practical marketing plan which will assist and benefit strategic planning processes. The implementation and delivery of the marketing plan will be demonstrated in its integrated format, and future action required to maintain marketing planning effectiveness will be included in suggested evaluation and review procedures. Original primary research will include interviews with senior college management, education officers, and governors of the college. Secondary research will take into account recent published work on the subjects of strategic and marketing planning in colleges, as well as established literature and articles on strategic and marketing planning in general as applied to both public and private organisations. Examples of best practice will be utilised.
Status: Sponsored project
Source of Grant: Northbrook College of Design and Technology – per annum £877
Date of Research: 1992-1994
KEYWORDS: *colleges of further education; educational administration; educational planning; management in education; marketing*

Nottingham Trent University

10/1112
Faculty of Education, Clifton Hall, Clifton Lane, Clifton, Nottingham NG11 8NS
01159 418418
Johnston, J. Mrs; Eland, S. Ms; Jackson, P. Mr
Improving attitudes to primary school science
Abstract: The project aims to develop a positive image of science in primary school parents and governors. An interactive workshop is being developed which can be used by schools in a variety of ways as part of a science evening. This is felt to be of great importance in supporting schools in their efforts to develop positive attitudes in children. The workshop will include simple resources and activity ideas for different areas of science and through it parents, governors, teachers and children can work together to solve simple problems and undertake specific tasks to the mutual benefit of individuals, education and science. The activities within the workshop have been designed as examples of good primary practice, in that they identify the dual nature of science (process and knowledge) with all activities involving the experience of science knowledge through initial curiosity and active participation.
Status: Sponsored project
Source of Grant: Royal Society, Committee on the Public Understanding of Science £2,030
Date of Research: 1993-1994
KEYWORDS: *attitudes; parent attitudes; primary education; school governors; science education; scientific attitudes*

10/1113
Faculty of Education, Clifton Hall, Clifton Lane, Clifton, Nottingham NG11 8NS
01159 418418
Bowen, R. Mr
Changes in the primary school curriculum resulting from the introduction of Technology
Abstract: The intention is to investigate the procedures being used to implement Technology into the curriculum of a selected group of primary schools in order to identify effective methodology.
Status: Individual research
Date of Research: 1990-continuing
KEYWORDS: *curriculum development; primary education; technology education*

10/1114
Faculty of Education, Clifton Hall, Clifton Lane, Clifton, Nottingham NG11 8NS
01159 418418
Dhingra, S. Ms; Dunkwu, K. Mr; Cooke, P. Mr; Bolla, M. Ms
Action for access – ethnic minorities into teaching
Abstract: The aims of the research are to: 1) investigate the existing barriers to teacher recruitment within the regional Asian and African-Caribbean communities; and 2) develop a model or models which could be used for the recruitment of ethnic minority teachers in this and other regions. This is a one year project in which the team will initially establish contacts with local ethnic minority communities and individuals. The barriers which deter entry into the teaching profession from these community groups will be investigated by research into attitudes and perspectives of children, students and teachers from these ethnic minority communities. The project aims to develop strategies to increase the recruitment into teaching of the target groups.
Status: Sponsored Research
Source of Grant: Higher Education Funding Council £61,500
Date of Research: 1993-1994
KEYWORDS: *ethnic groups; preservice teacher education; student recruitment; teacher recruitment; teaching profession*

10/1115
Faculty of Education, Clifton Hall, Clifton Lane, Clifton, Nottingham NG11 8NS
01159 418418
McAuley, S. Ms; *Supervisor:* Bloomfield, A. Dr; Phelps, A. Dr; Disney, A. Ms
Developing heritage education through the arts in the primary school
Abstract: To develop and evaluate a rationale and methodology for the teaching of heritage arts with primary school children making particular reference to an exemplar project – History in Action in Clifton Hall. It is intended to establish theoretical and practical strategies in order to acquire pedagogical, contextual and empirical understanding of the exemplar project, History in Action in Clifton Hall, and to secure its terms of reference in relation to the National Curriculum statutory orders and programmes of study at key stages 1 and 2 in the areas of the curriculum relevant to the study of heritage arts – visual art, music, dance, drama and history. It is necessary to pose four fundamental questions: 1) What is meant by the study of heritage arts in the primary school? 2) What knowledge areas and experiences must children be taught? 3) What teaching strategies and resource materials need to be employed? 4) What methods of evaluation can be used to assess the effectiveness and quality of the learning experience? The acquisition of theoretical understanding of the practice of heritage arts education will occur through the review of relevant literature relating to the child's experience of creative and aesthetic education as a means of understanding cultural transmission and re-creation of the past.
Status: Individual research
Date of Research: 1993-continuing
KEYWORDS: *arts education; cultural education; history; primary education*

10/1116
Faculty of Education, Clifton Hall, Clifton Lane, Clifton, Nottingham NG11 8NS
01159 418418
Howard, D. Mr; *Supervisor:* Hayes, M. Ms; Bassey, M. Dr; Swannell, M. Dr

Changes in the preferred learning styles of trainee nurses

Abstract: The aim is to study groups of trainee nurses of mixed academic ability, ages and social backgrounds, to establish an instrument for identifying their preferred learning styles and to compare this with their own descriptions of their learning styles using profiles as a means of assisting their preparations for practice. The objective is to: 1) Assist students at the end of their course to reflect upon their experience. The purpose of the reflections will be to: a) identify their own learning preferences, and how these might have altered during the course; b) assess how the students may have changed emotionally and socially as a result and whether a change in learning preferences coincided with social and emotional changes. 2) Compare the students' learning achievements: a) as described by themselves; b) their attitudes towards learning (measured by an instrument to be developed as part of the study), and other significant variables which include social background, past academic achievements, recency of previous learning and motivation for starting course. These data will be sifted for patterns, supplemented by data obtained from part (1) above. 3) Develop an attitudes and learning styles' instrument from the analysis of data, submit this to second cohort of students at start of course. 4) Identify the preferred learning style of each student and resubmit the instrument, at a time that will be decided from the first set of interviews, where it is indicated that most students' learning style would have changed. Compare the students' learning achievements, as described by themselves with their attitudes towards learning, as identified by the instrument. 5) Consolidate the results to provide a group profile of the preferred learning styles of individual students and student groups ascertaining whether particular students' preferred learning styles may change on educational courses.
Status: Individual research
Date of Research: 1993-continuing
KEYWORDS: learning activities; learning strategies; nurse education; study skills

10/1117
Faculty of Education, Clifton Hall, Clifton Lane, Clifton, Nottingham NG11 8NS
01159 418418
Marsh, C. Ms; *Supervisor:* Lofthouse, M. Dr; Hughes, C. Dr
How do children acquire ecological concepts?
Abstract: The aims are to investigate what children understand about the relationship between human beings and their environment, and to explore ways of improving the quality of such understanding. Specific objectives are to: 1) investigate the development of children's understanding of the relationship between human beings and their environment, in order to develop strategies through which education can assist in addressing major environmental issues; 2) assess the extent of individual differences in the development of ecological awareness; 3) explore whether new knowledge of major ecological issues can be gained by developing what Mead (1970) describes as 'prefigurational' cultures. Using an adaptation of Kelly's Repertory Grid (1955) techniques, data will be collected from a sample of children across the primary school age range in Nottinghamshire and in Massachusetts, USA, in order to elicit the types of cnstructs being used to describe ecological issues. Using open-ended stimulus stories and pictures children will write their own stories about ecological issues. The thesis will outline a theory of the development of children's ecological awareness, linked to the evaluation of strategies for improving present classroom practice.
Status: Individual research
Date of Research: 1993-continuing
KEYWORDS: concept formation; ecology; environmental education; physical environment

10/1118
Faculty of Education, Clifton Hall, Clifton Lane, Clifton, Nottingham NG11 8NS
01159 418418
Bowen, R. Mr; *Supervisor:* Kimbell, R. Prof.; Ovens, P. Dr
Improving aspects of performance in design and technology education for pupils, teachers and university students
Abstract: The aims of the project are to investigate how classroom practices influence the progression of children's learning in design and technology in primary school classrooms, and to apply this understanding to the work of practising and trainee teachers. The major aspect of the researcher's work is teaching undergraduate and inservice teacher education (INSET) courses in Design and Technology. The purpose of the research is to improve student and teacher classroom practice. It is expected that the research will improve: a) the researcher's teaching performance – because it will be based on better knowledge; b) the quality of the work of the Primary Design and Technology Curriculum Group because of the transmission of knowledge to the group via course planning and other meetings; c) the quality of Design and Technology teaching in the family of schools the researcher will be working with. There is concern, evidenced by personal contact with teachers and from Her Majesty's Inspectorate (HMI) Reports (1991, 1992) that, whilst there is good quality Design and Technology being undertaken in schools, the majority of the activity is 'one-off' in nature and lacks a coherent structure over the medium and long terms. This research intends to examine how teacher and pupil performance can be improved. It is intended to analyse the influence of differing classroom practices on the progression of children's learning, examine frameworks for improving performance and express considered opinions about the nature and intentions of the subject from a range of perspectives, the teacher, the child and the researcher.
Published Material: BOWEN, R. & WADE, W. (1993). 'Joining with industry: innovative curriculum materials for technology and science in primary schools'. Proceedings of the International Design and Technology Research and Curriculum Development (IDATER), Loughborough University, 1st-4th September, 1993.
Status: Individual research
Date of Research: 1993-continuing
KEYWORDS: design and technology; learning activities; teaching methods

10/1119
Faculty of Education, Clifton Hall, Clifton Lane, Clifton, Nottingham NG11 8NS
01159 418418
De Montfort University, Polhill Avenue, Bedford MK41 9EA
01234 351966
Plant, M. Mr; *Supervisor:* Ovens, P. Dr; Huckle, J. Mr
Towards a transformation of environmental education in higher education through action enquiry
Abstract: This research project has been established in response to a perceived need to critically examine educational processes in meeting the needs of the environment, particularly how the interaction between education and environmental issues is informed by political, economic and cultural interests. The main aims of this research programme are to: 1) critically evaluate action enquiry as a means to effective environmental education in higher education; 2) articulate an understanding of the role of the teacher educator in furthering the development of environmental education in higher education. These aims necessitate: 1) an analysis of the origins, processes and objectives of environmental education with special reference to teacher education; 2) an exploration of the social and cultural interpretations of the environment and the values attributed to it; and 3) the establishment of an epistemological framework for understanding the environment. The research strategy comprises three phases. Phase 1 critically examines educational processes in meeting the needs of the environment, particularly how the interaction between education and environmental issues is informed by political, economic and cultural interests. This examination will include an analysis of approaches to social enquiry, in particular those forms of collaborative action enquiry that may have potential for promoting improvements in education's response to environmental issues. Phase 2 is based on a collaborative action enquiry approach to environmental education through the design and implementation of a Masters Degree in Environmental Education. Phase 3 aims to formulate a conceptual and methodological framework for effective environmental education and to illuminate the role of the researcher in furthering the aims of environmental education.
Status: Sponsored project
Source of Grant: British Agrochemicals Association: Nottingham Project on Teaching Through Controversial Environmental Issues £20,000
Date of Research: 1992-continuing
KEYWORDS: environmental education; higher education

10/1120
Faculty of Education, Clifton Hall, Clifton Lane, Clifton, Nottingham NG11 8NS
01159 418418
De Montfort University, Polhill Avenue, Bedford MK41 9EA
01234 351966
Plant, M. Mr; *Supervisor:* Ovens, P. Dr; Huckle, J. Mr

BAA/Nottingham Project on Teaching Through Controversial Issues

Abstract: This project has been established to help teacher education students develop skills in handling controversial issues with a view to improving pupils' skills in this field, especially about issues related to the use of chemical sprays in agriculture. This project will necessitate collaboration with British Agrochemicals Association (BAA) to identify appropriate case study material, and with colleagues at Nottingham as well as with other teacher training institutions. The minimum outcome of the project will be a 'train-the-trainer' pack on how to teach controversial issues through case study and other material, thereby ensuring pupils have the intellectual resources and communication skills to contribute as informed citizens in debates about controversial issues. This pack provides examples of how tutors can enrich the professional development of their students through the opportunities afforded by controversial issues and to stress the need for active student involvement and flexibility. The activities and discussions are based on the authors' experience of working with primary and secondary initial teacher education students and teachers over several years.
Status: Sponsored project
Source of Grant: British Agrochemicals Association: Nottingham Project on Teaching Through Controversial Environmental Issues £20,000
Date of Research: 1992-1994
KEYWORDS: *agriculture; controversial issues – course content; environmental education; preservice teacher education*

10/1121

Faculty of Education, Clifton Hall, Clifton Lane, Clifton, Nottingham NG11 8NS
01159 418418
De Montfort University, Polhill Avenue, Bedford MK41 9EA
01234 351966
Firth, R. Mr; *Supervisor:* Ovens, P. Dr; Huckle, J. Mr
Education for environmental sustainability in schools: exploring a culture of teaching for social change through action research
Abstract: The project will address the relationship between institutional culture and the slowness of educational change, and in particular will consider the relationship between individual, institutional and the potential for social change. It involves a detailed case study of a primary school over two years using a collaborative school-based critical action research model with specific reference to environmental education. It will examine the usefulness of the 'cultural perspective' and teacher critical reflection in facilitating educational and social change, emphasising the need to link cultural interpretation, individual and collaborative action with structural imperatives, and the dialectical relationship between individuals and society.
Status: Sponsored project
Source of Grant: British Agrochemicals Association £20,000
Date of Research: 1993-continuing
KEYWORDS: *attitudes; conservation – environment; environmental education; social change*

10/1122

Faculty of Education, Clifton Hall, Clifton Lane, Clifton, Nottingham NG11 8NS
01159 418418
Sheffield University, Division of Education, 388 Glossop Road, Sheffield S10 2JA
01142 768555
Weston, V. Ms; *Supervisor:* Oglesby, K. Ms
Career development and biographies of women in senior management in further education colleges
Abstract: A previous research study in 1987 of 12 senior women managers in further education (FE) colleges provided various indicators of barriers to career progression. There are now substantially increased numbers of women managers, although these are still not represented in the proportions that can be found in lower levels of FE college structures, therefore this study aims to discover: (1) Whether such barriers are no longer in existence (whether there is incidence of positive discrimination). (2) If the more senior women represented have created positive role models. (3) Has the changes in college structures and organisation patterns benefited women whose management skills are now seen to be essential to colleges in the current environment of corporate status and team approaches to new systems and development and delivery of the curriculum.

Status: Individual research
Date of Research: 1990-1994
KEYWORDS: *colleges of further education; educational administration; women's employment*

10/1123

Faculty of Education, Clifton Hall, Clifton Lane, Clifton, Nottingham NG11 8NS
01159 418418
Sheffield University, Division of Education, 388 Glossop Road, Sheffield S10 2TN
01142 768555
Green, K. Ms; *Supervisor:* Rowlands, S. Mr
Improving the supervision of student research
Abstract: The major aim of the project is to find out more about what goes on during the process of supervision of student action research projects on B.Ed and M.Ed courses. The methodology used will be that of action research. Clearly some issues will arise at various stages of the proposed work but some of the initial questions which have been identified from a review of current practice are: 1) Do students and tutors have shared understandings of the nature of the supervision process? 2) Does a tutor know whether a student shares his/her understanding of what has taken place during the supervisory tutorial? 3) Does a tutor know which of the things said and done in tutorials are seen to be helpful by students in progressing their research? 4) Are there things which the tutor does and say which gets in the way of students' learning? The researcher proposes to interview selected students at the outset of their research to explore the nature of their work and their understanding of the supervision process and to examine to what extent do they share the tutor's understanding of the nature of the supervision process? All tutorials of selected students will be transcribed, recorded and analysed. Selected students will keep a personal diary relating to the supervision process, to be handed in only after work has been completed and marked. The researcher will keep a personal diary relating to the supervision process to record what she thinks has been achieved in each supervisory tutorial and any further reflections on the process. Final interviews will be conducted with students about the supervision process particularly discussing issues arising from their personal reflections, the researcher's personal reflections and from the analysis of the tutorials.
Status: Individual research
Date of Research: 1993-continuing
KEYWORDS: *student research; supervision; teacher-student relationship; tutorials*

Nottingham University

10/1124

Department of Adult Education, 14-22 Shakespeare Street, Nottingham NG1 4FJ
01159 515151
Sherman, I. Mr; Naylor, M. Mrs; Green, P. Ms; Vanaman, J. Ms; *Supervisor:* Jotham, R. Dr
The logistics of provision of vocational training in information technology for adult students with physical and sensory disabilities
Abstract: The aim is to establish and evaluate a model for the delivery of information technology (IT) training to disabled adults by direct experimentation. A key feature of the arrangement is that training operates in parallel with a workshop managed by disabled people with IT skills. The methodology involves regular consultation between staff, trainers and associated practitioners. The group of disabled people involved numbers approximately 70.
Published Material: A list of publications is available from the researchers.
Status: Sponsored project
Source of Grant: Nottingham Task Force; European Social Fund; Nottinghamshire County Council
Date of Research: 1988-1994
KEYWORDS: *adult vocational education; adults; computer literacy; disabilities; information technology; sheltered workshops; special educational needs; training centres*

10/1125
> Department of Adult Education, 14-22 Shakespeare Street,
> Nottingham NG1 4FJ
> 01159 515151
> Wood, A. Mr; *Supervisor:* Jotham, R. Dr

The role of information technology in the education of socially handicapped children
Abstract: Particular topics in numeracy and literacy areas are taught to groups of children in a special school for maladjusted children in formats which (a) do not use information technology (IT); and (b) use IT extensively. Observers, who are normally present in classes, record characteristics such as attention span systematically for individual children in order to establish primary data for comparison.
Status: Individual research
Date of Research: 1989-1993
KEYWORDS: *behaviour disorders; computer uses in education; information technology; special educational needs; special schools*

10/1126
> Department of Adult Education, 14-22 Shakespeare Street,
> Nottingham NG1 4FJ
> 01159 515151
> Leicester, D. Mr; Busby, M. Mrs; Green, P. Ms;
> *Supervisor:* Jotham, R. Dr

The use of information technology in adult basic education of students with physical and sensory handicaps
Abstract: Against a backcloth of computer courses for disabled adults in the University Adult Centre at Nottingham University, students whose educational needs lie primarily in the area of adult basic education, are worked with individually and/or in very small groups. Various teaching methods and materials are compared and contrasted, but the principle methodology is regular review of students' progress with tutors and Centre staff. The group of students under study numbers approximately 50.
Published Material: A complete list of publications is available from the researchers.
Status: Sponsored project
Source of Grant: Leverhulme Trust; Nottinghamshire County Council; Lincolnshire County Council; Derbyshire County Council
Date of Research: 1987-continuing
KEYWORDS: *adult basic education; adults; computer literacy; disabilities; information technology; special educational needs*

10/1127
> Department of Adult Education, 14-22 Shakespeare Street,
> Nottingham NG1 4FJ
> 01159 515151
> Sherman, I. Mr; Naylor, M. Mrs; Lamerton, P. Mrs; Ellis, M.
> Mrs; *Supervisor:* Jotham, R. Dr

The logistics of provision of courses in information technology for adult students with physical and sensory disabilities
Abstract: Centres with good disabled access have been equipped with computers and software for the provision of computer courses for disabled students and mixed groups of disabled and able-bodied students. As well as continually reviewing the logistics of such provision, including the need for special hardware aids, student progress is monitored and compared with progress of able-bodied adults attending similar computer courses at other centres. The number of disabled students involved in this educational programme is approximately 300.
Published Material: A list of publications is available from the researchers.
Status: Sponsored project
Source of Grant: Leverhulme Trust; Nottinghamshire County Council; Lincolnshire County Council; Derbyshire County Council
Date of Research: 1985-continuing
KEYWORDS: *adults; computer literacy; disabilities; information technology; special educational needs; training centres*

10/1128
> Department of Adult Education, 14-22 Shakespeare Street,
> Nottingham NG1 4FJ
> 01159 515151
> Jones, D. Dr; Stephens, M. Prof.

Adult education in the United Kingdom and China
Abstract: Working with colleagues at Shandung Teachers University, it is intended to carry out a comparative study of adult education in the United Kingdom and China which will examine: (a) theories and philosophies of adult education; (b) organisation and structure of adult education; (c) aims and purposes of adult education; (d) target groups; (e) institutions for adult education; (f) teaching methods; (g) developments and trends in adult education.
Status: Individual research
Date of Research: 1992-1993
KEYWORDS: *adult education; China; comparative education*

10/1129
> Department of Adult Education, 14-22 Shakespeare Street,
> Nottingham NG1 4FJ
> 01159 515151
> Yang, K-T. Mr; *Supervisor:* Jones, D. Dr; Stephens, M. Prof.

Analysis of the adult education problem in Taiwan, Republic of China: a comparative study of adult education between Taiwan and England and its implications in Taiwan
Abstract: This is a comparative study of university adult education in the United Kingdom and China. Questionnaires and semi-structured interviews will be used to collect data on attitudes towards university adult education. All departments of adult education in the United Kingdom will be contacted and a selection in China.
Status: Sponsored project
Source of Grant: Government of Taiwan
Date of Research: 1991-1994
KEYWORDS: *adult education; comparative education; Taiwan; United Kingdom; universities*

10/1130
> Department of Adult Education, 14-22 Shakespeare Street,
> Nottingham NG1 4FJ
> 01159 515151
> McCarthy, J. Mr; *Supervisor:* Morgan, W. Mr; Bayliss, F. Prof.

Adult employment training in Nottinghamshire: case studies
Abstract: Shortcomings in training are at the core of the National Skills and Training debate. What are the causes of these shortcomings? This enquiry attempts to answer this question and to indicate how firms local to the Nottinghamshire area seek to overcome them. Semi-structured interviews are undertaken with key providers and consumers of training. These are accompanied by a series of case studies, both of major employers and of small to medium sized industries
Published Material: McCARTHY, J., MORGAN, W.J. & BAYLISS, F.J. (1992). Adult employment training in Nottinghamshire. Nottingham: University of Nottingham, Department of Adult Education.
Status: Sponsored project
Source of Grant: National Westminster Bank Research Fund £18,000; Department of Employment £20,000
Date of Research: 1990-1993
KEYWORDS: *adult vocational education; employment; job skills; job training; work-education relationship*

10/1131
> Department of Adult Education, 14-22 Shakespeare Street,
> Nottingham NG1 4FJ
> 01159 515151
> Sherman, I. Mr; Barnes, K. Mr; *Supervisor:* Jotham, R. Dr

The potential of computer-mediated-communication for developing social and educational opportunities for adults with physical and sensory difficulties
Abstract: The aim is to establish a communication network for training and related activities between disabled centres and individual users in the East Midlands with links through the Joint Academic Network and the Packet Switch system to researchers, practitioners and other disabled people in the United Kingdom and worldwide. The efficient use of the network will be evaluated by monitoring traffic and by consultation with disabled users and professionals working with them.
Published Material: A list of publications is available from the researchers.
Status: Sponsored project
Source of Grant: Leverhulme Trust £55,000; Universities Funding Council £10,400
Date of Research: 1989-1993
KEYWORDS: *communications; computer networks; disabilities; training; wide area networks*

10/1132

Department of Adult Education, 14-22 Shakespeare Street, Nottingham NG1 4FJ
01159 515151
Elsdon, K. Prof.; Stewart, S. Mrs; Reynolds, J. Dr

Educational impact of voluntary organisations

Abstract: The project aims to investigate the learning effects of local voluntary organisations on their members as individuals, and through them on their catchment population. An intensive study is planned of a representative sample of about 25 organisations chosen to take account of factors such as purpose, activities, size, ethnicity, geographical area, sex and age range of members. Each study will rest on the organisation's records and structured interviews and questionnaires administered individually or in groups as appropriate. Independent sources of evidence in the community will also be tapped. The individual case studies will be published on completion and will form the basis of evidence on which the final report will rest; together they will also form a thesaurus of good practice. The analysis and interpretation of the case studies will be used to arrive at any general principles and practical applications.
Published Material: ELSDON, K.T. (1991). Adult learning in voluntary organisations: Vol 1: case studies 1 and 2. Nottingham: University of Nottingham, Department of Adult Education.; ELSDON, K.T. (1991). Voluntary organisations and the White Paper. In: Educational Centres Association Annual Report 1991.; ELSDON, K.T. (1992). Voluntary organisations, learning and democracy. Adult Education and Development; February.
Status: Sponsored project
Source of Grant: Universities Funding Council £18,900
Date of Research: 1990-continuing
KEYWORDS: *adult education; community; individual development; social change; voluntary agencies*

10/1133

Department of Adult Education, 14-22 Shakespeare Street, Nottingham NG1 4FJ
01159 515151
Jotham, R. Dr; Ellis, M. Mrs

Aspects of educational practice in the physical sciences and information technology

Abstract: The aim of this project is to evaluate, comment upon and improve educational practice in science and information technology. The methodology involves direct experimentation work with student groups, followed by discussion with students and tutors. The research also includes extensive studies of statistical information on the extent, diversity and logistics of provision of adult education in this general area.
Published Material: A list of publications is available from the researchers.
Status: Individual research
Date of Research: 1970-continuing
KEYWORDS: *adult education; educational practices; higher education; information technology; physical sciences; science education*

10/1134

Department of Adult Education, 14-22 Shakespeare Street, Nottingham NG1 4FJ
01159 515151
Henson, C. Rev.; *Supervisor:* Mackie, K. Dr; Parsons, W. Dr

The space within an interdisciplinary study of voluntary groups engaging with AIDS and HIV

Abstract: The aim of the research is to discover a model for adult education based on voluntary groups engaging with Acquired Immune Deficiency Syndrome (AIDS) and Human-Immunodeficiency Syndrome (HIV); and to understand the ethical and theological implications of this model. The research will include interviews with selected voluntary groups and a comparative study of educational philosophies.
Status: Individual research
Date of Research: 1989-1993
KEYWORDS: *acquired immune deficiency syndrome; adult education; ethics; sexually transmitted diseases; voluntary agencies*

10/1135

Department of Adult Education, 14-22 Shakespeare Street, Nottingham NG1 4FJ
01159 515151
Bo, J. Mr; *Supervisor:* Morgan, W. Mr; Muckle, J. Dr

An evaluation of current British policy concerning postgraduate overseas students

Abstract: The research is a study of overseas student issues from a host country perspective. It focuses on the 'managing' of the growth of incoming postgraduate students and on the extent to which the needs and obligations perceived and accepted by the policy making machinery shape the experience of students. The costs and benefits to the host country are considered in both immediate and longer terms.
Status: Sponsored project
Source of Grant: Overseas Research Studentship; British Council
Date of Research: 1990-1993
KEYWORDS: *educational policy; graduate study; higher education; overseas students*

10/1136

Department of Adult Education, 14-22 Shakespeare Street, Nottingham NG1 4FJ
01159 515151
Morgan, W. Mr

Adult employment training in four regions (East Midlands, South Wales, Bremen, and Baden Wurttemberg)

Abstract: The research concentrates upon: (i) the changing continuing education needs of the regions; (ii) the impact of the 1992 single market; and (iii) the possibility of a European model emerging from British-German experience.
Status: Sponsored project
Source of Grant: Universities Funding Council £55,000
Date of Research: 1990-1993
KEYWORDS: *adult education; comparative education; continuing education; European Community; Germany; United Kingdom; vocational education*

10/1137

Department of Adult Education, 14-22 Shakespeare Street, Nottingham NG1 4FJ
01159 515151
Cox, D. Mr

The mass media and the social construction of memory

Abstract: The research will explore the ways in which many parts of people's memories are socially derived and will especially focus on those parts that are dependent on vicarious experience, learned about via the mass media (although the research will not ignore the importance of inter-personal vicarious experience). Using a case study approach, the research will attempt to locate mass media influence in an historicised context. This is necessary because of: (a) the way we interpret present events will be affected by what we remember from the past; and (b) how we remember events from the past will be qualified by how new events are reported. As what we remember will also be filtered through the ideological positions of different people, then socially constructed memory has also to be seen in terms of ideological memory. The case studies chosen for the research will examine the reporting of various types of industrial relations issues in national daily newspapers, but will not use conventional content analysis techniques alone. There will be an attempt to refine other qualitative measures. The research will also consider issues in the education of adults, especially how students' memory resources can be channelled, and how they have to be critically questioned and interpreted, rather than being simply accepted as evidence.
Status: Individual research
Date of Research: 1988-continuing
KEYWORDS: *adult learning; mass media; memory*

10/1138

Department of Adult Education, 14-22 Shakespeare Street, Nottingham NG1 4FJ
01159 515151
Morgan, W. Mr

Political education, voluntary associations and civil society in state socialist countries

Abstract: The research seeks to identify and analyse the relationship of adult political education and voluntary associations to the emergence of civil society in state socialist countries. The key concepts will be defined theoretically and examined empirically through a series of related historical and sociological studies.
Published Material: MORGAN, W.R. (1989). 'Homo-Sovieticus – political education and civil society in the Soviet Union'. In:

MORGAN, W.P. (Ed). Proceedings of the Standing Conference of University Teachings and Research into the Education of Adults. Nottingham.; MORGAN, W.P. (1989). 'Workers adult education in the Soviet Union', Bulletin of the International Congress of University Adult Education, Vol 2, No 1, Spring 1989.
Status: Sponsored project
Source of Grant: British Council; Beatrice Webb Trust
Date of Research: 1989-continuing
KEYWORDS: adult education; citizenship education; political influences; social change; socialist countries; voluntary agencies

10/1139
> Department of Adult Education, 14-22 Shakespeare Street, Nottingham NG1 4FJ
> 01159 515151
> Thompson, E. Mrs; *Supervisor:* Morgan, W. Mr; Stock, A. Prof.

An international information and resources collection in adult education and training
Abstract: The aim of the research project is to establish an international information and bibliographical resources collection on adult education and training which will be of value to researchers engaged in international and comparative studies. The project involves the establishment of a database and production of a bibliography on comparative adult education and training.
Status: Sponsored project
Source of Grant: Universities Funding Council £15,000
Date of Research: 1990-continuing
KEYWORDS: adult education; adults; comparative education; continuing education; databases; vocational education

10/1140
> Department of Adult Education, 14-22 Shakespeare Street, Nottingham NG1 4FJ
> 01159 515151
> Wong, K. Mr; *Supervisor:* Morgan, W. Mr; Shipstone, D. Dr

Evaluation of the process of curriculum design of technical and vocational education in Hong Kong
Abstract: An evaluation of the process of curriculum design in technical and vocational education in Hong Kong will be undertaken. Special reference will be made to the interaction between education, training, employment and economic outcomes. It is also intended to identify present and likely difficulties, and to suggest ways of linking technical and vocational education with the general education system in order to ensure an adequate supply of competent technical personnel for the 1990s and beyond 1997.
Status: Individual research
Date of Research: 1989-1993
KEYWORDS: curriculum evaluation; economics-education relationship; Hong Kong; training; TVEI; work education relationship

10/1141
> Department of Adult Education, 14-22 Shakespeare Street, Nottingham NG1 4FJ
> 01159 515151
> Sutton, I. Dr

The value of field residential courses in the teaching of earth sciences
Abstract: The research is intended to investigate the value of field studies in the teaching of adults in the area of earth sciences. The study involves the investigation of the way field activities can be integrated into the teaching of earth sciences to adults with special reference to teaching methods, and day, weekend, longer residential and foreign study tours. The value of pre-course preparation for the field study is an important aspect of the research.
Status: Individual research
Date of Research: 1986-continuing
KEYWORDS: adult education; adult learning; earth science; field studies; field studies centres; study abroad

10/1142
> Department of Adult Education, 14-22 Shakespeare Street, Nottingham NG1 4FJ
> 01159 515151
> Associacao Portuguesa de Paralisia Cerebral, Rua Delfim Maia, 4300 Porto, Portugal
> Jotham, R. Dr; Da Cunha, A. Sr

Comparative study of information technology training for disabled people in Britain and Portugal
Abstract: A Portugese researcher will spend two months in the United Kingdom gathering information on the training of disabled people in information technology. This will be followed by gathering comparative data in Portugal and the results will be collated to generate a report which will be published in both English and Portugese.
Status: Sponsored project
Source of Grant: Gulbenkian Foundation £5,000
Date of Research: 1991-1993
KEYWORDS: adult vocational education; comparative education; disabilities; information technology; Portugal; special educational needs; training; United Kingdom

10/1143
> Department of Adult Education, 14-22 Shakespeare Street, Nottingham NG4 4FJ
> 01159 515151
> University of British Columbia, 5597 Iona Drive, Vancouver, Canada Riddell, B. Ms; *Supervisor:* Daines, J. Dr; Graham, B. Mr

Staff development in higher education
Abstract: This research is aimed at addressing the issue of teacher versus learner centred approaches to teaching/instruction. The research uses participants in 'instructor training' workshops as subjects. Using a case study method, it will seek to establish the antecedents and ongoing effects of training, experience and self-reflection upon teaching approaches. In particular it will seek to identify changes in values, attitudes and beliefs of participants towards more learner-centred approaches to university teaching.
Status: Individual research
Date of Research: 1990-1994
KEYWORDS: learner-centred methods; staff development; teaching process; universities; university teaching

10/1144
> Department of Psychology, University Park, Nottingham NG7 2RD
> 01159 515151
> Underwood, G. Prof.

Cognitive processes in reading and spelling
Abstract: The aim of the project is to identify the cognitive processes which enable us to read and spell – those processes through which written information must be transformed by the competent reader to reach understanding. Dependent measures of reading speed and accuracy are observed as a function of controlled variables. Measures are also used to observe eye movements. Experiments have been performed on skilled adult readers, young readers and latter with reading difficulties. Recognition of isolated words and the comprehension of coherent text have been investigated. The role of attention in recognition concerning isolated words has been studied and also the role of alternative processing routes (graphemic/phonological) by manipulating the orthographic regularity of the words presented. The role of regularity in spelling has also been investigated. Findings suggest that for children of 10+ and adults, attention is not essential for isolated word recognition but is for measuring of sentences. Good and poor readers do not differ in their ability to recognise the meanings of isolated words so much as in their ability to use the meanings after recognition. Individual differences in reading ability are more associated with post-recognition processes such as those involved in the use of working memory than with initial encoding. One of the researcher's interests is in the patterns of eye movements (saccades, regressive saccades and fixation durations) made by skilled readers who are comprehending sentences, with specific interest in the cognitive mechanisms of eye guidance. Computer-based learning support with classroom computers is currently being investigated. The questions being asked here are how can computers be used to enhance the cognitive processes involved in reading and spelling, and what uses can teachers make of classroom computers with children of different ability background?
Published Material: A list of publications is available from the researchers on request.
Status: Sponsored project
Source of Grant: Medical Research Council; Science and Engineering Research Council
Date of Research: 1979-continuing
KEYWORDS: cognitive processes; computer-assisted reading; reading comprehension; reading skills; spelling; word recognition

10/1145

Department of Psychology, Blind Mobility Research Unit, University Park, Nottingham NG7 2RD
01159 515151
Dodds, A. Dr; Doyle, A. Dr; Beggs, W. Dr; Flannigan, H. Ms; Ng, B. Ms; *Supervisor:* Howarth, C. Prof.
The mobility of blind and visually impaired persons
Abstract: The unit publishes its work in the national and international journals. Principal interests are investigation of the assessment of visual handicap and how trainers are taught to teach mobility of visually impaired people. A scale of adjustment is being developed.
Published Material: BEGGS, W.D.A. (1991). 'The psychological correlates of walking speed in the visually impaired', Ergonomics, Vol 34, No 1, pp.91-102.; BEGGS, W.D.A. (1990). 'Goal setting in sport'. In: GRAHAM-JONES, J. & HARDY. L. (Eds). Stress and performance in sport. Chichester: John Wiley & Sons.; DODDS, A.G. (1991). 'Psychological assessment and the rehabilitation process', New Beacon, LXXV (885), pp.101-106.; DODDS, A.G. (1991). 'The psychology of rehabilitation', British Journal of Visual Impairment, Vol 9, No 2, pp.38-40.; DODDS, A.G., BAILEY, P., PEARSON, A. & YATES, L. (1991). 'Psychological factors in acquired visual impairment: the development of a scale of adjustment', Journal of Visual Impairment and Blindess, Vol 85, No 7, pp.306-310. A full list of publications is available from the Blind Mobility Research Unit.
Status: Sponsored project
Source of Grant: Department of Health £186,000
Date of Research: 1960-continuing
KEYWORDS: *assessment; blindness; mobility aids; partial vision; special educational needs; travel training; visual impairments; visually handicapped mobility*

10/1146

Department of Psychology, Blind Mobility Research Unit, University Park, Nottingham NG7 2RD
01602 515151
Flannigan, H. Ms; Craig, D. Mr; *Supervisor:* Dodds, A. Dr
The development of a scale to measure psychological adjustment to sight loss
Abstract: A scale to measure psychological adjustment to sight loss has been developed in the form of a 50-item questionnaire. Sub-scales to measure anxiety, depression, self esteem, self-efficacy, locus of control, attitudes to sight loss, acceptance of blindness, and attributional style enable the assessment of psychological factors underlying emotional states. Psychometric analysis of a database comprising 469 clients presenting for rehabilitation has resulted in factorial validation of the questionnaire items. The instrument is able to identify clients experiencing psychological difficulties, and it is also sensitive to changes resulting from interventions. Lisrel structural modelling analysis has resulted in a model whereby the cognitive factors underlying emotional states can be related to those emotional states.
Published Material: DODDS, A.G., BAILEY, P., PEARSON, A. & YATES, L. (1991). 'Psychological factors in acquired impairment: the development of a scale of adjustment', Journal of Visual Impairment & Blindness, Vol 85, No 7, pp.306-310.; DODDS, A.G., NG, L. & YATES, L. (1992). 'Residential rehabilitation: 2 – psychological outcome of rehabilitation, New Beacon, LXXVI (902), pp.373-377.; DODDS, A.G., FLANNIGAN, H. & NG. L. (1993). 'The Nottingham Adjustment Scale: a validation study', International Journal of Rehabilitation Research, Vol 16, No 2, pp.177-184.; DODDS, A.G. (1993). Rehabilitating blind and visually impaired people: a psychological approach. London: Chapman & Hall.
Status: Sponsored project
Source of Grant: Department of Health: Health and Personal Social Services Research Programme
Date of Research: 1990-1993
KEYWORDS: *adaptive behaviour – of disabled; attitude measures; blindness; emotional adjustment; measurement techniques; rehabilitation; visual impairments*

10/1147

School of Education, University Park, Nottingham NG7 2RD
01159 515151
Thompson, W. Mr; *Supervisor:* Sands, M. Dr
The role of a change agent in the introduction of a new curriculum in technical teacher training
Abstract: The research stems from involvement as a consultant on a large project in an overseas country. This was to introduce a new teacher training curriculum into four faculties of technical/vocational teacher training, based upon common, core subjects/modules, that would apply in all faculties. It involved major structural and equipment refurbishment and the provision of new equipment. The basic method is the use of case studies based upon observation as a full participator. Curriculum documents, discussion papers, questionnaires, minutes of meetings, project documents, will be used as the database. Major themes to be considered will be the management of the project, role of consultancy and individual consultants, working methods of consultants, development of curriculum, development of faculty management resources and facilities. Comparison will be made with published accounts of other similar projects undertaken in overseas countries. From this an hypothesis about the role of change agents in similar situations will be generated.
Status: Individual research
Date of Research: 1990-1994
KEYWORDS: *change agents; curriculum development; preservice teacher education; TVEI*

10/1148

School of Education, University Park, Nottingham NG7 2RD
01159 515151
Goody, J. Mr; *Supervisor:* Shipstone, D. Dr; Selkirk, K. Dr
Technology for all: educational models for effective implementation
Abstract: Design and technology activity is cross-curricular. This, and its relatively recent appearance in schools' curricula, has made consensus and clarity concerning its nature difficult to achieve and the introduction of the National Curriculum has led to new interpretations. The study aims to establish a coherent theoretical framework to support the development of technology within the curriculum and to clarify the nature of technology and its role in education past, present and future. The problems to be addressed are: (1) defining technology; (2) describing the nature of technology; (3) investigation of the role of human values in technology education; (4) identifying fundamental aims and objectives; (5) developing a descriptive model to demonstrate the central ideas of technological activity; (6) determining current organisational structures; (7) identifying the principles of learning and teaching technology; (8) developing models for implementing 1-7 above; (9) critique of the National Curriculum Orders in relation to 1-8 above; (10) issues relating to assessment and evaluation. The methodology will include literature surveys; structured interviews, e.g. with practitioners working with students in the 5-18 age range; classroom observation and case studies.
Status: Individual research
Date of Research: 1990-continuing
KEYWORDS: *curriculum development; design education; National Curriculum; technology education*

10/1149

School of Education, University Park, Nottingham NG7 2RD
01159 515151
Whyte, G. Mr; *Supervisor:* Bennett, S. Mr; Shipstone, D. Dr
The enterprising college
Abstract: The aims of this research project are to: (1) propose an overall definition of the terms 'enterprise' and 'enterprising' and to identify the characteristics associated with enterprising people and their characteristics; (2) identify good practice in the techniques used by employers to develop an enterprising work force; (3) evolve a series of training events to enable managers to apply these techniques within further education and evaluate both the effectiveness of these techniques and the methods of importing them; (4) develop a mechanism for introducing enterprise approaches into the work of students and evaluate the effectiveness of these approaches; and (5) make recommendations for further applications of enterprise approaches within further education. This research requires the integration of academic disciplines in that it combines approaches to both educational research and to management development in the field of enterprise. The methodology falls into three distinct phases: (1) review of the literature; (2) project activity; and (3) evaluation.
Status: Individual research
Date of Research: 1991-continuing
KEYWORDS: *enterprise education; further education; work-education relationship*

10/1150

School of Education, University Park, Nottingham NG7 2RD
01159 515151
Parker-Jenkins, M. Dr
What is the experience of Muslim girls in a Muslim school in Britain?: An ethnographic study with proposals for change
Abstract: Muslims comprise the third largest religious group in Britain today, after Roman Catholics and Anglicans. Whilst multi-racial, multi-cultural and multi-lingual in nature, they are united by the faith dimension of their lives. The powerful revival of Islamic Fundamentalism of late has deeply affected the thinking of Muslim minority groups in the West. The education system has been criticised by Muslims, who see an incompatibility between values taught at home and those at school. The objective of this research is therefore to make a study of Muslim education as offered by a selected Muslim girls' independent school and to accumulate new and timely information. Other research aims are to examine the cognitive basis of Islamic education and the selection of knowledge. The research methodology is predominantly ethnographic with an indepth study of a girls' Muslim school and shorter studies of five other Muslim schools for comparative analysis. Following the traditions of ethnography, the research aims to examine the experience of Muslim girls in a Muslim school. Furthermore, proposals for change will be explored, and policy implications concerning the educational needs of Muslim children within the maintained school system.
Published Material: PARKER-JENKINS, M. (1990). 'Why Muslim needs won't disappear', New Era in Education, Vol 71, No 1, pp.14-16.
Status: Sponsored project
Source of Grant: Economic and Social Research Council £14,500
Date of Research: 1993-continuing
KEYWORDS: *Islamic education; Muslims; religion and education; religious cultural groups; women's education*

10/1151

School of Education, University Park, Nottingham NG7 2RD
01159 515151
Parker-Jenkins, M. Dr
What do Muslim children need from the education system?
Abstract: This case study of a Muslim girls' school in the Midlands will provide an insight into an unexplored area which has recently provoked educational debate here and abroad: the lack of understanding between the State educational system and the Muslim community. Adopting an ethnographic approach, the aim of the study is to examine educational provision in non-maintained Muslim schools and to consider the extent to which the maintained school sector is able to accommodate Muslim needs. The study involves 6 Muslim and 6 non-Muslim schools and is conducted by a small team comprising both Muslims and non-Muslims. Initial research of the Islamic Academy, Leicester; visits to other Muslim schools in Britain to provide comparative analysis; and to state schools with high numbers of Muslim children, followed by indepth interviewing of interested parties; educationalists; clergy; academics; and community leaders. Finally, the production of a report, study guide and articles for publication, offering practical solutions to the problems of educating Muslim children within State schools and in accordance with parents' religious convictions. The education system is presently being criticised by 'Muslims' who see an incompatibility between values taught at home and those at school. Although voluntary aided status may be granted to Muslim schools in the future, there will still be a large element of Muslim children who remain in regular maintained schools. Accommodating their educational needs will continue to be a pressing concern for educationalists and this research will provide a direct contribution to knowledge in the field of cultural diversity.
Published Material: PARKER-JENKINS, M. (1990). 'Muslin needs won't disappear', New Era in Education, Vol 17, No 1.; PARKER-JENKINS, M. (1990). 'Muslim educational needs', Multicultural Education Journal, (U.S.A.), Vol 8, No 2.; PARKER-JENKINS, M. (1990). 'Multiculturalism in British schools: lessons for Canada', Canadian School Executive', Vol 10, No 5.; PARKER-JENKINS, M. (1991). 'Muslim matters: exploring the educational needs of the Muslim child', New Community, Vol 17, No 4.
Status: Sponsored project
Source of Grant: Nottingham University Administered Funding Body £5,048
Date of Research: 1991-1993
KEYWORDS: *Islamic education; Muslims; religion and education; religious cultural groups; women's education*

10/1152

School of Education, University Park, Nottingham NG7 2RD
01159 515151
Day, C. Prof.; Ellis, C. Mr; Sutton, I. Dr
Investigating the effectiveness of continuing education
Abstract: Much research has focused upon developing continuing education provision in adult education, inservice training for teachers and industrial and professional training. The aim of this research is to examine critically these theories in practice, and to evaluate both independently and through comparison their effectiveness in terms of client/consumer expectations, relevance of course provision to client need and its effects on professional and institutional growth.
Status: Sponsored project
Source of Grant: Universities Funding Council £59,840
Date of Research: 1991-1994
KEYWORDS: *adult education; continuing education; industrial training; inservice teacher education; professional training; vocational education*

10/1153

School of Education, University Park, Nottingham NG7 2RD
01159 515151
Harrison, B. Mrs; *Supervisor:* Parsons, W. Dr; Hay, J. Dr
The interface of feminism, education and the Church: a study of power
Abstract: This research looks at definitions of power and at what are regarded as the structures of authority in the Church of England. A case has been made for the existence of patriarchy but little can be found on the mechanisms by which it works. This research proposes to look further into the theory of the management of complex organisations, and will involve working with a group from a church congregation on the language used for the experience of God. The management language used by church bureaucrats will also be studied. The researcher also may work with a group from another parish. Study sessions for clergy on inclusive language and the liturgy, have been conducted, and the aim is to provide material for a deanery synod to work with.
Status: Individual research
Date of Research: 1990-1994
KEYWORDS: *church and education; feminism; language usage; power structure; Protestant churches*

10/1154

School of Education, University Park, Nottingham NG7 2RD
01159 515151
Skelton, A. Mr; *Supervisor:* Murphy, R. Prof.; Murphy, E. Mrs
Low back pain in general practice: a new approach to patient education
Abstract: The study aims to provide the groundwork for the future development of educational strategies. These strategies will be used in general practice as part of the management and treatment of low back pain. 60 patients and 10 general practitioners (GPs) are taking part in the study. The patients are being asked about their low back pain (what they understand about it; how it has been managed and treated; their concerns and needs) using indepth interviews the GPs are being asked about their approach to management and treatment.
Status: Individual
Date of Research: 1991-1994
KEYWORDS: *doctor-patient relationship; medical services; pain; patient education; physical health*

10/1155

School of Education, University Park, Nottingham NG7 2RD
01159 515151
Phillips, R. Dr; Gillespie, J. Mr
Multimedia in the mathematics classroom
Abstract: This research follows up a major curriculum development project for the English National Curriculum Council (NCC) which produced interactive video materials to support mathematics teaching at key stages 3 and 4 (the 11 to 16 age group). Three double-sided laservision discs with supporting print material and software were completed by the Shell Centre and New Media during 1992. The package entitled 'The world of number' offers a rich and varied resource for teachers and their students to use, together with explicit suggestions for lesson activities. The present project is collecting data from seven schools which trialled the original development and agreed to continue as frequent users of the materials. The research

focuses on the mathematics departments in these schools and in particular on two teachers: one experienced and one inexperienced in using the materials. Through a mixture of classroom observation and interviews, the range of classroom activities supported by the materials is studied, including those that take place away from the equipment. A wide range of issues are under consideration including the merits of whole class and small group activities, the roles adopted by teachers and students, and the potential of the technology to support activities which are difficult or impossible to carry out in other ways. The research will collect teachers' views on the efficacy of the materials and any practical problems that arise in using them.
Published Material: NATIONAL CURRICULUM COUNCIL (1992). The world of number: an interactive video resource for teaching secondary mathematics. York: National Curriculum Council.; GILLESPIE, J. & PHILLIPS, R.J. (1992). 'The use of multimedia materials for modelling in the secondary mathematics classroom', Proceedings of Working Group 14, ICME -7, Quebec.; PHILLIPS, R.J. (1992). 'Gazing in the bright lights', Times Educational Supplement, 21 February, p.40.
Status: Individual research
Date of Research: 1992-1993
KEYWORDS: *classroom research; educational materials; educational technology; interactive video; mathematics education; multimedia approach*

10/1156
　　School of Education, University Park, Nottingham NG7 2RD
　　01159 515151
　　Ubuz, B. Miss; *Supervisor:* Phillips, R. Dr; Bibby, N. Mr
The effects of a computer based curriculum on the achievement of freshmen university students
Abstract: Calculus has held its importance in the core undergraduate mathematics curriculum. The Curriculum has often been reconsidered since the introduction of microcomputers in 1979. This investigation is about how microcomputers have been integrated into the teaching and learning of calculus concepts to improve students' understanding and to retain their understanding for the subsequent courses. This study is conducted on the necessity for students to acquire not only computational understanding but also conceptual understanding to analyse and solve routine or non-routine problems logically. Understanding the concept of integral appears to be difficult to a large proportion of students. This study investigates in some depth the effects of a particular computer-rich approach to the introductory teaching of integral calculus on students learning behaviours and mathematical performance.
Published Material: UBUZ, B., ERSOY, Y. & BERBEROGLU, G. (1992). 'Relative effectiveness of two methods of instruction on achievement in solving word problems in calculus'. In: Book of abstracts of short presentations (7th International Congress on Mathematical Education, 17-23 August 1992, Quebec).
Status: Individual research
Date of Research: 1992-continuing
KEYWORDS: *calculus education; computer uses in education; mathematics education; university students*

10/1157
　　School of Education, University Park, Nottingham NG7 2RD
　　01159 515151
　　Youngman, M. Dr
Careers of contract researchers in education
Abstract: The project comprised a quick, small-scale postal survey of all contract researchers working on Economic and Social Research Council (ESRC) projects in England and Wales. Replies from 44 researchers were received, a response rate of 80%. Data consisted of categorised career information, ratings of perceptions and open statements. The career data are tabulated in detail. Employing a classification into Career Development and Personal for the attitude and open data showed a negative perception of career and personal issues, but positive views on opportunites for development.
Published Material: YOUNGMAN, M.B. (1991). Careers of contract researchers in education: 1 – situations and perceptions. Swindon: Economic and Social Research Council.; YOUNGMAN, M.B. (1992). Careers of contract researchers in education: 2 – personal viewpoints. Swindon: Economic and Social Research Council.; YOUNGMAN, M.B. (1994). 'Career experiences of contract researchers in education', Research Papers in Education, Vol 9, No 3, pp.369-410.
Status: Sponsored project

Source of Grant: Economic and Social Research Council £2,455
Date of Research: 1991-1992
KEYWORDS: *careers; educational researchers*

10/1158
　　School of Education, University Park, Nottingham NG7 2RD
　　01159 515151
　　Skelton, A. Mr; *Supervisor:* Murphy, R. Prof.; O'Dowd, T. Dr
An educational analysis of patients' understanding of common rheumatic conditions
Abstract: The treatment and management of common conditions such as rheumatism depend upon a range of factors, including patients' understanding of their own condition and how it is being treated. It is argued that much could be done to improve the processes of patient education, and this study has been designed to provide a way of considering the way forward in more detail. The research is based on an indepth study of 60 patients and 10 general practitioners (GPs) and their individual perspectives on the patients' common rheumatic conditions. The aims of the research are to: (i) investigate patients' understanding of their own common rheumatological conditions in the context of their own lay health beliefs; (ii) study the consulting practice of general practitioners in relation to different patients presenting with common rheumatological conditions; (iii) provide the groundwork for the future development of educational materials, aids and methods, which will help to meet the identified needs of patients and their general practitioners. An intensive study will be made of a cohort of 60 patients, who are consulting their GPs about common rheumatological conditions. Patients will be chosen from the patients of the 10 participating GPs. Indepth interviews will be used to gain information from patients and GPs. Each patient will be interviewed twice, each GP once, for approximately 60 minutes. Interviews with patients will pursue the advice they have received about their condition, its prognosis, and their extent of satisfaction with the advice they have been given. Interviews with GPs will consider in general terms their approach to patients with common rheumatological conditions, as well as giving them opportunities to comment specifically on their own patients who have been chosen for inclusion in this study.
Status: Sponsored project
Source of Grant: Arthritis and Rheumatism Council £57,000
Date of Research: 1991-1994
KEYWORDS: *doctor-patient relationship; medical services; pain; patient education; physical health*

10/1159
　　School of Education, University Park, Nottingham NG7 2RD
　　01159 515151
　　Hadfield, M. Mr; McPherson, J. Mrs; *Supervisor:* Day, C. Prof.
Continuing education effectiveness project
Abstract: The project aims are: (a) to subject current provision in continuing education to a critical evaluation based on the differing notions of effectiveness used by providers, students and customers; (b) to investigate the actual and potential impact of such views upon course design and delivery; and (c) to consider the relationship between defining and recording educational outcomes. The project has recruited a range of institutes of higher education in England and Wales, which provide continuing education, either in the form of adult eduction or continuing professional development. The research is in three phases: Phase 1 (1991-1992) – A questionnaire survey identified the criteria used by staff and students to assess course effectiveness. Phase 2 (1992-1993) – Over one hundred preliminary interviews are being carried out with staff and students, in ten institutions, concerning how they view effectiveness, maintain it and how it influences course design and delivery. This work will be supported by parallel case studies, each focusing on a particular aspect of effectiveness. Phase 3 (1993-1994) – The project, working closely with 6-8 institutions, will research how to assist tutors/providers to enhance the effectiveness of their course provision. The interim report, due September 1993, will establish a range of criteria, against which, course effectiveness could be evaluated, with the case studies providing examples of good practice.
Status: Sponsored project
Source of Grant: Universities Funding Council £77,370
Date of Research: 1991-1994
KEYWORDS: *adult education; continuing education; course evaluation; professional continuing education; programme evaluation*

10/1160
School of Education, University Park, Nottingham NG7 2RD
01159 515151
Haw, K. Ms; *Supervisor:* Griffiths, M. Dr;
Parker-Jenkins, M. Dr
Muslim girls' schools: a conflict of interests?
Abstract: Many western feminists have begun to question whether girls benefit from co-education and whether more serious consideration should be given to the single sex alternative. Single sex schooling has been one of the most persistent demands of Muslims in this country since they became numerous and organised enough to make themselves heard, but to what extent does this make Muslims and western feminists natural allies in a common cause? The proposed research sets out to answer two questions which are themselves interlinked: (1) Were existing private secondary schools for Muslim girls established as a response to the foreclosure of options concerning local authority single sex provision in those localities? (2) Should western feminists object to these schools from 'anti-sexist' perspectives or are there any areas of agreement between them and Muslims concerning the ethos and purpose of these schools? Western feminists, it is claimed see single sex schools as a means of countering a bias towards males and encouraging women to respect other women in an atmosphere free from male domination and harrassment whereas Muslims seek to use them as a means of perpetuating traditional, patriarchal views concerning a woman's role in society. Therefore the dilemma that the establishment of schools for Muslim girls poses for the liberal anti-sexist/anti-racist and for over-arching equal opportunities policies is an integral part of this work. This piece of research gains its authority from the depth of insight made available through a broadly ethnographic approach by focusing on the everyday lives of pupils and teachers of a private Muslim girls' school and a maintained girls' school with a high proportion of Muslim students. At the same time sociological and historical factors, ideologies and discourses will be examined and analysed for they provide a crucial background, without which, the phenomena concerned would not exist in the form they do.
Published Material: HAW, K.F. (1991). 'Interactions of gender and race: a problem for teachers? a review of the emerging literature', Educational Research, Vol 33, No 1, pp.12-21.; PARKER-JENKINS, M. 'Why Muslim girls are more feminist in Muslim schools'. In: GRIFFITHS, M. & TROYNA, B. (Eds). Race, culture and education. Stoke: Trentham Books. (in press).; PARKER-JENKINS, M. & HAW, K.F. 'The educational needs of Muslim children in Britain: accommodation or neglect?'. In: VERTOVEC, S. (Ed). Muslims, Europeans, youth: reproducing ethnic and religious cultures. London: Pluto. (in press).
Status: Individual research
Date of Research: 1991-1994
KEYWORDS: *equal education; Islamic education; Muslims; religion and education; religious cultural groups; single sex schools; women's education*

10/1161
School of Education, University Park, Nottingham NG7 2RD
01159 515151
Nyirenda, D. Mr; *Supervisor:* Murphy, R. Prof.
A study of the implementation of the national curriculum in Malawi with emphasis on mathematics and science in standard three
Abstract: In 1987 the Ministry of Education and Culture in Malawi decided to have a review of the whole primary education curriculum. The review has been the most radical since independence in 1964. The most significant changes in the curriculum have been the reorganisation of subjects bringing in more integrated subjects and the suggestions put to teachers on teaching methods and teaching materials. These changes affect teachers as they have to reconcile their experiential background of teaching with the new ones proposed to them by the developers of the new materials. Problems may arise during the implementation which will need to be addressed in the early period of implementation. This study therefore focuses on the implementation of this revised curriculum, in particular mathematics and science. The intent is to identify factors that facilitate successful implementation of the innovations, and those that inhibit their implementation. This information when given to the curriculum developers at the Ministry of Education and Culture, will enable them to provide solutions to problem areas and reinforce existing good practices during the early period of the implementation of mathematics and science curriculum for primary schools.
Status: Individual research

Date of Research: 1992-1994
KEYWORDS: *curriculum development; Malawi; mathematics education; primary education; science education*

10/1162
School of Education, University Park, Nottingham NG7 2RD
01159 515151
Supervisor: Murphy, R. Prof.
Pupil assessments in the early years of secondary schooling in the United Kingdom and Ghana
Abstract: The research focuses on classroom assessment of pupils in the first two years of secondary schooling. The Education Reform Act 1988 brought about wide-ranging changes in pupils' assessment. The Act requires that pupils be assessed by their teachers at specific ages, and these results should be combined with externally assessed components and reported at the end of the year. In Ghana, the Continuous Assessment Scheme introduced in 1987 also places pupils' assessment on the teacher. The policy stated that internal assessment should constitute 40% of the child's overall marks while the externally assessed component takes 6%. However, in Ghana, the exact way in which the continuous assessment scheme operates has not been specified in the document. The research examines the impact of the policies in classroom teaching and pupil learning. Issues such as the competencies of teachers in assessment, that affect implementation processes, and the effect of the new assessment schemes on teachers' effectiveness and pupils' learning are identified for study. Teachers of mathematics and English were used for the classroom observation. In Nottingham, 12 teachers drawn from two secondary schools participated. Ten pupils from each school were interviewed. In Ghana, 18 teachers were randomly selected from 12 junior secondary schools for the case-study and 3 headteachers also participated in the study. A qualitative approach using a combination of case study, participant observation and interviewing were used for the collection of data. Analysis of the data is continuing and a final report will be produced.
Status: Individual research
Date of Research: 1990-1994
KEYWORDS: *assessment; assessment by teachers; comparative education; Ghana*

10/1163
School of Education, Centre for the Study of Human Relations, University Park, Nottingham NG7 2RD
01159 515151
Hall, E. Dr; Hall, C. Mrs
Outcomes of experiential learning
Abstract: This is an ongoing project which examines the outcomes of experiential interpersonal skills training programmes which have been developed over the years at the Centre for the Study of Human Relations at the University of Nottingham. A series of studies have been conducted, partly associated with four Ph.D students. All of the evaluations have involved experienced teachers who attended six-day residential courses or extended award bearing courses to gain an M.Ed. or an Advanced Diploma. Data has been collected before, during and up to three years after the courses. Data was collected using standardised questionnaires, interviews, diaries of critical incidents, outcomes of goal setting, learning journals and data collected during experiential exercises during the courses. A consistent pattern has emerged over several studies. The participants reported significant changes in both their personal and professional lives. These changes involved reports of reductions in stress, a greater sense of control over one's life and a shift to a more humanistic approach to discipline issues. These changes involved relationships with both students and colleagues. There was also a strong 'Sleeper effect' in several of the studies in which a significant improvement was obtained at the end of the course, followed by a much more substantial increase one year later. Further studies have involved the evaluation of the development of the same forms of training with students in schools.
Published Material: HALL, E., WOODHOUSE, D.A. & WOOSTER, A.D. (1984). 'An evaluation of inservice courses in human relations', British Journal of Inservice Education, Vol 11, No 1, pp.55-60.; HALL, E. & HALL, C.A. (1988). Human relations in education. London: Routledge.; HALL, E., HALL, C.A. & LEECH, A. (1990). A scripted fantasy in the classroom. London: Routledge.; HALL, C.A., & DELANEY, J. (1992). 'How a personal and social education programme can promote friendship in the infant class', Research in Education, No 47, pp.29-39.; HALL, E. (1994). 'The

social relational approach'. In: KUTNICK, P. & ROGERS, C. (Eds). Groups in schools. London: Cassell.
Status: Sponsored project
Source of Grant: Nottingham University: School of Education £4,000; Universities Funding Council £4,000; Enterprise in Higher Education £7,500
Date of Research: 1974-continuing
KEYWORDS: experiential learning; interpersonal competence; locus of control; outcomes of education; stress – psychological; student experience; teacher education

10/1164

School of Education, University Park, Nottingham NG7 2RD
01159 515151
Mid Trent College of Nursing and Midwifery, Headquarters 'A' Floor, Queens Medical Centre, Nottingham NG7 2UH
01159 421421
Chapple, M. Miss; *Supervisor:* Murphy, R. Prof.
A formative evaluation of the first two years of a new Bachelor of Nursing course
Abstract: The aim of this study is to evaluate the processes of teaching and learning within the first two years of a Bachelor of Nursing (BN) course with a view to monitoring and improving the process of education taking place. The study is addressing three questions: a) What are the students' views of the teaching processes and learning experiences during the foundation programme of the course? b) How do the students' views of these processes and experiences compare with those of staff (clinical and tutorial) who are involved with teaching and supporting learning? c) What is the context/learning milieu within which these teaching processes operate? An action research approach is being used in conjunction with responsive evaluation as described by Stake (Stake, R.A. (1988). 'An evolutionary view of educational improvements'. In: House, E.R. (Ed). New directions in educational evaluation. Lewes: Falmer Press.) The methods being employed include the nominal group technique as a form of student group evaluation at the end of each term: informal interviews/conversations; participant observation; field notes and student diaries. The first three cohorts of students are being interviewed once during the first two years of the course. The aim of these interviews is to obtain more detailed information about the students' views of the teaching and learning processes and to find out whether these correlate with data obtained during the formal formative and summative evaluations of the course.
Published Material: CHAPPLE, M., ALLCOCK, N. & WHARRAD, H.J. (1994). 'Bachelor Nursing students' experiences of learning biological sciences alongside medical students', Nurse Education Today, Vol 13, No 6, pp.426-434.
Status: Individual research
Date of Research: 1990-continuing
KEYWORDS: course evaluation; nurse education; student attitudes; teaching methods

10/1165

School of Education, University Park, Nottingham NG7 2RD
01159 515151
Mid Trent College of Nursing and Midwifery, Headquarters 'A' Floor, Queens Medical Centre, Nottingham NG7 2UH
01159 421421
Murphy, R. Prof.; Fraser, D. Mrs; Worth-Butler, M. Mrs
An outcome evaluation of the effectiveness of pre-registration midwifery programmes of education
Abstract: Midwifery education has recently seen the introduction of a new 'direct entry' (pre-registration) programme, alongside the traditional programme of midwifery education which required students to be previously registered as general nurses. Whilst many practitioners have welcomed the possibility of a more cost-effective programme which emphasises the 'normal' nature of midwifery, many have reservations about the competence of midwives trained through the programme, to care for a woman who has a medical, surgical or psychiatric problem. This project sets out to evaluate the effectiveness of the pre-registration programme in producing midwives who are competent to practise at the point of registration. Assessment tools currently being used in the programmes will be examined and used to develop a new assessment tool which will then be used to evaluate the outcomes of the pre-registration programme. A second phase of the study will involve looking at midwives who have trained through the pre-registration programme, one year on. Career intentions and patterns and intention rates will be examined

alongside a comparative assessment of their knowledge, attitudes and competences as midwives. Evidence regarding the effectiveness of the programme will be gathered through interviews, observations and document analysis.
Status: Sponsored project
Source of Grant: English National Board for Nursing, Midwifery and Health Visiting £150,000
Date of Research: 1993-continuing
KEYWORDS: medical education; nurses; obstetrics

10/1166

School of Education, University Park, Nottingham NG7 2RD
01159 515151
Mid Trent College of Nursing and Midwifery Headquarters, A Floor, Queens Medical Centre, Nottingham NG7 2UH
01602 421421
Fraser, D. Mrs; *Supervisor:* Murphy, R. Prof.
An evaluation of the non-midwifery placements in a three year pre-registration programme for the diploma in midwifery
Abstract: This study seeks to evaluate the effectiveness of the non-midwifery placements in a three year pre-registration programme for the diploma in midwifery. The development of these programmes has raised concerns, from some health care professionals, that these midwives will only be equipped to provide care when pregnancy and childbirth is normal. They need to be convinced that at the end of the programme, the students will be competent to provide midwifery care when a woman has a medical, surgical or psychiatric problem. The main focus of the study is to identify the learning experiences that best facilitate the acquisition of knowledge and skills needed to function as an autonomous, independent midwife practitioner. Given that there is a lack of consensus amongst midwives and doctors as to the value and effectiveness of learning experiences in acute general hospitals, the organisation of practice placements in this college has been based upon intuition rather than systematic enquiry. It therefore became evident that action research was needed to evaluate the implementation of this new programme. This should have the potential to influence the learning experiences for each 'case study' student as well as providing illuminative evidence for future curriculum decision making.
Status: Individual research
Date of Research: 1992-1994
KEYWORDS: medical education; obstetrics

Open University

10/1167

Institute of Educational Technology, Walton Hall, Milton Keynes MK7 6AA
01908 274066
Chambers, E. Ms; Durbridge, N. Ms
Distance education and the humanities
Abstract: This is an investigation of all aspects of adult students' encounters with distance courses in the Humanities. To date most research has been done into beginning students (i.e. those taking an interdisciplinary Foundation course) and those studying philosophy and music. The research covers: students' expectations of and attitudes to studying; students' acquisition of study skills; the particular problems facing students new to the study of philosophy (and, in 1995, literature and art history). The methods used are: survey questionnaires, large and small samples; interviews; small samples; institutional data (e.g. drop out, examination pass rates etc.).
Published Material: CHAMBERS, E.A. (1984). 'A project component in architectural history'. In: HENDERSON, E. & NATHENSON, M. (Eds). Independent learning in higher education. Englewood Cliffs, New Jersey: Prentice-Hall Inc.; CHAMBERS, E.A. & DURBRIDGE, N. (1987). 'Preparing for the examination', A102 An Arts Foundation Course, Units 31-32. Milton Keynes: Open University Press.; CHAMBERS, E.A. (1992). 'Workload and the quality of student learning', Studies in Higher Education, (in press).; CHAMBERS, E.A. (1991). 'Improving Foundation Level study at the Open University through Evaluation of student experience'. In: Proceedings of the CNAA Conference 'Academic Quality Assurance'. London: CNAA.
Status: Sponsored project
Source of Grant: Open University
Date of Research: 1975-continuing

KEYWORDS: adult students; distance education; humanities; mature students; open universities; student attitudes

10/1168

Institute of Educational Technology, Walton Hall, Milton Keynes MK7 6AA
01908 274066
Kirkup, G. Ms; Kirkwood, A. Mr; Jones, A. Dr
An evaluation of home computers in adult distance education
Abstract: An investigation of the effects of compulsory use of a personal computer students studying particular courses in the undergraduate programme of the Open University. Students were sampled during their studies in 1988, 1989, 1990 and 1991. Issues of interest include: access and availability of equipment; costs; the effect of introducing home based computing on study habits; content difficulty; and the impact on family of computer in home. Teaching staff are also researched to discover the effects on contact with students and teaching load. Research methods include: survey questionnaires at points in the year; interviews; and self-completion journals.
Published Material: KIRKWOOD, A. & KIRKUP, G. (1991). 'Access to computing for home-based students', Studies in Higher Education, Vol 16, No 3.; KIRKUP, G. (1991). 'Computer conferencing and gender', Computers in Adult Education and Training, Vol 2, No 2.; JONES, A., KIRKUP, G., KIRKWOOD, A. & MASON, R. (1992). Providing computing for distance learners: a strategy for home use', Computers and Education, No 18, pp.1-3.; KIRKUP, G., JONES, A. & KIRKWOOD, A. (1992). Personal computers for distance learning. London: Paul Chapman.
Status: Sponsored project
Source of Grant: Open University
Date of Research: 1988-1993
KEYWORDS: computer uses in education; distance education; microcomputers; open universities

10/1169

Institute of Educational Technology, Walton Hall, Milton Keynes MK7 6AA
01908 274066
Lefrere, P. Dr
The trainers' workbench
Abstract: The project aims at a partial codification, for proof of concept purposes, of open learning expertise, with a view to developing rule-based systems. A prototype system will provide on-the-job help with the design and evaluation of learning materials, including computer-assisted learning.
Status: Individual research
Date of Research: 1990-continuing
KEYWORDS: computer-assisted learning; educational materials; educational media; open education

10/1170

Institute of Educational Technology, Walton Hall, Milton Keynes MK7 6AA
01908 274066
Fitzgerald, D. Mr; *Supervisor:* Morgan, A. Dr
Qualitative thinking in tertiary education
Abstract: This research looks at approaches to teaching and consequent learning outcomes in tertiary education students, to investigate what techniques might be implemented in order to develop students' independence in thinking. The background work centres on research which suggests three fundamental approaches to learning (surface, strategic, deep) used by students. It will examine how it may be possible to aspire towards deep learning, i.e. how might critical thinking be instantiated into the learning process. How to think rather than what to know is the underlying rationale.
Status: Sponsored project
Source of Grant: Open University, per annum £5,000
Date of Research: 1991-1994
KEYWORDS: learning processes; learning strategies; teaching methods; tertiary education

10/1171

Institute of Educational Technology, Walton Hall, Milton Keynes MK7 6AA
01908 274066
Jones, A. Dr; Petre, M. Dr

Investigating effective reasoning models for students: what courses provide and what students concoct
Abstract: This research has two main aims: to investigate elements that contribute to the formation of mental models by novice users and to evaluate metaphors by which models are suggested. A further aim is to consider practical issues for designing instructional material for independent study. A pilot project will investigate instructional elements that contribute to the formation of mental models by novice users. Particular questions include: (1) Is there a generalisable set of initial information that obstructs learning if it is absent or encourages learning if it is offered at the outset? (2) Do the principle metaphors work; where do they break down, when and in what circumstances do users reject them? Practical issues for designing instructional material for independent study include the question of how people actually use the resources provided and when does the time it takes to become minimally competent with a system become prohibitive? The pilot study takes the form of a case study of a practical element of an Open University course. The domain is learning a computer application.
Status: Individual research
Date of Research: 1992-1994
KEYWORDS: computers; educational materials; metaphors; reasoning

10/1172

Institute of Educational Technology, Walton Hall, Milton Keynes MK7 6AA
01908 274066
Zand, H. Dr; Burt, G. Mr
Affect and learning mathematics
Abstract: Learners of mathematics experience a variety of emotions such as anxiety, raised/lowered self image, depression, elation, etc. In this project, the researchers have been studying the emotional experiences of mathematics learners and their influence on their ability to learn. The researchers are also interested in questions such as how affects exert their influence and the implications for teaching mathematics; how affects influence memory and mathematical insight.
Published Material: ZAND, H. & BURT, G.J. (1989). 'Social and emotional aspects of learning mathematics', Educational and Training Technology International, Vol 26, No 1.
Status: Individual research
Date of Research: 1986-continuing
KEYWORDS: affective behaviour; emotional response; mathematics; student behaviour

10/1173

Institute of Educational Technology, Walton Hall, Milton Keynes MK7 6AA
01908 274066
Burt, G. Mr
The curriculum as culture and ideology
Abstract: According to the common-sense view, education is about individual people 'learning' ideas and skills. It is an apolitical activity, which meets the needs of individuals and of society as a whole. The aim of the curriculum as culture and ideology project is to challenge this view. Education is not about people learning ideas and skills; it is about cultural ideas and practices taking possession of people. Education then is simply one of a number of arenas in which different cultures and ideologies with differential powers seek to promote themselves, and hence come into conflict. Cultures seek to promote themselves in every sphere of society. Hence cultures demand education about every social sphere. The aim of the research project is to study educational provision with a view to identifying the cultural and ideological promotions involved. Currently under study are the arenas of educational technology, educational computing, mathematics and technology education, management education and community education. Teaching materials in these areas involve cultural and ideological promotion relating to issues of gender, class, ethnicity, individualism, technicism and militarism. Proposals for how education might be redesigned to take account of this critique are also being developed.
Published Material: BURT, G.J. (1989). 'Social forces and school computing', British Journal of Educational Technology, Vol 20, No 2, pp.140-141.; BURT, G.J. (1989). 'Computers in schools as culture and ideology', International Council for Distance Education Bulletin, Vol 20, pp.19-24.; BURT, G.J. (1989). 'Beyond educational technology: the new discipline of cultural and ideological technology',

Research in Distance Education, Vol 1, No 3, pp.9-11.; BURT, G.J. (1989). 'The message behind the medium', Information Technology and Learning, December, pp.55-56.; BURT, G.J. (1991). 'Culture and ideology in the training literature', Educational Technology and Training International, Vol 28, No 3, pp.229-237. A full list of publications is available from the researcher.
Status: Individual research
Date of Research: 1988-continuing
KEYWORDS: cultural influences; curriculum; educational philosophy; ideology

10/1174

Institute of Educational Technology, Walton Hall, Milton Keynes MK7 6AA
01908 274066
Mason, R. Dr; Kaye, A. Mr
Computer conferencing in distance education
Abstract: The Open University pioneered the use of computer conferencing in mass distance education on its Information Technology course in 1988. The University is now looking to rewrite that course and to offer it to students throughout Europe. Computer conferencing will form a major component of the course, both as a medium for supporting students and as a means of presenting and maintaining the course. Through a series of pilot schemes and other small applications, the researchers are refining the use of this medium as a tool for distance education. Some of the areas under investigation are: (1) its integration with other media; (2) its use with world wide web; (3) its use as a tool for collaborative learning amongst students; and (4) its application to training and continuing education. The focus of research by Open University PhD students include: discourse analysis of conferencing interactions; and critical mass for successful conference interactions. The researchers are also investigating the design of conferencing systems and front ends to provide low cost, easy to use access for home-based students throughout Europe.
Published Material: MASON, R. & KAYE, A.R. (Eds). (1989). Mindweave: communication, computers and distance education. Oxford: Pergamon Press.; MASON, R. (1989). 'The use of computer networks in education and training', Report No OL87. Moorfoot, Sheffield: Training Agency.; KAYE, A.R. (Ed). (1992). Collaborative learning through computer conferencing. Heidelberg: Springer-Verlag.
Status: Sponsored project
Source of Grant: Training, Enterprise and Education Directorate; Economic and Social Research Council – studentships; European Community DELTA projects
Date of Research: 1990-continuing
KEYWORDS: distance education; international educational exchange; open universities; teleconferencing

10/1175

Institute of Educational Technology, Walton Hall, Milton Keynes MK7 6AA
01908 274066
Burt, G. Mr
Strategic management and development in educational organisation
Abstract: There is a growing attention to 'management' in educational organisations. However it is important that fashionable management ideas should not be accepted uncritically. The project studies the strategic process at the Open University noting the presence of structural and political dimensions. Special attention is given to studying the values and ethics dimensions.
Status: Individual research
Date of Research: 1990-continuing
KEYWORDS: educational planning; management in education; university administration

10/1176

Institute of Educational Technology, Walton Hall, Milton Keynes MK7 6AA
01908 274066
Taylor, M. Mrs; Valentine, C. Mr; *Supervisor:* Vincent, A. Dr
Access to teaching materials for visually impaired learners
Abstract: Compact disc versions (electronic and audio) of print course material from a number of Open University (OU) courses are being produced for students who are unable to use conventional print. The overall aim is to have OU preparatory packs, foundation courses,

selected post-foundation courses, and access-related packs available for students in these media by September 1996, and to have in place a mechanism for transformation to these media for all new courses from 1997 onwards. This approach is part of a long term strategy to provide disabled students with the choice of the most appropriate medium for course texts. The first courses have been made available to selected students 1994. Desktop or portable computers, with CD-ROM drives and appropriate enabling technologies, are being used by students to access modified versions of electronically published print materials. This modification involves the replacement of mark-up commands used for publishing through print and adding new mark-up commands that provide an appropriate layout of text for the CD-ROM delivery medium as well as taking into account that the text will be used with screenreaders (synthetic speech) or other enabling technologies. A retrieval program (ReadOut) has been developed that is compatible with enabling technologies, and allows for a more structured presentation of the course material and a higher level of interactivity.
Published Material: HAWKRIDGE, D. & VINCENT, T. (1992). Learning difficulties and computers: access to the curriculum. London: Jessica Kingsley.; TAYLOR, M.E. (1994). ReadOut. Internal Report for The Open University.
Status: Sponsored project
Source of Grant: Higher Education Funding Council for England; Guide Dogs for the Blind Association
Date of Research: 1993-continuing
KEYWORDS: blindness; computer uses in education; optical data discs; special educational needs; speech synthesisers; visual impairments

10/1177

Institute of Educational Technology, Walton Hall, Milton Keynes MK7 6AA
01908 274066
Whalley, P. Dr
Classroom based multimedia authoring tools
Abstract: The proposed project is concerned with children's use of the dynamic representations made possible by the newly available multimedia tools. With the micros affordable by schools, it is now possible to capture high quality colour images, sound, and short video clips. The purpose of this project is to develop an authoring tool for integrating these components which will be accessible to young children with a wide range of abilities, and to indicate ways in which it could enhance their work. Considerable success has already been achieved in the classroom with a prototype of the proposed system. The researchers intend to further refine the software to better incorporate video, and to provide detailed documentation as to how the various components of a dynamic document can be created, manipulated and finally assembled together. Technology, even if it is freely available, is of no use if it can not be integrated into classroom practice. The selection, organisation and presentation of learned materials is seen as a valuable part of current educational practice in British classrooms. Documenting how our software environment, together with paper based planning tools, can enable and extend these activities is seen as an important part of the project. Examples of completed projects on topics such as the 'rain cycle' and 'digestion' will be included, both in their final state and in the form of separate image and sound components.
Published Material: MOAR, M. (1992). 'The construction of dynamic documents by children', Proceedings of the East-West conference on emerging computer technologies in education, Moscow, April 1992.
Status: Individual research
Date of Research: 1992-continuing
KEYWORDS: animation; authoring aids – programming; computer assisted learning; computer uses in education; multimedia approach

10/1178

Institute of Educational Technology, Walton Hall, Milton Keynes MK7 6AA
01908 274066
Whalley, P. Dr; Williams, D. Dr
A 'virtual' microscope
Abstract: This project is concerned with developing a 'virtual' microscope which allows the student to choose, manipulate and examine rock samples on the computer screen. Embedding the 'virtual' microscope within a general multi-media database will provide the student with a powerful tool for enquiry and learning. The primary

problems that the researchers intend to tackle are pedagogic not technical – what does or does not aid student learning in the summer school environment, and how may computer-based materials be integrated with the other media being used. An important part of the project will be the developmental testing of the materials at Open University summer schools with the general aim of finding the right balance between questioning and support for the student. An immediate use of the materials will be to enrich the experience of the less mobile students attending these summer schools. Whilst other students go out collecting samples 'in the field', these students will be able to make detailed analyses of equivalent rock samples and consequently be able to make greater contributions to group discussions. A simple extension of the project on the lines of the well known 'Eco-Disc' project would allow the student to 'move' around computer based images and video clips of the hill or quarry and choose from where they would like a 'sample' to be taken. This would obviously empower disabled students to undertake courses and projects from which they would otherwise be blocked.
Status: Sponsored project
Source of Grant: Open University: Institute of Educational Technology £60,300
Date of Research: 1993-continuing
KEYWORDS: *computer-assisted learning; earth science; educational equipment; microscopes; simulation; special educational needs*

10/1179

Institute of Educational Technology, Walton Hall, Milton Keynes MK7 6AA
01908 274066
Whalley, P. Dr
An alternative metaphor for teaching control technology
Abstract: Control technology is viewed as a good way to provide practical experience of programmable systems that are familiar to children such as sliding doors, level crossings etc. Teachers using this technology usually also have the higher level goals of encouraging 'systems thinking' and general problem solving skills. Using a computer in this way to control physical micro-worlds can be an interesting and powerful educational experience. Unfortunately there is often a gulf between these aims and what happens in the classroom. The higher order goals are frequently lost in the struggle to cope with the presently available control technology environments. The project represents an attempt to create a graphic object-orientated control language for children. The underlying nature of environments like HyperTechnic is quite different from their procedural equivalents, and is in several ways intuitively more comprehensible. For example conditionals and loop-control are implicit in the way that the objects operate and do not have to be explicitly taught. The micro-worlds that the children are to explore and control are made up of plastic and cardboard models, rather than the purely screen-based, and hence necessarily more abstract, micro-worlds that are often provided for children. The immediate practical goal of this research is to evaluate to what extent the level of description and explanatory metaphors used to describe control technology problems affects children's understanding of them. A longer term aim is to foster understanding of how children comprehend the deeper conceptual problems underlying this form of task.
Published Material: WHALLEY, P. (1990). 'HyperTechnic – a graphic object-orientated control language'. Presented at the Seventh International Conference on Technology and Education, Brussels, March 1990.; WHALLEY, P. (1991). 'Level of description as a factor in children's interactions with computers'. Presented at the Fourth European Conference for Research on Learning and Instruction (EARLI), Turku, Finland, August 1991.; WHALLEY, P. (1992). 'An alternative metaphor for teaching control technology'. Proceedings of the 'East-West Conference on Emerging Computer Technologies in Education', Moscow, April 1992.; WHALLEY, P. (1993). 'Making control technology work in one classroom', British Journal of Educational Technology (in press).
Status: Individual research
Date of Research: 1990-continuing
KEYWORDS: *computer simulation; computer uses in education; control technology; logo; models*

10/1180

Institute of Educational Technology, Walton Hall, Milton Keynes MK7 6AA
01908 274066
Moar, M. Mr; *Supervisor:* Whalley, P. Dr

The construction of dynamic documents by children
Abstract: Project work seeks to encourage the pupils' freedom to investigate a subject. It requires the selection, organisation and presentation of learned materials and as such is seen as a valuable part of current educational practice in British classrooms. Typically, the end product of a project is a document consisting of text together with appropriate graphics. It is now possible however to produce dynamic computer based documents in the classroom, which incorporate moving images, text and sound. The thesis explores this possibility by looking briefly at the cognitive effects of producing media in an educational context and considering the representational qualities of such dynamic documents. The development of a methodology for dynamic document use based on conventional classroom practice is described, and suggestions for future research are made.
Published Material: MOAR, M. (1992). 'The construction of dynamic documents by children'. In: Proceedings of the 'East-West Conference on Emerging Computer Technologies for Education', Moscow, April 1992.
Status: Sponsored project
Source of Grant: Economic and Social Research Council
Date of Research: 1989-continuing
KEYWORDS: *animation; computer uses in education; pupil projects*

10/1181

Institute of Educational Technology, Walton Hall, Milton Keynes MK7 6AA
01908 274066
Issroff, K. Ms; *Supervisor:* Scanlon, E. Dr; Jones, A. Dr
Motivation and collaboration in computer-assisted learning of chemistry
Abstract: This research aims to investigate the motivation of secondary school students learning from computers in different learning situations. Motivation appears to change when students use computers for learning, especially when working collaboratively. In order to investigate the nature of this different motivation, quantitative and qualitative motivational indices can be measured. Quantitative indices refer to the students' behaviours during learning, while qualitative indices refer to their feelings and attitudes towards the learning. Studies of cooperative learning at the computer have focused predominantly on the cognitive aspects of the interaction and results have not been conclusive. By investigating the psychological environment which surrounds the computer, it may be possible to explain some aspects of the cooperative learning process. The main study involves 15 individuals and 30 pairs learning chemistry from a computer. There is pre- and post-testing of both cognitive and motivational factors and the sessions are video-taped for quantitative motivational indices. It is hoped that the results of this research will provide guidelines for designers of educational software, and educators in setting up effective computer-assisted learning situations and help us to understand the processes which occur when students work at the computer in different learning situations.
Published Material: ISSROFF, K. (1992). Cooperative computer-assisted learning. CITE Report No 173. Milton Keynes: Open University; Institute of Educational Technology.; ISSROFF, K. (1992). Motivation and computer-assisted learning. CITE Report No 174. Milton Keynes: Open University; Institute of Educational Technology.
Status: Sponsored project
Source of Grant: Economic and Social Research Council
Date of Research: 1991-continuing
KEYWORDS: *computer-assisted learning; computer uses in education; cooperative learning; human-computer interaction; learning processes*

10/1182

Institute of Educational Technology, Walton Hall, Milton Keynes MK7 6AA
01908 274066
Fitzgerald, D. Mr; *Supervisor:* Morgan, A. Dr
Teaching critical thinking through group discussion: does it foster a deep approach in teaching Psychology and Management Studies, to first year college students?
Abstract: The aim of this research is to reflect upon two issues: (1) The conceptualisation of the student in higher education as described by researchers in the last twenty years (Perry, Saljo, Marton). It is hoped both to use this framework (approaches to learning, and student conceptualisation of knowledge) to evaluate the teaching innovation as well as to reflect upon the conceptualisations themselves and their

strengths. (2) The teaching innovation itself deals with first year students in the social sciences and management studies as they experience thinking about thinking. Does it foster a deep approach to learning in the student? The method will be group discussion. The range of assessment tools to be used is yet to be fully decided as the research intends to be reflective and adaptable according to feedback on how the course is developing. Teaching will be an integral part of both courses. The courses are at the same university, with 65 students in both disciplines.

Status: Individual research
Date of Research: 1990-1994
KEYWORDS: critical thinking; group discussion; learning activities; teaching methods; university students

10/1183

Institute of Educational Technology, Walton Hall, Milton Keynes MK7 6AA
01908 274066
Queen Mary and Westfield College, Mile End Road, London E1 4NS
0181 980 4811
Bornat, R. Prof.; Reeves, S. Dr; O'Shea, T. Prof.; Fung, P. Dr
Cognitive skills in formal reasoning about programs
Abstract: The aim of the research is to test the hypothesis that with appropriate support, in particular with mechanical aids for symbolic calculation, a very much larger proportion of students can be made competent in formal techniques of reasoning about programs. In the Spring of 1991 and during the course of the academic year 1991 to 1992 a number of empirical studies were undertaken to assess the difficulties which students encounter in learning formal methods of reasoning. Information was obtained from 'diary' records kept by a selection of students. Exchanges on those electronic bulletin boards related to the programming course were noted and an informal electronic link was established between first year computer science students at Queen Mary & Westfield College (QMW) and investigators at the Open University (OU). Sets of data based on answers, given by students, to questions on their backgrounds, their motivations for studying computer science and their expectations of the course were combined with video and audio interviews of them discussing their work. The results of these empirical studies have been used as feedback to researchers at QMW. During this period, the project members at QMW have investigated what graphical tools are currently available to help students learn formal reasoning methods and have designed and developed their own computer-based tools. A series of empirical studies are being undertaken from 1992 to 1993, during which students will be observed using the graphical tools developed in the first phase of the project. These studies will serve as the basis of an evaluation of the help such tools afford to students and will contribute to the further refinement of the tools themselves.
Published Material: FUNG, P. & O'SHEA, T. 'Formal reasoning as a culture shock for computer science students'. In: Development in the Teaching of Computer Science. Proceedings of Conference at University of Kent, Canterbury, April, 1992, pp.26-34.; FUNG, P. & O'SHEA, T. 'Fear of formal reasoning'. In: Proceedings of the Fifth Psychology of Programming Workshop, Paris, 1992, December, pp.207-236.; FUNG, P. & O'SHEA, T. (1993). 'Computer science students' perceptions of learning formal reasoning methods', International Journal of Mathematical Education in Science and Technology, Vol 24, No 5, pp.749-759.; FUNG, P. & O'SHEA, T. (1994). 'Understanding why computer science students find formal reason frightening', Journal of Computer Assisted Learning, Vol 10, pp.240-250.
Status: Sponsored project
Source of Grant: Economic and Social Research Council; Science and Engineering Research Council; Medical Research Council
Date of Research: 1991-1994
KEYWORDS: cognitive development; computer programming; reasoning

10/1184

Mathematics Faculty, Centre for Mathematics Education, Walton Hall, Milton Keynes MK7 6AA
01908 274066
Galpin, B. Mr; Graham, A. Mr
Establishing the spreadsheet as a mathematical tool
Abstract: Starting from a personal interest in and use of the spreadsheet, the researchers are now working at the problem of promoting this software as a useful tool for doing mathematics at all levels. In

particular the intent is to research effective ways of bringing the software to the attention of teachers of mathematics, helping them reach the point where they can use the tool with confidence themselves, not only in their administrative work but also to enhance their own mathematical understanding. To this end a range of examples of spreadsheet applications which are appropriate for use by teachers at all levels will be collected and published.
Published Material: GRAHAM, A. & GALPIN, B. et al (1993). Supporting primary number work. Milton Keynes: Open University.
Status: Individual research
Date of Research: 1992-1993
KEYWORDS: computer uses in education; educational software; mathematics education; spreadsheets

10/1185

Mathematics Faculty, Centre for Mathematics Education, Walton Hall, Milton Keynes MK7 6AA
01908 274066
Galpin, B. Mr; Cooke, H. Mrs
Designated 20-day courses in mathematics
Abstract: Designated 20-day courses for primary coordinators have provided a new mode of inservice training. The Open University has been intimately involved with these courses, producing study materials specifically designed to enhance the personal mathematics competence and confidence of students on the courses. It has also been able to support those local education authorities (LEAs) wishing to run courses themselves by offering a framework of support and advice for the design, implementation and evaluation of the courses. Open University Liaison Advisers have taken a particular interest in researching factors which contribute to the effectiveness of the courses. In particular, an instrument known as a 'personal audit' has been used at the beginning of the courses and subsequently to encourage teachers to reflect on their own competencies. Research continues, aimed at developing this particular instrument and working with course tutors to identify other effective course components. Another strand of the research is to evaluate the role and effectiveness of distance learning materials in designated courses and other types of mathematics inservice provision.
Published Material: CENTRE FOR MATHEMATICS EDUCATION, OPEN UNIVERSITY. (1990). Supporting primary mathematics. Milton Keynes: Open University.; GALPIN, B. (1992). 'Twenty-day wonder', Times Educational Supplement, 21 February.
Status: Individual research
Date of Research: 1991-continuing
KEYWORDS: courses; inservice teacher education; mathematics education; primary school teachers

10/1186

Mathematics Faculty, Centre for Mathematics Education, Walton Hall, Milton Keynes MK7 6AA
01908 274066
Scott, H. Ms; Galpin, B. Mr; Portman, J. Ms; Graham, A. Mr; *Supervisor:* Mason, J. Prof.
Teachers, educators and advisers in mathematics (TEAM)
Abstract: The purpose of the project is to explore new directions of teacher professional development by generating a partnership between teacher, school, advisory service and tertiary institution. Teachers will pursue particular aspects of their practice in order to improve the learning of children. Participants (from 10 Northamptonshire schools) will provide mutual support in an action research mode working on: (1) giving brief-but-vivid descriptions of key incidents; (2) developing alternative strategies for interaction with pupils; (3) sharpening sensitivities to pupil thinking and to mathematical opportunities; (4) the purpose and possibilities in different mathematical tasks. The research will take place through cycles of group meetings, classroom observation and reflective review.
Status: Individual research
Date of Research: 1993-1994
KEYWORDS: mathematics teachers; teacher development; teaching methods

10/1187

Mathematics Faculty, Centre for Mathematics Education, Walton Hall, Milton Keynes MK7 6AA
01908 274066
Auckland University, Mathematics Education Unit, Auckland, New Zealand Graham, A. Mr; Reilly, I. Prof.

Using numbers and relationships
Abstract: This project shares the expertise of the Centre for Mathematics Education of the Open University and the Mathematics Education Unit of Auckland University. The main focus is the provision of foundation mathematics courses for the wide range of students who are entering tertiary education. In particular, the research will look at number and relationships and explore how student expectations, interests and the educational context of the course all play a part in how students develop understanding in these areas of basic mathematics. This will therefore involve research in the following aspects: (a) the access and enrolment in foundation courses for different gender, ethnic and socio-economic groups, looking at the reasons for unequal enrolment and producing course materials specific to the interests of particular groups of students; (b) investigating non-academic perceptions of and uses of number and relationships and how this can be taken account of in writing effective teaching materials; (c) the use of technology (particularly the graphics calculator and spreadsheets) to enhance the understanding of numbers and relationships.
Status: Sponsored project
Source of Grant: British Council
Date of Research: 1993-continuing
KEYWORDS: higher education; introductory courses; mathematics education; numbers; numeracy

10/1188
    School of Education, Walton Hall, Milton Keynes MK7 6AA
    01908 274066
    Tyler, S. Ms; *Supervisor:* Light, P. Prof.
Spatial cognition: children's pictorial representations
Abstract: Modern accounts of children's drawings still take intellectual/visual realism (or elaborations) as their focal point. The current research treats drawing as problem-solving, with solutions determined/constrained by factors such as lack of particular spatial concepts. However, Piaget's accounts of the child's construction of representational space, and his premise of perception in 2D are not accepted. Thus in the first experiments, which focused on inconsistencies in response when children are requested to draw an array in which one object is partly hidden by another, the dimensions of the objects were systematically varied (2D/3D). Results showed that children aged 4-7 years are sensitive to object dimensions. When 2D equivalents of 3D objects are used children are less likely to segregate either outlines or 2D cutouts when drawing or arranging materials on paper, than when the objects are 3D. They are able to arrange 2D materials so that one is partially hidden, provided the arrangement is made 'in space' so that many gaps can be left to represent object depth. They can also match arrays, using identical materials. The findings show that children's difficulties are confined to the 2D drawing surface, and that they have no problems with understanding simple spatial relationships, with allowing objects to be partially hidden, or with viewpoint. Other findings showed that children will treat 3D objects as 2D provided object depth is not an essential feature (as it is in spheres, cones etc.). A current experiment is investigating whether partial occlusion can be facilitated by triggering what may be schemas for drawing familiar objects – schemas that may be 2D in concept.
Status: Sponsored project
Source of Grant: Economic and Social Research Council £21,000
Date of Research: 1990-1993
KEYWORDS: cognitive ability; depth perception; drawing; problem solving; spatial ability; visual perception

10/1189
    School of Education, Walton Hall, Milton Keynes MK7 6AA
    01908 274066
    Bancroft, D. Dr
Temporal inference research project
Abstract: It is arguably the case that much human reasoning and problem solving rests on an understanding of the temporal inter-relations between events. Early and effective development of temporal understanding may then make a considerable contribution to wider cognitive skills. There has been a considerable amount of European laboratory based research investigation of the development of children's understanding of time. One outcome is the suggestion that the co-ordination of temporal concepts is problematic for children until late in childhood since it depends on considerable cognitive sophistication. Another possibility is that young children are capable of dealing with temporal concepts when not obstructed by 'interfering'

factors. There is also evidence from the psycholinguistic tradition which suggests that children use the language of 'time' effectively from a very early age. The aim of the project is to investigate children's ability to reason about, and manipulate the concepts of Order and Duration in order to resolve some of the theoretical issues and to identify means of encouraging the development of temporal reasoning. Children aged between 4 and 7 years are presented with temporal problems on a microcomputer. Children have either mouse or concept keyboard control of the computer, thus allowing a behavioural indication of comprehension. Results to date indicate that, although not all temporal problems are of equal complexity, children of this age are capable of producing sophisticated solutions and that this ability can be developed and promoted.
Status: Sponsored project
Source of Grant: Open University
Date of Research: 1987-continuing
KEYWORDS: cognitive development; reasoning; temporal integration; time perspective

10/1190
    School of Education, Walton Hall, Milton Keynes MK7 6AA
    01908 274066
    Edwards, R. Dr
Educational responses to adult employment
Abstract: The aim of this research is to critically examine the policies and practices which produce and respond to adult unemployment in contemporary society and the role of education and training discourse and programmes in overcoming and/or reproducing adult unemployment. This is pursued through desk research and interviews with policy makers, practitioners and participants in the field. Conclusions are always provisional, dependent on the changing constellation of policy and practice.
Published Material: EDWARDS, R. (1991). 'The Canadian jobs strategy', Unemployment Bulletin, Autumn, pp.8-13.; EDWARDS, R. (1991). 'The inevitable future? post-Fordism and open learning', Open Learning, Vol 6, No 2, pp.36-43.; EDWARDS, R. (1991). 'Guidance and unemployment in Canada', Adults Learning, Vol 2, No 10, pp.279-282.; EDWARDS, R. 'Winners and losers: the education and training of adults'. In: RAGGATT, P. & UNWIN, L. (Eds). Change and intervention: vocational education and training. London: Falmer Press.
Status: Sponsored project
Source of Grant: Canadian High Commission £1,800
Date of Research: 1990-1993
KEYWORDS: adult vocational education; employment patterns; training; unemployment

10/1191
    School of Education, Walton Hall, Milton Keynes MK7 6AA
    01908 274066
    Light, P. Prof.
Social interaction and cognitive development in school aged children
Abstract: An extensive programme of research (mostly in the form of small experimental projects) has addressed social aspects of children's cognitive development. Topics have encompassed social perspective taking, spatial perspective taking and drawing, conservation and logical reasoning. Current work is focused on the role of pragmatic schemes in deductive reasoning and the role of peer interaction in problem-solving, using computers.
Published Material: LIGHT, P. & PERRET-CLERMONG, A.N. (1989). 'Social context effects in reasoning and testing'. In: GELLATLY, A. et al (Eds). Cognition and social worlds. Oxford: Clarendon Press.; LIGHT, P. & BLAYE, A. (1990). 'Computer-based learning: the social dimensions'. In: FOOT, H.C., MORGAN, M.J. & SHUTE, R.H. (1990). Children helping children. Chichester: John Wiley & Sons Ltd.; LIGHT, P., GIROTTO, V. & LEGRENZI, P. (1990). 'Children's reasoning on conditional promises and permissions', Cognitive Development, No 5, pp.369-383.
Status: Sponsored project
Source of Grant: Economic and Social Resarch Council; Foundation Fyssen (Paris); Open University; Leverhulme Trust
Date of Research: 1979-continuing
KEYWORDS: cognitive development; interaction; peer groups; reasoning

10/1192

School of Education, Walton Hall, Milton Keynes MK7 6AA
01908 274066
McCormick, R. Dr

Problem solving in technology education

Abstract: The Problem Solving in Technology Education (PSTE) project team comprises Sara Hennessy, Bob McCormick and Patricia Murphy. The team is applying a situated learning perspective to technology education. This entails examining what kinds of 'problem solving' actually take place in technology classrooms, relating this to what teachers believe and communicate to pupils. Specifically, the researchers are investigating whether pupils are superficially following prescribed models of the design process. Key issues under investigation include: (1) the relationship between teachers' and children's agendas, perceptions and beliefs concerning Design and Technology (D&T) activities; (2) the influence of teachers' agendas on children's problem solving behaviour; (3) children's recognition of links across the component subject contexts, and between D&T activities and problem solving activities in the outside world. The work entails indepth observation of D&T activities and interviews with pupils and teachers, focusing on the nature of the planning, decision making and problem solving strategies that children use in designing and making an artifact, and in coping with problems which arise along the way. The results from the pilot work indicate that teachers are not always successfully communicating the design process and that perceived links between diverse activities are minimal. This work challenges the popular idea that 'problem solving' in technology denotes a holistic 'design-and-make' process. The team's position is that 'design-and-make' is instead a complex and iterative process of refining problems. Various kinds of tasks, and stages within them, present different problems which require different approaches.

Published Material: HENNESSY, S. & McCORMICK, R. (1993). 'The general problem solving process in technology education: myth or reality?'. In: BANKS, F. (Ed). Teaching technology. Open University Post-Graduate Certificate of Education Course E885 reader. London: Routledge.; HENNESSY, S., McCORMICK, R. & MURPHY, P. (1993). 'The myth of general problem solving capability: design and technology as an example', Curriculum Journal, Vol 4, No 1, pp.73-89.; McCORMICK, R., HENNESSY, S. & MURPHY, P. (1993). 'Problem-solving processes in technology education'. International Technology Education Association 55th Annual Conference, Charlotte, North Carolina, April 1993.; McCORMICK, R., HENNESSY, S. & MURPHY, P. (1993). 'A pilot study of children's problem-solving processes'. Proceedings of the International Conference on Design and Technology (IDATER), Loughborough, September 1993.; HENNESSY, S. (1993). 'Situated cognition and cognitive apprenticeship: implications for classroom learning', Studies in Science Education, Vol 22, p.1-41.

Status: Sponsored project
Source of Grant: Economic and Social Research Council £120,000
Date of Research: 1992-continuing
KEYWORDS: design and technology; learning strategies; problem solving; technology education

10/1193

School of Education, Walton Hall, Milton Keynes MK7 6AA
01908 274066
Faulkner, D. Dr; Miell, D. Dr

The effects of friendships and social isolation on young children's communication and collaborative learning

Abstract: This ongoing project began with an exploratory longitudinal study of 37, 4-5 year old children throughout their first term of formal schooling. A number of methods for examining the impact of early friendships on the children's success in settling into school were tested: pairs of friends and isolated children were observed over 11 weeks using a modified version of Sylva, Roy and Painter's (1980) Target Child observational system; interaction in the classroom was also recorded on video tape; teacher interviews took place at the beginning and end of term; children were interviewed about their friendships and were asked to take part in a communication game. Previous research would suggest that close enduring friendships foster the development of social skills, such as effective communication, negotiation, and social perspective taking. These skills are needed for effective entry into the wider peer culture of the primary school. The researchers predicted that children who started school in the company of a friend or friends would take less time to adjust to their new situation than children without friends, and that the former would have more sophisticated social and communicative skills. The results suggested that the methods employed were useful ones for

examining early friendships and children's behaviour and interactions in a range of school settings. The results also showed that children with friends had more success than children who were isolates, or merely acquaintances on a classroom communication game. The next phase of the project will extend this work to look at the effects of friendship on developing collaborative learning during the early years.

Status: Sponsored project
Source of Grant: Open University: Social Science Research Committee £1,000; Personal Research Fund (Dr D. Faulkner) £3,500
Date of Research: 1992-continuing
KEYWORDS: communication skills; early childhood education; friendship; infant school pupils; reception classes; social development; social isolation; young children

10/1194

School of Education, Walton Hall, Milton Keynes MK7 6AA
01908 274066
Bristol University, Senate House, Bristol BS8 1TH
01179 303030
Austin, J. Mr; *Supervisor:* Bell, R. Dr; Low-Beer, A. Dr

The preparatory school experience 1918-1940

Abstract: This is an historical study of the nature of preparatory school experience for boys and staff in the period between the wars. It will involve oral history methods as well as analysis of school magazines, autobiographies and other literary sources.

Status: Individual research
Date of Research: 1991-1994
KEYWORDS: boys; educational history; preparatory schools

10/1195

School of Education, Walton Hall, Milton Keynes MK7 6AA
01908 274066
Warwick University, Department of Education, Priory Street, Coventry CV1 5FB
01203 631313
Small, N. Mr; *Supervisor:* Bell, R. Dr; Bown, L. Prof.

The role of education for citizenship with reference to Zambia

Abstract: The research explores the informal area of education from which, and by which, adults develop a sense of identity at a national level. More positive is the idea and work of 'nation building' which can also arise from educational provision. The context is 'what counts as citizenship in States formed in the last century in former British colonial territories in east and central Africa?'. This offers a comparative background to the main focus on Zambia. Zambia was administered by a chartered company for about a quarter of a century; was the responsibility of the British Colonial Office for forty years as Northern Rhodesia; and has been an independent State in the Commonwealth for a quarter of a century. In that last period, it has faced particular external difficulties, reflecting circumstances in Southern Rhodesia (now Zimbabwe); and from its position economically with regard to South Africa. Internally, copper mining has been the major supplier of exports and of foreign exchange; but a decline in demand and a fall in price have seriously affected the robustness of the economy to finance the expansion of desired infrastructure, and social, health and educational development. The researcher hopes to review the role of education among adults, and indicate if and how it contributes to a commitment of a sense of identity with the State; and whether the adult as citizen is a concept that is consciously pursued by agencies formal and informal.

Status: Individual research
Date of Research: 1985-1994
KEYWORDS: citizenship; citizenship education; identity; nationalism; role of education; Zambia

10/1196

Science Faculty, Centre for Science Education, Walton Hall, Milton Keynes MK7 6AA
01908 274066
Sharp, G. Ms; *Supervisor:* West, R. Prof.; Whitelegg, E. Ms

Cognitive Acceleration in Science Education (CASE) related to age intervention and gender differentiation

Abstract: The project is to investigate a variety of science teaching intervention procedures with particular reference to age of intervention and gender differentiation, with the aim of discovering what types of intervention can be used to improve the science education of individual pupils within the 10 to 12 year old age range. The project

is looking in detail at one recent intervention programme the Cognitive Acceleration in Science Education (CASE) project, and comparing the effects of this to other intervention strategies, including inservice teacher education (INSET) on equal opportunities, primary science, collaborative learning methods, single sex teaching, etc. Much of the initial research will be to collate information on intervention strategies that have been used on a city, national and international basis. Whilst carrying out this research the project will use the 30 activity lessons as designed by Shayer et al with Year 7 pupils and will introduce the use of these materials at one of the feeder schools. The evaluation packs as provided by the CASE project will be used. New sets of evaluation and analysis documents will also be developed. Self-assessment, as well as group and individual interviews, will be used with pupils and teachers. The standard assessment tasks for the National Curriculum will be used with all the pupils and although these will be testing knowledge rather than cognitive understanding, they may be of some use.
Status: Individual research
Date of Research: 1993-continuing
KEYWORDS: intervention; science education; sex differences

10/1197
> Science Faculty, Centre for Science Education, Walton Hall, Milton Keynes MK7 6AA
> 01908 274066
> Hodgson, B. Dr; Murphy, P. Ms; Scanlon, E. Dr; Whitelegg, E. Ms

Collaborative learning and primary science (CLAPS)
Abstract: The aim of this work is to investigate the processes which occur in groups in primary classrooms tackling investigative science tasks and the way in which these processes can support the children's science learning. Based on a small scale exploration of the suitability of such tasks, the researchers found that it was possible to record these processes as pupils' work. The researchers now wish to undertake a naturalistic study following groups of eight and nine year old children undertaking investigative tasks as part of their normal science classroom work. Recent developments in the primary science curriculum and trends in classroom organisation make this study timely. The theoretical background to the study is the constructivist perspective on learning and an analysis of the role of conceptual conflict as part of the contribution made to children's learning by groupwork. Groups of four children will be videotaped and their conversation recorded as they work. The exploratory study suggests that such groupings, tasks and methods are suitable for study. The expected outcomes of the study are a description of the features of the task and the group composition which contribute to pupils' successful science learning, and the documentation of good practice for teachers of this age group.
Published Material: WHITELEGG, E., MURPHY, P., SCANLON, E. & HODGSON, B. (1992). 'Investigating collaboration in primary science classrooms: a gender perspective'. Vol 1. Proceedings of East and West European GASAT Conference, Eindhoven, Netherlands, October 1992.; WHITELEGG, E., MURPHY, P., SCANLON, E. & HODGSON, B. (1993). Group work on science investigations – do girls and boys do it differently. In: BENTLEY, D. & WATTS, M. (Eds). Primary science technology: practical alternatives. Buckingham: Open University Press.
Status: Sponsored project
Source of Grant: Open University £27,000
Date of Research: 1993-continuing
KEYWORDS: classroom observation techniques; group work; learning activities; science activities; science education

10/1198
> Science Faculty, Centre for Science Education, Walton Hall, Milton Keynes MK7 6AA
> 01908 274066
> Nottingham Trent University, Faculty of Education, Clifton Hall, Clifton Lane, Clifton, Nottingham NG11 8NS
> 01159 418418
> Tresman, S. Dr; Fox, D. Mr

How much science do teachers need to know to realise the potential of science in primary classrooms
Abstract: This project aims to investigate the question of how much science primary teachers need to know to realise the potential of their pupils. Since the introduction of the National Curriculum, there has been a substantial degree of inservice teacher education (INSET) in science for primary teachers, but little research into the nature, level and content of the science presented to teachers, and the impact of

this on their expectations of what they, and their pupils, can achieve in science. In a small scale study in 1992, Dennis Fox used reflective diaries to enable course participants on a 20-day science course to reflect on their experiences of the course and to share these reflections between course members. These shared reflections then formed the basis for developing involvement and progression through the science course. Phase 1 of the current project has widened the earlier project to include a further 6 groups, each of around 20 teachers. The central technique for obtaining information on how teachers are engaging with these programmes of training is a system of personal reflective diaries. The diaries, which are produced individually and remain anonymous within the group, become part of a group record for course members. The first wave of data is now being analysed according to the nature and frequency of style of response from participating teachers and course leaders. Phase 2 (1994/95) will follow some of these teachers back into school, and will use reflective diaries to establish the impact of their training on their science practice in the year following the INSET.
Published Material: TRESMAN, S. (1993). 'A new primary science project', Education in Science, No 152, p.27.; TRESMAN, S., FOX, D. & HODGKINSON, L. (1993). 'How much science do teachers need?', Primary Science Review, No 27, pp.26-27.; TRESMAN, S. & EDWARDS, D. (1993). 'Reflections on practice: some illustrations'. In: WHITELEGG, E. et al. Challenges and opportunities for science education. London: Chapman.
Status: Sponsored project
Source of Grant: Open University; Nottingham Trent University
Date of Research: 1993-continuing
KEYWORDS: inservice teacher education; primary school teachers; science education; teacher attitudes

10/1199
> North West Region, Chorlton House, 70 Manchester Road, Chorlton-cum-Hardy, Manchester M21 1PQ
> 0161 861 9823
> Underley Hall School, Kirkby Lonsdale, Carnforth LA6 2HE
> 01524 271206
> Litt, L. Dr; Pain, J. Dr

Asessment of handwriting and its relationship to spelling and reading in six and a half to seven and a half year old children
Abstract: The research arises from the development of a dictation test for use with top infant (six and a half to seven and a half year old) children. Data (total scores) is available for several thousand children. From these, a sub-sample of some 500 scripts is being analysed in detail so that comparisons may be made between handwriting characteristics and attainments in spelling and reading. Anomalies identified in these comparisons will be investigated on an individual basis to identify causal factors.
Status: Individual research
Date of Research: 1991-1993
KEYWORDS: handwriting; infant school pupils; reading; spelling; writing skills

Oxford Brookes University

10/1200
> School of Education, Wheatley Campus, Wheatley, Oxford OX33 1HX
> 01865 485930
> Howson, J. Mr

Readvertisement rates of senior staff posts in English state primary and secondary schools
Abstract: The survey aims to investigate staff turnover amongst headteachers and deputies in England's state schools. Readvertisement rates are a measure of the difficulty of appointing new headteachers. All posts advertised in the Times Educational Supplement are logged into a computer database which allows analysis on a range of variables including: school type, geographical location, religious affiliation or age range. The research is ongoing but there is evidence that readvertisement rates and turnover rates have fallen since the start of the recession. This coincided with the introduction of a new pay spine for headteachers. An annual report is published each January by the School of Education.
Status: Sponsored project
Source of Grant: Oxford Brookes University

Date of Research: 1984-continuing
KEYWORDS: *deputy head teachers; employment patterns; head teachers; teacher employment; teacher mobility; teacher recruitment; teacher supply and demand; teaching profession*

10/1201

School of Education, Wheatley Campus, Wheatley, Oxford OX33 1HX
01865 485930
Wellens, S. Dr; *Supervisor:* Silver, H. Prof.; Gaunt, D. Ms
Education/industry partnerships in England and Wales, and in the United States: a comparative analysis
Abstract: This study focuses on education/industry partnerships to analyse why differences in the political and governmental structures of England and Wales, and the United States, and differences in the policy process – rational in Britain and incremental in the United States – led to different systemic responses to similar economic, ideological and sociological pressures of the late 1970s and 1980s. It explains why industry in Britain sought to improve conditions through changing teaching and learning methods, while American business sought to reform the organisational and management structure of schools. Policial structures and methods of policy and decision making are compared to explain the differences in industry's approach to educational change in each country. The partnership focus then leads into a consideration of historical, governmental, political and other aspects, as well as educational policies, practices and contexts which affect the policy and decision making process. An examination is made of the role of the historical perspective in each country with particular attention to the differing concepts of vocationalism. The study concluded with a focus on the changes and trends in partnerships as well as related issues that emerged in both countries from 1990 to 1993 and suggests that the different responses demonstrated by the comparison of education/industry partnerships may be extended to other issues in education and beyond. The process of policy making in Britain and the United States is directly related to the way the governmental, political and other structures operate in each country.
Status: Individual research
Date of Research: 1990-1993
KEYWORDS: *comparative education; educational policy; industry-education relationship; politics-education relationship; United States of America*

10/1202

School of Education, Wheatley Campus, Wheatley, Oxford OX33 1HX
01865 485930
Harkin, J. Dr
Core skills in National Vocational Qualifications
Abstract: The project implemented the proposals of a national working party on core skills (National Curriculum Council (NCC), British Technician and Education Council (BTEC), National Council for Vocational Qualifications (NCVQ) etc). Four teams of tutors/trainers were selected from the following occupational areas, Engineering, Business Administration, Hairdressing, Health Care, to trial the core skills specifications with groups of learners. The outcomes of the project were fed back to the National Council for Vocational Qualifications in order to refine the core skills specifications, and to provide data to help form guidance to Examining Bodies.
Status: Sponsored project
Source of Grant: National Council for Vocational Qualifications £70,000
Date of Research: 1991-1993
KEYWORDS: *basic skills; National Vocational Qualifications; vocational education*

10/1203

School of Education, Wheatley Campus, Wheatley, Oxford OX33 1HX
01865 485930
Jones, C. Mrs; *Supervisor:* Wilson, M. Ms; Silver, H. Prof.; Measor, L. Dr
A longitudinal study of some factors influencing children's attitudes to science between the primary and secondary stages of education
Abstract: The proposed investigation will aim to evaluate children's attitudes to science, and the changes (if any), over a period of 4 years, between the primary and secondary stages of education. It will follow

on from the numerous research findings which have shown concern about science uptake in the later years of schooling and, particularly, the low uptake by girls in physical sciences. The investigation, to discover children's attitudes to science, will use structured mini-essays (at primary level); questionnaires; and interviews of children as they leave their primary school in July 1994, in the secondary school (after 1 term), and annually until age 14. It will take account of in-school and out-of-school factors and allow for an analysis of gender differences. Ideally, the survey will be extended so as to assess outcome (as measured by uptake of science components after age 16) at the end of National Curriculum key stage 4. The project proposes to use 3 primary schools in the area, each of which 'feed' about 60 children per annum into one large, coeducational comprehensive school at age 11. Expected sample size should be of the order of 150 children per annum.
Status: Individual research
Date of Research: 1994-continuing
KEYWORDS: *primary secondary education; pupil attitudes; science experiments; sex differences*

10/1204

School of Education, Wheatley Campus, Wheatley, Oxford OX33 1HX
01865 485930
Harkin, J. Dr
The effect of outcome-based programmes on communication in teaching and learning
Abstract: To investigate the patterns of communication in learning programmes where an outcome-based model is being used. Case studies will be conducted in a number of institutions of further and higher education. A collaborative approach will be used based on active participation by teachers and learners; observation, questionnaires and interviews will be employed. It is hoped to disseminate the results through publication.
Status: Sponsored project
Source of Grant: Oxford Brookes University £70,000
Date of Research: 1994-continuing
KEYWORDS: *communication research; competency-based education; further education; higher education; learning processes; teaching methods*

10/1205

School of Education, Wheatley Campus, Wheatley, Oxford OX33 1HX
01865 485930
Bentley, B. Mrs; Reid, D. Mrs
To examine the strengths and weaknesses of three different cueing strategies used with children who find reading difficult
Abstract: The study involves two schools and nine children in each school. The children are aged 7-10 years and each has been randomly allocated a teaching technique. The two researchers spent three hours per week in school working with the children on an individual basis. Each child had approximately a 15 minute training session which involved the child reading and the researcher employing the relevant technique to support the reading. At each session the child also does some related writing. Regular tape-recordings are made of each child reading and used as evidence of progress and for further analysis.
Status: Sponsored project
Source of Grant: Oxford Brookes University £2,120
Date of Research: 1993-1994
KEYWORDS: *oral reading; reading; reading difficulties; reading teaching*

10/1206

School of Education, Wheatley Campus, Wheatley, Oxford OX33 1HX
01865 485930
Supervisor: Thomas, G. Dr; Loxley, A. Mr
International comparison of special needs administration
Abstract: Comparisons will be made of administrative practice in the most developed integration schemes (for instance, those existing in Scandinavia and Italy and, to a lesser extent, USA), with those which have faced greater problems (for instance, in the UK). The relationship between that administrative practice and its outcome in terms of forms of assessment, waiting periods and ultimate degree of integration will be examined. For example, the discussion concerning strategic local arrangements for fostering integration in Massachusetts as

a means of realising the broader aims of US national legislation enacted in Public Law 94-142, is directly comparable to discussion currently occurring in this country about local arrangements to effect the broader aims of the Education Act 1981 in tandem with the Education Reform Act 1988, Local Management of Schools (LMS) and, Local Management of Special Schools (LMSS). This country's existing arrangements are widely taken to have been unsuccessful. Conclusions will be drawn about the importance or otherwise of administrative structures in effecting the realisation of policy, and the nature of those structures. Methodology will include documentary, bibliographic, and questionnaire. Results of the project will be disseminated to local authorities, via articles in relevant professional and refereed journals. In year 1 the researchers will examine in detail the comparative statistics on integration in Western Europe, North America and Australasia and publish these with commentaries on likely causes of difference. In year 2 examination of administrative procedures will be completed and these related to the year 1 statistics, and the conclusions published.
Status: Sponsored project
Source of Grant: Oxford Brookes University £20,000
Date of Research: 1994-continuing
KEYWORDS: *comparative education; educational administration; educational policy; Italy; mainstreaming; Scandinavia; special educational needs; support services*

10/1207
School of Education, Wheatley Campus, Wheatley, Oxford OX33 1HX
01865 485930
Brimblecombe, N. Ms; Ormston, M. Mr; Shaw, M. Ms
An investigation of the OFSTED inspection arrangements in schools, with particular reference to the effects on teachers
Abstract: A new system of school inspections was implemented by the Office for Standards in Education (OFSTED) in September 1993. A pilot study on the 'trial' inspections following the OFSTED format suggested areas for further study and resulted in the publication of a book on preparing for inspection. The research aims to identify the effects of, and responses to, inspection, in particular by schools, in order to enable the development of strategies for schools to prepare for the inspection process. The project is in several parts, looking at different areas and perspectives of the inspection process; the main focus being on schools. The study will include a national survey into the attitudes and experiences of teachers having an inspector in their classroom, follow-up indepth case studies into inspection in schools from the perspective of participants from a number of different areas, and an analysis and comparison of the inspection reports.
Published Material: ORMSTON, M. & SHAW, M. (1993). Inspection: a preparation guide for schools. Harlow: Longman.; ORMSTON, N. & SHAW, M. (1994). Inspection and the grant maintained school. Occasional Paper. High Wycombe: Grant Maintained Schools Centre.
Status: Sponsored project
Source of Grant: Oxford Brookes University
Date of Research: 1993-continuing
KEYWORDS: *educational change; inspection; teacher attitudes*

10/1208
School of Education, Wheatley Campus, Wheatley, Oxford OX33 1HX
01865 485930
Bines, H. Dr
The changing role of local education authorities in relation to special educational needs
Abstract: The role of local education authorities (LEAs) is rapidly changing as a result of legislation and government policies designed to devolve more responsibilities to schools within a quasi-market approach to education. Such changes will include policy and provision for special educational needs. This research will examine such developments, and their particular impact on perceptions held by LEA personnel, headteachers and practitioners in schools about the future role of LEAs in this new policy and organisational context. It will use interviews and questionnaires to examine such perceptions within one particular LEA in the first instance. Further comparison with another LEA may be developed from this particular case study. Issues to be explored will include: perceptions of the specific role and responsibilities of LEAs and schools; the consequent impact on policy, provision and practice; and the range of strategies and resources required to implement these new approaches.

Published Material: BINES, H. & THOMAS, G. 'From bureaucrats to advocates?: the changing role of LEAs', Support for Learning, Vol 9, No. 2. (in press).
Status: Sponsored project
Source of Grant: Oxford Brookes University
Date of Research: 1993-continuing
KEYWORDS: *educational administration; educational change; educational policy; local education authorities; special educational needs*

10/1209
School of Education, Wheatley Campus, Wheatley, Oxford OX33 1HX
01865 485930
Wilson, M. Ms
A comparative study of women in educational management in Europe
Abstract: This research project will investigate the disparity in the representations of women in educational management. It will draw together research carried out by key experts in Ireland, Greece, Spain, France, the Netherlands, Hungary, Sweden and the UK; present a European overview; and bring together policy recommendations. The project will draw on existing secondary research into patterns of recruitment and promotion. Where such data does not exist on a national scale, quantitative research in case-study institutions may be undertaken. Data will be supplemented by semi-structured interviews with women members of staff in promoted positions. At this stage, 8 interviews per country, totalling 64 interviews, are envisaged.
Status: Sponsored project
Source of Grant: Oxford Brookes University
Date of Research: 1994-continuing
KEYWORDS: *educational administration; Europe; management in education; teacher employment; teaching profession; women; women's employment*

10/1210
School of Education, Wheatley Campus, Wheatley, Oxford OX33 1HX
01865 485930
Reading University, Faculty of Education and Community Studies, Department of Arts and Humanities in Education, Bulmershe Court, Woodlands Avenue, Earley, Reading RG6 1HY
01734 875123
Maidlow, S. Ms; *Supervisor:* Kemp, A. Dr
The experiences and expectations of 'A' level music students related to their sex
Abstract: This work is directly related to the paradox wherein public music making is perceived, correctly, as being largely men's domain, whilst school music making is dominated by females at all levels. After piloting various qualitative approaches in local schools, Q-methodology was chosen for this research. This statistical, yet sensitive procedure, requires participants to sort printed statements into categories, indicating to what extent they agree or disagree with the sentiments expressed on the cards. With it the research has attempted to discover some of the ways in which 'A' level music students think of their past experiences as musicians, their present selves as they tackle 'A' level work, and their potential musical future. The hypothesis was that, by relating the differences in perception between members of the sample to their autobiographical details, clusters would fall more or less along the lines of girls/boys, those educated at state maintained/private schools, and, maybe, other 'A' level subjects. Apart from generating a psychological and biographical profile for the cohort as a whole, results from the students' response have been analysed by using quantitative statistical measures. When compared with the autobiographies of the constituents of each group, the only significant similarities which have been uncovered to date are, in decreasing order of strength, musical instruments played, birth ordinal position and parental occupation. In other words, none of the looked for psychological or sociological similarities are in evidence. The results do, however, speak eloquently for Q-methodology, which has the power to draw attention to unexpected aspects of participants' thinking.
Published Material: MAIDLOW, S. (1993). Music file, Series 6, No 1, September.
Status: Individual research
Date of Research: 1989-1994
KEYWORDS: *A level examinations; learner characteristics; music activities; music education; pupil attitudes; sex differences*

Oxford University

10/1211

Department for Continuing Education, Rewley House,
Wellington Square, Oxford OX1 2JA
01865 270376
Thomas, G. Dr
Scientific literacy
Abstract: The project builds on the national survey of public understanding of science carried out by the researcher and other collaborators in 1988. Its aim is to establish a framework for the public understanding of science which meets the (conflicting) aspirations of the scientific profession, the proponents of participatory democracy, economic utility, and cultural literacy.
Published Material: DURANT, J.R., EVANS, G.A. & THOMAS, G.P. (1989). 'The public understanding of science', Nature, Vol 340, pp.11-14.; DURANT, J., EVANS, G. & THOMAS, G. (1992). 'Public understanding of science in Britain: the role of medicine in the popular representation of science', Public Understanding of Science, Vol 1, pp.161-182.; THOMAS, G. (1993). 'Science in the public mind: a cause for concern?'. Schering Lecture No 15. Berlin: Schering Research Foundation.
Status: Individual research
Date of Research: 1988-continuing
KEYWORDS: attitudes; public opinion; scientific literacy

10/1212

Department of Educational Studies, 15 Norham Gardens,
Oxford OX2 6PY
01865 274024
McIntyre, D. Mr
Effective teaching and learning at National Curriculum key stage 3: teacher and pupil perspectives
Abstract: This research project is designed in two phases. The first phase is aimed at developing an understanding of teachers' thinking when they perceive themselves to be engaged in successful classroom teaching and a similar understanding of pupils' thinking when they perceive themselves to be engaged in successful classroom learning. The research is focused particularly on how teachers teach and how pupils learn so that pupils can understand subject knowledge and so that differences among pupils may be catered for. It uses the National Curriculum key stage 3 to provide a common framework while at the same time seeking to illuminate policy issues raised by National Curriculum arrangements. The second phase of the research will be aimed both at testing the value of the researchers' theoretical accounts of teachers' and pupils' thinking, by questioning their generalisability to other teachers and pupils, and also at testing the validity of theories derived from teachers' and pupils' accounts of their effective teaching and learning. Systematic observation, semi-structured interviewing of teachers and pupils, and yet to be determined procedures for assessing attainments will be used to explore the relationships among pupils' prior knowledge, teachers' preferred goals, teachers' pre-lesson planning and within-lesson thinking, teachers' overt behaviour, pupils' within-lesson perceptions, attention, motivation, attributions, and specific cognitive strategies, pupils' overt behaviour, and pupils' learning outcomes.
Status: Sponsored project
Source of Grant: Economic and Social Research Council £42,000
Date of Research: 1991-1994
KEYWORDS: learning strategies; National Curriculum; teacher effectiveness; teaching methods

10/1213

Department of Educational Studies, 15 Norham Gardens,
Oxford OX2 6PY
01865 274024
Judge, H. Dr
Teacher education in context
Abstract: This research will involve a cross-national study of the relationship of teacher education to higher education in France, the United States and Britain.
Published Material: JUDGE, H.G. (1988). 'Cross national perceptions of teachers', Comparative Education Review, Vol 32, No 2, pp.143-158.; JUDGE, H.G. (1990). 'The education of teachers in England and Wales'. In: GUMBERT, E. (Ed). Fit to teach: teacher education in international perspective. Georgia: Georgia State University.

Status: Sponsored project
Source of Grant: Spencer Foundation – Chicago £300,000
Date of Research: 1988-1993
KEYWORDS: comparative education; France; higher education; teacher education; United States of America

Peter Clyne Associates

10/1214

Education and Training Consultancy, 33 Altenburg Gardens,
London SW11 1JH
0171 228 5946
Clyne, P. Mr
Review of the use by the Preschool Playgroups Association of its grant from the Department for Education
Abstract: The objective of this study is to carry out an independent evaluation of the effectiveness of the work of the regional training and development officers and branch tutor organisers employed by the Preschool Playgroups Association and of the value of the Diploma in Playgroup Practice. The methods used include: (1) structured interviews with the staff concerned; (2) collection of job descriptions and training statistics; (3) visits to a range of training courses in different parts of the country; (4) visits to playgroups led by trained and untrained staff; and (5) reading and noting published curriculum and training materials.
Status: Sponsored project
Source of Grant: Department for Education £16,925
Date of Research: 1993-1993
KEYWORDS: child caregivers; play groups; preschool education; qualifications; training

Plymouth University

10/1215

Enterprise Unit, 92 Cobourg Street, Plymouth PL4 8AA
01752 232376
Davies, J. Mr
Mentors in education and training
Abstract: Mentors were introduced into Plymouth University's in-service Certificate in Education course in 1985 as a means of providing a link between the students' course of study and their place of work. As mentors have come to take an increasingly important role in education and training, so a need for mentor training has been identified. In order to design coherent training programmes, it is essential to have a clear view of the roles of both mentors and protégés. Through the literature, this research aims to clarify and identify established roles, to create a typology, and to suggest training programmes appropriate to the different roles.
Status: Sponsored project
Source of Grant: Plymouth University: Rolle Faculty of Education £750; Plymouth University: Enterprise in Higher Education £750
Date of Research: 1991-1993
KEYWORDS: inservice teacher education; mentors; training

10/1216

Department of Mathematics and Statistics, Centre for
Teaching Mathematics, Drake Circus, Plymouth PL4 8AA
01752 600600
May, W. Ms; *Supervisor:* Berry, J. Prof.; Mosley, P. Mrs
The effects of maturation on pupils' participation and achievement in mathematics
Abstract: The purpose of this research is to investigate if there are gender differences related to maturation and the participation and achievement of pupils in mathematics, particularly of associated absences and any related, psychological or physical factors.
Status: Individual research
Date of Research: 1992-continuing
KEYWORDS: individual development; mathematics achievement; mathematics education; pupil participation; sex difference

10/1217

Department of Psychology, Drake Circus, Plymouth PL4 8AA
01752 600600
Newstead, S. Prof.; Franklyn-Stokes, A. Dr

Academic dishonesty in students

Abstract: The purpose of the present project is to investigate the nature, frequency and causes of various forms of cheating behaviour. A general purpose questionnaire has been developed which has so far been given to staff and students at one 'new' and one 'old' university. The results indicate that staff underestimate the frequency of cheating compared to students, and this is especially marked with coursework. Staff also rated most types of cheating behaviour as more serious than did students, but there were exceptions to this, notably cheating in group projects. Among the students, there were also interesting differences between mature students and others, with mature students responding more like staff. Follow-up research will investigate self-reported frequency of cheating, the motives and causes of cheating, and cheating in other educational contexts.

Published Material: NEWSTEAD, S.E. & FRANKLYN-STOKES, A. (1993). 'Staff and student perceptions of the frequency and gravity of cheating behaviours'. Paper to be presented at the Annual Conference of the British Psychological Society, Blackpool, April.

Status: Individual research

Date of Research: 1992-continuing

KEYWORDS: *cheating; discipline problems; higher education; plagiarism; student behaviour*

10/1218

Faculty of Arts and Education, Rolle School of Education, Douglas Avenue, Exmouth EX8 2AT
01395 255309
Mackenzie, R. Mr; *Supervisor:* Hannan, A. Dr; Taylor, G. Dr

Educating teachers to be intellectuals: a study of an attempt to enable preservice primary teachers to develop as critically reflective practitioners

Abstract: The concept of the reflective practitioner has been explored and extended in a critical direction, and the investigation has been both conceptual and empirical. The case for teachers to act as transformative intellectuals rather than State technicians has been argued within the context of a post-modern period of cultural and legislative change in society and in relation to primary school practices developed beyond the ideological polarisations of the past period. The empirical part of the investigation is based on an attempt to incorporate the concept of teachers as intellectuals in a B Ed Educational Studies course component entitled 'Teachers and Children of the Future'. The course aims to support emerging teachers in developing a personal philosophy of education within collegial frameworks so that contemporary challenges should not swamp them personally or professionally. Action research and an ethnographic stance has been used to investigate the aims, content, pedagogy and outcomes of the course which 80 B Ed students have now completed. A smaller group of ex-students, now Newly Qualified Teachers (NQTs), are assisting a follow through into the first year of teaching: the aspiration is to compare and contrast the conceptual and empirical positions of the course with the experienced realities of being an NQT in the 1990s. The research stance has also been developed to incorporate a polyphonic post-modern account alongside autoethnography.

Status: Sponsored project

Source of Grant: Plymouth University £4,657.50

Date of Research: 1990-continuing

KEYWORDS: *intellectuals; preservice teacher education; probationary teachers; professional development; teacher role; teaching profession*

10/1219

Faculty of Arts and Education, Rolle School of Education, Douglas Avenue, Exmouth EX8 2AT
01395 255309
Graham, J. Mr

An investigation into the feasibility of presenting mathematics in the same form to pupils within National Curriculum key stages 2, 3 and 4

Abstract: Circular No. 17/91 (DES, 1991) states that "Teachers are required to teach with a view to pupils achieving levels of attainment within the ranges specified for that key stage." The aim of the research is to ascertain how realistic it is to present pupils in different key stages with common 'teaching materials' aimed at giving them opportunities to achieve common levels of attainment. It is envisaged that four different teaching 'units' will be employed and four different 'clusters' of schools will be sought comprising the following types: (a) primary – pupils aged 10/11, and middle – pupils aged 11 (key stage 2); (b) lower secondary – pupils aged 14 (key stage 3); (c) upper secondary – pupils aged 16 (key stage 4). In total, 16 groups/classes will be approached. The research will include a quantitative analysis of the effectiveness of the teaching materials used, using a two-way analysis of variance linked to a Latin square design.

Status: Sponsored project

Source of Grant: Plymouth University £2,546.50

Date of Research: 1993-continuing

KEYWORDS: *assessment; educational materials; mathematics achievement; mathematics education; National Curriculum*

10/1220

Faculty of Arts and Education, Rolle School of Education, Douglas Avenue, Exmouth EX8 2AT
01395 255309
Fisher, R. Mrs; *Supervisor:* Taylor, G. Dr; Clibbens, J. Dr; Hannan, A. Dr

A study of the role and practice of the teacher of reading at National Curriculum key stage 1

Abstract: The study aims to examine the decisions made by teachers of early reading as demonstrated by their responses to children. A pilot study examined the role of the teacher in four Reception/Year One classes and considered the relationship between what the teacher did to teach reading and what the children learned. This led to a further study of infant teachers in the classroom. Teachers were studied in their interactions with children in relation to literacy. They were then interviewed about their thinking at the time of interaction. This aimed to develop an understanding of the cognitive processes involved in the spontaneous decisions related to the teaching of reading made by teachers in the classroom.

Published Material: FISHER, R. (1992). Early Literacy and the Teacher. London: Hodder and Stoughton.; FISHER, R. (1993). 'Starting to read', Reading, Vol 27, No 1, Spring (in press).

Status: Individual research

Date of Research: 1991-continuing

KEYWORDS: *beginning reading; infant school education; reading teaching; teacher-pupil relationship; teaching methods*

10/1221

Faculty of Arts and Education, Rolle School of Education, Douglas Avenue, Exmouth EX8 2AT
01395 255309
Clark, V. Ms; *Supervisor:* Halstead, J. Dr; Hannan, A. Dr

Spiritual and moral development following childhood bereavement: an exploration

Abstract: The general principles established in the first section of the Education Reform Act 1988 (ERA) ensure that the education received "promotes the spiritual, moral (and) cultural...development of pupils at school and of society". Such developments, however, may be affected by personal rather than educational circumstances – such as the loss by death of a significant person in the child's life. Despite steady increase in research into the effects of bereavement in the adult population, less has been written about bereaved children's reactions and, in particular, of the links that may exist with spiritual and/or moral development. The aim of this research is: (a) to review the literature concerning spiritual, moral (and religious) development and bereavement reactions and to identify common themes, particularly regarding children; (b) to analyse the responses obtained through interviews and questionnaires from children, adolescents and adults concerning their thinking and behaviour following childhood/adolescent bereavement; and (c) to indicate what the implications of these findings are for the implementation of ERA. Respondents, who will be contacted through schools, colleges, bereavement counselling groups and national networks, will provide information through taped interviews and questionnaires, thus providing both breadth and depth of response. It is anticipated that some correlation between childhood bereavement and spiritual and/or moral thinking/development will appear, despite variations in its frequency and intensity and in individual awareness of it. Adults are likely to provide a longer term perspective of their development in this respect; children and adolescents, information as to how their educational life is/was affected by bereavement.

Status: Individual research

Date of Research: 1993-continuing

KEYWORDS: *adolescent development; bereavement; child development; death; moral development; religious attitudes*

10/1222

Faculty of Arts and Education, Rolle School of Education, Douglas Avenue, Exmouth EX8 2AT
01395 255309
Merryfield, A. Mr; *Supervisor:* Hannan, A. Dr; Lever, M. Mr

Expanding horizons: multicultural and international education in the South West of England

Abstract: The research examines one aspect of the relationship between a system of state education and the society which supports and funds it. The United Kingdom is a multicultural and multiracial society, one of many such societies in a diverse and changing world, but the National Curriculum introduced recently makes few specific references to this broader picture. Much will be left to the initiative of individual schools and teachers. The research looks at the effects of greater centralisation on the one hand, and the need for state schools to provide an education appropriate for all pupils on the other. It focuses on examples of good practice in multicultural and international education in what is mainly a 'white' area (the South West of England) and asks – is a more centralised curriculum necessarily a more relevant one, as the legislators claim?
Status: Sponsored project
Source of Grant: Plymouth University £19,000
Date of Research: 1992-continuing
KEYWORDS: *centralisation; educational practices; international education; multicultural education; National Curriculum*

10/1223

Faculty of Arts and Education, Rolle School of Education, Douglas Avenue, Exmouth EX8 2AT
01395 255309
Silver, H. Prof.

Good schools, effective schools: judgements and their history

Abstract: A study of the development of research interests in effective schools and school differences in the 1970s-1980s, in the United States and Britain, in a historical context. The investigation covers perceptions of what has constituted a good school, who has had the power to define what is good, and the criteria that have been used for different kinds of schooling. It considers the difference between 19th and earlier 20th century judgements about the quality of schooling and the research-based interest in effective schools after the decline in confidence in the outcomes of schooling in the late 1960s and early 1970s. It looks at the implementation of effective schools criteria in individual American states and in Congressional legislation in 1988. The study also examines alternatives to school reform based on the effective schools research – in the US essential and accelerated schools and forms of restructuring, and in the UK government-sponsored approaches to curricula and assessment. The study is mainly document-based, except for visits to Connecticut, Rhode Island and Washington DC to visit administrators and schools.
Published Material: SILVER, H. (1991). 'Poverty and effective schools', Journal of Education Policy, Vol 6, No 3, pp.271-285.; SILVER, H. (1991). Educational research and the policy environment: the case of 'effective schools', liber amoricum for H. Remak, Indiana University.; SILVER, H. (1994). Good schools, effective schools: judgments and their history. London: Cassell.
Status: Individual research
Date of Research: 1989-1993
KEYWORDS: *comparative education; educational history; educational quality; school effectiveness; United States of America*

10/1224

Faculty of Arts and Education, Rolle School of Education, Douglas Avenue, Exmouth EX8 2AT
01395 255309
Hayes, D. Mr; *Supervisor:* Hannan, A. Dr; Holt, D. Dr; Howarth, S. Mr

Decision-making and school policy: a case study of a primary school at a time of rapid change

Abstract: The case-study focuses upon the decision-making process within a primary school in the South West of England. It aims to provide a perspective on the involvement of staff and governors in the light of the rapidly changing circumstances created through government education legislation. Data have been gained during 1991 and 1992 through non-participant observation at staff meetings and governors' meetings, through formal and informal discussions with staff, and through familiarity with school management structures and procedures. Data analysis indicates that the rapidity of change has placed a considerable strain upon the headteacher and staff,
jeopardising the carefully designed management system established within the school, and creating insufficient opportunity for reflection upon, implementation, and subsequent amendment of decisions taken. The extent of teacher participation has varied according to the priority given to an issue by the staff and their beliefs about the genuineness of the consultation process. The need to act swiftly has sometimes obliged the headteacher to pre-empt full staff consultation by presenting, in consultation with governors and senior staff, a limited range of options or a single alternative, thereby limiting her preference for collaborative decision-making and collegial relations among staff.
Published Material: HAYES, D. (1993). 'Learning to live with the National Curriculum: a case-study of a headteacher's dilemmas', The Curriculum Journal, Vol 4, No 2, pp.201-213.; HAYES, D. (1994). 'A primary headteacher in search of a collaborative climate'. In: SOUTHWORTH, G. (Ed). Readings in primary school development. Basingstoke: Falmer Press.; HAYES, P. 'The primary head's tale', Educational Management and Administration. (in press).
Status: Sponsored project
Source of Grant: Plymouth University
Date of Research: 1991-1994
KEYWORDS: *change strategies; educational change; primary schools; school-based management; school organisation; staff-school relationship*

10/1225

Faculty of Arts and Education, Rolle School of Education, Douglas Avenue, Exmouth EX8 2AT
01395 255309
Mason, P. Mr; *Supervisor:* Hannan, A. Dr; Essex, S. Dr

The Learn to Travel School's Project

Abstract: This research has three aims: (1) To examine the claims made for introducing travel and tourism into the primary school curriculum. The research explores arguments about the importance of knowledge of travel and tourism in primary schools; and the use of travel and tourism as a vehicle for developing values and attitudes and acquiring skills. (2) To undertake action research in curriculum development in these areas by the design and implementation of a 'Learn to Travel School's Project'. This is an attempt to test, in practice, the ideas of the first aim. The researcher, with a group of teachers in Devon, will design, produce, implement and evaluate curriculum resources for the 'Learn to Travel School's Project'. (3) To evaluate the impact of this contribution to primary school children's education, in relation to the first aim. This will involve the use of questionnaire surveys with children; and interviews with children and teachers.
Published Material: MASON, P. (1992). Learn to travel: activities in travel and tourism for primary schools. Godalming: Worldwide Fund for Nature UK.
Status: Individual research
Date of Research: 1990-1994
KEYWORDS: *curriculum development; primary education; tourism; travel*

10/1226

Faculty of Arts and Education, Rolle School of Education, Douglas Avenue, Exmouth EX8 2AT
01395 255309
Dyer, A. Mr

Re-storying the landscape

Abstract: An environmental education project aimed at using all of the arts in the interpretation and discovery of the natural world. Children are encouraged to rediscover some of the stories about particular or nearby landscapes, or invent new ones. The experimental phase of the project took place at Killerton Park near Exeter in Devon, with a group of children taking part in a 'Dragon Quest'. A day visit programme has been developed and trialled for two years with over 100 schools. Workshops, conference and consultation presentations have been given throughout Britain and Europe. The results will be published in a handbook for teachers, leaders and parents.
Status: Sponsored project
Source of Grant: National Trust; Plymouth University, jointly £1,039
Date of Research: 1990-continuing
KEYWORDS: *environmental education; field studies; geographic location; local studies; story telling*

10/1227
Faculty of Arts and Education, Rolle School of Education,
Douglas Avenue, Exmouth EX8 2AT
01395 255309
Howarth, S. Mr; Jelly, S. Mrs
Curriculum management in the primary school: the curriculum coordinator and OFSTED inspection
Abstract: Comparatively little is known about the impact of recent legislation on curriculum management in the primary school at middle management level, particularly of the new Office for Standards in Education (OFSTED) procedures. With particular reference to science, the project aims to: 1) investigate, compare and contrast perceptions of the role of the curriculum coordinator held by coordinators themselves, and their headteachers; 2) identify implications for effective curriculum management in the primary school. The project will draw from semi-structured interviews with identified science coordinators, from large primary schools in the South West of England, their headteachers, and the framework for the inspection of schools. It is anticipated that results and conclusions will provide insights into the new inspection process and its relationship to school development.
Status: Sponsored project
Source of Grant: Plymouth University £1,525
Date of Research: 1993-1994
KEYWORDS: *curriculum development; educational administration; inspection; primary school curriculum; primary schools; school organisation*

10/1228
Faculty of Arts and Education, Rolle School of Education,
Douglas Avenue, Exmouth EX8 2AT
01395 255309
Lee, C. Mr; *Supervisor:* Hannan, A. Dr; Nias, J. Prof.
Teacher perceptions of bullying and its management
Abstract: The research of bullying has usually involved questionnaires set by the researcher. However, this piece of work will seek to use a variety of scenarios, followed by structured interviews, to gain access to teachers' views on the extent and management of the behaviour in their schools. The primary school, which has received less attention than the secondary sector, will be the principal focus of the work. Research will centre on: the behaviours that teachers consider to be bullying; the extent to which they see it as a problem in their schools; and the impact of the teacher's gender, age, experience and status within the school to determine any variations in the definition. There is a need to determine whether teachers build stereotypes of bullies and victims, and to examine their reactions to incidents reported to them. Management issues to be addressed include: perceived location and timing of bullying; efficacy of policies adopted; the amount of consideration that the school has given to the subject; and the degree to which this is seen as reflecting the extent of the problem. Teachers' attitudes towards their role and responsibility in the management of the matter will be considered. Teachers' views on a number of specific initiatives in the management of bullying, such as 'the no-blame approach', 'bully courts' and 'shared concern method', and their potential value to the primary school will be sought.
Status: Individual research
Date of Research: 1994-continuing
KEYWORDS: *antisocial behaviour; behaviour problems; bullying; discipline policy; discipline problems; teacher attitudes*

10/1229
Faculty of Arts and Education, Rolle School of Education,
Douglas Avenue, Exmouth EX8 2AT
01395 255309
Gill, J. Mrs; *Supervisor:* Halstead, J. Dr; Hannan, A. Dr
The nature and justifiability of the Act of Collective Worship in schools
Abstract: The act of collective worship continues to be a compulsory element in the daily organisation of all maintained schools, and this legal requirement, together with the current debate on the spiritual, moral and cultural development of children and young people, constitutes the contextual background within which this research is sited. Its aims are to: 1) examine the purpose, provision and implementation of the act of worship; 2) identify, explore and analyse its explicit and implicit features, together with the responses and perceptions of its participants; and 3) examine the issues raised, with particular reference to the development of spiritual, moral and cultural values, and the justification of its compulsory place in the curriculum of contemporary, secular and pluralist society. Data collection involves the use of observation, interview, questionnaire and case study; this includes material from both primary and secondary schools in rural and inner-city areas, and from the public and private sectors. The study will examine the overt content and context of the act of worship and the underlying values and attitudes which are transmitted, and seeks to identify the intentional and unintentional features of the hidden curriculum which are also present. Questions concerning the nature and purpose of the act of worship in a society which is both pluralist and secular, and which requires schools to provide pupils with a framework of religious and moral values, will be addressed.
Status: Individual research
Date of Research: 1993-continuing
KEYWORDS: *moral development; religion and education; religious attitudes; school worship; values education*

10/1230
Faculty of Arts and Education, Rolle School of Education,
Douglas Avenue, Exmouth EX8 2AT
01395 255309
Silver, H. Prof.
The role of external examiners in institutions accredited or credit-rated by the Open University
Abstract: The Open University accredits degree and other courses in some 25 institutions and credit-rates courses in a similar number of other institutions and organisations. The project was commissioned in order to consider the present and future roles of external examiners in the context of accreditation. The project involves: 1) visits to and interviews at half the institutions concerned; 2) interviews with a sample of the external examiners; and 3) scrutiny of examiners' reports and documentary evidence of institutional responses to external examiners' comments. The outcome will be a report to the Open University and to its associated institutions, and for wider circulation. Its findings will also contribute to the project on external examiners for the Higher Education Quality Council.
Status: Sponsored project
Source of Grant: Open University £34,000
Date of Research: 1993-1994
KEYWORDS: *accreditation – courses; accrediting authorities; assessment; educational quality; external examiners; higher education; open universities*

10/1231
Faculty of Arts and Education, Rolle School of Education,
Douglas Avenue, Exmouth EX8 2AT
01395 255309
Silver, H. Prof.
External examiners: possible futures
Abstract: Following a study for the Council for National Academic Awards in 1992-93 of the external examiner arrangements in higher education institutions, this project has been commissioned to consider possible future directions for the system and the contribution of external examining to quality assurance in higher education. A series of 'models' will be elaborated, the views of all higher education institutions canvassed (through those responsible for quality machineries), and the models and responses discussed with a sample of 10-12 institutions and professional and accrediting organisations. Interviews will be held with groups of external examiners. An analysis, with possible alternative proposals, will be produced as a report to be published by the Higher Education Quality Council in early 1995.
Status: Sponsored project
Source of Grant: Higher Education Quality Council £55,000
Date of Research: 1994-1994
KEYWORDS: *assessment; educational quality; external examiners; higher education; quality control*

10/1232
Faculty of Arts and Education, Rolle School of Education,
Douglas Avenue, Exmouth EX8 2AT
01395 255309
Revell, R. Mr; *Supervisor:* Nias, J. Prof.; Hannan, A. Dr
The day to day work of primary school headteachers: an ethnographic study
Abstract: The aim of the study is to provide insights into the day to day work of headteachers. The study examines the existing literature on headship and points to a need for detailed information and insights into primary headship. Ethnographic methods are used in the re-

search, including use of a one year journal of headship by the researcher, and semi-open interviews with headteachers. A total of 25 headteachers, from 4 local authorities, were interviewed. The respondents were an opportunity sample of headteachers. The study examines day to day headship in terms of: 1) respondents' experiences and impressions; 2) respondents' work each day; and 3) characteristics of respondents' work. The research finds a marked differentiation in headteachers' work, between the tasks of running the school and headteachers' personal work in shaping the school. There are contradictions and dilemmas for headteachers because of the differentiation in their work. These dilemmas are experienced in headteachers' thinking and decision-making, as well as in their feelings and emotions. The researcher suggests there are reasons for this differentiation to be found in the occupational culture of teaching.
Published Material: REVELL, R. (1993). 'Do we not bleed?: the affective nature of primary headship'. Paper presented at the British Educational Research Association Conference, Liverpool University, 1993.
Status: Individual research
Date of Research: 1988-1994
KEYWORDS: *head teachers; primary schools; teacher-administrator relationship; teacher role; teacher workload; teaching profession*

10/1233
    Faculty of Arts and Education, Rolle School of Education,
    Douglas Avenue, Exmouth EX8 2AT
    01395 255309
    Gerry, S. Ms; *Supervisor:* Dibbo, J. Mr; Halstead, J. Dr;
    Hannan, A. Dr
Health focused physical education: meeting the needs of the whole child
Abstract: Health focuses in physical education have tended to concentrate largely on the physical mechanisms of the body. This research is intended to challenge the established perspectives and will consider claims that if teaching in health focused physical education (HFPE) was holistic in conception and delivery, well-being would be promoted (Whitehead 1987). Despite a growing body of research pursuing a variety of themes to do with approaches to HFPE, there is as yet no research which focuses on the concept of monism. The project includes: 1) A survey of existing practice through case study analysis, having particular reference to the concept of personhood underlying the practice; 2) A discussion of the current perspectives of teaching HFPE in the primary sector which have a stress on the physiological dimension; 3) A detailed examination of the concept of monism in relation to the notions of: a) needs; b) the whole child and concept of personhood; c) health; d) well-being, both individually and via social context; and e) holistic education. The research will draw from the results of the above investigations in order to generate a new approach to HFPE, which may involve an element of action research to evaluate their impact on teaching and learning.
Status: Individual research
Date of Research: 1993-continuing
KEYWORDS: *health; health activities; holistic approach; physical education; well being*

10/1234
    Faculty of Arts and Education, Rolle School of Education,
    Douglas Avenue, Exmouth EX8 2AT
    01395 255309
    Hannan, A. Dr
The initial training of primary school teachers
Abstract: The work has involved two major surveys: the first early in 1992 gathered student and headteacher reaction to Kenneth Clarke's proposals for the reform of initial teacher training (ITT); and the second, in the summer of 1993 collected responses from headteachers, parents, students and tutors, to the proposals for primary ITT which (with the exception of the "mums' army" idea) became the new criteria for the accreditation of training arrangements in 1994. Both surveys took place in Devon, the first involving 358 students and 146 headteachers; and the second, 264 headteachers, 267 parents, 242 students and 50 tutors. Preliminary analysis of the quantitative data is complete and qualitative analysis of the open-ended 'further comments' is now underway.
Published Material: HANNAN, A. & NEWBY, M. (1993). 'Student teacher and headteacher views on current provision and proposals for the future of initial teacher education for primary schools', Collected Original Resources in Education, Vol 17, No 1, Fiche 1.; HANNAN, A. (1993). 'The initial training of primary school teachers: response

to the DFE (an interim report). Plymouth: Plymouth University, Faculty of Arts and Education.; HANNAN, A. (1994). 'Headteachers', parents', students' and tutors' responses to the reform of primary initial teacher education'. In: REID, I., CONSTABLE, H. & GRIFFITHS, R. (Eds). Teacher education reform: current research. London: Paul Chapman Publishing.; HANNAN, A. (1995). 'The case for school-led primary teacher training', Journal of Education for Teaching', Vol 21, No 1.
Status: Sponsored project
Source of Grant: Plymouth University
Date of Research: 1992-continuing
KEYWORDS: *educational change; parent attitudes; preservice teacher education; primary school teachers; student teacher attitudes; teacher attitudes; teaching profession*

10/1235
    Faculty of Arts and Education, Rolle School of Education,
    Douglas Avenue, Exmouth EX8 2AT
    01395 255309
    Jones, H. Mr; Holt, D. Dr; Clement, R. Prof.
Supporting primary teachers in teaching National Curriculum Art and Design
Abstract: The project is based upon the need to identify the readiness of primary schools to teach the National Curriculum in Art, to identify teachers' perceptions about the new legislation and the pattern of inservice support needed by schools to deliver their new responsibilities in the teaching of art in key stages 1 and 2. The project has undertaken a survey 'The Readiness of Primary Schools to Teach the National Curriculum in Art', based upon a questionnaire survey of 1,200 teachers in 500 primary schools in 22 different local education authorities (LEAs). The research findings have been published by the University of Plymouth and circulated to all higher education institutions and LEAs in England and Wales. The research findings have been published in 'The Journal for Art and Design Education' and disseminated through two national conferences. Copies of the research report are available from the Centre for the Study of the Arts in Primary Education at Plymouth. The project has used its research findings to identify primary school teachers' perceived priorities as to their needs for inservice training in the teaching of art and design. In response to these identified priorities, staff at the Centre for the Study of the Arts in Primary Education, working with four primary schools in Devon, have made three inservice training videos to support teachers' understanding of the way that children progress in making art in their primary schools. Further curriculum support materials are being developed in response to the research findings and the focus for further research is to be centred upon the development of continuity and progression in art teaching from primary schools to secondary schools.
Status: Sponsored project
Source of Grant: Calouste Gulbenkian Foundation £10,000; Hamlyn Foundation £10,000
Date of Research: 1992-1994
KEYWORDS: *art education; design education; inservice teacher education; National Curriculum; primary education; primary school teachers*

10/1236
    Faculty of Arts and Education, Rolle School of Education,
    Douglas Avenue, Exmouth EX8 2AT
    01395 255309
    University College of Swansea, Department of Education,
    Hendrefoilan, Swansea SA2 7NB
    01792 201231
    Whiting, C. Ms; *Supervisor:* Hannan, A. Dr; Halstead, J. Dr;
    Furlong, J. Prof.
School-based teacher training: a comparative case study of an Articled Teacher course and a one-year Post Graduate Certificate in Education (PGCE) course
Abstract: The aim of the study is to consider recent moves to develop school-based teacher training and in particular to carry out a comparative case study of the Articled Teacher course and a more traditional one-year Post Graduate Certificate of Education (PGCE) course based at the Faculty of Arts and Education, University of Plymouth, concentrating on the 1991 intake. The study will be an evaluation based on the 'illuminative' approach using participant observation, questionnaires and interviews. There are 12 Articled Teachers and 75 students on the one-year course, of which 12 will be studied in detail.

Status: Individual research
Date of Research: 1991-1994
KEYWORDS: *articled teachers; postgraduate certificate in education; preservice teacher education; student teachers; teacher education*

10/1237
>Faculty of Arts and Education, Rolle School of Education, Douglas Avenue, Exmouth EX8 2AT
>01395 255309
>University of the West of England, Frenchay Campus, Coldharbour Lane, Frenchay, Bristol BS16 1QY
>01179 656261
>Payne, G. Mrs; *Supervisor:* Hannan, A. Dr; Silver, H. Prof.; Menter, I. Mr

Competence-based teacher training for the primary years: a comparative approach
Abstract: The aim of the investigation is, generally, to contribute to our understanding of the management of change in initial teacher education. The specific aims are to: (1) analyse proposals over the past 10 years to change primary teacher training with particular reference to moves to introduce a competence-based approach; (2) undertake a national survey of how such change has been managed; (3) investigate indepth the experiences of a number of institutions selected to illustrate the range of responses; and (4) undertake a comparative study of two institutions in the process of adaptation. This research will focus on the management of change in initial teacher training (ITT) for the primary years, in particular on proposals for introducing competence-based training. Development of the research will be through a number of stages: (1) an analysis of the wide range of proposals over the past 10 years to change primary teacher training; (2) a national questionnaire survey of ITT providers (postal questionnaire to the 94 institutions offering ITT courses); (3) follow-up interviews with a selection of institutions; and (4) a comparative case study of the experience of change in two institutions.
Status: Individual research
Date of Research: 1992-continuing
KEYWORDS: *competency-based teacher education; preservice teacher education*

Portsmouth University

10/1238
>Academic Development Centre, University House, Winston Churchill Avenue, Portsmouth PO1 2UP
>01705 876543
>Brew, A. Dr

Curriculum assessment and Enterprise in Higher Education (EHE): a university-wide project
Abstract: The aims of this project are to investigate models of curriculum assessment appropriate to the aims and objectives of Enterprise in Higher Education (EHE) at the University of Portsmouth; to develop and evaluate a range of examples of good practice in different faculties and departments; and to disseminate information about them and guidelines for future developments throughout the University and elsewhere. One of the objectives of EHE at Portsmouth is 'to broaden the range of assessment procedures so as to ensure that performance in a wide range of skills and competencies contributes to the final award'. This raises the question of what forms of assessment are appropriate. The EHE aims of promoting a 'higher level of innovative, learner-directed education, in which students can 'learn to learn' in a flexible and adaptable way for the rest of their lives', and 'encouraging more open and flexible forms of learning which shall support the University's commitment to recruiting a wider range of student', point to changes in teaching methods which are supported by the current move in the University towards unitisation and semesterisation. New methods of teaching and learning demand that new forms of assessment are devised. There is, therefore, a need in the institution for knowledge and expertise in new modes of assessment. Detailed investigation as to what aspects of the students' learning experiences are to be assessed and how this is to be done is required. There are, already, examples of excellent work being done elsewhere in the assessment of transferable skills and the assessment of work placements, and it is not proposed to concentrate on these aspects at this stage. The project contributes to the less well researched area of curriculum assessment and will thus make a significant contribution to the knowledge and expertise in this University and also nationally and internationally. The expected outcomes of the project are: (1) An enhanced understanding of, and expertise in developing, new procedures for the assessment of students among participants. (2) Significant changes in assessment practices in line with EHE principles in at least three departments. (3) A manual providing guidance for future developments in curriculum assessment in the University. (4) A series of dissemination seminars, presentations and workshops given by participants to colleagues in their own departments and in other areas of the University. (5) Papers/articles in national and international journals.
Published Material: ROSBOTTOM, J. (1992). 'UNCLE enables peer assessment', Network: The newsletter of the Academic Development Centre, University of Portsmouth, December.
Status: Sponsored project
Source of Grant: Training, Enterprise and Education Directorate: Enterprise in Higher; Education Initiative £12,000
Date of Research: 1992-1994
KEYWORDS: *assessment; enterprise education; higher education; learning strategies; skill development; work-education relationship*

10/1239
>School of Educational Studies, Furze Lane, Milton, Portsmouth PO4 8LW
>01705 844500
>Southampton University, Faculty of Educational Studies, Centre for Language in Education, Highfield, Southampton SO9 5NH
>01703 595000
>Edwards, F. Mr; *Supervisor:* Brumfit, C. Prof.

Curriculum change and its effects on school departmental culture with particular reference to secondary school English
Abstract: The aims of this project are (1) An enquiry into the rationale for curriculum change in relation to the teaching of secondary school English as a consequence of the implementation of a National Curriculum for England and Wales. (2) An investigation of the effects such changes might have on the culture of secondary school English departments with particular reference to: programmes of study at National Curriculum key stages 3 and 4; teaching and learning styles; and methods of assessment. The introductory phase will offer a contextual overview of the recent imperatives which have driven and informed curriculum change in England and Wales since the 1944 Education Act. This will locate alongside a review of the development of English as a discrete discipline within the secondary school curriculum. The review will consider the numerous trends and tensions within the discipline which have characterised its operations during the recent past. A longitudinal case study will be undertaken of the work of an English department in a large co-educational comprehensive school in order to establish what, if any, are the effects of curriculum change upon the culture and operation of the department. This will involve consistent and regular contact with the department, both in classroom and organisational contexts and will involve the researcher in the role of participant observer. A variety of data gathering methods will be employed including document searches, field notes, classroom observations, questionnaires and interviews. Contact with the department will commence in September 1991 and will continue until the first National Curriculum assessment of English at National Curriculum key stage 4 in June, 1994.
Status: Individual research
Date of Research: 1991-continuing
KEYWORDS: *curriculum development; educational change; English studies curriculum; National Curriculum; secondary education*

10/1240
>Social Services Research and Information Unit, Kings Rooms, Bellevue Terrace, Portsmouth PO5 3AT
>01705 811504
>Portsmouth University, School of Educational Studies, Furze Lane, Milton, Portsmouth PO4 8LW
>01705 844500
>Lupton, C. Dr; Lawrence, B. Dr; Faupel, A. Mr; Hayden, C. Ms

Children excluded from primary schools in England and Wales
Abstract: The background to this research includes the legislative and other changes which have created increased pressure on schools and families, since the early 1980s. In particular the creation of an education 'market place' is likely to be increasingly problematic, in relation to meeting the needs of the less 'marketable' child. However, there is little reliable information about the real extent to which there

are pupils, particularly in the younger age groups, who are out of school for significant periods (weeks or months). Furthermore there has been no attempt to record the experience of exclusion from the point(s) of view of those most centrally involved. In conducting this sensitive study we aim to provide evidence of the difficulties schools and families are facing. The research also aims to inform the development of suitable support structures and alternative provisions for schools and families coping with troubled and/or troublesome children. The research will comprise the following three main stages: (1) a national profile: the compilation and analysis of existing data on school exclusions. Postal questionnaire to all local education authorities (LEAs) in England and Wales; (2) case study (local education authorities): four LEAs chosen to represent a range of policies and practices in relation to exclusion and special needs provision, as well as a range of geo-political and socio-economic profiles (England and Wales); and (3) case studies of excluded children: in each LEA, ten children, their parents and previous teacher(s) will be interviewed to ascertain their experiences of the process of exclusion.
Status: Sponsored project
Source of Grant: Economic and Social Research Council £95,320
Date of Research: 1993-continuing
KEYWORDS: *discipline policy; disruptive pupils; educational change; expulsion; primary schools; problem children; special educational needs; suspension*

Reading University

10/1241
Department of Agricultural Extension and Rural Development, 3 Earley Gate, Whiteknights Road, Reading RG6 2AH
01734 875123
Jones, G. Mr; White, J. Dr
Adapting to change: Further Education's response to a changing rural economy and the implications for staff development
Abstract: The background to the study is a confluence of a number of changes currently taking place which are affecting the provision and uptake of education and training for agriculture and related industries in the United Kingdom. On the one hand there is a decline in agriculture and a diversification of the rural economy, on the other there are changes in education policies and a decline in the proportion of 16-18 year olds in the population. Against this background of change this study set out to investigate staff development needs in agricultural colleges in England and Wales. It focuses on the role of agricultural colleges in a future rural economy and the type and amount of continuing professional development that should be undertaken by their staff. The findings are available for the consideration of any group or individual whose interests or responsibilities concern staff development in agricultural or further education colleges. It is offered as a review of the current scene in staff development, as a critique of current practices and methods and as a platform for putting forward suggestions to improve the situation. A report has been submitted to the Further Education Unit for the Department for Education.
Status: Sponsored project
Source of Grant: Further Education Unit for the Department of Education and Science; (PICKUP) £26,000
Date of Research: 1989-1992
KEYWORDS: *agricultural colleges; agricultural education; economic change; educational change; further education; staff development*

10/1242
Department of Linguistic Science, Whiteknights, Reading RG6 2AH
01734 875123
Kerswill, P. Dr; Williams, A. Dr
A new dialect in a new city: children's and adults' speech in Milton Keynes
Abstract: The research aims to examine the processes behind the formation of a new dialect in a city where the majority of the population originates from different parts of the country and to enquire how children develop 'sociolinguistic competence' – awareness of different accents and dialects in their community, and of their use. A range of sociolinguistic methods are used in the study of 48

children aged 4, 8 and 12.
Published Material: KERSWILL, P. & WILLIAMS, A. (1992). 'Some principles of dialect contact: evidence from the New Town of Milton Keynes'. In: WARBURTON, I. & INGHAM, R. (Eds). Working Papers 1992. Reading University, Department of Linguistic Science.
Status: Sponsored project
Source of Grant: Economic and Social Research Council £51,550
Date of Research: 1990-1993
KEYWORDS: *dialect studies; language variation; sociolinguistics*

10/1243
Department of Psychology, Whiteknights, Reading RG6 2AH
01734 875123
Henry, L. Dr; Norman, T. Miss
The development of visual memory strategies in children
Abstract: The aim of this research was to chart the development of verbal memory strategies in children. Previous research suggested that children progress from visual to verbal strategies of memory coding with age. However, this claim has not been adequately tested. The first stage of the present research has been to test this claim with a wide age range (5, 7, 9, and 11 year olds). Children recalled sequences of pictures which were either visually similar (they looked the same) or phonemically similar (they sounded the same). Recall for these types of pictures was contrasted with recall for control pictures which were neither visually nor phonemically similar. The results showed that all age groups were poorer at remembering phonemically similar pictures, suggesting that they all used verbal memory strategies. There was very little evidence for the use of visual memory strategies in any group. Further work with 4 year olds found that they did not appear to use any distinct strategy for remembering pictures. These findings conflicted with previous research which showed that five year olds used visual coding, and ongoing research is testing the competing claim of various hypotheses concerning the development of picture memory in children.
Status: Sponsored project
Source of Grant: Reading University Endowment £21,000
Date of Research: 1990-continuing
KEYWORDS: *child development; memorisation; phonemics; pictorial stimuli; verbal development; visual learning*

10/1244
Faculty of Education and Community Studies, Department of Arts and Humanities in Education, Bulmershe Court, Woodlands Avenue, Earley, Reading RG6 1HY
01734 875123
Pegg, L. Mrs; *Supervisor:* Kemp, A. Dr
National programme of training for primary school music consultants
Abstract: The purpose of the project is to provide a programme of inservice training for primary school music teachers who wish to develop consultancy skills. This training is offered on a national basis, organised in various locations throughout the country, and consists of four-week phased courses of the kind held at the University of Reading Music Education Centre since 1982. These courses offer teachers an updated view of recent developments in the primary music curriculum and training in the processes of consultancy work amongst colleagues. They also offer conferences for primary headteachers within their structure. A second important facet of the project will be the development of regional groups of music consultants to encourage on-going professional interchange and aftercare.
Published Material: SMITH, J. (1987). Music consultancy in Berkshire primary schools. Reading: Royal County of Berkshire Music Department.; KEMP, A.E. (1988). 'Towards national adoption of music consultancy in primary schools'. In: BARTON, M. & STEWART, A. (Eds). British Music Education Year Book 1988/89. London: Rhinehold.; KEMP, A.E. & WOOTTON-FREEMAN, S. (1988). 'New tasks for music in primary schools and teacher training', International Journal of Music Education, No 11, pp.21-24.; PEGG, L.J. (1992). 'If music is for all pupils then it must be for all teachers', Early Education, No 7, pp.8.; KEMP, A.E. (1993). 'School within communities; are music opportunities being missed?'. In: KEMP, A.E. & PEGG, L.J. Consultancy Matters. Reading: Reading University.
Status: Sponsored project
Source of Grant: Music Industries Association £75,000; Calouste Gulbenkian Foundation £15,000
Date of Research: 1988-1993
KEYWORDS: *consultants; inservice teacher education; music education; music teachers; primary school teachers*

10/1245
> Faculty of Education and Community Studies, Department of
> Arts and Humanities in Education, Bulmershe Court,
> Woodlands Avenue, Earley, Reading RG6 1HY
> 01734 875123
> Drever, M. Mrs; *Supervisor:* Richards, B. Dr

Teaching English in a multilingual classroom
Abstract: The research has two aims: (1) to carry out a survey of
strategies used by class teachers in the teaching of the English
language in a multilingual context, i.e. in a class composed of pupils
from more than one linguistic home background, including English
mother tongue, and (2) to suggest strategies which might benefit all
pupils in attaining a competent level of English performance in order
to cope with more sophisticated and subject specific language,
semantically and structurally, as they move up the curriculum. The
research will use classroom observation, interviews and questionnaires.
Status: Individual research
Date of Research: 1990-1993
*KEYWORDS: English; minority groups; multilingualism; teaching
methods*

10/1246
> Faculty of Education and Community Studies, Department of
> Arts and Humanities in Education, Bulmershe Court,
> Woodlands Avenue, Earley, Reading RG6 1HY
> 01734 875123
> Theale Green School, Bath Road, Reading RG7 5DA
> 01734 302741
> Kempe, A. Mr; Holroyd, R. Mr

Imaging
Abstract: The end product of the research will be four books for use
in top primary/lower secondary classrooms. Three pupil books will
contain a range of resources on three separate topics. Literature,
visual material, realia and research or creative tasks will be bound
together by a linking narrative for each of the three topics. An
accompanying teacher's book will outline how each individual resource may be used as part of an enactive learning programme and
suggest various strategies by which the resources may be combined
into dramatic structures. Within the whole project, there will be
opportunities to meet the stated attainment targets of English in the
National Curriculum document and some reference will also be made
to the history, science, and craft, design and technology (CDT)
documents. Most of the material is being trialled at a comprehensive
school in Reading. Other elements are being used on inservice teacher
education (INSET) courses and a programme of primary school
sessions. The final publications will hopefully provide the basis for
a more extensive and refined publishing programme aimed at meeting
the needs of the National Curriculum without destroying current good
practice.
Published Material: KEMPE, A. & HOLROYD, R. (1986). 'Team
teaching: cheap relief for a taxing problem', 2D Vol 6, No 1, pp.60-
71.; KEMPE, A. (1992). 'Enthusiastic beginners'. Drama, Vol 1, No
1, pp.13-16.
Status: Individual research
Date of Research: 1988-1993
*KEYWORDS: drama education; educational materials; English
studies curriculum; National Curriculum*

10/1247
> Faculty of Education and Community Studies, Department of
> Arts and Humanities in Education, Bulmershe Court,
> Woodlands Avenue, Earley, Reading RG6 1HY
> 01734 875123
> Fletcher-Campbell, F. Dr; *Supervisor:* Straughan, R. Dr

The caring school
Abstract: Most schools claim to be caring institutions but it is not
clear as to how this claim should be interpreted. The research analyses
accounts in the literature and as given by a small sample of secondary
headteachers. A philosophical analysis of the concept of the caring
school is then undertaken before practical recommendations for
schools' policy and practice are made.
Status: Individual research
Date of Research: 1988-1993
*KEYWORDS: educational environment; educational philosophy;
pastoral care – education; pupil-school relationship; pupil welfare*

10/1248
> Faculty of Education and Community Studies, Department of
> Arts and Humanities in Education, Bulmershe Court,
> Woodlands Avenue, Earley, Reading RG6 1HY
> 01734 875123
> Hall, J. Mr; *Supervisor:* Adelman, C. Prof.

**The development, implementation and evaluation of a model
of practice in art and design teacher education**
Abstract: This is a longitudinal study of a sample of beginning
teachers of art and design, following them through a one year postgraduate course of initial teacher education and into their first teaching appointments. The research will investigate the effectiveness of
the Post Graduate Certificate in Education (PGCE) Art and Design
Course at Reading University, and the processes through which
beginning teachers learn to teach and go on to develop and improve
their practice.
Published Material: HALL, J. (1991). 'The roles of practising
teachers and university lecturers in the initial training of teachers
of art and design', Journal of Art and Design Education, Vol 10,
No 3, pp.317-327.
Status: Individual research
Date of Research: 1991-continuing
*KEYWORDS: art; design; Postgraduate Certificate in Education;
preservice teacher education; probationary teachers; programme
effectiveness; student teachers*

10/1249
> Faculty of Education and Community Studies, Department of
> Arts and Humanities in Education, Bulmershe Court,
> Woodlands Avenue, Earley, Reading RG6 1HY
> 01734 875123
> Lee, F-J Mr; *Supervisor:* Straughan, R. Dr

**Emotivism, prescriptivism and moral education: some
significant implications for the development of moral
education in Taiwan**
Abstract: For Chinese, the core of traditional education has long been
how to cultivate the sound mind of pupils through some special
ceremonious disciplines. The exclusive and dominant criteria has
been Confucianism for about 2500 years since its establishment by
Confucius (551-479 BC). This traditional model of education is
mainly related to behaviour training and doctrines of specific virtue-
items. It therefore has less concern for developing pupils' moral
autonomy or enlightening their ability for making moral decisions or
judgments themselves. In view of the rapid changes in social structure
and the diverse concepts of values today, however, moral education
which is simply grounded on authority or heteronomy is doomed to
be insufficient and even controversial. On the other hand, the meta-
ethical theories, developed from the western world, by analysing
moral language and concepts and investigating the logical frameworks of moral argument and reasoning, aim to clarify those supporting claims beneath the traditional ethics. It is then considered that this
approach, which is different from Confucian approach, might contribute some significant implications for the development of moral
education in Taiwan. Since C.L. Stevenson's Emotivism and R.M.
Hare's Prescriptivism both play leading parts within this approach,
one of the main concerns of this study is to review and expound,
analyse and evaluate their ethical theories, and develop some important significance for moral education. The other major concern is to
utilise this significance and accordingly suggest some useful implications for the development of moral education. The objectives to be
achieved in this research could be summarised as follows: 1) to
investigate Emotivism and elaborate its related implications for moral
education; 2) to explore Prescriptivism and specify its implications
for moral education; 3) to discuss Confucianism and its influences on
the enterprise of moral education in Taiwan; and 4) to propose
recommendable ways to improve the theory and pratice of moral
education according to the research results.
Status: Individual research
Date of Research: 1991-1994
KEYWORDS: educational philosophy; moral education; Taiwan

10/1250
> Faculty of Education and Community Studies, Department of
> Arts and Humanities in Education, Bulmershe Court,
> Woodlands Avenue, Earley, Reading RG6 1HY
> 01734 875123
> Gathumbi, A. Mrs; *Supervisor:* Richards, B. Dr;
> Goodwyn, A. Mr

Verbal discourse events in a bilingual formal setting: instructional procedures in ESL classrooms in Kenyan secondary schools

Abstract: Kenyan English language teachers undergo pre-service and in-service training in the country's teacher training institutions, but there has not been any follow-up to find out what exactly goes on in the classrooms and the methods teachers use; therefore the effectiveness of the teacher training programmes is not known. Important as it is, classroom interaction research has been overlooked in Kenya. This is ironical bearing in mind that in recent years, claims have been made that standards of English are falling. It is important therefore that much more should be known about English language teaching in Kenya since it is the official language and the medium of instruction. The aims of this research are to: (1) reveal the practised teaching styles and the cognitive level of questions used by a sample of English language teachers in Kenya through the study of teacher-pupil interaction; (2) compare the teaching styles of in-service and non in-service English language teachers; and (3) make recommendations for teacher-training programmes, curriculum development, inspectorate and educational planning sectors. The target population for this study will comprise 17 English language teachers from public and private schools and their 500 Form 3 students. The sample will be selected from a rural and an urban district. There will be a pilot study before the main study. This will enable the researcher to become familiar with data collection procedures and to make adjustments where necessary. The methods to be used are: unstructured observation notes, video and audio recording of teacher-pupil discourse, a teachers' questionnaire, and a semi-structured pupils' interview.
Status: Sponsored project
Source of Grant: International Development Research Centre £31,200
Date of Research: 1991-1994
KEYWORDS: *English studies; English studies teachers; Kenya; teaching styles*

10/1251

Faculty of Education and Community Studies, Department of Arts and Humanities in Education, Bulmershe Court, Woodlands Avenue, Earley, Reading RG6 1HY
01734 875123
Wells, C. Mr; *Supervisor:* Kemp, A. Dr; Hopper, G. Mrs
The effects of information technology on the sequencing and development of concept acquisition, particularly in open ended, creative situations
Abstract: A preliminary study has been completed over a period of one year in a primary school with very good access to computer facilities. Work in creative areas, particularly in creative writing and in art, was monitored throughout the year – both with and without the use of the computer. Children from ages 5 to 11 were involved, though more detailed observations were made of a group of thirty, 9 to 10 year olds. This data, once analysed, will enable the focusing of particular sequencing and developmental trends in the main research.
Status: Individual research
Date of Research: 1990-1994
KEYWORDS: *computer uses in education; concept formation; creative development; learning processes*

10/1252

Faculty of Education and Community Studies, Department of Arts and Humanities in Education, Bulmershe Court, Woodlands Avenue, Earley, Reading RG6 1HY
01734 875123
Richards, B. Dr; Chambers, F. Dr; Richards, M. Mrs
Oral assessment in modern languages
Abstract: The project is a study of oral testing in French. The aim is to compare the reliability and validity of different assessment criteria currently used by GCSE examining groups and to investigate whether characteristics of teacher-examiners influence their ratings of candidates' performance. The main focus is on the assessment of 'free conversation'. The project involves: (1) a literature review; (2) a review of the syllabuses, administrative practices and marking schemes of the GCSE examining groups; (3) a survey of current practices in selected schools; (4) development of three sets of criteria for assessing free conversation which reflects different approaches used by examining groups; (5) obtaining tape recordings of 75 children who were examined in the 1990 GCSE examination. This sample represents the full range of oral marks awarded at GCSE; (6) selection of a sub-sample of 30 children from the above to represent the middle ability range; (7) preparation of two versions (two differ-

ent random orders) of a set of pre-recorded tapes of the 30 children completing a free conversation task; (8) piloting the three sets of assessment criteria and accompanying instructions and mark sheets; (9) assessment by four groups of six teachers representing native and non-native speakers in comprehensive and selective schools, of the 30 conversations on two separate occasions, one month apart; (10) assessment by 22 PGCE Modern Languages students of the 30 conversations; and (11) validation of the GCSE speaking task by using 15-year old children attending two schools in France.
Published Material: CHAMBERS, F. & RICHARDS, B.J. (1992). 'Criteria for oral assessment', Language Learning Journal, No 6, pp.5-9.; CHAMBERS, F. & RICHARDS, B.J. (1992). A deux (video-tape and accompanying notes). Reading: University of Reading, Department of Arts and Humanities in Education.; CHAMBERS, F. & RICHARDS, B.J. (1993). 'Oral assessment: the views of language teachers', Language Learning Journal, No 7, pp.22-26.; CHAMBERS, F. & RICHARDS, B.J. (1993). Native and non-native responses in oral interviews: implications for foreign language teachers and the assessment of oral performance. Departmental Working Paper. Reading: University of Reading, Department of Arts and Humanities in Education.; RICHARDS, B.J. & CHAMBERS, F. (1993). Oral assessment in modern languages: summary of findings. Working Paper No 1. Reading: University of Reading, Department of Arts and Humanities in Education.
Status: Sponsored project
Source of Grant: Reading University Research Endowment Fund £30,000
Date of Research: 1990-1993
KEYWORDS: *assessment; French; General Certificate of Secondary Education; modern language studies; oral tests*

10/1253

Faculty of Education and Community Studies, Department of Arts and Humanities in Education, Bulmershe Court, Earley, Reading RG6 1HY
01734 875123
Kempe, A. Mr
The uses of playscripts in the secondary school curriculum
Abstract: The research will involve collating the responses to a questionnaire sent to a sample of English and Drama departments in secondary schools around the country. The questionnaire will ascertain the range and type of playscripts held in stock and the appeal of newly advertised titles. Furthermore, the research will try to gauge recent shifts in trends regarding the use of playscripts as either a stimulus for creative drama work or as a means of delivering the National Curriculum Orders for English at key stage 3. It is envisaged that articles reporting the research will be submitted to national English and Drama publications.
Status: Individual research
Date of Research: 1993-1994
KEYWORDS: *drama education; English studies curriculum; National Curriculum; scripts; secondary education*

10/1254

Faculty of Education and Community Studies, Department of Arts and Humanities in Education, Bulmershe Court, Woodlands Avenue, Earley, Reading RG6 1HY
01734 875123
Parsons, M. Mr; *Supervisor:* Boorman, J. Dr; Green, E. Dr
'Will the true history ever reach the classrooms'. The myths of the Home Front UK in World War II
Abstract: This research comes about because the researcher's interest in the way the myths of the Second World War, especially with regard to the British Home Front, were being perpetuated in classroom lessons and school text books. The research uses primary and local sources to go beneath the surface and investigate what was actually taking place and not what the propaganda of the time, and some publishers of today, would like us to believe. The researcher has made extensive use of the Public Record Office and other County records; and also travelled to the west coast of the USA to see how they teach this period of history and what perceptions high school children have of the UK home front. A questionnaire about this period was sent to a number of schools in Berkshire. Future investigation will involve looking at evacuees who were sent to the colonies, and the local effects on small, isolated communities.
Status: Individual research
Date of Research: 1991-continuing
KEYWORDS: *history studies; war*

10/1255

Faculty of Education and Community Studies, Department of Education and Management Studies, Bulmershe Court, Woodlands Avenue, Earley, Reading RG6 1HY
01734 875123
Dawkins, J. Mr; *Supervisor:* Fidler, B. Dr

Local management of secondary schools in Berkshire – an evaluation

Abstract: The aim of this research is to monitor and evaluate the implementation of Local Management of Schools (LMS) in secondary schools in Berkshire to assess over the initial period if the quality of education in those schools has been enhanced by the provision of LMS. The researcher will aim to: (i) keep abreast of, and include current research in terms of a developing national perspective of the implementation of LMS; (ii) to detail within Berkshire the changes planned within the Local Education Authority as direct result of delegated budgets in secondary schools; (iii) evaluate (by means of a detailed case study of 3 secondary schools) the LMS pilot scheme; (iv) evaluate 3 further (non-pilot) schools as case studies; and (v) conclude whether the quality of education has been enhanced by the provision of LMS. Research will be carried out through questionnaires and follow up interviews of LEA officers and governors, teachers and administrators from at least six secondary schools.

Status: Sponsored project
Source of Grant: Berkshire Local Education Authority £450
Date of Research: 1989-1993
KEYWORDS: educational change; evaluation; local management of schools; school-based management; secondary schools

10/1256

Faculty of Education and Community Studies, Department of Education and Management Studies, Bulmershe Court, Woodlands Avenue, Earley, Reading RG6 1HY
01734 875123
Simpson, T. Mr; *Supervisor:* Fidler, B. Dr

Stress in primary headteachers following implementation of Local Management of Schools

Abstract: The aim of the investigation is to study the pressures on primary headteachers arising from their schools joining the Local Management of Schools scheme. A pressure which has been observed is lack of time to complete tasks and so a follow-up study is investigating whether the use of time management techniques reduces the pressures. Primary headteachers in one local education authority have completed questionnaires on stressors, mental health and coping skills, following finance being delegated to their school under Local Management of Schools. A follow-up study of a selected number to investigate time management techniques has also been carried out.

Status: Sponsored project
Source of Grant: Berkshire County Council grant and self funding
Date of Research: 1989-1994
KEYWORDS: change; head teachers; local management of schools; primary schools; role conflict; stress variables; time management

10/1257

Faculty of Education and Community Studies, Department of Education and Management Studies, Bulmershe Court, Woodlands Avenue, Earley, Reading RG6 1HY
01734 875123
De Montfort University, 37 Lansdown Road, Bedford
MK40 2BZ
01234 351966
Keiner, J. Ms; Grugeon, E. Mrs

Evaluation of the National Oracy Project

Abstract: The National Oracy Project was established to promote good practice in oral work across the curriculum and to develop appropriate modes of assessment for pupils aged 3 to 18 years. This evaluation of the National Oracy Project aims to explore the extent to which the Project's work fulfils its stated aims. A case study approach has been adopted, drawing on a selection of seven local authority consortia of teacher-based groups involved in the Project, in conjunction with studies of the National Project Team; its relationship with National Curriculum Council and other national educational policy bodies; and publications and other data emerging from the project. Methods used include analysis of published material and other documents; field visits and interviews; and participant observation. Results and conclusions will be published in a final report.

Status: Sponsored project

Source of Grant: National Curriculum Council £22,000
Date of Research: 1990-1993
KEYWORDS: oracy; oral language; programme evaluation; speech communication

10/1258

Faculty of Education and Community Studies, Department of Education and Management Studies, Bulmershe Court, Woodlands Avenue, Earley, Reading RG6 1HY
01734 875123
Singh, A. Dr; Spear, M. Dr

A local authority based demonstration trial of 'good practice' in road safety education

Abstract: The primary aim of the project is to develop, implement and evaluate policies of 'good practice' in road safety education for children aged 5-16. The initial phase of the project is being spent developing guidelines for the management and co-ordination of road safety education both at local authority and at school level in collaboration with educational advisers, teachers, road safety officers, health education officers and the police; and in conducting a pilot trial in one local authority. During the second phase of the research, the revised policy document will be implemented through inservice training in all the primary and secondary schools (about 130 schools) within the selected areas of the two trial authorities. The third phase of the research will be concerned with monitoring the implemented programmes closely in 20 primary and 10 secondary schools in order to assess the impact on educational outcomes over a given period of time, for example in pupils' knowledge, skills, attitudes, behaviour and future intentions regarding road safety. The research design will be quasi-experimental. The input, process and evaluation data will be obtained through visits, interviews, questionnaires, telephone calls, observation of lessons and unobtrusive observation of actual behaviour on the roads. The cost effectiveness of programmes including measures of changes in casualty rate will also be assessed. The final phase of the research will comprise feedback to the participants, dissemination of the findings and the production of a report designed to assist local authorities and schools in implementing such policy(ies) effectively and economically.

Status: Sponsored project
Source of Grant: Department of Transport: Transport and Road Research Laboratory £407,303
Date of Research: 1988-1993
KEYWORDS: safety education; traffic safety

10/1259

Faculty of Education and Community Studies, Department of Education and Management Studies, Bulmershe Court, Woodlands Avenue, Earley, Reading RG6 1HY
01734 875123
Newcastle upon Tyne University, Department of Psychology, Ridley Buildings, Newcastle upon Tyne
NE1 7RU
0191 222 6000
Stainthorp, R. Dr; *Supervisor:* Snowling, M. Prof.

A longitudinal study of the development of reading strategies in 7-11 year old children

Abstract: This research is a longitudinal study of a group of sixteen children from a mainstream primary school. The children's reading strategies were studied by means of a series of experiments during their time in National Curriculum key stage 2 (age 7-11 years). The experimental programme included a series of repeated measures tasks investigating word and non-word reading accuracy; the effects of context on word and non-word reading; lexical and phonological decision tasks using ordinary non-words and pseudo-homophones. Finally, the children were interviewed about their reading habits and asked to fill in a UK version of an Author Recognition Test. The results indicated that good readers were able to use a decoding strategy when reading from age 7, but that poor readers had difficulty in so doing. This lack of a decoding strategy appeared to hinder progress, particularly in the development of an extensive sight vocabulary.

Status: Individual research
Date of Research: 1988-1993
KEYWORDS: reading processes; reading skills; reading tests

10/1260

Faculty of Education and Community Studies, Department of Education and Management Studies, Bulmershe Court, Woodlands Avenue, Earley, Reading RG6 1HY
01734 875123
Copeland, I. Mr; *Supervisor:* Brehony, K. Dr; Ayles, R. Mrs

Change of entry criteria to special schools and/or units in the mid 1890s

Abstract: Entry to the first special schools and/or units was by educational criteria or by the judgement of headteachers and/or inspectors. This prevailed in the six or so special units established between 1890-1895. Then very quickly the criteria for entry became mental and through the judgement of schools' medical officers. At least two key players were doctors who were interested in and published material concerning the nature of the mind and its measurement. The research project asks if this transition was due to charismatic individuals or was part of a status struggle between the teaching and medical professions.

Status: Individual research
Date of Research: 1989-1994
KEYWORDS: educational history; special educational needs; special schools

10/1261

Faculty of Education and Community Studies, Department of Education and Management Studies, Bulmershe Court, Woodlands Avenue, Earley, Reading RG6 1HY
01734 875123
Cowan, B. Dr; *Supervisor:* Watson, K. Prof.

Transcending the myopic state – towards a new model of school marketing

Abstract: This thesis emanates from the belief that the marketing process in any organisation has significant potential for whole organisational development. It can create and sustain effective change mechanisms between parties, internal and external to the organisation, and above all synthesise the disparate, and often conflicting organisational targets and objectives, into achievable goals for both the short and long-term. State schools were propelled into the marketing arena during the 1980s by a number of factors. These ranged from the varied and incessant legislation of a Conservative government determined to make schools more accountable to their publics, to the falling rolls situation and Local Management of Schools, which put a price on each individual child. The underlying contention of this thesis is that schools are missing a valuable opportunity to take stock of their relationships with those having a stake in the education process and, furthermore, are diverting valuable resources to promotional activities without regard for the the impact and cost-effectiveness of such initiatives. Current literature on school marketing provides little guidance and is limited mainly to promoting 'fire-fighting' strategies for improving publicity and public relations. Through a consideration of marketing theory and research carried out in a number of commercial organisations, independent schools and colleges of further education, it is hoped to show the wider implications and potential of marketing for schools. Lessons learned from these contexts and the findings of research carried out into the marketing philosophies of eighty secondary schools, a survey of criteria employed by parents in selecting schools for their children and detailed case studies of the development of marketing thinking in two comprehensive schools serve to produce indicators for effective marketing policy and action. Related issues such as accountability, understanding customers' needs and perceptions, communication and the ethics of increasing competiton between schools, are addressed. Outcomes of this discussion contribute to the conceptualisation of marketing within an educational context and provide a more substantive foundation upon which a marketing model may be constructed. Schools, at present have a short-sighted view of marketing. This study seeks to encourage a transcendance of this myopia and lead readers to a state of greater enlightenment.

Status: Individual research
Date of Research: 1986-1992
KEYWORDS: educational change; institutional advancement; marketing

10/1262

Faculty of Education and Community Studies, Department of Education and Management Studies, Bulmershe Court, Woodlands Avenue, Earley, Reading RG6 1HY
01734 875123

Hull University, Department of Education, Hull HU6 7RX
01482 46311
Cowan, B. Dr; Wright, N. Mr

An investigation into the morale of teachers in secondary schools

Abstract: Previous research examined levels of morale and dissatisfaction among secondary school teachers. A further survey will provide a greater insight into the feelings expressed by respondents. The samples will be located in the north and south of England. The research was initiated by the frequent complaints of teachers and media coverage that teachers were suffering increased stress levels. The writers sought to determine whether this was the case and what factors contributed to such negative feelings. A detailed study of all the staff in one school has also been made.

Status: Individual research
Date of Research: 1992-1994
KEYWORDS: stress – psychological; teacher morale; teaching profession

10/1263

Faculty of Education and Community Studies, Department of Education and Management Studies, Bulmershe Court, Woodlands Avenue, Earley, Reading RG6 1HY
01734 875123
Fox-Lee, L. Mrs; *Supervisor:* Brehony, K. Dr

The Montessori movement and English elementary education 1909-1939

Abstract: The aim of the investigation is the evaluation of the reception of the Montessori system both at the level of the State educational apparatus and in elementary schools, with a view to the construction of a theoretical explanation for its trajectory. The methods used are documentary analysis and interviewing.

Status: Individual research
Date of Research: 1993-continuing
KEYWORDS: educational history; educational theories; elementary schools; Montessori method

10/1264

Faculty of Education and Community Studies, Department of Education and Management Studies, Bulmershe Court, Woodlands Avenue, Earley, Reading RG6 1HY
01734 875123
Stainthorp, R. Dr; Hughes, D. Mrs

Early fluent readers

Abstract: This research aims to study the cognitive processes, reading development, educational experiences and family environments of a group of 15 children identified as being able to read fluently before they begin formal schooling. The work is a partial replication of the work of Margaret Clark, conducted in the light of modern knowledge of children's reading development. The children, who are identified as fluent readers, will be monitored on a number of cognitive and reading tasks throughout their time in National Curriculum key stage 1. A further group of children matched for cognitive and linguistic development and socio-economic experience, but who are unable to read prior to school, will act as a control sample. Parental involvement in the project will include the keeping of event diaries.

Status: Sponsored project
Source of Grant: Reading University £45,000
Date of Research: 1993-continuing
KEYWORDS: child development; early reading; reading ability; young children

10/1265

Faculty of Education and Community Studies, Department of Education and Management Studies, Bulmershe Court, Woodlands Avenue, Earley, Reading RG6 1HY
01734 875123
Sellers, M. Mrs

Research and development of a postgraduate diploma in deaf studies and sign communication for higher education

Abstract: Access to higher education for some deaf students depends largely on the availability of 'communication facilitators' to enable them to participate to the highest level in their chosen course of study. The needs of deaf students vary widely and so a comprehensive range of support strategies is required – from note-taking and lip-speaking to the highly specialised sign interpreting specific to higher education. The demand for suitably qualified professionals has increased

to the point that there is now a national shortage of 'communication facilitators', particularly for those students who use sign language. However, currently there are no courses designed to prepare facilitators specifically for work with deaf students in higher education. In addition, there is evidence from interpreters already working in the field that they experience difficulties in applying British Sign Language (BSL) to much of the subject-specific terminology employed in higher education. The aims of the project are therefore to develop: 1) a course that will educate and train suitable persons (normally graduates) to be skilled in a variety of communication techniques, including sign language, appropriate for supporting students in higher education, within a framework of deaf awareness; 2) theoretical and practical strategies for overcoming the problem of interpreting the highly specialised vocabulary of higher education into British Sign Language.
Status: Sponsored project
Source of Grant: Higher Education Funding Council £32,500
Date of Research: 1993-1994
KEYWORDS: *deaf interpreting; deafness; graduate study; hearing impairments; higher education; interpreters; special educational needs*

10/1266
Faculty of Education and Community Studies, Department of Education and Management Studies, Bulmershe Court, Woodlands Avenue, Earley, Reading RG6 1HY
01734 875123
Sellers, M. Mrs; *Supervisor:* Postlethwaite, K. Dr
Home-based early intervention with hearing impaired children and their families
Abstract: Although there is a body of work on various aspects of the development of young hearing impaired children in relation to, for example, audiology and child language acquisition, there does not appear to be any significant literature on the 'whole' development of the hearing impaired child within the context of the family, particularly in relation to the provision of home-based early intervention. The present study therefore focuses on home-based early intervention. It locks into the broad theoretical area of child development, and is expected to contribute: 1) a comprehensive analysis of perceived needs and of current provision; 2) an understanding of professional and non-professional decision making in this area; 3) identification of 'best practice' and proposals for enhancement of provision; and 4) suggestions for further research.
Status: Individual research
Date of Research: 1992-continuing
KEYWORDS: *early childhood education; early experience; hearing impairments; intervention; parent participation; special educational needs*

10/1267
Faculty of Education and Community Studies, Department of Education and Management Studies, Bulmershe Court, Woodlands Avenue, Earley, Reading RG6 1HY
01734 875123
Taylor, B. Mrs; *Supervisor:* Fidler, B. Dr
The influence of the National Curriculum on continuity between infant and junior schools in one local education authority
Abstract: Questionnaires have been sent to a sample of Year 2 and Year 3 teachers in primary, infant and junior schools. The questionnaires asked about curricular, social and administrative continuity between schools or classes. The continuity of curriculum between separate schools appeared less good than between teachers in the same primary school. A case study of a linked infant and junior school trying to improve continuity is being studied. From this it is hoped that suggestions for improving continuity which have been tested can be assessed by other headteachers for their applicability to their situation. The aim of the investigation is to discover ways of improving continuity between separate infant and junior schools.
Status: Individual research
Date of Research: 1990-continuing
KEYWORDS: *developmental continuity; infant schools; junior schools; primary education; transfer pupils*

10/1268
Faculty of Education and Community Studies, Department of Education and Management Studies, Bulmershe Court, Woodlands Avenue, Earley, Reading RG6 1HY
01734 875123

Bristol University, School of Education, 35 Berkeley Square, Bristol BS8 1JA
01179 303030
McCulloch, M. Ms; *Supervisor:* Hoyle, E. Prof.
The management of change in higher education
Abstract: The research seeks to understand the changing relationship between the internal organisation of higher education institutions and their aims, reflecting on differences which may relate to the balance between teaching and research, between autonomy and accountability, between freedom to manage and bureaucracy. A case study of the merger between a predominantly teaching institution with a research/teaching institution will be used to illustrate the ways in which organisational structures and systems may be seen to facilitate different aims. The response of institutions to change is also examined in terms of the management and implementation of innovation in a turbulent external environment.
Status: Individual research
Date of Research: 1993-continuing
KEYWORDS: *educational administration; higher education; management in education*

10/1269
Faculty of Education and Community Studies, Department of Education and Management Studies, Bulmershe Court, Woodlands Avenue, Earley, Reading RG6 1HY
01734 875123
Rogers, A. Prof.
Women, literacy and income-generation
Abstract: Based on case studies in Kenya, Egypt, Bangladesh and India, this study looks at the relationship between income-generation and the teaching of literacy and the need for appropriate training of the literacy instructors so that more effective literacy instruction with women can be promoted.
Published Material: ROGERS, A. (1993). 'The world crisis in adult education: a case study from literacy', Compare, Vol 23, No 2, pp.159-175.
Status: Individual research
Date of Research: 1992-1994
KEYWORDS: *developing countries; literacy; women's education*

10/1270
Faculty of Education and Community Studies, Department of Education and Management Studies, Bulmershe Court, Woodlands Avenue, Earley, Reading RG6 1HY
01734 875123
Fox-Lee, L. Mrs; *Supervisor:* Brehony, K. Dr
The implementation of High/Scope and the Dalton Plan
Abstract: This is a comparative study of the implementation of two American educational programmes in England – High/Scope and the Dalton Plan. It includes the historical background to their adoption, and their presentation to a wider audience. Questions specifically address the measures of success adopted by each plan and the extent to which acceptance of outcomes was influenced by initial claims. 1) The involvement of parents in each programme, and the measures taken in each case to account for pupils' cultural backgrounds. 2) The relationship of ability and performance within these highly structured and specific programmes, also in relation to the programmes' short-term educational and long-term social goals.
Status: Individual research
Date of Research: 1993-continuing
KEYWORDS: *early childhood education; individualised methods; intervention; parent participation; teaching methods*

10/1271
Faculty of Education and Community Studies, Department of Science and Technology Education, Bulmershe Court, Woodlands Avenue, Earley, Reading RG6 1HY
01734 875123
Harries, D. Mr
The attitudes and confidence of primary school teachers regarding mathematics education
Abstract: Many people have a suspicious and wary attitude to mathematics, viewing it as a highly abstract and difficult subject to master, even though they make effective use of 'everyday' mathematics. Some primary teachers who are not mathematics specialists exhibit these attitudes, and appear to have high anxiety levels regarding their own mathematical abilities. This can lead to a sterile teaching ap-

proach, whereas the National Curriculum requires a variety of approaches in the teaching of mathematics, including practical and investigative work. This study is intended to provide more precise information about attitudes to mathematics amongst primary school teachers, and the nature of any problems that may arise. Such information can be used to inform Inservice Education of Teachers (INSET) planning and development. Initially a questionnaire survey of a local sample of teachers will be carried out. Further indepth work will be undertaken through selected individual interviews.
Status: Sponsored project
Source of Grant: Universities Funding Council £12,200
Date of Research: 1991-continuing
KEYWORDS: *inservice teacher education; mathematics; primary school teachers; teacher attitudes*

10/1272
Faculty of Education and Community Studies, Department of Science and Technology Education, Bulmershe Court, Woodlands Avenue, Earley, Reading RG6 1HY
01734 875123
Fisher, J. Ms; *Supervisor:* Postlethwaite, K. Dr
Early years classroom management: theories, beliefs and practice
Abstract: This research is concerned with the decisions which early years teachers make when selecting systems of classroom management, and what influences those decisions. A representative sample of early years practitioners are being interviewed about their personal theories and beliefs about early childhood education and the ways in which they organise and manage their early years classrooms to reflect their rationale. These interviews are revealing some common constraints which are impinging upon certain elements within generally held ideologies being put into practice. The intention of the second part of the research is to work for one academic year with one of these teachers and through observation, discussion and analysis to address the identified constraints. This second part is designed as an action research study and is intended to shed light on both the effects achieved and difficulties encountered when a university lecturer acts as consultant to an expert teacher. Such insights will be tested in a second cycle of action research with a different teacher.
Status: Individual research
Date of Research: 1992-continuing
KEYWORDS: *classroom management; early childhood education; infant school education; infant school teachers; reception classes*

10/1273
Faculty of Education and Community Studies, Department of Science and Technology Education, Bulmershe Court, Woodlands Avenue, Earley, Reading RG6 1HY
01734 875123
Yuven-Lafen, L. Mr; *Supervisor:* Malvern, D. Mr
Personal responses to physics: contrasting values in a developing country
Abstract: The central focus is the potential clash between traditional values in Cameroon societies and those which underpin physics as taught in schools following a curriculum essentially derived from those of the developed world. The methodology is based on questionnaires and interviews about critical incidents which explore solutions to social dilemmas where traditional values and authorities would suggest differences to the approaches favoured by science, technology and industrially based societies.
Status: Individual research
Date of Research: 1993-continuing
KEYWORDS: *Cameroon; physics education*

10/1274
Faculty of Education and Community Studies, Department of Science and Technology Education, Bulmershe Court, Woodlands Avenue, Earley, Reading RG6 1HY
01734 875123
Nji-Tima, R. Mr; *Supervisor:* Malvern, D. Mr
Criteria for 18+ examination courses in physics in Anglophone and Francophone Cameroon
Abstract: Cameroon has two education systems – the Anglophone and the Francophone derived from its twin colonial heritage. Harmonisation has proved not to be appropriate to the social circumstances and this research is investigating the possible application of subject based criteria as a means of establishing comparability between the curricula and examinations in physics at 18+ for the two

systems. Questionnaires and interviews of key personnel have been used to determine perceptions of significant attributes such as the dimensions of importance placed on topics within both courses and the purposes the courses are to serve.
Status: Individual research
Date of Research: 1990-1994
KEYWORDS: *Cameroon; physics education*

10/1275
Faculty of Education and Community Studies, Department of Science and Technology Education, Bulmershe Court, Woodlands Avenue, Earley, Reading RG6 1HY
01734 875123
Lock, N. Mr; McCulloch, M. Ms
Analysis of the complementary roles of teachers and tutors in the supervision of school-based initial teacher education
Abstract: This project is being developed in the context of Government policy initiatives in primary teacher education which seek to transfer a greater proportion of student time to school. The Faculty of Education and Community Studies at the University of Reading has innovative whole-school approach to mentorship with its development of Mentorship Primary Schools. This study seeks to locate the Faculty's mentorship programme in the emerging literature; examine in detail the interface of the theoretical and practical elements of the course; and help maintain quality control in student teacher learning. Following preparation programmes for tutors, students and whole-primary school staffs, students on school experience in the summer term of 1994 will be supervised in Mentorship Primary Schools by teachers and tutors committed to a new model of initial teacher education. This project aims to identify strengths and weaknesses in this model of mentorship. The research aims to: 1) analyse the role of the teacher, as mentor, in the whole school context; 2) identify and articulate the knowledge and skills required to perform these teacher roles effectively; 3) identify transferable skills between teachers' expertise and students' learning; 4) examine the role of university tutor in relation to teachers and students. The research methodology will include: 1) interviews with samples of University Group and Associate tutors, teachers who have acted as mentors and students who have undertaken their school experience in Mentorship Primary school; and 2) analysis of recorded conversations and discussions between mentors and students, tutors and students; mentors, tutors and students.
Published Material: McCULLOCH, M. & LOCK, N. (1992). 'Student teachers' school experience: the managerial implications for schools', Cambridge Journal of Education, Vol 22, No 1, pp.69-78.; McCULLOCH, M. (1993). 'What is involved in good school-based teacher education', Journal of Teacher Development, Vol 2, No 1, February, pp.39-45.
Status: Sponsored project
Source of Grant: Reading University £49,000
Date of Research: 1993-continuing
KEYWORDS: *mentors; preservice teacher education; school-based teacher education; student teacher supervisors*

10/1276
Faculty of Education and Community Studies, Department of Science and Technology Education, Bulmershe Court, Woodlands Avenue, Earley, Reading RG6 1HY
01734 875123
Orme, J. Mrs; *Supervisor:* Haggarty, L. Dr; Postlethwaite, K. Dr
Aspects of partnership model for teacher education: an enquiry into ways in which mathematics students learn
Abstract: The Reading University Secondary Postgraduate Certificate in Education (PGCE) course has developed a partnership model with local schools over the last three years. The resulting model has been informed by the notion of the 'Reflective Practitioner' and other literature on student teacher learning, in particular publications by Calderhead and by McIntyre. A major aspect of the model therefore is that of the student as an active learner, analysing their practice in terms of theory, research and the local context. A further element in this reflective learning is the student's own perspective of what makes a good mathematics teacher. This perspective is arrived at through a wide variety of experiences many of which are rooted in the student's past. These biographical or historical experiences also give rise to a personal agenda only part of which the student may acknowledge. The purpose of this study is to investigate student learning, and in particular to explore the role personal agendas play in this learning. The methodology is to be that of a naturalistic enquiry: an indepth

study of a small group of PGCE students who are planning to teach mathematics, with particular case studies of a subset of those students. The aim, using this methodology, is to develop a possible model of student teacher learning. The study will use a rich variety of data collection techniques including: analysis of the student's initial position statements, questionnaires, analysis of other written statements including student assignments, taped interviews, observation and the systematic collection of comments made in less structured settings.
Status: Individual research
Date of Research: 1993-continuing
KEYWORDS: learning strategies; mathematics teachers; preservice teacher education; school-based teacher education; student teachers

10/1277

Faculty of Education and Community Studies, Department of Science and Technology Education, Bulmershe Court, Woodlands Avenue, Earley, Reading RG6 1HY
01734 875123
Babila-Njingum, J. Mr; *Supervisor:* Malvern, D. Mr; Haggarty, L. Dr
Change in teaching and curriculum in mathematics for Anglophone Cameroon GCE
Abstract: The two main foci of the research are: 1) a study of the processes of change among Cameroonian mathematics teachers through action research of a group implementing mastery learning in secondary school mathematics; 2) investigation of various perceptions of the current mathematics curriculum for General Certificate of Education in Anglophone Cameroon.
Status: Individual research
Date of Research: 1991-1994
KEYWORDS: Cameroon; mathematics education

10/1278

Faculty of Education and Community Studies, Department of Science and Technology Education, Bulmershe Court, Woodlands Avenue, Earley, Reading RG6 1HY
01734 875123
Malvern, D. Mr; Townend, J. Mr; Fawcett, B. Mr
Reading University/Berkshire Local Education Authority induction project
Abstract: A twin track project combining enhancement of induction provision for newly qualified teachers in Berkshire with research into the characteristics of professional formation in early career. Surveys of headteachers, mentors and newly qualified teachers comparing actual provision with Government guidelines and investigating differing perceptions of need have been carried out. Current work concentrates on matching the Dreyfus model of professional development to competences developed for initial training and extending indicators of competence into the immediate post-qualifying period of professional employment.
Status: Sponsored project
Source of Grant: Department for Education; Berkshire Local Education Authority, jointly £120,000 per annum
Date of Research: 1992-continuing
KEYWORDS: competency-based teacher education; inservice teacher education; local education authorities; school-based teacher education; staff orientation; teacher development

10/1279

Reading and Language Information Centre, Bulmershe Court, Woodlands Avenue, Earley, Reading RG6 1HY
01734 875123
Abbas, S. Mrs
Access to Information on Multi-cultural Education Resources (AIMER)
Abstract: AIMER is a database project which offers students, teachers, advisers and others information on multicultural antiracist teaching materials. In recent years there has been a proliferation of booklets, packs and other resources produced within local education authorities (LEAs) and other organisations. AIMER acts as a clearing house for materials of this kind. In addition to a postal inquiry service, it publishes resource lists on a wide range of topics which are updated on an annual basis. It is possible either to buy individual resource lists or the whole set at a substantial discount in the form of a single volume, 'Photocopiable resources to support the multicultural dimension of the National Curriculum'. A publications list is available on request.

Date of Research: 1987-continuing
KEYWORDS: databases; multicultural education; resource materials

10/1280

Reading and Language Information Centre, Bulmershe Court, Woodlands Avenue, Earley, Reading RG6 1HY
01734 875123
Monaghan, F. Mr; *Supervisor:* Edwards, V. Dr
Language and mathematics: exploring polysemous vocabulary and conceptual understanding in secondary school mathematics at National Curriculum key stage 3
Abstract: The research project is concerned with children's understanding of polysemous vocabulary in mathematics and its role in their conceptual understanding. The project will aim to explore pupils at National Curriculum key stage 3, in an Inner London comprehensive school following an individualised learning scheme, namely Secondary Mathematics Individualised Learning Experience (SMILE). The pupils are mainly bilingual and cover the whole attainment range. A further aim is to develop specific materials that explore the ambiguities of polysemous vocabulary and provide students with a learner understanding of particular concepts (e.g. 'similarity' in describing shapes). The methodology will be largely ethnographic, drawing on analyses of transcripts of pupil interactions.
Status: Individual research
Date of Research: 1992-continuing
KEYWORDS: classroom communication; comprehension; mathematical concepts; mathematical vocabulary; mathematics education

10/1281

Reading and Language Information Centre, Bulmershe Court, Woodlands Avenue, Earley, Reading RG6 1HY
01734 875123
Edwards, V. Dr; Nwenmely, H. Ms
The teaching of Kweyol in the UK
Abstract: An investigation of the teaching of Kweyol in adult education in the UK, the implications for language maintenance and shift. The main aims of the research are: to provide new information on the French creole or Kweyol-speaking community in the UK; and to consider aspects of the teaching of Kweyol in adult education which have implications for language maintenance and shift.
Published Material: NWENMELY, H. & EDWARDS, V. (1992). 'The teaching of Kweyol in the UK: research practices in adult literacy', RaPAL Journal, Autumn.
Status: Sponsored project
Source of Grant: Economic and Social Research Council £70,000
Date of Research: 1991-1994
KEYWORDS: adult education; Creoles; mother tongue

10/1282

Reading and Language Information Centre, Bulmershe Court, Woodlands Avenue, Earley, Reading RG6 1HY
01734 875123
Thompson, A. Mrs; *Supervisor:* Edwards, V. Dr
Exploring bilingual support in the secondary school
Abstract: This classroom ethnographic research explores and looks into the use of a dual language approach to support bilingual second language learners in the mainstream secondary school classroom. Issues discussed include: code-switching; bilingual support pedagogy; professional development of bilingual support; integrating language and learning using two languages. The research aims to: critically examine the provision of bilingual support for second language pupils in the secondary school; to look at actual classroom practice; what factors affect the use of a dual language approach in mainstream secondary classrooms; and to point the way forward.
Published Material: THOMPSON, A. (1991). Exploring bilingual support in the secondary school. Hounslow: Hounslow Education Authority.
Status: Individual research
Date of Research: 1990-1994
KEYWORDS: bilingual education; bilingualism; English – second language; ethnic groups; language of instruction

10/1283

Reading and Language Information Centre, Bulmershe Court, Woodlands Avenue, Earley, Reading RG6 1HY
01734 875123

Callender, C. Ms; *Supervisor:* Edwards, V. Dr
Black teachers and black pupils: an investigation of teachers' style
Abstract: This ethnographic research project is designed to investigate the effects of teacher style on the achievement of black pupils. Eight teachers – six black and two white – in two London junior schools, were observed for a period of six months. The teachers were also video-recorded. Teachers and pupils have been interviewed to elicit their views on various issues arising from the observation and video-recording. The data are being analysed with a view to identifying features of a distinctive black teaching style and the implications of this style for black pupil achievement.
Status: Sponsored project
Source of Grant: Economic and Social Research Council £27,900
Date of Research: 1992-1994
KEYWORDS: *achievement; black pupils; black teachers; teacher behaviour; teacher-pupil relationship; teaching methods; teaching styles*

10/1284

Reading and Language Information Centre, Bulmershe Court, Woodlands Avenue, Earley, Reading RG6 1HY
01734 875123
Reading University, Department of Typography and Graphic Communication, No 2, Earley Gate, Whiteknights, Reading RG6 2AH
Blacksell, R. Ms; Chana, U. Ms; *Supervisor:* Walker, S. Dr; Edwards, V. Dr
Multilingual resources for children
Abstract: Multilingual Resources for Children is a two year research project at the University of Reading, based jointly in two departments: the Department of Arts and Humanities in Education and the Department of Typography and Graphic Communication. The project is concerned with the nature, availability and use of multilingual educational resources in the UK. In particular, the researchers want to review the different types of material available for use with children in primary schools. The research focuses on some of the main languages in the UK which use non-Latin scripts (Bengali, Gujerati, Punjabi, Urdu and Chinese). It will explore teachers' and children's preconceptions of such materials, as well as examining how these are designed and illustrated. The researchers hope to suggest ways of using such resources effectively in the classroom, as well as producing recommendations about ways they can be best designed and produced. Fieldwork for the project has been conducted in four mainstream and five community schools in the London area. These schools have a higher percentage of bilingual pupils, covering each of the project focus languages. The research is very much dependent on a team of project research workers, each a speaker of one of the project languages, and with a variety of experience in areas which include teaching, linguistics, publishing and typographic design.
Status: Sponsored project
Source of Grant: Reading University £40,950
Date of Research: 1992-1994
KEYWORDS: *bilingualism; multicultural education; multilingual materials; multilingualism*

Robert Gordon University

10/1285
School of Librarianship and Information Studies, 352 King Street, Aberdeen AB9 2TQ
01224 262000
Robertson, J. Miss; *Supervisor:* Williams, D. Dr
The application of computer aided learning to the development of information skills in further education
Abstract: The project seeks to examine the way in which further education (FE) students explore and utilise sources of information. The initial test group are National Diploma in Business Studies students at Telford College, Edinburgh and subsequently the students of similar courses in other Scottish FE colleges. A Hypertext system has been developed to guide students through information searches, and to log individual student's use of the system. These logs will be analysed to evaluate learning patterns.
Status: Individual research
Date of Research: 1990-1993

KEYWORDS: *computer-assisted learning; further education students; hypertext; information seeking; information sources*

10/1286
School of Librarianship and Information Studies, 352 King Street, Aberdeen AB9 2TQ
01224 262000
Johnson, I. Mr
Education for librarianship and information studies in Eastern Europe
Abstract: Visits were made to Schools of Librarianship and Information Studies in Bulgaria, the Czech Republic, Hungary, Poland, Romania, and the Slovak Republic in 1992 and 1993. The aim of the visits was to explore the developments necessary to support teaching of Librarianship and Information Studies in Eastern Europe. The specific needs identified may be summarised as follows: (1) Guidance in planning and developing modern curricula, and in conducting related manpower studies. (2) Guidance in teaching (and in making relevant in the local context): the principles and practice of management of libraries and information centres; the role of information in management and decision making; business information sources and services; public information services. (3) Improving the availability of learning resources. (4) An enhanced supply of up-to-date teaching materials in their own languages (including news about developments in libraries and information centres in their own countries). (5) An enhanced supply and continuing supply of foreign professional journals and monographs for staff research and for developing linguistic competences. (6) Upgrading of information technology, often requiring a substantial increase in the provision of hardware and appropriate software to equip students with the related skills, and appreciation of the potential of information technology so that they can play a pro-active role in transforming information work in their country. (7) Raising awareness of the standards of service expected in library services in market oriented circumstances. (8) Raising policy makers' awareness of potential problems such as those outlined above, and of the significance of libraries and information work for the economic, educational and social reconstruction which is taking place.
Published Material: JOHNSON, I.M. (1992). 'Librarianship and professional education in Poland', Focus on International and Comparative Librarianship, Vol 23, No 3, pp.84-88.; JOHNSON, I.M. (1993). 'Librarianship and professional education in Hungary', Focus on International and Comparative Librarianship, Vol 24, No 1, pp.14-17.; JOHNSON, I.M. 'Librarianship and professional education in Czechoslovakia', Focus on International and Comparative Librarianship (forthcoming).
Status: Sponsored project
Source of Grant: European Community: TEMPUS Office £2,500
Date of Research: 1992-1993
KEYWORDS: *developing countries; development education; Europe; information science; librarianship education*

10/1287
School of Librarianship and Information Studies, 352 King Street, Aberdeen AB9 2TQ
01224 262000
National Library of Scotland, Science Library Section, 33 Salisbury Place, Causeway End, Edinburgh EH9 1SL
0131 226 4531
Anderson, P. Mr; *Supervisor:* Johnson, I. Mr; Head, M. Mr; Bunch, A. Ms
Excessive publication in scholarly journals: an analysis of the implications for the scholarly communication process
Abstract: The pressure-to-publish experienced by researchers today can lead to potentially unethical behaviour in the form of excessive or wasteful publication. Researchers, caught up in the 'publish or perish' syndrome, are forced to produce articles in order to appear active, 'visible' and productive. Much of this new published information is of little real value, contributing little, if anything, to the research record. Repetitive publication of essentially the same information in different journals, the piecemeal publication, over time, of research results from a single study, and the combining of findings from separate and often inconsequential projects to form 'publishable' papers, are the three most evident forms of this abuse. The scholarly and academic community faces a growing crisis of confidence in terms of the true value of articles in scholarly journals.
Published Material: ANDERSON, P. (1993). 'Wasteful publication in scholarly journals: an analysis of the implications for the scholarly

communication process' (Research Report), Library and Information Research News, Vol 16, No 56, pp.21-25.
Status: Individual research
Date of Research: 1991-1994
KEYWORDS: *publications; research reports; researchers; writing for publication*

Roehampton Institute

10/1288
 Roehampton Lane, London SW15 5PU
 0181 392 3000
 Pinsent, P. Ms
Anti-racism and children's literature
Abstract: This investigation into racism/anti-racism in children's literature is based on a belief in the influence of literature in the formation of attitudes, and a conviction that children should not be provided with sub-standard writing simply because the attitudes displayed in it are acceptable. Those writers who incorporate positive attitudes towards equality within quality children's books need discovering and supporting. The research includes personal reading and the evaluation of fiction; the findings may be published.
Published Material: PINSENT, P. (1990). 'Anti-racism and children's literature', The School Librarian, Vol 38, No 2, pp.45-50, May.
Status: Individual research
Date of Research: 1989-continuing
KEYWORDS: *antiracism education; children's literature; fiction; racial attitudes*

10/1289
 Roehampton Lane, London SW15 5PU
 0181 392 3000
 Hunt, P. Ms
Annotated lists of quality children's fiction
Abstract: Teachers and parents of secondary school pupils are aware that there is a vast range of fiction available for young people today and yet many are frustrated by their lack of knowledge about what to offer to whom. The researcher intends to produce annotated book lists to help readers, and those who want to encourage reading, make informed choices. Booklets will be published which contain descriptions of at least forty books for each National Curriculum secondary school year group. Books commonly used as class readers will be the starting point for extension reading lists. Suggestions for suitable new class readers will be included.
Status: Sponsored project
Source of Grant: Higher Education Funding Council
Date of Research: 1993-1994
KEYWORDS: *books; children's literature; fiction; secondary school pupils*

10/1290
 Roehampton Lane, London SW15 5PU
 0181 392 3000
 Payne, M. Ms
Teaching art appreciation in the nursery school
Abstract: The research considered the response of nursery school children to art appreciation when it was introduced into their curriculum. It explains how art appreciation was integrated into an intercurriculum approach and 'taught' through activities that are a 'normal' part of a nursery school day such as mime, movement, telling stories, expressing feelings, games and puzzles. This work stemmed from a question as to whether appreciation is a means to learning and if young children develop in confidence and visual understanding as their awareness grows about the world of art 'outside the classroom'. The research aimed to discover how nursery school 3 and 4 year olds could be engaged in the activity; if their involvement could be sustained; which works of art attracted their interest; and whether the activity could be a vehicle for building positive attitudes with regard to multicultural issues. With such questions in mind a programme of activities in the sample school (Eastwood Nursery School, Aubyn Square, London SW15) and at the Tate Gallery was planned. The research has included 2 exhibitions: (1) Eastwood Nursery School at the Tate Gallery, an educational display of text and visual material detailing the educational value of the visit. Exhibited at the Tate

Gallery from September to December 1989; (2) Art Appreciation in a Multicultural Nursery School, an educational display – text and visuals. Exhibited at Spencer Park Teachers' Centre (ILEA), Summer 1989. Although the research is ongoing the findings suggest that critical appreciation of paintings and sculptures allows for reflective and physical participation, cognitive growth, observation, the development of vocabulary and can lead to children responding sensitively to stylistic similarities and being able to make cross references between paintings.
Published Material: PAYNE, M. (1989). 'Under fives at the Tate Gallery', Nursery World, Vol 89, No 3178.; PAYNE, M. (1990). 'Teaching art appreciation in the nursery school: its relevance for 3 and 4 year olds', Early Child Development and Care, Vol 61, pp.93-106.
Status: Individual research
Date of Research: 1989-continuing
KEYWORDS: *aesthetic education; art activities; art appreciation; nursery school education*

10/1291
 Roehampton Lane, London SW15 5PU
 0181 392 3000
 Wilkins, B. Miss; *Supervisor:* Welch, G. Prof.; Robinson, P. Mr
The teaching of traditional Japanese music in Japanese elementary and junior high schools, with special reference to the Shakuhachi (bamboo flute)
Abstract: The proposed research will be on the role of traditional Japanese music within the elementary and junior high school music curriculum. The research aims at a fuller understanding of the Japanese music curriculum and will examine ways in which more traditional Japanese music might be successfully introduced into the school curriculum, in the light of recent government papers on this subject. The research will be undertaken in Japanese schools in England and Japan, through participant observation and structured interviews. The resulting thesis will present a detailed understanding of certain aspects of traditional Japanese music, focusing on how it can be successfully taught in Japanese schools in line with the stated policy of promoting more creativity and interest in traditional music.
Status: Sponsored project
Source of Grant: Roehampton Institute £4,000
Date of Research: 1993-continuing
KEYWORDS: *Japan; music education*

10/1292
 Roehampton Lane, London SW15 5PU
 0181 392 3000
 Sangster, M. Ms; *Supervisor:* Rogers, L. Mr
Exploring mathematical thinking in the early years
Abstract: The aim is to closely examine young children's style of learning mathematics. By carefully examining their approach and developing understanding of pattern, it is hoped to identify some of the ways children build concepts, and particularly whether they are able to transfer this information to other areas of mathematics. Information will be collected by observation and interview.
Status: Individual research
Date of Research: 1993-continuing
KEYWORDS: *mathematical concepts; mathematics education; young children*

10/1293
 Roehampton Lane, London SW15 5PU
 0181 392 3000
 Alsop, S. Mr; *Supervisor:* Watts, M. Dr
An examination of the public awareness and understanding of radiation and radioactivity
Abstract: The importance of educating the general public in matters of science and technology has grown in recent years. The Public Understanding of Science is seen to be in need of particular redress. Not all attempts to raise public awareness and understanding have been successful. This study focuses on three 'slices' of the Public: 1) Training teachers; 2) The Public that use a hair salon in Clapham Common; 3) The Public living in an area of radiation concern – Cornwall and Devon. Slice (1) consists of a survey on X-rays, nuclear power, general radioactive and radiation awareness. Slice (2) consists of a survey focusing on sunbathing, and sun-care products. Slice (3) consists of a survey, semi-structured interview, and a number of set tasks on radon levels in homes.
Status: Individual research

Date of Research: 1991-continuing
KEYWORDS: attitudes; public opinion; radiation; risk; scientific literacy

10/1294
Roehampton Lane, London SW15 5PU
0181 392 3000
Taber, K. Mr; *Supervisor:* Watts, M. Dr
Development of A-level students' understanding of chemical bonding
Abstract: This project is looking at the development of students' ideas in the topic of chemical bonding. The research is focused at GCE A-level. The main research technique is semi-structured interview. The design is longitudinal in that the same students are interviewed at several stages of their course. The interviews are usually about one hour in length and are recorded on audio tape. The subjects are students in their researcher's college and are called co-learners. Instruments are also being developed to extend this small-scale study, so that findings may be compared with a larger sample of students from other institutions in the UK. In addition to interviews, triangulation is provided using Kelly's Triads and analysis of student course work. Student conversations regarding examination questions are also being recorded. Provisional findings are: 1) student misconceptions from GCSE work may survive an A-level course; 2) students may hold alternative ideas about ionic bonding of a 'psuedomolecular' nature.
Published Material: TABER, K.S. 'Misunderstanding the ionic bond: an alternative framework', Education in Chemistry. (in press).
Status: Individual research
Date of Research: 1993-continuing
KEYWORDS: chemical bonding; chemistry education; science education; scientific concepts

10/1295
Roehampton Lane, London SW15 5PU
0181 392 3000
Lee, S. Mrs; Wilkes, J. Mrs
Changing role of the school experience tutor
Abstract: As a result of the changes in initial teacher education, the role of the 'traditional' school experience supervisor (someone who has been seen as able to nurture, support and monitor the development of beginning teachers) may be difficult to sustain in the current climate. Initial teacher training, as described in the Department for Education (DFE) circular 14/93, may follow different models in the next decade but partnerships in, what the DFE describes as "schools centred education" will be a major feature. This project has been designed to explore: 1) Ways in which the traditional role of the school experience tutor have changed or are changing. 2) The professional development support required to manage the changing role/s. 3) Ways of implementing such support. A questionnaire was distributed to colleagues at Roehampton involved in school experience supervision in order to establish a common understanding of key features of the role of the school experience tutor (SET). The features listed on the questionnaire were found generally to be acceptable to colleagues. Interviews were held to identify: 1) existing patterns of support and induction for school experience (information-giving non-award/award bearing courses); and 2) areas for future developments re support for 1993/4/5. The project is on-going. The next stage requires: 1) monitoring the effectiveness of the models and 'pilots' which are operating currently, through interview and questionnaire; 2) providing proposals for increased support in the management of the changing role of the SET.
Status: Sponsored project
Source of Grant: Roehampton Institute £5,000
Date of Research: 1993-1994
KEYWORDS: preservice teacher education; school-based teacher education; student teacher supervisors; supervisors; teaching practice

10/1296
Roehampton Lane, London SW15 5PU
0181 392 3000
Shaughnessy, J. Miss; *Supervisor:* Jackson, P. Dr; Evans, R. Dr
A two-year study of students' progress and implications for training from PGCE to induction year
Abstract: The study will follow a cohort of Postgraduate Certificate in Education (PGCE) primary students through their training year and further into their experiences whilst in post. The research method will be an ethnographic approach involving frameworks that the students themselves develop and use in their job training, and the identification of the institutions' criteria for judgements of teacher competence.
Status: Individual research
Date of Research: 1994-continuing
KEYWORDS: followup studies; Postgraduate Certificate in Education; student teachers; teacher development

10/1297
Roehampton Lane, London SW15 5PU
0181 392 3000
Gura, P. Ms; *Supervisor:* Evans, R. Dr; Pound, L. Ms
Involving 3-5 year olds in reviewing and assessing their own achievements
Abstract: In 1985, the UK Government set up a National Steering Committee to advise on the implications of introducing records of achievement for all pupils of secondary school age. In its final report published in 1989 records of achievement were described as the core context for assessment. At the heart of this was placed the pupil's own contribution to the content and processes of assessment. A concluding recommendation was that there be 'urgent explication' of issues relating to the introduction of a coherent system (of records of achievement) for pupils aged 5-16. The present research will seek to establish a case for the extension of records of achievements yet further to include children of 3 to 5 years. At the centre of the enquiry will be children's own contribution. Accordingly, consideration will be given to the purpose, principles and practice of the adult/child 'review' of achievement during these early years. During 1993-94 observation, informal interviews with professional early childhood educators with experience of reviewing as an aspect of assessment, together with a study of reviews of achievement conducted with 3-5 year olds (access to be negotiated) will be undertaken. The report of these activities will provide the basis for the setting up of a practitioner research group in 1994-95, aimed at developing the research according to both individual and collective responses.
Status: Individual research
Date of Research: 1993-continuing
KEYWORDS: achievement; assessment; early childhood education; records of achievement; self evaluation – individuals; young children

10/1298
Roehampton Lane, London SW15 5PU
0181 392 3000
Lee, S. Mrs
Self-assessment in primary mathematics
Abstract: The intention was to begin to develop strategies for involving primary children in assessing their own performance and understanding of mathematics. Guidelines were distributed to participants suggesting possible starting points for work with children. Activities carried out with the children were monitored through feedback forms, interviews with students/teachers and visits to the schools. There was involvement in the project by students in Year 3 and Year 4 of a BA Qualified Teacher Status (QTS) Degree Programme, Postgraduate Certificate in Education (PGCE) students and experienced teachers. Main points from feedback received include: 1) self-assessment is worth pursuing; 2) it should be part of the overall assessment process; 3) its usefulness and success depends on developing a good rapport with the children and a common understanding of what is required. More specifically it was found that: 1) simply recording errors and considering their cause was insufficient; 2) discussion and completion of written records was more helpful; 3) discussion without self-assessment could lead to the teacher making the interpretation of what the child meant, losing the important self-analysis; 4) self-analysis came from developing clear targets and expectations with the children; and 5) successful involvement in self-assessment by the children has implications for the teacher's own professional development, in particular the level to which he/she is successfully 'matching' the tasks to the children's ability and providing a degree of challenge. The importance of agreeing targets is one of the strategies found to be valuable. This requires an understanding of what knowledge skills and learning are to be assessed and what would constitute evidence that this had taken place or that the agreed targets had been met. Further work is required to develop this.
Status: Sponsored project
Source of Grant: Roehampton Institute £300
Date of Research: 1993-1993
KEYWORDS: assessment; mathematics achievement; mathematics education; primary school pupils; self evaluation – individuals

10/1299
Roehampton Lane, London SW15 5PU
0181 392 3000
Udall, N. Mr; *Supervisor:* Bailey, G. Dr
Stimulating creativity in design education
Abstract: The research programme, although in its initial stages, focuses on particular techniques for stimulating the creativity of students in higher design education. These techniques were developed prior to the research programme, but have now formed the central core of the investigation. The programme develops a philosophical argument, backed up with experimental 'creativity' workshops, with design students, from British and Technician Education Council (BTEC) up to postgraduate level. A new model of creativity seems to be emerging, which tackles the dynamic imbalance between intellect and intuition from a new orientation.
Status: Individual research
Date of Research: 1993-continuing
KEYWORDS: creativity; design education

10/1300
Roehampton Lane, London SW15 5PU
0181 392 3000
Dodge, L. Ms; Lambert, J. Ms; *Supervisor:* Maxwell, S. Ms
Language development and social integration
Abstract: A language and social integration project, first piloted in 1992/93, is now in its second phase at Bromley-by-Bow Nursery in East London. The project funds young children from a multiethnic community to attend this day nursery based in a large and vibrant community centre. It arose out of a growing concern that children from the Bangladeshi community were educationally disadvantaged in school achievement and failed to attain high academic standards. This was seen to have long term implications for the community. Children join the project at age 18 months-2 years, and families are encouraged to join activities at the centre. Ten children were enrolled in 1992 and eight children in 1993. The social integration of children and their families into the life of the nursery and the centre is seen as crucial to the development of a knowledge and confidence in the English language, and to the children's later educational success. The role of the research team is to: 1) evaluate the development of the English language in the children as well as general confidence in the use of English by their families; and 2) evaluate the development of social integration of the children and their families into the life of the nursery and the centre. Methodology has included observational procedures, questionnaires and informal interviews.
Published Material: MAXWELL, S., LATHEY, G., DODGE, L. & GOODE, S. (1993). 'Language development and social integration in Bromley-by-Bow Nursery', Early Child Development and Care, Vol 92, pp.53-61.
Status: Sponsored project
Source of Grant: Home Office £6,000
Date of Research: 1993-1994
KEYWORDS: community centres; community education; community programmes; day care centres; English – second language; ethnic groups; racial integration; social integration

10/1301
Roehampton Lane, London SW15 5PU
0181 392 3000
Hewitt, J. Mr; Nunn, J. Ms
An evaluation of a new approach to secondary PGCE (school partnership)
Abstract: The South West London Teacher Education Consortium is a partnership of secondary schools from across the region and five higher education institutions (HEI's). The aims of the research are: 1) An evaluation of the Postgraduate Certificate in Education (PGCE) secondary course. 2) To compare the delivery of school-based teacher training in the 'Professional Development school' and the 'Accredited Assessment school'. 3) To evaluate the effectiveness of the partnership between members of the consortium. The research will be conducted in a sample of twelve schools. A mixture of questionnaires and interviews will be used with higher education tutors, student teachers and school-based mentors. The effectiveness of the partnership will be evaluated by means of an analysis of course documentation and the interviewing of members of the planning group and course directors from the five HEI's.
Status: Sponsored project
Source of Grant: Higher Education Funding Council £5,000
Date of Research: 1993-continuing
KEYWORDS: institutional cooperation; mentors; Postgraduate Certificate in Education; preservice teacher education; school-based teacher education

10/1302
Roehampton Lane, London SW15 5PU
0181 392 3000
Geddes, H. Ms; *Supervisor:* Best, R. Prof.
An investigation into the relationship between learning difficulties and social and emotional experiences
Abstract: The research proposal is founded in the belief that social and emotional experiences affect children's capacities to learn, and that there is a relationship between the nature of the learning difficulty and the particular life experience of the individual concerned. Source material is case files in Child Guidance Units, of children referred because of emotional and behavioural problems and with associated learning difficulties. This is confidential material made available by arrangement with area authorities. The sample will comprise some 100 cases where both family therapy and individual remedial educational therapy have been offered. The methods used will be ethnographic and qualitative. The sample will be examined and detailed information relating to learning difficulty, behaviour and life experience will be recorded. The psychoanalytic theory that will inform analysis of data will be 'Attachment Theory' (Bowlby). The hoped for outcome is a better understanding of the effects of life experiences such as abuse, loss and separation, on the learning process and educability of individuals, and to generate material that will inform the classroom teacher in the task of helping pupils with emotional and behavioural difficulties to learn more effectively.
Status: Individual research
Date of Research: 1993-continuing
KEYWORDS: behaviour problems; emotional problems; family problems; learning disabilities; problem children; social experience

10/1303
Roehampton Lane, London SW15 5PU
0181 392 3000
Jofili, Z. Ms; *Supervisor:* Watts, M. Dr
Transforming words into action: a study of the importance of experiencing the constructivist approach in science teachers' training in order to obtain qualitative changes in their classroom practices
Abstract: Considering that the results of research in science education frequently have not reached practice in classrooms, it is intended to investigate why this occurs and if the constructivist approach and an action-research methodology are both adequate for everyday classroom practice in secondary science teachers' views. By asking primary, secondary and university science teachers, the researcher finds that they are insecure about changing their classroom practice because they often feel frightened to lose class control. The research starts with four assumptions: 1) It is essential to provide opportunities to experience methods of teaching instead of only listening or reading about them, in order to obtain the involvement of teachers, the internalisation of concepts and consistent behaviour changes. 2) The support given by an inservice course would motivate teachers to develop and to test teaching units applying a constructivist approach. 3) The action-research methodology is a fairly good way for teachers to improve their classroom work. 4) If teachers feel that the results of applying the constructivist approach to be positive in classrooms during the project, they could feel stimulated to introduce it in their everyday classroom practice. So, it would be possible to make shorter the gap between scientific advances and practice in schools. The object of the research is to study ways of intervention into philosophy and practice of science teachers, aiming to change their understanding about the teaching/learning process by using the constructivist approach and action-research. The researcher intends to work with 20 secondary science teachers during 3 weeks using a constructivist approach in a training programme in a large town in north-eastern Brazil. All students will be required to elaborate their own research project approaching a constructivist model. They must choose a topic for developing during 1 or 2 months in two science classrooms at the same level. They will give different treatments fr each one (the usual and the constructivist approach) and they will evaluate the results. Three or four projects will be selected for follow-up. Tape-recorded interviews with these teachers will be carried out in order to compare their practice before and after the course and to collect their own opinions about it and on the use of the constructivist approach. Is it viable? Do they intend to implement its use in the everyday classroom? Research reports will be presented.

Published Material: JOFILI, Z. (1993). 'Entre o Construtivismo e uma boa pratica didatica'. Proceedings of 45 Reuniao Anual da SBPC (Sociedade Brasileira para o Progresso da Ciencia), São Paulo, July 1993, pp.340 B.6 Educacao.
Status: Individual research
Date of Research: 1992-continuing
KEYWORDS: *Brazil; science teachers; teaching methods*

10/1304

Roehampton Lane, London SW15 5PU
0181 392 3000
Collins, F. Ms
Annotated lists connected to National Curriculum History and Geography teaching
Abstract: The annotated lists relate to specific National Curriculum subjects, to support the teaching of literature alongside History and Geography. The first lists will be books connected to 'Britain since 1930' and 'The Victorians'. It will then go on to look at environmental issues, distant places and Britain. The lists will consist of books plus ideas of how to use these in the classroom.
Status: Sponsored project
Source of Grant: Higher Education Funding Council; Roehampton Institute
Date of Research: 1993-continuing
KEYWORDS: *books; children's literature; fiction; geography education; history studies*

10/1305

Roehampton Lane, London SW15 5PU
0181 392 3000
Smart, L. Mr; *Supervisor:* Evans, R. Dr
The development of project based learning in the English primary school
Abstract: The intention is to explore the concept of project based learning. This will include identifying where and when the term was first used in an educational context and the rationale originally given for it. An attempt will be made to trace its development in the English primary school over the last century and to consider the factors that have affected this development. An attempt will be made to examine the impact the recent changes, particularly the National Curriculum, have had on this form of curriculum organisation.
Status: Individual research
Date of Research: 1991-continuing
KEYWORDS: *curriculum development; discovery learning; educational history; primary education; projects – learning activities; pupil projects; teaching methods*

10/1306

Roehampton Lane, London SW15 5PU
0181 392 3000
Gifford, S. Ms; Gura, P. Ms
Number in early childhood
Abstract: The project has been prompted by recent developments that suggest that young children have a greater capacity to learn about numbers than has been appreciated by a Piagetian early years mathematics curriculum, which is now outdated compared to developments in literacy teaching. The aims are to develop and evaluate new initiatives in teaching three to five year olds about number. Methods involve collaborative action research in six nursery schools or classes, with long term child studies, and support visits by two Roehampton staff, with evaluation meetings twice termly.
Published Material: GIFFORD, S. (1993). 'What is an appropriate maths curriculum for three to six year olds?', Proceedings of SEMT 93, Charles University, Prague, 1993, pp.38-40.
Status: Sponsored project
Source of Grant: Roehampton Institute
Date of Research: 1993-continuing
KEYWORDS: *early childhood education; mathematics education; numbers; preschool education*

10/1307

Roehampton Lane, London SW15 5PU
0181 392 3000
Gifford, S. Ms; Wyllyams, B. Ms
Evaluation of profiles for Newly Qualified Teachers in Surrey and Kingston
Abstract: The Surrey new teacher competency profile arose from Grants for Education, Support and Training (GEST) Funding for Activity 27 in 1992 and was developed by a working party of experienced mentors, advisory teachers, an inspector and higher education representative. It aims to support professional development by means of a mentoring relationship, fostering self-critical reflection and a target-setting process by using a 'menu' of competences from which a focus is chosen, thus giving flexibility to suit individual teachers. The evaluation looked at these aims and processes and attempted to assess effectiveness through 20 interviews (midterm) and case studies throughout a year of six primary and secondary schools, with new and experienced mentors. The main findings are: 1) The profile is mainly useful in providing a focus for development and record of achievement. 2) All case study schools felt that new teachers had made more progress because of the profile than they would have done without it. 3) It was successful in terms of flexibility and in linking with appraisal and wider school professional development. 4) It was not successful in linking with initial teacher education experiences. The major factors affecting its success were a school's induction policy, which provided prioritised time for discussions, and the quality of mentoring, which had implications for mentor training and support. A Kingston evaluation is being carried out on similar lines.
Published Material: GIFFORD, S. (1992). 'The Surrey new teacher competency project', British Journal of In-service Education, Vol 18, No 3, pp.159-165.; GIFFORD, S. 'Design for a profile with pockets', Times Educational Supplement, January 15, 1993, pp.12-13.; GIFFORD, S. (1993). The Surrey new teacher competency profile: final report. London: Roehampton Institute.
Status: Sponsored project
Source of Grant: Surrey Local Education Authority; Kingston Local Education Authority
Date of Research: 1992-1994
KEYWORDS: *competency-based teacher education; mentors; profiles; teacher development; teaching profession*

10/1308

Roehampton Lane, London SW15 5PU
0181 392 3000
Wilton, P. Mr; *Supervisor:* Jackson, P. Dr
An investigation into links between the work of Sir Karl Popper and education
Abstract: The researcher will attempt to link Karl Popper's work on knowledge and the open society with education in order to provide a theory of education which transcends political ideologies and their concomitant theories of knowledge.
Status: Individual research
Date of Research: 1994-continuing
KEYWORDS: *educational theories; sociology of knowledge*

10/1309

Roehampton Lane, London SW15 5PU
0181 392 3000
Lathey, G. Ms; Hunt, P. Ms; Collins, F. Ms;
Supervisor: Reynolds, K. Dr
Contemporary juvenile reading habits
Abstract: This is a survey of what children read, when they read and how they choose books. The survey is being carried out in schools with pupils aged 5-16 years. A pilot study of 400 pupils has taken place and the findings published by the British Library.
Published Material: The Children's Literature Research Centre. (1994). Contemporary juvenile reading habits: a study of young people's reading at the end of the century. London: British Library.
Status: Sponsored project
Source of Grant: Higher Education Funding Council; British Library
Date of Research: 1993-continuing
KEYWORDS: *books; children's literature*

10/1310

Roehampton Lane, London SW15 5PU
0181 392 3000
Papazazis, A. Ms; *Supervisor:* Sergeant, D. Dr; Welch, G. Prof.
The implications for teaching resources and teacher training of the proposed introduction of a programme for music education in Greek primary schools
Abstract: The research is based on the formation of a systematic and active intervention in the music education of Greek children aged

between 6 and 12, plus the emphasis on the training of classroom teachers in music. The research includes an extensive report on the history and background of music in general education of Greece (from 1829 up to our times); a report with data on the educational system; questionnaires have been set to teacher education students, teachers and parents, on the questions regarding music education. Live observation of music teaching in schools will also be integrated in the research by means of video-taping some classrooms. Following analysis of the accumulated information, the researcher will develop an adapted school music curriculum (based on the UK model) for children aged between 6 and 12.
Status: Individual research
Date of Research: 1991-1994
KEYWORDS: Greece; music education

10/1311
Roehampton Lane, London SW15 5PU
0181 392 3000
Lodge, J. Mr; *Supervisor:* Evans, R. Dr; Watts, M. Dr
The concept keyboard in the primary curriculum
Abstract: The research will focus on how the overlay board is used in primary school classes asking such questions as: How many teachers use this device? Do they prepare their own overlays? What factors promote/inhibit the use of the concept keyboard?
Status: Individual research
Date of Research: 1993-continuing
KEYWORDS: computer keyboards; computer uses in education; concept keyboards; human computer interaction

10/1312
Roehampton Lane, London SW15 5PU
0181 392 3000
Robson, S. Mrs
An investigation of children's perspectives of play, work and learning
Abstract: This study looks at children's conceptions of play, work and learning, and in particular their ideas about what they do in school. It starts from the premise that, whilst much has been written about play and its place in young children's lives, it has tended to be from an adult perspective. Thus, the aim of this project is to talk with children themselves in an effort to elicit their views, and to enhance our understanding of children's concerns. Children aged four to five and a half, from 6 settings, are the subject of the study. Settings include nursery, reception classes, early years' units, and a workplace nursery. Data is being collected through observations, followed by extended discussions with individuals and groups of children. Photographs taken in the course of children's activities are also being used as stimulus for talk. Structured discussions are also being carried out with teachers, nursery nurses and welfare assistants, in order to elicit staff attitudes and intentions. Results so far have highlighted certain common features about children's conceptions: their tendency to see play as a social activity, largely unconnected with learning; and work as related to often seat-based teacher-initiated tasks. Some differences in attitudes across settings are also apparent, particularly in children's feelings about choice, and their freedom to choose. A model to account for children's apparent conception is being developed.
Published Material: ROBSON, S. (1993). 'Best of all I like choosing time: talking with children about play and work', Early Child Development and Care, Vol 92, pp.37-51.
Status: Sponsored project
Source of Grant: Higher Education Funding Council £1,431
Date of Research: 1992-1994
KEYWORDS: learning activities; play; pupil attitudes

10/1313
Roehampton Lane, London SW15 5PU
0181 392 3000
Best, R. Prof.
Teachers as active carers: international perspectives
Abstract: As part of the work of a network of researchers in Australia, New Zealand, Canada, Singapore, UK and elsewhere, this project investigates the caring roles of teachers, with particular reference to recent changes in the organisation of, and growing centralised influence over, the curriculum and teachers' work. Ethnographic case-studies of a junior school and a comprehensive school in south-eastern England have been carried out. Attention has been paid to teachers' and pupils' perceptions of their pastoral roles, their

perceived contribution to personal and social education, and to schools' pastoral policies and administrative systems. Data from interviews and observations are currently being subjected to content and dilemma analysis. One hundred and seventy questionnaires were received from UK teachers, using contacts through the National Association for Pastoral Care in Education (NAPCE). These have been coded and integrated with questionnaires from other countries in the network and submitted for processing by staff at Edith Cowan University, Western Australia.
Published Material: BEST, R. (1991). 'Teachers as active carers: international perspectives: a conference paper'. Proceedings of the British Educational Research Association Annual Conference, Nottingham, 1991.; BEST, R. (1993). 'Teachers' caring roles in an English junior school: a conference paper'. Proceedings of the British Educational Research Association Annual Conference, Liverpool, 1993.
Status: Sponsored project
Source of Grant: Roehampton Institute £1,431; Eastern Region Teacher Education Consortium £500; Anglia Polytechnic University £500
Date of Research: 1990-1994
KEYWORDS: comparative education; international educational exchange; pastoral care – education; teacher role

10/1314
Roehampton Lane, London SW15 5PU
0181 392 3000
White, P. Ms; *Supervisor:* Robinson, P. Mr; Welch, G. Prof.; Chiltern, E. Dr
The application of digital signal processing techniques to improved methods for the analysis and assessment of children's voices
Abstract: The spectral analysis of speech began with early experiments using analogue systems. More recently digital techniques have been developed which allow for greater manipulation of data, and even for real-time spectral and spectrographic displays of sounds. As early research tended to focus on the speech of adult males, the resulting technology has been modelled on the relatively low-pitched adult male voice. However, the adult female uses an average speaking fundamental frequency somewhat higher than males, and children use still higher frequencies. The harmonics of a sound with a high fundamental frequency are so widely spaced that the resonances (formants) of the vocal tract are poorly defined. This increases the likelihood of error in locating the centre frequency of formants (a commonly used measure). It can also be theorised that such limited acoustic information will result in a perceptual ambiguity of vowel sounds, and yet children's speech is not normally unintelligible. Perceptually, pitch is a very reliable cue towards age and sex identification, but it is not the only cue. The perceptual differences between voices are varied and often difficult to qualify (it may be easy to identify two voices as being different but not to say what those differences are). The initial aims of this research, therefore, are: 1) to review the literature relevant to the spectral analysis of high fundamental frequency sounds, and child voice in general; 2) to investigate the intelligibility and qualities of children's speech using perceptual studies; and 3) to investigate acoustically these aspects of children's voices.
Status: Individual research
Date of Research: 1993-continuing
KEYWORDS: speech; visible speech

10/1315
Roehampton Lane, London SW15 5PU
0181 392 3000
Alsop, S. Mr; Dock, G. Mr; Barbor, M. Mr
To examine the relationship between teachers' science content knowledge and general pedagogical knowledge when placed into 'action' in the primary classroom
Abstract: Over the past 5 years substantial doubt has been raised about primary school teachers' knowledge of scientific concepts by Her Majesty's Inspectorate (HMI) as well as by the Department for Education (DFE) and research. A course has been developed at Roehampton to provide students with a background knowledge of science. The principle underpinning this course is that teachers' subject knowledge is linked to the quality of children's classroom experiences. This study aims to look at how 6 students use their experiences of the course to plan and implement science-based activities in the classroom. The methodology will be case studies

involving semi-structured interviews about classroom instances stimulated by lesson evaluations.
Status: Sponsored project
Source of Grant: Roehampton Institute
Date of Research: 1993-1994
KEYWORDS: *preservice teacher education; primary school teachers; science education; science teachers; scientific concepts*

10/1316
> Roehampton Lane, London SW15 5PU
> 0181 392 3000
> Masters, B. Mr; *Supervisor:* Jackson, P. Dr

Steiner Education from founding principles to contemporary praxis: an evaluation of Steiner philosophy of education from its origins to the present day
Abstract: The thesis will examine and evaluate the educational philosophy of the Rudolf Steiner Waldorf schools movement. It will be in 3 parts: 1) A philosophical textual study of the Steiner archive documents; and their related critical commentaries will be used to develop a valid interpretation of the growth and development of Steiner's own philosophy of education. 2) The growth and development of the above from Steiner's death to the present day; with particular attention to continuity and change. 3) The contemporary praxis in the UK and abroad. Explanations will be given for the different practices encountered.
Status: Individual research
Date of Research: 1993-continuing
KEYWORDS: *Steiner Waldorf schools*

10/1317
> Roehampton Lane, London SW15 5PU
> 0181 392 3000
> Rogers, L. Mr

International cabri-geometre (1993-1994)
Abstract: This current phase is a continuation of a pilot project originally funded by the National Council for Educational Technology (NCET). The software has been created at Universite Joseph Fourier, Grenoble, France, for use in French secondary schools. It now has an international reputation and is used in many educational establishments in Europe and the USA. This project aims to consider and report on the possibilities of its use in English secondary schools, in the context of the National Curriculum and the place of geometry within it.
Published Material: ROGERS, L.F. (1992). 'Approaches to Cabri', Micromath, Vol 8, No 2, pp.25-26.; ROGERS, L.F. (1992). 'Nick', Micromath, Vol 8, No 2, pp.34-36.
Status: Sponsored project
Source of Grant: Roehampton Institute £4,862
Date of Research: 1993-1994
KEYWORDS: *computer uses in education; educational software; geometry; mathematics education*

10/1318
> Roehampton Lane, London SW15 5PU
> 0181 392 3000
> McCreery, E. Ms; *Supervisor:* Evans, R. Dr; Slee, N. Ms

Spiritual development and the education of young children
Abstract: The aim of the research is to investigate the role of schools in promoting spiritual development. It is grounded in the requirements of the Education Reform Act 1988 which requires schools to promote the spiritual development of children. The notion of the spiritual is notoriously difficult to define and an attempt will be made to discover how teachers interpret it for the classroom. Research will include interviews with teachers and practical work with children, taken from a small number of primary schools in the London area. From this a model for promoting spiritual development will be made, offering a way forward for teachers charged with the task within the education of young children.
Status: Individual research
Date of Research: 1993-continuing
KEYWORDS: *religious education; young children*

10/1319
> Roehampton Lane, London SW15 5PU
> 0181 392 3000
> Lathey, G. Ms; *Supervisor:* Reynolds, K. Dr; Evans, R. Dr

Recent autobiographical children's literature written in German and English on the subject of the Second World War
Abstract: The focus of the research is fictionalised autobiography, and the experiences of children in Britain and Germany as recollected in middle age. Differences and similarities between experiences and the writers' reconstruction of the past from a contemporary perspective, will be explored. The role of writing as therapy and cross-cultural links are to be examined from a range of theoretical perspectives. An analysis of the timing, audience and purpose of recent children's literature on the war years in both Britain and Germany will form an important concluding chapter to the study.
Status: Individual research
Date of Research: 1991-continuing
KEYWORDS: *autobiographies; children's literature; war*

10/1320
> Roehampton Lane, London SW15 5PU
> 0181 392 3000
> Lee, S-W. Mr; *Supervisor:* Evans, R. Dr

A study of the relevance of Friedrich Froebel to the Christian education of young children
Abstract: In the educational thought of Froebel, we are confronted with a panoramic view of the universe of knowledge and experience. Motivated by a profound grasp of the Creator-creature relationship in Christian theology, Froebel was able to provide a radical, holistic view of the task of Christian education. For Froebel, one's relationship to nature was nothing less than a religious communion, a drawing close to the Creator. Froebel's conception of God is big, comprehensive and cosmic. All truth, all knowledge, all reality is from God. Thus, in Froebel's educational theory, knowledge and truth have an inherently religious aspect. Humanity is made in the image of God, not to pursue its own ends, but to pursue a course of development according to the rules and laws of God. Education is not confined to just one compartment of human life; it must be free to address every part of the pupil's being, body, will, mind and spirit. Thus, education must span many subjects and embrace religion, science and art. The method of education must not be removed from real life but must engage the pupil at many levels of life and activity. Because education is such a holistic activity it cannot be dealt with in a compartment labelled 'school'. Parents are guardians of a sacred trust, responsible to God, to the child, and to all humanity. This is why Froebel placed such importance upon women. Upon women depends the welfare of the child, and thus the future welfare of the human race. Education is the process of coming to a knowledge of and love for this Triune Creator through His creation, via His holy institution of the family. Froebel has laid a most valuable foundation for Christian education theory; now, his shortcomings must be corrected and the insights of the intervening century must be added to his seminal work.
Status: Individual research
Date of Research: 1990-1993
KEYWORDS: *Christianity; religious education; young children*

10/1321
> Roehampton Lane, London SW15 5PU
> 0181 392 3000
> Harrison, J. Mr

The role of the imagination in children's mathematical learning
Abstract: The hypothesis behind the research is that the imagination can play an important role in children's mathematical learning, notably in task engagement, cognition and fulfilment. The research will use videotape to study children in imaginative play/simulations which have mathematical learning objectives, e.g. catering, shopping. Stimulus materials, e.g. pictures and stories, will be trialled and evaluated.
Status: Sponsored project
Source of Grant: Roehampton Institute
Date of Research: 1994-continuing
KEYWORDS: *imagination; mathematics education; pretend play; simulation*

10/1322
> Roehampton Lane, London SW15 5PU
> 0181 392 3000
> Rose, D. Mr; *Supervisor:* Best, R. Prof.; Whitty, G. Prof.

A consideration of the inherent conflict between local faith representation on Standing Advisory Council for Religious Education (SACRE) and the Agreed Syllabus requirements for the RE curriculum in schools

Abstract: The aims of the research are to: 1) explore the impact of plurality of faiths within England and Wales, and to consider how this is reflected in policy-making committees in relation to religious education (RE); 2) explore the mechanisms and rationale exercised for a 'faith' to be included in, or rejected from, religious education in the classroom as prescribed by the local Agreed Syllabus. The first part of the research was by questionnaire sent to every local education authority (LEA) in England and Wales. The data gleaned revealed specific anomalies which required further discussion. The next parts of the research will consider: 1) the nature of current legislation in relation to local representation; 2) the nature of the 'faiths' themselves – rationale for inclusion/rejection; and 3) the way forward, i.e. dealing with the anomalies.
Status: Individual research
Date of Research: 1993-continuing
KEYWORDS: religious cultural groups; religious education

10/1323

Roehampton Lane, London SW15 5PU
0181 392 3000
Welch, G. Prof.; Sergeant, D. Dr; White, P. Ms
Singing development in early childhood
Abstract: The aim of the research has been to chart the singing development of children during their first three years at school through a longitudinal study of 200 5 year olds; a comparative study of up to 800 children aged 3 to 12 years; and a study of trained male and female choristers. Child and personality profiles have also been taken for the longitudinal sample. There are many different foci within the study, including differences between trained and untrained voices, a study of age and gender differences, the perception and realisation of musical structures in song, the effect of social context on singing and a comparison between children's speaking and singing. Children's singing competences are assessed using a specially designed test battery and a range of song material. Subsequent data is subject to instrumental and panel analyses being recorded on digital tape and then edited at the project office. The third and final year's longitudinal data has just been completed and analysis is ongoing of the first two years' data.
Published Material: HOWARD, D.M., RUSH, C. & WELCH, G.F. (1991). 'A developmental continuum of singing ability: evidence from a study of five year old singing development', Early Child Development and Care, Vol 69, pp.107-119.; WHITE, P.J. & WELCH, G.F. (1992). 'A laryngographic study of the speaking and singing voices of young children'. Proceedings of the Institute of Acoustics Conference, Windermere, November 1992, Vol 14, No 6, pp.225-231.; WELCH, G.F. & WHITE, P.J. (1992). 'The developing voice: education and vocal efficiency – a physical perspective'. Proceedings of the Fourteenth ISME Research Seminar, Nogoya, Japan, July 18-24, 1992, pp.307-317.; WELCH, G.F. & MURAO, T. (Eds). (1994). Onchi and singing development: a cross-cultural perspective. London: David Fulton.
Status: Sponsored project
Source of Grant: Leverhulme Trust £100,000
Date of Research: 1990-continuing
KEYWORDS: music activities; music education; singing; young children

10/1324

Roehampton Lane, London SW15 5PU
0181 392 3000
Jackson, P. Dr
Distinctive approaches to early childhood education:
Montessori and Steiner
Abstract: In the light of the considerable body of evidence about early childhood education that has been developed over the past decade, Roehampton Institute commissioned an investigation into the philosophy, policies, practices and effects of two distinctive approaches: the Montessori and the Steiner (Waldorf). The project has a historical and philosophical section, a practical investigation involving nurseries and kindergarten nominated by the Montessori and Steiner foundations, and an evaluative conclusion.
Published Material: McAULEY, H. & JACKSON, P. (1992). Educating young children: a structural approach. London: David Fulton.; JACKSON, P.W. Distinctive approaches to early childhood education: Steiner and Montessori. London: Chapmans. (in press).
Status: Sponsored project
Source of Grant: Roehampton Institute
Date of Research: 1994-continuing

KEYWORDS: early childhood education; Montessori method; Steiner Waldorf schools; teaching methods

10/1325

Roehampton Lane, London SW15 5PU
0181 392 3000
Surrey University, Department of Educational Studies, Guildford GU2 5XH
01483 300800
Lee-Corbin, H. Mrs; *Supervisor:* Evans, R. Dr; Evans, K. Dr
The able child: why do some succeed whilst others fail?
Abstract: The research focuses on able children and the reasons why some succeed and others fail. A possible contributory reason for failure could be a mismatch in cognitive style between teacher and child. A grounded theory approach will be adopted to uncover other reasons for success or failure. Children studied will be Years 5 and 6 in primary schools. Three schools with differing intakes, have been selected. A battery of tests to determine attainment in English and Mathematics have been administered. Also tests to determine cognitive style (field independence and field dependence) have been given to teachers and pupils alike. Tests for verbal I.Q. and non-verbal I.Q. complete the battery of tests. Attainment tests will be repeated in July. The bulk of the research will be qualitative, based on observation and indepth interviews. Children, teachers and parents will be included.
Published Material: LEE-CORBIN, H. (1994). 'Teacher expectations and the able child', Early Child Development and Care, Vol 98, pp.73-78.
Status: Individual research
Date of Research: 1992-1994
KEYWORDS: academic achievement; achievement; cognitive style; failure; gifted; underachievement

10/1326

Roehampton Lane, London SW15 5PU
0181 392 3000
University of Utah, Salt Lake City, Utah 84112, USA
Durrant, C. Mr; *Supervisor:* Sergeant, D. Dr; Welch, G. Prof.; Cooksey, J. Prof.
Towards a definition of effective conducting
Abstract: The research arises from the teaching of postgraduate music students from a range of higher education institutions and an analysis of their skills in conducting. The art of conducting (if indeed it is an art) appears to receive little attention in a significant number of 3 year undergraduate music programmes across UK institutions, as evidenced by research amongst Postgraduate Certificate in Education (PGCE) music students at Roehampton (Durrant 1992). Most, if not all of these students will need to conduct choirs and other ensembles in their schools, and while they will normally have acquired a wide range and variety of musical skills through their training, evidence has highlighted a distinct weakness in their conducting compared with their other musical skills and knowledge. Data collected from higher education (HE) institutions in the UK confirm the supposition that few actually have any significant courses, compulsory or optional, as part of a 3 year programme. This apparently contrasts with the way conducting is approached in the USA, where research and other evidence would suggest that more attention is given to the philosophy, the technical and the communication aspects of conducting. This study seeks to determine what is teachable in conducting by examining and analysing good practice and from that evolve a rationale and philosophy for teaching in this area. In the research methodology the first stage (currently in progress) is to interview a selection of professional choral conductors and school choral conductors in order to establish any common ground in approach and priorities in choral conducting. This will be followed-up by interviews and observation schedules for a comparative study of a selection of choral conducting courses in UK and USA higher education institutions. Following analysis of the research, the intention will be to tease out definitions of effective conducting in relation to: 1) philosophical approaches; 2) specific musical and technical skills; and 3) personality/behavioural traits nd communication skills. Implications for a structured development of the training of music students in choral conducting in the UK will then be drawn.
Status: Individual research
Date of Research: 1992-continuing
KEYWORDS: music activities; music education; music teachers

Royal College of Nursing

10/1327
Institute of Advanced Nursing Education, 20 Cavendish Square, London W1M OAB
0171 409 3333
London University, Institute of Education, Department of Curriculum Studies, 20 Bedford Way, London WC1H 0AL
0171 580 1122
Thomson, S. Mrs; *Supervisor:* Maw, J. Miss
The effect of higher education upon the practice of post-registered nurses
Abstract: This project will use a case study format and will follow a cohort of students prior to entering one course, to completion of their studies. Methods will include questionnaire, semi-structured interview, non participant observation.
Status: Individual research
Date of Research: 1992-continuing
KEYWORDS: nurse education; nurses; outcomes of education

Royal Society of Arts

10/1328
Education Office, 8 John Adam Street, London WC2N 6EZ
0171 930 5115
Bastiani, J. Dr
Parents in a learning society
Abstract: The project is a two year research programme which focuses on the crucial roles of parents and families throughout their children's education. The project director works in ten schools, with groups of parents and staff. His work gives special emphasis to: a more integrated approach to home-school relations as children move through the phases of education; developing appropriate roles for the parents of older children; and working in partnerships focusing on careers education etc. In addition to the research being carried out in the project schools, a number of workshops will be organised and particular emphasis is being given to dissemination of ideas and experience.
Published Material: JONES, G. et al (1992). A willing partnership. London: Royal Society of Arts.; BASTIANI, J. (1992). Partners for learning (video). London: Royal Society of Arts.; BASTIANI, J. (1993). UK directory of home-school intiatives. London: Royal Society of Arts.
Status: Sponsored project
Source of Grant: Department of Employment; Private trusts and companies
Date of Research: 1993-continuing
KEYWORDS: family involvement; home-school relationship; parent participation; parent-pupil relationship

Ruskin College

10/1329
Ruskin Hall, Old Headington, Oxford OX3 9BZ
01865 63437
Bryant, R. Mr; Noble, M. Mr
Financial circumstances of adult/mature students
Abstract: This is a long-term evaluation of the financial circumstances of adult students at Ruskin College, with particular reference to students on the CQSW/Social Work course. The research aims to: (1) monitor the financial difficulties experienced by mature/adult students; (2) compile data on how financial problems impact upon recruitment and the course work of students; and (3) evaluate the impact of the student loans scheme on students at Ruskin.
Published Material: BRYANT, R. & NOBLE, M. (1988). Reflections on Social Work Education. Oxford: Ruskin College.; BRYANT, R. & NOBLE, M. (1989). Education on a Shoestring. Oxford: Ruskin College.
Status: Individual research
Date of Research: 1986-continuing

KEYWORDS: adult students; financial problems; mature students; student costs; student financial aid; student loans; student recruitment

Scottish Council for Research in Education

10/1330
15 St John Street, Edinburgh EH8 8JR
0131 557 2944
Black, H. Mr; Devine, M. Mrs; Fenwick, N. Ms; Gray, D. Mr; Mingard, S. Dr
Schools Assessment Research and Support Unit (SARSU)
Abstract: The Schools Assessment Research and Support Unit (SARSU) carries out a rolling programme of action research and exploratory studies in assessment. It also encourages the dissemination of research findings and provides a support service for local authorities' inservice staff development programmes in assessment.
Published Material: BLACK, H.D., DEVINE, M., TURNER, E. & HARRISON, C. (1988). Standard Grade Assessment: a support package for schools. Edinburgh: SCRE/SARSU; in collaboration with the Scottish Education Department.; BLACK, H.D. & DEVINE, M. (1988). Mathematics checkpoint 7: assessment materials for primary 7 pupils. Edinburgh: SCRE/SARSU.; TURNER, E., BLACK, H.D., HALL, J. & DEVINE, M. (1989). Technology in Home Economics. Edinbugh: SCRE/SARSU.; BLACK, H.D., DEVINE, M. & TURNER, E. (1989). Aspects of assessment: a primary perspective. Edinburgh SCRE/SARSU.; TURNER, E., BLACK, H.D. & DEVINE, M. (1990). Technology: an annotated bibliography. Edinburgh: SCRE/SARSU. A full list of publications is available from the researcher.
Status: Sponsored project
Source of Grant: Local authorities; Scottish Council for Research in Education; Scottish Office Education Department
Date of Research: 1983-1993
KEYWORDS: action research; assessment; educational research; school-based assessment

10/1331
15 St John Street, Edinburgh EH8 8JR
0131 557 2944
Thorpe, G. Mr; Docherty, G. Ms; Whitcombe, D. Mr; Bichard, A. Dr
Central Support Unit: the Assessment of Achievement Programme
Abstract: The Central Support Unit (CSU) has been funded by the Scottish Office Education Department to provide the technical support and infra-structure for its Assessment of Achievement Programme (AAP). The AAP is a systematic programme, designed to monitor pupil attainment. Individual teams with knowledge and expertise in the particular subject under study are established to have responsibility for the content-specific part of the projects. The CSU provides technical support to all projects across the subject spectrum. This support includes: advice on experimental design; sampling; liaison with schools; collation, distribution and collection of test materials; computing the desired analyses and advising on the statistics of these. Part of the general support of the AAP will incorporate the development and continuous updating of a set of guidelines for AAP projects. These guidelines will assist the project teams in the efficient design of their assessment programmes, will offer a repertoire of analytic approaches designed to enable the teams to extract different kinds of information from their data, and will make practical suggestions which will help to overcome anticipated difficulties.
Published Material: 'Noticeboard' – a newsletter for schools and Feedback booklets covering the 1989 science and 1990 mathematics surveys are available from the Scottish Council for Research in Education.
Status: Sponsored project
Source of Grant: Scottish Office Education Department
Date of Research: 1987-continuing
KEYWORDS: academic achievement; achievement rating; assessment; educational research

10/1332

15 St John Street, Edinburgh EH8 8JR
0131 557 2944
Munn, P. Mrs; Blair, A. Ms; Lowden, K. Mr; Powney, J. Dr;
McPake, J. Ms; Arney, N. Mr

Adult education: provision, guidance and progression

Abstract: The research will be carried out in four studies. It will provide a broad based national picture of opportunities for progression and of guidance while enabling more detailed information on adults' experiences and on the operation of particular systems to be collected. The four studies are: (1) case studies of adults' experiences of guidance, provision and progression, Scottish Council for Research in Education (SCRE) and Scottish Community Education Council (SCEC); (2) a survey of opportunities for progression, focusing particularly on inter-sector links and on links between formal and informal services, together with indepth analysis of opportunities for progression within one region; (3) a survey of guidance provision together with indepth analysis of a small number of new initiatives and an assessment of user experience (SCRE); and (4) a special study of adults in schools, investigating the opinions of adults and of the schools about the advantages of this form of provision (SCRE).
Status: Sponsored project
Source of Grant: Scottish Office Education Department £149,671
Date of Research: 1991-1993
KEYWORDS: access to education; adult education; adult students; community education; educational guidance; mature students; student attitudes

10/1333

15 St John Street, Edinburgh EH8 8JR
0131 557 2944
Black, H. Mr; Malcolm, H. Ms

Evaluation of the Lothian Region Technical and Vocational Education Initiative (TVEI) Extension

Abstract: The team provides an ongoing evaluation service to Lothian's Technical and Vocational Education Initiative (TVEI) Extension project – contact with the project being sustained through membership of the TVEI Evaluation Group. Evaluative studies and other services are negotiated throughout the lifetime of the evaluation. Three identified to date are: the project's school/college week; mechanisms for neighbourhood management group activity and ideas sharing; and curriculum auditing.
Published Material: MALCOLM, H. & JOHNSTONE, M. (1991). Working out? A study of the work experience module in secondary schools in Lothian. SCRE Project Report No 24. Edinburgh: Scottish Council for Research in Education. MALCOLM, H. (1991). 'Work out of school', SCRE Newsletter No 49, Autumn.; BLACK, H., MALCOLM, H. & BANKOWSKA, A. (1992). Furthering education? Links between schools and FE colleges in Lothian Regions. SCRE Research Report No 41. Edinburgh: Scottish Council for Research in Education.
Status: Sponsored project
Source of Grant: Lothian Region
Date of Research: 1989-1994
KEYWORDS: programme evaluation; TVEI

10/1334

15 St John Street, Edinburgh EH8 8JR
0131 557 2944
Devine, M. Mrs;

Health education and promotion in Scottish schools

Abstract: The main aim of the study is to examine how well the health education being delivered in Scottish primary and secondary schools is matched to the needs of pupils of different abilities and from different types of area and home background and to use the findings in a focused way to improve health education and health promotion in a few selected schools. Differing education authority policies on health education will also be taken into account in selecting schools.
Status: Sponsored project
Source of Grant: Scottish Office Education Department
Date of Research: 1993-continuing
KEYWORDS: health education; health promotion; pupil needs; Scotland

10/1335

15 St John Street, Edinburgh EH8 8JR
0131 557 2944
Harlen, W. Prof.

Primary teachers' understanding of concepts in science and technology

Abstract: The research is investigating factors relating primary teachers' understanding of relevant concepts to their practice in science and technology. Teachers' perceptions of their confidence in teaching these subjects is being explored through questionnaires and a small sample of P6 and P7 teachers will be interviewed to investigate their understanding of concepts in science and technology.
Status: Sponsored project
Source of Grant: Scottish Office Education Department £55,840
Date of Research: 1993-continuing
KEYWORDS: concept teaching; primary school teachers; science education; scientific concepts; technology education

10/1336

15 St John Street, Edinburgh EH8 8JR
0131 557 2944
Munn, P. Mrs

Pupils with social, emotional and behavioural difficulties

Abstract: The Scottish Office Education Department (SOED) is funding a national project as a follow-up to departmental and Regional initiatives on provision for pupils who are experiencing social, emotional and behavioural difficulties. The SOED has engaged the services of a number of experts working in this area. The Scottish Council for Research in Education (SCRE) is contributing to this work which will include a survey of relevant research findings and a national conference.
Published Material: MUNN, P. (Ed). (1994). 'Schooling with care? Developing provision for children and young people presenting social, emotional and behavioural difficulties'. Proceedings of SCRE Conference on pupils with social, emotional and behavioural difficulties, Edinburgh, December 1993. Edinburgh: SOED, Research and Intelligence Unit.
Status: Sponsored project
Source of Grant: Scottish Office Education Department: Top Slice Contract £10,000
Date of Research: 1993-1994
KEYWORDS: antisocial behaviour; behaviour problems; emotional problems; pupil problems; social behaviour; special educational needs

10/1337

15 St John Street, Edinburgh EH8 8JR
0171 557 2944
Powney, J. Dr

Teacher appraisal and equality

Abstract: The aim of the research study is to elucidate the main issues and concerns about appraisal and equal opportunities as identified by the Association of Teachers and Lecturers (ATL) membership. Broad research questions include: How does the actual process of appraisal being used in different education authorities and schools enhance or inhibit the implementation of equal opportunities policies? What does an analysis of those who are appraised and those who are the appraisers contribute to equal opportunities practices? What are participants' expectations of appraisal schemes? Are targets emerging from different appraisals yielding useful information about trends in equal opportunities for school staff?
Status: Sponsored project
Source of Grant: Association of Teachers and Lecturers
Date of Research: 1993-1993
KEYWORDS: equal opportunities – jobs; teacher development; teacher evaluation; teaching profession

10/1338

15 St John Street, Edinburgh EH8 8JR
0131 557 2944
Supervisor: Thorpe, G. Mr; Devine, M. Mrs

Third International Mathematics and Science Study (TIMSS) survey

Abstract: Over 50 countries are participating in the International Association for the Evaluation of Educational Achievement (IEA) Third International Mathematics and Science Study. The study has 3 main areas of investigation: 1) The intended curriculum based on an analysis of curriculum guidelines and textbooks; 2) The implemented curriculum using questionnaires for teachers and pupils; 3) The attained curriculum using tests of pupils' attainment.
Status: Sponsored project

Source of Grant: Scottish Office Education Department
Date of Research: 1993-continuing
KEYWORDS: *comparative education; curriculum development; international educational exchange; mathematics education; science education*

10/1339

15 St John Street, Edinburgh EH8 8JR
0131 557 2944
Munn, P. Mrs; Powney, J. Dr
Understanding values education in primary schools
Abstract: The study will explore the kinds of values taught, explicitly and implicitly, in primary schools; explore the ways in which values education takes place; and investigate teachers' and pupils' perceptions of the purposes of values education.
Status: Sponsored project
Source of Grant: Gordon Cook Foundation
Date of Research: 1993-continuing
KEYWORDS: *primary education; pupil attitudes; teacher attitudes; values education*

10/1340

15 St John Street, Edinburgh EH8 8JR
0131 557 2944
Supervisor: Harlen, W. Prof.
Consultation to the Northern Ireland Schools Examinations and Assessment Council (NISEAC) on the evaluation of the pilot key stages 2 and 3 assessments
Abstract: This consultation to the Northern Ireland Schools Examination and Assessment Council involves liaison with the steering committee and project manager in setting the detailed objectives, approving the methodology, reviewing progress and providing and commenting on the project's outcomes
Status: Sponsored project
Source of Grant: Northern Ireland Schools Examinations and Assessment Council £30,000
Date of Research: 1992-1994
KEYWORDS: *assessment; National Curriculum – Northern Ireland; school-based assessment*

10/1341

15 St John Street, Edinburgh EH8 8JR
0131 557 2944
Black, H. Mr
Evaluation of the Glasgow University Enterprise in Higher Education Initiative
Abstract: Glasgow University was one of the first round of Enterprise in Higher Education (EHE) projects. Glasgow EHE began in March 1989 and finished in February 1994. This project seeks to evaluate the impact of the activities which have taken place under the auspices of the initiative. In particular it will explore the extent to which: 1) the EHE initiative has secured effective links between the University and employers; 2) it has developed appropriate skills in students; 3) it has resulted in a more responsive curriculum. The results of the evaluation will be used to inform considerations of the University's future strategy in relation to the EHE initiative.
Status: Sponsored project
Source of Grant: Glasgow University; Scottish Enterprise, jointly £19,791
Date of Research: 1993-1993
KEYWORDS: *enterprise education; industry-higher education relationship*

10/1342

15 St John Street, Edinburgh EH8 8JR
0131 557 2944
Munn, P. Mrs
Adult literacy and numeracy
Abstract: The project will attempt to identify perceptions of need for adult literacy and numeracy and the adequacy of current provision. It will explore barriers to participation in existing provision, distinguishing situational barriers such as geography and mode of provision from attitudinal barriers such as social stigma. Data will be collected from a range of providers and from adult students themselves.
Status: Sponsored project

Source of Grant: Department of Education for Northern Ireland £30,000
Date of Research: 1993-1994
KEYWORDS: *adult basic education; adult education; adult literacy; adult students; numeracy*

10/1343

15 St John Street, Edinburgh EH8 8JR
0131 557 2944
Powney, J. Dr
Evaluation of headteacher review in Tayside Region
Abstract: The aim of this study is to elucidate the main issues, concerns and suggested improvements emerging from the first phase of the headteacher review in Tayside in order to improve the current headteacher guidelines.
Published Material: LOWDEN, K. & POWNEY, J. (1993). Evaluation of headteacher review in Tayside Region: a report of findings and recommendations. SCRE Research Report No 51. Edinburgh: Scottish Council for Research in Education.; LOWDEN, K. (1994). Developing headteacher management skills through performance review. SCRE Spotlight No 46. Edinburgh: Scottish Council for Research in Education.
Status: Sponsored project
Source of Grant: Tayside Region
Date of Research: 1993-1993
KEYWORDS: *head teachers; teacher development; teaching profession*

10/1344

15 St John Street, Edinburgh EH8 8JR
0131 557 2944
Powney, J. Dr
Effectiveness of Access courses: longitudinal study
Abstract: The aim of the project is to assess the effectiveness of science and social science access courses in preparing adults for degree level study. The research will provide a greater understanding of the strengths and weaknesses of access courses, as well as recommendations for good practice both in access courses themselves and in higher education responsiveness to access students. This is an extension of the project funded by the Leverhulme Trust.
Published Material: MUNN, P., JOHNSTONE, M. & LOWDEN, K. (1993). Students' perceptions of Access Courses: a survey. SCRE Research Report No 43. Edinburgh: Scottish Council for Research in Education.
Status: Sponsored project
Source of Grant: Scottish Office Education Department
Date of Research: 1994-continuing
KEYWORDS: *access programmes; access to education; adult students; higher education; mature students; programme evaluation; science education; social sciences*

10/1345

15 St John Street, Edinburgh EH8 8JR
0131 557 2944
Powney, J. Dr
Adult education: provision, guidance and progression. Study 3: educational guidance for adults in Scotland
Abstract: The Scottish Office Education Department is funding a large scale research project concerned with adult education in Scotland. The project is made up of four individual, yet related studies. This third study aims to: map existing guidance provision for adults; compare and contrast different approaches to provision and also to assess the effectiveness of different approaches in terms of adults who use guidance services.
Published Material: LOWDEN, K. & POWNEY, J. (1993). Where do we go from here: adult educational guidance in Scotland. SCRE Research Report No 48. Edinburgh: Scottish Council for Research in Education.
Status: Sponsored project
Source of Grant: Scottish Office Education Department
Date of Research: 1992-1993
KEYWORDS: *access to education; adult education; adult students; educational guidance; mature students; Scotland*

10/1346

15 St John Street, Edinburgh EH8 8JR
0131 557 2944
Black, H. Mr; Devine, M. Mrs

Evaluation of technology-based learning in medicine

Abstract: Evaluation of a three year project on technology-based learning in medicine. The project is to be carried out by a consortium of seven medical schools in the UK.

Status: Sponsored project
Source of Grant: Universities Funding Council
Date of Research: 1992-continuing
KEYWORDS: computer-assisted learning; computer uses in education; educational technology; medical education; medicine

10/1347

15 St John Street, Edinburgh EH8 8JR
0131 557 2944
Powney, J. Dr; Lowden, K. Mr

External evaluation of school health programme

Abstract: This is an evaluation (undertaken on behalf of the Greater Glasgow Health Board) of two schools programmes: 1) Drugs and Alcohol Education Programme; 2) Sexual Health Programme. The purpose of the evaluation is to provide insights into the effectiveness of each programme in achieving its objectives. This external evaluation will complement an internal evaluation being carried out as an integral part of the two youth health projects. The main aims of the evaluation are to: 1) examine acceptability and suitability of the two programmes for both teaching staff and pupils; 2) assess the success of the programmes in improving both pupil and teacher awareness and understanding of the subject matter; 3) assess the ability of both programmes to develop relevant skills in pupils (such as decision-making skills in various drug-related scenarios); 4) examine the extent to which the methods being piloted might have more widespread applicability in terms of use in other schools and in other health related programmes.

Published Material: LOWDEN, K. & POWNEY, J. (1994). Drugs, alcohol and sex education: a report on two innovative school-based programmes. SCRE Research Report No 59. Edinburgh: Scottish Council for Research in Education.
Status: Sponsored project
Source of Grant: Greater Glasgow Health Board
Date of Research: 1993-1994
KEYWORDS: alcohol education; drug education; health education; programme evaluation; sex education

10/1348

15 St John Street, Edinburgh EH8 8JR
0131 557 2944
Munn, P. Mrs

Economic and Social Research Council adult education research seminar series

Abstract: This aims to raise the profile of adult education research. A newsletter will be produced and seminars will take place three times a year. The work is carried out in collaboration with the Centre for Continuing Education of Edinburgh University.

Status: Sponsored project
Source of Grant: Economic and Social Research Council
Date of Research: 1993-1994
KEYWORDS: adult education; educational research

10/1349

15 St John Street, Edinburgh EH8 8JR
0131 557 2944
Hall, J. Dr; Fenwick, N. Ms

Evaluation of the further and higher education charter

Abstract: This project will evaluate the impact of the Further and Higher Education Charter on students and staff in higher education institutions and on employers who have contact with them. It will examine the quality and relevance of the information made available to client groups; the impact of the Charter on practice in higher education institutes; and the implementation of procedures designed to address problems, difficulties or grievances.

Status: Sponsored project
Source of Grant: Scottish Office Education Department
Date of Research: 1994-continuing
KEYWORDS: educational quality; further education; higher education; industry higher education relationship; institutional role; performance contracts; programme evaluation

10/1350

15 St John Street, Edinburgh EH8 8JR
0131 557 2944
Supervisor: Munn, P. Mrs

Scottish schools anti-bullying initiative

Abstract: The Scottish Schools Anti-Bullying (SSAB) Initiative: 1) provides advice to schools about anti-bullying strategies; 2) works with education authorities developing anti-bullying strategies; 3) provides information about anti-bullying strategies to interested parties within and without Scotland; and 4) carries out school-based studies, with the object of producing materials suitable for a range of audiences including schools, parents and student teachers.

Published Material: MELLOR, A. (1990). Bullying in Scottish secondary schools. SCRE Spotlight No 23. Edinburgh: Scottish Council for Research in Education.; MELLOR, A. (1994). Finding out about bullying. SCRE Spotlight No 43. Edinburgh: Scottish Council for Research in Education.
Status: Sponsored project
Source of Grant: Scottish Office Education Department
Date of Research: 1993-1994
KEYWORDS: bullying; discipline policy; discipline problems; Scotland

10/1351

15 St John Street, Edinburgh EH8 8JR
0131 557 2944
Black, H. Mr

TVEI skills: an evaluation

Abstract: The development of skills such as problem solving, working individually and in teams, communication and taking responsibility has been given considerable prominence by the Technical and Vocational Education Initiative (TVEI). The purpose of the project is to clarify the ways in which this development has been nurtured and to explore the views of teachers and young people as to its success. There are three main aspects of the study. The first is qualitative in nature, a small number of vignettes of interesting practice will be reported to provide practitioners with a range of ideas which they might wish to use in their own schools and classrooms. This will be followed by a survey of nationally representative sample of secondary schools and colleges of further education. Employers will also be surveyed for their views. The third aspect is to consider the extent to which the target skills are introduced and developed across special education in one authority.

Status: Sponsored project
Source of Grant: Scottish Office Education Department; TVEI Unit, jointly £35,000
Date of Research: 1993-1994
KEYWORDS: industry-education relationship; programme evaluation; skills; TVEI; vocational education

10/1352

15 St John Street, Edinburgh EH8 8JR
0131 557 2944
Powney, J. Dr

School development planning

Abstract: This project will monitor school development planning in action and so provide empirical evidence of strategies and solutions adopted. It will disseminate examples of effective practice and assist schools in their planning and evaluation.

Status: Sponsored project
Source of Grant: Scottish Office Education Department £19,405
Date of Research: 1992-1993
KEYWORDS: educational planning; school-based management

10/1353

15 St John Street, Edinburgh EH8 8JR
0131 557 2944
Black, H. Mr

Dental training guide: an evaluation

Abstract: Vocational training schemes aim to provide new graduates with the opportunity to refine their technical skills and develop a 'dentist's persona'. The Training Guide was developed to support the one-to-one training relationship between the recent graduate, the trainee, and the experienced general practitioner who had assumed the role of trainer. The evaluators found that the guide was less well used than it might have been, and considered ways in which a guide might fit into the 'socially-oriented' structure of the training year.

Published Material: BLACK, H., BANKOWSKA, A., WATSON,

G. (1992). The dental training guide: an evaluation. SCRE Research Report No 42. Edinburgh: Scottish Council for Research in Education.
Status: Sponsored project
Source of Grant: Scottish Council for Post Graduate Medical Education
Date of Research: 1992-1992
KEYWORDS: dental education; teaching guides

10/1354
15 St John Street, Edinburgh EH8 8JR
0131 557 2944
Munn, P. Mrs
Discipline support pack
Abstract: The aim of the project is to review the existing evidence concerning the establishment and maintenance of good discipline in schools and to use this as a basis for the production of a resource pack for use in primary and secondary schools in Scotland. This includes the trialling of the pack in a limited number of schools.
Published Material: MUNN, P., JOHNSTONE, M., WATSON, G. & EDWARDS, L. (1993). Action on discipline in the primary school: a support pack. Edinburgh: Scottish Council for Research in Education. MUNN, P., JOHNSTONE, M., WATSON, G. & EDWARDS, L. (1993). Action on discipline in the secondary school: a support pack. Edinburgh: Scottish Council for Research in Education.
Status: Sponsored project
Source of Grant: Scottish Office Education Department £20,631
Date of Research: 1992-1993
KEYWORDS: classroom discipline; discipline; discipline policy; educational materials

10/1355
15 St John Street, Edinburgh EH8 8JR
0131 557 2944
Black, H. Mr
Customers' views of further education lecturer training
Abstract: The research aims to explore and analyse the views of further education lecturers who have completed the Certificate in Education and further education qualifications in the last five years on the strengths, weaknesses and relevance of the courses. It will also provide a comparison of current Scottish provision in this area with equivalent courses in England and Wales.
Published Material: HALL, J. (1993). Customers' views of further education lecturer training. SCRE Research Report No 49. Edinburgh: Scottish Council for Research in Education. HALL, J. & MIMGARD, S. (1993). Training courses for further education college lecturers. SCRE Research Report No 50. Edinburgh: Scottish Council for Research in Education.
Status: Sponsored project
Source of Grant: Scottish Office Education Department: SCRE contract
Date of Research: 1992-1992
KEYWORDS: course evaluation; further education teachers; teacher attitudes; teacher education

10/1356
15 St John Street, Edinburgh EH8 8JR
0131 557 2944
Munn, P. Mrs
Adult education in the UK: policy, provision and practice
Abstract: Part of the process of developing a synthesis paper on adult education in European Community member states.
Published Material: BLAIR, A., McPAKE, J. & MUNN, P. (1993). Facing Goliath: adults' experiences of participation, guidance and progression in education. SCRE Research Report No 46. Edinburgh: Scottish Council for Research in Education.; MUNN, P., TETT, L. & ARNEY, N. (1993). Negotiating the labyrinth: progression opportunities for adult learners. SCRE Research Report No 47. Edinburgh: Scottish Council for Research in Education.; LOWDEN, K. & POWNEY, J. (1993). Where do we go from here? Adult educational guidance in Scotland. SCRE Research Report No 48. Edinburgh: Scottish Council for Research in Education.; BLAIR, A., MCPAKE, J. & MUNN, P. (1994). Adults in schools. SCRE Research Report No 58. Edinburgh: Sottish Council for Research in Education.
Status: Sponsored project
Source of Grant: European Community
Date of Research: 1991-1993
KEYWORDS: adult education

10/1357
15 St John Street, Edinburgh EH8 8JR
0131 557 2944
Harlen, W. Prof.; Powney, J. Dr
Provision for pre-fives in Scotland
Abstract: The research will examine a range of types of pre-school provision in relation to the implications for each setting of the 5-14 programme. Relevant aspects are: the curriculum; types of activitiy for pre-fives; record keeping; and home/school links. It will also consider how best to assess quality of different types of provision; how children with special needs are catered for; whether earlier diagnosis and intervention are leading to better adjustment and progress; the implications for subsequent support in schools; and the current costs/benefits (pros/cons) of the different provisions.
Status: Sponsored project
Source of Grant: Scottish Office Education Department £73,933
Date of Research: 1992-1994
KEYWORDS: early childhood education; preschool education; Scotland

10/1358
15 St John Street, Edinburgh EH8 8JR
0131 557 2944
Thorpe, G. Mr
Factors influencing entry to higher education
Abstract: The two main aims of this research are: 1) To assess the changes since 1991 in the social class and parental occupation of school leavers, determining the relationships between social class and measures of parental education with staying on at school, school qualifications, application to enter higher education, and entry to higher education. 2) To determine the best means of projecting entry to higher education.
Status: Sponsored project
Source of Grant: Scottish Office Education Department £15,470
Date of Research: 1992-1993
KEYWORDS: access to education; higher education; socioeconomic background; student recruitment

10/1359
15 St John Street, Edinburgh EH8 8JR
0131 557 2944
Munn, P. Mrs
Entry requirements for higher education
Abstract: This project aims to identify the formal published higher education entry (HE) requirements for a sample of faculties/courses covering both general entry requirements for each HE institution and the faculty requirements. It also aims to clarify the application of these rules and describe any arrangements for exemption from parts of courses for candidates with certain qualifications, e.g. HND or GCE 'A' levels. Finally, it will provide an indication of the incidence of special classes in HE to bring candidates up to an adequate level of attainment to cope on the mainstream course.
Status: Sponsored project
Source of Grant: Scottish Office Education Department
Date of Research: 1992-1993
KEYWORDS: access to education; admission criteria; higher education; student recruitment

10/1360
15 St John Street, Edinburgh EH8 8JR
0131 557 2944
Black, H. Mr
Evaluation of compacts in Scotland
Abstract: The compact initiative involves collaboration between education and industry. Its key elements include an enhancement of school industry links and the introduction of a 'job or training guarantee'. This offers young people a job or training leading to a job if they meet negotiated objectives. The project is investigating the experience of students, teachers and employers in the first two years of the programme.
Published Material: BLACK, H., FENWICK, N. & MINGARD, S. (1993). Compacts in Scotland: a first evaluation. Glasgow: Scottish Enterprise.
Status: Sponsored project
Source of Grant: Scottish Enterprise £23,796
Date of Research: 1991-1992
KEYWORDS: industry-education relationship; programme evaluation; school to work transition; vocational education; work-education relationship

10/1361
15 St John Street, Edinburgh EH8 8JR
0131 557 2944
Harlen, W. Prof.
Development programme 5-14: implementation of the guidelines on the curriculum and assessment in primary schools – an evaluation
Abstract: This project is one of four coordinated evaluation projects relating to the implementation of the 5-14 Development Programme. It focuses on the impact of the new curriculum on teachers, pupils and parents, gathering information through indepth visits to schools and a more widely spread questionnaire. The purpose is formative, providing information about strengths and weaknesses of various practices and building up descriptions of effective practice in particular circumstances.
Published Material: HARLEN, W. (1994). Implementing 5-14: a progress report. Interchange No 23. Edinburgh: Scottish Office Education Department.
Status: Sponsored project
Source of Grant: Scottish Office Education Department £107,936
Date of Research: 1991-continuing
KEYWORDS: assessment; curriculum development; primary secondary education; programme evaluation

10/1362
15 St John Street, Edinburgh EH8 8JR
0131 557 2944
Thorpe, G. Mr
Research services unit
Abstract: The Research Services Unit is analysing questionnaires for the Scottish Office Education Department on national assessment. The Unit has also conducted survey analyses for Wellpark Consultancy Services and provided a technical consultancy to the Psychological Corporation on the development of a new achievement test.
Status: Sponsored project
Source of Grant: Scottish Council for Research in Education
Date of Research: 1993-1994
KEYWORDS: educational research; statistical surveys

10/1363
15 St John Street, Edinburgh EH8 8JR
0131 557 2944
Powney, J. Dr
Monitoring the Moray House pilot PGCE (Secondary) course
Abstract: The main aims of the study are to describe some of the advantages and disadvantages of increasing school experience time and to identify the implications of this change for the different partners involved in pre-service teacher training.
Published Material: POWNEY, J., EDWARD, S., HOLROYD, C. & MARTIN, S. (1993). Monitoring the pilot: the Moray House Institute PGCE (Secondary). SCRE Research Report No 52. Edinburgh: Scottish Council for Research in Education.; POWNEY, J., EDWARD, S., HOLROYD, C. & MARTIN, S. (1993). Towards more school based training? Interchange No 20. Edinburgh: Scottish Council for Research in Education/Scottish Office Education Department.
Status: Sponsored project
Source of Grant: Scottish Office Education Department
Date of Research: 1992-1993
KEYWORDS: postgraduate certificate in education; preservice teacher education; teaching practice

10/1364
15 St John Street, Edinburgh EH8 8JR
0131 557 2944
Johnstone, M. Mrs
Teachers' workload and associated stress
Abstract: This project aims to provide: a snap-shot of teacher workload in different schools (i.e. nursery, primary, secondary) and at different levels of responsibility together with some breakdown of the workload in terms of context, time spent in various tasks, and potential stress.
Published Material: JOHNSTONE, M. (1993). Teachers workload and associated stress. SCRE Research Report No 53. Edinburgh: Scottish Council for Research in Education.; JOHNSTONE, M. (1993). Time and tasks: teacher workload and stress. SCRE Spotlight No 44. Edinburgh: Scottish Council for Research in Education.;

JOHNSTONE, M. (1993). Teachers' workload and associated stress. Edinburgh: Educational Institute of Scotland.
Status: Sponsored project
Source of Grant: Educational Institute of Scotland
Date of Research: 1992-1993
KEYWORDS: stress – psychological; teacher role; teacher workload; time management

10/1365
15 St John Street, Edinburgh EH8 8JR
0131 557 2944
Black, H. Mr
The teaching of foreign languages for vocational purposes in further education
Abstract: The overall aim is to identify evidence and analyse the effectiveness of different teaching approaches in order to provide practical advice for further education colleagues and others wishing to improve their provision. It will examine: 1) teaching approaches used in particular vocational contexts, eg catering, computing or engineering; 2) how foreign language skills for vocational purposes are assessed; 3) the evidence as to the effectiveness of different teaching approaches and those approaches considered most effective by lecturers and students.
Published Material: HALL, J. & BANKOWSKA, A. (1994). Vocational languages: foreign languages for vocational purposes in further and higher education. SCRE Research Report No 56. Edinburgh: Scottish Council for Research in Education.; HALL, J. & BANKOWSKA, A. (1994). Foreign languages for vocational purposes in further and higher education. Interchange No 25. Edinburgh: Scottish Office Education Department.
Status: Sponsored project
Source of Grant: Scottish Office Education Department £20,966
Date of Research: 1992-1993
KEYWORDS: further education; languages for specific purposes; modern language studies; second language teaching; vocational education

10/1366
15 St John Street, Edinburgh EH8 8JR
0131 557 2944
Munn, P. Mrs
Truancy in Scottish secondary schools
Abstract: This survey of attendance in secondary school was carried out as part of a national consultative exercise on truancy. It was based on a representative sample of one in eight Scottish secondary schools (50 schools) drawn up by the Scottish Division of the Scottish Office Education Department. This survey was complemented by a small number of case studies of schools' policies and practice.
Published Material: MUNN, P. & JOHNSTONE, M. (1992). Truancy and attendance in Scottish secondary schools. SCRE Spotlight No 38. Edinburgh: Scottish Council for Research in Education.
Status: Sponsored project
Source of Grant: Scottish Office Education Department; SCRE Contract Scottish Office Education Department £3,000
Date of Research: 1991-1992
KEYWORDS: attendance; pupil behaviour; Scotland; secondary schools; truancy

10/1367
15 St John Street, Edinburgh EH8 8JR
0131 557 2944
Black, H. Mr
5-14 diagnostic procedures
Abstract: As part of the 5-14 development programme, national guidelines on assessment have been issued (1991), and national tests in English language and mathematics were introduced in 1990. These were aimed primarily at improving teachers' assessments of children's progress for reporting to parents and to improve learning and teaching. This study will produce materials to help teachers identify what underlies pupils' performances so that they can build on strengths and overcome weaknesses. The project will review existing diagnostic materials and 'by building on existing research and teaching practice' will develop diagnostic units on selected aspects of learning in language, mathematics and science. Later stages of the project may cover other areas of the curriculum.
Published Material: BLACK, H.D. (1993). Taking a closer look at mathematics – around town: a resource pack for teachers. Edinburgh:

Scottish Council for Research in Education.; BLACK, H.D., DEVINE, M.S. & PEARSON, M. (1993). Taking a closer look at mathematics – space: fact and fiction: a resource pack for teachers. Edinburgh: Scottish Council for Research in Education.
Status: Sponsored project
Source of Grant: SCRE; Scottish Office Education Department, jointly £19,500
Date of Research: 1991-1993
KEYWORDS: achievement tests; assessment; primary-secondary education; school based assessment

10/1368
15 St John Street, Edinburgh EH8 8JR
0131 557 2944
Black, H. Mr
Health education in schools
Abstract: This project will review the nature and extent of provision for health education and health promotion in primary and secondary schools. It will also review the support available to schools from education authorities, health boards and other bodies.
Published Material: DEVINE, M. (1993). Encouraging healthy living: health education in Scottish schools. SCRE Spotlight No 41. Edinburgh: Scottish Council for Research in Education.; DEVINE, M., BLACK, H. & GRAY, D. (1993). Health education in Scottish schools: a survey of primary and secondary schools. SCRE Research Report No 44. Edinburgh: Scottish Council for Research in Education.
Status: Sponsored project
Source of Grant: Scottish Office Education Department; SCRE Contract
Date of Research: 1992-1993
KEYWORDS: health education; health promotion; pupil needs; Scotland

10/1369
15 St John Street, Edinburgh EH8 8JR
0131 557 2944
South Bank University, 103 Borough Road, London SE1 0AA
0171 928 8989
Powney, J. Dr; Farish, M. Ms; McPake, J. Ms; *Supervisor:* Weiner, G. Prof.
Equitable staffing policies in further and higher education
Abstract: This project will explore the strategies deployed by further and higher educational institutions committed to developing and implementing equitable staff policies and practices. Further it will disseminate examples of good practice for information to other institutions. The specific aims of the project are to: (1) develop understanding of the policies and practices which enhance the promotion of under-represented groups, e.g. female and black and ethnic minority staff in educational institutions; (2) encourage wider implementation and evaluation of such policies and practices; (3) develop understanding of processes of change by drawing together theoretical and emprical work in the fields of equal opportunities and the study of organisations; and (4) contribute to understanding and utilisation of evaluative case-study methodologies.
Published Material: FARISH, M., MCPAKE, J., POWNEY, J., & WEINER, G. Equal opportunities in colleges and universities: towards better practices. Buckingham: Open University Press. (in press).
Status: Sponsored project
Source of Grant: Economic and Social Research Council £36,930
Date of Research: 1991-1994
KEYWORDS: academic staff; academic staff promotion; employment opportunities; equal opportunities – jobs; further education; higher education

Sheffield Hallam University

10/1370
School of Urban and Regional Studies, Pond Street, Sheffield S1 1WB
01142 720911
York University, Department of Educational Studies, Heslington, York YO1 5DD
01904 430000
Grainger, N. Mr; *Supervisor:* Davies, I. Dr

European citizenship rights and higher education
Abstract: The research is in its initial stage, and a literature review is currently being undertaken of citizenship rights in Europe and educational issues. Preliminary questions include 'What are the rights and responsibilities of people working or seeking work in Europe?' This question leads to the issue – Are they the best? People have views on what their rights should be. The European Community view could be identified from its documentation. The views of experts would be sought on European higher education and citizenship and also the views of some students in the light of their experiences on exchanges, overseas placements etc. Following the above interviews or discussions, there would be an examination of implications for education, for example, types of education, and also possibly for other matters relating to vocational issues or culture identity. Issues which may be raised, could include those that students regard as essential for making their experiences more full in relation to concepts of European citizenship.
Status: Individual research
Date of Research: 1993-continuing
KEYWORDS: citizenship; Europe; higher education; overseas employment; overseas students

Sheffield University

10/1371
Department of Psychology, Sheffield S10 2TN
01142 768555
Boulton, M. Dr; Laver, R. Ms; Cowie, H. Dr;
Supervisor: Smith, P. Prof.
Prejudice, isolation and bullying: intervention in ethnically mixed classes
Abstract: Research has shown that racial prejudice, social isolation and bullying are far from uncommon during the middle school period. In a previous one year Economic and Social Research Council (ESRC) funded project, the research team found that prejudice could be ameliorated to some extent, and liking of peers increased, in classes where teachers were trained in and used cooperative group work (CGW). The central feature of this approach is the opportunity to learn through the expression and exploration of diverse ideas and the cooperative solution of problems, in groups formed across ethnic and gender barriers. In the present project, the CGW curriculum was refined and more focused in some respects, based on previous experience. An attempt was made to replicate the positive results of the previous study, using both quantitative and qualitative methods. In general, while some positive results were obtained, the research demonstrated the difficulty of cooperative group work with rejected or bullying pupils.
Published Material: BOULTON, M.J. & SMITH, P.K. (1991). 'Bullying and withdrawn children'. In: VARMA, V.P. (Ed). Truants from life: theory and therapy. London: David Fulton.; COWIE, H., BOULTON, M.J. & SMITH, P.K. (1992). 'Bullying: pupil relationships'. In: JONES, N. & JONES, E.B. (Eds). Learning to behave: curriculum and whole school management approaches to discipline. London: Kogan Page.; COWIE, H., SMITH, P.K., BOULTON, M. & LAVER, R. (1994). Cooperation in the multi-ethnic classroom. London: David Fulton.; SMITH, P.K., COWIE, H. & BERDONDINI, L. (1995). 'Cooperation and bullying'. In: KUTNICK, P. & ROGERS, C. (Eds). Groups in schools. Poole: Cassell.
Status: Sponsored project
Source of Grant: Economic and Social Research Council £82,496
Date of Research: 1990-1993
KEYWORDS: bullying; cooperation; ethnic relations; intergroup relations; intervention; middle school education; pupil behaviour; social isolation

10/1372
Department of Psychology, Sheffield S10 2TN
01142 768555
Smith, P. Prof.; Sharp, S. Ms; Ahmad, Y. Ms; Boulton, M. Dr; Cowie, H. Dr; Thompson, D. Dr
The DFE Sheffield Bullying Project: a follow up survey on bully/victim problems in one local education authority with monitoring and evaluation of the actions and interventions taken as a result of the survey
Abstract: The Department for Education (DFE) Sheffield Bullying

Project aims to identify through evaluation, ways in which schools can effectively tackle the problem of bullying. The project follows on from a survey which took place in November 1990 which monitored the nature and extent of bullying in 24 Sheffield schools (number of pupils = 6,758). Twenty three of these schools, (16 primary, 7 secondary) wished to continue with the intervention project. All of the schools have at a minimum developed a whole school anti-bullying policy which clarifies for staff, pupils and parents what bullying is and what can be done about it. Other interventions have also been explored. These include strategies for tackling bullying through the curriculum; strategies for working directly with bullies and victims; and strategies for enhancing the playground environment. Data gathered through regular monitoring, pupil and staff interviews and observation were combined with information gathered from a follow-up survey in November 1992 to indicate how successful schools have been in reducing levels of bullying, and which interventions work best. Results were encouraging with a substantial reduction in bullying in most schools. A Pack resulting from the project findings has been disseminated widely by the Department for Education.
Published Material: SHARP, S. & SMITH, P.K. (1991). 'Bullying in UK schools: the DES Sheffield Bullying Project', Early Child Development Care, No 77, pp.47-55.; COWIE, H. & SHARP, S. (1992). 'Students themselves tackle the problem of bullying', Pastoral Care in Education, Vol 10, No 4, pp.31-37.; COWIE, H., SHARP, S. & SMITH, P.K. (1992). 'Tackling bullying in schools: the method of common concern', Education Section Review, Vol 16, No 2, pp.55-57.; SHARP, S. & SMITH, P.K. (1993). 'Tackling bullying in the Sheffield Project'. In: TATTUM, D. (Ed.) Understanding and managing bullying. London: Heinemann.; SHARP, S. & SMITH, P.K. (Eds). (1994). Tackling bullying in your school: a practical handbook for teachers. London: Routledge.
Status: Sponsored project
Source of Grant: Department for Education £173,972
Date of Research: 1991-1993
KEYWORDS: *antisocial behaviour; behaviour problems; bullying; discipline; discipline policy; pupil behaviour*

10/1373
Department of Psychology, Sheffield S10 2TN
01142 768555
Mooney, S. Ms; Lewis, J. Mr; *Supervisor:* Smith, P. Prof.; Howard, S. Ms
Bullying and the dysfluent child in primary school
Abstract: Bullying has long been a matter of concern for schools in the UK; 27% of primary school children report being bullied 'at least sometimes'. Victims of bullying often suffer a loss of self-esteem and self-confidence and many are exposed to constant torment at school. Research carried out in 1992 found that children with special educational needs were bullied more than their mainstream peers. Children who bully may view certain characteristics as a pretext for bullying. One such pretext is stammering. Pupils who stammer appear to be easy targets for children who bully and they may find it difficult to adequately defend themselves, especially in distressful situations. They are also less likely to report incidents of bullying. Questionnaires completed by dysfluent individuals revealed that 85% were bullied at some period in their school lives, and that the bullying was most often related to their stammer. The aim of this project was to develop a package for teachers and speech and language therapists which focused on bullying and dysfluent children. If class pupils come to an understanding of the distress bullying causes, then the problem is more easily tackled. This would involve creating the correct class climate in which children feel secure enough to address such issues. The package provides information on bullying and stammering, although the main body of the pack comprises cooperative group work material. Based on the National Curriculum, these activities focus on topics such as self-esteem, trust building, empathy etc. Information is provided on assertiveness training and ways of tackling persistent bullying. The goal therefore is to change the class environment and to make teachers and pupils more aware of both bullying and stammering.
Published Material: MOONEY, S. & LEWIS, J. Bullying and the dysfluent child in primary school. A pack to help teachers with a dysfluent child in their class and speech and language therapists working with small groups of dysfluent children. London: Association for Stammerers. (in press).; MOONEY, S. & SMITH, P.K. 'Bullying and the child who stammers', British Journal of Special Education. (in press).
Status: Sponsored project

Source of Grant: Association for Stammerers £5,000
Date of Research: 1993-1994
KEYWORDS: *antisocial behaviour; behaviour modification; behaviour problems; bullying; classroom environment; intervention; speech handicaps; stuttering*

10/1374
Department of Psychology, Sheffield S10 2TN
01142 768555
Madsen, K. Ms; *Supervisor:* Smith, P. Prof.
Perceptions of bullying by children, teachers and parents
Abstract: Within the last few years much research has been done in the area of bullying but as yet no systematic analysis of persons' perceptions of the concept of 'bullying' has been carried out. This study is divided into two parts. The first is investigating: age differences, gender differences; bullying/victim perceived status; and people's perceptions of the concept of bullying. One hundred and fifty nine participants, aged 5/6, 9/10, 15/16 and 18-adult, were individually interviewed. They were asked to define the term bullying. Based on elements traditionally associated with the term 'bullying', twenty-six hypothetical scenarios were developed, and participants were asked whether or not they felt each was a bullying incident and why they had given that answer. Participants were then asked: 1) Who do you think can bully? 2) Who do you think can get bullied? 3) Why do you think people bully other people? 4) Can you give me some examples of bullying? Finally participants were again asked to define the term 'bullying'. A coding system based on content analysis and previous research ideas has been devised for each of the five questions. Age and gender differences have been examined. In the second part of the study, this methodology is being applied to compare teachers (n = 40) and parents (n = 40).
Published Material: MADSEN, K. & SMITH, P.K. (1993). 'Age x gender differences in participants' perception of the concept of the term 'bullying'. Poster presented at VIth European Conference on Developmental Psychology, University of Bonn, Germany, 1993.; MADSEN, K. & SMITH, P.K. (1994). 'Age x gender differences in participants' perception of why people bully'. Poster presented at the International Society for the Study of Behavioural Development XIIIth Biennial Meetings, Amsterdam, The Netherlands, 1994.; MADSEN, K. & SMITH, P.K. (1994). 'Teacher and parent perceptions of why people bully other people'. Paper presented at the Annual Conference of the Developmental Section of the British Psychological Section, University of Portsmouth, 1994.
Status: Individual research
Date of Research: 1992-continuing
KEYWORDS: *antisocial behaviour; attitudes; behaviour problems; bullying; parent attitudes; pupil attitudes; teacher attitudes*

10/1375
Department of Psychology, Sheffield S10 2TN
01142 768555
Eslea, M. Mr; *Supervisor:* Smith, P. Prof.
Pupils, parents and teachers: building a united opposition to bullying
Abstract: Between 1990 and 1992, seventeen primary schools took part in the Department for Education (DFE) funded Sheffield Bullying Project. They developed whole-school policies against bullying, and were supported in various other interventions. The current research is intended to investigate the long-term effectiveness of anti-bullying work in these schools, both in changing the nature and extent of bullying, and in changing attitudes to bullying and involving parents in anti-bullying work. Interviews were held with headteachers and other staff in twelve of the schools, describing the development of each anti-bullying policy, and the use of other interventions. Four schools then administered the Olweus questionnaire to all Year 3 to Year 6 pupils (n = 675), as they had done in 1990 and 1992. The results of this survey will be compared with both previous surveys, so that any differences in bullying behaviour or attitudes may be identified. Differences found may then be related to the anti-bullying work done, as described in the interviews, giving a measure of the relative effectiveness of the different policies and interventions. These findings will guide a second series of interviews, with a broader range of subjects including pupils, parents, lunchtime supervisors and other staff. It is intended to follow the new intake of pupils in September 1994 to examine the way each child (and their family) is introduced to the school's policy on bullying, and how their attitudes to bullying change.
Published Material: WHITNEY, I. & SMITH, P.K. (1993). 'A

survey of the nature and extent of bullying in junior/middle and secondary schools', Educational Research, Vol 35, No 1, pp.3-25.
Status: Individual research
Date of Research: 1993-continuing
KEYWORDS: antisocial behaviour; attitudes; bullying; discipline policy; parent attitudes; school policy; teacher attitudes

10/1376

Department of Psychology, Sheffield S10 2TN
01142 768555
Tapton Mount School for the Blind, 20 Manchester Road, Sheffield S10 5DG
01142 667151
Spencer, C. Dr; Blades, M. Dr; Ungar, S. Mr
Evaluation of mobility education for young blind children
Abstract: The researchers' previous work on the education for mobility of the visually handicapped has included: (1) development of spatial concepts; (2) the hierarchy of skills underlying successful mobility; (3) the evaluation of experimental programmes to improve aspects of training; and (4) the evaluation of tactile maps in learning a novel area. One such project – on the parental approach to independence and mobility skills for children prior to school – has led the researchers to embark upon the present project, which will study children through the years prior to entry to blind school, and their first few years of formal mobility training within the school. Research will be conducted in conjunction with Tapton Mount, the special school for the visually handicapped in Yorkshire and surrounding counties. The aim is to plan and test mobility training programmes designed to develop the child's techniques for (1) acquiring and storing knowledge of spatial layout; (2) updating one's position within a locale; and (3) applying systems of spatial concepts to plan routes. In 1994 an Economic and Social Research Council (ESRC) grant will extend this work into the training of blind adults.
Published Material: BLADES, M. & SPENCER, C.P. (1990). 'The development of 3-6 year olds' map using ability: the relative importance of landmarks and map alignment', Journal of Genetic Psychology, No 151, pp.181-194.; MORSLEY, K., SPENCER, C.P. & BAYBUTT, K. (1991). ' Is there any relationship between a child's body image and spatial skills?' British Journal of Visual Impairment, No 9, pp.41-43.; MORSLEY, K., SPENCER, C.P. & BAYBUTT, K. (1991). 'Two techniques for encouraging movement and exploration in the visually impaired child', British Journal of Visual Impairment, No 9, pp.75-78.; SPENCER, C., MORSLEY, K., UNGAR, S., PIKE, E. & BLADES, M. (1992). 'Developing the blind child's cognition of the environment: the role of direct experience and map given experience', Geoforum, No 23, pp.191-197.
Status: Sponsored project
Source of Grant: Economic and Social Research Council
Date of Research: 1990-1993
KEYWORDS: blindness; mobility aids; visual impairments; visually handicapped mobility

10/1377

Division of Education, 388 Glossop Road, Sheffield S10 2JA
01142 768555
Wilcox, B. Mr; *Supervisor:* Gray, J. Prof.
Assessing the effects of local education authority programmes to monitor and evaluate the quality of schooling
Abstract: The aims of the research are to: (1) obtain a national picture of the approaches to monitoring and evaluation being established by local education authorities (LEAs) with a view to developing a typology of approaches and to understanding their different rationales; (2) establish the perceived advantages, disadvantages, costs and benefits of these various approaches; and (3) explore the effects of different approaches represented in the typology on schools' practices and development, both in the short and medium term. The research methods involved are: (1) A questionnaire survey of LEAs in England and Wales directed at chief advisers/inspectors in order to establish the broad patterns of evaluation activities being undertaken. The survey will be carried out at the beginning of the project and again towards the end. (2) A panel study based on a one-in-five sample of chief advisers/inspectors. Individual interviews will be conducted on three occasions throughout the project. The study will play an important part in helping to understand the development of different approaches to evaluation, their rationales and their effectiveness in bringing about changes in schools. (3) Detailed case studies based on a number of primary and secondary schools, in different LEAs, which have recently undergone a major evaluation

exercise. Interviews will be carried out on those centrally involved (e.g. inspectors/advisers, teaching staff). Interviews will also be conducted on a second occasion approximately six months after the completion of the evaluation. Additionally for a sample of the secondary schools, a third stage of interviews will be included to assess any longer term effects of the evaluations.
Status: Sponsored project
Source of Grant: Economic and Social Research Council £106,470
Date of Research: 1991-1994
KEYWORDS: educational quality; inspection; institutional evaluation; local education authorities; school effectiveness

10/1378

Division of Education, 388 Glossop Road, Sheffield S10 2JA
01142 768555
Rudduck, J. Prof.; Harris, S. Dr
Making your way through secondary school: pupils' experiences of teaching and learning
Abstract: The project is one of a number of parallel research studies funded as part of the initiative 'Innovation and change in education: the quality of teaching and learning'. The broad aims of the research are to: (1) collect contextualised information about pupils' experiences of teaching and learning as they move through their final years of secondary schooling; (2) contribute to knowledge and understanding of the ways in which pupils perceive, make sense of and respond to the teaching and learning opportunities that their school provides. The specific aim is to examine pupils' experiences of and reactions to teaching and learning in relation to the concept of 'school career'. The research is being conducted in a single comprehensive school in three separate local education authorities (LEAs). It is developmental, using a longitudinal, interview based design and concentrates on one cohort of pupils in each school, who were 12 years old at the start of the research and will be 16 years at the end. The data is contextualised through information gathered in interviews with teachers, observation and the analysis of school records and documents. Fieldwork already undertaken over four terms has included: interviews with headteachers and members of senior management teams; interviews with the form tutor, subject teachers and pupils within the target classes, and interviews with the nominated school contact person. The researchers have also attended key events (e.g. parents' evenings) which affect their target group.
Published Material: HARRIS, S. & RUDDUCK, J. (1993). 'Establishing the seriousness of learning in the early years of secondary schooling', British Journal of Educational Psychology, (in press).
Status: Sponsored project
Source of Grant: Economic and Social Research Council £80,890
Date of Research: 1991-continuing
KEYWORDS: learning experience; pupil attitudes; pupil-school relationship; school effectiveness; secondary education; secondary school pupils; teaching process

10/1379

Division of Education, 388 Glossop Road, Sheffield S10 2JA
01142 768555
Leeds University, School of Education, Leeds LS2 9JT
01132 431751
Rudduck, J. Prof.; Taggart, L. Ms
Gender and equal opportunities in secondary schools
Abstract: The aim of the research was to identify secondary schools in urban areas which were seen to be making progress with gender at a whole-school level. Interviews were conducted with teachers (and, in some settings, with pupils) in five 'case study' schools, and with a range of teachers and advisors outside those schools whose experience was relevant to the concerns of the research. The report presents the stories told by different 'gender leaders' who took the initiative in developing a whole-school gender policy; yet also offers four profiles of different ways into the task of building a gender policy. The various threads are drawn together in one full study of the progress made – and the problems encountered – in one comprehensive school over a three year period. Major themes of the report are the tension between the individual in the institution and between accommodation and resistance.
Published Material: HARRIS, S. & RUDDUCK, J. (1991). Keeping gender on the agenda: a portfolio of material for students. Sheffield: University of Sheffield, Division of Education, QQSE Research Group.; RUDDUCK, J. (1993). Developing a gender policy in secondary schools. Milton Keynes: Open University Press.
Status: Sponsored project

Source of Grant: British Petroleum £38,000
Date of Research: 1990-1993
KEYWORDS: equal education; gender equality; school policy; secondary schools; whole school approach

10/1380
> Division of Education, 388 Glossop Road, Sheffield S10 2JA
> 01142 768555
> York University, Department of Economics and Related
> Studies, Heslington, York YO1 5DD
> 01904 430000
> Jesson, D. Mr; Mayston, D. Prof.

Developing models of educational accountability
Abstract: The research attempts to model the outputs of the secondary educational system using techniques drawn from the theory of production functions in economics. A major concern is to accommodate a wide variety of 'outputs', which, whilst including examination results, are capable of embracing other 'performance indicators'. The initial thrust has been to contrast the interpretations of previous studies using regression analysis with those obtained using data envelope analysis applied to inter-LEA studies. The phase now opening explores the potential at the intra-LEA level.
Published Material: JESSON, D., MAYSTON, D. & SMITH, P. (1987). 'Performance assessment in the education sector: educational and economic perspectives', Oxford Review of Education, Vol 13, No 3, pp.249-266.; JESSON, D. & MAYSTON, D. (1988). 'Developing models of educational accountability', Oxford Review of Education, Vol 14, No 3, pp.321-339.
Status: Sponsored project
Source of Grant: Sheffield University
Date of Research: 1987-continuing
KEYWORDS: accountability; educational quality; measurement; performance indicators; school effectiveness; secondary schools

South Bank University

10/1381
> Centre for Mathematics Education, 103 Borough Road,
> London SE1 0AA
> 0171 928 8989
> Vile, A. Mr; *Supervisor:* Lerman, S. Dr

A semiotic approach towards meaning in mathematics learning
Abstract: The aim of this project is to address the problem of meaning ascribed to mathematical concepts by mathematicians, teachers and learners both personally and socially. A theoretical framework will be developed, drawing on the work of structuralists, post-structuralists, socio-linguists and discourse analysts, that will bring together the process of internalization and the social nature of mathematical knowledge under a broad semiotic theory that describes the way in which mathematical knowledge, meaning and beliefs are assimilated. An ethnographic study of learning of mathematics by 13 year old pupils will be conducted to provide data for the analysis.
Status: Individual research
Date of Research: 1993-continuing
KEYWORDS: mathematical concepts; mathematics education

10/1382
> Centre for Mathematics Education, 103 Borough Road,
> London SE1 0AA
> 0171 928 8989
> Walker, K. Mr; *Supervisor:* Lerman, S. Dr

A socio-historical study of the development of individualized learning schemes in mathematics education, with particular reference to the Secondary Mathematics Individualized Learning Experiment (SMILE)
Abstract: The aims of the curriculum study are to document the historical development of individualized learning schemes in mathematics education, with particular reference to the Secondary Mathematics Individualized Learning Experiment (SMILE) in its social setting. The major objective of the project is the publication of a book, and associated papers, discussing the results of the research. This book will include: 1) What is SMILE? – an examination of the resources, methods and activities associated with the SMILE scheme. 2) The context of SMILE – a re-examination of developments in

British mathematics education 1900-1972 from the perspective of individualized learning. 3) The Kent mathematics project. 4) The start of SMILE (the first 5 years). 5) The growth of SMILE (issues and perspectives over the next 10 years) with curriculum analysis. 6) SMILE and the establishment (CSE, GCE, GCSE examinations and the National Curriculum). 7) SMILE in the classroom – issues and perspectives. 8) Individualized learning in the 1990's.
Published Material: WALKER, K.R. (1991). 'SMILE update'. Paper presented at the Pedagogic Text Analysis and Content Analysis Conference, Harnosand, Sweden, Nov 4-6, 1991.
Status: Individual research
Date of Research: 1991-1993
KEYWORDS: individualised methods; mathematics education; teaching methods

10/1383
> Centre for Mathematics Education, 103 Borough Road,
> London SE1 0AA
> 0171 928 8989
> London University, Institute of Education, 20 Bedford Way,
> London WC1H 0AL
> 0171 580 1122
> Finlow-Bates, K. Mr; *Supervisor:* Lerman, S. Dr;
> Morgan, C. Ms; Noss, R. Dr

Developing the notions of proof held by students, through the use of computers
Abstract: It is assumed that at the end of a degree in mathematics the students will have obtained an understanding of mathematical proof. This is despite the fact that proof is not usually explicitly taught at undergraduate level, and at secondary level is presented from a viewpoint different to that of the mathematics community. The project's aims are to investigate the potential use of the computer in developing first year undergraduate students' notions of proof, the design and evaluation of suitable teaching materials, and the development of a theory of 'learning of proof'. The project consists of four sections: 1) An evaluation and examination of philosophical, psychological, epistemological and sociological theories influencing current views of notions of proof. 2) A review of research on the role of computers in the teaching of mathematics, and the development of a methodology for the evaluation of educational computer software. 3) The design, piloting and evaluation of teaching materials. 4) The development of a theory of 'learning of proof'.
Status: Sponsored project
Source of Grant: South Bank University £21,000
Date of Research: 1992-continuing
KEYWORDS: computer microworlds; computer uses in education; mathematics education; proof – mathematics

10/1384
> Centre for Mathematics Education, 103 Borough Road,
> London SE1 0AA
> 0171 928 8989
> London University, King's College, Department of
> Education, Cornwall House Annexe, Waterloo Road,
> London SE1 3TY
> 0171 836 5454
> Winbourne, P. Mr; *Supervisor:* Lerman, S. Dr; Johnson, D. Prof.

Paradigm shifts in algebra: its nature, its learning, its teaching and its application
Abstract: Modern technology makes available new forms of representation and communication of mathematics which will influence the language and perception of mathematics and the nature of mathematical thinking. This research will first survey and discuss existing curricular paradigms. In particular, it will be concerned to survey current beliefs about the nature of algebra and of mathematical modelling. The research will build on previous work about the increasing accessibility, mediated by technology, of modelling activity and the important role that modelling should have in mathematics learning and seek to determine the level of algebraic understanding that is necessary for students to become effective modellers. Through modelling – particularly computer modelling – children can become metacognitively aware of learning processes and relate the modelling process in maths to the way we 'model' the world. The research will examine how technology can facilitate this metacognition drawing on Vygotsky's insights of the functioning of the zone of proximal development. The study and elucidation of changing curricular paradigms will parallel discussion of the development of mathematical thinking, from a historical, psychological and social perspective. An

additional question to be addressed is the neutrality or otherwise of technological development. This research will examine the implications of the existence of powerful tools such as symbol manipulators and graphical calculators for beliefs about learning and the nature of mathematics.
Status: Individual research
Date of Research: 1993-continuing
KEYWORDS: *algebra education; mathematical models; mathematics education*

10/1385
Department of Education, 103 Borough Road, London
SE1 0AA
0171 928 8989
Cambridge University, Department of Education, 17
Trumpington Street, Cambridge CB2 1QA
01223 332888
Weiner, G. Prof.; David, M. Prof.; Arnot, M. Dr
Educational reforms and gender equality in schools
Abstract: This is a one year study which involves three phases: 1) Re-analysis of existing data on gender, e.g. league tables, OFSTED and DFE statistics. 2) Survey of schools and local education authorities. A national sub-sample to gauge the impact of policy changes on gender issues. 3) Case studies of six local education authorities.
Status: Sponsored project
Source of Grant: Equal Opportunities Commission £30,000
Date of Research: 1994-continuing
KEYWORDS: *educational change; equal education; gender equality; school policy; sex differences*

10/1386
Department of Education, 103 Borough Road, London
SE1 0AA
0171 928 8989
Scottish Council for Research in Education, 15 St John Street, Edinburgh EH8 8JR
0131 557 2944
Weiner, G. Prof.; Powney, J. Dr
External evaluation of the Lambeth Technical and Vocational Education Initiative (TVEI)
Abstract: This two year project will comprise case studies of four schools involved in the Technical and Vocational Education Initiative (TVEI): a grant maintained school; a girls' secondary school; a special school; and a tuition centre. It will also include a further education college when it enters the scheme in 1994.
Status: Sponsored project
Source of Grant: Lambeth TVEI £33,000
Date of Research: 1993-continuing
KEYWORDS: *programme evaluation; TVEI*

Southampton University

10/1387
Department of Psychology, Highfield, Southampton SO9 5NH
01703 595000
Hewitt, J. Mr; *Supervisor:* Remington, B. Dr
Communication training via manual signing for non-speaking mentally handicapped children
Abstract: This is an ongoing research programme which aims to investigate the factors responsible for the development of effective communication in non-speaking children. Initially, the work focused both on children with a mental handicap and autistic children, but is now concerned primarily with mental handicap. Methods usually involve single-subject experimental designs. The role of receptive speech on expressive signing and the developments of novel sign combinations through specialised training methods have been investigated. The current interests of the research staff are in the communicative function of signing and symbol use and the investigation of transfer between requesting and naming functions.
Published Material: CLARKE, S., REMINGTON, B. & LIGHT, P. (1988). 'The role of referential speech in sign learning by mentally retarded children: A comparison of total communication and sign-alone training', Journal of Applied Behaviour Analysis, No 21, pp.419-426.; REMINGTON, B., WATSON, J. & LIGHT, P. (1990).

'Beyond the single sign: A matrix-based approach to teaching productive sign combinations', Mental Handicap Research, No 3, pp.33-50.; LIGHT, P., WATSON, J. & REMINGTON, B. (1990). 'Beyond the single sign II: The significance of sign order in a matrix-based approach to teaching productive sign combinations', Mental Handicap Research, No 3, pp.161-178.; REMINGTON, B. (1991). 'Why use single subject methods in AAC?'. In: BRODIN, J. & BJORCK-AKESSON, E. (Eds). Methodological issues in research in augmentative and alternative communication': Proceedings of the First International ISAAC Research Symposium in augmentative and alternative communication. Stockholm: Swedish Handicap Institute.; GOODMAN, J., & REMINGTON, B. (1991). 'Teaching communicative signing: Labelling, requesting and transfer of function'. In: REMINGTON, B. (Ed). The challenge of severe mental handicap: A behaviour analytic approach. Chichester: J. Wiley and Sons.
Status: Sponsored project
Source of Grant: Economic and Social Research Council
Date of Research: 1978-continuing
KEYWORDS: *communication aids – for disabled; communication disorders; manual communication; severe learning difficulties; sign language; special educational needs; symbolic language*

10/1388
Department of Sociology and Social Policy, Highfield, Southampton SO9 5NH
01703 595000
Shilling, C. Dr
Educational differentiation and social space
Abstract: Research consists firstly, of a review of the literature on the role of social space in educational differentiation with particular reference to the place of space in structuration theory. Secondly, an ethnographic study has been conducted into the use of space in two school libraries. Particular attention is given to teacher and pupil attempts to colonise and regulate this educational space.
Published Material: SHILLING, C. & COUSINS, F. (1990). 'Social use of the school library: the colonisation and regulation of educational space', British Journal of Sociology of Education, Vol 11, No 4, pp.411-430.; SHILLING, C. (1991). 'Social space, educational differentiation and gender inequalities', British Journal of Sociology of Education, Vol 12, No 1, pp.23-45.
Status: Individual research
Date of Research: 1990-1993
KEYWORDS: *equal education; personal space; school space*

10/1389
Department of Sociology and Social Policy, Highfield, Southampton SO9 5NH
01703 595000
London University, King's College, Centre for Educational Studies, Cornwall House Annexe, Waterloo Road, London SE1 3TY
0171 836 5454
Shilling, C. Dr; Ball, S. Prof.
New directions in education policy sociology
Abstract: 'New Directions in Education Policy Sociology' is a Nuffield Foundation funded conference taking place in March 1993. It is also intended that the Conference proceedings will (in part) contribute to a book, with the same title, addressing theoretical and methodological issues in the field of education policy sociology.
Status: Sponsored project
Source of Grant: Nuffield Foundation
Date of Research: 1993-1993
KEYWORDS: *educational policy; sociology of education*

10/1390
Faculty of Educational Studies, Centre for Language in Education, Highfield, Southampton SO9 5NH
01703 595000
Brumfit, C. Prof.; Mitchell, R. Dr
'Knowledge about language', language learning and the National Curriculum
Abstract: This project aims to investigate the nature of children's understanding of the nature of language and how it works, and how this is developed through experience of English/Modern Languages work in school. Teachers of English and Modern Languages have been encouraged by the Kingman Report, (Department of Education and Science Committee of Inquiry into the Teaching of English

Language (1988). Report of the Committee of Inquiry into the Teaching of English Language. London HMSO), the Language in the National Curriculum (LINC) programme, and National Curriculum programmes for their subjects, to pay more attention to developing children's knowledge about language. Traditionally however, teachers in the different language subjects have dealt with 'Knowledge about Language' (KAL) in rather different ways. Moreover, in spite of much debate, little is known about school age children's resulting knowledge and beliefs about the nature of language, and the relationship between such knowledge and the development of children's practical language skills. Fieldwork consists of case studies carried out during the school year 1991-92 in the English and Modern Languages departments of three Hampshire schools. A period of approximately 8 weeks is being spent in each school, spread over three terms. The focus is on pupils in Year 9; teachers of both subjects are being interviewed, and English/Modern Language classes are being observed and recorded, to learn how and when language matters are discussed, and in what terms. Children will also be interviewed, to explore their developing knowledge about language, and its relationship with classroom discussions and activities. The development of their language skills will also be monitored, through analysis of their day to day work, and possible links with their developing knowledge about language will be explored.
Status: Sponsored project
Source of Grant: Economic and Social Research Council £52,000
Date of Research: 1991-1993
KEYWORDS: *English studies; language skills; modern language studies*

10/1391
Faculty of Educational Studies, Centre for Language in Education, Highfield, Southampton SO9 5NH
01703 595000
Bilton, L. Miss; *Supervisor:* Mitchell, R. Dr
Adaptation in lecturing styles to audiences with English as a second language
Abstract: Lecturing to audiences in an overseas context where English is a foreign language is expanding, as new universities adopt English as the medium of instruction for science and technology. Expatriate lecturers are on the whole unprepared for their undergraduates' low level of English and consequently much of their effort in planning and delivering lectures is wasted. The aim of this research is to find out what goes on during lectures and where foreign students have particular difficulties in order to make recommendations about the adaptation of lecturing for audience needs.
Status: Individual research
Date of Research: 1989-1994
KEYWORDS: *English – second language; English for academic purposes; lecture method; overseas students; teaching styles*

10/1392
Faculty of Educational Studies, Centre for Language in Education, Highfield, Southampton SO9 5NH
01703 595000
Williams, S. Mr; *Supervisor:* Brumfit, C. Prof.
A longitudinal study of interpersonal affect in native speaker/non-native speaker interaction
Abstract: The reflexive relationship between affect and communication is implied by Berger, (BERGER, C.F. (1979). 'Beyond initial interaction: uncertainty, understanding and the development of interpersonal relationships'. In: HOWARD, G. & StCLAIR, R.N. (Eds). Language and Social Psychology. Oxford: Basil Blackwell), who suggests that communication over time is central to the development and disintegration of interpersonal relationships. This research concerns the association of interpersonal affect and various factors in native speaker (NS) non-native speaker (NNS) interaction in an academic setting. Both external and internal factors are examined, including (a) motivation; (b) discourse structure; (c) discourse quality; and (d) NNS fluency. It asks the following questions: (1) what sorts of speech events do formal conversation meetings comprise (e.g. how much is conversation and how much pedagogic discourse?); (2) are there (i) qualitative or (ii) NNS fluency differences between the conversation of dyads representing four kinds of scheme histories, namely those who, relative to other dyads, (a) get on and stop meeting; (b) get on and continue meeting; (c) do not get on and continue meeting and (d) do not get on and stop meeting. Recordings were made of a series of meetings from the English language conversation scheme organised by Southampton University Students Union.

Participants were requested to complete self-reflection sheets after each meeting and at regular intervals. The research also involved using Personal Construct Theory (PCT) repertory grids and a pragmatic oral test. The grids were used to track affective influences on the discourse, and the oral test to measure NNS language learning progress. Participants' own notions of a satisfactory conversation were also considered. Participants were also interviewed to discover language learning histories, the range of convenience of elicited PCT constructs and, at the end of the scheme, were asked for their retrospective impressions of the meetings. Transcriptions from the recordings are being analysed, and the findings will have implications for language learning and language teaching methodology.
Published Material: WILLIAMS, S. (1992). 'Playful – aloof': using personal construct theory as a measure of interpersonal affect in native speaker/non-native speaker conversation', Centre for Language in Education Occasional Paper. Southampton: University of Southampton.; WILLIAMS, S. (1992). 'The disqualified half': gender representation in a children's reading scheme'. In: BLUE, G. (Ed). Perspectives on reading, CLE Working Papers 2. Southampton: University of Southampton.
Status: Individual research
Date of Research: 1990-1993
KEYWORDS: *communication research; conversation; native speakers; second language learning; verbal communication*

10/1393
Faculty of Educational Studies, Centre for Language in Education, Highfield, Southampton SO9 5NH
01703 595000
Alansari, I. Mr; *Supervisor:* Brumfit, C. Prof.; Grenfell, M. Mr
Inservice training for English as a foreign language (EFL) teachers in Saudi Arabia
Abstract: Inservice training for English as a foreign language (EFL) teachers is becoming one of the main concerns to the Saudi educationalists. It intends to expand the knowledge of the teachers and keep them abreast with the new development in Saudi Arabian education. However, most of the inservice training activities are designed by people other than teachers. This descriptive study aims to design an inservice training (INSET) programme for secondary EFL teachers in Saudi Arabia. This programme is based on the identified INSET needs of these teachers as perceived by the teachers themselves, supervisors, school principals and specialists of teaching English as a second or other language (TESOL). It intends to seek the dissimilarities between the INSET provision in the Country on one hand and the identified needs of the secondary school EFL teachers on the other hand. These dissimilarities are eliminated by designing a substitutional theoretical INSET programme which meets the identified needs. This programme is designed by defining the main elements in terms of: objectives, materials and content, instructional methods, evaluation, and follow-up. A self-developed questionnaire, along with semi-structured interview, are used to identify the needs. The questionnaire consists of identifying seven areas: general education, language components, linguistic, methodology, pedagogy, culture, and INSET instructional methods. The investigation of the data will also take the form of interviews, conducted with small samples of the four groups of population.
Status: Individual research
Date of Research: 1992-continuing
KEYWORDS: *English – second language; inservice teacher education; Saudi Arabia; second language teaching*

10/1394
Faculty of Educational Studies, Centre for Language in Education, Highfield, Southampton SO9 5NH
01703 595000
Silveira, M. Miss; *Supervisor:* Mitchell, R. Dr
How can reading contribute to the development of English as a foreign language (EFL) in state education in Brazil?
Abstract: The research aims at analysing the role of reading in the development of English as a foreign language (EFL) in state education in Brazil. English has become of paramount importance in science and technology; thus, the ability to master the English language is nowadays a passport to reach better living standards. This research will look at the possibility of learning English by mainly focusing on the acquisition of reading skills. How can reading contribute to English? A limited time-table and lack of back-up materials are some of the underlying causes of low school achievement in foreign language teaching. An exclusive focus on oral skills has

proved inefficient. Oracity should not be the goal in the foreign language context where learners seek competence in writing and reading.

Status: Sponsored project
Source of Grant: Conselho Nacional de Desenvolvimento Cientifico e Tecnologico (CNPq – Brazil) – per month £747
Date of Research: 1992-continuing
KEYWORDS: *Brazil; English – second language; second language teaching*

10/1395

Faculty of Educational Studies, Centre for Language in Education, Highfield, Southampton SO9 5NH
01703 595000
Hamid, R. Mr; *Supervisor:* Brumfit, C. Prof.

A study of classroom practice in two Malaysian secondary schools in relation to perceived English language needs in the workplace
Abstract: Since English was relegated to the status of a second language, from that of a colonial language, Malaysia has been plagued with poor results in English, such that the aim of preparing school leavers to use English in work situations has become increasingly complex, more so as the country moves towards greater industrialisation. The research will study 'target needs' in the workplace through the use of a questionnaire survey and case studies of a small number of workers in contrasting occupations. On the basis of this information, school visits will be made covering one urban school with an ethnically mixed population and one rural school with a predominantly Malay population. Four classrooms will be observed and teachers interviewed in order to study 'process' needs. Selected pupils will also be interviewed to obtain information on their own 'subjective' needs. It is hoped that the study will throw some light on both expected target needs and process needs to enable the fashioning of programme objectives and programme content that are both meaningful and relevant.
Status: Individual research
Date of Research: 1991-1994
KEYWORDS: *English – second language; languages for specific purposes; Malaysia; second language learning*

10/1396

Faculty of Educational Studies, Centre for Language in Education, Highfield, Southampton SO9 5NH
01703 595000
Lee, Y. Mr; *Supervisor:* Mitchell, R. Dr

Developing English proficiency tests and achieving beneficial 'washback' on language teaching for communication in Korea
Abstract: Although the Korean education system is on the point of changing to accommodate communicative ideas of language teaching, many English teaching programmes are locked into the classifications imposed by the major examinations such as the standardised college entrance test of English. Since both teaching and testing are so closely interrelated that there could be a 'washback' effect of testing on language teaching and learning, it would be necessary to find an appropriate paradigm of language proficiency assessment which could implement English teaching for communication in the Korean context. At first, the research will investigate the basic considerations which underlie the practical development and use of language tests. It will specify the language abilities to be measured, define the nature of measurement and different purposes of language testing, and consider the context that determines the uses of language tests. In connection with some analyses of the current English tests, the researcher will also explore the testing methods that are used to measure a candidate's language proficiency in order to develop an appropriate proficiency test of English in Korea. Finally, further attempts will be made to see how the English proficiency test developed, by assessing the candidate's desired communicative competence, could achieve some beneficial 'washback' effect on English language teaching and learning for communication.
Status: Individual research
Date of Research: 1992-continuing
KEYWORDS: *communicative competence – languages; English – second language; Korea; language tests; second language teaching*

10/1397

Faculty of Educational Studies, Centre for Science Communication, Highfield, Southampton SO9 5NH
01703 595000
Ratcliffe, M. Mrs; Fullick, P. Mr; *Supervisor:* Kelly, P. Prof.

Issues in science and decision making
Abstract: With the implementation of the National Curriculum all pupils up to the age of 16 will be expected 'to study scientific controversies' and 'begin to understand the power and limitations of science in solving problems'. There is also a growing need to address the public understanding of science. The objectives of this research are: (1) To identify some of the features of the role of the individual in collective decision making, and to identify the particular thinking skills and capacities which individuals need in order to take decisions about science based issues. This objective to be met through – (a) literature search from fields of education, sociology, psychology and management; and (b) examination of case studies relating to decision making about science based issues in the public domain. (2) To examine, through action research in classrooms – (a) the ways in which pupils make decisions about aspects of science which affect them personally, and scientific issues which, at the time, may have only a marginal impact on their daily lives; and (b) the ways in which teachers manage this decision making process. Methodology will be observation in classes in the age range 14-18 in order to achieve objective 2. Techniques will include: observation schedules, video analysis, interviews and questionnaires involving both pupils and teachers. It is hoped to develop curriculum materials from this research.
Status: Sponsored project
Source of Grant: Southampton University: School of Education £3,000
Date of Research: 1992-1993
KEYWORDS: *decision making; National Curriculum; science education; scientific literacy*

10/1398

Faculty of Educational Studies, Centre for Science Communication, Highfield, Southampton SO9 5NH
01703 595000
Counihan, M. Dr; Fullick, P. Mr; Kelly, P. Prof.; Knight, D. Dr; Ratcliffe, M. Mrs

The interpretation and communication of science and technology in context
Abstract: This is a continuing programme of research covering the significance of science in society, the public understanding of science, the history of science and other topics. It is closely connected with the development of general courses on the nature of science for non-specialists.
Published Material: A full list of publications is available from the researcher.
Status: Sponsored project
Source of Grant: Southampton University
Date of Research: 1993-continuing
KEYWORDS: *science education; scientific literacy*

10/1399

Faculty of Educational Studies, Department of Adult and Continuing Education, Highfield, Southampton SO9 5NH
01703 595000
Counihan, M. Dr

Concepts in fundamental science: development, interpretation and communication
Abstract: This is a continuing programme of research on fundamental science in the context of adult education. It is concerned with the development and interpretation of concepts, their relevance, and their communication. The central focus is on cosmological and subnuclear phenomenon, and on how these matters can or should be interpreted to improve public understanding of science. The output from this research has taken the form of public course programmes, and is intended to be published in book form.
Status: Individual research
Date of Research: 1977-continuing
KEYWORDS: *adult education; science education*

10/1400

Faculty of Educational Studies, Department of Education, Highfield, Southampton SO9 5NH
01703 595000
Erben, M. Mr

Biography and education
Abstract: The aim of the research is to offer a disquisition on the meaning of biography. The will be realised by supporting a view that

the study of biography can develop a hermeneutical conceptualisation of how best knowledge that can be regarded as educational, is to be obtained and produced. Given that biography is a hermeneutical exercise the manner in which the objective slides into the subjective and vice versa will be developed as the protocol for a successful treatise upon biographical method. The work of Dilthey, Ricoeur, Sartre, Benjamin, Samuel Johnson, and Lacan will be examined to elaborate this exercise in cultural sociology.
Published Material: ERBEN, M. (1991). 'Geneology and sociology', Sociology, Vol 25, No 2, pp.275-292.
Status: Individual research
Date of Research: 1990-continuing
KEYWORDS: biographies; sociology

10/1401
Faculty of Educational Studies, Department of Health Education, Highfield, Southampton SO9 5NH
01703 595000
Castle, A. Mr; *Supervisor:* Weare, K. Ms
Assertion skills for radiographers
Abstract: In recent years the concept of assertion training has been the focus of growing interest as a way of enabling health professionals to improve their professional practice. This study attempted to determine whether, through the process of action research, an appropriate assertion training course could improve the assertive skills of student radiographers. Fifty-three students at the Southampton School of Radiography participated in the study over a period of three years by completing self-report assertion inventories and course evaluation exercises prior to, and on completion of an assertion training course. Control groups were established consisting of over two hundred students at other schools of radiography throughout the country. Self-report assertion inventory scores revealed that after assertion training students in Southampton had improved their assertive skills, and this was particularly evident when the performance of individual students was analysed. Students evaluated the courses as being very interesting and worthwhile exercises in the development of their interpersonal skills. It is suggested that enabling student radiographers to improve their assertive skills is an important step in their professional growth.
Status: Individual research
Date of Research: 1989-1992
KEYWORDS: assertiveness; health personnel; interpersonal competence; professional training; radiographers

10/1402
Faculty of Educational Studies, Department of Health Education, Highfield, Southampton SO9 5NH
01703 595000
Bidgood, S. Dr; *Supervisor:* Weare, K. Ms
The role of chiropractors in health education
Abstract: This research explores the role of chiropractors in health education. It aims to answer whether chiropractors should educate as well as treat their patients and if chiropractors do educate their patients in practise. The research hopes to suggest strategies for better initial and inservice training.
Published Material: BIDGOOD, S.J. (1988). A study to discover the health status at a college of chiropractic. Southampton: University of Southampton, Faculty of Educational Studies.
Status: Individual research
Date of Research: 1989-1994
KEYWORDS: allied health occupations; health education; patient education; preventive medicine

10/1403
Faculty of Educational Studies, Department of Health Education, Highfield, Southampton SO9 5NH
01703 595000
Royle, J. Mrs; *Supervisor:* Weare, K. Ms
Health promotion needs assessment
Abstract: The aim of this reserch is to discover how a Primary Health Care Team (PHCT) assesses health promotion needs and sets priorities based on the needs of the practice population. The main objective of the research is to identify the value of health promotion needs assessment. Definitions and philosophies of the concepts of health and need will be examined to provide a framework in which to explore the assessment of health promotion needs. The investigation will explore the issue of whether assessing health promotion needs is

an effective way of potentially improving the nation's health, and will develop a protocol for health promotion needs assessment by analysing the current methods of assessing these needs. A case study of a PHCT will be made using indepth interviews.
Status: Individual research
Date of Research: 1992-continuing
KEYWORDS: health education; health needs; needs assessment; primary health care

10/1404
Faculty of Educational Studies, Department of Health Education, Highfield, Southampton SO9 5NH
01703 595000
Box, V. Ms
United Kingdom primary health care cancer education/training audit
Abstract: The objectives of this research are: (i) Audit of multi-disciplinary cancer education training, topic and process, in statutory and voluntary agencies. (ii) Audit of existing resources for cancer education and prevention. (iii) Consultation with professionals about 'needs' in relation to cancer education. The methodology will involve: (a) interviewing of/by individuals at national, regional and district levels; (b) a questionnaire given to primary health care facilitators; and (c) focus group interviews with mixed groups of health professionals.
Status: Sponsored project
Source of Grant: Department of Health; Europe Against Cancer – jointly £20,000
Date of Research: 1992-1993
KEYWORDS: cancer education; health education; preventive medicine; primary health care

10/1405
Teaching Support and Media Services, Highfield, Southampton SO9 5NH
01703 595000
Smith, I. Mr; *Supervisor:* Allen, W. Mr
Optimising international links and exchange programmes between departments of photography
Abstract: This project is concerned with the study of links and exchanges as mechanisms for promoting a greater mutual understanding of the nature and structure of college and university courses in photography in Europe. The investigation involves case studies of selected interchange programmes, the establishment of a data base of European courses in photography and an analysis of the characteristics of photographic courses with a view to identifying the potential for a European Scheme for credit accumulation and transfer. The project has reached the stage of having produced a published data base of European courses in photography through the 'Photolink International' scheme which is supported by Kodak Limited and ERASMUS.
Published Material: SMITH, I.R. (1990). 'Directory of photographic education: A European survey', Photolink International.
Status: Sponsored project
Source of Grant: Kodak Limited; ERASMUS
Date of Research: 1988-1993
KEYWORDS: international educational exchange; photography

St Andrew's College of Education

10/1406
Duntocher Road, Bearsden, Glasgow G61 4QA
0141 943 1424
McGilp, J. Dr; Michael, M. Ms
The development of language through partnership and quality experiences
Abstract: The purpose of the study is threefold: (1) to provide different learning experience in language for pupils; (2) to involve parents and teacher in partnership; (3) to gain parent and pupil responses to the learning opportunities provided and to partnership. The study builds on extensive work carried out in the Australian Catholic University (Aquinas' Campus) by Dr McGilp. The research will be conducted in Clydebank. The researcher and headteacher have an established working relationship and with the senior stages teacher (P6) will collaboratively work with parents to establish partnership

through which to carry out the investigation. Qualitative and quantitative data will be obtained by questionnaire and interview. Improvements in pupil linguistic competence and the factors contributing to this will be recorded. The final published study will compare results with those in a paralleled Australian study.
Status: Sponsored project
Source of Grant: St Andrew's College of Education
Date of Research: 1993-1993
KEYWORDS: *language acquisition; language skills; learning experience; parent participation; parent-teacher cooperation*

10/1407
Duntocher Road, Bearsden, Glasgow G61 4QA
0141 943 1424
Kwiatkowski, H. Dr; Davis, R. Dr; Dixon, J. Mr; Elder, R. Mr
Partnership in the development and assessment of student teachers
Abstract: The nature of the core relationship among teacher, student and tutor and the context in which the relationship functions will be explored. From this the key factors in the relationship will be identified and a specification of roles in professional partnership as distinct from apprenticeship defined. The aims of the investigation are to determine: (i) the expectations of the participants in the partnership; (ii) the match among the expectations, needs of students and realities of placement; (iii) the key conditions in making partnership work; (iv) the nature of necessary 'contractual' understandings. Research methods will include: a review of literature followed by initial questionnaire survey; follow-up questionnaire applied to all three categories followed by interview, ethnographic observations and case studies; interviews with regional directors, observation of final placement. The expected outcome for shools will be a clear understanding of the roles of staff in the development and assessment of students together with a specification of their 'contractual' obligation. For the regions, the identification of procedures and commitments necessary to make partnership effective and clarification of how quality assurance is applied to ensure quality in the beginning teacher. For colleges, a clearer understanding of the roles of staff in developing and assessing students and of the complementary roles in partnership as well as guidance on where to target development and resources more effectively.
Status: Sponsored project
Source of Grant: Scottish Office Education Department; General Teaching Council; Tayside and Fife Regions – jointly £50,000
Date of Research: 1991-1992
KEYWORDS: *preservice teacher education; student teacher evaluation; student teacher supervisors; student teachers; teaching practice*

10/1408
Duntocher Road, Bearsden, Glasgow G61 4QA
0141 943 1424
Bourne, V. Mr; Blee, H. Mr; Barr, M. Ms; Webster, D. Mr; Dixon, J. Mr
Probationer teachers' views of college courses
Abstract: The investigation will determine how successfully the B.Ed course has been in preparing teachers for their first and second years of teaching. Strengths of the course will be identified together with suggestions for changes/additions as seen from probationer teachers' points of view. Areas for investigation will include: (1) the teacher's perception of competence and its origin; (2) the nature of the school induction programme; (3) the effectiveness of partnership between the school and St Andrew's College during B.Ed degree; (4) major gaps in course, e.g. language, positive behaviour, planning, classroom administration; (5) any difference between East/West/Tayside regions. A questionnaire will be issued to all students qualifying with a B.Ed degree from this college in the last two years. The response will be evaluated and summarised. Some interviews may be carried out to illuminate the questionnaire responses.
Status: Sponsored project
Source of Grant: St Andrew's College of Education £220
Date of Research: 1993-1993
KEYWORDS: *course evaluation; preservice teacher education; probationary teachers*

10/1409
Duntocher Road, Bearsden, Glasgow G61 4QA
0141 943 1424
Fraser, D. Mr

Evaluation of teacher placement
Abstract: The aim of the investigation is to determine the effectiveness of placement in industry in meeting the twin needs of teachers in relation to management and the curriculum. Much of the documented material in the field is exhortation, policy and rhetoric. The evaluation will be the first to go beyond description and aspiration to analysis of teachers' experience of placement. Initially a questionnaire will be sent to 1000 teachers in three Scottish Regions, this will be followed by an indepth documentary search and interview of approximately 50 teachers across the Regions. A report for Teacher Placement will be produced, which will be published nationally in 1993.
Status: Sponsored project
Source of Grant: Understanding British Industry: Teacher Placement Service £8,000
Date of Research: 1992-1992
KEYWORDS: *industrial secondments; industry-education relationship; teacher development*

10/1410
Duntocher Road, Bearsden, Glasgow G61 4QA
0141 943 1424
McKee, T. Mrs
Multicultural and anti-racist education
Abstract: The aims of the project are: (1) to carry out a review of existing College policies on multicultural and anti-racist education, and (2) to report on this and make recommendations for change where necessary. The analysis will be considered against Regional and National documentation relating to the same issues with a view to ensuring that College documentation and equality reflects these issues and prepares students for working in schools.
Status: Sponsored project
Source of Grant: St Andrew's College of Education £150
Date of Research: 1992-1992
KEYWORDS: *antiracism education; multicultural education; preservice teacher education*

10/1411
Duntocher Road, Bearsden, Glasgow G61 4QA
0141 943 1424
Ker, M. Mrs; Whyte, A. Mr
Using the school grounds
Abstract: The aims of this project are: (1) To evaluate the use of school grounds in Dunbarton Division; to compare this with recent research carried out elsewhere; and to help teachers in a selected group of schools to recognise the unique potential of each site, build on that, and challenge these teachers to fully exploit the grounds as a resource. (2) To devise strategies to assist these schools; improve the effective use of these environments involving the whole community; and to investigate the impact of these developments on pupil creativity. (3) To encourage interest in such development more widely. The project will involve students on the B.Ed 2 course 'Improving the College Grounds'. A questionnaire will be devised for students to use with pupils and teachers about their use of school grounds. The project will also involve working with the Educational Development Service, to promote the work in schools. Questionnaires and semi-structured interviews will be used in pilot schools. The outcomes of the project will include: instruments for evaluating and assessing impact of improved landscapes; a report with agenda for change; and training in the process of education authority art teachers.
Status: Sponsored project
Source of Grant: Dunbarton Division, Strathclyde £9,000; St Andrew's College of Education £120
Date of Research: 1992-1993
KEYWORDS: *campuses; educational facilities improvement; school space*

10/1412
Duntocher Road, Bearsden, Glasgow G61 4QA
0141 943 1424
Conroy, J. Mr; McClure, M. Sist.
Attitudes to religious education among college students
Abstract: The background to the research is that there has been a dearth of information as to the opinion of young adults about their school Religious Education (RE); and that there has been a national syllabus for RE extent for a number of years. The aims of the research are: (1) to discover (a) the effects of the National Syllabus on young college students; (b) the attitudes of young people in general; and (c)

the educational background against which attitudes develop; (2) To carry out comparative analysis with research completed in Europe and other parts of Britain. (3) To use the data as a springboard for a wider research project which goes beyond undergraduates. (4) To discover the efficacy of current pedagogies. The research methods will include a research questionnaire for all students; the development of a database; integration of the database using keyword/concept software; and statistical regression analysis.
Status: Sponsored project
Source of Grant: St Andrew's College of Education
Date of Research: 1992-1993
KEYWORDS: religious education; student attitudes

10/1413
Duntocher Road, Bearsden, Glasgow G61 4QA
0141 943 1424
McQueen, I. Ms
Flexible delivery of staff development
Abstract: The project was to provide information for Strathclyde Region on the provision currently available for staff development through flexible learning formats in order to meet increasing demands. The support such packages would require; the extent to which they were widely available; gaps in provision; the extent to which other authorities were generating packages; recommendations for future provision; and the creation of a database. The research involved a survey questionnaire, collation and cross referencing. The extended database was published in August 1992.
Status: Sponsored project
Source of Grant: Scottish Office Education Department; Strathclyde Region
Date of Research: 1991-1992
KEYWORDS: flexible learning; staff development

10/1414
Duntocher Road, Bearsden, Glasgow G61 4QA
0141 943 1424
Cooper, W. Mr
Control technology
Abstract: The aim of the project is to determine the extent to which upper primary school pupils are able to undertake control activities in the classroom. An action research approach will be used where pupils will be observed working on directed practical activity. Interviews of colleagues involved in the activities will also be undertaken together with evaluation of worksheets and achievement objectives.
Status: Sponsored project
Source of Grant: St Andrew's College of Education
Date of Research: 1992-1993
KEYWORDS: control technology; primary education

10/1415
Duntocher Road, Bearsden, Glasgow G61 4QA
0141 943 1424
Hutchison, M. Mrs
Science and technology in the primary school: implications of the Review and Development Group's Publication 3 (RDGP3) for curricular integration
Abstract: The aims of this research are to: (1) research existing practices in primary schools for the development of science and technology; (2) explore the problems which exist in integrating science within environmental studies in relation to the recommendations of 5-14 Review and Development Group 3; and (3) develop and pilot materials for a primary school programme in Science and Technology which will take account of existing practices and the recommendations of RDG3. The research will include: personal investigation of a sample of schools; evidence from Science and Technology Regional Organisation (SATRO); evidence from Strathclyde Regional Inspectorate; extended survey working with students as researchers in schools; design of materials; and piloting and evaluating materials. A report will be published with recommendations for policy and practice in relation to science and technology education in Scottish primary schools including specific targets and attainment levels with identified resources for achieving these.
Status: Sponsored project
Source of Grant: St Andrew's College of Education £440
Date of Research: 1992-continuing
KEYWORDS: primary education; science education; technology education

10/1416
Duntocher Road, Bearsden, Glasgow G61 4QA
0141 943 1424
McPhee, A. Mr; O'Dea, M. Mrs
The attainment of college students gaining entrance through the Scottish Wider Access Programme
Abstract: The aims of this project are: (i) to determine the attainment of Scottish Wider Access Programme (SWAP) students in College specified course objectives; and (ii) to determine the ability of SWAP students to cope with 'academic lifeskills' SWAP students will be assessed on pre-entry to College, then 'tested' during the course at two points. A control group with Scottish Certificate of Education (SCE) qualification will be established and similar investigations carried out. Results will be compared in an action research, case study approach. A report will be submitted which outlines the implications for SWAP students in College courses and for College delivery of courses. Evidence will be derived indicating whether SWAP students do indeed bring other skills to their course which complement the purely academic.
Status: Sponsored project
Source of Grant: St Andrew's College of Education
Date of Research: 1991-1992
KEYWORDS: academic achievement; access programmes; access to education; higher education; mature students; outcomes of education

10/1417
Duntocher Road, Bearsden, Glasgow G61 4QA
0141 943 1424
Naylor, A. Dr; Joyce, S. Mr
Values education in the primary curriclum
Abstract: The aim of the project is to develop materials and curricula which: (a) support the introduction of Values Education in Primary Schools; and (b) support the development of positive values and life skills in primary school children. The project is an action research one involving a range of activities which explore and analyse the effectiveness of various methods of introducing Values Education into primary schools. The focus is on active school-based (5-14) curriculum development activities with particular emphasis on: (a) Investigation and analysis of whole-school approaches to Values Education with a view to constructing a curriculum framework. (b) Preparation of appropriate resource materials for Values Education. (c) Piloting of curriculum materials and approaches to Values Education in the context of the National Guidelines (5-14). (d) Conducting a survey of developments in the primary curriculum in order to identify awareness of Values Education as it permeates the curriculum. All these developments will be conducted through a participative model with classroom teachers. (e) Establishing a working network of agencies involved in Values Education and exploring cooperative approaches. (f) An evaluation of the Gordon Cook Educational Plan in terms of (a) philosophy; (b) content; (c) process. A series of reports and publications for each of the stated activities will be produced.
Status: Sponsored project
Source of Grant: Gordon Cook Foundation £160,000
Date of Research: 1991-continuing
KEYWORDS: primary education; values education

10/1418
Duntocher Road, Bearsden, Glasgow G61 4QA
0141 943 1424
O'Brien, J. Mr; McGettrick, B. Prof.; McPhee, A. Mr;
McDonald, S. Mrs; Boyle, J. Mr; Blee, H. Mr; Luti, P.Mr
Valued forms of support for secondary school teachers in times of curriculum change and development
Abstract: The investigation examines the nature and type of support offered to teachers to facilitate curriculum change and educational development. The project will aim to identify those forms of support which have been regarded as essential, helpful and effective. It examines such initiatives as Standard Grade, Revised Higher and National Certificate. The main focus is on what can best be done centrally to: (1) provide materials and different forms of support; and (2) stimulate types of support which teachers find helpful. A triangulation approach to the illumination of the issues across a number of subjects will be used. The views and experiences of teachers in the subjects chosen will be considered in relation to three aspects of support for development: a focus on materials or subjects; a focus on school support; a focus on agencies. This will be achieved in workshop discussions, subsequent devising of a questionnaire; five case

studies; fifty schools sampled by questionnaire and structured interviews; interviews with a limited number of personnel from support agencies such as the Scottish Examination Board (SEB), Scottish Consultative Committee on the Curriculum (SCCC), Scottish Council for Educational Technology (SCET); and analysis of collected data. A report to the Scottish Office Education Department (SOED) will identify types of support viewed as valuable experiences for teachers; it may also indicate possible further investigations which could inform decision making on the support for curriculum development and change.
Status: Sponsored project
Source of Grant: Scottish Office Education Department £16,700
Date of Research: 1993-1993
KEYWORDS: curriculum development; secondary school teachers; teacher development

10/1419

Duntocher Road, Bearsden, Glasgow G61 4QA
0141 943 1424
Tiffney, A. Mrs
Drama as a curriculum stimulus in early education
Abstract: The aim of the project is to collate the evidence derived from previous activity in a number of nursery schools with a view to producing guidelines for using drama in pre-school situations.
Status: Sponsored project
Source of Grant: St Andrews's College of Education; Strathclyde Region £4,000
Date of Research: 1992-1992
KEYWORDS: drama; early childhood education; preschool education

10/1420

Duntocher Road, Bearsden, Glasgow G61 4QA
0141 943 1424
O'Brien, J. Mr
An evaluation of the operation of school boards
Abstract: This is a study of the origins of School Boards including philosophical, political and managerial aspects. One outcome of this study will be the production of training materials for School Board members.
Status: Sponsored project
Source of Grant: St Andrew's College of Education £400
Date of Research: 1990-continuing
KEYWORDS: educational administration; governing bodies; school boards – Scotland; school governors

10/1421

Duntocher Road, Bearsden, Glasgow G61 4QA
0141 943 1424
Mumford, J. Ms
Development of 5-14 Mathematics Programme
Abstract: The project aimed to find ways of illustrating how mathematics can be taught with particular reference to a current school text and in relation to 5-14 mathematics guidelines. The work included document analysis, participant observation and discussion of effective practice. A chapter for a book on 5-14 mathematics which contextualises the philosophy of the subject within current approaches resulted from the work.
Published Material: MUMFORD, J. (1993). 'Assessing with HBJ mathematics'. In: MENZIES, Y., MUMFORD, J. & SKINNER, G. Mathematics in context. London: Harcourt, Brace, Jovanovich.
Status: Sponsored project
Source of Grant: Collins Publishing
Date of Research: 1992-1993
KEYWORDS: mathematics education

10/1422

Duntocher Road, Bearsden, Glasgow G61 4QA
0141 943 1424
Gibson, D. Mr; Thomson, A. Mr
The Scottish Higher Education Funding Council (SHEFC) partnership project
Abstract: The project is to develop a flexible learning pack seeking to: strengthen the College's partnerships with schools and regional authorities; improve quality and effectiveness through the achievement of continuity of experience of student teachers from initial entry to College to the end of the probationary teaching period; and clarify

the roles and functions of all involved. The product of this work will be a resource covering: a shared undertanding of partnership; roles and responsibilities of teachers, college tutors, school mentors, and authority advisers; assessment and effective feedback; managing the partnership process. All students in all colleges of education and university departments of education, with responsibility for initial teacher training, will benefit from the pack, as will the partner schools associated with these institutions, and all schools employing probationary teachers, in both the primary and secondary sectors. Over a period of 15 months, the development of the pack will involve three phases: initial research into examples of good practice; the production of the package; and the piloting and evaluation of the materials. A development group will be formed at an early stage to steer and monitor the progress of the package, and a Committee for Partnership will arise from this group, to maintain activity in the partnerships built by the College. The package contents will contain interactive individual and group study materials appropriate to all the various facets of partnership, to be used by staff and students in colleges, by teachers and advisers in authority inservice sessions, and by teachers and senior staff in schools. It will include: CD-ROM disc; a video covering the probationary period (with cross-references to the CD-ROM); a video covering teaching practice (with cross-references to the CD-ROM); and supporting documentation.
Status: Sponsored project
Source of Grant: Scottish Higher Education Funding Council £7,000
Date of Research: 1994-1994
KEYWORDS: college-school cooperation; educational materials; flexible learning; material development; preservice teacher education

10/1423

Duntocher Road, Bearsden, Glasgow G61 4QA
0141 943 1424
Ker, M. Mrs; Adams, E. Ms
Development and use of school and college grounds
Abstract: The project aims to secure lasting and continuing improvements to the environmental quality of educational use of the land surrounding the College and the nation's schools for the benefit of teachers and children. In collaboration with Kilpatrick's Project, an evaluation of the current use and development of school grounds in the surrounding area will be undertaken.
Status: Sponsored project
Source of Grant: Strathclyde Regional Council; Rocol/Greenham Trading £300; Kilpatrick's Project £950; St Andrew's College £200; Centurian Scottish Brickworks £3,500
Date of Research: 1993-continuing
KEYWORDS: campuses; educational facilities improvement; school space

10/1424

Duntocher Road, Bearsden, Glasgow G61 4QA
0141 943 1424
Flood, M. Mrs; Lawson, D. Mr; Neilson, M. Miss
A study of the teaching and learning of biology, chemistry and physics at Standard Grade
Abstract: The teaching and learning of biology, physics and chemistry has been revolutionised by the introduction of Standard Grade. This encouraged schools in the direction of individualised learning. The aims of this project are: 1) to identify which packages for Standard Grade chemistry are in use in Strathclyde schools. 2) For those schools using Scottish Curriculum Consultative Council (SCCC) packages for the teaching of Standard Grade biology, chemistry and physics, to ascertain whether they are being used in their original or adapted format. 3) To ascertain the reasons why changes have been made. 4) To determine if schools are using a pupil centred learning approach in their teaching of the separate sciences at Standard Grade. 5) To identify how much class contact time is spent on pupil centred learning. 6) To determine teachers' views on a variety of issues (e.g. pupil progress, class management, stress levels, resource management, pupil and teacher satisfaction) concerning pupil centred learning. It is intended that a structured questionnaire which addresses the above aims will be produced and sent by post to all secondary schools in Strathclyde Region.
Status: Sponsored project
Source of Grant: Scottish Higher Education Funding Council £6,500
Date of Research: 1994-1994
KEYWORDS: biology education; chemistry education; learner centred methods; learning strategies; physics education; science education; teaching methods

10/1425

Duntocher Road, Bearsden, Glasgow G61 4QA
0141 943 1424
Gibson, D. Mr

"Profit" in staff development

Abstract: This project will be carried out in a consortium involving the Committee of Vice Chancellors and Principals, Scottish Council for Educational Technology; Glasgow University; Aberdeen University; and Glasgow College. The purpose of the investigation is to find appropriate mechanisms and strategies for developing student self-study packages utilising modern technologies and learning theories. The project will include: identification of good practice; design, production and trialling of modules; and dissemination of information and demonstrations. It will result in computer disc materials for interactive student learning and a report on the research.
Status: Sponsored project
Source of Grant: Universities Funding Council £570,000
Date of Research: 1992-continuing
KEYWORDS: educational technology; independent study; staff development

10/1426

Duntocher Road, Bearsden, Glasgow G61 4QA
0141 943 1424
Kwiatkowski, H. Dr; Dixon, J. Mr

Quality in placement for postgraduate student teachers

Abstract: The project will involve: 1) identification of an agreed view (with partners in schools) of quality experience for students on placement; 2) identification of indicates of quality on placement; 3) proposal procedures for monitoring of placement; 4) initial trialling of 2 and 3 above. The empirical study will use: questionnaires; personal constructs; techniques; interviews (structured); and structured trialling. The project will result in a report and internal guidance to college and school staff, and a published academic paper.
Status: Sponsored project
Source of Grant: St Andrew's College of Education £2,000
Date of Research: 1993-1994
KEYWORDS: educational quality; preservice teacher education; quality control; student teachers; teaching practice

10/1427

Duntocher Road, Bearsden, Glasgow G61 4QA
0141 943 1424
Bourne, V. Mr

The B.Ed. course as a preparation for teaching

Abstract: The research will investigate how successful the Bachelor of Education (B.Ed.) course has been in preparing teachers for their first and second years of teaching. It involved sending a questionnaire to B.Ed. students who have left during the past 2 years.
Status: Sponsored project
Source of Grant: St Andrew's College of Education £450
Date of Research: 1993-1994
KEYWORDS: B.Ed. degrees; course evaluation; graduate surveys; preservice teacher education

10/1428

Duntocher Road, Bearsden, Glasgow G61 4QA
0141 943 1424
Laing, A. Mr

Support for assessment. Expressive arts 5-14: art and design

Abstract: This project will build upon, within a Scottish context, the research at the University of Plymouth. The first phase is mainly data collection and will investigate the response of teachers in primary schools to the published national guidelines with the aim of addressing these difficulties and concerns, particularly in the area of assessment of pupil attainment.
Status: Sponsored project
Source of Grant: St Andrew's College of Education £500
Date of Research: 1993-1994
KEYWORDS: art education; assessment; design education

10/1429

Duntocher Road, Bearsden, Glasgow G61 4QA
0141 943 1424
Gibson, D. Mr; Thomson, A. Mr

Paediatric surgery and medicine course

Abstract: The project aims to develop open and flexible learning materials incorporating video, computer and text resources for undergraduate and postgraduate students in paediatric medicine and surgery. These materials will extend and vitalise a newly developed textbook written specifically for an existing course, freeing course staff from lectures and enabling them to increase the quality time they spend with students, while at the same time increasing student throughput. The materials will also act as a key resource in supported self-study activities associated with full-time and part-time courses.
Status: Sponsored project
Source of Grant: Glasgow University; Yorkhill Hospital Trust; Various pharmaceutical companies, jointly
Date of Research: 1993-continuing
KEYWORDS: educational materials; flexible learning; material development; medical education

10/1430

Duntocher Road, Bearsden, Glasgow G61 4QA
0141 943 1242
Thomson, A. Mr

AIDS interactive video

Abstract: This project is to develop an interactive video package dealing with the Acquired Immune Deficiency Sydrome (AIDS), sexuality and attitudes. Through a variety of media, it seeks to increase the user's knowledge of AIDS and associated diseases. The package makes use of interactive video, computer-based learning, paper-based resources, and peer-group interaction to support examination by young people and adults to their attitudes to AIDS, to sufferers and carriers of the disease, and to their own sexuality. Although there is a substantial amount of cognitive content in the materials, the greatest part of the activity of learners using the package is in terms of beliefs, feelings, perspectives, attitudes and relationships, and in the development of responsible behaviour. The materials are designed to be flexibly applied in a range of settings. It is expected that the package will be made available in a variety of public places for casual use by the general public. Additionally, small groups of learners will be able to work together on the materials, so that discussions between the participants can take place in a more structured way. Finally, in a tutor-led mode, a group is accompanied and supported by an experienced tutor, and all the materials on the disc are then accessible, some of which may be disturbing to users. A development group comprising individuals from St Andrew's College, the Scottish Community Education Council, and Northern College is working on the package.
Status: Sponsored project
Source of Grant: Smith Klein Beecham £9,000; Scottish Health Education Group £10,000; Lothian Region £5,000; Central Region £5,000
Date of Research: 1993-1994
KEYWORDS: acquired immune deficiency syndrome; educational materials; educational technology; health education; interactive video; material development; sex education

10/1431

Duntocher Road, Bearsden, Glasgow G61 4QA
0141 943 1424
McDonald, S. Mrs

A model for staff development in information technology within initial teacher training

Abstract: The Structure and Process in Teacher Education (SPRITE) initiative has given the College an opportunity to try out a new form of staff development in information technology (IT), targeting a group of staff working as a team towards a specific goal. The project involves one full-time equivalent post on IT staff development. A seconded teacher and a College staff member will focus on: 1) learning to make overlays for touch keyboard and creating overlays for a particular context; and 2) the location and piloting of resources on a theme for a class of 7 year olds.
Status: Sponsored project
Source of Grant: St Andrew's College of Education; Scottish Office Education Department
Date of Research: 1991-1993
KEYWORDS: information technology; staff development; teacher education

10/1432
Duntocher Road, Bearsden, Glasgow G61 4QA
0141 943 1424
Gibson, D. Mr; Thomson, A. Mr
Charles Rennie Mackintosh CD-ROM project
Abstract: This project aims to develop a comprehensive, high-technology visual and textual learning and teaching resource, covering the life and work of Charles Rennie Mackintosh. The materials will include photographs, drawings, articles, animations, and sound, and will be based on educational technology involving CD-ROM discs and Macintosh computers. This extensive resource will be able to be examined in both formal and informal settings: in a college or school, classes and individuals will be able to investigate aspects of Mackintosh's work in a structured way, while in an exhibition setting members of the general public will view the materials in a more casual, browsing mode. The development of this CD-ROM involves the collection, categorisation, conversion and annotation of photographs, drawings and articles, the writing of computer software and users' notes to link these resources together, the preparation of the data for the disc, and the production of the disc in appropriate quantities. A steering group of individuals from the interested organisations meet on a regular basis to oversee this work, adding expertise and direction to the project. The content and extent of the final product is being defined by this group, and the project is being managed in the College. The product of this work will be a CD-ROM package, comprising a CD-ROM disc, users' notes and additional materials. The development process will be published as a case study for future internal use. A by-product of the development procedure is a written specification for the materials which will be incorporated in the case study.
Status: Sponsored project
Source of Grant: Glasgow Museums; Hunterian Art Gallery; Glasgow School of Art, jointly £2,100; City of Glasgow £2,000; St Andrew's College of Education; Scottish Council for Educational Technology – jointly £4,500
Date of Research: 1993-1994
KEYWORDS: biographies; educational materials; educational technology; material development; optical data discs

10/1433
Duntocher Road, Bearsden, Glasgow G61 4QA
0141 943 1424
Bagnall, J. Mr
Partnership in primary religious education
Abstract: The study will be of a small number of Catholic primary schools in the East of Scotland, chosen in consultation with a diocesan and local authority advisers, and differing in features of size, catchment, number of parishes involved, and putative level of existing partnership. The information is gathered from church documents, by research reading, and a consultation from partnerships in the parishes, both by questionnaire and by documented interview.
Status: Sponsored project
Source of Grant: St Andrew's College of Education
Date of Research: 1993-1994
KEYWORDS: Catholic schools; church and education; primary schools; religious education

10/1434
Duntocher Road, Bearsden, Glasgow G61 4QA
0141 943 1424
McGonigal, J. Dr
Developing and assessing spoken English
Abstract: This is a complex area, where curriculum development work shades into research, since the strategies for supporting and assessing spoken work in English are largely unsystematised. The researcher is part of a small team attempting to help teachers assess spoken English within the context of national assessment. The research involves identifying problems; proposing solutions; and trialling these in a variety of schools in different regions. The outcomes of the research will include: staff development packages; types of examination papers; units of work in taped form; reports on trialling; articles and chapters arising from these activities; and conferences.
Status: Sponsored project
Source of Grant: St Andrew's College of Education
Date of Research: 1991-1994
KEYWORDS: assessment; English studies; oral English; school based assessment; speech communication

10/1435
Duntocher Road, Bearsden, Glasgow G61 4QA
0141 943 1424
McGonigal, J. Dr
Assessing competences in postgraduate secondary school experience
Abstract: The aim of this small project is to try out an alternative model of assessment documentation, within the postgraduate teacher education (secondary) course, in cooperation with principal teachers of English who are also using the new College format. The project will record and evaluate their perceptions of the case and use, and validity of the two methods.
Status: Sponsored project
Source of Grant: St Andrew's College of Education
Date of Research: 1993-1994
KEYWORDS: assessment; competency-based teacher education; preservice teacher education; student teacher evaluation; teaching practice

10/1436
Duntocher Road, Bearsden, Glasgow G61 4QA
0141 943 1424
Kieran, J. Dr
Museums and history
Abstract: Museum visits form part of the contribution to student college courses at St Andrew's College. The effect of these visits is being investigated to determine the contribution to students' learning and to the practice of teaching in schools, with particular reference to the guidelines for environmental studies for 5-14 year olds.
Status: Sponsored project
Source of Grant: St Andrew's College of Education
Date of Research: 1993-continuing
KEYWORDS: environmental education; history studies; museums; preservice teacher education

St Andrews University

10/1437
Department of Psychology, St Andrews, Fife KY16 9AJ
01334 76161
Craigie College of Education, Beech Grove, Ayr KA8 OSR
01292 260321
Holligan, C. Dr; *Supervisor:* Johnston, R. Dr
Segmentation ability and patterns of reading failure: the nature of the relationship
Abstract: The aim of this research is to examine: (a) how poor readers recognise words; (b) in what way this is qualitatively distinct from that of normal readers; and (c) why this leads to impaired nonword reading. A study is also being made of poor readers' memory difficulties, and the importance of visual skills to the early stages of reading development.
Status: Sponsored project
Source of Grant: Wellcome Trust £61,000
Date of Research: 1992-1993
KEYWORDS: dyslexia; reading difficulties; reading failure; reading skills; word recognition

Staff College

10/1438
Coombe Lodge, Blagdon, Bristol BS18 6RG
01761 462503
Civil, J. Mrs; *Supervisor:* Fineman, S. Dr
Effects of emotion and sexuality in the organizational processes of management
Abstract: This research will look at the effect of emotions and sexuality in the organizational processes of management. Particularly, appraisal, management, structures, interviews, promotions and divisions of labour.
Status: Individual research
Date of Research: 1990-1993

KEYWORDS: *administration; emotions; employment practices; sex differences; sexuality*

10/1439
>Coombe Lodge, Blagdon, Bristol BS18 6RG
>01761 462503
>Davies, P. Mr

Choice of further studies at the end of compulsory education
Abstract: The research was based around focus groups and telephone interviews with 396 young people who took GCSEs during 1992, concerning the significant demographic and attitudinal factors which influenced their choice of further studies.
Status: Sponsored project
Source of Grant: Commercial contract
Date of Research: 1992-1993
KEYWORDS: *choice of subjects; demography; further education; pupil attitudes; sixteen to nineteen education*

10/1440
>Coombe Lodge, Blagdon, Bristol BS18 6RG
>01761 462503
>Gray, L. Mr

The functions, purposes and contributions of national education management centres
Abstract: The project will examine the work of national education management centres, in part through visits to a sample of such centres. It will compare their purposes, and relationships to national and local government systems, and funding sources. It will also examine their functions, with relation to training, consultancy, research, curriculum and management development; their client groups; and their links with other management capabilities across the education sectors. The project will examine the feasibility of building an international network of such centres, will explore the likely costs and benefits, and will seek possible sources of funding for such a network.
Status: Sponsored project
Source of Grant: The Staff College
Date of Research: 1993-continuing
KEYWORDS: *management development; management in education; training centres*

10/1441
>Coombe Lodge, Blagdon, Bristol BS18 6RG
>01761 462503
>Warrender, A-M. Mrs; Havard, R. Mr

Investors in People in post-16 institutions
Abstract: The aim of this research is to identify: the extent to which post-16 institutions are committed to Investors in People; perceptions of connection with total quality management and British Standard 5750; and perceptions of support institutions have or are likely to receive from Training and Enterprise Councils. A survey report will be available from March 1993.
Status: Sponsored project
Source of Grant: The Staff College
Date of Research: 1992-1993
KEYWORDS: *colleges of further education; management in education; quality control; sixteen to nineteen education; staff development*

10/1442
>Coombe Lodge, Blagdon, Bristol BS18 6RG
>01761 462503
>Saunders, R. Mr; *Supervisor:* Gray, L. Mr

Design of a job evaluation system for use in further education corporations
Abstract: Incorporation of further education (FE) colleges will deprive them of the services of local authority job evaluation units. Equal Pay claims where support staff cite academic staff comparators become increasingly likely. This research aims to design and test a job evaluation system capable of measuring the comparative value of all the jobs in a further education corporation to produce an integrated salary structure. Relevant factors have been selected, defined and provisionally weighted by analysis of benchmark job descriptions obtained from four colleges. The resulting job evaluation manual now needs to be tested in practice by applying it to a range of jobs in one or more colleges. Outcomes will be described by papers in The Staff College Mendip Paper series.

Published Material: SAUNDERS, R.C. (1992). Job Analysis and the preparation of job descriptions. Mendip Paper No 37. Bristol: The Staff College.
Status: Sponsored project
Source of Grant: The Staff College
Date of Research: 1992-1994
KEYWORDS: *colleges of further education; comparable worth; employment practices; equal pay; job analysis; occupational information; salaries*

10/1443
>Coombe Lodge, Blagdon, Bristol BS18 6RG
>01761 462503
>Further Education Unit, Spring Gardens, Citadel Place,
>Tinworth Street, London SE11 5EH
>0171 962 1280
>Graystone, J. Mr; Reece, I. Mr; Bayliss, J. Ms; Evans, S. Ms;
>Warrender, A-M. Mrs; *Supervisor:* Coleman, J. Mrs

Further education governing bodies and their contribution to a quality learning service
Abstract: This project for the Further Education Unit (RP 716): (1) maps the current composition and characteristics of governing bodies in further education, with particular interest in their potential for an impact on curriculum issues; (2) identifies governors' current (a) expertise and experience, relevant to further education governance; and (b) individual commitment to curriculum issues and ways of working which contribute to the effectiveness of the college as a learning service; and (3) makes recommendations to further education (FE) colleges for incorporation, having regard for the wider responsibilities of governing bodies in the future. A short literature search was carried out, followed by a questionnaire completed by 214 FE colleges in England and Wales. Interviews were then held with over 50 governors from selected colleges, and five governing body meetings were observed.
Status: Sponsored project
Source of Grant: Further Education Unit; The Staff College
Date of Research: 1992-1993
KEYWORDS: *colleges of further education; educational quality; governing bodies*

Stirling University

10/1444
>Department of Education, Stirling FK9 4LA
>01786 467600
>Brown, S. Prof.; Drever, E. Mr; Swann, J. Dr

The Scottish educational reforms and teachers' theories of teaching and learning
Abstract: The Scottish reforms for curriculum, assessment and national testing for 5 to 14 year olds are likely to influence teachers' ideas about teaching and learning. In this context, the project explores teachers' assumptions about children's learning, how teachers interpret the differences among pupils (in the new atmosphere which emphasises 'attainment targets'), and the ways in which they cater for these differences. The work focuses on two curriculum areas within the new reforms: mathematics (which has national testing) and environmental studies (which does not). Twenty-one teachers in 8 schools are involved, with children aged 6+, 8+, 11+ and 13+. The research methods include classroom observation (responsive and systematic), interviews with teachers (open-ended and semi-structured), and analysis of curriculum documents and of other support. Particular attention is being paid to the impact of the reforms on teachers' goals. For instance, do they now emphasise 'progress' more than 'activity' goals? There is also concern with teachers' conceptions of how pupils influence these goals and the actions taken to achieve them. The project explores in depth: teachers' explicit use of 'attainment targets', their strategies of assessment and remediation, and evidence about how they think about children's learning.
Published Material: SWANN, J., BROWN, S., DREVER, E. & MCNALLY, J. (1993). 'A framework for analysing teachers' accounts of pupils and teaching', Research Intelligence, No 48, Winter, pp.5-6.
Status: Sponsored project
Source of Grant: Economic and Social Research Council £91,539
Date of Research: 1992-1994

KEYWORDS: assessment; curriculum development; educational change; environmental education; mathematics education; National Curriculum; scotland; teaching process

10/1445

Department of Education, Stirling FK9 4LA
01786 467600
Low, L. Mrs; Duffield, J. Mrs; Bankowska, A. Dr;
Supervisor: Brown, S. Prof.; Johnstone, R. Prof.

Evaluation of national pilot projects: foreign languages in primary schools (Scotland)

Abstract: As part of a major government initiative, pilot projects have been set up to test the feasibility of introducing foreign language teaching into the primary schools associated with twelve secondary schools. The commonest model involves collaboration between class teachers from P6 to P7 and visiting modern language teachers from the secondary school. The main aims of the evaluation are: (1) assessment of the linguistic attainments of children involved in the pilot projects including comparisons with those children not involved; (2) evaluation of the project courses including commentary on factors such as the nature of the course and pedagogical methods which influence the linguistic performance of the children involved. The first aim has involved speaking and listening assessments carried out with pairs of pupils in the foreign language. In 1991 these compared 'project' and 'non-project' pupils in S1 and S2. In 1992 attention was on progression from Primary 7 onwards with 'project' pupils only. Within class assessments carried out by teachers have also been analysed. The second aim has been addressed through an interview study with class teachers and others involved at every level in the management of the projects, and a lesson observation study of primary and secondary classes. The result of the evaluation remains confidential until April 1993. An extension, to September 1994, will investigate the gains in linguistic attainments of pupils commencing their foreign language at different stages in the primary school, effective teaching approaches and various wider implications for the organisation of primary and secondary schools.
Status: Sponsored project
Source of Grant: Scottish Office Education Department £172,901
Date of Research: 1991-1993
KEYWORDS: language proficiency; modern language studies; primary schools

10/1446

Department of Education, Stirling FK9 4LA
01786 467600
Simmons, M. Mr; Cope, P. Dr

Feedback: its effects on procedural and conceptual knowledge for problem solving strategies

Abstract: The aims of the research are to: (1) investigate the effects of changing the instructional environment on the problem-solving strategies of children using Logo microworlds; (2) measure the effect of such changes of strategy on the development of conceptual knowledge; (3) determine which aspects of conceptual knowledge relating to rotation and angle will enhance pupils' ability to solve simple geometry problems using a screen turtle; (4) investigate effective ways of teaching these aspects of rotation and angle. The background to this research is a general concern about the way in which young children interact with a Logo-based system. Effective use of Logo requires the development of mathematical knowledge about basic aspects of turtle geometry such as angle, rotation and distance. Such knowledge is a combination of both procedural and conceptual knowledge and although it is assumed that such knowledge can be developed through the use of Logo itself, this is by no means certain. Ideally, the development of knowledge about turtle geometry is one in which procedural knowledge and conceptual knowledge develop together. But in Logo the constant availability of feedback may have a profound effect on the development of knowledge. There are three phases to the study. Study 1 takes a sample of 60 children aged between 10 and 12. Groups are matched on the basis of a pre-test and thereafter are exposed to different kinds of feedback. Data collection is by taped transcripts and spooled output files. Study 2 takes the most appropriate principles of feedback found in Study 1 to develop structured Logo sessions. Study 3 compares computer based and non-computer based teaching strategies of angle and rotation concepts.
Published Material: COPE, P., SMITH, H. & SIMMONS, M. (1992). 'Misconceptions concerning rotation and angle in LOGO', Journal of Computer Assisted Learning, Vol 8, No 1, pp.16-24.; COPE, P. & SIMMONS, M. (1992). Children's exploration of rotation and angle in limited LOGO microworlds', Computers in Education, Vol 16, No 2, pp.133-141.; COPE, P. & SIMMONS, P. (1993). 'Angle and rotation: effects of different types of feedback on the quality of response', Educational Studies in Mathematics, Vol 24, No 2, pp.163-176.; COPE, P. & SIMMONS, M. 'Some effects of limited feedback on performance and problem-solving strategy in a LOGO microworld', Journal of Educational Psychology. (in press).
Status: Sponsored project
Source of Grant: Economic and Social Research Council £11,200
Date of Research: 1991-1994
KEYWORDS: computer uses in education; feedback; geometry; logo; mathematics education; problem solving

10/1447

Department of Education, Stirling FK9 4LA
01786 467600
Low, L. Mrs; Bankowska, A. Dr; Supervisor: Brown, S. Prof.; Johnstone, R. Prof.

Extension phase of the evaluation of national pilot projects: foreign languages in primary schools

Abstract: The extension phase of the evaluation has three strands: 1) assessment of the linguistic attainments of children involved in the primary and early secondary stages in pilot schools; 2) description of teaching and learning in project primary and secondary classes; 3) staff development needs. The first strand has involved speaking and listening assessments carried out with pairs of pupils in the foreign language to address the question of progression. The second strand has been addressed through an observation study; the third strand through interviews and questionnaires. In addition, three key topics are being addressed: continuity from primary to secondary; the role of instruction about language; and learner strategies. An interim report will be submitted at the end of January 1994. The full report will be completed by the end of November 1994.
Published Material: LOW, L., DUFFIELD, J., BROWN, S. & JOHNSTONE, D. (1993). Evaluating foreign languages in primary schools. Stirling: Scottish Centre for Information, Language, Teaching and Research.; LOW, L., DUFFIELD, J., JOHNSTONE, D., BROWN, S. & BANKOWSKA, A. (1993). Foreign languages in primary schools: the national pilot projects in Scotland. Interchange No 19. Edinburgh: Scottish Council for Educational Research/Scottish Office Education Department.
Status: Sponsored project
Source of Grant: Scottish Office Education Department £89,046
Date of Research: 1993-1994
KEYWORDS: language proficiency; modern language studies; primary schools

10/1448

Department of Education, Stirling FK9 4LA
01786 467600
Morris, B. Mr; Stronach, I. Prof.

Evaluation of the management of change: TVEI Tayside

Abstract: The research was commissioned by Tayside Region to assess the effectiveness of the approach to management of change adopted by Tayside Technical and Vocational Education Initiative (TVEI). The research was based on interviews (102) in seven case study schools and with TVEI and Regional personnel. The interim evaluation findings were incorporated into a report/questionnaire distributed to a stratified sample (72) of staff in an additional 9 schools for comment (86% return rate). Research findings include: 1) Tayside TVEI has sponsored a comprehensive work experience programme; contributed to the development of procedures for forward planning and allocation of resources in schools; and introduced information technology to a wide range of teachers and pupils. It has been less successful in influencing teaching styles and introducing profiling. 2) The creation of internal TVEI related school management posts has encouraged women into school management teams (albeit temporarily). 3) The departmental 'bidding' mechanism for allocating resources has tended to emphasise equipment purchase and to contain developments within subject boundaries. 4) Project 'responsiveness' has assisted acceptance in schools but created problems in establishing project identity and direction. 5) Where elements of TVEI were incorporated into policy, at school and Regional level ('led'), there was considerable impact. Where TVEI was 'licensed' to operate, development was 'patchy' and idiosyncratic. Decisions as to whether to 'license' or 'lead' were made throughout the system. 6) There is some evidence to suggest that change was being 'over reported' by school management and 'under reported' by some principal and classroom teachers.

Status: Sponsored project
Source of Grant: Tayside Regional Council £14,000
Date of Research: 1992-1993
KEYWORDS: change strategies; educational innovation; programme evaluation; TVEI

10/1449
　　　Department of Education, Stirling FK9 4LA
　　　01786 467600
　　　Stronach, I. Prof.; Riddell, S. Dr; Stephens, C. Dr
Evaluation of the Carisbrooke Day Centre for adults with profound learning disabilities
Abstract: The purpose of the evaluation is to develop an illuminative account of the Carisbrooke Centre. This account will aim to be formative, giving feedback to the Centre workers. It will also seek to understand and portray the work of the Centre to lay audiences unfamiliar with 'handicap' and unaware of the educational potential of such forms of support.
Published Material: STEPHENS, C. et al. (1994). Carisbrooke Day Centre: a description and independent evaluation. Stirling: Central Region/Research and Evaluation Service/Stirling: Univerity of Stirling, Department of Education.
Status: Sponsored project
Source of Grant: ENABLE £6,000
Date of Research: 1994-1994
KEYWORDS: adult day centres; learning disabilities; special educational needs

10/1450
　　　Department of Education, Stirling FK9 4LA
　　　01786 467600
　　　Stronach, I. Prof.; Morris, B. Mr; McNally, J. Mr
Evaluation of Fife Region staff appraisal and development scheme
Abstract: The evaluation of the teacher appraisal scheme is part-time and will involve a seconded teacher/evaluator in 1994. The intention is to provide formative evaluation throughout the development of the scheme, examining both the impact of the appraisal initiative and the management of the innovation.
Published Material: MORRIS, B. et al. (1993). Staff development and appraisal in Fife: 1st interim report. Stirling: Stirling University, Department of Education.; BLUNDELL, L. et al. (1994). Staff development and appraisal in Fife: 2nd interim report. Stirling: Stirling University, Department of Education/Stirling: Fife Region.
Status: Sponsored project
Source of Grant: Fife Region £30,000
Date of Research: 1993-continuing
KEYWORDS: programme evaluation; teacher development; teacher evaluation; teaching profession

10/1451
　　　Department of Education, Stirling FK9 4LA
　　　01786 467600
　　　Stronach, I. Prof.; Turner, E. Ms; Morris, B. Mr
Research and evaluation service
Abstract: The Evaluation Centre acts as a consultancy, research centre, and evaluation resource for Central Region, which annually contracts work to the Centre. Work currently underway includes: an evaluation of innovative support for pupils with behavioural problems; and research into the development of self-supported study.
Published Material: LAWSON, K. & STRONACH, I. (1993). Report on the Alloa Day Centre Project. Stirling: Stirling University, Department of Education/Stirling: Central Region/Research and Evaluation Service.; DONALD, P. et al. (1994). No problem here. Account of an action research project against racism. Stirling: Central Region/Research and Evaluation Service.; TURNER, E. et al. (1994). Supported study. Stirling: Central Region/Research and Evaluation Service.; TURNER, E. et al. (1994). Extension of school-based ITE: an evaluation. Stirling: Central Region/Research and Evaluation Service.
Status: Sponsored project
Source of Grant: Central Region £90,000
Date of Research: 1993-continuing
KEYWORDS: educational research; research and development centres

10/1452
　　　Department of Education, Stirling FK9 4LA
　　　01786 467600
　　　Lappas, N. Mr; *Supervisor:* Riddell, S. Dr; Brown S. Prof.
Policy and provision for children with specific learning difficulties in Scotland and Greece
Abstract: The research has been prompted by the European Unification and the following consequence of homogenising Member State policies. The comparison of two peripheral countries of the European Union will increase the self-awareness of each country in the area of the study, as well as enhance the collaboration and communication between Greece and Scotland, in the field of specific learning difficulties. The aims of the research are to describe and compare policies, current practice and provision. Furthermore, to investigate how teachers and parents construe specific learning difficulties, and to analyse the educational experiences of children with specific learning difficulties. Based on these, a broad European Union policy framework will be recommended. Analysis of documents, publications, literature and legislation will construct the initial part of the research. Key informants will be interviewed to explore factors which affect policy formation and implementation. Ten case studies, in each country, will then be conducted to investigate policy implementation. Teachers, parents and children will be interviewed and class observation will take place. Qualitative analysis will be used to identify key aspects of their perceptions of provision and the way in which this contrasts with official policy.
Status: Individual research
Date of Research: 1993-continuing
KEYWORDS: comparative education; Greece; learning disabilities; Scotland; special educational needs

10/1453
　　　Department of Education, Stirling FK9 4LA
　　　01786 467600
　　　Allan, J. Ms; *Supervisor:* Stronach, I. Prof.; Riddell, S. Dr
Experiences of pupils with special educational needs in mainstream schools
Abstract: The focus of the research is on pupils' experience of having a special educational need (SEN) and of being taught in mainstream schools. This involves: 1) analysis of discourses on SEN, in particular the Warnock Report and the HMI Report on children with learning difficulties in Scotland; 2) examination of the operation of records of needs in 8 schools; and 3) detailed case studies of 16 pupils in 8 schools. It is hoped that the three strands of the research will offer insight into the children's experiences and how these are constructed through the formal and informal discourses on SEN. The work of Foucault is considered relevant to both the methodology and the analytical framework which will be developed.
Status: Individual research
Date of Research: 1992-continuing
KEYWORDS: mainstreaming; pupil attitudes; pupil experience; special educational needs

10/1454
　　　Department of Education, Stirling FK9 4LA
　　　01786 467600
　　　Brown, S. Prof.; Duffield, J. Mrs; Riddell, S. Dr
School processes influencing pupil progress
Abstract: The project aims to study how school processes influence the learning of lower attaining pupils in schools rated as more or less effective overall. It uses a case study approach, based on two secondary schools in high socioeconomic circumstances and two in low. Teachers' perceptions of 'progress' and of 'below average attainment' are important determinants of the evidence sought, and these perceptions will be compared with 'official' interpretations of these terms. Data relating to children's progress is being collected through the schools' assessments, classroom observation, and standardised reading tests already carried out by the education authority. The gathering of evidence focuses on eight target pupils in each of the schools, and on English, mathematics and science. Pupils in two mixed ability entry classes are being followed for two years from arrival to entry to standard grade courses. The support provided by the school is being collected through: 1) interviews with key personnel and documentary analysis of policy documentation; and 2) in-depth interviews with target pupils about their perceptions of themselves as learners, their progress and the support received. Support in the classroom is being explored using classroom observation and post-lesson interviews with teachers.

Status: Sponsored project
Source of Grant: Economic and Social Research Council £97,731
Date of Research: 1992-continuing
KEYWORDS: academic achievement; educational practices; pupil improvement; secondary schools; support services; underachievement

10/1455

Department of Education, Stirling FK9 4LA
01786 467600
Allan, J. Ms; Supervisor: Brown, S. Prof.; Riddell, S. Dr

A comparative study of special educational needs provision in mainstream and special schools in Scotland

Abstract: The research aims to predict trends in the placement of children with special educational needs over the next 5-10 years. This will involve an analysis of relevant factors, such as national and regional policies, costs and the views of parents. The project will consider the implications for special schools of catering for fewer children with more complex needs. It will also examine the capacity of mainstream schools to meet the academic and social needs of children with significant learning difficulties. The research will include an analysis of available statistics and interviews with policy makers in each Scottish education authority. Detailed case studies of the financial and administrative arrangements for pupils with special educational needs will be conducted in two education authorities. There will also be sixteen case studies of mainstream and special schools, in which individual pupils will be shadowed.

Status: Sponsored project
Source of Grant: Scottish Office Education Department £82,000
Date of Research: 1992-1994
KEYWORDS: comparative analysis; educational policy; mainstreaming; special educational needs; special schools

10/1456

Department of Education, Stirling FK9 4LA
01786 467600
McNally, J. Mr

Evaluation and analysis of school-based experimental learning of beginning teachers

Abstract: Two cohorts of final teaching practice students (42 in all) were interviewed indepth about their experience in schools. It was found that the experience was predominantly affective, and depended on relationships with teaching colleagues and pupils taught. It also raised questions regarding the nature of teaching tips, received and developed, and makes tentative conclusions about how beginners learn to teach.

Status: Sponsored project
Source of Grant: Scottish Office Education Department £5,000; Stirling University £800
Date of Research: 1991-1994
KEYWORDS: preservice teacher education; student teachers; teaching experience; teaching practice

10/1457

Department of Education, Stirling FK9 4LA
01786 467600
McDaid, C. Ms; Supervisor: Riddell, S Dr; Brown, S. Prof.

The career experiences of job-sharing primary teachers in Scotland

Abstract: The first job-sharing scheme for teachers in Scotland was introduced by Strathclyde Regional Council in 1987. Although numbers participating in the scheme are still small, they have more than doubled since its introduction. The proposed research will investigate the career experiences of primary school teachers engaged in job sharing. Data will be gathered through a series of career history interviews with 30 promoted and unpromoted job-sharing primary teachers employed by one Scottish region. Semi-structured interviews will also be conducted with key informants at the Scottish Office Education Department, regional authorities, The General Teaching Council, and trade unions, in order to provide information on policy on job-sharing.

Status: Individual research
Date of Research: 1993-continuing
KEYWORDS: job sharing; part time teachers; primary school teachers; teaching profession

10/1458

Department of Education, Stirling FK9 4LA
01786 467600
Stronach, I. Prof.; Morris, B. Mr

Oral competencies of higher school leavers (OCHIL)

Abstract: The research is designed to explore the transition competencies of school leavers in Central Region, Scotland. The sample will be around 40 in the first instance, the methods ethnographic. The intention is to follow groups of well qualified school leavers (aged 17/18) through the transition from school to work. In addition, groups of young workers are being interviewed. The research will inform understanding of a hitherto neglected group of school leavers.

Status: Sponsored project
Source of Grant: Scottish Amicable; Forth Valley Enterprise, jointly £38,000
Date of Research: 1993-continuing
KEYWORDS: oracy; school leavers; school to work transition

10/1459

Department of Education, Stirling FK9 4LA
01786 467600
Stronach, I. Prof.; Turner, E. Ms; Waterhouse, S. Dr; Lloyd, J. Dr

Schools – industry links

Abstract: A national survey of schools-industry provision, based on interview, documentation and questionnaire. In addition, selected case studies of 'exemplary' and 'typical' practice. The project will attempt to generate largely qualitative accounts of costs and benefits of different types of initiative, and will, where possible, make recommendations for future policy.

Status: Sponsored project
Source of Grant: Scottish Office Education Department £46,000
Date of Research: 1992-1993
KEYWORDS: industry-education relationship; school to work transition; vocational education

Strathclyde University

10/1460

Careers Advisory Service, 26 Richmond Street, Glasgow G1 1XH
0141 552 4400
Graham, B. Miss

Mentoring and professional development

Abstract: The report gives an account of a pilot mentoring scheme designed to support a new programme of inservice professional development for the Association of Graduate Careers Advisory Services (AGCAS). The survey covers the purpose, structure and implementation of the scheme in Scotland in 1992 and reviews participants' experience of mentoring. The report also makes recommendations for the introduction of a scheme throughout the UK (subsequently implemented in 1993).

Published Material: GRAHAM, B. (1993). Mentoring and professional development. Manchester: Central Services Unit.
Status: Sponsored project
Source of Grant: Scottish Enterprise £14,400
Date of Research: 1991-1992
KEYWORDS: careers service; guidance personnel; mentors; professional development

10/1461

Department of Government, 16 Richmond Street, Glasgow G1 1XG
0141 552 4400
Furlong, A. Dr

Opportunity structures and the occupational and educational intentions of young people

Abstract: This project examines the components of opportunity structures through a quantitative analysis of the strength of factors associated with the development of occupational and educational intentions. It will study the ways in which young people's intentions reflect local opportunity structures by analysing differences within, and between, areas. In addition, through qualitative research, the project looks at ways young people negotiate opportunity structures and come to terms with change.

Status: Sponsored project
Source of Grant: Economic and Social Research Council £68,840
Date of Research: 1994-continuing
KEYWORDS: employment opportunities; labour market; learner educational objectives; occupational aspiration; opportunities; secondary school pupils; work-education relationship

10/1462

Department of Government, 16 Richmond Street, Glasgow G1 1XG
0141 552 4400
Furlong, A. Dr
The effects of opportunity structures and policy initiatives on the in-school development of occupational intentions
Abstract: A longitudinal study of pupils in 5 secondary schools which aims to examine the relationship between labour market structures and the in-school development of occupational and educational intentions of young people.
Status: Sponsored project
Source of Grant: Nuffield Foundation £4,720
Date of Research: 1991-continuing
KEYWORDS: career choice; employment opportunities; labour market; learner educational objectives; occupational aspiration; school to work transition; secondary school pupils; work-education relationship

10/1463

Department of Government, 16 Richmond Street, Glasgow G1 1XG
0141 442 4400
Kay, I. Ms
The partnership in education project
Abstract: The Partnership in Education Project (completed end October 1992), was set up to devise and disseminate ways of working with parents of young children, professionals, and community groups in order to empower local communities to support the cognitive and social development of young children, especially those living in deprived areas. The evaluation of the research has been both formative, contributing to project development, and summative, exploring languages and literacy outcomes for children whose parents became 'involved' in partnership work. It also ascertained from professionals the likelihood of sustained partnership between parents and inter-agency working. The project has worked in a number of neighbourhoods in different towns and villages in Strathclyde region, it has: provided inservice and preservice course modules for a wide range of professionals who work with young children and their families; has written guidelines and handbooks; and made videos to help others to work in a partnership mode.
Published Material: KAY, I. & STRUTHERS, S. (1988). The partnership in education project: a public report. Glasgow: Strathclyde Regional Council.; HALL, S., KAY, I. & STRUTHERS, S. (1992). The experience of partnership in education. Dereham, Norfolk: Peter Francis Publishers.
Status: Sponsored project
Source of Grant: Bernard Van Leer Foundation; Strathclyde Regional Council
Date of Research: 1983-1994
KEYWORDS: community programmes; community services; cooperative programmes; early childhood education; parent participation; young children

10/1464

Department of Psychology, Turnbull Building, 155 George Street, Glasgow G1 1RD
0141 552 4400
Howe, C. Dr; Tolmie, A. Dr
The development of hypothesis testing in children aged 9 to 14
Abstract: The research is an attempt to chart the development of hypothesis testing in physics as a function of pupil age, pupil gender, and subject domain. It begins with a descriptive phase with the aim of a detailed documentation of the difficulties pupils have in formulating and testing hypotheses. Pupils aged 9-14 are interviewed to ascertain the factors they regard as relevant to flotation in fluids, motion down an incline, the shape of shadows, and the pressure of water. They are then asked to plan, carry out and interpret tests to see if their beliefs are correct. The second part of the research is an intervention phase, addressing the receptivity of pupils to on-task guidance. Computer software has been designed which supports hypothesis testing in relation to the shape of shadows and the pressure of water. The research involves comparing the subsequent hypothesis testing skills of pupils who have worked with the software, against control pupils who work with software which offers no explicit support.
Published Material: HOLMIE, A., HOWE, C.J. & SOFRONIOU, N. (1993). 'Computer-supported hypothesis testing in primary and secondary school science'. Paper presented at CAL-93, York University.; HOWE, C.J., TOLMIE, A. & SOFRONIOU, N. (1993). 'Hypothesis testing in nine-to-fourteen-year-old children'. Paper presented at BPS Developmental Section Conference, Birmingham University.
Status: Sponsored project
Source of Grant: Economic and Social Research Council £46,795
Date of Research: 1992-1994
KEYWORDS: computer uses in education; hypothesis testing; physics education; science education

10/1465

Faculty of Education, Division of Business & Computer Education, Jordanhill Campus, Southbrae Drive, Glasgow G13 1PP
0141 950 3000
Kirkwood, M. Mrs
Programming in Scottish Standard Grade Computing Studies
Abstract: The aim of this project is to develop and trial individualised learning materials on programming in Scottish Standard Grade Computing Studies within the framework of a staff development project.
Status: Sponsored project
Source of Grant: Strathclyde University
Date of Research: 1990-1993
KEYWORDS: computer science education; material development

10/1466

Faculty of Education, Division of Business & Computer Education, Jordanhill Campus, Southbrae Drive, Glasgow G13 1PP
0141 950 3000
Northern College of Education, Computer Education Department, Dundee Campus, Gardyne Road, Dundee DD5 1NY
01382 464000
Munro, R. Mr; Lamont, M. Mrs
SPRITE (Supporting and Promoting Information Technology in Education)
Abstract: The aim of this project is to improve, enhance and encourage the use of information technology (IT) by college staff (throughout Scotland) and assist the permeation of IT use in college courses.
Status: Sponsored project
Source of Grant: Strathclyde University; Northern College; Scottish Office Education Department
Date of Research: 1991-1993
KEYWORDS: colleges; computer uses in education; information technology

10/1467

Faculty of Education, Division of Education and Psychology, Jordanhill Campus, Southbrae Drive, Glasgow G13 1PP
0141 950 3000
MacBeath, J. Dr; McAndrew, L. Ms
To evaluate the response of teacher, parents and pupils to new forms of reporting introduced in the 5-14 development programme
Abstract: This project will examine the usefulness of new styles of reporting to parents, their implication for teachers and the degree to which pupils find them helpful and formative.
Status: Sponsored project
Source of Grant: Scottish Office Education Department £111,000
Date of Research: 1991-continuing
KEYWORDS: assessment; parent-pupil relationship; profiles; school reports

10/1468

Faculty of Education, Division of Inservice Training, Jordanhill Campus, Southbrae Drive, Glasgow G13 1PP
0141 950 3000
McCall, C. Dr; Ellis, S. Mrs; Grant, M. Mrs; Hughes, A. Mrs

Philosophical inquiry in values education
Abstract: This project aims to disseminate the method of philosophical inquiry in values education and to use this in staff development in values education.
Status: Sponsored project
Source of Grant: Gordon Cook Foundation £40,000
Date of Research: 1991-1993
KEYWORDS: moral education; philosophy; values education

10/1469
　　　Faculty of Education, Division of Language and Literature, Jordanhill Campus, Southbrae Drive, Glasgow G13 1PP
　　　0141 950 3000
　　　Williams, W. Mr
Scottish Standard Grade Beginners Latin Course: design of a course book
Abstract: The aim of this project is to design a beginners Latin course book based on the elements of the Scottish Standard Grade.
Status: Sponsored project
Source of Grant: Strathclyde University £500
Date of Research: 1988-1993
KEYWORDS: educational materials; Latin; textbook preparation

10/1470
　　　Faculty of Education, Division of Special Educational Needs, Jordanhill Campus, Southbrae Drive, Glasgow G13 1PP
　　　0141 950 3000
　　　Hewitt, C. Mrs; Hamill, P. Mr; Robertson, P. Mrs
Below average attainment project
Abstract: This project aims to describe and evaluate the variety of services designed to support the progress of pupils with learning difficulties and social disadvantage.
Status: Sponsored project
Source of Grant: Scottish Office Education Department £69,638
Date of Research: 1991-1993
KEYWORDS: disadvantaged; moderate learning difficulties; special educational needs; support services

10/1471
　　　Faculty of Education, Scottish Centre for Children with Motor Impairment, Jordanhill Campus, Southbrae Drive, Glasgow G13 1PP
　　　0141 950 3000
　　　MacKay, G. Dr; McCartney, E. Miss; Cheseldine, S. Dr; McCool, S. Miss
Scottish Centre for Children with Motor Impairment
Abstract: This project will undertake evaluation of children's progress, development of curriculum, implementation of policy, and costs/benefits of the Scottish Centre for Children with Motor Impairment.
Status: Sponsored project
Source of Grant: Scottish Office Education Department £170,000
Date of Research: 1991-1994
KEYWORDS: motor development; special educational needs; special schools

Suffolk College of Higher and Further Education

10/1472
　　　Rope Walk, Ipswich IP4 1LT
　　　01473 255885
　　　Capey, C. Mrs; Broadbent, T. Rev.; Mojdehi, E. Ms; Barr, K. Mr; Thorpe, M. Rev.; *Supervisor:* Impey, R. Mr; Stott, D. Mr
Perceptions of equality of opportunity in a multicultural multifaith society – Ipswich
Abstract: The aim of this research is to investigate the religious dimensions of equal opportunities within local society generally, and in particular with regard to Suffolk College of Higher and Further Education. Ongoing consultation and cooperation will take place with the local (Ipswich) religious communities, identified through the local inter-faith network. The perspectives of groups outside the network will also be sought. Questions to be addressed include: (1)

Do all groups understand the same by 'equal opportunities'? (2) Do they think in terms of facilities or person potential? (3) Do they appreciate being seen as a distinct group? (4) What is the correlation between religious and cultural identities? Any questions posed need to be meaningful to the groups being consulted. The research team is seeking to identify their categories and concepts, therefore the first part of the process involves the compiling of a book (Faith in Focus in Ipswich (1993) which will be published by the College) in which as many groups as possible introduce themselves and explain their beliefs and values. Out of this cooperative venture a further dialogue should arise.
Status: Sponsored project
Source of Grant: Suffolk College of Higher and Further Education £2,200
Date of Research: 1992-1994
KEYWORDS: equal education; equal facilities; ethnic groups; minority groups; religious cultural groups

10/1473
　　　Rope Walk, Ipswich IP4 1LT
　　　01473 255885
　　　Cuff, D. Miss
Development of a learning environment audit tool
Abstract: This study is part of a joint project between health authorities and Suffolk College designed to develop quality measures for monitoring and evaluating the learning environment provided for student health visitors and district nurses. It is proposed to pilot three-quarters of the standards set by the Regional Standard Steering Group set up for this project. By piloting the standards developed the following null hypotheses will be tested: (1) The introduction of standards for the learning environment will have no effect on the quality of learning experiences offered in a placement; and (2) The introduction of standards will make no difference to the practice of community practice teachers.
Status: Sponsored project
Source of Grant: Suffolk College of Higher and Further Education £3,000
Date of Research: 1990-1992
KEYWORDS: health visitors; learning experience; nurse education; placement

10/1474
　　　Rope Walk, Ipswich IP4 1LT
　　　01473 255885
　　　Irwin, M. Mr
To analyse the effects of environmental change on the training requirements of non-life insurance brokers as a result of European integration
Abstract: In 1992 funding was received from the Further Education Unit to participate in a project researching into the effect of the Single Market on training for specific jobs. Work was carried out with reference to insurance brokers working in liability insurance. In 1993 sponsorship was received from Suffolk Training and Enterprise Council (TEC) and Exemplar Consultants to supplement a College commitment to extend this work. The aim of the project is to analyse the effects of environmental changes on the training requirements of non-life insurance brokers as a result of European integration. Within this aim, a number of sub-objectives exist: 1) To identify, describe and evaluate the environmental changes that have occurred, or are expected, as a result of European integration. 2) The current role and training of insurance brokers will be analysed and described. 3) The range and impact of European legislation on the occupation will be detailed. From this, an assessment will be made of the likely changes in the role and training requirements of brokers. Finally, an evaluation of the training plans, programmes and materials in the light of the previous findings will be made. In addition to desk-based research, structured interviews have taken place with leading figures in the UK insurance market. In the later stages of the project this will be supplemented by structured interviews with leading brokers and their representative organisations in selected European states.
Status: Sponsored project
Source of Grant: Suffolk Training and Enterprise Council £7,000; Exemplar Consultants £7,000; Suffolk College of Higher and Further Education
Date of Research: 1993-1994
KEYWORDS: insurance occupations; single European market; training

Sunderland University

10/1475
> School of Computing and Information Systems, Priestman
> Building, Green Terrace, Sunderland SR1 3SD
> 0191 515 2000
> Moscardini, A. Prof.; Curran, D. Dr; Middleton, W. Mr;
> Bloor, C. Dr; Prior, D. Mr

The use of computers to teach mathematics
Abstract: A laboratory has been set up for teaching mathematics to between 300-400 first year undergraduate engineering and science students. The laboratory has replaced a large amount of material previously taught by lectures. The work has also been extended to include teaching the mathematically unadapted and, more recently, teaching the disabled.
Published Material: MIDDLETON, W. (1990). 'Innovative applications of CAL to the teaching of the mathematically unadapted', Conference Proceedings, CAL 90, Barcelona.
Status: Sponsored project
Source of Grant: Training, Enterprise & Education Directorate
Date of Research: 1988-continuing
KEYWORDS: *computer assisted learning; computer uses in education; mathematics education*

10/1476
> School of Computing and Information Systems, Priestman
> Building, Green Terrace, Sunderland SR1 3SD
> 0191 515 2000
> Steward, A. Dr; Wyvill, M. Mr

Innovative teaching methods in computing
Abstract: The work entails a number of innovative approaches to the teaching of computing and mathematics including: peer assessment; industrial workshops; poster sessions; and presentation skills.
Status: Sponsored project
Source of Grant: Department of Employment: Enterprise in Higher Education £60,000
Date of Research: 1992-continuing
KEYWORDS: *computer science education; mathematics education; teaching methods*

10/1477
> School of Computing and Information Systems, Priestman
> Building, Green Terrace, Sunderland SR1 3SD
> 0191 515 2000
> Curran, D. Dr

The use of spreadsheets as a learning aid for the acquisition of statistical concepts
Abstract: Statistics appears in the curriculae of the majority of mathematics courses in higher education. Often the requirement to engage in substantial number crunching activities, using hand calculators obscures the basic underlying statistical concepts. Purpose designed statistical software is often overly sophisticated for teaching statistics at an elementary level, and often obscures the basic features of statistical computations. Spreadsheet programs are ideally suited to the implementation of the basic computational procedures used in statistics. Unlike the use of statistical packages, the use of spreadsheets reinforces the students' understanding of these computational procedures, whilst being more powerful than most hand-held calculators. A large proportion of statistical computations is suitable for spreadsheet implementation. The graphical capabilities of spreadsheets as well as making it easy to produce statistical diagrams, provide a powerful visual realisation of many statistical concepts. In addition routine processes can be easily mechanised by using the macro language of the spreadsheet. The principal aim of this proposal is to examine the advantages of using spreadsheets within statistics, both as a teaching and as a computational aid. A successful outcome of this project would be the validation of learning methods, which should enable students to obtain a firmer grasp of important concepts in a shorter time period than existing methods. A limited amount of open learning material will be produced to allow students to work through tutorial material in their own time.
Status: Sponsored project
Source of Grant: Sunderland University £900
Date of Research: 1991-1992
KEYWORDS: *computer uses in education; mathematics education; spreadsheets; statistics education*

10/1478
> School of Computing and Information Systems, Priestman
> Building, Green Terrace, Sunderland SR1 3SD
> 0191 515 2000
> Ramshaw, M. Mrs; Patience, S. Mrs

Problem based learning in relation to database packages
Abstract: The project will be aimed at one major topic area within the Micro Technology module in the first year of the HND Computer Studies for Women course at Sunderland University. The material developed will be available for other courses which use database packages. It has been reported by both Her Majesty's Inspectors (HMI's) and industrial placement supervisors that although students at the University have acquired computer related skills and knowledge, they lack the ability to apply these to problem solving. The material produced should develop and enhance the problem solving abilities and skills of the students, which could then be applied to all topic areas throughout their course and be carried beyond into their careers. From vast experience of teaching mature students, of whom are non-standard entrants, the researchers have found their lack of confidence exacerbated by their inexperience of using computers and the new environment in which they find themselves. This module is to be taught at the start of the course and on a block basis, thus gently introducing the student to the educational environment. It is hoped that the materials developed will not only improve their computing skills, but by learning to problem solve they will be encouraged to explore other subject areas with more confidence.
Status: Sponsored project
Source of Grant: Sunderland University £900
Date of Research: 1991-1992
KEYWORDS: *computer uses in education; problem solving*

10/1479
> School of Computing and Information Systems, Priestman
> Building, Green Terrace, Sunderland SR1 3SD
> 0191 515 2000
> Middleton, W. Mr

The development of computer algebra based learning material for a mathematics laboratory
Abstract: The project involves the development of a small suite of laboratory based tutorials using the computer algebra package DERIVE. The use of such packages in the teaching situation is growing rapidly on a national basis and in the view of the researchers it is essential that courses at Sunderland University are seen to be among the leaders in the field if it is to continue to attract students. The aim of the project is to provide the students with a learning resource which is relevant to as many courses as possible, and which can be used by the students, during their taught course in supervised laboratory sessions, and be followed-up during their own time and at their own pace. The teaching and learning process is at present changing rapidly as higher education institutions adapt themselves to the challenges posed by the ongoing demographic changes and the pressures brought about by the requirements of efficiency. In the area of service teaching, the problems can become both immediate and acute because of the increasingly general requirement that students be taught in large classes. While this does not automatically mean that students are disadvantaged, it does mean that staff have to give consideration to the pedagogical methods used and to the resources provided for the students. In a modern context, this implies that the power of the microcomputer should be placed in the hands of the teacher and the learner in order to enhance the teaching and learning process. Many of the students now entering the University are weak from a mathematical point of view, but in spite of this, they are motivated students who can do well in their chosen fields, often engineering or science. To achieve this goal they must be provided with the necessary help, encouragement, guidance and resources to cope with the more analytical aspects of their chosen course.
Status: Sponsored project
Source of Grant: Sunderland University £900
Date of Research: 1991-1992
KEYWORDS: *algebra education; computer assisted learning; mathematics education*

10/1480
> School of Education, Hammerton Hall, Gray Road,
> Sunderland SR2 8JB
> 0191 515 2000
> Mercer, D. Mr; *Supervisor:* Constable, H. Prof.

Job satisfaction on the part of secondary headteachers
Abstract: The research undertaken has involved the development of

a methodology suitable for the study, the carrying out of fieldwork based on this methodology and the development of the data obtained into the beginnings of a grounded theory of job satisfaction. In terms of the methodology, three approaches have been developed and made use of as a means of obtaining the data necessary to develop a grounded theory of job satisfaction, a methodological approach first fomulated by Glaser & Strauss. These three methods are Life History, Nominal Group Technique and Critical Incident Technique. Of these three, the Critical Incident Technique has proved to be the most productive in that after interviews with 39 secondary headteachers, important categories with regard to job satisfaction have begun to emerge, a crucial first step in the development of substantive and formal grounded theory. Examples of such categories are, for job satisfaction, a sense of personal achievement, the views of significant others, a sense of efficacy, and relations with governors. For job dissatisfaction, work pressure, role conflict, interpersonal relations and self esteem have been identified as being of importance. In total, twenty-three and twenty-nine respectively of such categories have appeared so far and the next process has begun of condensing these into 'themes'. The emergence of these themes is the second stage in the creation of a theoretical position which explains job satisfaction on the part of secondary headteachers. The future progress of the research is indicated by the degree to which the development of substantive theory has already begun. In this way it is anticipated that a formal theory of job satisfaction will emerge which will identify the key affective features of the job of headteacher. In view of the notable lack of research in this field, this will be a significant development which will increase understanding of a group which has a key part to play in our society.
Published Material: MERCER, D. & EVANS, B. (1991). 'Professional myopia: job satisfaction and the management of teachers', School Organisation, Vol 11, No 3, pp. 291-301.; MERCER, D. (1993). 'Job satisfaction and the headteacher: a nominal group approach', School Organisation, Vol 13, No 2, pp. 153-164.
Status: Individual research
Date of Research: 1990-continuing
KEYWORDS: *job satisfaction; stress – psychological; teacher attitudes; teaching profession*

10/1481
School of Education, Hammerton Hall, Gray Road, Sunderland SR2 8JB
0191 515 2000
Constable, H. Prof.; Meyer, W. Mr
The European dimension in inservice teacher education
Abstract: On 24 May 1988, the European Community Council adopted a resolution aimed at promoting and reinforcing the European Dimension in Education. The aim was to strengthen young people's sense of European identity, to improve their knowledge of the Community and to prepare them to take part in the future economic and social development of the Community. Certain sections of the resolution relate to inservice teacher education (INSET) and suggest that in this area the European Dimension might be fostered by providing courses and activities of an awareness-raising type and by opening up certain INSET activities to teachers from other European Community member states. As part of an investigation carried out by the Association for Teacher Education in Europe the University of Sunderland conducted a survey of UK and Irish INSET providers in order to establish the level and type of relevant INSET provision. It was found that in the UK provision of European Dimension INSET was strongest in the following regions: Scotland; Northern Ireland; Northern England; Yorkshire and Humberside; South-Western England. In Southern Ireland, work was generally limited both in extent and scope. In the UK, it was found that some of the most effective work was being done by groups of local education authorities working together in collaboration with higher education institutions and the Central Bureau for Educational Visits and Exchanges. Much depended on local and individual enthusiasm. There was a feeling in the field that the UK central government was failing to give a lead.
Published Material: CONSTABLE, H. & MEYER, W. (1994). The European dimension in inservice teacher education in the United Kingdom and Ireland. Sunderland: University of Sunderland, School of Education.
Status: Sponsored project
Source of Grant: European Commission Association
Date of Research: 1993-1993
KEYWORDS: *European Community; European studies; inservice teacher education; intercultural programmes*

10/1482
School of Education, Hammerton Hall, Gray Road, Sunderland SR2 8JB
0191 515 2000
Supervisor: Hufton, N. Mr; Ecclestone, K. Ms;
GNVQ's and pupils' careers
Abstract: The research aims to provide a description of the experience of pupils undertaking pilot study for General National Vocational Qualifications (GNVQ's). Pupils' reasons for choice, the role of the qualification in their educational experience, and the opportunities it avails to them will be monitored by interview and survey to provide an initial picture of features of an innovation in provision.
Status: Individual research
Date of Research: 1994-continuing
KEYWORDS: *educational experience; employment qualifications; national vocational qualifications; vocational education*

10/1483
School of Education, Hammerton Hall, Gray Road, Sunderland SR2 8JB
0191 515 2000
Constable, H. Prof.; Meyer, W. Mr
Evaluation of teacher and headteacher appraisal in Sunderland
Abstract: The 1986 Education Act contained enabling legislation for teacher appraisal and in December 1990 the Secretary of State for Education announced a national, compulsory scheme under which all teachers in service were to be appraised by the end of the 1994-95 school year. The School of Education of the University of Sunderland was commissioned by the Sunderland Local Education Authority (LEA) to evaluate the introduction and early stages of its appraisal scheme. The main research techniques were observations of appraisal inservice teacher education (INSET) sessions; interviews with teachers, headteachers, and LEA personnel; and the administering of a questionnaire to 500 teachers and headteachers. It was found that appraisal was generally favoured as a means of professional development and it was felt that the LEA had succeeded in introducing its scheme in a sensitive and efficient way. Fears were expressed that central government would act to bring in a strict accountability model of appraisal and would link appraisal to remuneration. Appraisal was found to be more popular with headteachers than with other teachers; and more popular in primary than in secondary schools. Appraisal was found useful in regard to clarifying roles and setting priorites but it was not thought that it would improve morale or equal opportunities. Fears were expressed about the confidentiality aspect and there was concern about the future availability of funding for cover and INSET requirements. A frequently expressed worry was that appraisal was a glutton for time.
Published Material: CONSTABLE, H. & MEYER, W. (1993). An evaluation of teacher and headteacher appraisal in Sunderland. Sunderland: University of Sunderland, School of Education.
Status: Sponsored project
Source of Grant: Sunderland Local Education Authority £4,800
Date of Research: 1992-1993
KEYWORDS: *academic staff development; head teachers; teacher evaluation; teaching profession*

10/1484
School of Education, Hammerton Hall, Gray Road, Sunderland SR2 8JB
0191 515 2000
Durham University, School of Education, Leazes Road, Durham DH1 1TA
0191 374 2000
Elliott, J. Mr; *Supervisor:* Coffield, F. Prof.
Locus of control beliefs in children with emotional and behavioural difficulties: an exploratory study
Abstract: The study examines control related beliefs of 240 children aged between nine and sixteen, and considers the implications of these beliefs for therapeutic intervention. All subjects have been referred to the educational psychology service because of perceived behavioural difficulties, and each child's behaviour is scored on nine behavioural dimensions. The data used for analysis are drawn from self-report scales, semi-structured interviews and case files. Both quantitative (using multivariate techniques) and qualitative modes of data analysis are employed and the stengths and weaknesses of each approach are noted. The research challenges many assumptions contained within the locus of control literature and highlights the difficulty of adopting findings from nomothetic research for the purpose of clinical intervention.

Status: Individual research
Date of Research: 1988-1993
KEYWORDS: *behaviour disorders; child psychiatry; emotional disturbances; locus of control*

10/1485
School of Education, Hammerton Hall, Gray Road,
Sunderland SR2 8JB
0191 515 2000
York University, Department of Educational Studies,
Heslington, York YO1 5DD
01904 430000
Shield, G. Mr; *Supervisor:* Kyriacou, C. Dr
Teaching and learning through a process model of technology education
Abstract: The work is concerned with an analysis of a process model of the teaching/learning of technology in secondary schools. It is a qualitative study based on case studies of ten technology departments in comprehensive schools in the north east of England. Provisional findings have indicated that the transmission of skills/knowledge takes place mainly through a didactic approach in a one to one situation. Teachers who are particularly skilled in the work, develop a teaching style which encourages a critical analytical approach, and affords opportunity for interaction between pupil and pupil, as well as between pupil and teacher. During the course of working a project, a teacher's role changes from one of instructor, or source of expertise, to that of 'facilitator'. This change in role accompanies the opportunity required by the pupil to consolidate his/her learning through introspective thought. A stimulating environment and provision of learning resource material appears to be valuable for successful learning to take place.
Status: Individual research
Date of Research: 1990-1994
KEYWORDS: *learning strategies; teaching methods; technology education*

Surrey University

10/1486
Department of Educational Studies, Guildford GU2 5XH
01483 300800
Desombre, T. Mr; *Supervisor:* Lathleen, J. Prof.; Denicolo, P. Dr
Role and preparation of Executive Directors of Nursing in the new National Health Service (NHS) (post 1990)
Abstract: The study identifies issues relating to the role of Executive Directors of Nursing in the new National Health Service (NHS) (post 1990). It identifies the function and competencies of these individuals and will suggest how these individuals should be prepared. The study uses a triangulation of research methods, but is based largely in the qualitative research paradigm.
Status: Individual research
Date of Research: 1992-continuing
KEYWORDS: *administrators; health personnel; health services; nursing*

10/1487
Department of Educational Studies, Guildford GU2 5XH
01483 300800
Denicolo, P. Dr
Developing techniques for professional self-appraisal for teachers using personal construct approaches
Abstract: In order to develop their professional competence teachers need to be able to evaluate their current practice and to have standards and skills in mind towards which they aim their development. This research seeks to evaluate and develop a variety of techniques, based in personal construct psychology, to help teachers to do this. The participants in the study are learner teachers of adults with a variety of different discipline bases undertaking a teacher training course at Surrey. They also have had a variety of past experience as teachers. This group comprises approximately 100 participants and is matched with a similar group at the University of the West Indies in Jamaica. Each participant completes a repertory grid, comparing their practice and professional personna with a range of teachers they have variously learnt from, and self-portrait as a teacher at the beginning,

middle and end of the course. They also note what they consider to be the most important constructs for defining a 'good teacher'. The grids are analysed and interpretations fed back to participants each time, but the self-portraits are collected to be interpreted at the end of the course. Synopses, using emergent categories, of the collated defining constructs between different groups of participants are produced each time for reflection and discussion. Interim results will be available in October 1993 when modifications will be considered.
Published Material: DENICOLO, P. & POPE, M. (1991). 'Developing constructive action: personal construct psychology, action research and professional development'. In: Zuber-Skerritt, O. (Ed). Action research for change and development. Aldershot: Avebury.
Status: Individual research
Date of Research: 1992-1994
KEYWORDS: *personal construct theory; self evaluation – individuals; teacher evaluation*

10/1488
Department of Educational Studies, Guildford GU2 5XH
01483 300800
Mulligan, J. Mr
Developing internal capacities in experiential learning
Abstract: The background to this research is related to the learning to learn challenges faced by experiential learners in assimilating and processing information before, during and after the learning event. The research has drawn on a variety of published sources, and on the experience of individual learners to identify and develop a model for discriminating and building the kinds of intra-personal behaviours used by successful experiential learners (or even learners more generally). This model has been developed and tested in a variety of informal settings and has been the focus of a series of workshops to elaborate the model and develop participant skills access to the various categories identified by the model. Refinement and extension of the model continues.
Published Material: MULLIGAN, J. (1992). 'Internal processes in experiential learning'. In: MULLIGAN, J. & GRIFFIN, G. (Eds). Empowerment through experiential learning: explanations of good practice. London: Kogan Page.; MULLIGAN, J. (1993). 'Activating internal processes in experiential learning'. In: BOWD, D., COHEN, R. & WALKER, D. (Eds). Using experience for learning. Milton Keynes: Open University Press.
Status: Individual research
Date of Research: 1990-continuing
KEYWORDS: *experiential learning; intellectual development; learning processes; learning strategies*

10/1489
Department of Educational Studies, Guildford GU2 5XH
01483 300800
Gregory, J. Ms; *Supervisor:* Lathleen, J. Prof.; Lucock, R. Dr
A grounded theory study of the education of hospital nurses: how education for interpersonal relations influences the way nurses relate to each other in the college and on the ward
Abstract: Working from a premise within humanistic education: that people will integrate professional and personal learning to be 'enabling' for others in professional practice, combined with the definition of nursing supplied by nurses in this study, that is: 'Nursing is about the quality of interpersonal relationships between nurses and patients'. This research focused on: (a) what constituted interpersonal relationships for the nurses studied; (b) how did the education of nurses address interpersonal relating; (c) how did the development of interpersonal relationships as therapeutic or enabling behaviour get practised among nurses themselves in educational and hospital ward practice. A grounded theory approach was used to discover the socio-psychological dimensions to how nurses related to each other. A purposive sample of 30 nurses was used from student to lecturers and trained ward staff. The method was indepth interviews, some non-participant observations and document searches. The main findings were that nurses felt ill equipped to form enabling (socio-psychological) relationships especially with each other. Socio-psychological training was given low priority with most lecturers feeling unable to teach the interpersonal curriculum experientially. The basic socio-psychological process found was a 'withholding of self as a way of self-management. Theoretical categories such as 'the professional shield', with over use of hierarchical power and fear of rejection were discussed. Finally there are some recommendations for nurse education to devise educational psychological learning contracting for interpersonal skills training, and that such training be

called psychosocial education to give it more prominence in the nursing curriculum.
Status: Individual research
Date of Research: 1989-1994
KEYWORDS: interpersonal relationship; nurse education

10/1490

Department of Educational Studies, Guildford GU2 5XH
01483 300800
Tjok-A-Tam Ms; *Supervisor:* Denicolo, P. Dr
Learning in action: developments in management education
Abstract: In the 1980's colleges of further and higher education were subject to a variety of pressures to develop their provision of management education. These pressures are reviewed in their historical context as a prelude and background to an exploration of the then current challenges for such education. Interviews with representatives of awarding bodies and colleges provide macro- and micro-level perspectives on these challenges. The process of Accreditation of Prior Learning (APL) now called by the Management Charter Initiative, the Crediting Competence Process, emerged as the potential means of facilitating flexible, work-based management education programmes. This view was reinforced by the results of telephone questionnaires and semi-structured interviews with senior human resource and line managers. The National Vocational Qualification (NVQ) initiatives (1988-1993) required such competence-based programmes, therefore an investigation was instituted into the changes required in management education, training and development (METD) so that it might respond appropriately. The development of the roles of staff/learners, as they attempt to support the effective learning of manager/learners, became a specific focus using an iterative, ethnomethodological approach incorporating constructivist techniques in a case study of a college undertaken immediately before and after the introduction of NVQ management programmes. This project argues that, to enable transformative learning by manager/learners through a process of emancipatory education, a complementary parallel process of critical, active reflection must be established for staff/learners within innovative educational programmes. This process should engage both teachers and managers in action learning to uncover the elements of reflection and to develop skills of reflection on reflection-in-action. To promote such development a strategic approach to the management of change is explored and elaborated to produce a model in which staff and organisational development ineract through the 'learning company' process so that a college and its individual members may continuously transform in order to survive and prosper into the 21st Century.
Published Material: TJOK-A-TAM, S. & DENICOLO, P. (1991). 'Using constructivist tools to develop understanding of lecturer thinking about the new initiatives in management education'. A paper presented at the 5th Conference of the International Study Association on Teacher Thinking. University of Surrey.; TJOK-A-TAM, S. (1991). 'The forgotten manager'. Management Charter Initiative (MCI) – An occasional paper, February.
Status: Individual research
Date of Research: 1988-1994
KEYWORDS: learning strategies; management studies

10/1491

Department of Educational Studies, Guildford GU2 5XH
01483 300800
Denicolo, P. Dr
Teaching for salient learning: actioning espoused theories in the face of perceived constraints
Abstract: Rapid developments in knowledge, technology and policy in educational institutions enforce reflection on practice, both by teachers and learners. Building on data and results from previous staff development work, this research will investigate firstly the relationship between espoused theories of teaching and learning, theories-in-use and perceived imposed theories held by teachers. Informal research suggests that, although such teachers recognise the value of developing transferable, learning-to-learn skills in their students, they nevertheless feel constrained in their teaching strategies by overloaded syllabi and the expectations (perceived) of the culture and systems in which they work. A literature review and an indepth investigation of this, using a Personal Construct Theory approach across a range of provision, will ground the consequent research in both theory and practice. The second phase will consist of pilot trials, implementing a series of specific teaching strategies which are congruent with espoused theories but which take account of practical

constraints. The results will be evaluated by triangulation of all participant views with comparisons of successful achievement between these and former students. The third phase will incorporate a similar study, using revised strategies from the second phase with a new group of students, to confirm and extend results and will also involve a follow-up study of the original student group to investigate the persistence of any new learning skills and their transfer to new learning situations. This will involve a variety of investigatory techniques with the original students and their new teachers as participants.
Status: Individual research
Date of Research: 1992-1994
KEYWORDS: learning strategies; learning theories; teaching methods

10/1492

Department of Educational Studies, Guildford GU2 5XH
01483 300800
Seidu, M. Mr; *Supervisor:* Black, T. Dr; Parnell, J. Dr
Information technology in nursing and nurse education
Abstract: The awareness of the ways in which computers can benefit the nursing care provided to National Health Service patients is growing rapidly. Many nurses are becoming familiar with using computers and some are actively involved in the development of computing systems. The National Health Service is currently involved in a number of projects which seek to aid nurses both in their role as managers of health service resources, and primarily to provide better levels of patient care. This study therefore seeks to investigate the impact of information technology on nursing, nursing care and also the education provisions for the use of this new technology. The specific aims of the project are: (1) To what extent does the use of information technology at the work place improve the efficiency of the care nurses deliver to patients? (2) What educational provisions are there to train nurses in the use of this new technology?
Status: Sponsored project
Source of Grant: Hillingdon Hospital, Department of Health Studies
Date of Research: 1991-1994
KEYWORDS: information technology; nurse education; nursing

10/1493

Department of Educational Studies, Guildford GU2 5XH
01483 300800
Miller, P. Rev.; *Supervisor:* Denicolo, P. Dr; Brownhill, R. Dr
The recognition and resolution of dilemma
Abstract: The intention is to study how well 16-19 year old students recognise and resolve dilemmas (either as these occur in everyday life, moral or political dilemmas, or in their chosen disciplines, e.g. history, physics, design or phsyical education). Dilemma can be defined negatively as choice or a situation requiring a choice between equally unfavourable alternatives ('in front the precipice, behind the wolf', 'between Scylla and Charybdis') or they can be stated more positively as perplexing predicaments which, from the perspective of the observer, have a number of equally valid solutions. The intention is to test the prima facie evidence that the ability to recognise, accept and resolve dilemmas is domain specific, rather than general. Secondly to discover whether it has a close relationship with postformal operational thought, relativist judgements or metasystematic and dialectical thinking. It is hoped that some light will be shed on the question which educational experiences are most supportive and relevant to the development of this ability.
Status: Individual research
Date of Research: 1991-continuing
KEYWORDS: decision making; problem solving; student attitudes

10/1494

Department of Educational Studies, Guildford GU2 5XH
01483 300800
Blamire-Prosser, J. Mrs; *Supervisor:* Jarvis, P. Prof.
Vocational education and training and the labour market: an economic curriculum model
Abstract: The research examines Government policies for Vocational Education and Training (VET) between 1981 and 1991 against changes in the labour market supply and demand and curriculum theories, notably vocationalism, core skills and competence-based curricula. Data sources include government reports, official papers and commentaries, and a case study into the effects of planning work-related further education in London in 1990. The research identifies characteristics derived from monetarism and the ideology

of market forces as: economy, efficiency and effectiveness. The main premise of the model is that a money-led curriculum serves and is subservient to, the requirements of the labour market and economic individualism. This justifies the value in Government policy placed on vocationalism, control by employers and changes to the organisation of the education and training system to reflect competitive commercialism. This gives rise to restructuring to create an internal market and the substitution of price mechanisms, consumerism and centralism for educational issues in planning the curriculum. The key issues are the tensions between public and private cost; scarcity and choice expressed by consumer preferences; price mechanisms operating on funding for institutions and courses; and the utility value of VET. The research redefines the curriculum model based on economy, efficiency, effectiveness and equity, reciprocal transfer of values between VET and the post-industrial labour market, and suggests alternative structures for both.
Status: Individual research
Date of Research: 1989-1993
KEYWORDS: *curriculum development; economics-education relationship; educational policy; labour market; politics education relationship; vocational education*

10/1495
Department of Educational Studies, Guildford GU2 5XH
01483 300800
Harwood, A. Mrs; *Supervisor:* Denicolo, P. Dr
The effects of institutional and curricula course changes in further education with regard to implications for staff development
Abstract: The introduction of National Vocational Qualifications and the requirements of business and technology education for competence-based learning have resulted in changes in the role of teaching staff as 'lecturers' to 'facilitators' of learning with a greater degree of work placement involvement and more flexible modes of operation. Institutional changes have also resulted in changes in role for staff in colleges of further education, requiring their involvement in costing, marketing, quality assurance; while at the same time experiencing reduced security of tenure. Both aspects of change require skills and abilities which were not necessarily part of 'traditional' teaching roles and, therefore, call for appropriate staff development.
Status: Individual research
Date of Research: 1991-1994
KEYWORDS: *educational change; further education; further education teachers; staff development*

10/1496
Department of Educational Studies, Guildford GU2 5XH
01483 300800
Guy, G. Mrs; *Supervisor:* Brownhill, R. Dr; Walters, N. Rev.
Religious education in the primary school post Education Reform Act 1988
Abstract: The main specific area of this research will be Religious Education (RE) in the primary school. This will be studied with particular reference to the Education Reform Act 1988. In particular the research will be related to the interpretation of RE within the intercultural and multicultural environment which currently exists in England. The research will be enquiry based on qualitative and quantitative surveys and data. The main objective will be to determine methodology for the teaching of RE and to define the influences of major world religions within the curriculum of primary schools. The research will be based on the following questions: (1) Is RE a necessary part of the curriculum? (2) If this is the case how should it be taught? (3) What should be the aims of RE? (4) If RE is problematic should it be removed from the education system.
Status: Individual research
Date of Research: 1991-continuing
KEYWORDS: *Education Reform Act 1988; multiculturalism; primary education; religious education*

10/1497
Department of Educational Studies, Guildford GU2 5XH
01483 300800
Thorp, H. Mrs; *Supervisor:* Evans, K. Dr; Brown, A. Dr
Training the Euro-Manager: curriculum implications for the 1990s
Abstract: The advent of the Single European Market in 1992 has generated interest in creating Euro-managers capable of responding

to this new business environment. The investigation looks at academic and corporate approaches to the development of these Euro-managers focusing on initiatives to create an innovative European business perspective. Methods include a survey of selected European Management Business Studies courses (undergraduate and Master of Business Administration (MBA) in the United Kingdom), and several small case studies comparing academic and corporate situations. It is envisaged that an Anglo-German study will be included in this part of the project design. Overall the aim of the investigation is to establish direction on curriculum implications for training.
Status: Individual research
Date of Research: 1990-1994
KEYWORDS: *business administration education; management studies; professional training; single European market*

10/1498
Department of Educational Studies, Guildford GU2 5XH
01483 300800
Dean, J. Dr; *Supervisor:* Hobrough, J. Dr
A study of effective advisory work in local education authorities
Abstract: This study of 4 widely differing local education authority (LEA) advisory teams, initially involved the working out of criteria by which judgements of effectiveness might be made. These were then incorporated into questionnaires which were sent to 100 headteachers and 200 teachers in each of the authorities. The questionnaires were complemented by interviews with groups of advisers, advisory teachers, primary and secondary headteachers and teachers whose schools had been inspected. Headteachers and teachers were also asked for their priorities for advisory work. In addition, there was a national survey of what was currently happening to advisory teams. Important findings included the fact that the team which separated inspection and advice did less well; the best team was very well managed but also had the highest staffing ratio; and that small teams were important in supporting people doing this work. There was a strong correlation between relationships with headteachers and teachers and successful inspection, advice and inservice work, and between knowledge, skill and experience and these three areas. The criteria offer a means by which other teams might evaluate their work.
Published Material: DEAN, J. (1991). The organisation of LEA inspectorate/advisory teams. Slough: National Foundation for Educational Research.; DEAN, J. (1992). Effectiveness in the advisory services. Slough: National Foundation for Educational Research.; DEAN, J. (1993). Headteachers' and teachers' priorities for advisory work and inspection. Slough: National Foundation for Educational Research.; DEAN, J. (1993). A survey of the organisation of LEA inspection and advisory services. Slough: National Foundation for Educational Research.; DEAN, J. (1994). What headteachers and teachers think about inspection. Slough: National Foundation for Educational Research. A full list is available from the researcher.
Status: Individual research
Date of Research: 1991-1993
KEYWORDS: *advisers; inservice teacher education; inspection; local education authorities; organisational effectiveness*

10/1499
Department of Educational Studies, Guildford GU2 5XH
01483 300800
Swan, R. Mr; *Supervisor:* Riggs, A. Ms; Brownhill, R. Dr
Perceptions of adult development and adult religious education by church leaders and church members: the implications of psychological theories of adult development, and the conflict between these areas
Abstract: The background to this research is the perception that psychological theories of adult development, and religious institutions' concepts of adult development are mostly incompatible. The project aims to sample some views of what ideal adult development is seen to be by individuals within religious groups (Christian); to critique these using James Fowler's work involving 'Stages of Faith', and other (psychological) theories such as Maslo and Ericson. The research will be qualitative and not seek to be generalisable to any great degree. It will test the range and depth of perception, to comment on it and apply the data to church documents detailing the 'ideal' congregation member.
Status: Individual research
Date of Research: 1992-continuing
KEYWORDS: *adult development; adult education; religion and education; religious education*

10/1500

Department of Educational Studies, Guildford GU2 5XH
01483 300800

Kearsley, M. Mr; *Supervisor:* James, D. Prof.; Tosey, P. Dr

Learning behaviour and value modification with particular reference to sales training

Abstract: Much time, effort and money is spent on developing skills (such as sales skills, presentation skills etc.) which are never put into practice by those trained because of internal beliefs and attitudes which have not changed. The aim of the project is to explore how internal beliefs are created and to explore how these may be changed so that behaviour is altered. This is an indepth study with volunteers from several major professional organisations and consultancies. It will include a survey/questionnaire of the total population, performance monitored over time, personal reflections and observations over 18 months.

Status: Individual research
Date of Research: 1992-continuing
KEYWORDS: attitudes; distributive trades education; salesmanship

10/1501

Department of Educational Studies, Guildford GU2 5XH
01483 300800

Marshall, M. Mrs; *Supervisor:* Lucock, R. Dr; Parnell, J. Dr

Professional development of diploma student nurses upon qualification

Abstract: The proposed research will address the issue of professional development in terms of continued/lifelong education and learning of diploma student nurses upon qualification. Little attention seems to have been paid to the professional development of nurses upon qualification. Previous studies focused mostly on nurses' career paths; career motivation and career patterns; opportunity for continuing education; and promotion prospects. A new curriculum for diploma nurses advocates a commitment to teach nurses how to learn to give them confidence and motivation to develop themselves during their nursing career. The proposed research therefore aims to ascertain how and to what extent these nurses are equipped to become responsible, self-directed lifelong learners. A cohort of students completing their diploma nursing course will be selected randomly and followed over a period of time. Data for analysis will be collected by self-completion questionnaires; semi-structured interviews and examination of educational documents.

Status: Individual research
Date of Research: 1992-continuing
KEYWORDS: lifelong learning; nurse education; nurses; professional continuing education; professional development

10/1502

Department of Educational Studies, Guildford GU2 5XH
01483 300800

Munro, L. Mrs; *Supervisor:* Hobrough, J. Dr; MaClaren, S. Mrs

The administration of oral medicines with special reference to food ingestion

Abstract: The aim of the study is to explore how often oral drugs are administered accurately in relation to food intake. Many drugs need to be given either before or after food. Failure to comply with this request may result in the drug being ineffective. The understanding of these issues by trained nurses will be explored. The curriculum will be analysed for content and teaching method in relation to pharmacology. The organisation of the wards will also be studied. It is anticipated that an educational intervention may be recommended as a result of the study.

Status: Individual research
Date of Research: 1993-continuing
KEYWORDS: medicine; nurse education; nurses; pharmacology

10/1503

Department of Educational Studies, Guildford GU2 5XH
01483 300800

Brown, A. Dr; Blackman, S. Dr

Evaluation of Young Engineers

Abstract: The project seeks to investigate key curricular issues concerning the operation of Young Engineers clubs. The evaluation will be illuminative, within initial investigations focusing on the operation of clubs in Hertfordshire, Hampshire and Surrey. Among the issues being investigated are the reasons for schools and teachers becoming involved in the initiative; the different patterns of commitment, achievement and progression of pupils; and any change or reinforcement of attitudes towards engineering.

Status: Sponsored project
Source of Grant: Standing Conference on Schools Science and Technology £12,000
Date of Research: 1992-1993
KEYWORDS: clubs; curriculum enrichment; engineering; engineers; industry-education relationship

10/1504

Department of Educational Studies, Guildford GU2 5XH
01483 300800

Brown, A. Dr; Germon, S. Ms

Widening access to higher education

Abstract: The research investigates admissions tutors' views on the qualities required of prospective entrants to higher education (HE). Ten admissions tutors from each of five subject areas (chemistry, business studies, sociology, engineering and history) were interviewed. Most tutors focused largely upon predicted or past academic attainment and often had difficulty weighing claims from students from different routes. However, from exceptional practice and commentary from admissions tutors and officers, coupled with extensive workshop discussions, it was possible to construct the basis of a more comprehensive framework for the HE admissions process. This involved the development of a grid to allow for a degree of integration in the factors upon which claims for admission to HE could be made from those following different routes aimed at entry into HE. The research promulgated a staff development process which was intended to stimulate debate about and make more explicit the criteria which should be used to determine entry into HE.

Published Material: BROWN, A.J. & BIMROSE, J. (1992). 'Skills and qualities required for entry into higher education in England: current practice and future policy'. Paper given at the 18th International Conference of the International Association for Education Assessment: admission to higher education, Dublin, September, 1992.
Status: Sponsored project
Source of Grant: Universities Funding Council £24,000
Date of Research: 1992-1993
KEYWORDS: access to education; admission criteria; admissions tutors; higher education; student recruitment

10/1505

Department of Educational Studies, Guildford GU2 5XH
01483 300800

Haines, T. Mrs; *Supervisor:* Black, T. Dr; Worle, B. Mr

The use and management of information technology in higher education in the United Kingdom

Abstract: The intention is to examine higher education: its purpose, effectiveness, efficiency, organisation and strategy with respect to information technology (IT). The holistic multidisciplinary approach focuses on conditions for effective and efficient management of information technology in institutions of higher education. It is of considerable interest that such knowledge-based industries are facilitated in sagacious IT use. A comparison of the 'new' and 'old' universities is being undertaken to consider the environmental influence on the synthesis of learning, learning management and IT. Sample survey work with needs analysis and appraisal of information strategies (and IT use) will be required. Suitable measures of IT effectiveness are intended to be developed.

Status: Individual research
Date of Research: 1992-continuing
KEYWORDS: computer uses in education; higher education; information technology

10/1506

Department of Educational Studies, Guildford GU2 5XH
01483 300800

Germon, S. Ms; *Supervisor:* Walters, N. Rev.

Needs analysis of staff development for volunteers in continuing education

Abstract: The project aims to use the experience of engaging with volunteers on a collaborative project, with the Community Education Department of the Open University, and Surrey Community Action Learning Programme, in order to research social policy implications, recruitment policy and process, initial training needs analysis for organisations and individual volunteers, progressional paths, and the interface between the volunteer and the professional. The objective

is to identify staff development programmes that meet the 'real' rather than perceived needs of the volunteer in adult continuing education. Methods include a case study of the collaborative project, questionnaire survey with managers of volunteers and volunteers themselves, (approximate sample size 200) followed by selective interviews.
Status: Sponsored project
Source of Grant: Universities Funding Council £21,486
Date of Research: 1992-1993
KEYWORDS: *community education; continuing education; staff development; training; voluntary service; volunteers*

10/1507
Department of Educational Studies, Guildford GU2 5XH
01483 300800
Costley, C. Ms; *Supervisor:* Tivers, J. Dr
Women, music and culture: equality issues in music education at National Curriculum key stage 3
Abstract: Case studies and action research are used to investigate the music education of girls at National Curriculum key stage 3 (ages 11-14), in five different secondary schools within one Greater London borough. Relevant literature indicates the significance of gender in European art music's history, musical aesthetics and education. Girls and women are found to have been excluded from certain musical roles. The study shows how European art music's history is rooted in a male ideology which proscribes a female musical role for women and how these meanings along with other more general gendered knowledge is transmitted in schools. The case studies include close observation, interviews and account gathering. This provides necessary background information for action research in which teachers become involved in the research, reflect on the issues, and make changes in their classrooms. Action research raises awareness amongst practitioners and contributes to further debate on the subject. The empirical research focuses on girls' experiences in the music classroom, with social class and race seen as other major explanations for differentiation in music education. The values, assumptions and previous experience of students, teachers, schools and the wider society are compared, and considered in relation to gendered disadvantage in music. The thesis concludes that it is possible to make education less gendered at National Curriculum key stage 3 in individual classrooms. However, there are wider institutional and societal influences which impede progress. A number of possible changes are proposed for the practice of holistic music education.
Published Material: COSTLEY, C. (1993). 'Music and gender at key stage three (11-14): an action research project', British Journal of Music Education, Vol 10, No 3, pp.197-203.
Status: Individual research
Date of Research: 1988-1994
KEYWORDS: *equal education; music; music education; sex differences*

10/1508
Department of Educational Studies, Guildford GU2 5XH
01483 300800
Evans, K. Dr; Brown, A. Dr
Technical and training mastery in the workplace
Abstract: This research aims to explore the issues involved in the implementation of attempts to develop people who combine both technical and training mastery in the workplace and to make recommendations on the development of a strategy which addresses delivery as well as policy issues. It is intended that the research findings should be of interest to both practitioners and policy makers. The researchers will investigate attempts to promote the development of 'key workers' – people who combine both technical and training mastery in the workplace. (This will cover both individual company initiatives and the attempt by City and Guilds of London Institute (CGLI) to develop a national system for accreditation of skilled 'masters'). It is also intended to identify factors significant in the success or failure of such initiatives with reference to selected international comparisons.
Status: Sponsored project
Source of Grant: Leverhulme Trust £37,650
Date of Research: 1991-1993
KEYWORDS: *industrial training; on the job training; trainers*

10/1509
Department of Educational Studies, Guildford GU2 5XH
01483 300800
Denicolo, P. Dr

Part-time research students: the integration of this role with others in their professional lives
Abstract: This research is yet in an embryonic stage and is derived from concerns about providing relevant and appropriate support for part-time research students in particular, although it may also produce results of significance to full-time research students. It is commonly accepted that research towards a higher degree is, inter alia, demanding, time-consuming, and requiring a high degree of motivation. Yet, a large number of part-time research students are mature and hence have many roles in life, personal and professional, which compete with their research student role. This research seeks to understand some of the effects that this role has on students' lives, in particular how it contributes to and constrains other roles. A personal construct theory approach (Kelly 1955) will be used to indicate commonalities of perspectives as well as to provide case studies which illuminate possible benefits, opportunities and difficulties derived from such an undertaking. Thus, it is speculated, the results will contribute to the provision of appropriate advice and support for prospective and current students.
Status: Individual research
Date of Research: 1993-continuing
KEYWORDS: *graduate study; mature students; part time students; student research*

10/1510
Department of Educational Studies, Guildford GU2 5XH
01483 300800
Frances Harrison College of Healthcare, St Luke's Hospital, Warren Road, Guildford GU1 3NT
Holmes, F. Mrs; *Supervisor:* Parnell, J. Dr; Lathleen, J. Prof.
An illuminative evaluation study of a Project 2000 Course
Abstract: This is an illuminative evaluation study of a Project 2000 course held in one of the demonstration colleges. It aims to illuminate the good and bad (if any) points about such a new, innovative nurse training programme. It was decided to study one cohort of students (100) throughout the 3 year training/education period and the following 6 months of post-registration. The methods used to date are quantitative and qualitative: interviews with teachers; classroom observations; background material; evaluations; examination and assessment results; questionnaires to practitioners and students; and critical incident recordings. The focus after the first 2 years is very much on teaching methods, learning styles and student centred learning.
Status: Individual research
Date of Research: 1990-continuing
KEYWORDS: *nurse education; programme evaluation*

10/1511
Department of Educational Studies, Guildford GU2 5XH
01483 300800
University of East London, Department of Psychology, Barking Campus, Longbridge Road, Dagenham RM8 2AS
0181 590 7722
Brown, A. Dr; Germon, S. Ms; Bimrose, J. Ms; Lagro, N. Ms
Competence for higher education
Abstract: The project was intended to inform the debate about policy and implementation of General National Vocational Qualifications (GNVQ). In particular, higher education (HE) admissions processes and practices were investigated with a view to the implications for the development and implementation of GNVQ. The following issues were considered: admissions tutors concerns; overall programme design; 'fit' with HE curricula; 'fit' with HE admissions strategy; importance of links between GNVQ provider and HE provider; monitoring future development. This was one part of a larger study on 'Widening access to HE'
Status: Sponsored project
Source of Grant: Further Education Unit £14,077
Date of Research: 1992-1992
KEYWORDS: *access to education; admission criteria; competency based education; higher education; National Vocational Qualifications*

Sussex University

10/1512

Institute of Continuing and Professional Education, Sussex
House, Falmer, Brighton BN1 9RH
01273 606755
Burke, J. Dr
**Research and development in National Vocational
Qualifications (NVQs) and the identification of various
competences in teaching and management**
Abstract: The objectives of this project are to: 1) pursue research and
development in competency-based learning in support of the emerging model of National Vocational Qualifications (NVQs); 2) publish,
disseminate and generally promote research and developments in
respect of the above area; and 3) provide consultancy to National
Vocational Qualifications on research and development on specific
projects. The major focus of the work in the first year was on generic
competences or core skills. Three papers, dealing with the reconcep-
tualisation of generic competence, and aspects of problem solving,
were published by the NCVQ. Subsequently, the focus of the research
has continued on generic competences, (a) supporting the work of the
NCVQ in collaboration with the National Curriculum Council (NCC)
and School Examinations and Assessment Council (SEAC), and
others, (b) working with the Open University Enterprise in Higher
Education Project, and (c) providing consultancy for School Management South's project on competency in educational management
(Director: Dr Tony Bailey, Project Director: Dr Peter Earley, National
Foundation for Educational Research). A fourth area of interest is
NVQs and Special Needs.
Published Material: BURKE, J. (1989). Competency-based education and training. London: Falmer Press.; BURKE, J. (1989). 'To-
wards a framework for problem solving as a common learning
outcome'. In JESSUP, G. Common learning outcomes: core skills in
A/AS levels and NVQs. London: National Council for Vocational
Qualifications (NCVQ R & D Report No 6).; BURKE, J. & JESSUP,
G. (1990). 'Assessment in NVQs: disentangling validity from reli-
ability in NVQs'. In: HORTON, T. Assessment debates. Open Uni-
versity Reader. London: Hodder and Stoughton.; BURKE, J. (1991).
Foreword to G. Jessup . Outcomes: NVQs and the emerging model
of education and training. London: Falmer Press.; A full list of
publications is available from the researcher.
Status: Sponsored project
Source of Grant: National Council for Vocational Qualifications
£93,000
Date of Research: 1989-continuing
*KEYWORDS: competency based education; minimum competences;
National Vocational Qualifications; skills*

10/1513

Institute of Continuing and Professional Education, Sussex
House, Falmer, Brighton BN1 9RH
01273 606755
Al-Rajab, E. Mr; *Supervisor:* Thomson, A. Dr
**Facilitating adult learning through continuing education: a
case study of the Centre for Community Service and
Continuing Education at Kuwait University**
Abstract: There is a lack of research on the relationship between the
principles of andragogical theory and adult higher education practice
in Kuwait. This study will attempt to address the void in the research
base and produce recommendations for improving education programme development and implementation. The study is designed to
examine the degree to which current practice at the Kuwait University
Center of Community Service and Continuing Education (CCS & CE)
reflects the use of the principles of andragogy in its community
service/continuing education programme. More specifically, the study
will: 1) examine the knowledge of, attitudes toward, and experience
with andragogy of key personnel; 2) identify the perceptions of the
personnel about andragogy and its application at the CCS & CE at
Kuwait University; and 3) consider the problems and issues in the
application of andragogy and its relevance to the CCS & CE at Kuwait
University. Finally, the purpose of this study is to make recommendations for the improvement of the community service/continuing education programme at the CCS & CE at Kuwait University.
Status: Individual research
Date of Research: 1993-continuing
*KEYWORDS: adult education; andragogy; continuing education;
Kuwait*

10/1514

Institute of Continuing and Professional Education, Sussex
House, Falmer, Brighton BN1 9RH
01273 606755
Stuart, M. Ms
Accreditation of prior learning: a pilot development scheme
Abstract: This project will build on appropriate knowledge and
experience of Accreditation of Prior Learning (APL) in order to
develop an APL system for the University of Sussex. An APL scheme
will be piloted with part-time students registered for award-bearing
courses and the part-time degree programme coordinated by the
Centre for Continuing Education (CCE), and will involve faculty
members, students and employers. Through information dissemination and the provision of staff development and training, the project
will ensure that University staff members, including teaching faculty
and admissions officers, are made aware of the nature and value of
APL. On the basis of the pilot, recommendations will be made about
the implementation of an APL scheme for the University as a whole.
The project has the following more specific aims: 1) Evaluate systems
of APL currently established within British higher education institutions. 2) Initiate a pilot scheme for APL based within CCE's award-
bearing courses and part-time degree programme. 3) Work with
relevant employers and professional bodies to design appropriate
forms of assessment for the APL scheme. 4) Monitor and evaluate
the pilot in order to establish and recommend good practice for a
University-wide APL scheme. 5) Prepare the ground for an APL
scheme throughout the University by disseminating information
about APL; and by working with the Staff Development Officer to
provide appropriate staff development events. 6) Raise awareness of
transferable "life skills" within higher education learning, and to
explore curriculum development in response to the potentials of APL.
Status: Sponsored project
Source of Grant: Enterprise in Higher Education £13,000
Date of Research: 1993-1994
*KEYWORDS: access to education; accreditation of prior learning;
experiential learning; higher education; transfer of learning*

10/1515

Institute of Continuing and Professional Education, Sussex
House, Falmer, Brighton BN1 9RH
01273 606755
Ryle, M. Mr
Group assessment: monitoring innovation
Abstract: Several award-bearing courses at the Centre for Continuing
Education (CCE) at Sussex University involve the formal assessment
of group projects, often using innovative media. The question of how
to define and carry out assessment of group work is of considerable
interest to the University and to students and employers. The project
aims to develop and evaluate CCE's methods of assessing group work
and to disseminate the results to a wide audience within the University
and among other higher education institutions (particularly in continuing education). The assessment of group work focuses on skills
and learning outcomes different from those evaluated by more traditional assessment methods. In particular, in group and team work
students are encouraged to develop the transferable skills of problem-
solving, planning, and effective communication. Group work also
frequently involves students in practical activities using innovative
media. Since assessment of group work focuses explicitly on the
extent and quality of students' involvement in the completion of
specified tasks, as well as on the quality of the 'product', these
transferable skills are foregrounded. The development of proven
methods of assessing group work will allow such work to figure more
largely and centrally in the curriculum of the University. The University Staff Development Team will disseminate knowledge about, and
facilitate discussion of, the methods for assessment of group work
which are developed in this project. Employers involved in the project
will include voluntary and commercial organisations, who will host
and deliver parts of the relevant courses and will be asked to participate in the evaluation of the assessment methods used.
Status: Sponsored project
Source of Grant: Enterprise in Higher Education £6,700
Date of Research: 1993-1994
KEYWORDS: assessment; group work

10/1516

Institute of Continuing and Professional Education, Sussex
House, Falmer, Brighton BN1 9RH
01273 606755

Thomson, A. Dr; *Supervisor:* Gray, F. Dr
The role of non-traditional partners in continuing education provision
Abstract: The general research aim was to examine the nature of liberal adult education provision by 'non-traditional' agencies (including voluntary bodies, charities, museums, arts centres, local societies and commercial tour operators). Specific aims were to examine the objectives, motives and target groups of non-traditional continuing education (CE) providers, the type and quality of provision; and the diversity of changing relationships between traditional (and specifically university CE departments) and non-traditional providers. The objectives were to clarify the array of provision and to assess the opportunities for, and limitations to, collaboration between mainstream and non-traditional providers. The project was pursued by way of three inter-connected case studies: 1) An historical investigation, based on documentary sources and secondary material, of the creation and development of the boundaries of adult continuing education in Britain throughout the 20th century, examining how certain providers have attained 'traditional' status while non-traditional agencies have sometimes challenged accepted boundaries. 2) An examination, via a postal questionnaire of English and Welsh university CE departments and indepth interviews with key individuals within selected departments, of the relationships of university CE centres with non-traditional partners, highlighting the value, potential and problems of collaboration. 3) A study of the evolution, from 1969 to 1992, of relationships between both traditional and non-traditional agencies in Sussex and the University of Sussex, Centre for Continuing Education. Research methods included questionnaires and face to face interviews.
Published Material: THOMSON, A. (1992). 'Sustaining the cutting edge: non-traditional partners in adult education provision'. Adults learning, Vol 3, No 6, pp.154-156.; THOMSON, A. (1992). 'New cultural contexts for university adult education: the potential of partnerships with non-traditional agencies'. In: MILLER, N. & WEST, L. Changing culture and adult learning. Canterbury: University of Kent at Canterbury, SCUTREA.; THOMSON, A. 'Non-traditional partners'. In: FIELDHOUSE, R. A new history of adult education. Leicester: National Institute for Adult and Continuing Education (NIACE). (in press).
Status: Sponsored project
Source of Grant: Universities Funding Council £30,000
Date of Research: 1991-1993
KEYWORDS: adult education; continuing education; liberal education; nontraditional education

10/1517
Institute of Continuing and Professional Education, Sussex House, Falmer, Brighton BN1 9RH
01273 606755
Holloway, G. Ms; Ambrose, P. Ms; Mayhew, G. Dr; *Supervisor:* Gray, F. Dr; Thomson, A. Dr
Accreditation and award-bearing courses as a challenge to liberal adult education
Abstract: This one year project sought to examine the major changes in university non-vocational continuing education resulting from the recent growth of accredited and award-bearing courses. In particular the project examined the historical and contemporary debates around the dichotomy, assessing whether liberal adult education (LAE) courses had different aims and objectives, curriculum, teaching methods, and student bodies, than accredited and award-bearing continuing education (CE) courses. The research was divided into discreet sections which followed on from each other: 1) A review of relevant historical developments and issues in university liberal adult education. 2) A documentary and postal questionnaire survey of university liberal adult education award-bearing and non-award-bearing provision. 3) Case studies based on interviews with key respondents – academic and administrative faculty in a selected number of CE departments throughout Britain – and focusing on the impact of, and responses to, recent funding and policy developments which are generally perceived to be a threat to LAE and of major significance in changing the character of traditional extra-mural provision. The subject of this project has particular relevance given the Higher Education Funding Council for England (HEFCE) proposed changes to the funding of LAE. The funding council review was published mid-way through the project, and resulted in an added impetus to, and change of direction in the research, a new and additional focus becoming an examination of how CE departments, faculty, tutors and students involved in LAE were responding to the likely changes.
Status: Sponsored project

Source of Grant: Higher Education Funding Council for England £21,000
Date of Research: 1993-1994
KEYWORDS: adult education; continuing education; liberal education

10/1518
Institute of Continuing and Professional Education, Sussex House, Falmer, Brighton BN1 9RH
01273 606755
Williams, R. Mr
Diversity within unity: an approach to education for the environment of Europe
Abstract: The project has two main aims: 1) To provide knowledge and understanding about the environmental state of Europe and to connect this with the converging economic, political and social policies being developed and implemented by the European Commission (EC). 2) To explore and examine the concept of the care and protection of the natural environment as a force for unification of the diverse peoples and cultures of Europe, but without diminishing or denying their separate and different identities. The project will take the form of a cooperative programme of research, involving people and institutions from selected member states of the EC. The programme will include critical evaluation of EC environmental policies and their implementation; and also case studies representing environmental issues and concerns together with an appropriate methodology for their implementation within educational systems.
Status: Sponsored project
Source of Grant: European Commission Directorate; World Wide Fund for Nature
Date of Research: 1992-continuing
KEYWORDS: environmental education; environmental research; Europe; European community

10/1519
Institute of Continuing and Professional Education, Sussex House, Falmer, Brighton BN1 9RH
01273 606755
Stephens, D. Dr
Culture as a frame of reference in education and development
Abstract: This research aims to provide a critique of current dominant, i.e. economic, frames of reference in education and development. A comprehensive review of secondary source literature in both Britain and North America will be followed by the development of a model of analysis which utilizes the concepts of culture and cultural identity. This model will then be applied to existing development projects in cultural contexts of which the author/researcher is familiar, e.g. Kenya, Sierra Leone, Nigeria. The research draws upon the researcher's masters and doctoral theses: Cultural Identity and Secondary Education in Sierra Leone, 1976 and Attitudes to Education Across Two Generations in Northern Nigeria, 1982. A book is projected.
Status: Individual research
Date of Research: 1992-continuing
KEYWORDS: cultural influences; developing countries; educational policy

10/1520
Institute of Continuing and Professional Education, Sussex House, Falmer, Brighton BN1 9RH
01273 606755
Lacey, C. Prof.; Williams, R. Mr
Education network for environment and development
Abstract: The project has two main purposes: 1) To build a network for collating information and analysing global change in the context of environmental and developmental systems and processes; 2) To change the provision of education so that it takes account of the importance of environment and development issues, and implements through curricular programmes appropriate knowledge, skills and values. The process for achieving these objectives is the stimulation of continuous and public debate, wherein new and creative ideas and critical thinking are brought to bear upon the impact of those systems and forces which shape the human predicament. Through a programme of research, through a series of seminars, and through the publication of a newsletter, occasional papers and books, the project intends to introduce into the debate forms of knowledge and radical perspectives as the means to renew educational approaches to global problems.

Published Material: LACEY, C. & WILLIAMS, R. (1987). Education, ecology and development: the case for an education network. London: Kogan Page/World Wide Fund for Nature.; LACEY, C. (1987). 'British charities and education'. Education Network for Environment and Development Occasional paper No 1. Brighton: Sussex University ENED.; LACEY, C. (1989). 'The world bank and the environment'. ENED Occasional paper No 2.; ABRAHAM, J., LACEY, C. & WILLIAMS, R. (1990). Deception, demonstration and debate: Toward a critical environment and development education. London: Kogan Page/World Wide Fund for Nature.; A full list of publications is available from the researcher.
Status: Sponsored project
Source of Grant: World Wide Fund for Nature
Date of Research: 1987-continuing
KEYWORDS: *environmental education; environmental research; global approach*

10/1521

Institute of Continuing and Professional Education, Sussex House, Falmer, Brighton BN1 9RH
01273 606755
Betts-Gosling, E. Ms; *Supervisor:* Yates, P. Dr
The healthy campus – health promotion in further education
Abstract: Maximisation of the physical and mental health of students would seem to be a vital pre-requisite for full learning potential to be achieved, yet few efforts have been made in further education colleges to determine what makes for the most suitable environment for this to occur. This study aims to identify essential factors in positive physical and mental health promotion and to establish strategies for their inclusion in the total college experience of a further education student. The study will have a particular focus towards the health development role played by that which is experienced outside the expressed curriculum. Thus, such things as extra-curricular opportunities, the facilities, environment and ethos of the college will form an important part of the research consideration.
Status: Individual research
Date of Research: 1991-1994
KEYWORDS: *colleges of further education; extracurricular activities; further education students; health promotion*

10/1522

Institute of Continuing and Professional Education, Sussex House, Falmer, Brighton BN1 9RH
01273 606755
Ryle, M. Mr
Issues in access to higher education
Abstract: Analysis and discussion of issues and developments in the design and delivery of Access to Higher Education courses, with a particular focus on: regional issues in South East England; questions of gender and appropriate curriculum; environmental education in Access; and collaboration in Access provision, especially the role of university continuing education departments.
Status: Individual research
Date of Research: 1990-continuing
KEYWORDS: *access programmes; access to education; continuing education; higher education*

10/1523

Institute of Continuing and Professional Education, Sussex House, Falmer, Brighton BN1 9RH
01273 606755
Ryle, M. Mr
Cultural studies and curriculum development in adult education
Abstract: This project involves: 1) discussion of the relation between 'cultural studies' and longer-established subjects/disciplines within the humanities, with especial reference to questions of teaching and learning; 2) dissemination/discussion articles on current and future course and curriculum development within the Centre for Continuing Education at Sussex University; and 3) theoretical articles and historical/genre-based research in literature and cultural studies.
Status: Individual research
Date of Research: 1992-continuing
KEYWORDS: *adult education; cultural education; curriculum development; humanities*

10/1524

Institute of Continuing and Professional Education, Sussex House, Falmer, Brighton BN1 9RH
01273 606755
Colclough, C. Dr; Lewin, K. Dr
Modelling the financing of Education for All
Abstract: This research is designed to explore the challenge created by the Jomtien Conference which committed many developing countries to pursue strategies for Education For All. In this work which follows on from a round table paper presented at the conference by the authors, the implications of resourcing Education for All are pursued in depth. The research explores the parameters, which are related to different levels of participation in developing countries, in the first cycle of the school system. It develops a computer simulation model to project forward enrolments and costs under different scenarios. A series of cost saving, cost shifting and quality enhancing reforms are introduced in order to explore the impact they have on the financial viability of Education for All strategies. The last part of the research explores the implications of these for the domestic financing of Education for All and needs for external assistance.
Published Material: COLCLOUGH, C. & LEWIN, K.M. (1993). Educating all the children: strategies for education in the south. Oxford: Oxford University Press
Status: Sponsored project
Source of Grant: UNICEF
Date of Research: 1990-1993
KEYWORDS: *developing countries; development aid; development education; financial support*

10/1525

Institute of Continuing and Professional Education, Sussex House, Falmer, Brighton BN1 9RH
01273 606755
Lacey, C. Prof.; Longman, D. Mr
An investigation of press reporting of environment and development issues, and the role of the press in public education
Abstract: An analysis of press reporting of environmental and development issues, with a view to understanding the processes which contributes to informing or educating public debate about issues that crucially affect the political and economic future of society. The research involves scanning a full-text-on-line database of the contents of four newspapers, to illustrate comparative patterns of newspaper coverage. Preliminary findings show that coverage of environment and development issues is highly selective; can contradict espoused editorial policy; and that frequently these issues receive less prominence as their political significance increases.
Status: Individual research
Date of Research: 1992-1993
KEYWORDS: *environmental education; news reporting; public opinion*

10/1526

Institute of Continuing and Professional Education, Sussex House, Falmer, Brighton BN1 9RH
01273 606755
Lewin, K. Dr
The implementation of basic education in China
Abstract: This research explores the implementation of 9 year compulsory education in the People's Republic of China. Three districts in different parts of China have been selected for close scrutiny. These areas include one close to Beijing in a peri-urban area amongst the 300 richest counties; the second area is in an interior province amongst the 300 poorest counties; and the third is amongst a national minority group in the south west of China. The researches involve both quantitative and qualitative data collection in the 3 case study areas. A particular strategy used has been to identify both rich and poor districts within each of the 3 main areas and contrast the development of provision on a number of dimensions. These include patterns of enrolment, gender differences in participation, financing of the development of universal primary education, the administrative and monitoring system that supports the implementation of the 9 year compulsory education law, and a variety of other interests which have emerged whilst the research has been taking place. The research provides a detailed and extensive account of problems which remain in the implementation of national policy and provides a uniquely detailed account of the situation in the 3 case study areas. A report on the project will be published by the International Institute of Educational Planning in association with UNICEF.

Status: Sponsored project
Source of Grant: UNICEF; British Council
Date of Research: 1990-1993
KEYWORDS: *China; educational policy; primary education*

10/1527

Institute of Continuing and Professional Education, Sussex
House, Falmer, Brighton BN1 9RH
01273 606755
Lewin, K. Dr

Dialogue for development: a policy review of the educational aid programme
Abstract: This research examines the activities and policy assumptions of the British Aid programme to education, specifically in relation to project aid. It reviews the existing basis for policy and analyses patterns of current disbursement. The research then identifies 6 key areas which will be definitive in formulating policy over the next decade. It then undertakes an analysis of the evidence of the effectiveness of educational aid in relation to 7 sectoral themes. Suggestions are given as to how the policy underlying the programme might best develop, and a model is created to assist with this.
Published Material: LEWIN, K. (1994). Education and development: the issues and the evidence. Educational development monographs. London: Overseas Development Administration.; LEWIN, K. (1994). 'British bilateral assistance to education: how much, to whom, and why', International Journal for Educational Development, Vol 14, No 2, pp.1-18.
Status: Sponsored project
Source of Grant: Overseas Development Administration; Foreign and Commonwealth Office
Date of Research: 1992-1992
KEYWORDS: *developing countries; development aid; development education*

10/1528

Institute of Continuing and Professional Education, Sussex
House, Falmer, Brighton BN1 9RH
01273 606755
Lewin, K. Dr

Implementing environmental and agricultural science curricula in Zimbabwe
Abstract: This project looks at the development of environmental and agricultural science in Zimbabwe. This area of the primary curriculum has been supported with German assistance over the last 10 years and the research was designed to establish the impact this assistance has had. A national survey was conducted along with a series of school case studies in four different parts of Zimbabwe. Analysis of this data produces a full picture of the extent to which the programme has been implemented.
Published Material: LEWIN, K., BAJAH et al. (1992). 'Teaching and learning in environmental agricultural science: meeting basic educational needs in Zimbabwe. An evaluation. Document 16/21 A/A. Bonn: German Foundation for International Development.; BHUNHU, N.D. (1992). 'Teaching and learning in environmental agricultural science: case studies of 16 primary schools in Zimbabwe. Document 16/50 C/A. Bonn: German Foundation for International Development.
Status: Sponsored project
Source of Grant: International Deutsche Stiftung für Internationale Entwickülung; Government of Zimbabwe
Date of Research: 1990-1992
KEYWORDS: *agricultural education; developing countries; environmental education; Zimbabwe*

10/1529

Institute of Continuing and Professional Education, Sussex
House, Falmer, Brighton BN1 9RH
01273 606755
Torrance, H. Dr

Teacher involvement in National Curriculum assessment
Abstract: A broad programme of work investigating teacher involvement in assessment for the National Curriculum along with specific studies of teacher involvement in Records of Achievement within Department for Education (DFE) funded pilot projects.
Published Material: TORRANCE, H. (1990). 'Records of achievement and formative assessment'. In: STAKE, R. Effects of changes in assessment policy. Hampton, Middx: JAI Press.; TORRANCE, H.

(1991). 'Researching the National Curriculum: the BERA task group on the curriculum', Journal of Curriculum Studies, Vol 23, No 4, pp.341-343.; TORRANCE, H. (1991). 'Evaluating SATS – the 1990 pilot', Cambridge Journal of Education, Vol 21, No 2, pp.129-140.; TORRANCE, H. (1992). 'Educational assessment and educational standards: towards an alternative view of quality'. In BROWN, P. & LAUDER, H. Education for economic survival: from Fordism to post-Fordism? London: Routledge.
Status: Individual research
Date of Research: 1990-continuing
KEYWORDS: *assessment by teachers; National Curriculum; records of achievement; school based assessment*

10/1530

Institute of Continuing and Professional Education, Sussex
House, Falmer, Brighton BN1 9RH
01273 606755
Wall, N. Mrs; Barnes, S. Mr

Nuffield economics and business studies project
Abstract: The researchers are members of a four-strong national team working full-time over 3 years to produce a new A-level course in Economics and Business Studies. This project arises from a perceived need to make a more explicit connection between Economics and business practice, and between Business Studies and economic ideas. The aim is to define a field of study within which students may specialise in either subject or gain a joint Economics/Business Studies A-level. However, all courses will include a core of integrated concepts linking both subjects. Outside the core, students will follow a modular pathway, choosing from a range of single subject and joint options. In the spirit of Nuffield projects, this project is planning a complete publishing programme of learning materials with extensive support for teachers. There will be thorough trialling of resources in partner schools/colleges, a major group of which are in East Sussex. It is intended that the course will be objective yet innovative. Students will gain a tight theoretical framework while testing its application to real resource management problems. The power of market forces will be explored, yet there will be serious coverage of social, environmental and ethical issues.
Status: Sponsored project
Source of Grant: Nuffield Foundation
Date of Research: 1991-1994
KEYWORDS: *a level examinations; business education; curriculum development; economics education*

10/1531

Institute of Continuing and Professional Education, Sussex
House, Falmer, Brighton BN1 9RH
01273 606755
Cooper, B. Dr; Torrance, H. Dr; *Supervisor:* Lacey, C. Prof.

Andhra Pradesh primary education project evaluation
Abstract: The project aims to improve the quality of primary education in the Indian state of Andhra Pradesh by implementing a child centred approach to learning in all primary schools. This approach is based on six principles: activity-based learning; practical work; group work; recognition of individual differences; use of the local environment; display of learners' and teachers' work. The role of the Sussex research team is to assist with the design, analysis and reporting of the project evaluation.
Published Material: LACEY, C., COOPER, B. & TORRANCE, H. (1993). 'Evaluating the Andhra Pradesh primary education project: problems of design and analysis', British Educational Research Journal, Vol 19, No 5, pp.535-554.
Status: Sponsored project
Source of Grant: Overseas Development Administration; British Council
Date of Research: 1986-continuing
KEYWORDS: *developing countries; development education; India; learning activities; primary education; teaching methods*

10/1532

Institute of Continuing and Professional Education, Sussex
House, Falmer, Brighton BN1 9RH
01273 606755
Cole, G. Mr; *Supervisor:* Eraut, M. Prof.

Assessing competence in higher level occupations
Abstract: This project studied existing and developing ways of assessing competence to practise in a variety of professions. An initial

survey of 30 groups was followed by case studies of 11 professions: architecture; chartered surveying; civil engineering; electrical engineering; nursing; optometry; social work; teaching in Scotland; management accountancy; industrial management; and personnel management. The report presents comparative data and discusses the principal issues arising. Two kinds of assessment evidence are distinguished: 1) evidence derived from observation and questioning directly from performance on-the-job, products arising from work or reports about that work; and 2) evidence of capabilities which enable performance such as the use of underpinning knowledge, personal skills and qualities, and professional thinking. Separate chapters of the report are devoted to standards and criteria, sources of evidence and assessment, and verification procedures. Issues discussed in the final chapter include the purposes of an assessment system, the role and character of standards, choosing appropriate sources of evidence, and the implementation of assessment policy.
Published Material: ERAUT, M. & COLE, G. (1993). 'Assessing competence in the professions'. Report No 11. Research and Development Series. Department of Employment, Strategy Unit.; ERAUT, M. & COLE, G. (1993). 'Assessment of competence in higher level occupations', Competence and Assessment Issue 21.; ERAUT, M. (1993). 'Implications for standards development', Competence and Assessment Issue 21.
Status: Sponsored project
Source of Grant: Department of Employment £47,000
Date of Research: 1991-1992
KEYWORDS: assessment; competence; job performance; professional occupations

10/1533

Institute of Continuing and Professional Education, Sussex House, Falmer, Brighton BN1 9RH
01273 606755
Lewis, M. Ms
Mentor development
Abstract: A group of 12 teachers were followed through a year of mentoring primary (PGCE) students. The project involved mentors working in pairs, visiting each other at work with students, engaging in discussion and regular meetings to identify issues and needs of newly appointed mentors. The aim of the project was to explore ways new mentors learned the skills of mentoring. An experienced mentor was paired with an inexperienced mentor. Mentors kept diaries and records, the project researcher observed the process in action, interviewed mentors, analysed records and diaries. Outcomes demonstrated: a) the need for support and training; b) the viability of the method used. Additionally, a range of issues and content considered relevant to mentoring and training needs were identified. Project findings are being analysed.
Status: Sponsored project
Source of Grant: Paul Hamlyn Foundation
Date of Research: 1991-1993
KEYWORDS: mentors; preservice teacher education; supervisory training; teaching practice

10/1534

Institute of Continuing and Professional Education, Sussex House, Falmer, Brighton BN1 9RH
01273 606755
Lewis, M. Ms
Career development of newly qualified teachers
Abstract: From 1991 data has been collected on newly qualified teachers in their first years of teaching using ex-students from Sussex University's post-graduate certificate in education (PGCE) course. The project aims to investigate what happens to graduates of the PGCE course, how they manage their first years of teaching, the issues that arise and their promotion patterns. Results will be used to: improve quality of PGCE provision; contribute to debates about primary PGCE training routes; consider inservice education of teachers (INSET) needs in the early years of teaching; and to provide data on "natural wastage" and promotion patterns. At the end of each year records are kept of first appointments. Students not in post by the end of the year are identified. Subsequent follow-up questionnaires relate to their experiences in their first years.
Status: Individual research
Date of Research: 1991-continuing
KEYWORDS: graduate employment; graduate surveys; probationary teachers; teacher development

10/1535

Institute of Continuing and Professional Education, Sussex House, Falmer, Brighton BN1 9RH
01273 606755
Payne, J. Dr; Boice, M. Mr; *Supervisor:* Lowerson, J. Rev.
Rural educational disadvantage and structures of provision for adults
Abstract: This two year project aimed to explore the structures of rural educational provision for adults, the factors influencing rural educational disadvantage, and the impact of recent government funding policies upon rural adult education. A particular theme of the project was to assess the extent to which patterns of disadvantage and structures of provision varied from locality to locality. Following contextual library research, which focused on a critical review of the existing literature, the major part of the project has concerned four case studies of rural East Sussex, Cornwall, Derbyshire and North Yorkshire. These areas were selected on the basis of factors such as political complexion and culture, relative remoteness or otherwise from major metropolitan areas, and population characteristics. The explicit decision was made to exclude both Wales and Scotland from the research. In all four cases a variety of quantitative and qualitative empirical information was gathered to help address and examine the major research themes. This information included official statistics, policy documents, research reports, interviews and discussions with key individuals, (i.e. policy makers, community leaders, adult education administrators) and adult students. The research will be published in the summer of 1994 in the form of a project report and articles submitted to relevant academic journals. Dissemination will also take the form of seminar presentation and conference papers.
Status: Sponsored project
Source of Grant: Higher Education Funding Council for England £21,000
Date of Research: 1993-1994
KEYWORDS: access to education; adult education; rural areas

10/1536

Institute of Continuing and Professional Education, Sussex House, Falmer, Brighton BN1 9RH
01273 606755
Willson, M. Mr; *Supervisor:* Lewin, K. Dr
The effectiveness of primary science inservice teacher education programmes on teaching styles and the learning process in the classroom
Abstract: The research will investigate the role of the primary science coordinator as change agent, particularly with respect to the introduction of the National Curriculum in Science in schools. It will evaluate the effectiveness of primary science inservice teacher education (INSET) programmes in assisting coordinators in this role and the effect they have on children's learning in science. The investigation will centre on 12 schools initially, with 4 or 5 schools used for detailed case studies at a later date. Methods used will be questionnaire and participant observation. The results of the studies will be made available to local education authorities.
Status: Individual research
Date of Research: 1990-1994
KEYWORDS: inservice teacher education; science education

10/1537

Institute of Continuing and Professional Education, Sussex House, Falmer, Brighton BN1 9RH
01273 606755
Sheridan, V. Ms; *Supervisor:* Kutnick, P. Dr
The Montessori method: links between theory and practice
Abstract: The study concentrates upon the links between theory and practice in Montessori schools based in the London area. It aims to investigate the interpretations of the Montessori approach as an educational method. Three basic areas have been identified concerning the practical aspects of a Montessori system: the materials; the social environment; and the teachers' role in class. The variety of approaches to these areas has been established by means of a questionnaire, which provided access to the views of a wide range of teachers. Analysis of the results has given a picture of the types of attitudes and interpretations prevalent among Montessori teachers today. In order to investigate further how these areas are approached in practice, and the different emphases and diversity therein, questionnaires will be followed by periods of classroom observation in a selection of schools, enriched and clarified by interviews with the teachers. The questionnaire results were analysed using SSPSX software.

Status: Individual research
Date of Research: 1987-1993
KEYWORDS: *early childhood education; Montessori method; nursery schools; preschool education*

10/1538

Institute of Continuing and Professional Education, Sussex House, Falmer, Brighton BN1 9RH
01273 606755
Great Ormond Street Hospital for Sick Children, Great Ormond Street, London WC1
0171 405 9200
Stephens, D. Dr; Lansdown, R. Dr
A case study investigation of the impact of introducing child-to-child approaches to health education upon the knowledge and practice of children, teachers and family members
Abstract: The project will involve working with teachers-as-researchers, using an action-research approach. It aims not only to assess the quality of children's learning in schools clustered around two selected teachers' colleges in India and Uganda, but also to evaluate the impact of their learning upon community health.
Status: Sponsored project
Source of Grant: Child to Child Trust; Stanley Thomas Johnson Foundation, Switzerland
Date of Research: 1992-continuing
KEYWORDS: *community benefits; developing countries; health education; India; peer teaching; Uganda*

10/1539

Institute of Continuing and Professional Education, Sussex House, Falmer, Brighton BN1 9RH
01273 606755
International Institute of Educational Planning,
7-9 rue Eugène Delacroix, 75116 Paris, France
Lewin, K. Dr; Caillods, F. Ms
Planning secondary science education in Malaysia
Abstract: The purpose of this project is to examine the planning of science education at secondary level in Malaysia. The International Institute of Educational Planning and the Education Planning and Research Division of the Ministry of Education Malaysia have collaborated in designing a joint project which has five main components. The first is a baseline study reviewing the existing status of science education in Malaysia; the second explores data on the interface between the science education system and opportunities in further and higher education and in anticipated demands from the labour market; the third consists of a survey on a national sample of schools located in four states comprehensively reviewing how science education development is taking place; the fourth consists of 13 school case studies where indepth and qualitative work is being undertaken to obtain a detailed picture illustrative of practice in science education; the final component is concerned with the analysis of performance data to identify areas of learning difficulty and patterns of differential achievement between groups of students.
Status: Sponsored project
Source of Grant: International Institute of Educational Planning; Malaysian Ministry of Education: Educational Planning and Research Division
Date of Research: 1990-1993
KEYWORDS: *Malaysia; science education*

10/1540

Institute of Continuing and Professional Education, Sussex House, Falmer, Brighton BN1 9RH
01273 606755
London University, Institute of Education, 20 Bedford Way, London WC1H 0AL
0171 580 1122
Hangzhou University, 34 Tian Mu Shan Road, Hangzhou, Zhejiang Province 310028, China
Lewin, K. Dr; Little, A. Prof.; Hui, X. Prof.; Ji Wei, Z. Prof.
Tracing the impact of the 1985 reforms in China
Abstract: The purpose of this research project is to explore the implementation of the 1985 educational reforms announced by the Central Committee of the Communist Party in the People's Republic of China. These reforms affect all levels of education. We have conducted research in several parts of China with a particular focus on Zhejiang Province. The research reviews the context in which the reform programme was announced and explores the rationale which underpinned it. It then examines the proposed reforms at the different levels of primary, secondary, teacher training, higher education, and charts progress with their implementation over the last 7 years. In addition we review other aspects of the reforms concerned with the assessment and selection system and curriculum development.
Published Material: LEWIN, K.M., LITTLE, A.W., HUI, X. & JI WEI, Z. (1994). Educational Innovation in China: tracing the impact of the 1985 educational reforms. London: Longman.
Status: Sponsored project
Source of Grant: British Council; University of Sussex; University of Hangzhou
Date of Research: 1987-1993
KEYWORDS: *China; educational change*

10/1541

Institute of Continuing and Professional Education, Sussex House, Falmer, Brighton BN1 9RH
01273 606755
Seychelles Polytechnic, PO Box 77, Mahe, Republic of Seychelles
Pennycuick, D. Dr; Stuart, J. Dr; Lacey, C. Prof.; Towner, E. Ms
Monitoring inservice and research programme: Seychelles B.Ed. project
Abstract: The Government of the Seychelles, in collaboration with the University of Sussex, established a split Batchelor of Education degree course (B.Ed) for Seychelles trainee teachers to equip them to teach in the Seychelles National Youth Service (NYS) and secondary schools. This course has been supported by a programme of monitoring, inservice and research, which included exchange visits by staff from Sussex and the Seychelles School of Education. A main objective of the research was to evaluate the effect of the training programme on the quality of education in NYS. It comprised four separate components, each undertaken collaboratively by Sussex staff and Seychellois educationists. While using a variety of research styles and methods, all contained an element of action research, in that most of the researchers were also involved in teaching on the B.Ed. course, and used the findings to improve the training programme both at Sussex and in Seychelles. Mathematics education was studied in October-December 1989 using multi-site case-study at NYS and primary levels. The first implementation of the Final Teaching Project (in which returning students must carry out and report on a reflective enquiry into their own teaching, before they can gain their degree) was evaluated in October-November 1990, using a responsive model. Teaching styles, teacher support, and school organisation at the NYS were studied before and after the Sussex graduates returned (February-March 1990, 1992), using classroom observation schedules and interviews. A small but significant shift in classroom practice was found. In October-December 1991 environmental education was surveyed at all educational levels and some inservice work carried out with teachers.
Published Material: A list of publications is available from the researcher.
Status: Sponsored project
Source of Grant: Overseas Development Agency £101,000
Date of Research: 1988-1993
KEYWORDS: *preservice teacher education; Seychelles*

10/1542

School of Cognitive and Computing Sciences, Sussex House, Falmer, Brighton BN1 9RH
01273 606755
Del Soldato, T. Dr; *Supervisor:* Du Boulay, J. Dr
Adapting tutoring systems to students' learning styles
Abstract: The purpose of this project is to investigate the possibilities of adapting computer-assisted instruction to students' learning styles. Usually tutoring systems adjust their instructional planning according to what knowledge the learner has acquired, neglecting how the student acquired such knowledge. Several aspects of learning systems (e.g. level of confidence, anxiety, independence vs. need of constant help, toleration to challenge) are being considered by the instructional planner, aiming to motivate the student and enrich the teaching interaction. As a result of this project, the core of a learning style adaptable tutoring system has been implemented.
Status: Sponsored project
Source of Grant: Brazilian Council for Scientific and Technological Development (CNPq)

Date of Research: 1989-1994
KEYWORDS: autoinstructional aids; cognitive style; computer assisted learning; computer uses in education; learning strategies; teaching machines

10/1543
School of Cognitive and Computing Sciences, Sussex House, Falmer, Brighton BN1 9RH
01273 606755
Puntambekar, S. Mrs; *Supervisor:* Du Bolay, B. Prof.; Sharples, M. Dr
Towards an intelligent tutoring system to train metacognitive skills in studying from texts
Abstract: Intelligent tutoring systems have traditionally been concerned with presenting a domain in a progressive way, having the student solve problems or answer questions and then providing feedback. Failure has almost always been interpreted as a lack of the necessary sub-skills. However, as research by metacognitive theorists has shown, this is not the only reason. Students are known to adopt wrong solution procedures, or fail to apply a skill because they do not have a good sense of what they know and how to use what they know effectively. Apart from the necessary learning skills, learners require an executive control mechanism that will plan and combine the necessary skills. The research applies some of the ideas put forth by theories of metacognition to the domain of studying from texts for students aged 14-16 and emphasises two main features of the system being built. Firstly, it is designed to teach general skills in the context of studying from texts, rather than the teaching of a specific domain. Secondly, it is concerned not only with the final state of learning, but with the various cognitive processes that make up the learning process. It will recognise and respond to these intermediate states thus improving the breadth of the available knowledge about the learner.
Status: Individual research
Date of Research: 1991-continuing
KEYWORDS: cognitive processes; computer assisted learning; learning processes; metacognition

10/1544
School of Cognitive and Computing Sciences, Sussex House, Falmer, Brighton BN1 9RH
01273 606755
Yuill, N. Dr
Adults' conceptions of the origin, development and modifiability of personality traits: the influence of studying psychology
Abstract: The project investigates the content of undergraduates' concepts of personality, and how the structure of these concepts may change as a result of studying psychology. Students of psychology will be questioned about their conceptions of personality traits when starting and after one year of their course, and their responses compared with non-psychology students, using a coding scheme adapted from research with children.
Status: Sponsored project
Source of Grant: Nuffield Foundation £2,290
Date of Research: 1992-1993
KEYWORDS: personality traits; psychology

10/1545
School of Cognitive and Computing Sciences, Sussex House, Falmer, Brighton BN1 9RH
01273 606755
Yuill, N. Dr; Oakhill, J. Dr; Garnham, A. Dr
Development of working memory in children
Abstract: This project aims to investigate the role of working memory in children's text comprehension. Recent research has shown that reading skills are highly reliant on working memory: the ability not just to store information, but also to perform manipulations on that information at the same time, as in mental arithmetic. Various tests of working memory have been developed for adults so as to identify its different components (linguistic, numerical and spatial) and to show how demands of storage are traded off against processing requirements. However, little is known about how working memory develops, and what influence this development has on the acquisition of reading skills. We will examine the development of the different components of working memory between the ages of 7 and 11, and the relation of working memory to reading skills. It is not known whether working memory becomes differentiated with age or whether distinct systems exist from an early age. The data will also

show whether working memory is related more closely to inferential skills than to memory for verbatim information, an assumption often made in work on children's text comprehension. A working memory test that seems not to be related to comprehension skills in adults is spatial working memory (i.e. memory for location). However, this aspect of memory may be related to developing text comprehension in children, because fluent readers develop 'place-keeping' skills that allow the selective reinspection of text, and children who are good readers are better at this reinspection than are poor ones. This conjecture will be tested by correlating spatial working memory skills with reading comprehension ability.
Status: Sponsored project
Source of Grant: University of Sussex £10,000
Date of Research: 1994-continuing
KEYWORDS: memory; reading skills

10/1546
School of Cognitive and Computing Sciences, Sussex House, Falmer, Brighton BN1 9RH
01273 606755
Yuill, N. Dr
The role of word-play in improving children's text comprehension
Abstract: This project aims to investigate whether making children aware of linguistic inferences by using word-play and riddles will improve text comprehension. Previous research has identified a group of 7-8 year old children who, although fluent readers, have noticeable difficulty with text comprehension. Although much is known about the specific deficits of such children, little research has been done on the most effective remedial techniques for them, and no-one has investigated the use of word-play as proposed here. Explicit instruction in inference skills, used for older children, is not suitable for young children, but it is important to address reading deficiencies as early in children's development as possible. A source of practice in making linguistic inferences not requiring explicit instruction are the word games that children engage in naturally at around this age. For example, some authors have shown how the everyday activity of rhyming games can help 5-6 year olds in learning to decode the written word because it increases their awarenes of sounds and corresponding letter patterns. In a similar way, it is possible that practice with 'plays on words' such as riddles and puns, is a way of fostering awareness of alternative meanings, and hence comprehension skills. The research involves assessing riddle comprehension of various types and developing a treatment programme to address comprehension skills in children who have either poor or good comprehension. Post-tests will be used to assess whether the training improves both specific and general comprehension skills.
Published Material: YUILL, N. & EASTON, K. (1993). 'The role of linguistic ambiguity in understanding and improving children's text comprehension'. Cognitive Science Research Paper No 296. Brighton: University of Sussex, School of Cognitive and Computing Sciences.
Status: Sponsored project
Source of Grant: University of Sussex £4,120
Date of Research: 1992-continuing
KEYWORDS: reading comprehension; reading games; word recognition

10/1547
School of Cognitive and Computing Sciences, Sussex House, Falmer, Brighton BN1 9RH
01273 606755
Direne, A. Mr; *Supervisor:* Sharples, M. Dr
Methodology and tools for designing concept tutoring systems
Abstract: The research describes how high-level knowledge about visual images should be represented and further interpreted through system-active and system-passive tutorial interactions. The ideas lend themselves to the design and implementation of intelligent tutoring systems aimed at the teaching of abnormalities in highly visual domains like medical radiology, magnetic resonance imaging and ultrasonography. Most past work in visual concept tutoring has concentrated on the theoretical principles of how humans acquire expertise in visual recognition. The few implementations there have been are domain-specific. A methodology has been developed for managing the complexity of tutoring systems design and a model of dialogue interpretation has been developed for implementing tutorial interactions. The method and the model are supported by computer-based tools that integrate the multi-layer environment, Representations for Understanding Images (RUI).

Status: Individual research
Date of Research: 1989-1993
KEYWORDS: *computer science; computer uses in education; visual perception*

Tavistock Institute of Human Relations

10/1548
Evaluation Development and Review Unit, The Tavistock Centre, 120 Belsize Lane, London NW3 5BA
0171 435 7111
Sommerlad, E. Dr; Moerkamp, T. Dr; Erlicher, L. Ms
Linking learning and work in youth training: a European partnership research project
Abstract: Funded by the European Commission under the PETRA initiative, this collaborative research project has been undertaken by researchers in three countries: the UK, the Netherlands and Italy. Its focus is on the workplace as a setting for learning, in particular the strategies for structured learning (on and off the job) which are intended to foster the development of transferable skills as part of broad occupational competence. Case studies of company-based training were undertaken in the three countries. The UK case study examines work-based learning in the water industry, drawing on qualitative data from a series of interviews in five different companies and more detailed investigation of youth training within two company settings.
Published Material: ERLICHER, L., MOERKAMP, T., & SOMMERLAD, E. (1993). Quality aspects of alternance in vocational education and training. London: The Tavistock Institute.
Status: Sponsored project
Source of Grant: European Commission: PETRA Initiative
Date of Research: 1991-1993
KEYWORDS: *off the job training; on the job training; skill development; training; transfer of training; work experience programmes*

10/1549
Evaluation Development and Review Unit, The Tavistock Centre, 120 Belsize Lane, London NW3 5BA
0171 435 7111
Stern, E. Mr; Sommerlad, E. Dr; Kelleher, J. Mr; Frade, C. Mr; Cullen, J. Dr
DELTA/ARTICULATE: distance and flexible learning technology innovation
Abstract: Telematic systems for flexible and distance learning (DELTA) is a strategic research and development programme supported by the European Commission. Its aim is to accelerate the design and implementation of learning technology solutions across Europe. Within DELTA, the Tavistock Institute's Evaluation Department and Review Unit leads an evaluation research consortium called ARTICULATE – The Evaluation of DELTA Pilot Applications. ARTICULATE is concerned with understanding the actual and potential contributions of learning technologies and with developing new methods for evaluating learning technology innovation through evaluating the DELTA Pilot Applications. The focus of evaluation is the role of the new media and technologies in life-long learning. The evaluation strategy combines a participative project-level evaluation, independent assessments and an over-arching quantitative and qualitative monitoring system.
Published Material: STERN, E. & KELLEHER, J. (1992). Evaluation of DELTA pilot applications: general orientation and approach. London: The Tavistock Institute.; CULLEN, J., KELLEHER, J. & STERN, E. (1992). DELTA pilots and development projects and their evaluation: ARTICULATE deliverable No. 2. London: The Tavistock Institute.; CULLEN, J., KELLEHER, J. & STERN, E. (1993). 'Evaluation in DELTA'. In: Journal of Computer Assisted Learning, Vol 9, No 2.
Status: Sponsored project
Source of Grant: European Commission: DELTA project
Date of Research: 1991-1994
KEYWORDS: *computer uses in education; distance education; educational media; educational technology; evaluation; flexible learning*

10/1550
Evaluation Development and Review Unit, The Tavistock Centre, 120 Belsize Lane, London NW3 5BA
0171 435 7111
Holly, L. Dr; Searle, C. Mr
Access and aspiration: oral history project to encourage young people of the inner city to gain entry to, and succeed in, higher education
Abstract: This research is based at Earl Marshal Comprehensive School which serves an area in the North East of Sheffield. This is a neighbourhood suffering from many of the features of a disadvantaged inner city area. However, this is also an area vibrant with a mix of communities. The School is multi-racial and multi-lingual, with a strong commitment to anti-racism and internationalism. Students include many Asian girls who are often discouraged from aspiring to higher education by the low expectations which are ingrained in this society in relation to class, gender and race. Some young women come from families where expectations for daughters continue to be related to domesticity and marriage. The aims of this action research study are three fold: 1) To encourage young women in the fourth year of study at Earl Marshal School to reflect on the influences from the wider society and from their families, which mould their lives. 2) To consider ways out of stereotypes and limitations whilst respecting those aspects of society and culture which sustain and support these young women. 3) To help the young women to develop the confidence to build on their achievements and lay the foundation for progress towards higher education if that is in their plans.
Status: Sponsored project
Source of Grant: Calouste Gulbenkian Foundation (UK branch) £4,000; Sheffield TVEI: 5,000
Date of Research: 1992-1993
KEYWORDS: *access to education; cultural background; equal education; ethnic groups; higher education; inner city; women's education*

Teesside University

10/1551
School of Computing and Mathematics, Interactive Systems Research Group, Borough Road, Middlesbrough, Cleveland TS1 3BA
01642 218121
Banerji, A. Mr; *Supervisor:* Barker, P. Prof.; Manji, K. Dr
Design of electronic performance support systems
Abstract: An Electronic Performance Support Systems (EPSS) is an approach to integrating hardware, software and end-user interfaces in order to produce more useful computer-based information delivery systems that embed various types of job performance aid. Essentially, an EPSS is intended to be a computer-based job performance aid that is able to provide 'just-in-time' (JIT) training and an enhanced interactive performance support environment. This environment provides various types of information, data, images, advice, assistance and guidance in order to permit an employee to perform his/her job with minimum support and intervention from others. The concept of JIT training is derived from the JIT inventory control methods adopted by the Japanese and accepted as a new productivity standard. It can be viewed as an evolution of computer based training (CBT) delivery stages – from 'off-the-job' training through 'prior-to-job-performance' training to the approach of learning while doing a job using an EPSS. Research into basic EPSS techniques has been taking place within the School of Computing and Mathematics at Teesside University. Interest in this area has arisen as a result of the School's organising research into the application of computer-based training and the development of interactive job performance aids. The objective of this current project is to investigate the potential utility of EPSS techniques and to formulate a set of design and fabrication guidelines to facilitate their creation within industrial and commercial environments. The four avenues of investigation currently explored involve the use of on-line help systems; full-text retrieval packages; expert systems; and intelligent simulation environments, in order to augment the use of CBT within the interactive work environment of an employee. This project will also explore the use of compact disc read-only memory (CD-Rom) as a means of embedding and delivering EPSS facilities to end-users.
Published Material: BANERJI, A.K. & SATHYAVASU, M.A. (1990). 'FEDS a computer aided learning approach for training in foregin exchange dealing', Proceedings of Indian Computing Con-

gress ICC 90, Hyderabad, Tata-McGraw Hill, New Delhi.; BARKER, P.G. (1991). 'Computer-based training in India', International Journal of Computers in Adult Education and Training, Vol 2, No 3, pp.213-224.; BARKER, P.G. 'Designing interactive learning systems', Educational & Training Technology International, Vol 27, No 2, pp.125-145, May.; BARKER, P.G. (1991). 'Developing competence through CBT', paper presented at AETT '91 International Conference, Polytechnic of Wales, Pontypridd, 2-5 April, 1991.
Status: Individual research
Date of Research: 1991-1994
KEYWORDS: computer assisted learning; educational technology; expert systems; optical data discs; training methods

10/1552
   School of Computing and Mathematics, Interactive Systems Research Group, Borough Road, Middlesbrough, Cleveland TS1 3BA
   01642 218121
   Richards, S. Mr; *Supervisor:* Barker, P. Prof.; Manji, K. Dr
End-user interfaces to electronic books
Abstract: The term 'electronic book' is a metaphor which is used to describe an application which aims to deliver information in an electronic form. The rapid advances in storage technologies, for example Compact Disc Read Only Memory (CD ROM) and Magneto Optical Rewritable Optical Disk (MOROD), have allowed such books to deliver huge quantities of information in a wide variety of presentation media forms. Such advances, along with the advances in digital information presentation; video and audio compression and decompression in real-time; high resolution colour display devices; and hypermedia information networks, can facilitate the creation of extremely rich and stimulating information delivery environments. The very newness of these technologies has meant that the full capabilities and potentials as applied to electronic books, has as yet not been fully investigated. The current research aims to develop extremely rich electronic book environments which are capable of tailoring the information which they deliver to individual user requirements. Information will be presented in the form of digital video, sound, animation, hypertext and hyperimages in order to assess the pedagogic impact of such information delivery strategies. This is to be effected by investigating the effectiveness of different page structures based upon the following models: simple page model; composite page model; overlay page model; and the viewport page model. Through the adoption of such a strategy it will then be possible to assess the efficacy of various page structures, presentation media and access techniques within learning and training environments.
Published Material: RICHARDS, S.M. & BARKER, P.G. (1991). 'Page structures for electronic books', Educational and Training Technology International, Vol 28, No 4, pp.291-301.
Status: Sponsored project
Source of Grant: Science and Engineering Research Council; Dean Associates
Date of Research: 1990-1993
KEYWORDS: computer assisted learning; electronic books; human-computer interaction; hypermedia; information technology; multimedia approach; optical data discs

10/1553
   School of Computing and Mathematics, Interactive Systems Research Group, Borough Road, Middlesbrough, Cleveland TS1 3BA
   01642 218121
   Lamont, C. Mr; *Supervisor:* Barker, P. Prof.; Manji, K. Dr
Human-computer interfaces to reactive graphical images
Abstract: A reactive graphical image is one that changes its form when pointed at by a computer user using a mouse or a touch screen. Such reactive graphical images can be combined with multimedia presentations (the blending of moving video, sound, and graphics in one display environment) to form the basis of effective interactive multimedia courseware for use in the computer based training (CBT) industries. Work has initially been undertaken to provide custom editors within the PC/PILOT and PROPI authoring environments. A custom editor is designed to enhance the authoring capability of a CBT production environment by allowing parameters to be embedded within a lesson to access external material and devices. Such methods can enhance the usability and training value of a CBT lesson. Initially, custom editors have been built to incorporate videodisc still images or moving video sequences into a lesson, and for displaying graphics images on a remote terminal. However, because videodisc

technology is based on analog data, it cannot effectively provide variable speed motion with continued sound synchronisation and effective graphics overlays. Thus the thrust of multimedia technology development is to provide all these features in one digital environment. Future custom editors will be built to take full advantage of this digital video interactive (DVI) technology. Once the full range of graphical custom editors has been designed and built, evaluations will be conducted to assess the quality of design and the usability of the products that are generated. Extensive end-user evaluations will also be conducted in order that a set of models and guidelines which reflect good design practice can be derived from the research.
Status: Sponsored project
Source of Grant: Science and Engineering Research Council; A.P. Chesters and Associates
Date of Research: 1990-1993
KEYWORDS: computer assisted learning; computer uses in education; educational software; interactive video

Thames Valley University

10/1554
   Faculty of Humanities and Languages, 1 The Grove, London W5 5DX
   0181 579 5000
   Durham University, School of Education, Leazes Road, Durham DH1 1TA
   0191 374 2000
   Roberts, C. Ms; Byram, M. Dr
Cultural studies in advanced language learning: the year abroad in under-graduate courses
Abstract: The aim of this research is to develop a more integrated approach to language and culture on four year language degree courses. At the Thames Valley University this will be done by introducing principles of ethnography in the second year of the degree course. Students will write ethnographies of the target culture while abroad, which will then be evaluated. Two language staff will learn ethnographic approaches and their learning will be documented. They will then develop a new course for the language students.
Status: Sponsored project
Source of Grant: Economic and Social Research Council £44,000
Date of Research: 1990-1993
KEYWORDS: cultural education; degree requirements; ethnography; higher education; second language learning; study abroad

The Advisory Council on Alcohol and Drug Education (TACADE)

10/1555
   1 Hulme Place, The Crescent, Salford, Greater Manchester M5 4QA
   0161 745 8925
   Dobson, B. Mr; Wright, L. Mrs; *Supervisor:* Lee, J. Mr
A collaborative study of the effective implementation of drug education in seven European countries
Abstract: The aim of the project is to promote effective approaches across Europe to the implementation of preventive drug misuse education in secondary schools. Its objectives are to: 1) identify how drug education is effectively implemented in a cross section of European countries; 2) follow up the recommendations of TACADE's Commission for European Community (CEC) funded feasibility study 'A comparison of the Delivery and Effectiveness of Drug Education in Belgium, the Netherlands and the United Kingdom' in respect of drug education implementation; 3) promote good practice in drug education implementation across Europe; 4) investigate the factors necessary for effective drug education implementation; 5) facilitate the sharing of experiences in drug education implementation between European countries; 6) report on a variety of experiences of drug education implementation; and 7) examine the commonality between a number of experiences of drug education implementation in a number of European countries. Research will include: 1) identification of National Representatives from each of

the seven countries included in the study, viz. Belgium, Germany, Italy, the Netherlands, Spain, Sweden and the United Kingdom; 2) collaborative identification of key implementation factors for drug education; 3) establishment of a trans-European network of participant schools; 4) school-based studies of drug education implementation; 5) analysis and documentation of findings; and 6) production of a final report, including guidelines on the effective implementation of drug education programmes.
Status: Sponsored project
Source of Grant: Commission of the European Community
Date of Research: 1993-continuing
KEYWORDS: *comparative education; drug education; health education*

Tidy Britain Group Schools Research Project

10/1556
Brighton University, Alfriston House, Falmer, Brighton BN1 9PH
01273 643115
Mares, C. Ms; Stephenson, R. Mr
Tidy Britain Group Schools Research Project
Abstract: The Tidy Britain Group Schools Research Project is funded by the Tidy Britain Group, which is grant aided by the Department of the Environment. The Tidy Britain Group works with local government, commerce, and local community groups to create a better environment, through improved practice in waste management and recycling, and the reduction of litter. Since 1973 the Group has sponsored a curriculum development research project, now located at Brighton University, which works with teachers and other educationalists to develop resources for schools. Over the years the Tidy Britain Group Schools Research Project has pilot-tested and produced a wide range of classroom materials and teachers' handbooks for many subjects and age ranges. These are all designed to provide resources to support existing curriculum studies and to introduce an element of environmental awareness and responsibility across all curriculum subjects. While the local environment litter and waste management are the starting point, the materials provide the basis for examining wider environmental issues on a national and global level. The Project has also developed materials for inservice and initial teacher training, and is involved in an Erasmus programme attempting to establish a methodology for introducing environmental responsibility and European awareness into initial teacher training throughout the European community.
Published Material: MARES, C. (1985). Our Europe: environmental awareness and language development through school exchanges. Wigan: Tidy Britain Group.; STEPHENSON, R. (1990). Waste issues – problem solving exercises in waste management. Wigan: Tidy Britain Group.; STEPHENSON, R. (1992). Materials and the environment (5 units: paper, glass, metals, plastics, wastes and resources). Wigan: Tidy Britain Group.; MARES, C. & STEPHENSON, R. (1992). Inside outside – an action plan for improving the primary school environment. Wigan: Tidy Britain Group.; STEPHENSON, R. (1993). Beating litter: a comprehensive environmental improvement programme for schools. Wigan: Tidy Britain Group. A full list of publications is available from the researcher.
Status: Sponsored project
Source of Grant: Tidy Britain Group £75,000
Date of Research: 1973-continuing
KEYWORDS: *curriculum development; environmental education; pollution; waste disposal*

Trinity and All Saints' College

10/1557
Brownberrie Lane, Horsforth, Leeds LS18 5HD
01132 584341
Rees, M. Dr
The provision of special schools for gifted children
Abstract: The aim of this research is to study the schools in the UK

which offer separate education to children with special gifts (music, dance, drama, athletics, academic subjects) and to attempt to assess the advantages and disadvantages of this type of schooling. The research will also attempt to compare provision for gifted children in the UK to that of other countries.
Status: Individual research
Date of Research: 1986-continuing
KEYWORDS: *comparative education; gifted; special schools*

Trinity College

10/1558
Carmarthen, Dyfed SA31 3EP
01267 237971
Francis, L. Prof.; Greer, J. Rev Dr
Secondary school pupils' attitudes towards science and religion (Northern Ireland)
Abstract: This project is re-analysing data collected from 2,000 secondary school pupils attending Catholic and Protestant schools in Northern Ireland in order to explore the relationship between attitudes to science, religion, creationism and scientism. Attitudes are measured by Likert type scales.
Status: Sponsored project
Source of Grant: Trinity College
Date of Research: 1992-continuing
KEYWORDS: *Northern Ireland; pupil attitudes; religious education; scientific attitudes; secondary school pupils*

10/1559
Carmarthen, Dyfed SA31 3EP
01267 237971
Francis, L. Prof.
Prayer and wellbeing
Abstract: This study explores the relationship between prayer and psychological wellbeing among a sample of 5,000 11-16 year old secondary school pupils. Wellbeing is measured as a Likert type inventory. Prayer is measured both by self-reported practice and by a scale of predisposition to pray.
Status: Sponsored project
Source of Grant: Trinity College
Date of Research: 1991-1994
KEYWORDS: *religion; secondary school pupils; well being*

10/1560
Carmarthen, Dyfed SA31 3EP
01267 237971
Francis, L. Prof.
The measurement of personality among primary school pupils
Abstract: The measurement of personality among primary school pupils has been sharpened by the development of the Revised Junior Eysenck Personality Questionnaire (JEPQ-R). As yet, however, no comparability study has reported on the empirical performance of these new scales alongside the earlier established measures. This project aims to explore the reliability and validity of the JEPQ-R among a sample of 800 primary school pupils.
Status: Sponsored project
Source of Grant: Trinity College
Date of Research: 1992-continuing
KEYWORDS: *personality measures; primary school pupils*

10/1561
Carmarthen, Dyfed SA31 3EP
01267 237971
Francis, L. Prof.; Lloyd Davies, B. Mrs
The development of a Welsh language edition of the Junior Eysenck Personality Questionnaire
Abstract: Since its development in 1975 the Junior Eysenck Personality Questionnaire (JEPQ) has been translated into a number of other languages. The aim of the present project is to develop and test empirically a Welsh language edition of the JEPQ for use among a secondary school population.
Status: Sponsored project
Source of Grant: Trinity College

Date of Research: 1992-continuing
KEYWORDS: *personality measures; welsh*

10/1562

Carmarthen, Dyfed SA31 3EP
01267 237971
Francis, L. Prof.
Denominational differences in secondary school pupils' attitudes towards substance use
Abstract: This project aims to compare the attitudes of churchgoing 13-15 year olds to smoking, alcohol, and drugs, according to the denomination attended. In order to build up a significant sample of churchgoing adolescents, the attitude inventory has been completed by 20,000 secondary school pupils.
Status: Sponsored project
Source of Grant: Trinity College
Date of Research: 1992-continuing
KEYWORDS: *drinking; drug abuse; pupil attitudes; religious attitudes; secondary school pupils; smoking; substance abuse*

10/1563

Carmarthen, Dyfed SA31 3EP
01267 237971
Francis, L. Prof.; Jones, S. Ms
School today: bullying, personality and values
Abstract: This study explores the relationship between personality, bullying, religious victimisation, self-concept and values among secondary school pupils in Wales. Personality is measured by the short form Revised Junior Eysenck Personality Questionnaire. Self-concept is measured by the Coopersmith Inventory. Two new Likert type scales have been developed to assess the tendency to be either bully or victim. Values are measured by a Likert instrument. So far 750 13-15 year olds have participated in a pilot project.
Status: Sponsored project
Source of Grant: Trinity College
Date of Research: 1993-continuing
KEYWORDS: *behaviour problems; bullying; personality; secondary school pupils; values*

10/1564

Carmarthen, Dyfed SA31 3EP
01267 237971
Francis, L. Prof.; Gibson, H. Prof.
The influence of Catholic schools on pupil attitudes towards Christianity
Abstract: This project aims to examine the attitudes of Catholic pupils towards Christianity and to compare the attitudes of those pupils educated in Catholic schools with those educated in non-denominational schools in Scotland. This project re-analyses data collected from over 6,000 pupils in Dundee.
Status: Sponsored project
Source of Grant: Trinity College
Date of Research: 1992-continuing
KEYWORDS: *christianity; pupil attitudes; religion; religious attitudes; roman catholic church*

10/1565

Carmarthen, Dyfed SA31 3EP
01267 237971
Francis, L. Prof.
Religion, sex and sex role identity
Abstract: While sex is consistently found to be a significant predictor of the dimensions of religiosity among children and adolescents as well as among adults, theoretical explanations for this finding remain confused. The aim of the present project is to explore the extent to which sex differences in religiosity can be accounted for in terms of the personality dimensions of masculinity and femininity proposed by Bem's Sex Role Inventory, rather than by the simple categorisation of gender, among a sample of 1,300 13-16 year olds.
Status: Sponsored project
Source of Grant: Trinity College
Date of Research: 1992-continuing
KEYWORDS: *pupil attitudes; religion; religious attitudes; secondary school pupils; sex differences; sex role*

10/1566

Carmarthen, Dyfed SA31 3EP
01267 237971
Francis, L. Prof.
Religion and self-concept
Abstract: This project aims to compare the empirical properties of three measures of self-concept and to explore the relationship between self-concept and religiosity among fifth year secondary school pupils on a database of 700 respondents.
Status: Sponsored project
Source of Grant: Trinity College
Date of Research: 1992-continuing
KEYWORDS: *pupil attitudes; religion; religious attitudes; secondary school pupils; self-concept*

10/1567

Carmarthen, Dyfed SA31 3EP
01267 237971
Francis, L. Prof.; Kay, W. Dr
Teenage religion and values today
Abstract: A modified form of the CENTYMCA Attitude Inventory developed by Leslie Francis in Teenagers and the Church (Collins, 1984) and Youth in Transit (Gower, 1982) is being completed by 20,000 13-15 year old pupils through state maintained and independent secondary schools in England and Wales. The inventory employs Likert type scales to measure religiosity, social, personal and moral values. The aim of the project is to explore the role of religion in shaping teenage values.
Published Material: FRANCIS, L.J. & MULLEN, K. (1993). 'Religiosity and attitudes towards drug use among 13-15 year olds in England', Addiction, Vol 88, pp.665-672.; FRANCIS, L.J. & KAY, W.K. The teenage soul. Leominster: Gracewing. (in press).
Status: Sponsored project
Source of Grant: Trinity College
Date of Research: 1990-continuing
KEYWORDS: *attitude measures; pupil attitudes; religion; religious attitudes; secondary school pupils; values*

Ulster University

10/1568

Coleraine Campus, Faculty of Education, Cromore Road, Coleraine, County Londonderry BT52 1SA
01265 44141
McGarvey, B. Prof.; Harper, D. Mr; Day, J. Mrs
Differentiated learning in science project
Abstract: The development and trials of schemes of work for the Northern Ireland Science Curriculum at key stages 1, 2 and 3. These schemes incorporate the principles of continuity, progression and differentiation.
Status: Sponsored project
Source of Grant: Northern Ireland Curriculum Council £213,378
Date of Research: 1992-1993
KEYWORDS: *curriculum development; differentiated curriculum; individualised methods; Northern Ireland; science education*

10/1569

Coleraine Campus, Faculty of Education, Cromore Road, Coleraine, County Londonderry BT52 1SA
01265 44141
Austin, R. Dr
Birth, marriage and death in Europe
Abstract: This project involves 16-18 year old students in a number of European countries. They are investigating the customs and traditions related to birth, marriage and death and the ways in which those rituals have evolved over the last three generations. By linking up with other schools in Europe, students are able to exchange data by fax or electronic mail (e-mail) and to contrast their own findings with those from a different culture.
Status: Individual research
Date of Research: 1993-continuing
KEYWORDS: *cross cultural studies; electronic mail; European studies; international education; social history; telecommunications*

10/1570

Coleraine Campus, Faculty of Education, Cromore Road,
Coleraine, County Londonderry BT52 1SA
01265 44141
Austin, R. Dr

The role of electronic mail in offering a European dimension in teacher training

Abstract: The project is examining the ways in which electronic mail (e-mail) can deliver a European dimension to students on a one year Postgraduate Certificate in Education (PGCE) course. A pilot study has been run at the University of Ulster in which students used e-mail to teach a class of 16 year olds in Oslo about Northern Ireland. This work brought together three cross-curricular themes for the Common Core Curriculum in Northern Ireland – Education for Mutual Understanding (EMU), Cultural Heritage and Information Technology, as well as offering a European dimension to the teacher trainees.

Status: Sponsored project
Source of Grant: European Commission
Date of Research: 1993-continuing
KEYWORDS: cross cultural studies; electronic mail; European studies; preservice teacher education; telecommunications

10/1571

Coleraine Campus, Faculty of Education, Cromore Road,
Coleraine, County Londonderry BT52 1SA
01265 44141
Austin, R. Dr

The role of electronic mail in modern language learning

Abstract: The project tested the language skills and level of cultural awareness of two groups of linked school pupils before and after an electronic mail (e-mail) project. The pupils in Northern Ireland were aged 14, while those in Germany were 14-16. Significant gains in language competence, cultural awareness and information technology skills were registered.

Published Material: AUSTIN, R. & MENDLICK, F. (1993). 'The role of electronic mail in cultural awareness and language development', ReCALL, Issue No 9, pp.19-23.; AUSTIN, R. & MENDLICK, F. 'Electronic mail in modern language development', Neusprachliche Mitteilungen aus Wissenschaft und Praxis. (in press).

Status: Sponsored project
Source of Grant: British Telecom
Date of Research: 1993-1993
KEYWORDS: cultural awareness; electronic mail; intercultural communication; language proficiency; modern language studies; telecommunications

10/1572

Coleraine Campus, Faculty of Education, Cromore Road,
Coleraine, County Londonderry BT52 1SA
01265 44141
Austin, R. Dr

The impact of computer conferencing on teaching and learning in history

Abstract: This project is studying the ways that computer conferencing in history can improve learning. In particular, it is examining how this form of interaction affects student motivation, appreciation of other perspectives, awareness of new research and the development of writing skills.

Published Material: AUSTIN, R. (1994). 'Computer conferencing in history: a pilot study at 16-18', Teaching History, No 75, April, pp.33-35.

Status: Sponsored project
Source of Grant: British Telecom
Date of Research: 1993-1994
KEYWORDS: computer uses in education; history studies; learning strategies; teaching methods; teleconferencing

10/1573

Coleraine Campus, Faculty of Education, Cromore Road,
Coleraine, County Londonderry BT52 1SA
01265 44141
McGarvey, B. Prof.; Morgan, V. Prof.; Marriott, S. Mr;
Abbott, L. Mrs

Differentiation in primary classrooms

Abstract: A study of existing provision for differentiation in primary classrooms, conducted through survey, interview and case study methods. 'Good practice' in differentiation will be investigated and associated problems identified. Implications for supporting differentiated learning will be discussed.

Status: Sponsored project
Source of Grant: Department of Education Northern Ireland
Date of Research: 1993-1994
KEYWORDS: differentiated curriculum; individualised methods; primary education; teaching methods

10/1574

Faculty of Education, Coleraine Campus, Cromore Road,
Coleraine, County Londonderry BT52 1SA
01265 44141
Mallon, P. Mr; *Supervisor:* McGarvey, B. Prof.

The impact of curriculum innovation in science in some small rural secondary schools

Abstract: The aim is to identify the range of issues which science teachers in small rural schools were facing in implementing the new Northern Ireland science curriculum at Key Stage 3. Open-ended case studies were conducted initially and then more focused case studies of four schools were carried out over a two-year period. The final report will describe the challenges which the new Science Curriculum is posing to small science departments and the responses being made.

Status: Individual research
Date of Research: 1988-1994
KEYWORDS: Northern Ireland; rural schools; science curriculum; science education; small schools

10/1575

Faculty of Education, Coleraine Campus, Cromore Road,
Coleraine, County Londonderry BT52 1SA
01265 44141
Austin, R. Dr

Junior Certificate History in the Republic of Ireland: purpose, problems and potential

Abstract: The aim of this study is to explore the ways in which a national curriculum change in the teaching of history in the Republic of Ireland is being implemented in the classroom. A sample of teachers are completing questionnaires, and resource materials are being designed, used and evaluated to measure student reaction to the proposed changes. The research is set in the wider context of the history of curriculum change in the Republic of Ireland and the perceived value and interest of history to young people.

Status: Individual research
Date of Research: 1991-continuing
KEYWORDS: curriculum development; history; Ireland

10/1576

Faculty of Education, Coleraine Campus, Cromore Road,
Coleraine, County Londonderry BT52 1SA
01265 44141
Chambers, M. Mrs; *Supervisor:* McGarvey, B. Prof.

Learning psychiatric nursing skills: the contribution of the ward environment

Abstract: The aim of this study is to ascertain those factors which facilitate student psychiatric nurses in the learning of psychiatric nursing skills. A pilot study of an open-ended nature was conducted on wards, using the Delphi technique, interview and participant observation. The main study involved more closely focused case studies of the learning experiences of eight students. The final report will compare and contrast the aims of the ward experience and the actual learning opportunities, and will discuss the roles of nursing and nurse education staff in supporting student learning on the ward.

Status: Individual research
Date of Research: 1987-1994
KEYWORDS: delphi technique; nurse education; psychiatric services

10/1577

Jordanstown Campus, Faculty of Education, Shore Road,
Whiteabbey, County Antrim BT37 0QB
01232 365131
Dallat, J. Dr; Robinson, A. Mr; Livingston, R. Dr;
MacGabhann, D. Mr; Abbott, L. Mrs; Frazer, G. Mrs

Video-conferencing

Abstract: This research examines: 1) the effectiveness of a recently-installed video-conferencing system at the University of Ulster; and 2) the effectiveness and the efficiency of video-conferencing as a

mode of teaching delivery in the context of independent, flexible and distance learning in higher education. The research evaluated the views and experiences of three different groups of postgraduate students (part-time), the majority being members of the teaching profession. The experiences and views of tutors were also evaluated and assessed. Data was collected by questionnaire and interview with all concerned. Interviews were conducted by an external evaluator and it was she who evaluated the students' experiences. Video-conferencing was shown to have positive effects on group cohesiveness and positively promoted independent learning. The sound system could however be problematic on occasions.
Published Material: DALLAT, J. et al. (1991). 'Videoconferencing in higher education'. International Conference Proceedings on Distance Education, Cambridge University, September 1991.; DALLAT, J. et al. (1992). Videoconferencing and the adult learner. Coleraine: University of Ulster.; DALLAT, J. et al. (1992). 'Video-conferencing at the University of Ulster', Open Learning, Vol 2, No 2, pp.14-22.; DALLAT, J. et al. (1992). 'The use of videoconferencing for teaching and learning', Research in Education, No 48, pp.92-102.; DALLAT, J. et al. (1993). Videoconferencing and community relations. Whiteabbey: University of Ulster at Jordanstown.
Status: Sponsored project
Source of Grant: Ulster University
Date of Research: 1990-1994
KEYWORDS: *distance education; interactive video; teaching methods; teleconferencing*

10/1578
> Jordanstown Campus, Faculty of Education, Shore Road,
> Whiteabbey, County Antrim BT37 0QB
> 01232 365131
> Hutchinson, B. Dr

Appraising appraisal: quality assurance and control in the University of Ulster
Abstract: A small scale qualitative research evaluation project investigating: the extent to which the recently established University staff appraisal scheme realised its intentions; the adequacy of the purposes and conceptions embedded in the appraisal scheme; the relationship between staff appraisal and other University-wide procedures. Documentary analysis and semi-structured, tape-recorded interviews were the main methods of investigation to supplement a critical review of literature. Findings: staff very much appreciated the appraisal interview; not many appraisals had been conducted along the devised themes suggested by management; this had more 'bad' effects than 'good' ones; no evidence to suggest that appraisal actually changed anything for the better – yet.
Published Material: HUTCHINSON, B. (1993). Appraising appraisal: quality assurance and control in the University of Ulster. Coleraine: University of Ulster.
Status: Sponsored project
Source of Grant: Ulster University at Jordanstown: Faculty of Education £2,600
Date of Research: 1991-1993
KEYWORDS: *academic staff evaluation; quality assurance; quality control; teacher evaluation; universities*

10/1579
> Jordanstown Campus, Faculty of Education, Shore Road,
> Newtownabbey, County Antrim BT37 OQB
> 01232 365131
> Crouch, C. Mr

Children and television
Abstract: The research aims to provide a broad picture of children's use and understanding of television. To date, children of primary school age (i.e. 7 to 11/12) preferences have been explored (sample of 3,700+ from Northern Ireland, England, Australia surveyed) and results have indicated early gender differences; females tending to prefer soap opera programmes increasingly by age. A second wave of research (sample of 1,000 Australian, circa 1,000 Northern Ireland 12 – 12/16 year olds) involves survey by questionnaire on a wide range of issues but with special emphasis on television and learning. These data remain to be analysed.
Published Material: CROUCH, C. (1989). 'Television and primary schoolchildren in Northern Ireland: 1: television programme preferences', Journal of Educational Television, Vol 15, No 13, pp.163-170.; CROUCH, C. (1989). 'Soap in the eyes: primary schoolgirl TV preferences', Metro: Media and Education Magazine, (Australia), No 81, pp.18-22, Summer.; CROUCH, C. (1991). 'The emergence of

soap: primary schoolchildren's TV preferences in Northern Ireland, England and Australia', Research in Education, No 46, pp.73-83, November.
Status: Individual research
Date of Research: 1988-continuing
KEYWORDS: *adolescents; children; television surveys; television viewing*

10/1580
> Jordanstown Campus, Faculty of Education, Shore Road,
> Whiteabbey, County Antrim BT37 0QB
> 01232 365131
> Hutchinson, B. Dr

Meeting the employment needs of the young unemployed
Abstract: The meeting the employment needs of the young unemployed (MENYU) project is supporting trainers of disadvantaged 16-25 year olds to develop improved strategies of delivering training programmes. Using an action research approach, trainers can shape the agenda and invite their trainees to participate in its determination. Trainers' experience of engagement in this process will be shared with a number of transnational European partners. It will also contribute to the development of a master's level distance learning course.
Status: Sponsored project
Source of Grant: European Social Fund
Date of Research: 1993-1994
KEYWORDS: *international educational exchange; programme development; trainers; training; youth employment; youth programmes*

10/1581
> Magee College, Faculty of Education, Northland Road,
> Derry, County Londonderry BT48 7JL
> 01504 265621
> North, R. Dr; Rae, G. Prof.; Brotherton, C. Prof.;
> Hashim, A. Prof.; Purcell, P. Prof.; Row, G. Mr

Interactivity in multimedia courseware
Abstract: An investigation into the use of multimedia in undergraduate statistical courseware using an experimental design.
Status: Sponsored project
Source of Grant: International Fund for Ireland
Date of Research: 1993-continuing
KEYWORDS: *computer assisted learning; educational software; multimedia approach; statistics education*

University College of North Wales

10/1582
> Department of Psychology, College Road, Bangor, Gwynedd
> LL57 2DG
> 01248 351151
> Miles, T. Prof.

Dyslexia and mathematics
Abstract: It is hypothesised that the mathematical difficulties of dyslexics are a consequence of the same anomaly of development which affects their literary skills. It has been shown (Pritchard, et al, 1989) that 15 dyslexic boys aged 12 to 14 had fewer 'number facts' available than a suitably matched control. Work is now in progress on the time needed by dyslexics and matched control to carry out different types of mathematical operations. Data on the mathematical performance of over 12,000 10 year-olds (Child Health and Education Study), including some dyslexics, are in the process of being analysed.
Published Material: MILES, T.R. (1989). 'Dyslexia and mathematics', Ace Reports, No 16, pp.16-20.; PRITCHARD, R.A., MILES, T.R., CHINN, S.J. & TAGGART, A.T. (1989). 'Dyslexia and knowledge of number facts', Links, Vol 14, No 3, pp.17-20.; MILES, T.R. & MILES, E. (Eds). (1991). Dyslexia and Mathematics. London: Routledge.
Status: Individual research
Date of Research: 1988-continuing
KEYWORDS: *dyslexia; learning disabilities; mathematics*

10/1583

School of Education, Deiniol Road, Bangor, Gwynedd
LL57 2UW
01248 351151
Baker, C. Dr
The effectiveness of bilingual education in Wales
Abstract: The project will look at the results of computer analysis of
the 1991 Census on the Welsh language studying spatial, age,
oracy/literacy trends alongside immigration/emigration and the effects on Welsh language educational provision. The major focus of
the project will be the relationship of these trends to Welsh medium
education and the implications for present and future educational
policy. The project will also include a historical perspective of the
growth of bilingual education in Wales 1939 – present; the National
Curriculum and Assessment and the implications for bilingual education in Wales; county policies for Welsh language in education and
the provision of Welsh medium teaching; recent conflicts and controversies over the Welsh language; perspectives of HMI reports on
Welsh medium teaching; Welsh medium curriculum development
projects; the provision of Welsh medium education in higher education and further education; Welsh language media and voluntary
bodies such as Urdd and Ysgolion Meithrin.
Status: Sponsored project
Source of Grant: University of Wales, Faculty of Education £5,000
Date of Research: 1992-continuing
*KEYWORDS: bilingual education; bilingualism; educational policy;
language policy; school effectiveness; Welsh; Welsh studies*

10/1584

School of Education, Deiniol Road, Bangor, Gwynedd
LL57 2UW
01248 351151
Williams, I. Prof.; Baker, C. Dr
**Evaluation of the National Curriculum assessment of Welsh
(GWASG)**
Abstract: The aim of this research is to carry out a comprehensive
and detailed evaluation of National Curriculum assessment in first
language (L1) and second language (L2) Welsh. The research issues
can be summarised as: (1) The validity and reliability of teacher
assessments (TA's). (2) Comparability, determining influences and
patterning in TA's. (3) Variability in teacher interpretations of TA's.
(4) Effects of aggregation on standard assessment task scores (SA's).
(5) The validity of SA's. (6) Effects of sampling of SA's on assessment outcomes. (7) Comparability, determining influences and patterning in SA's across time. (8) Relationships between assessments
and special educational needs pupils. (9) Relationships of assessments across key stages. (10) Quality of formative and summative
information provided by the assessments. The process and effectiveness of teachers recording assessments and reporting to parents. (11)
Effects of assessments on teaching and assessing L1 and L2 Welsh.
(12) Comparability of TA's and SA's. Stability in patterns of difference. Commonality bases. (13) Comparability of assessments from
two programmes at National Curriculum Key Stage 3. (14) The
manageability of assessments for teachers. (15) Patterns in the take-
up of non-statutory National Curriculum Key Stage 1 L2 Welsh
materials. (16) Relationship between standardisation of assessment
and School Examinations and Assessment Council (SEAC) (and
preferably local education authority) training and guidance. Three
approaches are being employed. These approaches may be termed
the statistical, the representative survey and the expert. First, the
assessment data require considerable statistical analysis to investigate
issues of validity, reliability, comparability across context and time,
patterns and relationships in the data. Second, there are issues requiring a wide-scale survey of teacher, classroom and school practices.
By stratified random sampling across Wales, a thoroughly representative elicitation of local procedures and individual viewpoints is
necessary. This is achieved by interviewing and questionnaires.
Third, the special insights of expert educationists provides a deep and
perceptive sensitivity to complement wide consensus viewpoints. A
careful and judicious 'purposeful sample' of experts will provide
detailed qualitative information to complement the quantitative statistical analysis and the part-qualitative/part-quantitative approach of
representative surveys. GWASG reports are available from SEAC.
Published Material: GWASG Report. KS3 Welsh First Language
Assessment (Cy): Analysis of Assessment Record Booklet Data.
Report for School Examinations and Assessment Council/Welsh
Office (October 1992).; GWASG Report. KS3 Welsh Second Lan-
guage Assessment (Ca): Analysis of Assessment Record Booklet
Data. Report for School Examinations and Assessment Coun-

cil/Welsh Office (October 1992).; GWASG Report. Evaluation of the
Bridges Assessment Pack for KS1 Second Language Welsh. Report
for School Examinations and Assessment Council/Welsh Office
(October 1992).; GWASG Report. KS1: An Analysis of Data from
Assessment Record Booklets. Report for School Examinations and
Assessment Council/Welsh Office (October 1992).; GWASG Re-
port. National Curriculum Assessment and Welsh Medium Educa-
tion: Trends in Recent Results. Report for School Examinations and
Assessment Council/Welsh Office (October 1992).
Status: Sponsored project
Source of Grant: The Welsh Office £338,000
Date of Research: 1992-1994
*KEYWORDS: assessment; mother tongue; National Curriculum;
school based assessment; second language learning; standard as-
sessment tasks; Welsh*

10/1585

School of Education, Deiniol Road, Bangor, Gwynedd
LL57 2UW
01248 351151
Rees, W. Dr
Counselling in different settings
Abstract: The aim of this research is to discover whether there is a
common core of counselling skills and approaches in different set-
tings. Interviews have been taped and transcribed with hospital
chaplains, hospital social workers, probation officers, drugs workers,
and student counsellors
Status: Individual research
Date of Research: 1992-1993
*KEYWORDS: counselling; counsellor characteristics; counsellor
performance; counsellors*

10/1586

School of English and Linguistics, College Road, Bangor,
Gwynedd LL57 2DG
01248 351151
Scholfield, P. Mr
**Vocabulary rate in course materials for English as a second or
foreign language**
Abstract: The research consists of analysing the rate of introduction
of new vocabulary items, lesson by lesson, in a sample of well known
course books for English as a second/foreign language. Using concepts of time series analysis, light is thrown on the patterns of rises
and falls to be found. The results are interpreted in the light of learner
needs and what the teacher can do when the rate in course materials
is inappropriate.
Published Material: SCHOLFIELD, P.J. (1991). 'Vocabulary rate in
course books: living with an unstable lexical economy', Proceedings
of 5th International Linguistics Symposium, Aristotle University,
Thessaloniki.
Status: Individual research
Date of Research: 1989-continuing
*KEYWORDS: educational materials; English – second language;
textbooks; vocabulary development*

10/1587

School of Sociology and Social Policy, College Road,
Bangor, Gwynedd LL57 2DG
01248 351151
Betts, S. Ms; Garland, P. Ms
Returning to learning: mature students in higher education
Abstract: This research investigates the transitions of students return-
ing to higher education. It considers the pathways and turning points
as well as the experiences of mature students in higher education.
Most importantly the research highlights gender differences in the
pathways and experiences of mature students and seeks to explain
these in the wider context of gender divisions in society.
Status: Sponsored project
Source of Grant: University College of North Wales: School of
Sociology and Social; Policy £2,000
Date of Research: 1990-continuing
KEYWORDS: higher education; mature students; sex differences

University College of Ripon and York St. John

10/1588

Department of Social Sciences, Lord Mayor's Walk, York
YO3 7EX
01904 656771
Forrest, L. Ms; Eagleton, M. Ms
What do young women need to know?
Abstract: This study springs from an awareness of a generation gap in Women's Studies. Most well-established practitioners are aged 40+, and most students are barely 20+. This action research project aims to explore three related questions: 1) How do young women (age 16-25) perceive feminism? 2) What material do young female students feel is appropriate for women's studies? 3) How can older Women's Studies teachers adapt their teaching to match these interests and needs? The main methods to be used will include questionnaires and interviews of a sample of approximately sixty female A level students not taking Women's studies and approximately forty female undergraduate Women's Studies students. Relevant literature and theory will be applied. In the spirit of action research and feminist praxis, curriculum developments and appropriate changes in pedagogy are the objectives.
Status: Individual research
Date of Research: 1993-continuing
KEYWORDS: age differences; feminism; women's studies

10/1589

Department of Social Sciences, Lord Mayor's Walk, York
YO3 7EX
01904 656771
Maynard, E. Ms; Pearsall, S. Mr
Male mature students in higher education: a comparison of the different experiences of higher education of male and female students
Abstract: This is an investigation of the experiences of male mature students compared to those of female mature students. Thirty male students and fifteen female students from two higher education insitutions were interviewed in depth. Particular attention was paid to the relationship between experiences in higher education and the work/home experiences which had preceded higher education. The researchers are also interested in the way in which home and academic life interacted, and the ultimate effects of the experience on individual students' perceptions of themselves and the world around them. Initial results suggest that male students tended to treat their studies as 'a job' and received a great deal of support from their families. Female students, usually due to greater domestic obligations, had a more fragmented work pattern, and received less support and encouragement from their families, especially their partners.
Status: Sponsored project
Source of Grant: University College of Ripon and York St. John £200
Date of Research: 1992-1994
KEYWORDS: educational experience; higher education; mature students; men; sex differences; student attitudes; women's education

University College of Swansea

10/1590

Centre for Applied Language Studies, Singleton Park,
Swansea SA2 8PP
01792 205678
Meara, P. Dr
Word recognition problems among Arabic-speaking learners of English
Abstract: The background of the research lies in the problems Arabic learners of English seem to have in distinguishing English words with similar consonant structure, e.g. broad/bread; curl/cereal. After several initial attempts to design test procedures which would replicate this type of error, a computer-based word-recognition test was developed in which firstly vowels and then secondly consonants were systematically deleted from word stimuli presented to the subjects. The test records response-times and error rates for each subject. Two initial experiments of this type indicated that there was a significant difference between the responses of, on the one hand, Arabic speaking subjects and on the other, native speakers and speakers of European languages written in Roman script. This difference was maintained in the final experiment where Arabic speaking subjects were compared with Japanese, Thai and European language speakers as well as native speakers of English, a total of 131 subjects. In spite of the overall significance of the results of the Arabic speaking group, there were considerable individual differences between subjects; this has prompted the final phase of the study in which it is hoped to design a simple diagnostic test to predict those subjects who are most likely to have word-handling difficulties of the type analysed here. Such a test would have considerable classroom value.
Published Material: RYAN, A. & MEARA, P. (1991). 'The case of the invisible vowels: Arabic speakers reading English words', Reading in a Foreign Language, Vol 7, No 2, pp.531-540.
Status: Individual research
Date of Research: 1987-1993
KEYWORDS: Arabs; English – second language; vowels; word recognition

10/1591

Centre for Applied Language Studies, Singleton Park,
Swansea SA2 8PP
01792 205678
Meara, P. Dr
Lexical behaviour in a second language
Abstract: This project comprises a group of linked studies aimed at improving our understanding of vocabulary acquisition in foreign languages. The project includes: (1) a large scale bibliographical survey; (2) development of lexical tests; and (3) a set of linked PhD projects on lexical difficulties of second language speakers.
Published Material: A list of publications is available from the researcher.
Status: Sponsored project
Source of Grant: Eurocentres; Longmans; TVEI; University of Oxford Local Examinations Delegacy; BBC English
Date of Research: 1981-continuing
KEYWORDS: second language learning; vocabulary development

10/1592

Department of Education, Hendrefoilan, Swansea SA2 7NB
01792 201231
Banks, F. Mr
An evaluation of distance learning Inservice Education of Teachers (INSET) in Wales
Abstract: The problems of geographical isolation and the small number of teachers requiring Inservice Education of Teachers (INSET) in some curriculum areas make distance learning an attractive option for many Welsh local education authorities. The study seeks to illuminate both effective course design and good practice in local education authority (LEA) management of teacher support. Teachers in Wales, from all LEAs, involved in (initially) one distance learning INSET programme have been interviewed about their perceived progress and satisfaction with the course, its delivery, and the extent to which they think the course will alter their practice. An attempt will be made to design an evaluation method which will include a longitudinal study of how teachers change over time following an INSET experience. They were asked to give factual details of patterns of study and use of the materials. The INSET coordinators from the corresponding LEAs have been asked to supply details of the support they are prepared to give to the teachers in terms of fees, expenses, free time, etc., and have been interviewed to gather their opinion of the effectiveness of the programmes.
Status: Sponsored project
Source of Grant: University of Wales: Faculty of Education £3,400
Date of Research: 1989-continuing
KEYWORDS: distance education; inservice teacher education; programme effectiveness; teacher attitudes; teacher development

10/1593

Department of Education, Hendrefoilan, Swansea SA2 7NB
01792 201231
Rowe, M. Mr; Tanner, H. Mr; Davies, L. Ms; Morgan-Jones, P. Mr; Prichard, J. Ms
Teacher competencies and professional development
Abstract: Action research is being conducted in Swansea, Aberystwyth and Bangor to develop a framework of competencies for

use in initial teacher education. Techniques and documentation are being developed to establish records of achievement for student teachers. The success of the competencies and records of achievement will then be evaluated.
Status: Sponsored project
Source of Grant: University of Wales
Date of Research: 1991-1993
KEYWORDS: *competence; competency based teacher education; preservice teacher education; records of achievement; student teachers*

10/1594
    Department of Education, Hendrefoilan, Swansea SA2 7NB
    01792 201231
    Tanner, H. Mr
The information technology in mathematics project
Abstract: This is a survey of the use of information technology for teaching mathematics in England and Wales. A network of schools has been set up to develop and trial materials and techniques for teaching elements from both the Mathematics and Information Technology (IT) National Curricula. It includes work on spreadsheets, logo and databases.
Status: Sponsored project
Source of Grant: University of Wales
Date of Research: 1989-continuing
KEYWORDS: *computer uses in education; information technology; mathematics education*

10/1595
    Department of Education, Hendrefoilan, Swansea SA2 7NB
    01792 201231
    Tanner, H. Mr
Teacher assessment of the National Curriculum
Abstract: A network of schools was established to conduct action research into the development of teacher assessment of the National Curriculum in key stage 3. Local education authority advisers were surveyed to establish the extent of guidance offered to teachers. Groups of teachers, trainers and advisers have been meeting to develop guidance materials.
Status: Sponsored project
Source of Grant: University of Wales; Association of Teachers of Mathematics
Date of Research: 1989-continuing
KEYWORDS: *assessment; National Curriculum; school based assessment*

10/1596
    Department of Education, Hendrefoilan, Swansea SA2 7NB
    01792 201231
    Hendley, D. Mr; Parkinson, J. Dr; Stables, A. Dr; Tanner, H. Mr; Thomas, B. Mrs
Pupil attitudes to English, Mathematics, Science, Technology and Welsh under the National Curriculum
Abstract: A questionnaire has been developed, using a Likert-type scale, to measure the attitudes of pupils in years 2 and 3 of secondary schools (years 8 and 9 of the National Curriculum) over a period of two years. The degree to which the implementation of the National Curriculum has affected attitudes will be ascertained.
Status: Individual research
Date of Research: 1991-continuing
KEYWORDS: *National Curriculum; pupil attitudes; secondary schools*

10/1597
    Department of Education, Hendrefoilan, Swansea SA2 7NB
    01792 201231
    Furlong, J. Prof.
The role of the mentor in initial teacher education
Abstract: This is an indepth study of the work of eight 'mentors' in different programmes of initial teacher education.
Status: Sponsored project
Source of Grant: Paul Hamlyn Foundation £14,000
Date of Research: 1992-1993
KEYWORDS: *mentors; preservice teacher education*

10/1598
    Department of Education, Hendrefoilan, Swansea SA2 7NB
    01792 201231
    Jephcote, M. Mr; *Supervisor:* Williams, M. Prof.
Economic awareness as a curriculum entitlement for Welsh pupils
Abstract: The study is to facilitate the development of economic awareness in primary and secondary schools in Wales. The project has curriculum development and curriculum research aspects. On the research side the focus is on the preparation of case studies of individual schools and upon pupils' cognitive growth.
Status: Sponsored project
Source of Grant: Welsh Office; Esme Fairbairn Trust
Date of Research: 1990-1993
KEYWORDS: *cross curricular approach; curriculum development; economics education; enterprise education; primary education; secondary education; Wales*

10/1599
    Department of Education, Hendrefoilan, Swansea SA2 7NB
    01792 201231
    Stables, A. Dr
Approaches to subject choice: an international survey of the research
Abstract: A book is in process, due to be published in 1995, which will survey research relating to the issue of subject and curriculum choice by pupils and students in the 14 – 19 age range. It will include detailed analysis of the author's research into subject choice at 14 and 16 in England and Wales. Issues addressed in the book will include gender and subject choice, school/college management and subject choice, the role of choice within the school/college curriculum, and the place of subject choice in varying social and educational contexts, including mixed and single-sex schools.
Published Material: HARVEY, T.J. & STABLES, A. (1984). 'Gender difference in subject preference and perception of subject importance among third year secondary school pupils in single-sex and mixed comprehensive schools', Educational Studies, Vol 10, No 3, pp. 243-253.; STABLES, A. (1986). 'Pupils' approaches to subject option choices: a study of differences between schools and between the sexes'. Unpublished PhD. Thesis. Bath: University of Bath.; STABLES, A. (1990).' Differences between pupils from mixed and single-sex schools in their enjoyment of school subjects and in their attitudes to science and to school', Educational Review, Vol 42, No 3, pp. 221-230.; STABLES, A. & STABLES, S. (1993). Students' approaches to A-level subject choices and perceptions of A-level subjects: a study of first year A-level students in a tertiary college. Occasional Paper No 8. Swansea: University College of Swansea, Department of Education.
Status: Individual research
Date of Research: 1993-continuing
KEYWORDS: *choice of subjects; pupil attitudes; pupil interests; sex differences*

10/1600
    Department of Education, Hendrefoilan, Swansea SA2 7NB
    01792 201231
    Furlong, J. Prof.; Sanders, S. Ms; Maynard, T. Ms
Effective mentoring in primary schools: a Welsh action research project
Abstract: The 'Effective Mentoring in Primary Schools' project is part of a larger project funded by the Esmee Fairbairn Charitable Trust, which is centred in six universities: Swansea, Oxford, Keele, Leicester and Manchester Metropolitan. The broad aims of the project are to examine the role of the mentor both in initial teacher education and the continuing professional development of teachers and also to explore the institutional implications of mentoring. In Swansea, we are particularly interested in exploring some of the content of mentoring – specifically, teachers' subject-matter knowlege – as well as the institutional arrangements that might be made to support mentoring in primary schools and their resource implications. Both of these issues will have fundamental importance with respect to the many small schools which predominate in Wales.
Status: Sponsored project
Source of Grant: Esmee Fairbairn Charitable Trust £35,000
Date of Research: 1993-1994
KEYWORDS: *mentors; preservice teacher education; primary schools; professional continuing education; teacher development*

10/1601

Department of Education, Hendrefoilan, Swansea SA2 7NB
01792 201231
Tanner, H. Mr; Jones, S. Mrs;
The practical applications of mathematics project phase 2: developing and evaluating a mathematical thinking skills course
Abstract: The research builds on the findings of 'The Use and Practical Applications of Mathematics' project funded by the Welsh Office, 1991/1992. The practical activities produced in phase one form the basis of a thinking skills course to accelerate pupils' cognitive development in mathematics. There are two strands to the course: 1) the development of a structured series of cognitive challenges to stimulate the progressive evolution of key skills in the areas of strategy, logic and communication; 2) the use and development of teaching techniques which will encourage the maturation of the metacognitive skills of planning, monitoring and evaluation. The aims of the research are to: 1) develop a structured series of cognitive challenges for use with pupils in National Curriculum key stage three; 2) devise instruments to assess pupils' cognitive development in mathematics; 3) evaluate the effect of the thinking skills course on pupils' mathematical development; 4) develop assessment strategies for use with these materials and to provide examples of pupils' assessed work suitable for use in National Curriculum key stage three. A network of six schools will conduct action research into the systematic development of mathematical thinking skills. The schools will develop and trial teaching strategies and materials supported by members of the project team. Experimental classes will be compared with matched control classes. The pupils will be tested before and after the course using specifically developed assessment instruments. The attitude of each group to mathematics will be monitored using a questionnaire.
Published Material: TANNER, H.F.R. & JONES, S.A. (1993). 'Developing metacognition through peer and self assessment'. In: BREITEIG, T. et al (Eds). Teaching and learning mathematics in context. Hemel Hempstead: Ellis Horwood.; TANNER, H.F.R. & JONES, S.A. (1993). Hands on maths. Swansea: University College of Swansea.
Status: Sponsored project
Source of Grant: The Welsh Office £22,500; University of Wales: Subject Panel £5,500
Date of Research: 1993-1994
KEYWORDS: *assessment; cognitive ability; mathematical models; mathematics education; metacognition*

University College of Wales, Aberystwyth

10/1602

Department of Education, PO Box 2, Aberystwyth
SY23 2AX
01970 623111
Lewis, G. Mr; *Supervisor:* Morris-Jones, R. Mr
Nature of second language teaching tasks in Welsh
Abstract: The purpose of the investigation is to consider the background to the use of tasks in second language teaching in Welsh. It then reviews what activities are included in current Welsh second language courses. Current practice in the use of tasks in the Welsh second language classroom will be considered. Specific areas of investigation will be attempting to measure the effectiveness of tasks and elements of pupils' task related motivation. The influence of assessment on the types of tasks used to teach Welsh as a second language will also be considered. Research methodology will comprise: reviewing current course material for Welsh as a second language; classroom observation; teacher questionnaires and interviews; and pupil interviews.
Status: Individual research
Date of Research: 1993-continuing
KEYWORDS: *second language teaching; teaching methods; Welsh*

10/1603

Department of Information and Library Studies, Llanbadarn Fawr, Aberystwyth, Dyfed SY23 3AS
01970 622189
Preston, G. Mrs; Barber, J. Mrs; *Supervisor:* Baggs, C. Mr

To initiate a distance learning undergraduate degree course in information and library studies
Abstract: In the light of current moves towards providing greater opportunities for mature adults with non-traditional educational qualifications to gain access to higher education, and the Universities Funding Council's (UFC) programme to encourage flexibility in course provision, it was proposed to set up a research and development programme to initiate a distance learning undergraduate degree course in information and library studies. The aim of the project is to investigate the scope and management of current distance learning provision; to evaluate the relative merits of different methods of course provision, including developments in educational technology; to look at methods of assessment for student-centred learning; and to develop quality control mechanisms appropriate for academic and professional validation. High attrition rates experienced in some models of distance learning provision make it important to assess how inherent problems such as student support and adequate resourcing may be overcome. This will lead to the design of a course aimed at mature non-traditional entrants currently or recently employed in a library or information environment, who wish to gain a professional qualification. The production of student-centred learning packages will involve research into developing Computer Assisted Learning (CAL) and video-conferencing to supplement traditional print-based materials.
Status: Sponsored project
Source of Grant: Universities Funding Council £63,100
Date of Research: 1992-1993
KEYWORDS: *distance education; flexible learning; information science; librarianship education; mature students*

University College Scarborough

10/1604

North Riding College, Filey Road, Scarborough YO11 3AZ
01732 362392
Payne-Ahmadi, E. Dr; Laidlaw, R. Mrs; Bayes, G. Miss
The impact of legislation on the development of the religious education curriculum in primary schools
Abstract: The research is investigating the effects of the Education Reform Act 1988 on the management of the religious education (RE) curriculum in primary schools. Specifically, the impact of new agreed syllabuses for religious education on the exercise of consultancy in RE in primary schools is being considered. This is a small scale project involving a questionnaire survey of county primary and voluntary controlled schools in a district of a large rural local education authority (LEA). Results are to be published in article form.
Status: Sponsored project
Source of Grant: University College Scarborough
Date of Research: 1993-1994
KEYWORDS: *Education Reform Act 1988; educational change; primary education; religious education*

University of Central England in Birmingham

10/1605

Centre for the Study of Quality in Higher Education, Perry Barr, Birmingham B42 2SU
0121 331 5000
Harvey, L. Dr; Burrows, A. Ms; Green, D. Prof.
Quality in higher education
Abstract: The Quality in Higher Education Project (QHE) is researching the nature of quality in higher education and how quality is assured and assessed. Criteria of quality have been identified from eight stakeholder groups through a variety of research techniques including structured questionnaires, indepth interviews, group-focused interviews, document analysis and literature review. The research is action research in the sense of continually feeding back results and reassessing and refining criteria, etc., on the basis of stakeholder reactions. The research has paid particular attention to student, staff and employer views, the latter through a series of small

projects culminating in the QHE employer satisfaction survey. Future work will address, in more detail than hitherto, international aspects of quality monitoring.
Published Material: HARVEY, L., BURROWS, A. & GREEN, D. (1993). Someone who can make an impression. Report of the employers' survey of qualities of higher education graduates. Birmingham: University of Central England in Birmingham.; HARVEY, L., BURROWS, A. & GREEN, D. (1993). 'Refining quality', Assessment and Evaluation in Higher Education, Vol 18, No 3, pp.9-34.; HARVEY, L., BURROWS, A. & GREEN, D. (1993). The quality assessors. 2nd Edition. Birmingham: University of Central England in Birmingham.; HARVEY, L., BURROWS, A., GREEN, D. & SMALLWOOD, P. (1993). The quality assurers. 2nd Edition. Birmingham: University of Central England in Birmingham.; HARVEY, L. (1993). Proceedings of the QHE quality assessment seminar, 21-22 January 1993. Birmingham: University of Central England in Birmingham. A full list of publications is available from the researcher.
Status: Sponsored project
Source of Grant: Government, Educational and Business Organisations, jointly £200,000
Date of Research: 1991-continuing
KEYWORDS: *educational quality; higher education; quality assurance; quality control*

10/1606

Faculty of Computing and Information Studies, School of Information Studies, Perry Barr, Birmingham B42 2SU
0121 331 5000
Bilston Community College, Green Lane Site, Wellington Road, Bilston, West Midlands WV14 6EW
01902 353929
Elkin, J. Prof.; Flatten, K. Dr; Frankel, A. Dr; Bill, A. Mr; Russell, A. Ms; *Supervisor:* Nankivell, C. Ms
The effectiveness of basic skills support in colleges of further education
Abstract: This is a joint project between the Centre for Information Research and Training at the University of Central England and the Quality and Equality Directorate at Bilston Community College. The approach to be used is based on a definition of effectiveness as the achievement of objectives which in turn depends upon the group whose objectives are being considered. The four main groups whose objectives need to be considered are: funding bodies; colleges; students; and teachers. The methodology of the project incorporates quantitative and qualitative measures of effectiveness and considers the objectives of all of the above groups. This approach will allow investigation of all the factors influencing effectiveness of basic skills support in further education (FE). The work is divided into seven phases: 1) Literature reviews at three points in the research to provide information on recent and current research into basic skills and FE nationwide. 2) A statistical survey of at least 30 FE colleges to provide the Adult Literacy and Basic Skills Unit (ALBSU) with information enabling comparisons to be drawn between colleges with differing levels of basic skills support, including information on non-completion and successful completion rates. 3) A management survey of basic skills support managers to identify measures of efficiency, comparing costs with other factors such as methods of delivery of basic skills support. This survey will be conducted using interviews in eight case study colleges. 4) A student survey to identify factors involved in successful completion of FE courses and the value of basic skills support to students. This study will involve interviews with leavers of FE courses at the eight case study colleges. 5) An audit of basic skills support activities which will develop performance indicators for a range of such activities. This will be carried out using an instrument such as the Further Education Unit (FEU) at eight case study colleges. 6) A staff survey which will focus on the identification of students in need of basic skills support. This will provide examples of practice and an evaluation of the consistency of practice. This will involve interviews and an evaluative exercise with basic skills teachers in FE. 7) All the information collected and analysed in the previous phases will be brought together and written up in two research reports. An interim report will be submitted in December 1994 and a final report in November 1995.
Status: Sponsored project
Source of Grant: Adult Literacy and Basic Skills Unit £75,830
Date of Research: 1994-continuing
KEYWORDS: *adult basic education; basic skills; colleges of further education; educational quality; further education; programme evaluation*

10/1607

Faculty of Computing and Information Studies, School of Information Studies, Perry Barr, Birmingham B42 2SU
0121 331 5000
Elkin, J. Prof.; Nankivell, C. Ms; Chivers, B. Ms; Reid, B. Mr; Markey, D. Mrs; *Supervisor:* Flatten, K. Dr
The value of library and information studies (LIS) school work placement
Abstract: This research will look at library and information studies (LIS) school placements in the UK. The research will examine the LIS placement from the perspective of the school, the employer and the student. The study will provide material for an open debate in the library and information profession on the role and value of placements. The research will enable LIS educators and employers alike to focus on how the placement experience can be improved, for the benefit of all parts of the profession. Work on this study began in 1993 when the British Association for Information and Library Education and Research (BAILER) expressed an interest in carrying forward the 1990 BLR&D Report with more study and coordination of LIS placements. BAILER followed this with funds to support the current project. The approach to the study is based on finding, by consensus, which valued characteristics are considered to be most important and satisfactory to three groups; placement coordinators; students; and employers. The results of these findings will form the basis of a report on which guidelines can be formulated for a model placement experience. The methodology incorporates qualitative measures to ensure that the most important valued characteristics are established. The work is divided into five phases: 1) Pilot questionnaires and placement workshop where placement coordinators will be asked to list the most valued characteristics of an ideal placement. These will then be scored for importance and satisfaction by the same coordinators. 2) Student questionnaires sent to three groups, (before, during and after placement), of randomly selected students at each of the LIS schools. They will be asked to score the valued characteristics identified by the placement coordinators and to answer questions resulting from the placement workshop. 3) Employer questionnaires sent to three groups (with a placement student; recently had a placement student; employers of LIS graduates) identified by the LIS schools. The employers will also be asked to score the valued characteristics and to answer questions resulting from the placement workshop. 4) Dissemination of the reports, statistical analysis and preparation of journal articles. 5) The establishing of guidelines will take place at a session at Under One UmbrelLA 3, Library Association in July 1995. All participating placement coordinators will be invited to attend this discussion and to assist in the task of building the results into guidelines for future LIS placement experience.
Status: Sponsored project
Source of Grant: University of Central England in Birmingham £9,239
Date of Research: 1994-continuing
KEYWORDS: *librarianship education; library schools; placement; professional education; work experience programmes*

10/1608

Faculty of Computing and Information Studies, School of Information Studies, Perry Barr, Birmingham B42 2SU
0121 331 5000
Elkin, J. Prof.; Nankivell, C. Ms; Green, L. Ms; Speake, L. Ms; *Supervisor:* Flatten, K. Dr
Development and evaluation of an information base for the Birmingham Drugs Prevention Initiative
Abstract: This project is designed to: 1) establish an information resource centre for the Birmingham Drugs Prevention Team; 2) measure the effectiveness of its resources; and 3) produce a literature guide matching client information needs with effective resources. Phase One is a three month consultancy and database construction period. Phase Two is the ongoing day-to-day operation of the Information Centre with attention to expanding the number of database records and adding evaluative entries. Phase Three concludes the project with an analysis of resource effectiveness and the writing of a literature guide and final research report.
Status: Sponsored project
Source of Grant: Home Office £11,000
Date of Research: 1994-1994
KEYWORDS: *drug education; information sources; libraries; prevention*

10/1609

Faculty of Education, Westbourne Road, Edgbaston,
Birmingham B15 3TN
0121 331 6100
Cavendish, M. Mr; *Supervisor:* Hellawell, D. Prof.; Hall, E. Miss

Going grant-maintained: a case study of change from a management perspective

Abstract: The intention is to carry out a research programme as a sequel to an earlier theoretical and reflective study of the processes of change and how they are managed. The investigation will cover the period from October 1990 to August 1993 during which the researcher's school became grant maintained. The aims are to: 1) focus on management processes during a period of institutional change from local education authority (LEA) status to grant maintained status; 2) provide evidence of the experience of the management of change which may be interpreted and used by other managers; 3) investigate management as a learning experience; and 4) identify some of the characteristics of effective and non-effective management practices.
Status: Individual research
Date of Research: 1992-continuing
KEYWORDS: educational administration; educational change; grant maintained schools; management in education; school based management

10/1610

Faculty of Education, Westbourne Road, Edgbaston,
Birmingham B15 3TN
0121 331 6100
Brooks, R. Ms; Duckworth, R. Ms;
Supervisor: Hellawell, D. Prof.

Social skills training in the classroom: effects on sociometric status

Abstract: The aims of this research are: (1) To present a review of current sociometric research and materials in the area of children's friendship choices and social adjustment in the classroom. (2) Use sociographic techniques to assess the patterns of specific friendship choices which exist in classes (e.g. popular children, reciprocated pairs, isolates, etc.). (3) Assess the personality and behavioural characteristics of specific 'types' of children (as identified in (2) using the Junior Eysenck and behavioural observations. (4) Intervene to coach the identified 'isolated' children in specific social skills, e.g. asking questions, offering directions to peers. (5) Ascertain what effect/s the social skill training (as in (4)) has on overall peer acceptance and popularity within the class. (6) Provide an indepth examination of individual isolates, including the perceptions of friendship, and reasons for sociometric choices made. (7) For individual isolates (as in (6)) examine the family structure, number of siblings, contact with other social networks (e.g. clubs, church) which affect their social experience and competence.
Status: Individual research
Date of Research: 1992-continuing
KEYWORDS: intergroup relations; pupil behaviour; social skills; sociometric techniques

10/1611

Faculty of Education, Westbourne Road, Edgbaston,
Birmingham B15 3TN
0121 331 6100
Cabral, B. Ms; *Supervisor:* Davis, D. Mr; Cherrington, D. Prof.

Towards a common form of assessment in drama as a methodology and as a performance art

Abstract: The aims of this research are to: (1) Search for a model of assessment for drama in education, both as a methodology and as a performance mode, which represents achievement in drama, not excluding the possibility of achievement in other subject matters as well. (2) Pinpoint the different ways both approaches deal with dramatic conventions and rules, and how these differences interfere in the assessment schemes. (3) Analyse the performance of the reader (audience, self-spectator) as a main element in assessment schemes. (4) Compare the assessment provided by the fellow student (audience) or by the student himself (self-spectator) with the one provided by the teacher. (5) Analyse the links between the plurality of audience assessment and the possibility of open-ended productions, i.e. a non-closed conclusion to the art-form.
Status: Sponsored project
Source of Grant: Ministry of Education, Brazil
Date of Research: 1992-continuing

KEYWORDS: assessment; audience response; drama education; dramatics

10/1612

Faculty of Education, Westbourne Road, Edgbaston,
Birmingham B15 3TN
0121 331 6100
Evans, M. Mr; *Supervisor:* Hellawell, D. Prof.; Eyles, J. Mrs; Seddon, J. Mrs

The management development needs of grant maintained schools and city technology colleges

Abstract: This research project will examine the management development needs of the staff at grant maintained schools and city technology colleges. A questionnaire will be used, together with a number of indepth interviews, with some of those completing the questionnaire. One aim of the research is to improve the inservice teacher education (INSET) provision in this area.
Status: Sponsored project
Source of Grant: University of Central England in Birmingham £20,000
Date of Research: 1993-1994
KEYWORDS: city technology colleges; grant maintained schools; inservice teacher education; management development; school based management; staff development

10/1613

Faculty of Education, Westbourne Road, Edgbaston,
Birmingham B15 3TN
0121 331 6100
Hudson, P. Mr; *Supervisor:* Farmer, M. Mr; Ager, R. Mr

The development and use of interactive learning packages in schools

Abstract: The research project aims to identify how the use of the Asymetrix Toolbook Authoring Package can assist teachers to extend and develop their own interest in information technology. The work will have both qualitative and quantitative elements and will focus upon staff in three schools: one infant; one junior; and one secondary. Schools will have considerable freedom in deciding the actual way in which they use interactive learning within their institution, and regular meetings will be held between the research team and the schools to ensure that perspectives are shared.
Status: Sponsored project
Source of Grant: University of Central England in Birmingham
Date of Research: 1993-1994
KEYWORDS: authoring aids – programming; computer assisted learning; computer software; computer uses in education; information technology; multimedia approach

10/1614

Faculty of Education, Westbourne Road, Edgbaston,
Birmingham B15 3TN
0121 331 6100
Hallan, V. Mr; *Supervisor:* Cherrington, D. Prof.; Rowley, K. Prof.

Children and racial stereotypes

Abstract: The aims of the investigation are to: 1) present a review of current research and materials in the area of primary school children's (aged 5 to 11 years) attitudes towards ethnic preference and choice; 2) further develop research materials to investigate children's ethnic preference and choice; 3) use supplementary questions to gain an insight into the possible influence of mass media and/or parents on children's (aged 4+) attitudes.
Status: Individual research
Date of Research: 1992-continuing
KEYWORDS: ethnic stereotypes; primary school pupils; pupil attitudes; racial attitudes

10/1615

Faculty of Education, Westbourne Road, Edgbaston,
Birmingham B15 3TN
0121 331 6100
Newman College, Genners Lane, Bartley Green,
Birmingham B32 3NT
0121 476 1181
Miller, S. Mr; Taylor, P. Prof.;
Supervisor: Hellawell, D. Prof.

The teacher education curriculum in the member states of the European Community
Abstract: The basis of the research was an initial survey of the existing literature and its reflective analysis. This was followed by two stages of empirical enquiry: the first was based on a structured questionnaire, the rationale for which was provided by the analysis of the research literature; the second was based on sample interviews in six member states of the European Community. Data for a final section of the research was based on the work undertaken by the European Community to foster between-country activities in the field of teacher education.
Published Material: HELLAWELL, D., MILLER, S. & TAYLOR, P. (1993). The teacher education curriculum in the member states of the European Community. Brussels: Association for Teacher Education in Europe.
Status: Sponsored project
Source of Grant: Commission of the European Communities, Brussels £20,000
Date of Research: 1991-1993
KEYWORDS: European Community; preservice teacher education; teacher education curriculum

University of Central Lancashire

10/1616
Department of Applied Biology, Preston PR1 2HE
01772 201201
Strettle, R. Dr
Transferable skills in undergraduate biological education
Abstract: The project aims to: 1) identify the transferable skills which are required by biological scientists; and 2) determine the importance of these skills to students at the University of Central Lancashire. The project has developed a list of skills required by scientists derived from a series of structured interviews with members of staff from the Department of Applied Biology. The list of skills has then been organised to produce a questionnaire which has been sent to past students from the Department. The questionnaire seeks to determine their views on how 'important' each one of the skills should be in their education and how well the skills were developed during their time at the University. Over 100 replies have been received and the information is being analysed to determine the views of the students.
Status: Sponsored project
Source of Grant: Enterprise in Higher Education
Date of Research: 1992-1994
KEYWORDS: biology education; science education; skills; transfer of learning

10/1617
Department of Built Environment, Preston PR1 2HE
01772 201201
Salford University, Department of Surveying, Salford M5 4WT
0161 745 5000
Lowe, D. Mr; *Supervisor:* Skitmore, R. Prof.
An investigation of the experiential factors affecting the development of the expert pre-tender estimator
Abstract: It is proposed to interview a sample of approximately sixty experienced quantity surveyors. This will involve: 1) establishing the preferred learning styles of a sample of 'experts' using Kolb's (1979) Learning Style Inventory; and Honey and Mumford's (1989) Learning Style Questionnaire in conjunction with the further development of the questionnaire utilised by Skitmore et al (1990) to determine whether there is a link between the utilization of the various learning style types and estimating accuracy; 2) developing the questionnaire used in (1) to incorporate specific questions used by Lowe (1992) in assessing how expertise is developed and how practitioners are stimulated to learn through their experiences; 3) developing a pre-tender cost estimating pro-forma that would enable practitioners to collate reference data based on experiental factors, introduce them to experiential learning theory and to carry out follow-up interviews after 12 months to assess any improvement in estimating accuracy; 4) producing a mechanism to improve estimating accuracy by developing the work of Ogunlana (1989, 1991) through the integration of data obtained using (1)-(3) above and experiential learning theory.
Published Material: LOWE, D.J. (1992). 'Experiential learning: a

factor in the development of an expert pre-tender estimator'. MSc Thesis. Salford: Salford University.; LOWE, D.J. (1993). 'Experiential learning in cost estimating'. Prepared for the Proceedings of the Centre for Advanced Surveying Studies, Salford University.; LOWE, D.J. (1993). 'Experiential learning: a factor in cost estimating'. Proceedings of the Association of Researchers in Construction Management 9th Annual Conference, Exeter College, Oxford University, 14-16 September 1993.; LOWE, D.J. & SKITMORE, R.M. 'Experiential learning: the development of an expert pre-tender estimator', Construction Management and Economics. (in press).
Status: Individual research
Date of Research: 1993-continuing
KEYWORDS: construction industry; experiential learning; learning activities; surveying education

10/1618
Department of Chemistry, Preston PR1 2HE
01772 201201
Haddon, K. Mr; Perz, R. Mr; *Supervisor:* Brattan, D. Dr; Smith, T. Prof.; Smith, C. Dr
Student based learning in chemistry
Abstract: Preparation, use of, and evaluation of student based learning materials, including text, video, and computer in physical and analytical chemistry. The main aims of this research are to evaluate a change to learning rather than teaching, to introduce transferable skills into the curriculum and to examine ways of increasing access to higher education. Evaluation involves interview, questionnaire and testing achievement of objectives.
Published Material: A full list of publications is available from the researchers.
Status: Sponsored project
Source of Grant: University of Central Lancashire £200; Erasmus £1,500; Enterprise in Higher Education £2,500
Date of Research: 1988-continuing
KEYWORDS: chemistry education; educational materials; learning strategies; multimedia approach; science education; skills; teaching methods; transfer of learning

10/1619
Department of Chemistry, Preston PR1 2HE
01772 201201
Dodd, J. Dr; *Supervisor:* Hart, A. Mrs
A competence framework in chemistry
Abstract: Recent change sin Business and Technician Education Council (BTEC) policy towards 'competences and transferable skills' call for an urgent response from course teams. The Faculty of Science at the University of Lancashire has granted the research a six-month secondment (February-August 1992) to make progress in this area. The aim of the project was to develop a competence framework, primarily (but not exclusively) for HND/HNC courses in chemistry – along with supporting materials and delivery systems. The activities involved liaison with other course teams in Faculty/University, and with the Faculty Support Group; visits to other institutions (to discover examples of good practice); consultation in industry to provide resource material, and to discuss joint assessment procedures in student placements and works based projects; and the development of related student centred learning materials. The outcomes of the research provided a coherent strategy for a competence framework in BTEC chemistry/science courses; the development of quality materials for use in teaching/learning situations; and the facilitating (and assessment) of transferable skills within the curriculum.
Status: Sponsored project
Source of Grant: Enterprise and Higher Education £2,500
Date of Research: 1992-1993
KEYWORDS: business and technician education council; chemistry education; competency-based education; science education; skills; transfer of learning

10/1620
Department of Computing, Preston PR1 2HE
01772 201201
Sheffield University, Division of Education, 388 Glossop Road, Sheffield S10 2JA
01142 768555
Mallatratt, J. Dr; *Supervisor:* Opie, C. Dr
Inservice education and training (INSET) to support information technology (IT) use across the secondary curriculum

Abstract: The research focused upon the effectiveness of Government policies aimed at supporting teachers to use information technology (IT) within the delivery of other subjects in the curriculum. The approach to the research was to follow the processes of formulation and implementation of national policies intended to affect inservice education and training (INSET) related to information technology. The main programmes included were the Local Education Authority Training Grants Scheme (LEATGS), the Education Support Grants (ESG) scheme and the Technical and Vocational Education Initiative (TVEI). The sample was comprised of five local education authorities (LEAs) within England and Wales, chosen to give variation in size and in nature (e.g. rural and urban). Within these authorities, twenty-nine schools were selected for detailed investigation. Approximately seventy key personnel, involved in the development and implementation of national, local and school policies, were identified and given extended interviews. Data was further triangulated by the use of a questionnaire with a simple random sample of 30% of the teachers in the selected schools. The research established that, although a significant amount of training had been delivered which was aimed at improving the capability of teachers to use IT within their own subject domains, much of the training had not been as effective as it might have been. The findings from previous studies into the correlates of effective INSET, appeared to have been ignored by some of the key personnel involved either in the design or delivery of IT-related INSET provision.
Published Material: MALLATRATT, J. (1990). 'A review of the effectiveness of national policies in the UK aimed at providing inservice training support to teachers to enable them to use computers in non-computing subjects'. Paper presented at EURIT 90, Herning, Denmark, April 1990.; MALLATRATT, J. (1990). 'Needs and provision: a consideration of the inservice education and training of teachers to use computers across the secondary school curriculum', Computer Education, No 64, pp.25-27.; MALLATRATT, J. (1992). 'Staff development (INSET) policies to support the use of IT across the curriculum: the good news'. Paper presented at IDATER 92, Loughborough University of Technology, September 1992.; MALLATRATT, J. (1993). 'The preparation of teachers to use information technology across the curriculum: a critique of the approaches in England and Wales'. Paper presented at IFIP WG 3.1/3.5 Open Conference: Information and Changes in Learning, Gmunden, Austria, June 1993.
Status: Individual research
Date of Research: 1987-1993
KEYWORDS: computer uses in education; information technology; inservice teacher education

10/1621

Department of Psychology, Preston PR1 2HE
01772 201201
Lancaster University, Department of Psychology, Cartmel College, Bailrigg, Lancaster LA1 4YW
01524 65201
Walker, P. Dr; Hitch, G. Prof.; Lewis, C. Dr
Cognitive impairments in children with arithmetical learning disabilities
Abstract: This project aims to discover why some children of normal intelligence have great difficulty with elementary arithmetic. In some cases arithmetical difficulties are associated with reading problems, in others they occur in isolation. The project will identify children with arithmetical learning disability and will investigate cognitive impairments in different subgroups using tasks designed to explore working memory, the part of the cognitive system responsible for storing and manipulating temporary information. The hypothesis is that children with specific arithmetical difficulties have impaired working memory for visuo-spatial information, whereas children with learning problems in both arithmetic and reading have impaired working memory for phonological information. These deficits will be analysed in relation to the way working memory normally develops in order to distinguish developmental lag from other kinds of abnormality. The researchers will test the prediction that different kinds of impairment to working memory are related to the kinds of difficulty children experience in simple arithmetic tasks. The results will contribute to diagnosis and assessment of arithmetical learning disabilities, and to the planning of more effective remediation.
Published Material: LEWIS, C., HITCH, G. & WALKER, P. (1994). 'The prevalence of specific arithmetic difficulties and specific reading difficulties in 9-10 year old boys and girls', Journal of Child Psychology and Psychiatry and Allied Disciplines, Vol 35, No 2, pp.283-292.

Status: Sponsored project
Source of Grant: Medical Research Council £80,000
Date of Research: 1990-1994
KEYWORDS: arithmetic; cognitive ability; learning disabilities

10/1622

Department of Psychology, Preston
01772 201201
Wolverhampton University, Department of Psychology, Molineux Street, Wolverhampton WV1 1SB
01902 321000
McDonald, M. Ms
Gender roles in adolescent girls
Abstract: A sample of 43 girls aged 10-15 years from the northwest of the United Kingdom were interviewed about their own, and other girls' preferences and choices regarding sports, school subjects, occupations and leisure interests. Their gender-role attitudes were also examined by means of two other methods: (1) responses to vignettes involving gender-role dilemmas; (2) repertory grids involving supplied and elicited elements. Grids were represented a year later to provide a limited longitudinal design. The interview data has been analysed separately in relation to the four topics. Quantitative analysis showed that the answers for both sports and school subjects departed from established stereotypes. There was little support for the hypothesis that gender-role activities become accentuated at adolescence. Qualitative analysis revealed a number of gender related themes in these answers. The remaining data from the project is being analysed. Supplementary studies have been provided by rating-scale investigations of the gender-stereotyping of school subjects (Archer & Freedman, 1989; Archer & Macrae, 1991), and the research has been integrated into more general theoretical work on gender-role development (Archer, 1984, 1989).
Published Material: ARCHER, J. & FREEDMAN, S. (1989). 'Gender-stereotypic perceptions of academic disciplines', British Journal of Educational Psychology, No 59, pp.306-313.; ARCHER, J. & MACDONALD, M. (1991). 'Gender roles and school subjects in adolescent girls', Educational Research, Vol 33, No 1.; ARCHER, J. (1989). 'Childhood gender roles: structure and development', The Psychologist, No 9, pp.367-370.; ARCHER, J. & MACDONALD, M. (1990). 'Gender roles and sports in adolescent girls', Leisure Studies, No 9, pp.225-240.
Status: Sponsored project
Source of Grant: University of Central Lancashire
Date of Research: 1984-1993
KEYWORDS: girls; sex differences; sex stereotypes

10/1623

Department of Social Work, Preston PR1 2HE
01772 201201
Parrott, L. Mr; Washington, J. Mr
The accreditation of work-based learning in social work education and training
Abstract: This project is to identify, measure and assess the learning in Psychology and Social Policy which can be acquired by social workers from work-based opportunities in social service agencies, and to develop a model of integrating these opportunities into the Diploma in Social Work Programmes curriculum within the University of Central Lancashire and its franchised colleges. This follows a similar research project into the work-based learning of Law. The current project commenced with a Work Book model of learning which had been successful in the earlier project. This has now been used in the learning and assessment of Social Policy. A different model of learning and assessment is being developed for Psychology. This is based on a Profiling model. The research project worked with 11 social work placements including social services, probation and voluntary agencies. A network group of practice teachers and tutors was formed as part of the research process. Two semi-structured interviews were conducted with each of the practice teachers. The results of these interviews were discussed at a number of group seminars held during the course of the project. The results of the research project are in the development for use of Work Book and Profiling models of learning and assessment which can be used in the current teaching of Diploma in Social Work Programmes.
Status: Sponsored project
Source of Grant: Training, Enterprise and Education Directorate
Date of Research: 1992-1994
KEYWORDS: competency based education; inservice education; on the job training; social work studies

University of East Anglia

10/1624

School of Education, Norwich NR4 7TJ
01603 456161
Somekh, B. Dr; Brown, A. Mr; Ebbutt, D. Mr

From competence to excellence (COMEX): a programme of work-based learning and accreditation

Abstract: The background to the project resides in the developing interest in the Assessment of Prior Experience Learning (APEL) in universities as exemplified by the work of the Learning from Experience Trust with various universities, and funded by the Department of Employment. The intensifying thrust towards work-based learning forms the other background thread. This project will develop a programme of work-based learning for an audience of office employees of varying seniority and managerial responsibility in a range of local public and private sector organisations. The programme will be enquiry-based and have an action focus such that it will contribute both to the development of the organisation and to the development of the individual student. Accreditation for the work of 'students' within the programme will be negotiated and developed by the project within the University of East Anglia and its various validating mechanisms on the basis of five levels of entry: Access; Foundation; Diploma; B.A.; and M.A. Among the intended outcomes would be: 1) the implementation of the programme for the first cohort of 40+ students; 2) a range of (replicable) support materials; 3) a costed breakdown of the various models of work-based learning that emerge; 4) a final report from the Project Directors; and 5) an evaluation report commissioned by the project to supplement evaluations produced by the Department of Employment.

Status: Sponsored project
Source of Grant: Department of Employment £170,000
Date of Research: 1994-continuing
KEYWORDS: accreditation of prior learning; experiential learning; higher education

10/1625

School of Education, Norwich NR4 7TJ
01603 456161
Brown, C. Mrs

Sex related differences in children's technological achievements in the middle years with special reference to the use of construction materials

Abstract: A study by the Assessment of Performance Unit (APU) showed that experience with construction materials was markedly different in boys and girls. The rise in scientific and technological work in the primary curriculum has made the study of its nature and extent essential. The current study follows on from an initial study in which the gender gap was documented over a period of four years. In this study the quantity and quality of models produced by pupils across the first school age range as a result of specific arrangements facilitating equal access to materials was monitored. Criteria for models made by each year group were drawn up to indicate the range of achievement. The criteria were used to support the teachers, not only in ensuring equal access to materials, but also to structure the work to enable the children to try to meet as many of the criteria as possible. Such structured opportunities were found to narrow the gender gap further than simply ensuring equal access for girls to the construction materials. Consequently a programme offering suggestions for learning opportunities with construction materials was devised for each class in the school. In 1990/91 a class of children who have received such structured opportunities throughout their entire time in the school were again monitored in their final year. The results showed that the gender gap had narrowed further but had not closed. It was decided therefore that the study of this cohort of children, for whom data exists from entry to school at 4+ years, should continue into the middle years. A second phase of data collection began in 1991/92 and findings from that academic year indicate that during that year the performance gap had closed according to the criteria used to assess implementation of science concepts in the models made. It was evident that in the variety of models made and the modification or origination of models the girls still lagged behind the boys. These aspects in addition to the implementation of science concepts will continue to be monitored as the cohort progresses through 1992/93/94.

Published Material: BROWN, C.A. (1989). 'Girls, boys and technology: getting to the roots of the problem: a study of differential achievement in the early years', School Science Review, Vol 71, No 255, pp.138-142.; BROWN, C.A. (1990). 'Girls, boys and technology: some observations of general progress and of gender related differences in achievement when using construction sets in the early years', School Science Review, Vol 71, No 257, pp.33-40.; BROWN, C.A. (1991). 'What are little girls made of? A study of technology in the early years', Educational Studies, Vol 17, No 1, pp.107-113.; BROWN, C.A. (1991). 'Using construction sets in a primary curriculum', Primary Science Review, No 17, pp.22-24.
Status: Sponsored project
Source of Grant: University of East Anglia
Date of Research: 1991-continuing
KEYWORDS: construction – process; construction materials; equal facilities; gender equality; primary education; science education; sex differences; technology education

10/1626

School of Education, Norwich NR4 7TJ
01603 456161
Ormell, C. Mr

Analysis of understanding as an educational aim and ways to detect its achievement

Abstract: The research is aimed at answering the question, 'how can we detect whether a child understands something, using objective behavioural methods?'. In most cases, 'understanding x' means 'having a fully assimilated model of x'. The chief assessment method consists of seeing whether children can apply the model swiftly and confidently to new circumstances. The central issue reduces to how to generate suitable 'new circumstances' in the numbers and variety required. To achieve reliability a lot of testing is needed, but this is only acceptable if the child's assessment experiences are also prime learning experiences. This means that the 'circumstances' used need to meet high standards of relevance, interest and memorability from the child's point of view. A major parameter is the degree to which the curriculum is 'liberal'. The more 'liberal' the curriculum the more distant its topics from the child's immediate experience. This makes it harder to devise appropriate 'new circumstances', but unless this problem can be solved, the production of behavioural tests for understanding will fail. The problem has been solved (see Ormell 1988, 1991) by the use of counter-factual and counter-fictional contexts. The project 'Children's application readiness with basic mathematics', applies the general methods devised in this project to the example of mathematics.

Published Material: ORMELL, C.P. (1988). 'Is there a future for liberal education?', Cambridge Journal of Education, Vol 18, No 2, pp.167-177.; ORMELL, C.P. (1991). Behavioural objectives in education. Geelong, Australia: Deakin University Press.; ORMELL, C.P. (1992). 'Behavioural objectives revisited', Educational Research, Vol 34, No 1, pp.23-33.; ORMELL, C.P. (1992). 'Is content good for your health?', Cambridge Journal of Education, Vol 22, No 2, pp.227-242.
Status: Individual research
Date of Research: 1978-continuing
KEYWORDS: behavioural objectives; comprehension; educational objectives; learning experience; test use

10/1627

School of Education, Norwich NR4 7TJ
01603 456161
Wright, D. Mr

Pupils as evaluators of textbooks

Abstract: Textbooks for pupils are reviewed by teachers, not by pupils. Pupils are encouraged nowadays in school to express opinions and to evaluate evidence. The research seeks to experiment with pupils as reviewers of textbooks and other school books. Pupils in the United Kingdom and Australia are invited to review textbooks and information books. Their written observations are incorporated into articles discussing this new approach. Teachers are involved in evaluating pupils' observations. Results and conclusions will be illuminative, not definitive. Ten provisional conclusions are included in publication (3) below. The findings have implications for teachers and for educational publishers.

Published Material: WRIGHT, D.R. (1987). 'A pupil's perspective on textbooks: issues of motivation and racism'. Internationale Schulbuchforschung, Vol 9, No 2, pp.137-142.; WRIGHT, D.R. (1988). 'Applied textbook research in geography'. In: GERBER, R. & LIDSTONE, J. (Eds). Skills in geographical education. International Geographical Union.; WRIGHT, D.R. (1990). 'The role of pupils in

textbook evaluation', Internationale Schulbuchforschung, Vol 12, No 4.
Status: Individual research
Date of Research: 1987-1994
KEYWORDS: observation; pupil attitudes; textbook evaluation; textbooks

10/1628
School of Education, Norwich NR4 7TJ
01603 456161
Cockburn, A. Dr
Teaching under pressure
Abstract: Stress in the teaching profession is reaching critical proportions, yet there is very little comprehensible and comprehensive help and advice for teachers. The aim of this study is to produce a practical and insightful guide for trainee, beginning and experienced teachers, on the sources, responses and possible solutions to the negative aspects of stress in their lives. Using a sample of local primary teachers and structured and clinical interview techniques, this investigation will examine teachers' experiences of stress, their awareness of its effects and how, if at all, they manage it.
Status: Sponsored project
Source of Grant: Nuffield Foundation £1,332
Date of Research: 1993-1993
KEYWORDS: stress – psychological; stress management; student teachers; teachers; teaching profession

10/1629
School of Education, Norwich NR4 7TJ
01603 456161
Bedford, H. Ms; *Supervisor:* Phillips, T. Mr; Schostak, J. Dr
The Three Year Degree Evaluation (TYDE) project: an evaluation of three year undergraduate nursing and midwifery programmes
Abstract: This national evaluation of three year undergraduate nursing and midwifery degrees responds to current concerns about the pressures experienced by staff and students in achieving academic and professional competence, and has implications for national policy making. To understand the real complexity of the educational process, the project focuses on the personal and social experiences of teaching and learning as well as on formal procedures and structures. In order to address current concerns adequately, the project makes appropriate comparisons with four year undergraduate nursing and midwifery programmes. The project employs the case study and evaluative approaches of interview, observation and document analysis, and data is being collected in two phases. During Phase 1, a strategy has been employed to ensure coverage. The research team conducted intensive periods of fieldwork in a number of institutions running three year degrees, and others offering four year degrees, gathering the views and experiences of students, educational staff and clinical staff involved in supporting students. In addition to these condensed fieldwork visits, all other institutions offering undergraduate nursing and/or midwifery degree programmes were approached to compile profiles of these courses. During Phase 2, a more indepth approach will be taken, exploring issues identified during the first phase. Fieldwork will be conducted on three year programmes and a selection of four year programmes. This will build upon the relationships established in the first phase, and will involve shadowing groups of students during their education, and new graduates as they start practice as registered practitioners.
Status: Sponsored project
Source of Grant: The English National Board for Nursing, Midwifery and Health Visiting £150,000
Date of Research: 1992-continuing
KEYWORDS: nurse education; obstetrics; programme evaluation

10/1630
School of Education, Norwich NR4 7TJ
01603 456161
Elliott, J. Prof.; Norris, N. Dr; Somekh, B. Dr; Pettigrew, M. Ms
Environment and school initiatives: an investigation of an international curriculum development programme
Abstract: An investigation of schools' attempts to initiate community focused environmental education curricula in Organisation for Economic Cooperation and Development (OECD) member states. It involves analysing case studies written by teachers, national reports on implementation issues, and policy documents, with a view to identifying and clarifying the major change issues and solutions proposed.
Published Material: ELLIOTT, J. (1991). 'Environmental education in Europe: innovation, marginalisation or assimilation'. In: Centre for Educational Research and Innovation/Organisation for Economic Cooperation and Development. Environment, schools and active learning. Paris: Organisation for Economic Cooperation and Development.; NORRIS, N., POSCH, P. & KELLY-LAINE, K. (1993). A review of environmental education policy in Norway 1993. Paris: Organisation for Economic Cooperation and Development.; NORRIS, N., EIDE, K. & KELLEY-LAINE, K. (1993). Environmental education policies in Finland: a review. Helsinki: Ministry of Education National Board of Education.; PETTIGREW, M. & SOMEKH, B. Evaluation and innovation in environmental education. Paris: Centre for Educational Research and Innovation/Organisation for Economic Cooperation and Development. (in press).
Status: Sponsored project
Source of Grant: Organisation for Economic Cooperation and Development
Date of Research: 1986-1994
KEYWORDS: comparative education; curriculum development; environmental education; school-community relationship

10/1631
School of Education, Norwich NR4 7TJ
01603 456161
Frankham, J. Ms
The HIV prevention needs of young gay men
Abstract: The research will consist of a 2-year longitudinal interview study of 60 young men living in 2 contrasting areas of the UK (Norfolk and Manchester). Specifically, the research will aim to: 1) document the experiences of young gay men in coming to terms with their identity and sexuality; 2) explore sexual decision-making and behaviour in relation to health choices; 3) examine the needs young gay men have for information, support and counselling with respect to their sexuality and sexual behaviour; 4) evaluate the barriers to the communication, use and impact of accurate information about Human Immunodeficiency Virus (HIV) and Acquired Immune Deficiency Syndrome (AIDS) and its relationship to sexual behaviour; 5) identify 'growth points' for breaking down such barriers and improving communication and support for young gay men. The project will produce, at minimum: 1) a major research report, aimed at statutory and voluntary bodies responsible for the provision of HIV and AIDS education for young gay men. This report would include case studies of some of the individuals involved in the study. 2) Recommendations about factors to be taken into account in future planning and provision for this group. 3) A condensed version of the report of the project. 4) A booklet containing condensed versions of the case studies.
Status: Sponsored project
Source of Grant: Aids Education and Research Trust (AVERT)
Date of Research: 1993-continuing
KEYWORDS: acquired immune deficiency syndrome; homosexuality; sex education; sexually transmitted diseases

10/1632
School of Education, Norwich NR4 7TJ
01603 456161
Bridges, D. Prof.; Elliott, J. Prof.
The use of a competence-based approach to learning, assessment and accreditation in specified higher education programmes
Abstract: An investigation of the feasibility of incorporating relevant national standards and National Vocational Qualifications (NVQs)/Scottish Vocational Qualifications (SVQs) in postgraduate initial teacher training programmes, and in higher education based professional education and training in the fields of health, engineering, and environmental science.
Status: Sponsored project
Source of Grant: Department of Employment
Date of Research: 1994-continuing
KEYWORDS: competency based education; higher education; National Vocational Qualifications; preservice teacher education; professional education; standards

10/1633

School of Education, Norwich NR4 7TJ
01603 456161
Elliott, J. Prof.; MacLure, M. Dr

Teachers as researchers in the context of award-bearing courses and research degrees

Abstract: This is an investigation of the claims made for teacher research. The project will use the study of exemplary cases cited by lecturers who are considered to promote excellence in this aspect of teacher education.
Status: Sponsored project
Source of Grant: Economic and Social Research Council £100,000
Date of Research: 1994-continuing
KEYWORDS: *educational research; educational researchers; research; teacher education*

10/1634

School of Education, Norwich NR4 7TJ
01603 456161
Norris, N. Dr; Pettigrew, M. Ms

Evaluation work and the profession of research

Abstract: The research is a continuation of a one year pilot project (1 May 1991 – 30 April 1992) funded by the Economic and Social Research Council (ESRC). The project aims to explore the recent experience of social policy and programme evaluation. It is addressing 5 questions: 1) In what ways is the conduct of research in the form of evaluations shaped by the judgemental purposes inherent in evaluation? 2) Has the research community's increasing commitment to evaluation work meant diminished public access to the knowledge generated by the community? 3) What kind of contractual obligations are drawn up between funding agencies and evaluations and what kind of relationships between the parties to the contract emerge as a consequence? 4) Are methodological and ethical compromises entailed in commissioned evaluative inquiry and, if so, what justifications are offered by researchers for them? 5) What strategies have developed in different research groups to take account of the changing political circumstances of social inquiry? The research design consists of 2 parallel activities: 1) a review of the literature and relevant documentation to establish what is already known about the conditions for evaluative inquiry with respect to the key questions outlined above; 2) the collection of testimony and further documentation from individual researchers, research centres and organisations about the key questions for the project. The strategy for the collection of testimony has consisted of: a) interviews with key people in research groups, centres, organisations and institutes, most, but not all, of whom have been university based; b) correspondence with the relevant heads of department across the social sciences (excluding economics) seeking written testimony from researchers and research groups; and c) correspondence with the relevant professional associations.
Published Material: PETTIGREW, M. & NORRIS, M. (1992). Expand and contract: the conditions of government sponsored social research. Norwich: University of East Anglia, Centre for Applied Research in Education.; PETTIGREW, M. 'Coming to terms with research: the contract business'. In: HALPIN, D & TROYNA, B. Researching education policy: ethical and methodological issues. London: Falmer. (in press).
Status: Sponsored project
Source of Grant: Economic and Social Research Council
Date of Research: 1991-1994
KEYWORDS: *educational research; research; social science research*

10/1635

School of Education, Norwich NR4 7TJ
01603 456161
Walker, B. Ms; *Supervisor:* MacDonald, B. Prof.

Young people's conversations about sex: a basis for peer education

Abstract: This project will investigate young people's conversations about sexuality. The aim is to increase our knowledge of the type of information exchanged between peers, its range and quality, and the circumstances under which such communication does or does not take place. The data will enable peer education programmes to be based on real types of interaction, therefore increasing their effectiveness. Unstructured interviews will be carried out with young people of both sexes between the ages of 13 and 23, both singly and in groups. Sample size = 60. Some of the sample will have experienced peer education, either as education or participant. They will be asked whether this experience has changed their conversations. The data will be correlated with a survey of teenage magazine problem pages.
Status: Sponsored project
Source of Grant: Norwich Health Authority
Date of Research: 1993-1994
KEYWORDS: *adolescents; conversation; peer groups; peer teaching; sexuality*

10/1636

School of Education, Norwich NR4 7TJ
01603 456161
Fox, J. Ms; Walker, B. Ms; *Supervisor:* Kushner, S. Dr

Young mothers' education project

Abstract: This was an evaluation of a small peer education project whereby young mothers were trained to run workshops in schools and youth clubs. The aims of the programme were to inform young people of the realities of young parenthood, and to provide information on contraception. Unstructured interviews were conducted with the organisers of the project, participants in 2 schools and 2 youth clubs, the young mothers themselves (5 of which were indepth interviews), and their youth/community workers. The evaluation considered the effectiveness of the training the young mothers received, the conduct of the workshops and their reception by the participants, and the effect of the programme on the young mothers. The evaluation concluded that the scheme was so small that it could only be viewed as a feasibility study and, as such, in spite of the inevitable tensions and uncertainties inherent in pioneering work of this kind, it would justify further support. The role of the youth/community workers was seen as important; the young mothers made personal gains as a result of involvement with the programme; and the programme, though small, was felt by the participants to be an improvement on current sex education provision – where it existed. However, the project relied heavily on the commitment of the youth/community workers involved and the enthusiasm of the volunteer young mothers whose idea it was.
Published Material: FOX, J., WALKER, B. & KUSHNER, S. (1993). It's not a bed of roses. Young mothers' education project evaluation report. Norwich: University of East Anglia, Centre for Applied Research in Education.
Status: Sponsored project
Source of Grant: Norwich Health Authority
Date of Research: 1993-1993
KEYWORDS: *community education; contraception; early parenthood; family planning; mothers; parenthood education; peer teaching; sex education*

10/1637

School of Education, Norwich NR4 7TJ
01603 456161
Husbands, C. Dr

Teacher development and school based teacher education

Abstract: The project links together 'mentors' involved in a school-based initial teacher education programme in programmes of action research focusing on: 1) the nature of student teacher learning; and 2) the relationships between course structures and observed outcomes.
Status: Sponsored project
Source of Grant: University of East Anglia £7,500
Date of Research: 1994-continuing
KEYWORDS: *mentors; preservice teacher education; student teachers; teacher development; teaching practice*

10/1638

School of Education, Norwich NR4 7TJ
01603 456161
McBride, R. Dr

The ideal context for the independent learner

Abstract: Using the methods of qualitative research, the research will investigate how students have engaged in distance learning courses. It will also investigate how students can be better supported, including the use of technological aids. A further interest is in the relationship between distance learning and the improvement of practice.
Status: Sponsored project
Source of Grant: University of East Anglia £8,000
Date of Research: 1994-1994
KEYWORDS: *distance education; independent study*

10/1639

School of Education, Norwich NR4 7TJ
01603 456161
MacDonald, B. Prof.; Stronach, I. Prof.; Kushner, S. Dr;
Norris, N. Dr; MacLure, M. Dr

The information technology and educational research policy evaluation

Abstract: This was a policy evaluation of the Economic and Social Research Council (ESRC) funding and the management and organisation of research initiatives. The evaluation was based on naturalistic, case-study methodology. It followed the principle that the evaluation of research policy has to be founded upon accounts of the experience of the research projects; i.e. that research evaluation and policy evaluation were inseparable. The themes illuminated and analysed in depth by the evaluation included: interdisciplinarity; research careers in the social sciences; the coordination of research initiatives and the process of refereeing; and selection and commissioning of research programmes.

Published Material: MACDONALD, B. & STRONACH, I. (1988). The InTER programme: the independent policy evaluation. InTER occasional publications 6/88. Lancaster: University of Lancaster, Department of Psychology.; STRONACH, I. & MACDONALD, B. (1989). Making a start: the origins of a research programme. A first report from the independent evaluators of the ESRC Research Programme Information Technology in Education (InTER). Norwich: University of East Anglia, Centre for Applied Research in Education.; STRONACH, I. & MACDONALD, B. (1991). Faces and future: an inquiry into the jobs, lives and careers of educational researchers in an ESRC initiative. A report from the independent evaluators of the ESRC Research Programme Information Technology in Education (InTER). Norwich: University of East Anglia, Centre for Applied Research in Education.; KUSHNER, S. (1991). ESRC initiatives and their coordinators: organising for innovation in the social sciences. A report from the independent evaluators of the ESRC Research Programme Information Technology in Education (InTER). Norwich: University of East Anglia, Centre for Applied Research in Education.; NORRIS, N., DAVIES, R., PETTIGREW, M. & KUSHNER, S. (1992). Research careers in the social sciences – a policy review paper for the ESRC. Commissioned by the ESRC's Research Resources Board. Mimeo. Norwich: University of East Anglia, Centre for Applied Research in Education. A full list of publications is available from the researcher.

Status: Sponsored project

Source of Grant: Economic and Social Research Council £150,000

Date of Research: 1988-1993

KEYWORDS: educational research; information technology; policy; research; research opportunities; social science research

10/1640

School of Education, Norwich NR4 7TJ
01603 456161
Georgetown College, Kentucky, KY 40324, USA
502 863 8011
Brown, G. Prof.; Shaw, G. Dr

Studies of Attention Disordered Hyperactive (ADHD) children

Abstract: A series of experiments is in progress to explore the cognitive skills of children with attention disorders and hyperactivity. In particular the research is investigating unusual facets of memory and high levels of non-verbal creativity in Attention Disordered Hyperactive (ADHD) children. There is also strong evidence of high levels of mixed laterality, left handedness and allergic conditions.

Published Material: SHAW, G.A. & BROWN, G. (1990). 'Laterality and creativity concomitants of attentional problems', Developmental Neuropsychology, Vol 6, No 1, pp.39-59.; SHAW, G.A. & BROWN, G. (1991). 'Laterality, implicit memory and attention disorders', Educational Studies, Vol 17, No 1, pp.15-23.; BROWN, G. (1991). 'Some more equal than others', The Vernon-Wall Lecture to the Education Section of the British Psychological Society, Blackpool, 1991.

Status: Sponsored project

Source of Grant: University of East Anglia; Georgetown College

Date of Research: 1989-1993

KEYWORDS: attention deficit disorders; cognitive ability; hyperactivity; learning disabilities; memory

10/1641

School of Education, Norwich NR4 7TJ
01603 456161

Suffolk College of Higher and Further Education, Rope Walk, Ipswich IP4 1LT
01473 255885
Suffolk and Great Yarmouth College of Nursing and Midwifery, Department of Nursing Studies, Education Centre, Ipswich Hospital, Heath Road, Ipswich IP4 5PD
Bedford, H. Ms; Robinson, J. Ms; *Supervisor:* Phillips, T. Mr; Schostak, J. Dr

Assessment of competencies in nursing and midwifery education (ACE Project)

Abstract: The project investigated the assessment of competencies in nursing and midwifery education, focusing upon the experiences of staff and students in classrooms and clinical areas. Through observation, interviewing and the collection of documentary evidence, it built up case studies of the structures and processes of assessment. It sought ways of understanding the complex nature of professional competence and asked whether current assessment practices were adequate for identifying and evaluating integrated theory and practice. It looked in particular at the collection, analysis and reflection upon evidence at the centre of the assessment process. Fieldwork was conducted in nine colleges of nursing/midwifery/health studies and their associated placement areas in three geographical regions of East Anglia, London and the North East. The project was conducted in two phases and progressive focusing was used to expose and explore the issues relevant to the assessment of competence on pre-registration nursing courses (Project 2000 and non diploma), and post-registration midwifery courses (diploma and non diploma). During the first phase, data was collected from all nine colleges to identify issues of national importance operating in local contexts. Issues relating to the whole of the assessment process were explored, including planning and design assessment experiences, monitoring and development. A grounded theory approach to data analysis enabled the generation of themes and issues to pursue in greater depth, in the second phase of the project, at a smaller number of fieldsites.

Published Material: BEDFORD, H., PHILLIPS, T., ROBINSON, J. & SCHOSTAK, J. (1992). The assessment of competencies in nursing and midwifery education and training (the ACE project): interim report. Norwich: University of East Anglia, School of Education.; BEDFORD, H., PHILLIPS, T., ROBINSON, J. & SCHOSTAK, J. (1993). Assessment of competencies in nursing and midwifery education and training (the ACE project). Research highlights 4. London: The English Board for Nursing, Midwifery and Health Visiting.; BEDFORD, H., PHILLIPS, T., ROBINSON, J. & SCHOSTAK, J. (1994). The assessment of competencies in nursing and midwifery education and training (the ACE project): final report. London: The English National Board for Nursing, Midwifery and Health Visiting.; BEDFORD, H., PHILLIPS, T., ROBINSON, J. & SCHOSTAK, J. (1994). The assessment of competencies in nursing and midwifery education and training (the ACE project): executive summary. London: The English National Board for Nursing, Midwifery and Health Visiting.

Status: Sponsored project

Source of Grant: The English National Board for Nursing, Midwifery and Health Visiting £95,000

Date of Research: 1991-1993

KEYWORDS: assessment; competence; nurse education; obstetrics

10/1642

School of Education, Norwich NR4 7TJ
01603 456161
University of Minia, Department of Education, El Minia,
Egypt Ormell, C. Mr; Abdel-Ghany, I. Dr

Children's 'application readiness with basic mathematics'

Abstract: 'Application Readiness' is a new idea in mathematics education. It signifies the condition in which a child has assimilated the applicative potency of a new mathematical concept so well that he/she is able spontaneously (without prompting or cueing) and unselfconsciously to recall and apply that concept to a practical situation needing that concept for its solution. The aims of the research are to clarify the idea of application readiness, to produce tests for it, to improve earlier tests, to trial such tests in schools and evaluate the results. Topics covered so far include basic (natural number) arithmetic up to 99 simple decimals and simple fractions. Recent research has centred on producing large numbers of 'rich, realistic contexts' of the kind needed to test for application readiness, including contexts where there is a mixed teaching/assessment use for the material.

Published Material: ABDEL-GHANY, I. & ORMELL, C.P. (1985). Problem solving with basic mathematics: ten lessons. University of

East Anglia: Mathematics Applicable Group.; ORMELL, C.P. (1989). 'Application readiness in mathematics at 10/11'. In: BLUM, W. et al. Applications and modelling in learning and teaching mathematics. Maths and its Applications Series. Chichester: Ellis Horwood.; ORMELL, C.P. (1989). 'Application readiness with fractions'. In: BLUM, W. et al. Modelling applications, and applied problem solving. Maths and its Applications Series. Chichester: Ellis Horwood.; ORMELL, C.P. (1991). 'Why story maths?', I.M.A. Bulletin.; ORMELL, C.P. (1992). Story maths. Adelaide, Australia: AAMT.
Status: Sponsored project
Source of Grant: Egyptian Bureau, London
Date of Research: 1981-continuing
KEYWORDS: *mathematical applications; mathematical concepts; mathematics education; test construction*

University of East London

10/1643
    Centre for Institutional Studies, Maryland House, Manbey Park Road, Stratford, London E15 1EY
    0181 590 7722
    Wright, M. Mr; *Supervisor:* Pratt, J. Prof.
Entrepreneurialism, education and training: a case study of South Bank Technopark
Abstract: The background for this research was the need for UK higher education institutions to find additional sources of finance in the 1980's, and to regenerate inner London. The aim of the project was to carry out a case study of South Bank Technopark, which was opened in December 1985 to promote new high technology firms in South London in collaboration with the Polytechnic of the South Bank (now South Bank University) and the Prudential Assurance Company. A pilot study plus intensive fieldwork via interviews and an archive search was undertaken. Preliminary results indicate that the Technopark is a unique institution which has acted as a nucleus of company development and job creation, and thus of inner city regeneration, in the local community. The Technopark has recorded this significant achievement in a short time by means of dedicated and innovative management, which has encouraged a wide variety of firms to locate in and grow on from the Technopark. The significant educational presence of the Polytechnic of the South Bank in the Technopark, as well as the variety and quality of the training provision within the institution, has also made an important contribution to the Technopark's success. This success has been confirmed by the use of the Technopark as a model for six other Technoparks which are under construction in six other UK cities.
Status: Individual research
Date of Research: 1986-1992
KEYWORDS: *entrepreneurship; industry-higher education relationship; science parks*

10/1644
    Centre for Institutional Studies, Maryland House, Manbey Park Road, Stratford, London E15 1EY
    0181 590 7722
    Supervisor: Locke, M. Mr
Governance in further and higher education
Abstract: The research is monitoring developments in structures and processes of governance in further and higher education, including the impact of legislative and environmental changes.
Published Material: LOCKE, M. (1989). 'Sweet charity', Management in Education, Vol 3, No 2, pp.7-8.; LOCKE, M. (1989). 'Can collegiality and entrepreneurialism exist together', Management in Education, Vol 3, No 4, pp.6-7.
Status: Sponsored project
Source of Grant: University of East London
Date of Research: 1991-continuing
KEYWORDS: *educational administration; educational change; further education; higher education*

10/1645
    Centre for Institutional Studies, Maryland House, Manbey Park Road, Stratford, London E15 1EY
    0181 590 7722
    Hillier, Y. Ms; *Supervisor:* Locke, M. Mr

Informal practitioner theory in adult basic education
Abstract: Adult basic education relies heavily on notions of 'good practice'. This study seeks to identify the elements of good practice used by practitioners in adult basic education and to relate these to adult education theory. This is in response to claims that practitioners do not take account of formal theory per se, but use informal theory to develop their practice. Thirty adult basic education practitioners, drawn from a sub-regional training group, will be interviewed using Kelly's Repertory Grid. This technique elicits constructs which will be used to identify underlying assumptions about 'good practice'. This will be used to create a formal statement of the informal theory.
Status: Individual research
Date of Research: 1990-1993
KEYWORDS: *adult basic education; adult educators; educational practices; teaching methods; theory-practice relationship*

10/1646
    Department of Education Studies, Barking Campus, Longbridge Road, Dagenham RM8 2AS
    0181 590 7722
    Corbett, J. Dr
Learning support provision in further education
Abstract: The background to this project is the development of integration in further education over the last decade. The researcher has examined the way in which provision and policy has developed, specifically in relation to the changing role of the special needs coordinator (Corbett and Barton, 1992). This project seeks to extend this research into a detailed investigation of current learning support provision and the form of its delivery. Thirty colleges of further education will be examined, through the use of a brief questionnaire, followed up by indepth interviews with ten of the colleges' learning support coordinators. In addition, there will be several case study illustrations which contextualise learning support in further education, as it relates to specific institutions, their history and ethos. The focus will be on the strategies which learning support coordinators have developed to cope with change.
Published Material: CORBETT, J. & BARTON, L. (1992). A struggle for choice: students with special needs in transition to adulthood. London: Routledge.; CORBETT, J. & BARTON, L. (1992). Facing challenges: the changing perspectives of special needs coordinators. London: SKILL (National Bureau for Students with Disabilities).
Status: Sponsored project
Source of Grant: University of East London
Date of Research: 1992-1994
KEYWORDS: *further education; mainstreaming; special educational needs; support services; support teachers*

University of North London

10/1647
    School of Teaching Studies, Marlborough Building, 383 Holloway Road, London N7 0RN
    0171 607 2789
    O'Keefe, D. Dr; Stoll, P. Mrs; Cole, H. Mrs
Truancy research project
Abstract: The present research covers 20 randomly selected local education authorities (LEAs) in England. In each of these, every fourth school is to be visited, to a total of 150 schools. In each school visited all year 10 and 11 pupils are surveyed through confidential and anonymous questionnaires. The aim is to uncover the incidence of truancy, especially Post Registration Truancy, and the incidence of alienation from the school curriculum. The analysis of the findings will be aided by those of a staff questionnaire aimed at uncovering the school ethos and socio-economic status. The most innovative factor in the research is the guiding expectation that truancy is essentially a sociological rather than a psychological phenomenon, and intimately related to the school curriculum.
Published Material: O'KEEFE, D. (1981). 'Truancy, industry and the school curriculum'. In: FLEW, et al (Eds). The Pied Pipers of Education. London: Social Affairs Unit.; O'KEEFE, D. & STOLL, P. (1989). Officially present. London: IEA Education Unit.
Status: Sponsored project
Source of Grant: Department of Education and Science £185,000
Date of Research: 1991-1993
KEYWORDS: *pupil behaviour; truancy*

10/1648

School of Teaching Studies, Marlborough Building,
383 Holloway Road, London N7 0RN
0171 607 2789
Dean, W. Ms; King, M. Ms; *Supervisor:* Ross, A. Prof.;
Hutchings, M. Ms

Technology at work

Abstract: Shell 'Technology at Work' is a research and curriculum development project, the aim of which is to produce teachers' packs of activities showing how large elements of the technology curriculum for National Curriculum key stage 1 and 2 can be studies using local workplaces as an experiential resource for children. The project is working closely with three local schools in development and trialling of the activities. A number of other local schools are involved in trialling the packs in prototype form.

Published Material: DEAN, W. Trial pack for 'Technology at Work' project: The school as a workplace: Teachers' guide.; DEAN, W. Trial pack for 'Technology at Work' project: The school as a workplace: Playtime.; DEAN, W. Trial pack for 'Technology at Work' project: The school as a workplace: The classroom.

Status: Sponsored project
Source of Grant: Shell Education Service (Shell UK) £117,000
Date of Research: 1990-1992
KEYWORDS: *curriculum development; educational materials; experiential learning; material development; primary education; technology education; work-education relationship*

10/1649

School of Teaching Studies, Marlborough Building,
383 Holloway Road, London N7 0RN
0171 607 2789
Ross, A. Prof.; Sims, L. Ms; Hutchings, M. Ms

Children's typologies of adult work and related concepts

Abstract: This project intends to make a longitudinal study of some 90 children, drawn from a variety of socio-economic backgrounds, drawing cohorts of four and seven year olds, and following these through for five years. Techniques to elicit information are being developed, and may include grid repertory techniques, semi-structured interviews, picture matching and role play. Various economic concepts will be explored, including that of adult work (using PAHL's classification), gender roles in workplaces, and others.

Status: Sponsored project
Source of Grant: University of North London £13,000
Date of Research: 1991-continuing
KEYWORDS: *attitude formation; childhood attitudes; primary school pupils; work attitudes*

10/1650

School of Teaching Studies, Marlborough Building,
383 Holloway Road, London N7 0RN
0171 607 2789
Merttens, R. Mrs; Vass, J. Mr

The Nuffield/IMPACT continuation project

Abstract: Inventing Mathematics for Parents and Children and Teachers (IMPACT) is a research and intervention project. Parents are involved in their children's learning of mathematics through the use of teacher designed take-home activities. The project runs in 24 local education authorities across England, Scotland and Wales, and is currently estimated to involve close to 1,000 schools. There is a diversity of research within, and relating to, IMPACT. This includes studies focussing upon: 1) the negotiation of the home/school boundary; 2) parents' attitudes to mathematics or schooling; 3) the child's negotiation of the mathematical task in the home; 4) child-tutoring of adults in mathematics; 5) teacher typifications of parents and participation in schooling; and 6) communications between home and school.

Published Material: MERTTENS, R. & VASS, J. (1990). Sharing mathematics cultures: Impact – Inventing Mathematics for Parents and Children and Teachers. London: Falmer Press.; MERTTENS, R. & VASS, J. Ruling the margins. London: Falmer Press. (in press).

Status: Sponsored project
Source of Grant: Tudor Trust £30,000; Barnet, Redbridge and Oxfordshire Local Education Authorities; Nuffield Foundation
Date of Research: 1991-1994
KEYWORDS: *home-school relationship; homework; learning activities; mathematics education; parent participation*

10/1651

School of Teaching Studies, Marlborough Building,
383 Holloway Road, London N7 0RN
0171 607 2789
Bath College of Higher Education, Newton Park, Newton St
Loe, Bath BA2 9BN
01225 873701
Hutchings, M. Ms; *Supervisor:* Ross, A. Prof.; Coulby, D. Dr

Children's perceptions of work and the sources of their understanding

Abstract: An investigation into primary aged children's thinking about work, examining (through semi-structured interviews) the way in which children draw on their experiences (in the home, school, community and through the media) and from them construct their understanding of work (including paid and unpaid work, and work at school).

Published Material: HUTCHINGS, M. (1989). Children's ideas about the world of work. London: Polytechnic of North London Press.; HUTCHINGS, M. (1990). 'Children's thinking about work'. In: ROSS, A. (Ed). Economic and industrial awareness in the primary school. London: Polytechnic of North London Press.

Status: Individual research
Date of Research: 1986-1993
KEYWORDS: *employment; primary school pupils; social cognition; work attitudes*

10/1652

School of Teaching Studies, Marlborough Building,
383 Holloway Road, London N7 0RN
0171 607 2789
Focus Consultancy Ltd, Bon Marshe Building, 444 Brixton
Road, London SW9 8EJ
0171 737 7155
Adler, A. Ms; *Supervisor:* Murray, A. Mr

Developing self-study materials to support teachers' understanding of scientific concepts

Abstract: The aim of this project is to develop self-study materials to support assessed course units in primary science education for the teacher training course at the University of North London, with possible future use for Inservice courses. The proposed approach is to develop materials which will support a specific concept area in science education. Target groups of staff and students will be identified with whom to pilot materials. These will be pre-tested groups to establish their understanding of key scientific concepts and relationships prior to use of self-study materials, and the materials will be introduced as part of course sessions dealing with a selected concept area. Post-testing of target groups will take place to identify any change in understanding of scientific concepts/relationships in the defined concept area, and feedback will be collected on other aspects of material e.g. clarity, ease of use, enjoyment etc. through 'attitude survey'. The findings will be collated and analysed before improvement is made on the materials. The approach will then be extended to other concept areas.

Status: Sponsored project
Source of Grant: Training, Enterprise and Education Directorate £18,090
Date of Research: 1991-1992
KEYWORDS: *educational material evaluation; educational materials; material development; science education; scientific attitudes; scientific literacy; supported self study; teacher education*

10/1653

School of Teaching Studies, Marlborough Building,
383 Holloway Road, London N7 0RN
0171 607 2789
Cambridge University, Homerton College, Cambridge
CB2 2PH
(see also under Homerton College)
01223 411141
Ross, A. Prof.; Hutchings, M. Ms; Ahier, J. Dr

The economic and industrial background, understanding and attitudes of student primary teachers

Abstract: This research investigated primary student teachers' demographic and other economic backgrounds, their understanding of economic and industrial awareness, and their attitude to teaching this area as a cross-curricular theme to primary aged children. 1,200 first year students from a sample of Bachelor of Education (B.Ed) and Postgraduate Certificate of Education (PGCE) courses in England,

Scotland and Wales completed a questionnaire, sixty of whom were subsequently interviewed at depth. Course leaders from seven institutions discussed the implications of the findings with the project team. Student teachers were found to have a much more varied background and age profile than had been assumed. Older students had a greater experience of everyday economic activities. Students were generally favourably disposed to teaching economic and industrial awareness in primary schools, but rated other cross-curricular themes as more important. Older students, students with children, PGCE students and those with more economic experiences were more in favour than those without these characteristics. These groups also had greater economic understanding themselves, although most students professed to be bemused by economics. A number of recommendations about initial teacher education courses were made.
Published Material: ROSS, A., AHIER, J. & HUTCHINGS, M. (1991). EATE Research Report No 1: 'Student primary teachers. their background, experience, attitude and understanding of economic and industrial matters', University of Bath: Enterprise Awareness and Teacher Education (Department of Employment).; ROSS, A. (1992). 'An investigation into the prior economic experiences of primary education students', Assessment and Evaluation in Higher Education, Vol 17, No 3. (in press). A full list of publications is available from the researchers.
Status: Sponsored project
Source of Grant: Enterprise Awareness and Teacher Education (EATE) £49,000
Date of Research: 1990-1991
KEYWORDS: *background; economics education; experience; industry-education relationship; preservice teacher education; student teacher attitudes; student teachers*

10/1654

School of Teaching Studies, Marlborough Building, 383 Holloway Road, London N7 0RN
0171 607 2789
University of Wales College of Cardiff, School of Education, Senghennydd Road, Cardiff CF2 4AG
01222 874000
Conolly, M. Mr; *Supervisor:* Davies, W. Prof.
Education, citizenship and the British state
Abstract: This research attempts to answer the question of why the State redistributes much of its revenue towards compulsory education. Most democratic states suggest that schooling is an enablement in democratic participation, can the same be said for the British State? The research examines the political and ideological forces which motivated the State to finance schooling from the 18th century until 1970. The method used involves the reading of texts (in particular, Governmental documents).
Status: Individual research
Date of Research: 1988-1994
KEYWORDS: *citizenship; educational finance; educational history; educational objectives; politics education relationship*

University of the West of England

10/1655

Department of Computer Studies and Mathematics, Frenchay Campus, Coldharbour Lane, Bristol BS16 1QY
01179 656261
Jukes, K. Prof.
A framework for enabling higher level information technology updating and continuous professional development of the existing regional workforce
Abstract: With demographic decline, rapid technological change, the use of information technology (IT) in all sectors of the market, and the impact of the downturn in the defence industry, the peace dividend and the recession, organisations have increasingly recognised the need to place effort into the continuing professional development (CPD) of the retained workforce. In IT and end-user support, historical skill shortages were historically plugged by personnel without formal training. Rapid changes in technology, tools and methodologies, and their strategic impact on competitiveness and the quality of information have led to a need to ensure staff have a firmer grounding in the subject. The University of the West of England has addressed this over recent years through the development of tailored training

programmes, part-time MSc's, part-time HNC/D programmes and top-ups to Degree level from HNC/D. Each of these areas has moved forward by modular provision and the development of credit rating structures. The project includes the following objectives: 1) the development of a formal network of employers and universities in the region to collaborate in providing modules for CPD with a range of levels, locations, and modes of delivery; 2) the setting up of access mechanisms to the network by other parties including small and medium sized enterprises (SMEs) and very small organisations; 3) fieldwork to research and establish requirements for and approaches to CPD; and 4) the establishment of a database of modules and providers, the database being in a variety of forms for effective access and use.
Status: Sponsored project
Source of Grant: Avon Training and Enterprise Council; Training, Enterprise and Education Directorate; Department of Employment, jointly £69,000
Date of Research: 1991-1993
KEYWORDS: *higher education; information technology; professional development*

10/1656

Faculty of Education, Redland Campus, Bristol BS6 6UZ
01179 741251
Attwood, G. Ms; *Supervisor:* Blunden, G. Dr; Bone, J. Mrs; Croll, P. Prof.
Understanding the colours of competence
Abstract: The main aim of the investigation is to identify the key educational issues concerning the use of competence based approaches to teaching and assessment and to identify situations and/or conditions which enable competence to be an effective measure of achievement. The research will include the collection of empirical evidence on the development, operation and effects of a competence based assessment scheme. The data will be collected by questionnaire from examination centres operating the Royal Society of Arts' Computer Literacy and Information Technology Scheme. There will also be interviews with senior examination board officers and tutors operating the scheme. The research will also include an evaluation of a range of competence based schemes as a means of measuring and recording achievement. The research will extend from an analysis of a skills-based competence assessment model to an investigtion of the use of competence as a measure of professional achievement. It is intended to carry out a study using the Delphi technique to compile a consensus view of the competence within a professional area of expertise and at this stage it is intended to use teacher education. The research evidence will offer a contribution to the literature and educational knowledge in the area of the 'competence' debate.
Status: Individual research
Date of Research: 1992-continuing
KEYWORDS: *assessment; competency based education*

10/1657

Faculty of Education, Redland Campus, Bristol BS6 6UZ
01179 741251
Blunden, G. Dr
Policy issues in the early provision of courses in non-advanced further education for women and girls
Abstract: The present research builds on the researcher's doctoral thesis (completed in 1983) which examined, by means of three historical case studies, the early development of non-advanced further education for women and girls in England. The current project explores policy issues of the control and governance of further education, especially in the light of the 1993 incorporation of further education colleges and the loss of local education authority control as providers. Through historical comparisons it examines the impact this might have on provision for women and girls in the post-16 sector.
Published Material: BLUNDEN, G. (1980). 'The whisky money and sexual inequality and non-advanced further education 1890-1903'. Paper 8/80 of Standing Conference on the Sociology of Further Education, Coombe Lodge, Blagdon, 1980.; BLUNDEN, G. (1981). 'Women and girls and non-advanced further education: some historical considerations'. In Transactions: Proceedings of the Annual Conference of the British Sociological Association, University College of Wales, Aberystwyth, 1981.; BLUNDEN, G. (1983). 'Typing in the tech: domesticity, ideology and women's place in further education'. In: GLEESON, D. (Ed). Youth training and the search for work. London: Routledge and Kegan Paul.; BLUNDEN, G.

(1984). 'Vocational education for women's work in England and Wales'. In: ACKER, S. (Ed) et al. World yearbook of education 1984: women and education. London: Kogan Page.
Status: Individual research
Date of Research: 1993-continuing
KEYWORDS: educational history; educational policy; further education; women's education

10/1658

Faculty of Education, Redland Campus, Bristol BS6 6UZ
01179 741251
Harnett, P. Mrs
Investigating children's understanding in primary history; progression in children's questioning of visual sources
Abstract: The research has built on earlier work which tried to analyse progression in children's historical understanding through using visual materials. Particular differences in the way children viewed pictures were noted and this has been explored more fully in the current research. A sample of sixty Year 4 and 5 children have been asked to select an historical picture from a range of source material. They have written questions about what they would like to know about the picture. Interviews with selected children will seek to ascertain how the children perceived the task and how they made their selection of particular questions which they wanted to raise. Differences in the details they have noted and the extent of their ability to use the pictures as an historical source and to raise historical questions are now being analysed. It is hoped that the data will provide a framework for discussion of the possible progression in children's historical thinking.
Published Material: HARNETT, P. (1990). 'Reading pictures, reading the past'. Paper presented at the Historical Association National Primary Conference, Bath, 1990.; HARNETT, P. (1991). 'Using pictures as evidence'. Primary Historian, Spring.; HARNETT, P. (1992). 'The visual dimension in teaching primary history'. Paper presented at the Primary History Conference, Exeter, 1992.; HARNETT, P. (1993). 'Identifying progression in children's understanding: the use of visual materials to assess primary school children's learning in history', Cambridge Journal of Education, Vol 23, No 2, pp.137-154.
Status: Sponsored project
Source of Grant: University of the West of England
Date of Research: 1993-1994
KEYWORDS: educational materials; history studies; pictorial stimuli; teaching methods; visual aids

10/1659

Faculty of Education, Redland Campus, Bristol BS6 6UZ
01179 741251
Kimber, D. Mr
Processes of assessing children's understanding of people, places and space. How do we assess children's learning in primary geography
Abstract: In the light of the National Curriculum, there has been increasing attention to the assessment of children's learning. The profile of geography within the primary curriculum has also been raised. The aim of this work is to investigate ways in which we can more effectively assess children's learning in geography, and also to gain insights into children's understanding of people and place. This small scale project will work with children in selected classes in 2 or 3 schools. Initially work will be with junior children; with infant children at a later stage. So far as is possible the research will be linked to ongoing work in the classroom. There will be discussions and feedback from teacher colleagues where appropriate.
Status: Sponsored project
Source of Grant: University of the West of England
Date of Research: 1994-continuing
KEYWORDS: assessment; geography education

10/1660

Faculty of Education, Redland Campus, Bristol BS6 6UZ
01179 741251
Robinson, G. Mr
An investigation into assertive discipline. Teachers' perceptions of assertive discipline and how these change with time
Abstract: There have been many articles published in the UK which support the increased use of assertive discipline. There has been only one critical UK article (Robinson, G.S. and Maines, B. 'Jumping on

the dated Wagon', Educational Psychology in Practice). The project will investigate teachers' perceptions of assertive discipline after initial training in the methods and how their perceptions change with time. Methods used will include questionnaires, interviewing and observation in classrooms.
Status: Sponsored project
Source of Grant: University of the West of England
Date of Research: 1994-continuing
KEYWORDS: classroom discipline; discipline

10/1661

Faculty of Education, Redland Campus, Bristol BS6 6UZ
01179 741251
Whitehead, J. Ms; Menter, I. Mr
Partnership and professionalism in initial teacher training
Abstract: The project is concerned with changes being brought about through the implementation of Department for Education (DFE) Circular 9/92, concerned with the training of teachers for the secondary school phase. The development of partnership arrangements between schools and higher education institutions (HEIs) is being examined. A principal aim is to analyse changes in conceptions of teacher professionalism which are being brought about. The first phase of the project consisted of an examination of documents produced by the Government, by teachers' professional associations and by HEIs. In the second phase, 2 or 3 case studies are being carried out within HEIs and some of their partner schools. Interim findings are that the significant changes in roles and responsibilities of teachers and higher education lecturers involve considerable redefinition of the nature of their work. Some of the changes appear to enhance professionalism, whilst others diminish it.
Status: Sponsored project
Source of Grant: University of the West of England £11,000
Date of Research: 1993-continuing
KEYWORDS: preservice teacher education; school based teacher education; teaching profession

10/1662

Faculty of Education, Redland Campus, Bristol BS6 6UZ
01179 741251
Robinson, G. Mr
An investigation into the use of a non-punitive method (No Blame Approach) in dealing with incidents of bullying
Abstract: The literature provides many strategies schools can use to reduce the incidents of bullying, but few strategies are suggested as to how schools can deal with incidents of bullying. This is a small scale investigation into how an infant, junior, secondary and special school implemented a non-punitive strategy in dealing with bullying incidents. All schools were given training in the 'No Blame Approach' and were asked to complete a report from detailing each use of the approach. This information was supplemented by interviewing a member of staff who had used the approach.
Status: Sponsored project
Source of Grant: University of the West of England
Date of Research: 1992-1994
KEYWORDS: behaviour problems; bullying; discipline policy; discipline problems

10/1663

Faculty of Education, Redland Campus, Bristol BS6 6UZ
01179 741251
Pollard, A. Prof.; Filer, A. Dr
Assessment and career in a primary school: a longitudinal ethnography
Abstract: National assessment procedures have generated much controversy since their introduction into schools in 1989. The assigning of numerical 'levels' to young children and comparisons of schools through 'league tables' being not least among the concerns. Virtually all of the research into this widely debated topic has, to date, been large in scale. Studies have, variously, sought insight into the reliability of classroom based assessment, into its impact on teachers' work and upon classroom environments on a nationwide basis. To complement this emerging broad picture, this detailed, longitudinal ethnography focuses on a group of ten children in one primary school class. The aim of the study is to generate insights into the impact of both ongoing teacher assessments and standard assessment tasks on the identity and the school careers of children as they move through the primary school. Children are being studied in the three social contexts

of classroom, playground and home. Observations are being made in classrooms and playground, with the additional use of video recordings and school records. Parents and children will be involved in contributing understandings through interviews and, in the case of parents, additionally through journal entries. Data already generated through Filer's PhD study will enable a longitudinal study to be made from Year 1 of the pupils careers, to Year 6. Comparisons will be made with findings from an existing Leverhulme funded longitudinal ethnography into pupil careers which is directed by Pollard and research by Filer and with findings from the Economic and Social Research Council (ESRC) funded Primary Assessment Curriculum and Experience project which draws on a national representative sample (Pollard et al 1994).
Published Material: FILER, A. (1993). Classroom contexts of assessment in a primary school. Unpublished PhD thesis. Bristol: University of the West of England.; POLLARD, A., BROADFOOT, P., CROLL, P., OSBORN, M. & ABBOTT, D. (1994). Changing English primary schools? London: Cassell.; POLLARD, A. & FILER, A. Identity and career in a primary school. London: Cassell. (in press).
Status: Sponsored project
Source of Grant: Economic and Social Research Council £66,510
Date of Research: 1989-continuing
KEYWORDS: assessment; longitudinal studies; primary education; primary school pupils; pupil-school relationship; school based assessment; standard assessment tasks

10/1664

Faculty of Education, Redland Campus, Bristol BS6 6UZ
01179 741251
Pollard, A. Prof.; Filer, A. Dr
Child careers in a primary school: an ethnographic study
Abstract: This study of pupil identity and career takes the form of a longitudinal ethnography, focusing on ten white, predominantly middle-class children, from their entry into primary school through to their leaving at age eleven. The study will attempt to relate the impact of social context and social relationships on primary school careers as pupils form and manage their identities, experiencing successes, disappointments and assessments to various kinds. Three major contexts, those of classroom, playground and home, are being studied. Interviews, observations, video recordings, documentary evidence, and journal entries by parents are being used to produce data on child relationships and developing identities. There are no existing sociological studies which take the pupil as the main unit of analysis and track the progressive impact of differentiation processes over a pupil career of many years. This study will broaden the concern for curriculum progression and coherence which underpins the introduction of the National Curriculum, to encompass issues related to continuity in pupil experience. It will provide new longitudinal insights concerning processes of social differentiation as they affect young children and complement an established literature on teacher career. Findings will help to inform a parallel Economic and Social Research Council (ESRC) funded longitudinal ethnography directed by Pollard and Filer concerned with assessment and pupil career. Findings from both will be related to the ESRC funded Primary Assessment and Curriculum project which draws on a national representative sample (Pollard et al 1994).
Published Material: POLLARD, A. (1992). 'Pupil learning and career in a primary school: the methodology of longitudinal ethnography'. Paper given at British Educational Research Association Conference, Stirling, 1992.; POLLARD, A., BROADFOOT, P., CROLL, P., OSBORN, M. & ABBOTT, D. (1994). Changing English primary schools? London: Cassell.; POLLARD, A. & FILER, A. Identity and career in a primary school. London: Cassell. (in press).
Status: Sponsored project
Source of Grant: Leverhulme Trust £32,300
Date of Research: 1987-1994
KEYWORDS: educational experience; longitudinal studies; primary education; primary school pupils; pupil-school relationship

10/1665

Faculty of Education, Redland Campus, Bristol BS6 6UZ
01179 741251
Pollard, A. Prof.
Learning, identity and social contexts: an ethnography of pupil learning in a primary school
Abstract: The research is concerned with the impact of social contexts and social relationships on the learning of children in an English

primary school. It takes the form of a longitudinal ethnography and focuses on the learning of ten white, predominantly middle-class children in one primary school since 1987. It will report on their learning from the ages of 5-7 years and will attempt to relate the impact of social contexts and social relationships on their identities to the way in which they approach learning tasks. Three major social contexts have been studied: classroom; playground, and home. Data on child relationships with teachers, peers, parents, and siblings has been collected using interviews, observations, video recordings, documentary evidence and journals of family life kept by parents. Explorations on these relationships at the micro level will be related to wider social and educational policies. Drawing on Vygotsky, L.S. (1962). Thought and Language. New York: Wiley and Vygotsky, L.S. (1978). Mind in Society. London: Harvard Press, Pollard argues that learning reflects specific social processes and relationships which are unique to the individual concerned and it is thus only partly amenable to the structuring of external conditions and requirements through national systems. A critique will thus be mounted of English education policies which have focused on curriculum, assessment and market-driven management styles whilst almost ignoring social contexts in schools, learning processes and the holistic needs of learners. Findings will be related to those from the Economic and Social Research Council (ESRC) funded by Primary Assessment, Curriculum and Experience project which draws on a national representative sample (Pollard et al 1994).
Published Material: POLLARD, A. (1990). 'Towards a sociology of learning in primary schools', British Journal of Sociology of Education, Vol 11, No 3, pp.241-256.; POLLARD, A. (1990). Learning in primary schools. London: Cassell.; POLLARD, A. (1992). 'Pupil learning and career in a primary school: the methodology of longitudinal ethnography'. Paper given at British Educational Research Association Conference, Stirling, 1992.; POLLARD, A., BROADFOOT, P., CROLL, P., OSBORN, M. & ABBOTT, D. (1994). Changing English primary schools. London: Cassell.
Status: Individual research
Date of Research: 1986-1994
KEYWORDS: home-school relationship; learning processes; primary school pupils; pupil-school relationship; social influences; sociology of education

10/1666

Faculty of Education, Redland Campus, Bristol BS6 6UZ
01179 741251
Newman, E. Ms
Learning materials in initial teacher training
Abstract: This research takes place within a particular educational context. The learning materials and the accompanying research are developing with reference to: 1) the Faculty of Education at the University of the West of England being committed to partnership with schools; 2) the move towards the greater involvement of schools in initial teacher training; 3) the move to modularised courses; and 4) continued innovation in the Faculty's approach to inservice teacher education (INSET). During the project, a trial package of learning materials has been produced. The impact of using the materials is being examined in connection with: a) student learning within the B.Ed. course; b) teachers and schools; c) tutors. This examination is focusing on: a) evaluating the effectiveness of the materials in supporting students; b) the potential role of such materials in developing partnership with schools; c) defining the role of the tutor in relation to student learning and school partnership; and d) the potential role of such materials in contributing to staff development.
Status: Sponsored project
Source of Grant: University of the West of England
Date of Research: 1993-1994
KEYWORDS: educational materials; preservice teacher education

10/1667

Faculty of Education, Redland Campus, Bristol BS6 6UZ
01179 741251
Menter, I. Mr; Muschamp, Y. Ms; Nicholls, P. Mr; Ozga, J. Prof.; Pollard, A. Prof.
Markets development and quality: the impact of market ideology on contemporary management systems and the achievement of quality in small service providers
Abstract: This is a joint Faculty of Education/Business School project developing a comparative study of organisational change in three service sectors: restaurants, nursing homes and primary schools. Based within a local education authority in the South of England, the

project is studying the market influences on the management of these institutions within a small city. In relation to schools the study will provide an evaluation of government policy of open enrolment, Local Management of Schools and the publication of school results which are designed to contribute to the creation of an educational market and the raising of standards.

Status: Sponsored project
Source of Grant: Polytechnics and Colleges Funding Council £62,000
Date of Research: 1992-continuing
KEYWORDS: educational administration; educational policy; local management of schools; management in education; organisational change

10/1668

Faculty of Education, Redland Campus, Bristol BS6 6UZ
01179 741251
Lewis, R. Dr

The development of a hypertext information and profiling information system for schools and colleges

Abstract: One of the key issues in teaching technology is the cross-curricular nature of the subject, clearly identified in the National Curriculum documentation; this together with the inherent breadth of technology makes it near impossible for schools to teach all the work within 'technology' time. The same issue can be identified in the provision of initial teacher education for technology teachers. The very essence of the subject is the application of knowledge, processes and techniques, drawn from any walk of life, to develop a solution to a particular need, normally to realise an opportunity for potential development. Information services of all kinds are used extensively in this work, but as yet little research has been undertaken into the monitoring of the subject with the very technology that is a part of the subject. The research will draw data from a sample of schools and apply information technology (IT) skills to the analysis of the curriculum, across all subjects, with a view to identifying cross-curricular opportunities, both real and latent, that exist. An information recording and retrieval system will be trialled; this will monitor a pupil's progress individually in technology in a cross-curricular manner. The application of IT should ensure that the strengths in a pupil's work are recognised, whilst identifying opportunity, but without emphasising non-attainment. Although focused initially within the subject of technology, this is a cross-curricular project concerned with teaching and learning; and it is anticipated that the findings will therefore be relevant across the whole school curriculum.

Status: Sponsored project
Source of Grant: University of the West of England £11,000
Date of Research: 1994-continuing
KEYWORDS: computer uses in education; cross curricular approach; hypertext; information technology; technology education

10/1669

Faculty of Education, Redland Campus, Bristol BS6 6UZ
01179 741251
Bristol University, School of Education, 35 Berkeley Square, Bristol BS8 1JA
01179 303030
Filer, A. Dr; *Supervisor:* Pollard, A. Prof.; Broadfoot, P. Prof.

Classroom contexts of assessment in a primary school

Abstract: The research is concerned with the provision for assessment related to the National Curriculum for England and Wales (Education Reform Act 1988). Through it, is presented a critique of some aspects of the provision with respect to teacher assessment. The focus of the study concerns the extent to which such assessments can be viewed as objective and comparable statements of the achievements of individuals and schools. An examination has been made of both formal, National Curriculum related, and informal assessments for a cohort of white, predominantly working class children as they moved through Years 1 to 3 of an English primary school. Data was collected from the three teaching environments using ethnographic methods. These included participant observation, teacher and pupil interviews and the use of documentary evidence. The research sets assessments in the context in which they were made. It examines the notion of assessment as a product of a teacher-created classroom context that is complex in its origins. Principal findings of the study are as follows: 1) There are fundamental and persistent differences between teachers in their classroom strategies that have an impact upon pupil responses and hence upon assessments made. 2) These fundamental differences between teachers are not addressed by governmental concerns for

systematising teacher assessment in the pursuit of comparability across sites of assessment. 3) Teacher assessments which appear 'objective' are the outcome of differentiating processes and contain within them a range of other pupil skills and attributes. 4) Teacher assessments are inevitably context-related.

Published Material: FILER, A. (1993). 'Contexts of assessment in a primary school classroom', British Educational Research Journal, Vol 19, No 1, pp.95-107.; FILER, A. (1993). 'The assessment of classroom language: challenging the rhetoric of 'objectivity', International Studies in Sociology of Education, Vol 2, No 2.; FILER, A. (1993). 'Teacher assessment: a sociological perspective'. Paper given at British Educational Research Association, Liverpool, 1993.; FILER, A. (1993). Classroom contexts of assessment in a primary school. Unpublished PhD thesis. Bristol: University of the West of England.
Status: Individual research
Date of Research: 1989-1993
KEYWORDS: assessment; National Curriculum; primary education; school-based assessment

10/1670

Faculty of Education, Redland Campus, Bristol BS6 6UZ
01179 741251
Open University, School of Education, Walton Hall, Milton Keynes MK7 6AA
01908 274066
Muschamp, Y. Ms; *Supervisor:* Pollard, A. Prof.; Woods, P. Prof.

Pupil self-assessment

Abstract: This action research project examines the way in which self-assessment can be used with young primary school children to enhance learning. It argues that teacher support in self-assessment can help children to develop meta-cognitive skills which further independence by enabling children to learn about learning. This teacher support is provided through the use of targets, the development of an assessment vocabulary and the compilation and review of individual portfolios or records of achievement.

Published Material: MUSCHAMP, Y. (1991). 'Pupil self-assessment'. In: NATIONAL PRIMARY CENTRE. Practical issues in primary education, No 8. Bristol: National Primary Centre (SW).; MUSCHAMP, Y. (1994). 'Target setting with young children'. In: POLLARD, A. & BOURNE, J. (Eds). Teaching and learning in the primary school. London: Routledge.
Status: Individual research
Date of Research: 1990-1994
KEYWORDS: achievement; assessment; primary school pupils; profiles; records of achievement; self evaluation – individuals

10/1671

Faculty of Education, Redland Campus, Bristol BS6 6UZ
01179 741251
Southampton University, School of Education, Highfield, Southampton SO9 5NH
01703 595000
James, D. Mr; *Supervisor:* Pollard, A. Prof.; Ozga, J. Prof.; Erben, M. Mr

A comparative and qualitative study of the learning experiences of non-traditional undergraduate students

Abstract: In the context of expansion, widened access and increasing numbers of mature students in post-binary higher education, this study makes use of indepth interviewing to allow a comparison between the accounts of mature students and tutors on social science programmes in two contrasting institutional settings. The main focus of these accounts is on learning experiences and on the articulation of home life and university life in the generation of particular experiences of 'studentship'. The focus on social practices means that methodologically, the study attempts to escape from the structure/agency dichotomy evident across earlier research in the particular field.

Published Material: JAMES, D. (1993). Admissions of the non-traditional. Redland papers, No 2. Bristol: University of the West of England.
Status: Individual research
Date of Research: 1990-continuing
KEYWORDS: higher education; learning experience; mature students; student experience

10/1672

Faculty of Education, Redland Campus, Bristol BS6 6UZ
01179 741251
University of Wales College of Cardiff, School of Education,
Senghennydd Road, Cardiff CF2 4AG
01222 874000
Lee, J. Mr; Fitz, J. Dr

Quality control in schools: the role of Her Majesty's Inspectorate (HMI) as policy makers in a climate of change

Abstract: In the context of change the main aim of the research is to explore the role of national inspection in England and Wales in the making of education policy. The specific objectives of the research are: 1) To investigate the practice of Her Majesty's Inspectors (HMIs) in maintaining quality and pursuing curriculum innovation. 2) To compare the practice of the Office for Standards in Education (OFSTED) with that of HMI in order to: a) explore the extent that theory and practice of instruction is proposed to schools; b) clarify the role of both in the creation and revision of the National Curriculum; and c) explore the role of both in the accreditation of an initial teacher training (ITT) curriculum. 3) To investigate the impact of OFSTED on teachers' perception of their professionalism. The empirical focus of the research will include: published and unpublished documents; interview data from retired members of HMI and members of OFSTED teams; and interview data from schools and teachers who have been inspected under the auspices of OFSTED.
Published Material: LEE, J. & FITZ, J. 'Constituting good practice: HMI and its influence on policy and pedagogy: some provisional findings'. In: DAVID, S. (Ed). Control and accountability in educational settings. London: Cassell (in press).
Status: Sponsored project
Source of Grant: University of the West of England
Date of Research: 1993-continuing
KEYWORDS: *educational policy; inspection; inspectors – of schools; quality control*

University of Wales College of Cardiff

10/1673

School of Education, Senghennydd Road, Cardiff CF2 4AG
01222 874000
Obeid, S. Mr; *Supervisor:* Nolan, R. Dr

Curriculum development in technical and vocational education in Saudi Arabia related to students' needs, perceptions and expectations

Abstract: This is a study that aims to determine the cause of student wastage in technical and vocational education institutes in Saudi Arabia as a basis of the need for curriculum development.
Status: Sponsored project
Source of Grant: Saudia Arabia Ministry of Education
Date of Research: 1991-1993
KEYWORDS: *Arab states; dropout research; student wastage; technical education; vocational education*

10/1674

School of Education, 42 Park Place, Cardiff CF1 3BB
01222 874000
Papatheodorou, T. Ms; *Supervisor:* Ramasut, A. Ms

Teachers' attitudes towards children's behaviour problems in nursery classes in Greece and management strategies used

Abstract: The study investigates teachers' attitudes towards children's behaviour problems in nursery classes in Greece and the management strategies used by them. The present research arose out of personal experiences as a nursery school teacher in Greece, together with data collected on behaviour problems in preschool children, which has now prompted this further investigation of teachers' attitudes and coping strategies. From a review of the relevant literature it was found that the age at which children begin to present behavioural problems in schools is getting lower, and that a significant proportion of children who have difficulties on entering school are still having difficulties later in their school life. Furthermore, it is believed that the way teachers view and treat children is of crucial significance in the matter of disruptive behaviour. Additionally, the notion for early intervention which currently dominates education

programmes – especially those of nursery education – makes the study of behaviour difficulties in early childhood an urgent and dominant issue in the field. The aims of the study are to examine: (1) the types and prevalence of children's behaviour problems, according to the degree of seriousness; (2) the factors associated with teachers' attitudes towards children's behaviour porblems; (3) how teachers manage children's behaviour problems; (4) what kind of help is available to nursery teachers, when children display serious and persistent behaviour problems; (5) how nursery teachers would like/wish to see their nursery school operating in order to prevent or to manage pupils' behaviour problems, more effectively; and (6) some of the theoretical and practical implications of the present study. For the purpose of the study, a questionnaire was constructed, with items elicited from nursery teachers in Greece. The sample of teachers (N=225) was selected from nursery schools located in large urban, small urban and rural areas. Factors such as the type of school and the socioeconomic status of the location were also taken into consideration. Each nursery teacher will complete the questionnaire for the two pupils whom they perceived to exhibit the most serious behaviour problems in their classroom. (Pupils sample N=450)
Status: Sponsored project
Source of Grant: Greek Government
Date of Research: 1991-continuing
KEYWORDS: *behaviour problems; classroom discipline; discipline; disruptive pupils; Greece; nursery school education; teacher attitudes*

10/1675

School of Education, Senghennydd Road, Cardiff CF2 4AG
01222 874000
Curtis, K. Ms; *Supervisor:* Donald, A. Dr

The role of adult basic education in the re-education of brain injured adults: an investigation into student specific re-learning programmes

Abstract: Although brain injuries are generally perceived to be the prerogative of the medical professions, this thesis presents a role for the adult basic education service in the re-education of dysphasic adults. The role model is the dysphasia project based in the Rhymney Valley district of Mid Glamorgan's community education service. Emphasis will be placed on the positive assessment of literacy and numeracy skills following brain injury and on student specific re-learning programmes devised for each client. Research methods adopted are literature surveys, interviews and study visits. The thesis includes: (1) an outline of the history of the adult basic education service in England and Wales; (2) an explanation of the causes of the condition known as dysphasia and its effects on language skills; (3) an explanation of the efficacy of dysphasia therapy: the vital role of volunteers, their induction and training for this specialised tuition; (4) an examination of the range of assessment procedures used by medical practitioners and their applicability to adult literacy and numeracy; (5) the assessments devised by the author for use with dysphasics; (6) an explanation of the need for student specific re-learning programmes and work materials, with particular reference to five case studies; and (7) an attempt to evaluate the success of dysphasia therapy and the ethical dilemma experienced by cross-professional approaches to re-education. The various chapters of the thesis combine to guide the educational practitioners along an avenue of rehabilitation not previously explored for sufferers of stroke or head injury.
Status: Individual research
Date of Research: 1991-continuing
KEYWORDS: *adult basic education; learning disabilities; neurological impairments; special educational needs; speech handicaps*

10/1676

School of Education, 42 Park Place, Cardiff CF1 3BB
01222 874000
Bird, J. Mr; *Supervisor:* Moss, G. Dr

An evaluation of information technology development strategies in South Glamorgan schools

Abstract: The introduction of the National Curriculum has meant a change of course for information technology (IT) education. Information Technology is now statutory and designed to be taught on a cross-curricular basis. The study will follow stages of implementation of IT into the curriculum. The research will be carried out at both primary and secondary levels and issues to be developed will be: local education authority (LEA) advisory roles; policy of school management; actual use; and attitudes of teachers. The research will need to be self-evolving in that the area is constantly undergoing change, and the pressures of time, resources and attitudinal difficulties.

Status: Individual research
Date of Research: 1991-1994
KEYWORDS: *cross curricular approach; curriculum development; information technology; National Curriculum*

10/1677
    School of Education, Senghennydd Road, Cardiff CF2 4AG
    01222 874000
    Loudon, M. Mrs; *Supervisor:* Allsobrook, D. Dr
Cardiff Collegiate Faculty of Education: provision of routes to graduate status for certificated teachers
Abstract: The research examines the significance of attainment of graduate status for participants – both providers and students.
Status: Individual research
Date of Research: 1985-1993
KEYWORDS: *B.Ed. degrees; graduates; student teachers; teacher certification; teacher education*

10/1678
    School of Education, Senghennydd Road, Cardiff CF2 4AG
    01222 874000
    Loudon, M. Mrs; Williamson, H. Dr;
    Supervisor: Davies, B. Prof.
Youth work curriculum in Wales
Abstract: The aim of this project is to inform the debate on the youth work curriculum in Wales. Twenty-five youth work settings were visited to elicit the views of youth workers and young people on current and future provision.
Status: Sponsored project
Source of Grant: Welsh Office £27,000
Date of Research: 1992-1993
KEYWORDS: *community organisations; youth; youth leaders; youth service*

10/1679
    School of Education, Senghennydd Road, Cardiff CF2 4AG
    01222 874000
    Howells, M. Miss; *Supervisor:* Donald, A. Dr
Training for the part-time youth service
Abstract: Most of the face-to-face work in the youth service is carried out by part-time workers. Therefore one way of ensuring good youth work is through the training of the part-time work force. This study describes the development of training for part-time youth work from the Albemarle report to the present, and sets it in the context of the aims of the youth service. Common elements in training are analysed. The social, economic and geographic background of Mid Glamorgan as an example, and the relationship of this with youth service provision are outlined. An investigation, based on a questionnaire and follow-up interview, of the perceptions of their training of 101 participants in the initial training course provided by the county over a period of four years is described. Issues such as the relationship between training and policies and practices; equal opportunities; and communications are discussed. Main findings were that for many of the respondents, the training increased self-confidence and paved the way to new opportunities in employment or in personal life; that the part-time workers concerned brought into the youth service a wide variety of skills which were not always used as fully as they might have been; and that, although there are interesting developments in new forms of training, course-based provision still has a valuable place.
Published Material: HOWELLS, M.J. & DONALD, A. (1992). The contribution made to the youth service by the interests and activities of part-time youth workers. Wales Youth Agency, Occasional Paper, March.
Status: Individual research
Date of Research: 1990-1993
KEYWORDS: *part time employment; training; youth service*

10/1680
    School of Education, 42 Park Place, Cardiff CF1 3BB
    01222 874000
    Edwards, M. Mr; *Supervisor:* Donald, A. Dr
The development, monitoring and evaluation of an advanced training course for part-time community education workers
Abstract: This action research/case study concerns the development, monitoring and evaluation of an advanced training course for part-

time youth and community workers in South East Wales. The study is designed to reflect on the participants' individual experiences in terms of personal and professional development in the circumstance of a Stage II training course. It attempts to place this innovative and unique course within the context of past and current local education authority training policy and practice. Qualitative data were gathered through participant observation; an analysis of student course journals; evaluation sheets; questionnaires; and tutor/participant meetings. The thesis concludes that there is a need for Welsh statutory youth services to consider the development of progressive training models based on consultation, negotiation and an acceptance of part-time youth worker training needs.
Published Material: LOUDON, M. & EDWARDS, M. (1989). 'The identification of inservice needs of part-time community education workers – a case study', Researching INSET, pp.104-109, September.
Status: Individual research
Date of Research: 1989-1993
KEYWORDS: *community organisations; training; youth leaders; youth service*

10/1681
    School of Education, 42 Park Place, Cardiff CF1 3BB
    01222 874000
    Rose, J. Mr; *Supervisor:* Donald, A. Dr
Youth work management policy to practice
Abstract: This study is an investigation into how youth work managers and full- and part-time youth workers within an identified local education authority translate their organisation's youth work policy into practice. It will be concerned with examining the consistency of practice throughout the organisation by trying to determine how quality standards are established and maintained for core elements of the youth work curriculum. It attempts to do this by identifying the political process by which policy is developed and then follows the interpretation of that policy through to the point of delivery with young people. Data are being collected from historical documents relating to policy discussion by the education sub-committee responsible for youth work; and through interviews with the chair of the relevant education sub-committee, assistant director of youth work, county adviser, part-time youth worker and young people. Questionnaires will also be used to obtain data from area youth workers, full-time youth workers, part-time youth workers and young people.
Status: Individual research
Date of Research: 1991-1993
KEYWORDS: *community organisations; policy; youth service*

10/1682
    School of Education, Senghennydd Road, Cardiff CF2 4AG
    01222 874000
    Al-Bassam, A. Mr; *Supervisor:* Richards, J. Dr
Educational resources allocation to primary schools in Saudi Arabia
Abstract: This is an investigation into the sources of education resources to state primary schools in Saudi Arabia, and the relationship with school quality.
Status: Sponsored project
Source of Grant: Saudi Arabian Government
Date of Research: 1991-1994
KEYWORDS: *educational finance; educational quality; primary schools; Saudi Arabia*

10/1683
    School of Education, Senghennydd Road, Cardiff CF2 4AG
    01222 874000
    Lapidot, R. Ms; *Supervisor:* Loudon, M. Mrs
Feminisation of teaching: a comparative study of Israel and Chile
Abstract: The mechanisms of feminisation will be examined and the effects on schools' socialising systems will be explored.
Status: Individual research
Date of Research: 1991-continuing
KEYWORDS: *Chile; comparative education; gender equality; Israel; women's education*

10/1684
    School of Education, 42 Park Place, Cardiff CF1 3BB
    01222 874000
    Gukhool, P. Ms; *Supervisor:* Aspinall, M. Ms

Social and psychological adjustment of educated married women in Mauritius
Abstract: The work concerns a study of the attitudes towards, and difficulties encountered by, educated working women in Mauritius. The investigation involved participatory observation, questionnaire and indepth questioning of some of the 120 respondents. These were women representing the different racial groups in Mauritius with the emphasis being upon those whose ancestors came from the Indian Sub-Continent, as for historic reasons family attitudes towards their participation in professional work has been slowest to change. Whilst it is being established that attitudes are changing, women are still meeting family and male hostility. However the actual results are not yet available.
Status: Individual research
Date of Research: 1987-1993
KEYWORDS: *gender equality; Mauritius; women's education; women's employment*

10/1685
School of Education, 42 Park Place, Cardiff CF1 3BB
01222 874000
Saunders, K. Ms; *Supervisor:* Aspinall, M. Ms
Women and education in Nepal
Abstract: The study examines teacher education and the structure of education in Nepal and questions whether policies will lead to equality in education and employment opportunities for girls and women. The research, spanning the years 1988-90, investigates the situation of female teachers living in Karnali Zone, a remote mountainous region of Mid-West Nepal. In addition, the lives of young girls from the Karnali area are highlighted. Restrictions in attendance at full-time formal school and the introduction of non-formal classes to meet the educational needs of 'out-of-school' girls are discussed. The researcher argues that traditional structures can obstruct equality and suggests that development agencies and educational policy makers sometimes perpetuate the status quo of inequality.
Status: Individual research
Date of Research: 1988-1993
KEYWORDS: *educational policy; equal education; gender equality; Nepal; women's education*

10/1686
School of Education, Senghennydd Road, Cardiff CF2 4AG
01222 874000
Nolan, R. Dr
Effectiveness of nurse teacher training related to experience since qualifying
Abstract: This project aims to determine how effective nurse teacher training at University of Wales College of Cardiff and elsewhere was in relation to experience. The sample comprises a random selection of nurse/midwifery teachers who qualified over the past four years taken from college records and via contacts from other centres.
Status: Individual research
Date of Research: 1992-1993
KEYWORDS: *nurse education; nurse teachers; programme effectiveness*

10/1687
School of Education, 42 Park Place, Cardiff CF1 3BB
01222 874000
Salkeld, T. Mrs; *Supervisor:* Sutton, R. Dr
The management of cross-curricular themes within the National Curriculum
Abstract: Currently there are five cross-curricular themes which have been identified as being the most pre-eminent and it is the management of these which is being researched. Curriculum Guidance No. 3 – 'The Whole Curriculum' (National Curriculum Council 1990) points to the importance of the themes being planned and coherent to ensure 'continuity and progression'. The aim of this research is to investigate how schools in Wales are managing staff, structures, teaching and learning to ensure cohesion. Questionnaires will be used to look at staffing structures and the methods used to manage the coordination of the themes. This in itself only indicates the presence of a framework and it will therefore also be necessary to research how learning is being managed. 'What takes place in the classroom?' will form an essential part of the research and will be investigated by a variety of methods. Interviews and questionnaires to both teachers and pupils will be used and examples of pupils' work will be sought.

It is recognised from the outset that in the current climate both schools and teachers may still be coming to grips with the necessary reorganisation to keep pace with the changes and therefore the findings of this research will not be finite, but will only reflect 'the current state of play'.
Published Material: SALKELD, T. & SUTTON, R.A. (1991). 'Introducing economic awareness', Economic Awareness, Vol 3, No 2, pp.22-25.
Status: Individual research
Date of Research: 1991-1994
KEYWORDS: *cross curricular approach; curriculum development; National Curriculum; school organisation; teaching methods; thematic approach*

10/1688
School of Education, Senghennydd Road, Cardiff CF2 4AG
01222 874000
Miller, G. Ms; *Supervisor:* Loudon, M. Mrs
Role, selection and preparation of unit head nurses
Abstract: The aim is to establish learning needs of head nurses. The study replicates that of Bergman et al 1980 in Israel. The application of role motivation theory will also be explored.
Status: Individual research
Date of Research: 1991-continuing
KEYWORDS: *nurse education; nurses*

10/1689
School of Education, Senghennydd Road, Cardiff CF2 4AG
01222 874000
Neary, M. Ms; Phillips, R. Ms; *Supervisor:* Davies, B. Prof.
The practitioner-teacher: a study in the introduction of mentors in the pre-registration nurse education programme
Abstract: The study has been commissioned by the Department of Health Research and Development Division on behalf of the Welsh Office Nursing Division. The rationale for the research therefore is to inform policy decision-making in order that policies on nursing practice and nurse education are based on empirical evidence. The study has two overall aims. Firstly, to explore how educationalists, managers and clinicians define and understand the role of the practitioner/teacher and secondly, to investigate the implementation and impact of the introduction of such student support systems. The nature and number of influences on the role of the practitioner/teacher and its enactment in different organisational contexts could not be clarified by a review of the literature. This factor, together with the customer's initial questions, required the use of both qualitative and quantitative methodologies. Initial qualitative methods (semi-structured focused interviews) are being complemented by quantitative instrumentation (student and mentor diaries and a questionnaire) thus pursuing data triangulation. Interviews are based on factors arising from the literature review and have been conducted with a range of staff, community-based and hospital-based, working in clinical areas throughout Wales where Project 2000 students will be placed during the Common Foundation Programme. The questionnaire content has been taken from the review of the literature and the initial data from the interviews and diaries. The research is being conducted on an all-Wales basis over a two year time period and is due for completion in February 1994.
Status: Sponsored project
Source of Grant: Department of Health £240,000
Date of Research: 1992-1994
KEYWORDS: *mentors; nurse education; nurse teachers*

10/1690
School of Education, 42 Park Place, Cardiff CF1 3BB
01222 874000
Kandeh, F. Mr; *Supervisor:* Sutton, R. Dr
Teaching, learning and educational technology: a case study of a sample of secondary schools in Sierra Leone
Abstract: Like most developing countries, Sierra Leone views a literate population with appropriate skills and relevant specialisms as a pre-requisite for national development. However, rapid population growth and a phenomenal expansion of both primary and secondary sectors, have in recent years continued to impose insurmountable strains on the weak and sick economy. Therefore much needs to be done to improve the efficiency and effectiveness of the teaching-learning process to justify government expenditure on education. This study finds that a growing level of inadequacies and constraints

restricting the teaching-learning process in general and in particular, the secondary sector of the educational system. Specific problems include: a) a growing degree of failure among candidates to satisfy examination requirements in primary and secondary examinations; b) the high rate of repeaters and dropouts – about 40% of pupils repeat or drop out before reaching form three of the secondary school system; c) a general dissatisfaction with secondary school products by employers. Using questionnaire and observation methods and a sample of form three secondary school pupils and teachers the research aims to determine: 1) the professional background, experience and qualification of teachers; 2) the attitudes of pupils towards learning; 3) to what extent availability of and in what ways audio-visual media are being used; 4) to what extent teachers employ the principles of educational technology in lesson planning and in the selection of appropriate teaching methodologies; 5) to what extent teachers in the sample have experience or have been trained in the use of various audio-visual media and attitudes towards its use; 6) the attitudes of teachers towards the application of a systematic approach to the design and development of lessons; and also their attitudes towards training for this.
Status: Individual research
Date of Research: 1989-1993
KEYWORDS: developing countries; educational improvement; secondary education; Sierra Leone

10/1691
School of Education, 42 Park Place, Cardiff CF1 3BB
01222 874000
Cardiff Institute of Higher Education, Faculty of Education, Cyncoed Centre, Cardiff CF2 6XZ
01222 551111
Rowlands, M. Mr; *Supervisor:* Sutton, R. Dr
Student teachers' conception of the nature of science and learning
Abstract: The aim of this research is to investigate any interrelationship between the construction of primary school student teachers' conceptions of the nature of science and the construction of their conceptions of teaching and learning. Case studies will be carried out of a small number of primary school student teachers during the period of their four-year teacher training course. Triangulation will be achieved by employing several techniques, including: observation of classroom interactions; interviews; and analysis of journals and teaching materials. Results will generate theories grounded in the data and illuminated by developments in the history, philosophy and sociology of science and science education.
Status: Individual research
Date of Research: 1992-continuing
KEYWORDS: philosophy of science; preservice teacher education; science education; scientific literacy; student teachers

10/1692
School of Education, Sengennhydd Road, Cardiff CF2 4AG
01222 874000
Nicosia General Hospital, School of Nursing, Nicosia
Antoniou, M. Miss; *Supervisor:* Nolan, R. Dr
The implications for nursing education in Cyprus commensurate with joining the European Community: a problem study
Abstract: The research aims to explore the changes required for nursing education in Cyprus commensurate with the EC directive re: nursing to be implemented in 1993. The study will compare nurse education in Cyprus with the changes in the United Kingdom in the implementation of Project 2000 and the need to conform to the EC directives as Cyprus has applied to join the European Community.
Status: Individual research
Date of Research: 1991-1994
KEYWORDS: change; Cyprus; nurse education

10/1693
School of Education, 42 Park Place, Cardiff CF1 3BB
01222 874000
University of Wales College of Medicine, Institute of Health Care Studies, Advanced Nursing Section, Heath Park, Cardiff CF4 4XW
01222 551111
Cardiff Institute of Higher Education, Faculty of Health and Community Studies, Llandaff Centre, Western Avenue, Cardiff CF5 2SG
01222 551111

Tope, R. Mrs; *Supervisor:* Sutton, R. Dr
Integrated interdisciplinary learning of the behavioural sciences in the health and social care professions: a feasibility study
Abstract: Integrated interdisciplinary education in health care and social care is a global issue. Maintaining health, preventing disease and caring for the sick is now so complex a problem that it is impossible for any single health profession to deliver quality care in isolation. In order to enhance an integrated interdisciplinary approach to health care a feasibility study has commenced which examines the behavioural sciences component within the curriculum of 14 health professions. Action research has been adopted as the appropriate methodology. To date a content analysis of the 14 curricula has been completed, which has revealed many potential areas for shared learning. A 'random' stratified sample of teaching staff (N=31) from each discipline, and a student from each year of each discipline (N=42) have been interviewed in order to ascertain their opinions of the potential for shared learning between all the professions. The information obtained from the literature review, the content analysis and the data generated from the structured interviews with the teaching staff and students has formed the basis of a questionnaire which will be distributed to all teaching staff (400) and all students (1,600) in March 1993. It is anticipated that the study will be completed by January 1994.
Status: Sponsored project
Source of Grant: S.E. Wales Inst. of Nursing and Midwifery Education and Cardiff Inst. of Higher Education £1,650; Smith & Nephew Education Scholarship £2,000; Welsh Office Grant £1,500
Date of Research: 1991-1994
KEYWORDS: behavioural sciences; health personnel; health services; interdisciplinary approach; medical education

Warwick University

10/1694
Centre for Education and Industry, Coventry CV4 7AL
01203 523523
Huddleston, P. Mrs; *Supervisor:* Woolhouse, J. Prof.;
Tomlinson, J. Prof.
The secondment of professional staff between education and industry
Abstract: The research is concerned with the professional development of outcomes of teacher secondments/placements into business and industry at both individual and institutional level. In particular, the impact of placement experiences on curriculum development is being investigated. The methodology includes questionnaire and personal interviews of teachers who have undertaken placements; longitudinal studies; core studies; and evaluation of placement studies.
Status: Sponsored project
Source of Grant: Goldsmiths' Company of London £165,000
Date of Research: 1988-1993
KEYWORDS: industrial secondments; industry-education relationship; teacher development

10/1695
Centre for Education and Industry, Coventry CV4 7AL
01203 523523
Richardson, W. Dr; Finegold, D. Dr
The education policies of large companies
Abstract: The project is an analysis of the education policies of large companies in the United Kingdom. Research methods include literature reviews (general and that of specific companies') and interviews with companies' managers. The research characterises the development of companies' education policies, how they are formulated and who is responsible for their operation. Analyses of results is presented in two ways: (a) stages of evolution in a company's relationship with education; (b) variables which shape company behaviour.
Published Material: RICHARDSON, W. & FINEGOLD, D. (1991). 'Making education our business', (interim report). Warwick: Warwick University.
Status: Sponsored project
Source of Grant: British Petroleum £100,000; Department for Education £12,500; Department of Employment £12,500
Date of Research: 1989-continuing
KEYWORDS: corporate education; industry-education relationship; labour force development

10/1696

Centre for Education and Industry, Coventry CV4 7AL
01203 523523
Richardson, W. Dr; Finegold, D. Dr

The relationship of curriculum and workplace change

Abstract: The research poses broad questions about the relationship between curriculum change and changes in skill deployment in the workplace. Specific stress is laid upon the need to incorporate research literature from a number of disciplines (political science, management studies, labour market studies, educational studies); and the main concern is closer analysis of the supply of skilled labour from education and the employers' demand for skilled labour.
Published Material: RICHARDSON, W. (1993). 'The changing nature of work: responses from education'. In WELLINGTON, J. (Ed). The education-work relationship for the future. London: Kogan Page.; RICHARDSON, W. (1994). 'School-business partnerships', The International Encyclopedia of Education. Oxford: Pergamon Press. (forthcoming).
Status: Sponsored project
Source of Grant: British Telecom; Department for Education; Department of Employment
Date of Research: 1990-continuing
KEYWORDS: *curriculum; employment; industry-education relationship; skills; work-education relationship*

10/1697

Centre for Education and Industry, Coventry CV4 7AL
01203 523523
Miller, A. Mr; *Supervisor:* Woolhouse, J. Prof.

Building effective school-business links

Abstract: In 1992 the Department for Education carried out a quantitative survey of school-business links during the 1991-92 academic year. The survey questionnaire was sent to a random sample of 865 primary and 554 secondary schools in England. At the same time a qualitative survey was commissioned from the Centre for Education and Industry, University of Warwick. A 'qualitative' questionnaire was sent to a 10% random sample of schools included in the main survey. The report based on the survey is unpublished and confidential to the Department. The second stage of the research involved joint visits by Her Majesty's Inspectorate (HMI) and researchers of the School Curriculum Industry Partnership Central Team to twenty schools. Six primary and six secondary schools were selected from the schools in the qualitative survey. They were supplemented with other schools identified by HMI as containing practice which would complement that found in the survey schools. Twenty case studies were written, based on the use of HMI criteria and methods of collecting evidence – interviews with staff and pupils; examination of samples of pupils' work and other documents; lesson observation; and interviews with business partners. The published report includes 'good practice' points that schools wishing to improve quality should consider, as well as numerous examples of good practice in school-business links.
Published Material: MILLER, A. (1993). Building effective school-business links: a practical guide to improving quality. London: Department for Education.
Status: Sponsored project
Source of Grant: Department for Education; Department of Employment; Esso PLC, jointly £75,000
Date of Research: 1991-1993
KEYWORDS: *cooperative programmes; industry-education relationship*

10/1698

Centre for Education and Industry, Coventry CV4 7AL
01203 523523
Richardson, W. Dr

Headteacher into industry programme: evaluation

Abstract: The Headteacher Into Industry programme is based at the University of Warwick. Since 1986 it has provided a structured, year-long secondment for headteachers and senior educationalists who wish to experience working for a major commercial or industrial organisation. During 1986-92, seventy-four participants went through the programme. The evaluation project is designed to assess the achievements of the programme and to identify themes for dissemination of practice. All participants will be surveyed by questionnaire and case material will be based around seven themes: 1) broadening the existing headteacher; 2) the potential headteacher; 3) school/college reorganisation and restructuring; 4) changing staff

roles and responsibilities; 5) the impact across a local education authority (LEA) or Training and Enterprise Council (TEC) area; 6) the impact on the company; and 7) 'knowledge transfer' between education and industry.
Status: Sponsored project
Source of Grant: Headteachers Into Industry Limited £10,000
Date of Research: 1993-1994
KEYWORDS: *head teachers; industrial secondments; industry education relationship; programme evaluation; secondments; teacher development*

10/1699

Centre for Education and Industry, Coventry CV4 7AL
01203 523523
Huddleston, P. Mrs; Anderson, J. Mrs

An evaluation of the pilot year of the School Associate Programme

Abstract: The evaluation commenced in January 1993 and covered two pilot School Associate Programmes in Essex and Durham. The focus of the evaluation: highlights potential strengths and weaknesses of the schemes; identifies good practice; and provides case study exemplars for dissemination. The evaluation involved a series of face-to-face interviews using semi-structured schedules with School Associates (business people working in schools), teacher mentors, headteachers, company training officers and project managers. Results highlight a wide range of practice and of opportunities for business people to work in schools. However, conclusions identify the need for appropriate recruitment, selection, induction and training of Associates. Management and ownership of the Programme by all parties is stressed and a need for better understanding of the culture of education and of business is important to maximise the potential of such exchanges.
Status: Sponsored project
Source of Grant: Paul Hamlyn Foundation £12,450
Date of Research: 1993-1993
KEYWORDS: *cooperative programmes; industry-education relationship; programme evaluation; secondments*

10/1700

Centre for Education and Industry, Coventry CV4 7AL
01203 523523
Woolhouse, J. Prof.; Richardson, W. Dr; Huddleston, P. Mrs

British Petroleum's 'Aiming for a College Education' initiative: evaluation

Abstract: British Petroleum's 'Aiming for a College Education' (ACE) initiative is a 5-year programme based in London, Glasgow and West Glamorgan. The initiative is designed to stimulate participation in post-compulsory education and training by young people in the three communities and to disseminate programme lessons nationally. The initiative, which runs from 1990-95, has a budget of three million pounds. Individual evaluations of the programmes in London and West Glamorgan will be carried out, and an evaluation of the entire initiative undertaken by researchers from Warwick University. Evaluation reports are available from the Centre for Education and Industry at the University.
Status: Sponsored project
Source of Grant: British Petroleum PLC £115,000
Date of Research: 1990-continuing
KEYWORDS: *access to education; further education; programme evaluation; sixteen to nineteen education*

10/1701

Centre for Education and Industry, Coventry CV4 7AL
01203 523523
Huddleston, P. Mrs; Anderson, J. Mrs

An evaluation of the Teacher Placement Service 1992-1994

Abstract: The study is concerned with an examination of the Teacher Placement Service and its operation in two English regions and in Wales. It looks at: pre-placement issues such as objective setting and selection of host organisation; developments in schools, both curricular and management; and at the cultural climate in which change is occurring. The main sources of data are responses from mailed-out questionnaires, semi-structured telephone interviews and a number of case studies. This longitudinal study tracks two cohorts of teachers (204 and 178 respectively) over a two-year period – before, immediately after, six months after, and one year after placement. Early results indicate that placements offer a wide variety of opportunities

to teachers for personal and professional development. Placements are still not being identified within the institutional development plan of schools, nor do they feature significantly in appraisal. There is evidence of curriculum development resulting from placements, and placements can offer training development opportunities for teachers wishing to deliver the new vocational qualifications.
Status: Sponsored project
Source of Grant: Department of Employment £37,510
Date of Research: 1992-1994
KEYWORDS: *industrial secondments; industry-education relationship; secondments; teacher development*

10/1702

Centre for Educational Development, Appraisal and
Research, Coventry CV4 7AL
01203 523523
Burgess, R. Prof.; Pole, C. Dr; Sprokkereef, A. Ms
Becoming a postgraduate science student
Abstract: This project examines postgraduate training in three disciplinary fields in the sciences: physics, mathematics, and engineering. The key issue to be addressed is: what is the process of becoming a postgraduate science student? Case study data will be collected regarding the first year of postgraduate training in nine departments in the United Kingdom, three in each discipline examined. The aims and objectives of the project are: (1) To provide data on the process of socialization in the first year of postgraduate study. Among the themes to be covered will be: student choice and selection; admission procedures; the selection and focusing of a research topic; taught course work; supervision; monitoring; and assessment. (2) To provide evidence on the range of postgraduate training in the light of the data obtained above. (3) To compare the different types of research training within and between disciplines. (4) To explore the implications of the research evidence for policy and practice regarding research training in the natural sciences in the United Kingdom. The main method of social investigation will be through unstructured interviews and observation. The research will result in nine departmental case studies; three disciplinary case studies; and a thematic report. In the latter comparisons will be made with the work conducted by the Centre for Educational Development, Appraisal and Research (CEDAR) on first year social science postgraduate students.
Status: Sponsored project
Source of Grant: Economic and Social Research Council
Date of Research: 1992-1994
KEYWORDS: *graduate study; graduates; science education*

10/1703

Centre for Educational Development, Appraisal and
Research, Coventry CV4 7AL
01203 523523
Burgess, R. Prof.; Morrison, M. Ms
Teaching and learning about food and nutrition in school: the nation's diet initiative
Abstract: The research is an exploratory case study on teaching and learning about food and nutrition in two primary and two secondary schools. The aim is to examine age, gender, ethnicity and social class in relation to food consumption. It will also contribute more broadly to studies on socialisation and attitude formation, and the use of case study methodology in the sociology of education. Included in the study will be an exploration of the implications of the research evidence for policy and practice on teaching and learning about food and nutrition in schools.
Status: Sponsored project
Source of Grant: Economic and Social Research Council
Date of Research: 1993-1994
KEYWORDS: *eating habits; food; health education; nutrition education*

10/1704

Centre for Educational Development, Appraisal and
Research, Coventry CV4 7AL
01203 523523
Burgess, R. Prof.; Galloway, S. Ms; Morrison, M. Ms
Supply teaching: an investigation of policy, processes and people in English schools
Abstract: The aims of the project are to investigate, at several levels, the provision of cover for teachers absent from their classes for a variety of reasons. The research involves identification of national

and local policies; examination of practice at institutional and classroom levels, and assessment of the impact and role of supply cover; and draws on the experiences of those closely involved, i.e. teachers, pupils, and supply staff.
Status: Sponsored project
Source of Grant: Leverhulme Trust £48,281
Date of Research: 1991-1992
KEYWORDS: *substitute teachers; teacher employment; teaching profession*

10/1705

Centre for Educational Development, Appraisal and
Research, Coventry CV4 7AL
01203 523523
Burgess, R. Prof.; Morrison, M. Ms; Scott, D. Dr
The role of the library in the primary school
Abstract: The central concern of this project is the role of the primary school library, and the extent to which it is being shaped by major curricular changes, new patterns of managing resources and developing educational philosophy. Quantitative and qualitative methods will be used to focus on the library as a resource to support the primary curriculum, and in relation to changing teaching and learning styles.
Status: Sponsored project
Source of Grant: The British Library £58,400
Date of Research: 1991-1992
KEYWORDS: *library role; primary schools; school libraries*

10/1706

Centre for Educational Development, Appraisal and
Research, Coventry CV4 7AL
01203 523523
Kehily, M. Ms; *Supervisor:* Burgess, R. Prof.
Schoolteacher appraisal
Abstract: The research project aims to be a qualitative study of schoolteacher appraisal as it has been implemented and developed in primary schools. It is anticipated that an indepth study of three schools will be conducted using a range of qualitative research methods, such as participant observation, interviews with teachers and headteachers, and analysis of school documents. The research project intends to produce course materials for teachers, based on the research evidence, to aid the professional development of teachers in this area.
Status: Sponsored project
Source of Grant: Warwick University
Date of Research: 1993-1994
KEYWORDS: *primary school teachers; teacher development; teacher evaluation; teaching profession*

10/1707

Centre for English Language Teaching, Coventry CV4 7AL
01203 523523
Nesi, H. Ms; Tsai, C. Ms
The development and evaluation of online computer-assisted language learning materials for English for academic purposes
Abstract: The proposed project is to build up a coherent package of English language learning materials which can be accessed by non-native speaker students via the Warwick University network. The programs intended for use are commercially produced, but will be 'authored' by the Centre for English Language Teaching (CELT) staff, with due regard for the students' subject specialisms and levels of expertise. It is anticipated that students will be introduced to the first phase of materials at the beginning of the 1992-1993 academic session, and the use made of the materials will then be monitored by means of Warwick University's Novell 1.12 Netware package, supplemented by questionnaires and interviews with selected subjects. The aim is to discover which types of Computer Assisted Language Learning (CALL) activity are (a) used most frequently; and (b) judged to be most effective by university-level learners of English for academic purposes. In further phases of the project the intention is to expand and modify the materials in accordance with these findings.
Status: Individual research
Date of Research: 1992-1993
KEYWORDS: *computer assisted language learning; English – second language; English for academic purposes; overseas students; second language learning*

10/1708
> Centre for English Language Teaching, Coventry CV4 7AL
> 01203 523523
> Karavas, E. Ms; *Supervisor:* Khan, J. Ms

English language teaching curriculum renewal in Greek secondary schools: the teachers' response
Abstract: The research focuses on the Greek English language teachers' response to a new English language course that was recently implemented in Greek secondary schools. The course is based on a weak version of the communicative learner-centred approach. The aims of the research are: a) to investigate the impact of the course on teachers' classroom behaviour; and b) to assess teachers' educational attitudes. Classroom observation and interviews are being used in order to fulfil the first aim. Questionnaires are being used in relation to the second aim.
Status: Individual research
Date of Research: 1990-1993
KEYWORDS: *English – second language; Greece*

10/1709
> Centre for Research in Ethnic Relations, Coventry CV4 7AL
> 01203 523523
> Taylor, P. Mr

Ethnic minorities in higher education
Abstract: The main aims of the project are to: (1) obtain greater knowledge of ethnic minority participation in higher education; (2) study the perceptions formed by these students; and (3) consider the role of higher education institutions in the continuation of discrimination. In order to pursue these aims several different institutions are being studied. Data obtained from various sources (including the Universities Central Council for Admissions (UCCA)) were used to study participation. Consideration of students' experiences and perceptions of higher education will be facilitated by interview and survey material. These studies are to be placed in the context of the institutional policies and practices which affect students, in particular ethnic minorities
Published Material: TAYLOR, P. (1992). 'Ethnic group data and application to higher education', Higher Education Quarterly, Autumn.; TAYLOR, P. (1992). 'Ethnic group data for university entry', Project report for the Committee of Vice-Chancellors and Principals, Coventry: Centre for Research in Ethnic Relations.
Status: Sponsored project
Source of Grant: Economic and Social Research Council
Date of Research: 1991-1993
KEYWORDS: *educational discrimination; ethnic groups; higher education; student recruitment*

10/1710
> Centre for Research in Ethnic Relations, Coventry CV4 7AL
> 01203 523523
> Hyder, K. Mrs

The effects of the Education Reform Act 1988 on black communities
Abstract: Pupils of Caribbean background have a long history of educational disadvantage in Britain. The main aim of the study is to examine developments in local authorities and their schools which arise from the Education Reform Act 1988 and which may further disadvantage black pupils. Advantages, disadvantages and the overall effect of the Act will be investigated using a questionnaire to be circulated to all local education authorities in 1993. A second aim of the study is to look in detail at the process of assessment. This is one of the few aspects of the Act with potential benefits for black pupils. The project will examine the hypothesis that the structures and networks developed for assessment will be used by authorities and schools to monitor and respond to inequalities. The third aim is to observe classroom teaching and assessment in order to clarify the more controversial causes of 'underachievement/achievement'. Particular attention will be paid to the role of teacher knowledge and awareness of black children's backgrounds and the mechanisms through which these inform teaching processes and influence academic success. For the second and third aims, the research will focus on a sample of Year Two learners in schools in two authorities. Research methods will include classroom observations and interviews of teachers, pupils and parents.
Status: Sponsored project
Source of Grant: Economic and Social Research Council
Date of Research: 1992-1993
KEYWORDS: *achievement; Afro Caribbean youth; assessment; black pupils; Education Reform Act 1988; equal education; ethnic groups; low achievement*

10/1711
> Department of Continuing Education, Continuing Education Research Centre, Coventry CV4 7AL
> 01203 523523
> Duke, C. Prof.

Continuing education and organisation change in universities
Abstract: This is a study of change in university continuing education in Britain as a window into change in higher education generally. The traditional, often marginalised, extramural departments are giving way to new structures and arrangements. Continuing education is gaining a much wider meaning and being 'mainstreamed' in policy and organisation. The research studies these trends and processes, and considers implications for higher education generally.
Published Material: DUKE, C. (1991). 'Restructuring for better service in continuing university education', New Education, Vol 13, No 1, pp.57-68.; DUKE, C. (1991). 'University continuing education: identities, prospects and perspectives'. In: FIELDHOUSE, R. (Ed). The organisation of Continuing Education in Universities. UDACE.; DUKE, C. (1991). 'Lifelong education and the universities of the United Kingdom', Higher Education in Europe, Vol XVI, No 1, pp.46-55.
Status: Sponsored project
Source of Grant: Universities Funding Council £30,000; Training, Enterprise & Education Directorate
Date of Research: 1990-1993
KEYWORDS: *adult education; continuing education; higher education; organisational change; universities*

10/1712
> Department of Continuing Education, Continuing Education Research Centre, Coventry CV4 7AL
> 01203 523523
> Leicester, M. Dr; Lovell, T. Ms

Race and continuing education
Abstract: In 1990, the Universities Funding Council for Adult Continuing Education received a report from its working party on education for minority ethnic communities. The research is concerned to monitor the extent to which University Departments of Continuing Education have responded to the recommendations of the report, and will also evaluate other identified initiatives designed to meet the needs of minority ethnic communities.
Status: Sponsored project
Source of Grant: Universities Funding Council
Date of Research: 1990-1992
KEYWORDS: *adult education; continuing education; equal education; minority groups*

10/1713
> Department of Continuing Education, Continuing Education Research Centre, Coventry CV4 7AL
> 01203 523523
> Field, J. Dr

The educational thinking of the environmentalist movement
Abstract: The study is concerned with three educational dimensions of the Green movement; (1) the formal policies for education developed by Green and environmentalist organisations; (2) the formal education provision offered to members and supporters within those organisations; and (3) the informal learning undertaken by members and supporters through their daily practice. Methodologically, the work uses a biographical approach to the individual, combined with documentary analysis. It is comparative in nature.
Published Material: FIELD, J. (1990). The educational policies of the West German Greens. London: Association for Recurrent Education.; FIELD, J. (Ed). (1991). Adult education and Die Grunen: extracts and commentary. University of Warwick: University of Warwick Discussion Papers in Continuing Education.
Date of Research: 1989-continuing
KEYWORDS: *conservation – environment; environmental education; pressure groups*

10/1714
> Department of Continuing Education, Continuing Education Research Centre, Coventry CV4 7AL
> 01203 523523
> Leicester, M. Dr; Lovell, T. Ms

Disability voice: towards an enabling education
Abstract: The aim of the project is to investigate the experience of

people with a range of 'disabilities', and the parents of special children, particularly their experience of education, continuing education and training. The investigation is by indepth interviews (about 30 and 10 respectively). The social theory of disability provides a theoretical framework. The researchers have relevant personal and professional experience. The intention is to produce a book drawing on the interview data which will contribute towards an enabling conception of education.
Status: Sponsored project
Source of Grant: Warwick University
Date of Research: 1993-1994
KEYWORDS: disabilities; equal education; special educational needs

10/1715

Department of Education, Coventry CV4 7AL
01203 523523
Abbott, I. Mr
The City Technology College initiative with particular reference to the establishment of a City Technology College on Teesside
Abstract: The study aims to assess the effectiveness and impact of a city technology college on the educational system of a deprived urban area, particularly the effect the college will have on the local education authority schools within the locality. The means of collecting data will include indepth interviews, observation and the use of questionnaires and surveys. Specifically extensive contacts have been made with the institutions and individuals involved in this process. It is expected that a wide range of issues will be identified including the role of the industrial sponsors, the position of the local authority, the effect on schools and colleges, the response of teachers and the impact on parents, pupils and staff involved in the college. The study will be looking at a rapidly developing area and it is expected that it will provide data which will be of use in determining future policy decisions.
Published Material: ABBOTT, I.D. (1991). 'British and American approaches to science and technology', Education and Training, Vol 33, No 1, pp.5-7.; ABBOTT, I.D. (1991). 'School industry links: an American perspective', Head Teachers Review, pp.10-12, Winter.
Status: Individual research
Date of Research: 1989-1993
KEYWORDS: city technology colleges; disadvantaged environment; industry-education relationship; school-community relationship

10/1716

Department of Education, Coventry CV4 7AL
01203 523523
Johnson, S. Mr; *Supervisor:* Gardner, P. Mr
The concept of skill and its implications for education
Abstract: A philosophical inquiry into the nature of skills, the dominance of skill-talk in contemporary education, and the ways skills are classified, with special concern for the nature and definition of basic, general, generic and transferable skills. The inquiry will also involve a consideration of thinking skills and critical thinking as well as the extent to which virtues can be reduced to and taught as skills.
Published Material:
Status: Individual research
Date of Research: 1988-1994
KEYWORDS: basic skills; critical thinking; educational philosophy; problem solving; skills; transfer of learning

10/1717

Department of Education, Coventry CV4 7AL
01203 523523
Lewis, A. Dr
Communication between non-handicapped children and pupils with severe learning difficulties
Abstract: This research is investigating the nature of communication between non-handicapped (NH) children and pupils with severe learning difficulties (SLD). The children interact in dyads or triads and each group comprises at least one NH and one SLD child. NH-SLD interaction has been video-recorded for approximately 60 minutes each week throughout a year of weekly integration sessions. Thirty-six NH children (ages ten years, one month to eleven years, one month at the start of the year) and nine pupils with SLD (ages twelve years, four months to fifteen years, eight months at the start of the year) have been involved. Analyses of data is being carried out utilising frameworks developed in an earlier study (Lewis and Carpenter, 1990; Lewis, 1990) involving younger children in NH-SLD dyads.

Published Material: LEWIS, A. (1990). 'Six and seven year old 'normal' children's talk to peers with severe learning difficulties', European Journal of Special Needs Education, Vol 5, No 1, pp.13-23.; LEWIS, A. & CARPENTER, B. (1990). 'Discourse, in an integrated school setting, between six and seven year old non-handicapped children and peers with severe learning difficulties'. In: FRASER, W.I. (Ed). Key issues in mental retardation. London: Routledge.; LEWIS, A. (1991). 'Entitled to learn together?'. In: ASHDOWN, R., CARPENTER, B. & BOVAIR, K. (Eds). Meeting the curriculum challenge. Lewes: Falmer Press.; LEWIS, A. (1994). Children's understanding of disability. London: Routledge.
Status: Sponsored project
Source of Grant: Warwick University: Research and Innovations Fund £1,300
Date of Research: 1990-1993
KEYWORDS: communication research; integration studies; severe learning difficulties; special educational needs; verbal communication

10/1718

Department of Education, Coventry CV4 7AL
01203 523523
Lewis, A. Dr
Primary school children's understanding of severe learning difficulties
Abstract: This research investigated non-handicapped (NH) children's understanding of the nature of severe learning difficulties (SLD). The literature on social cognition was reviewed in order to identify developmental changes during middle childhood in understanding about others. As a result of this review two questions about children's understanding of SLD were identified. These two questions were: which cues of SLD are salient for NH children, and do NH children recognise the irrevocability of SLD? Two age groups, 7 and 11 year olds, were selected for interview because research on social cognition (Aboud, 1988; Schneider, 1991) suggests that there will be marked differences between these two age groups in terms of their understanding of SLD. Nineteen 7 year olds (mean age seven years, two months) were interviewed individually. Thirty-two 11 year olds (mean age eleven years, one month) were interviewed in small friendship groups of four children. All children interviewed had participated in integration projects involving children with SLD. Findings indicated that the 7 year olds were confused about the nature of SLD and tended to believe that children with SLD had transitory sensory, but not cognitive, impairments. The 11 year olds also misunderstood the nature of SLD although they were clearer than the younger children about the irrevocability of SLD. For the 11 year olds, intra-SLD group, as well as inter group (SLD-NH), differences were recognised. These findings are consistent with research into the development of other aspects of social cognition, for example, children's understanding of gender and race.
Published Material: LEWIS, A. (1992). 'Group child interviews as a research tool', British Educational Research Journal, Vol 18, No 4, pp.413-421.; LEWIS, A. (1993). 'Integration, education and rights', British Educational Research Journal, Vol 19, No 3, pp.291-302.; LEWIS, A. (1993). 'Primary school children's understanding of severe learning difficulties', Educational Psychology, Vol 13, No 2, pp.133-145.; LEWIS, A. (1994). Children's understanding of disability. London: Routledge.
Status: Individual research
Date of Research: 1990-1993
KEYWORDS: children; comprehension; integration studies; severe learning difficulties; special educational needs

10/1719

Department of Education, Coventry CV4 7AL
01203 523523
Raban, B. Prof.
Evaluation of the National Curriculum core subjects (English) at key stages 1, 2 and 3
Abstract: The aim of this National Curriculum Council (NCC) monitoring programme is to ensure that problems which teachers are facing in implementing National Curriculum English are fully understood to discover: whether the difficulty lies in the Order; whether it is a question of teacher knowledge and understanding; or whether statement(s) of attainment are pitched inappropriately for pupils within a particular key stage. An analysis of the English Orders will provide a conceptual and practical framework for fieldwork in schools. Between 70-80 schools will be visited in 10 local education authorities (LEAs) throughout England. Teachers, parents and governors will be interviewed. Class-

rooms will be observed and school documents inspected. Access to key stage 1 standard assessment task data, examples of pupils' work and interviews with LEA personnel will form the body of evidence required to address the issues specified by the NCC.
Status: Sponsored project
Source of Grant: National Curriculum Council £377,000
Date of Research: 1991-1993
KEYWORDS: English studies curriculum; evaluation; monitoring; National Curriculum

10/1720
> Department of Education, Coventry CV4 7AL
> 01203 523523
> Richardson, W. Dr

Participation in education and training: age group 16-19
Abstract: A research seminar will convene on six occasions over two years. Six designated themes are identified: (1) determinants of individuals decisions; (2) qualifications as a predictor of post education destination; (3) funding structures; (4) the status of qualifications; (5) access; (6) quality in teaching and learning
Status: Sponsored project
Source of Grant: Economic and Social Research Council £7,500
Date of Research: 1992-1993
KEYWORDS: access to education; further education; sixteen to nineteen education; student participation; tertiary education; vocational education

10/1721
> Department of Education, Coventry CV4 7AL
> 01203 523523
> Packwood, A. Ms; *Supervisor:* Raban, B. Prof.

Metaphor as discourse strategy in teacher education
Abstract: A constructivist approach to metaphor has been used to develop an analytic framework. This is then being tested within the context of the discourse analysis of teachers in a classroom situation. The framework of metaphoric analysis will then be evaluated and refined.
Status: Individual research
Date of Research: 1991-1994
KEYWORDS: classroom communication; discourse analysis; metaphors; teacher education

10/1722
> Department of Education, Coventry CV4 7AL
> 01203 523523
> Troyna, B. Dr

Local Management of Schools and racial equality
Abstract: The research explores how the recent educational reforms have affected the status of (and commitment to) racial equality issues in a local education authority and a sample of its secondary schools.
Status: Sponsored project
Source of Grant: Commission for Racial Equality £33,000
Date of Research: 1992-1993
KEYWORDS: equal education; local management of schools; racial discrimination; racial integration; school based management; secondary schools

10/1723
> Department of Education, Coventry CV4 7AL
> 01203 523523
> Troyna, B. Dr; Siraj-Blatchford, I. Ms

Racial equality and initial teacher education
Abstract: Three case studies of initial teacher education institutions will be undertaken. Using multiple data collection procedures the research will try to establish the salience of racial equality in these institutions.
Status: Sponsored project
Source of Grant: Leverhulme Trust £33,000
Date of Research: 1993-1994
KEYWORDS: equal education; institutes of higher education; preservice teacher education; racial discrimination; racial integration

10/1724
> Department of Education, Coventry CV4 7AL
> 01203 523523
> Gardner, P. Mr

Ethical absolutism and education
Abstract: A consideration of the implications of ethical absolutism for moral education, especially in a multicultural society.
Published Material: GARDNER, P. (1992). 'Propositional attitudes and multicultural education, or believing others are mistaken'. In: HORTON, J. & NICHOLSON, P. (Eds). Tolerance: philosophy and practice. Aldershot: Avebury Press.; GARDNER, P. (1993). 'Ethical absolutism and moral education', Royal Institute of Philosophy Lectures. Cambridge: Cambridge University Press. (forthcoming).
Status: Individual research
Date of Research: 1992-continuing
KEYWORDS: ethics; moral education; multiculturalism; relativism – philosophy

10/1725
> Department of Education, Coventry CV4 7AL
> 01203 523523
> Gardner, P. Mr

Tolerance and education
Abstract: An inquiry into the nature, value and relevance of tolerance in education today.
Published Material: GARDNER, P. (1992). 'Propositional attitudes and multicultural education, or believing others are mistaken'. In: HORTON, J. & NICHOLSON, P. (Eds). Tolerance: philosophy and practice. Aldershot: Avebury Press.; GARDNER, P. (1993). 'Tolerance and education'. In: HORTON, J. (Ed). Liberalism, multiculturalism and toleration. London: Macmillan.
Status: Individual research
Date of Research: 1992-continuing
KEYWORDS: attitudes; educational principles

10/1726
> Department of Education, Coventry CV4 7AL
> 01203 523523
> Gardner, P. Mr; Pickering, J. Dr

Mature students and higher education
Abstract: Research into how mature students at university perceive younger undergraduates; how they get on in halls of residence; and how course selectors view mature students.
Published Material: GARDNER, P. & PICKERING, J. (1991). 'Learning with yuppies: or, on counselling mature students', Pastoral Care in Education, Vol 9, No 1, pp.13-19.; GARDNER, P. & PICKERING, J. (1992). 'Learning to live with Madonna: or mature students on campus', Pastoral Care in Education, Vol 10, No 4, pp.3-8.; PICKERING, J. & GARDNER, P. (1992). 'Access: a selector's perspective', Journal of Access Studies, Vol 7, No 2, pp.220-233.
Status: Individual research
Date of Research: 1992-continuing
KEYWORDS: access to education; higher education; mature students; student attitudes; student housing; student recruitment

10/1727
> Department of Education, Coventry CV4 7AL
> 01203 523523
> Sikes, P. Dr

Motherhood and teaching: a life history investigation
Abstract: Traditionally, it has been seen as 'natural' for women teachers to work with young children and to adopt a mother/teacher role. The research focuses on the perceptions and experiences of female primary school teachers and asks such questions as: how do mother teachers perceive their role; whether they felt there were any links between being a mother and being a teacher and if so what these are and whether or not they felt they affected the way they do their job. The research uses life history method. The sample consists of approximately 15 women. Around one-third are mature students with children on a teacher training course. The reason for including them is to discover whether motherhood had, in any way, motivated them to become teachers. The rest of the sample are practising teachers who were childless when they started teaching. As yet no conclusions have been formally drawn.
Status: Sponsored project
Source of Grant: Warwick University: Research and Innovations Fund £400
Date of Research: 1991-continuing
KEYWORDS: mothers; teacher attitudes; teacher background; teacher role; teaching profession; women teachers

10/1728

Department of Education, Coventry CV4 7AL
01203 523523
Phillips, G. Mr; *Supervisor:* Gardner, P. Mr

Moral principles and moral education

Abstract: An enquiry into the nature of objectivity in morality and moral education which includes a critical consideration of ethical subjectivism, relativism and proceduralism. The inquiry concentrates in the main on moral realism and considers the extent to which moral realism can withstand the objections of its critics and can provide an account of the provability and nature of moral knowledge and a secure foundation for moral education.

Published Material: PHILLIPS, G. (1991). 'Personal, social and moral education'. In: ENTWISTLE, N. (Ed) A Handbook of Educational Ideas. London: Croom Helm.

Status: Individual research
Date of Research: 1987-1993
KEYWORDS: *educational philosophy; ethics; moral education; moral values; realism; reasoning*

10/1729

Department of Education, Coventry CV4 7AL
01203 523523
Birke, L. Dr; Barr, J. Ms

Women and scientific literacy

Abstract: The project is mapping the extent of understanding in science and science policy among women with particular attention to ways in which women may have some scientific knowledge but do not identify it as such; and is identifying those issues within science which are of particular interest – actual and potential – to women who have no previous experience of higher education. Outcomes are oriented towards the development of policy and practice, and will be tested through a number of pilot courses.

Status: Sponsored project
Source of Grant: Universities Funding Council
Date of Research: 1990-continuing
KEYWORDS: *higher education; science education; scientific literacy; women*

10/1730

Department of Education, Coventry CV4 7AL
01203 523523
Brooks, V. Dr

An evaluation of the impact of Education 2000 on three Coventry schools

Abstract: Education 2000 is a charitable trust. Three Coventry schools submitted a successful bid to become one of its inner city initiatives. The Coventry project has targeted five areas for development in the schools: new technology; links with industry; staff development; the local community; and curriculum innovation. An independent evaluation of the impact of the project on the three schools is being undertaken using interviews with key project personnel and a whole-school evaluation exercise. All academic staff will contribute to this both individually and as part of a departmental/faculty response.

Status: Sponsored project
Source of Grant: Education 2000 in Coventry
Date of Research: 1993-1994
KEYWORDS: *educational innovation; programme evaluation; urban schools; whole school approach*

10/1731

Department of Education, Coventry CV4 7AL
01203 523523
Sikes, P. Dr

Coverage of equal opportunities in school-based initial teacher education

Abstract: Research suggests that equal opportunities receive limited coverage on initial teacher education (ITE) courses which are based in institutions of higher education (HEI). There is also considerable evidence to suggest that equal opportunities issues frequently are given marginal attention in schools and are even viewed with hostility by some teachers. This research is seeking to investigate views on equal opportunities held by students following a post graduate certificate in education (PGCE) course. It also looks at the input on equal opportunities they receive in their HEI and teaching practice schools. At present the research involves a cohort of approximately 200 students.

At one HEI around 170 of these students are on a school-based secondary PGCE course, the remainder are following a conventional primary PGCE course. Research methods include questionnaire, interview, non-participant observation and documentary analysis.

Status: Individual research
Date of Research: 1993-continuing
KEYWORDS: *equal education; postgraduate certificate in education; preservice teacher education; school based teacher education; student teacher attitudes*

10/1732

Department of Education, Coventry CV4 7AL
01203 523523
Lewis, A. Dr; Halpin, D. Dr

The implementation of the National Curriculum in special schools

Abstract: An exploration of the form and content of the National Curriculum as implemented in a cross-section of special schools (moderate learning difficulties (MLD), severe learning difficulties (SLD), and emotional and behaviour disorders (EBD) in three local education authorities. Data are being collected through interviews with headteachers and analyses of school documentation, notably school development plans and curricular policy statements. Analyses will focus on implicit underlying principles concerning the nature of special education.

Status: Sponsored project
Source of Grant: Warwick University £800
Date of Research: 1993-1994
KEYWORDS: *National Curriculum; special educational needs; special schools*

10/1733

Department of Education, Coventry CV4 7AL
01203 523523
Costley, D. Ms; *Supervisor:* Lewis, A. Dr

Special school curriculum and the National Curriculum

Abstract: This research aims to analyse the impact of the National Curriculum on the curriculum offered to, and experienced by, young people in special schools for pupils with moderate learning difficulties (MLD). It will focus specifically on pupils at key stage 4. Data collection will involve: 1) a questionnaire survey of a random sample of MLD schools in England; and 2) case studies of all the MLD schools (n=4) in one urban local education authority (LEA). Case study information will be collected through interviews with key personnel, parents and pupils, school and classroom observation and documentation analyses. From these data it is hoped to construct a theoretical model of the MLD school curriculum which will illuminate the process of curricular change in special education.

Status: Individual research
Date of Research: 1993-continuing
KEYWORDS: *moderate learning difficulties; National Curriculum; special educational needs; special schools*

10/1734

Department of Education, Coventry CV4 7AL
01203 523523
English, M. Miss; *Supervisor:* Lewis, A. Dr; Raban, B. Prof.

Young children's knowledge and application of language

Abstract: This is a comparative study of young children (age 4-8) involved in paired cooperative activities in infant school classes in England and Eire. The total sample for each country will comprise thirty-six children, twelve at each of three key age groups – 4, 6 and 8 years. Within each age group, six pairs of children will be observed during paired work on tasks routinely found in infant classrooms. Pairings will control for sex and friendship. Analyses of interaction will focus on the use of specific cooperative strategies. Findings will be related to the messages about cooperative learning embodied in key primary curriculum documents in England and Eire.

Status: Individual research
Date of Research: 1992-continuing
KEYWORDS: *child language; comparative education; group work; infant school pupils; verbal communication*

10/1735

Department of Education, Coventry CV4 7AL
01203 523523
Brooks, V. Dr

The role of mentoring in the revised postgraduate certificate in education (PGCE) secondary course at Warwick University
Abstract: Much of the existing work on mentoring is theoretical in nature. The aim of this study is to consider mentoring in practice by focusing on the experiences and perceptions of practising mentors. Fifteen interviews were conducted, ten with mentors and five with mentees. A five-page questionnaire was despatched to all of the mentors (approximately one hundred and forty) working in partnership with Warwick University on the Postgraduate Certificate in Education (Secondary) course. Two produced a 91% response rate.
Status: Sponsored project
Source of Grant: Comino Foundation
Date of Research: 1992-continuing
KEYWORDS: mentors; preservice teacher education; school based teacher education; student teacher supervisors

10/1736
Department of Education, Coventry CV4 7AL
01203 523523
Stirling, M. Mrs; *Supervisor:* Gardner, F. Dr;
Lloyd-Smith, M. Mr
Policy and provision for pupils excluded from school during the implementation of the Education Reform Act 1988
Abstract: A case study of patterns of exclusion in a single, large, metropolitan education authority. It will include an analysis of the way in which the legislation governing pupil exclusion has been: a) interpreted and b) affected by other legislation including the Education Reform Act 1988 and the Education Act 1993. An important focus of the research will be the alternative provision made for excluded pupils and the fate of those for whom no provision is available. Data will be obtained primarily from interviews with key professionals who are involved in the exclusion process and others who have direct contact with excludees (representatives of mainstream schools, educational psychology services, behaviour support teams, social services departments and local education authority officers).
Published Material: STIRLING, M. (1991). 'Absent with leave', Special Children, Vol 52, pp.10-13.; STIRLING, M. (1992). 'How many pupils are being excluded?', British Journal of Special Education, Vol 19, No 4, pp.128-130.
Status: Individual research
Date of Research: 1992-continuing
KEYWORDS: educational legislation; educational policy; educationally disadvantaged; expulsion; problem children; pupil alienation

10/1737
Department of Education, Coventry CV4 7AL
01203 523523
Hatcher, R. Mr; *Supervisor:* Troyna, B. Dr
Race relations in primary schools
Abstract: Race relations in the primary school remains a relatively unchartered territory for researchers. This project explores those relations through an ethnographic analysis of three mainly white primary schools. The children, who were in their final year of primary education at the time of the study, speak openly and frankly about the nature of their friendships within and outside their ethnic group.
Published Material: TROYNA, B. & HATCHER, R. (1991). 'Racist incidents in schools: a framework for analysis', Journal of Education Policy, Vol 6, No 1, pp.17-31.; TROYNA, B. & HATCHER, R. (1992). Racism in children's lives: study of mainly white primary schools. London: Routledge.; TROYNA, B. & HATCHER, R. (1992). 'It's only words: understanding 'racial' and racist incidents', New Community, Vol 18, No 3, pp.493-496.; HATCHER, R. & TROYNA, B. (1993). 'Racialisation and children'. In: CRICHLOW, W. & McCARTHY, C. (Eds). Race identity and representation in education. London: Routledge.
Status: Individual research
Date of Research: 1989-1994
KEYWORDS: ethnic relations; friendship; intergroup relations; primary schools; pupil attitudes; racial relations; whites

10/1738
Department of Education, Coventry CV4 7AL
01203 523523
Morris, A. Mr; *Supervisor:* Halpin, D. Dr
Pupil performance in Catholic schools
Abstract: Using data on examination performance in secondary schools in one West Midlands local education authority, as well as detailed case study work in two secondary Catholic schools in the same area, this investigation explores the extent to which the philosophy and practice of contrasting kinds of Catholic school contributes either way to academic output.
Status: Individual research
Date of Research: 1993-continuing
KEYWORDS: academic achievement; Catholic schools; school effectiveness

10/1739
Department of Education, Coventry CV4 7AL
01203 523523
Aitken, T. Mr; *Supervisor:* Gardner, F. Dr; Lloyd-Smith, M. Mr
School perceptions of the effects of the Education Reform Act 1988 on provision for pupils with emotional and behavioural difficulties
Abstract: An investigation into the extent to which provisions in the Education Reform Act 1988 (ERA), including Local Management of Schools (LMS) and league tables, are affecting schools' policies and practices for dealing with pupils who exhibit emotional and behavioural difficulties. Using existing data collected before the introduction of the ERA, a comparison will be made with current attitudes to disaffected and disruptive pupils and with decisions about whether to improve such pupils inside or outside the school. Quantitative and factual data will be collected from a sample of West Midlands secondary schools, and qualitative data obtained through interviews in a smaller sample involving headteachers, governors, pastoral heads, coordinators of special educational needs and newly-qualified teachers. It is intended to draw out the applications of this evidence for school policy and for the development of local education authority support services.
Status: Individual research
Date of Research: 1992-continuing
KEYWORDS: behaviour problems; disruptive pupils; Education Reform Act 1988; educational policy; emotional problems; problem children; school policy

10/1740
Department of Education, Coventry CV4 7AL
01203 523523
Lane, I. Mr; *Supervisor:* Bell, L. Dr
An analysis of the work of primary school headteachers
Abstract: This research is based on a series of questionnaires and interviews with primary headteachers which examines: 1) the changes brought about in their role by legislation post 1988; and 2) the strategies used to cope with and manage the changes.
Status: Individual research
Date of Research: 1987-continuing
KEYWORDS: educational administration; head teachers; primary schools; school based management; teacher role

10/1741
Department of Education, Coventry CV4 7AL
01203 523523
Daghistani, B. Mrs; *Supervisor:* David, T. Ms; Neill, S. Dr
Investigate and assess the impact of attendance at preschool education on pupil achievement at primary school level in Saudia Arabia
Abstract: The research entails a survey of the early years curriculum in different types of preschool provision in Saudi Arabia, and an analysis of the relationships between these curricula and the primary school curriculum.
Status: Individual research
Date of Research: 1990-continuing
KEYWORDS: preschool education; primary education; Saudi Arabia

10/1742
Department of Education, Coventry CV4 7AL
01203 523523
Davies, M. Ms; *Supervisor:* Halpin, D. Dr
Refocusing the future: the shape of local education authorities (LEAs) to come
Abstract: On the basis of data derived from a questionnaire survey of

eleven West Midlands local education authorities (LEAs), and detailed case studies of three of these, this investigation is designed to explore the different ways in which LEAs are responding to the policy changes included in the Education Reform Act of 1988 and the Education Act 1993.
Status: Individual research
Date of Research: 1992-continuing
KEYWORDS: *Education Reform Act 1988; educational change; educational legislation; educational policy; local education authorities*

10/1743
> Department of Education, Coventry CV4 7AL
> 01203 523523
> Abbott, I. Mr; Evans, L. Ms
Student and lecturer perceptions of the effectiveness of teaching on four undergraduate courses at Warwick University
Abstract: This research will investigate lecturers' and students' perceptions of the extent to which their courses are effective in meeting their respective needs and satisfying their preferences. In particular, it will explore the extent to which particular teaching methods are cost effective in terms of lecturers' time, and the feasibility and practical implications of identifying organisational strategies which fulfil this broad interpretation of effectiveness.
Status: Sponsored project
Source of Grant: Warwick University £2,000
Date of Research: 1993-1994
KEYWORDS: *course evaluation; educational quality; student evaluation of teacher performance; teacher effectiveness; teaching methods; universities*

10/1744
> Department of Education, Coventry CV4 7AL
> 01203 523523
> Abbott, I. Mr; Evans, L. Ms; Goodyear, R. Ms;
> Pritchard, A. Mr
A comparative study of two models of initial teacher education
Abstract: This is a two year, qualitative study which will use self-completion questionnaires and semi-structured interviews as data collecting techniques. The main aim of the research is to identify and compare the respective strengths and weaknesses, in relation to their contribution to teachers' professional development, of a school-administered model of initial teacher education (being piloted 1993-94) and a higher education administered model, as represented by two specific Postgraduate Certificate in Education (Secondary) courses.
Published Material: ABBOTT, I.D., EVANS, L., GOODYEAR, R. & PRITCHARD, A. (1993). 'A comparative study of two models of initial teacher education', Mentoring, Vol 1, No 2, pp.37-39.
Status: Sponsored project
Source of Grant: Association of Teachers and Lecturers £6,308
Date of Research: 1993-continuing
KEYWORDS: *postgraduate certificate in education; preservice teacher education; school based teacher education; student teachers*

10/1745
> Department of Education, Coventry CV4 7AL
> 01203 523523
> Pritchard, A. Mr; *Supervisor:* Eggleston, S. Prof.
The extent to which children's learning may be enhanced by the use of information technology
Abstract: The study: 1) examines literature; 2) identifies present information technology curriculum content in two sample schools; and 3) assesses consequences for learning enhancement.
Status: Individual research
Date of Research: 1993-continuing
KEYWORDS: *computer uses in education; information technology*

10/1746
> Department of Education, Coventry CV4 7AL
> 01203 523523
> Tufnell, R. Mr; *Supervisor:* Eggleston, S. Prof.
Technology education
Abstract: A report of the candidate's role in the national, government funded survey of assessment strategies for technology education for National Curriculum key stage 3 (ages 11-14). It describes test construction, piloting to 10 schools, trial to 50 schools and eventual widespread use, and reports and analyses findings.
Status: Individual research
Date of Research: 1991-continuing
KEYWORDS: *assessment; technology education*

10/1747
> Department of Education, Coventry CV4 7AL
> 01203 523523
> Crombie, R. Mr; *Supervisor:* Solity, J. Mr
Managing difficult behaviour in mainstream schools: changing the culture
Abstract: The research focuses on an evaluation of a behavioural support service. The service provides support of various kinds to children, families and schools in response to children's difficult behaviour in school. The overarching hypothesis is that by basing the structure and operation of the support service on clear aims, a theoretical foundation, empirical research information and a detailed analysis of context; its aims can be achieved in terms of: 1) explicit local authority objectives; 2) changing children's behaviour; 3) its context; and 4) enabling those involved to feel that their needs have been met optimally.
Status: Individual research
Date of Research: 1988-1994
KEYWORDS: *behaviour problems; disruptive pupils; problem children; support services*

10/1748
> Department of Education, Coventry CV4 7AL
> 01203 523523
> Solity, J. Mr
An investigation into the assessment procedures and criteria adopted by teachers to determine whether children have special educational needs
Abstract: The research is investigating the evidence used by teachers to determine whether children have special educational needs.
Status: Individual research
Date of Research: 1993-continuing
KEYWORDS: *diagnostic assessment; special educational needs*

10/1749
> Department of Education, Coventry CV4 7AL
> 01203 523523
> Solity, J. Mr
An investigation into the effects on reading progress of developing the phonological awareness of reception aged children
Abstract: The research is an experimental investigation into the effects on children's reading of providing different forms of phonological awareness training. Two different methods of developing phonological awareness are being used with reception aged children for a six month period. Their effects on a range of measures will then be evaluated.
Status: Individual research
Date of Research: 1993-1994
KEYWORDS: *early childhood education; phonics; reading; reading ability; reading skills*

10/1750
> Department of Education, Coventry CV4 7AL
> 01203 523523
> University of Wales College of Cardiff, School of Education,
> 42 Park Place, Cardiff CF1 3BB
> 01222 874000
> Halpin, D. Dr; Fitz, J. Dr
Self-governance, grant-maintained schools and educational identities
Abstract: The main aim of this research is to explore the extent to which self-governance arising from grant-maintained (GM) status has contributed to innovation and change within education. The specific objectives are: (1) To investigate the impact of self-governance on the distribution of power and control in GM school management structures and practices including its effects on specialisation within the division of labour amongst teaching and non-teaching staff in GM schools and teachers' perceptions of their work and professional status, and its consequences for relations between GM schools and their former local education authorities (LEAs). (2) To compare the management structures and practices found in GM schools with

those of other schools in order to: (a) explore the extent to which different forms of self-governance have consequences for the organisation to teaching and learning; and (b) clarify whether the educational experiences offered by GM schools arise from self-governance as much as from perceived financial advantages that GM status may afford. (3) To explore the extent to which organisational differences between GM and other schools foster diversity of pupil experience of schooling and contribute to differentiated and stratified educational identities.

Status: Sponsored project
Source of Grant: Economic and Social Research Council £72,000
Date of Research: 1992-1994
KEYWORDS: *educational practices; grant maintained schools; institutional autonomy; institutional characteristics; school based management*

10/1751

Department of Science Education, Coventry CV4 7AL
01203 523523
Harwood, D. Mr

The debriefing process in active learning

Abstract: Previous research has shown that the teacher becomes the focus of interaction in active learning whenever he or she is present with the teaching group. This research aims to study the nature of the teacher's statements and questions during the debriefing process and identify the effects they have upon pupil participation. Teachers who are experienced in active learning, have volunteered to participate. The 'debriefing' phase of the lesson will be videotaped and transcribed. As a result of collaboration between teacher and researcher, a commentary will be written to accompany the transcript. Guidelines for debriefing 'active learning' will be identified.

Published Material: HARWOOD, D.L. (1989). 'The nature of teacher-pupil interaction in the "Active Tutorial Work" approach: using interaction analysis to evaluate student-centred approaches', British Educational Research Journal, Vol 15, No 2, pp.177-194.; HARWOOD, D.L. (1991). 'Guidelines for debriefing active learning: an interim report'. Coventry: University of Warwick/Warwickshire Local Education Authority. (Available from the author).
Status: Sponsored project
Source of Grant: Warwickshire Local Education Authority £350
Date of Research: 1990-1993
KEYWORDS: *classroom communication; learning activities; teacher-pupil relationship; teacher role; teaching methods*

10/1752

International Centre for Education in Development, Coventry CV4 7AL
01203 523523
National Institute for Social and Economic Research, Windhoek, Namibia Preston, R. Dr

The integration of returned exiles, former combatants and other war-affected Namibians

Abstract: Independence in 1990 liberated Namibia from the apartheid regime of South Africa and brought an end to the civil strife of the past 30 years. Some 43,000 exiles returned to participate in building the new nation. The research combines cross-sectional community studies and a longitudinal tracer study of key individuals. It aims to compare the extent to which experiences during the struggles of those who went and those who stayed (fighters and non-fighters, men and women) have affected social and economic reintegration in rural and urban areas. In this, it will appraise the relevance of education in exile to opportunities on return and seek to identify policy that will facilitate economic integration and sustainable self-sufficiency. It will also attempt to locate differentiated repatriation within a theoretical framework of return migration.

Published Material: SIMON, D. & PRESTON, R. (1992). 'Return to the promised land: the repatriation and resettlement of Namibian refugees, 1989-1990'. In: BLACK, R. & ROBINSON, V. (Eds). Geography and refugees: patterns and processes of change. Chichester: Belhaven Press.
Status: Sponsored project
Source of Grant: European Commission £3,286
Date of Research: 1992-1992
KEYWORDS: *Namibia; refugees*

West London Institute

10/1753

College of Brunel University, Department of Education, Gordon House, 300 St Margaret's Road, Twickenham TW1 1PT
0181 891 0121
Gan, E. Mrs

Critical studies in art

Abstract: The project is a direct response to recent Department for Education legislation on the National Curriculum for Art in schools. Art is a foundation subject of the National Curriculum at key stages 1-3, and assessment in Art comprises two attainment targets (ATs). This project relates specifically to AT2: Knowledge and Understanding in Art, which entails the need to develop in pupils and teachers the skills of critical appraisal. The focus for the research is on the primary age range, and relates in particular to the use of art works in developing critical judgement and judgemental criteria in the appraisal of works of art. A questionnaire has been completed and returned by fifty-five primary teachers. Certain strands and themes have emerged from information received. One major implication here, (borne out by the 1993 published research report by the Centre for the Study of the Arts in Primary Education), is that AT2 in Art will require considerable inservice and development support for teachers, and that schools will need to make sufficient improvements to their reference and library provision in order to be able to meet the requirements of AT2. As a result of this, some schools and teachers in this sample will be followed up and interviews explored in a practical way. Resource-based tasks and materials will be tried out in schools in order to improve practice in this area. Work in schools will be monitored via video and photographic materials; transcripts will also be used. Archive research has taken place; using original source material has facilitated research into the historical background of art education and the status of art in state schools and also the training of teachers. Parallels with the present day National Curriculum are identified and compared.

Status: Sponsored project
Source of Grant: West London Institute £3,500
Date of Research: 1993-continuing
KEYWORDS: *aesthetic education; art activities; art appreciation; art education; criticism; National Curriculum*

10/1754

College of Brunel University, Department of Education, Gordon House, 300 St Margaret's Road, Twickenham TW1 1PT
0181 891 0121
Hilliman, P. Mrs; *Supervisor:* Sandow, S. Dr

An investigation into the management of change in a local education authority, with particular reference to special educational needs

Abstract: This study aims to elucidate the processes underlying a failed innovation and to identify the contributing factors. The analysis includes an examination of the interaction between the identification of the need for change, and the role of the education department. Interviews, reports and public documents provide sources for analysis.

Status: Individual research
Date of Research: 1991-1993
KEYWORDS: *educational change; educational innovation; local education authorities; special educational needs*

10/1755

College of Brunel University, Department of Education, Gordon House, 300 St Margaret's Road, Twickenham TW1 1PT
0181 891 0121
Exeter University, Northcote House, The Queen's Drive, Exeter EX4 4QJ
01392 263263
Koshy, V. Ms; *Supervisor:* Ernest, P. Dr

The implementation of the National Curriculum in mathematics: the effects of key stage 2 in primary schools

Abstract: The aims of the study are to: (1) find out to what extent changes have been made to the teaching and learning of mathematics in schools as a result of the implementation of the National Curriculum; (2) monitor classroom practice in schools at present, in the

National Curriculum context and compare it with what used to be the case, referring to curriculum development documents and surveys. The methodology employed includes questionnaires, interviews and case studies. From the data so far collected the following are noted: (1) there is a marked difference between the responses to questions supplied by teachers on inservice courses in mathematics, and teachers who are not; (2) there is increased awareness of investigative work; (3) group work is being attempted by teachers who use a variety of styles of groups; (4) assessment and record keeping seem to be an area of concern; (5) increased dependence on schemes.
Status: Individual research
Date of Research: 1990-1994
KEYWORDS: mathematics education; National Curriculum; primary education; teaching methods

10/1756
    College of Brunel University, Department of Education, Gordon House, 300 St Margaret's Road, Twickenham TW1 1PT
    0181 891 0121
    Kent University, Canterbury CT2 7NZ
    01227 764000
    Hinchcliffe, V. Mr; *Supervisor:* Forrester, M. Dr
The social cognitive development of children with severe learning difficulties
Abstract: This research involves questionnaires, observation and intervention studies to compare the social cognitive development of non-learning impaired and learning impaired children. Children's metalinguistic abilities and their use of mental state language is investigated. The research aims to point to useful teaching procedures for teachers of children with severe learning difficulties.
Status: Individual research
Date of Research: 1988-1993
KEYWORDS: cognitive development; severe learning difficulties; social cognition; special educational needs

10/1757
    College of Brunel University, Department of Education, Gordon House, 300 St Margaret's Road, Twickenham TW1 1PT
    0181 891 0121
    Leicester University, School of Education, University Road, Leicester LE1 7RH
    01162 522522
    McKenzie, J. Ms; *Supervisor:* Sandow, S. Dr; Fogelman, K. Prof.
Attendance, schools, families and learning processes
Abstract: Building on data collected from schools and from individuals, patterns of attendance among 'at-risk' groups of pupils in secondary schools are established. Interviews using repertory grid techniques will be conducted with pupils and families of pupils with poor attendance. An analysis is proposed which accepts the multi-layered and problematic nature of the relations between pupils, families and schools.
Status: Individual research
Date of Research: 1992-1994
KEYWORDS: attendance; educational attitudes; family influence; home-school relationship; truancy

10/1758
    College of Brunel University, Department of Education, Gordon House, 300 St Margaret's Road, Twickenham TW1 1PT
    0181 891 0121
    London University, Institute of Education, Department of International and Comparative Education, 20 Bedford Way, London WC1H 0AL
    0171 580 1122
    Garner, P. Dr; *Supervisor:* Jones, C. Mr
Disruptive behaviour in United Kingdom and United States schools: a comparative study
Abstract: This research uses 'pupil reality' to investigate disruptive behaviour in the UK and USA. Such a response is at the heart of a paradigm which might be best described as 'ecological', where the pupil is viewed as central to the microsystem. The research focuses upon two case studies (one each in the USA and UK). Pupils and their teachers are interviewed (unstructured) and other instruments include

critical biographies, diaries, and gathering formal documentary evidence. The research hopes to point to cross-cultural differences in the responses of disruptive pupils to their schooling.
Status: Individual research
Date of Research: 1988-1993
KEYWORDS: antisocial behaviour; comparative education; discipline problems; disruptive pupils; United States of America

10/1759
    College of Brunel University, Department of Education, Gordon House, 300 St Margaret's Road, Twickenham TW1 1PT
    0181 891 0121
    London University, Institute of Education, Department of English and Media Studies, 20 Bedford Way, London WC1H 0AL
    0171 580 1122
    Catt, R. Mr; *Supervisor:* Burgess, A. Dr
Speaking, listening and the English curriculum: examining oracy
Abstract: There is contention regarding both the National Curriculum programmes of study and the assessment arrangements for speaking and listening within the English curriculum, particularly at key stage 4. Drawing upon research conducted in secondary school classrooms, the researcher attempts to provide a critical examination of existing practice and argues for the development of a wider functional and social model of oracy.
Status: Individual research
Date of Research: 1991-1994
KEYWORDS: English studies curriculum; language skills; listening skills; National Curriculum; oracy; speech skills

10/1760
    College of Brunel University, Department of Education, Gordon House, 300 St Margaret's Road, Twickenham TW1 1PT
    0181 891 0121
    London University, King's College, Centre for Educational Studies, Cornwall House Annexe, Waterloo Road, London SE1 3TY
    0171 836 5454
    Blake, C. Mr; *Supervisor:* Walker, A. Dr
Assessment of affective religious studies in secondary schools
Abstract: This research examines several case studies in assessed Religious Studies in secondary schools, using the General Certificate of Secondary Education (GCSE) as the curricular context. Three assessment modes, written, oral and creative, are implemented and evaluated in each case, and interviews conducted with staff and students. The research aims to demonstrate the role of judgement in the assessment process, and to illustrate the tensions between good classroom practice and the aims of examination validity and reliability.
Status: Individual research
Date of Research: 1992-1994
KEYWORDS: assessment; religious education

10/1761
    College of Brunel University, Department of Education and Sport, Lancaster House, Borough Road, Isleworth TW7 5DU
    0181 891 0121
    Armour, K. Mrs
The ecology of physical education: an investigation into the 'life' of a physical education department
Abstract: Within an ethnographic, case study framework, this research uses observations, interviews and life history reflections to investigate the 'life' of a physical education department in a secondary school. The central focus is upon the four physical education teachers in the department, charting how they develop their personal understanding of the nature and purpose of physical education. These understandings are located in the broader context of the school and the conflicting perspectives of senior teachers, parents and pupils. In the final analysis, the ecological metaphor is found wanting and the dramatic nature of 'interacting scripts' for education and physical education is highlighted in the framework of the agent/structure debate.
Status: Individual research
Date of Research: 1988-1993
KEYWORDS: physical education; physical education teachers

Westminster College

10/1762
> North Hinksey, Oxford OX2 9AT
> 01865 247644
> Brighton University, Faculty of Education, Sport and
> Leisure, School of Education, Falmer, Brighton BN1 9PH
> 01273 600900
> London University, Institute of Education, Department of
> English and Media Studies, 20 Bedford Way, London
> WC1H 0AL
> 0171 580 1122
> Mitchell, H. Ms; *Supervisor:* Dombey, H. Dr;
> Meek-Spencer, M. Ms

A naturalistic study of early literacy
Abstract: Recent work has demonstrated the importance of involving parents in their children's reading, this includes a number of surveys conducted which show how many schools are involving parents in reading with their children but have not, however, examined closely the reading behaviours encouraged by parents. Other research has investigated the ways in which children reading at home with their parents, and at school with their teachers, are given different supporting strategies. This research, however, centres on children who had been in school for eighteen months, and in schools using reading schemes. It focuses on the development as readers of younger children, and the supporting strategies provided at home and at school. The subjects are twelve children in three local schools, with a close focus on one child in each school. There is a considerable amount of data collected at home and school for each of the three children. Analysis of the data will be carried out by a number of methods in order to establish a model of parent/child interaction and teacher/child interaction in psycholinguistic readings. Analysis of the tape recordings will be through a system of coded moves designed to indicate the nature of the interaction as it particularly relates to the development of reading behaviours. The analysis will take account of the socio-cultural settings of home and school, and will need to consider the ways in which literate behaviour is embedded within different social groups and the different significance accorded to it. The purpose of this study is to create a model of the reading process undertaken by the child in the home situation, and a similar model of the process in the school, enabling a deeper understanding of the nature of literacy as perceived by child, parent, and teacher. The intention is to clarify how teachers using the psycholinguistic approach can most profitably build on what parents perceive as their role, and further, how the dialogue between parents and teachers can be extended. No comparable stuy has so far been undertaken.
Published Material: MITCHELL, H. (1989). 'Vignettes', NATE News, Autumn 1989.
Status: Individual research
Date of Research: 1988-1994
KEYWORDS: beginning reading; literacy; parent participation; psycholinguistics; reading research; reading teaching

10/1763
> North Hinksey, Oxford OX2 9AT
> 01865 247644
> Oxford University, Department of Educational Studies,
> 15 Norham Gardens, Oxford OX2 6PY
> 01865 274024
> Palacio, D. Dr; Lenton, G. Dr; Summers, M. Mr;
> Kruger, C. Mr

Primary school teachers and science
Abstract: The aim of the project is to produce inservice materials for primary school teachers which will further develop their own understanding of those key conceptual areas of science which are known to be difficult, e.g. force, energy. A constructivist approach to the development of these materials has been adopted by the project team. Initially teachers' understanding in a particular conceptual area was elicited through one-to-one interviews (about 20 interviews per conceptual area) using a technique known as 'interview about instances'. The results of this phase of the project were then used to construct a questionnaire which was given to a larger sample of teachers (about 180 teachers per conceptual area). The results of this, the prevalence phase of the project, were used as a basis for the development of the inservice materials. These materials are designed for use by teachers, preferably in groups of four to five, without recourse to an 'expert' group leader or specialised science equipment.

Published Material: A full list of working papers and publications is available from the researchers.
Status: Sponsored project
Source of Grant: Leverhulme Trust £60,000; University of Oxford £2,500; Westminster College £2,500
Date of Research: 1989-continuing
KEYWORDS: educational materials; inservice teacher education; primary school teachers; science education; scientific concepts

10/1764
> North Hinksey, Oxford OX2 9AT
> 01865 247644
> Oxford University, Department of Educational Studies,
> 15 Norham Gardens, Oxford OX2 6PY
> 01865 274024
> Atkinson, S. Ms; *Supervisor:* McIntyre, D. Mr; Lewis, I. Mr

An action research study into the role of a mathematics coordinator in a primary school
Abstract: The role of the mathematics coordinator is explored in the context of school-based inservice education of teachers (INSET). The research looks at changes that took place in a primary school over three years; the ways that teachers coped with change; what the facilitating role of the coordinator involved; and when the facilitating was most successful. The nature of action research is discussed in relation to the feasibility of the concept of teacher-researcher and to the nature of the teacher's 'self' in a demanding situation.
Status: Individual research
Date of Research: 1985-1993
KEYWORDS: inservice teacher education; mathematics education; primary schools

Wolverhampton University

10/1765
> Walsall Campus, Gorway Road, Walsall WS1 3BD
> 01902 321000
> Philps, C. Mrs; *Supervisor:* Crocker, A. Prof.; Thomas, N. Mrs; Stanford, B. Mr

Comparative study of the language development of children with Down's Syndrome placed in mainstream and special schools
Abstract: This is a two-year longitudinal study of a sample of Down's children, half of whom are in mainstream schools and half of whom are in Moderate Learning Difficulty (MLD) schools. The baseline measurements are IQ, language development, social skills and family details. An analysis is to be made of expressive language heard in the context of classroom interaction, playground interaction and, possibly, family interaction with a view to testing the proposition that children placed in mainstream schools initiate more language than those in MLD schools.
Published Material: PHILPS, C. (1984). Elizabeth Joy: a mother's story. Oxford: Lion.; PHILPS, C. & ALEXANDER, P. (1991). Mummy, why have I got Down's Syndrome? Oxford: Lion.; PHILPS, C. & JONES, C. (1986). 'Parental role in portage: a consumer view'. In: DALEY, B. et al (Ed). Portage: the importance of parents. Windsor: NFER-Nelson.
Status: Sponsored project
Source of Grant: Down's Syndrome Association; Wolverhampton Polytechnic
Date of Research: 1990-1994
KEYWORDS: Down's Syndrome; expressive language; interaction; language acquisition; mainstreaming; special educational needs; special schools

10/1766
> Walsall Campus, Gorway Road, Walsall WS1 3BD
> 01902 321000
> Birley, G. Dr

University examinations in science 1870-1900
Abstract: This research will look at the content of science syllabuses and examination papers set by universities during the period 1870-1900, and relate this to examiners' interests and current scientific developments. The aim is to establish the role of the examinations and the extent to which the examination movement helped to codify scientific disciplines.

Status: Sponsored project
Source of Grant: Royal Society; Wolverhampton University
Date of Research: 1990-1993
KEYWORDS: educational history; examination syllabuses; science education; university examinations

10/1767
    Walsall Campus, Gorway Road, Walsall WS1 3BD
    01902 321000
    Jeavons, M. Mrs; *Supervisor:* Birley, G. Dr; Bentley, M. Mr
Academic underachievement of gifted children
Abstract: This is a qualitative study of the achievement of gifted children within mainstream primary education. The research will pinpoint perceptions of 'on-task behaviour' between gifted and non-gifted children, and relates this to child to child and child to teacher interaction using a non-participant observation method.
Status: Individual research
Date of Research: 1991-continuing
KEYWORDS: academic ability; academic failure; gifted; pupil behaviour; underachievement

10/1768
    Walsall Campus, Gorway Road, Walsall WS1 3BD
    01902 321000
    Harrison, R. Miss; *Supervisor:* Birley, G. Dr; Kowalski, R. Dr
The role of the college farm
Abstract: This is a study of how colleges of agriculture make use of their college farms both as aids to teaching agriculture and as working farms in their own right. A series of case studies have been conducted, examining the efficiency of the operation of such farms and relating this to the decision-making processes within the college farm organisations. This is determined by a modified method of the Aston Index.
Status: Individual research
Date of Research: 1991-1994
KEYWORDS: agricultural colleges; agricultural education; farms

10/1769
    Walsall Campus, Gorway Road, Walsall WS1 3BD
    01902 321000
    Birley, G. Dr
Nineteenth century science examinations in universities
Abstract: A study is being conducted of the content of examinations of the Universities of London, Oxford and Cambridge. An attempt is being made to identify how individual examiners were able to influence the scientific education of science (physical science) undergraduates by means of the examination system. It is intended that the results of this work will be fed into those of a previous study conducted by the author, into examinations in science carried out by the Science and Art Department.
Status: Sponsored project
Source of Grant: The Royal Society
Date of Research: 1991-continuing
KEYWORDS: educational history; examinations; science education; universities

10/1770
    Walsall Campus, Gorway Road, Walsall WS1 3BD
    01902 321000
    Kehoe, M. Mrs; *Supervisor:* Birley, G. Dr; Preston, J. Dr
Evaluation of the training needs of primary science teachers
Abstract: A survey is being undertaken in one large local education authority in order to establish the training needs of primary science teachers at key stage one of the National Curriculum. Programmes of training will then be arranged and implemented in response to the needs analysis; the effects of this training will be evaluated.
Status: Individual research
Date of Research: 1991-continuing
KEYWORDS: inservice teacher education; primary school teachers; science education; teacher development

10/1771
    Walsall Campus, Gorway Road, Walsall WS1 3BD
    01902 321000
    Tam, C. Mrs; *Supervisor:* Birley, G. Dr; Moreland, N. Dr; Pearl, L. Dr

An investigation of factors associated with high achievement in degree performance in higher education science students
Abstract: Using biographical information and basic information of socio-economic group, age, gender, etc., a study is being conducted of the outcomes of student learning against the inputs in order to determine what factors and study skills are associated with high achievement in science and technology undergraduates.
Status: Individual research
Date of Research: 1993-continuing
KEYWORDS: achievement; background; high achievement; individual characteristics; science education; undergraduate students

10/1772
    Walsall Campus, Gorway Road, Walsall WS1 3BD
    01902 321000
    Farley, K. Mr; *Supervisor:* Birley, G. Dr; Gomez, G. Dr
Implementing the National Curriculum History in primary schools
Abstract: This is an ethnographic study of three primary schools, in one local education authority, which will examine the effects upon the teaching of history following the introduction of the National Curriculum in history. Recent years have seen the development of process-based methods of teaching history in the primary school, and the study aims to discover the extent to which the introduction of new curricula has enabled this process to continue.
Status: Individual research
Date of Research: 1993-continuing
KEYWORDS: history; National Curriculum; primary education

10/1773
    Walsall Campus, Gorway Road, Walsall WS1 3BD
    01902 321000
    Evans, D. Mrs; *Supervisor:* Birley, G. Dr; Hyde, B. Miss
Professional practice and emotional development in the student nurse
Abstract: This research is studying the relationship between professional practice and the emotional development of the student nurse. It aims to test the assumption that psychological congruence will facilitate the integration of psychiatric theory and practice. On the basis of this study, a programme will be developed which, it is intended, will improve theory/practice integration. This programme will be evaluated.
Status: Individual research
Date of Research: 1993-continuing
KEYWORDS: emotional development; nurse education; nurses; professional development; student development

10/1774
    Walsall Campus, Gorway Road, Walsall WS1 3BD
    01902 321000
    Rotsides, C. Mr; *Supervisor:* Birley, G. Dr; Prudham, B. Mr
Education in Cyprus: comparisons with Greece and United Kingdom
Abstract: Surveys of Education Department personnel and of educationalists are being undertaken in Cyprus in order to examine the structure and mode of operation of their education system. It will then be compared with the systems in Greece and in the United Kingdom in order to establish what traditions have been imported into the educational system of Cyprus, and the compatibility of this educational system with the systems of Greece and the United Kingdom. This will indicate the degrees of adjustment which may be necessary as Cyprus prepares to join the European Union.
Status: Individual research
Date of Research: 1992-continuing
KEYWORDS: comparative education; Cyprus; educational policy; Greece; school systems

10/1775
    Walsall Campus, Gorway Road, Walsall WS1 3BD
    01902 321000
    Harrison, S. Mr; *Supervisor:* Birley, G. Dr; Mathias, J. Dr
Open and flexible learning systems in the National Health Service
Abstract: Flexible and open learning systems currently being introduced into the public service and National Health Service systems of Britain are being evaluated, against more traditional levels of delivery, in one hospital training school.

Status: Individual research
Date of Research: 1992-continuing
KEYWORDS: *flexible learning; medical schools; open education; teaching methods*

10/1776
Walsall Campus, Gorway Road, Walsall WS1 3BD
01902 321000
Han, M. Miss; *Supervisor:* Birley, G. Dr; Elliott, D. Mr
A longitudinal study of gifted children in Singapore
Abstract: This is an examination of a series of programmes for gifted children in Singapore. It involves the development and validation of selection tests and an evaluation of the effectiveness of the programmes.
Status: Individual research
Date of Research: 1993-continuing
KEYWORDS: *gifted; programme evaluation; Singapore*

10/1777
Walsall Campus, Gorway Road, Walsall WS1 3BD
01902 321000
Doherty, M. Mr; *Supervisor:* Birley, G. Dr; Moreland, N. Dr; Dudley, J. Mr
The managerial implications of General National Vocational Qualifications
Abstract: This research examines the introduction of the General National Vocational Qualification into the colleges of further and higher education. It looks at the implications for management and for the curriculum of such colleges.
Status: Individual research
Date of Research: 1992-continuing
KEYWORDS: *further education; higher education; National Vocational Qualifications; vocational education*

10/1778
Walsall Campus, Gorway Road, Walsall WS1 3BD
01902 321000
Delbridge, J. Mr; *Supervisor:* Birley, G. Dr; Dudley, J. Mr; Cleland, G. Mrs
The relationship between public education and industry
Abstract: This project examines both historical and current aspects of the schools-industry movement. Initially an examination using archive and published material is being undertaken of the inter-relationship between secondary schools and industry. Survey methods and case study methods are then being deployed to look at two initiatives in particular. These are the Schools Council Industry Project and the Teacher Placement Initiative. Respondents from both industry and education will be included in the survey.
Status: Sponsored project
Source of Grant: Wolverhampton University
Date of Research: 1993-continuing
KEYWORDS: *industrial secondments; industry-education relationship*

10/1779
Walsall Campus, Gorway Road, Walsall WS1 3BD
01902 321000
Bartlett, S. Mr; *Supervisor:* Birley, G. Dr; Mathias, J. Dr
Teacher appraisal in three case study secondary schools
Abstract: Case studies of three secondary schools are being undertaken to examine the operation of appraisal systems. Aspects to be examined include: organisational change; effects on appraisers; and the motivational change of appraisees.
Status: Individual research
Date of Research: 1992-continuing
KEYWORDS: *secondary school teachers; teacher development; teacher education; teaching profession*

10/1780
Walsall Campus, Gorway Road, Walsall WS1 3BD
01902 321000
Storey, S. Ms; O'Neill, M. Ms; *Supervisor:* Birley, G. Dr; Doherty, G. Prof; Moreland, N. Dr
Implementation of Total Quality Management in higher education
Abstract: This project examines the impact of the introduction of a

quality system in one higher education institution. It examines the management strategies employed and the resulting impact upon middle management, academic staff, secretarial staff and technical staff.
Status: Individual research
Date of Research: 1992-continuing
KEYWORDS: *educational administration; educational quality; higher education; institutes of higher education; quality assurance; quality control*

10/1781
Walsall Campus, Gorway Road, Walsall WS1 3BD
01902 321000
Jones, M. Mr
Teachers' development project evaluation
Abstract: A local initiative in 1990 by a Ciba plant in Manchester saw the development and publication of the 'Bicycle Pack': a resource for teaching science to primary school children. Packs were distributed to all U.K. schools, but many remained on teachers' book shelves even though the pack was widely regarded. During 1993 Ciba approached the Standing Conference on Schools' Science and Technology about updating and disseminating the pack as a partnership. The pack was rewritten to include resources for teaching technology in primary schools, a planning framework, and teachers' background information aimed at preventing the transmission of misconceptions. The effectiveness of the pack was also to be evaluated. This more coherent approach, supported by teacher training courses in the use of the pack, is now known as the Ciba Teacher Development Programme: Primary Science and Technology. The aims of the programme (forming the basis of the evaluation) are to: 1) make a significant contribution to the teaching of science and technology for the 21st century; 2) stimulate interest in science and technology, industry and the chemical industry in particular; and 3) present Ciba in a positive light, locally and nationally, to a broader audience. Research will include: contextual analysis of teacher needs in planning and teaching science and technology in primary schools; attendance at teachers training courses, and visits to a selection of schools whose staff have attended the training courses. It is planned to disseminate the pack to 6,000 schools in the three years up to 1996. Ten per cent of these schools will be selected for visits. The evaluation methods will include: observation and fieldnotes; questionnaires; critical incidence analyses; and interviews.
Status: Sponsored project
Source of Grant: Ciba (UK) Limited
Date of Research: 1993-continuing
KEYWORDS: *corporate support; educational materials; primary education; programme evaluation; science education; technology education*

10/1782
Wolverhampton Business School, Compton Park, Wolverhampton WV3 9DX
01902 321000
Williams, S. Ms; *Supervisor:* Birley, G. Dr; Davies, G. Dr
Assessment of action learning type sets as a management strategy
Abstract: This research examines the varied learning experiences of Master of Business Administration (MBA) students in relation to self-directed learning. It relates their learning experience to their progress and dilemmas on a personal development module which makes use of action learning type sets as a learning strategy.
Status: Individual research
Date of Research: 1993-continuing
KEYWORDS: *business administration education; learning activities; learning strategies; management studies*

Worcester College of Higher Education

10/1783
Henwick Grove, Worcester WR2 6AJ
01905 748080
Emery, H. Mrs; Picard, P. Ms; *Supervisor:* Phillipson, S. Mr

Pattern of teaching and learning at National Curriculum key stage 2

Abstract: The objectives are to be achieved by working with local education authority (LEA) inspection teams and eight individual case study schools in Hereford and Worcester, and Sandwell. They are to: 1) Develop a picture of the nature of teaching and learning in National Curriculum key stage 2 in the two LEAs, focusing particularly upon patterns of curriculum and classroom organisation in the case study schools. 2) Work in partnership with eight case study schools on key concerns they are developing in implementing the National Curriculum at key stage 2 and how the College can support them. Particularly focusing on developing mentoring for teaching experience placements, and developing initial teacher training (ITT) courses and inservice teacher education (INSET) provision. 3) Provide specific feedback on examples of teaching and learning in reading. 4) Provide staff development for members of the College's Later Primary Years Team by participating in the survey. The case study schools reflect a range of sizes, locations and patterns of organisation. At the end of the research a conference will be held for schools to share their development work with others.

Status: Sponsored project
Source of Grant: Worcester College of Higher Education £5,000
Date of Research: 1993-1993
KEYWORDS: *classroom research; learning strategies; National Curriculum; primary education; reading teaching; teaching methods*

10/1784

Henwick Grove, Worcester WR2 6AJ
01905 748080
Hudson, G. Dr; Glover, D. Dr

Evaluation of the Worcester College of Higher Education school-based Postgraduate Certificate in Education (PGCE) course

Abstract: The evaluation of a newly established one year postgraduate school-based secondary teacher training course. Worcester College of Higher Education has a long tradition of postgraduate training but the new course was designed to comply with the Government's requirements for postgraduate teacher training as set out in the Department for Education Circular 9/92 where some two-thirds of training had to be located within schools. The design has three phases: 1) Induction to schools. 2) Competency development. 3) Further professional development. Nearly 200 students are located within 7 clusters of schools, both secondary and independents, and colleges of further education (50 in total). The students' school-based experience is supervised by professional and subject mentors with links with Worcester College of Higher Education maintained through professional and subject tutors. Central to the evaluation is the students' experience of the whole course, i.e. in College and schools. Qualitative data is being collected on students' experiences by interviewing students from 3 clusters selected for their distinctiveness e.g. rural versus urban, secondary schools and colleges of further education, to ensure all types of institutional experience of the students is accounted for. Interviews will also be carried out with mentors, tutors and others concerned with the management of the course in Worcester College and its partner institutions. Two reports will be written on the Induction and Competency phases; a third and final report will be a review of the whole course including the Professional development phase.

Status: Sponsored project
Source of Grant: Worcester College of Higher Education
Date of Research: 1993-1994
KEYWORDS: *course evaluation; Postgraduate Certificate in Education; preservice teacher education; school based teacher education*

10/1785

Henwick Grove, Worcester WR2 6AJ
01905 748080
Ramsden, F. Mrs; Bruce, T. Mrs; Atkin, J. Ms; Dye, J. Mrs;
Georgeson, J. Mrs; Kelly, S. Mrs; Saunders, M. Mrs;
Supervisor: Pascal, C. Prof.

Effective early learning: an action plan for change

Abstract: There is now valid evidence that high quality early childhood education can have a significant and long-term effect on children's learning, and lead to gains in educational achievement throughout schooling and to more positive patterns of social behaviour, which will contribute to better citizenship in its broadest sense. However, the quality of learning currently available in many early childhood settings is poor. This project aims to develop a mechanism which might enhance the quality of provision in the wide range of settings for 3 and 4 year old children. The project has 3 key aims: 1) To evaluate and improve the quality of education for 3 and 4 year old children in a range of settings. 2) To develop and disseminate a 'Model of Evaluation and Development in Early Learning', which may be used as a cost-effective vehicle for workplace based training and development, and which is capable of widespread application. 3) To document the impact of the model on the effectiveness of early learning. These aims are achieved through the implementation of a 4 stage process: evaluation; action planning; development; and reflection. Methods to evaluate and develop the quality of learning provided in the settings include observations, documentary analysis, interviews, photographic analysis, professional biographies, journals and vignettes. In the first year, 13 case studies have been carried out in a range of early childhood settings, including reception classes, local education authority nurseries, local authority day nurseries, playgroups, workplace nurseries, and private nurseries. In the second year, the Model of Evaluation and Development will be disseminated through national nursery and support agencies to some 250+ settings. This will allow some comparative analysis of quality to take place. The project is now nearing completion of its first year of operation and results show a clear impact of the project methodology within the study settings.

Published Material: PASCAL, C. (1993). 'Capturing the quality of education provision for young children: a story of developing professionals and developing methodology', European Early Childhood Education Research Journal, Vol 1, No 1, pp.69-81.; PASCAL, C. & BERTRAM, A.D. (1994). Defining and assessing quality in the education of children from 4-7 years. Pedagogical monographs. Leuvan, Belgium: University of Leuvan.
Status: Sponsored project
Source of Grant: Esmee Fairbairn Charitable Foundation £90,000
Date of Research: 1993-continuing
KEYWORDS: *early childhood education; educational development; educational quality; preschool education; quality control*

10/1786

Henwick Grove, Worcester WR2 6AJ
01905 748080
Pascal, C. Prof.; Bertram, A. Mr

Development of local education authority (LEA) guidelines for admission to school

Abstract: This project was commissioned by Hereford and Worcester Local Education Authority with the aim of working collaboratively with a group of schools to develop a set of guidelines for the admission of children into school. Data was collected using interviews, observation and documentary analysis. The guidelines have been produced and are being used as part of a programme of school development and training.

Published Material: HEREFORD AND WORCESTER COUNTY COUNCIL. (1992). Learning together: a handbook for those involved with the education of young children. Worcester: Hereford and Worcester County Council.
Status: Sponsored project
Source of Grant: Hereford and Worcester Local Education Authority £2,000
Date of Research: 1991-1992
KEYWORDS: *admission criteria; local education authorities; school entrance age*

10/1787

Henwick Grove, Worcester WR2 6AJ
01905 748080
Pascal, C. Prof.; Bertram, A. Mr; Heaslip, P. Mr

A comparative directory of initial training for early years teachers

Abstract: This project was undertaken by the Association of Teacher Education in Europe (ATEE) Early Years Working Group based at Worcester. It aims to document the range, quality and characteristics of initial training for early years teachers in Europe. At a time of rapid change in Europe, it was felt there was a need for a comparative evidential base on teacher training for early years (defined as 0-8 years of age). Field workers have been appointed, with each contributing country presenting information on: 1) Structure of the educational system. 2) Terminology. 3) Current trends. 4) Names and addresses of universities with responsibility for training. 5) Names and addresses of bodies authorising courses. 6) Criteria used for authorising and approving training. 7) The different routes into teaching. 8) The status and level of such training. 9) Description of course requirements. 10) Content of courses. Entries for 11 European countries are now being updated, with 13 additional entries to include Eastern Europe. This is an essential data base from which others can draw conclusions.

Published Material: PASCAL, C., BERTRAM, A.D. & HEASLIP, P. (1991). ATEE comparative directory of initial training for early years teachers. Worcester: Association of Teacher Education in Europe, Early Years Working Group.; PASCAL, C., BERTRAM, A.D. & HEASLIP, P. (1992). 'The changing context of teacher education for the early years in Europe', Early Years, Vol 12, No 2, pp.7-12.; PASCAL, C. & BERTRAM, A.D. (1993). 'The education of young children and their teachers in Europe', European Early Childhood Education Research Journal, Vol 1, No 2, pp.27-38.

Status: Sponsored project
Source of Grant: European Commission £285
Date of Research: 1990-continuing
KEYWORDS: comparative education; directories; early childhood education; preservice teacher education

10/1788
  Henwick Grove, Worcester WR2 6AJ
  01905 748080
  Pascal, C. Prof.
Evaluating and improving the quality of educational provision for 3 and 4 year olds
Abstract: This three year research project aims to develop a model of evaluation and improvement for a variety of early childhood educational settings, including primary schools and classes, playgroups, private nurseries, family centres and childminders. Qualitative research instruments for evaluating quality will be developed and employed in constructing democratically illuminative case studies of the quality of educational provision in each setting. These case studies will be used to develop and implement an action plan for the improvement of quality. Research techniques employed include interviews, observations, diaries and documentary analysis.
Published Material: PASCAL, C. (1993). 'Capturing the quality of educational provision for young children: a story of developing professionals and developing methodology', European Early Childhood Education Research Journal, Vol 1, No 1, pp.5-11.
Status: Sponsored project
Source of Grant: Worcester College of Higher Education £45,000
Date of Research: 1992-continuing
KEYWORDS: early childhood education; educational development; educational quality; nursery schools; play groups; preschool education; quality control

10/1789
  Henwick Grove, Worcester WR2 6AJ
  01905 748080
  Wakefield, P. Mr; Ghaye, A. Dr
Successful schools
Abstract: This was a collaborative, action research project between Worcester College of Higher Education, the National Primary Centre, and Sandwell, Solihull, Walsall and Wolverhampton local education authorities (LEAs), which enabled all those in a school's community to get a better understanding of the factors and influences upon school success. Thirty-six schools in the four local education authorities in the West Midlands participated in the project. The three main features of the resulting report are: 1) That the 'voices' of children, teachers, LEA officers and other adults are reported and analysed. 2) The school findings are related to contemporary research on school improvement. 3) The presentation of eight features which our research tells us are characteristics of developing all successful schools.
Published Material: NATIONAL PRIMARY CENTRE. (1993). Disadvantaged but successful: successful schools. Oxford: National Primary Centre.
Status: Sponsored project
Source of Grant: Sandwell Local Education Authority; Solihull Local Education Authority; Walsall Local Education Authority; Wolverhampton Local Education Authority, jointly: £10,000
Date of Research: 1991-1993
KEYWORDS: educational quality; school effectiveness; success

10/1790
  Henwick Grove, Worcester WR2 6AJ
  01905 748080

O'Sullivan, F. Mr; McEwen, S. Ms; Olds, H. Ms; Owen, D. Mr; Russel, V. Mr; *Supervisor:* Ghaye, A. Dr
Evaluation of the impact of the development of school-based management using the MEDALS materials
Abstract: This evaluation is conducted in the context of the increasing autonomy of schools resulting from the Education Reform Act 1988 and in the light of a focus on management development in the Grants for Education and Training (GEST) programmes 1989-1992. Hereford and Worcester Local Education Authority (H & W LEA) is committed to a strategy for management development which suppports increasingly self-developing schools and which incorporates the following principles: 1) Participation in management development by all teachers. 2) The notion of continuous development. 3) The vital importance of school-based learning. 4) Action orientated development. 5) Continuous check on the quality of provision. The evaluation is being conducted by Worcester College of Higher Education (WCHE) in collaboration with H & W LEA and is of the implementation stage of a pilot Management Development Programme using the MEDALS (Hall, V. and Oldroyd, D. (1990). Management self-development – secondary. Bristol: National Development Centre for Educational Management and Policy) materials. The two main aims are: 1) to support individuals in the development of self-managing schools; and 2) to design and develop a process of training and support for implementation and evaluation. Twelve staff from ten schools are involved in the action-research and will receive training and support, including work on evaluation methodology. Data thus generated will result in feedback conferences and reports of progress in the individual schools plus overview reports which will incorporate additional data from the wider pilot group. The research asks: How far is the MEDALS process facilitating improvements in school-based management at the levels of the individual, the school and groups of schools in terms of thinking about management development, the practice of management development, and the context of supported self-managing schools.
Status: Sponsored project
Source of Grant: Hereford and Worcester Local Education Authority; Worcester College of Higher Education
Date of Research: 1993-continuing
KEYWORDS: educational administration; local management of schools; management in education; programme evaluation; school based management; teacher development

10/1791
  Henwick Grove, Worcester WR2 6AJ
  01905 748080
  Nottingham University, School of Education, University Park, Nottingham NG7 2RD
  01602 515151
  Bertram, A. Mr; *Supervisor:* Gammage, P. Prof.
Men as early childhood educators
Abstract: This project aims to explore the issues which encourage or prevent men from becoming early childhood educators. It will also explore the perceived benefits and limitations of men's involvement in children's early education. Case studies, questionnaires plus interviews will be used in this qualitative project.
Status: Individual research
Date of Research: 1992-continuing
KEYWORDS: early childhood education; men; sex differences

Y Coleg Normal

10/1792
  Ffordd Caergybi, Bangor, Gwynedd LL57 2PX
  01248 370171
  University College of North Wales, School of Education, Deiniol Road, Bangor, Gwynedd LL57 2UW
  01248 351151
  Williams, C. Mr; *Supervisor:* Baker, C. Dr; Jones, G. Mr
An assessment of teaching methodology in bilingual subject area situations in the secondary sector
Abstract: This is a study of successful teaching methods used in subject areas and within the bilingual (Welsh/English) context in the county of Gwynedd. The aim is to produce school based inservice training material based on good practice observed in the classroom, combined with recent research findings in the fields of: (1) language

across the curriculum in the bilingual setting; and (2) bilingual teaching. The research will involve observation across a sample of 120 lessons in years 7-9 and in 15-18 secondary schools within the authority, with videotaped evidence of approximately one-third of the lessons. These have been chosen on the basis of: (1) following a Welsh medium class for the whole day (in a variety of language medium settings); (2) following a group of Welsh learners for the whole day (either a whole teaching group or a smaller group within a bilingual class); and (3) observing a specifically stated policy for bilingual development, e.g. both languages within the same lesson, or bilingual development through modular monolingual teaching. Assessment of this variety of teaching methods in a range of bilingual situations will be included in the results and conclusions.
Status: Sponsored project
Source of Grant: Awdurdod Addysg Gwynedd £50,000
Date of Research: 1991-1994
KEYWORDS: *bilingual education; bilingual schools; secondary education; Welsh*

York University

10/1793

Department of Educational Studies, Heslington, York YO1 5DD
01904 430000
Davies, I. Dr; *Supervisor:* Lister, I. Prof.
Guidelines for political education
Abstract: There were three main sections to this research. Firstly, a combination of narrative and analysis which shows the early call for guidelines for political education, the West German example, Department of Education and Science (DES) and Local Education Authority (LEA) guidelines. The researcher sought to illuminate the nature of different guidelines, considering to what extent they addressed aims, content, methods, evaluation and suggesting how they related to the recommendations made by key political educators. Secondly, the research examined the perceptions of guidelines by the producers, the political educators, teachers and gatekeepers who may include headteachers, governors, and local education authority (LEA) officers and a sample of politicians. Finally, the research sought to enquire how the guidelines help practice and focus on the relation between reality and theory in a number of Local Education Authorities.
Published Material: DAVIES, I. (1988). 'Guidelines for political education', Social Science Teacher, Vol 18, No 2, pp.37-39.; DAVIES, I. (1993). 'The reform of education: how and why are documents produced for teachers and are they perceived to be of any value?', Curriculum, Vol 14, No 2, pp.114-123.; DAVIES, I. 'Whatever happened to political education?', Educational Review. (in press).
Status: Individual research
Date of Research: 1987-1993
KEYWORDS: *curriculum development; guidelines; political science studies*

10/1794

Department of Educational Studies, Heslington, York YO1 5DD
01904 430000
Stone, C. Mrs; *Supervisor:* Horbury, A. Dr
The implementation of the National Curriculum through topic work
Abstract: The thesis considers the implementation of the National Curriculum predominantly through topic work. The aim was to consider the impact of the National Curriculum on primary school teachers. The overall research strategy adopted was that of case study. The research took place in two schools in the North of England; a twenty-one class combined infant and junior school and a nine class infant school. Two days a week were spent at both these schools as a participant for a period of four terms. Data was collected through classroom observation, two rounds of lengthy semi-structured interviews in July 1990 and 1991 and from documentary materials. The data analysis revealed that topic work usage varied considerably from class to class and an emergent typology of topic work in the context of the National Curriculum is presented. It can be argued that through their attempts to implement the National Curriculum in this way the difficulties of acquiring 'clarity' are revealed. 'Clarity' in terms of this reform appears to be important at different levels: 1) in respect of the overall intentions of the Education Reform Act 1988; 2) in

relation to the National Curriculum itself; 3) in respect of their own practice and the changes required of them. At each of these levels there seems to be considerable barriers to the necessary process of clarification which, when taken together, create a formidable obstacle to reform. It therefore appears likely that although the National Curriculum may bring about change it may not produce reform.
Published Material: STONE, C.E. 'An emergent typology of topic work in the context of the National Curriculum', Journal of Teacher Development. (in press).
Status: Individual research
Date of Research: 1990-1993
KEYWORDS: *educational change; National Curriculum; projects – learning activities; pupil projects; teaching methods*

10/1795

Department of Educational Studies, Heslington, York YO1 5DD
01904 430000
Arnold, M. Mr; *Supervisor:* Millar, R. Dr
Teaching a scientific mental model: a case study using analogy to construct a model of thermal processes
Abstract: The research involves teaching a scientific mental model of thermal processes to early secondary school students, using a water flow analogy to introduce the idea of thermal equilibrium. The three ideas of heat, temperature and thermal equilibrium were progressively differentiated. A pilot study shows that students and adults use a basic 'on = hot, off = cold' model of thermal phenomena. A teaching approach to address this issue was developed with 180 year 8 and year 10 students, and subsequently taught to 90 year 8 students in normal science lessons. Written and observational data on the students' developing conceptions was obtained, and a sample of students interviewed, tape recorded and the transcripts analysed. Sixteen weeks later a written post-test was administered to determine the extent to which previously learned material had been retained. The water analogy enabled most students to understand thermal equilibrium more clearly, and this idea assists many students to differentiate heat and temperature within a model of thermal processes. Some students were able to extend the model to other systems in dynamic equilibrium. Teaching a coherent mental model in which the relevant concepts are inter-related appears to be a valuable technique for science education, and the use of analogy facilitates the understanding of the difficult concept of thermal equilibrium.
Published Material: MILLAR, R. & ARNOLD, M. (1987). 'Being constructive: an alternative approach to the teaching of introductory ideas in electricity', International Journal of Science Education, Vol 9, No 5, pp.553-563.
Status: Individual research
Date of Research: 1988-1993
KEYWORDS: *physics education; science education; scientific concepts; thermodynamics*

10/1796

Department of Educational Studies, Heslington, York YO1 5DD
01904 430000
Barker, V. Mrs; *Supervisor:* Millar, R. Dr
An investigation of students' ideas about 'A' level chemistry topics
Abstract: The aims of the project are three-fold: 1) To establish in what ways students' learning is influenced by the context-theory approach, as used by Salters' Advanced Chemistry (SAC). 2) To investigate the mental structures of chemistry developed by students who learn parts of many chemical ideas simultaneously (as SAC students would). 3) To find out how SAC students' chemical reasoning compares with that of students following traditional A-level courses. The SAC is being developed at the University of York and has a novel approach to teaching the content of a traditional A-level chemistry course. The SAC has a unit structure, each unit being written around an everyday context, from which the theoretical aspects of the subject are drawn. Traditionally, chemistry is taught by theoretical topic with the contexts as 'bolt-on' additions. Approximately 900 students, 550 SAC and 350 non-SAC students are being asked to complete a diagnostic set of questions compiled in a one-hour test three times during their A-level course. The students are attending 22 schools and colleges nationwide. Some students will be interviewed to confirm the validity of their written responses. The topics covered in the test include conservation of matter, energetics, chemical bonding, elements compounds and mixtures, reaction rates and entropy. Students' responses are being analysed for the types of frameworks used in answering the questions. Patterns across a range

of questions are being looked for. Comparisons will be made between SAC and non-SAC students.
Status: Sponsored project
Source of Grant: ICI; Shell, jointly £15,000
Date of Research: 1991-1994
KEYWORDS: *A level examinations; chemistry education; science education; teaching methods*

10/1797
Department of Educational Studies, Heslington, York YO1 5DD
01904 430000
Davies, I. Dr; Riley, M. Dr
Teaching and learning about interpretations of the recent European past in the secondary school
Abstract: The aim of the project is to explore the ways in which contributions are made in history classrooms, by teachers and pupils, to the development of European Citizenship. The research in Phase One will involve indepth interviews (tape-recorded, with each lasting about 30 or 40 minutes) with a sample of History teachers in the York area, and a questionnaire to a sample of pupils. A local education authority advisor responsible for History, together with one local representative from higher education will be interviewed. The aim of the interviews and questionnaire will be to explore issues concerning the problems and possibilities of teaching interpretations of History in the context of lessons on the recent European past. Qualitative data techniques will be used to analyse transcriptions of these tape-recordings. Teachers' perspectives on the key issues concerning the implementation of such work will be compared with the perspectives of the staff from the local education authority and higher education, and with an analysis of texts (teaching packs, non-statutory guidance and statutory regulations) published for use by teachers. In Phase Two, based on the findings of Phase One, a draft pack of teaching and learning materials will be created and presented to a sample of teachers. The materials will be revised in the light of teachers' comments and suggestions. In Phase Three the curriculum materials will be trialled in local schools. Research will take place on the practice related to these materials. Teachers will be asked to keep structured diaries; a sample of lessons will be observed; a sample of teachers will be interviewed; a sample of pupils will be interviewed; and a sample of pupil work will be analysed. In addition, a meeting will be held with teachers following the teaching of the lessons so as to allow for the collection of general feedback.
Status: Sponsored project
Source of Grant: York University £2,850
Date of Research: 1993-1994
KEYWORDS: *citizenship education; European history; history studies*

10/1798
Department of Educational Studies, Heslington, York YO1 5DD
01904 430000
Adams, J. Mrs; *Supervisor:* Campbell, R. Dr; Ramsden, J. Dr
Learning styles of children with special educational needs
Abstract: This study explores the idea of learning styles and is attempting to develop a learning styles inventory for children with special educational needs. The aim is to be able to tailor learning activities to the preferred learning styles of pupils.
Status: Individual research
Date of Research: 1991-continuing
KEYWORDS: *learning strategies; special educational needs*

10/1799
Department of Educational Studies, Heslington, York YO1 5DD
01904 430000
Peck, A. Mr
Modern languages in the National Curriculum
Abstract: Data will be collected via video-recording of language lessons, tape-recorded post-lesson interviews, and questionnaire. The method of investigation is the case study, revealing unique features of individual teachers' methodology. The analysis of language teaching methodology will help teachers through inservice teacher education (INSET) to make principled changes to their own teaching methods in a search for greater effectiveness. The intention is to develop language-based INSET courses for teams of teachers working within a school. It is expected that the programmes will be subject specific, school specific, arising out of the needs of particular teachers in the classroom, i.e. 'demand-led'. The same work is to be done in continental schools, so that British language teachers have the oppor-

tunity of further enriching their professional expertise by studying how teachers on the Continent tackle similar problems.
Published Material: PECK, A. (1988). Language teachers at work. Hemel Hempstead: Prentice-Hall.; PECK, A. (1990). 'Autonomous experimentation in language teaching: a case study of question and answer', The Language Teacher, Vol 3, No 1, pp.9-20.
Status: Sponsored project
Source of Grant: Higher Education Funding Council
Date of Research: 1992-continuing
KEYWORDS: *comparative education; language teachers; modern language studies; National Curriculum*

10/1800
Department of Educational Studies, Heslington, York YO1 5DD
01904 430000
Spurgeon, C. Mr; *Supervisor:* Lister, I. Prof.
Learning about citizenship issues through literature
Abstract: Responding to calls to infuse the teaching of citizenship into the curriculum, this study considers the possibilities for literary texts. Using an action research methodology, the learning outcomes of teaching selected texts in two English comprehensives are described and analysed. The first school, in which the initial research was executed, is described as a middle England school with a prosperous, predominantly middle class 95% white catchment. Texts taught included: M.D. Taylor's 'Roll of Thunder'; S.E. Hinton's 'The Outsiders'; A Camus' 'The Outsider'; and Joan Lingard's 'Across the Barricades'. The recorded learning outcomes included: empathetic gains; an awareness of the students' own privileged backgrounds; increased awareness of social and political issues; and some students displaying a desire to create a more just and fair society. The research also revealed some openly racist students, with perceptions of their own superiority. Similar and additional texts were used in the second school, which had a less privileged catchment. Interesting similarities, and social class-based differences, in attitudes and perceptions were noted. Overall findings suggest that literary texts can be profitably used, with appropriate pedagogies to enhance citizenship knowledge, attitudes and action.
Published Material: SPURGEON, C. (1991). 'Teaching about a citizenship issue through literature', Citizenship, Vol 2, No 1, pp.3-7.; SPURGEON, C. (1993). 'Re-teaching 'Animal Farm' in a post-communist world', Citizenship, Vol 3, No 1, pp.11-14.; SPURGEON, C. (1993). 'Re-teaching 'Roll of Thunder' alongside poetry by black American women', Multicultural teaching, Vol 11, No 2, pp.25-30.
Status: Individual research
Date of Research: 1990-1994
KEYWORDS: *citizenship education; human rights; literature studies; pupil attitudes; racial attitudes; social attitudes*

10/1801
Department of Educational Studies, Heslington, York YO1 5DD
01904 430000
Durham University, School of Education, Leazes Road, Durham DH1 1TA
0191 374 2000
Millar, R. Dr; Gott, R. Dr; Lubben, F. Mr; Duggan, S. Mrs
The interaction of children's conceptual and procedural knowledge in science
Abstract: The aims of the project are to: 1) develop and refine a model of children's reasoning in response to practical investigation tasks; 2) use this model to explore differences in pupils' peformance of investigations with age and increasing experience of school science, so as to characterise differences between novice and more expert performance; and 3) explore the interaction between children's conceptual and procedural knowledge in responding to investigation tasks. Seven pre-trialled science investigations have been given to groups and classes of children aged 9, 11 and 14. The performance of groups of children has been closely observed and recorded using an observation checklist. Groups have then been interviewed, using pre-trialled probes of conceptual and procedural knowledge relevant to the given investigation, to explore indepth their understanding of ideas which they might have drawn upon in addressing the task. Data takes the form of a detailed case-record of each group's performance and interview responses. In a second phase, written diagnostic questions are being used to provide a broader picture of children's understanding of key ideas associated with empirical evidence and its collection. Preliminary analysis of results shows differences in performance between 9 and 14 year olds, and suggests that certain aspects of children's responses are due as much to socialisation into

the school laboratory setting as to 'rational' decisions about data collection.
Status: Sponsored project
Source of Grant: Economic and Social Research Council £89,000
Date of Research: 1991-1993
KEYWORDS: *learning activities; practical science; science activities; science education*

10/1802

Department of Educational Studies, Heslington, York YO1 5DD
01904 430000
University of Swaziland, Faculty of Education, P/Bag 4, Kwaluseni, Swaziland, Southern Africa
010 268 54435
Lubben, F. Mr; Waddington, D. Prof.; Campbell, R. Dr; Dlamini, B. Mrs; Millar, R. Dr
Inservice support for a technological approach in science education
Abstract: The research explores the effectiveness of three approaches for increasing the relevance of the science curriculum in Swaziland (Southern Africa): 1) The inclusion of technological content in science; 2) An application-led lesson structure using instances from the students' own experience; 3) An emphasis on problem-solving tasks. Effective innovation in classroom practice depends on teacher ownership of the innovation and an increase in teacher confidence through well-planned inservice support. This project intends to: 1) develop and trial two units of teaching and learning science materials for early secondary school classes through practising teachers; 2) develop a package of in-service materials to support teacher induction; and 3) evaluate the effectiveness of the induction process in terms of a change in teaching approach. During two separate workshops, twelve teachers draft two units of about twelve lessons each, which are edited in readiness for a third (induction) workshop for all the participant teachers. Feedback on the class usage of the materials is collected through interviews and class observations. An induction course (including in-class support) is conducted for a new cohort of twenty teachers using an inservice teacher education (INSET) package, and the lesson materials. The effectiveness of the format and the content of the induction process is evaluated through questionnaires, interviews and observations. After six months the impact on classroom practice is documented, establishing a change in teachers' 'concerns'. The impact will be related to specific characteristics of the INSET package and the initial readiness for change of the individual participants.
Status: Sponsored project
Source of Grant: Overseas Development Administration £29,000
Date of Research: 1992-1994
KEYWORDS: *educational materials; inservice teacher education; science education; Swaziland*

10/1803

Department of Language and Linguistic Science, Heslington, York YO1 5DD
01904 430000
Verma, M. Mr; Firth, S. Ms; Corrigan, K. Ms
Working with bilingual children
Abstract: This two-year project is supported by grants from the Universities Funding Council and Humberside County Council. The primary aim of this pilot project is to describe the role and strategies of the Bilingual Support Teachers/Assistants/Instructors and/or the English as a Second Language (ESL) teachers in the education of bilingual children primarily in the reception class (language support: mother tongue and ESL, assessment and recording of learning and achievement). The purpose of this study is also to identify the needs of bilingual pupils and the bilingual support and/or ESL staff, and to develop inservice teacher education (INSET) for them. The proposed research has provisionally been divided into four parts: 1) a survey of good practice: teaching and assessment of bilingual children; 2) a sociolinguistic profile of the bilingual support/ESL staff; 3) a description of the cognitive and linguistic development of a select number of children over a period of three terms, and 4) development of INSET for primary school teachers. The data for (1) to (3) will be collected in selected local education authorities (LEAs). The research team will consist of the Director, the Research Assistant and a number of on-site and/or floating researchers. The research will be based on the sociolinguistic and ethnographic data that classroom observation, children's language, questionnaire data, interviews and analysis of published literature from LEAs will provide.
Status: Sponsored project

Source of Grant: Universities Funding Council £22,000; Humberside County Council £5,000
Date of Research: 1991-1994
KEYWORDS: *bilingual pupils; English – second language; language teachers; limited English speaking; second language teaching*

10/1804

Department of Language and Linguistic Science, Heslington, York YO1 5DD
01904 430000
Université Louis Pasteur, LADISIS, URA 668 – CNRS, Section Psycholinguistique, 12 rue Goethe, 67000 Strasbourg, France
00 33 88 35 82 04
Russell, J. Dr; Verma, M. Mr; *Supervisor:* Warner, A. Dr; Le Page, R. Prof.; Tabouret-Keller, A. Prof.
International group for the study of language standardisation and the vernacularisation of literacy
Abstract: Biennial workshops in 1986, 1988, 1990 and 1992 have brought together a group of people each actively concerned with vernacular education, especially in the former colonies of Britain and France, but also in Europe and the Americas. The results of this work are now being put into a book, Vernacular Literacy Revisited, to be published in 1995.
Status: Sponsored project
Source of Grant: ESRC £3,000; Nuffield Foundation £2,000; York University £600; CNRS – Paris £2,000; British Academy £2,000; British Council £1,500
Date of Research: 1986-continuing
KEYWORDS: *developing countries; language policy; language standardisation; literacy; mother tongue*

10/1805

Department of Psychology, Heslington, York YO1 5DD
01904 430000
McDougall, S. Ms; *Supervisor:* Ellis, A. Prof.; Hulme, C. Dr; Monk, A. Dr
Extent and correlates of variability among different groups of readers
Abstract: The study has two principal aims. The first aim is to investigate whether different groups of readers matched on reading age show the same or different patterns of reading performance when latency as well as accuracy, and variability, as well as central tendency are taken into consideration. This should resolve current controversy over the extent to which dyslexic reading performance follows simply from their reading age or includes a differential deficit in, for example, phonological processing. The groups concerned will be: (1) dyslexic children (high IQ) with specific and unexpected reading retardation; (2) poor readers (low IQ) with nonspecific learning difficulties; (3) precocious readers (high IQ) whose reading age is ahead of their chronological age; and (4) normal readers. If reading age is the sole determinant of group reading patterns, then these four groups should not differ from one another. The second aim is to discover whether different reading patterns related to different patterns of strength and weakness in performance on tasks which do not involve reading per se, but tap aspects of cognition which may be relevant to the acquisition of reading. Different patterns of strength and weakness in reading skill will be related to different patterns of strength and weakness in basic visual and phonological processes. A broader subsidiary aim of this project is to evaluate the extent to which information-processing accounts of a skill such as reading can also provide the dimensions for characterising individual differences in cognitive ability.
Status: Sponsored project
Source of Grant: Economic and Social Research Council £56,966
Date of Research: 1990-1993
KEYWORDS: *cognitive ability; dyslexia; reading difficulties; reading skills*

10/1806

Department of Psychology, Heslington, York YO1 5DD
01904 430000
Eames, C. Dr; *Supervisor:* Cox, M. Dr
Drawing ability in gifted and non-gifted autistic children
Abstract: The development of depth representation in the drawings of normal children is now beginning to be understood. This research project was carried out to see whether the development of depth

portrayal in the drawings of autistic children follows a 'normal' path. Comparing autistic children with Down's Syndrome children and normal children, matched on non-verbal mental age, it was found that autistic children are developmentally delayed in their depth representation rather than showing anomalous strategies of depth portrayal.
Published Material: EAMES, K. & COX, M.V. (1994). 'Visual realism in the drawings of autistic, Down's syndrome and normal children', British Journal of Developmental Psychology, Vol 12.
Status: Sponsored project
Source of Grant: Medical Research Council £13,680
Date of Research: 1989-1993
KEYWORDS: autism; Down's Syndrome; drawing; gifted; special educational needs; visual arts

10/1807
Department of Psychology, Heslington, York YO1 5DD
01904 430000
Eames, C. Dr; *Supervisor:* Cox, M. Dr
The teaching of drawing in the infants school: an evaluation of the 'negotiated drawing' method
Abstract: The aim was to evaluate the effectiveness of ten lessons based on a 'negotiated drawing' method devised by Grant Cooke, an advisory arts teacher. The programme was administered by Cooke to two classes of children aged from 5 to 7 years. The drawings were compared with those of children in three further conditions. It was predicted that those in the 'negotiated drawing' condition would improve most, since over and above the merits of the approach itself Cooke is almost an experienced art educator dealing with young children and, furthermore, is very enthusiastic about and committed to his own approach. In contrast, it was predicted that the drawings completed by the children taught in the normal way by their own classteachers would show least improvement. Similarly, it was predicted that the normal drawing lessons given by Cooke would not lead to a marked improvement in the children's drawings. Finally, an improvement in drawings was predicted when the lessons were given by a supply teacher specially trained in Cooke's approach. The results showed that children in all conditions improved their drawings over time. There was also evidence that the children in the two groups who completed the programme of 'negotiated drawing' improved their drawings more than the two groups who were given normal drawings lessons.
Published Material: COX, M.V., EAMES, K. & COOKE, G. (1994). 'The teaching of drawing in the infants' school: an evaluation of the negotiated drawing approach', The International Journal of Early Years Education, Vol 2.
Status: Sponsored project
Source of Grant: Leverhulme Trust £35,550
Date of Research: 1992-1994
KEYWORDS: art education; drawing; infant school education

10/1808
Department of Psychology, Heslington, York YO1 5DD
01904 430000
Newcastle upon Tyne University, Department of Psychology, Ridley Building, Newcastle upon Tyne NE1 7RU
0191 222 6000
Hulme, C. Dr; Snowling, M. Prof.; Smith, A. Mr; Bolt, G. Dr
A connectionist model of the development of visual word recognition
Abstract: The project will develop and evaluate a model of the processes involved in learning a sight vocabulary in the early stages of learning to read. The model will be evaluated and refined on the basis of data from studies of children's reading errors and will provide an explicit theoretical account of why good phonological skills aid the rapid learning of a sight vocabulary and how such learning may be impeded in dyslexic children. The research, which depends crucially on collaboration between different disciplines, will also contribute to the development of connectionist modelling techniques by advancing understanding of how to build a prior knowledge into such models, and in applying ideas taken from the study of self-organising neural maps to the modelling of higher level cognitive processes.
Published Material: HULME, C., SNOWLING, M. & QUINLAN, P. (1991). 'Connectionism and learning to read: steps towards a psychologically plausible model', Reading and Writing, Vol 3, pp.159-168.; RACK, J., HULME, C. & SNOWLING, M. (1993). 'Learning to read: a theoretical synthesis'. In: REESE, H. (Ed). Advances in child development and behavior: Vol 24. Orlando,

Florida: Academic Press.; SNOWLING, M., HULME, C., & GOULANDRIS, N. 'Word recognition in developmental dyslexia: a connectionist interpretation', Quarterly Journal of Experimental Psychology. (in press).; RACK, J, HULME, C., SNOWLING, M. & WIGHTMAN, J. 'The role of phonology in young children learning to read words: the direct mapping hypothesis', Journal of Experimental Child Psychology. (in press).
Status: Sponsored project
Source of Grant: Economic and Social Research Council; Medical Research Council; Science & Engineering Research Council, jointly £113,000
Date of Research: 1990-1994
KEYWORDS: beginning reading; dyslexia; sight method; word recognition

10/1809
Language Teaching Centre, Heslington, York YO1 5DD
01904 430000
Curtis, A. Mr; *Supervisor:* Kyriacou, C. Dr; Low, G. Mr
Language support systems of/for overseas students at British universities: the York case study
Abstract: As the number of non-native speakers of English at British universities increases, so too will the demands on language support systems. The research aims to investigate the changing language needs of postgraduate overseas students, both taught and research, as they go through their courses of study. This is the first longitudinal study of this area involving overseas students and their supervisors. Questionnaire data collection from 100 overseas students, was followed by indepth, tape-recorded interviews with 20 overseas students (undergraduates and postgraduates) from 14 departments. These interviews led to the identification of Peer Support Groups within academic speech communities and Language Learning/Language Use Contracts. In the second phase, 20 postgraduate overseas students and their supervisors have also been interviewed (audio-recorded). In the third and final phase, all students and their supervisors will be interviewed again to assess the changes in language demands and needs as the courses/research progress and develop. The research will relate the findings from the interviews to theories of: second language acquisition; learning in groups; peer support; speech communities; awareness of language needs; needs analysis; and language testing/assessment.
Status: Individual research
Date of Research: 1992-1994
KEYWORDS: English – second language; English for academic purposes; limited English speaking; overseas students; second language learning

10/1810
Language Teaching Centre, Heslington, York YO1 5DD
01904 43000
Universität Munchen, Lehrstuhl für die Didaktik der Englischen Sprache und Literatur, Schellingstrasse 3, D-8000 Munchen 40, Germany
02180 2995
Green, P. Mr; Hecht, Kh. Prof.
Learner language
Abstract: This was a project to investigate learner language and compare it at all stages with the language of native peers. The project involved German (and, for certain tasks, French, Hungarian, Italian and Swedish) school learners of English and English school pupils in performing communicative tasks in English (letter writing, oral and written narrative, and oral transaction) and completing tasks of grammatical and lexical competence. There were over 6000 pupil productions. The productions were analysed from the following standpoints: (1) linguistic form; (2) content; (3) communicative effectiveness; (4) strategies; (5) self correction/monitoring; (6) grammatical and lexical competence and performance; (7) development of communicative competence; (8) assessment/reactions by natives and non-natives. Conclusions were very varied.
Published Material: GREEN, P.S. & HECHT, Kh. (1985). 'Native and non-native evaluation of learners' errors in written discourse', System, Vol 13, No 2, pp.77-79.; GREEN, P.S. & HECHT, Kh. (1987). 'The influence of accuracy on communicative effectiveness', British Journal of Language Teaching, Vol 25, No 2, pp.79-84.; GREEN, P.S. & HECHT, Kh. (1988). 'The sympathetic native speaker – a GCSE role-play for the teacher', Modern Languages, Vol 69, No 1, pp.3-10.; GREEN, P.S. & HECHT, Kh. (1990). 'Investigating learners' language'. In: BRUMFIT, C.J. & MITCHELL, R.

(Eds). Research in the language classroom. Basingstoke: MacMillan.; GREEN, P.S. & HECHT, Kh. (1993). 'Language awareness of German pupils', Language Awareness, Vol 2, No 3, pp.125-142. A full list of publications is available from the researcher.
Status: Sponsored project
Source of Grant: British Council Academic Linking Scheme £600; European Community £1,400; EC Erasmus £1,400; York University £1,000; Leverhulme Trust £2,500
Date of Research: 1980-1993
KEYWORDS: comparative education; English; German; language tests; modern language studies; native speakers; second language teaching

10/1811

Language Teaching Centre, Heslington, York YO1 5DD
01904 430000
Low, G. Mr; *Supervisor:* Kyriacou, C. Dr
Questionnaire design project
Abstract: The object of the study is to explore the reactions of university students to linguistic aspects of the wording of Likert-type questionnaire items. Items of particular interest are those with 'AGREE/DISAGREE' as rating verbs and 'STRONGLY' or 'COM-PLETELY' as adverbs. Three tests have been designed, involving closer and closer approximations to the task of actually completing a questionnaire. They involve an acceptability test, an editing task and a think aloud protocol. In addition a test has been devised to establish empirically the levels of certain types of salience attached by subjects to sentences in a questionnaire-type environment.
Published Material: LOW, G.D. (1988). 'The semantics of questionnaire rating scales', Evaluation and Research in Education, Vol 2, No 2, pp.69-79.; LOW, G.D. (1991). 'Talking to questionnaires: pragmatic models in questionnaire design'. In: ADAMS, P., HEATON, B. & HOWARTH, P. (Eds). (1991). Review of English Language Teaching 1(2): Socio-Cultural Issues in English for Academic Purposes, pp.118-143. Modern English Publications in association with the British Council.; LOW, G., TASKER, I. & LU, H. (1991). 'The wording of bipolar attitude scales in Chinese', Educational Research, Vol 33, No 2, pp.141-150.; LOW, G. (1994). Verbal invisibility? The perception of intensifiers and hedges in questionnaire items. Applied Language Research Papers No 94/01. York: University of York, Department of Educational Studies.
Status: Individual research
Date of Research: 1986-continuing
KEYWORDS: Likert scales; linguistics; opinions; questionnaires; rating scales; semantics

Author Index

Abbas, S. Mrs 10/1279
Abbott, A. Ms 10/0935
Abbott, D. Ms 10/0153 10/0155
Abbott, I. Mr 10/1715 10/1743 10/1744
Abbott, L. Mrs 10/1573 10/1577
Abbott, P. Mr 10/0447
Abdel-Ghany, I. Dr 10/1642
Abdullah, S. Mr 10/0889
Abdulraman, A. Mr 10/0055
Abou El-Khir, M. Mr 10/0579
Abu-Jalala, F. Mrs 10/0290
Ackerman, J. Ms 10/0140
Ackland, J. Mr 10/0365
Adams, E. Ms 10/1423
Adams, J. Mrs 10/1798
Adams, T. Dr 10/0712
Adelman, C. Prof. 10/1248
Adler, A. Ms 10/1652
Adler, M. Mr 10/0345
Afzalnia, M. Mr 10/0520
Ager, D. Prof. 10/0031 10/0034
Ager, R. Mr 10/1613
Aggleton, P. Dr 10/0826 10/0827 10/0828
    10/0829 10/0831 10/0832
Ahier, J. Dr 10/1653
Ahmad, Y. Ms 10/1372
Ahmed, S. Mr 10/0985
Ahrens, P. Mrs 10/0461 10/0462
Ahuja, A. Mrs 10/0189
Ainley, P. Dr 10/0528 10/0529
Ainscow, M. Mr 10/0178 10/0179 10/0180
    10/0187 10/0189
Aird, E. Mrs 10/1093
Aitken, S. Dr 10/0325
Aitken, T. Mr 10/1739
Al Rawat, H. Dr 10/0898
Al-Alawi, K. Mr 10/0052
Al-Bassam, A. Mr 10/1682
Al-Rajab, E. Mr 10/1513
Al-Seaidy, H. Mr 10/0360
Al-Shehri, A. Dr 10/0701
Alansari, I. Mr 10/1393
Alaydarous, A. Mr 10/0487
Alcindor, L. Ms 10/0200
Aldrich, R. Dr 10/0769
Alexander, B. Ms 10/0531
Alexander, H. Mrs 10/0392
Alexopolou, E. Miss 10/0642
Alfrey, M. Mrs 10/0196
Alker, D. Mr 10/0574
Allan, J. Ms 10/1453 10/1455
Allen, J. Miss 10/0133
Allen, S. Prof. 10/0122 10/0123
Allen, W. Mr 10/1405
Allison, B. Prof. 10/0254 10/0255 10/0256
    10/0257 10/0259 10/0260
Allsobrook, D. Dr 10/1677
Allsop, L. Ms 10/0148
Alsford, V. Mrs 10/0171
Alsop, A. Mr 10/0913
Alsop, S. Mr 10/1293 10/1315
Alston, J. Dr 10/0917
Alston, P. Dr 10/0207 10/0208
Ambrose, P. Ms 10/1517
Amir, G. Mr 10/0981
Anamuah-Mensah, J. Dr 10/0594
Anderson, C. Mr 10/0334
Anderson, J. Mrs 10/1699 10/1701
Anderson, P. Mr 10/1287
Andrews, P. Mr 10/0950
Andrews, R. Dr 10/0472 10/0476 10/0485
Anghileri, J. Dr 10/0172
Anghilieri, N. Ms 10/0755
Annett, M. Dr 10/0659
Anning, A. Ms 10/0620

Antoniou, M. Miss 10/1692
ApThomas, J. Mr 10/0952 10/0957
Aplin, D. Dr 10/0961
Aplin, R. Mr 10/0664 10/0669
Archer, M. Mr 10/0938
Ariffin, S. Mrs 10/0422
Armitage, S. Ms 10/0570
Armour, K. Mrs 10/1761
Armstrong, D. Mr 10/0553
Armstrong, N. Dr 10/0351
Arney, N. Mr 10/1332
Arnold, M. Mr 10/1795
Arnot, M. Dr 10/1385
Arnott, M. Mrs 10/0345
Arnott, M. Ms 10/0076
Arthur, C. Ms 10/0941
Ashby, J. Mr 10/0998 10/1027
Ashby, P. Mrs 10/1022
Ashenden, C. Ms 10/0137
Asher, C. Dr 10/0649
Ashton, E. Miss 10/0297
Ashworth, A. Mr 10/0906
Asoko, H. Mrs 10/0589
Aspinall, M. Ms 10/1684 10/1685
Atherton, M. Ms 10/0962
Atkin, J. Ms 10/1785
Atkinson, S. Ms 10/1764
Attwood, G. Ms 10/1656
Aubrey, C. Ms 10/0306
Austin, J. Mr 10/1194
Austin, R. Dr 10/1569 10/1570 10/1571 10/1572
    10/1575
Austin, S. Mr 10/0134
Awiria, O. Mr 10/0298
Ayles, R. Mrs 10/1260
Ayres, D. Mr 10/0879

Babila-Njingum, J. Mr 10/1277
Baggs, C. Mr 10/1603
Bagilhole, B. Dr 10/0903
Bagley, C. Dr 10/0994
Bagnall, G. Dr 10/0315 10/0316 10/0321
Bagnall, J. Mr 10/1433
Bailey, G. Dr 10/1299
Baker, C. Dr 10/1583 10/1584 10/1792
Baker, C. Prof. 10/0377
Baker, K. Ms 10/1094
Baker, R. Mr 10/0611
Baldwin, S. Mrs 10/0907
Bale, J. Mr 10/0496
Ball, D. Mr 10/0585
Ball, S. Prof. 10/0220 10/0221 10/1389
Ballantyne, H. Mrs 10/0343
Bancroft, D. Dr 10/1189
Banerji, A. Mr 10/1551
Bankowska, A. Dr 10/1445 10/1447
Banks, F. Mr 10/1592
Barber, J. Mrs 10/1603
Barber, M. Prof. 10/0504 10/0516
Barbor, M. Mr 10/1315
Barker, P. Prof. 10/1551 10/1552 10/1553
Barker, T. Mr 10/0535
Barker, V. Mrs 10/1796
Barnes, E. Mrs 10/0921
Barnes, K. Mr 10/1131
Barnes, S. Dr 10/0151
Barnes, S. Mr 10/1530
Barnett, M. Prof. 10/0807 10/0844 10/0845
Barnett, R. Dr 10/0822
Baron, A-M. Dr 10/0646
Barr, A. Mr 10/0421 10/0422 10/0424
Barr, J. Ms 10/1729
Barr, K. Mr 10/1472
Barr, M. Ms 10/1408
Barr, N. Dr 10/0856

Barrett, E. Dr 10/0825
Barron, P. Mr 10/0435
Barrow, E. Ms 10/0001
Bartlett, S. Mr 10/1779
Barton, L. Prof. 10/0825
Bassett, J. Mr 10/0588
Bassey, M. Dr 10/1116
Bastiani, J. Dr 10/1328
Bastide, D. Mr 10/0137
Bates, R. Dr 10/0110
Batho, R. Mr 10/0212 10/0213
Bax, S. Mr 10/0198
Baxter, D. Mr 10/0020
Bayes, G. Miss 10/1604
Bayliss, F. Prof. 10/1130
Bayliss, J. Ms 10/1443
Beard, R. Dr 10/0110 10/0631
Beattie, N. Dr 10/0685 10/0690
Beattie, W. Mr 10/0284
Becher, T. Prof. 10/0166
Bedford, H. Ms 10/1629 10/1641
Bee, P. Ms 10/0853
Beggs, W. Dr 10/1145
Bell, F. Prof. 10/0392
Bell, L. Dr 10/0915 10/1740
Bell, R. Dr 10/1194 10/1195
Bendelow, G. Dr 10/0803
Benham, K. Ms 10/0954
Benn, C. Dr 10/0088
Bennett, A. Mr 10/0142
Bennett, H. Mr 10/0584
Bennett, J. Mr 10/0473
Bennett, R. Prof. 10/0855 10/0856
Bennett, S. Mr 10/1149
Bennett, S. Prof. 10/0359
Bentley, B. Mrs 10/1205
Bentley, M. Mr 10/1767
Benton, M. Dr 10/0212
Berdousi, E. Ms 10/0092
Beresford, C. Mr 10/0840
Bergin, S. Ms 10/0568
Berridge, D. Dr 10/0988
Berry, J. Mr 10/0077
Berry, J. Prof. 10/1216
Bertram, A. Mr 10/1786 10/1787 10/1791
Best, R. Prof. 10/1302 10/1313 10/1322
Betts, S. Ms 10/1587
Betts-Gosling, E. Ms 10/1521
Beveridge, M. Prof. 10/0141 10/0150
Beveridge, S. Dr 10/0646
Beverton, S. Dr 10/1101
Bibby, N. Mr 10/1156
Bichard, A. Dr 10/1331
Biddle, S. Dr 10/0351
Bidgood, S. Dr 10/1402
Biggs, M. Mr 10/0478
Bill, A. Mr 10/1606
Billington, J. Mr 10/0024
Bilton, L. Miss 10/1391
Bimrose, J. Ms 10/1511
Bines, H. Dr 10/1208
Bird, C. Ms 10/0842
Bird, D. Mr 10/0582
Bird, J. Mr 10/1676
Birke, L. Dr 10/1131
Birley, G. Dr 10/1766 10/1767 10/1768 10/1769
    10/1770 10/1771 10/1772 10/1773 10/1774
    10/1775 10/1776 10/1777 10/1778 10/1779
    10/1780 10/1782
Black, E. Ms 10/0139
Black, H. Mr 10/1330 10/1333 10/1341 10/1346
    10/1351 10/1353 10/1355 10/1360 10/1365
    10/1367 10/1368
Black, M. Ms 10/0942
Black, P. Miss 10/0197

Black, T. Dr 10/1492 10/1505
Blackburn, R. Dr 10/0176
Blackman, S. Dr 10/1503
Blacksell, R. Ms 10/1284
Blades, M. Dr 10/1376
Blair, A. Ms 10/1332
Blake, C. Mr 10/1760
Blake, D. Mr 10/0214
Blake, M. Mrs 10/0132
Blamire-Prosser, J. Mrs 10/1494
Blatchford, P. Dr 10/0758
Blease, D. Mr 10/0897
Blee, H. Mr 10/1408 10/1418
Blenkin, G. Ms 10/0708 10/0715
Bloomfield, A. Dr 10/1115
Bloor, C. Dr 10/1475
Blunden, G. Dr 10/1656 10/1657
Bo, J. Mr 10/1135
Boddington, G. Mr 10/0017
Boden, J. Mrs 10/0697
Boice, M. Mr 10/1535
Bolam, R. Prof. 10/0152 10/0156
Bolla, M. Ms 10/1114
Bolt, G. Dr 10/1808
Bolwell, L. Dr 10/0132 10/0133
Bone, J. Mrs 10/1656
Boohan, D. Mr 10/0834
Boorman, J. Dr 10/1254
Booth, A. Mr 10/0093
Booth, L. Ms 10/0284
Boreham, N. Prof. 10/0969 10/0970
Bornat, R. Prof. 10/1183
Botcherby, C. Miss 10/0446
Boulton, M. Dr 10/1371 10/1372
Bourne, V. Mr 10/1408 10/1427
Bovair, K. Mr 10/0095
Bowen, R. Mr 10/1113 10/1118
Bowker, P. Mr 10/0138
Bowl, R. Mr 10/0066
Bown, L. Prof. 10/1195
Box, V. Ms 10/1404
Boxall, V. Mrs 10/0207
Boyce-Tillman, J. Dr 10/0532
Boyd, B. Dr 10/0412
Boyes, E. Dr 10/0700
Boyle, B. Mr 10/0977 10/0978
Boyle, J. Mr 10/1418
Boyle, M-L. Miss 10/0248
Boyne, G. Dr 10/0377
Bozic, N. Mr 10/0104
Bradley, H. Mr 10/0183
Bradley, J. Dr 10/0989 10/0991 10/1013 10/1014
    10/1036 10/1037 10/1039 10/1048 10/1049
    10/1055 10/1057 10/1059 10/1060 10/1061
    10/1062 10/1063 10/1064 10/1068 10/1069
    10/1072 10/1073 10/1074 10/1075
Bramwell, A. Mrs 10/0584
Brannen, J. Dr 10/0852
Brattan, D. Dr 10/1618
Brauti, J. Mr 10/0148
Bray, R. Mr 10/0558
Breese, N. Mrs 10/1083
Breet, F. Ms 10/0286
Brehony, K. Dr 10/0569 10/1260 10/1263 10/1270
Brew, A. Dr 10/1238
Bridge, C. Mr 10/0201
Bridges, D. Prof. 10/1632
Brimblecombe, N. Ms 10/1207
Brna, P. Dr 10/0324
Broadbent, T. Rev. 10/1472
Broadfoot, P. Prof. 10/0036 10/0153 10/0154
    10/0155 10/1669
Broadhead, P. Dr 10/0647
Brook, D. Mr 10/0437 10/0438
Brookes, K. Mr 10/0482
Brooks, G. Dr 10/1031 10/1047 10/1048 10/1049
    10/1050 10/1051 10/1084
Brooks, R. Ms 10/1610
Brooks, V. Dr 10/1730 10/1735
Brosnan, T. Mr 10/0836 10/0837
Brotherton, C. Prof. 10/1581
Brown S. Prof. 10/1452
Brown, A. Dr 10/0931 10/0987 10/1497 10/1503
    10/1504 10/1508 10/1511
Brown, A. Mr 10/1624
Brown, C. Mrs 10/1625
Brown, G. Prof. 10/0193 10/1640
Brown, M. Mrs 10/0666
Brown, M. Prof. 10/0188 10/0735
Brown, S. Dr 10/0954 10/0955

Brown, S. Prof. 10/1444 10/1445 10/1447
    10/1454 10/1455 10/1457
Brownhill, R. Dr 10/1493 10/1496 10/1499
Bruce, T. Mrs 10/1785
Brumfit, C. Prof. 10/1239 10/1390 10/1392
    10/1393 10/1395
Bruntlett, S. Mr 10/0257 10/0258
Bryant, A. Miss 10/0902
Bryant, B. Prof. 10/0725
Bryant, R. Mr 10/1329
Buchan, A. Miss 10/0624
Buckingham, D. Mr 10/0762
Bull, J. Ms 10/0851
Bull, S. Miss 10/0324
Bullock, A. Dr 10/0075 10/0076
Bullock, K. Ms 10/0049 10/0051
Bunch, A. Ms 10/1287
Burgess, A. Dr 10/1759
Burgess, R. Mr 10/0497
Burgess, R. Prof. 10/1099 10/1702 10/1703
    10/1704 10/1705 10/1706
Burgess, T. Dr 10/0761
Burghes, D. Prof. 10/0360
Burke, J. Dr 10/1512
Burnett, F. Dr 10/0531
Burns, M. Mrs 10/0676
Burrows, A. Ms 10/1605
Burt, G. Mr 10/1172 10/1173 10/1175
Burton, D. Dr 10/0578
Busby, M. Mrs 10/1126
Bush, T. Prof. 10/0672 10/0673 10/0674
Busher, H. Dr 10/0887 10/0888 10/0891
Butler, G. Mr 10/0157
Byard, M. Mr 10/0593
Bynner, J. Prof. 10/0232
Byram, M. Dr 10/0286 10/0290 10/0292 10/0293
    10/0295 10/0308 10/0309 10/1554

Cabral, B. Ms 10/1611
Caillods, F. Ms 10/1539
Cale, L. Mrs 10/0307
Callender, C. Ms 10/1283
Came, F. Mr 10/0138
Cameron, C. Ms 10/0851
Cameron, L. Ms 10/0655
Campbell, A. Ms 10/0944
Campbell, D. Dr 10/0005
Campbell, P. Mr 10/0430
Campbell, R. Dr 10/1798 10/1802
Campbell, R. Prof. 10/0463
Candappa, M. Mr 10/0851
Canen, A. Mrs 10/0423
Cant, R. Mr 10/0200
Capey, C. Mrs 10/1472
Capizzi, E. Ms 10/0225 10/0226
Carhart, J. Rev. 10/0208
Carr, M. Dr 10/0535
Carr-Hill, R. Prof. 10/0339
Carre, C. Dr 10/0374
Carroll, R. Mr 10/0983
Carter, D. Mr 10/0615
Carter, J. Ms 10/0227 10/0231
Carter, K. Ms 10/0934
Castle, A. Mr 10/1401
Catt, R. Mr 10/1759
Cavanagh, J. Mr 10/0413
Cavanagh, S. Prof. 10/1100
Cavendish, M. Mr 10/1609
Chambers, E. Ms 10/1167
Chambers, F. Dr 10/1252
Chambers, G. Mr 10/0608 10/0616 10/0649
Chambers, J. Ms 10/0050
Chambers, M. Mrs 10/1576
Chan, Y. Ms 10/0974
Chana, U. Ms 10/1284
Chandler, W. Mr 10/0488
Chapple, M. Miss 10/1164
Charles, L. Mrs 10/0025
Charlton, A. Dr 10/0205
Charlwood, A. Mr 10/0163
Chatfield, J. Mrs 10/0697
Cherrington, D. Prof. 10/1611 10/1614
Cheseldine, S. Dr 10/1471
Child, D. Prof. 10/0611
Chiltern, E. Dr 10/1314
Chitty, C. Dr 10/0088
Chivers, B. Ms 10/1607
Christie, T. Prof. 10/0927 10/0976 10/0977
    10/0979
Christophers, U. Mrs 10/1007 10/1019 10/1023

    10/1054
Churcher, J. Mr 10/0912
Civil, J. Mrs 10/1438
Clark, J. Mr 10/0281
Clark, N. Miss 10/0197
Clark, U. Ms 10/1097
Clark, V. Ms 10/1221
Clarke, G. Ms 10/0143
Clarke, J. Mr 10/0684
Clausen, T. Dr 10/1053
Clayton, A. Dr 10/0157 10/0158
Clayton, A. Mr 10/0436
Cleaver, H. Mrs 10/0243
Cleland, G. Mrs 10/1778
Clement, R. Prof. 10/1235
Cleves, I. Mr 10/0054
Clibbens, J. Dr 10/1220
Clifford, J. Ms 10/0489
Clift, S. Dr 10/0197
Cline, T. Mr 10/0907
Cloke, C. Dr 10/0047
Clowes, P. Mr 10/0887
Clyne, P. Mr 10/0710 10/1214
Coben, D. Ms 10/0710
Cockburn, A. Dr 10/1628
Cockett, M. Mr 10/0942 10/0956
Cockett, P. Ms 10/0944
Coe, B. Mr 10/0259
Coe, J. Mr 10/0196
Coffield, F. Prof. 10/1484
Colclough, C. Dr 10/1524
Colclough, P. Mr 10/0505
Cole, G. Mr 10/1532
Cole, H. Mrs 10/1647
Coleman, H. Mr 10/0656
Coleman, J. Mrs 10/1443
Coleman, M. Mrs 10/0672 10/0673 10/0674
Coleman, P. Mr 10/0644
Coles, J. Mrs 10/0614
Colley, A. Dr 10/0662
Collins, F. Ms 10/1304 10/1309
Collins, J. Mrs 10/0646
Conolly, M. Mr 10/1654
Conroy, J. Mr 10/1412
Constable, H. Ms 10/0620
Constable, H. Prof. 10/1480 10/1481 10/1483
Conti-Ramsden, G. Dr 10/0972
Cook, G. Dr 10/0655
Cook, M. Mrs 10/0094
Cook, P. Mr 10/0289
Cooke, A. Mr 10/0266 10/0267
Cooke, H. Mrs 10/1185
Cooke, P. Mr 10/1114
Cooksey, J. Prof. 10/1326
Cooper, B. Dr 10/0218 10/0445 10/1531
Cooper, C. Dr 10/0957
Cooper, M. Dr 10/0443
Cooper, W. Mr 10/1414
Cope, P. Dr 10/1446
Copeland, I. Mr 10/1260
Copley, T. Mr 10/0357
Corbett, J. Dr 10/1646
Corbett, P. Mr 10/0206
Cordingley, P. Ms 10/0162
Cornelius, M. Mr 10/0299
Corrigan, K. Ms 10/1803
Cosford, B. Mr 10/0452
Costello, J. Mr 10/0893
Costley, C. Ms 10/1507
Costley, D. Ms 10/1733
Cotton, J. Mrs 10/0285
Cotton, P. Ms 10/0301
Coulby, D. Dr 10/0038 10/1651
Counihan, M. Dr 10/1398 10/1399
Courtenay, D. Ms 10/1000
Cousins, J. Ms 10/0364
Cowan, B. Dr 10/1261 10/1262
Cowan, R. Dr 10/0748 10/0749
Cowie, H. Dr 10/1371 10/1372
Cox, B. Dr 10/0718
Cox, D. Mr 10/1137
Cox, M. Dr 10/1806 10/1807
Coyle, P. Mr 10/0047
Craig, D. Mr 10/1146
Cremin, P. Mr 10/0534
Cresswell, M. Mr 10/0030
Crocker, A. Prof. 10/1765
Croft, A. Dr 10/0586
Croll, P. Prof. 10/0153 10/0155 10/1656
Crombie, R. Mr 10/1747

Crook, D. Mr 10/0663
Cross, V. Mrs 10/0073
Crossley, M. Dr 10/0142 10/0143 10/0144
Crouch, C. Mr 10/1579
Crowley, K. Mr 10/0861
Crowther, N. Mr 10/0454
Croxford, L. Ms 10/0311
Crozier-Smith, D. Mr 10/0019
Crystal, L. Dr 10/0911 10/0915
Cuff, D. Miss 10/1473
Cullen, J. Dr 10/1549
Curran, D. Dr 10/1475 10/1477
Curtis, A. Mr 10/1809
Curtis, K. Ms 10/1675
Cutland, N. Prof. 10/0250

D'Arcy, J. Mr 10/1108
D'Armenia, M. Ms 10/0234
Da Cunha, A. Sr 10/1142
Dadds, M. Dr 10/0182
Daghistani, B. Mrs 10/1741
Daines, J. Dr 10/1143
Dallat, J. Dr 10/1577
Daniels, H. Dr 10/0755
Daniels, R. Mr 10/0699
Daniels, S. Mrs 10/0652
Darby, D. Mr 10/0974
Darling, J. Dr 10/0002 10/0003 10/0004
Davenport, A. Mr 10/1106
Davey, B. Mr 10/0529
David, M. Prof. 10/0163 10/1385
David, T. Ms 10/1741
Davidson, J. Dr 10/0527
Davies, B. Prof. 10/1678 10/1689
Davies, C. Mr 10/0378 10/0379
Davies, G. Dr 10/1782
Davies, I. Dr 10/1370 10/1793 10/1797
Davies, J. Mr 10/1215
Davies, J. Mrs 10/0965 10/0971 10/1109
Davies, J. Prof. 10/0015
Davies, L. Dr 10/0074 10/0084
Davies, L. Ms 10/1593
Davies, M. Ms 10/1742
Davies, P. Mr 10/0963 10/0964 10/0977 10/0978
    10/1439
Davies, P. Ms 10/0225 10/0226 10/0227 10/0228
    10/0229 10/0230 10/0231
Davies, R. Dr 10/0211
Davies, W. Mr 10/0378
Davies, W. Prof. 10/1654
Davis, A. Dr 10/0288
Davis, D. Mr 10/1611
Davis, J. Mr 10/0331
Davis, M. Dr 10/0272 10/0274 10/0281
Davis, M. Mr 10/0958
Davis, N. Dr 10/0369 10/0370 10/0371
Davis, R. Dr 10/1407
Dawkins, J. Mr 10/1255
Day, C. Prof. 10/1152 10/1159
Day, D. Mr 10/0147
Day, J. Mrs 10/1568
De La Gorgendiere, L. Dr 10/0344
DeJonckheere, S. Ms 10/0935
Dean, D.Mr 10/0978
Dean, J. Dr 10/1498
Dean, W. Mr 10/1648
Dee, L. Ms 10/0751 10/1069
Deem, R. Prof. 10/0536 10/0569
Del Soldato, T. Dr 10/1542
Delap, M. Dr 10/0030
Delbridge, J. Mr 10/1778
Delve, R. Mr 10/0373
Demaine, J. Dr 10/0868 10/0869 10/0870 10/0871
    10/0877 10/0878 10/0880 10/0894 10/0895
    10/0896
Demetre, J. Dr 10/0759
Demsetz, E. Ms 10/0617
Denicolo, P. Dr 10/0987 10/1486 10/1487
    10/1490 10/1491 10/1493 10/1495 10/1509
Denley, P. Dr 10/0040
Denscombe, M. Dr 10/0261
Derby, J. Mrs 10/0207
Derbyshire, G. Mr 10/1083
Derricott, R. Mr 10/0696 10/0701
Desforges, C. Prof. 10/0358 10/0361 10/0364
    10/0374 10/1106
Desombre, T. Mr 10/1486
Devine, M. Mrs 10/1330 10/1334 10/1338
    10/1346
Devlin, T. Mr 10/0916

Dexter, G. Mr 10/0287
Dhingra, S. Ms 10/1114
Dibbo, J. Mr 10/1233
Dickie, S. Ms 10/0335
Dickinson, A. Mr 10/0765 10/0768
Dickinson, L. Mr 10/0456
Dickinson, N. Ms 10/0462
Dickson, P. Mr 10/1001 10/1045 10/1078
    10/1079 10/1080 10/1088
Digby, B. Mr 10/0977
Dillon, M. Mr 10/0905
Ding, D. Mr 10/0555
Diniz, F. Mr 10/0453
Direne, A. Mr 10/1547
Disney, A. Ms 10/1115
Dixon, J. Mr 10/1407 10/1408 10/1426
Dlamini, B. Mrs 10/1802
Dobson, B. Mr 10/1555
Dobson, N. Mr 10/0664
Docherty, G. Ms 10/1331
Dock, G. Mr 10/1315
Dodd, J. Dr 10/1619
Dodds, A. Dr 10/1145 10/1146
Dodge, L. Ms 10/1300
Doggett, A. Ms 10/0435
Doherty, G. Prof 10/1780
Doherty, M. Mr 10/1777
Dombey, H. Dr 10/0135 10/0136 10/1762
Donald, A. Dr 10/1675 10/1679 10/1680 10/1681
Donn, G. Dr 10/0327 10/0331 10/0332
Donnelly, J. Dr 10/0590 10/0591 10/0612
    10/0623 10/0624 10/0625 10/0634 10/0650
Dorn, L. Dr 10/0106
Dorn, N. Dr 10/0492
Douglas, F. Mr 10/0484
Douglas, G. Dr 10/0104
Down, B. Dr 10/0170
Doxford, P. Ms 10/0850
Doyle, A. Dr 10/1145
Drake, F. Dr 10/0637
Drame, M. Mr 10/0456
Drane, J. Mrs 10/0671
Draper, J. Mrs 10/0452
Draper, M. Mr 10/0436
Dray, A. Dr 10/0028
Drever, E. Mr 10/1444
Drever, M. Mrs 10/1245
Driver, R. Prof. 10/0590 10/0591 10/0592
    10/0596 10/0626 10/0637 10/0642
Drysdale, D. Dr 10/1018
Du Bolay, B. Prof. 10/1543
Du Boulay, J. Dr 10/1542
Dubowitz, L. Dr 10/0745 10/0760
Duckett, H. Ms 10/0915
Duckworth, R. Ms 10/1610
Dudley, J. Mr 10/1777 10/1778
Duffield, B. Mr 10/0579
Duffield, J. Mrs 10/1445 10/1454
Duffield, R. Mr 10/0912
Duffin, J. Mrs 10/0249
Duggan, S. Mrs 10/1801
Duke, C. Prof. 10/0789 10/1711
Duncan, D. Ms 10/1099
Duncan, E. Dr 10/0392
Dunford, J. Dr 10/0647
Dunkwu, K. Mr 10/1114
Dunn, W. Mr 10/0394 10/0408 10/0425 10/0789
Dunne, J. Mr 10/0165
Dunnett, A. Mrs 10/0452
Dupre, A. Mr 10/0534
Durbridge, N. Ms 10/1167
Durojaiye, S. Dr 10/0203
Durrant, C. Mr 10/1326
Dye, J. Mrs 10/1785
Dyer, A. Mr 10/1226
Dyer, C. Dr 10/0329 10/0332 10/0333
Dyer, D. Mr 10/0739
Dyson, J. Mr 10/0987

Eade, F. Mr 10/0346
Eagleton, M. Ms 10/1588
Eames, C. Dr 10/1806 10/1807
Earley, P. Mr 10/0996 10/1039 10/1068
Eason, S. Mr 10/0030
Eastwood, J. Ms 10/0261
Ebbutt, D. Mr 10/1624
Ecclestone, K. Ms 10/1482
Edgar, B. Ms 10/0945
Edwards, F. Mr 10/1239
Edwards, J. Mrs 10/0670

Edwards, M. Mr 10/1680
Edwards, R. Dr 10/0380 10/0381 10/0387 10/1190
Edwards, V. Dr 10/0346 10/1280 10/1281
    10/1282 10/1283 10/1284
Eggleston, S. Prof. 10/1745 10/1746
Eichener, V. Dr 10/0124
El-Laithy, S. Mrs 10/0872
Eland, S. Ms 10/1112
Elder, R. Mr 10/1407
Elkin, J. Prof. 10/1606 10/1607 10/1608
Elliott, D. Mr 10/1776
Elliott, J. Mr 10/1484
Elliott, J. Prof. 10/1630 10/1632 10/1633
Ellis, A. Prof. 10/1805
Ellis, C. Mr 10/1152
Ellis, M. Mrs 10/1127 10/1133
Ellis, S. Mr 10/0927
Ellis, S. Mrs 10/1468
Ellis, S. Ms 10/1096
Ellis, V. Mrs 10/0207
Elsdon, K. Prof. 10/1132
Emara, H. Mrs 10/0424
Emery, H. Mrs 10/1783
Emmett, T. Dr 10/0028
English, M. Miss 10/1734
Eno, R. Mr 10/0060
Entwistle, D. Dr 10/0338
Entwistle, N. Prof. 10/0325 10/0326 10/0330
    10/0334 10/0335 10/0336 10/0337 10/0338
    10/0340
Eraut, M. Prof. 10/1532
Erben, M. Mr 10/1400 10/1671
Erlicher, L. Ms 10/1548
Ernest, P. Dr 10/0355 10/1755
Eslea, M. Mr 10/1375
Esp, D. Mr 10/0809
Essex, S. Dr 10/1225
Evans, C. Ms 10/1073
Evans, D. Mr 10/0013 10/0016 10/0018 10/0024
Evans, D. Mrs 10/1773
Evans, J. Dr 10/0217 10/0223 10/0902
Evans, J. Ms 10/0746 10/0752 10/0756
Evans, K. Dr 10/1325 10/1497 10/1508
Evans, L. Ms 10/1743 10/1744
Evans, M. Mr 10/1612
Evans, R. Dr 10/1296 10/1297 10/1305 10/1311
    10/1318 10/1319 10/1320 10/1325
Evans, R. Mr 10/0023
Evans, S. Dr 10/1053
Evans, S. Ms 10/1443
Evans, W. Mr 10/0077
Evershed, J. Mr 10/0136
Eyles, J. Mrs 10/1612

Faber, D. Mrs 10/0702
Falkingham, J. Miss 10/0856
Fallows, S. Dr 10/0904 10/0905 10/0906
Farish, M. Ms 10/1369
Farley, K. Mr 10/1772
Farmer, M. Mr 10/1613
Farrel, V. Mr 10/0112
Farrell, C. Miss 10/0377
Faulkner, D. Dr 10/1193
Faupel, A. Mr 10/1240
Fawcett, B. Mr 10/1278
Feiler, A. Mr 10/0037
Fenner, R. Mr 10/0048
Fenton, M. Mr 10/0018
Fenwick, G. Mr 10/0675
Fenwick, N. Ms 10/1330 10/1349
Ferguson, J. Ms 10/0211
Ferguson, S. Mr 10/0689 10/0692
Fernandes, C. Mr 10/1048 10/1050
Fidler, B. Dr 10/0914 10/1255 10/1256 10/1267
Fidler, I. Miss 10/0678
Field, D. Dr 10/1098
Field, J. Dr 10/0119 10/0120 10/0125 10/1713
Fielder, A. Prof. 10/0106
Fielding, M. Mr 10/0180
Fields, J. Miss 10/0490
Filer, A. Dr 10/1663 10/1664 10/1669
Finch, J. Prof. 10/0536
Finegold, D. Dr 10/1695 10/1696
Fineman, S. Dr 10/1438
Fines, J. Dr 10/0352
Finlow-Bates, K. Mr 10/1383
Firth, R. Mr 10/1121
Firth, S. Ms 10/1803
Fish, J. Mr 10/0865
Fisher, G. Mr 10/0440

Fisher, J. Ms 10/1272
Fisher, K. Dr 10/0116
Fisher, R. Mrs 10/1220
Fitz, J. Dr 10/1672 10/1750
Fitz-Gibbon, C. Prof. 10/1087
Fitzgerald, D. Mr 10/1170 10/1182
Fitzgerald, M. Ms 10/0021 10/0022
Flannigan, H. Ms 10/1145 10/1146
Flatten, K. Dr 10/1606 10/1607 10/1608
Flavell, R. Dr 10/0764
Fleetwood-Walker, P. Dr 10/0033
Fleming, S. Dr 10/0131
Fleming, W. Mr 10/0033
Fletcher, J. Dr 10/0032
Fletcher-Campbell, F. Dr 10/1013 10/1014
    10/1015 10/1016 10/1017 10/1018 10/1247
Flett, M. Dr 10/0001
Flintoff, A. Dr 10/0585
Flood, M. Mrs 10/1424
Florian, L. Dr 10/0186 10/0191
Flynn, S. Mrs 10/0238
Fogelman, K. Prof. 10/0663 10/0666 10/0670
    10/1757
Foreman, N. Dr 10/0660 10/0661
Forrest, L. Ms 10/1588
Forrester, K. Dr 10/0597 10/0601
Forrester, M. Dr 10/1756
Forth, I. Mr 10/0222
Foster, E. Dr 10/0648
Fowler, C. Dr 10/0033
Fox, C. Dr 10/0134 10/0135 10/0136
Fox, D. Mr 10/1198
Fox, J. Ms 10/1636
Fox, K. Dr 10/0351
Fox-Lee, L. Mrs 10/0850 10/1263 10/1270
Foxman, D. Mr 10/1031 10/1047 10/1052
    10/1084 10/1085
Frade, C. Mr 10/1549
Francis, E. Mrs 10/0451
Francis, H. Prof. 10/0750
Francis, L. Prof. 10/1558 10/1559 10/1560
    10/1561 10/1562 10/1563 10/1564 10/1565
    10/1566 10/1567
Francis, M. Mrs 10/1082
Francis, M. Ms 10/0653
Frank, F. Ms 10/0564
Frankel, A. Dr 10/1606
Frankham, J. Ms 10/1631
Frankland, J. Ms 10/0448 10/0449
Franklyn-Stokes, A. Dr 10/1217
Fraser, A. Dr 10/0283
Fraser, D. Mr 10/1409
Fraser, D. Mrs 10/1165 10/1166
Fraser, R. Prof. 10/0282
Frazer, G. Mrs 10/1577
Frederickson, N. Ms 10/0862
French, M. Mr 10/0296
Froud, K. Ms 10/1021 10/1029
Fulcher, G. Mr 10/0224
Fullerton, D. Ms 10/0806 10/0818
Fullick, P. Mr 10/1397 10/1398
Fulton, O. Prof. 10/0545 10/0555 10/0558
    10/0559 10/0565
Fung, P. Dr 10/1183
Furlong, A. Dr 10/1461 10/1462
Furlong, J. Prof. 10/0825 10/1236 10/1597
    10/1600
Furnham, A. Prof. 10/0862

Gaine, C. Mr 10/0220
Galbraith, J. Mrs 10/1086
Gallacher, S. Dr 10/1035 10/1043
Galloway, D. Prof. 10/0303 10/0304 10/0550
    10/0553
Galloway, S. Ms 10/1704
Galpin, B. Mr 10/1184 10/1185 10/1186
Galton, M. Prof. 10/0668
Gamble, A. Mr 10/0104
Gammage, P. Prof. 10/1791
Gan, E. Mrs 10/1753
Gardiner, J. Ms 10/0599
Gardner, F. Dr 10/1736 10/1739
Gardner, P. Mr 10/1716 10/1724 10/1725 10/1726
    10/1728
Garland, P. Ms 10/1587
Garner, P. Dr 10/1758
Garnham, A. Dr 10/1545
Garrick, R. Mrs 10/0632
Garrigan, P. Ms 10/0692
Garven, F. Mrs 10/0392

Gates, J. Mrs 10/0294
Gathumbi, A. Mrs 10/1250
Gatrell, M. Mrs 10/0215
Gaunt, D. Ms 10/1201
Geale, J. Mr 10/0575
Geddes, H. Ms 10/1302
George, R. Ms 10/0216
Georgeson, J. Ms 10/1785
Germon, S. Ms 10/1504 10/1506 10/1511
Gerry, S. Ms 10/1233
Gewirtz, D. Ms 10/0973
Ghaye, A. Dr 10/1789 10/1790
Gibb, A. Prof. 10/0285
Gibbs, L. Ms 10/0711
Gibbs, W. Mr 10/0621 10/0630
Gibson, D. Mr 10/1422 10/1425 10/1429 10/1432
Gibson, F. Mr 10/0937
Gibson, H. Prof. 10/1564
Gibson, R. Dr 10/0181
Gifford, S. Ms 10/1306 10/1307
Gilchrist, D. Ms 10/0585
Gilding, D. Dr 10/0126
Gill, J. Mrs 10/1229
Gillespie, J. Mr 10/1155
Gillett, R. Dr 10/0657 10/0658
Gilliland, J. Mr 10/0287 10/0289 10/0298
    10/0301 10/0302 10/0305
Gipps, C. Prof. 10/0727 10/0729 10/0732 10/0733
    10/0735
Glandon, N. Dr 10/0118
Gleeson, D. Prof. 10/0497 10/0498 10/0499
    10/0511
Glendinning, A. Mr 10/0003 10/0004 10/0011
Glennerster, H. Prof. 10/0856
Glover, D. Dr 10/0504 10/0514 10/0674 10/1784
Goddard, W. Mr 10/0445
Godwin, J. Mrs 10/0062
Golby, M. Dr 10/0210 10/0354 10/0366 10/0367
    10/0373
Goldstein, H. Prof. 10/0775
Gomez, G. Dr 10/1772
Gonzalez, B. Mr 10/0483
Goodger, B. Dr 10/0441
Goodger, J. Dr 10/0441
Gooding, S. Ms 10/0196
Goodlad, S. Dr 10/0717
Goodwin, A. Mr 10/0943 10/0956
Goodwyn, A. Mr 10/1250
Goody, J. Mr 10/1148
Goodyear, P. Dr 10/0547 10/0548 10/0566
Goodyear, R. Ms 10/1744
Gordon, F. Mrs 10/0006
Gordon, P. Prof. 10/0766 10/0767 10/0768
Gorman, T. Dr 10/1049 10/1052
Gornal, L. Ms 10/0386
Gorwood, B. Dr 10/0480 10/0483 10/0486
Goswami, U. Dr 10/0174
Gott, R. Dr 10/1801
Gough, G. Dr 10/0504
Goulandris, N. Dr 10/0864
Grace, G. Prof. 10/0291
Graham, A. Mr 10/1184 10/1186 10/1187
Graham, B. Miss 10/1460
Graham, B. Mr 10/1143
Graham, J. Mr 10/1219
Graham, S. Mrs 10/0053
Grahame, J. Ms 10/0762
Grainger, N. Mr 10/1370
Grant, F. Ms 10/0342
Grant, M. Dr 10/0138
Grant, M. Mrs 10/1468
Grant, N. Prof. 10/0398 10/0399 10/0400 10/0401
    10/0405 10/0417 10/0418 10/0419 10/0420
    10/0421 10/0422 10/0423 10/0424 10/0426
    10/0430 10/0431
Gray, D. Mr 10/1330
Gray, F. Dr 10/1516 10/1517
Gray, J. Prof. 10/1377
Gray, L. Mr 10/1440 10/1442
Graystone, J. Mr 10/1443
Greaney, J. Dr 10/0103 10/0107
Green, A. Dr 10/0797
Green, D. Prof. 10/1605
Green, E. Dr 10/1254
Green, J. Ms 10/0934 10/0946
Green, K. Ms 10/1123
Green, L. Ms 10/1608
Green, M. Mrs 10/0240
Green, P. Mr 10/1810
Green, P. Ms 10/1124 10/1126

Greenhough, P. Ms 10/0362
Greer, J. RevDr 10/1558
Gregor, P. Dr 10/0284
Gregory, E. Dr 10/0706 10/0716
Gregory, J. Ms 10/1489
Grenfell, M. Mr 10/0222 10/1393
Griffiths, M. Dr 10/1160
Griffiths, M. Mr 10/0986
Griffiths, T. Mr 10/0679 10/0680
Grimshaw, R. Dr 10/0988
Gronow, S. Mr 10/0382 10/0383
Grugeon, E. Mrs 10/0248 10/1257
Guest, K. Mr 10/0905
Guise, S. Ms 10/0029
Gukhool, P. Ms 10/1684
Gundara, J. Dr 10/0720 10/0721
Gura, P. Ms 10/1297 10/1306
Gutteridge, K. Dr 10/0932 10/0945
Guy, G. Mrs 10/1496

Haddon, K. Mr 10/1618
Hadfield, M. Mr 10/1159
Haggarty, L. Dr 10/1276 10/1277
Hagues, N. Mr 10/1000
Hailey, A. Ms 10/0916
Haines, C. Dr 10/0744
Haines, T. Mrs 10/1505
Hall, A. Dr 10/0581
Hall, C. Mrs 10/0533 10/1163
Hall, E. Dr 10/1163
Hall, E. Miss 10/1609
Hall, J. Dr 10/1349
Hall, J. Mr 10/0718 10/1248
Hall, K. Mr 10/0696
Hall, N. Mr 10/0940 10/0941
Hallan, V. Mr 10/1614
Halpin, D. Dr 10/1732 10/1738 10/1742 10/1750
Halsall, R. Mr 10/0934
Halstead, J. Dr 10/1221 10/1229 10/1233 10/1236
Hamid, R. Mr 10/1395
Hamill, P. Mr 10/1470
Hamilton, D. Dr 10/0425
Hamilton, D. Prof. 10/0691
Hamilton, J. Dr 10/0457
Hamilton, M. Dr 10/0564 10/0568 10/0577
Hammersley, P. Rev. 10/0099
Han, M. Miss 10/1776
Hancock, R. Mr 10/0438
Hanley, V. Dr 10/0214
Hann, K. Dr 10/0836 10/0837
Hannan, A. Dr 10/1218 10/1220 10/1221 10/1222
    10/1224 10/1225 10/1228 10/1229 10/1232
    10/1233 10/1234 10/1236 10/1237
Hanson, S. Mr 10/0071
Harber, C. Dr 10/0074 10/0084
Harden, R. Prof. 10/0269 10/0270 10/0271
    10/0272 10/0273 10/0281
Hardman, F. Mr 10/1105
Hardman, M. Dr 10/0191
Hargreaves, D. Dr 10/0662
Hargreaves, D. Prof. 10/0187
Hargreaves, E. Ms 10/0998
Hargreaves, L. Dr 10/0668
Harkin, J. Dr 10/1202 10/1204
Harland, J. Dr 10/0989 10/1005 10/1060 10/1061
    10/1062 10/1063 10/1064
Harland, L. Ms 10/0437 10/0438 10/0439 10/0733
Harlen, W. Prof. 10/0111 10/1335 10/1340
    10/1357 10/1361
Harnett, P. Mrs 10/1658
Harnor, M. Mr 10/0939 10/0954 10/0955
Harper, D. Mr 10/1568
Harri-Augstein, S. Dr 10/0159 10/0160
Harries, D. Mr 10/1271
Harries, T. Mr 10/0039
Harris, A. Dr 10/0050 10/0051 10/0056
Harris, A. Ms 10/0045
Harris, D. Prof. 10/0159 10/1084
Harris, J. Dr 10/0089 10/0094
Harris, N. Prof. 10/0169 10/0170
Harris, R. Mr 10/0114
Harris, S. Dr 10/1378
Harris, S. Mrs 10/1001 10/1040 10/1041 10/1042
    10/1058 10/1085
Harrison, B. Mrs 10/1153
Harrison, I. Mr 10/0976 10/0979
Harrison, J. Mr 10/1321
Harrison, M. Dr 10/0605
Harrison, R. Miss 10/1768
Harrison, S. Mr 10/1775

Harrop, S. Mrs 10/0693 10/0695
Hart, A. Mrs 10/1619
Hart, J. Dr 10/0344
Hart, S. Ms 10/0180
Hartley, J. Dr 10/0263 10/0264 10/0265
Hartley, J. Prof. 10/0520 10/0521 10/0526
Harvey, J. Miss 10/0891
Harvey, L. Dr 10/1605
Harvey, R. Dr 10/0906
Harvey, T. Dr 10/0041
Harwood, A. Mrs 10/1495
Harwood, D. Mr 10/1751
Hashim, A. Prof. 10/1581
Hassan, F. Mr 10/0309
Hatch, G. Mrs 10/0932 10/0950
Hatcher, R. Mr 10/1737
Havard, R. Mr 10/1441
Haw, K. Ms 10/1160
Hawker, J. Mrs 10/1079 10/1088
Hawkins, P. Prof. 10/0386
Hawthorn, R. Ms 10/1091
Hay, J. Dr 10/1153
Hayden, C. Ms 10/1240
Hayden, M. Ms 10/0046
Hayes, D. Mr 10/0644 10/1224
Hayes, M. Ms 10/1116
Hayler, S. Mr 10/1111
Haynes, G. Mrs 10/0372
Hayward, L. Ms 10/0433
Hazlewood, P. Mr 10/0356
Head, J. Dr 10/0443 10/0854
Head, M. Mr 10/1287
Healy, M. Ms 10/0633 10/0650
Heames, R. Mrs 10/0240
Heaney, S. Ms 10/0210
Heaslip, P. Mr 10/1787
Heath, S. Ms 10/0544
Heathcote, G. Dr 10/0918
Hecht, Kh. Prof. 10/1810
Hegarty, J. Dr 10/0522
Hegarty, P. Dr 10/0573
Hegarty, P. Mrs 10/0573
Hegarty, S. Dr 10/1043
Hellawell, D. Prof. 10/1609 10/1610 10/1612 10/1615
Helsby, G. Ms 10/0538 10/0562 10/0563
Hemmings, N. Mr 10/0924
Henderson, S. Dr 10/0492 10/0745 10/0747
    10/0759 10/0760
Hendley, D. Mr 10/1596
Hendry, L. Prof. 10/0010
Henkel, M. Ms 10/0166
Henkhuzens, Z. Ms 10/1053
Henry, L. Dr 10/1243
Henson, C. Rev. 10/1134
Hentschke, L. Dr 10/0793
Hesford, L. Mrs 10/0693
Hesketh, A. Mrs 10/0270
Heverin, A. Ms 10/0853
Hewitt, C. Mrs 10/1470
Hewitt, J. Mr 10/1301 10/1387
Hewitt, R. Dr 10/0843
Heywood, D. Mr 10/0937
Hibberd, P. Prof. 10/0382 10/0383
Hicks, C. Dr 10/0073
Hill, A. Dr 10/0524
Hill, D. Mr 10/0219
Hill, E. Mrs 10/0101 10/0103
Hill, J. Mrs 10/0171
Hillier, Y. Ms 10/1645
Hilliman, P. Mrs 10/1754
Hilpert, U. Prof. 10/0124
Hinchcliffe, V. Mr 10/1756
Hind, A. Ms 10/0731
Hindley, C. Prof. 10/0722
Hinton, J. Dr 10/0460
Hinton, R. Dr 10/0876 10/0884 10/0886 10/0900
Hitch, G. Prof. 10/1621
Hobrough, J. Dr 10/1498 10/1502
Hodgkinson, K. Mr 10/0888 10/0892
Hodgson, B. Dr 10/1197
Hodgson, J. Ms 10/0647
Hodkinson, H. Mrs 10/0926
Hodkinson, P. Mr 10/0926
Hodkinson, S. Mr 10/0736 10/0962 10/0963
    10/0964
Hogbin, J. Mr 10/0938
Holder, K. Mr 10/0593
Holland, D. Ms 10/0346
Holland, J. Dr 10/0798 10/0799 10/0800 10/0805
    10/0817 10/0818 10/0820

Holliday, A. Dr 10/0198
Holligan, C. Dr 10/1437
Holloway, G. Ms 10/1517
Holly, L. Dr 10/1550
Holmes, F. Mrs 10/1510
Holroyd, C. Mr 10/0394
Holroyd, R. Mr 10/1246
Holt, D. Dr 10/1224 10/1235
Hood, P. Ms 10/0906
Hooper, J. Ms 10/1088
Hopkins, D. Dr 10/0178 10/0187
Hopkins, S. Dr 10/0111
Hopper, G. Ms 10/1251
Horbury, A. Dr 10/1794
Hornby, G. Mr 10/0474
Hough, J. Prof. 10/0882 10/0883 10/0890
Howard, D. Mr 10/1116
Howard, S. Ms 10/1373
Howarth, C. Ms 10/0956
Howarth, C. Prof. 10/1145
Howarth, S. Mr 10/1224 10/1227
Howe, C. Dr 10/1464
Howe, M. Prof. 10/0527
Howell, D. Dr 10/0796
Howells, M. Miss 10/1679
Howieson, C. Ms 10/0311 10/0314 10/0318
    10/0321
Howlett, K. Mr 10/0194
Howson, J. Mr 10/1200
Hoyle, E. Prof. 10/0149 10/1268
Hoyles, C. Prof. 10/0779 10/0788
Huckle, J. Mr 10/1119 10/1120 10/1121
Huddart, D. Dr 10/0679 10/0680
Huddleston, P. Mrs 10/1694 10/1699 10/1700
    10/1701
Hudson, G. Dr 10/1784
Hudson, P. Mr 10/1613
Hufton, N. Mr 10/1482
Huggins, M. Mr 10/0567
Hughes, A. Mrs 10/1468
Hughes, C. Dr 10/1117
Hughes, D. Mrs 10/1264
Hughes, J. Mr 10/0717
Hughes, M. Dr 10/0353 10/0358 10/0362 10/0364
    10/0366 10/0367 10/0374
Hughes, T. Mr 10/0383
Hui, X. Prof. 10/1540
Hull, B. Mrs 10/0727
Hull, J. Prof. 10/0090 10/0097 10/0098 10/0099
Hull, T. Mr 10/0100 10/0102
Hulme, C. Dr 10/1805 10/1808
Humes, W. Dr 10/0404 10/0405 10/0406 10/0414
    10/0415 10/0416 10/0427 10/0428 10/0429
Humphreys, G. Prof. 10/0102
Humphries, B. Dr 10/0928
Hunt, M. Dr 10/0173
Hunt, M. Mr 10/0946
Hunt, P. Ms 10/0853 10/1289 10/1309
Hurry, J. Dr 10/0849 10/0850
Hurst, V. Ms 10/0708 10/0715
Husbands, C. Dr 10/1637
Hussain, N. Ms 10/0170
Hustler, D. Mr 10/0933 10/0934 10/0956
Hutchings, M. Ms 10/1648 10/1649 10/1651
    10/1653
Hutchinson, B. Dr 10/1578 10/1580
Hutchison, D. Mr 10/1011 10/1034 10/1052
    10/1076 10/1077 10/1086 10/1087
Hutchison, M. Mrs 10/1415
Hyde, B. Miss 10/1773
Hyde, M. Mr 10/0198
Hyder, K. Mrs 10/1710

Impey, R. Mr 10/1472
Indoe, D. Mr 10/0205
Ineson, E. Dr 10/0929
Ingham, A. Dr 10/0440 10/0442
Inman, S. Ms 10/0824
Irving, B. Mr 10/0894
Irwin, M. Mr 10/1474
Isa, P. Mrs 10/0526
Issroff, K. Ms 10/1181
Iwano, M. Miss 10/0252

Jackson, A. Dr 10/0464
Jackson, C. Ms 10/0552
Jackson, D. Mr 10/0147
Jackson, P. Dr 10/1296 10/1308 10/1316 10/1324
Jackson, P. Mr 10/1112
Jackson, S. Dr 10/0208

Jacques, K. Ms 10/0211 10/0221 10/0825
James, A. Mr 10/0379
James, B. Ms 10/0492
James, C. Dr 10/0049
James, D. Mr 10/1671
James, D. Prof. 10/1500
James, J. Mr 10/0601
James, J. Ms 10/0205
James, L. Dr 10/0925
James, M. Mr 10/0923
James, P. Dr 10/0681
Jamieson, I. Prof. 10/0042 10/0043 10/0049
    10/0050 10/0051 10/0057
Jamison, J. Mr 10/1004 10/1029 10/1030 10/1032
Jangira, N. Prof. 10/0189
Jarman, J. Dr 10/0176
Jarvis, P. Prof. 10/1494
Jeavons, M. Mrs 10/1767
Jelly, S. Mrs 10/1227
Jenkins, E. Prof. 10/0612 10/0622 10/0623
    10/0624 10/0625 10/0634 10/0635 10/0637
    10/0651
Jenkins, H. Prof. 10/0014 10/0017 10/0019
    10/0023 10/0024 10/0025
Jennings, M. Mr 10/0214
Jephcote, M. Mr 10/1598
Jesson, D. Mr 10/1380
Jessop, T. Ms 10/0533
Ji Wei, Z. Prof. 10/1540
Jiang, L. Mr 10/0382
Jiya, M. Mrs 10/0630
Job, D. Mr 10/0741
Jofili, Z. Ms 10/1303
John, M. Prof. 10/0357
Johnson, D. Prof. 10/1384
Johnson, F. Ms 10/1024 10/1029 10/1032 10/1043
Johnson, G. Mr 10/0160
Johnson, I. Mr 10/1286 10/1287
Johnson, M. Mr 10/0504 10/0942
Johnson, P. Dr 10/0936
Johnson, R. Mr 10/0548
Johnson, S. Mr 10/1716
Johnston, J. Mrs 10/1112
Johnston, K. Ms 10/0694
Johnston, R. Dr 10/1437
Johnstone, M. Mrs 10/1364
Johnstone, R. Prof. 10/1445 10/1447
Jolleff, N. Ms 10/0493
Jones, A. Dr 10/1168 10/1171 10/1181
Jones, C. Dr 10/0308 10/1758
Jones, C. Mrs 10/1203
Jones, C. Ms 10/0684
Jones, D. Dr 10/1128 10/1129
Jones, D. Mr 10/0242
Jones, E. Ms 10/0998
Jones, G. Dr 10/0319
Jones, G. Mr 10/0233 10/1241 10/1792
Jones, H. Mr 10/1235
Jones, H. Ms 10/0627
Jones, L. Mr 10/0447
Jones, L. Ms 10/0714
Jones, Ll. Ms 10/1008
Jones, M. Miss 10/0535
Jones, M. Mr 10/1781
Jones, S. Mrs 10/1601
Jones, S. Ms 10/1563
Jordan, R. Ms 10/0466
Jotham, R. Dr 10/1124 10/1125 10/1126 10/1127
    10/1131 10/1133 10/1142
Jowett, S. Ms 10/1071 10/1072 10/1073 10/1074
    10/1075
Jowitt, J. Mr 10/0121 10/0124
Joyce, S. Mr 10/1417
Judge, H. Dr 10/1213
Jukes, K. Prof. 10/1655

Kambouri, M. Dr 10/0750
Kandeh, F. Mr 10/1690
Kang, B. Mr 10/0566
Karavas, E. Ms 10/1708
Kaskaris, I. Mr 10/0264
Kay, I. Ms 10/1463
Kay, W. Dr 10/1567
Kaye, A. Mr 10/1174
Kearsley, M. Mr 10/1500
Keating, I. Ms 10/0920
Keenan, A. Prof. 10/0450
Kehily, M. Ms 10/1706
Kehoe, M. Mrs 10/1770
Keiner, J. Ms 10/1257

Kelleher, J. Mr 10/1549
Kelly, M. Mr 10/0952 10/0957
Kelly, P. Prof. 10/1397 10/1398
Kelly, S. Mrs 10/1785
Kemp, A. Dr 10/1210 10/1244 10/1251
Kempa, R. Prof. 10/0929
Kempe, A. Mr 10/1246 10/1253
Kendall, L. Mrs 10/1018 10/1077 10/1086
Kendrick, A. Dr 10/0283
Kennaway, A. Prof. 10/0259
Kennedy, B. Ms 10/0850
Kennett, D. Mr 10/0360
Kenny, C. Miss 10/0115
Kent, A. Mr 10/0845
Kent, D. Mr 10/0593 10/0595
Ker, M. Mrs 10/1411 10/1423
Kerswill, P. Dr 10/1242
Keys, W. Dr 10/1017 10/1018 10/1038 10/1039
    10/1040 10/1041 10/1042 10/1058 10/1070
    10/1071
Khan, J. Ms 10/1708
Kidd, J. Dr 10/1091
Kieran, J. Dr 10/1436
Kiger, A. Dr 10/0005 10/0006 10/0011
Killeen, J. Mr 10/1091
Kim, J. Mr 10/0508
Kimbell, R. Prof. 10/1118
Kimber, D. Mr 10/1659
Kinder, K. Ms 10/0989 10/0996 10/1060 10/1061
    10/1062 10/1063 10/1064
King, E. Ms 10/0168
King, J. Mr 10/0115
King, K. Prof. 10/0327 10/0328 10/0332 10/0339
King, M. Ms 10/1648
Kingdon, R. Mr 10/0384
Kinmont, A. Mrs 10/0535
Kirk, R. Ms 10/0395
Kirkham, J. Mr 10/0410
Kirkman, C. Mr 10/0371
Kirkup, G. Ms 10/1168
Kirkwood, A. Mr 10/1168
Kirkwood, M. Mrs 10/1465
Knight, D. Dr 10/1398
Knight, P. Dr 10/0546 10/0557 10/0563 10/0567
Knott, M. Dr 10/1086
Knowler, J. Prof. 10/0389
Knowles, I. Mr 10/0452
Knox, E. Prof. 10/0064
Kogan, M. Prof. 10/0161 10/0162 10/0163
    10/0164 10/0165 10/0166
Konting, M. Mr 10/0557
Koshy, V. Ms 10/1755
Koumi, I. Miss 10/0141
Kowalski, R. Dr 10/1768
Kress, G. Prof. 10/0135 10/0136 10/0761 10/0839
Kruger, C. Mr 10/1763
Kurup, P. Mr 10/0587
Kushner, S. Dr 10/1636 10/1639
Kutnick, P. Dr 10/1537
Kwiatkowski, H. Dr 10/1407 10/1426
Kyeleve, J. Mr 10/0980
Kyeyune, R. Mr 10/0198
Kyle, J. Dr 10/0140 10/0147
Kypreou, I. Ms 10/0256
Kyriacou, C. Dr 10/1485 10/1809 10/1811

Lacey, C. Prof. 10/1520 10/1525 10/1531 10/1541
Lacey, P. Mrs 10/0083
Lagro, N. Ms 10/1511
Laidlaw, J. Miss 10/0269
Laidlaw, R. Mrs 10/1604
Laing, A. Mr 10/1428
Laing, S. Dr 10/0134
Lakin, J. Mr 10/0235
Lamb, J. Dr 10/0311 10/0312 10/0313 10/0315
    10/0316 10/0320
Lambert, J. Ms 10/1300
Lamerton, P. Mrs 10/1127
Lamont, C. Mr 10/1553
Lamont, M. Mrs 10/1466
Lanade, J. Mr 10/0481
Lancey, K. Mr 10/0203
Lane, I. Mr 10/1740
Langrish, J. Dr 10/0943
Lansdell, J. Ms 10/0215
Lansdown, R. Dr 10/1538
Lapidot, R. Ms 10/1683
Lappas, N. Mr 10/1452
Latham, J. Mr 10/0678
Lathey, G. Ms 10/1309 10/1319

Lathleen, J. Prof. 10/1486 10/1489 10/1510
Laver, R. Ms 10/1371
Law, I. Dr 10/0605
Law, W. Dr 10/1091
Lawrance, R. Mr 10/0058 10/0059 10/0061
    10/0063
Lawrence, B. Dr 10/1240
Laws, C. Mr 10/0217
Lawson, D. Mr 10/1424
Lawton, D. Prof. 10/0728
Layton, L. Mrs 10/0078
Lazonby, J. Dr 10/1089
Le Metais, J. Dr 10/0161 10/1045
Le Page, R. Prof. 10/1804
Lea, M. Ms 10/0530
Leach, F. Dr 10/0339
Leach, J. Mr 10/0596 10/0626 10/0637
Leaman, O. Dr 10/0681 10/0684
Leask, M. Ms 10/0247
Lee, B. Ms 10/1001 10/1013
Lee, C. Mr 10/1228
Lee, F-J Mr 10/1249
Lee, J. Mr 10/1555 10/1672
Lee, M. Dr 10/0128 10/0492
Lee, P. Mr 10/0765 10/0767
Lee, S-W. Mr 10/1320
Lee, S. Mrs 10/1295 10/1298
Lee, Y. Mr 10/1396
Lee-Corbin, H. Mrs 10/1325
Lefrere, P. Dr 10/1169
Leger, E. Ms 10/0636
Leicester, D. Mr 10/1126
Leicester, M. Dr 10/1712 10/1714
Leitch, A. Mrs 10/0389
Leitch, C. Miss 10/1108
Lenton, G. Dr 10/1763
Leo, E. Ms 10/0205
Lerman, S. Dr 10/1381 10/1382 10/1383 10/1384
Lever, M. Mr 10/1222
Lewin, K. Dr 10/1524 10/1526 10/1527 10/1528
    10/1536 10/1539 10/1540
Lewis, A. Dr 10/1717 10/1718 10/1732 10/1733
    10/1734
Lewis, C. Dr 10/1621
Lewis, G. Mr 10/1008 10/1019 10/1033 10/1065
    10/1602
Lewis, I. Mr 10/0612 10/1764
Lewis, J. Mr 10/1373
Lewis, M. Mrs 10/0375
Lewis, M. Ms 10/1533 10/1534
Lewis, R. Dr 10/1668
Lewis, T. Mr 10/1008 10/1083
Light, P. Prof. 10/1188 10/1191
Light, R. Mr 10/0572
Lindsay, A. Mr 10/0225 10/0231
Lindsay, G. Mr 10/0270
Lines, A. Mrs 10/1011 10/1019
Lines, D. Mr 10/0738 10/0739
Lingard, D. Mr 10/0932
Lister, C. Dr 10/1102
Lister, I. Prof. 10/1793 10/1800
Litt, L. Dr 10/1199
Little, A. Prof. 10/0773 10/1540
Littlewood, P. Mr 10/0434
Livingston, R. Dr 10/1577
Lloyd Davies, B. Mrs 10/1561
Lloyd, J. Dr 10/1459
Lloyd, P. Mr 10/1109
Lloyd-Smith, M. Mr 10/1736 10/1739
Lock, N. Mr 10/1275
Lock, R. Dr 10/0087
Locke, M. Mr 10/1644 10/1645
Lockley, P. Mr 10/0950
Lockwood, A. Ms 10/0244
Loder, C. Ms 10/0794
Lodge, J. Mr 10/1311
Lofthouse, M. Dr 10/0667 10/0671 10/0912
    10/1117
Long, J. Mr 10/0579 10/0580
Longman, D. Mr 10/1525
Loudon, M. Mrs 10/1677 10/1678 10/1683
    10/1688
Loumidis, K. Mr 10/0524
Lovell, T. Ms 10/1712 10/1714
Lovie, A. Dr 10/0702
Low, G. Mr 10/1809 10/1811
Low, L. Mrs 10/1445 10/1447
Low-Beer, A. Dr 10/1194
Lowden, K. Mr 10/1332 10/1347
Lowe, D. Mr 10/1617

Lowerson, J. Rev. 10/1535
Loxley, A. Mr 10/0057 10/1206
Loynes, A. Mr 10/0914
Lubben, F. Mr 10/1801 10/1802
Lucock, R. Dr 10/1489 10/1501
Ludlow, M. Mrs 10/0953
Lung, M. Mr 10/0016
Lunt, I. Ms 10/0746 10/0752 10/0756
Lunt, P. Dr 10/0208
Lupton, C. Dr 10/1240
Luti, P.Mr 10/1418
Lynas, W. Dr 10/0960
Lyon, D. Ms 10/0068 10/0072

Ma, S. Miss 10/0285
MaCaskill, C. Mrs 10/0833
MaClaren, S. Mrs 10/1502
MacArthur, C. Dr 10/0064
MacBeath, J. Dr 10/1467
MacBeth, A. Dr 10/0409 10/0432
MacDonald, A. Ms 10/0993 10/1011 10/1067
MacDonald, B. Prof. 10/0190 10/1635 10/1639
MacGabhann, D. Mr 10/1577
MacGilchrist, B. Mrs 10/0770 10/0771 10/0772
    10/0840
MacKay, G. Dr 10/1471
MacKenzie, M. Mr 10/0402 10/0403 10/0410
    10/0411 10/0412 10/0413 10/0423 10/0428
    10/0430
MacLeod, M. Mr 10/0679
MacLure, M. Dr 10/1633 10/1639
MacPherson, K. Ms 10/0041
Mace, J. Ms 10/0706 10/0707
Machell, J. Ms 10/0549
Macintyre, C. Dr 10/0459
Mackenzie, R. Mr 10/1218
Mackie, K. Dr 10/1134
Macrory, G. Ms 10/0948
Madsen, K. Ms 10/1374
Mahmood, Z. Dr 10/0393
Mahmoud, T. Mr 10/0304
Maidlow, S. Ms 10/1210
Maisch, M. Ms 10/0029
Majid, M. Mrs 10/0583
Major, D. Mr 10/0208
Malcolm, H. Ms 10/1333
Malcolm, J. Ms 10/0599 10/0627
Malewski, M. Dr 10/0125
Mallatratt, J. Dr 10/1620
Mallon, F. Mr 10/1574
Malvern, D. Mr 10/1273 10/1274 10/1277
    10/1278
Manji, K. Dr 10/1551 10/1552 10/1553
Manning, J. Miss 10/0090
Marangou, A. Mrs 10/0145
Marchant, J. Mr 10/0012
Mardle, G. Mr 10/0505 10/0514
Mares, C. Ms 10/1556
Marker, W. Mr 10/0411
Markey, D. Mrs 10/1607
Marques, L. Mr 10/0502
Marriott, J. Prof. 10/0606 10/0607 10/0614
    10/0636 10/0654
Marriott, S. Mr 10/1573
Marry, R. Dr 10/0913
Marsden, W. Prof. 10/0688
Marsh, C. Ms 10/1117
Marshall, L. Mrs 10/0164
Marshall, M. Mrs 10/1501
Marshall, P. Mr 10/0858
Marsland, J. Mr 10/0127
Martin, D. Mr 10/0680
Martin, J. Mrs 10/0096 10/0667
Martin, J. Ms 10/0086
Martin, P. Mr 10/0580 10/0583
Martin, W. Ms 10/0135
Martland, J. Mr 10/0687
Mason, H. Mrs 10/0100
Mason, J. Dr 10/0544
Mason, J. Prof. 10/1186
Mason, K. Mr 10/1002 10/1053
Mason, M. Mrs 10/0683
Mason, P. Mr 10/1225
Mason, R. Dr 10/0252 10/0253 10/0256 10/0258
    10/0261 10/1174
Massey, A. Mr 10/0697
Masters, B. Mr 10/1316
Masterton, T. Mr 10/0455
Matheson, D. Dr 10/0417
Mathias, J. Dr 10/1775 10/1779

Matthews, B Mr 10/0709
Matthews, M. Dr 10/0201
Maughan, C. Mr 10/0253
Mauthner, M. Ms 10/0817
Maw, J. Miss 10/1327
Mawer, M. Mr 10/0474
Maxwell, S. Ms 10/1300
May, W. Ms 10/1216
Mayall, B. Dr 10/0804 10/0813 10/0815 10/0823
Maychell, K. Ms 10/0991 10/1037 10/1038
    10/1056 10/1070
Mayes, J. Ms 10/0435
Mayhew, G. Dr 10/1517
Maynard, E. Ms 10/1589
Maynard, T. Ms 10/1600
Mayston, D. Prof. 10/1380
McAleer, J. Dr 10/0269
McAndrew, L. Ms 10/1467
McAuley, J. Mr 10/0610
McAuley, S. Ms 10/1115
McBride, R. Dr 10/1638
McCall, C. Dr 10/1468
McCall, S. Mr 10/0082
McCarthy, J. Mr 10/1130
McCartney, E. Miss 10/1471
McCarty, C. Mr 10/0697
McClelland, V. Prof. 10/0470 10/0475 10/0479
    10/0484 10/0487 10/0489
McClements, R. Mr 10/0126
McClure, M. Sist. 10/1412
McConachie, H. Dr 10/0493 10/0494
McCool, S. Miss 10/1471
McCormick, R. Dr 10/1192
McCreery, E. Ms 10/1318
McCulloch, G. Prof. 10/0551 10/0554 10/0563
McCulloch, M. Ms 10/1268 10/1275
McDaid, C. Ms 10/1457
McDonald, M. Ms 10/1622
McDonald, S. Mrs 10/1418 10/1431
McDougall, S. Ms 10/1805
McEntee, L. Dr 10/0140
McEwen, S. Ms 10/1790
McGarvey, B. Prof. 10/1568 10/1573 10/1574
    10/1576
McGettrick, B. Prof. 10/1418
McGilp, J. Dr 10/1406
McGivney, V. Dr 10/1092 10/1093
McGonigal, J. Dr 10/1434 10/1435
McGrath, S. Mr 10/0339
McGuiness, J. Mr 10/0287 10/0291 10/0298
    10/0301
McGurk, H. Prof. 10/0846 10/0849
McHugh, G. Ms 10/0560 10/0564
McIntyre, D. Mr 10/1212 10/1764
McKay, K. Ms 10/0450
McKee, T. Mrs 10/1410
McKenzie, J. Ms 10/1757
McKeown, P. Ms 10/0096
McKinlay, R. Dr 10/0282
McLaughlin, C. Ms 10/0185
McLean, L. Miss 10/1107
McLean, M. Dr 10/0247
McLean, M. Mrs 10/0511
McMahon, A. Ms 10/0156
McMahon, J. Miss 10/1108
McManus, I. Dr 10/0719
McMichael, P. Dr 10/0456
McNally, J. Mr 10/1450 10/1456
McNamara, D. Prof. 10/0469
McNay, I. Prof. 10/0024
McNorton, M. Ms 10/0388
McPake, J. Ms 10/1332 10/1369
McPhee, A. Mr 10/1416 10/1418
McPherson, A. Prof. 10/0310 10/0311 10/0312
    10/0313 10/0315 10/0316 10/0317 10/0320
    10/0322 10/0323 10/0330
McPherson, J. Mrs 10/1159
McQueen, A. Mr 10/0207
McQueen, I. Ms 10/1413
McQueen, R. Mr 10/0390
Meadows, S. Dr 10/0141 10/0145 10/0146
Meakin, D. Mr 10/0686
Meara, P. Dr 10/1590 10/1591
Measor, L. Dr 10/1203
Meek-Spencer, M. Ms 10/1762
Mellar, H. Dr 10/0778
Melrose, J. Miss 10/0901
Mennell, D. Ms 10/0681
Menter, I. Mr 10/1237 10/1661 10/1667
Menzies, I. Mrs 10/0157 10/0158

Mercer, D. Mr 10/1480
Merrett, F. Dr 10/0085
Merriman, L. Mrs 10/1098
Merry, R. Dr 10/0260
Merryfield, A. Mr 10/1222
Merttens, R. Mrs 10/1650
Meyer, W. Mr 10/1481 10/1483
Michael, M. Ms 10/1406
Middleton, L. Ms 10/0311 10/0312 10/0313
    10/0315 10/0316
Middleton, W. Mr 10/1475 10/1479
Midgley, C. Ms 10/0236 10/0237
Miell, D. Dr 10/1193
Miles, C. Dr 10/0087
Miles, S. Ms 10/0825
Miles, T. Prof. 10/1582
Millar, D. Dr 10/0596 10/1795 10/1796 10/1801
    10/1802
Millar, S. Ms 10/0325
Millar, W. Dr 10/0863
Miller, A. Mr 10/1697
Miller, C. Ms 10/0093
Miller, D. Mr 10/0510 10/0512 10/0513
Miller, G. Ms 10/1688
Miller, N. Dr 10/0958
Miller, P. Rev. 10/1493
Miller, S. Miss 10/0978
Miller, S. Mr 10/1615
Millham, S. Prof. 10/0243
Millican, J. Ms 10/0346
Milloy, N. Dr 10/0660
Mingard, S. Dr 10/1330
Mirelman, H. Ms 10/0850
Mitchell, C. Miss 10/0374
Mitchell, G. Dr 10/0122 10/0123
Mitchell, H. Ms 10/1762
Mitchell, R. Dr 10/1088 10/1390 10/1391
    10/1394 10/1396
Mitchell, S. Ms 10/0472 10/0485
Mittler, P. Prof. 10/0966
Moar, M. Mr 10/1180
Modgil, S. Dr 10/0137
Modiba, M. Ms 10/0505
Moerkamp, T. Dr 10/1548
Mojdehi, E. Ms 10/1472
Monaghan, F. Mr 10/1280
Monaghan, J. Dr 10/0619
Moncur, D. Mr 10/0613
Monk, A. Dr 10/1805
Monk, E. Mrs 10/0393
Mooney, A. Ms 10/0846
Mooney, S. Ms 10/1373
Moorcroft-Cuckle, P. Dr 10/0647
Moore, C. Ms 10/0345
Moore, J. Dr 10/0109 10/0468
Moore, L. Dr 10/0448 10/0449
Moore, M. Dr 10/0091 10/0092
Moore, T. Prof. 10/0722
Moreland, N. Dr 10/1771 10/1777 10/1780
Morgan, A. Dr 10/1170 10/1182
Morgan, C. Dr 10/0052 10/0053
Morgan, C. Ms 10/1383
Morgan, S. Mr 10/0025
Morgan, V. Prof. 10/1573
Morgan, W. Mr 10/1130 10/1135 10/1136
    10/1138 10/1139 10/1140
Morgan-Jones, P. Mr 10/1593
Morris, A. Mr 10/0811 10/1738
Morris, B. Mr 10/1448 10/1450 10/1451 10/1458
Morris, C. Dr 10/0284
Morris, J. Mr 10/0330
Morris, M. Miss 10/1003 10/1012 10/1019
    10/1065
Morris-Jones, R. Mr 10/1602
Morrison, D. Mr 10/0407
Morrison, K. Mr 10/0302
Morrison, M. Ms 10/1703 10/1704 10/1705
Mortimore, J. Mrs 10/0841
Mortimore, P. Prof. 10/0730 10/0731 10/0734
    10/0840 10/0841
Moscardini, A. Prof. 10/1475
Moschovaki, E. Miss 10/0146
Mosley, P. Miss 10/1216
Moss, G. Dr 10/1676
Moss, G. Ms 10/0763
Moss, P. Mr 10/0851
Moss, W. Ms 10/0568
Mouhoubi, R. Ms 10/0418
Muckle, J. Dr 10/1135
Mulholland, H. Dr 10/0268 10/0275 10/0276

    10/0277 10/0278 10/0279 10/0280 10/0282
Mulligan, J. Mr 10/1488
Mullins, P. Ms 10/0677
Mumford, J. Ms 10/1421
Munn, P. Mrs 10/0322 10/0345 10/1332 10/1336
    10/1339 10/1342 10/1348 10/1350 10/1354
    10/1356 10/1359 10/1366
Munro, J. Mr 10/0409
Munro, L. Mrs 10/1502
Munro, R. Mr 10/1466
Munton, A. Dr 10/0846
Murdoch, H. Ms 10/0089
Murji, K. Mr 10/0492
Murphy, E. Mrs 10/1154
Murphy, P. Ms 10/1197
Murphy, R. Prof. 10/1154 10/1158 10/1161
    10/1162 10/1164 10/1165 10/1166
Murray, A. Mr 10/1652
Murray, R. Dr 10/0118
Murray, R. Mr 10/0265
Muschamp, Y. Ms 10/1667 10/1670
Mushi, P. Mr 10/0595

Naftalin, I. Ms 10/0952
Nagata, T. Mr 10/0259
Nakase, A. Prof. 10/0258
Nankivell, C. Ms 10/1606 10/1607 10/1608
Napuk, A. Mrs 10/0335
Naylor, A. Dr 10/1417
Naylor, M. Mrs 10/1124 10/1127
Naylor, S. Mr 10/0949
Neale, F. Miss 10/0266
Neale, P. Mrs 10/0604
Neary, I. Prof. 10/0347
Neary, M. Ms 10/1689
Neather, E. Mr 10/0368
Neill, S. Dr 10/1741
Neilson, M. Miss 10/1424
Nesi, H. Ms 10/1707
Neville, C. Mr 10/0118
Nevison, D. Mr 10/0856
New, S. Ms 10/0569
Newberry-Tarrier, S. Mrs 10/0522
Newell, A. Prof. 10/0284
Newman, E. Ms 10/1666
Newstead, K. Ms 10/0172
Newstead, S. Prof. 10/1217
Newton, L. Mrs 10/1104
Ng, B. Ms 10/1145
Nherera, C. Dr 10/0773
Nias, J. Prof. 10/0190 10/1228 10/1232
Nichol, B. Dr 10/0958 10/1110
Nichol, J. Dr 10/0352
Nicholls, G. Dr 10/0195
Nicholls, P. Mr 10/0519 10/1667
Nisbet, J. Prof. 10/0007 10/0008
Nisbet, P. Mr 10/0325
Nixon, J. Dr 10/0096
Nji-Tima, R. Mr 10/1274
Nobes, G. Dr 10/0853
Noble, J. Mrs 10/0138
Noble, M. Mr 10/1329
Nolan, R. Dr 10/1673 10/1686 10/1692
Norman, M. Ms 10/0112
Norman, T. Miss 10/1243
Normand, D. Mr 10/0335
Norris, N. Dr 10/1630 10/1634 10/1639
North, R. Dr 10/1581
North, T. Mr 10/0972
Norwich, B. Dr 10/0746 10/0752 10/0753
    10/0755 10/0757
Noss, R. Dr 10/1383
Noyes, P. Dr 10/0206
Nunes, T. Dr 10/0723 10/0725 10/0726
Nunn, J. Ms 10/1301
Nwaokolo, P. Mr 10/0556
Nwenmely, H. Ms 10/1281
Nyirenda, D. Mr 10/1161

O'Brien, J. Mr 10/0432 10/1418 10/1420
O'Dea, M. Mrs 10/1416
O'Dowd, T. Dr 10/1158
O'Hanlon, C. Dr 10/0090
O'Keefe, D. Dr 10/1647
O'Mahony, C. Ms 10/0568
O'Neill, M. Ms 10/1780
O'Neill, S. Ms 10/0525
O'Rourke, R. Ms 10/0586
O'Shea, T. Prof. 10/1183

O'Sullivan, F. Mr 10/1790
O'Sullivan, T. Mr 10/0251
Oakhill, J. Dr 10/1545
Oakley, A. Prof. 10/0801 10/0802 10/0803
    10/0804 10/0805 10/0806 10/0810 10/0815
    10/0818 10/0820 10/0852
Obeid, S. Mr 10/1673
Ogborn, J. Prof. 10/0778 10/0834 10/0835
    10/0836 10/0837 10/0839
Oglesby, K. Ms 10/1122
Okazaki, T. Mr 10/0347
Okpanachi, J. Mr 10/0474
Olds, H. Ms 10/1790
Olek, H. Mrs 10/0373
Oliver, L. Ms 10/0492
Oliver, M. Prof. 10/0442
Opie, C. Dr 10/1620
Orme, J. Mrs 10/1276
Ormell, C. Mr 10/1626 10/1642
Ormston, M. Mr 10/1207
Orsini-Jones, M. Mrs 10/0242
Orton, A. Dr 10/0609 10/0610 10/0613 10/0615
    10/0621 10/0628 10/0630 10/0632
Orton, J. Mrs 10/0628
Osborn, M. Ms 10/0139 10/0153 10/0154 10/0155
Ovens, P. Dr 10/1118 10/1119 10/1120 10/1121
Owen, C. Mr 10/0734 10/0851
Owen, D. Mr 10/1790
Owen, G. Mr 10/0370
Owen, L. Ms 10/0955
Owen, M. Mrs 10/0267
Ozga, J. Prof. 10/0517 10/0518 10/0519 10/1667
    10/1671

Packer, Rh. Miss 10/0379
Packwood, A. Ms 10/1721
Paechter, C. Dr 10/0854
Pain, H. Dr 10/0324
Pain, J. Dr 10/1199
Palacio, D. Dr 10/1763
Palmer, J. Dr 10/0300
Palmer, J. Ms 10/0946
Palmerone, W. Ms 10/0938
Papatheodorou, T. Ms 10/1674
Papazazis, A. Ms 10/1310
Parker, J. Dr 10/0937
Parker-Jenkins, M. Dr 10/1150 10/1151 10/1160
Parkhouse, P. Mr 10/0509
Parkinson, F. Ms 10/0684
Parkinson, J. Dr 10/1596
Parnell, J. Dr 10/1492 10/1501 10/1510
Parrott, L. Mr 10/1623
Parry, G. Mr 10/0228
Parsons, C. Dr 10/0194
Parsons, M. Mr 10/1254
Parsons, W. Dr 10/1134 10/1153
Pascal, C. Prof. 10/1785 10/1786 10/1787 10/1788
Passey, D. Mr 10/0571
Pastor, C. Prof. 10/0092
Paterson, L. Dr 10/0310 10/0311
Pathak, S. Ms 10/1015 10/1017 10/1038
Patience, S. Mrs 10/1478
Paton, R. Mr 10/0218
Payne, G. Mrs 10/1237
Payne, J. Dr 10/0597 10/1535
Payne, M. Ms 10/1290
Payne, S. Ms 10/1075
Payne-Ahmadi, E. Dr 10/1604
Peacock, A. Dr 10/0126 10/0363 10/1106
Peacock, M. Dr 10/0631
Pearce, J. Ms 10/0692 10/0694
Pearl, L. Dr 10/1771
Pearsall, S. Mr 10/1589
Pearson, L. Dr 10/0064
Pearson, M. Dr 10/0116
Peck, A. Mr 10/1799
Peckett, J. Ms 10/0946
Peel, J. Dr 10/0676
Peer, L. Ms 10/0917
Pegg, L. Mrs 10/1244
Pegg, R. Dr 10/0208
Penney, D. Miss 10/0902
Pennington, L. Ms 10/0493 10/0494
Penny, A. Dr 10/0533
Pennycuick, D. Dr 10/1541
Percy, K. Dr 10/0575 10/0576 10/0577 10/0578
Percy, S. Ms 10/0327
Pereiro, J. Rev. 10/0479
Perfect, H. Mr 10/0451
Perkin, R. Dr 10/0579

Perz, R. Mr 10/1618
Petre, M. Dr 10/1171
Petrie, P. Dr 10/0848
Pettigrew, M. Ms 10/1630 10/1634
Phelps, A. Dr 10/1115
Philip, K. Ms 10/0009 10/0010
Phillips, A. Prof. 10/0224
Phillips, G. Mr 10/1728
Phillips, R. Dr 10/1155 10/1156
Phillips, R. Ms 10/1689
Phillips, S. Ms 10/0944 10/0945
Phillips, T. Dr 10/0112
Phillips, T. Mr 10/1629 10/1641
Phillipson, S. Mr 10/1783
Philps, C. Mrs 10/1765
Picard, P. Ms 10/1783
Piccoli, M. Mrs 10/1086
Pickard, A. Dr 10/0938 10/0947
Pickering, J. Dr 10/1726
Pickford, A. Mr 10/0209
Pimm, D. Mr 10/0467
Pinel, A. Mr 10/0223
Pinsent, P. Ms 10/1288
Piotrowski, J. Mrs 10/0968
Plant, M. Mr 10/1119 10/1120
Platt, C. Mrs 10/0157
Playle, R. Ms 10/0448 10/0449
Plewis, I. Mr 10/0847
Plimmer, F. Ms 10/0382
Pocklington, K. Mr 10/0156
Poland, G. Ms 10/0848 10/0853
Pole, C. Dr 10/1702
Pollard, A. Prof. 10/0153 10/0154 10/0155
    10/0519 10/1663 10/1664 10/1665 10/1667
    10/1669 10/1670 10/1671
Ponsford, A-S. Mrs 10/0035
Porter, J. Dr 10/0682
Portman, J. Dr 10/1186
Postle, M. Dr 10/0574
Postlethwaite, K. Dr 10/1266 10/1272 10/1276
Pound, L. Ms 10/1297
Powell, G. Mr 10/0500 10/0515
Powell, R. Dr 10/0052 10/0053
Powell, R. Mr 10/1008 10/1082 10/1083
Powell, S. Dr 10/0466
Powney, J. Dr 10/1332 10/1337 10/1339 10/1343
    10/1344 10/1345 10/1347 10/1352 10/1357
    10/1363 10/1369 10/1386
Pozzi, S. Mr 10/0780
Pratt, J. Prof. 10/1643
Preece, P. Dr 10/0348 10/0350 10/0362
Prenton, K. Mr 10/0109
Preston, C. Mrs 10/1085
Preston, C. Mrs 10/1603
Preston, J. Dr 10/1770
Preston, R. Dr 10/1752
Price, A. Mr 10/0378
Prichard, J. Ms 10/1593
Priestley, J. Dr 10/0491
Prior, D. Mr 10/1475
Pritchard, A. Mr 10/1744 10/1745
Pritchard, J. Mrs 10/0241
Procter, P. Mrs 10/0951
Prophet, R. Mr 10/0587
Prout, A. Dr 10/0823
Prudham, B. Mr 10/1774
Pumfrey, P. Prof. 10/0921 10/0965 10/0967
    10/0968
Puntambekar, S. Mrs 10/1543
Purcell, P. Prof. 10/1581

Qattous, K. Mr 10/0293
Qualter, A. Dr 10/0698
Quicke, J. Dr 10/0117

Raab, C. Mr 10/0345
Raban, B. Prof. 10/1719 10/1721 10/1734
Race, P. Prof. 10/0387 10/0388
Rae, G. Prof. 10/1581
Raffe, D. Prof. 10/0311 10/0312 10/0313 10/0314
    10/0315 10/0316 10/0317 10/0320 10/0321
Rainer, J. Mr 10/0942
Rainey, N. Mrs 10/1108
Rajan, L. Ms 10/0810
Rajanaorison, A. Mr 10/0420
Ramasut, A. Ms 10/1674
Ramsden, F. Mrs 10/1785
Ramsden, J. Dr 10/1798
Ramshaw, M. Mrs 10/1478
Ranson, S. Prof. 10/0081 10/0096

Ratcliffe, M. Mrs 10/1397 10/1398
Ratcliffe, S. Ms 10/1025 10/1032 10/1066
    10/1067
Ray, R. Dr 10/0978
Redfern, E. Dr 10/0652
Reece, D. Mr 10/0062
Reece, I. Mr 10/1443
Reed, M. Mr 10/0150
Reeder, D. Dr 10/0663
Rees, M. Dr 10/1557
Rees, W. Dr 10/1585
Reese, R. Mr 10/0468
Reeve, J. Miss 10/0097
Reeves, C. Mr 10/0443
Reeves, S. Dr 10/1183
Reid, B. Mr 10/1607
Reid, D. Mrs 10/1205
Reid, D. Prof. 10/0984 10/0985
Reid, G. Mr 10/0453 10/0460
Reid, I. Prof. 10/0867
Reilly, I. Prof. 10/1187
Remington, B. Dr 10/1387
Revell, R. Mr 10/1232
Reynolds, J. Dr 10/1132
Reynolds, J. Dr 10/1309 10/1319
Ribbins, P. Dr 10/0081
Rice, J. Mrs 10/0251
Richards, B. Dr 10/1245 10/1250 10/1252
Richards, C. Dr 10/0238 10/0239
Richards, J. Dr 10/1682
Richards, M. Mrs 10/1252
Richards, P. Dr 10/0047 10/0048 10/0054
Richards, P. Prof. 10/0719
Richards, S. Mr 10/1552
Richardson, J. Prof. 10/0167 10/0168
Richardson, K. Dr 10/0389
Richardson, S. Mr 10/0873
Richardson, W. Dr 10/1695 10/1696 10/1698
    10/1700 10/1720
Richmond, J. Mr 10/0080
Richmond, M. Mr 10/0471
Ricketts, I. Dr 10/0284
Riddell, B. Ms 10/1143
Riddell, S Dr 10/1457
Riddell, S. Dr 10/1449 10/1452 10/1453 10/1454
    10/1455
Riddoch, M. Dr 10/0102
Ridgway, J. Mr 10/0571
Ridout, M. Mr 10/1081
Riggs, A. Ms 10/1499
Riley, M. Dr 10/1797
Rimmershaw, R. Dr 10/0541 10/0542
Risager, K. Ms 10/0308
Riseborough, G. Mr 10/0947
Ritchie, R. Mr 10/0040
Rix, C. Mr 10/0248
Roberts, A. Mr 10/0790
Roberts, C. Ms 10/1554
Roberts, K. Prof. 10/0703
Roberts, R. Ms 10/0114 10/0677
Robertson, C. Dr 10/0323
Robertson, D. Mr 10/0208
Robertson, J. Miss 10/1285
Robertson, P. Mrs 10/1470
Robinson, A. Mr 10/1577
Robinson, A. Mrs 10/0940 10/0941
Robinson, G. Mr 10/1660 10/1662
Robinson, J. Ms 10/1641
Robinson, P. Mr 10/0654 10/1291 10/1314
Robinson, S. Ms 10/0202
Robson, M. Ms 10/0289
Robson, S. Mrs 10/1312
Rodger, R. Ms 10/0935
Rodney, C. Mr 10/0241
Rodrigues, S. Dr 10/1010 10/1044
Rogers, A. Prof. 10/0346 10/1269
Rogers, C. Dr 10/0543 10/0550 10/0552 10/0562
Rogers, L. Mr 10/0899 10/1292 10/1317
Rogers, S. Ms 10/0386
Rogerson, E. Mrs 10/0271
Roper, E. Mr 10/0580 10/0581 10/0584
Roper, T. Mr 10/0619 10/0650
Rose, A. Miss 10/0953
Rose, D. Mr 10/1322
Rose, J. Mr 10/1681
Ross, A. Prof. 10/1648 10/1649 10/1651 10/1653
Ross, K. Dr 10/0066 10/0068
Ross, R. Ms 10/0112 10/0113
Ross, S. Dr 10/0106
Rotsides, C. Mr 10/1774

Rouse, M. Mr 10/0184 10/0186 10/0191
Rovira-Garza, N. Miss 10/0884
Row, G. Mr 10/1581
Rowe, M. Mr 10/1593
Rowland, L. Ms 10/0846
Rowland, T. Mr 10/0467
Rowlands, M. Mr 10/0937 10/1691
Rowlands, S. Mr 10/1123
Rowley, K. Prof. 10/1614
Royle, J. Mrs 10/1403
Ruddock, G. Dr 10/1027 10/1053 10/1081
    10/1084
Ruddock, R. Mr 10/0958
Rudduck, J. Prof. 10/1378 10/1379
Russ, J. Ms 10/0056
Russel, V. Mr 10/1790
Russell, A. Ms 10/1606
Russell, J. Dr 10/1804
Russell, T. Mr 10/0697 10/0698
Russell, V. Mr 10/0498 10/0499
Ryan, C. Dr 10/0534
Ryan, M. Mr 10/0171
Ryle, M. Mr 10/1515 10/1522 10/1523

Saeedi,N. Mrs 10/0860
Sainsbury, M. Dr 10/0997 10/0998
Sainsbury, S. Ms 10/0001
Salih, L. Mrs 10/0890
Salkeld, T. Mrs 10/1687
Salt, S. Mr 10/1084
Salveson, P. Dr 10/0603
Sambili, H. Dr 10/0561
Sammons, P. Dr 10/0731 10/0734
Sampson, J. Mr 10/0246
Sanders, S. Ms 10/1600
Sandow, S. Dr 10/1754 10/1757
Sands, M. Dr 10/1147
Sang, J. Mr 10/0496
Sangster, M. Ms 10/1292
Saran, R. Dr 10/0809
Sarkar, R. Mrs 10/0426
Satterly, D. Dr 10/0151
Saunders, C. Ms 10/0251
Saunders, D. Mr 10/0384 10/0385 10/0387
    10/0388
Saunders, K. Ms 10/1685
Saunders, L. Ms 10/1003 10/1035
Saunders, M. Dr 10/0538 10/0549 10/0556
    10/0560 10/0561 10/0563 10/0565
Saunders, M. Mrs 10/1785
Saunders, R. Mr 10/1442
Savage, J. Mrs 10/0361
Savage, J. Ms 10/0840
Scanlon, E. Dr 10/1181 10/1197
Schagen, I. Dr 10/1034 10/1035
Schagen, S. Dr 10/1011 10/1024 10/1025 10/1066
Scharf, M. Dr 10/0019
Schiavone, T. Mr 10/0977 10/0978
Schilling, M. Dr 10/0697 10/0699
Schofield, A. Ms 10/0947
Scholfield, P. Mr 10/1586
Schostak, J. Dr 10/1629 10/1641
Schwarzenberger, R. Prof. 10/0901
Scott, D. Dr 10/1705
Scott, H. Ms 10/1186
Scott, P. Mr 10/0589 10/0590 10/0591 10/0596
    10/0617
Scott, W. Dr 10/0055
Scrivener, S. Dr 10/0865
Seale, J. Mrs 10/0522
Searl, J. Dr 10/0340 10/0341 10/0342 10/0343
Searle, C. Mr 10/1550
Seddon, J. Mrs 10/1612
Seeley, M. Rev. 10/0065
Seidu, M. Mr 10/1492
Self, T. Mr 10/1049
Selkirk, K. Dr 10/1148
Sellers, M. Mrs 10/1265 10/1266
Sepehr, H. Dr 10/0159
Serafingos, J. Mr 10/0543
Sergeant, D. Dr 10/1310 10/1323 10/1326
Sexton, T. Mr 10/1111
Seymour, R. Mr 10/0923 10/0924 10/0925
Shain, F. Ms 10/0505
Shanley, E. Dr 10/0419
Sharma, C. Mr 10/0476 10/0490
Sharp, A. Dr 10/0581 10/0584
Sharp, C. Ms 10/1036 10/1055 10/1056 10/1057
    10/1059
Sharp, G. Ms 10/1196

Sharp, S. Ms 10/1372
Sharpe, K. Dr 10/0199
Sharples, M. Dr 10/1543 10/1547
Shaughnessy, J. Miss 10/1296
Shaw, G. Dr 10/1640
Shaw, M. Dr 10/0582
Shaw, M. Ms 10/1207
Shepherd, D. Ms 10/0879
Shepherson, D. Mr 10/0079
Sheridan, V. Ms 10/1537
Sherman, I. Mr 10/1124 10/1127 10/1131
Shield, G. Mr 10/1485
Shilling, C. Dr 10/1388 10/1389
Shiobara, M. Ms 10/0792
Shipstone, D. Dr 10/1140 10/1148 10/1149
Shorrocks, D. Dr 10/0110 10/0638 10/0643
    10/0652 10/0653
Shucksmith, J. Mrs 10/0009 10/0011
Shute, C. Dr 10/0261
Siann, G. Dr 10/0391
Sikes, P. Dr 10/1727 10/1731
Silcock, P. Dr 10/1095
Silto, W. Mr 10/0766
Silveira, M. Miss 10/1394
Silver, H. Prof. 10/1201 10/1203 10/1223
    10/1230 10/1231 10/1237
Simco, N. Dr 10/0537
Simkin, C. Ms 10/1024
Simmons, C. Mr 10/0881 10/0898
Simmons, M. Mr 10/1446
Simms, B. Dr 10/0035
Simpson, A. Mr 10/0249 10/0250 10/0455
Simpson, L. Miss 10/1102
Simpson, T. Mr 10/1256
Sims, D. Mr 10/0995 10/1005 10/1028 10/1030
    10/1054
Sims, L. Ms 10/1649
Sinclair, N. Miss 10/0415
Sinclair, R. Dr 10/0988
Singh, A. Dr 10/1258
Siraj-Blatchford, I. Ms 10/1723
Sizmur, S. Mr 10/0998
Skelton, M. Mr 10/1154 10/1158
Skelton, F. Ms 10/0416
Skidmore, G. Ms 10/0346
Skidmore, P. Ms 10/0695
Skinner, G. Mr 10/0973 10/0975
Skitmore, R. Prof. 10/1617
Slater, F. Dr 10/0741
Sleap, M. Mr 10/0307
Slee, N. Ms 10/1318
Sloboda, J. Prof. 10/0525 10/0527
Slowey, M. Prof. 10/0431
Sluckin, A. Mrs 10/0660
Small, N. Mr 10/1195
Smart, L. Mr 10/1305
Smedley, D. Mr 10/0872
Smith, A. Mr 10/1808
Smith, C. Mr 10/0095 10/0326 10/0448 10/0449
Smith, C. Ms 10/0245
Smith, I. Mr 10/1405
Smith, J. Mr 10/0475
Smith, J. Ms 10/0245
Smith, L. Dr 10/0537
Smith, M. Dr 10/0853
Smith, M. Mr 10/0303
Smith, M. Mrs 10/0067
Smith, P. Dr 10/0990 10/0992 10/0999 10/1026
Smith, P. Mrs 10/0919
Smith, P. Prof. 10/1371 10/1372 10/1373 10/1374
    10/1375
Smith, R. Mr 10/0294 10/0297
Smith, S. Mrs 10/0171
Smith, T. Prof. 10/1618
Smith, C. Dr 10/1618
Smyth, J. Dr 10/0273
Snape, J. Dr 10/1100
Snowling, M. Prof. 10/0864 10/1103 10/1259
    10/1808
Solity, J. Mr 10/1747 10/1748 10/1749
Somekh, B. Dr 10/1624 10/1630
Somers, J. Mr 10/0349
Sommerlad, E. Dr 10/1548 10/1549
South, N. Dr 10/0492
Southworth, A. Mrs 10/0639
Southworth, G. Dr 10/0178 10/0190
Spackman, A. Dr 10/0267
Spalding, R. Mr 10/0677
Sparkes, A. Dr 10/0370 10/0926
Speake, L. Ms 10/1608

Spear, M. Dr 10/1258
Spence, B. Dr 10/0478 10/0481
Spencer, C. Dr 10/1376
Speth, C. Dr 10/0336
Sprokkereef, A. Ms 10/1702
Spurgeon, C. Mr 10/1800
Stables, A. Dr 10/1596 10/1599
Stafford, C. Dr 10/0175
Stainthorp, R. Dr 10/1259 10/1264
Stainton, R. Mr 10/1094
Stanesby, C. Mrs 10/1067
Stanford, B. Mr 10/1765
Staniforth, J. Mr 10/0937
Stanisstreet, M. Dr 10/0700
Stanley, N. Mr 10/0683
Stapa, S. Mrs 10/0421
Statham, J. Dr 10/0851
Stears, D. Mr 10/0197
Steedman, J. 10/0232
Steeg, T. Mr 10/0982
Steele, G. Dr 10/0600 10/0602
Steele, J. Mr 10/0305
Stein-Davies, M. Mrs 10/0914
Steiner, M. Ms 10/0930
Stephens, C. Dr 10/1449
Stephens, D. Dr 10/1519 10/1538
Stephens, M. Prof. 10/1128 10/1129
Stephens, W. Dr 10/0640 10/0641
Stephenson, H. Ms 10/0246
Stephenson, R. Mr 10/1556
Stern, E. Mr 10/1549
Steward, A. Dr 10/1476
Stewart, R. Mr 10/0687 10/0692
Stewart, S. Mrs 10/1132
Stirling, M. Mrs 10/1736
Stock, A. Prof. 10/0959 10/1139
Stockdale, C. Mr 10/0296
Stokes, I. Ms 10/0928
Stoll, P. Mrs 10/1647
Stone, C. Mrs 10/1794
Stone, J. Mrs 10/0082
Stones, E. Prof. 10/0108
Stoney, S. Dr 10/0994 10/0995 10/1003 10/1005
    10/1006 10/1007 10/1009 10/1011 10/1019
    10/1020 10/1021 10/1022 10/1023 10/1024
    10/1028 10/1043 10/1054 10/1065
Storey, S. Ms 10/1780
Stothard, S. Dr 10/1103
Stott, D. Mr 10/1472
Stradling, R. Dr 10/0993 10/1004 10/1025
    10/1029 10/1030 10/1032 10/1035 10/1066
    10/1067
Strahan, H. Ms 10/0938
Strand, S. Dr 10/0704
Straughan, R. Dr 10/1247 10/1249
Street, B. Dr 10/0346
Street-Porter, R. Ms 10/0436
Strettle, R. Dr 10/1616
Stronach, I. Prof. 10/1448 10/1449 10/1450
    10/1451 10/1453 10/1458 10/1459 10/1639
Stuart, J. Dr 10/1541
Stuart, J. Mrs 10/0260
Stuart, M. Ms 10/1514
Sugden, D. Prof. 10/0608 10/0645 10/0646
    10/0650
Summerfield, P. Dr 10/0539 10/0544
Summers, M. Mr 10/1763
Sutherland, A. Miss 10/1107 10/1108
Sutherland, E. Ms 10/0325
Sutherland, R. Dr 10/0039 10/0774 10/0777
    10/0781 10/0782 10/0783
Sutton, I. Dr 10/1141 10/1152
Sutton, R. Dr 10/1687 10/1690 10/1691 10/1693
Swan, D. Miss 10/0174
Swan, R. Mr 10/1499
Swann, J. Dr 10/1444
Swannell, M. Dr 10/1116
Swanwick, K. Prof. 10/0791 10/0792 10/0793
Sweeney, S. Mr 10/0044
Swinnerton, B. Dr 10/0651
Sylva, K. Prof. 10/0724 10/0850
Symonds, G. Mr 10/0060
Syson, A. Dr 10/0239

Tabberer, R. Mr 10/1010 10/1044 10/1045
    10/1046
Taber, K. Mr 10/1294
Tabi, T. Mr 10/0143
Tabouret-Keller, A. Prof. 10/1804
Taggart, L. Ms 10/1379

Tait, H. Dr 10/0336 10/0337
Talbot, M. Prof. 10/0583 10/0585
Talbot, S. Ms 10/0975
Tallack, M. Mrs 10/0020
Tam, C. Mrs 10/1771
Tann, J. Prof. 10/0065 10/0067 10/0068 10/0069
  10/0070 10/0071 10/0072
Tanner, H. Mr 10/1593 10/1594 10/1595 10/1596
  10/1601
Tate, A. Dr 10/1047
Taylor, B. Mrs 10/1267
Taylor, G. Dr 10/1218 10/1220
Taylor, M. Miss 10/0994 10/1009 10/1019
  10/1020 10/1029 10/1067
Taylor, M. Mr 10/0030
Taylor, M. Mrs 10/1176
Taylor, P. Mr 10/0957 10/1709
Taylor, P. Ms 10/0437 10/0438
Taylor, P. Prof. 10/1615
Taylor, R. Mr 10/0198
Taylor, R. Prof. 10/0598 10/0600 10/0602
Taylorson, D. Dr 10/0920
Thody, A. Dr 10/0908 10/0909 10/0910 10/0911
  10/0912 10/0913 10/0914 10/0915
Thomas, B. Mrs 10/1596
Thomas, D. Mr 10/0111
Thomas, G. Dr 10/1206 10/1211
Thomas, H. Dr 10/0075 10/0076 10/0079 10/0080
  10/0081 10/0086 10/0841
Thomas, H. Mr 10/0014 10/0143
Thomas, J. Mr 10/0874 10/0875 10/0885
Thomas, L. Dr 10/0736 10/0737 10/0740 10/0743
Thomas, L. Prof. 10/0160
Thomas, N. Mrs 10/1765
Thomas, P. Mr 10/0201
Thomas, R. Mr 10/0582
Thomas, R. Ms 10/0376
Thomas, S. Dr 10/0730 10/0731 10/0734
Thompson, A. Mrs 10/1282
Thompson, D. Dr 10/1372
Thompson, D. Mr 10/0501 10/0502 10/0503
Thompson, E. Mrs 10/1139
Thompson, J. Prof. 10/0044 10/0046
Thompson, K. Miss 10/1108
Thompson, L. Ms 10/0286
Thompson, Q. Mr 10/0234 10/0235
Thompson, W. Mr 10/1147
Thomson, A. Dr 10/1513 10/1516 10/1517
Thomson, A. Mr 10/1422 10/1429 10/1430
  10/1432
Thomson, G. Dr 10/0328 10/0331
Thomson, L. Mrs 10/0271
Thomson, S. Mrs 10/1327
Thorne, C. Mr 10/0601
Thornton, M. Dr 10/0465
Thorp, H. Mrs 10/1497
Thorpe, G. Mr 10/1331 10/1338 10/1358 10/1362
Thorpe, M. Rev. 10/1472
Threadingham, M. Mrs 10/0533
Threlfall, J. Dr 10/0632 10/0653
Thumpston, G. Ms 10/0709
Tickle, S. Mrs 10/0857
Tiffney, A. Mrs 10/1419
Tikly, L. Mr 10/0414
Tinkler, P. Dr 10/0540
Tinklin, T. Ms 10/0450
Tivers, J. Dr 10/1507
Tjok-A-Tam Ms 10/1490
Tobin, M. Dr 10/0101 10/0103 10/0104 10/0105
  10/0106 10/0107
Tod, J. Ms 10/0447
Todd, F. Dr 10/0604
Todd, N. Mr 10/0900
Tolley, J. Ms 10/0506
Tolly, B. Dr 10/0922
Tolmie, A. Dr 10/1464
Tomley, D. Mr 10/0665
Tomlins, B. Dr 10/1005 10/1022 10/1084 10/1089
Tomlinson, A. Prof. 10/0131
Tomlinson, J. Prof. 10/1694
Tomlinson, P. Dr 10/0608 10/0617 10/0631
  10/0642
Tomlinson, S. Prof. 10/0713
Tope, R. Mrs 10/1693
Topping, M. Mr 10/0522
Torrance, H. Dr 10/1529 10/1531
Tosey, P. Dr 10/1500
Towler, L. Ms 10/0036
Townend, J. Mr 10/1278
Towner, E. Ms 10/1541

Townsend, R. Ms 10/0437
Townson, M. Dr 10/0033
Towse, P. Mr 10/0587 10/0594
Toy, K. Mr 10/0507
Trafford, V. Dr 10/0012 10/0013 10/0014
  10/0016 10/0017 10/0018 10/0019 10/0023
Treadwell, P. Mr 10/0233
Tresman, S. Dr 10/1198
Treweek, J. Mr 10/0043
Triadafillidis, T. Mr 10/0340
Trimble, J. Ms 10/1052
Trotter, A. Mrs 10/0359
Trowler, P. Mr 10/0565
Troyna, B. Dr 10/1722 10/1723 10/1737
Trueman, M. Mr 10/0523
Tsai, C. Ms 10/1707
Tufnell, R. Mr 10/1746
Tuohy, A. Dr 10/0390
Turner, E. Ms 10/1451 10/1459
Turner, H. Ms 10/0810
Turner, S. Dr 10/0838
Turnock, J. Mr 10/0922
Twigger, D. Mr 10/0592
Twining, J. Mr 10/0446
Twitchin, R. Mr 10/1005
Tyers, J. Mr 10/0255
Tyler, K. Mr 10/0866
Tyler, S. Ms 10/1188
Tymms, P. Mr 10/0452 10/0458

Ubuz, B. Miss 10/1156
Udall, N. Mr 10/1299
Underhay, S. Mrs 10/0997
Underwood, G. Prof. 10/1144
Ungar, S. Mr 10/1376
Upton, C. Dr 10/0032
Upton, G. Prof. 10/0078 10/0083 10/0094
  10/0095
Utley, A. Ms 10/0645
Uzoigwe, F. Mrs 10/0482

Valentine, C. Mr 10/1176
Valentine, E. Dr 10/0858
Vallance, T. Mr 10/0204
Valli, Y. Miss 10/0583
Van den Brink Budgen, R. Dr 10/0905
Van der Lely, H. Dr 10/0705
Vanaman, J. Ms 10/1124
Vass, J. Mr 10/1650
Veltman, M. Ms 10/0847
Verma, G. Prof. 10/0973 10/0974 10/0975
Verma, R. Mr 10/1803 10/1804
Vile, A. Mr 10/1381
Vincent, A. Dr 10/1176
Vincent, C. Dr 10/0719
Vincent, C. Ms 10/0756
Vosho, M. Mr 10/0369

Waddington, D. Prof. 10/1089 10/1802
Wade, B. Dr 10/0091 10/0092
Wain, G. Mr 10/0588 10/0619
Wakefield, A. Ms 10/1061 10/1063
Wakefield, P. Mr 10/1789
Wakelin, M. Mrs 10/0495
Walker, A. Dr 10/1760
Walker, B. Ms 10/1635 10/1636
Walker, K. Mr 10/0951 10/1382
Walker, L. Ms 10/0408
Walker, M. Mr 10/0169
Walker, P. Dr 10/1621
Walker, S. Dr 10/1284
Wall, B. Ms 10/0673
Wall, N. Mrs 10/1530
Wallace, G. Dr 10/0262
Wallace, M. Dr 10/0149 10/0152
Walsh, A. Ms 10/0188
Walsh, S. Ms 10/0687
Walters, M. Mrs 10/1110
Walters, N. Rev. 10/1496 10/1506
Walton, I. Ms 10/1056 10/1075
Walton, R. Mr 10/0622
Wanjala, E. Mr 10/0621
Warburton, P. Mr 10/0307
Warburton, T. Mr 10/0563
Ward, C. Mrs 10/0446
Ward, K. Mr 10/0597 10/0603
Ware, J. Mrs 10/1006
Warner, A. Dr 10/1804
Warner, M. Mr 10/0477
Warrender, A-M. Mrs 10/1441 10/1443

Warwick, I. Mr 10/0819 10/0826
Washington, J. Mr 10/1623
Wasp, D. Mr 10/0444
Waterhouse, S. Dr 10/1459
Watson, K. Prof. 10/1261
Watson, P. Mr 10/0618 10/0636
Watson-Broughton, A. Mrs 10/0357
Watt, J. Dr 10/0001 10/0002 10/0007
Watts, A. Mr 10/1090 10/1091
Watts, M. Dr 10/1293 10/1294 10/1303 10/1311
Watts, P. Mr 10/0095
Waugh, D. Mr 10/0480 10/0486
Weale, A. Mr 10/0241
Weare, K. Ms 10/0202 10/1401 10/1402 10/1403
Webb, S. Ms 10/0227
Webster, A. Dr 10/0026 10/0027 10/0037
  10/0145 10/0150
Webster, D. Dr 10/0491
Webster, D. Mr 10/1408
Webster, D. Rev. 10/0473 10/0477
Wedell, K. Prof. 10/0746 10/0752 10/0753
Weindling, R. Mr 10/0156
Weiner, G. Prof. 10/1369 10/1385 10/1386
Weir, C. Dr 10/0863
Weiyuan, Z. Mr 10/0328
Welch, G. Prof. 10/1291 10/1310 10/1314
  10/1323 10/1326
Welch, S. Ms 10/0581 10/0582
Welford, A. Mr 10/0623 10/0625 10/0650
Wellens, S. Dr 10/1201
Wells, C. Mr 10/1251
Wells, P. Mr 10/1096
Wells, R. Ms 10/0173
West, L. Mr 10/0530 10/0531
West, M. Mr 10/0178
West, R. Prof. 10/1196
West-Burnham, J. Mr 10/0673 10/0925
Weston, P. Mrs 10/1011 10/1012 10/1022
  10/1061 10/1067 10/1089
Weston, V. Ms 10/1122
Whalley, P. Dr 10/1177 10/1178 10/1179
  10/1180
Whetton, C. Mr 10/0990 10/0992 10/0999
  10/1002 10/1007 10/1026 10/1084
Whitcombe, D. Mr 10/1331
White, J. Dr 10/1241
White, P. Ms 10/1314 10/1323
White, S. Mr 10/0669
Whitebread, D. Mr 10/0177
Whitehead, D. Dr 10/0742
Whitehead, J. Dr 10/0129 10/0130
Whitehead, J. Ms 10/1661
Whitehead, M. Dr 10/0244 10/0471
Whitehead, M. Ms 10/0715
Whitelaw, S. Ms 10/0650
Whitelegg, E. Ms 10/1196 10/1197
Whiteley, M. Ms 10/0946
Whiting, C. Ms 10/1236
Whittaker, J. Mr 10/0117
Whitty, G. Prof. 10/0219 10/0819 10/0821
  10/0824 10/0825 10/0826 10/0827 10/0828
  10/0829 10/0830 10/0831 10/0832 10/1322
Whyte, A. Mr 10/1411
Whyte, G. Mr 10/1149
Wicks, P. Dr 10/0855
Widdows, S. Mr 10/0347
Wikeley, F. Mrs 10/0366 10/0372
Wilcox, B. Mr 10/1377
Wild, G. Dr 10/0876
Wild, P. Dr 10/0873 10/0889 10/0892 10/0897
  10/0899
Wilding, J. Dr 10/0857 10/0858 10/0859 10/0860
  10/0861
Wildman, S. Mr 10/0241
Wilenius, F. Mr 10/1069
Wilkes, J. Mrs 10/1295
Wilkin, A. Mrs 10/1049 10/1063
Wilkins, B. Miss 10/1291
Wilkinson, H. Miss 10/0536
Wilkinson, J. Dr 10/0395 10/0396 10/0397
  10/0407 10/0426 10/0433
Willcocks, J. Mr 10/0643
Williams, A. Dr 10/1242
Williams, C. Mr 10/1792
Williams, C. Prof. 10/0393
Williams, D. Dr 10/1178 10/1285
Williams, G. Dr 10/0436
Williams, G. Prof. 10/0794 10/0795 10/0816
Williams, I. Prof. 10/1584
Williams, J. Dr 10/0192 10/0980 10/0981

Williams, M. Mrs 10/1082
Williams, M. Prof. 10/1598
Williams, R. Mr 10/0629 10/0639 10/0648
  10/1518 10/1520
Williams, S. Mr 10/1392
Williams, S. Ms 10/1782
Williams, T. Mr 10/0383
Williams, V. Ms 10/0491
Williams, W. Mr 10/1469
Williamson, H. Dr 10/1678
Williamson, J. Mr 10/1105
Willson, M. Mr 10/1536
Wilson, M. Ms 10/1203 10/1209
Wilson, P. Dr 10/0661
Wilton, P. Mr 10/1308
Winbourne, P. Mr 10/1384
Winch, C. Dr 10/1096 10/1098
Winter, R. Prof. 10/0029
Winther-Jensen, Th. Dr 10/0431
Wisbeach, A. Ms 10/0493
Withnall, A. Ms 10/0576 10/0577 10/0578
Wolf, A. Mrs 10/0754 10/0776 10/0783 10/0784
  10/0785 10/0786 10/0787 10/0789
Woll, B. Dr 10/0148
Wong, K. Mr 10/1140

Wood, A. Mr 10/1125
Wood, D. Mr 10/0943
Wood, S. Mrs 10/0131
Wood-Robinson, C. Mr 10/0626 10/0637
Woodcock, G. Dr 10/0695
Woodcock, M. Miss 10/0953
Woodrow, D. Mr 10/0950
Woods, P. Prof. 10/1670
Wooldridge, I. Mrs 10/0246
Woolhouse, J. Prof. 10/1694 10/1697 10/1700
Worle, B. Mr 10/1505
Worth-Butler, M. Mrs 10/1165
Wortley, A. Mrs 10/0664
Wragg, C. Ms 10/0365 10/0372
Wragg, E. Prof. 10/0356 10/0365 10/0371 10/0372
Wray, D. Mr 10/0375
Wrennall, M. Mr 10/0390
Wright, A. Mr 10/0239
Wright, C. Dr 10/0666
Wright, D. Mr 10/1627
Wright, J. Mrs 10/0061
Wright, L. Mrs 10/1555
Wright, M. Mr 10/1643
Wright, N. Mr 10/0488 10/1262
Wright, S. Dr 10/0031

Wright, Y. Miss 10/0978
Wringe, C. Dr 10/0495 10/0506 10/0507 10/0508
Wyllyams, B. Ms 10/1307
Wyvill, M. Mr 10/1476

Yang, K-T. Mr 10/1129
Yates, P. Dr 10/0137 10/1521
Yekta, Z. Mrs 10/0419
Yeomans, D. Mr 10/0629
Yeomans, R. Mr 10/0246
Young, A. Miss 10/0034
Young, M. Dr 10/0773 10/0807 10/0808 10/0811
  10/0812 10/0814
Young, P. Dr 10/0756
Youngman, M. Dr 10/0177 10/1157
Yue, N. Dr 10/0715
Yuill, N. Dr 10/1544 10/1545 10/1546
Yuven-Lafen, L. Mr 10/1273

Zachos, I. Mr 10/0615
Zand, H. Dr 10/1172
Zec, P. Mr 10/0973
Zeng, J. Ms 10/0580
Zukas, M. Ms 10/0599
Zuke, L. Ms 10/0850

Subject Index

'A' LEVEL EXAMINATIONS
10/0053 learning strategies; modern language studies; sixteen to nineteen education
10/0255 design education; learner characteristics; student attitudes
10/0458 accountability; examination results; outcomes of education; performance indicators; programme effectiveness; school effectiveness
10/1210 learner characteristics; music activities; music education; pupil attitudes; sex differences
10/1530 business education; curriculum development; economics education
10/1796 chemistry education; science education; teaching methods

ABILITY
10/0348 learning; mixed ability; pacing; time factors – learning
10/0612 projects – learning activities; pupil projects; secondary education; technology education
10/0620 design and technology; National Curriculum; primary education; technology education
10/0722 child development; developmental continuity; longitudinal studies; personality development
10/1044 computer uses in education; gifted; information technology; primary school pupils
10/1067 class organisation; grouping – teaching purposes; mixed ability; pupil placement; streaming; teaching methods

ABILITY TESTS
10/0972 language handicaps; learning disabilities; mathematical ability; mathematics education; numbers; special educational needs
10/1026 diagnostic assessment; intelligence tests; special educational needs

ACADEMIC ABILITY
10/1767 academic failure; gifted; pupil behaviour; underachievement

ACADEMIC ACHIEVEMENT
10/0003 choice of subjects; sex differences
10/0031 bilingualism; diglossia; ethnic groups; language usage
10/0056 equal education; school effectiveness; underachievement; urban schools
10/0105 blindness; cognitive development; longitudinal studies; outcomes of education; partial vision; special schools; visual impairments
10/0323 higher education; school effectiveness; secondary schools
10/0520 cognitive ability; listening skills; reading achievement; television research; television viewing
10/0531 access programmes; higher education; mature students; nontraditional education; performance
10/0559 educational experience; higher education; mature students; student attitudes
10/0652 achievement; birth; performance; school entrance age
10/0867 performance factors; scaling; school effectiveness; social environment; socioeconomic influences
10/1325 achievement; cognitive style; failure; gifted; underachievement
10/1331 achievement rating; assessment; educational research

10/1416 access programmes; access to education; higher education; mature students; outcomes of education
10/1454 educational practices; pupil improvement; secondary schools; support services; underachievement
10/1738 Catholic schools; school effectiveness

ACADEMIC ASPIRATION
10/0526 locus of control; Malaysia; motivation tests; student motivation

ACADEMIC FAILURE
10/0336 higher education; intervention; student problems; underachievement
10/1767 academic ability; gifted; pupil behaviour; underachievement

ACADEMIC RECORDS
10/0358 parent aspiration; parent-school relationship; school based assessment

ACADEMIC STAFF
10/0528 ethnic groups; higher education; mature students; middle class students; student attitudes; student experience; working class
10/0903 employment opportunities; equal opportunities – jobs; higher education; universities; women teachers; women's employment
10/1068 further education teachers; higher education; stress – psychological; teacher workload
10/1106 higher education; inservice teacher education; preservice teacher education; teacher educators
10/1369 academic staff promotion; employment opportunities; equal opportunities – jobs; further education; higher education

ACADEMIC STAFF DEVELOPMENT
10/0263 educational policy; inservice teacher education; professional development; Scotland
10/1483 head teachers; teacher evaluation; teaching profession

ACADEMIC STAFF EVALUATION
10/1578 quality assurance; quality control; teacher evaluation; universities

ACADEMIC STAFF PROMOTION
10/1369 academic staff; employment opportunities; equal opportunities – jobs; further education; higher education

ACCESS PROGRAMMES
10/0118 higher education; mature students; men; student experience
10/0225 adult education; databases
10/0226 adult education; mature students; student development
10/0267 access to education; adult education; comparative education; higher education; mature students
10/0530 access to education; higher education; mature students; nontraditional education; student motivation
10/0531 academic achievement; higher education; mature students; nontraditional education; performance
10/0599 continuing education; educational benefits; educational objectives; women's education
10/1344 access to education; adult students;

higher education; mature students; programme evaluation; science education; social sciences
10/1416 academic achievement; access to education; higher education; mature students; outcomes of education
10/1522 access to education; continuing education; higher education

ACCESS TO EDUCATION
10/0001 community education; mothers; preschool education; young children
10/0007 disadvantaged environment; educational innovation; educationally disadvantaged; Scotland
10/0018 parent choice; secondary schools; selection
10/0024 Canada natives; educational policy; qualifications
10/0043 adult education; adult learning; basic skills; mature students; self evaluation – individuals
10/0090 disabilities; higher education; special educational needs; student needs; universities; university admission
10/0121 adult education; continuing education; lifelong learning
10/0123 higher education; nontraditional education; student counselling; student health and welfare
10/0170 equal education; higher education; Pakistan; women's education
10/0176 equal education; gender equality; higher education; social class
10/0227 finance occupations; mature students; professional education
10/0229 adult education; Germany; higher education; mature students; student participation
10/0230 adult education; France; higher education; mature students; student participation
10/0267 access programmes; adult education; comparative education; higher education; mature students
10/0310 educational change; further education; higher education; sixteen to nineteen education
10/0317 further education; higher education; programme evaluation
10/0367 Education Reform Act 1988; parent choice; primary schools
10/0408 dropout research; higher education; nontraditional education; summer schools; university admission; university preparation
10/0425 higher education; summer schools; transition education; university admission; university preparation
10/0442 accessibility – for disabled; disabilities; equal education; higher education; student recruitment
10/0530 access programmes; higher education; mature students; nontraditional education; student motivation
10/0536 parent choice; special educational needs
10/0565 credit transfer; educational change; higher education
10/0580 equal education; ethnic groups; higher education; student experience; student recruitment
10/0934 higher education; programme evaluation; records of achievement; student records
10/0986 adult basic education; adult learning; intelligence differences; multiple disabilities; severe learning difficulties
10/1074 admission criteria; enrolment; open entry; parent choice; secondary schools

10/1093 adult education; retraining; women's education
10/1332 adult education; adult students; community education; educational guidance; mature students; student attitudes
10/1344 access programmes; adult students; higher education; mature students; programme evaluation; science education; social sciences
10/1345 adult education; adult students; educational guidance; mature students; Scotland
10/1358 higher education; socioeconomic background; student recruitment
10/1359 admission criteria; higher education; student recruitment
10/1416 academic achievement; access programmes; higher education; mature students; outcomes of education
10/1504 admission criteria; admissions tutors; higher education; student recruitment
10/1511 admission criteria; competency based education; higher education; National Vocational Qualifications
10/1514 accreditation of prior learning; experiential learning; higher education; transfer of learning
10/1522 access programmes; continuing education; higher education
10/1535 adult education; rural areas
10/1550 cultural background; equal education; ethnic groups; higher education; inner city; women's education
10/1700 further education; programme evaluation; sixteen to nineteen education
10/1720 further education; sixteen to nineteen education; student participation; tertiary education; vocational education
10/1726 higher education; mature students; student attitudes; student housing; student recruitment

ACCESS TO INFORMATION
10/0842 information needs; parent-school relationship

ACCESSIBILITY – FOR DISABLED
10/0442 access to education; disabilities; equal education; higher education; student recruitment

ACCIDENTS
10/0953 comparative education; European Community; food standards; health education; nutrition education; safety education

ACCOUNTABILITY
10/0458 'A' level examinations; examination results; outcomes of education; performance indicators; programme effectiveness; school effectiveness
10/1380 educational quality; measurement; performance indicators; school effectiveness; secondary schools

ACCOUNTANCY EDUCATION
10/0987 business education; research; teaching methods

ACCREDITATION – COURSES
10/1230 accrediting authorities; assessment; educational quality; external examiners; higher education; open universities

ACCREDITATION OF PRIOR LEARNING
10/0784 assessment; National Vocational Qualifications; training and enterprise councils; vocational education
10/1514 access to education; experiential learning; higher education; transfer of learning
10/1624 experiential learning; higher education

ACCREDITING AUTHORITIES
10/1230 accreditation – courses; assessment; educational quality; external examiners; higher education; open universities

ACHIEVEMENT
10/0113 assessment; experiential learning; further education; National Vocational Qualifications; prior learning

10/0129 failure; motivation; sports
10/0130 sports
10/0525 motivation; music education; musical instruments
10/0652 academic achievement; birth; performance; school entrance age
10/0734 educational quality; performance factors; performance indicators; school effectiveness
10/0750 adult basic education; adult dropouts; basic skills; dropout research
10/0965 National Curriculum; primary education; reading achievement
10/0971 mathematics education; National Curriculum; primary education; reading achievement
10/1048 comparative testing; reading ability; reading achievement; reading research
10/1055 birth; local education authorities; school entrance age
10/1058 achievement tests; assessment; comparative education; mathematics education; science education
10/1076 classroom environment; performance factors; statistical analysis
10/1077 educational quality; examination results; outcomes of education; performance factors; performance indicators; school effectiveness
10/1283 black pupils; black teachers; teacher behaviour; teacher-pupil relationship; teaching methods; teaching styles
10/1297 assessment; early childhood education; records of achievement; self evaluation – individuals; young children
10/1325 academic achievement; cognitive style; failure; gifted; underachievement
10/1670 assessment; primary school pupils; profiles; records of achievement; self evaluation – individuals
10/1710 Afro Caribbean youth; assessment; black pupils; Education Reform Act 1988; equal education; ethnic groups; low achievement
10/1771 background; high achievement; individual characteristics; science education; undergraduate students

ACHIEVEMENT RATING
10/1331 academic achievement; assessment; educational research

ACHIEVEMENT TESTS
10/1053 assessment; mathematics achievement; mathematics education; National Curriculum
10/1058 achievement; assessment; comparative education; mathematics education; science education
10/1367 assessment; primary secondary education; school based assessment

ACQUIRED IMMUNE DEFICIENCY SYNDROME
10/0009 health education; parent participation; peer teaching; sex education
10/0197 health education; health promotion; sexuality; sexually transmitted diseases; tourism; travel
10/0492 drug abuse; drug education; health education; welfare services
10/0798 health education; sex education; sexuality; sexually transmitted diseases
10/0799 health education; sex education; sexuality; sexually transmitted diseases
10/0800 health education; sex education; sexuality; sexually transmitted diseases
10/0818 health education; sex education; sexually transmitted diseases
10/0819 health education; sex education; sexually transmitted diseases; youth
10/0826 health education; homeless people
10/0827 evaluation; health education; training
10/0828 health education; secondary schools
10/0829 educational materials; health education
10/0830 nurse education; nurses; sexually transmitted diseases
10/0831 health education; homosexuality; sex education; sexuality; sexually transmitted diseases
10/0879 health education; sex education
10/1056 educational materials; nurses; sexually

transmitted diseases
10/1134 adult education; ethics; sexually transmitted diseases; voluntary agencies
10/1430 educational materials; educational technology; health education; interactive video; material development; sex education
10/1631 homosexuality; sex education; sexually transmitted diseases

ACTION RESEARCH
10/1330 assessment; educational research; school based assessment

ACTIVITIES
10/0664 comparative education; France; outdoor pursuits; physical education

ADAPTIVE BEHAVIOUR – OF DISABLED
10/1146 attitude measures; blindness; emotional adjustment; measurement techniques; rehabilitation; visual impairments

ADAPTIVE TESTING
10/1034 assessment; attainment tests; computer assisted testing; National Curriculum; test validity

ADMINISTRATION
10/1438 emotions; employment practices; sex differences; sexuality

ADMINISTRATOR ROLE
10/0671 educational change; head teachers; management in education; role conflict; secondary schools; teacher role

ADMINISTRATORS
10/0049 educational administration; management in education; teacher-administrator relationship
10/0517 educational administration; further education; higher education; management in education; women; women's employment
10/0952 educational administration; head teachers; management development; management in education
10/1486 health personnel; health services; nursing

ADMISSION CRITERIA
10/0719 medical schools; medical students; selective admission
10/1074 access to education; enrolment; open entry; parent choice; secondary schools
10/1359 access to education; higher education; student recruitment
10/1504 access to education; admissions tutors; higher education; student recruitment
10/1511 access to education; competency based education; higher education; National Vocational Qualifications
10/1786 local education authorities; school entrance age

ADMISSIONS TUTORS
10/1504 access to education; admission criteria; higher education; student recruitment

ADOLESCENT ATTITUDES
10/0967 adolescent development; adolescents; educational attitudes; interests; personality development; social development; vocational interests

ADOLESCENT DEVELOPMENT
10/0967 adolescent attitudes; adolescents; educational attitudes; interests; personality development; social development; vocational interests
10/1221 bereavement; child development; death; moral development; religious attitudes

ADOLESCENTS
10/0852 family influence; health; smoking
10/0955 electroencephalograph; epilepsy; handicap identification
10/0967 adolescent attitudes; adolescent development; educational attitudes; interests; personality development; social development; vocational interests
10/0974 Chinese; cultural background; ethnic groups; ethnicity; Hong Kong; migrants

10/1579 children; television surveys; television viewing
10/1635 conversation; peer groups; peer teaching; sexuality

ADULT BASIC EDUCATION
10/0568 open education
10/0750 achievement; adult dropouts; basic skills; dropout research
10/0986 access to education; adult learning; intelligence differences; multiple disabilities; severe learning difficulties
10/1126 adults; computer literacy; disabilities; information technology; special educational needs
10/1342 adult education; adult literacy; adult students; numeracy
10/1606 basic skills; colleges of further education; educational quality; further education; programme evaluation
10/1645 adult educators; educational practices; teaching methods; theory-practice relationship
10/1675 learning disabilities; neurological impairments; special educational needs; speech handicaps

ADULT COUNSELLING
10/1090 career counselling; Europe; European Community; vocational guidance

ADULT DAY CENTRES
10/0066 caregivers; educational needs; services; special educational needs
10/1449 learning disabilities; special educational needs

ADULT DEVELOPMENT
10/1499 adult education; religion and education; religious education

ADULT DROPOUTS
10/0750 achievement; adult basic education; basic skills; dropout research

ADULT EDUCATION
10/1356 adult education
10/0043 access to education; adult learning; basic skills; mature students; self evaluation – individuals
10/0098 capitalism; Christianity; church and education; religious education; secularisation
10/0119 life style; participation
10/0121 access to education; continuing education; lifelong learning
10/0125 citizenship; comparative education; consumer economics; educational policy; Poland
10/0225 access programmes; databases
10/0226 access programmes; mature students; student development
10/0228 databases; further education; higher education; mature students
10/0229 access to education; Germany; higher education; mature students; student participation
10/0230 access to education; France; higher education; mature students; student participation
10/0266 community education; rural areas
10/0267 access programmes; access to education; comparative education; higher education; mature students
10/0296 educational history; mechanics institutes
10/0430 comparative education; lifelong learning; mature students; people's universities; Scandinavia
10/0431 comparative education; Denmark; lifelong learning; mature students; people's universities
10/0576 older adults
10/0577 life skills; numeracy; older adults
10/0578 adult learning; caregivers; disabilities; independent study; lifelong learning
10/0586 creative writing
10/0597 labour force development; works schools
10/0598 Canada; comparative education; continuing education
10/0600 educational history; India
10/0602 educational history; social history; working class

10/0606 biographies; educational history; extension education; universities; working class
10/0607 educational history; educational policy; extension education; working class
10/0614 comparative education; educational history; extension education
10/0627 continuing education; educational finance; educational policy; European Community; financial support
10/0695 educational broadcasting; educational radio; local radio; mass media; radio
10/0766 continuing education; educational history
10/0959 comparative education; continuing education; cultural differences; Europe; lifelong learning
10/1054 adult learning; guidance; lifelong learning
10/1093 access to education; retraining; women's education
10/1128 China; comparative education
10/1129 comparative education; Taiwan; United Kingdom; universities
10/1132 community; individual development; social change; voluntary agencies
10/1133 educational practices; higher education; information technology; physical sciences; science education
10/1134 acquired immune deficiency syndrome; ethics; sexually transmitted diseases; voluntary agencies
10/1136 comparative education; continuing education; European Community; Germany; United Kingdom; vocational education
10/1138 citizenship education; political influences; social change; socialist countries; voluntary agencies
10/1139 adults; comparative education; continuing education; databases; vocational education
10/1141 adult learning; earth science; field studies; field studies centres; study abroad
10/1152 continuing education; industrial training; inservice teacher education; professional training; vocational education
10/1159 continuing education; course evaluation; professional continuing education; programme evaluation
10/1281 Creoles; mother tongue
10/1332 access to education; adult students; community education; educational guidance; mature students; student attitudes
10/1342 adult basic education; adult literacy; adult students; numeracy
10/1345 access to education; adult students; educational guidance; mature students; Scotland
10/1348 educational research
10/1399 science education
10/1499 adult development; religion and education; religious education
10/1513 andragogy; continuing education; Kuwait
10/1516 continuing education; liberal education; nontraditional education
10/1517 continuing education; liberal education
10/1523 cultural education; curriculum development; humanities
10/1535 access to education; rural areas
10/1711 continuing education; higher education; organisational change; universities
10/1712 continuing education; equal education; minority groups

ADULT EDUCATION TEACHERS
10/0710 adult educators; professional development

ADULT EDUCATORS
10/0710 adult education teachers; professional development
10/1645 adult basic education; educational practices; teaching methods; theory-practice relationship

ADULT LEARNING
10/0043 access to education; adult education; basic skills; mature students; self evaluation – individuals
10/0151 human-computer interaction; learning strategies; secretaries; word processing

10/0578 adult education; caregivers; disabilities; independent study; lifelong learning
10/0986 access to education; adult basic education; intelligence differences; multiple disabilities; severe learning difficulties
10/1054 adult education; guidance; lifelong learning
10/1137 mass media; memory
10/1141 adult education; earth science; field studies; field studies centres; study abroad

ADULT LITERACY
10/0232 basic skills; cohort analysis; numeracy
10/0706 home-school relationship; literacy; literacy education; mother tongue; native speakers; primary education; teaching methods
10/1342 adult basic education; adult education; adult students; numeracy

ADULT STUDENTS
10/1167 distance education; humanities; mature students; open universities; student attitudes
10/1329 financial problems; mature students; student costs; student financial aid; student loans; student recruitment
10/1332 access to education; adult education; community education; educational guidance; mature students; student attitudes
10/1342 adult basic education; adult education; adult literacy; numeracy
10/1344 access programmes; access to education; higher education; mature students; programme evaluation; science education; social sciences
10/1345 access to education; adult education; educational guidance; mature students; Scotland

ADULT VOCATIONAL EDUCATION
10/0318 followup studies; outcomes of education; retraining; women's education; women's employment
10/1124 adults; computer literacy; disabilities; information technology; sheltered workshops; special educational needs; training centres
10/1130 employment; job skills; job training; work-education relationship
10/1142 comparative education; disabilities; information technology; Portugal; special educational needs; training; United Kingdom
10/1190 employment patterns; training; unemployment

ADULTS
10/1124 adult vocational education; computer literacy; disabilities; information technology; sheltered workshops; special educational needs; training centres
10/1126 adult basic education; computer literacy; disabilities; information technology; special educational needs
10/1127 computer literacy; disabilities; information technology; special educational needs; training centres
10/1139 adult education; comparative education; continuing education; databases; vocational education

ADVISERS
10/1498 inservice teacher education; inspection; local education authorities; organisational effectiveness

ADVISORY COMMITTEES
10/0796 higher education; policy formation; politics-education relationship; universities

AESTHETIC EDUCATION
10/1290 art activities; art appreciation; nursery school education
10/1753 art activities; art appreciation; art education; criticism; National Curriculum

AESTHETIC VALUES
10/0485 literary criticism; literature studies

AFFECTIVE BEHAVIOUR
10/1172 emotional response; mathematics; student behaviour

AFRO CARIBBEAN YOUTH
10/1710 achievement; assessment; black pupils; Education Reform Act 1988; equal education; ethnic groups; low achievement

AGE DIFFERENCES
10/1017 educational economics; educational finance; resource allocation
10/1588 feminism; women's studies

AGENCY COOPERATION
10/0397 child caregivers; community services; day care centres; early childhood education; programme evaluation; quality control

AGRICULTURAL COLLEGES
10/1241 agricultural education; economic change; educational change; further education; staff development
10/1768 agricultural education; farms

AGRICULTURAL EDUCATION
10/1241 agricultural colleges; economic change; educational change; further education; staff development
10/1528 developing countries; environmental education; Zimbabwe
10/1768 agricultural colleges; farms

AGRICULTURE
10/1120 controversial issues – course content; environmental education; preservice teacher education

AIR POLLUTION
10/0700 conservation – environment; environmental education; misconceptions; scientific concepts; secondary school pupils

ALCOHOL EDUCATION
10/1036 drinking; health education
10/1347 drug education; health education; programme evaluation; sex education

ALGEBRA
10/0039 computer uses in education; logo; low achievement; mathematics education
10/0613 cognitive processes; comprehension; mathematical formulas; mathematics education
10/0619 calculators; computer uses in education; mathematics education; secondary education
10/0621 Kenya; mathematics education; pupil problems
10/0777 computer uses in education; mathematics education; symbols – mathematics

ALGEBRA EDUCATION
10/0780 computer uses in education; mathematics education; problem solving
10/1384 mathematical models; mathematics education
10/1479 computer assisted learning; mathematics education

ALGERIA
10/0418 bilingualism; comparative education; Gaelic; language policy; mother tongue; Scotland

ALLIED HEALTH OCCUPATIONS
10/1402 health education; patient education; preventive medicine

AMBIGUITY
10/0537 class activities; preservice teacher education; student teachers; teaching practice; teaching styles

ANDRAGOGY
10/1513 adult education; continuing education; Kuwait

ANIMATION
10/1177 authoring aids – programming; computer assisted learning; computer uses in education; multimedia approach
10/1180 computer uses in education; pupil projects

ANTIRACISM EDUCATION
10/0220 probationary teachers; racial attitudes; student teacher attitudes; student teachers; teacher education
10/0880 ethnic groups; multicultural education
10/0994 Education Reform Act 1988; educational planning; equal education; local education authorities; multicultural education
10/1288 children's literature; fiction; racial attitudes
10/1410 multicultural education; preservice teacher education

ANTISOCIAL BEHAVIOUR
10/0095 discipline; disruptive pupils; pupil behaviour; pupil placement
10/0243 behaviour problems; delinquency prevention; longitudinal studies; secondary school pupils; transfer pupils
10/1228 behaviour problems; bullying; discipline policy; discipline problems; teacher attitudes
10/1336 behaviour problems; emotional problems; pupil problems; social behaviour; special educational needs
10/1372 behaviour problems; bullying; discipline; discipline policy; pupil behaviour
10/1373 behaviour modification; behaviour problems; bullying; classroom environment; intervention; speech handicaps; stuttering
10/1374 attitudes; behaviour problems; bullying; parent attitudes; pupil attitudes; teacher attitudes
10/1375 attitudes; bullying; discipline policy; parent attitudes; school policy; teacher attitudes
10/1758 comparative education; discipline problems; disruptive pupils; United States of America

APTITUDE
10/0905 assessment; critical thinking; higher education; mature students; prediction of success; selection; student evaluation

ARAB STATES
10/0290 English – second language; second language teaching
10/0293 English – second language; English for specific purposes; programme evaluation
10/0309 cultural awareness; English – second language; foreign culture; native speakers; second language learning
10/0478 developing countries; development education; educational policy
10/0872 English – second language; higher education
10/1673 dropout research; student wastage; technical education; vocational education

ARABIC
10/0347 Chinese languages; educational materials; Japanese; nonwestern languages; second language learning

ARABS
10/1590 English – second language; vowels; word recognition

ARCHITECTURAL EDUCATION
10/0097 blindness; educational equipment; special educational needs; visual impairments

AREA
10/0723 concept formation; mathematics education; measurement equipment

ARGUMENT
10/0472 criticism; higher education; sixth form education; writing processes; writing skills

ARITHMETIC
10/0609 mathematical ability; mathematics education; problem solving; teacher education; teaching methods
10/0618 cognitive style; mathematics education; mature students; secondary school pupils
10/0748 cognitive development; number concepts; numbers; numeracy; primary education
10/1621 cognitive ability; learning disabilities

ARITHMETIC AND NUMBER EDUCATION
10/0188 calculators; mathematics education; primary education

ART
10/0254 databases; design; information sources; research
10/0491 religious education
10/0572 art history; cognitive development; cross curricular approach; mathematics; spatial ability
10/1248 design; Postgraduate Certificate in Education; preservice teacher education; probationary teachers; programme effectiveness; student teachers

ART ACTIVITIES
10/0020 art education; criticism; cross curricular approach
10/1290 aesthetic education; art appreciation; nursery school education
10/1753 aesthetic education; art appreciation; art education; criticism; National Curriculum

ART APPRECIATION
10/1290 aesthetic education; art activities; nursery school education
10/1753 aesthetic education; art activities; art education; criticism; National Curriculum

ART EDUCATION
10/0020 art activities; criticism; cross curricular approach
10/0252 Japan
10/0256 assessment; comparative education; degrees – academic; fine arts; Greece
10/0257 computer assisted design; computer uses in education; design education
10/0260 criticism; intellectual development; reasoning
10/0811 dance; music; sixteen to nineteen education; theatre arts
10/0951 photography; visual arts
10/1235 design education; inservice teacher education; National Curriculum; primary education; primary school teachers
10/1428 assessment; design education
10/1753 aesthetic education; art activities; art appreciation; criticism; National Curriculum
10/1807 drawing; infant school education

ART HISTORY
10/0572 art; cognitive development; cross curricular approach; mathematics; spatial ability

ARTICLED TEACHERS
10/1236 postgraduate certificate in education; preservice teacher education; student teachers; teacher education

ARTIFICIAL INTELLIGENCE
10/0548 computer assisted learning; educational materials; material development

ARTISTS
10/0253 peripatetic teachers; training

ARTS
10/1060 attitudes; culture; mass media; music; participation; sports; theatre arts
10/1062 arts education; attitudes; culture; leisure time; participation; youth

ARTS EDUCATION
10/0258 computer uses in education; cultural education; handicrafts; museums; visual arts
10/1062 arts; attitudes; culture; leisure time; participation; youth
10/1115 cultural education; history; primary education

ASIANS
10/0426 bilingualism; ethnic groups; language maintenance; language policy; minority groups; mother tongue
10/0583 ethnic groups; parent participation; parent-school relationship

ASPIRATION

10/0101 life style; skills; special educational needs; visual impairments; vocational education

10/1071 attitudes; health; pupil attitudes; pupil behaviour; secondary school pupils; sex education; social attitudes

ASSERTIVENESS

10/1083 attainment tests; National Curriculum; standard assessment tasks; Welsh studies

10/1401 health personnel; interpersonal competence; professional training; radiographers

ASSESSMENT

10/0729 10/0030 evaluation; examinations; moderation – marking; National Curriculum

10/0036 primary schools; profiles; pupil responsibility; records of achievement; school reports; self evaluation – individuals

10/0044 music education; National Curriculum

10/0113 achievement; experiential learning; further education; National Vocational Qualifications; prior learning

10/0138 examinations; General Certificate of Secondary Education; low achievement; special educational needs

10/0153 educational change; infant school curriculum; infant school education; National Curriculum; primary school teachers; pupil attitudes

10/0155 educational change; National Curriculum; primary education; primary school curriculum; primary school teachers; pupil attitudes

10/0256 art education; comparative education; degrees – academic; fine arts; Greece

10/0268 competence; examinations; medical education; medicine; physicians

10/0282 competence; examinations; medical education; medicine; physicians

10/0335 attainment tests; English studies; language tests; Scotland

10/0361 classroom observation techniques; teacher response

10/0381 higher education; learner centred curriculum; self evaluation – individuals; teaching methods

10/0387 higher education; learner centred methods; open education; self evaluation – individuals; teaching methods

10/0392 clinical experience; medical education; physical therapy

10/0446 computer assisted testing; computer uses in education; National Vocational Qualifications

10/0588 first schools; infant schools; mathematics curriculum; mathematics teachers; standard assessment tasks

10/0623 National Curriculum; school based assessment; science education

10/0624 General Certificate of Secondary Education; practical science; science activities; science education

10/0625 General Certificate of Secondary Education; practical science; science activities; science education

10/0638 mathematics education; National Curriculum; school based assessment

10/0692 competency based education; group work; higher education; teaching methods

10/0699 National Curriculum; school based assessment; science education

10/0704 pupil development; pupil evaluation; reception classes; school entrance age; screening tests

10/0730 educational quality; National Curriculum; school effectiveness

10/0735 National Curriculum; primary schools; standard assessment tasks

10/0751 colleges of further education; diagnostic assessment; disabilities; further education; moderate learning difficulties; special educational needs

10/0776 job skills; mastery tests; retention – psychology; vocational education

10/0784 accreditation of prior learning; National Vocational Qualifications; training and enterprise councils; vocational education

10/0785 job skills; National Vocational

Qualifications; Scottish vocational qualifications; verbal tests

10/0822 educational quality; higher education

10/0889 data processing; expert systems

10/0905 aptitude; critical thinking; higher education; mature students; prediction of success; selection; student evaluation

10/0927 National Curriculum

10/0964 assessment by teachers; geography education; National Curriculum

10/0977 assessment by teachers; attainment tests; geography education; National Curriculum; standard assessment tasks

10/0978 attainment tests; English studies; geography education; mathematics education; National Curriculum – Northern Ireland; Northern Ireland; science education

10/0979 electrical engineering

10/0983 examinations; physical education

10/0992 memory; spatial ability

10/0997 English studies; National Curriculum; reading achievement; standard assessment tasks; writing skills

10/0998 mathematics achievement; National Curriculum; primary education; science education; standard assessment tasks

10/1000 item banks; screening tests; test items; test selection; tests

10/1002 core curriculum; English studies; mathematics education; National Curriculum; science education

10/1008 attainment tests; National Curriculum; standard assessment tasks; Welsh studies

10/1013 learning disabilities; low achievement; moderate learning difficulties; special educational needs

10/1027 early childhood education; mathematical concepts; mathematics education; mathematics tests; school entrance age

10/1033 attainment tests; differential performance; second language learning

10/1034 adaptive testing; attainment tests; computer assisted testing; National Curriculum; test validity

10/1050 programme evaluation; reading ability; reading achievement

10/1053 achievement tests; mathematics achievement; mathematics education; National Curriculum

10/1058 achievement; achievement tests; comparative education; mathematics education; science education

10/1082 attainment tests; National Curriculum; standard assessment tasks; Welsh studies

10/1084 English studies; evaluation; mathematics education; National Curriculum; science education; secondary education; technology education

10/1145 blindness; mobility aids; partial vision; special educational needs; travel training; visual impairments; visually handicapped mobility

10/1162 assessment by teachers; comparative education; Ghana

10/1219 educational materials; mathematics achievement; mathematics education; National Curriculum

10/1230 accreditation – courses; accrediting authorities; educational quality; external examiners; higher education; open universities

10/1231 educational quality; external examiners; higher education; quality control

10/1238 enterprise education; higher education; learning strategies; skill development; work-education relationship

10/1252 French; General Certificate of Secondary Education; modern language studies; oral tests

10/1297 achievement; early childhood education; records of achievement; self evaluation – individuals; young children

10/1298 mathematics achievement; mathematics education; primary school pupils; self evaluation – individuals

10/1330 action research; educational research; school based assessment

10/1331 academic achievement; achievement rating; educational research

10/1340 National Curriculum – Northern Ireland; school based assessment

10/1361 curriculum development; primary secondary education; programme evaluation

10/1367 achievement tests; primary secondary education; school based assessment

10/1428 art education; design education

10/1434 English studies; oral English; school based assessment; speech communication

10/1435 competency based teacher education; preservice teacher education; student teacher evaluation; teaching practice

10/1444 curriculum development; educational change; environmental education; mathematics education; National Curriculum; Scotland; teaching process

10/1467 parent-pupil relationship; profiles; school reports

10/1515 group work

10/1532 competence; job performance; professional occupations

10/1584 mother tongue; National Curriculum; school based assessment; second language learning; standard assessment tasks; Welsh

10/1595 National Curriculum; school based assessment

10/1601 cognitive ability; mathematical models; mathematics education; metacognition

10/1611 audience response; drama education; dramatics

10/1641 competence; nurse education; obstetrics

10/1656 competency based education

10/1659 geography education

10/1663 longitudinal studies; primary education; primary school pupils; pupil-school relationship; school based assessment; standard assessment tasks

10/1669 National Curriculum; primary education; school based assessment

10/1670 achievement; primary school pupils; profiles; records of achievement; self evaluation – individuals

10/1710 achievement; Afro Caribbean youth; black pupils; Education Reform Act 1988; equal education; ethnic groups; low achievement

10/1746 technology education

10/1760 religious education

ASSESSMENT BY TEACHERS

10/0964 assessment; geography education; National Curriculum

10/0977 assessment; attainment tests; geography education; National Curriculum; standard assessment tasks

10/1162 assessment; comparative education; Ghana

10/1529 National Curriculum; records of achievement; school based assessment

ATTAINMENT TESTS

10/0335 assessment; English studies; language tests; Scotland

10/0977 assessment; assessment by teachers; geography education; National Curriculum; standard assessment tasks

10/0978 assessment; English studies; geography education; mathematics education; National Curriculum – Northern Ireland; Northern Ireland; science education

10/1008 assessment; National Curriculum; standard assessment tasks; Welsh studies

10/1033 assessment; differential performance; second language learning

10/1034 adaptive testing; assessment; computer assisted testing; National Curriculum; test validity

10/1082 assessment; National Curriculum; standard assessment tasks; Welsh studies

10/1083 assertiveness; National Curriculum; standard assessment tasks; Welsh studies

ATTENDANCE

10/0322 discipline; discipline problems; pupil attitudes; secondary schools; teacher attitudes

10/1063 discipline problems; disruptive pupils; expulsion; truancy

10/1107 attendance patterns; Northern Ireland; pupil behaviour; truancy

10/1366 pupil behaviour; Scotland; secondary schools; truancy

10/1757 educational attitudes; family influence; home-school relationship; truancy

ATTENDANCE PATTERNS
10/0127 business education; course evaluation; examination results; outcomes of education; sandwich courses; undergraduate study
10/1107 attendance; Northern Ireland; pupil behaviour; truancy

ATTENTION
10/0859 attention deficit disorders; concentration; hyperactivity
10/0863 cognitive development; early experience; infant behaviour; learning; neurological impairments

ATTENTION DEFICIT DISORDERS
10/0859 attention; concentration; hyperactivity
10/1640 cognitive ability; hyperactivity; learning disabilities; memory

ATTITUDE CHANGE
10/0676 motivation techniques; pupil needs; self concept; self esteem

ATTITUDE FORMATION
10/0681 bereavement; childhood attitudes; death
10/1649 childhood attitudes; primary school pupils; work attitudes

ATTITUDE MEASURES
10/0452 institutes of higher education; institutional environment; organisational climate; student attitudes; teacher attitudes
10/1146 adaptive behaviour – of disabled; blindness; emotional adjustment; measurement techniques; rehabilitation; visual impairments
10/1567 pupil attitudes; religion; religious attitudes; secondary school pupils; values

ATTITUDES
10/0523 computer literacy; computers; sex differences
10/0915 higher education; quality assurance
10/1060 arts; culture; mass media; music; participation; sports; theatre arts
10/1062 arts; arts education; culture; leisure time; participation; youth
10/1071 aspiration; health; pupil attitudes; pupil behaviour; secondary school pupils; sex education; social attitudes
10/1112 parent attitudes; primary education; school governors; science education; scientific attitudes
10/1121 conservation – environment; environmental education; social change
10/1211 public opinion; scientific literacy
10/1293 public opinion; radiation; risk; scientific literacy
10/1374 antisocial behaviour; behaviour problems; bullying; parent attitudes; pupil attitudes; teacher attitudes
10/1375 antisocial behaviour; bullying; discipline policy; parent attitudes; school policy; teacher attitudes
10/1500 distributive trades education; salesmanship
10/1725 educational principles

AUDIENCE RESPONSE
10/1611 assessment; drama education; dramatics

AUDIOVISUAL AIDS
10/0948 educational media; language acquisition; second language teaching; teaching methods; videodiscs

AUDIOVISUAL EDUCATION
10/0343 calculators; equipment; mathematics education; undergraduate students

AUTHORING AIDS – PROGRAMMING
10/1177 animation; computer assisted learning; computer uses in education; multimedia approach
10/1613 computer assisted learning; computer software; computer uses in education; information technology; multimedia approach

AUTHORS
10/0541 cooperation; writing – composition

AUTISM
10/0466 cognitive ability; curriculum research; social cognition
10/1806 Down's Syndrome; drawing; gifted; special educational needs; visual arts

AUTOBIOGRAPHIES
10/1319 children's literature; war

AUTOINSTRUCTIONAL AIDS
10/1542 cognitive style; computer assisted learning; computer uses in education; learning strategies; teaching machines

B ED DEGREES
10/0435 preservice teacher education; science curriculum; science education
10/0573 participant satisfaction; preservice teacher education; probationary teachers; student teachers; teaching experience
10/1427 course evaluation; graduate surveys; preservice teacher education
10/1677 graduates; student teachers; teacher certification; teacher education

BACKGROUND
10/1653 economics education; experience; industry-education relationship; preservice teacher education; student teacher attitudes; student teachers
10/1771 achievement; high achievement; individual characteristics; science education; undergraduate students

BASIC SKILLS
10/0043 access to education; adult education; adult learning; mature students; self evaluation – individuals
10/0232 adult literacy; cohort analysis; numeracy
10/0750 achievement; adult basic education; adult dropouts; dropout research
10/0754 educational research
10/1028 building trades education; construction – process; construction industry; course evaluation; National Vocational Qualifications; technical education; vocational education
10/1047 cross curricular approach; National Curriculum; secondary education
10/1051 communication skills; numeracy
10/1202 National Vocational Qualifications; vocational education
10/1606 adult basic education; colleges of further education; educational quality; further education; programme evaluation
10/1716 critical thinking; educational philosophy; problem solving; skills; transfer of learning

BEGINNING READING
10/0463 early reading; oral reading; reading skills; teacher-pupil relationship
10/1220 infant school pupils; reading teaching; teacher-pupil relationship; teaching methods
10/1762 literacy; parent participation; psycholinguistics; reading research; reading teaching
10/1808 dyslexia; sight method; word recognition

BEHAVIOUR
10/0089 deaf blind; disabilities; motor reactions; multiple disabilities; sensory deprivation

BEHAVIOUR DISORDERS
10/0159 classroom communication; conversation; learning activities; literacy education; special educational needs
10/0553 emotional disturbances; special educational needs; statements – special educational needs
10/0988 emotional disturbances; special educational needs; special schools
10/1125 computer uses in education; information technology; special educational needs; special schools
10/1484 child psychiatry; emotional disturbances; locus of control

BEHAVIOUR MODIFICATION
10/0094 behaviour problems; severe learning

difficulties; special education teachers; special educational needs; special schools
10/1373 antisocial behaviour; behaviour problems; bullying; classroom environment; intervention; speech handicaps; stuttering

BEHAVIOUR PROBLEMS
10/0063 discipline problems; disruptive pupils; infant school pupils; primary school pupils; problem children; surveys
10/0085 classroom discipline; classroom management; pupil behaviour; teacher behaviour; teacher-pupil relationship
10/0094 behaviour modification; severe learning difficulties; special education teachers; special educational needs; special schools
10/0243 antisocial behaviour; delinquency prevention; longitudinal studies; secondary school pupils; transfer pupils
10/0298 comparative education; discipline; disruptive pupils; Kenya; secondary schools
10/0660 elective mutism; inhibition; psychopathology; speech communication
10/0853 bullying; family influence; home environment; parent-child relationship; parent-pupil relationship; punishment; pupil behaviour
10/0907 communication disorders; elective mutism; problem children
10/0913 discipline policy; discipline problems; disruptive pupils; primary secondary education; problem children; transfer pupils
10/1228 antisocial behaviour; bullying; discipline policy; discipline problems; teacher attitudes
10/1302 emotional problems; family problems; learning disabilities; problem children; social experience
10/1336 antisocial behaviour; emotional problems; pupil problems; social behaviour; special educational needs
10/1372 antisocial behaviour; bullying; discipline; discipline policy; pupil behaviour
10/1373 antisocial behaviour; behaviour modification; bullying; classroom environment; intervention; speech handicaps; stuttering
10/1374 antisocial behaviour; attitudes; bullying; parent attitudes; pupil attitudes; teacher attitudes
10/1563 bullying; personality; secondary school pupils; values
10/1662 bullying; discipline policy; discipline problems
10/1674 classroom discipline; discipline; disruptive pupils; Greece; nursery school education; teacher attitudes
10/1739 disruptive pupils; Education Reform Act 1988; educational policy; emotional problems; problem children; school policy
10/1747 disruptive pupils; problem children; support services

BEHAVIOURAL OBJECTIVES
10/1626 comprehension; educational objectives; learning experience; test use

BEHAVIOURAL SCIENCES
10/1693 health personnel; health services; interdisciplinary approach; medical education

BELIEFS
10/0477 Christianity; mental retardation; religious education; special educational needs

BELIZE
10/0142 developing countries; development education; educational quality; primary education
10/0144 developing countries; educational materials; material development; textbooks

BEREAVEMENT
10/0681 attitude formation; childhood attitudes; death
10/1221 adolescent development; child development; death; moral development; religious attitudes

BILINGUAL EDUCATION
10/0401 minority groups; multicultural education; multiculturalism

10/1282 bilingualism; English – second language; ethnic groups; language of instruction
10/1583 bilingualism; educational policy; language policy; school effectiveness; Welsh; Welsh studies
10/1792 bilingual schools; secondary education; Welsh

BILINGUAL EDUCATION PROGRAMMES
10/0716 English – second language; ethnic groups; home-school relationship; literacy education; parent participation; reading teaching; second language learning

BILINGUAL PUPILS
10/0917 cognitive ability; dyslexia; language acquisition; language handicaps; learning disabilities; special educational needs
10/1803 English – second language; language teachers; limited English speaking; second language teaching

BILINGUAL SCHOOLS
10/1792 bilingual education; secondary education; Welsh

BILINGUALISM
10/0031 academic achievement; diglossia; ethnic groups; language usage
10/0192 lexicology; word recognition
10/0418 Algeria; comparative education; Gaelic; language policy; mother tongue; Scotland
10/0426 Asians; ethnic groups; language maintenance; language policy; minority groups; mother tongue
10/1282 bilingual education; English – second language; ethnic groups; language of instruction
10/1284 multicultural education; multilingual materials; multilingualism
10/1583 bilingual education; educational policy; language policy; school effectiveness; Welsh; Welsh studies

BIOGRAPHICAL INVENTORIES
10/0527 music activities; musical ability; musicians

BIOGRAPHIES
10/0606 adult education; educational history; extension education; universities; working class
10/1400 sociology
10/1432 educational materials; educational technology; material development; optical data discs

BIOLOGICAL SCIENCES
10/0280 computer assisted learning; medical education

BIOLOGY EDUCATION
10/1424 chemistry education; learner centred methods; learning strategies; physics education; science education; teaching methods
10/1616 science education; skills; transfer of learning

BIOTECHNOLOGY
10/0087 genetic engineering; pupil attitudes; science education

BIRTH
10/0652 academic achievement; achievement; performance; school entrance age
10/1055 achievement; local education authorities; school entrance age

BLACK PUPILS
10/1283 achievement; black teachers; teacher behaviour; teacher-pupil relationship; teaching methods; teaching styles
10/1710 achievement; Afro Caribbean youth; assessment; Education Reform Act 1988; equal education; ethnic groups; low achievement

BLACK TEACHERS
10/1283 achievement; black pupils; teacher behaviour; teacher-pupil relationship; teaching

methods; teaching styles

BLACKS
10/0928 ethnic groups; social work teachers

BLINDNESS
10/0082 braille; learning disabilities; literacy education; raised line drawings; sensory aids; special educational needs
10/0097 architectural education; educational equipment; special educational needs; visual impairments
10/0100 tactual perception; tactual visual tests; tests; visual impairments
10/0102 maps; memory; raised line drawings; spatial ability; tactile adaptation; visual impairments
10/0103 braille; reading teaching; sensory aids; tactile adaptation; tactual perception
10/0104 computer assisted reading; computer software; computer system design; educational materials; partial vision; visual impairments
10/0105 academic achievement; cognitive development; longitudinal studies; outcomes of education; partial vision; special schools; visual impairments
10/0106 child development; infants; visual impairments; young children
10/0107 braille; reading tests; visual impairments
10/0876 communication problems; higher education; nonverbal communication; special educational needs; visual impairments
10/0886 low vision aids; microcomputers; sensory aids; tactile adaptation; visual impairments
10/1102 concept formation; number concepts; quantity concepts
10/1145 assessment; mobility aids; partial vision; special educational needs; travel training; visual impairments; visually handicapped mobility
10/1146 adaptive behaviour – of disabled; attitude measures; emotional adjustment; measurement techniques; rehabilitation; visual impairments
10/1176 computer uses in education; optical data discs; special educational needs; speech synthesisers; visual impairments
10/1376 mobility aids; visual impairments; visually handicapped mobility

BODY IMAGE
10/0202 eating habits; food; health; self concept

BOOKS
10/0091 early childhood education; early experience; early reading; infants; parent participation
10/0675 children's literature; fiction; poetry; primary school pupils; reading; reading material selection
10/0761 secondary schools
10/0936 children as writers; children's literature; literacy; picture books
10/1289 children's literature; fiction; secondary school pupils
10/1304 children's literature; fiction; geography education; history studies
10/1309 children's literature

BOTSWANA
10/0587 language of instruction; languages for specific purposes; science education; scientific vocabulary; second language learning

BOYS
10/1194 educational history; preparatory schools

BRAILLE
10/0082 blindness; learning disabilities; literacy education; raised line drawings; sensory aids; special educational needs
10/0103 blindness; reading teaching; sensory aids; tactile adaptation; tactual perception
10/0107 blindness; reading tests; visual impairments

BRAIN HEMISPHERE FUNCTIONS
10/0659 dyslexia; handedness; lateral dominance; reading difficulties; visual perception

BRAZIL
10/0423 comparative education; public opinion; teacher role
10/1303 science teachers; teaching methods
10/1394 English – second language; second language teaching

BUDGETING
10/1038 educational administration; educational finance; local management of schools; school based management

BUILDING TRADES EDUCATION
10/0995 construction – process; construction industry; cross curricular approach; technical education; vocational education
10/1028 basic skills; construction – process; construction industry; course evaluation; National Vocational Qualifications; technical education; vocational education

BULLYING
10/0853 behaviour problems; family influence; home environment; parent-child relationship; parent-pupil relationship; punishment; pupil behaviour
10/1228 antisocial behaviour; behaviour problems; discipline policy; discipline problems; teacher attitudes
10/1350 discipline policy; discipline problems; Scotland
10/1371 cooperation; ethnic relations; intergroup relations; intervention; middle school education; pupil behaviour; social isolation
10/1372 antisocial behaviour; behaviour problems; discipline; discipline policy; pupil behaviour
10/1373 antisocial behaviour; behaviour modification; behaviour problems; classroom environment; intervention; speech handicaps; stuttering
10/1374 antisocial behaviour; attitudes; behaviour problems; parent attitudes; pupil attitudes; teacher attitudes
10/1375 antisocial behaviour; attitudes; discipline policy; parent attitudes; school policy; teacher attitudes
10/1563 behaviour problems; personality; secondary school pupils; values
10/1662 behaviour problems; discipline policy; discipline problems

BUSINESS ADMINISTRATION EDUCATION
10/1497 management studies; professional training; Single European Market
10/1782 learning activities; learning strategies; management studies

BUSINESS AND TECHNICIAN EDUCATION COUNCIL
10/1619 chemistry education; competency based education; science education; skills; transfer of learning

BUSINESS EDUCATION
10/0127 attendance patterns; course evaluation; examination results; outcomes of education; sandwich courses; undergraduate study
10/0570 computer simulation; computer uses in education; management studies
10/0738 curriculum development; economics education; sixteen to nineteen education
10/0739 curriculum development; inservice teacher education
10/0963 curriculum development; economics education; teacher attitudes; teacher development
10/0987 accountancy education; research; teaching methods
10/1530 'A' level examinations; curriculum development; economics education

CALCULATORS
10/0188 arithmetic and number education; mathematics education; primary education
10/0343 audiovisual education; equipment; mathematics education; undergraduate students
10/0619 algebra; computer uses in education; mathematics education; secondary education

CALCULUS EDUCATION
10/1156 computer uses in education;
mathematics education; university students

CAMEROON
10/0286 cross curricular approach; English –
second language; language of instruction;
mathematics education
10/1273 physics education
10/1274 physics education
10/1277 mathematics education

CAMPUSES
10/1411 educational facilities improvement;
school space
10/1423 educational facilities improvement;
school space

CANADA
10/0598 adult education; comparative education;
continuing education

CANADA NATIVES
10/0019 ethnic groups; indigenous populations;
newly qualified teachers; teacher background;
teacher induction; teaching profession
10/0024 access to education; educational policy;
qualifications

CANCER EDUCATION
10/0803 health education; pupil attitudes
10/1404 health education; preventive medicine;
primary health care

CAPITALISM
10/0098 adult education; Christianity; church and
education; religious education; secularisation

CAREER CHOICE
10/1462 employment opportunities; labour
market; learner educational objectives;
occupational aspiration; school to work
transition; secondary school pupils; work-
education relationship

CAREER COUNSELLING
10/0321 guidance; secondary schools; vocational
guidance
10/0328 China; comparative education; Scotland;
vocational guidance
10/0391 ethnic groups; minority groups;
secondary school pupils; vocational guidance
10/0956 outcomes of education; pupil attitudes;
school leavers; school to work transition;
transition education; TVEI; work-education
relationship
10/1007 evaluation methods; guidance
objectives; measurement techniques;
vocational guidance
10/1090 adult counselling; Europe; European
Community; vocational guidance
10/1091 career education; vocational guidance

CAREER DEVELOPMENT
10/0376 institutes of higher education; teacher
evaluation; teaching profession; women
teachers; women's employment
10/0450 engineering education; engineers;
training; work-education relationship
10/1022 career education; career planning;
school to work transition; vocational guidance

CAREER EDUCATION
10/0558 higher education; vocational guidance
10/1019 careers service; school to work
transition; vocational guidance
10/1022 career development; career planning;
school to work transition; vocational guidance
10/1065 careers service; school to work
transition; vocational guidance; Wales
10/1091 career counselling; vocational guidance

CAREER LADDERS
10/0072 careers; equal opportunities – jobs;
france; job training; work education
relationship

CAREER PLANNING
10/0051 individual development; planning;
profiles

10/1022 career development; career education;
school to work transition; vocational guidance

CAREERS
10/0072 career ladders; equal opportunities –
jobs; France; job training; work-education
relationship
10/1157 educational researchers

CAREERS SERVICE
10/1019 career education; school to work
transition; vocational guidance
10/1065 career education; school to work
transition; vocational guidance; Wales
10/1460 guidance personnel; mentors;
professional development

CAREGIVERS
10/0066 adult day centres; educational needs;
services; special educational needs
10/0578 adult education; adult learning;
disabilities; independent study; lifelong
learning
10/1015 child caregivers; residential schools;
special schools; training

CARTOONS
10/0949 educational materials; science education

CATHOLIC SCHOOLS
10/0470 church and education; church-state
relationship; educational history; educational
policy; Roman Catholic church
10/1433 church and education; primary schools;
religious education
10/1738 academic achievement; school
effectiveness

CATHOLICS
10/0067 clergy; priests; professional education;
religious education; theological education

CENTRALISATION
10/1222 educational practices; international
education; multicultural education; National
Curriculum

CEREBRAL PALSY
10/0035 driver education
10/0645 mobility aids; neurological impairments;
psychomotor skills; special educational
needs
10/0747 disabilities; motor reactions; perceptual
handicaps; perceptual motor coordination;
special educational needs

CHANGE
10/0364 child language; classroom management;
teacher attitudes
10/0471 comparative education; democracy;
development education; politics-education
relationship
10/1256 head teachers; local management of
schools; primary schools; role conflict; stress
variables; time management
10/1692 Cyprus; nurse education

CHANGE AGENTS
10/1147 curriculum development; preservice
teacher education; TVEI

CHANGE STRATEGIES
10/0187 educational environment; educational
research; organisational change; research
methodology
10/1224 educational change; primary schools;
school based management; school
organisation; staff-school relationship
10/1448 educational innovation; programme
evaluation; TVEI

CHEATING
10/1217 discipline problems; higher education;
plagiarism; student behaviour

CHEMICAL BONDING
10/1294 chemistry education; science education;
scientific concepts

CHEMISTRY EDUCATION
10/1089 science education; sixteen to nineteen
education
10/1294 chemical bonding; science education;
scientific concepts
10/1424 biology education; learner centred
methods; learning strategies; physics
education; science education; teaching
methods
10/1618 educational materials; learning
strategies; multimedia approach; science
education; skills; teaching methods; transfer of
learning
10/1619 Business and Technician Education
Council; competency based education; science
education; skills; transfer of learning
10/1796 'A' level examinations; science
education; teaching methods

CHILD CARE GIVERS
10/0848 community services; play; play centres;
recreational activities

CHILD CAREGIVERS
10/0397 agency cooperation; community
services; day care centres; early childhood
education; programme evaluation; quality
control
10/0846 child minding; day care; day care
centres; preschool children; quality control
10/1015 caregivers; residential schools; special
schools; training
10/1214 play groups; preschool education;
qualifications; training

CHILD DEVELOPMENT
10/0064 cognitive ability; health education;
intellectual development; intelligence quotient;
pregnancy; smoking
10/0106 blindness; infants; visual impairments;
young children
10/0722 ability; developmental continuity;
longitudinal studies; personality development
10/0745 motor development; neurological
impairments; perceptual handicaps; premature
infants; special educational needs
10/1221 adolescent development; bereavement;
death; moral development; religious attitudes
10/1243 memorisation; phonemics; pictorial
stimuli; verbal development; visual learning
10/1264 early reading; reading ability; young
children

CHILD LANGUAGE
10/0248 classroom communication; language of
instruction; language research; primary school
pupils; science education
10/0364 change; classroom management; teacher
attitudes
10/0655 figurative language; metaphors
10/1734 comparative education; group work;
infant school pupils; verbal communication

CHILD MINDING
10/0846 child caregivers; day care; day care
centres; preschool children; quality control

CHILD PSYCHIATRY
10/1484 behaviour disorders; emotional
disturbances; locus of control

CHILD PSYCHOLOGY
10/0351 exercise; health; physical activities;
physical activity level

CHILD REARING
10/0396 children at risk; community services;
family programmes; programme evaluation;
quality control
10/0810 parent-child relationship; parenthood
education; parenting skills; voluntary agencies

CHILD WELFARE
10/0283 community services; residential care;
Scotland; social services; social work

CHILDHOOD ATTITUDES
10/0681 attitude formation; bereavement; death
10/1649 attitude formation; primary school
pupils; work attitudes

CHILDREN
10/0823 sociology
10/1579 adolescents; television surveys; television viewing
10/1718 comprehension; integration studies; severe learning difficulties; special educational needs

CHILDREN ACT 1989
10/0851 day care; early childhood education; legislation; local government; preschool education; social services

CHILDREN AS WRITERS
10/0134 group work; narration; primary school pupils; story telling; writing – composition
10/0936 books; children's literature; literacy; picture books

CHILDREN AT RISK
10/0395 community services; day care; family problems; family relationship
10/0396 child rearing; community services; family programmes; programme evaluation; quality control

CHILDREN'S LITERATURE
10/0146 early childhood education; reading aloud to others; story reading; teacher-pupil relationship
10/0173 comics – publications; educational history; girls; popular culture; sex role; textbooks; women's education
10/0675 books; fiction; poetry; primary school pupils; reading; reading material selection
10/0936 books; children as writers; literacy; picture books
10/1288 antiracism education; fiction; racial attitudes
10/1289 books; fiction; secondary school pupils
10/1304 books; fiction; geography education; history studies
10/1309 books
10/1319 autobiographies; war

CHILE
10/1683 comparative education; gender equality; Israel; women's education

CHINA
10/0328 career counselling; comparative education; Scotland; vocational guidance
10/0382 housing; professional education
10/1128 adult education; comparative education
10/1526 educational policy; primary education
10/1540 educational change

CHINESE
10/0974 adolescents; cultural background; ethnic groups; ethnicity; Hong Kong; migrants

CHINESE LANGUAGES
10/0347 Arabic; educational materials; Japanese; nonwestern languages; second language learning

CHOICE OF SUBJECTS
10/0003 academic achievement; sex differences
10/0562 course selection – students; science education; sex differences; sixteen to nineteen education
10/1439 demography; further education; pupil attitudes; sixteen to nineteen education
10/1599 pupil attitudes; pupil interests; sex differences

CHRISTIANITY
10/0098 adult education; capitalism; church and education; religious education; secularisation
10/0137 primary schools; religious education
10/0477 beliefs; mental retardation; religious education; special educational needs
10/1320 religious education; young children
10/1564 pupil attitudes; religion; religious attitudes; Roman Catholic church

CHURCH AND EDUCATION
10/0098 adult education; capitalism; Christianity; religious education; secularisation
10/0099 religious education; theological education

10/0470 Catholic schools; church-state relationship; educational history; educational policy; Roman Catholic church
10/0475 church-state relationship; educational history; educational legislation; nonconformity; religion and education
10/1153 feminism; language usage; power structure; Protestant churches
10/1433 Catholic schools; primary schools; religious education

CHURCH–EDUCATION RELATIONSHIP
10/0479 educational history; educational philosophy
10/0922 educational history; educational legislation; financial support; free education; school governors

CHURCH–STATE RELATIONSHIP
10/0470 Catholic schools; church and education; educational history; educational policy; Roman Catholic church
10/0475 church and education; educational history; educational legislation; nonconformity; religion and education

CITIZENSHIP
10/0125 adult education; comparative education; consumer economics; educational policy; Poland
10/1195 citizenship education; identity; nationalism; role of education; Zambia
10/1370 Europe; higher education; overseas employment; overseas students
10/1654 educational finance; educational history; educational objectives; politics-education relationship

CITIZENSHIP EDUCATION
10/0670 cross curricular approach; National Curriculum
10/0868 National Curriculum
10/0895 comparative education; politics-education relationship
10/0930 global approach; teacher education
10/1138 adult education; political influences; social change; socialist countries; voluntary agencies
10/1195 citizenship; identity; nationalism; role of education; Zambia
10/1797 European history; history studies
10/1800 human rights; literature studies; pupil attitudes; racial attitudes; social attitudes

CITY TECHNOLOGY COLLEGES
10/0447 dyslexia; educational materials; learning disabilities; special educational needs; teaching methods
10/0841 school personnel; support staff; teacher aides
10/1612 grant maintained schools; inservice teacher education; management development; school based management; staff development
10/1715 disadvantaged environment; industry-education relationship; school community relationship

CLASS ACTIVITIES
10/0537 ambiguity; preservice teacher education; student teachers; teaching practice; teaching styles

CLASS ORGANISATION
10/1067 ability; grouping – teaching purposes; mixed ability; pupil placement; streaming; teaching methods

CLASS SIZE
10/0656 English – second language; second language learning; second language teaching

CLASSROOM COMMUNICATION
10/0159 behaviour disorders; conversation; learning activities; literacy education; special educational needs
10/0248 child language; language of instruction; language research; primary school pupils; science education
10/0467 concept teaching; mathematical concepts; mathematics education

10/0643 primary school teachers; teacher behaviour; teacher-pupil relationship; verbal communication
10/0732 feedback; infant school education; infant school teachers; teacher-pupil relationship; teacher response
10/1280 comprehension; mathematical concepts; mathematical vocabulary; mathematics education
10/1721 discourse analysis; metaphors; teacher education
10/1751 learning activities; teacher-pupil relationship; teacher role; teaching methods

CLASSROOM DISCIPLINE
10/0085 behaviour problems; classroom management; pupil behaviour; teacher behaviour; teacher-pupil relationship
10/1354 discipline; discipline policy; educational materials
10/1660 discipline
10/1674 behaviour problems; discipline; disruptive pupils; Greece; nursery school education; teacher attitudes

CLASSROOM ENVIRONMENT
10/0862 mainstreaming; moderate learning difficulties; pupil attitudes; pupil behaviour; social behaviour; special educational needs
10/0942 classroom management; drama education; primary schools; pupil behaviour
10/1076 achievement; performance factors; statistical analysis
10/1373 antisocial behaviour; behaviour modification; behaviour problems; bullying; intervention; speech handicaps; stuttering

CLASSROOM MANAGEMENT
10/0085 behaviour problems; classroom discipline; pupil behaviour; teacher behaviour; teacher-pupil relationship
10/0364 change; child language; teacher attitudes
10/0365 classroom research; primary schools
10/0372 classroom observation techniques; teacher evaluation; teaching profession
10/0650 preservice teacher education; student teachers
10/0942 classroom environment; drama education; primary schools; pupil behaviour
10/1272 early childhood education; infant school education; infant school teachers; reception classes

CLASSROOM OBSERVATION TECHNIQUES
10/0361 assessment; teacher response
10/0372 classroom management; teacher evaluation; teaching profession
10/1197 group work; learning activities; science activities; science education

CLASSROOM RESEARCH
10/0365 classroom management; primary schools
10/0847 curriculum research; Education Reform Act 1988; educational change; educational experience; infant schools; mathematics education
10/1155 educational materials; educational technology; interactive video; mathematics education; multimedia approach
10/1783 learning strategies; National Curriculum; primary education; reading teaching; teaching methods

CLERGY
10/0065 continuing education; learning processes; professional education; religious education; theological education
10/0067 Catholics; priests; professional education; religious education; theological education

CLIMATE
10/0637 global approach; physical environment; scientific attitudes; social attitudes

CLINICAL EXPERIENCE
10/0069 distance education; pharmaceutical education; pharmacists; professional training; programme evaluation
10/0073 medical education; outcomes of education

10/0279 medical education; medical students
10/0392 assessment; medical education; physical therapy

CLUBS
10/1503 curriculum enrichment; engineering; engineers; industry-education relationship

CLUMSY CHILDREN
10/0760 perceptual motor coordination; psychomotor skills; special educational needs

CLUSTER GROUPING
10/0746 educational cooperation; special educational needs; special schools
10/0752 educational cooperation; special educational needs; special schools

COGNITIVE ABILITY
10/0064 child development; health education; intellectual development; intelligence quotient; pregnancy; smoking
10/0362 computer assisted learning; interaction; logo; turtles – robots
10/0466 autism; curriculum research; social cognition
10/0487 creative thinking; Saudi Arabia
10/0520 academic achievement; listening skills; reading achievement; television research; television viewing
10/0858 gifted; memory
10/0917 bilingual pupils; dyslexia; language acquisition; language handicaps; learning disabilities; special educational needs
10/1188 depth perception; drawing; problem solving; spatial ability; visual perception
10/1601 assessment; mathematical models; mathematics education; metacognition
10/1621 arithmetic; learning disabilities
10/1640 attention deficit disorders; hyperactivity; learning disabilities; memory
10/1805 dyslexia; reading difficulties; reading skills

COGNITIVE DEVELOPMENT
10/0105 academic achievement; blindness; longitudinal studies; outcomes of education; partial vision; special schools; visual impairments
10/0572 art; art history; cross curricular approach; mathematics; spatial ability
10/0748 arithmetic; number concepts; numbers; numeracy; primary education
10/0749 comprehension; heat; primary education; science education; temperature
10/0863 attention; early experience; infant behaviour; learning; neurological impairments
10/1183 computer programming; reasoning
10/1189 reasoning; temporal integration; time perspective
10/1191 interaction; peer groups; reasoning
10/1756 severe learning difficulties; social cognition; special educational needs

COGNITIVE PROCESSES
10/0167 cognitive psychology; epistemology; higher education; learning processes; memory
10/0177 cognitive style; learning strategies; problem solving
10/0288 learning processes; learning theories; mathematics education
10/0369 computer games
10/0610 cognitive style; field dependence-independence; learning; mathematics; teaching styles
10/0613 algebra; comprehension; mathematical formulas; mathematics education
10/0628 mathematics education; National Curriculum; pattern recognition
10/0661 mainstreaming; spatial ability; special educational needs
10/0969 decision making; professional education
10/0970 decision making; professional autonomy
10/1144 computer assisted reading; reading comprehension; reading skills; spelling; word recognition
10/1543 computer assisted learning; learning processes; metacognition

COGNITIVE PSYCHOLOGY
10/0167 cognitive processes; epistemology; higher education; learning processes; memory

COGNITIVE STYLE
10/0177 cognitive processes; learning strategies; problem solving
10/0610 cognitive processes; field dependence-independence; learning; mathematics; teaching styles
10/0618 arithmetic; mathematics education; mature students; secondary school pupils
10/1325 academic achievement; achievement; failure; gifted; underachievement
10/1542 autoinstructional aids; computer assisted learning; computer uses in education; learning strategies; teaching machines

COHORT ANALYSIS
10/0232 adult literacy; basic skills; numeracy
10/0320 followup studies; longitudinal studies; school leavers; school to work transition; Scotland; sixteen to nineteen education; youth
10/1011 programme evaluation; school leavers; school to work transition; sixteen to nineteen education; TVEI
10/1061 curriculum development; National Curriculum – Northern Ireland; Northern Ireland; pupil attitudes

COLLEGE ADMINISTRATION
10/0023 colleges of further education; educational administration; further education; institutional administration; organisational change

COLLEGE EFFECTIVENESS
10/0546 higher education; outcomes of education; universities and colleges
10/1087 educational quality; further education; institutional characteristics; performance factors; performance indicators

COLLEGE-SCHOOL COOPERATION
10/1422 educational materials; flexible learning; material development; preservice teacher education

COLLEGES
10/1466 computer uses in education; information technology

COLLEGES OF FURTHER EDUCATION
10/0023 college administration; educational administration; further education; institutional administration; organisational change
10/0564 community colleges; course evaluation; European Community; international programmes
10/0740 industry-further education relationship; staff development; work experience programmes
10/0751 assessment; diagnostic assessment; disabilities; further education; moderate learning difficulties; special educational needs
10/1111 educational administration; educational planning; management in education; marketing
10/1122 educational administration; women's employment
10/1441 management in education; quality control; sixteen to nineteen education; staff development
10/1442 comparable worth; employment practices; equal pay; job analysis; occupational information; salaries
10/1443 educational quality; governing bodies
10/1521 extracurricular activities; further education students; health promotion
10/1606 adult basic education; basic skills; educational quality; further education; programme evaluation

COMICS – PUBLICATIONS
10/0173 children's literature; educational history; girls; popular culture; sex role; textbooks; women's education

COMMONWEALTH OF INDEPENDENT STATES
10/0399 Communist education; educational change; ideology; politics-education relationship; social change; USSR

COMMUNICATION AIDS – FOR DISABLED
10/0325 disabilities; educational materials; special educational needs
10/0493 communication disorders; programme evaluation; special educational needs; workshops
10/0961 deafness; hearing aids; hearing impairments; psychological evaluation
10/1387 communication disorders; manual communication; severe learning difficulties; sign language; special educational needs; symbolic language

COMMUNICATION DISORDERS
10/0493 communication aids – for disabled; programme evaluation; special educational needs; workshops
10/0907 behaviour problems; elective mutism; problem children
10/1387 communication aids – for disabled; manual communication; severe learning difficulties; sign language; special educational needs; symbolic language

COMMUNICATION PROBLEMS
10/0876 blindness; higher education; nonverbal communication; special educational needs; visual impairments

COMMUNICATION RESEARCH
10/0817 family involvement; health education
10/1204 competency based education; further education; higher education; learning processes; teaching methods
10/1392 conversation; native speakers; second language learning; verbal communication
10/1717 integration studies; severe learning difficulties; special educational needs; verbal communication

COMMUNICATION SKILLS
10/0251 competency based education; humanities; minimum competencies; modular courses; open education
10/0287 counselling techniques; counsellor training; course evaluation
10/0494 nonverbal communication; physical disabilities; severe disabilities; special educational needs; speech handicaps
10/0611 deafness; hearing impairments; hearing therapy; special schools; total communication
10/0843 listening skills; National Curriculum; speech communication
10/1051 basic skills; numeracy
10/1193 early childhood education; friendship; infant school pupils; reception classes; social development; social isolation; young children

COMMUNICATIONS
10/0547 distance education; networks; open education; teleconferencing
10/1131 computer networks; disabilities; training; wide area networks

COMMUNICATIVE COMPETENCE – LANGUAGES
10/1396 English – second language; Korea; language tests; second language teaching

COMMUNIST EDUCATION
10/0399 Commonwealth of Independent States; educational change; ideology; politics-education relationship; social change; USSR

COMMUNITY
10/1132 adult education; individual development; social change; voluntary agencies

COMMUNITY BENEFITS
10/1538 developing countries; health education; India; peer teaching; Uganda

COMMUNITY CENTRES
10/1300 community education; community programmes; day care centres; English – second language; ethnic groups; racial integration; social integration

COMMUNITY COLLEGES
10/0564 colleges of further education; course evaluation; European Community; international programmes

COMMUNITY DEVELOPMENT
10/0603 community programmes

COMMUNITY EDUCATION
10/0001 access to education; mothers; preschool education; young children
10/0266 adult education; rural areas
10/1300 community centres; community programmes; day care centres; English – second language; ethnic groups; racial integration; social integration
10/1332 access to education; adult education; adult students; educational guidance; mature students; student attitudes
10/1506 continuing education; staff development; training; voluntary service; volunteers
10/1636 contraception; early parenthood; family planning; mothers; parenthood education; peer teaching; sex education

COMMUNITY ORGANISATIONS
10/0380 databases; student projects
10/1678 youth; youth leaders; youth service
10/1680 training; youth leaders; youth service
10/1681 policy; youth service

COMMUNITY PROGRAMMES
10/0603 community development
10/1300 community centres; community education; day care centres; English – second language; ethnic groups; racial integration; social integration
10/1463 community services; cooperative programmes; early childhood education; parent participation; young children

COMMUNITY SERVICES
10/0283 child welfare; residential care; Scotland; social services; social work
10/0395 children at risk; day care; family problems; family relationship
10/0396 child rearing; children at risk; family programmes; programme evaluation; quality control
10/0397 agency cooperation; child caregivers; day care centres; early childhood education; programme evaluation; quality control
10/0848 child care givers; play; play centres; recreational activities
10/0935 day care; early childhood education; local government; nursery school curriculum; nursery schools; preschool education; young children
10/1463 community programmes; cooperative programmes; early childhood education; parent participation; young children

COMPARABLE WORTH
10/1442 colleges of further education; employment practices; equal pay; job analysis; occupational information; salaries

COMPARATIVE ANALYSIS
10/1455 educational policy; mainstreaming; special educational needs; special schools

COMPARATIVE EDUCATION
10/0034 modern language studies; pupil attitudes
10/0092 disabilities; mainstreaming; pupil attitudes; special educational needs; special schools
10/0124 economic change; economics-education relationship; Germany; industry-education relationship; structural unemployment; training; work-education relationship
10/0125 adult education; citizenship; consumer economics; educational policy; Poland
10/0143 Ghana; higher education; modular courses; universities
10/0154 educational change; France; primary school teachers; teacher attitudes; teaching profession
10/0179 educational materials; mainstreaming; special educational needs; teacher education

10/0198 English – second language; international educational exchange; second language teaching
10/0199 France; primary education
10/0224 core curriculum; National Curriculum; Netherlands; Zambia
10/0247 educational quality
10/0256 art education; assessment; degrees – academic; fine arts; Greece
10/0267 access programmes; access to education; adult education; higher education; mature students
10/0292 cultural education; educational materials; second language learning; teaching methods
10/0298 behaviour problems; discipline; disruptive pupils; Kenya; secondary schools
10/0301 creativity; France; handwriting; writing research; writing skills
10/0308 cultural awareness; Denmark; Europe; modern language studies
10/0314 curriculum development; European Community; modular courses; vocational education
10/0328 career counselling; China; Scotland; vocational guidance
10/0374 mathematics education; primary education
10/0398 educational policy; educational practices; international education
10/0400 educational history; educational policy; Scotland
10/0411 educational history; educational policy; Scotland; teacher education
10/0418 Algeria; bilingualism; Gaelic; language policy; mother tongue; Scotland
10/0423 Brazil; public opinion; teacher role
10/0430 adult education; lifelong learning; mature students; people's universities; Scandinavia
10/0431 adult education; Denmark; lifelong learning; mature students; people's universities
10/0440 distance education; higher education; international educational exchange; learning activities; Netherlands; teaching methods; telecommunications
10/0471 change; democracy; development education; politics-education relationship
10/0534 European studies; preservice teacher education
10/0598 adult education; Canada; continuing education
10/0614 adult education; educational history; extension education
10/0664 activities; France; outdoor pursuits; physical education
10/0685 educational history; educational theories; progressive education
10/0689 industry-education relationship; United States of America; work-education relationship
10/0786 France; mathematics achievement; trainees
10/0881 cross cultural studies; educational attitudes; pupil attitudes; Saudi Arabia
10/0895 citizenship education; politics-education relationship
10/0953 accidents; European Community; food standards; health education; nutrition education; safety education
10/0959 adult education; continuing education; cultural differences; Europe; lifelong learning
10/1040 mathematics education; science education
10/1043 educational research; Europe; international educational exchange; research and development
10/1058 achievement; achievement tests; assessment; mathematics education; science education
10/1079 language policy; modern language curriculum; modern language studies; second language teaching; secondary education
10/1128 adult education; China
10/1129 adult education; Taiwan; United Kingdom; universities
10/1136 adult education; continuing education; European Community; Germany; United Kingdom; vocational education
10/1139 adult education; adults; continuing education; databases; vocational education
10/1142 adult vocational education; disabilities;

information technology; Portugal; special educational needs; training; United Kingdom
10/1162 assessment; assessment by teachers; Ghana
10/1201 educational policy; industry-education relationship; politics-education relationship; United States of America
10/1206 educational administration; educational policy; Italy; mainstreaming; Scandinavia; special educational needs; support services
10/1213 France; higher education; teacher education; United States of America
10/1223 educational history; educational quality; school effectiveness; United States of America
10/1313 international educational exchange; pastoral care – education; teacher role
10/1338 curriculum development; international educational exchange; mathematics education; science education
10/1452 Greece; learning disabilities; Scotland; special educational needs
10/1555 drug education; health education
10/1557 gifted; special schools
10/1630 curriculum development; environmental education; school-community relationship
10/1683 Chile; gender equality; Israel; women's education
10/1734 child language; group work; infant school pupils; verbal communication
10/1758 antisocial behaviour; discipline problems; disruptive pupils; United States of America
10/1774 Cyprus; educational policy; Greece; school systems
10/1787 directories; early childhood education; preservice teacher education
10/1799 language teachers; modern language studies; National Curriculum
10/1810 English; German; language tests; modern language studies; native speakers; second language teaching

COMPARATIVE TESTING
10/1048 achievement; reading ability; reading achievement; reading research

COMPETENCE
10/0160 competency based teacher education; discussion – teaching technique; personal construct theory; repertory grid test; teacher effectiveness
10/0268 assessment; examinations; medical education; medicine; physicians
10/0282 assessment; examinations; medical education; medicine; physicians
10/1532 assessment; job performance; professional occupations
10/1593 competency based teacher education; preservice teacher education; records of achievement; student teachers
10/1641 assessment; nurse education; obstetrics

COMPETENCY BASED EDUCATION
10/0025 management development
10/0029 degrees – academic; inservice education; professional education
10/0251 communication skills; humanities; minimum competencies; modular courses; open education
10/0394 education courses; higher education; masters' courses; qualifications; standards
10/0692 assessment; group work; higher education; teaching methods
10/0789 higher education; masters courses; National Vocational Qualifications; qualifications; standards
10/1204 communication research; further education; higher education; learning processes; teaching methods
10/1511 access to education; admission criteria; higher education; National Vocational Qualifications
10/1512 minimum competencies; National Vocational Qualifications; skills
10/1619 Business and Technician Education Council; chemistry education; science education; skills; transfer of learning
10/1623 inservice education; on the job training; social work studies
10/1632 higher education; National Vocational

Qualifications; preservice teacher education; professional education; standards
10/1656 assessment

COMPETENCY BASED TEACHER EDUCATION
10/0160 competence; discussion – teaching technique; personal construct theory; repertory grid test; teacher effectiveness
10/0919 mentors; profiles; teacher development
10/0933 educational research; teacher education
10/1237 preservice teacher education
10/1278 inservice teacher education; local education authorities; school based teacher education; staff orientation; teacher development
10/1307 mentors; profiles; teacher development; teaching profession
10/1435 assessment; preservice teacher education; student teacher evaluation; teaching practice
10/1593 competence; preservice teacher education; records of achievement; student teachers

COMPREHENSION
10/0326 learning
10/0338 essays; examination techniques; higher education; learning strategies; review – reexamination; study skills; writing – composition
10/0502 earth science; oceanography; physical sciences; plate tectonics
10/0509 philosophy of science; science education; scientific concepts; student attitudes
10/0596 science education; scientific concepts; scientific literacy
10/0613 algebra; cognitive processes; mathematical formulas; mathematics education
10/0626 ecology education; science education; scientific concepts
10/0749 cognitive development; heat; primary education; science education; temperature
10/0767 explanation; historiography; history; imagination
10/0768 computer assisted learning; computer uses in education; history; thinking skills
10/0941 punctuation; writing skills; written language
10/1280 classroom communication; mathematical concepts; mathematical vocabulary; mathematics education
10/1626 behavioural objectives; educational objectives; learning experience; test use
10/1718 children; integration studies; severe learning difficulties; special educational needs

COMPREHENSIVE SCHOOLS
10/0088 secondary schools
10/0663 educational change; educational history; secondary education

COMPUTER ASSISTED DESIGN
10/0257 art education; computer uses in education; design education
10/0865 computer graphics; drawing

COMPUTER ASSISTED LANGUAGE LEARNING
10/0324 educational software; models
10/1707 English – second language; English for academic purposes; overseas students; second language learning

COMPUTER ASSISTED LEARNING
10/0028 computer uses in education; earth science; educational software
10/0238 dyslexia; interactive video; learning disabilities; multimedia approach
10/0239 design education; hypermedia
10/0273 computer uses in education; individualised methods; information technology; medical education
10/0280 biological sciences; medical education
10/0362 cognitive ability; interaction; logo; turtles – robots
10/0548 artificial intelligence; educational materials; material development
10/0566 computer system design; computer uses in education

10/0582 computer uses in education; expert systems; management studies
10/0718 computer uses in education; educational software; management studies
10/0768 comprehension; computer uses in education; history; thinking skills
10/0860 computer uses in education; concept keyboards; human-computer interaction; learning disabilities; special educational needs; touch screens
10/1169 educational materials; educational media; open education
10/1177 animation; authoring aids – programming; computer uses in education; multimedia approach
10/1178 earth science; educational equipment; microscopes; simulation; special educational needs
10/1181 computer uses in education; cooperative learning; human-computer interaction; learning processes
10/1285 further education students; hypertext; information seeking; information sources
10/1346 computer uses in education; educational technology; medical education; medicine
10/1475 computer uses in education; mathematics education
10/1479 algebra education; mathematics education
10/1542 autoinstructional aids; cognitive style; computer uses in education; learning strategies; teaching machines
10/1543 cognitive processes; learning processes; metacognition
10/1551 educational technology; expert systems; optical data discs; training methods
10/1552 electronic books; human-computer interaction; hypermedia; information technology; multimedia approach; optical data discs
10/1553 computer uses in education; educational software; interactive video
10/1581 educational software; multimedia approach; statistics education
10/1613 authoring aids – programming; computer software; computer uses in education; information technology; multimedia approach

COMPUTER ASSISTED READING
10/0104 blindness; computer software; computer system design; educational materials; partial vision; visual impairments
10/1144 cognitive processes; reading comprehension; reading skills; spelling; word recognition

COMPUTER ASSISTED TESTING
10/0446 assessment; computer uses in education; National Vocational Qualifications
10/1034 adaptive testing; assessment; attainment tests; National Curriculum; test validity

COMPUTER GAMES
10/0369 cognitive processes

COMPUTER GRAPHICS
10/0865 computer assisted design; drawing

COMPUTER KEYBOARDS
10/1311 computer uses in education; concept keyboards; human-computer interaction

COMPUTER LITERACY
10/0305 computer uses in education; information technology; preservice teacher education
10/0523 attitudes; computers; sex differences
10/1124 adult vocational education; adults; disabilities; information technology; sheltered workshops; special educational needs; training centres
10/1126 adult basic education; adults; disabilities; information technology; special educational needs
10/1127 adults; disabilities; information technology; special educational needs; training centres

COMPUTER MICROWORLDS
10/1383 computer uses in education; mathematics education; proof – mathematics

COMPUTER NETWORKS
10/1131 communications; disabilities; training; wide area networks

COMPUTER PROGRAMMING
10/1183 cognitive development; reasoning

COMPUTER SCIENCE
10/1547 computer uses in education; visual perception

COMPUTER SCIENCE EDUCATION
10/1465 material development
10/1476 mathematics education; teaching methods

COMPUTER SIMULATION
10/0390 computer uses in education; industrial psychology; psychology
10/0570 business education; computer uses in education; management studies
10/1179 computer uses in education; control technology; logo; models

COMPUTER SOFTWARE
10/0104 blindness; computer assisted reading; computer system design; educational materials; partial vision; visual impairments
10/0195 educational materials; energy education; material development; science education
10/0284 computer uses in education; learning disabilities; special educational needs; spelling; writing difficulties
10/0906 computer uses in education; higher education; performance indicators; quality control
10/1085 computer uses in education; educational software; information technology; technology education
10/1613 authoring aids – programming; computer assisted learning; computer uses in education; information technology; multimedia approach

COMPUTER SYSTEM DESIGN
10/0104 blindness; computer assisted reading; computer software; educational materials; partial vision; visual impairments
10/0522 computer uses in education; severe learning difficulties; special educational needs
10/0566 computer assisted learning; computer uses in education

COMPUTER USES IN EDUCATION
10/0028 computer assisted learning; earth science; educational software
10/0039 algebra; logo; low achievement; mathematics education
10/0047 information networks; information technology; telecommunications
10/0213 English studies curriculum; information technology; optical data discs
10/0257 art education; computer assisted design; design education
10/0258 arts education; cultural education; handicrafts; museums; visual arts
10/0273 computer assisted learning; individualised methods; information technology; medical education
10/0284 computer software; learning disabilities; special educational needs; spelling; writing difficulties
10/0304 gifted; individualised methods; Jordan; mathematics; primary education
10/0305 computer literacy; information technology; preservice teacher education
10/0353 feedback; interaction; learning processes; peer teaching; teacher-pupil relationship
10/0371 information technology; National Curriculum
10/0390 computer simulation; industrial psychology; psychology
10/0446 assessment; computer assisted testing; National Vocational Qualifications
10/0464 group work; microcomputers; primary schools; problem solving
10/0468 information technology; research reports; theses
10/0490 English – second language; second language learning

10/0512 information technology; mathematics education; microcomputers; secondary schools

10/0513 information technology; mathematics education; secondary schools

10/0522 computer system design; severe learning difficulties; special educational needs

10/0566 computer assisted learning; computer system design

10/0570 business education; computer simulation; management studies

10/0571 cross curricular approach; curriculum development; information technology

10/0582 computer assisted learning; expert systems; management studies

10/0619 algebra; calculators; mathematics education; secondary education

10/0631 secondary school pupils; word processing; writing skills

10/0662 gender equality; humanities; information technology; sex differences

10/0683 optical data discs

10/0718 computer assisted learning; educational software; management studies

10/0768 comprehension; computer assisted learning; history; thinking skills

10/0777 algebra; mathematics education; symbols – mathematics

10/0779 data processing; databases; material development; primary schools

10/0780 algebra education; mathematics education; problem solving

10/0781 imagery; mathematics education

10/0782 mathematics education; symbols – mathematics; trigonometry; visualisation

10/0788 educational software; mathematics education; symbols – mathematics; visual learning

10/0860 computer assisted learning; concept keyboards; human-computer interaction; learning disabilities; special educational needs; touch screens

10/0873 educational administration; information technology; local management of schools; management systems; school based management

10/0897 open education; preservice teacher education

10/0899 practical science; science education

10/0906 computer software; higher education; performance indicators; quality control

10/0950 information technology; mathematics education; preservice teacher education; student teachers; teacher attitudes

10/1010 information technology; literature reviews

10/1030 curriculum development; information technology; microcomputers

10/1041 information technology; school policy

10/1044 ability; gifted; information technology; primary school pupils

10/1085 computer software; educational software; information technology; technology education

10/1125 behaviour disorders; information technology; special educational needs; special schools

10/1156 calculus education; mathematics education; university students

10/1168 distance education; microcomputers; open universities

10/1176 blindness; optical data discs; special educational needs; speech synthesisers; visual impairments

10/1177 animation; authoring aids – programming; computer assisted learning; multimedia approach

10/1179 computer simulation; control technology; logo; models

10/1180 animation; pupil projects

10/1184 educational software; mathematics education; spreadsheets

10/1251 concept formation; creative development; learning processes

10/1311 computer keyboards; concept keyboards; human-computer interaction

10/1317 educational software; geometry; mathematics education

10/1346 computer assisted learning; educational technology; medical education; medicine

10/1383 computer microworlds; mathematics education; proof – mathematics

10/1446 feedback; geometry; logo; mathematics education; problem solving

10/1464 hypothesis testing; physics education; science education

10/1466 colleges; information technology

10/1475 computer assisted learning; mathematics education

10/1477 mathematics education; spreadsheets; statistics education

10/1478 problem solving

10/1505 higher education; information technology

10/1542 autoinstructional aids; cognitive style; computer assisted learning; learning strategies; teaching machines

10/1547 computer science; visual perception

10/1549 distance education; educational media; educational technology; evaluation; flexible learning

10/1553 computer assisted learning; educational software; interactive video

10/1572 history studies; learning strategies; teaching methods; teleconferencing

10/1594 information technology; mathematics education

10/1613 authoring aids – programming; computer assisted learning; computer software; information technology; multimedia approach

10/1620 information technology; inservice teacher education

10/1668 cross curricular approach; hypertext; information technology; technology education

10/1745 information technology

COMPUTERS

10/0523 attitudes; computer literacy; sex differences

10/1171 educational materials; metaphors; reasoning

COMPUTERS USES IN EDUCATION

10/1181 computer assisted learning; cooperative learning; human-computer interaction; learning processes

CONCENTRATION

10/0859 attention; attention deficit disorders; hyperactivity

CONCEPT FORMATION

10/0591 learning theories; science education; scientific concepts

10/0592 longitudinal studies; science education; scientific concepts

10/0723 area; mathematics education; measurement equipment

10/1102 blindness; number concepts; quantity concepts

10/1117 ecology; environmental education; physical environment

10/1251 computer uses in education; creative development; learning processes

CONCEPT KEYBOARDS

10/0860 computer assisted learning; computer uses in education; human-computer interaction; learning disabilities; special educational needs; touch screens

10/1311 computer keyboards; computer uses in education; human-computer interaction

CONCEPT TEACHING

10/0467 classroom communication; mathematical concepts; mathematics education

10/1335 primary school teachers; science education; scientific concepts; technology education

CONSERVATION – ENVIRONMENT

10/0300 environmental education; natural resources

10/0700 air pollution; environmental education; misconceptions; scientific concepts; secondary school pupils

10/1121 attitudes; environmental education; social change

10/1713 environmental education; pressure groups

CONSERVATISM

10/0402 politics-education relationship; Scotland

CONSTRUCTION – PROCESS

10/0995 building trades education; construction industry; cross curricular approach; technical education; vocational education

10/1028 basic skills; building trades education; construction industry; course evaluation; National Vocational Qualifications; technical education; vocational education

10/1625 construction materials; equal facilities; gender equality; primary education; science education; sex differences; technology education

CONSTRUCTION INDUSTRY

10/0995 building trades education; construction – process; cross curricular approach; technical education; vocational education

10/1028 basic skills; building trades education; construction – process; course evaluation; National Vocational Qualifications; technical education; vocational education

10/1617 experiential learning; learning activities; surveying education

CONSTRUCTION MATERIALS

10/1625 construction – process; equal facilities; gender equality; primary education; science education; sex differences; technology education

CONSULTANTS

10/1244 inservice teacher education; music education; music teachers; primary school teachers

CONSUMER ECONOMICS

10/0125 adult education; citizenship; comparative education; educational policy; Poland

10/0165 educational administration; educational change; educational finance; educational policy; politics-education relationship

CONSUMER EDUCATION

10/0962 cross curricular approach; National Curriculum

CONTINUING EDUCATION

10/0065 clergy; learning processes; professional education; religious education; theological education

10/0121 access to education; adult education; lifelong learning

10/0575 lifelong learning; professional continuing education; professional development

10/0598 adult education; Canada; comparative education

10/0599 access programmes; educational benefits; educational objectives; women's education

10/0627 adult education; educational finance; educational policy; European Community; financial support

10/0766 adult education; educational history

10/0959 adult education; comparative education; cultural differences; Europe; lifelong learning

10/1136 adult education; comparative education; European Community; Germany; United Kingdom; vocational education

10/1139 adult education; adults; comparative education; databases; vocational education

10/1152 adult education; industrial training; inservice teacher education; professional training; vocational education

10/1159 adult education; course evaluation; professional continuing education; programme evaluation

10/1506 community education; staff development; training; voluntary service; volunteers

10/1513 adult education; andragogy; Kuwait

10/1516 adult education; liberal education; nontraditional education

10/1517 adult education; liberal education

10/1522 access programmes; access to education; higher education

10/1711 adult education; higher education; organisational change; universities
10/1712 adult education; equal education; minority groups

CONTRACEPTION
10/1636 community education; early parenthood; family planning; mothers; parenthood education; peer teaching; sex education

CONTROL TECHNOLOGY
10/1179 computer simulation; computer uses in education; logo; models
10/1414 primary education

CONTROVERSIAL ISSUES – COURSE CONTENT
10/1120 agriculture; environmental education; preservice teacher education

CONVERSATION
10/0159 behaviour disorders; classroom communication; learning activities; literacy education; special educational needs
10/0193 language; speech communication; verbal communication
10/1392 communication research; native speakers; second language learning; verbal communication
10/1635 adolescents; peer groups; peer teaching; sexuality

COOPERATION
10/0541 authors; writing – composition
10/0567 developmental continuity; history; National Curriculum; primary secondary education
10/0668 National Curriculum; rural schools; small schools
10/1371 bullying; ethnic relations; intergroup relations; intervention; middle school education; pupil behaviour; social isolation

COOPERATIVE EDUCATION
10/1003 school to work transition; vocational education; work-education relationship

COOPERATIVE LEARNING
10/0180 staff development; teacher development
10/1181 computer assisted learning; computer uses in education; human-computer interaction; learning processes

COOPERATIVE PROGRAMMES
10/0026 corporate support; industry-higher education relationship; research
10/0533 mentors; preservice teacher education
10/1463 community programmes; community services; early childhood education; parent participation; young children
10/1697 industry-education relationship
10/1699 industry-education relationship; programme evaluation; secondments

COORDINATORS
10/0370 information technology; secondary schools; staff role

CORE CURRICULUM
10/0224 comparative education; National Curriculum; Netherlands; Zambia
10/0923 curriculum development; educational administration; educational change; educational development; interdisciplinary approach; National Curriculum
10/1002 assessment; English studies; mathematics education; National Curriculum; science education

CORPORATE EDUCATION
10/1695 industry-education relationship; labour force development

CORPORATE SUPPORT
10/0026 cooperative programmes; industry-higher education relationship; research
10/0164 employers; enterprise education; industry-higher education relationship; transfer of learning
10/1781 educational materials; primary

education; programme evaluation; science education; technology education

COST EFFECTIVENESS
10/0882 developing countries; educational economics; educational finance; efficiency

COUNSELLING
10/1585 counsellor characteristics; counsellor performance; counsellors

COUNSELLING SERVICES
10/0712 higher education; pastoral care – education; student counselling; student needs
10/1110 higher education; mature students; student counselling

COUNSELLING TECHNIQUES
10/0287 communication skills; counsellor training; course evaluation

COUNSELLOR CHARACTERISTICS
10/1585 counselling; counsellor performance; counsellors

COUNSELLOR PERFORMANCE
10/1585 counselling; counsellor characteristics; counsellors

COUNSELLOR TRAINING
10/0287 communication skills; counselling techniques; course evaluation

COUNSELLORS
10/1585 counselling; counsellor characteristics; counsellor performance

COURSE CONTENT
10/0242 educational materials; Italian; modern language studies; multimedia approach

COURSE EVALUATION
10/0127 attendance patterns; business education; examination results; outcomes of education; sandwich courses; undergraduate study
10/0240 educational quality
10/0250 degrees – academic; mathematics education; student attitudes
10/0287 communication skills; counselling techniques; counsellor training
10/0564 colleges of further education; community colleges; European Community; international programmes
10/0654 economics-education relationship; educational administration; educational economics; entrepreneurship; further education
10/1023 educational quality; higher education; performance indicators; quality control; student attitudes; teacher effectiveness; universities
10/1028 basic skills; building trades education; construction – process; construction industry; National Vocational Qualifications; technical education; vocational education
10/1159 adult education; continuing education; professional continuing education; programme evaluation
10/1164 nurse education; student attitudes; teaching methods
10/1355 further education teachers; teacher attitudes; teacher education
10/1408 preservice teacher education; probationary teachers
10/1427 B Ed degrees; graduate surveys; preservice teacher education
10/1743 educational quality; student evaluation of teacher performance; teacher effectiveness; teaching methods; universities
10/1784 Postgraduate Certificate in Education; preservice teacher education; school based teacher education

COURSE SELECTION – STUDENTS
10/0562 choice of subjects; science education; sex differences; sixteen to nineteen education

COURSES
10/1185 inservice teacher education; mathematics education; primary school teachers

CREATIVE DEVELOPMENT
10/1251 computer uses in education; concept formation; learning processes

CREATIVE THINKING
10/0487 cognitive ability; Saudi Arabia

CREATIVE WRITING
10/0077 English studies curriculum; literary genres; National Curriculum; writing – composition; writing skills
10/0586 adult education

CREATIVITY
10/0301 comparative education; France; handwriting; writing research; writing skills
10/1299 design education

CREDIT TRANSFER
10/0565 access to education; educational change; higher education

CREDITS
10/0208 experiential learning; industry-higher education relationship; job placement; work-education relationship
10/1005 school to work transition; training; Training and Enterprise Councils; vocational education; vocational guidance

CREOLES
10/1281 adult education; mother tongue

CRIME PREVENTION
10/0303 delinquency; discipline problems; expulsion; programme evaluation; truancy

CRITICAL READING
10/0542 reading; student development; study skills; writing – composition; writing skills

CRITICAL THINKING
10/0701 experiential learning; medical education; professional continuing education; professional development; reflective teaching
10/0905 aptitude; assessment; higher education; mature students; prediction of success; selection; student evaluation
10/1182 group discussion; learning activities; teaching methods; university students
10/1716 basic skills; educational philosophy; problem solving; skills; transfer of learning

CRITICISM
10/0020 art activities; art education; cross curricular approach
10/0260 art education; intellectual development; reasoning
10/0472 argument; higher education; sixth form education; writing processes; writing skills
10/1753 aesthetic education; art activities; art appreciation; art education; National Curriculum

CROSS CULTURAL STUDIES
10/0881 comparative education; educational attitudes; pupil attitudes; Saudi Arabia
10/1569 electronic mail; European studies; international education; social history; telecommunications
10/1570 electronic mail; European studies; preservice teacher education; telecommunications

CROSS CURRICULAR APPROACH
10/0020 art activities; art education; criticism
10/0083 special education teachers; special educational needs; support services; team teaching
10/0244 National Curriculum; physical education
10/0286 Cameroon; English – second language; language of instruction; mathematics education
10/0571 computer uses in education; curriculum development; information technology
10/0572 art; art history; cognitive development; mathematics; spatial ability
10/0670 citizenship education; National Curriculum
10/0678 multicultural education; National Curriculum; primary education

10/0682 curriculum development; environmental education; National Curriculum; polymers
10/0736 curriculum development; economics education; enterprise education; teacher education
10/0821 curriculum development; Northern Ireland
10/0832 curriculum development; educational quality; National Curriculum
10/0962 consumer education; National Curriculum
10/0995 building trades education; construction – process; construction industry; technical education; vocational education
10/1047 basic skills; National Curriculum; secondary education
10/1598 curriculum development; economics education; enterprise education; primary education; secondary education; Wales
10/1668 computer uses in education; hypertext; information technology; technology education
10/1676 curriculum development; information technology; National Curriculum
10/1687 curriculum development; National Curriculum; school organisation; teaching methods; thematic approach

CULTURAL ACTIVITIES
10/0038 curriculum; European Community; sciences

CULTURAL AWARENESS
10/0295 English – second language; German; modern language studies; textbook evaluation
10/0308 comparative education; Denmark; Europe; modern language studies
10/0309 Arab states; English – second language; foreign culture; native speakers; second language learning
10/0420 international education
10/1571 electronic mail; intercultural communication; language proficiency; modern language studies; telecommunications

CULTURAL BACKGROUND
10/0974 adolescents; Chinese; ethnic groups; ethnicity; Hong Kong; migrants
10/0981 mathematics education; probability
10/1550 access to education; equal education; ethnic groups; higher education; inner city; women's education

CULTURAL DIFFERENCES
10/0959 adult education; comparative education; continuing education; Europe; lifelong learning

CULTURAL EDUCATION
10/0258 arts education; computer uses in education; handicrafts; museums; visual arts
10/0292 comparative education; educational materials; second language learning; teaching methods
10/1115 arts education; history; primary education
10/1523 adult education; curriculum development; humanities
10/1554 degree requirements; ethnography; higher education; second language learning; study abroad

CULTURAL INFLUENCES
10/0720 gypsies; minority group children; performance factors; travellers – itinerants
10/0721 gypsies; minority group children; performance factors; travellers – itinerants
10/1173 curriculum; educational philosophy; ideology
10/1519 developing countries; educational policy

CULTURE
10/1060 arts; attitudes; mass media; music; participation; sports; theatre arts
10/1062 arts; arts education; attitudes; leisure time; participation; youth

CURRICULUM
10/0038 cultural activities; European Community; sciences
10/0150 literacy education; reading skills; secondary school curriculum; writing skills
10/1173 cultural influences; educational philosophy; ideology

10/1696 employment; industry-education relationship; skills; work-education relationship

CURRICULUM DEVELOPMENT
10/0139 educational change; National Curriculum; primary education; primary school teachers; primary schools; teacher role; teacher workload
10/0217 individualism; physical education; teaching methods; theory-practice relationship
10/0314 comparative education; European Community; modular courses; vocational education
10/0327 educational assessment; educational change; English studies; Scotland
10/0349 drama; educational materials; learning experience
10/0445 educational history; secondary education; technical education
10/0451 sixteen to nineteen education; values education
10/0456 educational materials; English – second language; second language teaching; Senegal
10/0510 information technology; mathematics education; secondary education
10/0571 computer uses in education; cross curricular approach; information technology
10/0630 geometry; mathematics education; secondary education; South Africa
10/0679 environmental education; higher education
10/0682 cross curricular approach; environmental education; National Curriculum; polymers
10/0686 educational philosophy; individual development; moral education; physical education; religious education
10/0698 National Curriculum; science education
10/0714 developmental continuity; primary secondary education
10/0736 cross curricular approach; economics education; enterprise education; teacher education
10/0737 economics education; sixteen to nineteen education
10/0738 business education; economics education; sixteen to nineteen education
10/0739 business education; inservice teacher education
10/0812 sixteen to nineteen education
10/0821 cross curricular approach; Northern Ireland
10/0832 cross curricular approach; educational quality; National Curriculum
10/0923 core curriculum; educational administration; educational change; educational development; interdisciplinary approach; National Curriculum
10/0945 low achievement; moderate learning difficulties; special educational needs; underachievement
10/0963 business education; economics education; teacher attitudes; teacher development
10/0966 National Curriculum; severe learning difficulties; special educational needs
10/0982 mathematics education; science education; technology education
10/1001 developmental continuity; local education authorities; National Curriculum; primary secondary education; transfer pupils
10/1004 European Community; European studies; local education authorities
10/1030 computer uses in education; information technology; microcomputers
10/1061 cohort analysis; National Curriculum – Northern Ireland; Northern Ireland; pupil attitudes
10/1113 primary education; technology education
10/1147 change agents; preservice teacher education; TVEI
10/1148 design education; National Curriculum; technology education
10/1161 Malawi; mathematics education; primary education; science education
10/1225 primary education; tourism; travel
10/1227 educational administration; inspection; primary education; primary schools; school organisation
10/1239 educational change; English studies

curriculum; National Curriculum; secondary education
10/1305 discovery learning; educational history; primary education; projects – learning activities; pupil projects; teaching methods
10/1338 comparative education; international educational exchange; mathematics education; science education
10/1361 assessment; primary secondary education; programme evaluation
10/1418 secondary school teachers; teacher development
10/1444 assessment; educational change; environmental education; mathematics education; National Curriculum; Scotland; teaching process
10/1494 economics-education relationship; educational policy; labour market; politics-education relationship; vocational education
10/1523 adult education; cultural education; humanities
10/1530 'A' level examinations; business education; economics education
10/1556 environmental education; pollution; waste disposal
10/1568 differentiated curriculum; individualised methods; Northern Ireland; science education
10/1575 history; Ireland
10/1598 cross curricular approach; economics education; enterprise education; primary education; secondary education; Wales
10/1630 comparative education; environmental education; school-community relationship
10/1648 educational materials; experiential learning; material development; primary education; technology education; work-education relationship
10/1676 cross curricular approach; information technology; National Curriculum
10/1687 cross curricular approach; National Curriculum; school organisation; teaching methods; thematic approach
10/1793 guidelines; political science studies

CURRICULUM ENRICHMENT
10/1503 clubs; engineering; engineers; industry-education relationship

CURRICULUM EVALUATION
10/0275 medical education
10/1140 economics-education relationship; Hong Kong; training; TVEI; work-education relationship

CURRICULUM RESEARCH
10/0466 autism; cognitive ability; social cognition
10/0847 classroom research; Education Reform Act 1988; educational change; educational experience; infant schools; mathematics education
10/1024 National Vocational Qualifications; sixteen to nineteen education; sixth form education; vocational education

CYPRUS
10/1692 change; nurse education
10/1774 comparative education; educational policy; Greece; school systems

DANCE
10/0811 art education; music; sixteen to nineteen education; theatre arts

DANCE EDUCATION
10/0245 interactive video

DATA PROCESSING
10/0779 computer uses in education; databases; material development; primary schools
10/0889 assessment; expert systems

DATABASES
10/0225 access programmes; adult education
10/0228 adult education; further education; higher education; mature students
10/0254 art; design; information sources; research
10/0262 local management of schools; research
10/0380 community organisations; student projects
10/0779 computer uses in education; data processing; material development; primary schools

10/0806 intervention; pupil welfare
10/0844 information technology; National Curriculum; technology education
10/1139 adult education; adults; comparative education; continuing education; vocational education
10/1279 multicultural education; resource materials

DAY CARE
10/0395 children at risk; community services; family problems; family relationship
10/0846 child caregivers; child minding; day care centres; preschool children; quality control
10/0851 Children Act 1989; early childhood education; legislation; local government; preschool education; social services
10/0935 community services; early childhood education; local government; nursery school curriculum; nursery schools; preschool education; young children

DAY CARE CENTRES
10/0397 agency cooperation; child caregivers; community services; early childhood education; programme evaluation; quality control
10/0846 child caregivers; child minding; day care; preschool children; quality control
10/1300 community centres; community education; community programmes; English – second language; ethnic groups; racial integration; social integration

DEAF BLIND
10/0089 behaviour; disabilities; motor reactions; multiple disabilities; sensory deprivation

DEAF INTERPRETING
10/1265 deafness; graduate study; hearing impairments; higher education; interpreters; special educational needs

DEAFNESS
10/0140 language acquisition; sign language
10/0147 distance education; material development; sign language; special educational needs
10/0148 sign language
10/0611 communication skills; hearing impairments; hearing therapy; special schools; total communication
10/0960 hearing impairments; special educational needs
10/0961 communication aids – for disabled; hearing aids; hearing impairments; psychological evaluation
10/1265 deaf interpreting; graduate study; hearing impairments; higher education; interpreters; special educational needs

DEATH
10/0681 attitude formation; bereavement; childhood attitudes
10/1221 adolescent development; bereavement; child development; moral development; religious attitudes

DECISION MAKING
10/0969 cognitive processes; professional education
10/0970 cognitive processes; professional autonomy
10/1397 National Curriculum; science education; scientific literacy
10/1493 problem solving; student attitudes

DEGREE REQUIREMENTS
10/1554 cultural education; ethnography; higher education; second language learning; study abroad

DEGREES – ACADEMIC
10/0029 competency based education; inservice education; professional education
10/0250 course evaluation; mathematics education; student attitudes
10/0256 art education; assessment; comparative education; fine arts; Greece
10/0993 main subjects; Postgraduate Certificate in Education; preservice teacher education

10/1098 medicine; professional education; undergraduate students

DELINQUENCY
10/0303 crime prevention; discipline problems; expulsion; programme evaluation; truancy

DELINQUENCY PREVENTION
10/0243 antisocial behaviour; behaviour problems; longitudinal studies; secondary school pupils; transfer pupils

DELPHI TECHNIQUE
10/1576 nurse education; psychiatric services

DEMOCRACY
10/0471 change; comparative education; development education; politics-education relationship

DEMOGRAPHY
10/1439 choice of subjects; further education; pupil attitudes; sixteen to nineteen education

DENMARK
10/0308 comparative education; cultural awareness; Europe; modern language studies
10/0431 adult education; comparative education; lifelong learning; mature students; people's universities

DENTAL EDUCATION
10/1353 teaching guides

DENTISTRY
10/0281 medical education

DEPARTMENTS
10/0731 differential performance; examination results; outcomes of education; school effectiveness; secondary schools

DEPTH PERCEPTION
10/1188 cognitive ability; drawing; problem solving; spatial ability; visual perception

DEPUTY HEAD TEACHERS
10/1200 employment patterns; head teachers; teacher employment; teacher mobility; teacher recruitment; teacher supply and demand; teaching profession

DESIGN
10/0254 art; databases; information sources; research
10/1248 art; Postgraduate Certificate in Education; preservice teacher education; probationary teachers; programme effectiveness; student teachers

DESIGN AND TECHNOLOGY
10/0620 ability; National Curriculum; primary education; technology education
10/0854 sex differences; teaching profession
10/1118 learning activities; teaching methods
10/1192 learning strategies; problem solving; technology education

DESIGN EDUCATION
10/0239 computer assisted learning; hypermedia
10/0255 'A' level examinations; learner characteristics; student attitudes
10/0257 art education; computer assisted design; computer uses in education
10/0259 designers; spatial ability; visualisation
10/1148 curriculum development; National Curriculum; technology education
10/1235 art education; inservice teacher education; National Curriculum; primary education; primary school teachers
10/1299 creativity
10/1428 art education; assessment

DESIGNERS
10/0259 design education; spatial ability; visualisation

DEVELOPING COUNTRIES
10/0021 development education; environmental education

10/0074 educational administration; educational environment; educational finance
10/0084 educational administration; educational policy; politics-education relationship; school systems
10/0109 educational improvement; inservice teacher education; Pakistan; primary education; programme evaluation
10/0142 Belize; development education; educational quality; primary education
10/0144 Belize; educational materials; material development; textbooks
10/0344 development education; Ghana
10/0346 development education; educational materials; literacy; material development; reading materials
10/0461 English – second language; second language teaching
10/0478 Arab states; development education; educational policy
10/0773 vocational education; Zimbabwe
10/0882 cost effectiveness; educational economics; educational finance; efficiency
10/1269 literacy; women's education
10/1286 development education; Europe; information science; librarianship education
10/1519 cultural influences; educational policy
10/1524 development aid; development education; financial support
10/1527 development aid; development education
10/1528 agricultural education; environmental education; Zimbabwe
10/1531 development education; India; learning activities; primary education; teaching methods
10/1538 community benefits; health education; India; peer teaching; Uganda
10/1690 educational improvement; secondary education; Sierra Leone
10/1804 language policy; language standardisation; literacy; mother tongue

DEVELOPMENT AID
10/1524 developing countries; development education; financial support
10/1527 developing countries; development education

DEVELOPMENT EDUCATION
10/0021 developing countries; environmental education
10/0142 Belize; developing countries; educational quality; primary education
10/0344 developing countries; Ghana
10/0346 developing countries; educational materials; literacy; material development; reading materials
10/0471 change; comparative education; democracy; politics-education relationship
10/0478 Arab states; developing countries; educational policy
10/1286 developing countries; Europe; information science; librarianship education
10/1524 developing countries; development aid; financial support
10/1527 developing countries; development aid
10/1531 developing countries; India; learning activities; primary education; teaching methods

DEVELOPMENT PLANS
10/0647 educational planning; planning; primary schools; whole school approach
10/0840 educational administration; planning; primary schools

DEVELOPMENTAL CONTINUITY
10/0181 English literature; higher education; sixteen to nineteen education; teaching methods
10/0443 physical activity level; physical education; primary secondary education
10/0444 primary secondary education
10/0567 cooperation; history; National Curriculum; primary secondary education
10/0714 curriculum development; primary secondary education
10/0722 ability; child development; longitudinal studies; personality development
10/1001 curriculum development; local education authorities; National Curriculum; primary secondary education; transfer pupils

10/1267 infant schools; junior schools; primary education; transfer pupils

DIAGNOSTIC ASSESSMENT

10/0751 assessment; colleges of further education; disabilities; further education; moderate learning difficulties; special educational needs

10/1026 ability tests; intelligence tests; special educational needs

10/1748 special educational needs

DIALECT STUDIES

10/1242 language variation; sociolinguistics

DIFFERENTIAL PERFORMANCE

10/0731 departments; examination results; outcomes of education; school effectiveness; secondary schools

10/1033 assessment; attainment tests; second language learning

DIFFERENTIATED CURRICULUM

10/0041 English studies curriculum; learning disabilities; low achievement; mainstreaming; special educational needs

10/0677 individual needs; mainstreaming; National Curriculum; special educational needs

10/1568 curriculum development; individualised methods; Northern Ireland; science education

10/1573 individualised methods; primary education; teaching methods

DIGLOSSIA

10/0031 academic achievement; bilingualism; ethnic groups; language usage

DIRECTORIES

10/1006 educational research; environmental education

10/1020 moral education; reference materials; values education

10/1787 comparative education; early childhood education; preservice teacher education

DISABILITIES

10/0089 behaviour; deaf blind; motor reactions; multiple disabilities; sensory deprivation

10/0090 access to education; higher education; special educational needs; student needs; universities; university admission

10/0092 comparative education; mainstreaming; pupil attitudes; special educational needs; special schools

10/0325 communication aids – for disabled; educational materials; special educational needs

10/0442 access to education; accessibility – for disabled; equal education; higher education; student recruitment

10/0474 mainstreaming; moderate learning difficulties; Nigeria; physical education; special educational needs

10/0578 adult education; adult learning; caregivers; independent study; lifelong learning

10/0747 cerebral palsy; motor reactions; perceptual handicaps; perceptual motor coordination; special educational needs

10/0751 assessment; colleges of further education; diagnostic assessment; further education; moderate learning difficulties; special educational needs

10/1069 further education; further education students; literature reviews; moderate learning difficulties; special educational needs

10/1124 adult vocational education; adults; computer literacy; information technology; sheltered workshops; special educational needs; training centres

10/1126 adult basic education; adults; computer literacy; information technology; special educational needs

10/1127 adults; computer literacy; information technology; special educational needs; training centres

10/1131 communications; computer networks; training; wide area networks

10/1142 adult vocational education; comparative education; information technology; Portugal; special educational needs; training; United Kingdom

10/1714 equal education; special educational needs

DISADVANTAGED

10/1470 moderate learning difficulties; special educational needs; support services

DISADVANTAGED ENVIRONMENT

10/0007 access to education; educational innovation; educationally disadvantaged; Scotland

10/1715 city technology colleges; industry-education relationship; school-community relationship

DISCIPLINE

10/0095 antisocial behaviour; disruptive pupils; pupil behaviour; pupil placement

10/0298 behaviour problems; comparative education; disruptive pupils; Kenya; secondary schools

10/0322 attendance; discipline problems; pupil attitudes; secondary schools; teacher attitudes

10/1354 classroom discipline; discipline policy; educational materials

10/1372 antisocial behaviour; behaviour problems; bullying; discipline policy; pupil behaviour

10/1660 classroom discipline

10/1674 behaviour problems; classroom discipline; disruptive pupils; Greece; nursery school education; teacher attitudes

DISCIPLINE POLICY

10/0913 behaviour problems; discipline problems; disruptive pupils; primary secondary education; problem children; transfer pupils

10/1228 antisocial behaviour; behaviour problems; bullying; discipline problems; teacher attitudes

10/1240 disruptive pupils; educational change; expulsion; primary schools; problem children; special educational needs; suspension

10/1350 bullying; discipline problems; Scotland

10/1354 classroom discipline; discipline; educational materials

10/1372 antisocial behaviour; behaviour problems; bullying; discipline; pupil behaviour

10/1375 antisocial behaviour; attitudes; bullying; parent attitudes; school policy; teacher attitudes

10/1662 behaviour problems; bullying; discipline problems

DISCIPLINE PROBLEMS

10/0063 behaviour problems; disruptive pupils; infant school pupils; primary school pupils; problem children; surveys

10/0303 crime prevention; delinquency; expulsion; programme evaluation; truancy

10/0322 attendance; discipline; pupil attitudes; secondary schools; teacher attitudes

10/0913 behaviour problems; discipline policy; disruptive pupils; primary-secondary education; problem children; transfer pupils

10/1063 attendance; disruptive pupils; expulsion; truancy

10/1217 cheating; higher education; plagiarism; student behaviour

10/1228 antisocial behaviour; behaviour problems; bullying; discipline policy; teacher attitudes

10/1350 bullying; discipline policy; Scotland

10/1662 behaviour problems; bullying; discipline policy

10/1758 antisocial behaviour; comparative education; disruptive pupils; United States of America

DISCOURSE ANALYSIS

10/1721 classroom communication; metaphors; teacher education

DISCOVERY LEARNING

10/1305 curriculum development; educational history; primary education; projects – learning activities; pupil projects; teaching methods

DISCUSSION

10/0709 group work; interaction; intergroup education; learning activities

DISCUSSION – TEACHING TECHNIQUE

10/0160 competence; competency based teacher education; personal construct theory; repertory grid test; teacher effectiveness

DISRUPTIVE PUPILS

10/0063 behaviour problems; discipline problems; infant school pupils; primary school pupils; problem children; surveys

10/0095 antisocial behaviour; discipline; pupil behaviour; pupil placement

10/0298 behaviour problems; comparative education; discipline; Kenya; secondary schools

10/0913 behaviour problems; discipline policy; discipline problems; primary-secondary education; problem children; transfer pupils

10/1063 attendance; discipline problems; expulsion; truancy

10/1240 discipline policy; educational change; expulsion; primary schools; problem children; special educational needs; suspension

10/1674 behaviour problems; classroom discipline; discipline; Greece; nursery school education; teacher attitudes

10/1739 behaviour problems; Education Reform Act 1988; educational policy; emotional problems; problem children; school policy

10/1747 behaviour problems; problem children; support services

10/1758 antisocial behaviour; comparative education; discipline problems; United States of America

DISTANCE EDUCATION

10/0069 clinical experience; pharmaceutical education; pharmacists; professional training; programme evaluation

10/0093 language handicaps; special education teachers; special educational needs; speech handicaps; teacher development

10/0147 deafness; material development; sign language; special educational needs

10/0269 institutional evaluation; medical services; professional continuing education

10/0271 nurse education; professional continuing education; professional development

10/0276 medical education; programme evaluation

10/0436 educational media; infant school teachers; inservice education; international educational exchange; Sweden; telecommunications

10/0440 comparative education; higher education; international educational exchange; learning activities; Netherlands; teaching methods; telecommunications

10/0547 communications; networks; open education; teleconferencing

10/0898 open universities; Saudi Arabia; women's education

10/1167 adult students; humanities; mature students; open universities; student attitudes

10/1168 computer uses in education; microcomputers; open universities

10/1174 international educational exchange; open universities; teleconferencing

10/1549 computer uses in education; educational media; educational technology; evaluation; flexible learning

10/1577 interactive video; teaching methods; teleconferencing

10/1592 inservice teacher education; programme effectiveness; teacher attitudes; teacher development

10/1603 flexible learning; information science; librarianship education; mature students

10/1638 independent study

DISTRIBUTIVE TRADES EDUCATION

10/0601 National Vocational Qualifications; retailing; training; vocational education

10/1500 attitudes; salesmanship

DOCTOR-PATIENT RELATIONSHIP

10/1154 medical services; pain; patient education; physical health

10/1158 medical services; pain; patient education; physical health

DOWN'S SYNDROME
10/0884 mainstreaming; special educational needs
10/1765 expressive language; interaction; language acquisition; mainstreaming; special educational needs; special schools
10/1806 autism; drawing; gifted; special educational needs; visual arts

DRAMA
10/0349 curriculum development; educational materials; learning experience
10/1419 early childhood education; preschool education

DRAMA EDUCATION
10/0579 dramatics; learning processes; primary education; theatre arts
10/0942 classroom environment; classroom management; primary schools; pupil behaviour
10/1246 educational materials; English studies curriculum; National Curriculum
10/1253 English studies curriculum; National Curriculum; scripts; secondary education
10/1611 assessment; audience response; dramatics

DRAMATICS
10/0579 drama education; learning processes; primary education; theatre arts
10/1611 assessment; audience response; drama education

DRAWING
10/0865 computer assisted design; computer graphics
10/1188 cognitive ability; depth perception; problem solving; spatial ability; visual perception
10/1806 autism; Down's Syndrome; gifted; special educational needs; visual arts
10/1807 art education; infant school education

DRINKING
10/1036 alcohol education; health education
10/1562 drug abuse; pupil attitudes; religious attitudes; secondary school pupils; smoking; substance abuse

DRIVER EDUCATION
10/0035 cerebral palsy

DROPOUT RESEARCH
10/0122 dropouts; enrolment; higher education; student behaviour
10/0408 access to education; higher education; nontraditional education; summer schools; university admission; university preparation
10/0750 achievement; adult basic education; adult dropouts; basic skills
10/1673 Arab states; student wastage; technical education; vocational education

DROPOUTS
10/0122 dropout research; enrolment; higher education; student behaviour

DRUG ABUSE
10/0492 acquired immune deficiency syndrome; drug education; health education; welfare services
10/1562 drinking; pupil attitudes; religious attitudes; secondary school pupils; smoking; substance abuse

DRUG EDUCATION
10/0492 acquired immune deficiency syndrome; drug abuse; health education; welfare services
10/0849 health education; life skills; primary education
10/1347 alcohol education; health education; programme evaluation; sex education
10/1555 comparative education; health education
10/1608 information sources; libraries; prevention

DYSLEXIA
10/0174 reading difficulties
10/0238 computer assisted learning; interactive video; learning disabilities; multimedia approach
10/0447 city technology colleges; educational materials; learning disabilities; special educational needs; teaching methods
10/0453 learning disabilities; reading difficulties; special educational needs; teacher education
10/0659 brain hemisphere functions; handedness; lateral dominance; reading difficulties; visual perception
10/0864 language handicaps; reading difficulties
10/0917 bilingual pupils; cognitive ability; language acquisition; language handicaps; learning disabilities; special educational needs
10/1437 reading difficulties; reading failure; reading skills; word recognition
10/1582 learning disabilities; mathematics
10/1805 cognitive ability; reading difficulties; reading skills
10/1808 beginning reading; sight method; word recognition

EARLY CHILDHOOD EDUCATION
10/0091 books; early experience; early reading; infants; parent participation
10/0145 Greece; preschool to primary transition; primary school pupils; school readiness
10/0146 children's literature; reading aloud to others; story reading; teacher-pupil relationship
10/0306 infant school teachers; mathematics education; reception classes
10/0377 nursery school education; preschool education; regional characteristics; regional planning
10/0397 agency cooperation; child caregivers; community services; day care centres; programme evaluation; quality control
10/0484 Ireland; Montessori method; play groups; preschool education
10/0632 mathematics education; pattern recognition; play; young children
10/0715 preschool education
10/0724 preschool education
10/0851 Children Act 1989; day care; legislation; local government; preschool education; social services
10/0914 governing bodies; nursery schools; parent attitudes; parent-school relationship; preschool education; school governors
10/0920 mothers; nursery schools; parent participation
10/0935 community services; day care; local government; nursery school curriculum; nursery schools; preschool education; young children
10/1027 assessment; mathematical concepts; mathematics education; mathematics tests; school entrance age
10/1193 communication skills; friendship; infant school pupils; reception classes; social development; social isolation; young children
10/1266 early experience; hearing impairments; intervention; parent participation; special educational needs
10/1270 individualised methods; intervention; parent participation; teaching methods
10/1272 classroom management; infant school education; infant school teachers; reception classes
10/1297 achievement; assessment; records of achievement; self evaluation – individuals; young children
10/1306 mathematics education; numbers; preschool education
10/1324 Montessori method; Steiner Waldorf schools; teaching methods
10/1357 preschool education; Scotland
10/1419 drama; preschool education
10/1463 community programmes; community services; cooperative programmes; parent participation; young children
10/1537 Montessori method; nursery schools; preschool education
10/1749 phonics; reading; reading ability; reading skills
10/1787 educational development; educational quality; preschool education; quality control
10/1787 comparative education; directories; preservice teacher education
10/1788 educational development; educational quality; nursery schools; play groups; preschool education; quality control
10/1791 men; sex differences

EARLY EXPERIENCE
10/0091 books; early childhood education; early reading; infants; parent participation
10/0863 attention; cognitive development; infant behaviour; learning; neurological impairments
10/1266 early childhood education; hearing impairments; intervention; parent participation; special educational needs

EARLY PARENTHOOD
10/1636 community education; contraception; family planning; mothers; parenthood education; peer teaching; sex education

EARLY READING
10/0091 books; early childhood education; early experience; infants; parent participation
10/0196 home-school relationship; reading achievement; reading difficulties
10/0463 beginning reading; oral reading; reading skills; teacher-pupil relationship
10/1264 child development; reading ability; young children

EARTH SCIENCE
10/0028 computer assisted learning; computer uses in education; educational software
10/0501 educational history; geology education; physical sciences; science education
10/0502 comprehension; oceanography; physical sciences; plate tectonics
10/0503 educational materials; material development; National Curriculum; physical sciences; science education
10/0680 environmental education; learning activities
10/0741 laboratories; laboratory experiments; physical environment; physical geography; simulated environment
10/0845 geography education; inservice teacher education; National Curriculum
10/1141 adult education; adult learning; field studies; field studies centres; study abroad
10/1178 computer assisted learning; educational equipment; microscopes; simulation; special educational needs

EATING HABITS
10/0202 body image; food; health; self concept
10/1703 food; health education; nutrition education

ECOLOGY
10/1117 concept formation; environmental education; physical environment

ECOLOGY EDUCATION
10/0626 comprehension; science education; scientific concepts

ECONOMIC CHANGE
10/0120 comparative education; economics-education relationship; Germany; industry-education relationship; structural unemployment; training; work-education relationship
10/0703 educational needs; educational policy; Poland; social change; youth
10/1241 agricultural colleges; agricultural education; educational change; further education; staff development

ECONOMIC FACTORS
10/0519 educational quality; management in education; marketing; primary schools

ECONOMICS EDUCATION
10/0736 cross curricular approach; curriculum development; enterprise education; teacher education
10/0737 curriculum development; sixteen to nineteen education
10/0738 business education; curriculum development; sixteen to nineteen education
10/0742 secondary school pupils
10/0963 business education; curriculum development; teacher attitudes; teacher development
10/1025 industry-education relationship; money management

10/1066 life skills; money management;
volunteers
10/1530 'A' level examinations; business
education; curriculum development
10/1598 cross curricular approach; curriculum
development; enterprise education; primary
education; secondary education; Wales
10/1653 background; experience; industry-
education relationship; preservice teacher
education; student teacher attitudes; student
teachers

ECONOMICS-EDUCATION RELATIONSHIP
10/0124 comparative education; economic
change; Germany; industry-education
relationship; structural unemployment;
training; work-education relationship
10/0654 course evaluation; educational
administration; educational economics;
entrepreneurship; further education
10/0856 educational benefits; educational
finance; employment opportunities; outcomes
of education; rewards; work-education
relationship
10/1140 curriculum evaluation; Hong Kong;
training; TVEI; work-education relationship
10/1494 curriculum development; educational
policy; labour market; politics-education
relationship; vocational education

EDUCATION COURSES
10/0394 competency based education; higher
education; masters courses; qualifications;
standards

EDUCATION REFORM ACT 1988
10/0080 local management of schools; school
size; small schools
10/0081 educational administration; educational
change; educational finance; grant maintained
schools; open entry; parent choice; school
based management
10/0357 religion and education; school worship;
symbolism
10/0367 access to education; parent choice;
primary schools
10/0473 individual development; moral
education; National Curriculum; primary
schools; religious education; social
development
10/0486 educational change; educational
legislation; educational planning; primary
schools; school size; small schools
10/0713 educational change; educational policy;
politics-education relationship
10/0847 classroom research; curriculum
research; educational change; educational
experience; infant schools; mathematics
education
10/0883 educational change; educational
development; educational planning;
educational policy; government role; local
education authorities
10/0924 educational administration; educational
change; local management of schools; school
based management; secondary schools
10/0994 antiracism education; educational
planning; equal education; local education
authorities; multicultural education
10/1496 multiculturalism; primary education;
religious education
10/1604 educational change; primary education;
religious education
10/1710 achievement; Afro Caribbean youth;
assessment; black pupils; equal education;
ethnic groups; low achievement
10/1739 behaviour problems; disruptive pupils;
educational policy; emotional problems;
problem children; school policy
10/1742 educational change; educational
legislation; educational policy; local education
authorities

EDUCATION SUPPORT GRANTS
10/0497 inservice teacher education; programme
evaluation; TVEI

EDUCATION VOUCHERS
10/0878 educational change; educational policy;
politics-education relationship

EDUCATIONAL ADMINISTRATION
10/0015 universities; university administration
10/0017 local education authorities
10/0023 college administration; colleges of further
education; further education; institutional
administration; organisational change
10/0049 administrators; management in
education; teacher-administrator relationship
10/0057 educational change; educational policy;
school based management; special educational
needs; support services
10/0074 developing countries; educational
environment; educational finance
10/0081 Education Reform Act 1988;
educational change; educational finance; grant
maintained schools; open entry; parent choice;
school based management
10/0084 developing countries; educational
policy; politics-education relationship; school
systems
10/0086 educational finance; educational
software; resource allocation; school
effectiveness
10/0096 educational change; educational policy;
governance; local education authorities;
management in education; politics-education
relationship
10/0152 educational change; management teams;
school based management; secondary schools
10/0162 educational change; educational policy;
governance; governing bodies; local education
authorities; management in education
10/0165 consumer economics; educational
change; educational finance; educational
policy; politics-education relationship
10/0235 local management of schools; school
based management; small schools
10/0345 educational change; local management
of schools; parent participation; school based
management; school boards – Scotland; school
governing bodies
10/0354 school governing bodies; school governors
10/0356 secondary schools; teacher evaluation
10/0386 head teachers; management in
education; sex differences; teaching
profession; women's employment
10/0406 teacher morale; teaching profession
10/0410 organisational theories
10/0428 educational policy; management in
education; politics-education relationship;
Scotland
10/0432 school boards – Scotland; school
governing bodies; Scotland
10/0517 administrators; further education; higher
education; management in education; women;
women's employment
10/0551 educational history; educational policy;
public education; secondary education;
tripartite system
10/0654 course evaluation; economics-education
relationship; educational economics;
entrepreneurship; further education
10/0669 National Curriculum; preservice teacher
education; school effectiveness; secondary
schools
10/0672 grant maintained schools; local
management of schools; management in
education; school based management
10/0674 educational change; grant maintained
schools; management in education; school
based management
10/0756 local management of schools; school
based management; special educational needs
10/0770 educational materials; management
development; management in education;
material development
10/0771 educational materials; management
development; management in education;
material development
10/0772 educational materials; management in
education; material development
10/0809 governance; head teachers; school
governing bodies; school governors
10/0840 development plans; planning; primary
schools
10/0870 educational change; local management
of schools; school based management
10/0873 computer uses in education; information
technology; local management of schools;
management systems; school based management

10/0888 institutional cooperation; local
management of schools
10/0908 educational history; management in
education
10/0909 educational administrators; local
education authorities; management in
education
10/0912 governing bodies; head teachers;
management in education; school governors
10/0923 core curriculum; curriculum
development; educational change; educational
development; interdisciplinary approach;
National Curriculum
10/0924 Education Reform Act 1988; educational
change; local management of schools; school
based management; secondary schools
10/0952 administrators; head teachers;
management development; management in
education
10/0957 governing bodies; primary schools;
school governors
10/0989 inservice teacher education; local
education authorities
10/1014 educational finance; local management
of schools; mainstreaming; resource
allocation; school based management; special
educational needs
10/1038 budgeting; educational finance; local
management of schools; school based
management
10/1039 local management of schools; school
based management; school governing bodies;
school governors
10/1111 colleges of further education;
educational planning; management in
education; marketing
10/1122 colleges of further education; women's
employment
10/1206 comparative education; educational
policy; Italy; mainstreaming; Scandinavia;
special educational needs; support services
10/1208 educational change; educational policy;
local education authorities; special educational
needs
10/1209 Europe; management in education;
teacher employment; teaching profession;
women; women's employment
10/1227 curriculum development; inspection;
primary school curriculum; primary schools;
school organisation
10/1268 higher education; management in
education
10/1420 governing bodies; school boards –
Scotland; school governors
10/1609 educational change; grant maintained
schools; management in education; school
based management
10/1644 educational change; further education;
higher education
10/1667 educational policy; local management of
schools; management in education;
organisational change
10/1740 head teachers; primary schools; school
based management; teacher role
10/1780 educational quality; higher education;
institutes of higher education; quality
assurance; quality control
10/1790 local management of schools;
management in education; programme
evaluation; school based management; teacher
development

EDUCATIONAL ADMINISTRATORS
10/0909 educational administration; local
education authorities; management in
education

EDUCATIONAL ASSESSMENT
10/0327 curriculum development; educational
change; English studies; Scotland

EDUCATIONAL ATTITUDES
10/0881 comparative education; cross cultural
studies; pupil attitudes; Saudi Arabia
10/0967 adolescent attitudes; adolescent
development; adolescents; interests;
personality development; social development;
vocational interests
10/1757 attendance; family influence; home-
school relationship; truancy

EDUCATIONAL BENEFITS

10/0599 access programmes; continuing education; educational objectives; women's education

10/0856 economics-education relationship; educational finance; employment opportunities; outcomes of education; rewards; work-education relationship

EDUCATIONAL BROADCASTING

10/0695 adult education; educational radio; local radio; mass media; radio

10/1057 educational radio; educational television; radio; television

EDUCATIONAL CHANGE

10/0057 educational administration; educational policy; school based management; special educational needs; support services

10/0076 head teachers; local management of schools; school based management

10/0081 Education Reform Act 1988; educational administration; educational finance; grant maintained schools; open entry; parent choice; school based management

10/0096 educational administration; educational policy; governance; local education authorities; management in education; politics-education relationship

10/0139 curriculum development; National Curriculum; primary education; primary school teachers; primary schools; teacher role; teacher workload

10/0149 educational policy; mass media effects; press opinion; public opinion

10/0152 educational administration; management teams; school based management; secondary schools

10/0153 assessment; infant school curriculum; infant school education; National Curriculum; primary school teachers; pupil attitudes

10/0154 comparative education; France; primary school teachers; teacher attitudes; teaching profession

10/0155 assessment; National Curriculum; primary education; primary school curriculum; primary school teachers; pupil attitudes

10/0161 educational policy; politics-education relationship

10/0162 educational administration; educational policy; governance; governing bodies; local education authorities; management in education

10/0165 consumer economics; educational administration; educational finance; educational policy; politics-education relationship

10/0310 access to education; further education; higher education; sixteen to nineteen education

10/0327 curriculum development; educational assessment; English studies; Scotland

10/0345 educational administration; local management of schools; parent participation; school based management; school boards – Scotland; school governing bodies

10/0399 Commonwealth of Independent States; communist education; ideology; politics-education relationship; social change; USSR

10/0415 educational history; Scotland

10/0480 primary schools

10/0486 Education Reform Act 1988; educational legislation; educational planning; primary schools; school size; small schools

10/0516 educational history; educational policy

10/0563 secondary education; secondary school curriculum; secondary school teachers; teacher role; teaching profession

10/0565 access to education; credit transfer; higher education

10/0585 educational policy; educationally disadvantaged; equal education; politics-education relationship; secondary schools

10/0629 longitudinal studies; TVEI

10/0663 comprehensive schools; educational history; secondary education

10/0671 administrator role; head teachers; management in education; role conflict; secondary schools; teacher role

10/0674 educational administration; grant maintained schools; management in education; school based management

10/0713 Education Reform Act 1988; educational policy; politics-education relationship

10/0769 educational history; educational policy

10/0847 classroom research; curriculum research; Education Reform Act 1988; educational experience; infant schools; mathematics education

10/0870 educational administration; local management of schools; school based management

10/0878 education vouchers; educational policy; politics-education relationship

10/0883 Education Reform Act 1988; educational development; educational planning; educational policy; government role; local education authorities

10/0896 governing bodies; local management of schools; school based management; school governors

10/0902 local management of schools; National Curriculum; physical education; sports

10/0923 core curriculum; curriculum development; educational administration; educational development; interdisciplinary approach; National Curriculum

10/0924 Education Reform Act 1988; educational administration; local management of schools; school based management; secondary schools

10/0947 educational legislation; educational policy; primary schools; urban schools

10/1094 inspection; secondary schools; teacher attitudes

10/1095 National Curriculum; primary schools

10/1207 inspection; teacher attitudes

10/1208 educational administration; educational policy; local education authorities; special educational needs

10/1224 change strategies; primary schools; school based management; school organisation; staff-school relationship

10/1234 parent attitudes; preservice teacher education; primary school teachers; student teacher attitudes; teacher attitudes; teaching profession

10/1239 curriculum development; English studies curriculum; National Curriculum; secondary education

10/1240 discipline policy; disruptive pupils; expulsion; primary schools; problem children; special educational needs; suspension

10/1241 agricultural colleges; agricultural education; economic change; further education; staff development

10/1255 evaluation; local management of schools; school based management; secondary schools

10/1261 institutional advancement; marketing

10/1385 equal education; gender equality; school policy; sex differences

10/1444 assessment; curriculum development; environmental education; mathematics education; National Curriculum; Scotland; teaching process

10/1495 further education; further education teachers; staff development

10/1540 China

10/1604 Education Reform Act 1988; primary education; religious education

10/1609 educational administration; grant maintained schools; management in education; school based management

10/1644 educational administration; further education; higher education

10/1742 Education Reform Act 1988; educational legislation; educational policy; local education authorities

10/1754 educational innovation; local education authorities; special educational needs

10/1794 National Curriculum; projects – learning activities; pupil projects; teaching methods

EDUCATIONAL COOPERATION

10/0746 cluster grouping; special educational needs; special schools

10/0752 cluster grouping; special educational needs; special schools

EDUCATIONAL DEVELOPMENT

10/0379 language of instruction; language policy; mother tongue; Wales; Welsh; Welsh speaking schools

10/0816 higher education; prediction; universities

10/0883 Education Reform Act 1988; educational change; educational planning; educational policy; government role; local education authorities

10/0923 core curriculum; curriculum development; educational administration; educational change; interdisciplinary approach; National Curriculum

10/1785 early childhood education; educational quality; preschool education; quality control

10/1788 early childhood education; educational quality; nursery schools; play groups; preschool education; quality control

EDUCATIONAL DISCRIMINATION

10/1709 ethnic groups; higher education; student recruitment

EDUCATIONAL ECONOMICS

10/0654 course evaluation; economics-education relationship; educational administration; entrepreneurship; further education

10/0882 cost effectiveness; developing countries; educational finance; efficiency

10/0890 educational finance; Sudan

10/1017 age differences; educational finance; resource allocation

EDUCATIONAL ENVIRONMENT

10/0074 developing countries; educational administration; educational finance

10/0187 change strategies; educational research; organisational change; research methodology

10/0460 institutional environment; stress – psychological; stress management; stress variables; teacher morale

10/0916 pastoral care – education; school organisation

10/1247 educational philosophy; pastoral care – education; pupil-school relationship; pupil welfare

EDUCATIONAL EQUIPMENT

10/0097 architectural education; blindness; special educational needs; visual impairments

10/1178 computer assisted learning; earth science; microscopes; simulation; special educational needs

EDUCATIONAL EXPERIENCE

10/0559 academic achievement; higher education; mature students; student attitudes

10/0847 classroom research; curriculum research; Education Reform Act 1988; educational change; infant schools; mathematics education

10/1482 employment qualifications; National Vocational Qualifications; vocational education

10/1589 higher education; mature students; men; sex differences; student attitudes; women's education

10/1664 longitudinal studies; primary education; primary school pupils; pupil-school relationship

EDUCATIONAL FACILITIES IMPROVEMENT

10/1411 campuses; school space

10/1423 campuses; school space

EDUCATIONAL FINANCE

10/0012 fund raising; income; money management; school funds; secondary schools

10/0014 financial support; universities; university administration

10/0074 developing countries; educational administration; educational environment

10/0075 financial policy; financial support; local management of schools

10/0079 educational planning; local education authorities

10/0081 Education Reform Act 1988; educational administration; educational change; grant maintained schools; open entry; parent choice; school based management

10/0086 educational administration; educational software; resource allocation; school effectiveness

10/0163 educational policy; higher education; local education authorities

10/0165 consumer economics; educational administration; educational change; educational policy; politics-education relationship
10/0627 adult education; continuing education; educational policy; European Community; financial support
10/0856 economics-education relationship; educational benefits; employment opportunities; outcomes of education; rewards; work-education relationship
10/0882 cost effectiveness; developing countries; educational economics; efficiency
10/0890 educational economics; Sudan
10/1014 educational administration; local management of schools; mainstreaming; resource allocation; school based management; special educational needs
10/1017 age differences; educational economics; resource allocation
10/1038 budgeting; educational administration; local management of schools; school based management
10/1654 citizenship; educational history; educational objectives; politics-education relationship
10/1682 educational quality; primary schools; Saudi Arabia

EDUCATIONAL GUIDANCE
10/0132 higher education; student counselling
10/1332 access to education; adult education; adult students; community education; mature students; student attitudes
10/1345 access to education; adult education; adult students; mature students; Scotland

EDUCATIONAL HISTORY
10/0640 10/0691
10/0032 institutional administration; universities
10/0173 children's literature; comics – publications; girls; popular culture; sex role; textbooks; women's education
10/0265 management in education; Scotland
10/0296 adult education; mechanics' institutes
10/0330 educational research; Scotland
10/0400 comparative education; educational policy; Scotland
10/0405 Scotland
10/0409 parent participation; parent-school relationship
10/0411 comparative education; educational policy; Scotland; teacher education
10/0414 educational policy; politics-education relationship; South Africa
10/0415 educational change; Scotland
10/0416 educational psychology; educational theories
10/0445 curriculum development; secondary education; technical education
10/0470 Catholic schools; church and education; church-state relationship; educational policy; Roman Catholic Church
10/0475 church and education; church-state relationship; educational legislation; nonconformity; religion and education
10/0479 church-education relationship; educational philosophy
10/0500 educational theories; philosophy
10/0501 earth science; geology education; physical sciences; science education
10/0516 educational change; educational policy
10/0539 training; women's education; women's employment
10/0551 educational administration; educational policy; public education; secondary education; tripartite system
10/0554 educational policy; educational principles; school systems; secondary education; secondary modern schools; tripartite system; working class
10/0600 adult education; India
10/0602 adult education; social history; working class
10/0606 adult education; biographies; extension education; universities; working class
10/0607 adult education; educational policy; extension education; working class
10/0614 adult education; comparative education; extension education

10/0635 science education
10/0651 primary education; science curriculum; science education
10/0663 comprehensive schools; educational change; secondary education
10/0667 Jamaica; preservice teacher education
10/0685 comparative education; educational theories; progressive education
10/0688 head teachers
10/0693 higher education; professional education; universities; women's education; women's employment
10/0702 France; intelligence tests; psychological testing; psychology
10/0766 adult education; continuing education
10/0769 educational change; educational policy
10/0874 educational psychology; teacher education
10/0875 preservice teacher education
10/0908 educational administration; management in education
10/0922 church-education relationship; educational legislation; financial support; free education; school governors
10/1194 boys; preparatory schools
10/1223 comparative education; educational quality; school effectiveness; United States of America
10/1260 special educational needs; special schools
10/1263 educational theories; elementary schools; Montessori method
10/1305 curriculum development; discovery learning; primary education; projects – learning activities; pupil projects; teaching methods
10/1654 citizenship; educational finance; educational objectives; politics-education relationship
10/1657 educational policy; further education; women's education
10/1766 examination syllabuses; science education; university examinations
10/1769 examinations; science education; universities

EDUCATIONAL IMPROVEMENT
10/0109 developing countries; inservice teacher education; Pakistan; primary education; programme evaluation
10/0178 educational innovation; educational quality; school effectiveness
10/1690 developing countries; secondary education; Sierra Leone

EDUCATIONAL INNOVATION
10/0007 access to education; disadvantaged environment; educationally disadvantaged; Scotland
10/0178 educational improvement; educational quality; school effectiveness
10/0412 educational policy; middle school education; Scotland
10/1448 change strategies; programme evaluation; TVEI
10/1730 programme evaluation; urban schools; whole school approach
10/1754 educational change; local education authorities; special educational needs

EDUCATIONAL LEGISLATION
10/0475 church and education; church-state relationship; educational history; nonconformity; religion and education
10/0486 Education Reform Act 1988; educational change; educational planning; primary schools; school size; small schools
10/0922 church-education relationship; educational history; financial support; free education; school governors
10/0947 educational change; educational policy; primary schools; urban schools
10/1736 educational policy; educationally disadvantaged; expulsion; problem children; pupil alienation
10/1742 Education Reform Act 1988; educational change; educational policy; local education authorities

EDUCATIONAL MATERIAL EVALUATION
10/0274 educational materials; medical education
10/1652 educational materials; material development; science education; scientific attitudes; scientific literacy; supported self study; teacher education

EDUCATIONAL MATERIALS
10/0054 industry-education relationship; mathematics education
10/0104 blindness; computer assisted reading; computer software; computer system design; partial vision; visual impairments
10/0144 Belize; developing countries; material development; textbooks
10/0179 comparative education; mainstreaming; special educational needs; teacher education
10/0195 computer software; energy education; material development; science education
10/0242 course content; Italian; modern language studies; multimedia approach
10/0272 learning strategies; medical education; medical students
10/0274 educational material evaluation; medical education
10/0292 comparative education; cultural education; second language learning; teaching methods
10/0307 exercise; health activities; health promotion; heart rate; physical activities; primary school pupils
10/0325 communication aids – for disabled; disabilities; special educational needs
10/0346 developing countries; development education; literacy; material development; reading materials
10/0347 Arabic; Chinese languages; Japanese; nonwestern languages; second language learning
10/0349 curriculum development; drama; learning experience
10/0447 City Technology Colleges; dyslexia; learning disabilities; special educational needs; teaching methods
10/0454 environmental education; outdoor education; publications; resource materials
10/0455 environmental education; publications; social studies
10/0456 curriculum development; English – second language; second language teaching; Senegal
10/0503 earth science; material development; National Curriculum; physical sciences; science education
10/0521 educational media; low vision aids; printing; textbooks
10/0548 artificial intelligence; computer assisted learning; material development
10/0770 educational administration; management development; management in education; material development
10/0771 educational administration; management development; management in education; material development
10/0772 educational administration; management in education; material development
10/0813 guides; health education; nurse education; nurses; smoking
10/0829 acquired immune deficiency syndrome; health education
10/0949 cartoons; science education
10/1056 acquired immune deficiency syndrome; nurses; sexually transmitted diseases
10/1155 classroom research; educational technology; interactive video; mathematics education; multimedia approach
10/1169 computer assisted learning; educational media; open education
10/1171 computers; metaphors; reasoning
10/1219 assessment; mathematics achievement; mathematics education; National Curriculum
10/1246 drama education; English studies curriculum; National Curriculum
10/1354 classroom discipline; discipline; discipline policy
10/1422 college-school cooperation; flexible learning; material development; preservice teacher education
10/1429 flexible learning; material development; medical education

10/1430 acquired immune deficiency syndrome; educational technology; health education; interactive video; material development; sex education

10/1432 biographies; educational technology; material development; optical data discs

10/1469 Latin; textbook preparation

10/1586 English – second language; textbooks; vocabulary development

10/1618 chemistry education; learning strategies; multimedia approach; science education; skills; teaching methods; transfer of learning

10/1648 curriculum development; experiential learning; material development; primary education; technology education; work-education relationship

10/1652 educational material evaluation; material development; science education; scientific attitudes; scientific literacy; supported self study; teacher education

10/1658 history studies; pictorial stimuli; teaching methods; visual aids

10/1666 preservice teacher education

10/1763 inservice teacher education; primary school teachers; science education; scientific concepts

10/1781 corporate support; primary education; programme evaluation; science education; technology education

10/1802 inservice teacher education; science education; Swaziland

EDUCATIONAL MEDIA

10/0126 learner centred methods; learning resources centres; management development; management studies; multimedia approach

10/0436 distance education; infant school teachers; inservice education; international educational exchange; Sweden; telecommunications

10/0521 educational materials; low vision aids; printing; textbooks

10/0762 mass media; material development; production techniques

10/0948 audiovisual aids; language acquisition; second language teaching; teaching methods; videodiscs

10/1169 computer assisted learning; educational materials; open education

10/1549 computer uses in education; distance education; educational technology; evaluation; flexible learning

EDUCATIONAL NEEDS

10/0066 adult day centres; caregivers; services; special educational needs

10/0703 economic change; educational policy; poland; social change; youth

EDUCATIONAL OBJECTIVES

10/0495 institutional evaluation; organisational effectiveness; performance indicators

10/0506 French; modern language studies

10/0508 educational philosophy; quality of life; well being

10/0599 access programmes; continuing education; educational benefits; women's education

10/1626 behavioural objectives; comprehension; learning experience; test use

10/1654 citizenship; educational finance; educational history; politics-education relationship

EDUCATIONAL PHILOSOPHY

10/0355 mathematics

10/0479 church-education relationship; educational history

10/0508 educational objectives; quality of life; well being

10/0686 curriculum development; individual development; moral education; physical education; religious education

10/0931 linguistics; mathematics education

10/1173 cultural influences; curriculum; ideology

10/1247 educational environment; pastoral care – education; pupil-school relationship; pupil welfare

10/1249 moral education; Taiwan

10/1716 basic skills; critical thinking; problem solving; skills; transfer of learning

10/1728 ethics; moral education; moral values; realism; reasoning

EDUCATIONAL PLANNING

10/0079 educational finance; local education authorities

10/0486 Education Reform Act 1988; educational change; educational legislation; primary schools; school size; small schools

10/0518 educational policy; policy formation; policy makers

10/0647 development plans; planning; primary schools; whole school approach

10/0883 Education Reform Act 1988; educational change; educational development; educational policy; government role; local education authorities

10/0994 antiracism education; Education Reform Act 1988; equal education; local education authorities; multicultural education

10/1111 colleges of further education; educational administration; management in education; marketing

10/1175 management in education; university administration

10/1352 school based management

EDUCATIONAL POLICY

10/0024 access to education; Canada natives; qualifications

10/0057 educational administration; educational change; school based management; special educational needs; support services

10/0084 developing countries; educational administration; politics-education relationship; school systems

10/0096 educational administration; educational change; governance; local education authorities; management in education; politics-education relationship

10/0125 adult education; citizenship; comparative education; consumer economics; Poland

10/0149 educational change; mass media effects; press opinion; public opinion

10/0161 educational change; politics-education relationship

10/0162 educational administration; educational change; governance; governing bodies; local education authorities; management in education

10/0163 educational finance; higher education; local education authorities

10/0165 consumer economics; educational administration; educational change; educational finance; politics-education relationship

10/0263 academic staff development; inservice teacher education; professional development; Scotland

10/0331 educational practices; physical education; sports

10/0332 India; primary education

10/0398 comparative education; educational practices; international education

10/0400 comparative education; educational history; Scotland

10/0411 comparative education; educational history; Scotland; teacher education

10/0412 educational innovation; middle school education; Scotland

10/0414 educational history; politics-education relationship; South Africa

10/0427 politics-education relationship; Scotland

10/0428 educational administration; management in education; politics-education relationship; Scotland

10/0470 Catholic schools; church and education; church-state relationship; educational history; Roman Catholic Church

10/0478 Arab states; developing countries; development education

10/0505 equal education; gender equality; nondiscriminatory education

10/0516 educational change; educational history

10/0518 educational planning; policy formation; policy makers

10/0551 educational administration; educational history; public education; secondary education; tripartite system

10/0554 educational history; educational principles; school systems; secondary education; secondary modern schools; tripartite system; working class

10/0585 educational change; educationally disadvantaged; equal education; politics-education relationship; secondary schools

10/0607 adult education; educational history; extension education; working class

10/0627 adult education; continuing education; educational finance; European Community; financial support

10/0703 economic change; educational needs; Poland; social change; youth

10/0713 Education Reform Act 1988; educational change; politics-education relationship

10/0753 special educational needs

10/0757 seminars; special educational needs

10/0769 educational change; educational history

10/0877 politics-education relationship

10/0878 education vouchers; educational change; politics-education relationship

10/0883 Education Reform Act 1988; educational change; educational development; educational planning; government role; local education authorities

10/0947 educational change; educational legislation; primary schools; urban schools

10/1135 graduate study; higher education; overseas students

10/1201 comparative education; industry-education relationship; politics-education relationship; United States of America

10/1206 comparative education; educational administration; Italy; mainstreaming; Scandinavia; special educational needs; support services

10/1208 educational administration; educational change; local education authorities; special educational needs

10/1389 sociology of education

10/1455 comparative analysis; mainstreaming; special educational needs; special schools

10/1494 curriculum development; economics-education relationship; labour market; politics-education relationship; vocational education

10/1519 cultural influences; developing countries

10/1526 China; primary education

10/1583 bilingual education; bilingualism; language policy; school effectiveness; Welsh; Welsh studies

10/1657 educational history; further education; womens education

10/1667 educational administration; local management of schools; management in education; organisational change

10/1672 inspection; inspectors – of schools; quality control

10/1685 equal education; gender equality; nepal; womens education

10/1736 educational legislation; educationally disadvantaged; expulsion; problem children; pupil alienation

10/1739 behaviour problems; disruptive pupils; Education Reform Act 1988; emotional problems; problem children; school policy

10/1742 Education Reform Act 1988; educational change; educational legislation; local education authorities

10/1774 comparative education; Cyprus; Greece; school systems

EDUCATIONAL PRACTICES

10/0331 educational policy; physical education; sports

10/0398 comparative education; educational policy; international education

10/1133 adult education; higher education; information technology; physical sciences; science education

10/1222 centralisation; international education; multicultural education; National Curriculum

10/1454 academic achievement; pupil improvement; secondary schools; support services; underachievement

10/1645 adult basic education; adult educators; teaching methods; theory-practice relationship

10/1750 grant maintained schools; institutional autonomy; institutional characteristics; school based management

EDUCATIONAL PRINCIPLES
10/0554 educational history; educational policy; school systems; secondary education; secondary modern schools; tripartite system; working class
10/1725 attitudes

EDUCATIONAL PSYCHOLOGY
10/0416 educational history; educational theories
10/0874 educational history; teacher education

EDUCATIONAL QUALITY
10/0116 National Vocational Qualifications; performance indicators; vocational education
10/0142 Belize; developing countries; development education; primary education
10/0178 educational improvement; educational innovation; school effectiveness
10/0240 course evaluation
10/0247 comparative education
10/0383 industry-higher education relationship; quality control; vocational education; work-education relationship
10/0413 quality assurance; school effectiveness; secondary schools
10/0433 hearing impairments; mainstreaming; peripatetic teachers; special educational needs; support teachers; teacher effectiveness
10/0504 outcomes of education; parent-school relationship; school effectiveness; success
10/0519 economic factors; management in education; marketing; primary schools
10/0529 higher education; institutional role; performance contracts
10/0730 assessment; National Curriculum; school effectiveness
10/0734 achievement; performance factors; performance indicators; school effectiveness
10/0795 higher education; teacher effectiveness
10/0822 assessment; higher education
10/0832 cross curricular approach; curriculum development; National Curriculum
10/0925 management in education; school based management
10/1023 course evaluation; higher education; performance indicators; quality control; student attitudes; teacher effectiveness; universities
10/1035 evaluation criteria; institutional evaluation; performance indicators; school effectiveness
10/1077 achievement; examination results; outcomes of education; performance factors; performance indicators; school effectiveness
10/1087 college effectiveness; further education; institutional characteristics; performance factors; performance indicators
10/1223 comparative education; educational history; school effectiveness; United States of America
10/1230 accreditation – courses; accrediting authorities; assessment; external examiners; higher education; open universities
10/1231 assessment; external examiners; higher education; quality control
10/1349 further education; higher education; industry-higher education relationship; institutional role; performance contracts; programme evaluation
10/1377 inspection; institutional evaluation; local education authorities; school effectiveness
10/1380 accountability; measurement; performance indicators; school effectiveness; secondary schools
10/1426 preservice teacher education; quality control; student teachers; teaching practice
10/1443 colleges of further education; governing bodies
10/1605 higher education; quality assurance; quality control
10/1606 adult basic education; basic skills; colleges of further education; further education; programme evaluation
10/1682 educational finance; primary schools; Saudi Arabia
10/1743 course evaluation; student evaluation of teacher performance; teacher effectiveness; teaching methods; universities
10/1780 educational administration; higher education; institutes of higher education;

quality assurance; quality control
10/1785 early childhood education; educational development; preschool education; quality control
10/1788 early childhood education; educational development; nursery schools; play groups; preschool education; quality control
10/1789 school effectiveness; success

EDUCATIONAL RADIO
10/0695 adult education; educational broadcasting; local radio; mass media; radio
10/1057 educational broadcasting; educational television; radio; television

EDUCATIONAL RESEARCH
10/0008 Scotland
10/0187 change strategies; educational environment; organisational change; research methodology
10/0330 educational history; Scotland
10/0754 basic skills
10/0933 competency based teacher education; teacher education
10/1006 directories; environmental education
10/1043 comparative education; Europe; international educational exchange; research and development
10/1086 performance; statistical data
10/1330 action research; assessment; school based assessment
10/1331 academic achievement; achievement rating; assessment
10/1348 adult education
10/1362 statistical surveys
10/1451 research and development centres
10/1633 educational researchers; research; teacher education
10/1634 research; social science research
10/1639 information technology; policy; research; research opportunities; social science research

EDUCATIONAL RESEARCHERS
10/1157 careers
10/1633 educational research; research; teacher education

EDUCATIONAL RESOURCES
10/0236 environmental education; information needs; information sources
10/0237 environmental education; information needs; information sources
10/0791 music education; National Curriculum

EDUCATIONAL SOFTWARE
10/0028 computer assisted learning; computer uses in education; earth science
10/0086 educational administration; educational finance; resource allocation; school effectiveness
10/0324 computer assisted language learning; models
10/0718 computer assisted learning; computer uses in education; management studies
10/0788 computer uses in education; mathematics education; symbols – mathematics; visual learning
10/1085 computer software; computer uses in education; information technology; technology education
10/1184 computer uses in education; mathematics education; spreadsheets
10/1317 computer uses in education; geometry; mathematics education
10/1553 computer assisted learning; computer uses in education; interactive video
10/1581 computer assisted learning; multimedia approach; statistics education

EDUCATIONAL TECHNOLOGY
10/1155 classroom research; educational materials; interactive video; mathematics education; multimedia approach
10/1346 computer assisted learning; computer uses in education; medical education; medicine
10/1425 independent study; staff development
10/1430 acquired immune deficiency syndrome; educational materials; health education; interactive video; material development; sex education

10/1432 biographies; educational materials; material development; optical data discs
10/1549 computer uses in education; distance education; educational media; evaluation; flexible learning
10/1551 computer assisted learning; expert systems; optical data discs; training methods

EDUCATIONAL TELEVISION
10/1057 educational broadcasting; educational radio; radio; television

EDUCATIONAL THEORIES
10/0108 learning theories; psychology; teacher education; teaching experience; teaching practice; teaching process
10/0264 sociology of education
10/0302 primary school curriculum
10/0416 educational history; educational psychology
10/0500 educational history; philosophy
10/0685 comparative education; educational history; progressive education
10/1263 educational history; elementary schools; Montessori method
10/1308 sociology of knowledge

EDUCATIONALLY DISADVANTAGED
10/0007 access to education; disadvantaged environment; educational innovation; Scotland
10/0585 educational change; educational policy; equal education; politics-education relationship; secondary schools
10/1736 educational legislation; educational policy; expulsion; problem children; pupil alienation

EFFICIENCY
10/0882 cost effectiveness; developing countries; educational economics; educational finance

ELECTIVE MUTISM
10/0660 behaviour problems; inhibition; psychopathology; speech communication
10/0907 behaviour problems; communication disorders; problem children

ELECTRICAL ENGINEERING
10/0979 assessment

ELECTRICITY
10/0617 learning processes; physics education; science education; sixth form education

ELECTROENCEPHALOGRAPH
10/0955 adolescents; epilepsy; handicap identification

ELECTRONIC BOOKS
10/1552 computer assisted learning; human-computer interaction; hypermedia; information technology; multimedia approach; optical data discs

ELECTRONIC MAIL
10/1569 cross cultural studies; European studies; international education; social history; telecommunications
10/1570 cross cultural studies; European studies; preservice teacher education; telecommunications
10/1571 cultural awareness; intercultural communication; language proficiency; modern language studies; telecommunications

ELEMENTARY SCHOOLS
10/1263 educational history; educational theories; Montessori method

EMOTIONAL ADJUSTMENT
10/1146 adaptive behaviour – of disabled; attitude measures; blindness; measurement techniques; rehabilitation; visual impairments

EMOTIONAL DEVELOPMENT
10/1773 nurse education; nurses; professional development; student development

EMOTIONAL DISTURBANCES
10/0553 behaviour disorders; special educational

needs; statements – special educational needs
10/0988 behaviour disorders; special educational
needs; special schools
10/1484 behaviour disorders; child psychiatry;
locus of control

EMOTIONAL PROBLEMS
10/1302 behaviour problems; family problems;
learning disabilities; problem children; social
experience
10/1336 antisocial behaviour; behaviour
problems; pupil problems; social behaviour;
special educational needs
10/1739 behaviour problems; disruptive pupils;
Education Reform Act 1988; educational
policy; problem children; school policy

EMOTIONAL RESPONSE
10/1172 affective behaviour; mathematics;
student behaviour

EMOTIONS
10/1438 administration; employment practices;
sex differences; sexuality

EMPLOYER ATTITUDES
10/0299 graduate employment; graduates;
mathematical ability; numeracy;
work-education relationship

EMPLOYER SUPPORTED DAY CARE
10/0708 evaluation methods; institutional
evaluation; self evaluation – groups

EMPLOYERS
10/0164 corporate support; enterprise education;
industry-higher education relationship; transfer
of learning
10/0231 financial support; professional
continuing education; sponsorship; staff
development

EMPLOYMENT
10/1130 adult vocational education; job skills;
job training; work-education relationship
10/1651 primary school pupils; social cognition;
work attitudes
10/1696 curriculum; industry-education
relationship; skills; work-education relationship

EMPLOYMENT OPPORTUNITIES
10/0856 economics-education relationship;
educational benefits; educational finance;
outcomes of education; rewards;
work-education relationship
10/0903 academic staff; equal opportunities –
jobs; higher education; universities; women
teachers; women's employment
10/1369 academic staff; academic staff
promotion; equal opportunities – jobs; further
education; higher education
10/1461 labour market; learner educational
objectives; occupational aspiration;
opportunities; secondary school pupils;
work-education relationship
10/1462 career choice; labour market; learner
educational objectives; occupational
aspiration; school to work transition;
secondary school pupils; work-education
relationship

EMPLOYMENT PATTERNS
10/1190 adult vocational education; training;
unemployment
10/1200 deputy head teachers; head teachers;
teacher employment; teacher mobility; teacher
recruitment; teacher supply and demand;
teaching profession

EMPLOYMENT PRACTICES
10/1438 administration; emotions; sex
differences; sexuality
10/1442 colleges of further education;
comparable worth; equal pay; job analysis;
occupational information; salaries

EMPLOYMENT QUALIFICATIONS
10/0787 National Vocational Qualifications;
vocational education
10/1482 educational experience; National

Vocational Qualifications; vocational
education

ENERGY EDUCATION
10/0195 computer software; educational
materials; material development; science
education
10/0834 physics education; science education

ENGINEERING
10/1503 clubs; curriculum enrichment;
engineers; industry-education relationship

ENGINEERING EDUCATION
10/0450 career development; engineers; training;
work-education relationship
10/0783 mathematical models; mathematics
education; spreadsheets

ENGINEERS
10/0450 career development; engineering
education; training; work-education relationship
10/1503 clubs; curriculum enrichment;
engineering; industry-education relationship

ENGLISH
10/1245 minority groups; multilingualism;
teaching methods
10/1810 comparative education; German;
language tests; modern language studies;
native speakers; second language teaching

ENGLISH – SECOND LANGUAGE
10/0052 Oman; second language teaching
10/0198 comparative education; international
educational exchange; second language
teaching
10/0222 language proficiency; language teachers;
second language teaching
10/0286 Cameroon; cross curricular approach;
language of instruction; mathematics education
10/0290 Arab states; second language teaching
10/0293 Arab states; English for specific
purposes; programme evaluation
10/0295 cultural awareness; German; modern
language studies; textbook evaluation
10/0309 Arab states; cultural awareness; foreign
culture; native speakers; second language
learning
10/0421 Malaysia; secondary schools
10/0422 Malaysia; secondary schools
10/0424 higher education; language of
instruction; Saudi Arabia
10/0456 curriculum development; educational
materials; second language teaching; Senegal
10/0461 developing countries; second language
teaching
10/0490 computer uses in education; second
language learning
10/0644 inservice teacher education; language
teachers; second language teaching; Thailand
10/0656 class size; second language learning;
second language teaching
10/0716 bilingual education programmes; ethnic
groups; home-school relationship; literacy
education; parent participation; reading
teaching; second language learning
10/0764 Mozambique; radio; second language
learning
10/0872 Arab states; higher education
10/1282 bilingual education; bilingualism; ethnic
groups; language of instruction
10/1300 community centres; community
education; community programmes; day care
centres; ethnic groups; racial integration;
social integration
10/1391 English for academic purposes; lecture
method; overseas students; teaching styles
10/1393 inservice teacher education; Saudi
Arabia; second language teaching
10/1394 Brazil; second language teaching
10/1395 languages for specific purposes;
Malaysia; second language learning
10/1396 communicative competence –
languages; Korea; language tests; second
language teaching
10/1586 educational materials; textbooks;
vocabulary development
10/1590 Arabs; vowels; word recognition
10/1707 computer assisted language learning;

English for academic purposes; overseas
students; second language learning
10/1708 Greece
10/1803 bilingual pupils; language teachers;
limited English speaking; second language
teaching
10/1809 English for academic purposes; limited
English speaking; overseas students; second
language learning

ENGLISH FOR ACADEMIC PURPOSES
10/1391 English – second language; lecture
method; overseas students; teaching styles
10/1707 computer assisted language learning;
English – second language; overseas students;
second language learning
10/1809 English – second language; limited
English speaking; overseas students; second
language learning

ENGLISH FOR SPECIFIC PURPOSES
10/0293 Arab states; English – second language;
programme evaluation

ENGLISH LITERATURE
10/0181 developmental continuity; higher
education; sixteen to nineteen education;
teaching methods
10/0212 English studies curriculum; literature
studies

ENGLISH STUDIES
10/0327 curriculum development; educational
assessment; educational change; Scotland
10/0335 assessment; attainment tests; language
tests; Scotland
10/0978 assessment; attainment tests; geography
education; mathematics education; National
Curriculum – Northern Ireland; Northern
Ireland; science education
10/0997 assessment; National Curriculum;
reading achievement; standard assessment
tasks; writing skills
10/1002 assessment; core curriculum;
mathematics education; National Curriculum;
science education
10/1084 assessment; evaluation; mathematics
education; National Curriculum; science
education; secondary education; technology
education
10/1097 language teachers; National Curriculum
10/1105 grammar; student teachers
10/1250 English studies teachers; Kenya;
teaching styles
10/1390 language skills; modern language studies
10/1434 assessment; oral English; school based
assessment; speech communication

ENGLISH STUDIES CURRICULUM
10/0041 differentiated curriculum; learning
disabilities; low achievement; mainstreaming;
special educational needs
10/0077 creative writing; literary genres;
National Curriculum; writing – composition;
writing skills
10/0212 English literature; literature studies
10/0213 computer uses in education; information
technology; optical data discs
10/1239 curriculum development; educational
change; National Curriculum; secondary
education
10/1246 drama education; educational materials;
National Curriculum
10/1253 drama education; National Curriculum;
scripts; secondary education
10/1719 evaluation; monitoring; National
Curriculum
10/1759 language skills; listening skills; National
Curriculum; oracy; speech skills

ENGLISH STUDIES TEACHERS
10/1250 English studies; Kenya; teaching styles

ENROLMENT
10/0122 dropout research; dropouts; higher
education; student behaviour
10/1074 access to education; admission criteria;
open entry; parent choice; secondary schools

ENTERPRISE EDUCATION
10/0164 corporate support; employers; industry-higher education relationship; transfer of learning
10/0285 industry-education relationship; learning strategies; motivation; skill development; transfer of learning
10/0545 higher education; programme evaluation; work-education relationship
10/0555 industry-higher education relationship; institutes of higher education
10/0648 industrial secondments; industry-education relationship; placement; preservice teacher education; student teachers
10/0736 cross curricular approach; curriculum development; economics education; teacher education
10/0937 industrial secondments; industry-education relationship; preservice teacher education; science teachers; student teachers
10/1149 further education; work-education relationship
10/1238 assessment; higher education; learning strategies; skill development; work-education relationship
10/1341 industry-higher education relationship
10/1598 cross curricular approach; curriculum development; economics education; primary education; secondary education; Wales

ENTREPRENEURSHIP
10/0654 course evaluation; economics-education relationship; educational administration; educational economics; further education
10/1643 industry-higher education relationship; science parks

ENVIRONMENTAL EDUCATION
10/0021 developing countries; development education
10/0022 geography
10/0236 educational resources; information needs; information sources
10/0237 educational resources; information needs; information sources
10/0300 conservation – environment; natural resources
10/0454 educational materials; outdoor education; publications; resource materials
10/0455 educational materials; publications; social studies
10/0679 curriculum development; higher education
10/0680 earth science; learning activities
10/0682 cross curricular approach; curriculum development; National Curriculum; polymers
10/0700 air pollution; conservation – environment; misconceptions; scientific concepts; secondary school pupils
10/1006 directories; educational research
10/1021 pupil attitudes; secondary school pupils
10/1117 concept formation; ecology; physical environment
10/1119 higher education
10/1120 agriculture; controversial issues – course content; preservice teacher education
10/1121 attitudes; conservation – environment; social change
10/1226 field studies; geographic location; local studies; story telling
10/1436 history studies; museums; preservice teacher education
10/1444 assessment; curriculum development; educational change; mathematics education; National Curriculum; Scotland; teaching process
10/1518 environmental research; Europe; European Community
10/1520 environmental research; global approach
10/1525 news reporting; public opinion
10/1528 agricultural education; developing countries; Zimbabwe
10/1556 curriculum development; pollution; waste disposal
10/1630 comparative education; curriculum development; school-community relationship
10/1713 conservation – environment; pressure groups

ENVIRONMENTAL RESEARCH
10/1518 environmental education; Europe; European Community
10/1520 environmental education; global approach

EPILEPSY
10/0939 higher education; student attitudes; student health and welfare
10/0954 special educational needs; special schools; statements – special educational needs
10/0955 adolescents; electroencephalograph; handicap identification

EPISTEMOLOGY
10/0167 cognitive processes; cognitive psychology; higher education; learning processes; memory

EQUAL EDUCATION
10/0056 academic achievement; school effectiveness; underachievement; urban schools
10/0170 access to education; higher education; Pakistan; women's education
10/0176 access to education; gender equality; higher education; social class
10/0442 access to education; accessibility – for disabled; disabilities; higher education; student recruitment
10/0505 educational policy; gender equality; nondiscriminatory education
10/0544 gender equality; transition education; TVEI
10/0580 access to education; ethnic groups; higher education; student experience; student recruitment
10/0585 educational change; educational policy; educationally disadvantaged; politics-education relationship; secondary schools
10/0605 ethnic groups; student recruitment; university admission
10/0894 TVEI
10/0994 antiracism education; Education Reform Act 1988; educational planning; local education authorities; multicultural education
10/1160 islamic education; Muslims; religion and education; religious cultural groups; single sex schools; women's education
10/1379 gender equality; school policy; secondary schools; whole school approach
10/1385 educational change; gender equality; school policy; sex differences
10/1388 personal space; school space
10/1472 equal facilities; ethnic groups; minority groups; religious cultural groups
10/1507 music; music education; sex differences
10/1550 access to education; cultural background; ethnic groups; higher education; inner city; women's education
10/1685 educational policy; gender equality; Nepal; women's education
10/1710 achievement; Afro Caribbean youth; assessment; black pupils; Education Reform Act 1988; ethnic groups; low achievement
10/1712 adult education; continuing education; minority groups
10/1714 disabilities; special educational needs
10/1722 local management of schools; racial discrimination; racial integration; school based management; secondary schools
10/1723 institutes of higher education; preservice teacher education; racial discrimination; racial integration
10/1731 postgraduate certificate in education; preservice teacher education; school based teacher education; student teacher attitudes

EQUAL FACILITIES
10/1472 equal education; ethnic groups; minority groups; religious cultural groups
10/1625 construction – process; construction materials; gender equality; primary education; science education; sex differences; technology education

EQUAL OPPORTUNITIES – JOBS
10/0004 gender equality; promotion – occupational; teaching profession; women teachers; women's employment
10/0072 career ladders; careers; France; job

training; work-education relationship
10/0903 academic staff; employment opportunities; higher education; universities; women teachers; women's employment
10/1337 teacher development; teacher evaluation; teaching profession
10/1369 academic staff; academic staff promotion; employment opportunities; further education; higher education

EQUAL PAY
10/1442 colleges of further education; comparable worth; employment practices; job analysis; occupational information; salaries

EQUIPMENT
10/0343 audiovisual education; calculators; mathematics education; undergraduate students

ERROR ANALYSIS – LANGUAGE
10/0378 second language learning; Welsh

ESSAYS
10/0338 comprehension; examination techniques; higher education; learning strategies; review – reexamination; study skills; writing – composition

ETHICS
10/0128 sports; sportsmanship; values
10/1134 acquired immune deficiency syndrome; adult education; sexually transmitted diseases; voluntary agencies
10/1724 moral education; multiculturalism; relativism – philosophy
10/1728 educational philosophy; moral education; moral values; realism; reasoning

ETHNIC GROUPS
10/0019 Canada natives; indigenous populations; newly qualified teachers; teacher background; teacher induction; teaching profession
10/0031 academic achievement; bilingualism; diglossia; language usage
10/0216 preservice teacher education
10/0391 career counselling; minority groups; secondary school pupils; vocational guidance
10/0426 Asians; bilingualism; language maintenance; language policy; minority groups; mother tongue
10/0528 academic staff; higher education; mature students; middle class students; student attitudes; student experience; working class
10/0580 access to education; equal education; higher education; student experience; student recruitment
10/0583 Asians; parent participation; parent-school relationship
10/0605 equal education; student recruitment; university admission
10/0666 multicultural education; primary schools
10/0716 bilingual education programmes; English – second language; home-school relationship; literacy education; parent participation; reading teaching; second language learning
10/0880 antiracism education; multicultural education
10/0928 blacks; social work teachers
10/0973 ethnic relations; intergroup relations; multiculturalism; racial relations; school policy; secondary schools
10/0974 adolescents; Chinese; cultural background; ethnicity; Hong Kong; migrants
10/0975 minority groups; multiculturalism; primary schools; voluntary schools
10/1114 preservice teacher education; student recruitment; teacher recruitment; teaching profession
10/1282 bilingual education; bilingualism; English – second language; language of instruction
10/1300 community centres; community education; community programmes; day care centres; English – second language; racial integration; social integration
10/1472 equal education; equal facilities; minority groups; religious cultural groups
10/1550 access to education; cultural background; equal education; higher education; inner city; women's education

10/1709 educational discrimination; higher education; student recruitment
10/1710 achievement; Afro Caribbean youth; assessment; black pupils; Education Reform Act 1988; equal education; low achievement

ETHNIC ORIGINS
10/0060 mother tongue; pupils; religion; surveys

ETHNIC RELATIONS
10/0973 ethnic groups; intergroup relations; multiculturalism; racial relations; school policy; secondary schools
10/1371 bullying; cooperation; intergroup relations; intervention; middle school education; pupil behaviour; social isolation
10/1737 friendship; intergroup relations; primary schools; pupil attitudes; racial relations; whites

ETHNIC STEREOTYPES
10/1614 primary school pupils; pupil attitudes; racial attitudes

ETHNICITY
10/0974 adolescents; Chinese; cultural background; ethnic groups; Hong Kong; migrants

ETHNOGRAPHY
10/1554 cultural education; degree requirements; higher education; second language learning; study abroad

EUROPE
10/0204 international education; international educational exchange
10/0308 comparative education; cultural awareness; Denmark; modern language studies
10/0959 adult education; comparative education; continuing education; cultural differences; lifelong learning
10/1009 international educational exchange; values education
10/1043 comparative education; educational research; international educational exchange; research and development
10/1090 adult counselling; career counselling; European Community; vocational guidance
10/1209 educational administration; management in education; teacher employment; teaching profession; women; women's employment
10/1286 developing countries; development education; information science; librarianship education
10/1370 citizenship; higher education; overseas employment; overseas students
10/1518 environmental education; environmental research; European Community

EUROPEAN COMMUNITY
10/0038 cultural activities; curriculum; sciences
10/0314 comparative education; curriculum development; modular courses; vocational education
10/0564 colleges of further education; community colleges; course evaluation; international programmes
10/0574 Germany; teacher mobility; teacher transfer; training
10/0604 professional associations; professional continuing education; qualifications; Single European Market
10/0627 adult education; continuing education; educational finance; educational policy; financial support
10/0953 accidents; comparative education; food standards; health education; nutrition education; safety education
10/1004 curriculum development; European studies; local education authorities
10/1090 adult counselling; career counselling; Europe; vocational guidance
10/1136 adult education; comparative education; continuing education; Germany; United Kingdom; vocational education
10/1481 European studies; inservice teacher education; intercultural programmes
10/1518 environmental education; environmental research; Europe
10/1615 preservice teacher education; teacher education curriculum

EUROPEAN HISTORY
10/1797 citizenship education; history studies

EUROPEAN STUDIES
10/0534 comparative education; preservice teacher education
10/1004 curriculum development; European Community; local education authorities
10/1481 European Community; inservice teacher education; intercultural programmes
10/1569 cross cultural studies; electronic mail; international education; social history; telecommunications
10/1570 cross cultural studies; electronic mail; preservice teacher education; telecommunications

EVALUATION
10/0030 assessment; examinations; moderation – marking; National Curriculum
10/0827 acquired immune deficiency syndrome; health education; training
10/0991 inspection; local education authorities; monitoring
10/1084 assessment; English studies; mathematics education; National Curriculum; science education; secondary education; technology education
10/1255 educational change; local management of schools; school based management; secondary schools
10/1549 computer uses in education; distance education; educational media; educational technology; flexible learning
10/1719 English studies curriculum; monitoring; National Curriculum

EVALUATION CRITERIA
10/1035 educational quality; institutional evaluation; performance indicators; school effectiveness

EVALUATION METHODS
10/0708 employer supported day care; institutional evaluation; self evaluation – groups
10/1007 career counselling; guidance objectives; measurement techniques; vocational guidance

EXAMINATION RESULTS
10/0058 institutional evaluation; performance indicators
10/0127 attendance patterns; business education; course evaluation; outcomes of education; sandwich courses; undergraduate study
10/0407 school effectiveness; secondary schools
10/0458 'A' level examinations; accountability; outcomes of education; performance indicators; programme effectiveness; school effectiveness
10/0731 departments; differential performance; outcomes of education; school effectiveness; secondary schools
10/1077 achievement; educational quality; outcomes of education; performance factors; performance indicators; school effectiveness

EXAMINATION SYLLABUSES
10/1766 educational history; science education; university examinations

EXAMINATION TECHNIQUES
10/0338 comprehension; essays; higher education; learning strategies; review – reexamination; study skills; writing – composition

EXAMINATIONS
10/0030 assessment; evaluation; moderation – marking; National Curriculum
10/0138 assessment; General Certificate of Secondary Education; low achievement; special educational needs
10/0268 assessment; competence; medical education; medicine; physicians
10/0282 assessment; competence; medical education; medicine; physicians
10/0983 assessment; physical education
10/1769 educational history; science education; universities

EXERCISE
10/0307 educational materials; health activities; health promotion; heart rate; physical activities; primary school pupils
10/0351 child psychology; health; physical activities; physical activity level

EXPERIENCE
10/1653 background; economics education; industry-education relationship; preservice teacher education; student teacher attitudes; student teachers

EXPERIENTIAL LEARNING
10/0045 preservice teacher education; prior learning; social work studies
10/0113 achievement; assessment; further education; National Vocational Qualifications; prior learning
10/0208 credits; industry-higher education relationship; job placement; work-education relationship
10/0701 critical thinking; medical education; professional continuing education; professional development; reflective teaching
10/0866 interpersonal competence; learning experience; preservice teacher education; student teachers; workshops
10/1163 interpersonal competence; locus of control; outcomes of education; stress – psychological; student experience; teacher education
10/1488 intellectual development; learning processes; learning strategies
10/1514 access to education; accreditation of prior learning; higher education; transfer of learning
10/1617 construction industry; learning activities; surveying education
10/1624 accreditation of prior learning; higher education
10/1648 curriculum development; educational materials; material development; primary education; technology education; work-education relationship

EXPERT SYSTEMS
10/0582 computer assisted learning; computer uses in education; management studies
10/0889 assessment; data processing
10/1551 computer assisted learning; educational technology; optical data discs; training methods

EXPLANATION
10/0767 comprehension; historiography; history; imagination
10/0778 reasoning; research methodology
10/0835 physical environment; public opinion; reasoning; scientific attitudes; scientific literacy
10/0839 science education

EXPRESSIVE LANGUAGE
10/1765 Down's Syndrome; interaction; language acquisition; mainstreaming; special educational needs; special schools

EXPULSION
10/0194 primary school pupils; pupil experience; suspension
10/0303 crime prevention; delinquency; discipline problems; programme evaluation; truancy
10/1063 attendance; discipline problems; disruptive pupils; truancy
10/1240 discipline policy; disruptive pupils; educational change; primary schools; problem children; special educational needs; suspension
10/1736 educational legislation; educational policy; educationally disadvantaged; problem children; pupil alienation

EXTENSION EDUCATION
10/0606 adult education; biographies; educational history; universities; working class
10/0607 adult education; educational history; educational policy; working class
10/0614 adult education; comparative education; educational history

EXTERNAL EXAMINERS
10/1230 accreditation – courses; accrediting authorities; assessment; educational quality; higher education; open universities
10/1231 assessment; educational quality; higher education; quality control

EXTRACURRICULAR ACTIVITIES
10/1521 colleges of further education; further education students; health promotion

FAILURE
10/0129 achievement; motivation; sports
10/1325 academic achievement; achievement; cognitive style; gifted; underachievement

FAMILY ATTITUDES
10/0801 family health; health education; sex education; sexuality

FAMILY HEALTH
10/0801 family attitudes; health education; sex education; sexuality
10/0802 family influence; smoking
10/0805 family influence; health education

FAMILY INCOME
10/0319 family influence; financial support; parent-child relationship; parent role; youth

FAMILY INFLUENCE
10/0319 family income; financial support; parent-child relationship; parent role; youth
10/0802 family health; smoking
10/0805 family health; health education
10/0852 adolescents; health; smoking
10/0853 behaviour problems; bullying; home environment; parent-child relationship; parent-pupil relationship; punishment; pupil behaviour
10/1757 attendance; educational attitudes; home-school relationship; truancy

FAMILY INVOLVEMENT
10/0817 communication research; health education
10/1049 family programmes; literacy; parent participation; reading skills; writing skills
10/1328 home-school relationship; parent participation; parent-pupil relationship

FAMILY LIFE
10/0175 nationalism; religion; state schools

FAMILY PLANNING
10/1636 community education; contraception; early parenthood; mothers; parenthood education; peer teaching; sex education

FAMILY PROBLEMS
10/0395 children at risk; community services; day care; family relationship
10/1302 behaviour problems; emotional problems; learning disabilities; problem children; social experience

FAMILY PROGRAMMES
10/0396 child rearing; children at risk; community services; programme evaluation; quality control
10/1049 family involvement; literacy; parent participation; reading skills; writing skills

FAMILY RELATIONSHIP
10/0395 children at risk; community services; day care; family problems

FARMS
10/1768 agricultural colleges; agricultural education

FEEDBACK
10/0353 computer uses in education; interaction; learning processes; peer teaching; teacher-pupil relationship
10/0726 group work; mathematics education; problem solving
10/0732 classroom communication; infant school education; infant school teachers; teacher-pupil relationship; teacher response
10/1446 computer uses in education; geometry; logo; mathematics education; problem solving

FEMINISM
10/1153 church and education; language usage; power structure; Protestant churches
10/1588 age differences; women's studies

FICTION
10/0675 books; children's literature; poetry; primary school pupils; reading; reading material selection
10/1288 antiracism education; children's literature; racial attitudes
10/1289 books; children's literature; secondary school pupils
10/1304 books; children's literature; geography education; history studies

FIELD DEPENDENCE-INDEPENDENCE
10/0610 cognitive processes; cognitive style; learning; mathematics; teaching styles

FIELD STUDIES
10/1141 adult education; adult learning; earth science; field studies centres; study abroad
10/1226 environmental education; geographic location; local studies; story telling

FIELD STUDIES CENTRES
10/1141 adult education; adult learning; earth science; field studies; study abroad

FIGURATIVE LANGUAGE
10/0655 child language; metaphors

FINANCE OCCUPATIONS
10/0227 access to education; mature students; professional education

FINANCIAL POLICY
10/0075 educational finance; financial support; local management of schools

FINANCIAL PROBLEMS
10/1329 adult students; mature students; student costs; student financial aid; student loans; student recruitment

FINANCIAL SUPPORT
10/0014 educational finance; universities; university administration
10/0075 educational finance; financial policy; local management of schools
10/0231 employers; professional continuing education; sponsorship; staff development
10/0234 inner city; investment; training; youth leaders; youth service
10/0319 family income; family influence; parent-child relationship; parent role; youth
10/0627 adult education; continuing education; educational finance; educational policy; European Community
10/0922 church-education relationship; educational history; educational legislation; free education; school governors
10/1524 developing countries; development aid; development education

FINE ARTS
10/0256 art education; assessment; comparative education; degrees – academic; Greece

FIRE SERVICE
10/0048 learning strategies; professional education; teaching methods

FIRST SCHOOLS
10/0588 assessment; infant schools; mathematics curriculum; mathematics teachers; standard assessment tasks

FLEXIBLE LEARNING
10/1413 staff development
10/1422 college-school cooperation; educational materials; material development; preservice teacher education
10/1429 educational materials; material development; medical education
10/1549 computer uses in education; distance education; educational media; educational technology; evaluation
10/1603 distance education; information science;

librarianship education; mature students
10/1775 medical schools; open education; teaching methods

FOLLOWUP STUDIES
10/0318 adult vocational education; outcomes of education; retraining; women's education; women's employment
10/0320 cohort analysis; longitudinal studies; school leavers; school to work transition; Scotland; sixteen to nineteen education; youth
10/1296 postgraduate certificate in education; student teachers; teacher development

FOOD
10/0202 body image; eating habits; health; self concept
10/1703 eating habits; health education; nutrition education

FOOD STANDARDS
10/0953 accidents; comparative education; European Community; health education; nutrition education; safety education

FORCE
10/0622 museums; science activities; science education; science teaching centres; scientific concepts

FOREIGN CULTURE
10/0309 Arab states; cultural awareness; English – second language; native speakers; second language learning

FRANCE
10/0072 career ladders; careers; equal opportunities – jobs; job training; work-education relationship
10/0154 comparative education; educational change; primary school teachers; teacher attitudes; teaching profession
10/0199 comparative education; primary education
10/0230 access to education; adult education; higher education; mature students; student participation
10/0301 comparative education; creativity; handwriting; writing research; writing skills
10/0664 activities; comparative education; outdoor pursuits; physical education
10/0702 educational history; intelligence tests; psychological testing; psychology
10/0786 comparative education; mathematics achievement; trainees
10/1213 comparative education; higher education; teacher education; United States of America

FREE EDUCATION
10/0922 church-education relationship; educational history; educational legislation; financial support; school governors

FRENCH
10/0506 educational objectives; modern language studies
10/0616 German; modern language studies; National Curriculum
10/1088 modern language studies
10/1252 assessment; General Certificate of Secondary Education; modern language studies; oral tests

FRIENDSHIP
10/1193 communication skills; early childhood education; infant school pupils; reception classes; social development; social isolation; young children
10/1737 ethnic relations; intergroup relations; primary schools; pupil attitudes; racial relations; whites

FUND RAISING
10/0012 educational finance; income; money management; school funds; secondary schools

FURTHER EDUCATION
10/0011 higher education; sixteen to nineteen education; student health and welfare; student needs

10/0023 college administration; colleges of further education; educational administration; institutional administration; organisational change
10/0112 open education; teaching methods
10/0113 achievement; assessment; experiential learning; National Vocational Qualifications; prior learning
10/0114 special educational needs; support services
10/0115 higher education; information retrieval; information systems; optical data discs; search strategies; student attitudes
10/0117 mainstreaming; severe learning difficulties; special educational needs; support services
10/0228 adult education; databases; higher education; mature students
10/0310 access to education; educational change; higher education; sixteen to nineteen education
10/0311 higher education; school to work transition; unemployment; vocational education; youth employment
10/0317 access to education; higher education; programme evaluation
10/0417 Switzerland
10/0517 administrators; educational administration; higher education; management in education; women; women's employment
10/0654 course evaluation; economics-education relationship; educational administration; educational economics; entrepreneurship
10/0684 industry-further education relationship; training; vocational education
10/0751 assessment; colleges of further education; diagnostic assessment; disabilities; moderate learning difficulties; special educational needs
10/0794 higher education; independent colleges; private education; private universities
10/0900 mainstreaming; special educational needs; visual impairments
10/1069 disabilities; further education students; literature reviews; moderate learning difficulties; special educational needs
10/1087 college effectiveness; educational quality; institutional characteristics; performance factors; performance indicators
10/1149 enterprise education; work-education relationship
10/1204 communication research; competency based education; higher education; learning processes; teaching methods
10/1241 agricultural colleges; agricultural education; economic change; educational change; staff development
10/1349 educational quality; higher education; industry-higher education relationship; institutional role; performance contracts; programme evaluation
10/1365 languages for specific purposes; modern language studies; second language teaching; vocational education
10/1369 academic staff; academic staff promotion; employment opportunities; equal opportunities – jobs; higher education
10/1439 choice of subjects; demography; pupil attitudes; sixteen to nineteen education
10/1495 educational change; further education teachers; staff development
10/1606 adult basic education; basic skills; colleges of further education; educational quality; programme evaluation
10/1644 educational administration; educational change; higher education
10/1646 mainstreaming; special educational needs; support services; support teachers
10/1657 educational history; educational policy; women's education
10/1700 access to education; programme evaluation; sixteen to nineteen education
10/1720 access to education; sixteen to nineteen education; student participation; tertiary education; vocational education
10/1777 higher education; National Vocational Qualifications; vocational education

FURTHER EDUCATION STUDENTS
10/1069 disabilities; further education; literature reviews; moderate learning difficulties; special educational needs

10/1096 higher education; literacy; reading skills; writing skills
10/1285 computer assisted learning; hypertext; information seeking; information sources
10/1521 colleges of further education; extracurricular activities; health promotion

FURTHER EDUCATION TEACHERS
10/1068 academic staff; higher education; stress – psychological; teacher workload
10/1355 course evaluation; teacher attitudes; teacher education
10/1495 educational change; further education; staff development

GAELIC
10/0418 Algeria; bilingualism; comparative education; language policy; mother tongue; Scotland

GENDER EQUALITY
10/0002 head teachers; sex stereotypes; teaching profession; women teachers; women's employment
10/0004 equal opportunities – jobs; promotion – occupational; teaching profession; women teachers; women's employment
10/0176 access to education; equal education; higher education; social class
10/0505 educational policy; equal education; nondiscriminatory education
10/0544 equal education; transition education; TVEI
10/0662 computer uses in education; humanities; information technology; sex differences
10/1379 equal education; school policy; secondary schools; whole school approach
10/1385 educational change; equal education; school policy; sex differences
10/1625 construction – process; construction materials; equal facilities; primary education; science education; sex differences; technology education
10/1683 Chile; comparative education; Israel; women's education
10/1684 Mauritius; women's education; women's employment
10/1685 educational policy; equal education; Nepal; women's education

GENERAL CERTIFICATE OF SECONDARY EDUCATION
10/0138 assessment; examinations; low achievement; special educational needs
10/0624 assessment; practical science; science activities; science education
10/0625 assessment; practical science; science activities; science education
10/1252 assessment; French; modern language studies; oral tests

GENETIC ENGINEERING
10/0087 biotechnology; pupil attitudes; science education

GEOGRAPHIC CONCEPTS
10/0201 geography education; primary education

GEOGRAPHIC LOCATION
10/1226 environmental education; field studies; local studies; story telling

GEOGRAPHY
10/0022 environmental education

GEOGRAPHY EDUCATION
10/0201 geographic concepts; primary education
10/0483 Gibraltar
10/0687 mathematics education; navigation; orientation; orienteering; outdoor pursuits; primary education
10/0845 earth science; inservice teacher education; National Curriculum
10/0964 assessment; assessment by teachers; National Curriculum
10/0977 assessment; assessment by teachers; attainment tests; National Curriculum; standard assessment tasks
10/0978 assessment; attainment tests; English studies; mathematics education; National

Curriculum – Northern Ireland; Northern Ireland; science education
10/1304 books; childrens literature; fiction; history studies
10/1659 assessment

GEOLOGY EDUCATION
10/0501 earth science; educational history; physical sciences; science education

GEOMETRY
10/0630 curriculum development; mathematics education; secondary education; South Africa
10/1317 computer uses in education; educational software; mathematics education
10/1446 computer uses in education; feedback; logo; mathematics education; problem solving

GEOMETRY EDUCATION
10/0615 Greece; mathematics education; problem solving

GERMAN
10/0295 cultural awareness; English – second language; modern language studies; textbook evaluation
10/0616 French; modern language studies; National Curriculum
10/1810 comparative education; English; language tests; modern language studies; native speakers; second language teaching

GERMANY
10/0124 comparative education; economic change; economics-education relationship; industry-education relationship; structural unemployment; training; work-education relationship
10/0229 access to education; adult education; higher education; mature students; student participation
10/0574 European Community; teacher mobility; teacher transfer; training
10/1136 adult education; comparative education; continuing education; European Community; United Kingdom; vocational education

GHANA
10/0143 comparative education; higher education; modular courses; universities
10/0344 developing countries; development education
10/0594 industry-education relationship; science education
10/1162 assessment; assessment by teachers; comparative education

GIBRALTAR
10/0483 geography education

GIFTED
10/0304 computer uses in education; individualised methods; Jordan; mathematics; primary education
10/0858 cognitive ability; memory
10/1044 ability; computer uses in education; information technology; primary school pupils
10/1325 academic achievement; achievement; cognitive style; failure; underachievement
10/1557 comparative education; special schools
10/1767 academic ability; academic failure; pupil behaviour; underachievement
10/1776 programme evaluation; Singapore
10/1806 autism; Down's Syndrome; drawing; special educational needs; visual arts

GIRLS
10/0173 childrens literature; comics – publications; educational history; popular culture; sex role; textbooks; women's education
10/0540 leisure time; recreational activities; women's studies
10/1622 sex differences; sex stereotypes

GLOBAL APPROACH
10/0637 climate; physical environment; scientific attitudes; social attitudes
10/0930 citizenship education; teacher education
10/1520 environmental education; environmental research

GOVERNANCE
10/0096 educational administration; educational
change; educational policy; local education
authorities; management in education;
politics-education relationship
10/0162 educational administration; educational
change; educational policy; governing bodies;
local education authorities; management in
education
10/0809 educational administration; head
teachers; school governing bodies; school
governors

GOVERNING BODIES
10/0162 educational administration; educational
change; educational policy; governance; local
education authorities; management in
education
10/0896 educational change; local management
of schools; school based management; school
governors
10/0912 educational administration; head
teachers; management in education; school
governors
10/0914 early childhood education; nursery
schools; parent attitudes; parent school
relationship; preschool education; school
governors
10/0957 educational administration; primary
schools; school governors
10/1420 educational administration; school
boards – Scotland; school governors
10/1443 colleges of further education;
educational quality

GOVERNMENT – ADMINISTRATIVE BODY
10/0404 home-school relationship; industry-
education relationship

GOVERNMENT ROLE
10/0883 Education Reform Act 1988;
educational change; educational development;
educational planning; educational policy; local
education authorities

GRADUATE EMPLOYMENT
10/0299 employer attitudes; graduates;
mathematical ability; numeracy;
work-education relationship
10/1534 graduate surveys; probationary teachers;
teacher development

GRADUATE STUDY
10/0166 higher education; student recruitment
10/1135 educational policy; higher education;
overseas students
10/1265 deaf interpreting; deafness; hearing
impairments; higher education; interpreters;
special educational needs
10/1509 mature students; part time students;
student research
10/1702 graduates; science education

GRADUATE SURVEYS
10/1427 B Ed degrees; course evaluation;
preservice teacher education
10/1534 graduate employment; probationary
teachers; teacher development

GRADUATES
10/0299 employer attitudes; graduate
employment; mathematical ability; numeracy;
work-education relationship
10/1677 B Ed degrees; student teachers; teacher
certification; teacher education
10/1702 graduate study; science education

GRAMMAR
10/0725 morphology – languages; semantics;
spelling; syntax
10/1105 English studies; student teachers

GRANT MAINTAINED SCHOOLS
10/0081 Education Reform Act 1988;
educational administration; educational
change; educational finance; open entry;
parent choice; school based management
10/0672 educational administration; local
management of schools; management in
education; school based management

10/0674 educational administration; educational
change; management in education; school
based management
10/1609 educational administration; educational
change; management in education; school
based management
10/1612 city technology colleges; inservice
teacher education; management development;
school based management; staff development
10/1750 educational practices; institutional
autonomy; institutional characteristics; school
based management

GREECE
10/0141 self concept; self esteem
10/0145 early childhood education; preschool to
primary transition; primary school pupils;
school readiness
10/0256 art education; assessment; comparative
education; degrees – academic; fine arts
10/0543 mathematics education; mathematics
teachers; teacher education
10/0615 geometry education; mathematics
education; problem solving
10/1310 music education
10/1452 comparative education; learning
disabilities; Scotland; special educational needs
10/1674 behaviour problems; classroom
discipline; discipline; disruptive pupils;
nursery school education; teacher attitudes
10/1708 English – second language
10/1774 comparative education; Cyprus;
educational policy; school systems

GROUP BEHAVIOUR
10/0958 group dynamics; group work

GROUP DISCUSSION
10/0642 group work; physics education; science
education
10/1182 critical thinking; learning activities;
teaching methods; university students

GROUP DYNAMICS
10/0958 group behaviour; group work

GROUP WORK
10/0134 children as writers; narration; primary
school pupils; story telling; writing –
composition
10/0342 mathematics education
10/0464 computer uses in education;
microcomputers; primary schools; problem
solving
10/0642 group discussion; physics education;
science education
10/0692 assessment; competency based
education; higher education; teaching methods
10/0709 discussion; interaction; intergroup
education; learning activities
10/0726 feedback; mathematics education;
problem solving
10/0958 group behaviour; group dynamics
10/1052 learning activities; reading
improvement; reading strategies
10/1197 classroom observation techniques;
learning activities; science activities; science
education
10/1515 assessment
10/1734 child language; comparative education;
infant school pupils; verbal communication

GROUPING – TEACHING PURPOSES
10/1067 ability; class organisation; mixed ability;
pupil placement; streaming; teaching methods

GUIDANCE
10/0321 career counselling; secondary schools;
vocational guidance
10/1054 adult education; adult learning; lifelong
learning

GUIDANCE OBJECTIVES
10/1007 career counselling; evaluation methods;
measurement techniques; vocational guidance

GUIDANCE PERSONNEL
10/1460 careers service; mentors; professional
development

GUIDELINES
10/1793 curriculum development; political
science studies

GUIDES
10/0813 educational materials; health education;
nurse education; nurses; smoking
10/1059 music activities; music education

GYPSIES
10/0720 cultural influences; minority group
children; performance factors; travellers –
itinerants
10/0721 cultural influences; minority group
children; performance factors; travellers –
itinerants

HANDEDNESS
10/0659 brain hemisphere functions; dyslexia;
lateral dominance; reading difficulties; visual
perception

HANDICAP IDENTIFICATION
10/0955 adolescents; electroencephalograph;
epilepsy

HANDICRAFTS
10/0258 arts education; computer uses in
education; cultural education; museums; visual
arts

HANDWRITING
10/0301 comparative education; creativity;
France; writing research; writing skills
10/0744 motor development; perceptual motor
coordination; reading; speech
10/1199 infant school pupils; reading; spelling;
writing skills

HEAD TEACHERS
10/0002 gender equality; sex stereotypes;
teaching profession; women teachers;
women's employment
10/0076 educational change; local management
of schools; school based management
10/0156 mentors; programme evaluation;
teaching profession
10/0183 management in education; mentors
10/0190 primary schools; school organisation;
teaching profession
10/0291 leadership; leadership styles; local
management of schools; management in
education; school based management
10/0386 educational administration; management
in education; sex differences; teaching
profession; women's employment
10/0633 teacher evaluation
10/0671 administrator role; educational change;
management in education; role conflict;
secondary schools; teacher role
10/0673 mentors; middle management;
professional continuing education; teacher
development; teaching profession
10/0688 educational history
10/0809 educational administration; governance;
school governing bodies; school governors
10/0910 management development; managerial
occupations; mentors
10/0912 educational administration; governing
bodies; management in education; school
governors
10/0952 administrators; educational
administration; management development;
management in education
10/1200 deputy head teachers; employment
patterns; teacher employment; teacher
mobility; teacher recruitment; teacher supply
and demand; teaching profession
10/1232 primary schools; teacher administrator
relationship; teacher role; teacher workload;
teaching profession
10/1256 change; local management of schools;
primary schools; role conflict; stress variables;
time management
10/1343 teacher development; teaching
profession
10/1483 academic staff development; teacher
evaluation; teaching profession
10/1698 industrial secondments;
industry-education relationship; programme

evaluation; secondments; teacher development
10/1740 educational administration; primary schools; school based management; teacher role

HEALTH
10/0202 body image; eating habits; food; self concept
10/0351 child psychology; exercise; physical activities; physical activity level
10/0852 adolescents; family influence; smoking
10/1071 aspiration; attitudes; pupil attitudes; pupil behaviour; secondary school pupils; sex education; social attitudes
10/1233 health activities; holistic approach; physical education; well being

HEALTH ACTIVITIES
10/0307 educational materials; exercise; health promotion; heart rate; physical activities; primary school pupils
10/1233 health; holistic approach; physical education; well being

HEALTH EDUCATION
10/0009 acquired immune deficiency syndrome; parent participation; peer teaching; sex education
10/0064 child development; cognitive ability; intellectual development; intelligence quotient; pregnancy; smoking
10/0197 acquired immune deficiency syndrome; health promotion; sexuality; sexually transmitted diseases; tourism; travel
10/0270 medical services; patient education; pharmacists; pharmacy
10/0448 health promotion; primary schools
10/0449 health promotion; primary schools
10/0492 acquired immune deficiency syndrome; drug abuse; drug education; welfare services
10/0798 acquired immune deficiency syndrome; sex education; sexuality; sexually transmitted diseases
10/0799 acquired immune deficiency syndrome; sex education; sexuality; sexually transmitted diseases
10/0800 acquired immune deficiency syndrome; sex education; sexuality; sexually transmitted diseases
10/0801 family attitudes; family health; sex education; sexuality
10/0803 cancer education; pupil attitudes
10/0804 heart disorders
10/0805 family health; family influence
10/0813 educational materials; guides; nurse education; nurses; smoking
10/0815 primary education
10/0817 communication research; family involvement
10/0818 acquired immune deficiency syndrome; sex education; sexually transmitted diseases
10/0819 acquired immune deficiency syndrome; sex education; sexually transmitted diseases; youth
10/0820 sex education; youth
10/0824 health promotion; secondary schools
10/0826 acquired immune deficiency syndrome; homeless people
10/0827 acquired immune deficiency syndrome; evaluation; training
10/0828 acquired immune deficiency syndrome; secondary schools
10/0829 acquired immune deficiency syndrome; educational materials
10/0831 acquired immune deficiency syndrome; homosexuality; sex education; sexuality; sexually transmitted diseases
10/0838 local education authorities; nutrition education; school meals
10/0849 drug education; life skills; primary education
10/0879 acquired immune deficiency syndrome; sex education
10/0918 inservice teacher education; professional development
10/0953 accidents; comparative education; European Community; food standards; nutrition education; safety education
10/1029 health promotion; programme evaluation
10/1032 parent attitudes; sex education
10/1036 alcohol education; drinking

10/1072 secondary schools; sex education
10/1334 health promotion; pupil needs; Scotland
10/1347 alcohol education; drug education; programme evaluation; sex education
10/1368 health promotion; pupil needs; Scotland
10/1402 allied health occupations; patient education; preventive medicine
10/1403 health needs; needs assessment; primary health care
10/1404 cancer education; preventive medicine; primary health care
10/1430 acquired immune deficiency syndrome; educational materials; educational technology; interactive video; material development; sex education
10/1538 community benefits; developing countries; India; peer teaching; Uganda
10/1555 comparative education; drug education
10/1703 eating habits; food; nutrition education

HEALTH NEEDS
10/1403 health education; needs assessment; primary health care

HEALTH PERSONNEL
10/1401 assertiveness; interpersonal competence; professional training; radiographers
10/1486 administrators; health services; nursing
10/1693 behavioural sciences; health services; interdisciplinary approach; medical education

HEALTH PROMOTION
10/0197 acquired immune deficiency syndrome; health education; sexuality; sexually transmitted diseases; tourism; travel
10/0307 educational materials; exercise; health activities; heart rate; physical activities; primary school pupils
10/0448 health education; primary schools
10/0449 health education; primary schools
10/0824 health education; secondary schools
10/1029 health education; programme evaluation
10/1334 health education; pupil needs; Scotland
10/1368 health education; pupil needs; Scotland
10/1521 colleges of further education; extracurricular activities; further education students

HEALTH SERVICES
10/1486 administrators; health personnel; nursing
10/1693 behavioural sciences; health personnel; interdisciplinary approach; medical education

HEALTH VISITORS
10/1473 learning experience; nurse education; placement

HEARING AIDS
10/0961 communication aids – for disabled; deafness; hearing impairments; psychological evaluation

HEARING IMPAIRMENTS
10/0433 educational quality; mainstreaming; peripatetic teachers; special educational needs; support teachers; teacher effectiveness
10/0611 communication skills; deafness; hearing therapy; special schools; total communication
10/0960 deafness; special educational needs
10/0961 communication aids – for disabled; deafness; hearing aids; psychological evaluation
10/1265 deaf interpreting; deafness; graduate study; higher education; interpreters; special educational needs
10/1266 early childhood education; early experience; intervention; parent participation; special educational needs

HEARING THERAPY
10/0611 communication skills; deafness; hearing impairments; special schools; total communication

HEART DISORDERS
10/0804 health education

HEART RATE
10/0307 educational materials; exercise; health activities; health promotion; physical activities; primary school pupils

HEAT
10/0749 cognitive development; comprehension; primary education; science education; temperature

HELPLESSNESS
10/0550 motivation; self esteem; special educational needs

HEURISTICS
10/0111 learning processes; primary education; teaching methods

HIGH ACHIEVEMENT
10/1771 achievement; background; individual characteristics; science education; undergraduate students

HIGHER EDUCATION
10/0011 further education; sixteen to nineteen education; student health and welfare; student needs
10/0016 nurse education
10/0090 access to education; disabilities; special educational needs; student needs; universities; university admission
10/0115 further education; information retrieval; information systems; optical data discs; search strategies; student attitudes
10/0118 access programmes; mature students; men; student experience
10/0122 dropout research; dropouts; enrolment; student behaviour
10/0123 access to education; nontraditional education; student counselling; student health and welfare
10/0132 educational guidance; student counselling
10/0143 comparative education; Ghana; modular courses; universities
10/0163 educational finance; educational policy; local education authorities
10/0166 graduate study; student recruitment
10/0167 cognitive processes; cognitive psychology; epistemology; learning processes; memory
10/0168 learning experience; mature students
10/0170 access to education; equal education; Pakistan; women's education
10/0176 access to education; equal education; gender equality; social class
10/0181 developmental continuity; English literature; sixteen to nineteen education; teaching methods
10/0200 mature students; student attitudes; student needs
10/0228 adult education; databases; further education; mature students
10/0229 access to education; adult education; Germany; mature students; student participation
10/0230 access to education; adult education; France; mature students; student participation
10/0267 access programmes; access to education; adult education; comparative education; mature students
10/0310 access to education; educational change; further education; sixteen to nineteen education
10/0311 further education; school to work transition; unemployment; vocational education; youth employment
10/0317 access to education; further education; programme evaluation
10/0323 academic achievement; school effectiveness; secondary schools
10/0336 academic failure; intervention; student problems; underachievement
10/0337 learning strategies; learning theories; student attitudes; teaching methods
10/0338 comprehension; essays; examination techniques; learning strategies; review – reexamination; study skills; writing – composition
10/0341 learning motivation; learning strategies; mathematics achievement; sixteen to nineteen education; undergraduate study
10/0381 assessment; learner centred curriculum; self evaluation – individuals; teaching methods
10/0385 profiles; records of achievement; resumes – personal; self evaluation – individuals; skill development

10/0387 assessment; learner centred methods; open education; self evaluation – individuals; teaching methods
10/0388 learner characteristics; learning experience; learning strategies; student experience
10/0389 learning strategies; study skills; undergraduate students
10/0393 stress – psychological; stress management; stress variables; student health and welfare
10/0394 competency based education; education courses; masters' courses; qualifications; standards
10/0408 access to education; dropout research; nontraditional education; summer schools; university admission; university preparation
10/0424 English – second language; language of instruction; Saudi Arabia
10/0425 access to education; summer schools; transition education; university admission; university preparation
10/0440 comparative education; distance education; international educational exchange; learning activities; Netherlands; teaching methods; telecommunications
10/0442 access to education; accessibility – for disabled; disabilities; equal education; student recruitment
10/0472 argument; criticism; sixth form education; writing processes; writing skills
10/0489 religion and education; religious education; universities
10/0517 administrators; educational administration; further education; management in education; women; women's employment
10/0528 academic staff; ethnic groups; mature students; middle class students; student attitudes; student experience; working class
10/0529 educational quality; institutional role; performance contracts
10/0530 access programmes; access to education; mature students; nontraditional education; student motivation
10/0531 academic achievement; access programmes; mature students; nontraditional education; performance
10/0545 enterprise education; programme evaluation; work-education relationship
10/0546 college effectiveness; outcomes of education; universities and colleges
10/0549 prior learning; transfer of learning
10/0558 career education; vocational guidance
10/0559 academic achievement; educational experience; mature students; student attitudes
10/0565 access to education; credit transfer; educational change
10/0580 access to education; equal education; ethnic groups; student experience; student recruitment
10/0636 mature students; stress – psychological; stress variables
10/0679 curriculum development; environmental education
10/0692 assessment; competency based education; group work; teaching methods
10/0693 educational history; professional education; universities; women's education; women's employment
10/0712 counselling services; pastoral care – education; student counselling; student needs
10/0789 competency based education; masters' courses; National Vocational Qualifications; qualifications; standards
10/0794 further education; independent colleges; private education; private universities
10/0795 educational quality; teacher effectiveness
10/0796 advisory committees; policy formation; politics-education relationship; universities
10/0816 educational development; prediction; universities
10/0822 assessment; educational quality
10/0869 student evaluation of teacher performance; teacher effectiveness
10/0872 Arab states; English – second language
10/0876 blindness; communication problems; nonverbal communication; special educational needs; visual impairments
10/0903 academic staff; employment opportunities; equal opportunities – jobs;

universities; women teachers; women's employment
10/0904 open education
10/0905 aptitude; assessment; critical thinking; mature students; prediction of success; selection; student evaluation
10/0906 computer software; computer uses in education; performance indicators; quality control
10/0915 attitudes; quality assurance
10/0934 access to education; programme evaluation; records of achievement; student records
10/0939 epilepsy; student attitudes; student health and welfare
10/1023 course evaluation; educational quality; performance indicators; quality control; student attitudes; teacher effectiveness; universities
10/1068 academic staff; further education teachers; stress – psychological; teacher workload
10/1096 further education students; literacy; reading skills; writing skills
10/1106 academic staff; inservice teacher education; preservice teacher education; teacher educators
10/1110 counselling services; mature students; student counselling
10/1119 environmental education
10/1133 adult education; educational practices; information technology; physical sciences; science education
10/1135 educational policy; graduate study; overseas students
10/1187 introductory courses; mathematics education; numbers; numeracy
10/1204 communication research; competency based education; further education; learning processes; teaching methods
10/1213 comparative education; France; teacher education; United States of America
10/1217 cheating; discipline problems; plagiarism; student behaviour
10/1230 accreditation – courses; accrediting authorities; assessment; educational quality; external examiners; open universities
10/1231 assessment; educational quality; external examiners; quality control
10/1238 assessment; enterprise education; learning strategies; skill development; work-education relationship
10/1265 deaf interpreting; deafness; graduate study; hearing impairments; interpreters; special educational needs
10/1268 educational administration; management in education
10/1344 access programmes; access to education; adult students; mature students; programme evaluation; science education; social sciences
10/1349 educational quality; further education; industry-higher education relationship; institutional role; performance contracts; programme evaluation
10/1358 access to education; socioeconomic background; student recruitment
10/1359 access to education; admission criteria; student recruitment
10/1369 academic staff; academic staff promotion; employment opportunities; equal opportunities – jobs; further education
10/1370 citizenship; Europe; overseas employment; overseas students
10/1416 academic achievement; access programmes; access to education; mature students; outcomes of education
10/1504 access to education; admission criteria; admissions tutors; student recruitment
10/1505 computer uses in education; information technology
10/1511 access to education; admission criteria; competency based education; National Vocational Qualifications
10/1514 access to education; accreditation of prior learning; experiential learning; transfer of learning
10/1522 access programmes; access to education; continuing education
10/1550 access to education; cultural background; equal education; ethnic groups; inner city; women's education

10/1554 cultural education; degree requirements; ethnography; second language learning; study abroad
10/1587 mature students; sex differences
10/1589 educational experience; mature students; men; sex differences; student attitudes; women's education
10/1605 educational quality; quality assurance; quality control
10/1624 accreditation of prior learning; experiential learning
10/1632 competency based education; National Vocational Qualifications; preservice teacher education; professional education; standards
10/1644 educational administration; educational change; further education
10/1655 information technology; professional development
10/1671 learning experience; mature students; student experience
10/1709 educational discrimination; ethnic groups; student recruitment
10/1711 adult education; continuing education; organisational change; universities
10/1726 access to education; mature students; student attitudes; student housing; student recruitment
10/1729 science education; scientific literacy; women
10/1777 further education; National Vocational Qualifications; vocational education
10/1780 educational administration; educational quality; institutes of higher education; quality assurance; quality control

HISTORIOGRAPHY
10/0767 comprehension; explanation; history; imagination

HISTORY
10/0352 National Curriculum; primary education
10/0567 cooperation; developmental continuity; National Curriculum; primary secondary education
10/0765 history studies; National Curriculum; teaching methods
10/0767 comprehension; explanation; historiography; imagination
10/0768 comprehension; computer assisted learning; computer uses in education; thinking skills
10/1115 arts education; cultural education; primary education
10/1575 curriculum development; Ireland
10/1772 National Curriculum; primary education

HISTORY STUDIES
10/0488 National Curriculum; oral history; small schools
10/0641 local history; National Curriculum
10/0765 history; National Curriculum; teaching methods
10/1254 war
10/1304 books; children's literature; fiction; geography education
10/1436 environmental education; museums; preservice teacher education
10/1572 computer uses in education; learning strategies; teaching methods; teleconferencing
10/1658 educational materials; pictorial stimuli; teaching methods; visual aids
10/1797 citizenship education; European history

HOLISTIC APPROACH
10/1233 health; health activities; physical education; well being

HOME ENVIRONMENT
10/0853 behaviour problems; bullying; family influence; parent-child relationship; parent-pupil relationship; punishment; pupil behaviour

HOME-SCHOOL RELATIONSHIP
10/0196 early reading; reading achievement; reading difficulties
10/0404 government – administrative body; industry-education relationship
10/0706 adult literacy; literacy; literacy education; mother tongue; native speakers; primary education; teaching methods

10/0716 bilingual education programmes; English – second language; ethnic groups; literacy education; parent participation; reading teaching; second language learning
10/1328 family involvement; parent participation; parent-pupil relationship
10/1650 homework; learning activities; mathematics education; parent participation
10/1665 learning processes; primary school pupils; pupil-school relationship; social influences; sociology of education
10/1757 attendance; educational attitudes; family influence; truancy

HOMELESS PEOPLE
10/0826 acquired immune deficiency syndrome; health education

HOMEWORK
10/1650 home-school relationship; learning activities; mathematics education; parent participation

HOMOSEXUALITY
10/0831 acquired immune deficiency syndrome; health education; sex education; sexuality; sexually transmitted diseases
10/1631 acquired immune deficiency syndrome; sex education; sexually transmitted diseases

HONG KONG
10/0974 adolescents; Chinese; cultural background; ethnic groups; ethnicity; migrants
10/1140 curriculum evaluation; economics-education relationship; training; TVEI; work-education relationship

HOTEL AND CATERING EDUCATION
10/0929 hotel management education; selection

HOTEL MANAGEMENT EDUCATION
10/0929 hotel and catering education; selection

HOUSING
10/0382 China; professional education

HUMAN-COMPUTER INTERACTION
10/0151 adult learning; learning strategies; secretaries; word processing
10/0277 interactive video; medical education
10/0860 computer assisted learning; computer uses in education; concept keyboards; learning disabilities; special educational needs; touch screens
10/1181 computer assisted learning; computer uses in education; cooperative learning; learning processes
10/1311 computer keyboards; computer uses in education; concept keyboards
10/1552 computer assisted learning; electronic books; hypermedia; information technology; multimedia approach; optical data discs

HUMAN RIGHTS
10/1800 citizenship education; literature studies; pupil attitudes; racial attitudes; social attitudes

HUMANITIES
10/0251 communication skills; competency based education; minimum competencies; modular courses; open education
10/0662 computer uses in education; gender equality; information technology; sex differences
10/1167 adult students; distance education; mature students; open universities; student attitudes
10/1523 adult education; cultural education; curriculum development

HYPERACTIVITY
10/0859 attention; attention deficit disorders; concentration
10/1640 attention deficit disorders; cognitive ability; learning disabilities; memory

HYPERMEDIA
10/0239 computer assisted learning; design education

10/0476 literary criticism; literature studies; multimedia approach
10/1552 computer assisted learning; electronic books; human-computer interaction; information technology; multimedia approach; optical data discs

HYPERTEXT
10/1285 computer assisted learning; further education students; information seeking; information sources
10/1668 computer uses in education; cross curricular approach; information technology; technology education

HYPOTHESIS TESTING
10/1464 computer uses in education; physics education; science education

IDENTITY
10/1195 citizenship; citizenship education; nationalism; role of education; Zambia

IDEOLOGY
10/0399 Commonwealth of Independent States; Communist education; educational change; politics-education relationship; social change; USSR
10/1173 cultural influences; curriculum; educational philosophy

IMAGERY
10/0781 computer uses in education; mathematics education

IMAGINATION
10/0767 comprehension; explanation; historiography; history
10/1321 mathematics education; pretend play; simulation

INCIDENTAL LEARNING
10/0763 literacy; mass media; popular culture

INCOME
10/0012 educational finance; fund raising; money management; school funds; secondary schools

INDEPENDENT COLLEGES
10/0794 further education; higher education; private education; private universities

INDEPENDENT SCHOOLS
10/0891 marketing; parent choice

INDEPENDENT STUDY
10/0578 adult education; adult learning; caregivers; disabilities; lifelong learning
10/1425 educational technology; staff development
10/1638 distance education

INDIA
10/0189 mainstreaming; special educational needs; teacher education
10/0332 educational policy; primary education
10/0333 literacy; nomads
10/0600 adult education; educational history
10/1531 developing countries; development education; learning activities; primary education; teaching methods
10/1538 community benefits; developing countries; health education; peer teaching; Uganda

INDIGENOUS POPULATIONS
10/0019 Canada natives; ethnic groups; newly qualified teachers; teacher background; teacher induction; teaching profession

INDIVIDUAL CHARACTERISTICS
10/1771 achievement; background; high achievement; science education; undergraduate students

INDIVIDUAL DEVELOPMENT
10/0051 career planning; planning; profiles
10/0473 Education Reform Act 1988; moral education; National Curriculum; primary schools; religious education; social development

10/0686 curriculum development; educational philosophy; moral education; physical education; religious education
10/1132 adult education; community; social change; voluntary agencies
10/1216 mathematics achievement; mathematics education; pupil participation; sex difference

INDIVIDUAL NEEDS
10/0061 pupils; special educational needs; surveys
10/0062 language proficiency; pupils; surveys
10/0677 differentiated curriculum; mainstreaming; National Curriculum; special educational needs

INDIVIDUAL TEACHING
10/0334 small group teaching; teaching methods; tutorials; university teaching

INDIVIDUALISED METHODS
10/0273 computer assisted learning; computer uses in education; information technology; medical education
10/0304 computer uses in education; gifted; Jordan; mathematics; primary education
10/1270 early childhood education; intervention; parent participation; teaching methods
10/1382 mathematics education; teaching methods
10/1568 curriculum development; differentiated curriculum; Northern Ireland; science education
10/1573 differentiated curriculum; primary education; teaching methods

INDIVIDUALISM
10/0217 curriculum development; physical education; teaching methods; theory-practice relationship

INDUSTRIAL PSYCHOLOGY
10/0390 computer simulation; computer uses in education; psychology

INDUSTRIAL SECONDMENTS
10/0042 industry-education relationship; preservice teacher education; teacher development
10/0593 industry-education relationship; teacher development
10/0648 enterprise education; industry-education relationship; placement; preservice teacher education; student teachers
10/0937 enterprise education; industry-education relationship; preservice teacher education; science teachers; student teachers
10/1409 industry-education relationship; teacher development
10/1694 industry-education relationship; teacher development
10/1698 head teachers; industry-education relationship; programme evaluation; secondments; teacher development
10/1701 industry-education relationship; secondments; teacher development
10/1778 industry-education relationship

INDUSTRIAL TRAINING
10/0797 job training
10/1152 adult education; continuing education; inservice teacher education; professional training; vocational education
10/1508 on the job training; trainers

INDUSTRY-EDUCATION RELATIONSHIP
10/0042 industrial secondments; preservice teacher education; teacher development
10/0050 Training and Enterprise Councils
10/0054 educational materials; mathematics education
10/0120 National Vocational Qualifications; work attitudes; work-education relationship
10/0124 comparative education; economic change; economics-education relationship; Germany; structural unemployment; training; work-education relationship
10/0285 enterprise education; learning strategies; motivation; skill development; transfer of learning
10/0404 government – administrative body;

home-school relationship
10/0593 industrial secondments; teacher development
10/0594 Ghana; science education
10/0648 enterprise education; industrial secondments; placement; preservice teacher education; student teachers
10/0689 comparative education; United States of America; work-education relationship
10/0743 teacher development; work experience programmes
10/0855 local education authorities; school to work transition; vocational education
10/0911 management development; mentors; work-education relationship
10/0937 enterprise education; industrial secondments; preservice teacher education; science teachers; student teachers
10/1025 economics education; money management
10/1201 comparative education; educational policy; politics-education relationship; United States of America
10/1351 programme evaluation; skills; TVEI; vocational education
10/1360 programme evaluation; school to work transition; vocational education; work-education relationship
10/1409 industrial secondments; teacher development
10/1459 school to work transition; vocational education
10/1503 clubs; curriculum enrichment; engineering; engineers
10/1653 background; economics education; experience; preservice teacher education; student teacher attitudes; student teachers
10/1694 industrial secondments; teacher development
10/1695 corporate education; labour force development
10/1696 curriculum; employment; skills; work-education relationship
10/1697 cooperative programmes
10/1698 head teachers; industrial secondments; programme evaluation; secondments; teacher development
10/1699 cooperative programmes; programme evaluation; secondments
10/1701 industrial secondments; secondments; teacher development
10/1715 city technology colleges; disadvantaged environment; school-community relationship
10/1778 industrial secondments

INDUSTRY-FURTHER EDUCATION RELATIONSHIP
10/0684 further education; training; vocational education
10/0740 colleges of further education; staff development; work experience programmes

INDUSTRY-HIGHER EDUCATION RELATIONSHIP
10/0026 cooperative programmes; corporate support; research
10/0027 intellectual property; patents; research
10/0164 corporate support; employers; enterprise education; transfer of learning
10/0208 credits; experiential learning; job placement; work-education relationship
10/0383 educational quality; quality control; vocational education; work-education relationship
10/0555 enterprise education; institutes of higher education
10/1109 management studies; placement; work experience
10/1341 enterprise education
10/1349 educational quality; further education; higher education; institutional role; performance contracts; programme evaluation
10/1643 entrepreneurship; science parks

INFANT BEHAVIOUR
10/0863 attention; cognitive development; early experience; learning; neurological impairments

INFANT SCHOOL CURRICULUM
10/0153 assessment; educational change; infant school education; National Curriculum;

primary school teachers; pupil attitudes

INFANT SCHOOL EDUCATION
10/0153 assessment; educational change; infant school curriculum; National Curriculum; primary school teachers; pupil attitudes
10/0732 classroom communication; feedback; infant school teachers; teacher-pupil relationship; teacher response
10/1220 beginning reading; reading teaching; teacher-pupil relationship; teaching methods
10/1272 classroom management; early childhood education; infant school teachers; reception classes
10/1807 art education; drawing

INFANT SCHOOL PUPILS
10/0063 behaviour problems; discipline problems; disruptive pupils; primary school pupils; problem children; surveys
10/0999 nursery school pupils; reading; reading readiness; reception classes; tests
10/1193 communication skills; early childhood education; friendship; reception classes; social development; social isolation; young children
10/1199 handwriting; reading; spelling; writing skills
10/1734 child language; comparative education; group work; verbal communication

INFANT SCHOOL TEACHERS
10/0306 early childhood education; mathematics education; reception classes
10/0436 distance education; educational media; inservice education; international educational exchange; Sweden; telecommunications
10/0727 National Curriculum; professional recognition; teaching profession
10/0732 classroom communication; feedback; infant school education; teacher-pupil relationship; teacher response
10/1272 classroom management; early childhood education; infant school education; reception classes

INFANT SCHOOLS
10/0588 assessment; first schools; mathematics curriculum; mathematics teachers; standard assessment tasks
10/0847 classroom research; curriculum research; Education Reform Act 1988; educational change; educational experience; mathematics education
10/1267 developmental continuity; junior schools; primary education; transfer pupils

INFANTS
10/0091 books; early childhood education; early experience; early reading; parent participation
10/0106 blindness; child development; visual impairments; young children

INFORMATION NEEDS
10/0236 educational resources; environmental education; information sources
10/0237 educational resources; environmental education; information sources
10/0842 access to information; parent-school relationship

INFORMATION NETWORKS
10/0047 computer uses in education; information technology; telecommunications

INFORMATION RETRIEVAL
10/0115 further education; higher education; information systems; optical data discs; search strategies; student attitudes

INFORMATION SCIENCE
10/1286 developing countries; development education; Europe; librarianship education
10/1603 distance education; flexible learning; librarianship education; mature students

INFORMATION SEEKING
10/0375 literacy; primary education; reading skills; writing skills
10/0833 information technology; National

Curriculum; optical data discs; technology education
10/1285 computer assisted learning; further education students; hypertext; information sources

INFORMATION SOURCES
10/0236 educational resources; environmental education; information needs
10/0237 educational resources; environmental education; information needs
10/0254 art; databases; design; research
10/0329 international education
10/1285 computer assisted learning; further education students; hypertext; information seeking
10/1608 drug education; libraries; prevention

INFORMATION SYSTEMS
10/0115 further education; higher education; information retrieval; optical data discs; search strategies; student attitudes

INFORMATION TECHNOLOGY
10/0047 computer uses in education; information networks; telecommunications
10/0209 preservice teacher education; student teachers; teaching practice
10/0213 computer uses in education; English studies curriculum; optical data discs
10/0273 computer assisted learning; computer uses in education; individualised methods; medical education
10/0305 computer literacy; computer uses in education; preservice teacher education
10/0370 coordinators; secondary schools; staff role
10/0371 computer uses in education; National Curriculum
10/0468 computer uses in education; research reports; theses
10/0510 curriculum development; mathematics education; secondary education
10/0512 computer uses in education; mathematics education; microcomputers; secondary schools
10/0513 computer uses in education; mathematics education; secondary schools
10/0571 computer uses in education; cross curricular approach; curriculum development
10/0662 computer uses in education; gender equality; humanities; sex differences
10/0833 information seeking; National Curriculum; optical data discs; technology education
10/0844 databases; National Curriculum; technology education
10/0873 computer uses in education; educational administration; local management of schools; management systems; school based management
10/0892 preservice teacher education; student teachers; teaching practice
10/0950 computer uses in education; mathematics education; preservice teacher education; student teachers; teacher attitudes
10/1010 computer uses in education; literature reviews
10/1030 computer uses in education; curriculum development; microcomputers
10/1041 computer uses in education; school policy
10/1044 ability; computer uses in education; gifted; primary school pupils
10/1085 computer software; computer uses in education; educational software; technology education
10/1101 National Curriculum; oracy; teacher attitudes
10/1124 adult vocational education; adults; computer literacy; disabilities; sheltered workshops; special educational needs; training centres
10/1125 behaviour disorders; computer uses in education; special educational needs; special schools
10/1126 adult basic education; adults; computer literacy; disabilities; special educational needs
10/1127 adults; computer literacy; disabilities; special educational needs; training centres

10/1133 adult education; educational practices; higher education; physical sciences; science education
10/1142 adult vocational education; comparative education; disabilities; Portugal; special educational needs; training; United Kingdom
10/1431 staff development; teacher education
10/1466 colleges; computer uses in education
10/1492 nurse education; nursing
10/1505 computer uses in education; higher education
10/1552 computer assisted learning; electronic books; human-computer interaction; hyper-media; multimedia approach; optical data discs
10/1594 computer uses in education; mathematics education
10/1613 authoring aids – programming; computer assisted learning; computer software; computer uses in education; multimedia approach
10/1620 computer uses in education; inservice teacher education
10/1639 educational research; policy; research; research opportunities; social science research
10/1655 higher education; professional development
10/1668 computer uses in education; cross curricular approach; hypertext; technology education
10/1676 cross curricular approach; curriculum development; National Curriculum
10/1745 computer uses in education

INHIBITION
10/0660 behaviour problems; elective mutism; psychopathology; speech communication

INNER CITY
10/0234 financial support; investment; training; youth leaders; youth service
10/1550 access to education; cultural background; equal education; ethnic groups; higher education; women's education

INSERVICE EDUCATION
10/0029 competency based education; degrees – academic; professional education
10/0436 distance education; educational media; infant school teachers; international educational exchange; Sweden; telecommunications
10/1623 competency based education; on the job training; social work studies

INSERVICE TEACHER EDUCATION
10/0040 preservice teacher education; primary education; science education; student teachers
10/0109 developing countries; educational improvement; Pakistan; primary education; programme evaluation
10/0182 primary school teachers; teacher development
10/0205 programme evaluation; pupil development; self concept
10/0263 academic staff development; educational policy; professional development; Scotland
10/0373 international educational exchange; international programmes; Poland; preservice teacher education; teacher education
10/0497 education support grants; programme evaluation; TVEI
10/0511 TVEI
10/0644 English – second language; language teachers; second language teaching; Thailand
10/0739 business education; curriculum development
10/0837 material development; primary education; science education
10/0845 earth science; geography education; National Curriculum
10/0918 health education; professional development
10/0944 professional development; teacher development; teaching profession
10/0989 educational administration; local education authorities
10/1106 academic staff; higher education; preservice teacher education; teacher educators
10/1152 adult education; continuing education; industrial training; professional training; vocational education
10/1185 courses; mathematics education; primary school teachers
10/1198 primary school teachers; science education; teacher attitudes
10/1215 mentors; training
10/1235 art education; design education; National Curriculum; primary education; primary school teachers
10/1244 consultants; music education; music teachers; primary school teachers
10/1271 mathematics; primary school teachers; teacher attitudes
10/1278 competency based teacher education; local education authorities; school based teacher education; staff orientation; teacher development
10/1393 English – second language; Saudi Arabia; second language teaching
10/1481 European Community; European studies; intercultural programmes
10/1498 advisers; inspection; local education authorities; organisational effectiveness
10/1536 science education
10/1592 distance education; programme effectiveness; teacher attitudes; teacher development
10/1612 city technology colleges; grant maintained schools; management development; school based management; staff development
10/1620 computer uses in education; information technology
10/1763 educational materials; primary school teachers; science education; scientific concepts
10/1764 mathematics education; primary schools
10/1770 primary school teachers; science education; teacher development
10/1802 educational materials; science education; Swaziland

INSPECTION
10/0498 inspectors – of schools; local education authorities
10/0991 evaluation; local education authorities; monitoring
10/1046 inspectors – of schools; parent attitudes
10/1094 educational change; secondary schools; teacher attitudes
10/1207 educational change; teacher attitudes
10/1227 curriculum development; educational administration; primary school curriculum; primary schools; school organisation
10/1377 educational quality; institutional evaluation; local education authorities; school effectiveness
10/1498 advisers; inservice teacher education; local education authorities; organisational effectiveness
10/1672 educational policy; inspectors – of schools; quality control

INSPECTORS – OF SCHOOLS
10/0498 inspection; local education authorities
10/1046 inspection; parent attitudes
10/1672 educational policy; inspection; quality control

INSTITUTES OF HIGHER EDUCATION
10/0376 career development; teacher evaluation; teaching profession; women teachers; women's employment
10/0452 attitude measures; institutional environment; organisational climate; student attitudes; teacher attitudes
10/0514 mentors; preservice teacher education; school based teacher education; student teacher supervisors
10/0555 enterprise education; industry-higher education relationship
10/1723 equal education; preservice teacher education; racial discrimination; racial integration
10/1780 educational administration; educational quality; higher education; quality assurance; quality control

INSTITUTIONAL ADMINISTRATION
10/0013 TVEI
10/0023 college administration; colleges of further education; educational administration; further education; organisational change
10/0032 educational history; universities

INSTITUTIONAL ADVANCEMENT
10/0366 marketing; parent choice; parent-school relationship; selection
10/1261 educational change; marketing

INSTITUTIONAL AUTONOMY
10/1750 educational practices; grant maintained schools; institutional characteristics; school based management

INSTITUTIONAL CHARACTERISTICS
10/1087 college effectiveness; educational quality; further education; performance factors; performance indicators
10/1750 educational practices; grant maintained schools; institutional autonomy; school based management

INSTITUTIONAL COOPERATION
10/0888 educational administration; local management of schools
10/1016 mainstreaming; special educational needs; special schools
10/1301 mentors; Postgraduate Certificate in Education; preservice teacher education; school based teacher education

INSTITUTIONAL ENVIRONMENT
10/0452 attitude measures; institutes of higher education; organisational climate; student attitudes; teacher attitudes
10/0460 educational environment; stress – psychological; stress management; stress variables; teacher morale

INSTITUTIONAL EVALUATION
10/0058 examination results; performance indicators
10/0186 mainstreaming; special educational needs; whole school approach
10/0191 mainstreaming; special educational needs; United States of America; whole school approach
10/0269 distance education; medical services; professional continuing education
10/0495 educational objectives; organisational effectiveness; performance indicators
10/0708 employer supported day care; evaluation methods; self evaluation – groups
10/1035 educational quality; evaluation criteria; performance indicators; school effectiveness
10/1377 educational quality; inspection; local education authorities; school effectiveness

INSTITUTIONAL ROLE
10/0529 educational quality; higher education; performance contracts
10/1349 educational quality; further education; higher education; industry-higher education relationship; performance contracts; programme evaluation

INSURANCE OCCUPATIONS
10/1474 single European market; training

INTEGRATION STUDIES
10/1717 communication research; severe learning difficulties; special educational needs; verbal communication
10/1718 children; comprehension; severe learning difficulties; special educational needs

INTELLECTUAL DEVELOPMENT
10/0064 child development; cognitive ability; health education; intelligence quotient; pregnancy; smoking
10/0260 art education; criticism; reasoning
10/1488 experiential learning; learning processes; learning strategies

INTELLECTUAL PROPERTY
10/0027 industry-higher education relationship; patents; research

INTELLECTUALS
10/1218 preservice teacher education;

probationary teachers; professional development; teacher role; teaching profession

INTELLIGENCE DIFFERENCES
10/0986 access to education; adult basic education; adult learning; multiple disabilities; severe learning difficulties

INTELLIGENCE QUOTIENT
10/0064 child development; cognitive ability; health education; intellectual development; pregnancy; smoking

INTELLIGENCE TESTS
10/0702 educational history; France; psychological testing; psychology
10/1026 ability tests; diagnostic assessment; special educational needs

INTERACTION
10/0353 computer uses in education; feedback; learning processes; peer teaching; teacher-pupil relationship
10/0362 cognitive ability; computer assisted learning; logo; turtles – robots
10/0709 discussion; group work; intergroup education; learning activities
10/1191 cognitive development; peer groups; reasoning
10/1765 Down's Syndrome; expressive language; language acquisition; mainstreaming; special educational needs; special schools

INTERACTIVE VIDEO
10/0360
10/0238 computer assisted learning; dyslexia; learning disabilities; multimedia approach
10/0245 dance education
10/0277 human-computer interaction; medical education
10/1155 classroom research; educational materials; educational technology; mathematics education; multimedia approach
10/1430 acquired immune deficiency syndrome; educational materials; educational technology; health education; material development; sex education
10/1553 computer assisted learning; computer uses in education; educational software
10/1577 distance education; teaching methods; teleconferencing

INTERCULTURAL COMMUNICATION
10/1571 cultural awareness; electronic mail; language proficiency; modern language studies; telecommunications

INTERCULTURAL PROGRAMMES
10/1481 European Community; European studies; inservice teacher education

INTERDISCIPLINARY APPROACH
10/0923 core curriculum; curriculum development; educational administration; educational change; educational development; National Curriculum
10/1693 behavioural sciences; health personnel; health services; medical education

INTERESTS
10/0967 adolescent attitudes; adolescent development; adolescents; educational attitudes; personality development; social development; vocational interests

INTERGROUP EDUCATION
10/0709 discussion; group work; interaction; learning activities

INTERGROUP RELATIONS
10/0973 ethnic groups; ethnic relations; multiculturalism; racial relations; school policy; secondary schools
10/1371 bullying; cooperation; ethnic relations; intervention; middle school education; pupil behaviour; social isolation
10/1610 pupil behaviour; social skills; sociometric techniques
10/1737 ethnic relations; friendship; primary schools; pupil attitudes; racial relations; whites

INTERNATIONAL EDUCATION
10/0046 international programmes; international schools
10/0204 Europe; international educational exchange
10/0329 information sources
10/0398 comparative education; educational policy; educational practices
10/0420 cultural awareness
10/1222 centralisation; educational practices; multicultural education; National Curriculum
10/1569 cross cultural studies; electronic mail; European studies; social history; telecommunications

INTERNATIONAL EDUCATIONAL EXCHANGE
10/0198 comparative education; English – second language; second language teaching
10/0204 Europe; international education
10/0373 inservice teacher education; international programmes; Poland; preservice teacher education; teacher education
10/0436 distance education; educational media; infant school teachers; inservice education; Sweden; telecommunications
10/0440 comparative education; distance education; higher education; learning activities; Netherlands; teaching methods; telecommunications
10/1009 Europe; values education
10/1043 comparative education; educational research; Europe; research and development
10/1174 distance education; open universities; teleconferencing
10/1313 comparative education; pastoral care – education; teacher role
10/1338 comparative education; curriculum development; mathematics education; science education
10/1405 photography
10/1580 programme development; trainers; training; youth employment; youth programmes

INTERNATIONAL PROGRAMMES
10/0046 international education; international schools
10/0373 inservice teacher education; international educational exchange; Poland; preservice teacher education; teacher education
10/0564 colleges of further education; community colleges; course evaluation; European Community
10/1078 modern language studies; programme evaluation; second language learning; student exchange programmes

INTERNATIONAL SCHOOLS
10/0046 international education; international programmes

INTERPERSONAL COMPETENCE
10/0866 experiential learning; learning experience; preservice teacher education; student teachers; workshops
10/1163 experiential learning; locus of control; outcomes of education; stress – psychological; student experience; teacher education
10/1401 assertiveness; health personnel; professional training; radiographers

INTERPERSONAL RELATIONSHIP
10/1489 nurse education

INTERPRETERS
10/1265 deaf interpreting; deafness; graduate study; hearing impairments; higher education; special educational needs

INTERVENTION
10/0336 academic failure; higher education; student problems; underachievement
10/0806 databases; pupil welfare
10/1196 science education; sex differences
10/1266 early childhood education; early experience; hearing impairments; parent participation; special educational needs
10/1270 early childhood education; individualised methods; parent participation; teaching methods

10/1371 bullying; cooperation; ethnic relations; intergroup relations; middle school education; pupil behaviour; social isolation
10/1373 antisocial behaviour; behaviour modification; behaviour problems; bullying; classroom environment; speech handicaps; stuttering

INTRODUCTORY COURSES
10/1187 higher education; mathematics education; numbers; numeracy

INVESTMENT
10/0234 financial support; inner city; training; youth leaders; youth service

IRAN
10/0419 nurse education

IRELAND
10/0484 early childhood education; Montessori method; play groups; preschool education
10/1575 curriculum development; history

ISLAMIC EDUCATION
10/1150 Muslims; religion and education; religious cultural groups; women's education
10/1151 Nuslims; religion and education; religious cultural groups; women's education
10/1160 equal education; Muslims; religion and education; religious cultural groups; single sex schools; women's education

ISRAEL
10/1683 Chile; comparative education; gender equality; women's education

ITALIAN
10/0242 course content; educational materials; modern language studies; multimedia approach

ITALY
10/1206 comparative education; educational administration; educational policy; mainstreaming; Scandinavia; special educational needs; support services

ITEM BANKS
10/1000 assessment; screening tests; test items; test selection; tests

JAMAICA
10/0667 educational history; preservice teacher education

JAPAN
10/0252 art education
10/1291 music education

JAPANESE
10/0347 Arabic; Chinese languages; educational materials; non western languages; second language learning
10/0790 postgraduate certificate in education; second language teaching

JAPANESE STUDIES
10/0535 primary education

JOB ANALYSIS
10/1442 colleges of further education; comparable worth; employment practices; equal pay; occupational information; salaries

JOB PERFORMANCE
10/1532 assessment; competence; professional occupations

JOB PLACEMENT
10/0208 credits; experiential learning; industry-higher education relationship; work-education relationship

JOB SATISFACTION
10/1480 stress – psychological; teacher attitudes; teaching profession

JOB SHARING
10/1457 part time teachers; primary school teachers; teaching profession

JOB SKILLS
10/0776 assessment; mastery tests; retention – psychology; vocational education
10/0785 assessment; National Vocational Qualifications; Scottish Vocational Qualifications; verbal tests
10/1130 adult vocational education; employment; job training; work-education relationship

JOB TRAINING
10/0072 career ladders; careers; equal opportunities – jobs; France; work-education relationship
10/0797 industrial training
10/1092 part time employment; temporary employment; training
10/1130 adult vocational education; employment; job skills; work-education relationship

JORDAN
10/0304 computer uses in education; gifted; individualised methods; mathematics; primary education

JUDO
10/0441 physical activities; sports

JUNIOR SCHOOLS
10/1267 developmental continuity; infant schools; primary education; transfer pupils

KENYA
10/0298 behaviour problems; comparative education; discipline; disruptive pupils; secondary schools
10/0496 sports
10/0561 school leavers; school to work transition; unemployment; vocational education; youth employment
10/0621 algebra; mathematics education; pupil problems
10/1250 English studies; English studies teachers; teaching styles

KOREA
10/1396 communicative competence – languages; English – second language; language tests; second language teaching

KUWAIT
10/1513 adult education; andragogy; continuing education

LABORATORIES
10/0741 earth science; laboratory experiments; physical environment; physical geography; simulated environment

LABORATORY EXPERIMENTS
10/0741 earth science; laboratories; physical environment; physical geography; simulated environment

LABOUR FORCE DEVELOPMENT
10/0597 adult education; works schools
10/1695 corporate education; industry-education relationship

LABOUR MARKET
10/1108 Northern Ireland; probationary teachers; teacher employment; teacher recruitment; teaching profession
10/1461 employment opportunities; learner educational objectives; occupational aspiration; opportunities; secondary school pupils; work-education relationship
10/1462 career choice; employment opportunities; learner educational objectives; occupational aspiration; school to work transition; secondary school pupils; work-education relationship
10/1494 curriculum development; economics-education relationship; educational policy; politics-education relationship; vocational education

LANGUAGE
10/0193 conversation; speech communication; verbal communication

LANGUAGE ACQUISITION
10/0140 deafness; sign language
10/0705 language handicaps; learning disabilities; psycholinguistics
10/0917 bilingual pupils; cognitive ability; dyslexia; language handicaps; learning disabilities; special educational needs
10/0948 audiovisual aids; educational media; second language teaching; teaching methods; videodiscs
10/1406 language skills; learning experience; parent participation; parent-teacher cooperation
10/1765 Down's Syndrome; expressive language; interaction; mainstreaming; special educational needs; special schools

LANGUAGE ATTITUDES
10/0608 language teachers; learning motivation; modern language studies

LANGUAGE HANDICAPS
10/0093 distance education; special education teachers; special educational needs; speech handicaps; teacher development
10/0705 language acquisition; learning disabilities; psycholinguistics
10/0864 dyslexia; reading difficulties
10/0917 bilingual pupils; cognitive ability; dyslexia; language acquisition; learning disabilities; special educational needs
10/0972 ability tests; learning disabilities; mathematical ability; mathematics education; numbers; special educational needs
10/1073 speech handicaps; speech therapy

LANGUAGE MAINTENANCE
10/0426 Asians; bilingualism; ethnic groups; language policy; minority groups; mother tongue

LANGUAGE OF INSTRUCTION
10/0248 child language; classroom communication; language research; primary school pupils; science education
10/0286 Cameroon; cross curricular approach; English – second language; mathematics education
10/0379 educational development; language policy; mother tongue; Wales; Welsh; Welsh speaking schools
10/0424 English – second language; higher education; Saudi Arabia
10/0587 Botswana; languages for specific purposes; science education; scientific vocabulary; second language learning
10/1282 bilingual education; bilingualism; English – second language; ethnic groups

LANGUAGE POLICY
10/0379 educational development; language of instruction; mother tongue; Wales; Welsh; Welsh speaking schools
10/0418 Algeria; bilingualism; comparative education; Gaelic; mother tongue; Scotland
10/0426 Asians; bilingualism; ethnic groups; language maintenance; minority groups; mother tongue
10/1079 comparative education; modern language curriculum; modern language studies; second language teaching; secondary education
10/1583 bilingual education; bilingualism; educational policy; school effectiveness; Welsh; Welsh studies
10/1804 developing countries; language standardisation; literacy; mother tongue

LANGUAGE PROFICIENCY
10/0062 individual needs; pupils; surveys
10/0222 English – second language; language teachers; second language teaching
10/1445 modern language studies; primary schools
10/1447 modern language studies; primary schools
10/1571 cultural awareness; electronic mail; intercultural communication; modern language studies; telecommunications

LANGUAGE RESEARCH
10/0248 child language; classroom communication; language of instruction; primary school pupils; science education

LANGUAGE SKILLS
10/0206 literacy; oracy; reading skills; special educational needs; spelling; writing skills
10/1390 English studies; modern language studies
10/1406 language acquisition; learning experience; parent participation; parent-teacher cooperation
10/1759 English studies curriculum; listening skills; National Curriculum; oracy; speech skills

LANGUAGE STANDARDISATION
10/1804 developing countries; language policy; literacy; mother tongue

LANGUAGE TEACHERS
10/0222 English – second language; language proficiency; second language teaching
10/0608 language attitudes; learning motivation; modern language studies
10/0644 English – second language; inservice teacher education; second language teaching; Thailand
10/1097 English studies; National Curriculum
10/1799 comparative education; modern language studies; National Curriculum
10/1803 bilingual pupils; English – second language; limited English speaking; second language teaching

LANGUAGE TESTS
10/0335 assessment; attainment tests; English studies; Scotland
10/1396 communicative competence – languages; English – second language; Korea; second language teaching
10/1810 comparative education; English; German; modern language studies; native speakers; second language teaching

LANGUAGE USAGE
10/0031 academic achievement; bilingualism; diglossia; ethnic groups
10/0135 role playing; young children
10/0136 role playing; young children
10/1153 church and education; feminism; power structure; Protestant churches

LANGUAGE VARIATION
10/1242 dialect studies; sociolinguistics

LANGUAGES FOR SPECIFIC PURPOSES
10/0587 Botswana; language of instruction; science education; scientific vocabulary; second language learning
10/1365 further education; modern language studies; second language teaching; vocational education
10/1395 English – second language; Malaysia; second language learning

LATERAL DOMINANCE
10/0659 brain hemisphere functions; dyslexia; handedness; reading difficulties; visual perception

LATIN
10/1469 educational materials; textbook preparation

LEADERSHIP
10/0291 head teachers; leadership styles; local management of schools; management in education; school based management
10/0437 performance indicators; seminars; small group teaching; teacher effectiveness; teaching methods; university teaching
10/0438 seminars; small group teaching; teaching methods; university teaching

LEADERSHIP STYLES
10/0291 head teachers; leadership; local management of schools; management in education; school based management

LEARNER CENTRED CURRICULUM
10/0381 assessment; higher education; self
evaluation – individuals; teaching methods

LEARNER CENTRED METHODS
10/0126 educational media; learning resources
centres; management development;
management studies; multimedia approach
10/0387 assessment; higher education; open
education; self evaluation – individuals;
teaching methods
10/1143 staff development; teaching process;
universities; university teaching
10/1424 biology education; chemistry education;
learning strategies; physics education; science
education; teaching methods

LEARNER CHARACTERISTICS
10/0255 'A' level examinations; design
education; student attitudes
10/0388 higher education; learning experience;
learning strategies; student experience
10/1210 'A' level examinations; music activities;
music education; pupil attitudes; sex differences

LEARNER EDUCATIONAL OBJECTIVES
10/1461 employment opportunities; labour
market; occupational aspiration; opportunities;
secondary school pupils; work-education
relationship
10/1462 career choice; employment
opportunities; labour market; occupational
aspiration; school to work transition;
secondary school pupils; work-education
relationship

LEARNING
10/0218 music; music education
10/0326 comprehension
10/0348 ability; mixed ability; pacing; time
factors – learning
10/0610 cognitive processes; cognitive style;
field dependence-independence; mathematics;
teaching styles
10/0863 attention; cognitive development; early
experience; infant behaviour; neurological
impairments

LEARNING ACTIVITIES
10/0159 behaviour disorders; classroom
communication; conversation; literacy
education; special educational needs
10/0215 learning processes; mathematics
education
10/0340 mathematical applications; mathematics
education; secondary education
10/0440 comparative education; distance
education; higher education; international
educational exchange; Netherlands; teaching
methods; telecommunications
10/0680 earth science; environmental education
10/0709 discussion; group work; interaction;
intergroup education
10/1052 group work; reading improvement;
reading strategies
10/1116 learning strategies; nurse education;
study skills
10/1118 design and technology; teaching methods
10/1182 critical thinking; group discussion;
teaching methods; university students
10/1197 classroom observation techniques; group
work; science activities; science education
10/1312 play; pupil attitudes
10/1531 developing countries; development
education; India; primary education; teaching
methods
10/1617 construction industry; experiential
learning; surveying education
10/1650 home-school relationship; homework;
mathematics education; parent participation
10/1751 classroom communication; teacher-pupil
relationship; teacher role; teaching methods
10/1782 business administration education;
learning strategies; management studies
10/1801 practical science; science activities;
science education

LEARNING DISABILITIES
10/0041 differentiated curriculum; English
studies curriculum; low achievement;

mainstreaming; special educational needs
10/0082 blindness; braille; literacy education;
raised line drawings; sensory aids; special
educational needs
10/0238 computer assisted learning; dyslexia;
interactive video; multimedia approach
10/0284 computer software; computer uses in
education; special educational needs; spelling;
writing difficulties
10/0447 city technology colleges; dyslexia;
educational materials; special educational
needs; teaching methods
10/0453 dyslexia; reading difficulties; special
educational needs; teacher education
10/0705 language acquisition; language
handicaps; psycholinguistics
10/0860 computer assisted learning; computer
uses in education; concept keyboards;
human-computer interaction; special
educational needs; touch screens
10/0917 bilingual pupils; cognitive ability;
dyslexia; language acquisition; language
handicaps; special educational needs
10/0972 ability tests; language handicaps;
mathematical ability; mathematics education;
numbers; special educational needs
10/1013 assessment; low achievement; moderate
learning difficulties; special educational needs
10/1103 reading comprehension; reading
difficulties; special educational needs
10/1302 behaviour problems; emotional
problems; family problems; problem children;
social experience
10/1449 adult day centres; special educational
needs
10/1452 comparative education; Greece;
Scotland; special educational needs
10/1582 dyslexia; mathematics
10/1621 arithmetic; cognitive ability
10/1640 attention deficit disorders; cognitive
ability; hyperactivity; memory
10/1675 adult basic education; neurological
impairments; special educational needs;
speech handicaps

LEARNING EXPERIENCE
10/0168 higher education; mature students
10/0349 curriculum development; drama;
educational materials
10/0388 higher education; learner characteristics;
learning strategies; student experience
10/0866 experiential learning; interpersonal
competence; preservice teacher education;
student teachers; workshops
10/1378 pupil attitudes; pupil-school
relationship; school effectiveness; secondary
education; secondary school pupils; teaching
process
10/1406 language acquisition; language skills;
parent participation; parent-teacher cooperation
10/1473 health visitors; nurse education;
placement
10/1626 behavioural objectives; comprehension;
educational objectives; test use
10/1671 higher education; mature students;
student experience

LEARNING MOTIVATION
10/0341 higher education; learning strategies;
mathematics achievement; sixteen to nineteen
education; undergraduate study
10/0457 modern language studies; Scotland;
second language teaching
10/0608 language attitudes; language teachers;
modern language studies

LEARNING PROCESSES
10/0065 clergy; continuing education;
professional education; religious education;
theological education
10/0111 heuristics; primary education; teaching
methods
10/0167 cognitive processes; cognitive psychology;
epistemology; higher education; memory
10/0215 learning activities; mathematics
education
10/0249 mathematics education; thinking skills
10/0288 cognitive processes; learning theories;
mathematics education
10/0353 computer uses in education; feedback;

interaction; peer teaching; teacher-pupil
relationship
10/0579 drama education; dramatics; primary
education; theatre arts
10/0617 electricity; physics education; science
education; sixth form education
10/1170 learning strategies; teaching methods;
tertiary education
10/1181 computer assisted learning; computer
uses in education; cooperative learning;
human-computer interaction
10/1204 communication research; competency
based education; further education; higher
education; teaching methods
10/1251 computer uses in education; concept
formation; creative development
10/1488 experiential learning; intellectual
development; learning strategies
10/1543 cognitive processes; computer assisted
learning; metacognition
10/1665 home-school relationship; primary
school pupils; pupil-school relationship; social
influences; sociology of education

LEARNING RESOURCES CENTRES
10/0126 educational media; learner centred
methods; management development;
management studies; multimedia approach

LEARNING STRATEGIES
10/0005 medical education; nurse education;
predictive measurement
10/0048 fire service; professional education;
teaching methods
10/0053 'A' level examinations; modern
language studies; sixteen to nineteen education
10/0151 adult learning; human-computer
interaction; secretaries; word processing
10/0177 cognitive processes; cognitive style;
problem solving
10/0272 educational materials; medical
education; medical students
10/0285 enterprise education; industry-education
relationship; motivation; skill development;
transfer of learning
10/0337 higher education; learning theories;
student attitudes; teaching methods
10/0338 comprehension; essays; examination
techniques; higher education; review –
reexamination; study skills; writing –
composition
10/0341 higher education; learning motivation;
mathematics achievement; sixteen to nineteen
education; undergraduate study
10/0388 higher education; learner characteristics;
learning experience; student experience
10/0389 higher education; study skills;
undergraduate students
10/0581 learning theories; preservice teacher
education; student teachers
10/0857 study skills
10/1116 learning activities; nurse education;
study skills
10/1170 learning processes; teaching methods;
tertiary education
10/1192 design and technology; problem solving;
technology education
10/1212 National Curriculum; teacher
effectiveness; teaching methods
10/1238 assessment; enterprise education; higher
education; skill development; work-education
relationship
10/1276 mathematics teachers; preservice teacher
education; school based teacher education;
student teachers
10/1424 biology education; chemistry education;
learner centred methods; physics education;
science education; teaching methods
10/1485 teaching methods; technology
education
10/1488 experiential learning; intellectual
development; learning processes
10/1490 management studies
10/1491 learning theories; teaching methods
10/1542 autoinstructional aids; cognitive style;
computer assisted learning; computer uses in
education; teaching machines
10/1572 computer uses in education; history
studies; teaching methods; teleconferencing
10/1618 chemistry education; educational

materials; multimedia approach; science education; skills; teaching methods; transfer of learning
10/1782 business administration education; learning activities; management studies
10/1783 classroom research; National Curriculum; primary education; reading teaching; teaching methods
10/1798 special educational needs

LEARNING THEORIES
10/0108 educational theories; psychology; teacher education; teaching experience; teaching practice; teaching process
10/0288 cognitive processes; learning processes; mathematics education
10/0337 higher education; learning strategies; student attitudes; teaching methods
10/0581 learning strategies; preservice teacher education; student teachers
10/0591 concept formation; science education; scientific concepts
10/1491 learning strategies; teaching methods

LECTURE METHOD
10/1391 English – second language; English for academic purposes; overseas students; teaching styles

LEGISLATION
10/0851 Children Act 1989; day care; early childhood education; local government; preschool education; social services

LEISURE TIME
10/0540 girls; recreational activities; women's studies
10/1062 arts; arts education; attitudes; culture; participation; youth

LETTERS – CORRESPONDENCE
10/0940 writing – composition; writing exercises; writing skills

LEXICOLOGY
10/0192 bilingualism; word recognition

LIBERAL EDUCATION
10/1516 adult education; continuing education; nontraditional education
10/1517 adult education; continuing education

LIBRARIANSHIP EDUCATION
10/1286 developing countries; development education; Europe; information science
10/1603 distance education; flexible learning; information science; mature students
10/1607 library schools; placement; professional education; work experience programmes

LIBRARIES
10/1608 drug education; information sources; prevention

LIBRARY ROLE
10/1705 primary schools; school libraries

LIBRARY SCHOOLS
10/1607 librarianship education; placement; professional education; work experience programmes

LICENSED TEACHERS
10/0560 preservice teacher education; programme evaluation; teacher qualifications; teaching profession

LIFE SKILLS
10/0577 adult education; numeracy; older adults
10/0849 drug education; health education; primary education
10/1066 economics education; money management; volunteers

LIFE STYLE
10/0101 aspiration; skills; special educational needs; visual impairments; vocational education
10/0119 adult education; participation

LIFELONG LEARNING
10/0121 access to education; adult education; continuing education
10/0430 adult education; comparative education; mature students; people's universities; Scandinavia
10/0431 adult education; comparative education; Denmark; mature students; people's universities
10/0575 continuing education; professional continuing education; professional development
10/0578 adult education; adult learning; caregivers; disabilities; independent study
10/0959 adult education; comparative education; continuing education; cultural differences; Europe
10/1054 adult education; adult learning; guidance
10/1501 nurse education; nurses; professional continuing education; professional development

LIKERT SCALES
10/1811 linguistics; opinions; questionnaires; rating scales; semantics

LIMITED English SPEAKING
10/1803 bilingual pupils; English – second language; language teachers; second language teaching
10/1809 English – second language; English for academic purposes; overseas students; second language learning

LINGUISTICS
10/0931 educational philosophy; mathematics education
10/1811 Likert scales; opinions; questionnaires; rating scales; semantics

LISTENING SKILLS
10/0520 academic achievement; cognitive ability; reading achievement; television research; television viewing
10/0843 communication skills; National Curriculum; speech communication
10/1759 English studies curriculum; language skills; National Curriculum; oracy; speech skills

LITERACY
10/0206 language skills; oracy; reading skills; special educational needs; spelling; writing skills
10/0333 India; nomads
10/0346 developing countries; development education; educational materials; material development; reading materials
10/0375 information seeking; primary education; reading skills; writing skills
10/0706 adult literacy; home-school relationship; literacy education; mother tongue; native speakers; primary education; teaching methods
10/0707 memory; older adults; oral history; personal narratives
10/0763 incidental learning; mass media; popular culture
10/0936 books; children as writers; children's literature; picture books
10/1049 family involvement; family programmes; parent participation; reading skills; writing skills
10/1096 further education students; higher education; reading skills; writing skills
10/1269 developing countries; women's education
10/1762 beginning reading; parent participation; psycholinguistics; reading research; reading teaching
10/1804 developing countries; language policy; language standardisation; mother tongue

LITERACY EDUCATION
10/0082 blindness; braille; learning disabilities; raised line drawings; sensory aids; special educational needs
10/0150 curriculum; reading skills; secondary school curriculum; writing skills
10/0159 behaviour disorders; classroom communication; conversation; learning activities; special educational needs

10/0706 adult literacy; home-school relationship; literacy; mother tongue; native speakers; primary education; teaching methods
10/0716 bilingual education programmes; English – second language; ethnic groups; home-school relationship; parent participation; reading teaching; second language learning

LITERARY CRITICISM
10/0476 hypermedia; literature studies; multimedia approach
10/0485 aesthetic values; literature studies

LITERARY GENRES
10/0077 creative writing; English studies curriculum; National Curriculum; writing – composition; writing skills

LITERATURE REVIEWS
10/1010 computer uses in education; information technology
10/1069 disabilities; further education; further education students; moderate learning difficulties; special educational needs

LITERATURE STUDIES
10/0212 English literature; English studies curriculum
10/0476 hypermedia; literary criticism; multimedia approach
10/0485 aesthetic values; literary criticism
10/1800 citizenship education; human rights; pupil attitudes; racial attitudes; social attitudes

LOCAL EDUCATION AUTHORITIES
10/0017 educational administration
10/0079 educational finance; educational planning
10/0096 educational administration; educational change; educational policy; governance; management in education; politics-education relationship
10/0162 educational administration; educational change; educational policy; governance; governing bodies; management in education
10/0163 educational finance; educational policy; higher education
10/0184 mainstreaming; primary schools; special educational needs; teacher development
10/0498 inspection; inspectors – of schools
10/0639 programme evaluation; TVEI
10/0838 health education; nutrition education; school meals
10/0855 industry-education relationship; school to work transition; vocational education
10/0883 Education Reform Act 1988; educational change; educational development; educational planning; educational policy; government role
10/0909 educational administration; educational administrators; management in education
10/0989 educational administration; inservice teacher education
10/0991 evaluation; inspection; monitoring
10/0994 antiracism education; Education Reform Act 1988; educational planning; equal education; multicultural education
10/0996 preservice teacher education; probationary teachers; teacher development; teacher education; teacher induction
10/1001 curriculum development; developmental continuity; National Curriculum; primary secondary education; transfer pupils
10/1004 curriculum development; European Community; European studies
10/1018 maintenance grants; student financial aid; tuition grants
10/1037 voluntary service; youth leaders; youth service
10/1055 achievement; birth; school entrance age
10/1070 voluntary agencies; youth leaders; youth service
10/1208 educational administration; educational change; educational policy; special educational needs
10/1278 competency based teacher education; inservice teacher education; school based teacher education; staff orientation; teacher development
10/1377 educational quality; inspection; institutional evaluation; school effectiveness

10/1498 advisers; inservice teacher education; inspection; organisational effectiveness

10/1742 Education Reform Act 1988; educational change; educational legislation; educational policy

10/1754 educational change; educational innovation; special educational needs

10/1786 admission criteria; school entrance age

LOCAL GOVERNMENT

10/0851 Children Act 1989; day care; early childhood education; legislation; preschool education; social services

10/0935 community services; day care; early childhood education; nursery school curriculum; nursery schools; preschool education; young children

LOCAL HISTORY

10/0641 history studies; National Curriculum

LOCAL MANAGEMENT OF SCHOOLS

10/0075 educational finance; financial policy; financial support

10/0076 educational change; head teachers; school based management

10/0080 Education Reform Act 1988; school size; small schools

10/0235 educational administration; school based management; small schools

10/0262 databases; research

10/0291 head teachers; leadership; leadership styles; management in education; school based management

10/0345 educational administration; educational change; parent participation; school based management; school boards – Scotland; school governing bodies

10/0569 parent participation; participative decision making; school based management; school governing bodies; school governors

10/0672 educational administration; grant maintained schools; management in education; school based management

10/0756 educational administration; school based management; special educational needs

10/0870 educational administration; educational change; school based management

10/0873 computer uses in education; educational administration; information technology; management systems; school based management

10/0888 educational administration; institutional cooperation

10/0896 educational change; governing bodies; school based management; school governors

10/0902 educational change; National Curriculum; physical education; sports

10/0924 Education Reform Act 1988; educational administration; educational change; school based management; secondary schools

10/1014 educational administration; educational finance; mainstreaming; resource allocation; school based management; special educational needs

10/1038 budgeting; educational administration; educational finance; school based management

10/1039 educational administration; school based management; school governing bodies; school governors

10/1255 educational change; evaluation; school based management; secondary schools

10/1256 change; head teachers; primary schools; role conflict; stress variables; time management

10/1667 educational administration; educational policy; management in education; organisational change

10/1722 equal education; racial discrimination; racial integration; school based management; secondary schools

10/1790 educational administration; management in education; programme evaluation; school based management; teacher development

LOCAL RADIO

10/0695 adult education; educational broadcasting; educational radio; mass media; radio

LOCAL STUDIES

10/1226 environmental education; field studies; geographic location; story telling

LOCUS OF CONTROL

10/0526 academic aspiration; Malaysia; motivation tests; student motivation

10/0968 mainstreaming; primary schools; self esteem; socialisation; special educational needs

10/1163 experiential learning; interpersonal competence; outcomes of education; stress – psychological; student experience; teacher education

10/1484 behaviour disorders; child psychiatry; emotional disturbances

LOGO

10/0039 algebra; computer uses in education; low achievement; mathematics education

10/0362 cognitive ability; computer assisted learning; interaction; turtles – robots

10/1179 computer simulation; computer uses in education; control technology; models

10/1446 computer uses in education; feedback; geometry; mathematics education; problem solving

LONG RANGE PLANNING

10/0059 prediction; pupil numbers; regional planning

LONGITUDINAL STUDIES

10/0105 academic achievement; blindness; cognitive development; outcomes of education; partial vision; special schools; visual impairments

10/0243 antisocial behaviour; behaviour problems; delinquency prevention; secondary school pupils; transfer pupils

10/0320 cohort analysis; followup studies; school leavers; school to work transition; Scotland; sixteen to nineteen education; youth

10/0592 concept formation; science education; scientific concepts

10/0629 educational change; TVEI

10/0722 ability; child development; developmental continuity; personality development

10/0758 pupil attitudes; school activities; self evaluation – individuals; sixteen to nineteen education

10/1663 assessment; primary education; primary school pupils; pupil-school relationship; school based assessment; standard assessment tasks

10/1664 educational experience; primary education; primary school pupils; pupil-school relationship

LOW ACHIEVEMENT

10/0039 algebra; computer uses in education; logo; mathematics education

10/0041 differentiated curriculum; English studies curriculum; learning disabilities; mainstreaming; special educational needs

10/0138 assessment; examinations; General Certificate of Secondary Education; special educational needs

10/0901 mathematics achievement; mathematics education

10/0945 curriculum development; moderate learning difficulties; special educational needs; underachievement

10/1013 assessment; learning disabilities; moderate learning difficulties; special educational needs

10/1710 achievement; Afro Caribbean youth; assessment; black pupils; Education Reform Act 1988; equal education; ethnic groups

LOW VISION AIDS

10/0521 educational materials; educational media; printing; textbooks

10/0886 blindness; microcomputers; sensory aids; tactile adaptation; visual impairments

MAIN SUBJECTS

10/0993 degrees – academic; Postgraduate Certificate in Education; preservice teacher education

MAINSTREAMING

10/0041 differentiated curriculum; English studies curriculum; learning disabilities; low achievement; special educational needs

10/0092 comparative education; disabilities; pupil attitudes; special educational needs; special schools

10/0117 further education; severe learning difficulties; special educational needs; support services

10/0179 comparative education; educational materials; special educational needs; teacher education

10/0184 local education authorities; primary schools; special educational needs; teacher development

10/0186 institutional evaluation; special educational needs; whole school approach

10/0189 India; special educational needs; teacher education

10/0191 institutional evaluation; special educational needs; United States of America; whole school approach

10/0359 secondary education; special educational needs; support services

10/0433 educational quality; hearing impairments; peripatetic teachers; special educational needs; support teachers; teacher effectiveness

10/0474 disabilities; moderate learning difficulties; Nigeria; physical education; special educational needs

10/0646 pupil needs; school effectiveness; special educational needs

10/0661 cognitive processes; spatial ability; special educational needs

10/0677 differentiated curriculum; individual needs; National Curriculum; special educational needs

10/0862 classroom environment; moderate learning difficulties; pupil attitudes; pupil behaviour; social behaviour; special educational needs

10/0884 Down's Syndrome; special educational needs

10/0900 further education; special educational needs; visual impairments

10/0968 locus of control; primary schools; self esteem; socialisation; special educational needs

10/1014 educational administration; educational finance; local management of schools; resource allocation; school based management; special educational needs

10/1016 institutional cooperation; special educational needs; special schools

10/1206 comparative education; educational administration; educational policy; Italy; Scandinavia; special educational needs; support services

10/1453 pupil attitudes; pupil experience; special educational needs

10/1455 comparative analysis; educational policy; special educational needs; special schools

10/1646 further education; special educational needs; support services; support teachers

10/1765 Down's Syndrome; expressive language; interaction; language acquisition; special educational needs; special schools

MAINTENANCE GRANTS

10/1018 local education authorities; student financial aid; tuition grants

MALAWI

10/1161 curriculum development; mathematics education; primary education; science education

MALAYSIA

10/0421 English – second language; secondary schools

10/0422 English – second language; secondary schools

10/0526 academic aspiration; locus of control; motivation tests; student motivation

10/0557 secondary school teachers; teacher behaviour; teacher effectiveness; teaching styles

10/1395 English – second language; languages for specific purposes; second language learning

10/1539 science education

MALAYSIANS
10/0985 secondary schools; teacher evaluation

MANAGEMENT DEVELOPMENT
10/0025 competency based education
10/0126 educational media; learner centred
methods; learning resources centres;
management studies; multimedia approach
10/0770 educational administration; educational
materials; management in education; material
development
10/0771 educational administration; educational
materials; management in education; material
development
10/0910 head teachers; managerial occupations;
mentors
10/0911 industry-education relationship;
mentors; work-education relationship
10/0952 administrators; educational
administration; head teachers; management in
education
10/1440 management in education; training centres
10/1612 city technology colleges; grant
maintained schools; inservice teacher
education; school based management; staff
development

MANAGEMENT IN EDUCATION
10/0049 administrators; educational
administration; teacher-administrator
relationship
10/0096 educational administration; educational
change; educational policy; governance; local
education authorities; politics-education
relationship
10/0162 educational administration; educational
change; educational policy; governance;
governing bodies; local education authorities
10/0183 head teachers; mentors
10/0265 educational history; Scotland
10/0291 head teachers; leadership; leadership
styles; local management of schools; school
based management
10/0386 educational administration; head
teachers; sex differences; teaching profession;
women's employment
10/0428 educational administration; educational
policy; politics-education relationship; Scotland
10/0507 teacher evaluation; teacher role
10/0517 administrators; educational
administration; further education; higher
education; women; women's employment
10/0519 economic factors; educational quality;
marketing; primary schools
10/0671 administrator role; educational change;
head teachers; role conflict; secondary
schools; teacher role
10/0672 educational administration; grant
maintained schools; local management of
schools; school based management
10/0674 educational administration; educational
change; grant maintained schools; school
based management
10/0770 educational administration; educational
materials; management development; material
development
10/0771 educational administration; educational
materials; management development; material
development
10/0772 educational administration; educational
materials; material development
10/0887 professional personnel
10/0908 educational administration; educational
history
10/0909 educational administration; educational
administrators; local education authorities
10/0912 educational administration; governing
bodies; head teachers; school governors
10/0925 educational quality; school based
management
10/0952 administrators; educational
administration; head teachers; management
development
10/1111 colleges of further education;
educational administration; educational
planning; marketing
10/1175 educational planning; university
administration

10/1209 educational administration; Europe;
teacher employment; teaching profession;
women; women's employment
10/1268 educational administration; higher
education
10/1440 management development; training
centres
10/1441 colleges of further education; quality
control; sixteen to nineteen education; staff
development
10/1609 educational administration; educational
change; grant maintained schools; school
based management
10/1667 educational administration; educational
policy; local management of schools;
organisational change
10/1790 educational administration; local
management of schools; programme
evaluation; school based management; teacher
development

MANAGEMENT STUDIES
10/0126 educational media; learner centred
methods; learning resources centres;
management development; multimedia
approach
10/0570 business education; computer
simulation; computer uses in education
10/0582 computer assisted learning; computer
uses in education; expert systems
10/0718 computer assisted learning; computer
uses in education; educational software
10/1109 industry-higher education relationship;
placement; work experience
10/1490 learning strategies
10/1497 business administration education;
professional training; Single European Market
10/1782 business administration education;
learning activities; learning strategies

MANAGEMENT SYSTEMS
10/0873 computer uses in education; educational
administration; information technology; local
management of schools; school based
management

MANAGEMENT TEAMS
10/0152 educational administration; educational
change; school based management; secondary
schools

MANAGERIAL OCCUPATIONS
10/0910 head teachers; management
development; mentors

MANUAL COMMUNICATION
10/1387 communication aids – for disabled;
communication disorders; severe learning
difficulties; sign language; special educational
needs; symbolic language

MAPS
10/0102 blindness; memory; raised line
drawings; spatial ability; tactile adaptation;
visual impairments

MARKETING
10/0366 institutional advancement; parent
choice; parent-school relationship; selection
10/0519 economic factors; educational quality;
management in education; primary schools
10/0696 secondary schools
10/0891 independent schools; parent choice
10/1111 colleges of further education;
educational administration; educational
planning; management in education
10/1261 educational change; institutional
advancement

MASS MEDIA
10/0695 adult education; educational broadcasting;
educational radio; local radio; radio
10/0762 educational media; mass media; material
development; production techniques
10/0763 incidental learning; literacy; popular
culture
10/0836 primary school teachers; public opinion;
science teachers; scientific attitudes; scientific
literacy; television
10/1060 arts; attitudes; culture; music;

participation; sports; theatre arts
10/1080 media studies
10/1137 adult learning; memory

MASS MEDIA EFFECTS
10/0149 educational change; educational policy;
press opinion; public opinion

MASTERS' COURSES
10/0394 competency based education; education
courses; higher education; qualifications;
standards
10/0789 competency based education; higher
education; National Vocational Qualifications;
qualifications; standards

MASTERY TESTS
10/0776 assessment; job skills; retention –
psychology; vocational education

MATERIAL DEVELOPMENT
10/0144 Belize; developing countries;
educational materials; textbooks
10/0147 deafness; distance education; sign
language; special educational needs
10/0195 computer software; educational
materials; energy education; science education
10/0346 developing countries; development
education; educational materials; literacy;
reading materials
10/0503 earth science; educational materials;
National Curriculum; physical sciences;
science education
10/0548 artificial intelligence; computer assisted
learning; educational materials
10/0762 educational media; mass media;
production techniques
10/0770 educational administration; educational
materials; management development;
management in education
10/0771 educational administration; educational
materials; management development;
management in education
10/0772 educational administration; educational
materials; management in education
10/0779 computer uses in education; data
processing; databases; primary schools
10/0837 inservice teacher education; primary
education; science education
10/1422 college-school cooperation; educational
materials; flexible learning; preservice teacher
education
10/1429 educational materials; flexible learning;
medical education
10/1430 acquired immune deficiency syndrome;
educational materials; educational technology;
health education; interactive video; sex
education
10/1432 biographies; educational materials;
educational technology; optical data discs
10/1465 computer science education
10/1648 curriculum development; educational
materials; experiential learning; primary
education; technology education;
work-education relationship
10/1652 educational material evaluation;
educational materials; science education;
scientific attitudes; scientific literacy;
supported self study; teacher education

MATHEMATICAL ABILITY
10/0299 employer attitudes; graduate
employment; graduates; numeracy;
work-education relationship
10/0609 arithmetic; mathematics education;
problem solving; teacher education; teaching
methods
10/0972 ability tests; language handicaps;
learning disabilities; mathematics education;
numbers; special educational needs

MATHEMATICAL APPLICATIONS
10/0340 learning activities; mathematics
education; secondary education
10/1642 mathematical concepts; mathematics
education; test construction

MATHEMATICAL CONCEPTS
10/0467 classroom communication; concept
teaching; mathematics education

10/1027 assessment; early childhood education; mathematics education; mathematics tests; school entrance age
10/1280 classroom communication; comprehension; mathematical vocabulary; mathematics education
10/1292 mathematics education; young children
10/1381 mathematics education
10/1642 mathematical applications; mathematics education; test construction

MATHEMATICAL FORMULAS
10/0613 algebra; cognitive processes; comprehension; mathematics education

MATHEMATICAL MODELS
10/0783 engineering education; mathematics education; spreadsheets
10/0980 mathematics education
10/1384 algebra education; mathematics education
10/1601 assessment; cognitive ability; mathematics education; metacognition

MATHEMATICAL VOCABULARY
10/1280 classroom communication; comprehension; mathematical concepts; mathematics education

MATHEMATICS
10/0304 computer uses in education; gifted; individualised methods; Jordan; primary education
10/0355 educational philosophy
10/0572 art; art history; cognitive development; cross curricular approach; spatial ability
10/0610 cognitive processes; cognitive style; field dependence-independence; learning; teaching styles
10/1172 affective behaviour; emotional response; student behaviour
10/1271 inservice teacher education; primary school teachers; teacher attitudes
10/1582 dyslexia; learning disabilities

MATHEMATICS ACHIEVEMENT
10/0341 higher education; learning motivation; learning strategies; sixteen to nineteen education; undergraduate study
10/0786 comparative education; France; trainees
10/0901 low achievement; mathematics education
10/0998 assessment; National Curriculum; primary education; science education; standard assessment tasks
10/1053 achievement tests; assessment; mathematics education; National Curriculum
10/1081 mathematics education; primary education
10/1216 individual development; mathematics education; pupil participation; sex difference
10/1219 assessment; educational materials; mathematics education; National Curriculum
10/1298 assessment; mathematics education; primary school pupils; self evaluation – individuals

MATHEMATICS ANXIETY
10/0172 mathematics education; teaching methods

MATHEMATICS CURRICULUM
10/0588 assessment; first schools; infant schools; mathematics teachers; standard assessment tasks

MATHEMATICS EDUCATION
10/1421 mathematics education
10/0039 algebra; computer uses in education; logo; low achievement
10/0054 educational materials; industry-education relationship
10/0172 mathematics anxiety; teaching methods
10/0188 arithmetic and number education; calculators; primary education
10/0215 learning activities; learning processes
10/0249 learning processes; thinking skills
10/0250 course evaluation; degrees – academic; student attitudes
10/0286 Cameroon; cross curricular approach; English – second language; language of instruction
10/0288 cognitive processes; learning processes; learning theories

10/0306 early childhood education; infant school teachers; reception classes
10/0340 learning activities; mathematical applications; secondary education
10/0342 group work
10/0343 audiovisual education; calculators; equipment; undergraduate students
10/0374 comparative education; primary education
10/0467 classroom communication; concept teaching; mathematical concepts
10/0469 mentors; National Curriculum; preservice teacher education; student teacher supervisors; teaching practice
10/0510 curriculum development; information technology; secondary education
10/0512 computer uses in education; information technology; microcomputers; secondary schools
10/0513 computer uses in education; information technology; secondary schools
10/0543 Greece; mathematics teachers; teacher education
10/0609 arithmetic; mathematical ability; problem solving; teacher education; teaching methods
10/0613 algebra; cognitive processes; comprehension; mathematical formulas
10/0615 geometry education; Greece; problem solving
10/0618 arithmetic; cognitive style; mature students; secondary school pupils
10/0619 algebra; calculators; computer uses in education; secondary education
10/0621 algebra; Kenya; pupil problems
10/0628 cognitive processes; National Curriculum; pattern recognition
10/0630 curriculum development; geometry; secondary education; South Africa
10/0632 early childhood education; pattern recognition; play; young children
10/0638 assessment; National Curriculum; school based assessment
10/0653 number concepts; numbers
10/0687 geography education; navigation; orientation; orienteering; outdoor pursuits; primary education
10/0717 peer influence; peer teaching; science education; student volunteers; technology education
10/0723 area; concept formation; measurement equipment
10/0726 feedback; group work; problem solving
10/0774 science education; spreadsheets
10/0777 algebra; computer uses in education; symbols – mathematics
10/0780 algebra education; computer uses in education; problem solving
10/0781 computer uses in education; imagery
10/0782 computer uses in education; symbols – mathematics; trigonometry; visualisation
10/0783 engineering education; mathematical models; spreadsheets
10/0788 computer uses in education; educational software; symbols – mathematics; visual learning
10/0847 classroom research; curriculum research; Education Reform Act 1988; educational change; educational experience; infant schools
10/0893 special educational needs
10/0901 low achievement; mathematics achievement
10/0931 educational philosophy; linguistics
10/0950 computer uses in education; information technology; preservice teacher education; student teachers; teacher attitudes
10/0971 achievement; National Curriculum; primary education; reading achievement
10/0972 ability tests; language handicaps; learning disabilities; mathematical ability; numbers; special educational needs
10/0978 assessment; attainment tests; English studies; geography education; National Curriculum – Northern Ireland; Northern Ireland; science education
10/0980 mathematical models
10/0981 cultural background; probability
10/0982 curriculum development; science education; technology education

10/1002 assessment; core curriculum; English studies; National Curriculum; science education
10/1027 assessment; early childhood education; mathematical concepts; mathematics tests; school entrance age
10/1040 comparative education; science education
10/1053 achievement tests; assessment; mathematics achievement; National Curriculum
10/1058 achievement; achievement tests; assessment; comparative education; science education
10/1081 mathematics achievement; primary education
10/1084 assessment; English studies; evaluation; National Curriculum; science education; secondary education; technology education
10/1155 classroom research; educational materials; educational technology; interactive video; multimedia approach
10/1156 calculus education; computer uses in education; university students
10/1161 curriculum development; Malawi; primary education; science education
10/1184 computer uses in education; educational software; spreadsheets
10/1185 courses; inservice teacher education; primary school teachers
10/1187 higher education; introductory courses; numbers; numeracy
10/1216 individual development; mathematics achievement; pupil participation; sex difference
10/1219 assessment; educational materials; mathematics achievement; National Curriculum
10/1277 Cameroon
10/1280 classroom communication; comprehension; mathematical concepts; mathematical vocabulary
10/1292 mathematical concepts; young children
10/1298 assessment; mathematics achievement; primary school pupils; self evaluation – individuals
10/1306 early childhood education; numbers; preschool education
10/1317 computer uses in education; educational software; geometry
10/1321 imagination; pretend play; simulation
10/1338 comparative education; curriculum development; international educational exchange; science education
10/1381 mathematical concepts
10/1382 individualised methods; teaching methods
10/1383 computer microworlds; computer uses in education; proof – mathematics
10/1384 algebra education; mathematical models
10/1444 assessment; curriculum development; educational change; environmental education; National Curriculum; Scotland; teaching process
10/1446 computer uses in education; feedback; geometry; logo; problem solving
10/1475 computer assisted learning; computer uses in education
10/1476 computer science education; teaching methods
10/1477 computer uses in education; spreadsheets; statistics education
10/1479 algebra education; computer assisted learning
10/1594 computer uses in education; information technology
10/1601 assessment; cognitive ability; mathematical models; metacognition
10/1642 mathematical applications; mathematical concepts; test construction
10/1650 home-school relationship; homework; learning activities; parent participation
10/1755 National Curriculum; primary education; teaching methods
10/1764 inservice teacher education; primary schools

MATHEMATICS TEACHERS
10/0543 Greece; mathematics education; teacher education
10/0588 assessment; first schools; infant schools;

mathematics curriculum; standard assessment tasks
10/1186 teacher development; teaching methods
10/1276 learning strategies; preservice teacher education; school based teacher education; student teachers

MATHEMATICS TESTS
10/1027 assessment; early childhood education; mathematical concepts; mathematics education; school entrance age

MATURE STUDENTS
10/0043 access to education; adult education; adult learning; basic skills; self evaluation – individuals
10/0118 access programmes; higher education; men; student experience
10/0168 higher education; learning experience
10/0200 higher education; student attitudes; student needs
10/0226 access programmes; adult education; student development
10/0227 access to education; finance occupations; professional education
10/0228 adult education; databases; further education; higher education
10/0229 access to education; adult education; Germany; higher education; student participation
10/0230 access to education; adult education; France; higher education; student participation
10/0267 access programmes; access to education; adult education; comparative education; higher education
10/0430 adult education; comparative education; lifelong learning; peoples universities; Scandinavia
10/0431 adult education; comparative education; Denmark; lifelong learning; people's universities
10/0528 academic staff; ethnic groups; higher education; middle class students; student attitudes; student experience; working class
10/0530 access programmes; access to education; higher education; nontraditional education; student motivation
10/0531 academic achievement; access programmes; higher education; nontraditional education; performance
10/0559 academic achievement; educational experience; higher education; student attitudes
10/0618 arithmetic; cognitive style; mathematics education; secondary school pupils
10/0636 higher education; stress – psychological; stress variables
10/0905 aptitude; assessment; critical thinking; higher education; prediction of success; selection; student evaluation
10/1099 preservice teacher education; student behaviour; student teacher attitudes; student teachers; women's education
10/1110 counselling services; higher education; student counselling
10/1167 adult students; distance education; humanities; open universities; student attitudes
10/1329 adult students; financial problems; student costs; student financial aid; student loans; student recruitment
10/1332 access to education; adult education; adult students; community education; educational guidance; student attitudes
10/1344 access programmes; access to education; adult students; higher education; programme evaluation; science education; social sciences
10/1345 access to education; adult education; adult students; educational guidance; Scotland
10/1416 academic achievement; access programmes; access to education; higher education; outcomes of education
10/1509 graduate study; part time students; student research
10/1587 higher education; sex differences
10/1591 educational experience; higher education; men; sex differences; student attitudes; women's education
10/1603 distance education; flexible learning; information science; librarianship education
10/1671 higher education; learning experience; student experience
10/1726 access to education; higher education;

student attitudes; student housing; student recruitment

MAURITIUS
10/1684 gender equality; women's education; women's employment

MEASUREMENT
10/1380 accountability; educational quality; performance indicators; school effectiveness; secondary schools

MEASUREMENT EQUIPMENT
10/0723 area; concept formation; mathematics education

MEASUREMENT TECHNIQUES
10/1007 career counselling; evaluation methods; guidance objectives; vocational guidance
10/1146 adaptive behaviour – of disabled; attitude measures; blindness; emotional adjustment; rehabilitation; visual impairments

MECHANICS INSTITUTES
10/0296 adult education; educational history

MEDIA STUDIES
10/1080 mass media

MEDICAL EDUCATION
10/0005 learning strategies; nurse education; predictive measurement
10/0073 clinical experience; outcomes of education
10/0169 surgery
10/0268 assessment; competence; examinations; medicine; physicians
10/0272 educational materials; learning strategies; medical students
10/0273 computer assisted learning; computer uses in education; individualised methods; information technology
10/0274 educational material evaluation; educational materials
10/0275 curriculum evaluation
10/0276 distance education; programme evaluation
10/0277 human-computer interaction; interactive video
10/0279 clinical experience; medical students
10/0280 biological sciences; computer assisted learning
10/0281 dentistry
10/0282 assessment; competence; examinations; medicine; physicians
10/0392 assessment; clinical experience; physical therapy
10/0701 critical thinking; experiential learning; professional continuing education; professional development; reflective teaching
10/1165 nurses; obstetrics
10/1166 obstetrics
10/1346 computer assisted learning; computer uses in education; educational technology; medicine
10/1429 educational materials; flexible learning; material development
10/1693 behavioural sciences; health personnel; health services; interdisciplinary approach

MEDICAL SCHOOLS
10/0719 admission criteria; medical students; selective admission
10/1775 flexible learning; open education; teaching methods

MEDICAL SERVICES
10/0269 distance education; institutional evaluation; professional continuing education
10/0270 health education; patient education; pharmacists; pharmacy
10/0278 training
10/1154 doctor-patient relationship; pain; patient education; physical health
10/1158 doctor-patient relationship; pain; patient education; physical health

MEDICAL STUDENTS
10/0272 educational materials; learning strategies; medical education

10/0279 clinical experience; medical education
10/0719 admission criteria; medical schools; selective admission

MEDICINE
10/0268 assessment; competence; examinations; medical education; physicians
10/0282 assessment; competence; examinations; medical education; physicians
10/1098 degrees – academic; professional education; undergraduate students
10/1346 computer assisted learning; computer uses in education; educational technology; medical education
10/1502 nurse education; nurses; pharmacology

MEMORISATION
10/1243 child development; phonemics; pictorial stimuli; verbal development; visual learning

MEMORY
10/0102 blindness; maps; raised line drawings; spatial ability; tactile adaptation; visual impairments
10/0167 cognitive processes; cognitive psychology; epistemology; higher education; learning processes
10/0707 literacy; older adults; oral history; personal narratives
10/0858 cognitive ability; gifted
10/0984 pictorial stimuli; science education; visual learning
10/0990 perceptual development; spatial ability
10/0992 assessment; spatial ability
10/1137 adult learning; mass media
10/1545 reading skills
10/1640 attention deficit disorders; cognitive ability; hyperactivity; learning disabilities

MEN
10/0118 access programmes; higher education; mature students; student experience
10/1589 educational experience; higher education; mature students; sex differences; student attitudes; women's education
10/1791 early childhood education; sex differences

MENTAL RETARDATION
10/0477 beliefs; Christianity; religious education; special educational needs

MENTORS
10/0010 youth leaders; youth service
10/0133 teacher development; teacher education; teacher induction
10/0156 head teachers; programme evaluation; teaching profession
10/0183 head teachers; management in education
10/0214 Postgraduate Certificate in Education; preservice teacher education; school based teacher education; student teacher attitudes; teacher attitudes
10/0246 preservice teacher education; primary school teachers; secondary school teachers
10/0439 preservice teacher education; student teacher supervisors; teaching practice
10/0469 mathematics education; National Curriculum; preservice teacher education; student teacher supervisors; teaching practice
10/0514 institutes of higher education; preservice teacher education; school based teacher education; student teacher supervisors
10/0533 cooperative programmes; preservice teacher education
10/0673 head teachers; middle management; professional continuing education; teacher development; teaching profession
10/0910 head teachers; management development; managerial occupations
10/0911 industry-education relationship; management development; work-education relationship
10/0919 competency based teacher education; profiles; teacher development
10/0938 preservice teacher education; student teacher supervisors; supervision; supervisory methods; teaching practice
10/1215 inservice teacher education; training
10/1275 preservice teacher education; school

based teacher education; student teacher
supervisors
10/1301 institutional cooperation; Postgraduate
Certificate in Education; preservice teacher
education; school based teacher education
10/1307 competency based teacher education;
profiles; teacher development; teaching
profession
10/1460 careers service; guidance personnel;
professional development
10/1533 preservice teacher education;
supervisory training; teaching practice
10/1597 preservice teacher education
10/1600 preservice teacher education; primary
schools; professional continuing education;
teacher development
10/1637 preservice teacher education; student
teachers; teacher development; teaching
practice
10/1689 nurse education; nurse teachers
10/1735 preservice teacher education; school
based teacher education; student teacher
supervisors

METACOGNITION
10/1543 cognitive processes; computer assisted
learning; learning processes
10/1601 assessment; cognitive ability;
mathematical models; mathematics education

METAPHORS
10/0655 child language; figurative language
10/1171 computers; educational materials;
reasoning
10/1721 classroom communication; discourse
analysis; teacher education

MICROCOMPUTERS
10/0464 computer uses in education; group work;
primary schools; problem solving
10/0512 computer uses in education; information
technology; mathematics education; secondary
schools
10/0886 blindness; low vision aids; sensory aids;
tactile adaptation; visual impairments
10/1030 computer uses in education; curriculum
development; information technology
10/1168 computer uses in education; distance
education; open universities

MICROSCOPES
10/1178 computer assisted learning; earth
science; educational equipment; simulation;
special educational needs

MIDDLE CLASS STUDENTS
10/0528 academic staff; ethnic groups; higher
education; mature students; student attitudes;
student experience; working class

MIDDLE MANAGEMENT
10/0673 head teachers; mentors; professional
continuing education; teacher development;
teaching profession

MIDDLE SCHOOL EDUCATION
10/0412 educational innovation; educational
policy; Scotland
10/1371 bullying; cooperation; ethnic relations;
intergroup relations; intervention; pupil
behaviour; social isolation

MIGRANTS
10/0974 adolescents; Chinese; cultural
background; ethnic groups; ethnicity; Hong
Kong

MINIMUM COMPETENCES
10/0251 communication skills; competency
based education; humanities; modular courses;
open education
10/1512 competency based education; National
Vocational Qualifications; skills

MINORITY GROUP CHILDREN
10/0720 cultural influences; gypsies;
performance factors; travellers – itinerants
10/0721 cultural influences; gypsies;
performance factors; travellers – itinerants

MINORITY GROUPS
10/0391 career counselling; ethnic groups;
secondary school pupils; vocational guidance
10/0401 bilingual education; multicultural
education; multiculturalism
10/0426 Asians; bilingualism; ethnic groups;
language maintenance; language policy;
mother tongue
10/0975 ethnic groups; multiculturalism; primary
schools; voluntary schools
10/1245 English; multilingualism; teaching
methods
10/1472 equal education; equal facilities; ethnic
groups; religious cultural groups
10/1712 adult education; continuing education;
equal education

MISCONCEPTIONS
10/0700 air pollution; conservation –
environment; environmental education;
scientific concepts; secondary school pupils

MIXED ABILITY
10/0348 ability; learning; pacing; time factors –
learning
10/1067 ability; class organisation; grouping –
teaching purposes; pupil placement; streaming;
teaching methods

MOBILITY AIDS
10/0645 cerebral palsy; neurological
impairments; psychomotor skills; special
educational needs
10/1145 assessment; blindness; partial vision;
special educational needs; travel training;
visual impairments; visually handicapped
mobility
10/1376 blindness; visual impairments; visually
handicapped mobility

MODELS
10/0324 computer assisted language learning;
educational software
10/0658 predictive validity; probability;
statistical inference
10/0775 research tools; statistical analysis
10/1179 computer simulation; computer uses in
education; control technology; logo

MODERATE LEARNING DIFFICULTIES
10/0474 disabilities; mainstreaming; Nigeria;
physical education; special educational needs
10/0524 problem solving; severe learning
difficulties; social skills; special educational
needs
10/0751 assessment; colleges of further
education; diagnostic assessment; disabilities;
further education; special educational needs
10/0862 classroom environment; mainstreaming;
pupil attitudes; pupil behaviour; social
behaviour; special educational needs
10/0945 curriculum development; low
achievement; special educational needs;
underachievement
10/1013 assessment; learning disabilities; low
achievement; special educational needs
10/1069 disabilities; further education; further
education students; literature reviews; special
educational needs
10/1470 disadvantaged; special educational
needs; support services
10/1733 National Curriculum; special
educational needs; special schools

MODERATION – MARKING
10/0030 assessment; evaluation; examinations;
National Curriculum

MODERN LANGUAGE CURRICULUM
10/1079 comparative education; language policy;
modern language studies; second language
teaching; secondary education

MODERN LANGUAGE STUDIES
10/0034 comparative education; pupil attitudes
10/0053 'A' level examinations; learning
strategies; sixteen to nineteen education
10/0242 course content; educational materials;
Italian; multimedia approach
10/0295 cultural awareness; English – second

language; German; textbook evaluation
10/0308 comparative education; cultural
awareness; Denmark; Europe
10/0368 preservice teacher education; student
teachers
10/0457 learning motivation; Scotland; second
language teaching
10/0462 primary education; problems; second
language teaching; teaching methods
10/0506 educational objectives; French
10/0608 language attitudes; language teachers;
learning motivation
10/0616 French; German; National Curriculum
10/0649 special educational needs
10/1078 international programmes; programme
evaluation; second language learning; student
exchange programmes
10/1079 comparative education; language policy;
modern language curriculum; second language
teaching; secondary education
10/1088 French
10/1252 assessment; French; General Certificate
of Secondary Education; oral tests
10/1365 further education; languages for specific
purposes; second language teaching;
vocational education
10/1390 English studies; language skills
10/1445 language proficiency; primary schools
10/1447 language proficiency; primary schools
10/1571 cultural awareness; electronic mail;
intercultural communication; language
proficiency; telecommunications
10/1799 comparative education; language
teachers; National Curriculum
10/1810 comparative education; English;
German; language tests; native speakers;
second language teaching

MODULAR COURSES
10/0143 comparative education; Ghana; higher
education; universities
10/0251 communication skills; competency
based education; humanities; minimum
competencies; open education
10/0314 comparative education; curriculum
development; European Community;
vocational education

MONEY MANAGEMENT
10/0012 educational finance; fund raising;
income; school funds; secondary schools
10/1025 economics education;
industry-education relationship
10/1066 economics education; life skills;
volunteers

MONITORING
10/0991 evaluation; inspection; local education
authorities
10/1719 English studies curriculum; evaluation;
National Curriculum

MONTESSORI METHOD
10/0484 early childhood education; Ireland; play
groups; preschool education
10/1263 educational history; educational
theories; elementary schools
10/1324 early childhood education; Steiner
Waldorf schools; teaching methods
10/1537 early childhood education; nursery
schools; preschool education

MORAL DEVELOPMENT
10/1221 adolescent development; bereavement;
child development; death; religious attitudes
10/1229 religion and education; religious
attitudes; school worship; values education

MORAL EDUCATION
10/0473 Education Reform Act 1988; individual
development; National Curriculum; primary
schools; religious education; social
development
10/0686 curriculum development; educational
philosophy; individual development; physical
education; religious education
10/1020 directories; reference materials; values
education
10/1249 educational philosophy; Taiwan
10/1468 philosophy; values education

10/1724 ethics; multiculturalism; relativism – philosophy
10/1728 educational philosophy; ethics; moral values; realism; reasoning

MORAL VALUES
10/1728 educational philosophy; ethics; moral education; realism; reasoning

MORPHOLOGY – LANGUAGES
10/0725 grammar; semantics; spelling; syntax

MOTHER TONGUE
10/0060 ethnic origins; pupils; religion; surveys
10/0379 educational development; language of instruction; language policy; Wales; Welsh; Welsh speaking schools
10/0418 Algeria; bilingualism; comparative education; Gaelic; language policy; Scotland
10/0426 Asians; bilingualism; ethnic groups; language maintenance; language policy; minority groups
10/0706 adult literacy; home-school relationship; literacy; literacy education; native speakers; primary education; teaching methods
10/1281 adult education; Creoles
10/1584 assessment; National Curriculum; school based assessment; second language learning; standard assessment tasks; Welsh
10/1804 developing countries; language policy; language standardisation; literacy

MOTHERS
10/0001 access to education; community education; preschool education; young children
10/0920 early childhood education; nursery schools; parent participation
10/1636 community education; contraception; early parenthood; family planning; parenthood education; peer teaching; sex education
10/1727 teacher attitudes; teacher background; teacher role; teaching profession; women teachers

MOTIVATION
10/0129 achievement; failure; sports
10/0285 enterprise education; industry-education relationship; learning strategies; skill development; transfer of learning
10/0525 achievement; music education; musical instruments
10/0550 helplessness; self esteem; special educational needs
10/0552 sex differences; sexual identity; teacher-pupil relationship

MOTIVATION TECHNIQUES
10/0676 attitude change; pupil needs; self concept; self esteem

MOTIVATION TESTS
10/0526 academic aspiration; locus of control; Malaysia; student motivation

MOTOR DEVELOPMENT
10/0203 primary school pupils; sex differences
10/0744 handwriting; perceptual motor coordination; reading; speech
10/0745 child development; neurological impairments; perceptual handicaps; premature infants; special educational needs
10/1471 special educational needs; special schools

MOTOR REACTIONS
10/0089 behaviour; deaf blind; disabilities; multiple disabilities; sensory deprivation
10/0747 cerebral palsy; disabilities; perceptual handicaps; perceptual motor coordination; special educational needs

MOVEMENT EDUCATION
10/0792 music education; psychomotor skills

MOZAMBIQUE
10/0764 English – second language; radio; second language learning

MULTICULTURAL EDUCATION
10/0401 bilingual education; minority groups; multiculturalism

10/0666 ethnic groups; primary schools
10/0678 cross curricular approach; National Curriculum; primary education
10/0880 antiracism education; ethnic groups
10/0994 antiracism education; Education Reform Act 1988; educational planning; equal education; local education authorities
10/1222 centralisation; educational practices; international education; National Curriculum
10/1279 databases; resource materials
10/1284 bilingualism; multilingual materials; multilingualism
10/1410 antiracism education; preservice teacher education

MULTICULTURALISM
10/0401 bilingual education; minority groups; multicultural education
10/0973 ethnic groups; ethnic relations; intergroup relations; racial relations; school policy; secondary schools
10/0975 ethnic groups; minority groups; primary schools; voluntary schools
10/1496 Education Reform Act 1988; primary education; religious education
10/1724 ethics; moral education; relativism – philosophy

MULTILINGUAL MATERIALS
10/1284 bilingualism; multicultural education; multilingualism

MULTILINGUALISM
10/1245 English; minority groups; teaching methods
10/1284 bilingualism; multicultural education; multilingual materials

MULTIMEDIA APPROACH
10/0126 educational media; learner centred methods; learning resources centres; management development; management studies
10/0238 computer assisted learning; dyslexia; interactive video; learning disabilities
10/0242 course content; educational materials; Italian; modern language studies
10/0476 hypermedia; literary criticism; literature studies
10/1155 classroom research; educational materials; educational technology; interactive video; mathematics education
10/1177 animation; authoring aids – programming; computer assisted learning; computer uses in education
10/1552 computer assisted learning; electronic books; human-computer interaction; hypermedia; information technology; optical data discs
10/1581 computer assisted learning; educational software; statistics education
10/1613 authoring aids – programming; computer assisted learning; computer software; computer uses in education; information technology
10/1618 chemistry education; educational materials; learning strategies; science education; skills; teaching methods; transfer of learning

MULTIPLE DISABILITIES
10/0089 behaviour; deaf blind; disabilities; motor reactions; sensory deprivation
10/0986 access to education; adult basic education; adult learning; intelligence differences; severe learning difficulties

MUSEUMS
10/0258 arts education; computer uses in education; cultural education; handicrafts; visual arts
10/0622 force; science activities; science education; science teaching centres; scientific concepts
10/1436 environmental education; history studies; preservice teacher education

MUSIC
10/0218 learning; music education
10/0811 art education; dance; sixteen to nineteen education; theatre arts

10/1060 arts; attitudes; culture; mass media; participation; sports; theatre arts
10/1507 equal education; music education; sex differences

MUSIC ACTIVITIES
10/0527 biographical inventories; musical ability; musicians
10/1059 guides; music education
10/1210 'A' level examinations; learner characteristics; music education; pupil attitudes; sex differences
10/1323 music education; singing; young children
10/1326 music education; music teachers

MUSIC APPRECIATION
10/0793 music education

MUSIC EDUCATION
10/0044 assessment; National Curriculum
10/0207 National Curriculum; primary school teachers
10/0218 learning; music
10/0525 achievement; motivation; musical instruments
10/0532 musical composition; sex differences
10/0791 educational resources; National Curriculum
10/0792 movement education; psychomotor skills
10/0793 music appreciation
10/1059 guides; music activities
10/1210 'A' level examinations; learner characteristics; music activities; pupil attitudes; sex differences
10/1244 consultants; inservice teacher education; music teachers; primary school teachers
10/1291 Japan
10/1310 Greece
10/1323 music activities; singing; young children
10/1326 music activities; music teachers
10/1507 equal education; music; sex differences

MUSIC TEACHERS
10/0711 professional development; professional training; teacher education
10/1244 consultants; inservice teacher education; music education; primary school teachers
10/1326 music activities; music education

MUSICAL ABILITY
10/0527 biographical inventories; music activities; musicians
10/0861 phonology; reading ability

MUSICAL COMPOSITION
10/0532 music education; sex differences

MUSICAL INSTRUMENTS
10/0525 achievement; motivation; music education

MUSICIANS
10/0527 biographical inventories; music activities; musical ability

MUSLIMS
10/1150 Islamic education; religion and education; religious cultural groups; women's education
10/1151 Islamic education; religion and education; religious cultural groups; women's education
10/1160 equal education; Islamic education; religion and education; religious cultural groups; single sex schools; women's education

NAMIBIA
10/1752 refugees

NARRATION
10/0134 children as writers; group work; primary school pupils; story telling; writing – composition

NATIONAL CURRICULUM
10/0030 assessment; evaluation; examinations; moderation – marking
10/0044 assessment; music education
10/0077 creative writing; English studies curriculum; literary genres; writing – composition; writing skills

10/0139 curriculum development; educational change; primary education; primary school teachers; primary schools; teacher role; teacher workload
10/0153 assessment; educational change; infant school curriculum; infant school education; primary school teachers; pupil attitudes
10/0155 assessment; educational change; primary education; primary school curriculum; primary school teachers; pupil attitudes
10/0207 music education; primary school teachers
10/0224 comparative education; core curriculum; Netherlands; Zambia
10/0233 physical education; primary education
10/0244 cross curricular approach; physical education
10/0352 history; primary education
10/0363 parent attitudes; parent-school relationship; primary education; science education
10/0371 computer uses in education; information technology
10/0469 mathematics education; mentors; preservice teacher education; student teacher supervisors; teaching practice
10/0473 Education Reform Act 1988; individual development; moral education; primary schools; religious education; social development
10/0488 history studies; oral history; small schools
10/0503 earth science; educational materials; material development; physical sciences; science education
10/0567 cooperation; developmental continuity; history; primary secondary education
10/0616 French; German; modern language studies
10/0620 ability; design and technology; primary education; technology education
10/0623 assessment; school based assessment; science education
10/0628 cognitive processes; mathematics education; pattern recognition
10/0634 school based assessment; secondary education; technology education
10/0638 assessment; mathematics education; school based assessment
10/0641 history studies; local history
10/0668 cooperation; rural schools; small schools
10/0669 educational administration; preservice teacher education; school effectiveness; secondary schools
10/0670 citizenship education; cross curricular approach
10/0677 differentiated curriculum; individual needs; mainstreaming; special educational needs
10/0678 cross curricular approach; multicultural education; primary education
10/0682 cross curricular approach; curriculum development; environmental education; polymers
10/0698 curriculum development; science education
10/0699 assessment; school based assessment; science education
10/0727 infant school teachers; professional recognition; teaching profession
10/0730 assessment; educational quality; school effectiveness
10/0735 assessment; primary schools; standard assessment tasks
10/0765 history; history studies; teaching methods
10/0791 educational resources; music education
10/0832 cross curricular approach; curriculum development; educational quality
10/0833 information seeking; information technology; optical data discs; technology education
10/0843 communication skills; listening skills; speech communication
10/0844 databases; information technology; technology education
10/0845 earth science; geography education; inservice teacher education
10/0868 citizenship education
10/0902 educational change; local management of schools; physical education; sports
10/0923 core curriculum; curriculum development; educational administration;

educational change; educational development; interdisciplinary approach
10/0927 assessment
10/0962 consumer education; cross curricular approach
10/0964 assessment; assessment by teachers; geography education
10/0965 achievement; primary education; reading achievement
10/0966 curriculum development; severe learning difficulties; special educational needs
10/0971 achievement; mathematics education; primary education; reading achievement
10/0977 assessment; assessment by teachers; attainment tests; geography education; standard assessment tasks
10/0997 assessment; English studies; reading achievement; standard assessment tasks; writing skills
10/0998 assessment; mathematics achievement; primary education; science education; standard assessment tasks
10/1001 curriculum development; developmental continuity; local education authorities; primary secondary education; transfer pupils
10/1002 assessment; core curriculum; English studies; mathematics education; science education
10/1008 assessment; attainment tests; standard assessment tasks; Welsh studies
10/1034 adaptive testing; assessment; attainment tests; computer assisted testing; test validity
10/1047 basic skills; cross curricular approach; secondary education
10/1053 achievement tests; assessment; mathematics achievement; mathematics education
10/1064 pupil attitudes; relevance – education
10/1082 assessment; attainment tests; standard assessment tasks; Welsh studies
10/1083 assertiveness; attainment tests; standard assessment tasks; Welsh studies
10/1084 assessment; English studies; evaluation; mathematics education; science education; secondary education; technology education
10/1095 educational change; primary schools
10/1097 English studies; language teachers
10/1101 information technology; oracy; teacher attitudes
10/1148 curriculum development; design education; technology education
10/1212 learning strategies; teacher effectiveness; teaching methods
10/1219 assessment; educational materials; mathematics achievement; mathematics education
10/1222 centralisation; educational practices; international education; multicultural education
10/1235 art education; design education; inservice teacher education; primary education; primary school teachers
10/1239 curriculum development; educational change; English studies curriculum; secondary education
10/1246 drama education; educational materials; English studies curriculum
10/1253 drama education; English studies curriculum; scripts; secondary education
10/1397 decision making; science education; scientific literacy
10/1444 assessment; curriculum development; educational change; environmental education; mathematics education; Scotland; teaching process
10/1529 assessment by teachers; records of achievement; school based assessment
10/1584 assessment; mother tongue; school based assessment; second language learning; standard assessment tasks; Welsh
10/1595 assessment; school based assessment
10/1596 pupil attitudes; secondary schools
10/1669 assessment; primary education; school based assessment
10/1676 cross curricular approach; curriculum development; information technology
10/1687 cross curricular approach; curriculum development; school organisation; teaching methods; thematic approach
10/1719 English studies curriculum; evaluation; monitoring

10/1732 special educational needs; special schools
10/1733 moderate learning difficulties; special educational needs; special schools
10/1753 aesthetic education; art activities; art appreciation; art education; criticism
10/1755 mathematics education; primary education; teaching methods
10/1759 English studies curriculum; language skills; listening skills; oracy; speech skills
10/1772 history; primary education
10/1783 classroom research; learning strategies; primary education; reading teaching; teaching methods
10/1794 educational change; projects – learning activities; pupil projects; teaching methods
10/1799 comparative education; language teachers; modern language studies

NATIONAL CURRICULUM – NORTHERN IRELAND
10/0978 assessment; attainment tests; English studies; geography education; mathematics education; Northern Ireland; science education
10/1061 cohort analysis; curriculum development; Northern Ireland; pupil attitudes
10/1340 assessment; school based assessment

NATIONAL ORGANISATIONS
10/0429 professional associations; Scotland; teaching profession

NATIONAL VOCATIONAL QUALIFICATIONS
10/0113 achievement; assessment; experiential learning; further education; prior learning
10/0116 educational quality; performance indicators; vocational education
10/0120 industry-education relationship; work attitudes; work-education relationship
10/0446 assessment; computer assisted testing; computer uses in education
10/0601 distributive trades education; retailing; training; vocational education
10/0728 qualifications; vocational education
10/0784 accreditation of prior learning; assessment; Training and Enterprise Councils; vocational education
10/0785 assessment; job skills; Scottish Vocational Qualifications; verbal tests
10/0787 employment qualifications; vocational education
10/0789 competency based education; higher education; masters' courses; qualifications; standards
10/1024 curriculum research; sixteen to nineteen education; sixth form education; vocational education
10/1028 basic skills; building trades education; construction – process; construction industry; course evaluation; technical education; vocational education
10/1202 basic skills; vocational education
10/1482 educational experience; employment qualifications; vocational education
10/1511 access to education; admission criteria; competency based education; higher education
10/1512 competency based education; minimum competencies; skills
10/1632 competency based education; higher education; preservice teacher education; professional education; standards
10/1777 further education; higher education; vocational education

NATIONALISM
10/0175 family life; religion; state schools
10/1195 citizenship; citizenship education; identity; role of education; Zambia

NATIVE SPEAKERS
10/0309 Arab states; cultural awareness; English – second language; foreign culture; second language learning
10/0706 adult literacy; home-school relationship; literacy; literacy education; mother tongue; primary education; teaching methods
10/1392 communication research; conversation; second language learning; verbal communication
10/1810 comparative education; English; German; language tests; modern language studies; second language teaching

NATURAL RESOURCES
10/0300 conservation – environment; environmental education

NAVIGATION
10/0687 geography education; mathematics education; orientation; orienteering; outdoor pursuits; primary education

NEEDS ASSESSMENT
10/1403 health education; health needs; primary health care

NEPAL
10/1685 educational policy; equal education; gender equality; women's education

NETHERLANDS
10/0224 comparative education; core curriculum; National Curriculum; Zambia
10/0440 comparative education; distance education; higher education; international educational exchange; learning activities; teaching methods; telecommunications

NETWORKS
10/0547 communications; distance education; open education; teleconferencing

NEUROLOGICAL IMPAIRMENTS
10/0645 cerebral palsy; mobility aids; psychomotor skills; special educational needs
10/0745 child development; motor development; perceptual handicaps; premature infants; special educational needs
10/0863 attention; cognitive development; early experience; infant behaviour; learning
10/1675 adult basic education; learning disabilities; special educational needs; speech handicaps

NEWLY QUALIFIED TEACHERS
10/0019 Canada natives; ethnic groups; indigenous populations; teacher background; teacher induction; teaching profession

NEWS REPORTING
10/1525 environmental education; public opinion

NIGERIA
10/0474 disabilities; mainstreaming; moderate learning difficulties; physical education; special educational needs
10/0481 parent-school relationship; parent-teacher associations; secondary schools
10/0482 women's education
10/0556 professional recognition; status need; teacher attitudes; teachers; teaching profession

NOMADS
10/0333 India; literacy

NON WESTERN LANGUAGES
10/0347 Arabic; Chinese languages; educational materials; Japanese; second language learning

NONCONFORMITY
10/0475 church and education; church-state relationship; educational history; educational legislation; religion and education

NONDISCRIMINATORY EDUCATION
10/0505 educational policy; equal education; gender equality

NONTRADITIONAL EDUCATION
10/0123 access to education; higher education; student counselling; student health and welfare
10/0408 access to education; dropout research; higher education; summer schools; university admission; university preparation
10/0530 access programmes; access to education; higher education; mature students; student motivation
10/0531 academic achievement; access programmes; higher education; mature students; performance
10/1516 adult education; continuing education; liberal education

NONVERBAL COMMUNICATION
10/0494 communication skills; physical disabilities; severe disabilities; special educational needs; speech handicaps
10/0876 blindness; communication problems; higher education; special educational needs; visual impairments

NORTHERN IRELAND
10/0821 cross curricular approach; curriculum development
10/0978 assessment; attainment tests; English studies; geography education; mathematics education; National Curriculum – Northern Ireland; science education
10/1031 reading ability; reading research
10/1061 cohort analysis; curriculum development; National Curriculum – Northern Ireland; pupil attitudes
10/1107 attendance; attendance patterns; pupil behaviour; truancy
10/1108 labour market; probationary teachers; teacher employment; teacher recruitment; teaching profession
10/1558 pupil attitudes; religious education; scientific attitudes; secondary school pupils
10/1568 curriculum development; differentiated curriculum; individualised methods; science education
10/1574 rural schools; science curriculum; science education; small schools

NUMBER CONCEPTS
10/0653 mathematics education; numbers
10/0748 arithmetic; cognitive development; numbers; numeracy; primary education
10/1102 blindness; concept formation; quantity concepts

NUMBERS
10/0653 mathematics education; number concepts
10/0748 arithmetic; cognitive development; number concepts; numeracy; primary education
10/0972 ability tests; language handicaps; learning disabilities; mathematical ability; mathematics education; special educational needs
10/1187 higher education; introductory courses; mathematics education; numeracy
10/1306 early childhood education; mathematics education; preschool education

NUMERACY
10/0232 adult literacy; basic skills; cohort analysis
10/0299 employer attitudes; graduate employment; graduates; mathematical ability; work-education relationship
10/0577 adult education; life skills; older adults
10/0748 arithmetic; cognitive development; number concepts; numbers; primary education
10/1051 basic skills; communication skills
10/1187 higher education; introductory courses; mathematics education; numbers
10/1342 adult basic education; adult education; adult literacy; adult students

NURSE EDUCATION
10/0005 learning strategies; medical education; predictive measurement
10/0006 nurses
10/0016 higher education
10/0241 professional education
10/0271 distance education; professional continuing education; professional development
10/0419 Iran
10/0813 educational materials; guides; health education; nurses; smoking
10/0830 acquired immune deficiency syndrome; nurses; sexually transmitted diseases
10/1075 professional education
10/1100 nurses; stress – psychological
10/1116 learning activities; learning strategies; study skills
10/1164 course evaluation; student attitudes; teaching methods
10/1327 nurses; outcomes of education
10/1473 health visitors; learning experience; placement
10/1489 interpersonal relationship

10/1492 information technology; nursing
10/1501 lifelong learning; nurses; professional continuing education; professional development
10/1502 medicine; nurses; pharmacology
10/1510 programme evaluation
10/1576 Delphi technique; psychiatric services
10/1629 obstetrics; programme evaluation
10/1641 assessment; competence; obstetrics
10/1686 nurse teachers; programme effectiveness
10/1688 nurses
10/1689 mentors; nurse teachers
10/1692 change; Cyprus
10/1773 emotional development; nurses; professional development; student development

NURSE TEACHERS
10/1686 nurse education; programme effectiveness
10/1689 mentors; nurse education

NURSERY SCHOOL CURRICULUM
10/0935 community services; day care; early childhood education; local government; nursery schools; preschool education; young children

NURSERY SCHOOL EDUCATION
10/0377 early childhood education; preschool education; regional characteristics; regional planning
10/1290 aesthetic education; art activities; art appreciation
10/1674 behaviour problems; classroom discipline; discipline; disruptive pupils; Greece; teacher attitudes

NURSERY SCHOOL PUPILS
10/0999 infant school pupils; reading; reading readiness; reception classes; tests

NURSERY SCHOOLS
10/0078 phonology; preschool children; preschool education; speech handicaps
10/0914 early childhood education; governing bodies; parent attitudes; parent-school relationship; preschool education; school governors
10/0920 early childhood education; mothers; parent participation
10/0935 community services; day care; early childhood education; local government; nursery school curriculum; preschool education; young children
10/1537 early childhood education; Montessori method; preschool education
10/1788 early childhood education; educational development; educational quality; play groups; preschool education; quality control

NURSES
10/0006 nurse education
10/0813 educational materials; guides; health education; nurse education; smoking
10/0830 acquired immune deficiency syndrome; nurse education; sexually transmitted diseases
10/1056 acquired immune deficiency syndrome; educational materials; sexually transmitted diseases
10/1100 nurse education; stress – psychological
10/1165 medical education; obstetrics
10/1327 nurse education; outcomes of education
10/1501 lifelong learning; nurse education; professional continuing education; professional development
10/1502 medicine; nurse education; pharmacology
10/1688 nurse education
10/1773 emotional development; nurse education; professional development; student development

NURSING
10/1486 administrators; health personnel; health services
10/1492 information technology; nurse education

NUTRITION EDUCATION
10/0838 health education; local education authorities; school meals

10/0953 accidents; comparative education; European Community; food standards; health education; safety education
10/1703 eating habits; food; health education

OBSERVATION
10/1627 pupil attitudes; textbook evaluation; textbooks

OBSTETRICS
10/1165 medical education; nurses
10/1166 medical education
10/1629 nurse education; programme evaluation
10/1641 assessment; competence; nurse education

OCCUPATIONAL ASPIRATION
10/1461 employment opportunities; labour market; learner educational objectives; opportunities; secondary school pupils; work-education relationship
10/1462 career choice; employment opportunities; labour market; learner educational objectives; school to work transition; secondary school pupils; work-education relationship

OCCUPATIONAL INFORMATION
10/1442 colleges of further education; comparable worth; employment practices; equal pay; job analysis; salaries

OCEANOGRAPHY
10/0502 comprehension; earth science; physical sciences; plate tectonics

OFF THE JOB TRAINING
10/1548 on the job training; skill development; training; transfer of training; work experience programmes

OLDER ADULTS
10/0576 adult education
10/0577 adult education; life skills; numeracy
10/0707 literacy; memory; oral history; personal narratives

OMAN
10/0052 English – second language; second language teaching

ON THE JOB TRAINING
10/0814 teacher development
10/1508 industrial training; trainers
10/1548 off the job training; skill development; training; transfer of training; work experience programmes
10/1623 competency based education; inservice education; social work studies

OPEN EDUCATION
10/0112 further education; teaching methods
10/0251 communication skills; competency based education; humanities; minimum competencies; modular courses
10/0387 assessment; higher education; learner centred methods; self evaluation – individuals; teaching methods
10/0547 communications; distance education; networks; teleconferencing
10/0568 adult basic education
10/0897 computer uses in education; preservice teacher education
10/0904 higher education
10/1169 computer assisted learning; educational materials; educational media
10/1775 flexible learning; medical schools; teaching methods

OPEN ENTRY
10/0081 Education Reform Act 1988; educational administration; educational change; educational finance; grant maintained schools; parent choice; school based management
10/1074 access to education; admission criteria; enrolment; parent choice; secondary schools

OPEN UNIVERSITIES
10/0898 distance education; Saudi Arabia; women's education

10/1167 adult students; distance education; humanities; mature students; student attitudes
10/1168 computer uses in education; distance education; microcomputers
10/1174 distance education; international educational exchange; teleconferencing
10/1230 accreditation – courses; accrediting authorities; assessment; educational quality; external examiners; higher education

OPINIONS
10/1811 Likert scales; linguistics; questionnaires; rating scales; semantics

OPPORTUNITIES
10/1461 employment opportunities; labour market; learner educational objectives; occupational aspiration; secondary school pupils; work-education relationship

OPTICAL DATA DISCS
10/0115 further education; higher education; information retrieval; information systems; search strategies; student attitudes
10/0213 computer uses in education; English studies curriculum; information technology
10/0683 computer uses in education
10/0833 information seeking; information technology; National Curriculum; technology education
10/1176 blindness; computer uses in education; special educational needs; speech synthesisers; visual impairments
10/1432 biographies; educational materials; educational technology; material development
10/1551 computer assisted learning; educational technology; expert systems; training methods
10/1552 computer assisted learning; electronic books; human-computer interaction; hypermedia; information technology; multimedia approach

ORACY
10/0206 language skills; literacy; reading skills; special educational needs; spelling; writing skills
10/1101 information technology; National Curriculum; teacher attitudes
10/1257 oral language; programme evaluation; speech communication
10/1458 school leavers; school to work transition
10/1759 English studies curriculum; language skills; listening skills; National Curriculum; speech skills

ORAL ENGLISH
10/1434 assessment; English studies; school based assessment; speech communication

ORAL HISTORY
10/0488 history studies; National Curriculum; small schools
10/0707 literacy; memory; older adults; personal narratives

ORAL LANGUAGE
10/1257 oracy; programme evaluation; speech communication

ORAL READING
10/0463 beginning reading; early reading; reading skills; teacher-pupil relationship
10/1205 reading; reading difficulties; reading teaching

ORAL TESTS
10/1252 assessment; French; General Certificate of Secondary Education; modern language studies

ORGANISATIONAL CHANGE
10/0023 college administration; colleges of further education; educational administration; further education; institutional administration
10/0187 change strategies; educational environment; educational research; research methodology
10/1667 educational administration; educational policy; local management of schools; management in education

10/1711 adult education; continuing education; higher education; universities

ORGANISATIONAL CLIMATE
10/0452 attitude measures; institutes of higher education; institutional environment; student attitudes; teacher attitudes

ORGANISATIONAL EFFECTIVENESS
10/0495 educational objectives; institutional evaluation; performance indicators
10/1498 advisers; inservice teacher education; inspection; local education authorities

ORGANISATIONAL THEORIES
10/0410 educational administration

ORIENTATION
10/0687 geography education; mathematics education; navigation; orienteering; outdoor pursuits; primary education

ORIENTEERING
10/0687 geography education; mathematics education; navigation; orientation; outdoor pursuits; primary education

OUTCOMES OF EDUCATION
10/0073 clinical experience; medical education
10/0105 academic achievement; blindness; cognitive development; longitudinal studies; partial vision; special schools; visual impairments
10/0127 attendance patterns; business education; course evaluation; examination results; sandwich courses; undergraduate study
10/0313 performance indicators; school effectiveness; school leavers; secondary schools
10/0318 adult vocational education; followup studies; retraining; women's education; women's employment
10/0458 'A' level examinations; accountability; examination results; performance indicators; programme effectiveness; school effectiveness
10/0504 educational quality; parent-school relationship; school effectiveness; success
10/0546 college effectiveness; higher education; universities and colleges
10/0731 departments; differential performance; examination results; school effectiveness; secondary schools
10/0856 economics-education relationship; educational benefits; educational finance; employment opportunities; rewards; work-education relationship
10/0956 career counselling; pupil attitudes; school leavers; school to work transition; transition education; TVEI; work-education relationship
10/1077 achievement; educational quality; examination results; performance factors; performance indicators; school effectiveness
10/1163 experiential learning; interpersonal competence; locus of control; stress – psychological; student experience; teacher education
10/1327 nurse education; nurses
10/1416 academic achievement; access programmes; access to education; higher education; mature students

OUTDOOR EDUCATION
10/0454 educational materials; environmental education; publications; resource materials

OUTDOOR PURSUITS
10/0664 activities; comparative education; France; physical education
10/0687 geography education; mathematics education; navigation; orientation; orienteering; primary education

OVERSEAS EMPLOYMENT
10/1370 citizenship; Europe; higher education; overseas students

OVERSEAS STUDENTS
10/1135 educational policy; graduate study; higher education

10/1370 citizenship; Europe; higher education; overseas employment

10/1391 English – second language; English for academic purposes; lecture method; teaching styles

10/1707 computer assisted language learning; English – second language; English for academic purposes; second language learning

10/1809 English – second language; English for academic purposes; limited English speaking; second language learning

PACING
10/0348 ability; learning; mixed ability; time factors – learning

PAIN
10/1154 doctor-patient relationship; medical services; patient education; physical health

10/1158 doctor-patient relationship; medical services; patient education; physical health

PAKISTAN
10/0109 developing countries; educational improvement; inservice teacher education; primary education; programme evaluation

10/0170 access to education; equal education; higher education; women's education

PARENT ASPIRATION
10/0358 academic records; parent-school relationship; school based assessment

PARENT ATTITUDES
10/0363 National Curriculum; parent-school relationship; primary education; science education

10/0914 early childhood education; governing bodies; nursery schools; parent-school relationship; preschool education; school governors

10/1032 health education; sex education

10/1046 inspection; inspectors – of schools

10/1112 attitudes; primary education; school governors; science education; scientific attitudes

10/1234 educational change; preservice teacher education; primary school teachers; student teacher attitudes; teacher attitudes; teaching profession

10/1374 antisocial behaviour; attitudes; behaviour problems; bullying; pupil attitudes; teacher attitudes

10/1375 antisocial behaviour; attitudes; bullying; discipline policy; school policy; teacher attitudes

PARENT-CHILD RELATIONSHIP
10/0319 family income; family influence; financial support; parent role; youth

10/0810 child rearing; parenthood education; parenting skills; voluntary agencies

10/0853 behaviour problems; bullying; family influence; home environment; parent-pupil relationship; punishment; pupil behaviour

PARENT CHOICE
10/0018 access to education; secondary schools; selection

10/0081 Education Reform Act 1988; educational administration; educational change; educational finance; grant maintained schools; open entry; school based management

10/0366 institutional advancement; marketing; parent-school relationship; selection

10/0367 access to education; Education Reform Act 1988; primary schools

10/0536 access to education; special educational needs

10/0891 independent schools; marketing

10/1074 access to education; admission criteria; enrolment; open entry; secondary schools

PARENT CONTROL
10/0434 parent-school relationship; school boards – Scotland; school governing bodies

PARENT PARTICIPATION
10/0009 acquired immune deficiency syndrome; health education; peer teaching; sex education

10/0091 books; early childhood education; early experience; early reading; infants

10/0345 educational administration; educational change; local management of schools; school based management; school boards – Scotland; school governing bodies

10/0409 educational history; parent-school relationship

10/0569 local management of schools; participative decision making; school based management; school governing bodies; school governors

10/0583 Asians; ethnic groups; parent-school relationship

10/0716 bilingual education programmes; English – second language; ethnic groups; home-school relationship; literacy education; reading teaching; second language learning

10/0920 early childhood education; mothers; nursery schools

10/1049 family involvement; family programmes; literacy; reading skills; writing skills

10/1266 early childhood education; early experience; hearing impairments; intervention; special educational needs

10/1270 early childhood education; individualised methods; intervention; teaching methods

10/1328 family involvement; home-school relationship; parent-pupil relationship

10/1406 language acquisition; language skills; learning experience; parent-teacher cooperation

10/1463 community programmes; community services; cooperative programmes; early childhood education; young children

10/1650 home-school relationship; homework; learning activities; mathematics education

10/1762 beginning reading; literacy; psycholinguistics; reading research; reading teaching

PARENT-PUPIL RELATIONSHIP
10/0853 behaviour problems; bullying; family influence; home environment; parent-child relationship; punishment; pupil behaviour

10/1328 family involvement; home-school relationship; parent participation

10/1467 assessment; profiles; school reports

PARENT ROLE
10/0319 family income; family influence; financial support; parent-child relationship; youth

PARENT-SCHOOL RELATIONSHIP
10/0358 academic records; parent aspiration; school based assessment

10/0363 National Curriculum; parent attitudes; primary education; science education

10/0366 institutional advancement; marketing; parent choice; selection

10/0409 educational history; parent participation

10/0434 parent control; school boards – Scotland; school governing bodies

10/0481 Nigeria; parent-teacher associations; secondary schools

10/0504 educational quality; outcomes of education; school effectiveness; success

10/0583 Asians; ethnic groups; parent participation

10/0842 access to information; information needs

10/0914 early childhood education; governing bodies; nursery schools; parent attitudes; preschool education; school governors

PARENT-TEACHER ASSOCIATIONS
10/0481 Nigeria; parent-school relationship; secondary schools

PARENT-TEACHER COOPERATION
10/1406 language acquisition; language skills; learning experience; parent participation

PARENTHOOD EDUCATION
10/0810 child rearing; parent-child relationship; parenting skills; voluntary agencies

10/1636 community education; contraception; early parenthood; family planning; mothers; peer teaching; sex education

PARENTING SKILLS
10/0810 child rearing; parent-child relationship; parenthood education; voluntary agencies

PART TIME EMPLOYMENT
10/1092 job training; temporary employment; training

10/1679 training; youth service

PART TIME STUDENTS
10/1509 graduate study; mature students; student research

PART TIME TEACHERS
10/1457 job sharing; primary school teachers; teaching profession

PARTIAL VISION
10/0104 blindness; computer assisted reading; computer software; computer system design; educational materials; visual impairments

10/0105 academic achievement; blindness; cognitive development; longitudinal studies; outcomes of education; special schools; visual impairments

10/1145 assessment; blindness; mobility aids; special educational needs; travel training; visual impairments; visually handicapped mobility

PARTICIPANT SATISFACTION
10/0573 B Ed degrees; preservice teacher education; probationary teachers; student teachers; teaching experience

PARTICIPATION
10/0119 adult education; life style

10/1060 arts; attitudes; culture; mass media; music; sports; theatre arts

10/1062 arts; arts education; attitudes; culture; leisure time; youth

PARTICIPATIVE DECISION MAKING
10/0569 local management of schools; parent participation; school based management; school governing bodies; school governors

PASTORAL CARE – EDUCATION
10/0712 counselling services; higher education; student counselling; student needs

10/0916 educational environment; school organisation

10/1247 educational environment; educational philosophy; pupil-school relationship; pupil welfare

10/1313 comparative education; international educational exchange; teacher role

PATENTS
10/0027 industry-higher education relationship; intellectual property; research

PATIENT EDUCATION
10/0270 health education; medical services; pharmacists; pharmacy

10/1154 doctor-patient relationship; medical services; pain; physical health

10/1158 doctor-patient relationship; medical services; pain; physical health

10/1402 allied health occupations; health education; preventive medicine

PATTERN RECOGNITION
10/0628 cognitive processes; mathematics education; National Curriculum

10/0632 early childhood education; mathematics education; play; young children

PEER EVALUATION
10/0071 pharmacists; pharmacy; self evaluation – individuals

PEER GROUPS
10/1191 cognitive development; interaction; reasoning

10/1635 adolescents; conversation; peer teaching; sexuality

PEER INFLUENCE
10/0717 mathematics education; peer teaching;

science education; student volunteers; technology education

PEER TEACHING
10/0009 acquired immune deficiency syndrome; health education; parent participation; sex education
10/0353 computer uses in education; feedback; interaction; learning processes; teacher-pupil relationship
10/0384 role models; student-school relationship; wales
10/0717 mathematics education; peer influence; science education; student volunteers; technology education
10/1538 community benefits; developing countries; health education; India; Uganda
10/1635 adolescents; conversation; peer groups; sexuality
10/1636 community education; contraception; early parenthood; family planning; mothers; parenthood education; sex education

PEOPLE'S UNIVERSITIES
10/0430 adult education; comparative education; lifelong learning; mature students; Scandinavia
10/0431 adult education; comparative education; Denmark; lifelong learning; mature students

PERCEPTUAL DEVELOPMENT
10/0990 memory; spatial ability

PERCEPTUAL HANDICAPS
10/0745 child development; motor development; neurological impairments; premature infants; special educational needs
10/0747 cerebral palsy; disabilities; motor reactions; perceptual motor coordination; special educational needs

PERCEPTUAL MOTOR COORDINATION
10/0744 handwriting; motor development; reading; speech
10/0747 cerebral palsy; disabilities; motor reactions; perceptual handicaps; special educational needs
10/0759 self concept; special educational needs
10/0760 clumsy children; psychomotor skills; special educational needs

PERFORMANCE
10/0531 academic achievement; access programmes; higher education; mature students; nontraditional education
10/0652 academic achievement; achievement; birth; school entrance age
10/1086 educational research; statistical data

PERFORMANCE CONTRACTS
10/0529 educational quality; higher education; institutional role
10/0946 preservice teacher education; records of achievement; school based teacher education; student teachers; teacher development; teaching profession
10/1349 educational quality; further education; higher education; industry-higher education relationship; institutional role; programme evaluation

PERFORMANCE FACTORS
10/0720 cultural influences; gypsies; minority group children; travellers – itinerants
10/0721 cultural influences; gypsies; minority group children; travellers – itinerants
10/0734 achievement; educational quality; performance indicators; school effectiveness
10/0867 academic achievement; scaling; school effectiveness; social environment; socioeconomic influences
10/1076 achievement; classroom environment; statistical analysis
10/1077 achievement; educational quality; examination results; outcomes of education; performance indicators; school effectiveness
10/1087 college effectiveness; educational quality; further education; institutional characteristics; performance indicators

PERFORMANCE INDICATORS
10/0058 examination results; institutional evaluation
10/0116 educational quality; National Vocational Qualifications; vocational education
10/0313 outcomes of education; school effectiveness; school leavers; secondary schools
10/0437 leadership; seminars; small group teaching; teacher effectiveness; teaching methods; university teaching
10/0458 'A' level examinations; accountability; examination results; outcomes of education; programme effectiveness; school effectiveness
10/0495 educational objectives; institutional evaluation; organisational effectiveness
10/0734 achievement; educational quality; performance factors; school effectiveness
10/0906 computer software; computer uses in education; higher education; quality control
10/1023 course evaluation; educational quality; higher education; quality control; student attitudes; teacher effectiveness; universities
10/1035 educational quality; evaluation criteria; institutional evaluation; school effectiveness
10/1077 achievement; educational quality; examination results; outcomes of education; performance factors; school effectiveness
10/1087 college effectiveness; educational quality; further education; institutional characteristics; performance factors
10/1380 accountability; educational quality; measurement; school effectiveness; secondary schools

PERIPATETIC TEACHERS
10/0253 artists; training
10/0433 educational quality; hearing impairments; mainstreaming; special educational needs; support teachers; teacher effectiveness

PERSONAL CONSTRUCT THEORY
10/0160 competence; competency based teacher education; discussion – teaching technique; repertory grid test; teacher effectiveness
10/1487 self evaluation – individuals; teacher evaluation

PERSONAL NARRATIVES
10/0707 literacy; memory; older adults; oral history

PERSONAL SPACE
10/1388 equal education; school space

PERSONALITY
10/1563 behaviour problems; bullying; secondary school pupils; values

PERSONALITY DEVELOPMENT
10/0722 ability; child development; developmental continuity; longitudinal studies
10/0967 adolescent attitudes; adolescent development; adolescents; educational attitudes; interests; social development; vocational interests

PERSONALITY MEASURES
10/1560 primary school pupils
10/1561 Welsh

PERSONALITY TRAITS
10/1544 psychology

PHARMACEUTICAL EDUCATION
10/0069 clinical experience; distance education; pharmacists; professional training; programme evaluation
10/0070 pharmacists; professional training
10/0976 pharmacists; professional development

PHARMACISTS
10/0069 clinical experience; distance education; pharmaceutical education; professional training; programme evaluation
10/0070 pharmaceutical education; professional training
10/0071 peer evaluation; pharmacy; self evaluation – individuals
10/0270 health education; medical services; patient education; pharmacy

10/0976 pharmaceutical education; professional development

PHARMACOLOGY
10/1502 medicine; nurse education; nurses

PHARMACY
10/0071 peer evaluation; pharmacists; self evaluation – individuals
10/0270 health education; medical services; patient education; pharmacists

PHILOSOPHY
10/0500 educational history; educational theories
10/1468 moral education; values education

PHILOSOPHY OF SCIENCE
10/0509 comprehension; science education; scientific concepts; student attitudes
10/1691 preservice teacher education; science education; scientific literacy; student teachers

PHONEMICS
10/1243 child development; memorisation; pictorial stimuli; verbal development; visual learning

PHONICS
10/0850 reading difficulties; reading teaching; remedial reading
10/1749 early childhood education; reading; reading ability; reading skills

PHONOLOGY
10/0078 nursery schools; preschool children; preschool education; speech handicaps
10/0861 musical ability; reading ability

PHOTOGRAPHY
10/0951 art education; visual arts
10/1405 international educational exchange

PHYSICAL ACTIVITIES
10/0307 educational materials; exercise; health activities; health promotion; heart rate; primary school pupils
10/0351 child psychology; exercise; health; physical activity level
10/0441 judo; sports

PHYSICAL ACTIVITY LEVEL
10/0351 child psychology; exercise; health; physical activities
10/0443 developmental continuity; physical education; primary secondary education

PHYSICAL DISABILITIES
10/0494 communication skills; nonverbal communication; severe disabilities; special educational needs; speech handicaps

PHYSICAL EDUCATION
10/0217 curriculum development; individualism; teaching methods; theory-practice relationship
10/0233 National Curriculum; primary education
10/0244 cross curricular approach; National Curriculum
10/0331 educational policy; educational practices; sports
10/0443 developmental continuity; physical activity level; primary secondary education
10/0474 disabilities; mainstreaming; moderate learning difficulties; Nigeria; special educational needs
10/0664 activities; comparative education; france; outdoor pursuits
10/0686 curriculum development; educational philosophy; individual development; moral education; religious education
10/0902 educational change; local management of schools; National Curriculum; sports
10/0983 assessment; examinations
10/1233 health; health activities; holistic approach; well being
10/1761 physical education teachers

PHYSICAL EDUCATION TEACHERS
10/0131 preservice teacher education; socialisation; teacher educators
10/1761 physical education

PHYSICAL ENVIRONMENT
10/0637 climate; global approach; scientific attitudes; social attitudes
10/0741 earth science; laboratories; laboratory experiments; physical geography; simulated environment
10/0835 explanation; public opinion; reasoning; scientific attitudes; scientific literacy
10/1117 concept formation; ecology; environmental education

PHYSICAL GEOGRAPHY
10/0741 earth science; laboratories; laboratory experiments; physical environment; simulated environment

PHYSICAL HEALTH
10/1154 doctor-patient relationship; medical services; pain; patient education
10/1158 doctor-patient relationship; medical services; pain; patient education

PHYSICAL SCIENCES
10/0501 earth science; educational history; geology education; science education
10/0502 comprehension; earth science; oceanography; plate tectonics
10/0503 earth science; educational materials; material development; National Curriculum; science education
10/1133 adult education; educational practices; higher education; information technology; science education

PHYSICAL THERAPY
10/0392 assessment; clinical experience; medical education

PHYSICIANS
10/0268 assessment; competence; examinations; medical education; medicine
10/0282 assessment; competence; examinations; medical education; medicine

PHYSICS EDUCATION
10/0617 electricity; learning processes; science education; sixth form education
10/0642 group discussion; group work; science education
10/0834 energy education; science education
10/1273 Cameroon
10/1274 Cameroon
10/1424 biology education; chemistry education; learner centred methods; learning strategies; science education; teaching methods
10/1464 computer uses in education; hypothesis testing; science education
10/1795 science education; scientific concepts; thermodynamics

PICTORIAL STIMULI
10/0984 memory; science education; visual learning
10/1243 child development; memorisation; phonemics; verbal development; visual learning
10/1658 educational materials; history studies; teaching methods; visual aids

PICTURE BOOKS
10/0936 books; children as writers; children's literature; literacy

PLACEMENT
10/0648 enterprise education; industrial secondments; industry-education relationship; preservice teacher education; student teachers
10/0932 preservice teacher education; primary schools; secondary schools; student teachers; teaching practice
10/1109 industry-higher education relationship; management studies; work experience
10/1473 health visitors; learning experience; nurse education
10/1607 librarianship education; library schools; professional education; work experience programmes

PLAGIARISM
10/1217 cheating; discipline problems; higher education; student behaviour

PLANNING
10/0051 career planning; individual development; profiles
10/0647 development plans; educational planning; primary schools; whole school approach
10/0665 Postgraduate Certificate in Education; teacher education
10/0840 development plans; educational administration; primary schools

PLATE TECTONICS
10/0502 comprehension; earth science; oceanography; physical sciences

PLAY
10/0632 early childhood education; mathematics education; pattern recognition; young children
10/0848 child care givers; community services; play centres; recreational activities
10/1312 learning activities; pupil attitudes

PLAY CENTRES
10/0848 child care givers; community services; play; recreational activities

PLAY GROUPS
10/0484 early childhood education; ireland; Montessori method; preschool education
10/1214 child caregivers; preschool education; qualifications; training
10/1788 early childhood education; educational development; educational quality; nursery schools; preschool education; quality control

POETRY
10/0675 books; children's literature; fiction; primary school pupils; reading; reading material selection

POLAND
10/0125 adult education; citizenship; comparative education; consumer economics; educational policy
10/0373 inservice teacher education; international educational exchange; international programmes; preservice teacher education; teacher education
10/0703 economic change; educational needs; educational policy; social change; youth

POLICY
10/1639 educational research; information technology; research; research opportunities; social science research
10/1681 community organisations; youth service

POLICY FORMATION
10/0518 educational planning; educational policy; policy makers
10/0796 advisory committees; higher education; politics-education relationship; universities

POLICY MAKERS
10/0518 educational planning; educational policy; policy formation

POLITICAL ATTITUDES
10/0871 social attitudes; teacher attitudes; teacher education; teacher educators

POLITICAL INFLUENCES
10/0219 politics-education relationship; teacher education
10/1138 adult education; citizenship education; social change; socialist countries; voluntary agencies

POLITICAL SCIENCE STUDIES
10/1793 curriculum development; guidelines

POLITICS-EDUCATION RELATIONSHIP
10/0084 developing countries; educational administration; educational policy; school systems
10/0096 educational administration; educational change; educational policy; governance; local education authorities; management in education
10/0161 educational change; educational policy
10/0165 consumer economics; educational administration; educational change; educational finance; educational policy
10/0219 political influences; teacher education
10/0399 Commonwealth of Independent States; Communist education; educational change; ideology; social change; USSR
10/0402 conservatism; Scotland
10/0414 educational history; educational policy; South Africa
10/0427 educational policy; Scotland
10/0428 educational administration; educational policy; management in education; Scotland
10/0471 change; comparative education; democracy; development education
10/0585 educational change; educational policy; educationally disadvantaged; equal education; secondary schools
10/0713 Education Reform Act 1988; educational change; educational policy
10/0796 advisory committees; higher education; policy formation; universities
10/0877 educational policy
10/0878 education vouchers; educational change; educational policy
10/0895 citizenship education; comparative education
10/1201 comparative education; educational policy; industry-education relationship; United States of America
10/1494 curriculum development; economics-education relationship; educational policy; labour market; vocational education
10/1654 citizenship; educational finance; educational history; educational objectives

POLLUTION
10/1556 curriculum development; environmental education; waste disposal

POLYMERS
10/0682 cross curricular approach; curriculum development; environmental education; National Curriculum

POPULAR CULTURE
10/0173 children's literature; comics – publications; educational history; girls; sex role; textbooks; women's education
10/0763 incidental learning; literacy; mass media

PORTUGAL
10/1142 adult vocational education; comparative education; disabilities; information technology; special educational needs; training; United Kingdom

POSTGRADUATE CERTIFICATE IN EDUCATION
10/0214 mentors; preservice teacher education; school based teacher education; student teacher attitudes; teacher attitudes
10/0350 preservice teacher education; student attitudes; student teacher evaluation; teacher behaviour; teaching practice
10/0665 planning; teacher education
10/0694 preservice teacher education; school based teacher education
10/0790 Japanese; second language teaching
10/0993 degrees – academic; main subjects; preservice teacher education
10/1236 articled teachers; preservice teacher education; student teachers; teacher education
10/1248 art; design; preservice teacher education; probationary teachers; programme effectiveness; student teachers
10/1296 followup studies; student teachers; teacher development
10/1301 institutional cooperation; mentors; preservice teacher education; school based teacher education
10/1363 preservice teacher education; teaching practice
10/1731 equal education; preservice teacher education; school based teacher education; student teacher attitudes
10/1744 preservice teacher education; school based teacher education; student teachers
10/1784 course evaluation; preservice teacher education; school based teacher education

POWER STRUCTURE
10/1153 church and education; feminism; language usage; Protestant churches

PRACTICAL SCIENCE
10/0624 assessment; General Certificate of Secondary Education; science activities; science education
10/0625 assessment; General Certificate of Secondary Education; science activities; science education
10/0899 computer uses in education; science education
10/1801 learning activities; science activities; science education

PREDICTION
10/0059 long range planning; pupil numbers; regional planning
10/0816 educational development; higher education; universities

PREDICTION OF SUCCESS
10/0905 aptitude; assessment; critical thinking; higher education; mature students; selection; student evaluation

PREDICTIVE MEASUREMENT
10/0005 learning strategies; medical education; nurse education

PREDICTIVE VALIDITY
10/0658 models; probability; statistical inference

PREGNANCY
10/0064 child development; cognitive ability; health education; intellectual development; intelligence quotient; smoking

PREMATURE INFANTS
10/0745 child development; motor development; neurological impairments; perceptual handicaps; special educational needs

PREPARATORY SCHOOLS
10/1194 boys; educational history

PRESCHOOL CHILDREN
10/0078 nursery schools; phonology; preschool education; speech handicaps
10/0846 child caregivers; child minding; day care; day care centres; quality control

PRESCHOOL EDUCATION
10/0001 access to education; community education; mothers; young children
10/0078 nursery schools; phonology; preschool children; speech handicaps
10/0377 early childhood education; nursery school education; regional characteristics; regional planning
10/0484 early childhood education; Ireland; Montessori method; play groups
10/0715 early childhood education
10/0724 early childhood education
10/0851 Children Act 1989; day care; early childhood education; legislation; local government; social services
10/0914 early childhood education; governing bodies; nursery schools; parent attitudes; parent-school relationship; school governors
10/0935 community services; day care; early childhood education; local government; nursery school curriculum; nursery schools; young children
10/1214 child caregivers; play groups; qualifications; training
10/1306 early childhood education; mathematics education; numbers
10/1357 early childhood education; Scotland
10/1419 drama; early childhood education
10/1537 early childhood education; Montessori method; nursery schools
10/1741 primary education; Saudi Arabia
10/1785 early childhood education; educational development; educational quality; quality control
10/1788 early childhood education; educational development; educational quality; nursery schools; play groups; quality control

PRESCHOOL TO PRIMARY TRANSITION
10/0145 early childhood education; Greece; primary school pupils; school readiness

PRESERVICE TEACHER EDUCATION
10/0040 inservice teacher education; primary education; science education; student teachers
10/0042 industrial secondments; industry-education relationship; teacher development
10/0045 experiential learning; prior learning; social work studies
10/0131 physical education teachers; socialisation; teacher educators
10/0209 information technology; student teachers; teaching practice
10/0210 primary school teachers; probationary teachers; professional development; student teachers; teaching profession
10/0211 professional development; teacher attitudes; teacher development; teaching profession
10/0214 mentors; Postgraduate Certificate in Education; school based teacher education; student teacher attitudes; teacher attitudes
10/0216 ethnic groups
10/0221 school based teacher education; teacher attitudes
10/0246 mentors; primary school teachers; secondary school teachers
10/0305 computer literacy; computer uses in education; information technology
10/0350 Postgraduate Certificate in Education; student attitudes; student teacher evaluation; teacher behaviour; teaching practice
10/0368 modern language studies; student teachers
10/0373 inservice teacher education; international educational exchange; international programmes; Poland; teacher education
10/0435 B Ed degrees; science curriculum; science education
10/0439 mentors; student teacher supervisors; teaching practice
10/0459 stress – psychological; stress variables; student teachers; teaching experience; teaching practice
10/0469 mathematics education; mentors; National Curriculum; student teacher supervisors; teaching practice
10/0514 institutes of higher education; mentors; school based teacher education; student teacher supervisors
10/0515 teacher educators
10/0533 cooperative programmes; mentors
10/0534 comparative education; European studies
10/0537 ambiguity; class activities; student teachers; teaching practice; teaching styles
10/0560 licensed teachers; programme evaluation; teacher qualifications; teaching profession
10/0573 B Ed degrees; participant satisfaction; probationary teachers; student teachers; teaching experience
10/0581 learning strategies; learning theories; student teachers
10/0648 enterprise education; industrial secondments; industry-education relationship; placement; student teachers
10/0650 classroom management; student teachers
10/0667 educational history; Jamaica
10/0669 educational administration; National Curriculum; school effectiveness; secondary schools
10/0694 Postgraduate Certificate in Education; school based teacher education
10/0825 school based teacher education
10/0866 experiential learning; interpersonal competence; learning experience; student teachers; workshops
10/0875 educational history
10/0892 information technology; student teachers; teaching practice
10/0897 computer uses in education; open education
10/0932 placement; primary schools; secondary schools; student teachers; teaching practice
10/0937 enterprise education; industrial secondments; industry-education relationship; science teachers; student teachers

10/0938 mentors; student teacher supervisors; supervision; supervisory methods; teaching practice
10/0943 school based teacher education; science education; science teachers; student teachers
10/0946 performance contracts; records of achievement; school based teacher education; student teachers; teacher development; teaching profession
10/0950 computer uses in education; information technology; mathematics education; student teachers; teacher attitudes
10/0993 degrees – academic; main subjects; Postgraduate Certificate in Education
10/0996 local education authorities; probationary teachers; teacher development; teacher education; teacher induction
10/1099 mature students; student behaviour; student teacher attitudes; student teachers; women's education
10/1104 probationary teachers; student teachers; teaching profession
10/1106 academic staff; higher education; inservice teacher education; teacher educators
10/1114 ethnic groups; student recruitment; teacher recruitment; teaching profession
10/1120 agriculture; controversial issues – course content; environmental education
10/1147 change agents; curriculum development; TVEI
10/1218 intellectuals; probationary teachers; professional development; teacher role; teaching profession
10/1234 educational change; parent attitudes; primary school teachers; student teacher attitudes; teacher attitudes; teaching profession
10/1236 articled teachers; Postgraduate Certificate in Education; student teachers; teacher education
10/1237 competency based teacher education
10/1248 art; design; Postgraduate Certificate in Education; probationary teachers; programme effectiveness; student teachers
10/1275 mentors; school based teacher education; student teacher supervisors
10/1276 learning strategies; mathematics teachers; school based teacher education; student teachers
10/1295 school based teacher education; student teacher supervisors; supervisors; teaching practice
10/1301 institutional cooperation; mentors; Postgraduate Certificate in Education; school based teacher education
10/1315 primary school teachers; science education; science teachers; scientific concepts
10/1363 Postgraduate Certificate in Education; teaching practice
10/1407 student teacher evaluation; student teacher supervisors; student teachers; teaching practice
10/1408 course evaluation; probationary teachers
10/1410 antiracism education; multicultural education
10/1422 college-school cooperation; educational materials; flexible learning; material development
10/1426 educational quality; quality control; student teachers; teaching practice
10/1427 B Ed degrees; course evaluation; graduate surveys
10/1435 assessment; competency based teacher education; student teacher evaluation; teaching practice
10/1436 environmental education; history studies; museums
10/1456 student teachers; teaching experience; teaching practice
10/1533 mentors; supervisory training; teaching practice
10/1541 Seychelles
10/1570 cross cultural studies; electronic mail; European studies; telecommunications
10/1593 competence; competency based teacher education; records of achievement; student teachers
10/1597 mentors
10/1600 mentors; primary schools; professional continuing education; teacher development
10/1615 European Community; teacher education curriculum

10/1632 competency based education; higher education; National Vocational Qualifications; professional education; standards
10/1637 mentors; student teachers; teacher development; teaching practice
10/1653 background; economics education; experience; industry-education relationship; student teacher attitudes; student teachers
10/1661 school based teacher education; teaching profession
10/1666 educational materials
10/1691 philosophy of science; science education; scientific literacy; student teachers
10/1723 equal education; institutes of higher education; racial discrimination; racial integration
10/1731 equal education; Postgraduate Certificate in Education; school based teacher education; student teacher attitudes
10/1735 mentors; school based teacher education; student teacher supervisors
10/1744 Postgraduate Certificate in Education; school based teacher education; student teachers
10/1784 course evaluation; Postgraduate Certificate in Education; school based teacher education
10/1787 comparative education; directories; early childhood education

PRESS OPINION
10/0149 educational change; educational policy; mass media effects; public opinion

PRESSURE GROUPS
10/1713 conservation – environment; environmental education

PRETEND PLAY
10/1321 imagination; mathematics education; simulation

PREVENTION
10/1608 drug education; information sources; libraries

PREVENTIVE MEDICINE
10/1402 allied health occupations; health education; patient education
10/1404 cancer education; health education; primary health care

PREWRITING
10/0110 writing – composition; writing research; writing skills; young children

PRIESTS
10/0067 Catholics; clergy; professional education; religious education; theological education
10/0068 professional education; religious education; theological education; women

PRIMARY EDUCATION
10/0037 reading difficulties; reading teaching; remedial programmes; remedial reading; special educational needs
10/0040 inservice teacher education; preservice teacher education; science education; student teachers
10/0109 developing countries; educational improvement; inservice teacher education; Pakistan; programme evaluation
10/0111 heuristics; learning processes; teaching methods
10/0139 curriculum development; educational change; National Curriculum; primary school teachers; primary schools; teacher role; teacher workload
10/0142 Belize; developing countries; development education; educational quality
10/0155 assessment; educational change; National Curriculum; primary school curriculum; primary school teachers; pupil attitudes
10/0188 arithmetic and number education; calculators; mathematics education
10/0199 comparative education; France
10/0201 geographic concepts; geography education

10/0233 National Curriculum; physical education
10/0297 religious education
10/0304 computer uses in education; gifted; individualised methods; Jordan; mathematics
10/0332 educational policy; India
10/0352 history; National Curriculum
10/0363 National Curriculum; parent attitudes; parent-school relationship; science education
10/0374 comparative education; mathematics education
10/0375 information seeking; literacy; reading skills; writing skills
10/0462 modern language studies; problems; second language teaching; teaching methods
10/0535 Japanese studies
10/0579 drama education; dramatics; learning processes; theatre arts
10/0620 ability; design and technology; National Curriculum; technology education
10/0651 educational history; science curriculum; science education
10/0678 cross curricular approach; multicultural education; National Curriculum
10/0687 geography education; mathematics education; navigation; orientation; orienteering; outdoor pursuits
10/0706 adult literacy; home-school relationship; literacy; literacy education; mother tongue; native speakers; teaching methods
10/0748 arithmetic; cognitive development; number concepts; numbers; numeracy
10/0749 cognitive development; comprehension; heat; science education; temperature
10/0815 health education
10/0837 inservice teacher education; material development; science education
10/0849 drug education; health education; life skills
10/0965 achievement; National Curriculum; reading achievement
10/0971 achievement; mathematics education; National Curriculum; reading achievement
10/0998 assessment; mathematics achievement; National Curriculum; science education; standard assessment tasks
10/1081 mathematics achievement; mathematics education
10/1112 attitudes; parent attitudes; school governors; science education; scientific attitudes
10/1113 curriculum development; technology education
10/1115 arts education; cultural education; history
10/1161 curriculum development; Malawi; mathematics education; science education
10/1225 curriculum development; tourism; travel
10/1235 art education; design education; inservice teacher education; National Curriculum; primary school teachers
10/1267 developmental continuity; infant schools; junior schools; transfer pupils
10/1305 curriculum development; discovery learning; educational history; projects – learning activities; pupil projects; teaching methods
10/1339 pupil attitudes; teacher attitudes; values education
10/1414 control technology
10/1415 science education; technology education
10/1417 values education
10/1496 Education Reform Act 1988; multiculturalism; religious education
10/1526 China; educational policy
10/1531 developing countries; development education; India; learning activities; teaching methods
10/1573 differentiated curriculum; individualised methods; teaching methods
10/1598 cross curricular approach; curriculum development; economics education; enterprise education; secondary education; Wales
10/1604 Education Reform Act 1988; educational change; religious education
10/1625 construction – process; construction materials; equal facilities; gender equality; science education; sex differences; technology education
10/1648 curriculum development; educational materials; experiential learning; material development; technology education; work-

education relationship
10/1663 assessment; longitudinal studies; primary school pupils; pupil-school relationship; school based assessment; standard assessment tasks
10/1664 educational experience; longitudinal studies; primary school pupils; pupil-school relationship
10/1669 assessment; National Curriculum; school based assessment
10/1741 preschool education; Saudi Arabia
10/1755 mathematics education; National Curriculum; teaching methods
10/1772 history; National Curriculum
10/1781 corporate support; educational materials; programme evaluation; science education; technology education
10/1783 classroom research; learning strategies; National Curriculum; reading teaching; teaching methods

PRIMARY HEALTH CARE
10/1403 health education; health needs; needs assessment
10/1404 cancer education; health education; preventive medicine

PRIMARY SCHOOL CURRICULUM
10/0155 assessment; educational change; National Curriculum; primary education; primary school teachers; pupil attitudes
10/0302 educational theories
10/1227 curriculum development; educational administration; inspection; primary schools; school organisation

PRIMARY SCHOOL PUPILS
10/0063 behaviour problems; discipline problems; disruptive pupils; infant school pupils; problem children; surveys
10/0134 children as writers; group work; narration; story telling; writing – composition
10/0145 early childhood education; Greece; preschool to primary transition; school readiness
10/0157 pupil attitudes; safety education; traffic safety
10/0194 expulsion; pupil experience; suspension
10/0203 motor development; sex differences
10/0248 child language; classroom communication; language of instruction; language research; science education
10/0307 educational materials; exercise; health activities; health promotion; heart rate; physical activities
10/0675 books; children's literature; fiction; poetry; reading; reading material selection
10/1042 pupil attitudes; secondary school pupils
10/1044 ability; computer uses in education; gifted; information technology
10/1298 assessment; mathematics achievement; mathematics education; self evaluation – individuals
10/1560 personality measures
10/1614 ethnic stereotypes; pupil attitudes; racial attitudes
10/1649 attitude formation; childhood attitudes; work attitudes
10/1651 employment; social cognition; work attitudes
10/1663 assessment; longitudinal studies; primary education; pupil-school relationship; school based assessment; standard assessment tasks
10/1664 educational experience; longitudinal studies; primary education; pupil-school relationship
10/1665 home-school relationship; learning processes; pupil-school relationship; social influences; sociology of education
10/1670 achievement; assessment; profiles; records of achievement; self evaluation – individuals

PRIMARY SCHOOL TEACHERS
10/0139 curriculum development; educational change; National Curriculum; primary education; primary schools; teacher role; teacher workload
10/0153 assessment; educational change; infant

school curriculum; infant school education; National Curriculum; pupil attitudes

10/0154 comparative education; educational change; France; teacher attitudes; teaching profession

10/0155 assessment; educational change; National Curriculum; primary education; primary school curriculum; pupil attitudes

10/0182 inservice teacher education; teacher development

10/0207 music education; National Curriculum

10/0210 preservice teacher education; probationary teachers; professional development; student teachers; teaching profession

10/0223 teacher behaviour; teacher development; teacher role; teaching methods

10/0246 mentors; preservice teacher education; secondary school teachers

10/0294 professional development; teacher attitudes

10/0465 primary schools; sex differences; teacher role; teaching profession

10/0643 classroom communication; teacher behaviour; teacher-pupil relationship; verbal communication

10/0836 mass media; public opinion; science teachers; scientific attitudes; scientific literacy; television

10/1185 courses; inservice teacher education; mathematics education

10/1198 inservice teacher education; science education; teacher attitudes

10/1234 educational change; parent attitudes; preservice teacher education; student teacher attitudes; teacher attitudes; teaching profession

10/1235 art education; design education; inservice teacher education; National Curriculum; primary education

10/1244 consultants; inservice teacher education; music education; music teachers

10/1271 inservice teacher education; mathematics; teacher attitudes

10/1315 preservice teacher education; science education; science teachers; scientific concepts

10/1335 concept teaching; science education; scientific concepts; technology education

10/1457 job sharing; part time teachers; teaching profession

10/1706 teacher development; teacher evaluation; teaching profession

10/1763 educational materials; inservice teacher education; science education; scientific concepts

10/1770 inservice teacher education; science education; teacher development

PRIMARY SCHOOLS

10/0036 assessment; profiles; pupil responsibility; records of achievement; school reports; self evaluation – individuals

10/0137 Christianity; religious education

10/0139 curriculum development; educational change; National Curriculum; primary education; primary school teachers; teacher role; teacher workload

10/0171 school librarians; school libraries

10/0184 local education authorities; mainstreaming; special educational needs; teacher development

10/0190 head teachers; school organisation; teaching profession

10/0365 classroom management; classroom research

10/0367 access to education; Education Reform Act 1988; parent choice

10/0448 health education; health promotion

10/0449 health education; health promotion

10/0464 computer uses in education; group work; microcomputers; problem solving

10/0465 primary school teachers; sex differences; teacher role; teaching profession

10/0473 Education Reform Act 1988; individual development; moral education; National Curriculum; religious education; social development

10/0480 educational change

10/0486 Education Reform Act 1988; educational change; educational legislation; educational planning; school size; small schools

10/0519 economic factors; educational quality; management in education; marketing

10/0647 development plans; educational planning; planning; whole school approach

10/0666 ethnic groups; multicultural education

10/0735 assessment; National Curriculum; standard assessment tasks

10/0755 special educational needs; support services

10/0779 computer uses in education; data processing; databases; material development

10/0840 development plans; educational administration; planning

10/0932 placement; preservice teacher education; secondary schools; student teachers; teaching practice

10/0942 classroom environment; classroom management; drama education; pupil behaviour

10/0947 educational change; educational legislation; educational policy; urban schools

10/0957 educational administration; governing bodies; school governors

10/0968 locus of control; mainstreaming; self esteem; socialisation; special educational needs

10/0975 ethnic groups; minority groups; multiculturalism; voluntary schools

10/1095 educational change; National Curriculum

10/1224 change strategies; educational change; school based management; school organisation; staff-school relationship

10/1227 curriculum development; educational administration; inspection; primary school curriculum; school organisation

10/1232 head teachers; teacher administrator relationship; teacher role; teacher workload; teaching profession

10/1240 discipline policy; disruptive pupils; educational change; expulsion; problem children; special educational needs; suspension

10/1256 change; head teachers; local management of schools; role conflict; stress variables; time management

10/1433 Catholic schools; church and education; religious education

10/1445 language proficiency; modern language studies

10/1447 language proficiency; modern language studies

10/1600 mentors; preservice teacher education; professional continuing education; teacher development

10/1682 educational finance; educational quality; Saudi Arabia

10/1705 library role; school libraries

10/1737 ethnic relations; friendship; intergroup relations; pupil attitudes; racial relations; whites

10/1764 educational administration; head teachers; school based management; teacher role

10/1764 inservice teacher education; mathematics education

PRIMARY-SECONDARY EDUCATION

10/0443 developmental continuity; physical activity level; physical education

10/0444 developmental continuity

10/0567 cooperation; developmental continuity; history; National Curriculum

10/0714 curriculum development; developmental continuity

10/0913 behaviour problems; discipline policy; discipline problems; disruptive pupils; problem children; transfer pupils

10/1001 curriculum development; developmental continuity; local education authorities; National Curriculum; transfer pupils

10/1203 pupil attitudes; science experiments; sex differences

10/1361 assessment; curriculum development; programme evaluation

10/1367 achievement tests; assessment; school based assessment

PRINTING

10/0521 educational materials; educational media; low vision aids; textbooks

PRIOR LEARNING

10/0045 experiential learning; preservice teacher education; social work studies

10/0113 achievement; assessment; experiential learning; further education; National Vocational Qualifications

10/0549 higher education; transfer of learning

PRIVATE EDUCATION

10/0794 further education; higher education; independent colleges; private universities

PRIVATE UNIVERSITIES

10/0794 further education; higher education; independent colleges; private education

PROBABILITY

10/0658 models; predictive validity; statistical inference

10/0981 cultural background; mathematics education

PROBATIONARY TEACHERS

10/0210 preservice teacher education; primary school teachers; professional development; student teachers; teaching profession

10/0220 antiracism education; racial attitudes; student teacher attitudes; student teachers; teacher education

10/0573 B Ed degrees; participant satisfaction; preservice teacher education; student teachers; teaching experience

10/0996 local education authorities; preservice teacher education; teacher development; teacher education; teacher induction

10/1104 preservice teacher education; student teachers; teaching profession

10/1108 labour market; Northern Ireland; teacher employment; teacher recruitment; teaching profession

10/1218 intellectuals; preservice teacher education; professional development; teacher role; teaching profession

10/1248 art; design; Postgraduate Certificate in Education; preservice teacher education; programme effectiveness; student teachers

10/1408 course evaluation; preservice teacher education

10/1534 graduate employment; graduate surveys; teacher development

PROBLEM CHILDREN

10/0063 behaviour problems; discipline problems; disruptive pupils; infant school pupils; primary school pupils; surveys

10/0907 behaviour problems; communication disorders; elective mutism

10/0913 behaviour problems; discipline policy; discipline problems; disruptive pupils; primary secondary education; transfer pupils

10/1240 discipline policy; disruptive pupils; educational change; expulsion; primary schools; special educational needs; suspension

10/1302 behaviour problems; emotional problems; family problems; learning disabilities; social experience

10/1736 educational legislation; educational policy; educationally disadvantaged; expulsion; pupil alienation

10/1739 behaviour problems; disruptive pupils; Education Reform Act 1988; educational policy; emotional problems; school policy

10/1747 behaviour problems; disruptive pupils; support services

PROBLEM SOLVING

10/0177 cognitive processes; cognitive style; learning strategies

10/0464 computer uses in education; group work; microcomputers; primary schools

10/0524 moderate learning difficulties; severe learning difficulties; social skills; special educational needs

10/0609 arithmetic; mathematical ability; mathematics education; teacher education; teaching methods

10/0615 geometry education; Greece; mathematics education

10/0726 feedback; group work; mathematics education

10/0780 algebra education; computer uses in education; mathematics education

10/1188 cognitive ability; depth perception; drawing; spatial ability; visual perception
10/1192 design and technology; learning strategies; technology education
10/1446 computer uses in education; feedback; geometry; logo; mathematics education
10/1478 computer uses in education
10/1493 decision making; student attitudes
10/1716 basic skills; critical thinking; educational philosophy; skills; transfer of learning

PROBLEMS
10/0462 modern language studies; primary education; second language teaching; teaching methods

PRODUCTION TECHNIQUES
10/0762 educational media; mass media; material development

PROFESSIONAL ASSOCIATIONS
10/0429 national organisations; Scotland; teaching profession
10/0604 European Community; professional continuing education; qualifications; Single European Market

PROFESSIONAL AUTONOMY
10/0970 cognitive processes; decision making

PROFESSIONAL CONTINUING EDUCATION
10/0231 employers; financial support; sponsorship; staff development
10/0269 distance education; institutional evaluation; medical services
10/0271 distance education; nurse education; professional development
10/0575 continuing education; lifelong learning; professional development
10/0604 European Community; professional associations; qualifications; Single European Market
10/0673 head teachers; mentors; middle management; teacher development; teaching profession
10/0701 critical thinking; experiential learning; medical education; professional development; reflective teaching
10/1159 adult education; continuing education; course evaluation; programme evaluation
10/1501 lifelong learning; nurse education; nurses; professional development
10/1600 mentors; preservice teacher education; primary schools; teacher development

PROFESSIONAL DEVELOPMENT
10/0210 preservice teacher education; primary school teachers; probationary teachers; student teachers; teaching profession
10/0211 preservice teacher education; teacher attitudes; teacher development; teaching profession
10/0263 academic staff development; educational policy; inservice teacher education; Scotland
10/0271 distance education; nurse education; professional continuing education
10/0294 primary school teachers; teacher attitudes
10/0575 continuing education; lifelong learning; professional continuing education
10/0701 critical thinking; experiential learning; medical education; professional continuing education; reflective teaching
10/0710 adult education teachers; adult educators
10/0711 music teachers; professional training; teacher education
10/0918 health education; inservice teacher education
10/0944 inservice teacher education; teacher development; teaching profession
10/0976 pharmaceutical education; pharmacists
10/1218 intellectuals; preservice teacher education; probationary teachers; teacher role; teaching profession
10/1460 careers service; guidance personnel; mentors
10/1501 lifelong learning; nurse education; nurses; professional continuing education
10/1655 higher education; information technology

PROFESSIONAL EDUCATION
10/0029 competency based education; degrees – academic; inservice education
10/0048 fire service; learning strategies; teaching methods
10/0065 clergy; continuing education; learning processes; religious education; theological education
10/0067 Catholics; clergy; priests; religious education; theological education
10/0068 priests; religious education; theological education; women
10/0227 access to education; finance occupations; mature students
10/0241 nurse education
10/0382 China; housing
10/0693 educational history; higher education; universities; women's education; women's employment
10/0969 cognitive processes; decision making
10/1075 nurse education
10/1098 degrees – academic; medicine; undergraduate students
10/1607 librarianship education; library schools; placement; work experience programmes
10/1632 competency based education; higher education; National Vocational Qualifications; preservice teacher education; standards

PROFESSIONAL OCCUPATIONS
10/1532 assessment; competence; job performance

PROFESSIONAL PERSONNEL
10/0887 management in education

PROFESSIONAL RECOGNITION
10/0556 Nigeria; status need; teacher attitudes; teachers; teaching profession
10/0727 infant school teachers; National Curriculum; teaching profession

PROFESSIONAL TRAINING
10/0069 clinical experience; distance education; pharmaceutical education; pharmacists; programme evaluation
10/0070 pharmaceutical education; pharmacists
10/0711 music teachers; professional development; teacher education
10/1152 adult education; continuing education; industrial training; inservice teacher education; vocational education
10/1401 assertiveness; health personnel; interpersonal competence; radiographers
10/1497 business administration education; management studies; Single European Market

PROFILES
10/0036 assessment; primary schools; pupil responsibility; records of achievement; school reports; self evaluation – individuals
10/0051 career planning; individual development; planning
10/0385 higher education; records of achievement; resumes – personal; self evaluation – individuals; skill development
10/0919 competency based teacher education; mentors; teacher development
10/1307 competency based teacher education; mentors; teacher development; teaching profession
10/1467 assessment; parent-pupil relationship; school reports
10/1670 achievement; assessment; primary school pupils; records of achievement; self evaluation – individuals

PROGRAMME DEVELOPMENT
10/1580 international educational exchange; trainers; training; youth employment; youth programmes

PROGRAMME EFFECTIVENESS
10/0458 'A' level examinations; accountability; examination results; outcomes of education; performance indicators; school effectiveness
10/1248 art; design; Postgraduate Certificate in Education; preservice teacher education; probationary teachers; student teachers
10/1592 distance education; inservice teacher education; teacher attitudes; teacher development
10/1686 nurse education; nurse teachers

PROGRAMME EVALUATION
10/0069 clinical experience; distance education; pharmaceutical education; pharmacists; professional training
10/0109 developing countries; educational improvement; inservice teacher education; Pakistan; primary education
10/0156 head teachers; mentors; teaching profession
10/0205 inservice teacher education; pupil development; self concept
10/0276 distance education; medical education
10/0293 Arab states; English – second language; English for specific purposes
10/0303 crime prevention; delinquency; discipline problems; expulsion; truancy
10/0317 access to education; further education; higher education
10/0396 child rearing; children at risk; community services; family programmes; quality control
10/0397 agency cooperation; child caregivers; community services; day care centres; early childhood education; quality control
10/0493 communication aids – for disabled; communication disorders; special educational needs; workshops
10/0497 education support grants; inservice teacher education; TVEI
10/0538 TVEI
10/0545 enterprise education; higher education; work-education relationship
10/0560 licensed teachers; preservice teacher education; teacher qualifications; teaching profession
10/0639 local education authorities; TVEI
10/0934 access to education; higher education; records of achievement; student records
10/1011 cohort analysis; school leavers; school to work transition; sixteen to nineteen education; TVEI
10/1012 Training and Enterprise Councils; training credits; vocational education
10/1029 health education; health promotion
10/1050 assessment; reading ability; reading achievement
10/1078 international programmes; modern language studies; second language learning; student exchange programmes
10/1159 adult education; continuing education; course evaluation; professional continuing education
10/1257 oracy; oral language; speech communication
10/1333 TVEI
10/1344 access programmes; access to education; adult students; higher education; mature students; science education; social sciences
10/1347 alcohol education; drug education; health education; sex education
10/1349 educational quality; further education; higher education; industry-higher education relationship; institutional role; performance contracts
10/1351 industry-education relationship; skills; TVEI; vocational education
10/1360 industry-education relationship; school to work transition; vocational education; work-education relationship
10/1361 assessment; curriculum development; primary secondary education
10/1386 TVEI
10/1448 change strategies; educational innovation; TVEI
10/1450 teacher development; teacher evaluation; teaching profession
10/1510 nurse education
10/1606 adult basic education; basic skills; colleges of further education; educational quality; further education
10/1629 nurse education; obstetrics
10/1698 head teachers; industrial secondments; industry-education relationship; secondments; teacher development

10/1699 cooperative programmes; industry-education relationship; secondments

10/1700 access to education; further education; sixteen to nineteen education

10/1730 educational innovation; urban schools; whole school approach

10/1776 gifted; Singapore

10/1781 corporate support; educational materials; primary education; science education; technology education

10/1790 educational administration; local management of schools; management in education; school based management; teacher development

PROGRESSIVE EDUCATION
10/0685 comparative education; educational history; educational theories

PROJECTS – LEARNING ACTIVITIES
10/0612 ability; pupil projects; secondary education; technology education

10/1305 curriculum development; discovery learning; educational history; primary education; pupil projects; teaching methods

10/1794 educational change; National Curriculum; pupil projects; teaching methods

PROMOTION – OCCUPATIONAL
10/0004 equal opportunities – jobs; gender equality; teaching profession; women teachers; women's employment

PROOF – MATHEMATICS
10/1383 computer microworlds; computer uses in education; mathematics education

PROTESTANT CHURCHES
10/1153 church and education; feminism; language usage; power structure

PSYCHIATRIC SERVICES
10/1576 Delphi technique; nurse education

PSYCHOLINGUISTICS
10/0705 language acquisition; language handicaps; learning disabilities

10/1762 beginning reading; literacy; parent participation; reading research; reading teaching

PSYCHOLOGICAL EVALUATION
10/0961 communication aids – for disabled; deafness; hearing aids; hearing impairments

PSYCHOLOGICAL TESTING
10/0702 educational history; France; intelligence tests; psychology

PSYCHOLOGY
10/0108 educational theories; learning theories; teacher education; teaching experience; teaching practice; teaching process

10/0390 computer simulation; computer uses in education; industrial psychology

10/0702 educational history; France; intelligence tests; psychological testing

10/1544 personality traits

PSYCHOMOTOR SKILLS
10/0645 cerebral palsy; mobility aids; neuro-logical impairments; special educational needs

10/0760 clumsy children; perceptual motor coordination; special educational needs

10/0792 movement education; music education

PSYCHOPATHOLOGY
10/0660 behaviour problems; elective mutism; inhibition; speech communication

PUBLIC EDUCATION
10/0551 educational administration; educational history; educational policy; secondary education; tripartite system

PUBLIC OPINION
10/0149 educational change; educational policy; mass media effects; press opinion

10/0423 Brazil; comparative education; teacher role

10/0835 explanation; physical environment; reasoning; scientific attitudes; scientific literacy

10/0836 mass media; primary school teachers; science teachers; scientific attitudes; scientific literacy; television

10/1211 attitudes; scientific literacy

10/1293 attitudes; radiation; risk; scientific literacy

10/1525 environmental education; news reporting

PUBLICATIONS
10/0454 educational materials; environmental education; outdoor education; resource materials

10/0455 educational materials; environmental education; social studies

10/1287 research reports; researchers; writing for publication

PUNCTUATION
10/0941 comprehension; writing skills; written language

PUNISHMENT
10/0853 behaviour problems; bullying; family influence; home environment; parent-child relationship; parent-pupil relationship; pupil behaviour

PUPIL ALIENATION
10/1736 educational legislation; educational policy; educationally disadvantaged; expulsion; problem children

PUPIL ATTITUDES
10/0034 comparative education; modern language studies

10/0087 biotechnology; genetic engineering; science education

10/0092 comparative education; disabilities; mainstreaming; special educational needs; special schools

10/0153 assessment; educational change; infant school curriculum; infant school education; National Curriculum; primary school teachers

10/0155 assessment; educational change; National Curriculum; primary education; primary school curriculum; primary school teachers

10/0157 primary school pupils; safety education; traffic safety

10/0322 attendance; discipline; discipline problems; secondary schools; teacher attitudes

10/0758 longitudinal studies; school activities; self evaluation – individuals; sixteen to nineteen education

10/0803 cancer education; health education

10/0862 classroom environment; mainstreaming; moderate learning difficulties; pupil behaviour; social behaviour; special educational needs

10/0881 comparative education; cross cultural studies; educational attitudes; Saudi Arabia

10/0956 career counselling; outcomes of education; school leavers; school to work transition; transition education; TVEI; work-education relationship

10/1021 environmental education; secondary school pupils

10/1042 primary school pupils; secondary school pupils

10/1061 cohort analysis; curriculum development; National Curriculum – Northern Ireland; Northern Ireland

10/1064 National Curriculum; relevance – education

10/1071 aspiration; attitudes; health; pupil behaviour; secondary school pupils; sex education; social attitudes

10/1203 primary secondary education; science experiments; sex differences

10/1210 'A' level examinations; learner characteristics; music activities; music education; sex differences

10/1312 learning activities; play

10/1339 primary education; teacher attitudes; values education

10/1374 antisocial behaviour; attitudes; behaviour problems; bullying; parent attitudes; teacher attitudes

10/1378 learning experience; pupil-school relationship; school effectiveness; secondary education; secondary school pupils; teaching process

10/1439 choice of subjects; demography; further education; sixteen to nineteen education

10/1453 mainstreaming; pupil experience; special educational needs

10/1558 Northern Ireland; religious education; scientific attitudes; secondary school pupils

10/1562 drinking; drug abuse; religious attitudes; secondary school pupils; smoking; substance abuse

10/1564 Christianity; religion; religious attitudes; Roman Catholic Church

10/1565 religion; religious attitudes; secondary school pupils; sex differences; sex role

10/1566 religion; religious attitudes; secondary school pupils; self concept

10/1567 attitude measures; religion; religious attitudes; secondary school pupils; values

10/1596 National Curriculum; secondary schools

10/1599 choice of subjects; pupil interests; sex differences

10/1614 ethnic stereotypes; primary school pupils; racial attitudes

10/1627 observation; textbook evaluation; textbooks

10/1737 ethnic relations; friendship; intergroup relations; primary schools; racial relations; whites

10/1800 citizenship education; human rights; literature studies; racial attitudes; social attitudes

PUPIL BEHAVIOUR
10/0085 behaviour problems; classroom discipline; classroom management; teacher behaviour; teacher-pupil relationship

10/0095 antisocial behaviour; discipline; disruptive pupils; pupil placement

10/0853 behaviour problems; bullying; family influence; home environment; parent-child relationship; parent-pupil relationship; punishment

10/0862 classroom environment; mainstreaming; moderate learning difficulties; pupil attitudes; social behaviour; special educational needs

10/0942 classroom environment; classroom management; drama education; primary schools

10/1071 aspiration; attitudes; health; pupil attitudes; secondary school pupils; sex education; social attitudes

10/1107 attendance; attendance patterns; Northern Ireland; truancy

10/1366 attendance; Scotland; secondary schools; truancy

10/1371 bullying; cooperation; ethnic relations; intergroup relations; intervention; middle school education; social isolation

10/1372 antisocial behaviour; behaviour problems; bullying; discipline; discipline policy

10/1610 intergroup relations; social skills; sociometric techniques

10/1647 truancy

10/1767 academic ability; academic failure; gifted; underachievement

PUPIL DEVELOPMENT
10/0205 inservice teacher education; programme evaluation; self concept

10/0704 assessment; pupil evaluation; reception classes; school entrance age; screening tests

PUPIL EVALUATION
10/0704 assessment; pupil development; reception classes; school entrance age; screening tests

PUPIL EXPERIENCE
10/0194 expulsion; primary school pupils; suspension

10/1453 mainstreaming; pupil attitudes; special educational needs

PUPIL IMPROVEMENT
10/1454 academic achievement; educational practices; secondary schools; support services; underachievement

PUPIL INTERESTS
10/1599 choice of subjects; pupil attitudes; sex differences

PUPIL NEEDS
10/0646 mainstreaming; school effectiveness; special educational needs
10/0676 attitude change; motivation techniques; self concept; self esteem
10/1334 health education; health promotion; Scotland
10/1368 health education; health promotion; Scotland

PUPIL NUMBERS
10/0059 long range planning; prediction; regional planning

PUPIL PARTICIPATION
10/1216 individual development; mathematics achievement; mathematics education; sex difference

PUPIL PLACEMENT
10/0095 antisocial behaviour; discipline; disruptive pupils; pupil behaviour
10/1067 ability; class organisation; grouping – teaching purposes; mixed ability; streaming; teaching methods

PUPIL PROBLEMS
10/0621 algebra; Kenya; mathematics education
10/1336 antisocial behaviour; behaviour problems; emotional problems; social behaviour; special educational needs

PUPIL PROJECTS
10/0612 ability; projects – learning activities; secondary education; technology education
10/1180 animation; computer uses in education
10/1305 curriculum development; discovery learning; educational history; primary education; projects – learning activities; teaching methods
10/1794 educational change; National Curriculum; projects – learning activities; teaching methods

PUPIL RESPONSIBILITY
10/0036 assessment; primary schools; profiles; records of achievement; school reports; self evaluation – individuals

PUPIL-SCHOOL RELATIONSHIP
10/1247 educational environment; educational philosophy; pastoral care – education; pupil welfare
10/1378 learning experience; pupil attitudes; school effectiveness; secondary education; secondary school pupils; teaching process
10/1663 assessment; longitudinal studies; primary education; primary school pupils; school based assessment; standard assessment tasks
10/1664 educational experience; longitudinal studies; primary education; primary school pupils
10/1665 home-school relationship; learning processes; primary school pupils; social influences; sociology of education

PUPIL WELFARE
10/0806 databases; intervention
10/1247 educational environment; educational philosophy; pastoral care – education; pupil-school relationship

PUPILS
10/0060 ethnic origins; mother tongue; religion; surveys
10/0061 individual needs; special educational needs; surveys
10/0062 individual needs; language proficiency; surveys

QUALIFICATIONS
10/0024 access to education; Canada natives; educational policy
10/0394 competency based education; education courses; higher education; masters' courses; standards

10/0604 European Community; professional associations; professional continuing education; Single European Market
10/0728 National Vocational Qualifications; vocational education
10/0789 competency based education; higher education; masters' courses; National Vocational Qualifications; standards
10/0807 technology education
10/1214 child caregivers; play groups; preschool education; training

QUALITY ASSURANCE
10/0413 educational quality; school effectiveness; secondary schools
10/0915 attitudes; higher education
10/1578 academic staff evaluation; quality control; teacher evaluation; universities
10/1605 educational quality; higher education; quality control
10/1780 educational administration; educational quality; higher education; institutes of higher education; quality control

QUALITY CONTROL
10/0383 educational quality; industry-higher education relationship; vocational education; work-education relationship
10/0396 child rearing; children at risk; community services; family programmes; programme evaluation
10/0397 agency cooperation; child caregivers; community services; day care centres; early childhood education; programme evaluation
10/0846 child caregivers; child minding; day care; day care centres; preschool children
10/0906 computer software; computer uses in education; higher education; performance indicators
10/1023 course evaluation; educational quality; higher education; performance indicators; student attitudes; teacher effectiveness; universities
10/1231 assessment; educational quality; external examiners; higher education
10/1426 educational quality; preservice teacher education; student teachers; teaching practice
10/1441 colleges of further education; management in education; sixteen to nineteen education; staff development
10/1578 academic staff evaluation; quality assurance; teacher evaluation; universities
10/1605 educational quality; higher education; quality assurance
10/1672 educational policy; inspection; inspectors – of schools
10/1780 educational administration; educational quality; higher education; institutes of higher education; quality assurance
10/1785 early childhood education; educational development; educational quality; preschool education
10/1788 early childhood education; educational development; educational quality; nursery schools; play groups; preschool education

QUALITY OF LIFE
10/0508 educational objectives; educational philosophy; well being

QUANTITY CONCEPTS
10/1102 blindness; concept formation; number concepts

QUESTIONNAIRES
10/1811 Likert scales; linguistics; opinions; rating scales; semantics

RACIAL ATTITUDES
10/0220 antiracism education; probationary teachers; student teacher attitudes; student teachers; teacher education
10/1288 antiracism education; children's literature; fiction
10/1614 ethnic stereotypes; primary school pupils; pupil attitudes
10/1800 citizenship education; human rights; literature studies; pupil attitudes; social attitudes

RACIAL DISCRIMINATION
10/1722 equal education; local management of schools; racial integration; school based management; secondary schools
10/1723 equal education; institutes of higher education; preservice teacher education; racial integration

RACIAL INTEGRATION
10/1300 community centres; community education; community programmes; day care centres; English – second language; ethnic groups; social integration
10/1722 equal education; local management of schools; racial discrimination; school based management; secondary schools
10/1723 equal education; institutes of higher education; preservice teacher education; racial discrimination

RACIAL RELATIONS
10/0973 ethnic groups; ethnic relations; intergroup relations; multiculturalism; school policy; secondary schools
10/1737 ethnic relations; friendship; intergroup relations; primary schools; pupil attitudes; whites

RADIATION
10/1293 attitudes; public opinion; risk; scientific literacy

RADIO
10/0695 adult education; educational broadcasting; educational radio; local radio; mass media
10/0764 English – second language; Mozambique; second language learning
10/1057 educational broadcasting; educational radio; educational television; television

RADIOGRAPHERS
10/1401 assertiveness; health personnel; interpersonal competence; professional training

RAISED LINE DRAWINGS
10/0082 blindness; braille; learning disabilities; literacy education; sensory aids; special educational needs
10/0102 blindness; maps; memory; spatial ability; tactile adaptation; visual impairments

RATING SCALES
10/1811 Likert scales; linguistics; opinions; questionnaires; semantics

READING
10/0542 critical reading; student development; study skills; writing – composition; writing skills
10/0675 books; children's literature; fiction; poetry; primary school pupils; reading material selection
10/0744 handwriting; motor development; perceptual motor coordination; speech
10/0999 infant school pupils; nursery school pupils; reading readiness; reception classes; tests
10/1199 handwriting; infant school pupils; spelling; writing skills
10/1205 oral reading; reading difficulties; reading teaching
10/1749 early childhood education; phonics; reading ability; reading skills

READING ABILITY
10/0861 musical ability; phonology
10/1031 Northern Ireland; reading research
10/1048 achievement; comparative testing; reading achievement; reading research
10/1050 assessment; programme evaluation; reading achievement
10/1264 child development; early reading; young children
10/1749 early childhood education; phonics; reading; reading skills

READING ACHIEVEMENT
10/0196 early reading; home-school relationship; reading difficulties

10/0520 academic achievement; cognitive
ability; listening skills; television research;
television viewing
10/0965 achievement; National Curriculum;
primary education
10/0971 achievement; mathematics education;
National Curriculum; primary education
10/0997 assessment; English studies; National
Curriculum; standard assessment tasks; writing
skills
10/1048 achievement; comparative testing;
reading ability; reading research
10/1050 assessment; programme evaluation;
reading ability

READING ALOUD TO OTHERS
10/0146 children's literature; early childhood
education; story reading; teacher-pupil
relationship

READING COMPREHENSION
10/1103 learning disabilities; reading difficulties;
special educational needs
10/1144 cognitive processes; computer assisted
reading; reading skills; spelling; word
recognition
10/1546 reading games; word recognition

READING DIFFICULTIES
10/0037 primary education; reading teaching;
remedial programmes; remedial reading;
special educational needs
10/0174 dyslexia
10/0196 early reading; home-school relationship;
reading achievement
10/0453 dyslexia; learning disabilities; special
educational needs; teacher education
10/0659 brain hemisphere functions; dyslexia;
handedness; lateral dominance; visual
perception
10/0850 phonics; reading teaching; remedial
reading
10/0864 dyslexia; language handicaps
10/1103 learning disabilities; reading
comprehension; special educational needs
10/1205 oral reading; reading; reading teaching
10/1437 dyslexia; reading failure; reading skills;
word recognition
10/1805 cognitive ability; dyslexia; reading skills

READING FAILURE
10/1437 dyslexia; reading difficulties; reading
skills; word recognition

READING GAMES
10/1546 reading comprehension; word
recognition

READING IMPROVEMENT
10/1052 group work; learning activities; reading
strategies

READING MATERIAL SELECTION
10/0675 books; children's literature; fiction;
poetry; primary school pupils; reading

READING MATERIALS
10/0346 developing countries; development
education; educational materials; literacy;
material development

READING PROCESSES
10/1259 reading skills; reading tests

READING READINESS
10/0999 infant school pupils; nursery school
pupils; reading; reception classes; tests

READING RESEARCH
10/1031 Northern Ireland; reading ability
10/1048 achievement; comparative testing;
reading ability; reading achievement
10/1762 beginning reading; literacy; parent
participation; psycholinguistics; reading
teaching

READING SKILLS
10/0150 curriculum; literacy education;
secondary school curriculum; writing skills
10/0206 language skills; literacy; oracy; special

educational needs; spelling; writing skills
10/0375 information seeking; literacy; primary
education; writing skills
10/0463 beginning reading; early reading; oral
reading; teacher-pupil relationship
10/1049 family involvement; family
programmes; literacy; parent participation;
writing skills
10/1096 further education students; higher
education; literacy; writing skills
10/1144 cognitive processes; computer assisted
reading; reading comprehension; spelling;
word recognition
10/1259 reading processes; reading tests
10/1437 dyslexia; reading difficulties; reading
failure; word recognition
10/1545 memory
10/1749 early childhood education; phonics;
reading; reading ability
10/1805 cognitive ability; dyslexia; reading
difficulties

READING STRATEGIES
10/1052 group work; learning activities; reading
improvement

READING TEACHING
10/0037 primary education; reading difficulties;
remedial programmes; remedial reading;
special educational needs
10/0103 blindness; braille; sensory aids; tactile
adaptation; tactual perception
10/0716 bilingual education programmes;
English – second language; ethnic groups;
home-school relationship; literacy education;
parent participation; second language learning
10/0850 phonics; reading difficulties; remedial
reading
10/1205 oral reading; reading; reading difficulties
10/1220 beginning reading; infant school
education; teacher-pupil relationship; teaching
methods
10/1762 beginning reading; literacy; parent
participation; psycholinguistics; reading
research
10/1783 classroom research; learning strategies;
National Curriculum; primary education;
teaching methods

READING TESTS
10/0107 blindness; braille; visual impairments
10/1259 reading processes; reading skills

REALISM
10/1728 educational philosophy; ethics; moral
education; moral values; reasoning

REASONING
10/0260 art education; criticism; intellectual
development
10/0778 explanation; research methodology
10/0835 explanation; physical environment;
public opinion; scientific attitudes; scientific
literacy
10/1171 computers; educational materials;
metaphors
10/1183 cognitive development; computer
programming
10/1189 cognitive development; temporal
integration; time perspective
10/1191 cognitive development; interaction; peer
groups
10/1728 educational philosophy; ethics; moral
education; moral values; realism

RECEPTION CLASSES
10/0306 early childhood education; infant school
teachers; mathematics education
10/0704 assessment; pupil development; pupil
evaluation; school entrance age; screening tests
10/0999 infant school pupils; nursery school
pupils; reading; reading readiness; tests
10/1193 communication skills; early childhood
education; friendship; infant school pupils;
social development; social isolation; young
children
10/1272 classroom management; early childhood
education; infant school education; infant
school teachers

RECORDS OF ACHIEVEMENT
10/0036 assessment; primary schools; profiles;
pupil responsibility; school reports; self
evaluation – individuals
10/0385 higher education; profiles; resumes –
personal; self evaluation – individuals; skill
development
10/0934 access to education; higher education;
programme evaluation; student records
10/0946 performance contracts; preservice
teacher education; school based teacher
education; student teachers; teacher
development; teaching profession
10/1297 achievement; assessment; early
childhood education; self evaluation –
individuals; young children
10/1529 assessment by teachers; National
Curriculum; school based assessment
10/1593 competence; competency based teacher
education; preservice teacher education;
student teachers
10/1670 achievement; assessment; primary
school pupils; profiles; self evaluation –
individuals

RECREATIONAL ACTIVITIES
10/0540 girls; leisure time; women's studies
10/0848 child care givers; community services;
play; play centres

REFERENCE MATERIALS
10/1020 directories; moral education; values
education

REFLECTIVE TEACHING
10/0701 critical thinking; experiential learning;
medical education; professional continuing
education; professional development

REFUGEES
10/1752 Namibia

REGIONAL CHARACTERISTICS
10/0377 early childhood education; nursery
school education; preschool education;
regional planning

REGIONAL PLANNING
10/0059 long range planning; prediction; pupil
numbers
10/0377 early childhood education; nursery
school education; preschool education;
regional characteristics

REHABILITATION
10/1146 adaptive behaviour – of disabled;
attitude measures; blindness; emotional
adjustment; measurement techniques; visual
impairments

RELATIVISM – PHILOSOPHY
10/1724 ethics; moral education; multiculturalism

RELEVANCE – EDUCATION
10/1064 National Curriculum; pupil attitudes

RELIGION
10/0060 ethnic origins; mother tongue; pupils;
surveys
10/0175 family life; nationalism; state schools
10/1559 secondary school pupils; well being
10/1564 Christianity; pupil attitudes; religious
attitudes; Roman Catholic Church
10/1565 pupil attitudes; religious attitudes;
secondary school pupils; sex differences; sex role
10/1566 pupil attitudes; religious attitudes;
secondary school pupils; self concept
10/1567 attitude measures; pupil attitudes;
religious attitudes; secondary school pupils;
values

RELIGION AND EDUCATION
10/0357 Education Reform Act 1988; school
worship; symbolism
10/0403 Scotland
10/0475 church and education; church-state
relationship; educational history; educational
legislation; nonconformity
10/0489 higher education; religious education;
universities

10/1150 Islamic education; Muslims; religious cultural groups; women's education
10/1151 Islamic education; Muslims; religious cultural groups; women's education
10/1160 equal education; Islamic education; Muslims; religious cultural groups; single sex schools; women's education
10/1229 moral development; religious attitudes; school worship; values education
10/1499 adult development; adult education; religious education

RELIGIOUS ATTITUDES
10/1221 adolescent development; bereavement; child development; death; moral development
10/1229 moral development; religion and education; school worship; values education
10/1562 drinking; drug abuse; pupil attitudes; secondary school pupils; smoking; substance abuse
10/1564 Christianity; pupil attitudes; religion; Roman Catholic Church
10/1565 pupil attitudes; religion; secondary school pupils; sex differences; sex role
10/1566 pupil attitudes; religion; secondary school pupils; self concept
10/1567 attitude measures; pupil attitudes; religion; secondary school pupils; values

RELIGIOUS CULTURAL GROUPS
10/1150 Islamic education; Muslims; religion and education; women's education
10/1151 Islamic education; Muslims; religion and education; women's education
10/1160 equal education; Islamic education; Muslims; religion and education; single sex schools; women's education
10/1322 religious education
10/1472 equal education; equal facilities; ethnic groups; minority groups

RELIGIOUS EDUCATION
10/0065 clergy; continuing education; learning processes; professional education; theological education
10/0067 Catholics; clergy; priests; professional education; theological education
10/0068 priests; professional education; theological education; women
10/0098 adult education; capitalism; Christianity; church and education; secularisation
10/0099 church and education; theological education
10/0137 Christianity; primary schools
10/0297 primary education
10/0473 Education Reform Act 1988; individual development; moral education; National Curriculum; primary schools; social development
10/0477 beliefs; Christianity; mental retardation; special educational needs
10/0489 higher education; religion and education; universities
10/0491 art
10/0686 curriculum development; educational philosophy; individual development; moral education; physical education
10/1318 young children
10/1320 Christianity; young children
10/1322 religious cultural groups
10/1412 student attitudes
10/1433 Catholic schools; church and education; primary schools
10/1496 Education Reform Act 1988; multiculturalism; primary education
10/1499 adult development; adult education; religion and education
10/1558 Northern Ireland; pupil attitudes; scientific attitudes; secondary school pupils
10/1604 Education Reform Act 1988; educational change; primary education
10/1760 assessment

REMEDIAL PROGRAMMES
10/0037 primary education; reading difficulties; reading teaching; remedial reading; special educational needs

REMEDIAL READING
10/0037 primary education; reading difficulties;

reading teaching; remedial programmes; special educational needs
10/0850 phonics; reading difficulties; reading teaching

REPERTORY GRID TEST
10/0160 competence; competency based teacher education; discussion – teaching technique; personal construct theory; teacher effectiveness

RESEARCH
10/0026 cooperative programmes; corporate support; industry-higher education relationship
10/0027 industry-higher education relationship; intellectual property; patents
10/0254 art; databases; design; information sources
10/0262 databases; local management of schools
10/0987 accountancy education; business education; teaching methods
10/1633 educational research; educational researchers; teacher education
10/1634 educational research; social science research
10/1639 educational research; information technology; policy; research opportunities; social science research

RESEARCH AND DEVELOPMENT
10/1043 comparative education; educational research; Europe; international educational exchange

RESEARCH AND DEVELOPMENT CENTRES
10/1451 educational research

RESEARCH METHODOLOGY
10/0187 change strategies; educational environment; educational research; organisational change
10/0657 sample size
10/0778 explanation; reasoning

RESEARCH OPPORTUNITIES
10/1639 educational research; information technology; policy; research; social science research

RESEARCH REPORTS
10/0468 computer uses in education; information technology; theses
10/1287 publications; researchers; writing for publication

RESEARCH TOOLS
10/0775 models; statistical analysis

RESEARCHERS
10/1287 publications; research reports; writing for publication

RESIDENTIAL CARE
10/0283 child welfare; community services; Scotland; social services; social work

RESIDENTIAL SCHOOLS
10/1015 caregivers; child caregivers; special schools; training

RESOURCE ALLOCATION
10/0086 educational administration; educational finance; educational software; school effectiveness
10/1014 educational administration; educational finance; local management of schools; mainstreaming; school based management; special educational needs
10/1017 age differences; educational economics; educational finance

RESOURCE MATERIALS
10/0454 educational materials; environmental education; outdoor education; publications
10/1279 databases; multicultural education

RESUMES – PERSONAL
10/0385 higher education; profiles; records of achievement; self evaluation – individuals; skill development

RETAILING
10/0601 distributive trades education; National Vocational Qualifications; training; vocational education

RETENTION – PSYCHOLOGY
10/0776 assessment; job skills; mastery tests; vocational education

RETRAINING
10/0318 adult vocational education; followup studies; outcomes of education; women's education; women's employment
10/1093 access to education; adult education; women's education

REVIEW – REEXAMINATION
10/0338 comprehension; essays; examination techniques; higher education; learning strategies; study skills; writing – composition

REWARDS
10/0856 economics-education relationship; educational benefits; educational finance; employment opportunities; outcomes of education; work-education relationship

RISK
10/1293 attitudes; public opinion; radiation; scientific literacy

ROLE CONFLICT
10/0671 administrator role; educational change; head teachers; management in education; secondary schools; teacher role
10/1256 change; head teachers; local management of schools; primary schools; stress variables; time management

ROLE MODELS
10/0384 peer teaching; student school relationship; Wales

ROLE OF EDUCATION
10/1195 citizenship; citizenship education; identity; nationalism; Zambia

ROLE PLAYING
10/0135 language usage; young children
10/0136 language usage; young children

ROMAN CATHOLIC CHURCH
10/0470 Catholic schools; church and education; church-state relationship; educational history; educational policy
10/1564 Christianity; pupil attitudes; religion; religious attitudes

RURAL AREAS
10/0266 adult education; community education
10/1535 access to education; adult education

RURAL SCHOOLS
10/0668 cooperation; National Curriculum; small schools
10/1574 Northern Ireland; science curriculum; science education; small schools

SAFETY EDUCATION
10/0157 primary school pupils; pupil attitudes; traffic safety
10/0158 Scotland; secondary education; traffic safety
10/0953 accidents; comparative education; European Community; food standards; health education; nutrition education
10/1258 traffic safety

SALARIES
10/1442 colleges of further education; comparable worth; employment practices; equal pay; job analysis; occupational information

SALESMANSHIP
10/1500 attitudes; distributive trades education

SAMPLE SIZE
10/0657 research methodology

SANDWICH COURSES
10/0127 attendance patterns; business education; course evaluation; examination results; outcomes of education; undergraduate study

SAUDI ARABIA
10/0424 English – second language; higher education; language of instruction
10/0487 cognitive ability; creative thinking
10/0881 comparative education; cross cultural studies; educational attitudes; pupil attitudes
10/0898 distance education; open universities; women's education
10/1393 English – second language; inservice teacher education; second language teaching
10/1682 educational finance; educational quality; primary schools
10/1741 preschool education; primary education

SCALING
10/0867 academic achievement; performance factors; school effectiveness; social environment; socioeconomic influences

SCANDINAVIA
10/0430 adult education; comparative education; lifelong learning; mature students; people's universities
10/1206 comparative education; educational administration; educational policy; Italy; mainstreaming; special educational needs; support services

SCHOOL ACTIVITIES
10/0758 longitudinal studies; pupil attitudes; self evaluation – individuals; sixteen to nineteen education

SCHOOL BASED ASSESSMENT
10/0358 academic records; parent aspiration; parent-school relationship
10/0623 assessment; National Curriculum; science education
10/0634 National Curriculum; secondary education; technology education
10/0638 assessment; mathematics education; National Curriculum
10/0699 assessment; National Curriculum; science education
10/1330 action research; assessment; educational research
10/1340 assessment; National Curriculum – Northern Ireland
10/1367 achievement tests; assessment; primary-secondary education
10/1434 assessment; English studies; oral English; speech communication
10/1529 assessment by teachers; National Curriculum; records of achievement
10/1584 assessment; mother tongue; National Curriculum; second language learning; standard assessment tasks; Welsh
10/1595 assessment; National Curriculum
10/1663 assessment; longitudinal studies; primary education; primary school pupils; pupil-school relationship; standard assessment tasks
10/1669 assessment; National Curriculum; primary education

SCHOOL BASED MANAGEMENT
10/0057 educational administration; educational change; educational policy; special educational needs; support services
10/0076 educational change; head teachers; local management of schools
10/0081 Education Reform Act 1988; educational administration; educational change; educational finance; grant maintained schools; open entry; parent choice
10/0152 educational administration; educational change; management teams; secondary schools
10/0235 educational administration; local management of schools; small schools
10/0291 head teachers; leadership; leadership styles; local management of schools; management in education
10/0345 educational administration; educational change; local management of schools; parent participation; school boards – Scotland; school governing bodies

10/0569 local management of schools; parent participation; participative decision making; school governing bodies; school governors
10/0672 educational administration; grant maintained schools; local management of schools; management in education
10/0674 educational administration; educational change; grant maintained schools; management in education
10/0756 educational administration; local management of schools; special educational needs
10/0870 educational administration; educational change; local management of schools
10/0873 computer uses in education; educational administration; information technology; local management of schools; management systems
10/0896 educational change; governing bodies; local management of schools; school governors
10/0924 Education Reform Act 1988; educational administration; educational change; local management of schools; secondary schools
10/0925 educational quality; management in education
10/1014 educational administration; educational finance; local management of schools; mainstreaming; resource allocation; special educational needs
10/1038 budgeting; educational administration; educational finance; local management of schools
10/1039 educational administration; local management of schools; school governing bodies; school governors
10/1224 change strategies; educational change; primary schools; school organisation; staff-school relationship
10/1255 educational change; evaluation; local management of schools; secondary schools
10/1352 educational planning
10/1609 educational administration; educational change; grant maintained schools; management in education
10/1612 city technology colleges; grant maintained schools; inservice teacher education; management development; staff development
10/1722 equal education; local management of schools; racial discrimination; racial integration; secondary schools
10/1740 educational administration; head teachers; primary schools; teacher role
10/1750 educational practices; grant maintained schools; institutional autonomy; institutional characteristics
10/1790 educational administration; local management of schools; management in education; programme evaluation; teacher development

SCHOOL BASED TEACHER EDUCATION
10/0214 mentors; Postgraduate Certificate in Education; preservice teacher education; student teacher attitudes; teacher attitudes
10/0221 preservice teacher education; teacher attitudes
10/0514 institutes of higher education; mentors; preservice teacher education; student teacher supervisors
10/0694 Postgraduate Certificate in Education; preservice teacher education
10/0825 preservice teacher education
10/0943 preservice teacher education; science education; science teachers; student teachers
10/0946 performance contracts; preservice teacher education; records of achievement; student teachers; teacher development; teaching profession
10/1275 mentors; preservice teacher education; student teacher supervisors
10/1276 learning strategies; mathematics teachers; preservice teacher education; student teachers
10/1278 competency based teacher education; inservice teacher education; local education authorities; staff orientation; teacher development
10/1295 preservice teacher education; student teacher supervisors; supervisors; teaching practice
10/1301 institutional cooperation; mentors; Postgraduate Certificate in Education;

preservice teacher education
10/1661 preservice teacher education; teaching profession
10/1731 equal education; Postgraduate Certificate in Education; preservice teacher education; student teacher attitudes
10/1735 mentors; preservice teacher education; student teacher supervisors
10/1744 Postgraduate Certificate in Education; preservice teacher education; student teachers
10/1784 course evaluation; Postgraduate Certificate in Education; preservice teacher education

SCHOOL BOARDS – SCOTLAND
10/0345 educational administration; educational change; local management of schools; parent participation; school based management; school governing bodies
10/0432 educational administration; school governing bodies; Scotland
10/0434 parent control; parent-school relationship; school governing bodies
10/1420 educational administration; governing bodies; school governors

SCHOOL-COMMUNITY RELATIONSHIP
10/1630 comparative education; curriculum development; environmental education
10/1715 city technology colleges; disadvantaged environment; industry-education relationship

SCHOOL EFFECTIVENESS
10/0056 academic achievement; equal education; underachievement; urban schools
10/0086 educational administration; educational finance; educational software; resource allocation
10/0178 educational improvement; educational innovation; educational quality
10/0313 outcomes of education; performance indicators; school leavers; secondary schools
10/0323 academic achievement; higher education; secondary schools
10/0407 examination results; secondary schools
10/0413 educational quality; quality assurance; secondary schools
10/0458 'A' level examinations; accountability; examination results; outcomes of education; performance indicators; programme effectiveness
10/0504 educational quality; outcomes of education; parent-school relationship; success
10/0646 mainstreaming; pupil needs; special educational needs
10/0669 educational administration; National Curriculum; preservice teacher education; secondary schools
10/0730 assessment; educational quality; National Curriculum
10/0731 departments; differential performance; examination results; outcomes of education; secondary schools
10/0734 achievement; educational quality; performance factors; performance indicators
10/0867 academic achievement; performance factors; scaling; social environment; socioeconomic influences
10/1035 educational quality; evaluation criteria; institutional evaluation; performance indicators
10/1045 teacher attitudes; teacher effectiveness; teacher workload; time management
10/1077 achievement; educational quality; examination results; outcomes of education; performance factors; performance indicators
10/1223 comparative education; educational history; educational quality; United States of America
10/1377 educational quality; inspection; institutional evaluation; local education authorities
10/1378 learning experience; pupil attitudes; pupil-school relationship; secondary education; secondary school pupils; teaching process
10/1380 accountability; educational quality; measurement; performance indicators; secondary schools
10/1583 bilingual education; bilingualism; educational policy; language policy; Welsh; Welsh studies

10/1738 academic achievement; Catholic schools
10/1789 educational quality; success

SCHOOL ENTRANCE AGE
10/0652 academic achievement; achievement; birth; performance
10/0704 assessment; pupil development; pupil evaluation; reception classes; screening tests
10/1027 assessment; early childhood education; mathematical concepts; mathematics education; mathematics tests
10/1055 achievement; birth; local education authorities
10/1786 admission criteria; local education authorities

SCHOOL FUNDS
10/0012 educational finance; fund raising; income; money management; secondary schools

SCHOOL GOVERNING BODIES
10/0345 educational administration; educational change; local management of schools; parent participation; school based management; school boards – Scotland
10/0354 educational administration; school governors
10/0432 educational administration; school boards – Scotland; Scotland
10/0434 parent control; parent-school relationship; school boards – Scotland
10/0569 local management of schools; parent participation; participative decision making; school based management; school governors
10/0809 educational administration; governance; head teachers; school governors
10/1039 educational administration; local management of schools; school based management; school governors

SCHOOL GOVERNORS
10/0354 educational administration; school governing bodies
10/0569 local management of schools; parent participation; participative decision making; school based management; school governing bodies
10/0809 educational administration; governance; head teachers; school governing bodies
10/0896 educational change; governing bodies; local management of schools; school based management
10/0912 educational administration; governing bodies; head teachers; management in education
10/0914 early childhood education; governing bodies; nursery schools; parent attitudes; parent-school relationship; preschool education
10/0922 church-education relationship; educational history; educational legislation; financial support; free education
10/0957 educational administration; governing bodies; primary schools
10/1039 educational administration; local management of schools; school based management; school governing bodies
10/1112 attitudes; parent attitudes; primary education; science education; scientific attitudes
10/1420 educational administration; governing bodies; school boards – Scotland

SCHOOL LEAVERS
10/0312 school to work transition; Scotland; secondary education; surveys
10/0313 outcomes of education; performance indicators; school effectiveness; secondary schools
10/0315 school to work transition; sixteen to nineteen education; surveys; youth
10/0316 school to work transition; sixteen to nineteen education; surveys; youth
10/0320 cohort analysis; followup studies; longitudinal studies; school to work transition; Scotland; sixteen to nineteen education; youth
10/0561 Kenya; school to work transition; unemployment; vocational education; youth employment
10/0956 career counselling; outcomes of education; pupil attitudes; school to work

transition; transition education; TVEI; work-education relationship
10/1011 cohort analysis; programme evaluation; school to work transition; sixteen to nineteen education; TVEI
10/1458 oracy; school to work transition

SCHOOL LIBRARIANS
10/0171 primary schools; school libraries

SCHOOL LIBRARIES
10/0171 primary schools; school librarians
10/1705 library role; primary schools

SCHOOL MEALS
10/0838 health education; local education authorities; nutrition education

SCHOOL ORGANISATION
10/0190 head teachers; primary schools; teaching profession
10/0916 educational environment; pastoral care – education
10/1224 change strategies; educational change; primary schools; school based management; staff-school relationship
10/1227 curriculum development; educational administration; inspection; primary school curriculum; primary schools
10/1687 cross curricular approach; curriculum development; National Curriculum; teaching methods; thematic approach

SCHOOL PERSONNEL
10/0841 city technology colleges; support staff; teacher aides

SCHOOL POLICY
10/0973 ethnic groups; ethnic relations; intergroup relations; multiculturalism; racial relations; secondary schools
10/1041 computer uses in education; information technology
10/1375 antisocial behaviour; attitudes; bullying; discipline policy; parent attitudes; teacher attitudes
10/1379 equal education; gender equality; secondary schools; whole school approach
10/1385 educational change; equal education; gender equality; sex differences
10/1739 behaviour problems; disruptive pupils; Education Reform Act 1988; educational policy; emotional problems; problem children

SCHOOL READINESS
10/0145 early childhood education; Greece; preschool to primary transition; primary school pupils

SCHOOL REPORTS
10/0036 assessment; primary schools; profiles; pupil responsibility; records of achievement; self evaluation – individuals
10/1467 assessment; parent-pupil relationship; profiles

SCHOOL SIZE
10/0080 Education Reform Act 1988; local management of schools; small schools
10/0486 Education Reform Act 1988; educational change; educational legislation; educational planning; primary schools; small schools

SCHOOL SPACE
10/1388 equal education; personal space
10/1411 campuses; educational facilities improvement
10/1423 campuses; educational facilities improvement

SCHOOL SYSTEMS
10/0084 developing countries; educational administration; educational policy; politics-education relationship
10/0554 educational history; educational policy; educational principles; secondary education; secondary modern schools; tripartite system; working class
10/1774 comparative education; Cyprus; educational policy; Greece

SCHOOL TO WORK TRANSITION
10/0311 further education; higher education; unemployment; vocational education; youth employment
10/0312 school leavers; Scotland; secondary education; surveys
10/0315 school leavers; sixteen to nineteen education; surveys; youth
10/0316 school leavers; sixteen to nineteen education; surveys; youth
10/0320 cohort analysis; followup studies; longitudinal studies; school leavers; Scotland; sixteen to nineteen education; youth
10/0561 Kenya; school leavers; unemployment; vocational education; youth employment
10/0855 industry-education relationship; local education authorities; vocational education
10/0926 training; training credits; youth employment
10/0956 career counselling; outcomes of education; pupil attitudes; school leavers; transition education; TVEI; work-education relationship
10/1003 cooperative education; vocational education; work-education relationship
10/1005 credits; training; Training and Enterprise Councils; vocational education; vocational guidance
10/1011 cohort analysis; programme evaluation; school leavers; sixteen to nineteen education; TVEI
10/1019 career education; careers service; vocational guidance
10/1022 career development; career education; career planning; vocational guidance
10/1065 career education; careers service; vocational guidance; Wales
10/1360 industry-education relationship; programme evaluation; vocational education; work-education relationship
10/1458 oracy; school leavers
10/1459 industry-education relationship; vocational education
10/1462 career choice; employment opportunities; labour market; learner educational objectives; occupational aspiration; secondary school pupils; work-education relationship

SCHOOL WORSHIP
10/0357 Education Reform Act 1988; religion and education; symbolism
10/1229 moral development; religion and education; religious attitudes; values education

SCIENCE ACTIVITIES
10/0622 force; museums; science education; science teaching centres; scientific concepts
10/0624 assessment; General Certificate of Secondary Education; practical science; science education
10/0625 assessment; General Certificate of Secondary Education; practical science; science education
10/1197 classroom observation techniques; group work; learning activities; science education
10/1801 learning activities; practical science; science education

SCIENCE CURRICULUM
10/0435 B Ed degrees; preservice teacher education; science education
10/0651 educational history; primary education; science education
10/1574 Northern Ireland; rural schools; science education; small schools

SCIENCE EDUCATION
10/0040 inservice teacher education; preservice teacher education; primary education; student teachers
10/0087 biotechnology; genetic engineering; pupil attitudes
10/0195 computer software; educational materials; energy education; material development
10/0248 child language; classroom communication; language of instruction; language research; primary school pupils
10/0363 National Curriculum; parent attitudes; parent-school relationship; primary education

10/0435 B Ed degrees; preservice teacher education; science curriculum
10/0501 earth science; educational history; geology education; physical sciences
10/0503 earth science; educational materials; material development; National Curriculum; physical sciences
10/0509 comprehension; philosophy of science; scientific concepts; student attitudes
10/0562 choice of subjects; course selection – students; sex differences; sixteen to nineteen education
10/0587 Botswana; language of instruction; languages for specific purposes; scientific vocabulary; second language learning
10/0589 scientific concepts; teaching methods
10/0590 scientific concepts; sociology of education; teaching methods
10/0591 concept formation; learning theories; scientific concepts
10/0592 concept formation; longitudinal studies; scientific concepts
10/0594 Ghana; industry-education relationship
10/0596 comprehension; scientific concepts; scientific literacy
10/0617 electricity; learning processes; physics education; sixth form education
10/0622 force; museums; science activities; science teaching centres; scientific concepts
10/0623 assessment; National Curriculum; school based assessment
10/0624 assessment; General Certificate of Secondary Education; practical science; science activities
10/0625 assessment; General Certificate of Secondary Education; practical science; science activities
10/0626 comprehension; ecology education; scientific concepts
10/0635 educational history
10/0642 group discussion; group work; physics education
10/0651 educational history; primary education; science curriculum
10/0698 curriculum development; National Curriculum
10/0699 assessment; National Curriculum; school based assessment
10/0717 mathematics education; peer influence; peer teaching; student volunteers; technology education
10/0749 cognitive development; comprehension; heat; primary education; temperature
10/0774 mathematics education; spreadsheets
10/0834 energy education; physics education
10/0837 inservice teacher education; material development; primary education
10/0839 explanation
10/0899 computer uses in education; practical science
10/0943 preservice teacher education; school based teacher education; science teachers; student teachers
10/0949 cartoons; educational materials
10/0978 assessment; attainment tests; English studies; geography education; mathematics education; National Curriculum – Northern Ireland; Northern Ireland
10/0982 curriculum development; mathematics education; technology education
10/0984 memory; pictorial stimuli; visual learning
10/0998 assessment; mathematics achievement; National Curriculum; primary education; standard assessment tasks
10/1002 assessment; core curriculum; English studies; mathematics education; National Curriculum
10/1040 comparative education; mathematics education
10/1058 achievement; achievement tests; assessment; comparative education; mathematics education
10/1084 assessment; English studies; evaluation; mathematics education; National Curriculum; secondary education; technology education
10/1089 chemistry education; sixteen to nineteen education
10/1112 attitudes; parent attitudes; primary education; school governors; scientific attitudes

10/1133 adult education; educational practices; higher education; information technology; physical sciences
10/1161 curriculum development; Malawi; mathematics education; primary education
10/1196 intervention; sex differences
10/1197 classroom observation techniques; group work; learning activities; science activities
10/1198 inservice teacher education; primary school teachers; teacher attitudes
10/1294 chemical bonding; chemistry education; scientific concepts
10/1315 preservice teacher education; primary school teachers; science teachers; scientific concepts
10/1335 concept teaching; primary school teachers; scientific concepts; technology education
10/1338 comparative education; curriculum development; international educational exchange; mathematics education
10/1344 access programmes; access to education; adult students; higher education; mature students; programme evaluation; social sciences
10/1397 decision making; National Curriculum; scientific literacy
10/1398 scientific literacy
10/1399 adult education
10/1415 primary education; technology education
10/1424 biology education; chemistry education; learner centred methods; learning strategies; physics education; teaching methods
10/1464 computer uses in education; hypothesis testing; physics education
10/1536 inservice teacher education
10/1539 Malaysia
10/1568 curriculum development; differentiated curriculum; individualised methods; Northern Ireland
10/1574 Northern Ireland; rural schools; science curriculum; small schools
10/1616 biology education; skills; transfer of learning
10/1618 chemistry education; educational materials; learning strategies; multimedia approach; skills; teaching methods; transfer of learning
10/1619 Business and Technician Education Council; chemistry education; competency based education; skills; transfer of learning
10/1625 construction – process; construction materials; equal facilities; gender equality; primary education; sex differences; technology education
10/1652 educational material evaluation; educational materials; material development; scientific attitudes; scientific literacy; supported self study; teacher education
10/1691 philosophy of science; preservice teacher education; scientific literacy; student teachers
10/1702 graduate study; graduates
10/1729 higher education; scientific literacy; women
10/1763 educational materials; inservice teacher education; primary school teachers; scientific concepts
10/1766 educational history; examination syllabuses; university examinations
10/1769 educational history; examinations; universities
10/1770 inservice teacher education; primary school teachers; teacher development
10/1771 achievement; background; high achievement; individual characteristics; undergraduate students
10/1781 corporate support; educational materials; primary education; programme evaluation; technology education
10/1795 physics education; scientific concepts; thermodynamics
10/1796 'A' level examinations; chemistry education; teaching methods
10/1801 learning activities; practical science; science activities
10/1802 educational materials; inservice teacher education; Swaziland

SCIENCE EXPERIMENTS
10/1203 primary secondary education; pupil attitudes; sex differences

SCIENCE PARKS
10/1643 entrepreneurship; industry-higher education relationship

SCIENCE TEACHERS
10/0836 mass media; primary school teachers; public opinion; scientific attitudes; scientific literacy; television
10/0937 enterprise education; industrial secondments; industry-education relationship; preservice teacher education; student teachers
10/0943 preservice teacher education; school based teacher education; science education; student teachers
10/1303 Brazil; teaching methods
10/1315 preservice teacher education; primary school teachers; science education; scientific concepts

SCIENCE TEACHING CENTRES
10/0622 force; museums; science activities; science education; scientific concepts

SCIENCES
10/0038 cultural activities; curriculum; European Community

SCIENTIFIC ATTITUDES
10/0637 climate; global approach; physical environment; social attitudes
10/0835 explanation; physical environment; public opinion; reasoning; scientific literacy
10/0836 mass media; primary school teachers; public opinion; science teachers; scientific literacy; television
10/1112 attitudes; parent attitudes; primary education; school governors; science education
10/1558 Northern Ireland; pupil attitudes; religious education; secondary school pupils
10/1652 educational material evaluation; educational materials; material development; science education; scientific literacy; supported self study; teacher education

SCIENTIFIC CONCEPTS
10/0509 comprehension; philosophy of science; science education; student attitudes
10/0589 science education; teaching methods
10/0590 science education; sociology of education; teaching methods
10/0591 concept formation; learning theories; science education
10/0592 concept formation; longitudinal studies; science education
10/0596 comprehension; science education; scientific literacy
10/0622 force; museums; science activities; science education; science teaching centres
10/0626 comprehension; ecology education; science education
10/0700 air pollution; conservation – environment; environmental education; misconceptions; secondary school pupils
10/1294 chemical bonding; chemistry education; science education
10/1315 preservice teacher education; primary school teachers; science education; science teachers
10/1335 concept teaching; primary school teachers; science education; technology education
10/1763 educational materials; inservice teacher education; primary school teachers; science education
10/1795 physics education; science education; thermodynamics

SCIENTIFIC LITERACY
10/0596 comprehension; science education; scientific concepts
10/0835 explanation; physical environment; public opinion; reasoning; scientific attitudes
10/0836 mass media; primary school teachers; public opinion; science teachers; scientific attitudes; television
10/1211 attitudes; public opinion

10/1293 attitudes; public opinion; radiation; risk
10/1397 decision making; National Curriculum; science education
10/1398 science education
10/1652 educational material evaluation; educational materials; material development; science education; scientific attitudes; supported self study; teacher education
10/1691 philosophy of science; preservice teacher education; science education; student teachers
10/1729 higher education; science education; women

SCIENTIFIC VOCABULARY
10/0587 Botswana; language of instruction; languages for specific purposes; science education; second language learning

SCOTLAND
10/0007 access to education; disadvantaged environment; educational innovation; educationally disadvantaged
10/0008 educational research
10/0158 safety education; secondary education; traffic safety
10/0263 academic staff development; educational policy; inservice teacher education; professional development
10/0265 educational history; management in education
10/0283 child welfare; community services; residential care; social services; social work
10/0312 school leavers; school to work transition; secondary education; surveys
10/0320 cohort analysis; followup studies; longitudinal studies; school leavers; school to work transition; sixteen to nineteen education; youth
10/0327 curriculum development; educational assessment; educational change; English studies
10/0328 career counselling; China; comparative education; vocational guidance
10/0330 educational history; educational research
10/0335 assessment; attainment tests; English studies; language tests
10/0400 comparative education; educational history; educational policy
10/0402 conservatism; politics-education relationship
10/0403 religion and education
10/0405 educational history
10/0411 comparative education; educational history; educational policy; teacher education
10/0412 educational innovation; educational policy; middle school education
10/0415 educational change; educational history
10/0418 Algeria; bilingualism; comparative education; Gaelic; language policy; mother tongue
10/0427 educational policy; politics-education relationship
10/0428 educational administration; educational policy; management in education; politics-education relationship
10/0429 national organisations; professional associations; teaching profession
10/0432 educational administration; school boards – Scotland; school governing bodies
10/0457 learning motivation; modern language studies; second language teaching
10/1334 health education; health promotion; pupil needs
10/1345 access to education; adult education; adult students; educational guidance; mature students
10/1350 bullying; discipline policy; discipline problems
10/1357 early childhood education; preschool education
10/1366 attendance; pupil behaviour; secondary schools; truancy
10/1368 health education; health promotion; pupil needs
10/1444 assessment; curriculum development; educational change; environmental education; mathematics education; National Curriculum; teaching process
10/1452 comparative education; Greece; learning disabilities; special educational needs

SCOTTISH VOCATIONAL QUALIFICATIONS
10/0785 assessment; job skills; National Vocational Qualifications; verbal tests

SCREENING TESTS
10/0704 assessment; pupil development; pupil evaluation; reception classes; school entrance age
10/1000 assessment; item banks; test items; test selection; tests

SCRIPTS
10/1253 drama education; English studies curriculum; National Curriculum; secondary education

SEARCH STRATEGIES
10/0115 further education; higher education; information retrieval; information systems; optical data discs; student attitudes

SECOND LANGUAGE LEARNING
10/0292 comparative education; cultural education; educational materials; teaching methods
10/0309 Arab states; cultural awareness; English – second language; foreign culture; native speakers
10/0347 Arabic; Chinese languages; educational materials; Japanese; non western languages
10/0378 error analysis – language; Welsh
10/0490 computer uses in education; English – second language
10/0587 Botswana; language of instruction; languages for specific purposes; science education; scientific vocabulary
10/0656 class size; English – second language; second language teaching
10/0716 bilingual education programmes; English – second language; ethnic groups; home-school relationship; literacy education; parent participation; reading teaching
10/0764 English – second language; Mozambique; radio
10/1033 assessment; attainment tests; differential performance
10/1078 international programmes; modern language studies; programme evaluation; student exchange programmes
10/1392 communication research; conversation; native speakers; verbal communication
10/1395 English – second language; languages for specific purposes; Malaysia
10/1554 cultural education; degree requirements; ethnography; higher education; study abroad
10/1584 assessment; mother tongue; National Curriculum; school based assessment; standard assessment tasks; Welsh
10/1591 vocabulary development
10/1707 computer assisted language learning; English – second language; English for academic purposes; overseas students
10/1809 English – second language; English for academic purposes; limited English speaking; overseas students

SECOND LANGUAGE TEACHING
10/0052 English – second language; Oman
10/0198 comparative education; English – second language; international educational exchange
10/0222 English – second language; language proficiency; language teachers
10/0290 Arab states; English – second language
10/0456 curriculum development; educational materials; English – second language; Senegal
10/0457 learning motivation; modern language studies; Scotland
10/0461 developing countries; English – second language
10/0462 modern language studies; primary education; problems; teaching methods
10/0644 English – second language; inservice teacher education; language teachers; Thailand
10/0656 class size; English – second language; second language learning
10/0790 Japanese; Postgraduate Certificate in Education
10/0948 audiovisual aids; educational media; language acquisition; teaching methods; videodiscs

10/1079 comparative education; language policy; modern language curriculum; modern language studies; secondary education
10/1365 further education; languages for specific purposes; modern language studies; vocational education
10/1393 English – second language; inservice teacher education; Saudi Arabia
10/1394 Brazil; English – second language
10/1396 communicative competence – languages; English – second language; Korea; language tests
10/1602 teaching methods; Welsh
10/1803 bilingual pupils; English – second language; language teachers; limited English speaking
10/1810 comparative education; English; German; language tests; modern language studies; native speakers

SECONDARY EDUCATION
10/0158 safety education; Scotland; traffic safety
10/0312 school leavers; school to work transition; Scotland; surveys
10/0340 learning activities; mathematical applications; mathematics education
10/0359 mainstreaming; special educational needs; support services
10/0445 curriculum development; educational history; technical education
10/0510 curriculum development; information technology; mathematics education
10/0551 educational administration; educational history; educational policy; public education; tripartite system
10/0554 educational history; educational policy; educational principles; school systems; secondary modern schools; tripartite system; working class
10/0563 educational change; secondary school curriculum; secondary school teachers; teacher role; teaching profession
10/0612 ability; projects – learning activities; pupil projects; technology education
10/0619 algebra; calculators; computer uses in education; mathematics education
10/0630 curriculum development; geometry; mathematics education; South Africa
10/0634 National Curriculum; school based assessment; technology education
10/0663 comprehensive schools; educational change; educational history
10/1047 basic skills; cross curricular approach; National Curriculum
10/1079 comparative education; language policy; modern language curriculum; modern language studies; second language teaching
10/1084 assessment; English studies; evaluation; mathematics education; National Curriculum; science education; technology education
10/1239 curriculum development; educational change; English studies curriculum; National Curriculum
10/1253 drama education; English studies curriculum; National Curriculum; scripts
10/1378 learning experience; pupil attitudes; pupil-school relationship; school effectiveness; secondary school pupils; teaching process
10/1598 cross curricular approach; curriculum development; economics education; enterprise education; primary education; Wales
10/1690 developing countries; educational improvement; Sierra Leone
10/1792 bilingual education; bilingual schools; Welsh

SECONDARY MODERN SCHOOLS
10/0554 educational history; educational policy; educational principles; school systems; secondary education; tripartite system; working class

SECONDARY SCHOOL CURRICULUM
10/0150 curriculum; literacy education; reading skills; writing skills
10/0563 educational change; secondary education; secondary school teachers; teacher role; teaching profession

SECONDARY SCHOOL PUPILS
10/0243 antisocial behaviour; behaviour problems; delinquency prevention; longitudinal studies; transfer pupils
10/0289 stress – psychological; stress management
10/0391 career counselling; ethnic groups; minority groups; vocational guidance
10/0618 arithmetic; cognitive style; mathematics education; mature students
10/0631 computer uses in education; word processing; writing skills
10/0700 air pollution; conservation – environment; environmental education; misconceptions; scientific concepts
10/0742 economics education
10/1021 environmental education; pupil attitudes
10/1042 primary school pupils; pupil attitudes
10/1071 aspiration; attitudes; health; pupil attitudes; pupil behaviour; sex education; social attitudes
10/1289 books; childrens literature; fiction
10/1378 learning experience; pupil attitudes; pupil-school relationship; school effectiveness; secondary education; teaching process
10/1461 employment opportunities; labour market; learner educational objectives; occupational aspiration; opportunities; work-education relationship
10/1462 career choice; employment opportunities; labour market; learner educational objectives; occupational aspiration; school to work transition; work-education relationship
10/1558 Northern Ireland; pupil attitudes; religious education; scientific attitudes
10/1559 religion; well being
10/1562 drinking; drug abuse; pupil attitudes; religious attitudes; smoking; substance abuse
10/1563 behaviour problems; bullying; personality; values
10/1565 pupil attitudes; religion; religious attitudes; sex differences; sex role
10/1566 pupil attitudes; religion; religious attitudes; self concept
10/1567 attitude measures; pupil attitudes; religion; religious attitudes; values

SECONDARY SCHOOL TEACHERS
10/0246 mentors; preservice teacher education; primary school teachers
10/0557 Malaysia; teacher behaviour; teacher effectiveness; teaching styles
10/0563 educational change; secondary education; secondary school curriculum; teacher role; teaching profession
10/1418 curriculum development; teacher development
10/1779 teacher development; teacher education; teaching profession

SECONDARY SCHOOLS
10/0012 educational finance; fund raising; income; money management; school funds
10/0018 access to education; parent choice; selection
10/0088 comprehensive schools
10/0152 educational administration; educational change; management teams; school based management
10/0298 behaviour problems; comparative education; discipline; disruptive pupils; Kenya
10/0313 outcomes of education; performance indicators; school effectiveness; school leavers
10/0321 career counselling; guidance; vocational guidance
10/0322 attendance; discipline; discipline problems; pupil attitudes; teacher attitudes
10/0323 academic achievement; higher education; school effectiveness
10/0356 educational administration; teacher evaluation
10/0370 coordinators; information technology; staff role
10/0407 examination results; school effectiveness
10/0413 educational quality; quality assurance; school effectiveness
10/0421 English – second language; Malaysia
10/0422 English – second language; Malaysia
10/0481 Nigeria; parent-school relationship; parent-teacher associations

10/0512 computer uses in education; information technology; mathematics education; microcomputers
10/0513 computer uses in education; information technology; mathematics education
10/0585 educational change; educational policy; educationally disadvantaged; equal education; politics-education relationship
10/0669 educational administration; National Curriculum; preservice teacher education; school effectiveness
10/0671 administrator role; educational change; head teachers; management in education; role conflict; teacher role
10/0696 marketing
10/0731 departments; differential performance; examination results; outcomes of education; school effectiveness
10/0761 books
10/0824 health education; health promotion
10/0828 acquired immune deficiency syndrome; health education
10/0924 Education Reform Act 1988; educational administration; educational change; local management of schools; school based management
10/0932 placement; preservice teacher education; primary schools; student teachers; teaching practice
10/0973 ethnic groups; ethnic relations; intergroup relations; multiculturalism; racial relations; school policy
10/0985 Malaysians; teacher evaluation
10/1072 health education; sex education
10/1074 access to education; admission criteria; enrolment; open entry; parent choice
10/1094 educational change; inspection; teacher attitudes
10/1255 educational change; evaluation; local management of schools; school based management
10/1366 attendance; pupil behaviour; Scotland; truancy
10/1379 equal education; gender equality; school policy; whole school approach
10/1380 accountability; educational quality; measurement; performance indicators; school effectiveness
10/1454 academic achievement; educational practices; pupil improvement; support services; underachievement
10/1596 National Curriculum; pupil attitudes
10/1722 equal education; local management of schools; racial discrimination; racial integration; school based management

SECONDMENTS
10/1698 head teachers; industrial secondments; industry-education relationship; programme evaluation; teacher development
10/1699 cooperative programmes; industry-education relationship; programme evaluation
10/1701 industrial secondments; industry-education relationship; teacher development

SECRETARIES
10/0151 adult learning; human-computer interaction; learning strategies; word processing

SECULARISATION
10/0098 adult education; capitalism; Christianity; church and education; religious education

SELECTION
10/0018 access to education; parent choice; secondary schools
10/0366 institutional advancement; marketing; parent choice; parent-school relationship
10/0905 aptitude; assessment; critical thinking; higher education; mature students; prediction of success; student evaluation
10/0929 hotel and catering education; hotel management education

SELECTIVE ADMISSION
10/0719 admission criteria; medical schools; medical students

SELF CONCEPT
10/0141 Greece; self esteem
10/0202 body image; eating habits; food; health
10/0205 inservice teacher education; programme evaluation; pupil development
10/0676 attitude change; motivation techniques; pupil needs; self esteem
10/0759 perceptual motor coordination; special educational needs
10/1566 pupil attitudes; religion; religious attitudes; secondary school pupils

SELF ESTEEM
10/0141 Greece; self concept
10/0550 helplessness; motivation; special educational needs
10/0676 attitude change; motivation techniques; pupil needs; self concept
10/0968 locus of control; mainstreaming; primary schools; socialisation; special educational needs

SELF EVALUATION – GROUPS
10/0708 employer supported day care; evaluation methods; institutional evaluation

SELF EVALUATION – INDIVIDUALS
10/0036 assessment; primary schools; profiles; pupil responsibility; records of achievement; school reports
10/0043 access to education; adult education; adult learning; basic skills; mature students
10/0071 peer evaluation; pharmacists; pharmacy
10/0381 assessment; higher education; learner centred curriculum; teaching methods
10/0385 higher education; profiles; records of achievement; resumes – personal; skill development
10/0387 assessment; higher education; learner centred methods; open education; teaching methods
10/0758 longitudinal studies; pupil attitudes; school activities; sixteen to nineteen education
10/1297 achievement; assessment; early childhood education; records of achievement; young children
10/1298 assessment; mathematics achievement; mathematics education; primary school pupils
10/1487 personal construct theory; teacher evaluation
10/1670 achievement; assessment; primary school pupils; profiles; records of achievement

SEMANTICS
10/0725 grammar; morphology – languages; spelling; syntax
10/1811 Likert scales; linguistics; opinions; questionnaires; rating scales

SEMINARS
10/0437 leadership; performance indicators; small group teaching; teacher effectiveness; teaching methods; university teaching
10/0438 leadership; small group teaching; teaching methods; university teaching
10/0757 educational policy; special educational needs

SENEGAL
10/0456 curriculum development; educational materials; English – second language; second language teaching

SENSORY AIDS
10/0082 blindness; braille; learning disabilities; literacy education; raised line drawings; special educational needs
10/0103 blindness; braille; reading teaching; tactile adaptation; tactual perception
10/0886 blindness; low vision aids; microcomputers; tactile adaptation; visual impairments

SENSORY DEPRIVATION
10/0089 behaviour; deaf blind; disabilities; motor reactions; multiple disabilities

SERVICES
10/0066 adult day centres; caregivers; educational needs; special educational needs

SEVERE DISABILITIES
10/0494 communication skills; nonverbal communication; physical disabilities; special educational needs; speech handicaps

SEVERE LEARNING DIFFICULTIES
10/0094 behaviour modification; behaviour problems; special education teachers; special educational needs; special schools
10/0117 further education; mainstreaming; special educational needs; support services
10/0522 computer system design; computer uses in education; special educational needs
10/0524 moderate learning difficulties; problem solving; social skills; special educational needs
10/0966 curriculum development; National Curriculum; special educational needs
10/0986 access to education; adult basic education; adult learning; intelligence differences; multiple disabilities
10/1387 communication aids – for disabled; communication disorders; manual communication; sign language; special educational needs; symbolic language
10/1717 communication research; integration studies; special educational needs; verbal communication
10/1718 children; comprehension; integration studies; special educational needs
10/1756 cognitive development; social cognition; special educational needs

SEX DIFFERENCE
10/1216 individual development; mathematics achievement; mathematics education; pupil participation

SEX DIFFERENCES
10/0003 academic achievement; choice of subjects
10/0203 motor development; primary school pupils
10/0386 educational administration; head teachers; management in education; teaching profession; women's employment
10/0465 primary school teachers; primary schools; teacher role; teaching profession
10/0523 attitudes; computer literacy; computers
10/0532 music education; musical composition
10/0552 motivation; sexual identity; teacher-pupil relationship
10/0562 choice of subjects; course selection – students; science education; sixteen to nineteen education
10/0662 computer uses in education; gender equality; humanities; information technology
10/0854 design and technology; teaching profession
10/1196 intervention; science education
10/1203 primary-secondary education; pupil attitudes; science experiments
10/1210 'A' level examinations; learner characteristics; music activities; music education; pupil attitudes
10/1385 educational change; equal education; gender equality; school policy
10/1438 administration; emotions; employment practices; sexuality
10/1507 equal education; music; music education
10/1565 pupil attitudes; religion; religious attitudes; secondary school pupils; sex role
10/1587 higher education; mature students
10/1589 educational experience; higher education; mature students; men; student attitudes; women's education
10/1599 choice of subjects; pupil attitudes; pupil interests
10/1622 girls; sex stereotypes
10/1625 construction – process; construction materials; equal facilities; gender equality; primary education; science education; technology education
10/1791 early childhood education; men

SEX EDUCATION
10/0009 acquired immune deficiency syndrome; health education; parent participation; peer teaching
10/0798 acquired immune deficiency syndrome; health education; sexuality; sexually transmitted diseases

10/0799 acquired immune deficiency syndrome; health education; sexuality; sexually transmitted diseases
10/0800 acquired immune deficiency syndrome; health education; sexuality; sexually transmitted diseases
10/0801 family attitudes; family health; health education; sexuality
10/0818 acquired immune deficiency syndrome; health education; sexually transmitted diseases
10/0819 acquired immune deficiency syndrome; health education; sexually transmitted diseases; youth
10/0820 health education; youth
10/0831 acquired immune deficiency syndrome; health education; homosexuality; sexuality; sexually transmitted diseases
10/0879 acquired immune deficiency syndrome; health education
10/1032 health education; parent attitudes
10/1071 aspiration; attitudes; health; pupil attitudes; pupil behaviour; secondary school pupils; social attitudes
10/1072 health education; secondary schools
10/1347 alcohol education; drug education; health education; programme evaluation
10/1430 acquired immune deficiency syndrome; educational materials; educational technology; health education; interactive video; material development
10/1631 acquired immune deficiency syndrome; homosexuality; sexually transmitted diseases
10/1636 community education; contraception; early parenthood; family planning; mothers; parenthood education; peer teaching

SEX ROLE
10/0173 children's literature; comics – publications; educational history; girls; popular culture; textbooks; women's education
10/1565 pupil attitudes; religion; religious attitudes; secondary school pupils; sex differences

SEX STEREOTYPES
10/0002 gender equality; head teachers; teaching profession; women teachers; women's employment
10/1622 girls; sex differences

SEXUAL IDENTITY
10/0552 motivation; sex differences; teacher-pupil relationship

SEXUALITY
10/0197 acquired immune deficiency syndrome; health education; health promotion; sexually transmitted diseases; tourism; travel
10/0798 acquired immune deficiency syndrome; health education; sex education; sexually transmitted diseases
10/0799 acquired immune deficiency syndrome; health education; sex education; sexually transmitted diseases
10/0800 acquired immune deficiency syndrome; health education; sex education; sexually transmitted diseases
10/0801 family attitudes; family health; health education; sex education
10/0831 acquired immune deficiency syndrome; health education; homosexuality; sex education; sexually transmitted diseases
10/1438 administration; emotions; employment practices; sex differences
10/1635 adolescents; conversation; peer groups; peer teaching

SEXUALLY TRANSMITTED DISEASES
10/0197 acquired immune deficiency syndrome; health education; health promotion; sexuality; tourism; travel
10/0798 acquired immune deficiency syndrome; health education; sex education; sexuality
10/0799 acquired immune deficiency syndrome; health education; sex education; sexuality
10/0800 acquired immune deficiency syndrome; health education; sex education; sexuality
10/0818 acquired immune deficiency syndrome; health education; sex education

10/0819 acquired immune deficiency syndrome; health education; sex education; youth
10/0830 acquired immune deficiency syndrome; nurse education; nurses
10/0831 acquired immune deficiency syndrome; health education; homosexuality; sex education; sexuality
10/1056 acquired immune deficiency syndrome; educational materials; nurses
10/1134 acquired immune deficiency syndrome; adult education; ethics; voluntary agencies
10/1631 acquired immune deficiency syndrome; homosexuality; sex education

SEYCHELLES
10/1541 preservice teacher education

SHELTERED WORKSHOPS
10/1124 adult vocational education; adults; computer literacy; disabilities; information technology; special educational needs; training centres

SIERRA LEONE
10/1690 developing countries; educational improvement; secondary education

SIGHT METHOD
10/1808 beginning reading; dyslexia; word recognition

SIGN LANGUAGE
10/0140 deafness; language acquisition
10/0147 deafness; distance education; material development; special educational needs
10/0148 deafness
10/1387 communication aids – for disabled; communication disorders; manual communication; severe learning difficulties; special educational needs; symbolic language

SIMULATED ENVIRONMENT
10/0741 earth science; laboratories; laboratory experiments; physical environment; physical geography

SIMULATION
10/1178 computer assisted learning; earth science; educational equipment; microscopes; special educational needs
10/1321 imagination; mathematics education; pretend play

SINGAPORE
10/1776 gifted; programme evaluation

SINGING
10/1323 music activities; music education; young children

SINGLE EUROPEAN MARKET
10/0604 European Community; professional associations; professional continuing education; qualifications
10/1474 insurance occupations; training
10/1497 business administration education; management studies; professional training

SINGLE SEX SCHOOLS
10/1160 equal education; Islamic education; Muslims; religion and education; religious cultural groups; women's education

SIXTEEN TO NINETEEN EDUCATION
10/0011 further education; higher education; student health and welfare; student needs
10/0053 'A' level examinations; learning strategies; modern language studies
10/0181 developmental continuity; English literature; higher education; teaching methods
10/0310 access to education; educational change; further education; higher education
10/0315 school leavers; school to work transition; surveys; youth
10/0316 school leavers; school to work transition; surveys; youth
10/0320 cohort analysis; followup studies; longitudinal studies; school leavers; school to work transition; Scotland; youth
10/0341 higher education; learning motivation;

learning strategies; mathematics achievement; undergraduate study

10/0451 curriculum development; values education

10/0562 choice of subjects; course selection – students; science education; sex differences

10/0737 curriculum development; economics education

10/0738 business education; curriculum development; economics education

10/0758 longitudinal studies; pupil attitudes; school activities; self evaluation – individuals

10/0808 vocational education

10/0811 art education; dance; music; theatre arts

10/0812 curriculum development

10/1011 cohort analysis; programme evaluation; school leavers; school to work transition; TVEI

10/1024 curriculum research; National Vocational Qualifications; sixth form education; vocational education

10/1089 chemistry education; science education

10/1439 choice of subjects; demography; further education; pupil attitudes

10/1441 colleges of further education; management in education; quality control; staff development

10/1700 access to education; further education; programme evaluation

10/1720 access to education; further education; student participation; tertiary education; vocational education

SIXTH FORM EDUCATION

10/0472 argument; criticism; higher education; writing processes; writing skills

10/0617 electricity; learning processes; physics education; science education

10/1024 curriculum research; National Vocational Qualifications; sixteen to nineteen education; vocational education

SKILL DEVELOPMENT

10/0285 enterprise education; industry-education relationship; learning strategies; motivation; transfer of learning

10/0385 higher education; profiles; records of achievement; resumes – personal; self evaluation – individuals

10/1238 assessment; enterprise education; higher education; learning strategies; work-education relationship

10/1548 off the job training; on the job training; training; transfer of training; work experience programmes

SKILLED WORKERS

10/0595 Tanzania; training; vocational education

SKILLS

10/0101 aspiration; life style; special educational needs; visual impairments; vocational education

10/1351 industry-education relationship; programme evaluation; TVEI; vocational education

10/1512 competency based education; minimum competencies; National Vocational Qualifications

10/1616 biology education; science education; transfer of learning

10/1618 chemistry education; educational materials; learning strategies; multimedia approach; science education; teaching methods; transfer of learning

10/1619 business and technician education council; chemistry education; competency based education; science education; transfer of learning

10/1696 curriculum; employment; industry-education relationship; work-education relationship

10/1716 basic skills; critical thinking; educational philosophy; problem solving; transfer of learning

SMALL BUSINESSES

10/0339 vocational education

SMALL GROUP TEACHING

10/0334 individual teaching; teaching methods; tutorials; university teaching

10/0437 leadership; performance indicators; seminars; teacher effectiveness; teaching methods; university teaching

10/0438 leadership; seminars; teaching methods; university teaching

SMALL SCHOOLS

10/0080 Education Reform Act 1988; local management of schools; school size

10/0235 educational administration; local management of schools; school based management

10/0486 Education Reform Act 1988; educational change; educational legislation; educational planning; primary schools; school size

10/0488 history studies; National Curriculum; oral history

10/0668 cooperation; National Curriculum; rural schools

10/1574 Northern Ireland; rural schools; science curriculum; science education

SMOKING

10/0064 child development; cognitive ability; health education; intellectual development; intelligence quotient; pregnancy

10/0802 family health; family influence

10/0813 educational materials; guides; health education; nurse education; nurses

10/0852 adolescents; family influence; health

10/1562 drinking; drug abuse; pupil attitudes; religious attitudes; secondary school pupils; substance abuse

SOCIAL ATTITUDES

10/0637 climate; global approach; physical environment; scientific attitudes

10/0871 political attitudes; teacher attitudes; teacher education; teacher educators

10/1071 aspiration; attitudes; health; pupil attitudes; pupil behaviour; secondary school pupils; sex education

10/1800 citizenship education; human rights; literature studies; pupil attitudes; racial attitudes

SOCIAL BEHAVIOUR

10/0862 classroom environment; mainstreaming; moderate learning difficulties; pupil attitudes; pupil behaviour; special educational needs

10/1336 antisocial behaviour; behaviour problems; emotional problems; pupil problems; special educational needs

SOCIAL CHANGE

10/0399 Commonwealth of Independent States; Communist education; educational change; ideology; politics-education relationship; USSR

10/0703 economic change; educational needs; educational policy; Poland; youth

10/1121 attitudes; conservation – environment; environmental education

10/1132 adult education; community; individual development; voluntary agencies

10/1138 adult education; citizenship education; political influences; socialist countries; voluntary agencies

SOCIAL CLASS

10/0176 access to education; equal education; gender equality; higher education

SOCIAL COGNITION

10/0466 autism; cognitive ability; curriculum research

10/1651 employment; primary school pupils; work attitudes

10/1756 cognitive development; severe learning difficulties; special educational needs

SOCIAL DEVELOPMENT

10/0473 Education Reform Act 1988; individual development; moral education; National Curriculum; primary schools; religious education

10/0967 adolescent attitudes; adolescent development; adolescents; educational attitudes; interests; personality development; vocational interests

10/1193 communication skills; early childhood education; friendship; infant school pupils; reception classes; social isolation; young children

SOCIAL ENVIRONMENT

10/0867 academic achievement; performance factors; scaling; school effectiveness; socioeconomic influences

SOCIAL EXPERIENCE

10/1302 behaviour problems; emotional problems; family problems; learning disabilities; problem children

SOCIAL HISTORY

10/0602 adult education; educational history; working class

10/1569 cross cultural studies; electronic mail; European studies; international education; telecommunications

SOCIAL INFLUENCES

10/1665 home-school relationship; learning processes; primary school pupils; pupil-school relationship; sociology of education

SOCIAL INTEGRATION

10/1300 community centres; community education; community programmes; day care centres; English – second language; ethnic groups; racial integration

SOCIAL ISOLATION

10/1193 communication skills; early childhood education; friendship; infant school pupils; reception classes; social development; young children

10/1371 bullying; cooperation; ethnic relations; intergroup relations; intervention; middle school education; pupil behaviour

SOCIAL SCIENCE RESEARCH

10/1634 educational research; research

10/1639 educational research; information technology; policy; research; research opportunities

SOCIAL SCIENCES

10/1344 access programmes; access to education; adult students; higher education; mature students; programme evaluation; science education

SOCIAL SERVICES

10/0283 child welfare; community services; residential care; Scotland; social work

10/0851 Children Act 1989; day care; early childhood education; legislation; local government; preschool education

SOCIAL SKILLS

10/0524 moderate learning difficulties; problem solving; severe learning difficulties; special educational needs

10/1610 intergroup relations; pupil behaviour; sociometric techniques

SOCIAL STUDIES

10/0455 educational materials; environmental education; publications

SOCIAL WORK

10/0283 child welfare; community services; residential care; Scotland; social services

SOCIAL WORK STUDIES

10/0045 experiential learning; preservice teacher education; prior learning

10/1623 competency based education; inservice education; on the job training

SOCIAL WORK TEACHERS

10/0928 blacks; ethnic groups

SOCIALISATION

10/0131 physical education teachers; preservice teacher education; teacher educators

10/0968 locus of control; mainstreaming; primary schools; self esteem; special educational needs

SOCIALIST COUNTRIES
10/1138 adult education; citizenship education; political influences; social change; voluntary agencies

SOCIOECONOMIC BACKGROUND
10/1358 access to education; higher education; student recruitment

SOCIOECONOMIC INFLUENCES
10/0867 academic achievement; performance factors; scaling; school effectiveness; social environment

SOCIOLINGUISTICS
10/1242 dialect studies; language variation

SOCIOLOGY
10/0823 children
10/1400 biographies

SOCIOLOGY OF EDUCATION
10/0264 educational theories
10/0590 science education; scientific concepts; teaching methods
10/1389 educational policy
10/1665 home-school relationship; learning processes; primary school pupils; pupil-school relationship; social influences

SOCIOLOGY OF KNOWLEDGE
10/1308 educational theories

SOCIOMETRIC TECHNIQUES
10/1610 intergroup relations; pupil behaviour; social skills

SOUTH AFRICA
10/0414 educational history; educational policy; politics-education relationship
10/0630 curriculum development; geometry; mathematics education; secondary education

SPATIAL ABILITY
10/0102 blindness; maps; memory; raised line drawings; tactile adaptation; visual impairments
10/0259 design education; designers; visualisation
10/0572 art; art history; cognitive development; cross curricular approach; mathematics
10/0661 cognitive processes; mainstreaming; special educational needs
10/0990 memory; perceptual development
10/0992 assessment; memory
10/1188 cognitive ability; depth perception; drawing; problem solving; visual perception

SPECIAL EDUCATION TEACHERS
10/0083 cross curricular approach; special educational needs; support services; team teaching
10/0093 distance education; language handicaps; special educational needs; speech handicaps; teacher development
10/0094 behaviour modification; behaviour problems; severe learning difficulties; special educational needs; special schools

SPECIAL EDUCATIONAL NEEDS
10/0037 primary education; reading difficulties; reading teaching; remedial programmes; remedial reading
10/0041 differentiated curriculum; English studies curriculum; learning disabilities; low achievement; mainstreaming
10/0057 educational administration; educational change; educational policy; school based management; support services
10/0061 individual needs; pupils; surveys
10/0066 adult day centres; caregivers; educational needs; services
10/0082 blindness; braille; learning disabilities; literacy education; raised line drawings; sensory aids
10/0083 cross curricular approach; special education teachers; support services; team teaching
10/0090 access to education; disabilities; higher education; student needs; universities; university admission

10/0092 comparative education; disabilities; mainstreaming; pupil attitudes; special schools
10/0093 distance education; language handicaps; special education teachers; speech handicaps; teacher development
10/0094 behaviour modification; behaviour problems; severe learning difficulties; special education teachers; special schools
10/0097 architectural education; blindness; educational equipment; visual impairments
10/0101 aspiration; life style; skills; visual impairments; vocational education
10/0114 further education; support services
10/0117 further education; mainstreaming; severe learning difficulties; support services
10/0138 assessment; examinations; General Certificate of Secondary Education; low achievement
10/0147 deafness; distance education; material development; sign language
10/0159 behaviour disorders; classroom communication; conversation; learning activities; literacy education
10/0179 comparative education; educational materials; mainstreaming; teacher education
10/0184 local education authorities; mainstreaming; primary schools; teacher development
10/0186 institutional evaluation; mainstreaming; whole school approach
10/0189 India; mainstreaming; teacher education
10/0191 institutional evaluation; mainstreaming; United States of America; whole school approach
10/0206 language skills; literacy; oracy; reading skills; spelling; writing skills
10/0284 computer software; computer uses in education; learning disabilities; spelling; writing difficulties
10/0325 communication aids – for disabled; disabilities; educational materials
10/0359 mainstreaming; secondary education; support services
10/0433 educational quality; hearing impairments; mainstreaming; peripatetic teachers; support teachers; teacher effectiveness
10/0447 city technology colleges; dyslexia; educational materials; learning disabilities; teaching methods
10/0453 dyslexia; learning disabilities; reading difficulties; teacher education
10/0474 disabilities; mainstreaming; moderate learning difficulties; Nigeria; physical education
10/0477 beliefs; Christianity; mental retardation; religious education
10/0493 communication aids – for disabled; communication disorders; programme evaluation; workshops
10/0494 communication skills; nonverbal communication; physical disabilities; severe disabilities; speech handicaps
10/0522 computer system design; computer uses in education; severe learning difficulties
10/0524 moderate learning difficulties; problem solving; severe learning difficulties; social skills
10/0536 access to education; parent choice
10/0550 helplessness; motivation; self esteem
10/0553 behaviour disorders; emotional disturbances; statements – special educational needs
10/0645 cerebral palsy; mobility aids; neurological impairments; psychomotor skills
10/0646 mainstreaming; pupil needs; school effectiveness
10/0649 modern language studies
10/0661 cognitive processes; mainstreaming; spatial ability
10/0677 differentiated curriculum; individual needs; mainstreaming; National Curriculum
10/0733 support teachers; teachers
10/0745 child development; motor development; neurological impairments; perceptual handicaps; premature infants
10/0746 cluster grouping; educational cooperation; special schools
10/0747 cerebral palsy; disabilities; motor reactions; perceptual handicaps; perceptual motor coordination

10/0751 assessment; colleges of further education; diagnostic assessment; disabilities; further education; moderate learning difficulties
10/0752 cluster grouping; educational cooperation; special schools
10/0753 educational policy
10/0755 primary schools; support services
10/0756 educational administration; local management of schools; school based management
10/0757 educational policy; seminars
10/0759 perceptual motor coordination; self concept
10/0760 clumsy children; perceptual motor coordination; psychomotor skills
10/0860 computer assisted learning; computer uses in education; concept keyboards; human-computer interaction; learning disabilities; touch screens
10/0862 classroom environment; mainstreaming; moderate learning difficulties; pupil attitudes; pupil behaviour; social behaviour
10/0876 blindness; communication problems; higher education; nonverbal communication; visual impairments
10/0884 Down's Syndrome; mainstreaming
10/0893 mathematics education
10/0900 further education; mainstreaming; visual impairments
10/0917 bilingual pupils; cognitive ability; dyslexia; language acquisition; language handicaps; learning disabilities
10/0945 curriculum development; low achievement; moderate learning difficulties; underachievement
10/0954 epilepsy; special schools; statements – special educational needs
10/0960 deafness; hearing impairments
10/0966 curriculum development; National Curriculum; severe learning difficulties
10/0968 locus of control; mainstreaming; primary schools; self esteem; socialisation
10/0972 ability tests; language handicaps; learning disabilities; mathematical ability; mathematics education; numbers
10/0988 behaviour disorders; emotional disturbances; special schools
10/1013 assessment; learning disabilities; low achievement; moderate learning difficulties
10/1014 educational administration; educational finance; local management of schools; mainstreaming; resource allocation; school based management
10/1016 institutional cooperation; mainstreaming; special schools
10/1026 ability tests; diagnostic assessment; intelligence tests
10/1069 disabilities; further education; further education students; literature reviews; moderate learning difficulties
10/1103 learning disabilities; reading comprehension; reading difficulties
10/1124 adult vocational education; adults; computer literacy; disabilities; information technology; sheltered workshops; training centres
10/1125 behaviour disorders; computer uses in education; information technology; special schools
10/1126 adult basic education; adults; computer literacy; disabilities; information technology
10/1127 adults; computer literacy; disabilities; information technology; training centres
10/1142 adult vocational education; comparative education; disabilities; information technology; Portugal; training; United Kingdom
10/1145 assessment; blindness; mobility aids; partial vision; travel training; visual impairments; visually handicapped mobility
10/1176 blindness; computer uses in education; optical data discs; speech synthesisers; visual impairments
10/1178 computer assisted learning; earth science; educational equipment; microscopes; simulation
10/1206 comparative education; educational administration; educational policy; Italy; mainstreaming; Scandinavia; support services

10/1208 educational administration; educational change; educational policy; local education authorities
10/1240 discipline policy; disruptive pupils; educational change; expulsion; primary schools; problem children; suspension
10/1260 educational history; special schools
10/1265 deaf interpreting; deafness; graduate study; hearing impairments; higher education; interpreters
10/1266 early childhood education; early experience; hearing impairments; intervention; parent participation
10/1336 antisocial behaviour; behaviour problems; emotional problems; pupil problems; social behaviour
10/1387 communication aids – for disabled; communication disorders; manual communication; severe learning difficulties; sign language; symbolic language
10/1449 adult day centres; learning disabilities
10/1452 comparative education; Greece; learning disabilities; Scotland
10/1453 mainstreaming; pupil attitudes; pupil experience
10/1455 comparative analysis; educational policy; mainstreaming; special schools
10/1470 disadvantaged; moderate learning difficulties; support services
10/1471 motor development; special schools
10/1646 further education; mainstreaming; support services; support teachers
10/1675 adult basic education; learning disabilities; neurological impairments; speech handicaps
10/1714 disabilities; equal education
10/1717 communication research; integration studies; severe learning difficulties; verbal communication
10/1718 children; comprehension; integration studies; severe learning difficulties
10/1732 National Curriculum; special schools
10/1733 moderate learning difficulties; National Curriculum; special schools
10/1748 diagnostic assessment
10/1754 educational change; educational innovation; local education authorities
10/1756 cognitive development; severe learning difficulties; social cognition
10/1765 Down's Syndrome; expressive language; interaction; language acquisition; mainstreaming; special schools
10/1798 learning strategies
10/1806 autism; Down's Syndrome; drawing; gifted; visual arts

SPECIAL SCHOOLS
10/0092 comparative education; disabilities; mainstreaming; pupil attitudes; special educational needs
10/0094 behaviour modification; behaviour problems; severe learning difficulties; special education teachers; special educational needs
10/0105 academic achievement; blindness; cognitive development; longitudinal studies; outcomes of education; partial vision; visual impairments
10/0611 communication skills; deafness; hearing impairments; hearing therapy; total communication
10/0746 cluster grouping; educational cooperation; special educational needs
10/0752 cluster grouping; educational cooperation; special educational needs
10/0954 epilepsy; special educational needs; statements – special educational needs
10/0988 behaviour disorders; emotional disturbances; special educational needs
10/1015 caregivers; child caregivers; residential schools; training
10/1016 institutional cooperation; mainstreaming; special educational needs
10/1125 behaviour disorders; computer uses in education; information technology; special educational needs
10/1260 educational history; special educational needs
10/1455 comparative analysis; educational policy; mainstreaming; special educational needs
10/1471 motor development; special educational needs

10/1557 comparative education; gifted
10/1732 National Curriculum; special educational needs
10/1733 moderate learning difficulties; National Curriculum; special educational needs
10/1765 Down's Syndrome; expressive language; interaction; language acquisition; mainstreaming; special educational needs

SPEECH
10/0744 handwriting; motor development; perceptual motor coordination; reading
10/1314 visible speech

SPEECH COMMUNICATION
10/0193 conversation; language; verbal communication
10/0660 behaviour problems; elective mutism; inhibition; psychopathology
10/0843 communication skills; listening skills; National Curriculum
10/1257 oracy; oral language; programme evaluation
10/1434 assessment; English studies; oral English; school based assessment

SPEECH HANDICAPS
10/0078 nursery schools; phonology; preschool children; preschool education
10/0093 distance education; language handicaps; special education teachers; special educational needs; teacher development
10/0494 communication skills; nonverbal communication; physical disabilities; severe disabilities; special educational needs
10/1073 language handicaps; speech therapy
10/1373 antisocial behaviour; behaviour modification; behaviour problems; bullying; classroom environment; intervention; stuttering
10/1675 adult basic education; learning disabilities; neurological impairments; special educational needs

SPEECH SKILLS
10/1759 English studies curriculum; language skills; listening skills; National Curriculum; oracy

SPEECH SYNTHESISERS
10/1176 blindness; computer uses in education; optical data discs; special educational needs; visual impairments

SPEECH THERAPY
10/0261 speech training; therapists; training methods
10/1073 language handicaps; speech handicaps

SPEECH TRAINING
10/0261 speech therapy; therapists; training methods

SPELLING
10/0206 language skills; literacy; oracy; reading skills; special educational needs; writing skills
10/0284 computer software; computer uses in education; learning disabilities; special educational needs; writing difficulties
10/0725 grammar; morphology – languages; semantics; syntax
10/0921 writing skills; writing teaching
10/1144 cognitive processes; computer assisted reading; reading comprehension; reading skills; word recognition
10/1199 handwriting; infant school pupils; reading; writing skills

SPONSORSHIP
10/0231 employers; financial support; professional continuing education; staff development

SPORTS
10/0128 ethics; sportsmanship; values
10/0129 achievement; failure; motivation
10/0130 achievement
10/0331 educational policy; educational practices; physical education
10/0441 judo; physical activities
10/0496 Kenya

10/0902 educational change; local management of schools; National Curriculum; physical education
10/1060 arts; attitudes; culture; mass media; music; participation; theatre arts

SPORTSMANSHIP
10/0128 ethics; sports; values

SPREADSHEETS
10/0774 mathematics education; science education
10/0783 engineering education; mathematical models; mathematics education
10/1184 computer uses in education; educational software; mathematics education
10/1477 computer uses in education; mathematics education; statistics education

STAFF DEVELOPMENT
10/0033 support staff
10/0180 cooperative learning; teacher development
10/0231 employers; financial support; professional continuing education; sponsorship
10/0740 colleges of further education; industry-further education relationship; work experience programmes
10/1143 learner centred methods; teaching process; universities; university teaching
10/1241 agricultural colleges; agricultural education; economic change; educational change; further education
10/1413 flexible learning
10/1425 educational technology; independent study
10/1431 information technology; teacher education
10/1441 colleges of further education; management in education; quality control; sixteen to nineteen education
10/1495 educational change; further education; further education teachers
10/1506 community education; continuing education; training; voluntary service; volunteers
10/1612 city technology colleges; grant maintained schools; inservice teacher education; management development; school based management

STAFF ORIENTATION
10/1278 competency based teacher education; inservice teacher education; local education authorities; school based teacher education; teacher development

STAFF ROLE
10/0370 coordinators; information technology; secondary schools

STAFF-SCHOOL RELATIONSHIP
10/1224 change strategies; educational change; primary schools; school based management; school organisation

STANDARD ASSESSMENT TASKS
10/0588 assessment; first schools; infant schools; mathematics curriculum; mathematics teachers
10/0735 assessment; National Curriculum; primary schools
10/0977 assessment; assessment by teachers; attainment tests; geography education; National Curriculum
10/0997 assessment; English studies; National Curriculum; reading achievement; writing skills
10/0998 assessment; mathematics achievement; National Curriculum; primary education; science education
10/1008 assessment; attainment tests; National Curriculum; Welsh studies
10/1082 assessment; attainment tests; National Curriculum; Welsh studies
10/1083 assertiveness; attainment tests; National Curriculum; Welsh studies
10/1584 assessment; mother tongue; National Curriculum; school based assessment; second language learning; Welsh
10/1663 assessment; longitudinal studies;

primary education; primary school pupils; pupil-school relationship; school based assessment

STANDARDS
10/0394 competency based education; education courses; higher education; masters' courses; qualifications
10/0789 competency based education; higher education; masters' courses; National Vocational Qualifications; qualifications
10/1632 competency based education; higher education; National Vocational Qualifications; preservice teacher education; professional education

STATE SCHOOLS
10/0175 family life; nationalism; religion

STATEMENTS – SPECIAL EDUCATIONAL NEEDS
10/0553 behaviour disorders; emotional disturbances; special educational needs
10/0954 epilepsy; special educational needs; special schools

STATISTICAL ANALYSIS
10/0775 models; research tools
10/1076 achievement; classroom environment; performance factors

STATISTICAL DATA
10/1086 educational research; performance

STATISTICAL INFERENCE
10/0658 models; predictive validity; probability

STATISTICAL SURVEYS
10/1362 educational research

STATISTICS EDUCATION
10/1477 computer uses in education; mathematics education; spreadsheets
10/1581 computer assisted learning; educational software; multimedia approach

STATUS NEED
10/0556 Nigeria; professional recognition; teacher attitudes; teachers; teaching profession

STEINER WALDORF SCHOOLS
10/1316 10/1324 early childhood education; Montessori method; teaching methods

STORY READING
10/0146 children's literature; early childhood education; reading aloud to others; teacher-pupil relationship

STORY TELLING
10/0134 children as writers; group work; narration; primary school pupils; writing – composition
10/1226 environmental education; field studies; geographic location; local studies

STREAMING
10/1067 ability; class organisation; grouping – teaching purposes; mixed ability; pupil placement; teaching methods

STRESS – PSYCHOLOGICAL
10/0289 secondary school pupils; stress management
10/0393 higher education; stress management; stress variables; student health and welfare
10/0459 preservice teacher education; stress variables; student teachers; teaching experience; teaching practice
10/0460 educational environment; institutional environment; stress management; stress variables; teacher morale
10/0636 higher education; mature students; stress variables
10/1068 academic staff; further education teachers; higher education; teacher workload
10/1100 nurse education; nurses
10/1163 experiential learning; interpersonal competence; locus of control; outcomes of education; student experience; teacher education

10/1262 teacher morale; teaching profession
10/1364 teacher role; teacher workload; time management
10/1480 job satisfaction; teacher attitudes; teaching profession
10/1628 stress management; student teachers; teachers; teaching profession

STRESS MANAGEMENT
10/0289 secondary school pupils; stress – psychological
10/0393 higher education; stress – psychological; stress variables; student health and welfare
10/0460 educational environment; institutional environment; stress – psychological; stress variables; teacher morale
10/1628 stress – psychological; student teachers; teachers; teaching profession

STRESS VARIABLES
10/0393 higher education; stress – psychological; stress management; student health and welfare
10/0459 preservice teacher education; stress – psychological; student teachers; teaching experience; teaching practice
10/0460 educational environment; institutional environment; stress – psychological; stress management; teacher morale
10/0636 higher education; mature students; stress – psychological
10/1256 change; head teachers; local management of schools; primary schools; role conflict; time management

STRUCTURAL UNEMPLOYMENT
10/0124 comparative education; economic change; economics-education relationship; Germany; industry-education relationship; training; work-education relationship

STUDENT ATTITUDES
10/0115 further education; higher education; information retrieval; information systems; optical data discs; search strategies
10/0200 higher education; mature students; student needs
10/0250 course evaluation; degrees – academic; mathematics education
10/0255 'A' level examinations; design education; learner characteristics
10/0337 higher education; learning strategies; learning theories; teaching methods
10/0350 Postgraduate Certificate in Education; preservice teacher education; student teacher evaluation; teacher behaviour; teaching practice
10/0452 attitude measures; institutes of higher education; institutional environment; organisational climate; teacher attitudes
10/0509 comprehension; philosophy of science; science education; scientific concepts
10/0528 academic staff; ethnic groups; higher education; mature students; middle class students; student experience; working class
10/0559 academic achievement; educational experience; higher education; mature students
10/0939 epilepsy; higher education; student health and welfare
10/1023 course evaluation; educational quality; higher education; performance indicators; quality control; teacher effectiveness; universities
10/1164 course evaluation; nurse education; teaching methods
10/1167 adult students; distance education; humanities; mature students; open universities
10/1332 access to education; adult education; adult students; community education; educational guidance; mature students
10/1412 religious education
10/1493 decision making; problem solving
10/1589 educational experience; higher education; mature students; men; sex differences; women's education
10/1726 access to education; higher education; mature students; student housing; student recruitment

STUDENT BEHAVIOUR
10/0122 dropout research; dropouts; enrolment; higher education

10/1099 mature students; preservice teacher education; student teacher attitudes; student teachers; women's education
10/1172 affective behaviour; emotional response; mathematics
10/1217 cheating; discipline problems; higher education; plagiarism

STUDENT COSTS
10/1329 adult students; financial problems; mature students; student financial aid; student loans; student recruitment

STUDENT COUNSELLING
10/0123 access to education; higher education; nontraditional education; student health and welfare
10/0132 educational guidance; higher education
10/0712 counselling services; higher education; pastoral care – education; student needs
10/1110 counselling services; higher education; mature students

STUDENT DEVELOPMENT
10/0226 access programmes; adult education; mature students
10/0542 critical reading; reading; study skills; writing – composition; writing skills
10/1773 emotional development; nurse education; nurses; professional development

STUDENT EVALUATION
10/0905 aptitude; assessment; critical thinking; higher education; mature students; prediction of success; selection

STUDENT EVALUATION OF TEACHER PERFORMANCE
10/0869 higher education; teacher effectiveness
10/1743 course evaluation; educational quality; teacher effectiveness; teaching methods; universities

STUDENT EXCHANGE PROGRAMMES
10/1078 international programmes; modern language studies; programme evaluation; second language learning

STUDENT EXPERIENCE
10/0118 access programmes; higher education; mature students; men
10/0388 higher education; learner characteristics; learning experience; learning strategies
10/0528 academic staff; ethnic groups; higher education; mature students; middle class students; student attitudes; working class
10/0580 access to education; equal education; ethnic groups; higher education; student recruitment
10/1163 experiential learning; interpersonal competence; locus of control; outcomes of education; stress – psychological; teacher education
10/1671 higher education; learning experience; mature students

STUDENT FINANCIAL AID
10/1018 local education authorities; maintenance grants; tuition grants
10/1329 adult students; financial problems; mature students; student costs; student loans; student recruitment

STUDENT HEALTH AND WELFARE
10/0011 further education; higher education; sixteen to nineteen education; student needs
10/0123 access to education; higher education; nontraditional education; student counselling
10/0393 higher education; stress – psychological; stress management; stress variables
10/0939 epilepsy; higher education; student attitudes

STUDENT HOUSING
10/1726 access to education; higher education; mature students; student attitudes; student recruitment

STUDENT LOANS
10/1329 adult students; financial problems;

mature students; student costs; student financial aid; student recruitment

STUDENT MOTIVATION
10/0526 academic aspiration; locus of control; Malaysia; motivation tests
10/0530 access programmes; access to education; higher education; mature students; nontraditional education

STUDENT NEEDS
10/0011 further education; higher education; sixteen to nineteen education; student health and welfare
10/0090 access to education; disabilities; higher education; special educational needs; universities; university admission
10/0200 higher education; mature students; student attitudes
10/0712 counselling services; higher education; pastoral care – education; student counselling

STUDENT PARTICIPATION
10/0229 access to education; adult education; Germany; higher education; mature students
10/0230 access to education; adult education; France; higher education; mature students
10/1720 access to education; further education; sixteen to nineteen education; tertiary education; vocational education

STUDENT PROBLEMS
10/0336 academic failure; higher education; intervention; underachievement

STUDENT PROJECTS
10/0380 community organisations; databases

STUDENT RECORDS
10/0934 access to education; higher education; programme evaluation; records of achievement

STUDENT RECRUITMENT
10/0166 graduate study; higher education
10/0442 access to education; accessibility – for disabled; disabilities; equal education; higher education
10/0580 access to education; equal education; ethnic groups; higher education; student experience
10/0605 equal education; ethnic groups; university admission
10/1114 ethnic groups; preservice teacher education; teacher recruitment; teaching profession
10/1329 adult students; financial problems; mature students; student costs; student financial aid; student loans
10/1358 access to education; higher education; socioeconomic background
10/1359 access to education; admission criteria; higher education
10/1504 access to education; admission criteria; admissions tutors; higher education
10/1709 educational discrimination; ethnic groups; higher education
10/1726 access to education; higher education; mature students; student attitudes; student housing

STUDENT RESEARCH
10/1123 supervision; teacher-student relationship; tutorials
10/1509 graduate study; mature students; part time students

STUDENT-SCHOOL RELATIONSHIP
10/0384 peer teaching; role models; wales

STUDENT TEACHER ATTITUDES
10/0214 mentors; Postgraduate Certificate in Education; preservice teacher education; school based teacher education; teacher attitudes
10/0220 antiracism education; probationary teachers; racial attitudes; student teachers; teacher education
10/1099 mature students; preservice teacher education; student behaviour; student teachers; women's education

10/1234 educational change; parent attitudes; preservice teacher education; primary school teachers; teacher attitudes; teaching profession
10/1653 background; economics education; experience; industry-education relationship; preservice teacher education; student teachers
10/1731 equal education; Postgraduate Certificate in Education; preservice teacher education; school based teacher education

STUDENT TEACHER EVALUATION
10/0350 Postgraduate Certificate in Education; preservice teacher education; student attitudes; teacher behaviour; teaching practice
10/1407 preservice teacher education; student teacher supervisors; student teachers; teaching practice
10/1435 assessment; competency based teacher education; preservice teacher education; teaching practice

STUDENT TEACHER SUPERVISORS
10/0439 mentors; preservice teacher education; teaching practice
10/0469 mathematics education; mentors; National Curriculum; preservice teacher education; teaching practice
10/0514 institutes of higher education; mentors; preservice teacher education; school based teacher education
10/0938 mentors; preservice teacher education; supervision; supervisory methods; teaching practice
10/1275 mentors; preservice teacher education; school based teacher education
10/1295 preservice teacher education; school based teacher education; supervisors; teaching practice
10/1407 preservice teacher education; student teacher evaluation; student teachers; teaching practice
10/1735 mentors; preservice teacher education; school based teacher education

STUDENT TEACHERS
10/0040 inservice teacher education; preservice teacher education; primary education; science education
10/0209 information technology; preservice teacher education; teaching practice
10/0210 preservice teacher education; primary school teachers; probationary teachers; professional development; teaching profession
10/0220 antiracism education; probationary teachers; racial attitudes; student teacher attitudes; teacher education
10/0368 modern language studies; preservice teacher education
10/0459 preservice teacher education; stress – psychological; stress variables; teaching experience; teaching practice
10/0537 ambiguity; class activities; preservice teacher education; teaching practice; teaching styles
10/0573 B Ed degrees; participant satisfaction; preservice teacher education; probationary teachers; teaching experience
10/0581 learning strategies; learning theories; preservice teacher education
10/0648 enterprise education; industrial secondments; industry-education relationship; placement; preservice teacher education
10/0650 classroom management; preservice teacher education
10/0866 experiential learning; interpersonal competence; learning experience; preservice teacher education; workshops
10/0892 information technology; preservice teacher education; teaching practice
10/0932 placement; preservice teacher education; primary schools; secondary schools; teaching practice
10/0937 enterprise education; industrial secondments; industry-education relationship; preservice teacher education; science teachers
10/0943 preservice teacher education; school based teacher education; science education; science teachers
10/0946 performance contracts; preservice teacher education; records of achievement;

school based teacher education; teacher development; teaching profession
10/0950 computer uses in education; information technology; mathematics education; preservice teacher education; teacher attitudes
10/1099 mature students; preservice teacher education; student behaviour; student teacher attitudes; women's education
10/1104 preservice teacher education; probationary teachers; teaching profession
10/1105 English studies; grammar
10/1236 articled teachers; Postgraduate Certificate in Education; preservice teacher education; teacher education
10/1248 art; design; Postgraduate Certificate in Education; preservice teacher education; probationary teachers; programme effectiveness
10/1276 learning strategies; mathematics teachers; preservice teacher education; school based teacher education
10/1296 followup studies; Postgraduate Certificate in Education; teacher development
10/1407 preservice teacher education; student teacher evaluation; student teacher supervisors; teaching practice
10/1426 educational quality; preservice teacher education; quality control; teaching practice
10/1456 preservice teacher education; teaching experience; teaching practice
10/1593 competence; competency based teacher education; preservice teacher education; records of achievement
10/1628 stress – psychological; stress management; teachers; teaching profession
10/1637 mentors; preservice teacher education; teacher development; teaching practice
10/1653 background; economics education; experience; industry-education relationship; preservice teacher education; student teacher attitudes
10/1677 B Ed degrees; graduates; teacher certification; teacher education
10/1691 philosophy of science; preservice teacher education; science education; scientific literacy
10/1744 Postgraduate Certificate in Education; preservice teacher education; school based teacher education

STUDENT VOLUNTEERS
10/0717 mathematics education; peer influence; peer teaching; science education; technology education

STUDENT WASTAGE
10/1673 Arab states; dropout research; technical education; vocational education

STUDY ABROAD
10/1141 adult education; adult learning; earth science; field studies; field studies centres
10/1554 cultural education; degree requirements; ethnography; higher education; second language learning

STUDY SKILLS
10/0338 comprehension; essays; examination techniques; higher education; learning strategies; review – reexamination; writing – composition
10/0389 higher education; learning strategies; undergraduate students
10/0542 critical reading; reading; student development; writing – composition; writing skills
10/0857 learning strategies
10/1116 learning activities; learning strategies; nurse education

STUTTERING
10/1373 antisocial behaviour; behaviour modification; behaviour problems; bullying; classroom environment; intervention; speech handicaps

SUBSTANCE ABUSE
10/1562 drinking; drug abuse; pupil attitudes; religious attitudes; secondary school pupils; smoking

SUBSTITUTE TEACHERS
10/1704 teacher employment; teaching profession

SUCCESS
10/0504 educational quality; outcomes of education; parent-school relationship; school effectiveness
10/1789 educational quality; school effectiveness

SUDAN
10/0055 technical education; vocational education
10/0890 educational economics; educational finance

SUMMER SCHOOLS
10/0408 access to education; dropout research; higher education; nontraditional education; university admission; university preparation
10/0425 access to education; higher education; transition education; university admission; university preparation

SUPERVISION
10/0938 mentors; preservice teacher education; student teacher supervisors; supervisory methods; teaching practice
10/1123 student research; teacher student relationship; tutorials

SUPERVISORS
10/1295 preservice teacher education; school based teacher education; student teacher supervisors; teaching practice

SUPERVISORY METHODS
10/0938 mentors; preservice teacher education; student teacher supervisors; supervision; teaching practice

SUPERVISORY TRAINING
10/1533 mentors; preservice teacher education; teaching practice

SUPPORT SERVICES
10/0057 educational administration; educational change; educational policy; school based management; special educational needs
10/0083 cross curricular approach; special education teachers; special educational needs; team teaching
10/0114 further education; special educational needs
10/0117 further education; mainstreaming; severe learning difficulties; special educational needs
10/0359 mainstreaming; secondary education; special educational needs
10/0755 primary schools; special educational needs
10/1206 comparative education; educational administration; educational policy; Italy; mainstreaming; Scandinavia; special educational needs
10/1454 academic achievement; educational practices; pupil improvement; secondary schools; underachievement
10/1470 disadvantaged; moderate learning difficulties; special educational needs
10/1646 further education; mainstreaming; special educational needs; support teachers
10/1747 behaviour problems; disruptive pupils; problem children

SUPPORT STAFF
10/0033 staff development
10/0841 city technology colleges; school personnel; teacher aides

SUPPORT TEACHERS
10/0433 educational quality; hearing impairments; mainstreaming; peripatetic teachers; special educational needs; teacher effectiveness
10/0733 special educational needs; teachers
10/1646 further education; mainstreaming; special educational needs; support services

SUPPORTED SELF STUDY
10/1652 educational material evaluation; educational materials; material development;

science education; scientific attitudes; scientific literacy; teacher education

SURGERY
10/0169 medical education

SURVEYING EDUCATION
10/1617 construction industry; experiential learning; learning activities

SURVEYS
10/0060 ethnic origins; mother tongue; pupils; religion
10/0061 individual needs; pupils; special educational needs
10/0062 individual needs; language proficiency; pupils
10/0063 behaviour problems; discipline problems; disruptive pupils; infant school pupils; primary school pupils; problem children
10/0312 school leavers; school to work transition; Scotland; secondary education
10/0315 school leavers; school to work transition; sixteen to nineteen education; youth
10/0316 school leavers; school to work transition; sixteen to nineteen education; youth

SUSPENSION
10/0194 expulsion; primary school pupils; pupil experience
10/1240 discipline policy; disruptive pupils; educational change; expulsion; primary schools; problem children; special educational needs

SWAZILAND
10/1802 educational materials; inservice teacher education; science education

SWEDEN
10/0436 distance education; educational media; infant school teachers; inservice education; international educational exchange; telecommunications

SWITZERLAND
10/0417 further education

SYMBOLIC LANGUAGE
10/1387 communication aids – for disabled; communication disorders; manual communication; severe learning difficulties; sign language; special educational needs

SYMBOLISM
10/0357 Education Reform Act 1988; religion and education; school worship

SYMBOLS – MATHEMATICS
10/0777 algebra; computer uses in education; mathematics education
10/0782 computer uses in education; mathematics education; trigonometry; visualisation
10/0788 computer uses in education; educational software; mathematics education; visual learning

SYNTAX
10/0725 grammar; morphology – languages; semantics; spelling

TACTILE ADAPTATION
10/0102 blindness; maps; memory; raised line drawings; spatial ability; visual impairments
10/0103 blindness; braille; reading teaching; sensory aids; tactual perception
10/0886 blindness; low vision aids; microcomputers; sensory aids; visual impairments

TACTUAL PERCEPTION
10/0100 blindness; tactual visual tests; tests; visual impairments
10/0103 blindness; braille; reading teaching; sensory aids; tactile adaptation

TACTUAL VISUAL TESTS
10/0100 blindness; tactual perception; tests; visual impairments

TAIWAN
10/1129 adult education; comparative education; United Kingdom; universities
10/1249 educational philosophy; moral education

TANZANIA
10/0595 skilled workers; training; vocational education

TEACHER-ADMINISTRATOR RELATIONSHIP
10/0049 administrators; educational administration; management in education
10/1232 head teachers; primary schools; teacher role; teacher workload; teaching profession

TEACHER AIDES
10/0841 city technology colleges; school personnel; support staff

TEACHER ATTITUDES
10/0154 comparative education; educational change; France; primary school teachers; teaching profession
10/0211 preservice teacher education; professional development; teacher development; teaching profession
10/0214 mentors; Postgraduate Certificate in Education; preservice teacher education; school based teacher education; student teacher attitudes
10/0221 preservice teacher education; school based teacher education
10/0294 primary school teachers; professional development
10/0322 attendance; discipline; discipline problems; pupil attitudes; secondary schools
10/0364 change; child language; classroom management
10/0452 attitude measures; institutes of higher education; institutional environment; organisational climate; student attitudes
10/0556 Nigeria; professional recognition; status need; teachers; teaching profession
10/0871 political attitudes; social attitudes; teacher education; teacher educators
10/0950 computer uses in education; information technology; mathematics education; preservice teacher education; student teachers
10/0963 business education; curriculum development; economics education; teacher development
10/1045 school effectiveness; teacher effectiveness; teacher workload; time management
10/1094 educational change; inspection; secondary schools
10/1101 information technology; National Curriculum; oracy
10/1198 inservice teacher education; primary school teachers; science education
10/1207 educational change; inspection
10/1228 antisocial behaviour; behaviour problems; bullying; discipline policy; discipline problems
10/1234 educational change; parent attitudes; preservice teacher education; primary school teachers; student teacher attitudes; teaching profession
10/1271 inservice teacher education; mathematics; primary school teachers
10/1339 primary education; pupil attitudes; values education
10/1355 course evaluation; further education teachers; teacher education
10/1374 antisocial behaviour; attitudes; behaviour problems; bullying; parent attitudes; pupil attitudes
10/1375 antisocial behaviour; attitudes; bullying; discipline policy; parent attitudes; school policy
10/1480 job satisfaction; stress – psychological; teaching profession
10/1592 distance education; inservice teacher education; programme effectiveness; teacher development
10/1674 behaviour problems; classroom discipline; discipline; disruptive pupils; greece; nursery school education
10/1727 mothers; teacher background; teacher role; teaching profession; women teachers

TEACHER BACKGROUND
10/0019 Canada natives; ethnic groups; indigenous populations; newly qualified teachers; teacher induction; teaching profession
10/1727 mothers; teacher attitudes; teacher role; teaching profession; women teachers

TEACHER BEHAVIOUR
10/0085 behaviour problems; classroom discipline; classroom management; pupil behaviour; teacher-pupil relationship
10/0223 primary school teachers; teacher development; teacher role; teaching methods
10/0350 Postgraduate Certificate in Education; preservice teacher education; student attitudes; student teacher evaluation; teaching practice
10/0557 Malaysia; secondary school teachers; teacher effectiveness; teaching styles
10/0643 classroom communication; primary school teachers; teacher-pupil relationship; verbal communication
10/1283 achievement; black pupils; black teachers; teacher-pupil relationship; teaching methods; teaching styles

TEACHER CERTIFICATION
10/1677 B Ed degrees; graduates; student teachers; teacher education

TEACHER DEVELOPMENT
10/0042 industrial secondments; industry-education relationship; preservice teacher education
10/0093 distance education; language handicaps; special education teachers; special educational needs; speech handicaps
10/0133 mentors; teacher education; teacher induction
10/0180 cooperative learning; staff development
10/0182 inservice teacher education; primary school teachers
10/0184 local education authorities; mainstreaming; primary schools; special educational needs
10/0211 preservice teacher education; professional development; teacher attitudes; teaching profession
10/0223 primary school teachers; teacher behaviour; teacher role; teaching methods
10/0584 teacher effectiveness; teacher evaluation; teaching profession
10/0593 industrial secondments; industry-education relationship
10/0673 head teachers; mentors; middle management; professional continuing education; teaching profession
10/0743 industry-education relationship; work experience programmes
10/0814 on the job training
10/0919 competency based teacher education; mentors; profiles
10/0944 inservice teacher education; professional development; teaching profession
10/0946 performance contracts; preservice teacher education; records of achievement; school based teacher education; student teachers; teaching profession
10/0963 business education; curriculum development; economics education; teacher attitudes
10/0996 local education authorities; preservice teacher education; probationary teachers; teacher education; teacher induction
10/1186 mathematics teachers; teaching methods
10/1278 competency based teacher education; inservice teacher education; local education authorities; school based teacher education; staff orientation
10/1296 followup studies; Postgraduate Certificate in Education; student teachers
10/1307 competency based teacher education; mentors; profiles; teaching profession
10/1337 equal opportunities – jobs; teacher evaluation; teaching profession
10/1343 head teachers; teaching profession
10/1409 industrial secondments; industry-education relationship
10/1418 curriculum development; secondary school teachers

10/1450 programme evaluation; teacher evaluation; teaching profession
10/1534 graduate employment; graduate surveys; probationary teachers
10/1592 distance education; inservice teacher education; programme effectiveness; teacher attitudes
10/1600 mentors; preservice teacher education; primary schools; professional continuing education
10/1637 mentors; preservice teacher education; student teachers; teaching practice
10/1694 industrial secondments; industry-education relationship
10/1698 head teachers; industrial secondments; industry-education relationship; programme evaluation; secondments
10/1701 industrial secondments; industry-education relationship; secondments
10/1706 primary school teachers; teacher evaluation; teaching profession
10/1770 inservice teacher education; primary school teachers; science education
10/1779 secondary school teachers; teacher education; teaching profession
10/1790 educational administration; local management of schools; management in education; programme evaluation; school based management

TEACHER EDUCATION
10/0108 educational theories; learning theories; psychology; teaching experience; teaching practice; teaching process
10/0133 mentors; teacher development; teacher induction
10/0179 comparative education; educational materials; mainstreaming; special educational needs
10/0189 India; mainstreaming; special educational needs
10/0219 political influences; politics-education relationship
10/0220 antiracism education; probationary teachers; racial attitudes; student teacher attitudes; student teachers
10/0373 inservice teacher education; international educational exchange; international programmes; Poland; preservice teacher education
10/0411 comparative education; educational history; educational policy; Scotland
10/0453 dyslexia; learning disabilities; reading difficulties; special educational needs
10/0543 Greece; mathematics education; mathematics teachers
10/0609 arithmetic; mathematical ability; mathematics education; problem solving; teaching methods
10/0665 planning; Postgraduate Certificate in Education
10/0711 music teachers; professional development; professional training
10/0736 cross curricular approach; curriculum development; economics education; enterprise education
10/0871 political attitudes; social attitudes; teacher attitudes; teacher educators
10/0874 educational history; educational psychology
10/0885 universities
10/0930 citizenship education; global approach
10/0933 competency based teacher education; educational research
10/0996 local education authorities; preservice teacher education; probationary teachers; teacher development; teacher induction
10/1163 experiential learning; interpersonal competence; locus of control; outcomes of education; stress – psychological; student experience
10/1213 comparative education; France; higher education; United States of America
10/1236 articled teachers; Postgraduate Certificate in Education; preservice teacher education; student teachers
10/1355 course evaluation; further education teachers; teacher attitudes
10/1431 information technology; staff development

10/1633 educational research; educational researchers; research
10/1652 educational material evaluation; educational materials; material development; science education; scientific attitudes; scientific literacy; supported self study
10/1677 B Ed degrees; graduates; student teachers; teacher certification
10/1721 classroom communication; discourse analysis; metaphors
10/1779 secondary school teachers; teacher development; teaching profession

TEACHER EDUCATION CURRICULUM
10/1615 European Community; preservice teacher education

TEACHER EDUCATORS
10/0131 physical education teachers; preservice teacher education; socialisation
10/0515 preservice teacher education
10/0871 political attitudes; social attitudes; teacher attitudes; teacher education
10/1106 academic staff; higher education; inservice teacher education; preservice teacher education

TEACHER EFFECTIVENESS
10/0160 competence; competency based teacher education; discussion – teaching technique; personal construct theory; repertory grid test
10/0185 teacher evaluation
10/0433 educational quality; hearing impairments; mainstreaming; peripatetic teachers; special educational needs; support teachers
10/0437 leadership; performance indicators; seminars; small group teaching; teaching methods; university teaching
10/0557 Malaysia; secondary school teachers; teacher behaviour; teaching styles
10/0584 teacher development; teacher evaluation; teaching profession
10/0795 educational quality; higher education
10/0869 higher education; student evaluation of teacher performance
10/1023 course evaluation; educational quality; higher education; performance indicators; quality control; student attitudes; universities
10/1045 school effectiveness; teacher attitudes; teacher workload; time management
10/1212 learning strategies; National Curriculum; teaching methods
10/1743 course evaluation; educational quality; student evaluation of teacher performance; teaching methods; universities

TEACHER EMPLOYMENT
10/1108 labour market; Northern Ireland; probationary teachers; teacher recruitment; teaching profession
10/1200 deputy head teachers; employment patterns; head teachers; teacher mobility; teacher recruitment; teacher supply and demand; teaching profession
10/1209 educational administration; Europe; management in education; teaching profession; women; women's employment
10/1704 substitute teachers; teaching profession

TEACHER EVALUATION
10/0185 teacher effectiveness
10/0356 educational administration; secondary schools
10/0372 classroom management; classroom observation techniques; teaching profession
10/0376 career development; institutes of higher education; teaching profession; women teachers; women's employment
10/0507 management in education; teacher role
10/0584 teacher development; teacher effectiveness; teaching profession
10/0633 head teachers
10/0985 Malaysians; secondary schools
10/1337 equal opportunities – jobs; teacher development; teaching profession
10/1450 programme evaluation; teacher development; teaching profession
10/1483 academic staff development; head teachers; teaching profession

10/1487 personal construct theory; self evaluation – individuals
10/1578 academic staff evaluation; quality assurance; quality control; universities
10/1706 primary school teachers; teacher development; teaching profession

TEACHER INDUCTION
10/0019 Canada natives; ethnic groups; indigenous populations; newly qualified teachers; teacher background; teaching profession
10/0133 mentors; teacher development; teacher education
10/0996 local education authorities; preservice teacher education; probationary teachers; teacher development; teacher education

TEACHER MOBILITY
10/0574 European Community; Germany; teacher transfer; training
10/1200 deputy head teachers; employment patterns; head teachers; teacher employment; teacher recruitment; teacher supply and demand; teaching profession

TEACHER MORALE
10/0406 educational administration; teaching profession
10/0460 educational environment; institutional environment; stress – psychological; stress management; stress variables
10/1262 stress – psychological; teaching profession

TEACHER-PUPIL RELATIONSHIP
10/0085 behaviour problems; classroom discipline; classroom management; pupil behaviour; teacher behaviour
10/0146 children's literature; early childhood education; reading aloud to others; story reading
10/0353 computer uses in education; feedback; interaction; learning processes; peer teaching
10/0463 beginning reading; early reading; oral reading; reading skills
10/0552 motivation; sex differences; sexual identity
10/0643 classroom communication; primary school teachers; teacher behaviour; verbal communication
10/0732 classroom communication; feedback; infant school education; infant school teachers; teacher response
10/1220 beginning reading; infant school education; reading teaching; teaching methods
10/1283 achievement; black pupils; black teachers; teacher behaviour; teaching methods; teaching styles
10/1751 classroom communication; learning activities; teacher role; teaching methods

TEACHER QUALIFICATIONS
10/0560 licensed teachers; preservice teacher education; programme evaluation; teaching profession

TEACHER RECRUITMENT
10/1108 labour market; Northern Ireland; probationary teachers; teacher employment; teaching profession
10/1114 ethnic groups; preservice teacher education; student recruitment; teaching profession
10/1200 deputy head teachers; employment patterns; head teachers; teacher employment; teacher mobility; teacher supply and demand; teaching profession

TEACHER RESPONSE
10/0361 assessment; classroom observation techniques
10/0732 classroom communication; feedback; infant school education; infant school teachers; teacher-pupil relationship

TEACHER ROLE
10/0139 curriculum development; educational change; National Curriculum; primary education; primary school teachers; primary schools; teacher workload

10/0223 primary school teachers; teacher behaviour; teacher development; teaching methods
10/0423 Brazil; comparative education; public opinion
10/0465 primary school teachers; primary schools; sex differences; teaching profession
10/0507 management in education; teacher evaluation
10/0563 educational change; secondary education; secondary school curriculum; secondary school teachers; teaching profession
10/0671 administrator role; educational change; head teachers; management in education; role conflict; secondary schools
10/1218 intellectuals; preservice teacher education; probationary teachers; professional development; teaching profession
10/1232 head teachers; primary schools; teacher-administrator relationship; teacher workload; teaching profession
10/1313 comparative education; international educational exchange; pastoral care – education
10/1364 stress – psychological; teacher workload; time management
10/1727 mothers; teacher attitudes; teacher background; teaching profession; women teachers
10/1740 educational administration; head teachers; primary schools; school based management
10/1751 classroom communication; learning activities; teacher-pupil relationship; teaching methods

TEACHER-STUDENT RELATIONSHIP
10/1123 student research; supervision; tutorials

TEACHER SUPPLY AND DEMAND
10/1200 deputy head teachers; employment patterns; head teachers; teacher employment; teacher mobility; teacher recruitment; teaching profession

TEACHER TRANSFER
10/0574 European Community; Germany; teacher mobility; training

TEACHER WORKLOAD
10/0139 curriculum development; educational change; National Curriculum; primary education; primary school teachers; primary schools; teacher role
10/1045 school effectiveness; teacher attitudes; teacher effectiveness; time management
10/1068 academic staff; further education teachers; higher education; stress – psychological
10/1232 head teachers; primary schools; teacher-administrator relationship; teacher role; teaching profession
10/1364 stress – psychological; teacher role; time management

TEACHERS
10/0556 Nigeria; professional recognition; status need; teacher attitudes; teaching profession
10/0733 special educational needs; support teachers
10/1628 stress – psychological; stress management; student teachers; teaching profession

TEACHING EXPERIENCE
10/0108 educational theories; learning theories; psychology; teacher education; teaching practice; teaching process
10/0459 preservice teacher education; stress – psychological; stress variables; student teachers; teaching practice
10/0573 B Ed degrees; participant satisfaction; preservice teacher education; probationary teachers; student teachers
10/1456 preservice teacher education; student teachers; teaching practice

TEACHING GUIDES
10/1353 dental education

TEACHING MACHINES
10/1542 autoinstructional aids; cognitive style; computer assisted learning; computer uses in education; learning strategies

TEACHING METHODS
10/0048 fire service; learning strategies; professional education
10/0111 heuristics; learning processes; primary education
10/0112 further education; open education
10/0172 mathematics anxiety; mathematics education
10/0181 developmental continuity; English literature; higher education; sixteen to nineteen education
10/0217 curriculum development; individualism; physical education; theory-practice relationship
10/0223 primary school teachers; teacher behaviour; teacher development; teacher role
10/0292 comparative education; cultural education; educational materials; second language learning
10/0334 individual teaching; small group teaching; tutorials; university teaching
10/0337 higher education; learning strategies; learning theories; student attitudes
10/0381 assessment; higher education; learner centred curriculum; self evaluation – individuals
10/0387 assessment; higher education; learner centred methods; open education; self evaluation – individuals
10/0437 leadership; performance indicators; seminars; small group teaching; teacher effectiveness; university teaching
10/0438 leadership; seminars; small group teaching; university teaching
10/0440 comparative education; distance education; higher education; international educational exchange; learning activities; Netherlands; telecommunications
10/0447 city technology colleges; dyslexia; educational materials; learning disabilities; special educational needs
10/0462 modern language studies; primary education; problems; second language teaching
10/0589 science education; scientific concepts
10/0590 science education; scientific concepts; sociology of education
10/0609 arithmetic; mathematical ability; mathematics education; problem solving; teacher education
10/0692 assessment; competency based education; group work; higher education
10/0706 adult literacy; home-school relationship; literacy; literacy education; mother tongue; native speakers; primary education
10/0765 history; history studies; National Curriculum
10/0948 audiovisual aids; educational media; language acquisition; second language teaching; videodiscs
10/0987 accountancy education; business education; research
10/1067 ability; class organisation; grouping – teaching purposes; mixed ability; pupil placement; streaming
10/1118 design and technology; learning activities
10/1164 course evaluation; nurse education; student attitudes
10/1170 learning processes; learning strategies; tertiary education
10/1182 critical thinking; group discussion; learning activities; university students
10/1186 mathematics teachers; teacher development
10/1204 communication research; competency based education; further education; higher education; learning processes
10/1212 learning strategies; National Curriculum; teacher effectiveness
10/1220 beginning reading; infant school education; reading teaching; teacher-pupil relationship
10/1245 English; minority groups; multilingualism
10/1270 early childhood education; individualised methods; intervention; parent participation

10/1283 achievement; black pupils; black teachers; teacher behaviour; teacher-pupil relationship; teaching styles
10/1303 Brazil; science teachers
10/1305 curriculum development; discovery learning; educational history; primary education; projects – learning activities; pupil projects
10/1324 early childhood education; Montessori method; Steiner Waldorf schools
10/1382 individualised methods; mathematics education
10/1424 biology education; chemistry education; learner centred methods; learning strategies; physics education; science education
10/1476 computer science education; mathematics education
10/1485 learning strategies; technology education
10/1491 learning strategies; learning theories
10/1531 developing countries; development education; India; learning activities; primary education
10/1572 computer uses in education; history studies; learning strategies; teleconferencing
10/1573 differentiated curriculum; individualised methods; primary education
10/1577 distance education; interactive video; teleconferencing
10/1602 second language teaching; Welsh
10/1618 chemistry education; educational materials; learning strategies; multimedia approach; science education; skills; transfer of learning
10/1645 adult basic education; adult educators; educational practices; theory-practice relationship
10/1658 educational materials; history studies; pictorial stimuli; visual aids
10/1687 cross curricular approach; curriculum development; National Curriculum; school organisation; thematic approach
10/1743 course evaluation; educational quality; student evaluation of teacher performance; teacher effectiveness; universities
10/1751 classroom communication; learning activities; teacher-pupil relationship; teacher role
10/1755 mathematics education; National Curriculum; primary education
10/1775 flexible learning; medical schools; open education
10/1783 classroom research; learning strategies; National Curriculum; primary education; reading teaching
10/1794 educational change; National Curriculum; projects – learning activities; pupil projects
10/1796 'A' level examinations; chemistry education; science education

TEACHING PRACTICE
10/0108 educational theories; learning theories; psychology; teacher education; teaching experience; teaching process
10/0209 information technology; preservice teacher education; student teachers
10/0350 Postgraduate Certificate in Education; preservice teacher education; student attitudes; student teacher evaluation; teacher behaviour
10/0439 mentors; preservice teacher education; student teacher supervisors
10/0459 preservice teacher education; stress – psychological; stress variables; student teachers; teaching experience
10/0469 mathematics education; mentors; National Curriculum; preservice teacher education; student teacher supervisors
10/0537 ambiguity; class activities; preservice teacher education; student teachers; teaching styles
10/0892 information technology; preservice teacher education; student teachers
10/0932 placement; preservice teacher education; primary schools; secondary schools; student teachers
10/0938 mentors; preservice teacher education; student teacher supervisors; supervision; supervisory methods
10/1295 preservice teacher education; school based teacher education; student teacher supervisors; supervisors

10/1363 Postgraduate Certificate in Education; preservice teacher education
10/1407 preservice teacher education; student teacher evaluation; student teacher supervisors; student teachers
10/1426 educational quality; preservice teacher education; quality control; student teachers
10/1435 assessment; competency based teacher education; preservice teacher education; student teacher evaluation
10/1456 preservice teacher education; student teachers; teaching experience
10/1533 mentors; preservice teacher education; supervisory training
10/1637 mentors; preservice teacher education; student teachers; teacher development

TEACHING PROCESS
10/0108 educational theories; learning theories; psychology; teacher education; teaching experience; teaching practice
10/1143 learner centred methods; staff development; universities; university teaching
10/1378 learning experience; pupil attitudes; pupil-school relationship; school effectiveness; secondary education; secondary school pupils
10/1444 assessment; curriculum development; educational change; environmental education; mathematics education; National Curriculum; Scotland

TEACHING PROFESSION
10/0002 gender equality; head teachers; sex stereotypes; women teachers; women's employment
10/0004 equal opportunities – jobs; gender equality; promotion – occupational; women teachers; women's employment
10/0019 Canada natives; ethnic groups; indigenous populations; newly qualified teachers; teacher background; teacher induction
10/0154 comparative education; educational change; France; primary school teachers; teacher attitudes
10/0156 head teachers; mentors; programme evaluation
10/0190 head teachers; primary schools; school organisation
10/0210 preservice teacher education; primary school teachers; probationary teachers; professional development; student teachers
10/0211 preservice teacher education; professional development; teacher attitudes; teacher development
10/0372 classroom management; classroom observation techniques; teacher evaluation
10/0376 career development; institutes of higher education; teacher evaluation; women teachers; women's employment
10/0386 educational administration; head teachers; management in education; sex differences; women's employment
10/0406 educational administration; teacher morale
10/0429 national organisations; professional associations; Scotland
10/0465 primary school teachers; primary schools; sex differences; teacher role
10/0556 Nigeria; professional recognition; status need; teacher attitudes; teachers
10/0560 licensed teachers; preservice teacher education; programme evaluation; teacher qualifications
10/0563 educational change; secondary education; secondary school curriculum; secondary school teachers; teacher role
10/0584 teacher development; teacher effectiveness; teacher evaluation
10/0673 head teachers; mentors; middle management; professional continuing education; teacher development
10/0727 infant school teachers; National Curriculum; professional recognition
10/0854 design and technology; sex differences
10/0944 inservice teacher education; professional development; teacher development
10/0946 performance contracts; preservice teacher education; records of achievement; school based teacher education; student teachers; teacher development

10/1104 preservice teacher education; probationary teachers; student teachers
10/1108 labour market; Northern Ireland; probationary teachers; teacher employment; teacher recruitment
10/1114 ethnic groups; preservice teacher education; student recruitment; teacher recruitment
10/1200 deputy head teachers; employment patterns; head teachers; teacher employment; teacher mobility; teacher recruitment; teacher supply and demand
10/1209 educational administration; Europe; management in education; teacher employment; women; women's employment
10/1218 intellectuals; preservice teacher education; probationary teachers; professional development; teacher role
10/1232 head teachers; primary schools; teacher-administrator relationship; teacher role; teacher workload
10/1234 educational change; parent attitudes; preservice teacher education; primary school teachers; student teacher attitudes; teacher attitudes
10/1262 stress – psychological; teacher morale
10/1307 competency based teacher education; mentors; profiles; teacher development
10/1337 equal opportunities – jobs; teacher development; teacher evaluation
10/1343 head teachers; teacher development
10/1450 programme evaluation; teacher development; teacher evaluation
10/1457 job sharing; part time teachers; primary school teachers
10/1480 job satisfaction; stress – psychological; teacher attitudes
10/1483 academic staff development; head teachers; teacher evaluation
10/1628 stress – psychological; stress management; student teachers; teachers
10/1661 preservice teacher education; school based teacher education
10/1704 substitute teachers; teacher employment
10/1706 primary school teachers; teacher development; teacher evaluation
10/1727 mothers; teacher attitudes; teacher background; teacher role; women teachers
10/1779 secondary school teachers; teacher development; teacher education

TEACHING STYLES
10/0537 ambiguity; class activities; preservice teacher education; student teachers; teaching practice
10/0557 Malaysia; secondary school teachers; teacher behaviour; teacher effectiveness
10/0610 cognitive processes; cognitive style; field dependence-independence; learning; mathematics
10/1250 English studies; English studies teachers; Kenya
10/1283 achievement; black pupils; black teachers; teacher behaviour; teacher-pupil relationship; teaching methods
10/1391 English – second language; English for academic purposes; lecture method; overseas students

TEAM TEACHING
10/0083 cross curricular approach; special education teachers; special educational needs; support services

TECHNICAL EDUCATION
10/0055 Sudan; vocational education
10/0445 curriculum development; educational history; secondary education
10/0995 building trades education; construction – process; construction industry; cross curricular approach; vocational education
10/1028 basic skills; building trades education; construction – process; construction industry; course evaluation; National Vocational Qualifications; vocational education
10/1673 Arab states; dropout research; student wastage; vocational education

TECHNOLOGY EDUCATION
10/0612 ability; projects – learning activities; pupil projects; secondary education

10/0620 ability; design and technology; National Curriculum; primary education
10/0634 National Curriculum; school based assessment; secondary education
10/0717 mathematics education; peer influence; peer teaching; science education; student volunteers
10/0807 qualifications
10/0833 information seeking; information technology; National Curriculum; optical data discs
10/0844 databases; information technology; National Curriculum
10/0982 curriculum development; mathematics education; science education
10/1084 assessment; English studies; evaluation; mathematics education; National Curriculum; science education; secondary education
10/1085 computer software; computer uses in education; educational software; information technology
10/1113 curriculum development; primary education
10/1148 curriculum development; design education; National Curriculum
10/1192 design and technology; learning strategies; problem solving
10/1335 concept teaching; primary school teachers; science education; scientific concepts
10/1415 primary education; science education
10/1485 learning strategies; teaching methods
10/1625 construction – process; construction materials; equal facilities; gender equality; primary education; science education; sex differences
10/1648 curriculum development; educational materials; experiential learning; material development; primary education; work-education relationship
10/1668 computer uses in education; cross curricular approach; hypertext; information technology
10/1746 assessment
10/1781 corporate support; educational materials; primary education; programme evaluation; science education

TELECOMMUNICATIONS
10/0047 computer uses in education; information networks; information technology
10/0436 distance education; educational media; infant school teachers; inservice education; international educational exchange; Sweden
10/0440 comparative education; distance education; higher education; international educational exchange; learning activities; Netherlands; teaching methods
10/1569 cross cultural studies; electronic mail; European studies; international education; social history
10/1570 cross cultural studies; electronic mail; European studies; preservice teacher education
10/1571 cultural awareness; electronic mail; intercultural communication; language proficiency; modern language studies

TELECONFERENCING
10/0547 communications; distance education; networks; open education
10/1174 distance education; international educational exchange; open universities
10/1572 computer uses in education; history studies; learning strategies; teaching methods
10/1577 distance education; interactive video; teaching methods

TELEVISION
10/0836 mass media; primary school teachers; public opinion; science teachers; scientific attitudes; scientific literacy
10/1057 educational broadcasting; educational radio; educational television; radio

TELEVISION RESEARCH
10/0520 academic achievement; cognitive ability; listening skills; reading achievement; television viewing

TELEVISION SURVEYS
10/1579 adolescents; children; television viewing

TELEVISION VIEWING
10/0520 academic achievement; cognitive ability; listening skills; reading achievement; television research
10/1579 adolescents; children; television surveys

TEMPERATURE
10/0749 cognitive development; comprehension; heat; primary education; science education

TEMPORAL INTEGRATION
10/1189 cognitive development; reasoning; time perspective

TEMPORARY EMPLOYMENT
10/1092 job training; part time employment; training

TERTIARY EDUCATION
10/1170 learning processes; learning strategies; teaching methods
10/1720 access to education; further education; sixteen to nineteen education; student participation; vocational education

TEST CONSTRUCTION
10/1642 mathematical applications; mathematical concepts; mathematics education

TEST ITEMS
10/1000 assessment; item banks; screening tests; test selection; tests

TEST SELECTION
10/1000 assessment; item banks; screening tests; test items; tests

TEST USE
10/1626 behavioural objectives; comprehension; educational objectives; learning experience

TEST VALIDITY
10/1034 adaptive testing; assessment; attainment tests; computer assisted testing; National Curriculum

TESTS
10/0100 blindness; tactual perception; tactual visual tests; visual impairments
10/0999 infant school pupils; nursery school pupils; reading; reading readiness; reception classes
10/1000 assessment; item banks; screening tests; test items; test selection

TEXTBOOK EVALUATION
10/0295 cultural awareness; English – second language; German; modern language studies
10/1627 observation; pupil attitudes; textbooks

TEXTBOOK PREPARATION
10/1469 educational materials; Latin

TEXTBOOKS
10/0144 Belize; developing countries; educational materials; material development
10/0173 children's literature; comics – publications; educational history; girls; popular culture; sex role; women's education
10/0521 educational materials; educational media; low vision aids; printing
10/1586 educational materials; English – second language; vocabulary development
10/1627 observation; pupil attitudes; textbook evaluation

THAILAND
10/0644 English – second language; inservice teacher education; language teachers; second language teaching

THEATRE ARTS
10/0579 drama education; dramatics; learning processes; primary education
10/0811 art education; dance; music; sixteen to nineteen education
10/1060 arts; attitudes; culture; mass media; music; participation; sports

THEMATIC APPROACH
10/1687 cross curricular approach; curriculum development; National Curriculum; school organisation; teaching methods

THEOLOGICAL EDUCATION
10/0065 clergy; continuing education; learning processes; professional education; religious education
10/0067 Catholics; clergy; priests; professional education; religious education
10/0068 priests; professional education; religious education; women
10/0099 church and education; religious education

THEORY-PRACTICE RELATIONSHIP
10/0217 curriculum development; individualism; physical education; teaching methods
10/1645 adult basic education; adult educators; educational practices; teaching methods

THERAPISTS
10/0261 speech therapy; speech training; training methods

THERMODYNAMICS
10/1795 physics education; science education; scientific concepts

THESES
10/0468 computer uses in education; information technology; research reports

THINKING SKILLS
10/0249 learning processes; mathematics education
10/0768 comprehension; computer assisted learning; computer uses in education; history

TIME FACTORS – LEARNING
10/0348 ability; learning; mixed ability; pacing

TIME MANAGEMENT
10/1045 school effectiveness; teacher attitudes; teacher effectiveness; teacher workload
10/1256 change; head teachers; local management of schools; primary schools; role conflict; stress variables
10/1364 stress – psychological; teacher role; teacher workload

TIME PERSPECTIVE
10/1189 cognitive development; reasoning; temporal integration

TOTAL COMMUNICATION
10/0611 communication skills; deafness; hearing impairments; hearing therapy; special schools

TOUCH SCREENS
10/0860 computer assisted learning; computer uses in education; concept keyboards; human-computer interaction; learning disabilities; special educational needs

TOURISM
10/0197 acquired immune deficiency syndrome; health education; health promotion; sexuality; sexually transmitted diseases; travel
10/1225 curriculum development; primary education; travel

TRAFFIC SAFETY
10/0157 primary school pupils; pupil attitudes; safety education
10/0158 safety education; Scotland; secondary education
10/1258 safety education

TRAINEES
10/0786 comparative education; France; mathematics achievement

TRAINERS
10/1508 industrial training; on the job training
10/1580 international educational exchange; programme development; training; youth employment; youth programmes

TRAINING

10/0124 comparative education; economic change; economics-education relationship; Germany; industry-education relationship; structural unemployment; work-education relationship

10/0234 financial support; inner city; investment; youth leaders; youth service

10/0253 artists; peripatetic teachers

10/0278 medical services

10/0450 career development; engineering education; engineers; work-education relationship

10/0539 educational history; women's education; women's employment

10/0574 European Community; Germany; teacher mobility; teacher transfer

10/0595 skilled workers; Tanzania; vocational education

10/0601 distributive trades education; National Vocational Qualifications; retailing; vocational education

10/0684 further education; industry-further education relationship; vocational education

10/0827 acquired immune deficiency syndrome; evaluation; health education

10/0926 school to work transition; training credits; youth employment

10/1005 credits; school to work transition; Training and Enterprise Councils; vocational education; vocational guidance

10/1015 caregivers; child caregivers; residential schools; special schools

10/1092 job training; part time employment; temporary employment

10/1131 communications; computer networks; disabilities; wide area networks

10/1140 curriculum evaluation; economics-education relationship; Hong Kong; TVEI; work-education relationship

10/1142 adult vocational education; comparative education; disabilities; information technology; Portugal; special educational needs; United Kingdom

10/1190 adult vocational education; employment patterns; unemployment

10/1214 child caregivers; play groups; preschool education; qualifications

10/1215 inservice teacher education; mentors

10/1474 insurance occupations; Single European Market

10/1506 community education; continuing education; staff development; voluntary service; volunteers

10/1548 off the job training; on the job training; skill development; transfer of training; work experience programmes

10/1580 international educational exchange; programme development; trainers; youth employment; youth programmes

10/1679 part time employment; youth service

10/1680 community organisations; youth leaders; youth service

TRAINING AND ENTERPRISE COUNCILS

10/0050 industry-education relationship

10/0784 accreditation of prior learning; assessment; National Vocational Qualifications; vocational education

10/1005 credits; school to work transition; training; vocational education; vocational guidance

10/1012 programme evaluation; training credits; vocational education

TRAINING CENTRES

10/1124 adult vocational education; adults; computer literacy; disabilities; information technology; sheltered workshops; special educational needs

10/1127 adults; computer literacy; disabilities; information technology; special educational needs

10/1440 management development; management in education

TRAINING CREDITS

10/0926 school to work transition; training; youth employment

10/1012 programme evaluation; Training and Enterprise Councils; vocational education

TRAINING METHODS

10/0261 speech therapy; speech training; therapists

10/1551 computer assisted learning; educational technology; expert systems; optical data discs

TRANSFER OF LEARNING

10/0164 corporate support; employers; enterprise education; industry-higher education relationship

10/0285 enterprise education; industry-education relationship; learning strategies; motivation; skill development

10/0549 higher education; prior learning

10/1514 access to education; accreditation of prior learning; experiential learning; higher education

10/1616 biology education; science education; skills

10/1618 chemistry education; educational materials; learning strategies; multimedia approach; science education; skills; teaching methods

10/1619 Business and Technician Education Council; chemistry education; competency based education; science education; skills

10/1716 basic skills; critical thinking; educational philosophy; problem solving; skills

TRANSFER OF TRAINING

10/1548 off the job training; on the job training; skill development; training; work experience programmes

TRANSFER PUPILS

10/0243 antisocial behaviour; behaviour problems; delinquency prevention; longitudinal studies; secondary school pupils

10/0913 behaviour problems; discipline policy; discipline problems; disruptive pupils; primary-secondary education; problem children

10/1001 curriculum development; developmental continuity; local education authorities; National Curriculum; primary secondary-education

10/1267 developmental continuity; infant schools; junior schools; primary education

TRANSITION EDUCATION

10/0425 access to education; higher education; summer schools; university admission; university preparation

10/0544 equal education; gender equality; TVEI

10/0956 career counselling; outcomes of education; pupil attitudes; school leavers; school to work transition; TVEI; work-education relationship

TRAVEL

10/0197 acquired immune deficiency syndrome; health education; health promotion; sexuality; sexually transmitted diseases; tourism

10/1225 curriculum development; primary education; tourism

TRAVEL TRAINING

10/1145 assessment; blindness; mobility aids; partial vision; special educational needs; visual impairments; visually handicapped mobility

TRAVELLERS – ITINERANTS

10/0720 cultural influences; gypsies; minority group children; performance factors

10/0721 cultural influences; gypsies; minority group children; performance factors

TRIGONOMETRY

10/0782 computer uses in education; mathematics education; symbols – mathematics; visualisation

TRIPARTITE SYSTEM

10/0551 educational administration; educational history; educational policy; public education; secondary education

10/0554 educational history; educational policy; educational principles; school systems; secondary education; secondary modern schools; working class

TRUANCY

10/0303 crime prevention; delinquency; discipline problems; expulsion; programme evaluation

10/1063 attendance; discipline problems; disruptive pupils; expulsion

10/1107 attendance; attendance patterns; Northern Ireland; pupil behaviour

10/1366 attendance; pupil behaviour; Scotland; secondary schools

10/1647 pupil behaviour

10/1757 attendance; educational attitudes; family influence; home-school relationship

TUITION GRANTS

10/1018 local education authorities; maintenance grants; student financial aid

TURTLES – ROBOTS

10/0362 cognitive ability; computer assisted learning; interaction; logo

TUTORIALS

10/0334 individual teaching; small group teaching; teaching methods; university teaching

10/1123 student research; supervision; teacher-student relationship

TVEI

10/0499 TVEI

10/0013 institutional administration

10/0497 education support grants; inservice teacher education; programme evaluation

10/0511 inservice teacher education

10/0538 programme evaluation

10/0544 equal education; gender equality; transition education

10/0629 educational change; longitudinal studies

10/0639 local education authorities; programme evaluation

10/0894 equal education

10/0956 career counselling; outcomes of education; pupil attitudes; school leavers; school to work transition; transition education; work-education relationship

10/1011 cohort analysis; programme evaluation; school leavers; school to work transition; sixteen to nineteen education

10/1140 curriculum evaluation; economics-education relationship; Hong Kong; training; work-education relationship

10/1147 change agents; curriculum development; preservice teacher education

10/1333 programme evaluation

10/1351 industry-education relationship; programme evaluation; skills; vocational education

10/1386 programme evaluation

10/1448 change strategies; educational innovation; programme evaluation

UGANDA

10/1538 community benefits; developing countries; health education; India; peer teaching

UNDERACHIEVEMENT

10/0056 academic achievement; equal education; school effectiveness; urban schools

10/0336 academic failure; higher education; intervention; student problems

10/0945 curriculum development; low achievement; moderate learning difficulties; special educational needs

10/1325 academic achievement; achievement; cognitive style; failure; gifted

10/1454 academic achievement; educational practices; pupil improvement; secondary schools; support services

10/1767 academic ability; academic failure; gifted; pupil behaviour

UNDERGRADUATE STUDENTS

10/0343 audiovisual education; calculators; equipment; mathematics education

10/0389 higher education; learning strategies; study skills

10/1098 degrees – academic; medicine; professional education

10/1771 achievement; background; high achievement; individual characteristics; science education

UNDERGRADUATE STUDY
10/0127 attendance patterns; business education; course evaluation; examination results; outcomes of education; sandwich courses
10/0341 higher education; learning motivation; learning strategies; mathematics achievement; sixteen to nineteen education

UNEMPLOYMENT
10/0311 further education; higher education; school to work transition; vocational education; youth employment
10/0561 Kenya; school leavers; school to work transition; vocational education; youth employment
10/1190 adult vocational education; employment patterns; training

UNITED KINGDOM
10/1129 adult education; comparative education; Taiwan; universities
10/1136 adult education; comparative education; continuing education; European Community; Germany; vocational education
10/1142 adult vocational education; comparative education; disabilities; information technology; Portugal; special educational needs; training

UNITED STATES OF AMERICA
10/0191 institutional evaluation; mainstreaming; special educational needs; whole school approach
10/0689 comparative education; industry-education relationship; work-education relationship
10/1201 comparative education; educational policy; industry-education relationship; politics-education relationship
10/1213 comparative education; France; higher education; teacher education
10/1223 comparative education; educational history; educational quality; school effectiveness
10/1758 antisocial behaviour; comparative education; discipline problems; disruptive pupils

UNIVERSITIES
10/0014 educational finance; financial support; university administration
10/0015 educational administration; university administration
10/0032 educational history; institutional administration
10/0090 access to education; disabilities; higher education; special educational needs; student needs; university admission
10/0143 comparative education; Ghana; higher education; modular courses
10/0489 higher education; religion and education; religious education
10/0606 adult education; biographies; educational history; extension education; working class
10/0693 educational history; higher education; professional education; women's education; women's employment
10/0796 advisory committees; higher education; policy formation; politics-education relationship
10/0816 educational development; higher education; prediction
10/0885 teacher education
10/0903 academic staff; employment opportunities; equal opportunities – jobs; higher education; women teachers; women's employment
10/1023 course evaluation; educational quality; higher education; performance indicators; quality control; student attitudes; teacher effectiveness
10/1129 adult education; comparative education; Taiwan; United Kingdom
10/1143 learner centred methods; staff development; teaching process; university teaching
10/1578 academic staff evaluation; quality assurance; quality control; teacher evaluation
10/1711 adult education; continuing education; higher education; organisational change

10/1743 course evaluation; educational quality; student evaluation of teacher performance; teacher effectiveness; teaching methods
10/1769 educational history; examinations; science education

UNIVERSITIES AND COLLEGES
10/0546 college effectiveness; higher education; outcomes of education

UNIVERSITY ADMINISTRATION
10/0014 educational finance; financial support; universities
10/0015 educational administration; universities
10/1175 educational planning; management in education

UNIVERSITY ADMISSION
10/0090 access to education; disabilities; higher education; special educational needs; student needs; universities
10/0408 access to education; dropout research; higher education; nontraditional education; summer schools; university preparation
10/0425 access to education; higher education; summer schools; transition education; university preparation
10/0605 equal education; ethnic groups; student recruitment

UNIVERSITY EXAMINATIONS
10/1766 educational history; examination syllabuses; science education

UNIVERSITY PREPARATION
10/0408 access to education; dropout research; higher education; nontraditional education; summer schools; university admission
10/0425 access to education; higher education; summer schools; transition education; university admission

UNIVERSITY STUDENTS
10/1156 calculus education; computer uses in education; mathematics education
10/1182 critical thinking; group discussion; learning activities; teaching methods

UNIVERSITY TEACHING
10/0334 individual teaching; small group teaching; teaching methods; tutorials
10/0437 leadership; performance indicators; seminars; small group teaching; teacher effectiveness; teaching methods
10/0438 leadership; seminars; small group teaching; teaching methods
10/1143 learner centred methods; staff development; teaching process; universities

URBAN SCHOOLS
10/0056 academic achievement; equal education; school effectiveness; underachievement
10/0947 educational change; educational legislation; educational policy; primary schools
10/1730 educational innovation; programme evaluation; whole school approach

USSR
10/0399 Commonwealth of Independent States; Communist education; educational change; ideology; politics-education relationship; social change

VALUES
10/0128 ethics; sports; sportsmanship
10/1563 behaviour problems; bullying; personality; secondary school pupils
10/1567 attitude measures; pupil attitudes; religion; religious attitudes; secondary school pupils

VALUES EDUCATION
10/0451 curriculum development; sixteen to nineteen education
10/1009 Europe; international educational exchange
10/1020 directories; moral education; reference materials
10/1229 moral development; religion and education; religious attitudes; school worship

10/1339 primary education; pupil attitudes; teacher attitudes
10/1417 primary education
10/1468 moral education; philosophy

VERBAL COMMUNICATION
10/0193 conversation; language; speech communication
10/0643 classroom communication; primary school teachers; teacher behaviour; teacher-pupil relationship
10/1392 communication research; conversation; native speakers; second language learning
10/1717 communication research; integration studies; severe learning difficulties; special educational needs
10/1734 child language; comparative education; group work; infant school pupils

VERBAL DEVELOPMENT
10/1243 child development; memorisation; phonemics; pictorial stimuli; visual learning

VERBAL TESTS
10/0785 assessment; job skills; National Vocational Qualifications; Scottish Vocational Qualifications

VIDEODISCS
10/0948 audiovisual aids; educational media; language acquisition; second language teaching; teaching methods

VISIBLE SPEECH
10/1314 speech

VISUAL AIDS
10/1658 educational materials; history studies; pictorial stimuli; teaching methods

VISUAL ARTS
10/0258 arts education; computer uses in education; cultural education; handicrafts; museums
10/0951 art education; photography
10/1806 autism; Down's Syndrome; drawing; gifted; special educational needs

VISUAL IMPAIRMENTS
10/0097 architectural education; blindness; educational equipment; special educational needs
10/0100 blindness; tactual perception; tactual visual tests; tests
10/0101 aspiration; life style; skills; special educational needs; vocational education
10/0102 blindness; maps; memory; raised line drawings; spatial ability; tactile adaptation
10/0104 blindness; computer assisted reading; computer software; computer system design; educational materials; partial vision
10/0105 academic achievement; blindness; cognitive development; longitudinal studies; outcomes of education; partial vision; special schools
10/0106 blindness; child development; infants; young children
10/0107 blindness; braille; reading tests
10/0876 blindness; communication problems; higher education; nonverbal communication; special educational needs
10/0886 blindness; low vision aids; microcomputers; sensory aids; tactile adaptation
10/0900 further education; mainstreaming; special educational needs
10/1145 assessment; blindness; mobility aids; partial vision; special educational needs; travel training; visually handicapped mobility
10/1146 adaptive behaviour – of disabled; attitude measures; blindness; emotional adjustment; measurement techniques; rehabilitation
10/1176 blindness; computer uses in education; optical data discs; special educational needs; speech synthesisers
10/1376 blindness; mobility aids; visually handicapped mobility

VISUAL LEARNING
10/0788 computer uses in education; educational
software; mathematics education; symbols –
mathematics
10/0984 memory; pictorial stimuli; science
education
10/1243 child development; memorisation;
phonemics; pictorial stimuli; verbal development

VISUAL PERCEPTION
10/0659 brain hemisphere functions; dyslexia;
handedness; lateral dominance; reading
difficulties
10/1188 cognitive ability; depth perception;
drawing; problem solving; spatial ability
10/1547 computer science; computer uses in
education

VISUALISATION
10/0259 design education; designers; spatial
ability
10/0782 computer uses in education;
mathematics education; symbols –
mathematics; trigonometry

VISUALLY HANDICAPPED MOBILITY
10/1145 assessment; blindness; mobility aids;
partial vision; special educational needs; travel
training; visual impairments
10/1376 blindness; mobility aids; visual
impairments

VOCABULARY DEVELOPMENT
10/1586 educational materials; English – second
language; textbooks
10/1591 second language learning

VOCATIONAL EDUCATION
10/0055 Sudan; technical education
10/0101 aspiration; life style; skills; special
educational needs; visual impairments
10/0116 educational quality; National Vocational
Qualifications; performance indicators
10/0311 further education; higher education;
school to work transition; unemployment;
youth employment
10/0314 comparative education; curriculum
development; European Community; modular
courses
10/0339 small businesses
10/0383 educational quality; industry-higher
education relationship; quality control;
work-education relationship
10/0561 Kenya; school leavers; school to work
transition; unemployment; youth employment
10/0595 skilled workers; Tanzania; training
10/0601 distributive trades education; National
Vocational Qualifications; retailing; training
10/0684 further education; industry-further
education relationship; training
10/0728 National Vocational Qualifications;
qualifications
10/0773 developing countries; Zimbabwe
10/0776 assessment; job skills; mastery tests;
retention – psychology
10/0784 accreditation of prior learning;
assessment; National Vocational Qualifications;
Training and Enterprise Councils
10/0787 employment qualifications; National
Vocational Qualifications
10/0808 sixteen to nineteen education
10/0855 industry-education relationship; local
education authorities; school to work transition
10/0995 building trades education; construction –
process; construction industry; cross curricular
approach; technical education
10/1003 cooperative education; school to work
transition; work-education relationship
10/1005 credits; school to work transition;
training; Training and Enterprise Councils;
vocational guidance
10/1012 programme evaluation; Training and
Enterprise Councils; training credits
10/1024 curriculum research; National
Vocational Qualifications; sixteen to nineteen
education; sixth form education
10/1028 basic skills; building trades education;
construction – process; construction industry;
course evaluation; National Vocational
Qualifications; technical education

10/1136 adult education; comparative education;
continuing education; European Community;
Germany; United Kingdom
10/1139 adult education; adults; comparative
education; continuing education; databases
10/1152 adult education; continuing education;
industrial training; inservice teacher education;
professional training
10/1202 basic skills; National Vocational
Qualifications
10/1351 industry-education relationship;
programme evaluation; skills; TVEI
10/1360 industry-education relationship;
programme evaluation; school to work
transition; work-education relationship
10/1365 further education; languages for specific
purposes; modern language studies; second
language teaching
10/1459 industry-education relationship; school
to work transition
10/1482 educational experience; employment
qualifications; National Vocational
Qualifications
10/1494 curriculum development; economics-
education relationship; educational policy;
labour market; politics-education relationship
10/1673 Arab states; dropout research; student
wastage; technical education
10/1720 access to education; further education;
sixteen to nineteen education; student
participation; tertiary education
10/1777 further education; higher education;
National Vocational Qualifications

VOCATIONAL GUIDANCE
10/0321 career counselling; guidance; secondary
schools
10/0328 career counselling; China; comparative
education; Scotland
10/0391 career counselling; ethnic groups;
minority groups; secondary school pupils
10/0558 career education; higher education
10/1005 credits; school to work transition;
training; Training and Enterprise Councils;
vocational education
10/1007 career counselling; evaluation methods;
guidance objectives; measurement
techniques
10/1019 career education; careers service; school
to work transition
10/1022 career development; career education;
career planning; school to work transition
10/1065 career education; careers service; school
to work transition; Wales
10/1090 adult counselling; career counselling;
Europe; European Community
10/1091 career counselling; career education

VOCATIONAL INTERESTS
10/0967 adolescent attitudes; adolescent
development; adolescents; educational
attitudes; interests; personality development;
social development

VOLUNTARY AGENCIES
10/0810 child rearing; parent-child relationship;
parenthood education; parenting skills
10/1070 local education authorities; youth
leaders; youth service
10/1132 adult education; community; individual
development; social change
10/1134 acquired immune deficiency syndrome;
adult education; ethics; sexually transmitted
diseases
10/1138 adult education; citizenship education;
political influences; social change; socialist
countries

VOLUNTARY SCHOOLS
10/0975 ethnic groups; minority groups;
multiculturalism; primary schools

VOLUNTARY SERVICE
10/1037 local education authorities; youth
leaders; youth service
10/1506 community education; continuing
education; staff development; training;
volunteers

VOLUNTEERS
10/1066 economics education; life skills; money
management
10/1506 community education; continuing
education; staff development; training;
voluntary service

VOWELS
10/1590 Arabs; English – second language; word
recognition

WALES
10/0379 educational development; language of
instruction; language policy; mother tongue;
Welsh; Welsh speaking schools
10/0384 peer teaching; role models; student-
school relationship
10/1065 career education; careers service; school
to work transition; vocational guidance
10/1598 cross curricular approach; curriculum
development; economics education; enterprise
education; primary education; secondary
education

WAR
10/1254 history studies
10/1319 autobiographies; children's literature

WASTE DISPOSAL
10/1556 curriculum development; environmental
education; pollution

WELFARE SERVICES
10/0492 acquired immune deficiency syndrome;
drug abuse; drug education; health education

WELL BEING
10/0508 educational objectives; educational
philosophy; quality of life
10/1233 health; health activities; holistic
approach; physical education
10/1559 religion; secondary school pupils

WELSH
10/0378 error analysis – language; second
language learning
10/0379 educational development; language of
instruction; language policy; mother tongue;
Wales; Welsh speaking schools
10/1561 personality measures
10/1583 bilingual education; bilingualism;
educational policy; language policy; school
effectiveness; Welsh studies
10/1584 assessment; mother tongue; National
Curriculum; school based assessment; second
language learning; standard assessment tasks
10/1602 second language teaching; teaching
methods
10/1792 bilingual education; bilingual schools;
secondary education

WELSH SPEAKING SCHOOLS
10/0379 educational development; language of
instruction; language policy; mother tongue;
wales; Welsh

WELSH STUDIES
10/1008 assessment; attainment tests; National
Curriculum; standard assessment tasks
10/1082 assessment; attainment tests; National
Curriculum; standard assessment tasks
10/1083 assertiveness; attainment tests; National
Curriculum; standard assessment tasks
10/1583 bilingual education; bilingualism;
educational policy; language policy; school
effectiveness; Welsh

WHITES
10/1737 ethnic relations; friendship; intergroup
relations; primary schools; pupil attitudes;
racial relations

WHOLE SCHOOL APPROACH
10/0186 institutional evaluation; mainstreaming;
special educational needs
10/0191 institutional evaluation; mainstreaming;
special educational needs; United States of
America
10/0647 development plans; educational
planning; planning; primary schools

10/1379 equal education; gender equality; school policy; secondary schools
10/1730 educational innovation; programme evaluation; urban schools

WIDE AREA NETWORKS
10/1131 communications; computer networks; disabilities; training

WOMEN
10/0068 priests; professional education; religious education; theological education
10/0517 administrators; educational administration; further education; higher education; management in education; women's employment
10/1209 educational administration; Europe; management in education; teacher employment; teaching profession; women's employment
10/1729 higher education; science education; scientific literacy

WOMEN TEACHERS
10/0002 gender equality; head teachers; sex stereotypes; teaching profession; women's employment
10/0004 equal opportunities – jobs; gender equality; promotion – occupational; teaching profession; women's employment
10/0376 career development; institutes of higher education; teacher evaluation; teaching profession; women's employment
10/0903 academic staff; employment opportunities; equal opportunities – jobs; higher education; universities; women's employment
10/1727 mothers; teacher attitudes; teacher background; teacher role; teaching profession

WOMEN'S EDUCATION
10/0170 access to education; equal education; higher education; Pakistan
10/0173 children's literature; comics – publications; educational history; girls; popular culture; sex role; textbooks
10/0318 adult vocational education; followup studies; outcomes of education; retraining; women's employment
10/0482 Nigeria
10/0539 educational history; training; women's employment
10/0599 access programmes; continuing education; educational benefits; educational objectives
10/0693 educational history; higher education; professional education; universities; women's employment
10/0898 distance education; open universities; Saudi Arabia
10/1093 access to education; adult education; retraining
10/1099 mature students; preservice teacher education; student behaviour; student teacher attitudes; student teachers
10/1150 Islamic education; Muslims; religion and education; religious cultural groups
10/1151 Islamic education; Muslims; religion and education; religious cultural groups
10/1160 equal education; Islamic education; Muslims; religion and education; religious cultural groups; single sex schools
10/1269 developing countries; literacy
10/1550 access to education; cultural background; equal education; ethnic groups; higher education; inner city
10/1589 educational experience; higher education; mature students; men; sex differences; student attitudes
10/1657 educational history; educational policy; further education
10/1683 Chile; comparative education; gender equality; Israel
10/1684 gender equality; Mauritius; women's employment
10/1685 educational policy; equal education; gender equality; Nepal

WOMEN'S EMPLOYMENT
10/0002 gender equality; head teachers; sex stereotypes; teaching profession; women teachers

10/0004 equal opportunities – jobs; gender equality; promotion – occupational; teaching profession; women teachers
10/0318 adult vocational education; followup studies; outcomes of education; retraining; women's education
10/0376 career development; institutes of higher education; teacher evaluation; teaching profession; women teachers
10/0386 educational administration; head teachers; management in education; sex differences; teaching profession
10/0517 administrators; educational administration; further education; higher education; management in education; women
10/0539 educational history; training; women's education
10/0693 educational history; higher education; professional education; universities; women's education
10/0903 academic staff; employment opportunities; equal opportunities – jobs; higher education; universities; women teachers
10/1122 colleges of further education; educational administration
10/1209 educational administration; Europe; management in education; teacher employment; teaching profession; women
10/1684 gender equality; Mauritius; women's education

WOMEN'S STUDIES
10/0540 girls; leisure time; recreational activities
10/1588 age differences; feminism

WORD PROCESSING
10/0151 adult learning; human-computer interaction; learning strategies; secretaries
10/0631 computer uses in education; secondary school pupils; writing skills

WORD RECOGNITION
10/0192 bilingualism; lexicology
10/1144 cognitive processes; computer assisted reading; reading comprehension; reading skills; spelling
10/1437 dyslexia; reading difficulties; reading failure; reading skills
10/1546 reading comprehension; reading games
10/1590 Arabs; English – second language; vowels
10/1808 beginning reading; dyslexia; sight method

WORK ATTITUDES
10/0120 industry-education relationship; National Vocational Qualifications; work-education relationship
10/1649 attitude formation; childhood attitudes; primary school pupils
10/1651 employment; primary school pupils; social cognition

WORK-EDUCATION RELATIONSHIP
10/0072 career ladders; careers; equal opportunities – jobs; France; job training
10/0120 industry-education relationship; National Vocational Qualifications; work attitudes
10/0124 comparative education; economic change; economics-education relationship; Germany; industry-education relationship; structural unemployment; training
10/0208 credits; experiential learning; industry-higher education relationship; job placement
10/0299 employer attitudes; graduate employment; graduates; mathematical ability; numeracy
10/0383 educational quality; industry-higher education relationship; quality control; vocational education
10/0450 career development; engineering education; engineers; training
10/0545 enterprise education; higher education; programme evaluation
10/0689 comparative education; industry-education relationship; United States of America
10/0856 economics-education relationship; educational benefits; educational finance; employment opportunities; outcomes of education; rewards

10/0911 industry-education relationship; management development; mentors
10/0956 career counselling; outcomes of education; pupil attitudes; school leavers; school to work transition; transition education; TVEI
10/1003 cooperative education; school to work transition; vocational education
10/1130 adult vocational education; employment; job skills; job training
10/1140 curriculum evaluation; economics education relationship; Hong Kong; training; TVEI
10/1149 enterprise education; further education
10/1238 assessment; enterprise education; higher education; learning strategies; skill development
10/1360 industry-education relationship; programme evaluation; school to work transition; vocational education
10/1461 employment opportunities; labour market; learner educational objectives; occupational aspiration; opportunities; secondary school pupils
10/1462 career choice; employment opportunities; labour market; learner educational objectives; occupational aspiration; school to work transition; secondary school pupils
10/1648 curriculum development; educational materials; experiential learning; material development; primary education; technology education
10/1696 curriculum; employment; industry-education relationship; skills

WORK EXPERIENCE
10/1109 industry-higher education relationship; management studies; placement

WORK EXPERIENCE PROGRAMMES
10/0740 colleges of further education; industry-further education relationship; staff development
10/0743 industry-education relationship; teacher development
10/1548 off the job training; on the job training; skill development; training; transfer of training
10/1607 librarianship education; library schools; placement; professional education

WORKING CLASS
10/0528 academic staff; ethnic groups; higher education; mature students; middle class students; student attitudes; student experience
10/0554 educational history; educational policy; educational principles; school systems; secondary education; secondary modern schools; tripartite system
10/0602 adult education; educational history; social history
10/0606 adult education; biographies; educational history; extension education; universities
10/0607 adult education; educational history; educational policy; extension education

WORKS SCHOOLS
10/0597 adult education; labour force development

WORKSHOPS
10/0493 communication aids – for disabled; communication disorders; programme evaluation; special educational needs
10/0866 experiential learning; interpersonal competence; learning experience; preservice teacher education; student teachers

WRITING – COMPOSITION
10/0077 creative writing; English studies curriculum; literary genres; National Curriculum; writing skills
10/0110 prewriting; writing research; writing skills; young children
10/0134 children as writers; group work; narration; primary school pupils; story telling
10/0338 comprehension; essays; examination techniques; higher education; learning strategies; review – reexamination; study skills
10/0541 authors; cooperation

10/0542 critical reading; reading; student development; study skills; writing skills

10/0940 letters – correspondence; writing exercises; writing skills

WRITING DIFFICULTIES

10/0284 computer software; computer uses in education; learning disabilities; special educational needs; spelling

WRITING EXERCISES

10/0940 letters – correspondence; writing – composition; writing skills

WRITING FOR PUBLICATION

10/1287 publications; research reports; researchers

WRITING PROCESSES

10/0472 argument; criticism; higher education; sixth form education; writing skills

WRITING RESEARCH

10/0110 prewriting; writing – composition; writing skills; young children

10/0301 comparative education; creativity; France; handwriting; writing skills

WRITING SKILLS

10/0077 creative writing; English studies curriculum; literary genres; National Curriculum; writing – composition

10/0110 prewriting; writing – composition; writing research; young children

10/0150 curriculum; literacy education; reading skills; secondary school curriculum

10/0206 language skills; literacy; oracy; reading skills; special educational needs; spelling

10/0301 comparative education; creativity; France; handwriting; writing research

10/0375 information seeking; literacy; primary education; reading skills

10/0472 argument; criticism; higher education; sixth form education; writing processes

10/0542 critical reading; reading; student development; study skills; writing – composition

10/0631 computer uses in education; secondary school pupils; word processing

10/0921 spelling; writing teaching

10/0940 letters – correspondence; writing – composition; writing exercises

10/0941 comprehension; punctuation; written language

10/0997 assessment; English studies; National Curriculum; reading achievement; standard assessment tasks

10/1049 family involvement; family programmes; literacy; parent participation; reading skills

10/1096 further education students; higher education; literacy; reading skills

10/1199 handwriting; infant school pupils; reading; spelling

WRITING TEACHING

10/0921 spelling; writing skills

WRITTEN LANGUAGE

10/0941 comprehension; punctuation; writing skills

YOUNG CHILDREN

10/0001 access to education; community education; mothers; preschool education

10/0106 blindness; child development; infants; visual impairments

10/0110 prewriting; writing – composition; writing research; writing skills

10/0135 language usage; role playing

10/0136 language usage; role playing

10/0632 early childhood education; mathematics education; pattern recognition; play

10/0935 community services; day care; early childhood education; local government; nursery school curriculum; nursery schools; preschool education

10/1193 communication skills; early childhood education; friendship; infant school pupils; reception classes; social development; social isolation

10/1264 child development; early reading; reading ability

10/1292 mathematical concepts; mathematics education

10/1297 achievement; assessment; early childhood education; records of achievement; self evaluation – individuals

10/1318 religious education

10/1320 Christianity; religious education

10/1323 music activities; music education; singing

10/1463 community programmes; community services; cooperative programmes; early childhood education; parent participation

YOUTH

10/0315 school leavers; school to work transition; sixteen to nineteen education; surveys

10/0316 school leavers; school to work transition; sixteen to nineteen education; surveys

10/0319 family income; family influence; financial support; parent-child relationship; parent role

10/0320 cohort analysis; follow-up studies; longitudinal studies; school leavers; school to work transition; Scotland; sixteen to nineteen education

10/0703 economic change; educational needs; educational policy; Poland; social change

10/0819 acquired immune deficiency syndrome; health education; sex education; sexually transmitted diseases

10/0820 health education; sex education

10/1062 arts; arts education; attitudes; culture; leisure time; participation

10/1678 community organisations; youth leaders; youth service

YOUTH EMPLOYMENT

10/0311 further education; higher education; school to work transition; unemployment; vocational education

10/0561 Kenya; school leavers; school to work transition; unemployment; vocational education

10/0926 school to work transition; training; training credits

10/1580 international educational exchange; programme development; trainers; training; youth programmes

YOUTH LEADERS

10/0010 mentors; youth service

10/0234 financial support; inner city; investment; training; youth service

10/1037 local education authorities; voluntary service; youth service

10/1070 local education authorities; voluntary agencies; youth service

10/1678 community organisations; youth; youth service

10/1680 community organisations; training; youth service

YOUTH PROGRAMMES

10/1580 international educational exchange; programme development; trainers; training; youth employment

YOUTH SERVICE

10/0010 mentors; youth leaders

10/0234 financial support; inner city; investment; training; youth leaders

10/1037 local education authorities; voluntary service; youth leaders

10/1070 local education authorities; voluntary agencies; youth leaders

10/1678 community organisations; youth; youth leaders

10/1679 part time employment; training

10/1680 community organisations; training; youth leaders

10/1681 community organisations; policy

ZAMBIA

10/0224 comparative education; core curriculum; National Curriculum; Netherlands

10/1195 citizenship; citizenship education; identity; nationalism; role of education

ZIMBABWE

10/0773 developing countries; vocational education

10/1528 agricultural education; developing countries; environmental education

10/1528 agricultural education; developing countries; environmental education